Measures for Clinical Practice and Research

Measures for Clinical Practice and Research

A SOURCEBOOK

Fifth Edition

VOLUME 2

Adults

KEVIN CORCORAN   JOEL FISCHER

OXFORD
UNIVERSITY PRESS
2013

OXFORD
UNIVERSITY PRESS

Oxford University Press is a department of the University of Oxford.
It furthers the University's objective of excellence in research, scholarship,
and education by publishing worldwide.

Oxford   New York
Auckland   Cape Town   Dar es Salaam   Hong Kong   Karachi
Kuala Lumpur   Madrid   Melbourne   Mexico City   Nairobi
New Delhi   Shanghai   Taipei   Toronto

With offices in
Argentina   Austria   Brazil   Chile   Czech Republic   France   Greece
Guatemala   Hungary   Italy   Japan   Poland   Portugal   Singapore
South Korea   Switzerland   Thailand   Turkey   Ukraine   Vietnam

ISBN 978–0–19–977859–1

9 8 7 6 5 4 3 2 1

Printed in the United States of America
on acid-free paper

*To Art Vandalay, architect of dreams,
and to Renee and Schmoopie
for virtually everything else.*
JF

*To my current wife, who will
always be my girlfriend.*
KC

Contents

Part 2 Instruments for Practice and Research

Volume 2
Instruments for Adults

Volume 1
Instruments for Couples

Volume 1
Instruments for Families

Volume 1
Instruments for Children

Instruments Cross-Indexed
by Problem Area

(Instruments in **boldface** are in Volume 1, and those in standard type are in Volume 2.)

ANXIETY AND FEAR (also see Mood, Phobias)

ASSERTIVENESS (also see Anxiety, Inter personal Behavior)

BELIEFS (Rational and Irrational)

COPING

COUPLE RELATIONSHIP (see Marital/Couple Relationship)

DEATH CONCERNS

DEPRESSION AND GRIEF (also see Mood, Suicide)

GERIATRIC (also see listings under problem areas)

GUILT (also see Anxiety, Beliefs)

GENERAL HEALTH AND MENTAL HEALTH ISSUES

HOPE

IDENTITY

IMPULSIVITY

INTERPERSONAL BEHAVIOR (also see related issues)

[INTERPERSONAL BEHAVIOR (also see related issues)]

LOCUS OF CONTROL

SOCIAL SUPPORT

STRESS

SUICIDE (also see Depression, Satisfaction with Life)

TREATMENT ISSUES

SUBSTANCE ABUSE

Foreword

In 1987, when I composed the foreword for the first edition of this book, I attempted some prognosticating, as follows:

> Historians of behavioral science reviewing progress in the provision of human services at some point in the future will have to confront a curious issue. They will note that the twentieth century witnessed the development of a science of human behavior. They will also note that from mid-century on, clinicians treating behavioral and emotional disorders began relying more heavily on the systematic application of theories and facts emanating from this science to emotional and behavioral problems. They will make observations on various false starts in the development of our therapeutic techniques, and offer reasons for the initial acceptance of these "false starts" in which clinicians or practitioners would apply exactly the same intervention or style of intervention to every problem that came before them. But in the last analysis historians will applaud the slow but systematic development of ever more powerful specific procedures and techniques devised to deal successfully with the variety of specific emotional and behavioral problems. This will be one of the success stories of the twentieth century.
>
> Historians will also note a curious paradox which they will be hard pressed to explain. They will write that well into the 1990s and 2000s few practitioners or clinicians evaluated the effects of their new treatments in any systematic way. Rather, whatever the behavioral or emotional problem, they would simply ask clients from time to time how they were feeling or how they were doing. Sometimes this would be followed by reports in an official chart or record duly noting clients' replies. If families or married couples were involved, a report from only one member of the interpersonal system would often suffice. Occasionally, these attempts at "evaluation" would reach peaks of quantifiable objectivity by presenting the questions in somewhat different ways, such as "how are you feeling or doing compared to a year ago when you first came to see me?"
>
> Historians will point out wryly that this practice would be analogous to physicians periodically asking patients with blood infections or fractures "how are you feeling" without bothering to analyze blood samples or take X-rays. "How could this have been?" they will ask. In searching for answers they will examine records of clinical practice in the late twentieth century and find that the most usual response from clinicians was that

they were simply too busy to evaluate what they were doing. But the real reason, astute historians will note, is that they never learned how.

Now another generation has passed and the ascendance of empirically supported treatments as well as the fundamental necessity of assessing what we do has become apparent to educational and healthcare policy makers and practitioners alike. "Accountability" has become the watchword, and sophisticated measures of functioning and change have appeared under a variety of names, with perhaps "outcomes measurement" the most common label. Most practitioners now fully appreciate the ultimate logic and wisdom of evaluating what they do and, indeed, the curricula of all human service providers contain detailed coursework in this area. In addition, numerous books have appeared detailing the science and process of measurement. For many applied scientists who are now collaborating with practitioners directly in the field, these outcomes measures comprise the heart and soul of ascertaining the "effectiveness" or generalizability of interventions and procedures developed in applied and scientific centers. Under the name of "services research" or "effectiveness research" practitioners who measure what they do are making substantial contributions to our science and our practice.

Central to this task have been compendiums of instruments that pass methodological muster and are appropriate for use in a wide range of settings. Corcoran is one of the first to put together in one source such a compendium in the form of a description of the essentials of measurement accompanied by the most up-to-date and satisfactory measures of change for almost any problem a practitioner might encounter. In this the fifth edition, he continues with their extraordinarily successful endeavor, which enables practitioners to choose the most appropriate measurement instrument for problems they encounter in a matter of minutes. This book should be on the shelf of every practitioner working in a human service setting. Through the use of this book, practitioners will not only continue to meet the ever increasing demands for accountability, but will also satisfy their own desires for objective, quantifiable indications of progress in a manner that can be accomplished in no more than several minutes. As I predicted over 25 years ago, "the value of this book will increase," and that continues to be the case.

David H. Barlow, Ph.D., ABPP
Professor of Psychology and Psychiatry
Director of the Center for Anxiety
and Related Disorders at Boston University

Preface to the fifth edition

The purpose of this book, like the earlier editions, is to provide practitioners and students with a large variety of instruments that they can use to help them monitor and evaluate their practice, and for researchers interested in clinical outcomes. These instruments were specifically selected because they measure most of the common problems seen in clinical practice, they are very short, easy to score and administer, and most of all because we believe they will actually help you in your deliverance of human services. This edition, as was the case for the 2nd through the 4th editions, comes in two volumes. Volume 1contains measures for couple, families, and children. Volume 2 contains measures for adults with individual problems outside the family or couple context. This edition includes a number of new instruments, but we have intentionally tried to keep this to about 50 in order not to make the books so big that they would cost too much. Now the books contain over 550 measurement tools immediately available for clinical practice and research.

The most significant difference of the 5th edition from the earlier ones and we believe a considerable improvement, is the attention paid to the "Availability" section of each review. We have tried, and we have succeeded, at locating over 98% of all the authors, emails addresses. When the idea for *Measures for Clinical Practice* was first conceptualized by us in 1983 or 1984 (We cannot remember which year in particular), we did not have high speed computers or the internet and, of course, there was no such thing as "email." We did have the prototype which was called "bitnet" which stood for bits of information networked together. It all started with the need for scientists in northern southern California to be able to communicate with computers. Bitnet was only available to the military and to academics. Few academics used it, although we and Walter Hudson did in 1983 with dot-matrix tracker-pulled printers, as there was no such thing a computer screen. Video-conference from a smart phone was dreams of young men, and while it is common-place today, it will soon be replace with holographic conferencing and three-dimensional virtual classrooms.; even the most advance technology is temporary. While nearly comical today in comparison to the era of immediacy and the e-generation, seemed like a miracle then, and it was. It was the embryo to where we are today where it seems everybody has an email address and probably a social network page or two.

These advances have result in the vast majority of those instrument that are not available for copying from these books to be accessed very easily. If we could not locate an email address, which was only difficult for folks working in medical schools, we were able to locate a telephone number. We have intentionally avoided referencing Facebook or other social networks because we believe they will change dramatically and fairly quickly. While Facebook may have nearly one billion members, the same generation that gave it life, that is juniors and seniors in college, are beginning to realize that those pictures from spring break in Mexico may not help land that job in the downtown firm. We believe Facebook is in for a virtual world of change, so we have tried to avoid providing social network pages. When all that was available, we reluctantly provided a few, but only if there was no alternative.

As a consequence of the task, and it was herculean, using *Measures for Clinical Practice* should not be easier. Well, of course it could be easier if we had apps, but that is for the next edition, although apps would exist by then. In the meantime, we hope this improvement helps you use measures in your clinical practice.

But why?

We know through our own practices, and the practice of students and colleagues, how difficult it sometimes is to be clear about where you are going with a client and whether or not you actually get there. We also realize the frustration of trying to help a client be specific about a particular problem rather than leaving the problem ill-defined in some global, vague—and therefore far less useful—way. Without knowing precisely what needs to be changed in treatment, then little change is likely.

These essentially are problems in *measurement*: being able to be as clear as possible about what you and the clients are attempting to change. Without a clear definition on the problem, the typical frustrations of practice multiplied many times. We believe the instruments presented in these volumes will help relieve many of the frustrations you may have experienced in attempting to be precise about clients' problems. We also hope that we will be able to overcome the old and erroneous myth of clinical practice that "most of our clients' problems really aren't measurable." After nearly three decades of collecting instruments for clinical practice, we know this is not true. We hope to show you that the conditions seen in clinical practice are easily measured, and just how to go about using measures in your routine clinical practice.

Practitioners in all the human services –psychology, social work, counseling, psychiatry, nursing, and substance abuse workers—increasingly are being held accountable for monitoring and evaluating their practice. One of the simplest yet most productive ways of doing this is to have available a large number of instruments that measure the wide range of problems practitioners typically face. With a wide range of instruments, you simply select the one most appropriate for the problem of the client, whether individual, couple, group, or family, and use that instrument to monitor the course of treatment with your client.

There are a huge number of instruments relevant to clinical practice and more are becoming available all the time. Unfortunately, these instruments are widely scattered throughout the literature in journals, books and on the internet. With these volumes, we hope to save you the time, energy, and aggravation required to go to the literature t o find and select the best instrument. These volumes not only provide information about each of the instruments, copies are included so you can immediately determine their utility for your practice. With that purpose in mind, we have provided information as to where you can obtain copies of the instruments if you want to use them. Many of the authors have kindly granted permission for the reader to copy the instruments from these volumes.

These books are addressed to members of all the human services and helping professions who are engaged in clinical or therapeutic work and research with individuals –adults and children alike—, couples, groups, or families. Further, we believe the instruments contained in these books will be useful to practitioners from all theoretical orientations who are interested in monitoring and evaluating their practice. Indeed, one of the great appeals of these instruments is that they are not limited to use by adherents of only one of even a few clinical schools of thought or theoretical orientations. If you believe that an instrument is useful to being able to keep track of change in your client's condition over the course of treatment, then we think these books are for you.

Although we do not mean to oversimplify the task, we do believe these books can be useful to students and practitioners with very little experience in using measurement tools in their routine or daily clinical practice. Of course, we will provide information on how to use these instruments in your practice, including relevant data on norms and scoring for useful interpretation.

We hope these books will prove useful to you. Most of all, we hope they will help you enhance your effectiveness and efficiency of your practice. We hope these books help you help others.

ORGANIZATION OF THE BOOKS

Volume 1 includes an introduction to the basic principles of measurement, an overview of different types of measures, and an introduction to the rapid assessment inventories included in these books: how they were selected, how to administer and score them, and how t o avoid errors in their use. Volume 1 also contains descriptions and reviews of each instrument as well as copies of the instrument for use with couples, families and children. Volume 2 contains measures for use with adults whose problems or conditions of concern are not focused on the family or couple relationship.

In both volumes, the measures are listed alphabetically. However, for more help in finding the best instrument that is designed for a particular problem area, consult the third part of the table of contents. We present the instruments cross–indexed by the problem area. Thus, if you need an instrument for evaluating your client's anxiety, you could look under the heading "Anxiety" in the table of contents and see which instruments were designed for measuring the clinical condition. We hope this will facilitate the selection process and eventually the likelihood of using rapid assessment tools in clinical practice.

Instruments for Practice and Research

Introduction to Volume 2

Volume 2 of this book, unlike Volume 1, consists exclusively of measures you can use in your practice. In the first part of Volume 1, we reviewed the role of measurement to help in monitoring your client's progress and in evaluating your effectiveness. Our discussion included an overview of the basic principles of reliable and valid measures, the principles related to using measures in practice, and issues regarding interpreting scores. We also discussed some of the different types of measures, including the advantages and disadvantages of rapid assessment instruments (RAI) which are the focus of this book. While we believe this type of measurement is particularly valuable, we know that there may be times when you will want other measurement tools as well as additional rapid assessment instruments. To this end we presented information on determining what to measure within the context of practice, how to locate measures, and pertinent questions you might ask when evaluating what measure to use. Finally, we presented some guidelines for you to consider when administering instruments.

We now turn to the rationale and procedures we used to locate and select the instruments presented in both volumes. We have not included all rapid assessment instruments in existence, but we believe that the measures that are included cover most of the client problem areas commonly encountered in practice.

The primary rationale for including an instrument in these volumes was that it measures some specific client problem or treatment goal relevant to clinical practice. Thus, we excluded certain instruments that we believed just were not relevant to treatment. For example, a measure of one's personal epistemology was not included because this is not a frequently seen clinical problem.

We also excluded instruments that measure *practitioner* behaviors that might occur during your interventions. While there is indeed a growing concern for measuring what you do as a clinician, we believe you are more likely to want to measure particular *client* problems or treatment goals. This, after all, is one of the best ways to monitor practice.

We also decided to include mainly self-report instruments that can be used for rapid assessment. While numerous other types of measurement are available, as we discussed in Chapter 3 of Volume 1, we believe you are more likely to monitor your practice with those on which your client directly reports his or her perceptions, feelings, or experiences. Not only are clients often the best source of this information, but RAIs can be used in conjunction with your own clinical assessment.

In the same vein, we have included only those instruments that are relatively short. While there is no concrete agreement on how short an instrument should be in order to be used for rapid completion and scoring, we have included mainly those that are 50 items or less. There are a few, however, that are somewhat longer than 50 items; we included these because shorter measures were not available for that particular problem, because the instrument has subscales that can be used for rapid assessment, or because the instrument can be completed quickly despite its length.

Finally, most of the instruments we include have some evidence of reliability and/or validity. All have some practice utility, providing information that will help you monitor your client's progress and evaluate your effectiveness. In order to facilitate your use of these instruments to monitor practice, we have used a standardized format to critique each instrument to help you make judgments about which instruments would be best for your particular purposes. Like many measures in the behavioral and social sciences, some of those included here lack convincing reliability, validity, or other important data. This is not to imply that no data were available, just that more is needed to be thoroughly convincing. When you use one of these instruments, even one with sufficient reliability and validity data for that matter, we hope you will approach it with a judicious degree of caution and your own critique.

LOCATING THE INSTRUMENTS

In order to locate measurement tools, we began with a computer literature search. Additionally, we identified key volumes and journals that pertained to measurement in practice and reviewed them for appropriate instruments. (See Volume 1, Chapter 5, Tables 5.2 and 5.3.) For the journals we identified, all volumes were reviewed from 1974, except the *Journal of Clinical Psychology* and the *Journal of Personality Assessment*, which were reviewed from 1964 through 2011. For journals that first appeared later than 1974, all volumes were reviewed.

THE FINAL SELECTION

Whenever possible, we have tried to include more than one instrument to measure a problem, not only to provide a choice, but because different instruments tap different aspects of a problem. For example, you will notice there are several measures of anxiety. One of these may be more appropriate for use with a given client than others. Finally, there are obviously more instruments available to measure certain types of problems than other types. For example, relatively few measures are available to assess children, because children tend to have more difficulty in filling out self-report instruments than adults. Thus, while we included as many self-report RAIs as we could, we also included some observer rating scales for children. In this and a few other areas as well, where the nature of the people or problem suggests that self-report measures may be difficult to administer, observer rating scales may be an appropriate substitute.

In this volume, we have focused solely on measures for adults where the problem does not seem primarily concerned with other family members. We recognize that categorizing measures this way—adult measures in this volume and measures for couples, families, and children in Volume 1—leaves something to be desired. There is obvious overlap among many of the categories for several problems. Nevertheless, we hope this organization of the two volumes will make selection of measures for your practice as smooth as possible.

In sum, we have not included all available self-report rapid assessment instruments. For example, a few that we would have chosen to include, such as the Beck Depression Inventory (Beck et al., 1961), were not available for reproduction. However, we believe the instruments we have chosen cover most of the client problem areas commonly encountered in practice. Nevertheless, we must stress that other measures are available, and you should consider using them in conjunction with the RAIs included here. We hope the instruments presented in these two volumes will get you started and help you develop more measurement tools for use in monitoring clients and evaluating your practice effectiveness.

Instruments for Adults

Accepting the Past/Reminiscing about the Past (ACPAST/REM)

PURPOSE To measure acceptance of and reminiscence about the past as correlates of depressive symptoms.

AUTHORS Darcy A. Santor and David C. Zuroff

DESCRIPTION The ACPAST/REM is a 27-item scale comprising two components: acceptance of the past as a predictor of depressive symptoms and reminiscence of the past, which discriminates the evaluation of past experiences from the act of thinking about past experiences. The main component of the ACPAST/REM is the acceptance component, which is hypothesized as a core component of Erik Erikson's ego-integrity construct. Accepting the past involves how individuals evaluate and reflect on past experience and is conceptualized as one source of self-worth central to many formulations of depression. Thus, accepting the past is conceptualized as an internal representation of one's past as satisfying. Items on the scale related to accepting the past are marked with an "A" after the item, and items related to reminiscing about the past are marked with an "R." The ACPAST/REM provides an important conceptualization of the cognitive perspective on the internalization of past events and how they influence a person's assessment of the past. Thus the ACPAST/REM represents a potentially useful measure for cognitive practitioners attempting to help clients in reevaluating or restructuring their cognitions about the past.

NORMS The ACPAST/REM was initially studied with a sample of 84 Canadian citizens age 55 or over who were retired from McGill University. The largest single ethnic group was British. The modal age was 66 to 70; 65% of respondents were female and 35% were male. On the ACPAST, the mean for women was 87 (SD = 15) and for men the mean was 95 (SD = 13); this difference was statistically significant. On the REM, the mean for women was 39 (SD = 10) and for men the mean was 37 (SD = 10); this difference was not significant.

SCORING The ACPAST/REM is easily scored by summing items on each of the two components, being certain to reverse-score all items marked with a negative sign in the parentheses following each item.

RELIABILITY The ACPAST/REM has fair internal consistencies with alphas reported as greater than .70 for both scales. Data on stability were not reported.

VALIDITY The ACPAST was not significantly correlated with the REM. The ACPAST was significantly correlated in predicted directions with Ego-Integrity, with depression as measured by the CES-D, with negative affectivity as measured by the Negative Affectivity Scale and with physical symptoms, while the REM was not correlated with any of these scales. Neither scale was affected by social desirability response bias. Regression analysis revealed that Accepting the Past predicted depressive symptoms mainly in individuals reporting high negative affectivity.

PRIMARY REFERENCE Santor, D. A., and Zuroff, D. C. (1994). Depressive symptoms: Effects of negative affectivity and failing to accept the past, *Journal of Personality Assessment*, 63, 294–312.

AVAILABILITY Dr. Darcy A. Santor, Department of Psychiatry, Dalhousie University, Halifax, Nova Scotia, Canada, B3H 2E2. Email: dsantor@IS.dal.CA.

Here are some statements regarding the way you may feel about your past. Read each of the following statements and tell us whether you agree or disagree *and* to what extent. If you *strongly agree*, circle "7"; if you *strongly disagree*, circle "1." If you are *uncertain or don't know*, circle "4." Use whatever number is correct for the way that you feel. Think about each of the questions carefully before answering.

1	2	3	4	5	6	7
Strongly disagree	Disagree		Not certain/ don't know		Agree	Strongly agree

1. Thinking about my past brings more pain than pleasure. (A–)   1 2 3 4 5 6 7
2. I would rather talk about the present than about things from the past. (R–)   1 2 3 4 5 6 7
3. I feel comfortable talking about things I've done in the past. (A+)   1 2 3 4 5 6 7
4. Sometimes I have the feeling that I've never had the chance to live. (A–)   1 2 3 4 5 6 7
5. The difficult parts of my past I just ignore. (R–)   1 2 3 4 5 6 7
6. There are things from my past that I will have to set right, before I will be truly happy. (A–)   1 2 3 4 5 6 7
7. I do not think about experiences from the past very often. (R–)   1 2 3 4 5 6 7
8. There are things about my past that frighten me. (A–)   1 2 3 4 5 6 7
9. I tend to ignore the difficult parts of my past rather than dealing with them. (R–)   1 2 3 4 5 6 7
10. Although my past experiences are important to me, I prefer not to think about them. (R–)   1 2 3 4 5 6 7
11. There are some disappointments in my life that I will never be able to accept. (A–)   1 2 3 4 5 6 7
12. Some personal experiences from earlier on are still too difficult to think about. (A–)   1 2 3 4 5 6 7
13. Generally, I feel contented with the way my life has turned out. (A+)   1 2 3 4 5 6 7
14. There are things about my life that I have difficulty accepting. (A–)   1 2 3 4 5 6 7
15. I have not led a very meaningful life. (A–)   1 2 3 4 5 6 7
16. I look back on the things I've done with a sense of satisfaction. (A+)   1 2 3 4 5 6 7
17. I have no desire to think about my past. (R–)   1 2 3 4 5 6 7
18. I often think about past experiences. (R+)   1 2 3 4 5 6 7
19. All in all, I am comfortable with the choices I've made in the past. (A+)   1 2 3 4 5 6 7
20. When I look back on my past, I have a feeling of fulfillment. (A+)   1 2 3 4 5 6 7
21. I like to reminisce about my past. (R+)   1 2 3 4 5 6 7
22. I still feel angry about certain childhood experiences. (A–)   1 2 3 4 5 6 7

23. I try to remember as much from my past as I possibly can, both the good experiences and the bad experiences. (R+) 1 2 3 4 5 6 7

24. I have not rejected my past, nor have I accepted it, I just leave my past alone. (R−) 1 2 3 4 5 6 7

25. I don't worry about things that happened a long time ago. (A−) 1 2 3 4 5 6 7

26. I often tell others about experiences from my past. (R+) 1 2 3 4 5 6 7

27. I generally feel contented with what I have done so far in life. (A+) 1 2 3 4 5 6 7

Acculturation Rating Scale for Mexican Americans—II (ARSMA-II)

PURPOSE To assess acculturation processes.

AUTHORS Israel Cuellar, Bill Arnold, and Roberto Maldonado

DESCRIPTION The ARSMA-II comprises two scales designed to measure acculturation by measuring cultural orientation as well as modes of acculturation. The first scale contains 30 items from which are derived a Mexican orientation subscale (MOS) and an Anglo orientation subscale (AOS) which yield a multidimensional configuration with two acculturation modes, integration and assimilation. The second scale, called the marginality scale, has 18 items which in conjunction with Scale 1 produce scores to measure separation and marginalization as modes of acculturation. Both scales are written in English and in Spanish. Each scale can be administered, scored, and interpreted individually. Scale 1 allows subjects to obtain high or low scores with each culture (Anglo orientation and Mexican orientation) independent of the other. Scale 2, the marginality scale, allows subjects to indicate the difficulty they have in accepting aspects of each of three cultural groups (Anglo, Mexican, and Mexican American) independently. The scales can be used to reliably assess cultural diversity, to better understand an individual client's psychological makeup regarding acculturation, ethnocultural, and identity characteristics; they have relevance for clinical assessment practices in cross-cultural contexts especially in the provision of culturally competent services.

NORMS The ARSMA-II was studied with 479 university students who represented five generation levels of Mexicans, Mexican Americans, and white non-Hispanics. Subjects were drawn from groups varying in socioeconomic status and proportionately representing both genders (43% male, 48% female, 10% missing gender data). The mean education level was between one and two years of college; mean SES on a 9-point scale was 5. The original article discusses a variety of means and standard deviations for the two scales including mean acculturation scores, mean Anglo orientation scores, mean Mexican orientation scores, and a variety of acculturative types, including cut-off points for each of the acculturation types. A typology of acculturative types was generated using six categories ranging from "traditional Mexican" to "assimilated," and the cut-off scores for each of these categories is provided in the original article. The overall means and standard deviations obtained for the ARSMA-II scales are: AOS mean = 3.82 (SD = .57), MOS mean = 3.28 (SD = .84), marginality mean = 41.31 (SD = 12.19), Anglo marginality mean = 4.70 (SD = 5.28), Mexican marginality mean = 13.98 (SD = 5.68), and Mexican American marginality mean = 12.61 (SD = 4.73).

SCORING Scale 1 of ARSMA-II comprises a 13-item Anglo orientation subscale (AOS) (items 2, 4, 7, 9, 10, 13, 15, 16, 19, 23, 25, 27, and 30) and a Mexican orientation subscale (MOS) of 17 items (items 1, 3, 5, 6, 8, 11, 12, 14, 17, 18, 20, 21, 22, 24, 26, 28, and 29). The sum of the AOS is divided by 13 to obtain a mean score for that subscale. The sum of the MOS is divided by 17 to obtain a mean for that subscale. The MOS mean is subtracted from the AOS mean to obtain a linear acculturation score that represents an individual score along a continuum from very Mexican-oriented to very Anglo-oriented. Scale 2, the marginality scale (MARG), has a total of 18 items which are added to obtain a marginality score that reflects total difficulty accepting Anglo, Mexican, and Mexican-American ideas, beliefs, customs, and values. The MARG comprises three subscales reflecting difficulty accepting one's own as well as other cultures. The three subscales are Anglo marginality composed of items 1–6, Mexican marginality composed of items 6–12, and Mexican-American marginality which is composed of items 13–18. The score for each of the MARG's three subscales is the sum of the six items for that subscale. The original article lists a variety of cutting criteria used to generate subtypes based on an individual score on all of the scales and subscales of the ARSMA-II.

RELIABILITY All scales and subscales with the exception of the Mexican marginality subscale have good to excellent reliability, with a coefficient alpha ranging from .83 to .91 (alpha for Mexican marginality was .68). All scales had good to excellent test-retest reliability at 1-week intervals with the correlations ranging from .72 for Anglo marginality to .96 for the MOS.

VALIDITY The ARSMA-II has excellent concurrent validity with a correlation of .89 between the scores of ARSMA-II and the original ARSMA, which has established validity as a measure of acculturation. Scores on the ARSMA-II also showed good predictive validity in that there was a proportional increase in acculturation scores with acculturation toward Anglo culture based on a correlation between acculturation and generational status. Factor analysis of the 17 item MOS and the 13 item AOS also showed good factorial validity.

PRIMARY REFERENCE Cuellar, I., Arnold, B., and Maldonado, R. (1995). Acculturation rating scale for Mexican Americans—II: A revision of the original ARSMA scale, *Hispanic Journal of Behavioral Sciences*, 17, 275–304. Reprinted with permission of the authors and Sage Publications.

AVAILABILITY Sage Publications Incorporated, *Hispanic Journal of Behavioral Sciences*, 2455 Teller Road, Thousand Oaks, CA 91320.

ENGLISH VERSION

Name: _____

Male: _____ Female: _____

Age: _____ DOB: _____ / _____ / _____

Marital Status: _____

What is your religious preference? _____

(a) Last grade you completed in school: *Circle your choice*

1. = Elementary–6
2. = 7–8
3. = 9–12
4. = 1–2 years of college
5. = 3–4 years of college
6. = College graduate and higher

(b) In what country? _____

Circle the generation that best applies to *you*. Circle only one.

1. 1st generation = You were born in Mexico or other country.

2. 2nd generation = You were born in USA; either parent born in Mexico or other country.

3. 3rd generation = You were born in USA, both parents born in USA and all grandparents born in Mexico or other country.

4. 4th generation = You and your parents born in USA and at least one grandparent born in Mexico or other country with remainder born in the USA.

5. 5th generation = You and your parents born in the USA and all grandparents born in the USA.

SCALE 1—ENGLISH VERSION

Circle a number between 1 and 5 next to each item that best applies.

	Not at all	Very little or not very often or	Moderately	Much or very often	Extremely often or almost always
1. I speak Spanish	1	2	3	4	5
2. I speak English	1	2	3	4	5
3. I enjoy speaking Spanish	1	2	3	4	5
4. I associate with Anglos	1	2	3	4	5

continued

	Not at all	Very little or not very often	Moderately	Much or very often	Extremely often or almost always
5. I associate with Mexicans and/or Mexican Americans	1	2	3	4	5
6. I enjoy listening to Spanish language music	1	2	3	4	5
7. I enjoy listening to English language music	1	2	3	4	5
8. I enjoy Spanish language TV	1	2	3	4	5
9. I enjoy English language TV	1	2	3	4	5
10. I enjoy English language movies	1	2	3	4	5
11. I enjoy Spanish language movies	1	2	3	4	5
12. I enjoy reading (e.g., books in Spanish)	1	2	3	4	5
13. I enjoy reading (e.g., books in English)	1	2	3	4	5
14. I write (e.g., letters in Spanish)	1	2	3	4	5
15. I write (e.g., letters in English)	1	2	3	4	5
16. My thinking is done in the English language	1	2	3	4	5
17. My thinking is done in the Spanish language	1	2	3	4	5
18. My contact with Mexico has been	1	2	3	4	5
19. My contact with the USA has been	1	2	3	4	5
20. My father identifies or identified himself as 'Mexicano'	1	2	3	4	5
21. My mother identifies or identified herself as 'Mexicana'	1	2	3	4	5
22. My friends, while I was growing up, were of Mexican origin	1	2	3	4	5
23. My friends, while I was growing up, were of Anglo origin	1	2	3	4	5
24. My family cooks Mexican foods	1	2	3	4	5
25. My friends now are of Anglo origin	1	2	3	4	5
26. My friends now are of Mexican origin	1	2	3	4	5
27. I like to identify myself as an Anglo American	1	2	3	4	5
28. I like to identify myself as a Mexican American	1	2	3	4	5
29. I like to identify myself as a Mexican	1	2	3	4	5
30. I like to identify myself as an American	1	2	3	4	5

Nombre: _____

Masculino: _____ Femenino: _____

Edad: _____ Día de Nacimiento: _____

Estado Civil: _____

Cual es su religión predilecta? _____

(a) ¿Hasta que grado fué a la escuela?
Indique con un círculo la respuesta

        1. = Primaria–6
        2. = Secundaria 7–8
        3. = Preparatoria 9–12
        4. = Universidad o Colegio 1–2 años
        5. = Universidad o Colegio 3–4 años
        6. = Graduado, o grado mas alto de Colegio o Universidad

(b) ¿En que país? _____

Indique con un círculo el numero de la generación que considere adecuada para *usted*. Dé solamente una repuesta.

1. 1a. generación = Usted nació en México o otro país [no en los Estados Unidos (USA)].

2. 2a. generación = Usted nació en los Estados Unidos Americanos (USA), sus padres nacieron en México o en otro país.

3. 3a. generación = Usted nació en los Estados Unidos Americanos (USA), sus padres tambien nacieron en los Estados Unidos (USA) y sus abuelos nacieron en México o en otro país.

4. 4a. generación = Usted nació en los Estados Unidos Americanos (USA), sus padres nacieron en los Estados Unidos Americanos (USA) y por lo menos uno de sus abuelos nació en México o algun otro país.

5. 5a. generación = Usted y sus padres y todos sus abuelos nacieron en los Estados Unidos (USA).

SCALE 1—VERSION EN ESPANOL

Marque con un círculo el numero entre 1 y 5 a la respuesta que sea más adecuada para usted.

	Nada	Un poquito o aveces	Moderato	Mucho o muy frecuente	Muchísimo o casi todo siempre
1. Yo hablo Español	1	2	3	4	5
2. Yo hablo Inglés	1	2	3	4	5
3. Me gusta hablar en Español	1	2	3	4	5
4. Me asocio con Anglos	1	2	3	4	5

continued

	Nada	Un poquito o aveces	Moderato	Mucho o muy frecuente	Muchísimo o casi todo siempre
5. Yo me asocio con Mexicanos o con Norte Americanos	1	2	3	4	5
6. Me gusta la musica Mexicana (musica en idioma Español)	1	2	3	4	5
7. Me gusta la musica de idioma Inglés	1	2	3	4	5
8. Me gusta ver programas en la televisión que sean en Español	1	2	3	4	5
9. Me gusta ver programas en la televisión que sean en Inglés	1	2	3	4	5
10. Me gusta ver peliculas en Inglés	1	2	3	4	5
11. Me gusta ver películas en Español	1	2	3	4	5
12. Me gusta leer (e.g., libros en Español)	1	2	3	4	5
13. Me gusta leer (e.g., libros en Inglés)	1	2	3	4	5
14. Escribo (e.g., cartas en Español)	1	2	3	4	5
15. Escribo (e.g., cartas en Inglés)	1	2	3	4	5
16. Mis piensamientos ocurren en el idioma Inglés	1	2	3	4	5
17. Mis piensamientos ocurren en el idioma Español	1	2	3	4	5
18. Mi contacto con Mexico ha sido	1	2	3	4	5
19. Mi contacto con los Estados Unidos Americanos ha sido	1	2	3	4	5
20. Mi padre se identifica (o se identificaba) como Mexicano	1	2	3	4	5
21. Mi madre se identifica (o se identificaba) como Mexicana	1	2	3	4	5
22. Mis amigos(as) de mí niñez eran de origen Mexicano	1	2	3	4	5
23. Mis amigos(as) de mí niñez eran de origen Anglo Americano	1	2	3	4	5
24. Mi familia cocina comidas Mexicanas	1	2	3	4	5
25. Mis amigos recientes son Anglo Americanos	1	2	3	4	5
26. Mis amigos recientes son Mexicanos	1	2	3	4	5
27. Me gusta identificarme como Anglo Americano	1	2	3	4	5
28. Me gusta identificarme como Norte Americano* (México-Americano)	1	2	3	4	5
29. Me gusta identificarme como Mexicano	1	2	3	4	5

	Nada	Un poquito o aveces	Moderato	Mucho o muy frecuente	Muchísimo o casi todo siempre
30. Me gusta identificarme como un(a) Americano(a)	1	2	3	4	5

* Estado unidenses de origen Mexicano

SCALE 2—ENGLISH VERSION

Use the scale below to answer questions 1–18 below.

	Not at all	Very little or not very often	Moderately	Much or very often	Extremely often or almost always
1. I have difficulty accepting some ideas held by Anglos	1	2	3	4	5
2. I have difficulty accepting certain attitudes held by Anglos	1	2	3	4	5
3. I have difficulty accepting some behaviors exhibited by Anglos	1	2	3	4	5
4. I have difficulty accepting some values held by some Anglos	1	2	3	4	5
5. I have difficulty accepting certain practices and customs commonly found in some Anglos	1	2	3	4	5
6. I have, or think I would have, difficulty accepting Anglos as close personal friends	1	2	3	4	5
7. I have difficulty accepting ideas held by some Mexicans	1	2	3	4	5
8. I have difficulty accepting certain attitudes held by Mexicans	1	2	3	4	5
9. I have difficulty accepting some behaviors exhibited by Mexicans	1	2	3	4	5
10. I have difficulty accepting some values held by some Mexicans	1	2	3	4	5
11. I have difficulty accepting certain practices and customs commonly found in some Mexicans	1	2	3	4	5
12. I have, or think I would have, difficulty accepting Mexicans as close personal friends	1	2	3	4	5
13. I have difficulty accepting ideas held by some Mexican Americans	1	2	3	4	5

continued

	Not at all	Very little or not very often	Moderately	Much or very often	Extremely often or almost always
14. I have difficulty accepting certain attitudes held by Mexican Americans	1	2	3	4	5
15. I have difficulty accepting some behaviors exhibited by Mexican Americans	1	2	3	4	5
16. I have difficulty accepting some values held by Mexican Americans	1	2	3	4	5
17. I have difficulty accepting certain practices and customs commonly found in some Mexican Americans	1	2	3	4	5
18. I have, or think I would have, difficulty accepting Mexican Americans as close personal friends	1	2	3	4	5

SCALE 2—VERSION EN ESPANOL

Utilice la escala que sigue para contestar preguntas 1–18.

	Nada	Un poquito o aveces	Moderato	Mucho o muy frecuente	Muchísimo o casi todo el tiempo
1. Tengo dificultad aceptando ideas de algunos Anglo Americanos	1	2	3	4	5
2. Tengo dificultad aceptando ciertas actitudes de los Anglo Americanos	1	2	3	4	5
3. Tengo dificultad aceptando algunos comportamientos de los Anglo Americanos	1	2	3	4	5
4. Tengo dificultad aceptando algunos valores que tienen los Anglo Americanos	1	2	3	4	5
5. Tengo dificultad aceptando ciertas costumbres entre algunos Anglo Americanos	1	2	3	4	5
6. Tengo, o creo que sí tuviera, dificultad aceptando Anglo Americanos como buenos amigos	1	2	3	4	5
7. Tengo dificultad aceptando ideas de algunos Mexicanos	1	2	3	4	5
8. Tengo dificultad aceptando ciertas actitudes de algunos Mexicanos	1	2	3	4	5

	Nada	Un poquito o aveces	Moderato	Mucho o muy frecuente	Muchísimo o casi todo el tiempo
9. Tengo dificultad aceptando algunos comportamientos de los Mexicanos	1	2	3	4	5
10. Tengo dificultad aceptando algunos valores que tienen los Mexicanos	1	2	3	4	5
11. Tengo dificultad aceptando ciertas costumbres entre algunos Mexicanos	1	2	3	4	5
12. Tengo, o creo que sí tuviera, dificultad aceptando a Mexicanos como buenos amigos	1	2	3	4	5
13. Tengo dificultad aceptando ideas de algunos Mexico-Americanos*	1	2	3	4	5
14. Tengo dificultad aceptando ciertas actitudes de algunos Mexico-Americanos*	1	2	3	4	5
15. Tengo dificultad aceptando algunos comportamientos de los Mexico-Americanos*	1	2	3	4	5
16. Tengo dificultad aceptando algunos valores que tienen Mexico-Americanos*	1	2	3	4	5
17. Tengo dificultad aceptando ciertas costumbres entre algunos Mexico-Americanos*	1	2	3	4	5
18. Tengo, o creo que sí tuviera, dificultad aceptando Mexico-Americanos* como buenos amigos	1	2	3	4	5

* Estadounidenses de origen Mexicano

Achievement Anxiety Test (AAT)

PURPOSE To measure anxiety about academic achievement.

AUTHORS Richard Alpert and Ralph N. Haber

DESCRIPTION The AAT is a 19-item instrument designed to measure anxiety about academic achievement. The AAT consists of two separate scales, a "facilitating scale" (items 2, 6, 8, 9, 10, 12, 15, 16, 18) which assesses anxiety as a motivator, and a "debilitating scale" (remainder of items) which assesses the degree to which anxiety interferes with performance. The two scales are administered on one questionnaire but scored separately. The value of these scales is in their specificity, both in defining the two aspects of anxiety, and in measuring anxiety specifically related to academic achievement. The AAT predicts academic performance, particularly verbal aptitude, more accurately than do the general anxiety scales.

NORMS The AAT was developed with several samples of undergraduate introductory psychology students. The total number of subjects was 323, with no other demographic data reported, although it appeared that respondents were male. The mean score on the facilitating scale was 27.28, and on the debilitating scale, 26.33.

SCORING The two subscales are scored separately with scores on each of the items summed to produce the overall score. Each item has a different response category, although all are on 5-point scales indicating the degree to which the statement applies to the respondent. Items 8, 10, and 12 from the facilitating scale are reverse-scored as are items 3, 4, 13, 17, and 19 from the debilitating scale.

RELIABILITY The AAT has excellent stability: ten-week test-retest correlations of .83 for the facilitating and .87 for the debilitating scale, and eight-month test-retest correlations of .75 for the facilitating scale and .76 for the debilitating scale. No internal consistency information was reported.

VALIDITY The AAT has good criterion-related validity, correlating significantly with several measures of academic performance. Both subscales also are correlated with verbal aptitude. The AAT also has good predictive validity, significantly predicting grade point averages.

PRIMARY REFERENCE Alpert, R., and Haber, R. N. (1960). Anxiety in academic achievement situations, *Journal of Abnormal and Social Psychology*, 61, 207–215. Instrument reproduced with permission of the American Psychological Association.

AVAILABILITY May be copied from this volume.

Please circle the number for each item that comes closest to describing you on a sliding scale from "1" to "5."

1. Nervousness while taking an exam or test hinders me from doing well.

    Always   Never
    1   2   3   4   5

2. I work most effectively under pressure, as when the task is very important.

    Always   Never
    1   2   3   4   5

3. In a course where I have been doing poorly, my fear of a bad grade cuts down my efficiency.

    Never   Always
    1   2   3   4   5

4. When I am poorly prepared for an exam or test, I get upset, and do less well than even my restricted knowledge should allow.

    This never   This practic-
    happens   ally always
    to me   happens to me
    1   2   3   4   5

5. The more important the examination, the less well I seem to do.

    Always   Never
    1   2   3   4   5

6. While I may (or may not) be nervous before taking an exam, once I start, I seem to forget to be nervous.

    I always   I am always
    forget   nervous
    1   2   3   4   5

7. During exams or tests, I block on questions to which I know the answers, even though I remember them as soon as the exam is over.

    This always   I never block
    happens   on questions to
    to me   which I know
                                                the answers
    1   2   3   4   5

8. Nervousness while taking a test helps me do better.

    It never helps   It often helps
    1   2   3   4   5

9. When I start a test, nothing is able to distract me.

    This is always   This is never
    true of me   true of me
    1   2   3   4   5

10. In courses in which the total grade is based mainly on one exam, I seem to do better than other people.

Never				Always
1	2	3	4	5

11. I find that my mind goes blank at the beginning of an exam, and it takes me a few minutes before I can function.

I almost always blank out at first				I never blank out at first
1	2	3	4	5

12. I look forward to exams.

Never				Always
1	2	3	4	5

13. I am so tired from worrying about an exam, that I find I almost don't care how well I do by the time I start the test.

I never feel this way				I almost always feel this way
1	2	3	4	5

14. Time pressure on an exam causes me to do worse than the rest of the group under similar conditions.

Time pressure always seems to make me do worse than others on an exam				Time pressure never seems to make me do worse than others on an exam
1	2	3	4	5

15. Although "cramming" under preexamination tension is not effective for most people, I find that if the need arises, I can learn material immediately before an exam, even under considerable pressure, and successfully retain it to use on the exam.

I am always able to use the "crammed" material successfully				I am never able to use the "crammed" material successfully
1	2	3	4	5

16. I enjoy taking a difficult exam more than an easy one.

Always				Never
1	2	3	4	5

17. I find myself reading exam questions without understanding them and I must go back over them so that they will make sense.

Never				Always
1	2	3	4	5

18. The more important the exam or test, the better I seem to do.

This is true of me				This is not true of me
1	2	3	4	5

19. When I don't do well on a difficult item at the beginning of an exam, it tends to upset me so that I block on every easy question later on.

This never happens to me				This almost always happens to me
1	2	3	4	5

Activity-Feeling Scale II (AFS-II)

PURPOSE To measure organismic needs and motivation.

AUTHOR Johnmarshall Reeve

DESCRIPTION This 16-item instrument measures organismic needs which theoretically give rise to intrinsic motivation. There are four organismic needs: competence, self-determination, relatedness, and curiosity. Tension is antithetical to motivation. Competence refers to one's perceived capability for achievement. Self-determination refers to one's internal locus of causality. Relatedness concerns the emotional bonds and attachments between persons. Curiosity concerns seeking information and dispels moments of uncertainty. Tension, in contrast, diminishes motivation. In completing the scales, clients are asked to rate their affective reactions to a target activity, such as work or recreational activity. This allows one to use the AFS-II for specific problems when a client may lack motivation, such as problems related to procrastination. Clinicians may also find the AFS-II useful in evaluating a client's motivation in treatment or their response to various homework assignments. The AFS-II consists of four subscales for each of the intrinsic needs and for tension.

NORMS Specific norms are difficult to report because scores vary according to the activity being evaluated. A sample of 50 college students exposed to an intrinsically motivating activity reported means (and standard deviations) for competence, self-determination, relatedness, curiosity, and tension of 4.45 (1.45), 5.52 (.99), 2.12 (1.26), 3.85 (.79), and 3.80 (1.73), respectively.

SCORING Respondents indicate their degree of agreement to any particular stimulus recorded on the scale. Scores are the sum of each item score averaged by the number of items. Competence is composed of "capable" + "competent" + "achieving." Self-determination is composed of "offered choices what to do" + "that my participation is voluntary" + "my decision to continue is voluntary" + "forced to participate" (which is reverse-scored). Relatedness is composed of "involved with friends" + "part of a team" + "brotherly/sisterly." Curiosity is composed of "curious" + "want to know more about it" + "stimulated." Tension is composed of "pressured" + "stressed" + "uptight." Scale scores range from 1 to 7 with higher scores reflecting stronger intrinsic needs.

RELIABILITY Reliability has been estimated with Cronbach's alpha from seven studies. The average internal consistency for each subscale was: competence, .85; self-determination, .70; relatedness, .79; curiosity, .72; and tension .92. Test-retest reliability over a one-hour period was estimated in two studies as follows: competence, .52 and .68; self-determination, .64 and .62; relatedness, .65 and .59; curiosity, .66 and .62; tension, .61 and .63. Additional and similar coefficients of stability over five consecutive weeks are reported from a sample of students in an introductory psychology class. The moderate test-retest coefficients suggest that intrinsic needs are "states" as opposed to enduring aspects of the individual ("traits").

VALIDITY Validity has been tested with factorial validity with the subscales showing modest intercorrelations, ranging from .09 to .34. Predictive validity was estimated by correlating AFS-II scales with self-report and behavioral measures of intrinsic motivation in three separate studies. There were strong correlations between AFS-II scales and the self-report measures, ranging from .22 to .77, but only moderate correlations with the behavioral measures, ranging from .12 to .36. Construct validity has been shown by differences in competence scores for subjects in an experiment that manipulated success and failure where subjects receiving an objective source of competence information reported significantly greater perceived competence than those receiving information suggesting incompetence. Similar construct validity results are reported for the self-determination, relatedness, and curiosity scales. Validity also has been estimated by determining the emotional correlates of each scale. Competence is correlated with positive emotions and enjoyment and inversely with negative emotions. These results suggest the emotional consequence of competence is enjoyment, while the emotional experience of incompetence is distress. Fairly similar associations are reported for the other scales, although there were some complex relationships between the needs and emotionality.

PRIMARY REFERENCES Reeve, J., and Robinson, D. T. (1987). Toward a reconceptualization of intrinsic motivation: Correlates and factor structure of the activity-feeling scale, *Journal of Social Behavior and Personality*, 2, 23–36. Chang-way, L., and Reeve, J. (1989). *Manual for the Activity-Feeling Scale II* (submitted for publication).

AVAILABILITY Johnmarshall Reeve, College of Education, The University of Iowa, Iowa City, IA 52242. Email: johnmarshall@uiowa.edu.

The items listed below ask how puzzle-solving makes you feel at the present time. For each item, circle a number near 7 if you strongly agree that puzzle-solving makes you feel that way. Circle a number near 1 if you strongly disagree that puzzle-solving makes you feel that way. If you agree and disagree equally that puzzle-solving makes you feel that way, then circle a number near 4.

(Target Activity) Makes Me Feel:

	Strongly disagree			Agree and disagree equally			Strongly agree
Capable	1	2	3	4	5	6	7
Offered choices what to do	1	2	3	4	5	6	7
Curious	1	2	3	4	5	6	7
Part of a team	1	2	3	4	5	6	7
Stressed	1	2	3	4	5	6	7
Involved with friends	1	2	3	4	5	6	7
Stimulated	1	2	3	4	5	6	7
Pressured	1	2	3	4	5	6	7
Competent	1	2	3	4	5	6	7
Want to know more about it	1	2	3	4	5	6	7
That my participation is voluntary	1	2	3	4	5	6	7
My decision to continue is voluntary	1	2	3	4	5	6	7
Uptight	1	2	3	4	5	6	7
Achieving	1	2	3	4	5	6	7
Brotherly/sisterly	1	2	3	4	5	6	7
Forced to participate	1	2	3	4	5	6	7

Acute Stress Disorder Scale (ASDS)

PURPOSE To measure acute stress.

AUTHORS Richard A. Bryant, Michelle L. Moulds, and Rachel M. Guthrie

DESCRIPTION The ASDS is a 19-item scale designed to index Acute Stress Disorder (ASD) and predict Post Traumatic Stress Disorder (PTSD). ASD is a disorder that was new to DSM-IV; research shows that people who respond to acute stress according to the several DSM criteria of ASD will suffer within two years from PTSD in 75 to 80% of the cases. Thus, a measure to identify ASD is very important to have available for practitioners and researchers alike. The ASDS is comprised of four subscales based on factor analysis. These subscales correspond to most of the DSM criteria for ASD. The subscales are: Dissociation (D; 5 items); Reexperiencing (R; 4 items); Avoidance (A; 4 items); and Intrusion/Arousal (IA; 6 items) (individual items on the subscales are available in the Primary Reference).

NORMS The ASDS was developed in a series of studies in Australia involving almost 300 respondents. In one study, 65 men and 34 women with a mean age of 31.59 years (SD = 11.28) participated. All respondents had survived accidents or nonsexual assault. The sample was comprised of 65 white respondents, 12 Asian, and 22 respondents of Mediterranean descent. The mean score for this sample was 44.93 (SD = 22.4). However, for those respondents diagnosed with ASD, the mean was 65.11 (SD = 14.74) compared to 36.97 (SD = 19.54) for those without ASD.

SCORING The ASDS is easily scored by summing items for the subscale and total scores. Higher scores indicate greater magnitude of the problem. A cut-off score on the total scale is 56, over which clients are most likely to develop PTSD.

RELIABILITY The ASDS has excellent internal consistency with an alpha of .96 for the entire scale, and alphas of .84, .87, .92, and .93 for D, R, A, and IA, respectively. The ASDS also has excellent 2- to 7-day stability with a test-retest correlation of .94 for the total scale and correlations of .85 to .94 for the subscales.

VALIDITY The ASDS has established excellent convergent, known-groups, and predictive validity. The ASDS is correlated significantly with a number of valid measures of psychopathology such as the Beck Anxiety Inventory. The ASDS distinguishes between those with and without ASD. And the ASDS also can predict with 91% accuracy, using the cut-off of 56, those who will develop PTSD.

PRIMARY REFERENCE Bryant, R. A., Moulds, M. L., and Guthrie, R. M. (2000). Acute Stress Disorder Scale: A self-report measure of Acute Stress Disorder, *Psychological Assessment,* 12, 61–68. Instrument reproduced with permission of Dr. Bryant.

AVAILABILITY Dr. Richard A. Bryant, School of Psychology, University of New South Wales, NSW 2052, Australia. Email: r.bryant@unsw.edu.au.

Name: Date:

Briefly describe your recent traumatic experience:

Did the experience frighten you?   Yes   or   No

Please answer each of these questions about how you have felt since the event. Circle one number next to each question to indicate how you have felt.

1   *Not at all*
2   *Mildly*
3   *Medium*
4   *Quite a bit*
5   *Very much*

During or after the trauma, did you ever feel numb or distant from your emotions?
During or after the trauma, did you ever feel in a daze?
During or after the trauma, did things around you ever feel unreal or dreamlike?
During or after the trauma, did you ever feel distant from your normal self or like you were watching it happen from outside?
Have you been unable to recall important aspects of the trauma?
Have memories of the trauma kept entering your mind?
Have you had bad dreams or nightmares about the trauma?
Have you felt as if the trauma was about to happen again?
Do you feel very upset when you are reminded of the trauma?
Have you tried not to think about the trauma?
Have you tried not to talk about the trauma?
Have you tried to avoid situations or people that remind you of the trauma?
Have you tried not to feel upset or distressed about the trauma?
Have you had trouble sleeping since the trauma?
Have you felt more irritable since the trauma?
Have you had difficulty concentrating since the trauma?
Have you become more alert to danger since the trauma?
Have you become jumpy since the trauma?
When you are reminded of the trauma, do you sweat or tremble or does your heart beat fast?

Adherence Determinants Questionnaire (ADQ)

PURPOSE To measure adherence to cancer regimens.

AUTHORS M. Robin DiMatteo, et al.

DESCRIPTION The ADQ is a 38-item questionnaire designed to assess patient adherence to cancer control regimens. Patient nonadherence to medical treatment is a widespread phenomenon, occurring in many settings with prevalence rates that range up to 93% of patients. Noncompliance is a particularly important issue with life-threatening diseases such as cancer. The ADQ was designed to provide opportunities for practitioners to develop a focus for intervention with patients who may be noncompliant, and to evaluate whether interventions are successful in increasing compliance or adherence to medical regimens. The ADQ measures seven elements of patients' adherence to medical treatment and prevention; these seven elements are divided into subscales as presented on the actual questionnaire and include interpersonal aspects of care, perceived utility (benefits/costs and efficacy), perceived severity, perceived susceptibility, subjective norms, intentions, and supports/barriers.

NORMS The ADQ was developed in a series of studies with patients in a number of different medical treatment programs including abnormal pap smears, a rehabilitation program, a head and neck cancer study program, and a low-fat diet program. A total of 316 people participated across the four studies. Subjects were of mixed ethnicity, predominantly female, and had a wide age range across the four individual studies. Demographic data are available in the original article. The means on the subscales were as follows: interpersonal aspects of care 32.99 (SD = 4.53); perceived utility 33.82 (SD = 3.71); severity 11.06 (SD = 2.87); susceptibility 10.97 (SD = 2.87); subjective norms 4.18 (SD = 5.17); intentions 17.53 (SD = 2.35); supports barriers 14.81 (SD = 2.70). The scale can also be transformed to a 0–100 range so that all scales are on the same metric. These data are available in the original article.

SCORING All the subscales except for subjective norms are scored the same way by summing individual item scores. Thus, for the first two subscales the range is from 8 to 40; for the remainder of the subscales, except for subjective norms, the range is from 4 to 20. The subjective norms score is the sum of three multiplicative items: (item 25 × item 26) + (item 27 × item 28) + (item 29 × item 30); this produces a range from −18 to +18.

RELIABILITY The ADQ has fair internal consistency with alphas that range from .63 to .94 and a median alpha of .76. Data on stability were not reported.

VALIDITY The ADQ has fair to good validity as determined by several evaluations of the subscales in regression analyses as related to a number of characteristics of adherence. Responses on the ADQ are not affected by social desirability response set.

PRIMARY REFERENCE DiMatteo, M. R., et al. (1993). Patient adherence to cancer control regimens: Scale development and initial validation, *Psychological Assessment*, 5, 102–112.

AVAILABILITY Dr. M. Robin DiMatteo, Department of Psychology-075, University of California, Riverside, CA, 92521-0426. Email: robin.dimatteo@ucr.edu.

In the space provided to the left, please indicate how much you agree or disagree with each statement using the following scale:

1 = Strongly disagree
2 = Disagree
3 = Neither agree nor disagree
4 = Agree
5 = Strongly agree

___ 1. The doctors and other health professionals sometimes ignore what I tell them.
___ 2. The doctors and other health professionals listen carefully to what I have to say.
___ 3. The doctors and other health professionals answer all my questions.
___ 4. Sometimes the doctors and other health professionals use medical terms without explaining what they mean.
___ 5. I trust that the doctors and other health professionals have my best interest at heart.
___ 6. The doctors and other health professionals act like I'm wasting their time.
___ 7. The doctors and other health professionals treat me in a very friendly and courteous manner.
___ 8. The doctors and other health professionals show little concern for me.
___ 9. The benefits of my treatment plan outweigh any difficulty I might have in following it.
___ 10. My treatment plan is too much trouble for what I get out of it.
___ 11. Because my treatment plan is too difficult, it is not worth following.
___ 12. Following my treatment plan is better for me than not following my treatment plan.
___ 13. Following my treatment plan will help me to be healthy.
___ 14. I'll be just as healthy if I avoid my treatment plan.
___ 15. I believe that my treatment plan will help to prevent my getting cancer again.
___ 16. It's hard to believe that my treatment plan will help me.
___ 17. There are many diseases more severe than the kind of cancer I have.
___ 18. The kind of cancer I have is not as bad as people say.
___ 19. The kind of cancer I have is a terrible disease.
___ 20. There is little hope for people with the kind of cancer that I have.
___ 21. The chances I might develop cancer again are pretty high.
___ 22. I expect to be free of cancer in the future.
___ 23. No matter what I do, there's a good chance of developing cancer again.
___ 24. My body will fight off cancer in the future.
___ 25. Members of my immediate family think I should follow my treatment plan.
___ 26. I want to do what members of my immediate family think I should do about my treatment plan.
___ 27. My close friends think I should follow my treatment plan.
___ 28. I want to do what my close friends think I should do about my treatment plan.
___ 29. My relatives think I should follow my treatment plan.
___ 30. I want to do what my relatives think I should do about my treatment plan.
___ 31. I have made a commitment to my treatment plan.
___ 32. Following my treatment plan is not in my plans.

_____ 33. I intend to follow my treatment plan.
_____ 34. I have no intention of following my treatment plan.
_____ 35. Lots of things get in the way of following my treatment plan.
_____ 36. I need more assistance in order to follow my treatment plan.
_____ 37. I get the help I need to carry out my treatment plan.
_____ 38. I am able to deal with any problems in following my treatment plan.

Adult Health Concerns Questionnaire (HCQ)

PURPOSE To measure psychiatric symptoms.

AUTHORS Richard L. Spoth and David M. Dush

DESCRIPTION The HCQ is a 55-item psychiatric symptom checklist. The items on the HCQ were derived from the DSM III-R. Its brief format and simplicity of structure make it very easy to use. Factor analysis reveals 10 factors, described in the original article. The HCQ has a two-level response format: respondents first underline any concern that applies to them and then rate the underlined items on a 5-point Likert-type scale regarding severity. Use of the HCQ without the distress ratings is not recommended. The HCQ is designed as a tool for clinical use especially for diagnosis and assessment. Subsequent research may reveal the HCQ to be equally useful as a tool to evaluate therapeutic outcomes.

NORMS The HCQ was studied initially with two samples, the first involving 167 in- and outpatients referred to a psychology service in a private, nonprofit general hospital (with a mean age of 38 and 64% female), and the second, another 82 patients referred to the psychology service plus 32 patients attending a headache pain clinic and 15 college students. Actual norms are not presented, although means for the 10 most frequently (.95 to 1.90) and 10 least frequently (.09 to .35) checked items were reported.

SCORING Two scores can be obtained from the HCQ. The first is a simple total of all items underlined. The second is a total distress score, a simple sum of distress ratings for all items underlined.

RELIABILITY No actual data other than the results of the factor analysis were provided.

VALIDITY The HCQ has fair concurrent validity, with several scales of the MMPI being correlated with both number of items completed on the HCQ and the total distress score. Only one scale on the Psychological Screening Inventory (Neuroticism) was correlated with the total distress score on the HCQ.

PRIMARY REFERENCE Spoth, R. L., and Dush, D. M. (1988). The Adult Health Concerns Questionnaire: A psychiatric symptoms checklist, *Innovations in Clinical Practice: A Sourcebook*, 7, 289–297.

AVAILABILITY May be copied from this volume.

Part One: Please *underline* any of the following concerns that apply to you.

___ Marital stress	___ Too much alcohol
___ Other family problems	___ Feel negative about the future
___ Other relationship problems	___ Hard to make friends
___ Problems at work/school	___ Feeling lonely
___ Health problems	___ Sexual problems
___ Financial problems	___ Less energy than usual
___ Legal problems	___ More energy than usual
___ Sad/depressed	___ Very talkative
___ Loss of appetite	___ Restless/can't sit still
___ Loss of weight	___ Nervous/tense
___ Gain of weight	___ Panicky
___ Difficulty sleeping	___ Shaky/trembling
___ Difficulty concentrating	___ Hard to trust anyone
___ Quick change of moods	___ Problems controlling my thoughts
___ Dwelling on problems	___ Upset stomach
___ Problems with breathing	___ Sweating
___ Hot or cold spells	___ Light headed/dizzy
___ Problems controlling anger or urges	___ Too much worry
___ Feeling suicidal	___ Too many fears
___ Feeling worthless	___ Feeling guilty
___ Drawing away from people	___ Feeling angry/frustrated
___ Lack of interest/enjoyment	___ Memory problems
___ Nightmares	___ See/hear strange things
___ Feel ignored/abandoned	___ Feel used by people
___ Too much pain	___ Feel others are out to get me
___ Confused	___ Watched/talked about by others
___ Laugh without reason	___ Other
___ Too many drugs	

Part Two: In front of each concern underlined, please rate its *severity* as:

1 = Mildly distressing
2 = Moderate
3 = Serious
4 = Severe
5 = Very severely distressing

Adult Self-Expression Scale (ASES)

PURPOSE To measure assertiveness in adults.

AUTHORS Melvin L. Gay, James G. Hollandsworth, Jr., and John P. Galassi

DESCRIPTION This 48-item assertiveness instrument was developed from the College Self-Expression Scale (an assertiveness measure for college students) along with a pool of 106 additional items. Items were selected according to rigorous psychometric standards, including item-total correlations and item discrimination. The instrument contains 25 positively worded items and 23 negatively worded items. The content of the ASES items reflects specific verbal assertive behavior in particular interpersonal situations where assertion may be problematic. Consequently, in addition to the rapid assessment of assertion, the ASES is useful in isolating situations where a client has difficulty asserting him/herself.

NORMS Means and standard deviation are reported for a sample of 464 community college students, ranging in ages from 18 to 60 years of age (mean = 25.38). For males ($n = 192$), the mean was 118.56 and the standard deviation was 18.57. For females ($n = 268$), the mean was 114.78 and the standard deviation was 21.22. Married respondents had a mean of 118.47 with a standard deviation of 19.62, while singles had a mean of 114.26 and a standard deviation of 20.60. A sample of 32 people seeking counseling services had a mean of 101.81 and a standard deviation of 26.99.

SCORING Items 7, 8, 9, 10, 11, 12, 13, 15, 16, 17, 19, 20, 22, 25, 28, 29, 32, 35, 36, 43, 44, 47, and 48 are reverse-scored. All item scores are then summed for a total score. Scores range from zero to 192 with higher scores reflecting higher levels of assertiveness.

RELIABILITY Test-retest reliability was determined for a two-week period ($r = .88$) and for a five-week period ($r = .91$), which suggests the ASES is a stable measure of assertiveness. Data on internal consistency were not available.

VALIDITY Concurrent validity is evidenced with correlations between the ASES and measures of defensiveness, self-consciousness, lability, achievement, dominance, affiliation, heterosexuality, exhibition, autonomy, and aggression. Scores on the ASES were also associated with anxiety and locus of control. A sample of persons seeking counseling services had significantly lower scores than the sample of community college students.

PRIMARY REFERENCE Gay, M. L., Hollandsworth, J. G., and Galassi, J. P. (1975). An assertiveness inventory for adults, *Journal of Counseling Psychology*, 22, 340–344. Instrument reproduced with permission of John Galassi.

AVAILABILITY May be copied from this volume.

The following inventory is designed to provide information about the way in which you express yourself. Please answer the questions by writing a number from 0 to 4 in the space to the left of each item. Your answer should indicate how you generally express yourself in a variety of situations. If a particular situation does not apply to you, answer as you think you would respond in that situation. Your answer should *not* reflect how you feel you ought to act or how you would like to act. Do not deliberate over any individual question. Please work quickly. Your first response to the question is probably your most accurate one.

$$0 = \text{Almost always or always}$$
$$1 = \text{Usually}$$
$$2 = \text{Sometimes}$$
$$3 = \text{Seldom}$$
$$4 = \text{Never or rarely}$$

1. Do you ignore it when someone pushes in front of you in line?
2. Do you find it difficult to ask a friend to do a favor for you?
3. If your boss or supervisor makes what you consider to be an unreasonable request, do you have difficulty saying no?
4. Are you reluctant to speak to an attractive acquaintance of the opposite sex?
5. Is it difficult for you to refuse unreasonable requests from your parents?
6. Do you find it difficult to accept compliments from your boss or supervisor?
7. Do you express your negative feelings to others when it is appropriate?
8. Do you freely volunteer information or opinions in discussions with people whom you do not know very well?
9. If there was a public figure whom you greatly admired and respected at a large social gathering, would you make an effort to introduce yourself?
10. How often do you openly express justified feelings of anger to your parents?
11. If you have a friend of whom your parents do not approve, do you make an effort to help them get to know one another better?
12. If you were watching a TV program in which you were very interested and a close relative was disturbing you, would you ask them to be quiet?
13. Do you play an important part in deciding how you and your close friends spend your leisure time together?
14. If you are angry at your spouse/boyfriend/girlfriend, is it difficult for you to tell him/her?
15. If a friend who is supposed to pick you up for an important engagement calls fifteen minutes before he/she is supposed to be there and says that he/she cannot make it, do you express your annoyance?
16. If you approve of something your parents do, do you express your approval?
17. If in a rush you stop by a supermarket to pick up a few items, would you ask to go before someone in the check-out line?
18. Do you find it difficult to refuse the requests of others?
19. If your boss or supervisor expresses opinions with which you strongly disagree, do you venture to state your own point of view?
20. If you have a close friend whom your spouse/boyfriend/girlfriend dislikes and constantly criticizes, would you inform him/her that you disagree and tell him/her of your friend's assets?

___ 21. Do you find it difficult to ask favors of others?

___ 22. If food which is not to your satisfaction was served in a good restaurant, would you bring it to the waiter's attention?

___ 23. Do you tend to drag out your apologies?

___ 24. When necessary, do you find it difficult to ask favors of your parents?

___ 25. Do you insist that others do their fair share of the work?

___ 26. Do you have difficulty saying no to salesmen?

___ 27. Are you reluctant to speak up in a discussion with a small group of friends?

___ 28. Do you express anger or annoyance to your boss or supervisor when it is justified?

___ 29. Do you compliment and praise others?

___ 30. Do you have difficulty asking a close friend to do an important favor even though it will cause him/her some inconvenience?

___ 31. If a close relative makes what you consider to be an unreasonable request, do you have difficulty saying no?

___ 32. If your boss or supervisor makes a statement that you consider untrue, do you question it aloud?

___ 33. If you find yourself becoming fond of a friend, do you have difficulty expressing these feelings to that person?

___ 34. Do you have difficulty exchanging a purchase with which you are dissatisfied?

___ 35. If someone in authority interrupts you in the middle of an important conversation, do you request that the person wait until you have finished?

___ 36. If a person of the opposite sex whom you have been wanting to meet directs attention to you at a party, do you take the initiative in beginning the conversation?

___ 37. Do you hesitate to express resentment to a friend who has unjustifiably criticized you?

___ 38. If your parents wanted you to come home for a weekend visit and you had made important plans, would you change your plans?

___ 39. Are you reluctant to speak up in a discussion or debate?

___ 40. If a friend who has borrowed $5.00 from you seems to have forgotten about it, is it difficult for you to remind this person?

___ 41. If your boss or supervisor teases you to the point that it is no longer fun, do you have difficulty expressing your displeasure?

___ 42. If your spouse/boyfriend/girlfriend is blatantly unfair, do you find it difficult to say something about it to him/her?

___ 43. If a clerk in a store waits on someone who has come in after you when you are in a rush, do you call his attention to the matter?

___ 44. If you lived in an apartment and the landlord failed to make certain repairs after it had been brought to his attention, would you insist on it?

___ 45. Do you find it difficult to ask your boss or supervisor to let you off early?

___ 46. Do you have difficulty verbally expressing love and affection to your spouse/boyfriend/girlfriend?

___ 47. Do you readily express your opinions to others?

___ 48. If a friend makes what you consider to be an unreasonable request, are you able to refuse?

Affect Balance Scale (ABS)

PURPOSE To measure psychological well-being.

AUTHORS Norman Bradburn and E. Noll

DESCRIPTION The ABS is a 10-item instrument designed to measure psychological well-being, especially mood state or happiness. The current version was modified from the original. The ABS is an extensively studied scale with excellent data on its applicability in a broad range of situations and cultures. The current version yields scores on two distinct conceptual dimensions, positive affect (items 1, 3, 5, 7, and 9) and negative affect (items 2, 4, 6, 8, and 10). The ABS is highly recommended as a brief, easy to score and administer measure of psychological well-being in a variety of populations.

NORMS Data are not available.

SCORING The ABS is easily scored by summing item responses for the two subscales and the total scale score; numbers on the scale are assigned to each score as indicated on the instrument (e.g., a "yes" on item 1 is assigned a score of 3).

RELIABILITY The ABS has shown good to excellent internal consistency in a number of studies with alphas that consistently exceed .80.

VALIDITY The ABS has extensive data on concurrent, predictive, and construct validity. It is correlated in predicted directions with numerous measures including the Depression Adjective Checklist, reports of levels of activities and response to illness among the elderly, life satisfaction, and social interaction.

PRIMARY REFERENCE Bradburn, N. M., and Noll, E. (1969). *The Structure of Psychological Well-Being*. Chicago: Aldine.

AVAILABILITY Primary reference, or may be copied from this volume.

We are interested in the way people are feeling these days. Please circle "yes" or "no" for each item.

During the past few weeks, did you ever feel:

Yes (3)	No (2)	1.	Particularly excited or interested in something?
Yes (6)	No (5)	2.	So restless that you couldn't sit long in a chair?
Yes (9)	No (8)	3.	Proud because someone complimented you on something you had done?
Yes (3)	No (2)	4.	Very lonely or remote from other people?
Yes (6)	No (5)	5.	Pleased about having accomplished something?
Yes (9)	No (8)	6.	Bored?
Yes (3)	No (2)	7.	On top of the world?
Yes (6)	No (5)	8.	Depressed or very unhappy?
Yes (9)	No (8)	9.	That things were going your way?
Yes (3)	No (2)	10.	Upset because someone criticized you?

Aggression Inventory (AI)

PURPOSE To measure aggressive behavioral characteristics or traits.

AUTHOR Brian A. Gladue

DESCRIPTION This 30-item instrument is designed to measure different aggressive traits. Respondents rate the items on a five-point scale, ranging from "does not apply at all to me" to "applies exactly to me." The AI consists of four subscales: physical aggression (PA = 9 + 11 + 12 + 13); verbal aggression (VA = 3 + 4 + 6 + 7 + 8 + 16 + 21); impulsive/impatient (II = 15 + 18 + 20 + 24 + 25 + 28 + 30); and avoidance (Avoid = 17 + 22). Because of possible gender differences in many aspects of aggression, scores on the AI must be considered separately for women and men. For example, factor analyses provide differences in terms of the explained variance of the construct of aggression for the assembly of subscales. For men the pattern of explained variance was PA (32.6%); VA (12.7%); II (8.4%); and Avoid (4.9%). For women the pattern was VA (33.9%); II (15.2%); PA (5.6%); and Avoid (5.3%).

NORMS The AI was studied with 960 undergraduates enrolled in introductory psychology classes. This population was primarily Caucasian (96%) and consisted of 517 male and 443 female young adults (mean age = 20.4 years, ranging from 18 to 34). For males the mean subscale scores were PA = 2.34; VA = 3.04; II = 2.80; Avoid = 2.85. For females the subscale mean scores were PA = 1.82; VA = 2.58; II = 2.68; and Avoid = 3.06.

SCORING The subscales are scored by summing the item responses and then dividing by the number of items for the particular subscale. Scores range from 1 to 5 with higher scores reflecting more aggression.

RELIABILITY The AI has fair to good internal consistency. For men the alpha coefficients were PA = .82; VA = .81; II = .80 and .65 for Avoid. For women the alpha coefficients were PA = .70; VA = .76; II = .76; and .70 for Avoid. Data on stability were not reported.

VALIDITY The validity of the AI subscale has been supported by factor analysis and differences between men and women. The latter serves to suggest the AI has fair known-groups validity where men and women significantly differed on each subscale and on all but six of the individual items.

PRIMARY REFERENCE Gladue, B. A. (1991). Qualitative and quantitative sex differences in self-reported aggressive behavior characteristics, *Psychological Reports*, 68, 675–684. Instrument reproduced with permission of Brian A. Gladue and *Psychological Reports*.

AVAILABILITY Dr. Brian A. Gladue, University of North Texas, Health Science Center. Email: Brian.Gladue@unthsc.edu.

Each statement in this questionnaire asks about you, how you interact with other people or how you typically respond in a variety of situations. For each statement please select the response which applies BEST to YOU. Please record the applicable response for each item on the space next to it. Using the following rating scale select the response which applies BEST to YOU, and record it in the space next to each item.

1 = Does NOT apply AT ALL to me
2 = Applies SOMEWHAT to me
3 = Applies FAIRLY WELL to me
4 = Applies WELL to me
5 = Applies EXACTLY to me

___ 1. I enjoy working with my hands doing repetitive tasks.
___ 2. I admire people who can walk away from a fight or argument.
___ 3. When a person is unfair to me I get angry and protest.
___ 4. When a person tries to "cut ahead" of me in a line, I firmly tell him not to do so.
___ 5. Whenever I have trouble understanding a problem, I ask others for advice.
___ 6. When a person criticizes me, I tend to answer back and protest.
___ 7. When a person tries to boss me around, I resist strongly.
___ 8. I think it is OK to make trouble for an annoying person.
___ 9. I get into fights with other people.
___ 10. When a person criticizes or negatively comments on my clothing or hair, I tell him/her it is none of their business.
___ 11. I really admire persons who know how to fight with their fists or body (not using any weapons).
___ 12. When another person hassles or shoves me, I try to give him/her a good shove or punch.
___ 13. When another person picks a fight with me, I fight back.
___ 14. I prefer to listen to rock-and-roll instead of classical music.
___ 15. I become easily impatient and irritable if I have to wait.
___ 16. When another person is mean or nasty to me, I try to get even with him/her.
___ 17. Whenever someone is being unpleasant, I think it is better to be quiet than to make a fuss.
___ 18. Others say that I lose patience easily.
___ 19. I consider myself to be an authority figure for some people.
___ 20. More often than others, I seem to do things that I regret later.
___ 21. If a person insults me, I insult him/her back.
___ 22. I prefer to get out of the way and stay out of trouble whenever somebody is hassling me.
___ 23. When I am on bad terms with a person, it usually ends up in a fight.
___ 24. I become easily impatient if I have to keep doing the same thing for a long time.
___ 25. It often happens that I act too hastily.
___ 26. Whenever I build something new, I read the instruction booklet before doing anything.

___ 27. I really admire persons who know how to fight with weapons.
___ 28. I often act before I have had the time to think.
___ 29. When I am very angry with someone, I yell at them.
___ 30. When I have to make up my mind, I usually do it quickly.

Aggression Questionnaire (AQ)

PURPOSE To measure four aspects of aggression.

AUTHORS Arnold H. Buss and Mark Perry

DESCRIPTION This 29-item instrument measures four aspects of aggression: physical aggression (PA: items 1, 5, 9, 13, 17, 21, 24, 26, 28), verbal aggression (VA: items 2, 6, 10, 14, 18), anger (A: items 3, 7, 11, 15, 19, 22, 29), and hostility (H: items 4, 8, 12, 16, 20, 23, 25, 27). The AQ is a refinement of the Hostility Inventory. a widely used instrument developed by the first author over thirty years ago. The AQ was developed from a pool of 52 items, many of which were from the original Hostility Inventory, by means of principal component factor analysis and confirmatory factor analysis. The instrument allows one to assess not only how aggressive one is by using total scores, but also how that aggression is manifested, which is determined by the subscale scores.

NORMS For a sample of 612 undergraduate males, the AQ subscale had the following means (and standard deviations): PA = 24.3 (7.7), VA = 15.2 (3.9), A = 17.0 (5.6), H = 21.2 (5.5); the mean for the total score for this sample was 77.8 with a standard deviation of 16.5. From a sample of 641 female college students the means (and standard deviations) for the subscales were PA = 17.9 (6.6), VA = 13.5 (3.9), A = 16.7 (5.8), and H = 20.2 (6.3); total scores had a mean of 68.2 and a standard deviation of 17.0.

SCORING Items 24 and 29 are first reverse-scored. Subscale scores are the sum of the item scores for those items in the subscale. A total score is the sum of all item scores and ranges from 29 to 145. Higher scores reflect more aggression.

RELIABILITY The internal consistency of the AQ is very good. Alpha coefficients were .85, .72, .83, and .77 for the PA, VA, A, and H subscales. Total scores had an alpha of .89. The AQ is a stable instrument with good test-retest reliability; over a nine-week period the test-retest correlations were .80, .76, .72, and .72 for the PA, VA, A, and H subscales and .80 for total scores.

VALIDITY Scores on the AQ were moderately correlated with each other. However, when the variance in the correlations due to the anger score was partialed out, correlations were not significant; this supports the theoretical validity of the AQ in that the associations between physical aggression, verbal aggression, and hostility are due to their connection with anger. Scores also have good concurrent validity, with no significant association between the PA and VA and emotionality, but strong correlations between emotionality and the A and H subscales. Scores on all four subscales correlated with impulsiveness, competition, and assertiveness, although noticeably lower correlations were found between assertiveness and PA and H subscales. Construct validity was evidenced with correlations between the AQ and peer observations of aggression, sociability, and shyness.

PRIMARY REFERENCE Buss, A. H., and Perry, M. (1992). The Aggression Questionnaire, *Journal of Personality and Social Psychology*, 63, 452–459. Instrument reproduced with permission of Arnold Buss and the American Psychological Association.

AVAILABILITY May be copied from this volume.

For the following items please rate how characteristic each is of you. Using the following rating scale record your answer in the space to the left of each item.

> 1 = Extremely uncharacteristic of me
> 2 = Somewhat uncharacteristic of me
> 3 = Only slightly characteristic of me
> 4 = Somewhat characteristic of me
> 5 = Extremely characteristic of me

___ 1. Once in a while I can't control the urge to strike another person.
___ 2. I tell my friends openly when I disagree with them.
___ 3. I flare up quickly but get over it quickly.
___ 4. I am sometimes eaten up with jealousy.
___ 5. Given enough provocation, I may hit another person.
___ 6. I often find myself disagreeing with people.
___ 7. When frustrated, I let my irritation show.
___ 8. At times I feel I have gotten a raw deal out of life.
___ 9. If somebody hits me, I hit back.
___ 10. When people annoy me, I may tell them what I think of them.
___ 11. I sometimes feel like a powder keg ready to explode.
___ 12. Other people always seem to get the breaks.
___ 13. I get into fights a little more than the average person.
___ 14. I can't help getting into arguments when people disagree with me.
___ 15. Some of my friends think I'm a hothead.
___ 16. I wonder why sometimes I feel so bitter about things.
___ 17. If I have to resort to violence to protect my rights, I will.
___ 18. My friends say that I'm somewhat argumentative.
___ 19. Sometimes I fly off the handle for no good reason.
___ 20. I know that "friends" talk about me behind my back.
___ 21. There are people who pushed me so far that we came to blows.
___ 22. I have trouble controlling my temper.
___ 23. I am suspicious of overly friendly strangers.
___ 24. I can think of no good reason for ever hitting a person.
___ 25. I sometimes feel that people are laughing at me behind my back.
___ 26. I have threatened people I know.
___ 27. When people are especially nice, I wonder what they want.
___ 28. I have become so mad that I have broken things.
___ 29. I am an even-tempered person.

Agoraphobic Cognitions Questionnaire (ACQ)

PURPOSE To measure catastrophic thinking in agoraphobia.

AUTHORS Dianne L. Chambless, G. Craig Caputo, Priscilla Bright, and Richard Gallagher

DESCRIPTION The ACQ is a 14-item instrument (with an optional fifteenth item) designed to measure thoughts concerning negative consequences of experiencing anxiety. The ACQ was developed on the basis of interviews with clients being treated for agoraphobia. The ACQ comprises two factors physical consequences and social/behavioral consequences. However, the total score can be used as an overall measure. The ACQ actually measures "fear of fear" and, as such, is a very important tool for use in evaluating treatment programs for agoraphobia.

NORMS The ACQ was studied initially with 173 clients applying for treatment at the Agoraphobia and Anxiety Programs at Temple University. The sample had been agoraphobic for a median of eight years; 80% were female. The mean ACQ score was 2.32 (SD = .66).

SCORING The ACQ is easily scored by averaging responses across the individual items.

RELIABILITY The ACQ has good internal consistency, with an alpha of .80. It also has good stability, with a one-month test-retest correlation of .75.

VALIDITY The ACQ has good concurrent validity, correlating with the Beck Depression Inventory, the neuroticism score of the Eysenck Personality Questionnaire, and the State-Trait Anxiety Inventory. The ACQ also has good known-groups validity, distinguishing among agoraphobics, "normals," and clients with other depression and anxiety disorders. The ACQ also is sensitive to changes due to treatment.

PRIMARY REFERENCE Chambless, D. L., Caputo, G. C., Bright, P., and Gallagher, R. (1984). Assessment of fear in agoraphobics: The Body Sensations Questionnaire and the Agoraphobics Questionnaire, *Journal of Consulting and Clinical Psychology*, 52, 1090–1097.

AVAILABILITY Dr. Dianne Chambless, Department of Psychology, University of Pennsylvania, Philadelphia, PA 19104. Email: dcamb@psych.upenn.edu.

ACQ

Below are some thoughts or ideas that may pass through your mind when you are nervous or frightened. Please indicate how often each thought occurs when you are nervous. Rate from 1–5 using the scale below.

> 1 = Thought never occurs
> 2 = Thought rarely occurs
> 3 = Thought occurs during half of the times I am nervous
> 4 = Thought usually occurs
> 5 = Thought always occurs when I am nervous

___ 1. I am going to throw up.
___ 2. I am going to pass out.
___ 3. I must have a brain tumor.
___ 4. I will have a heart attack.
___ 5. I will choke to death.
___ 6. I am going to act foolish.
___ 7. I am going blind.
___ 8. I will not be able to control myself.
___ 9. I will hurt someone.
___ 10. I am going to have a stroke.
___ 11. I am going to go crazy.
___ 12. I am going to scream.
___ 13. I am going to babble or talk funny.
___ 14. I will be paralyzed by fear.
___ 15. Other ideas not listed (Please describe and rate them)

_____

Alcohol Beliefs Scale (ABS)

PURPOSE To measure beliefs and expectations about alcohol's effect.

AUTHORS Gerard J. Connors and Stephen A. Maisto

DESCRIPTION This 29-item instrument assesses one's beliefs about the effects of alcohol and its usefulness. The ABS is composed of two parts. Part A contains 17 items assessing the impact of different amounts of alcohol on behaviors and affect. This portion of the instrument assesses four domains of alcohol's effect: control issues (CI; items 1, 8, 11, 15); sensations (SEN; items 5, 7, 9, 13); capability issues (CAP; items 2, 6, 10, 12, 14, 17); and social issues (SI; items 3, 4, 16). Part B consists of 12 items where a respondent indicates how useful the consumption of different doses of alcohol would be, such as in self-medication or in order to forget worries. Part B has three factors or subscales: useful for feeling better (FB: items 4, 8, 9, 10); useful for feeling in charge (FC: items 1, 5, 6, 12); useful for relieving emotional distress (RED; items 3, 7, 11). These subscales may be useful in monitoring change, in treatment planning, or when the goals of treatment include cognitive restructuring.

NORMS From a sample of 420 male drinkers including 250 inpatient alcoholics, 79 problem drinkers, and 81 non-problem drinkers, the means (and standard deviations) for CI were .03 (2.11), −.49 (1.91), −.55 (1.32), respectively. The mean CAP scores were −.43 (1.78), −.66 (1.72), and −1.03 (1.31) for alcoholics, problem drinkers, and non-problem drinkers, respectively. Norms for the other subscales are not reported.

SCORING Part A is scored on an eleven-point rating scale from "strong decrease in the behavior or feeling" (−5) to "strong increase in the behavior or feeling" (+5). This rating is made for three different quantities of alcohol consumption. Part B instructs a respondent to note the usefulness of the three levels of alcohol consumption over a four-hour period. Again, an eleven-point scale is used ranging from "not at all useful" (0) to "very useful" (10). Scale scores are the total of item scores divided by the number of subscale items. Scores range from −5 to +5 for the subscales in Part A, and 0 to 11 for those in Part B.

RELIABILITY Data on reliability were not available for the ABS.

VALIDITY The ABS has demonstrated known-groups validity, distinguishing among groups of alcoholic addicts, problem drinkers, and drinkers with no problems. There were also differences on the responses due to different doses of alcohol. Non-problem drinkers expected greater impairment on control issues and capability issues subscales than problem drinkers; in turn, addicts reported less impairment than the problem drinkers. Usefulness (Part B) also differed based on amount of alcohol consumed.

PRIMARY REFERENCE Connors, G. J., and Maisto, S. A. (1988). Alcohol Beliefs Scale. In M. Hersen and A. S. Bellack (eds.), *Dictionary of Behavioral Assessment Techniques*, pp. 24–26. New York: Pergamon Press. Instrument reproduced with permission of Gerard J. Connors.

AVAILABILITY Dr. Gerard J. Connors, Research Institute on Addictions, University of Buffalo, Buffalo, New York at NY 14203. Email: connors@ria.buffalo.edu.

Please answer the questions in Parts A and B below using the following definition of 1 standard drink. One (1) standard drink contains either 1 oz. spirits (hard liquor), or 12 oz. of beer, or 4 oz. table wine (12%).

We want you to answer every question on this form using three different levels of drinking. Those levels are (1) after consuming 1–3 standard drinks, (2) after 4–6 standard drinks, and (3) when "drunk."

Before starting, please indicate here how many standard drinks it takes to make you feel "drunk": _____ standard drinks.

PART A

Please rate the extent to which 1–3 standard drinks, 4–6 standard drinks, and "drunkenness" will cause, *for you*, a decrease or increase in the following behaviors and feelings over a four-hour period (including time spent drinking). Use the following scale to indicate your ratings, which are to be written in the appropriate spaces for each question.

−5	−4	−3	−2	−1	0	1	2	3	4	5

Strong decrease in the behavior or feeling	No change in the behavior or feeling	Strong increase in the behavior or feeling

Behavior or Feeling	1–3 Standard drinks	4–6 Standard drinks	When "drunk"
1. Feeling in control of a situation	—	—	—
2. Stress	—	—	—
3. Elation	—	—	—
4. Interacting in groups	—	—	—
5. Depression	—	—	—
6. Making decisions	—	—	—
7. Nonsocial anxiety (e.g., caused by wild animals or sickness)	—	—	—
8. Feeling powerful	—	—	—
9. Light-headed	—	—	—
10. Speed at which you react to something	—	—	—
11. Problem solving	—	—	—
12. Thinking clearly	—	—	—
13. Head spinning	—	—	—
14. Ability to drive a car	—	—	—
15. Judgment	—	—	—
16. Feelings of courage	—	—	—
17. Estimation of the passage of time	—	—	—

PART B

Rate the extent to which *you* feel 1–3 standard drinks, 4–6 standard drinks, and "drunkenness" are useful for the following reasons over a four-hour period (including drinking time). Use the following scale to make your ratings:

	0	1	2	3	4	5	6	7	8	9	10	

| Not at all | | | | Moderately useful | | | | | | Very useful | |

"Reason" to Drink	1–3 Standard drinks	4–6 Standard drinks	When "drunk"
1. Increase the effects of other drugs	—	—	—
2. Be more sociable	—	—	—
3. Relieve depression	—	—	—
4. Get in a better mood	—	—	—
5. Increase courage	—	—	—
6. Be aggressive	—	—	—
7. Escape stress	—	—	—
8. Feel happy	—	—	—
9. Become disinhibited	—	—	—
10. Feel you have more control over what's happening	—	—	—
11. Forget worries	—	—	—
12. Attract attention to yourself	—	—	—

Alcohol Outcome Expectancies Scale (AOES)

PURPOSE To measure alcohol outcome expectancies.

AUTHORS Barbara C. Leigh and Alan W. Stacy

DESCRIPTION The AOES is a 34-item scale designed to measure alcohol outcome expectancies—that is, the beliefs that people hold about the effects of alcohol on their behavior, moods, and emotions. Previous research has shown these expectancies are correlated with drinking behavior in adolescents and in adults and may play a role in the initiation and maintenance of dysfunctional drinking of alcohol. The authors undertook two studies to develop this instrument using an elegant structural equation modeling analysis to determine the extent to which specific indicator factors of expectancies were subsumed under higher-order global factors. The analysis revealed two global factors: one of positive effects and the other of negative effects. Each of the global factors had several subfactors revealed through the structural equation modeling. The subfactors for positive expectancies were: social facilitation (items 1, 20, 23, 26, 28, and 32); fun (items 5, 7, 10, 14, 17, and 24); sex (items 16, 22, 25, and 29); and tension reduction (items 21, 31, and 34). The subfactors for negative expectancies were: social (items 2, 8, and 18); emotional (items 4, 12, and 27); physical (items 13, 15, 30, and 33); and cognitive performance (items 3, 6, 9, 11, and 19).

NORMS The AOES was studied with 588 introductory psychology students (266 males and 322 females) with a mean age of 20. The sample was 65% white and 25% Asian. While standard deviations and intercorrelations were provided for all items, no overall means and standard deviations for the subscales were provided in the original article.

SCORING The AOES items are on 6-point likelihood scales with endpoints from "no chance" = 1 to "certain to happen" = 6. Scores are a simple sum of the scores within each subscale.

RELIABILITY The AOES has excellent internal consistency and test-retest reliability. The alpha for positive effects was .94 and for negative effects, .88. Stability was very good with test-retest reliability of .87 over a one-week interval.

VALIDITY The AOES has very good discriminant and convergent validity, thereby producing good construct validity. The global factors of positive and negative expectancy were equally related to actual alcohol use; however, specific subfactors of positive expectancy were additional significant predictors of drinking.

PRIMARY REFERENCE Leigh, B. C., and Stacy, A. W. (1993). Alcohol outcome expectancies: Scale construction and predictive utility in higher order confirmatory models, *Psychological Assessment*, 5, 216–229. Reprinted by permission of the authors.

AVAILABILITY May be copied from this volume.

Here is a list of some effects or consequences that some people experience after drinking alcohol. How likely is it that these things happen to *you* when you drink alcohol? Please record the number that best describes how drinking alcohol would affect you, using the following scale:

1 = No chance
2 = Very unlikely
3 = Unlikely
4 = Likely
5 = Very likely
6 = Certain to happen

(If you do not drink at all, you can still fill this out: just answer it according to what you think would happen to you if you *did* drink.)

___ 1. I am more accepted socially
___ 2. I become aggressive
___ 3. I am less alert
___ 4. I feel ashamed of myself
___ 5. I enjoy the buzz
___ 6. I become clumsy or uncoordinated
___ 7. I feel happy
___ 8. I get into fights
___ 9. I have problems driving
___ 10. I have a good time
___ 11. I can't concentrate
___ 12. I feel guilty
___ 13. I feel sick
___ 14. It is fun
___ 15. I get a hangover
___ 16. I have more desire for sex
___ 17. I feel pleasant physical effects
___ 18. I get mean
___ 19. I have problems with memory and concentration
___ 20. I am more outgoing
___ 21. It takes away my negative moods and feelings
___ 22. I become more sexually active
___ 23. It is easier for me to socialize
___ 24. I feel good
___ 25. I am more sexually responsive
___ 26. I am able to talk more freely
___ 27. I feel sad or depressed
___ 28. I am friendlier
___ 29. I am more sexually assertive
___ 30. I feel more social
___ 31. I get a headache
___ 32. I feel less stressed
___ 33. I experience unpleasant physical effects
___ 34. I am able to take my mind off my problems

Alcohol Use Disorders Identification Test (AUDIT)

PURPOSE To identify persons with hazardous or harmful alcohol use.

AUTHORS Thomas Babor, John Higgins-Biddle, John Saunders and Maristela Monteiro

DESCRIPTION The AUDIT is a 10-item instrument designed by the World Health Organization to assess excessive alcohol consumption. It was developed in 1989 and has had world-wide use by health and mental health providers. There are volumes of empirical support for the psychometrics and utility of the AUDIT that are summarized in the primary reference below. The use of the AUDIT has been so extensive it is available in a number of different languages and it is also available in an interview format. The AUDIT may be used as a total score or with three subscales: Hazardous Alcohol Use (HzAU; items 1–3), Dependence Symptoms (DS; items 4–6) and Harmful Alcohol Use (HAU; items 7–10). While only taking 3 to 4 minutes to complete using either the self-report or interview forms, the AUDIT may be shortened by having respondents answer only 9 and 10, if their response on item 1 zero. Alternatively, if a respondent scores zero on items 2 and 3, and then he or she only need answer 9 and 10.

NORMS There are numerous normative data for the AUDIT. Scores from 8 to 15 indicate there is medium level of alcohol problems; scores from 16 to 19 indicate a high level of alcohol problems and 20 or above indicate a need for future evaluation for alcohol dependency.

SCORING Total scores are the sum of all item scores. Subscale scores are the sum of the items noted above.

RELIABILITY The AUDIT has very good reliability with internal consistency coefficients from numerous studies exceeding. 80.

VALIDITY The validity of the AUDIT has been supported in numerous studies, time and again. They are too numerous to summarize in any detail. In general, there is consistently very strong support for the validity of this instrument, such as correlating .88 with the Michigan Alcohol Screening Test (reprinted in this volume).

PRIMARY REFERENCE Babor, T. F., Higgins-Biddle, J. C., Saunders, J. B. and Monteiro, M. G. (2001). Alcohol Use Disorders Identification Test: Guidelines for use in primary care. (2nd. ed). Geneva, Switzerland: WHO (also available at the WHO website).

AVAILABILITY In public domain, but may not be used for commercial purposes. Inquires should be directed to the Department of Mental Health and Substance Dependency, WHO, CH-121 Geneva 27, Switzerland.

THE ALCOHOL USE DISORDERS IDENTIFICATION TEST: SELF-REPORT VERSION

PATIENT: Because alcohol use can affect your health and can interfere with certain medications and treatments, it is important that we ask some questions about your use of alcohol. Your answers will remain confidential so please be honest.

Place an X in one box that best describes your answer to each question.

Questions	0	1	2	3	4	
1. Hew often do you have a drink containing alcohol?	Never	Monthly or less	2-4 times a month	2-3 times a week	4 or more times a week	
2. How many drinks containing alcohol do you have on a typical day when you are drinking?	1 or 2	3 or 4	5 or 6	7 to 9	10 or more	
3. How often do you have six or more drinks on one occasion?	Never	Less than monthly	Monthly	Weekly	Daily or almost daily	
4. How often during the last year have you found that you were not able to stop drinking once you had started?	Never	Less than monthly	Monthly	Weekly	Daily or almost daily	
5. How often during the last year have you failed to do what was normally expected of you because of drinking?	Never	Less than monthly	Monthly	Weekly	Daily or almost daily	
6. How often during the last year have you needed a first drink in the morning to get yourself going after a heavy drinking session?	Never	Less than monthly	Monthly	Weekly	Daily or almost daily	

7. How often during the last year have you had a feeling of guilt or remorse after drinking?	Never	Less than monthly	Monthly	Weekly	Daily or almost daily	
8. How often during the last year have you been unable to remember what happened the night before because of your drinking?	Never	Less than monthly	Monthly	Weekly	Daily or almost daily	
9. Have you or someone else been injured because of your drinking?	No		Yes, but not in the last year		Yes, during the last year	
10. Has a relative, friend, doctor, or other health care worker been concerned about your drinking or suggested you cut down?	No		Yes, but not in the last year		Yes, during the last year	
					Total	

Anger Idioms Scale (AIS)

PURPOSE To measure idioms of anger.

AUTHORS Robert G. Malgady, Lloyd H. Rogler, and Dharma E. Cortes

DESCRIPTION The AIS is an 11-item scale designed to measure cultural expression of psychiatric symptoms, in particular, idioms of anger among Puerto Ricans. The scale was developed out of a need for research to clarify the cultural roots of expressive symptomatology. The authors utilized cultural consultants who noted that idioms of anger are salient in the conception of mental health among low income, inner-city Puerto Ricans in the United States. The AIS comprises three factors: aggressive (items 1, 2, 3, 4); assertive (items 5, 6, 7); and vindictive (items 8, 9, 10, 11).

NORMS The AIS was developed with a pool of 128 clinical subjects who were selected from the medical records of adult Puerto Rican clients in a local community mental health center (mean age = 43.5) and 403 nonclinical subjects from a sample of adult Puerto Ricans in the New York metropolitan area. Of the 531 subjects 41.5% were male, 32.4% were married, and 34.5% were born in the United States. Means and standard deviations were not presented in the primary reference.

SCORING The AIS is easily scored by summing individual item scores for the total scale and the subscales after reverse-scoring item 11.

RELIABILITY The AIS has fair internal consistency with an alpha of .75. No data on stability were reported.

VALIDITY The AIS has good concurrent validity with the total scale and all three subscales correlated significantly with depressive symptoms as measured by the Center for Epidemiological Studies Depression Scale. The total score and all three subscales also are significantly correlated with anxiety symptoms as measured by the trait anxiety scale from the State-Trait Anxiety Inventory.

PRIMARY REFERENCE Malgady, R. G., Rogler, L. H., and Cortes, D. E. (1996). Cultural expression of psychiatric symptoms: Idioms of anger among Puerto Ricans, *Psychological Assessment*, 8, 265–268.

AVAILABILITY May be copied from this volume.

Please indicate how much you disagree or agree with each statement below by writing the number in the space to the left of each item.

1 = Strongly disagree
2 = Disagree
3 = Agree
4 = Strongly agree

____ 1. At times, it is difficult to control my temper.
____ 2. I often feel I have so many problems that I don't know where to begin solving them.
____ 3. If I get angry, it usually takes me some time to cool down.
____ 4. At times, I have hit someone in anger.
____ 5. In any sort of fight, it pays to get the first blow in.
____ 6. I have to step on people's fingers to get to the top of the ladder; so much the worse for them for getting in my way.
____ 7. If someone is rude to me, I usually answer back.
____ 8. If someone stabs me in the back, I feel I have to pay them back in kind.
____ 9. It pays to remember who your enemies are.
____ 10. There are times when I feel like picking a fight with someone.
____ 11. If a salesclerk does not wait on me properly, I usually say nothing.

Anxiety Depression Distress Inventory-27 (ADDI-27)

PURPOSE To measure symptoms of anxiety, depression and distress from the tripartite model.

AUTHORS Augustine Osman, Stacey Freedenthal, Peter Gutierrez, Jane Wong, Ashley Emmerich and Gregorio Lozano

DESCRIPTION The ADDI-27 is a 27-item inventory designed to measure the internalized symptoms of depression, anxiety and general distress. It was derived from the Mood and Anxiety Symptoms Questionnaire, and greatly improved. The ADDI-27 was developed in three excellent studies using exploratory and confirmatory factor analysis, and has three distinguishable scales: depression, but as defined by the absence of Positive Affect (PA), Somatic Anxiety (SA), and General Distress (GD). These measures are the operationalization of the tripartite model of affect, which generally speaking attempts to address the large overlap between depression and anxiety in clinical samples and the general population. The model asserts that the conditions are the internalization of positive affect, such as happiness or optimism, where depression is the absence of positive affect The other two affects are anxious arousal, which is more of a somatic experience, and negative affect; negative affect tends to account for the overlap in the two distinguishable conditions of depression and anxiety. While the ADDI-27 has three separate subscales, it seems to work best as a complete inventory as you can more accurately monitor change in depression and anxiety within the context of your client's negative affect.

NORMS A sample of 112 male and 118 female adolescent patients from a state psychiatric inpatient hospital were divided into two groups based on the mental health diagnoses: internalizers, which include conditions such as depression and bi-polar disorders, and externalizers, which included conditions such as conduct disorders and oppositional defiance. Internalizers had a mean (and standard deviation) of 21.19 (6.68), 27.59 (7.85), and 27.68 (8.72) for the SA, GD and PA scales. Externalizers had means and (standard deviations) of 17.05 (4.58), 24.81 (6.07) and 29.29 (7.79) for the SA, GD and PA scales.

SCORING Scores are the sum of each of the individual items. PA scores are 4 + 9 + 10 + 11 + 13 + 17 + 19 + 21 + 26. GD scores are 1 + 2 + 3 +5 + 6 + 7 + 12 + 22 + 25. And SA scores are 8 +14 +15 + 16 + 18 + 20 + 23 + 24 + 27. Scale scores range from 9 to 45.

RELIABILITY The scales of ADDI have excellent internal consistency with coefficients above .80 on all three scales and from all three studies. The highest internal consistency coefficient was .92.

VALIDITY The ADDI has very strong evidence of the instruments' validity. Scores correlated with the original Mood and Anxiety Questionnaire, scores on the Beck Depression Inventory, the Beck Anxiety Inventory, the Positive and Negative Affect Scale, the State-Trait Depression Scale, the Symptom Assessment-45 Questionnaire, and the Depression, Anxiety and Stress scale which is included in this volume. The three scales have excellent evidence of known-groups validity as scores distinguished between internalizers and externalizers.

PRIMARY REFERENCE Osman, A., Freedenthal, S., Gutierrez, P. M., Wong, J. L, Emmerich, A. and Lozano, G. (2011). The Anxiety Depression Distress Inventory-27 (ADDI-27): A short version of the Mood and Anxiety Symptom Questionnaire-90. *Journal of Pinical Psychology.* 67, 591–608.

AVAILABILITY Augustine Osman, Ph.D., Department of Psychology, The University of Texas at San Antonio, San Antonio: Texas 78249-0652. Email: augustine. osman@utsa.edu.

ADDI-27

INSTRUCTIONS: Below is a list of feelings, sensations, problems, and experiences that people sometimes have. Please read each item and then circle the appropriate choice to the right of that item. Use the choice that best describes how much you have felt or experienced things this way during the past two weeks, including today. Use the scale to the right when answering.

Item	Not at all	A little bit	Moderately	Quite a bit	Extremely
1. Felt sad	1	2	3	4	5
2. Felt discouraged	1	2	3	4	5
3. Felt worthless	1	2	3	4	5
4. Felt really happy	1	2	3	4	5
5. Felt nervous	1	2	3	4	5
6. Felt hopeless	1	2	3	4	5
7. Blamed myself for a lot of things	1	2	3	4	5
8. Felt numbness or tingling in my body	1	2	3	4	5
9. Felt like I had accomplished a lot	1	2	3	4	5
10. Felt like I had a lot of interesting things to do	1	2	3	4	5
11. Felt like I had a lot to look forward to	1	2	3	4	5
12. Felt like a failure	1	2	3	4	5
13. Was proud of myself	1	2	3	4	5
14. Felt dizzy or lightheaded	1	2	3	4	5
15. Was short of breath	1	2	3	4	5
16. Hands were shaky	1	2	3	4	5
17. Felt really "up" lively	1	2	3	4	5
18. Had a very dry mouth	1	2	3	4	5
19. Felt confident about myself	1	2	3	4	5
20. Muscles twitched or trembled	1	2	3	4	5
21. Felt like I had a lot of energy	1	2	3	4	5
22. Was disappointed in myself	1	2	3	4	5
23. Heart was racing or pounding	1	2	3	4	5
24. Was trembling or shaking	1	2	3	4	5
25. Worried a lot about things	1	2	3	4	5
26. Felt really good about myself	1	2	3	4	5
27. Had trouble swallowing	1	2	3	4	5

Argumentativeness Scale (ARG)

PURPOSE To measure argumentativeness.

AUTHORS Dominic A. Infante and Andrew S. Rancer

DESCRIPTION The ARG is a 20-item scale designed to measure the tendency to argue about controversial issues (or argumentativeness). Argumentativeness is viewed as a generally stable trait which predisposes the individual in communication situations to advocate positions on controversial issues and to attack verbally the positions other people take on those issues. Ten of the items indicate a tendency to approach argumentative situations and ten involve the tendency to avoid argumentative situations. The ARG is considered useful for examining communication and social conflict and dysfunctional communication. Both areas have implications for clinical practice in that high scores on the ARG may identify the incessant arguer whose behavior impairs interpersonal relations while very low scores may identify people who almost never dispute an issue and are compliant and/or easily manipulated. Thus, the ARG may prove useful particularly in couple and family counseling.

NORMS A series of studies largely involving over 800 students in undergraduate communication courses formed the basis for much of the research on the ARG. No demographic data are reported nor are actual norms.

SCORING Scores for each item ranging from 1 to 5 are totaled separately for the two dimensions. The total score for the tendency to avoid argumentative situations (items 1, 3, 5, 6, 8, 10, 12, 14, 16, 19) is subtracted from the total score for the tendency to approach argumentative situations (2, 4, 7, 9, 11, 13, 15, 17, 18, 20) to provide an overall score for the argumentativeness trait.

RELIABILITY The ARG has good to excellent internal consistency, with the approach dimension (ARG ap) having a coefficient alpha of .91 and the avoidance dimension (ARG av) having an alpha of .86. The ARG also is a stable instrument with an overall ARG test-retest reliability (one week) of .91 and test-retest reliabilities of .87 for ARG ap and .86 for ARG av.

VALIDITY The ARG has fairly good concurrent validity, correlating significantly and in the expected direction with three other measures of communication predispositions. In addition, the ARG significantly correlates with friends' ratings of argumentativeness. Further, the ARG has some degree of construct validity in accurately predicting a series of behavioral choices which should and should not correlate with argumentativeness.

PRIMARY REFERENCE Infante, D. A., and Rancer, A. S. (1982). A conceptualization and measure of argumentativeness, *Journal of Personality Assessment*, 46, 72–80. Instrument reproduced with permission of Dominic A. Infante and the *Journal of Personality Assessment*.

AVAILABILITY May be copied from this volume.

This questionnaire contains statements about arguing controversial issues. Indicate how often each statement is true for you personally by placing the appropriate number in the blank to the left of the statement. If the statement is *almost never true* for you, place a "1" in the blank. If the statement is *rarely true* for you, place a "2" in the blank. If the statement is *occasionally true* for you, place a "3" in the blank. If the statement is *often true* for you, place a "4" in the blank. If the statement is *almost always true* for you, place a "5" in the blank.

___ 1. While in an argument, I worry that the person I am arguing with will form a negative impression of me.
___ 2. Arguing over controversial issues improves my intelligence.
___ 3. I enjoy avoiding arguments.
___ 4. I am energetic and enthusiastic when I argue.
___ 5. Once I finish an argument I promise myself that I will not get into another.
___ 6. Arguing with a person creates more problems for me than it solves.
___ 7. I have a pleasant, good feeling when I win a point in an argument.
___ 8. When I finish arguing with someone I feel nervous and upset.
___ 9. I enjoy a good argument over a controversial issue.
___ 10. I get an unpleasant feeling when I realize I am about to get into an argument.
___ 11. I enjoy defending my point of view on an issue.
___ 12. I am happy when I keep an argument from happening.
___ 13. I do not like to miss the opportunity to argue a controversial issue.
___ 14. I prefer being with people who rarely disagree with me.
___ 15. I consider an argument an exciting intellectual challenge.
___ 16. I find myself unable to think of effective points during an argument.
___ 17. I feel refreshed and satisfied after an argument on a controversial issue.
___ 18. I have the ability to do well in an argument.
___ 19. I try to avoid getting into arguments.
___ 20. I feel excitement when I expect that a conversation I am in is leading to an argument.

Arousability Predisposition Scale (APS)

PURPOSE To measure the tendency toward insomnia.

AUTHOR Stanley Coren

DESCRIPTION This 12-item instrument is designed to assess cognitive arousal that is predictive of sleep disturbance. The point of departure for the instrument is that insomnia is not simply the result of the relatively immediate predormital time period, but a trait or behavioral predisposition for sleep disturbance. The APS was developed from a pool of 314 items, and reduced to 70 based on face validity, and finally to 12 items which were predictive of sleep disturbance. While an item or two may appear to reflect somatic arousal, the APS is intended to tap cognitive arousal as a predictor of sleep disruption. The APS is truly a rapid assessment instrument, taking only 2 or 3 minutes to complete.

NORMS Normative data are available from a sample of 786 university students, 479 females and 307 males. The average scores were 37.6 for women and 34.5 for men. Scores ranged from 20 to 51, although the scale's score range is 12 to 60.

SCORING Total score on the APS is the sum of the 12 items scores. "Never" is scored 1 and "Always" scored 5. Higher scores indicate more cognitive arousal which is likely to interfere with sleep.

RELIABILITY The APS has good internal consistency, with an alpha coefficient of .84 from one sample and .83 from another. This is very good reliability for a 12-item instrument. Stability data were not available.

VALIDITY The APS has strong evidence to support its validity. Scores on the APS correlate with sleep disruption, and six specific aspects of disruption: frequency of night awakenings, frequency of nightmares, dormital restlessness, early morning awakening, delayed onset of sleep, and the subjective experience of feeling tired upon arising. These correlations were found for a sample of 196 and cross-validated with a sample of 693 college students. There is evidence the APS is sensitive to measuring change. High scores on the APS were associated with more physiological arousal than was found for persons with low APS scores.

PRIMARY REFERENCES Coren, S. (1988). Prediction of insomnia from arousability scores: Scale development and cross-validation, *Behavioural Research and Therapy*, 26, 415–420. Coren, S. (1990). The arousal predisposition scale: Normative data, *Bulletin of Psychonomic Society*, 28, 551–552.

AVAILABILITY Professor Stanley Coren, Department of Psychology, University of British Columbia, 2136 West Mall, Vancouver, BC V67 1Y7 Canada. Email: scoren@psych.ubc.edu.

This questionnaire deals with a number of common behaviors and self-perceptions. For each question you should select the response which best describes you and your behaviors. You can select from among the following response alternatives:

1 = Never (or almost never)
2 = Seldom
3 = Occasionally
4 = Frequently
5 = Always (or almost always)

All that you need to do is write the number which corresponds to your choice.

___ 1. I am a calm person.
___ 2. I get flustered if I have several things to do at once.
___ 3. Sudden changes of any kind produce an immediate emotional effect on me.
___ 4. Strong emotions carry over for one or two hours after I leave the situation which caused them.
___ 5. I am restless and fidgety.
___ 6. My mood is quickly influenced by entering new places.
___ 7. I get excited easily.
___ 8. I find that my heart keeps beating fast for a while after I have been "stirred up."
___ 9. I can be emotionally moved by what other people consider to be simple things.
___ 10. I startle easily.
___ 11. I am easily frustrated.
___ 12. I tend to remain excited or moved for a long period of time after seeing a good movie.

Ascription of Responsibility Questionnaire (ARQ)

PURPOSE To measure willingness to ascribe specific responsibility.

AUTHORS A. Ralph Hakstian and Peter Suedfeld

DESCRIPTION The ARQ is a 40-item instrument designed to measure one's ascription of responsibility. Conceptually, ascription of responsibility is similar to locus of responsibility and locus of control. The ARQ is composed of four subscales: traditional focused (TF: items 1, 5, 14, 18, 22, 26, 29, 31, 33, 39) reflects ascription of responsibility to traditional authority such as parents and schools and is closely related to conservatism; diffused responsibility (DR: items = 2, 6, 8, 11, 15, 19, 23, 27, 30, 34, 36, 38) is the tendency to see social groups as the locus of authority; exercised responsibility (ER: items = 3, 9, 12, 16, 20, 24, 40) assesses how much a person has exercised authority; and individual focused responsibility (IFR: items 4, 7, 10, 13, 17, 21, 25, 28, 32, 35, 37) reflects belief in more inner-directed individualistic ethics.

NORMS Normative data are available from a sample of 654 university undergraduates. There are no normative differences between women and men. The TF had a mean of 46.65 and a standard deviation of 10.53. For the DF the mean was 56.13 and standard deviation was 9.03. For ER the figures are 36.67 and 6.76, and for IFR the mean and standard deviations were 56.91 and 7.93.

SCORING After reverse-scoring item 12, scores for each subscale are simply the sums of the scores on designated items. In order to maintain a common score range, the summed score may be divided by the number of subscale items. This will produce a score range from 1 to 7, with higher scores reflecting more ascription of responsibility.

RELIABILITY The subscales have modest internal consistency. From two studies of college students, alpha coefficients ranged from .56 to .76 and averaged .68. The test-retest coefficient of stability for a one-week period ranged from .74 to .90, and averaged .84.

VALIDITY Concurrent validity was evidenced by correlations with scores on conceptually related scales. The ARQ scores did not correlate with Rotter's Locus of Control Scale. Some evidence of known-groups validity is available as seen in differences in TF scores for Catholics and Protestants compared to respondents with no religious affiliation.

PRIMARY REFERENCE Hakstian, A. R., Suedfeld, P., Ballard, E. J., and Rank, D. S. (1986). The Ascription of Responsibility Questionnaire: Development and empirical extensions, *Journal of Personality Assessment*, 50, 229–247. Instrument reproduced with permission of A. Ralph Hakstian.

AVAILABILITY May be copied from this volume.

Indicate the extent to which you are in agreement with each item by putting one number next to the item.

7 = Agree strongly
6 = Agree somewhat
5 = Agree slightly
4 = Neither agree nor disagree
3 = Disagree slightly
2 = Disagree somewhat
1 = Disagree strongly

___ 1. I have always respected my parents highly.
___ 2. Fate plays an important role in our lives.
___ 3. I have a lot of responsibility in my present job and extracurricular activities.
___ 4. Most people on welfare are lazy.
___ 5. I attended church often as a child.
___ 6. All old people should get a pension.
___ 7. Ability should be rewarded.
___ 8. The state is responsible for the well-being of its citizens.
___ 9. I enjoy taking charge of things.
___ 10. Good behavior should be rewarded, bad behavior punished.
___ 11. As a student, I would feel students should have a say in which professors receive tenure.
___ 12. I prefer following rather than leading.
___ 13. Every sane individual is responsible for his every action.
___ 14. My family and I are very close.
___ 15. Our country should take the first step toward world disarmament.
___ 16. I often make suggestions.
___ 17. Robbery with violence should be severely punished.
___ 18. My parents were always willing to give me advice on things that were important to me.
___ 19. Students should decide how they want their teachers to evaluate their knowledge of the course.
___ 20. I was given a lot of responsibility as a child.
___ 21. Your personality is what you make it.
___ 22. Pornography should be censored to protect the innocent.
___ 23. As a student, I would feel that what I study should be completely up to me.
___ 24. I have often been a group leader.
___ 25. Society should reward only merit.
___ 26. Human destiny is ordained by a Supreme Being.
___ 27. When a country has done its utmost, but does not have the resources to maintain itself, it is the responsibility of other countries to come to its aid.
___ 28. Justice is better than mercy.
___ 29. People can be controlled by supernatural forces.
___ 30. As a teacher, I would feel it is my job to make sure none of my students fails my course.
___ 31. I enjoyed going to church.

___ 32. If a child insists on having a pet, he should be responsible for its care.
___ 33. Heaven is the reward for those who have followed the precepts of their belief.
___ 34. All decisions should be made by groups.
___ 35. Parents should not financially support offspring who could make a living for themselves.
___ 36. Students should have equal representation at all levels of school administration concerning any policy.
___ 37. Society does not owe you a living.
___ 38. Students should be responsible for the evaluation and firing of teachers.
___ 39. My parents attended church often when I was a child.
___ 40. I have held many positions of responsibility in the past in my job(s) and extracurricular activities.

Assertion Inventory (AI)

PURPOSE To measure three aspects of assertiveness.

AUTHORS Eileen Gambrill and Cheryl Richey

DESCRIPTION This versatile 40-item instrument measures three aspects of assertion: discomfort with assertion (DAI), response probability (RP) of engaging in assertive behavior, and identification of situations (IS) where assertion needs improvement. In order to calculate scores on all three scales, each item must be answered three times. However, any one of the three scores can be used. The measure can also be used to characterize a client as "assertive," "unassertive," "anxious performer," and "doesn't care." This typology is helpful in selecting an intervention which best fits the type of assertion problem of the client. Finally, in terms of known gender differences on assertion, the AI compares favorably with other assertion instruments by having a balance between negative and positive assertive behaviors.

NORMS Normative data are available on samples of college students in Berkeley and Seattle ($N = 608$). The mean DAI, RP, and IS scores were 93.9, 103.8, and 10.1, respectively.

SCORING DAI scores and RP scores are the sums of the ratings on each item in the respective columns. The IS score is the total number of items circled. Client profiles are determined by categorizing scores from the DAI and RP scores as follows:

		RP Scores	
		≤ 104	≥ 105
DAI Score	≥ 96	Unassertive	Anxious performer
	≤ 95	Doesn't care	Assertive

For example, if a client's DAI score is greater than or equal to 96 and the RP score is greater than or equal to 105, the client's problem would be considered unassertive. The AI can also be scored as eleven factors reflecting specific situations of discomfort (see primary reference).

RELIABILITY The AI has very good stability, with test-retest correlations of .87 and .81 for DAI scores and RP scores respectively. Data on internal consistency were not available.

VALIDITY The validity support of the AI is very strong. Tests of known-groups validity illustrate that scores discriminate between clinical and "normal" samples. The instrument also is sensitive to change, as demonstrated by differences between pre- and posttherapy scores.

PRIMARY REFERENCE Gambrill, E. D., and Richey, C. A. (1975). An assertion inventory for use in assessment and research, *Behavior Therapy*, 6, 550–561. Instrument reproduced with permission of Cheryl A. Richey.

AVAILABILITY Email: gambrill@berkeley.edu.

Many people experience difficulty in handling interpersonal situations requiring them to assert themselves in some way, for example, turning down a request or asking a favor. Please indicate your degree of discomfort or anxiety in the space provided before each situation listed below. Use the following scale to indicate degree of discomfort.

1 = None
2 = A little
3 = A fair amount
4 = Much
5 = Very much

Then, go over the list a second time and indicate after each item the probability or likelihood of responding as described if actually presented with the situation.* For example, if you rarely apologize when you are at fault, you would mark "4" after that item. Use the following scale to indicate response probability:

1 = Always do it
2 = Usually do it
3 = Do it about half the time
4 = Rarely do it
5 = Never do it

Please indicate the situations you would like to handle more assertively by placing a circle around the item number.

* Note: It is important to assess your discomfort ratings apart from your response probability. Otherwise, one may influence the other. To prevent this, place a piece of paper over your discomfort ratings while responding to the situation a second time for response probability.

Degree of Discomfort	Situation	Response Probability
___	1. Turn down a request to borrow your car	___
___	2. Compliment a friend	___
___	3. Ask a favor of someone	___
___	4. Resist sales pressure	___
___	5. Apologize when you are at fault	___
___	6. Turn down a request for a meeting or date	___
___	7. Admit fear and request consideration	___
___	8. Tell a person with whom you are intimately involved when he or she says or does something that bothers you	___
___	9. Ask for a raise	___
___	10. Admit ignorance in some area	___
___	11. Turn down a request to borrow money	___
___	12. Ask personal questions	___
___	13. Turn off a talkative friend	___
___	14. Ask for constructive criticism	___
___	15. Initiate a conversation with a stranger	___

Degree of Discomfort	Situation	Response Probability
——	16. Compliment a person you are romantically involved with or interested in	——
——	17. Request a meeting or a date with a person	——
——	18. Your initial request for a meeting is turned down and you ask the person again at a later time	——
——	19. Admit confusion about a point under discussion and ask for clarification	——
——	20. Apply for a job	——
——	21. Ask whether you have offended someone	——
——	22. Tell someone that you like him or her	——
——	23. Request expected service when such is not forthcoming, for example, in a restaurant	——
——	24. Discuss openly with a person his or her criticism of your behavior	——
——	25. Return defective items in a store or restaurant	——
——	26. Express an opinion that differs from that of the person with whom you are talking	——
——	27. Resist sexual overtures when you are not interested	——
——	28. Tell a person when you feel that he or she has done something that is unfair to you	——
——	29. Accept a date	——
——	30. Tell someone good news about yourself	——
——	31. Resist pressure to drink	——
——	32. Resist a significant person's unfair demand	——
——	33. Quit a job	——
——	34. Resist pressure to use drugs	——
——	35. Discuss openly with a person his or her criticism of your work	——
——	36. Request the return of a borrowed item	——
——	37. Receive compliments	——
——	38. Continue to converse with someone who disagrees with you	——
——	39. Tell a friend or co-worker when he or she says or does something that bothers you	——
——	40. Ask a person who is annoying you in a public situation to stop	——

Assertion Questionnaire in Drug Use (AQ-D)

PURPOSE To measure assertion in drug users.

AUTHORS Dale A. Callner and Steven M. Ross

DESCRIPTION The AQ-D is a 40-item instrument designed to measure assertion in heavy drug users, particularly males. Six assertion content areas were selected as most relevant to drug users: positive feedback (+F: items 1, 7, 13, 19, 26, 32), negative feedback (−F: items 2, 8, 14, 20, 27, 33), drug (D: items 3, 9, 15, 21, 28, 37), authority (A: items 4, 10, 16, 22, 29, 38), heterosexual (H: items 5, 11, 17, 23, 30, 35), and general assertiveness (Gen.: items 6, 12, 18, 24, 25, 31, 34, 36, 39, 40). This measure is seen as particularly useful in work with substance abusers where assertion or social skills training is a major intervention.

NORMS The AQ-D was studied initially with 16 male veterans who were inpatients in a drug abuse program (age range from 18 to 25), and 16 age-matched veterans who were not drug users and were solicited from the community. The drug use group had a mean of 8.5 years of education, and the nondrug-use group had a mean of 9.4 years. All subjects were either divorced or married. No actual norms were presented.

SCORING Respondents rate each item on the AQ-D on a 4-point scale with items summed for scores on the content area scales or total scales. The total score can range from −80 to +80, the Gen subscale (10 items) from −20 to +20, and the remaining content areas (six items each) from −12 to +12. High positive scores represent extreme assertive ratings, and high negative scores represent extreme nonassertive ratings.

RELIABILITY The AQ-D has very good stability, with a seven-day test-retest correlation of .86. No data on internal consistency were presented.

VALIDITY The AQ-D has excellent concurrent validity, with correlations ranging from .71 to .95 with self-ratings of assertion and behavioral ratings of role plays.

PRIMARY REFERENCE Callner, D. A., and Ross, S. M. (1976). The reliability and validity of three measures of assertion in a drug addict population, *Behavior Therapy*, 7, 659–667. Instrument reprinted by permission of publisher and authors.

AVAILABILITY Dr. Steven M. Ross, Department of Psychiatry, 74 University of Utah, Salt Lake City, UT 84148. Telephone: 801.585.1575. Email: steven.ross@hsc.utah.edu.

Please record your response to each item in the space to the left using the following scale:

-2 = Never descriptive of me
-1 = Usually not descriptive of me
$+1$ = Usually descriptive of me
$+2$ = Always descriptive of me

____ 1. When someone says something nice to me, I have a hard time taking their compliment.
____ 2. I usually avoid complaining about the poor service in a restaurant.
____ 3. I have no trouble telling friends not to bring drugs over to my house.
____ 4. If I disagreed with the director of the drug program on something he said, I probably would not openly express my opinions.
____ 5. I never have a hard time getting up enough nerve to call up girls to ask them out for dates.
____ 6. In general, I believe that the only way to make new friends is to get out and find them yourself.
____ 7. I have a problem with telling someone that I like them.
____ 8. I have a hard time criticizing others even when I know that they are wrong and I am right.
____ 9. If I knew of a person on the ward taking drugs on the sly, I probably would not bring it up in a group meeting.
____ 10. I never feel shaky and overly nervous when I think of asking a boss for a raise.
____ 11. In general, I am outgoing and aggressive with girls that I take out.
____ 12. I usually take the lead when with a group of friends.
____ 13. I often don't say some of the nice things that I am thinking about some people.
____ 14. Anyone attempting to push ahead of me in a line is in for a good battle.
____ 15. When it comes to drugs, I have a hard time turning them down, even when I really want to.
____ 16. I usually hesitate to make phone calls to business establishments and institutions.
____ 17. I usually wait for the girl to make physical advances towards me before I make physical advances towards her.
____ 18. I believe that following the lead of others is more desirable than leading them yourself.
____ 19. I never have a hard time saying nice things and complimenting other people.
____ 20. If someone took the parking place that I had been waiting for, I would be mad, but I would probably drive off without saying anything.
____ 21. Drugs allow me to be more aggressive and outgoing than I normally would be.
____ 22. If a policeman started to give me a ticket for speeding, I would try to talk him out of it.
____ 23. I have little trouble in starting a conversation with girls that I have just met or been introduced to.
____ 24. Most people seem to be more aggressive and assertive than I am.
____ 25. I never avoid asking questions for fear of sounding stupid.
____ 26. If one of my friends was very depressed, I would go up and try to make him feel better.

___ 27. During an argument, I usually keep my real feelings bottled up inside and do not express them.
___ 28. If I were at a good party and a person that I just met offered me some free drugs, I would turn him down without any trouble.
___ 29. If I were applying for a job that I had a lot of experience for, and the employer told me that I didn't have enough experience, I would try to convince him that I did.
___ 30. Showing affection with girls has been a problem for me.
___ 31. I tend to let my feelings be known rather than keeping them bottled up inside of me.
___ 32. I never get embarrassed whenever I try to give someone a compliment.
___ 33. If I stopped at the laundry to pick up my shirts and the clerk told me that some of them had been lost, I probably would just walk out and not say anything.
___ 34. I am open and frank about my feelings.
___ 35. I am afraid of asking girls out because I would feel rejected if they refused.
___ 36. To be honest, people often take advantage of me.
___ 37. I have no problem turning down drugs when they are offered to me.
___ 38. In general, I get overly nervous whenever I have to talk to people in authority positions.
___ 39. I would not describe myself as shy.
___ 40. In general, I don't hesitate to openly express my opinions when in a group of people.

Assertion Self-Statement Test—Revised (ASST-R)

PURPOSE To measure self-statements in relation to assertiveness.

AUTHORS Richard G. Heimberg, Emil J. Chiauzzi, Robert E. Becker, and Rita Madrazo-Peterson

DESCRIPTION The ASST-R is a 24-item instrument designed to assess the role of self-statements in assertive (or nonassertive) behaviors. Self-statements are assumed to have a crucial role in affecting assertiveness and unassertiveness, especially by cognitive and cognitive-behavior therapists. The ASST-R was devised to be used to teach these self-statements and to assess the relationship to assertiveness. The ASST-R consists of 12 positive and 12 negative self-statements. The ASST-R is viewed as a useful measure for teaching cognitive changes in problems involving nonassertive behavior.

NORMS The ASST-R was studied with three samples including 12 psychiatric patients of mixed diagnosis randomly selected from a mental health clinic in Albany, New York; 16 "normal" adults from the center's nonprofessional staff; and 20 college students from undergraduate psychology courses at SUNY-Albany. The means for positive self-statements were: students = 44, "normal" adults = 39, psychiatric patients = 33. The means for negative self-statements were: students = 27, "normal" adults = 23, psychiatric patients = 37.

SCORING Each item is rated for frequency on a 5-point scale, and the individual items are summed for scores on the positive and negative dimensions. Total scores are not used. Positive items = 3, 5, 6, 9, 13, 14–16, 19, 21–23. Negative items = 1, 2, 4, 7, 8, 10–12, 17, 18, 20, 24.

RELIABILITY No data were reported.

VALIDITY The ASST-R has good known-groups validity, significantly discriminating between patients and the other two groups on negative and positive statements. There also was a significant difference between subjects evaluated as high and low in assertion on negative self-statements (but not positive statements).

PRIMARY REFERENCE Heimberg, R. G., Chiauzzi, E. J., Becker, R. E., and Madrazo-Peterson, R. (1983). Cognitive mediation of assertive behavior: An analysis of the self-statement patterns of college students, psychiatric patients, and normal adults, *Cognitive Therapy and Research*, 7, 455–464.

AVAILABILITY Dr. Richard Heimberg, Department of Psychology, Temple University, 1701 North 13th Street, Philadelphia, PA 19122-6085. Email: heimberg@temple.edu.

It is obvious that people think a variety of things when they are responding in different situations. These thoughts, along with feelings, determine what kind of responses a person will make.

Below is a list of things which you may have thought to yourself at some time while responding in the assertive situations. Read each item and decide how frequently you may have been thinking a similar thought during the assertive situations.

Circle a number from 1 to 5 for each item. The scale is interpreted as follows:

1 = *Hardly ever* had the thought
2 = *Rarely* had the thought
3 = *Sometimes* had the thought
4 = *Often* had the thought
5 = *Very often* had the thought

Please answer as honestly as possible.

1. I was thinking that I was too nervous to say what I felt.

   1   2   3   4   5

2. I was thinking that the other person would suspect some ulterior motive if I said anything.

   1   2   3   4   5

3. I was thinking that the other person should respect an honest expression of feelings.

   1   2   3   4   5

4. I was thinking that many people fail to get involved or stand up for themselves in similar situations, so there is nothing wrong with my keeping quiet.

   1   2   3   4   5

5. I was thinking that I could benefit by expressing myself.

   1   2   3   4   5

6. I was thinking that I should act in accord with what I think is right.

   1   2   3   4   5

7. I was thinking that if I could avoid this situation, I could somehow relieve my discomfort.

   1   2   3   4   5

8. I was thinking that it would be selfish of me to let my own feelings be known.

   1   2   3   4   5

9. I was thinking that I could express myself in a calm, relaxed way.

   1   2   3   4   5

10. I was thinking that I would appear incompetent or inadequate if I tried to take a stand.

    1   2   3   4   5

11. I was thinking that something bad would happen to me if I tried to express myself.

1	2	3	4	5

12. I was thinking that the other person wouldn't like me if I offered my opinion.

1	2	3	4	5

13. I was thinking that my opinions and decisions should be respected if they are reasonable.

1	2	3	4	5

14. I was thinking that since letting my feelings be known was an effective course of action in the past, I should do likewise now.

1	2	3	4	5

15. I was thinking that I would only be hurting myself by not expressing myself.

1	2	3	4	5

16. I was thinking that future interactions with the other person might be damaged if I didn't say what I felt now.

1	2	3	4	5

17. I was thinking that since similar past experiences resulted in failure or ineffectiveness, I shouldn't bother to do anything now.

1	2	3	4	5

18. I was thinking that I would probably feel guilty later if I refused to do the person a favor.

1	2	3	4	5

19. I was thinking that there didn't seem to be a good reason why I shouldn't speak my mind.

1	2	3	4	5

20. I was thinking that I would become embarrassed if I let my feelings be known.

1	2	3	4	5

21. I was thinking that if I didn't state my opinion now, it might cause problems later on.

1	2	3	4	5

22. I was thinking that my views are important.

1	2	3	4	5

23. I was thinking that if I didn't speak up, it would interfere with my plans.

1	2	3	4	5

24. I was thinking that a friendly person would not impose his/her views in this situation.

1	2	3	4	5

Assertive Job-Hunting Survey (AJHS)

PURPOSE To measure self-reported job-hunting assertiveness.

AUTHOR Heather A. Becker

DESCRIPTION The AJHS is a 25-item questionnaire designed to assess assertiveness in hunting for jobs—that is, the extent to which the respondent acts on his or her environment to procure information, establish contact persons in organizations, and so on. Developed originally from a pool of 35 items based on the job-hunting literature, the items on the complete instrument were designed to reflect all aspects of job-hunting including resumé writing, contacting prospective employees, soliciting recommendations, and interviewing. The AJHS can be used in classes or assertive training groups, as an outcome measure, to stimulate discussion of job-hunting assertiveness, and as a research tool for investigating correlates of assertiveness in job hunting.

NORMS Norms for the AJHS were established on 190 college students who had applied at a university center for career planning or job assistance. (Several hundred other students also have been studied.) The norm group included 50% men and 50% women, and represented all classifications from freshman to graduate students and a wide range of academic areas. Mean responses for each item are available in the primary reference; the overall mean score was 105.55. Scores for subgroups of students are not provided.

SCORING Items 1, 2, 4, 5, 7, 8, 10–12, 14, 15, 17, 19, 20, 22–25 are reverse-scored on the 6-point scales, with all responses then summed. This provides a range of 25 to 150, with higher scores indicating more assertive responses.

RELIABILITY The AJHS has good internal consistency, with a coefficient alpha of .82. The instrument also has good stability, with a two-month test-retest reliability of .77.

VALIDITY The AJHS established a form of concurrent validity, with a significant correlation between previous job-hunting experience and scores on the AJHS. The AJHS also is sensitive to change, showing significant pre- to posttest changes in two assertive job-hunting classes. No other validity data were reported.

PRIMARY REFERENCE Becker, H. A. (1980). The Assertive Job-Hunting Survey, *Measurement and Evaluation in Guidance*, 13, 43–48. Instrument reproduced with permission of Heather Becker.

AVAILABILITY Dr. Heather Becker, The University of Texas, Austin, TX 78701-1499. Email: heatherbecker@mail.utexas.edu.

For each of the following items, please indicate to the left of the item how likely you would be to respond in a job-hunting situation using the scale below.

1 = Very unlikely
2 = Rather unlikely
3 = Unlikely
4 = Likely
5 = Rather likely
6 = Very likely

___ 1.   Would mention only paid work experience
___ 2.   Reluctant to ask for more information
___ 3.   Would ask employers if they knew of other employers
___ 4.   Downplay my qualifications
___ 5.   Would rather use an employment agency
___ 6.   Would contact employee to learn more about organization
___ 7.   Hesitate to ask questions when interviewed
___ 8.   Avoid contacting employers because they're too busy
___ 9.   Would leave or arrange another appointment
___ 10. Experienced employment counselor knows best
___ 11. If employer too busy, would stop trying to contact
___ 12. Getting job largely luck
___ 13. Would directly contact employer, rather than personnel
___ 14. Reluctant to contact employer unless there's opening
___ 15. Would not apply unless had all qualifications
___ 16. Would not ask for a second interview
___ 17. Reluctant to contact employer unless there's opening
___ 18. Would ask employer how to improve chances for another position
___ 19. Feel uncomfortable asking friends for job leads
___ 20. Better take whatever job I can get
___ 21. If personnel didn't refer me, directly contact the person
___ 22. Would rather interview with recruiters
___ 23. Figure there's nothing else to do
___ 24. Check out openings before deciding what to do
___ 25. Reluctant to contact someone I don't know for information

Assertiveness Self-Report Inventory (ASRI)

PURPOSE To measure assertiveness.

AUTHORS Sharon D. Herzberger, Esther Chan, and Judith Katz

DESCRIPTION The ASRI is a 25-item instrument specifically developed to overcome criticisms of other measures of assertiveness: it is specific, in that items indicate the behavior, situation, and other people involved; it focuses on behavioral and affective dimensions of assertiveness; it is relatively short; it is broadly conceptualized; and details about development of the items for the scale are reported. The ASRI is simple to administer and to score. Items were generated by upper-level psychology students who were studying test construction and the construct of assertiveness. Those items that were not strongly endorsed in a preliminary study, that were correlated with social desirability, or that were not significantly correlated with the total score were dropped, leaving these 25 items.

NORMS Initial work on the ASRI has been conducted with college students and not on clinical populations. A series of studies was conducted with 268 students (96 males and 172 females). Mean scores for males in different testing sessions ranged from 9.54 to 10.63 and for females from 9.81 to 10.71. There were no significant male-female differences.

SCORING The total score is derived simply by adding the total number of "true" responses for items 1, 3, 4, 9, 13, 15, 16, 18–20, 22, 24 to "false" responses for remaining items.

RELIABILITY The ASRI has good stability with a five-week test-retest correlation of .81. Data were not reported on internal consistency.

VALIDITY The ASRI has good concurrent validity, correlating significantly with the Rathus Assertiveness Schedule. Further, the ASRI was not significantly correlated with subscales of the Buss-Durkee Aggression Inventory, suggesting that assertiveness and aggression are independent constructs. The ASRI also significantly predicted respondents' assertive solutions to specific dilemmas and peer-rated assertiveness, thus suggesting fair predictive validity.

PRIMARY REFERENCE Herzberger, S. D., Chan, E., and Katz, J. (1984). The development of an assertiveness self-report inventory, *Journal of Personality Assessment*, 48, 317–323. Instrument reproduced with permission of Sharon D. Herzberger and the *Journal of Personality Assessment*.

AVAILABILITY May be copied from this volume.

Read each question carefully and answer all 25 of them. Circle either "True" (T) or "False" (F), whichever most represents your viewpoint.

T F 1. When my date has acted rudely at a party, I don't hesitate to let him/her know I don't like it.

T F 2. I feel guilty after I ask my neighbor to be quiet after midnight on a weeknight.

T F 3. After eating an excellent meal at a restaurant, I do not hesitate to compliment the chef.

T F 4. If I were stood up on a date I would tell the person who stood me up that I felt angry.

T F 5. When I get a terrible haircut and my hair stylist/barber asks me how I like it, I say I like it.

T F 6. I would feel self-conscious asking a question in a large lecture class.

T F 7. I usually let my friends have a larger portion of food at social gatherings and take a smaller one for myself.

T F 8. When on a date I act cheerful, even though I am depressed, so as not to upset my date's mood.

T F 9. I feel justified when I send improperly cooked food back to the kitchen in a restaurant.

T F 10. When people I don't know wear nice outfits, I hesitate to compliment them.

T F 11. I'm not likely to tell my date that I am irritated when he/she pays more attention to others and ignores me.

T F 12. I tip a consistent percentage to a waitress despite receiving poor service.

T F 13. When an interviewer cancels an appointment for the third time I tell him/her that I am annoyed.

T F 14. When a roommate makes a mess I would rather clean it up myself than confront him/her about it.

T F 15. If I received a call late at night from a casual acquaintance, I would say I was sleeping and ask not to be called so late.

T F 16. When people use my car and don't refill the tank, I let them know I feel unfairly treated.

T F 17. I find it difficult to ask a favor of a stranger.

T F 18. If my stereo were stolen, I wouldn't regret reporting it to the police even if I suspected a friend.

T F 19. If I were going out with friends for an evening and my boyfriend/girlfriend did not want me to, I would do it anyway.

T F 20. I feel comfortable engaging in discussions in a group.

T F 21. I feel guilty when my boyfriend/girlfriend wants to go to a movie but we go where I wanted to instead.

T F 22. When my roommate consistently fails to take an accurate telephone message, I let him/her know I'm upset.

T F 23. When people use abusive language around me, I ignore it even though it bothers me.

T F 24. If someone makes loud noises when I am studying at the library I will express my discontent.

T F 25. I feel guilty telling my boyfriend/girlfriend that I have to do homework this evening instead of seeing him/her.

Assertiveness Self-Statement Test (ASST)

PURPOSE To measure cognitions related to assertion.

AUTHORS R. M. Schwartz and J. M. Gottman

DESCRIPTION The ASST is a 32-item instrument designed to measure cognitions—defined as self-statements—in assertion-related problems. The ASST is designed to be situation-specific rather than global and to be used when the cognitions are active in short-term memory to minimize distortion. Thus, recent situations that called for assertive behaviors can be focused on for each administration of the ASST. The ASST has two subscales relevant to the refusal of unreasonable requests: positive self-statements that facilitate (or make it easier to refuse) a request (items: 4, 5, 7, 9, 10, 12, 16, 17, 20, 23, 24, 26, 28, 30–32) and negative self-statements that interfere (or make it harder to refuse) with a request (items: 1–3, 6, 8, 11, 13–15, 18, 19, 21, 22, 25, 27, 29).

NORMS The ASST was studied initially with undergraduate students. No other demographic data are available nor are actual norms.

SCORING The ASST is easily scored by summing individual items for each of the subscales. The range for each subscale is from 16 to 80.

RELIABILITY The ASST has fair internal consistency, with an alpha of .78. No data on stability are available.

VALIDITY The ASST has good construct validity, consistently demonstrating that functional and dysfunctional groups differ in their frequency of positive and negative self-statements, and show predictable changes in self-statements (mainly a reduction in negative) as a result of psychotherapy. The ASST also has good concurrent validity, with correlations between negative self-statements and a measure of cognitive complexity and the Irrational Beliefs Test, and between the positive subscale and self-efficacy scores.

PRIMARY REFERENCE Schwartz, R. M., and Gottman, J. M. (1976). Toward a task analysis of assertive behavior, *Journal of Consulting and Clinical Psychology*, 44, 910–920.

AVAILABILITY May be copied from this volume.

It is obvious that people think a variety of things when they are responding in different situations. These thoughts, along with feelings, determine what kind of responses a person will make.

Below is a list of things which you may have thought to yourself at some time while responding in the assertive situations. Read each item and decide how frequently you may have been thinking a similar thought during the assertive situations.

Circle a number from 1 to 5 for each item. The scale is interpreted as follows:

1 = *Hardly ever* had the thought
2 = *Rarely* had the thought
3 = *Sometimes* had the thought
4 = *Often* had the thought
5 = *Very often* had the thought

Please answer as honestly as possible.

1. I was thinking that it was not worth the hassle to refuse.

    1   2   3   4   5

2. I was worried about what the other person would think about me if I refused.

    1   2   3   4   5

3. I was thinking that I would probably feel guilty later if I refused to do the person a favor.

    1   2   3   4   5

4. I was thinking that it is not my responsibility to help people I hardly know.

    1   2   3   4   5

5. I was thinking that there didn't seem to be a good reason why I should say yes.

    1   2   3   4   5

6. I was thinking that it was my responsibility to help those who need me.

    1   2   3   4   5

7. I was thinking that I just don't feel like saying yes.

    1   2   3   4   5

8. I was worried that the person might become angry if I refused.

    1   2   3   4   5

9. I was thinking that this request is an unreasonable one.

    1   2   3   4   5

10. I was thinking that the person could ask someone else.

    1   2   3   4   5

11. I was thinking that it is better to help others than to be self-centered.

    1   2   3   4   5

12. I was thinking that I will be happy later if I don't commit myself to something I don't want to do.

        1   2   3   4   5

13. I was thinking that I would get embarrassed if I refused.

        1   2   3   4   5

14. I was concerned that the person would think I was selfish if I refused.

        1   2   3   4   5

15. I was thinking that this person really seems to need me.

        1   2   3   4   5

16. I was thinking that I am perfectly free to say no.

        1   2   3   4   5

17. I was thinking that if I don't say no now, I'll end up doing something I don't want to do.

        1   2   3   4   5

18. I was thinking that it is always good to be helpful to other people.

        1   2   3   4   5

19. I was thinking that the person might be hurt or insulted if I refused.

        1   2   3   4   5

20. I was thinking that this person should take care of his/her own business.

        1   2   3   4   5

21. I was thinking that this request sounds pretty reasonable.

        1   2   3   4   5

22. I was thinking that people will dislike me if I always refuse.

        1   2   3   4   5

23. I was thinking that my own plans are too important.

        1   2   3   4   5

24. I was thinking that I don't have to please this person by giving in to his/her request.

        1   2   3   4   5

25. I was thinking that it is morally wrong to refuse someone who needs help.

        1   2   3   4   5

26. I was thinking that if I commit myself, it will interfere with my plans.

        1   2   3   4   5

27. I was thinking that a friendly person would not refuse in this situation.

        1   2   3   4   5

28. I was thinking that I am too busy now to say yes.

        1   2   3   4   5

29. I was afraid that there would be a scene if I said no.

1	2	3	4	5

30. I was thinking that since I hardly know the person, why should I go out of my way for him/her.

1	2	3	4	5

31. I was thinking that it doesn't matter what the person thinks of me.

1	2	3	4	5

32. I was thinking that this request is an imposition on me.

1	2	3	4	5

Auditory Hallucinations Questionnaire (AHQ)

PURPOSE To measure auditory hallucinations.

AUTHORS Harry H. Hustig and R. Julian Hafner

DESCRIPTION The AHQ is a 9-item instrument (plus open-ended questions) that measures the presence and characteristics of auditory hallucinations. The AHQ also measures respondents' delusions and mood. The AHQ is filled out as a diary, three times a day at 8 A.M., 2 P.M., and 8 P.M. The first part of the diary requests respondents to write down their two most prominent delusions (referred to in the first two items). The remainder of the questionnaire is then filled out in response to those two delusions. The AHQ has been used successfully with respondents diagnosed as schizophrenic, with persistent auditory hallucinations. Although each of the 9 scales is typically used as a separate scale, it may also be possible to use a total score for all scales (sum of 9 item responses) or to derive three scores, one for delusions (first 2 scales), one for hallucinations (next 4 scales), and one for mood (last 3 scales).

NORMS The AHQ was studied initially with 12 individuals, all diagnosed as schizophrenic, with auditory hallucinations that persisted over 12 months. Eleven subjects were women (mean age of 32.6 years) whose auditory hallucinations had persisted for a mean of 4.5 years, and all reported persistent paranoid delusions of at least 2 years' duration. All respondents were receiving neuroleptic medication. Mean scores for the nine scale items, in order of their presentation on the instrument, for one week, were: truthfulness of delusions = 2.8, 2.8; quality of hallucinations = 2.9, 2.2, 2.8, 3.1; mood = 2.9, 3.0; and clarity = 2.2. The mean for all 9 scales was 2.74 (total score 24.7).

RELIABILITY Reliability for the AHQ was determined by correlating scores made at the same time on seven occasions over 20 days, a type of test-retest reliability. The two belief scales (1 and 2) had a mean correlation of .84, the loudness of hallucination scale had a mean correlation of .71, and the other scales had a mean correlation exceeding .74, suggesting good stability.

VALIDITY A type of concurrent validity was determined by correlating each scale with all the others. This correlation matrix showed consistent significant relationships over time between quality of auditory relationships, mood, and strength of delusional beliefs.

PRIMARY REFERENCE Hustig, H. H., and Hafner, R. J. (1990). Persistent auditory hallucinations and their relationship to delusions and mood, *Journal of Nervous and Mental Disease*, 178, 264–267. Instrument reprinted with permission of publisher and authors.

AVAILABILITY May be copied from this volume.

AHQ

PLEASE START COMPLETING THIS SHEET AT ABOUT 8:00 A.M.

DATE: _____ Time at which you started filling in this page _____

PLEASE WRITE DOWN YOUR TWO MOST PROMINENT BELIEFS

Belief 1. _____

_____

Belief 2. _____

_____

Please remind yourself of *Belief 1*. Now, rate your belief as it is *right now* by circling the correct number:

Scale 1.	1	2	3	4	5
	This is definitely true	This is very likely to be true	This is probably true	I am not sure if this is true	This is probably not true

Please remind yourself of *Belief 2*. Now, rate it in the same way:

Scale 1.	1	2	3	4	5
	This is definitely true	This is very likely to be true	This is probably true	I am not sure if this is true	This is probably not true

NOW, PLEASE DESCRIBE YOUR VOICES

Right now, my voices are saying: _____

_____

_____

THESE VOICES ARE:

Scale 3.	1	2	3	4	5
	Very loud	Fairly loud	Average	Fairly quiet	Very quiet

Scale 4.	1	2	3	4	5
	Very clear	Fairly clear	Average	Fairly mumbled	Very mumbled

Scale 5.	1	2	3	4	5
	Very distressing	Fairly distressing	Neutral	Fairly comforting	Very comforting

Scale 6.

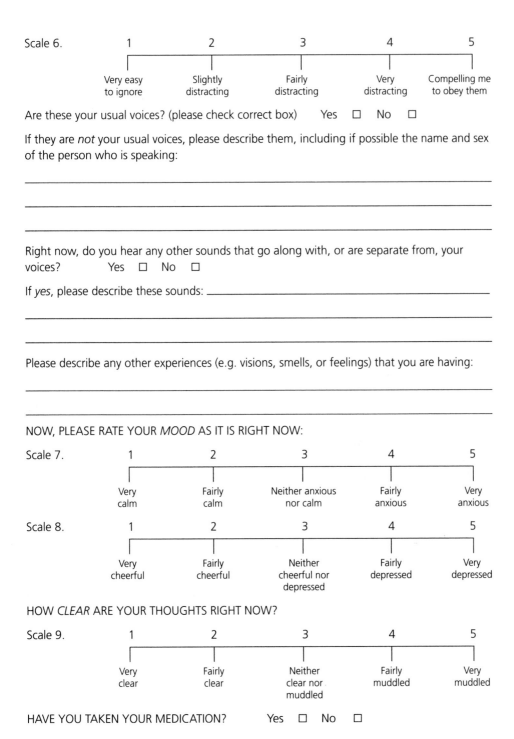

1	2	3	4	5
Very easy to ignore	Slightly distracting	Fairly distracting	Very distracting	Compelling me to obey them

Are these your usual voices? (please check correct box)   Yes ☐   No ☐

If they are *not* your usual voices, please describe them, including if possible the name and sex of the person who is speaking:

_____

_____

_____

Right now, do you hear any other sounds that go along with, or are separate from, your voices?   Yes ☐   No ☐

If *yes*, please describe these sounds: _____

_____

_____

Please describe any other experiences (e.g. visions, smells, or feelings) that you are having:

_____

_____

NOW, PLEASE RATE YOUR *MOOD* AS IT IS RIGHT NOW:

Scale 7.

1	2	3	4	5
Very calm	Fairly calm	Neither anxious nor calm	Fairly anxious	Very anxious

Scale 8.

1	2	3	4	5
Very cheerful	Fairly cheerful	Neither cheerful nor depressed	Fairly depressed	Very depressed

HOW *CLEAR* ARE YOUR THOUGHTS RIGHT NOW?

Scale 9.

1	2	3	4	5
Very clear	Fairly clear	Neither clear nor muddled	Fairly muddled	Very muddled

HAVE YOU TAKEN YOUR MEDICATION?   Yes ☐   No ☐

Authoritarianism Scale (AS)

PURPOSE To measure authoritarian behavior.

AUTHOR Patrick C. L. Heaven

DESCRIPTION The AS (Revised F-scale) is a 35-item instrument designed to measure authoritarianism. Much work has been done on the authoritarian personality using the original F-scale (Adorno et al., 1950). That scale, however, does not predict authoritarian behavior, but rather is most likely a measure of potential fascism. The AS was developed to address this limitation and two other weaknesses: the unilateral wording of items and a response set to particular items. The AS focuses on the multifaceted nature of authoritarianism and the items represent authoritarian behaviors. By presenting a balance of negatively and positively worded items, an acquiescent response set is controlled. The scale can be used as a short form by deleting items 3, 6, 8, 9, 10, 11, 15, 16, 17, 18, 22, 24, 26, 31, and 35; this is the recommended form for the non-Australian client.

NORMS The AS was developed on four separate samples from New South Wales, Australia: two samples of randomly selected adults ($n = 456$) who were in their middle 40s; 48 experienced police officers, whose average age was 31.1 with a standard deviation of 6.24 years; and a purposive sample of adults ($n = 49$). Few data are presented on the samples' scores except for the police officers and a subsample of adults matched with the police according to gender, age, and level of education. The average score for police was 75.71 with a standard deviation of 7.37. The matched subsample's average score was 69.85 with a standard deviation of 10.98.

SCORING Scoring is not fully described in the primary reference. Each item is rated on the degree to which the respondent agrees. A 5-item scale can be used for responses, giving a range of scores from 35 to 165. Items 5–9, 12–14, 22–24, 31 are reverse-scored. Higher scores reflect more authoritarianism.

RELIABILITY The internal consistency of the AS ranged from .70 to .83 for the sample of police officers and randomly selected adults, respectively. The internal consistency for the 20-item short form was .79, which was based on the sample of adults.

VALIDITY Research on known-groups validity suggests the AS discriminates police officers' scores from the matched sample of adults. The purposive sample of 49 adults had scores on the AS which correlated with 11 behavioral dimensions of authoritarianism as rated by two close friends.

PRIMARY REFERENCE Heaven, P. C. L. (1985). Construction and validation of a measure of authoritarian personality, *Journal of Personality Assessment*, 49, 545–551.

AVAILABILITY May be copied from this volume.

Rate each item in terms of how much you agree with the content. Please use the following scale and record your responses in the space to the left of the item.

1 = Almost never
2 = Rarely
3 = Occasionally
4 = Frequently
5 = Almost always

___ 1. Does the idea of being a leader attract you?
___ 2. Do you tend to feel quite confident on occasions when you are directing the activities of others?
___ 3. Do you try to get yourself into positions of authority when you can?
___ 4. Do you think you would make a good officer in the army?
___ 5. Do you think you would make a poor military leader?
___ 6. I would not vote for a political party that advocates racial discrimination.
___ 7. Is being comfortable more important to you than getting ahead?
___ 8. Are you satisfied to be no better than most other people at your job?
___ 9. I am easily convinced by the opinions of others.
___ 10. I agree with South Africa's Apartheid Policy.
___ 11. Do you tend to boss people around?
___ 12. Do you dislike having to tell others what to do?
___ 13. If you are told to take charge of some situation, does this make you feel uncomfortable?
___ 14. Would you rather take orders than give them?
___ 15. Do you tend to be the one who makes the decisions at home?
___ 16. Do you like to have the last word in an argument or discussion?
___ 17. If ever a Falkland-type situation arose in Australia, I'd volunteer to fight.
___ 18. I enjoy and feel good wearing a military uniform.
___ 19. Do you tend to plan ahead for your job or career?
___ 20. Is "getting on in life" important to you?
___ 21. Are you an ambitious person?
___ 22. Are you inclined to read of the successes of others rather than do the work of making yourself a success?
___ 23. Are you inclined to take life as it comes without much planning?
___ 24. Would it upset you a lot to see a child or animal suffer?
___ 25. Do you have enemies who want to harm you?
___ 26. Do you tend to dominate the conversation?
___ 27. Are you argumentative?
___ 28. Are there several people who keep trying to avoid you?
___ 29. I often find myself disagreeing with people.
___ 30. I can't help getting into arguments when people disagree with me.
___ 31. Even when my anger is aroused, I don't use strong language.
___ 32. If somebody annoys me, I am apt to tell him/her what I think.
___ 33. When people yell at me I yell back.
___ 34. When arguing, I tend to raise my voice.
___ 35. Would you like other people to be afraid of you?

Authority Behavior Inventory (ABI)

PURPOSE To measure acceptance of authority.

AUTHOR Ken Rigby

DESCRIPTION This 24-item instrument measures the acceptance of authority in the form of a behavioral inventory. As a concept, the acceptance of authority is different from accepting or liking people in general. It is similar to the notion of "authoritarian submission" found in the California F Scale. The Rokeach Dogmatism Scale, and other attitude scales. As a behavioral inventory, instead of an attitude scale, the ABI is based on observable and verifiable actions or events. The current version of the ABI was developed from an earlier 14-item instrument. A respondent with higher acceptance of authority is generally considered pro-authority, is likely to follow rules, and tends to obey social demands that include the legal obligation to conform. This could encompass such activities as obeying traffic regulations and refraining from illegal drug and alcohol abuse. Clinicians may find this instrument useful with rebellious youngsters or juvenile delinquents. The relation of the ABI to antisocial personality is apparent; however, the honesty of the responses must be taken into consideration.

NORMS The ABI has norms on a sample of social work students ($n = 100$) and nonstudents in the general public ($n = 100$) from Australia. The mean scores were 68.64 for the students and 75.78 for nonstudents. A separate sample of nonstudents had a similar mean (74.85). The mean ABI scores were not different between women and men.

SCORING Scores are the total of each item score. Items 2, 5, 8, 9, 12, 14, 15, 17, 18, 19, 21, and 24 are reverse-scored. Scores range from 24 to 200, with higher scores indicating more positive orientation toward acceptance of authority.

RELIABILITY Reliability was first determined by the item-total correlation. All items were significantly correlated with total scores, with a range from .12 to .67. The ABI also has good internal consistency, with an alpha of .84. From the second sample of nonstudent respondents, the alpha was .90. Date on stability are not available.

VALIDITY Validity was estimated by correlating scores on the ABI items with a corresponding item when a rater independently evaluated the respondent. Respondents' scores were significantly correlated with the rater's evaluation, with correlations ranging from .23 to .88. Similarly, a separate study of 150 respondents found correlations between ABI scores and ratings of perceived authority by a rater who knew the person. Total scores on the ABI were significantly correlated with a measure of attitude towards authority .71 for students and .77 for nonstudents, which supports the ABI's concurrent validity. Respondents perceived as more pro-authority had significantly higher ABI scores than subjects perceived as less pro-authority. This supports the instrument's known-groups validity. Similarly, differences were found on the ABI scores by membership in different political parties.

PRIMARY REFERENCE Rigby, K. (1987). An authority behavior inventory, *Journal of Personality Assessment*, 51, 615–625. Instrument reproduced with permission of Ken Rigby and Lawrence Erlbaum Associates, Inc.

AVAILABILITY Dr. Ken Rigby, Division of Education, Arts, and Social Science, University of South Australia, Adelaide, SA, 50001 Australia. Email: Ken.Rigby@unisa.edu.au.

This questionnaire is intended to assess the frequency with which you *behave* in certain ways. Answer each question as carefully as you can by placing a number on the space by each one as follows:

1 = Never
2 = Rarely
3 = Occasionally
4 = Frequently
5 = Very frequently

—— 1. Do you listen attentively to what older people say about how you should behave?
—— 2. Do you question the judgment of umpires or referees when you think they have made an incorrect decision?
—— 3. When a person in authority whom you trust tells you to do something, do you do it, even though you can't see the reason for it?
—— 4. Do you criticize people who are rude to their superiors?
—— 5. Do you encourage young people to do what they want to do, even when it is against the wishes of their parents?
—— 6. When you go to work, do you dress so as to be acceptable to the people who run the place?
—— 7. Do you treat experts with respect even when you don't think much of them personally?
—— 8. Do you support left-wing, radical policies?
—— 9. Do you take part in demonstrations to show your opposition to policies you do not like?
—— 10. Do you express approval for the work of school teachers?
—— 11. Do you go to church?
—— 12. Do you make fun of the police?
—— 13. When things are bad, do you look for guidance from someone wiser than yourself?
—— 14. Do you sympathize with rebels?
—— 15. When you are in a hurry, do you break the speed limit or encourage your driver to do so, if it seems reasonably safe?
—— 16. Do you follow doctor's orders?
—— 17. Do you question what you hear on the news?
—— 18. Do you cross the road against the pedestrian traffic lights?
—— 19. Do you ask for a "second opinion" when you feel uncertain about a doctor's advice?
—— 20. Do you stand when they play the national anthem in public?
—— 21. Do you express contempt for politicians?
—— 22. Do you get annoyed when people sneer at those in authority?
—— 23. Do you show special respect for people in high positions?
—— 24. Do you speak up against your boss or person in charge when he or she acts unfairly?

Automatic Thoughts Questionnaire (ATQ)

PURPOSE To measure cognitive self-statements of depression.

AUTHORS Philip C. Kendall and Steven D. Hollon

DESCRIPTION This ATQ is a 30-item instrument that measures the frequency of automatic negative statements about the self. Such negative covert statements play an important role in the development, maintenance and treatment of various psychopathologies, including depression. ATQ taps four aspects of these automatic thoughts: personal maladjustment and desire for change (PMDC), negative self-concepts and negative expectations (NSNE), low self-esteem (LSE), and Helplessness. The instrument is particularly noteworthy as it was designed to measure change in cognition due to clinical interventions.

NORMS The ATQ was developed on a sample of 312 undergraduates. The sample had an average age of 20.22 with a standard deviation of 4.34 years. From this sample subjects were categorized as depressed or nondepressed based on scores from the Beck Depression Inventory and Minnesota Multiphasic Personality Inventory Depression scale. The average ATQ score for the depressed subsample was 79.64 with a standard deviation of 22.29. The average score for the nondepressed sample was 48.57 with a standard deviation of 10.89.

SCORING Items are rated on the frequency of occurrence from "not at all" to "all the time." Total scores are the sum of all 30 items. Items on each factor are: PMDC: 7, 10, 14, 20, 26; NSNE: 2, 3, 9, 21, 23, 24, 28; LSE: 17, 18; Helplessness: 29, 30.

RELIABILITY The instrument has excellent internal consistency with an alpha coefficient of .97. No information was available for test-retest reliability.

VALIDITY The 30 items of the ATQ were selected from a pool of 100, and all significantly discriminated depressed from nondepressed subjects. This finding was repeated with another sample of depressed and nondepressed subjects. The instrument also has good concurrent validity, correlating with two measures of depression, the Beck Depression Inventory and the MMPI Depression Scale. Contrary to the initial prediction, scores were highly correlated with anxiety.

PRIMARY REFERENCE Hollon, S. D., and Kendall, P. C. (1980). Cognitive self-statements in depression: Development of an Automatic Thoughts Questionnaire, *Cognitive Therapy and Research*, 4, 383–395. Instrument reproduced with permission of Philip C. Kendall.

AVAILABILITY Dr. Philip C. Kendall, Division of Clinical Psychology, Temple University, Philadelphia, PA 19122. Email: pkendall@temple.edu.

Listed below are a variety of thoughts that pop into people's heads. Please read each thought and indicate how frequently, if at all, the thought occurred to you *over the last week*. Please read each item carefully and fill in the blank with the appropriate number, using the following scale:

1 = Not at all
2 = Sometimes
3 = Moderately often
4 = Often
5 = All the time

___ 1.   I feel like I'm up against the world.
___ 2.   I'm no good.
___ 3.   Why can't I ever succeed?
___ 4.   No one understands me.
___ 5.   I've let people down.
___ 6.   I don't think I can go on.
___ 7.   I wish I were a better person.
___ 8.   I'm so weak.
___ 9.   My life's not going the way I want it to.
___ 10.   I'm so disappointed in myself.
___ 11.   Nothing feels good anymore.
___ 12.   I can't stand this anymore.
___ 13.   I can't get started.
___ 14.   What's wrong with me?
___ 15.   I wish I were somewhere else.
___ 16.   I can't get things together.
___ 17.   I hate myself.
___ 18.   I'm worthless.
___ 19.   I wish I could just disappear.
___ 20.   What's the matter with me?
___ 21.   I'm a loser.
___ 22.   My life is a mess.
___ 23.   I'm a failure.
___ 24.   I'll never make it.
___ 25.   I feel so helpless.
___ 26.   Something has to change.
___ 27.   There must be something wrong with me.
___ 28.   My future is bleak.
___ 29.   It's just not worth it.
___ 30.   I can't finish anything.

Autonomy Preference Index (API)

PURPOSE To measure autonomy.

AUTHORS John Ende et al.

DESCRIPTION The API is a 23-item scale designed to assess patients' preferences for two dimensions of autonomy, their desire to make medical decisions and their desire to be informed. In an era of increasing emphasis on medical ethics, patient autonomy is viewed as key to ethical practice. Thus, a scale measuring preferences for autonomy is thought to be useful to ethicists and practitioners. The API is comprised of two scales: a 15-item scale on Decision-Making (items 1–15) and an 8-item scale on Information Seeking (items 16–23).

NORMS The API was developed with a sample of 312 patients in a hospital-based primary care clinic in Boston, of whom 192 were female. Approximately similar percentages of patients were in three of four age groupings, 26–50, 51–65 and over 65, with only 4% between the ages of 18–25. 55% of respondents were white, 39% were African American, 2% were Hispanic and 11% other ethnicities. 42% of the sample was married with the remainder spread over other categories of marital status. 38% had 12 years of education or less, and 55% were retired or otherwise not employed outside the home. The mean score on Decision-Making was 33.2 (SD = 12.6). The mean score on Preference for Information Seeking was 79.5 (SD = 11.5).

SCORING The two subscales of the API are scored separately. Each is arranged to be scored from 0 to 100 so that 100 equals a high preference for decision-making and information-seeking, 50 is neutral and 0 indicates a very low preference for either aspect of autonomy. The following items are reverse-scored: 1, 3, 5, and 20.

RELIABILITY The API has good internal consistency with both subscales having an alpha of .82. The API also has excellent stability with 2-week test-retest reliabilities of .84 for Decision-Making and .83 for Information-Seeking.

VALIDITY The API has some degree of concurrent validity for the Decision-Making scale with a significant correlation with a separate global item on patient preferences for control of their medical care. The API also has some degree of criterion-related validity with a significantly higher score on Decision-Making for highly motivated diabetic patients compared to a sample from the general population.

PRIMARY REFERENCE Ende, J., et al. (1989). Measuring patients' desire for autonomy, *Journal of General Internal Medicine, 4*, 23–30. Instrument reproduced with permission of Dr. Jack Ende.

AVAILABILITY Jack Ende, M.D., Presbyterian Medical Center, University of Pennsylvania, 39th and Market Streets, Philadelphia, PA 19104. Email: Ende@mail.med.upenn.edu.

In this section we would like to know how you feel about some general health related issues. There are no right or wrong answers. We are only interested in your opinions.

Please check the box which indicates how strongly you agree, or disagree, with each statement.

	Strongly Disagree	Disagree	Neither Agree Nor Disagree	Agree	Strongly Agree
1. The important medical decisions should be made by the doctor, not the patient.	☐	☐	☐	☐	☐
2. Patients should go along with the doctor's advice even if they disagree with it.	☐	☐	☐	☐	☐
3. Hospitalized patients should not be making decisions about their own medical care.	☐	☐	☐	☐	☐
4. Patients should feel free to make decisions about everyday medical problems.	☐	☐	☐	☐	☐
5. If you were sick, as your illness became worse, you would want the doctor to take greater control.	☐	☐	☐	☐	☐
6. Patients should decide how frequently they need a check-up.	☐	☐	☐	☐	☐

In this section, three medical problems are described. Each problem is followed by some statements related to decision-making.

Please check the box which indicates how you would feel about each statement if you actually had the medical problem which is described.

A. Suppose you developed a sore throat, stuffy nose, and cough which lasted three days. You are about to call the doctor on the telephone. Who should make the following decision, you or the doctor?

	You Alone	Mostly You	The Doctor And You Equally	Mostly The Doctor	The Doctor Alone
7. Whether you should be seen by the doctor.	☐	☐	☐	☐	☐
8. If a chest X-ray should be taken.	☐	☐	☐	☐	☐
9. If you should try taking cough syrup.	☐	☐	☐	☐	☐

B. Suppose you went to the doctor for a routine physical examination and he or she found that everything was all right except that your blood pressure was high (170/100). Who should make the following decisions?

	You Alone	Mostly You	The Doctor And You Equally	Mostly The Doctor	The Doctor Alone
10. When the next visit to check your blood pressure should be.	☐	☐	☐	☐	☐
11. Whether you should take some time off from work to relax.	☐	☐	☐	☐	☐
12. Whether you should be treated with medication or diet.	☐	☐	☐	☐	☐

C. Suppose you had an attack of severe chest pain that lasted for almost an hour, frightening you enough so that you went to the emergency room. In the emergency room the doctors discover that you are having a heart attack. Your own doctor is called and you are taken up to the intensive care unit. Who should make the following decisions?

	You Alone	Mostly You	The Doctor And You Equally	Mostly The Doctor	The Doctor Alone
13. How often the nurses should wake you up to check your temperature and blood pressure.	☐	☐	☐	☐	☐
14. Whether you may have visitors aside from your immediate family.	☐	☐	☐	☐	☐
15. Whether a cardiologist should be consulted.	☐	☐	☐	☐	☐

The next eight questions refer to your experiences with medical care.

	Strongly Disagree	Disagree	Neither Agree Nor Disagree	Agree	Strongly Agree
16. As you become sicker you should be told more and more about your illness.	☐	☐	☐	☐	☐
17. You should understand completely what is happening inside your body as a result of your illness.	☐	☐	☐	☐	☐
18. Even if the news is bad, you should be well informed.	☐	☐	☐	☐	☐
19. Your doctor should explain the purpose of your laboratory tests.	☐	☐	☐	☐	☐
20. You should be given information only when you ask for it.	☐	☐	☐	☐	☐
21. It is important for you to know all the side effects of your medication.	☐	☐	☐	☐	☐

	Strongly Disagree	Disagree	Neither Agree Nor Disagree	Agree	Strongly Agree
22. Information about your illness is as important to you as treatment.	☐	☐	☐	☐	☐
23. When there is more than one method to treat a problem, you should be told about each one.	☐	☐	☐	☐	☐

Bakker Assertiveness-Aggressiveness Inventory (AS-AGI)

PURPOSE To measure two dimensions of assertion.

AUTHORS Cornelis B. Bakker, Marianne K. Bakker-Rabdau, and Saul Breit

DESCRIPTION This 36-item inventory measures assertiveness in terms of two components necessary for social functioning: the ability to refuse unreasonable requests ("assertiveness" AS), and the ability to take the initiative, make requests, or ask for favors ("aggressiveness" AG). In this measure aggressiveness differs from hostility, tending to relate more to being responsible and taking the initiative in social situations. The two instruments can also be used separately as 18-item measures.

NORMS Normative data are available from seven different samples. From a sample of 250 college students, males had average AS and AG scores of 48.83 and 51.07, respectively, while female scores were 47.69 for the AS and 52.37 for the AG. A sample of 17 male city employee supervisors, with an average age of 40.1 with a standard deviation of 6.3 years, had AS scores of 43.85 and 47.88 for the AG. From a sample of students seeking assertiveness training the average AS and AG scores were 55.0 and 58.67 respectively, for males and 54.85 and 58.60 for females; the average ages of these males and females were 39.0 and 43.4, respectively. Additional normative data on nurses, X-ray technicians and employees of a city water department are reported in the primary reference.

SCORING Each item is rated on a 5-point scale from "almost always" to "almost never" according to the likelihood the respondent would behave in the specified manner. Each scale is scored separately. Those items with a plus sign before the alternative are reverse-scored as follows: 1 becomes 5, 2 becomes 4, 4 becomes 2, and 5 becomes 1. The item responses for each scale are summed with a range from 18 to 90. Higher scores indicate that the individual is less likely to exhibit assertiveness or aggressiveness.

RELIABILITY These scales have been shown to be fairly reliable in terms of internal consistency and test-retest reliability. Internal consistency was estimated from a split-half procedure and was .73 for the AS scale and .80 for AG scale. Test-retest correlations were .75 for the AS and .88 for AG over a six-week period.

VALIDITY Item analysis of all 36 items indicated that scores on each correlated highly with the score on the subscale of which it is a part. Research on known-groups validity indicated that both scales discriminated between a client and college sample. The scales are sensitive to measuring change as AS and AG scores changed subsequent to assertiveness training.

PRIMARY REFERENCE Bakker, C. B., Bakker-Rabdau, M. K., and Breit, S. (1978). The measurement of assertiveness and aggressiveness, *Journal of Personality Assessment*, 42, 277–284. Instrument reproduced with permission of C. B. Bakker and the *Journal of Personality Assessment*.

AVAILABILITY C. B. Bakker, M.D., Department of Psychiatry, Adult Development Program, Sacred Heart Medical Center, West 101 Eighth Avenue, Spokane, WA 99220. Telephone: 509.474.4818.

Below are several different situations. Each is followed by one way of responding. Your task is to read each question and indicate how likely you are to respond in that way, according to the following scale:

$$1 = \text{Almost always}$$
$$2 = \text{Frequently}$$
$$3 = \text{Occasionally}$$
$$4 = \text{Sometimes}$$
$$5 = \text{Almost never}$$

Record your answers in the space to the left of each item.

AS Items

___ 1. You have set aside the evening to get some necessary work done. Just as you get started some friends drop over for a social visit.
  – You welcome them in and postpone what you had planned to do.

___ 2. You are standing in line when someone pushes ahead of you.
  + You tell the person to get back in line behind you.

___ 3. A friend or relative asks to borrow your car or other valuable property but you would prefer not to lend it to them.
  – You lend it to them anyway.

___ 4. A person who has kept you waiting before is late again for an appointment.
  – You ignore it and act as if nothing has happened.

___ 5. Someone has, in your opinion, treated you unfairly or incorrectly.
  + You confront the person directly concerning this.

___ 6. Friends or neighbors fail to return some items they have borrowed from you.
  + You keep after them until they return them.

___ 7. Others put pressure on you to drink, smoke pot, take drugs, or eat too much.
  + You refuse to yield to their pressure.

___ 8. Another person interrupts you while you are speaking.
  – You wait until the other is finished speaking before you go on with your story.

___ 9. You are asked to carry out a task that you do not feel like doing.
  + You tell the other that you don't want to do it.

___ 10. Your sexual partner has done something that you do not like.
  – You act as if nothing bothersome has happened.

___ 11. A salesperson has spent a great deal of time showing you merchandise but none of it is exactly what you want.
  – You buy something anyway.

___ 12. You are invited to a party or other social event, which you would rather not attend.
  – You accept the invitation.

___ 13. In a concert or a movie theater a couple next to you distracts you with their conversation.
  + You ask them to be quiet or move somewhere else.

___ 14. In a restaurant you receive food that is poorly prepared.
  + You ask the waiter or waitress to replace it.

_____ 15. You receive incorrect or damaged merchandise from a store.
+ You return the merchandise.
_____ 16. A person who seems a lot worse off than you asks you for something you could easily do without but you don't like to.
– You give the person what he/she asks for.
_____ 17. Someone gives you—unasked for—a negative appraisal of your behavior.
+ You tell the other you are not interested.
_____ 18. Friends or parents try to get information from you that you consider personal.
– You give them the information they want.

AG Items

_____ 19. You have been appointed to a newly formed committee.
+ You take a leadership role.
_____ 20. You are in a bus or plane sitting next to a person you have never met.
+ You strike up a conversation.
_____ 21. You are a guest in a home of a new acquaintance. The dinner was so good you would like a second helping.
+ You go ahead and take a second helping.
_____ 22. You are being interviewed for a job you really want to get.
– You undersell yourself.
_____ 23. You are meeting or greeting several people.
+ You make physical contact with each other in turn either by hugging, putting an arm around their shoulders, or slapping their backs.
_____ 24. You have observed that someone has done an excellent job at something.
– You don't tell that person about it.
_____ 25. In a store or restaurant the personnel are very busy and many customers seem to be waiting a long time for service.
+ You manage to get service ahead of other customers.
_____ 26. You observe someone behave in a suspicious manner.
– You don't do anything because it is none of your business.
_____ 27. You have parked your car but notice that you do not have the correct change for the parking meter.
+ You ask a passer-by for the change.
_____ 28. Someone has done or said something that arouses your curiosity.
– You refrain from asking questions.
_____ 29. You have observed certain behaviors of a friend or acquaintance that you think need to be changed. You tell the other person about this as soon as possible.
+ You tell the other person about this as soon as possible.
_____ 30. You would like to get a raise but your boss has said nothing about it.
– You wait for your boss to bring the matter up.
_____ 31. During a social visit with a group of friends everyone participates actively in the conversation.
+ You dominate the conversation most of the time.
_____ 32. During a discussion you believe that you have something worthwhile to contribute.
+ You don't bother to state it unless the others ask you to give your opinion.
_____ 33. You have an opportunity to participate in a lively, no-holds-barred debate.
– You remain a listener rather than participate.

___ 34. You want a favor done by a person you do not know too well.
    – You prefer to do without rather than ask that person.

___ 35. You have moved into a new neighborhood or started a new job and you would like to make social contacts.
    – You wait for others to introduce themselves.

___ 36. You see an opportunity to get ahead but know it will take a great deal of energy.
    + You take the opportunity and forge ahead.

Barnett Liking of Children Scale (BLOCS)

PURPOSE To measure attitudes toward children.

AUTHORS Mark A. Barnett and Christina S. Sinisi

DESCRIPTION The BLOCS is a 14-item instrument designed to assess the extent to which individuals have a favorable attitude toward children. The BLOCS measures general attitudes of people like parents and teachers whose attitudes could be associated with a broad range of beliefs and behaviors about children and childbearing. The BLOCS is seen as a viable measure for examining the way an individual's tendency to like or dislike children may influence his or her interactions with children in areas as diverse as teaching and child maltreatment.

NORMS The BLOCS was studied initially with several different samples involving a total of 284 undergraduate students of whom 145 were males and 139 females. No other demographic data were reported. Females report significantly greater liking of children than males with means that range from 80.66 to 81.23 for females and 72.02 to 74.35 for males.

SCORING The BLOCS is easily scored by reverse-scoring items 3, 6, 10, and 13 and then summing individual items for a total score. The higher the score, the more positive the attitude toward children.

RELIABILITY The BLOCS has excellent internal consistency, with an alpha of .93. The BLOCS also has excellent stability, with a one-week test-retest reliability coefficient of .91.

VALIDITY The BLOCS has good concurrent validity, correlating significantly with several subscales of the Hereford Childbearing Scale and with a number of independent statements of childbearing attitudes.

PRIMARY REFERENCE Barnett, M. A., and Sinisi, C. S. (1990). The initial validation of a Liking of Children Scale, *Journal of Personality Assessment*, 55, 161–167.

AVAILABILITY May be copied from this volume.

BLOCS

Please indicate the extent to which you agree or disagree with each of the following statements by circling the appropriate number under each statement.

Strongly disagree			Neither disagree nor agree			Strongly agree
1	2	3	4	5	6	7

1. Watching little children play gives me pleasure.

1	2	3	4	5	6	7

2. I enjoy getting to know a child.

1	2	3	4	5	6	7

3. I do not like talking with young children.

1	2	3	4	5	6	7

4. I enjoy holding little children.

1	2	3	4	5	6	7

5. I feel happy when I make a child smile.

1	2	3	4	5	6	7

6. I do not like being around children.

1	2	3	4	5	6	7

7. I enjoy watching children play in a park.

1	2	3	4	5	6	7

8. Time seems to go by quickly when I interact with children.

1	2	3	4	5	6	7

9. I like to listen to children talk to one another.

1	2	3	4	5	6	7

10. Children are annoying.

1	2	3	4	5	6	7

11. I enjoy trying to make a child smile.

1	2	3	4	5	6	7

12. Children are likable once you get to know them.

1	2	3	4	5	6	7

13. It bothers me when children get loud and active.

1	2	3	4	5	6	7

14. I like children.

1	2	3	4	5	6	7

Barratt Impulsiveness Scale 11 (BIS-11)

PURPOSE To measure impulsivity.

AUTHOR Ernest S. Barratt

DESCRIPTION This 30-item instrument assesses impulsivity as a trait independent of anxiety. The BIS was originally developed in the late 1950s and has had nearly four decades of attention by researchers. The BIS, in fact, has been revised eleven times. There are three subscales of the BIS: impulsive non-planning (INP: items 1*, 3, 5*, 8*, 11*, 14, 17*, 20, 22*, 25, 28, and 30), motor impulsivity (MI: items 2, 6*, 9, 12, 15, 18, 21, 23, 26, and 29), and attentional impulsivity (AI: items 4, 7*, 10*, 13*, 16, 19*, 24, and 27). The INP subscale reflects a present orientation and lack of consideration for the future. The MI defines acting on the spur of the moment. The AI subscale reflects impulsivity in focusing on the task at hand. The BIS also may be used as a total scale score of impulsivity. Items on the BIS were selected on two criteria: significant correlation between the item and total scale scores, and the ability of the item to differentiate between respondents with high and low scores.

NORMS Normative data are available for the total BIS scores from various samples. Undergraduate males ($n = 130$) had a mean of 63.72 and a standard deviation of 10.16. Female substance abuse patients ($n = 54$) had a mean of 69.78 and a standard deviation of 10.51, while male substance abuse patients ($n = 110$) had a mean of 69.0 and a standard deviation of 10.21. Female patients with psychiatric disorders at discharge ($n = 45$) had a mean of 72.78 and a standard deviation of 13.43, while male patients ($n = 39$) had a mean of 69.74 and a standard deviation of 11.54. Male inmates from a maximum security facility had a mean of 76.3 and a standard deviation of 11.86.

SCORING The BIS is accompanied with scoring templates, which greatly facilitates the task of scoring. Each item is rated from Rarely/Never (scored as 1) to Almost always/Always (scored as a 4). Subscale scores are the summation of the individual items after reverse-scoring items marked with an asterisk above. Scores range from 12 to 48 for the INP, 10 to 40 for the MI, and 8 to 32 for the IA.

RELIABILITY The reliability of the BIS is first supported with the inclusion criterion that items correlated with total scores and differentiate high from low scores on the total BIS. The internal consistency of the BIS ranges from .79 to .83 for a number of samples.

VALIDITY There is considerable evidence of the validity of the BIS. Scores on the three subscales were moderately correlated, suggesting the subscales are tapping a similar construct. Scores also correlate with a measure of disinhibition, a subscale of sensation seeking behaviors. Scores on the BIS correlated with psychoticism for a sample of inpatient psychiatric patients. Scores on the BIS differentiate undergraduates from substance abuse patients and psychiatric patients. Undergraduate males were significantly different in impulsivity scores than men in a secured correctional facility. These differences support the known-groups validity of BIS.

PRIMARY REFERENCE Patton, J. H., Stanford, M. S., and Barratt, E. S. (1995). Factor structure of the Barratt Impulsivity Scale, *Journal of Clinical Psychology*, 51, 768–774.

AVAILABILITY May be copied from this volume.

People differ in the ways they act and think in different situations. This is a test to measure some of the ways in which you act and think. Read each statement and darken the appropriate circle on the right side of the page. Do not spend too much time on any statement. Answer quickly and honestly.

	Rarely/Never (1)	Occasionally (2)	Often (3)	Almost always/Always (4)
1. I plan tasks carefully.	O	O	O	O
2. I do things without thinking.	O	O	O	O
3. I am happy-go-lucky.	O	O	O	O
4. I have "racing" thoughts.	O	O	O	O
5. I plan trips well ahead of time.	O	O	O	O
6. I am self-controlled.	O	O	O	O
7. I concentrate easily.	O	O	O	O
8. I save regularly.	O	O	O	O
9. I find it hard to sit still for long periods of time.	O	O	O	O
10. I am a careful thinker.	O	O	O	O
11. I plan for job security.	O	O	O	O
12. I say things without thinking.	O	O	O	O
13. I like to think about complex problems.	O	O	O	O
14. I change jobs.	O	O	O	O
15. I act "on impulse."	O	O	O	O
16. I get easily bored when solving thought problems.	O	O	O	O
17. I have regular medical/dental checkups.	O	O	O	O
18. I act on the spur of the moment.	O	O	O	O
19. I am a steady thinker.	O	O	O	O
20. I change where I live.	O	O	O	O
21. I buy things on impulse.	O	O	O	O
22. I finish what I start.	O	O	O	O
23. I walk and move fast.	O	O	O	O
24. I solve problems by trial-and-error.	O	O	O	O
25. I spend or charge more than I earn.	O	O	O	O
26. I talk fast.	O	O	O	O
27. I have outside thoughts when thinking.	O	O	O	O
28. I am more interested in the present than the future.	O	O	O	O
29. I am restless at lectures or talks.	O	O	O	O
30. I plan for the future.	O	O	O	O

Belief in Personal Control Scale (BPCS)

PURPOSE To measure personal control.

AUTHOR Joy L. Berrenberg

DESCRIPTION The BPCS is a 45-item instrument designed to measure three dimensions of personal control: general external control (F1) assesses the extent to which an individual believes his or her outcomes are self-produced (internality) or produced by fate or others (externality). The exaggerated control dimension (F2) measures an extreme and unrealistic belief in personal control. The God-mediated dimension (F3) measures the belief that God can be enlisted in the achievement of outcomes (distinguishing between individuals who believe they have no control over their outcomes and those who believe they control outcomes through God). Items on the three subscales are indicated on the measure itself.

NORMS The BPCS was studied with several samples of students for a total of 404 (169 males and 235 females). Of this group, all were undergraduates except for 48 seminary graduate students and 34 psychology graduate students. For the undergraduates, means for general external control were 68.91 (SD = 8.35), for exaggerated internal control were 55.57 (SD = 7.56), and for God-mediated control were 28.27 (SD = 11.43).

SCORING The BPCS is easily scored by summing items for each subscale score. Items marked with an asterisk are reverse-scored so that higher scores mean more internal control (F1), a more exaggerated belief in control (F2), and less belief in God as a mediator of control (F3).

RELIABILITY The BPCS has very good to excellent internal consistency, with alphas of .85 (F1), .88 (F2), and .97 (F3). The BPCS has very good stability, with four-week test-retest correlations of .81 (F1), .85 (F2), and .93 (F3).

VALIDITY The BPCS has excellent construct validity, with correlations in the expected directions with several other measures including Internal-External Locus of Control, the Taylor Manifest Anxiety Scale, the Feelings of Inadequacy Scale, and the Mania and Depression Scales. The 45-item BPCS is also highly correlated with an earlier 85-item version (factors correlate from .85 to .95).

PRIMARY REFERENCE Berrenberg, J. L. (1987). The Belief in Personal Control Scale: A measure of God-mediated and exaggerated control, *Journal of Personality Assessment*, 51, 194–206.

AVAILABILITY Dr. Joy Berrenberg, Department of Psychology, University of Colorado, CB 173, PO Box 173364, Denver, CO 80217-3364. Telephone: 303.556.8350. Email: joy.berrenberg@ucdenver.edu.

This questionnaire consists of items describing possible perceptions you may have of yourself, others, and life in general. Please respond to each of the statements below by indicating the extent to which that statement describes your beliefs. For each statement circle the number that best describes your feelings.

1 = Always true
2 = Often true
3 = Sometimes true
4 = Rarely
5 = Never true

Scoring
Key

*F2	1.	I can make things happen easily.	1	2	3	4	5
F1	2.	Getting what you want is a matter of knowing the right people.	1	2	3	4	5
F1	3.	My behavior is dictated by the demands of society.	1	2	3	4	5
*F2	4.	If I just keep trying, I can overcome any obstacle.	1	2	3	4	5
F3	5.	I can succeed with God's help.	1	2	3	4	5
F1	6.	I find that luck plays a bigger role in my life than my ability.	1	2	3	4	5
*F2	7.	If nothing is happening, I go out and make it happen.	1	2	3	4	5
*F2	8.	I am solely responsible for the outcomes in my life.	1	2	3	4	5
F3	9.	I rely on God to help me control my life.	1	2	3	4	5
*F2	10.	Regardless of the obstacles, I refuse to quit trying.	1	2	3	4	5
F1	11.	My success is a matter of luck.	1	2	3	4	5
F1	12.	Getting what you want is a matter of being in the right place at the right time.	1	2	3	4	5
*F2	13.	I am able to control effectively the behavior of others.	1	2	3	4	5
F3	14.	If I need help, I know that God is there for me.	1	2	3	4	5
F1	15.	I feel that other people have more control over my life than I do.	1	2	3	4	5
F1	16.	There is little that I can do to change my destiny.	1	2	3	4	5
*F2	17.	I feel that I control my life as much as is humanly possible.	1	2	3	4	5

F3	18.	God rewards me if I obey his laws.	1	2	3	4	5
F1	19.	I am not the master of my own fate.	1	2	3	4	5
*F2	20.	I continue to strive for a goal long after others would have given up.	1	2	3	4	5
F1	21.	Most things in my life I just can't control.	1	2	3	4	5
F3	22.	God helps me to control my life.	1	2	3	4	5
*F2	23.	I have more control over my life than other people have over theirs.	1	2	3	4	5
*F2	24.	I actively strive to make things happen for myself.	1	2	3	4	5
F1	25.	Other people hinder my ability to direct my life.	1	2	3	4	5
F1	26.	What happens to me is a matter of good or bad fortune.	1	2	3	4	5
*F2	27.	When something stands in my way, I go around it.	1	2	3	4	5
*F2	28.	I can be whatever I want to be.	1	2	3	4	5
*F2	29.	I know how to get what I want from others.	1	2	3	4	5
F1	30.	Fate can be blamed for my failures.	1	2	3	4	5
F3	31.	With God's help, I can be whatever I want to be.	1	2	3	4	5
F1	32.	I am the victim of circumstances beyond my control.	1	2	3	4	5
F1	33.	I can control my own thoughts.	1	2	3	4	5
*F2	34.	There is nothing that happens to me that I don't control.	1	2	3	4	5
*F2	35.	Whenever I run up against some obstacle, I strive even harder to overcome it and reach my goal.	1	2	3	4	5
F3	36.	By placing my life in God's hands, I can accomplish anything.	1	2	3	4	5
F1	37.	I am at the mercy of my physical impulses.	1	2	3	4	5
F1	38.	In this life, what happens to me is determined by my fate.	1	2	3	4	5
F3	39.	My actions are the result of God working through me.	1	2	3	4	5
F1	40.	I am the victim of social forces.	1	2	3	4	5
*F2	41.	Controlling my life involves mind over matter.	1	2	3	4	5
*F2	42.	When I want something, I assert myself in order to get it.	1	2	3	4	5
F1	43.	The unconscious mind, over which I have no control, directs my life.	1	2	3	4	5
F3	44.	If I really want something, I pray to God to bring it to me.	1	2	3	4	5
F1	45.	I am not really in control of the outcomes in my life.	1	2	3	4	5

Beliefs Associated with Childhood Sexual Abuse (BACSA)

PURPOSE To measure beliefs associated with sexual abuse.

AUTHORS Derek Jehu, Carole Klassen, and Marjorie Gazan

DESCRIPTION The BACSA is a 17-item instrument designed to measure common distorted beliefs associated with childhood sexual abuse. The instrument actually was developed to be used to depict changes in clients who are receiving cognitive therapy to restructure distorted beliefs that could contribute to mood disturbances such as guilt, low self-esteem, and sadness.

NORMS No norms were reported. Initial testing of the instrument was conducted on 25 women who previously had been sexually abused. No demographic data are available.

SCORING The BACSA is scored by simply totaling the scores (0–4) on the 5-point scale, producing a potential range of 0 to 68 with higher scores suggesting a greater degree of distortion that is clinically significant. A cut-off point of 15 (one standard deviation below the mean of 30.82 for 11 clients) is suggested, with clients scoring above 15 presumably having clinically significant distorted beliefs.

RELIABILITY The BACSA has excellent short-term stability, with a one-week test-retest correlation of .93. No data were provided on internal consistency.

VALIDITY The authors report good face validity and fair concurrent validity, with a .55 (p < .01) correlation with the Beck Depression Inventory.

PRIMARY REFERENCE Jehu, D., Klassen, C., and Gazan, M. (1986). Cognitive restructuring of distorted beliefs associated with childhood sexual abuse, *Journal of Social Work and Human Sexuality*, 4, 49–69.

AVAILABILITY Dr. Derek Jehu, Department of Psychology, University of Leicester, Leicester, LE17RH, England. Telephone: +44(0) 116.229.7198; Fax: +44(0) 116.229.7196.

Please circle one number from 0 to 4 that best indicates how strongly you believe each statement to be true in your own case. Please answer according to what you really believe yourself, not what you think you should believe.

0 = Absolutely untrue
1 = Mostly untrue
2 = Partly true, partly untrue
3 = Mostly true
4 = Absolutely true

1. I must be an extremely rare woman to have experienced sex with an older person I was a child.	0	1	2	3	4
2. I am worthless and bad.	0	1	2	3	4
3. You can't depend on women; they are all weak and useless creatures.	0	1	2	3	4
4. No man can be trusted.	0	1	2	3	4
5. I must have permitted sex to happen because I wasn't forced into it.	0	1	2	3	4
6. I don't have the right to deny my body to any man who demands it.	0	1	2	3	4
7. Anyone who knows what happened to me sexually will not want anything more to do with me.	0	1	2	3	4
8. I must have been seductive and provocative when I was young.	0	1	2	3	4
9. It doesn't matter what happens to me in my life.	0	1	2	3	4
10. No man could care for me without a sexual relationship.	0	1	2	3	4
11. It is dangerous to get close to anyone because they always betray, exploit, or hurt you.	0	1	2	3	4
12. I must have been responsible for sex when I was young because it went on for so long.	0	1	2	3	4
13. I will never be able to lead a normal life; the damage is permanent.	0	1	2	3	4
14. Only bad, worthless guys would be interested in me.	0	1	2	3	4
15. It must be unnatural to feel any pleasure during molestation.	0	1	2	3	4
16. I am inferior to other people because I did not have normal experiences.	0	1	2	3	4
17. I've already been used so it doesn't matter if other men use me.	0	1	2	3	4

Bidimensional Acculturation Scale for Hispanics (BAS)

PURPOSE To measure acculturation.

AUTHORS Gerardo Marin and Raymond J. Gamba

DESCRIPTION The BAS is a 24-item instrument designed to measure acculturation among Hispanics. The BAS provides an acculturation score for two major cultural dimensions (Hispanic and non-Hispanic) in an attempt to avoid the methodological problems of other acculturation scales that assume acculturation is unidimensional. The scale has three language-related factors: the language use subscale (items 1–6); the linguistic proficiency subscale (items 7–18); and the electronic media subscale (items 19–24). The BAS provides two scores by cultural dimension as well as a biculturation score which would be indicated by high scores in both cultural domains (Hispanic and non-Hispanic). The scale works equally well with Mexican Americans and Central Americans. Respondents should be allowed to choose to answer the BAS in English or in Spanish. Therefore, two identical linguistic versions should be made available to each respondent.

NORMS The scale was initially developed with a random sample of 254 adult Hispanic residents of San Francisco, California, who were interviewed over the telephone. Female respondents made up 53.9% of the sample; the mean age was 37.3 years with an average of 10.4 years of formal education. Respondents born outside of the United States made up 79.5% of the sample, with 19.7% having arrived in the United States within the five years prior to the survey. Respondents classified as first-generation Hispanics (born outside the United States) made up 79.9% of the sample. Actual means and standard deviations were not provided in the original article.

SCORING The items from the three subscales should be presented to respondents in random order. There are 12 items for each cultural domain, with response scales varying across items. The answers to the 12 items measuring each cultural domain should be averaged across items for each respondent. Each respondent should be assigned two scores: one for the average of the 12 items making up the Hispanic domain (items 4–6, 13–18, and 22–24) and another score for the 12 items forming the non-Hispanic domain (items 1–3, 7–12, and 19–21). The scores for each item are on a Likert-type scale ranging from 1 to 4; the possible total score range is from 1 to 4 for each cultural domain with the two scores used to define the level of acculturation of the respondent. A score of 2.5 can be used as a cut-off score to indicate low or high level of adherence to each cultural domain, and scores above 2.5 in both cultural domains can be interpreted as indicating biculturalism. The response categories for the items are as follows (with Spanish responses in parentheses): items 1–6 and 19–24 are "almost always" = 4 (casi siempre); "often" = 3 (frecuentemente); "sometimes" = 2 (algunas veces); and "almost never" = 1 (casi nunca). The response categories for items 7–18 are: "very well" = 4 (muy bien); "well" = 3 (bien); "poorly" = 2 (no muy bien); and "very poorly" = 1 (muy mal).

RELIABILITY The BAS has good to excellent internal consistency. The alpha for the combined score of the three subscales for the Hispanic domain was .90 and for the non-Hispanic domain was .96. The alpha for the subscales ranges from .81 to .97. No data on stability were provided in the original article.

VALIDITY The BAS has very good concurrent validity. The subscales and combined overall scores were validated by correlating them with variables used previously by researchers developing other acculturation scales. These variables are generation status, length of residence in the United States, amount of formal education, age at arrival in the United States, proportion of respondents' life lived in the United States, ethnic self-identification, and correlation with the score obtained from the Short Acculturation Scale for Hispanics. All scales and subscales showed moderate to high correlations with all the variables (with the exception of the electronic media subscales) with residence in the United States and proportion of life in the United States. The BAS has equal validity for Central Americans and for Mexican Americans.

PRIMARY REFERENCE Marin, G., and Gamba, R. J. (1996). A new measurement of acculturation for Hispanics: The bidimensional acculturation scale for Hispanics (BAS), *Hispanic Journal of Behavioral Sciences*, 18, 297–316.

AVAILABILITY May be copied from this volume.

ENGLISH VERSION

Circle a number between 4 and 1 that best applies for each item.

Language Use Subscale

	Almost always	Often	Sometimes	Almost never
1. How often do you speak English?	4	3	2	1
2. How often do you speak in English with your friends?	4	3	2	1
3. How often do you think in English?	4	3	2	1
4. How often do you speak Spanish?	4	3	2	1
5. How often do you speak in Spanish with your friends?	4	3	2	1
6. How often do you think in Spanish?	4	3	2	1

Linguistic Proficiency Subscale

	Very well	Well	Poorly	Very poorly
7. How well do you speak English?	4	3	2	1
8. How well do you read in English?	4	3	2	1
9. How well do you understand television programs in English?	4	3	2	1
10. How well do you understand radio programs in English?	4	3	2	1
11. How well do you write in English?	4	3	2	1
12. How well do you understand music in English?	4	3	2	1
13. How well do you speak Spanish?	4	3	2	1
14. How well do you read in Spanish?	4	3	2	1
15. How well do you understand television programs in Spanish?	4	3	2	1
16. How well do you understand radio programs in Spanish?	4	3	2	1
17. How well do you write in Spanish?	4	3	2	1
18. How well do you understand music in Spanish?	4	3	2	1

Electronic Media Subscale

	Almost always	Often	Sometimes	Almost never
19. How often do you watch television programs in English?	4	3	2	1
20. How often do you listen to radio programs in English?	4	3	2	1

	Almost always	Often	Sometimes	Almost never
21. How often do you listen to music in English?	4	3	2	1
22. How often do you watch television programs in Spanish?	4	3	2	1
23. How often do you listen to radio programs in Spanish?	4	3	2	1
24. How often do you listen to music in Spanish?	4	3	2	1

SPANISH VERSION

Marque con un círculo el numero entre 4 y 1 a la respuesta que sea más adecuada para usted.

Language Use Subscale

	Casi siempre	Frecuentemente	Algunas veces	Casi nunca
1. ¿Con qué frecuencia habla usted inglés?	4	3	2	1
2. ¿Con qué frecuencia habla usted en inglés con sus amigos?	4	3	2	1
3. ¿Con qué frecuencia piensa usted en inglés?	4	3	2	1
4. ¿Con qué frecuencia habla usted español?	4	3	2	1
5. ¿Con qué frecuencia habla usted en español con sus amigos?	4	3	2	1
6. ¿Con qué frecuencia piensa usted en español?	4	3	2	1

Linguistic Proficiency Subscale

	Muy bien	Bien	No muy bien	Muy mal
7. ¿Qué tan bien habla usted inglés?	4	3	2	1
8. ¿Qué tan bien lee usted en inglés?	4	3	2	1
9. ¿Qué tan bien entiende usted los programas de televisión en inglés?	4	3	2	1
10. ¿Qué tan bien entiende usted los programas de radio en inglés?	4	3	2	1
11. ¿Qué tan bien escribe usted en inglés?	4	3	2	1
12. ¿Qué tan bien entiende usted música en inglés?	4	3	2	1
13. ¿Qué tan bien habla usted español?	4	3	2	1
14. ¿Qué tan bien lee usted en español?	4	3	2	1
15. ¿Qué tan bien entiende usted los programas de televisión en español?	4	3	2	1

	Muy bien	Bien	No muy bien	Muy mal
16. ¿Qué tan bien entiende usted los programas de radio en español?	4	3	2	1
17. ¿Qué tan bien escribe usted en español?	4	3	2	1
18. ¿Qué tan bien entiende usted música en español?	4	3	2	1

Electronic Media Subscale

	Casi siempre	Frecuente-mente	Algunas veces	Casi nunca
19. ¿Con qué frecuencia ve usted programas de televisión en inglés?	4	3	2	1
20. ¿Con qué frecuencia escucha usted programas de radio en inglés?	4	3	2	1
21. ¿Con qué frecuencia escucha usted música en inglés?	4	3	2	1
22. ¿Con qué frecuencia ve usted programas de televisión en español?	4	3	2	1
23. ¿Con qué frecuencia escucha usted programas de radio en español?	4	3	2	1
24. ¿Con qué frecuencia escucha usted música en español?	4	3	2	1

Body Image Assessment Scale-Body Dimensions (BIAS-BD)

PURPOSE To measure body image and body dissatisfaction

AUTHORS Rick Gardner, Leah Jappe and Lisa Gardner

PURPOSE The BIAS-BD is a 2-item scale consisting of 17 male contour-line figures and 17 female contour- figures which measures one perceived Body Size (BS), Ideal Size (IS) and Body Dissatisfaction (BD). Each figure is drawn to reflect known anthropometric body dimensions. The figures reflect body sizes ranging from 60% below average to 140% above the average for the American population, and each figure is 5% above or below the adjacent figure. The BIAS-BD is particularly useful for patients with eating disorders, including obesity. It is also useful for participants in stress management programs and health promotion programs. Both men and women tend to overestimate their body size when compared to their known Body Mass Index (BMI) and females overestimate this more than males. Since the BIAS-BD is based on well-known body dimensions, its accuracy is an improvement over some other measures of body image.

NORMS For a sample of 207 undergraduates the mean BMI score was 22.57 for females with a standard deviation of 3.93. For males the mean BMI was 23.49 with a standard deviation of 4.5. The average BD scores was .45 with a standard deviation of .26 for the combined sample and .58 (sd = .52) for men and .40 (sd = .29) for women. The national norms for the BMI had an mean of 27.8 for men and 28.2 for women.

SCORING Scores on the BS and IS are the percentage score of the selected figure, converted to BMI scores based on well-established national norms from the general population. Percentage scores are transformed into BMI scores follows: 60% = 16.68, 65% = 18.0, 70% = 19.5, 75% = 20.75, 80% = 21.95, 85% = 23.5, 90% = 24.81, 95% = 26.5, 100% = 27.8, 105% = 29.2, 110% = 30.6, 115% = 32.0, 120% = 33.3, 125% = 35.0, 130% = 36.3, 135% = 37.6, 140% = 38.92 for men. For women the BMI scores were 16.92, 18.25, 19.57, 20.9, 22.5, 23.8, 25.5, 26.8, 28.2, 30.2, 35.5, 32.85, 34.2, 35.5, 36.8, 38.15 and 39.48 for each of the percentage noted with males. These BMI scores are approximate due to small rounding errors. Scores on the BD are the differences between IS and BS BMI scores.

RELIABILITY The BIAS-BD has very good test retest reliability over a two-week period. The correlations were .86, .72 sand .81 for the BS, IS and BD, respectively.

VALIDITY One estimate of the accuracy is the fact that each figure is based on well-established anthropometric body dimensions. Additionally, concurrent validity is supported by the correlation between BAIS-BD scores and known BMI for the 207 undergraduates, which was .76.

PRIMARY Reference Gardner, R. M., Jappe, L M. and Gardner, L (2009). Development and validation of a new figural drawing scale for body-image assessment: The BIAS-BD. *Journal of Clinical Psychology.* 65, 113–122.

AVAILABILITY Rick M. Gardner, Ph.D., Department of Psychology, University of Colorado, Campus Box 173, POB 173364 Denver, CO 80217. Email: rick.gardner@ucdenver.edu.

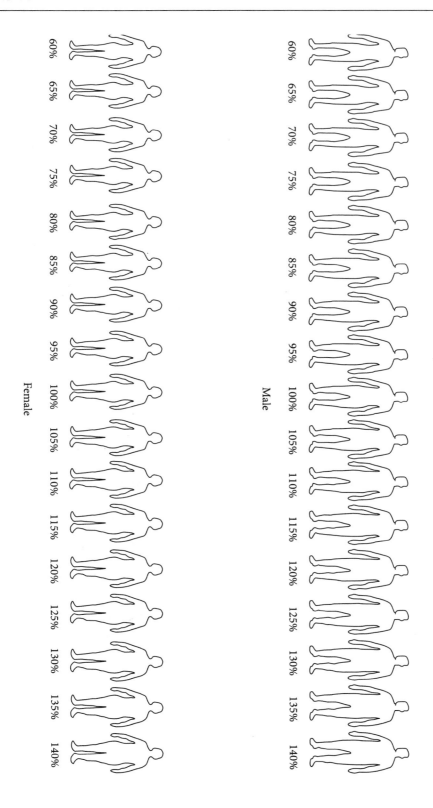

Body Image Avoidance Questionnaire (BIAQ)

PURPOSE To measure behavioral tendencies that frequently accompany body-image disturbance.

AUTHORS James C. Rosen, Debra Srebnik, Elaine Saltzberg, and Sally Wendt

DESCRIPTION The BIAQ is a 19-item instrument designed to measure behavioral tendencies that often accompany body-image disturbance. In particular, the questionnaire deals with avoidance of situations that provoke concern about physical appearance, such as avoidance of physical intimacy, social outings, and tight-fitting clothes. Since these avoidance behaviors are common in persons with body dissatisfaction and since there are no measures of this component of the problem, the authors interviewed 40 randomly selected female residents of a university dormitory and categorized commonly reported complaints of behavioral changes associated with negative body image into the items of this questionnaire. The measure is viewed as useful for targeting changes in avoidance of these situations as a result of treatment.

NORMS The BIAQ was tested with a sample of 353 female introductory psychology students with a mean age of 19.7 years and a mean deviation from normal weight (according to charts of the Metropolitan Life Insurance Company) of 2.01%. The mean score on the BIAQ was 31.5 with a standard deviation of 13.9 and a range of 1 to 74.

SCORING The BIAQ is scored by simply totaling the scores on the individual, 6-point items, providing a potential range of scores from 0 to 94. Although the BIAQ comprises four factors derived through factor analysis (clothing, social activities, eating at restaurants, and grooming and weight), these factors are not scored separately.

RELIABILITY The BIAQ has excellent internal consistency, with a Cronbach's alpha of .89, and is very stable with a two-week, test-retest reliability coefficient of .87.

VALIDITY The BIAQ has fair to good concurrent validity, with a low but significant correlation of .22 with body size estimation, a correlation of .78 with the Body Shape Questionnaire, and correlations of .68 and .63 with the Shape Concern and Weight Concern scales respectively. The BIAQ has good known-groups validity, significantly distinguishing between clinical (bulimia nervosa) and nonclinical populations. Finally, the BIAQ has been shown to be sensitive to changes in clients with body-image disturbance.

PRIMARY REFERENCE Rosen, J. C., Srebnik, D., Saltzberg, E., and Wendt, S. (1991). Development of a Body Image Avoidance Questionnaire, *Psychological Assessment*, 3, 32–37. Instrument reprinted by permission of authors and publisher.

AVAILABILITY Dr. J. C. Rosen, Department of Psychology, University of Vermont, Burlington, VT 05405. Email: james.rosen@uvm.edu.

BIAQ

Circle the number which best describes how often you engage in these behaviors at the present time.

	Always	Usually	Often	Some-times	Rarely	Never
1. I wear baggy clothes.	5	4	3	2	1	0
2. I wear clothes I do not like.	5	4	3	2	1	0
3. I wear darker color clothing.	5	4	3	2	1	0
4. I wear a special set of clothing, e.g., my "fat clothes."	5	4	3	2	1	0
5. I restrict the amount of food I eat.	5	4	3	2	1	0
6. I only eat fruits, vegetables, and other low calorie foods.	5	4	3	2	1	0
7. I fast for a day or longer.	5	4	3	2	1	0
8. I do not go out socially if I will be "checked out."	5	4	3	2	1	0
9. I do not go out socially if the people I am with will discuss weight.	5	4	3	2	1	0
10. I do not go out socially if the people I am with are thinner than me.	5	4	3	2	1	0
11. I do not go out socially if it involves eating.	5	4	3	2	1	0
12. I weigh myself.	5	4	3	2	1	0
13. I am inactive.	5	4	3	2	1	0
14. I look at myself in the mirror.	5	4	3	2	1	0
15. I avoid physical intimacy.	5	4	3	2	1	0
16. I wear clothes that will divert attention from my weight.	5	4	3	2	1	0
17. I avoid going clothes shopping.	5	4	3	2	1	0
18. I don't wear "revealing" clothes (e.g., bathing suits, tank tops, or shorts).	5	4	3	2	1	0
19. I get dressed up or made up.	5	4	3	2	1	0

Body Sensations Questionnaire (BSQ)

PURPOSE To measure physical sensations in agoraphobia.

AUTHORS Dianne L. Chambless, G. Craig Caputo, Priscilla Bright, and Richard Gallagher

DESCRIPTION The BSQ is an 18-item instrument designed to measure body sensations associated with agoraphobia. The items on the BSQ were generated from interviews with clients and therapists involved in an agoraphobia treatment program. The BSQ contains items that clients report to be disturbing that are associated with anxiety. The BSQ can be used to help assess agoraphobia and to monitor changes due to treatment.

NORMS The BSQ was studied initially with 175 clients applying for treatment at the Agoraphobia and Anxiety Program at Temple University; 80% were female and the sample had been agoraphobic for a median of eight years. The mean age of the group was 37.64. The mean score was 3.05 (SD = .86).

SCORING The BSQ is easily scored by summing the individual item ratings and dividing by the number of items rated.

RELIABILITY The BSQ has very good internal consistency, with an alpha of .87. It also has good stability, with a one-month test-retest correlation of .67.

VALIDITY The BSQ has very good concurrent validity, correlating with other measures of agoraphobia and several measures of psychopathology such as the Beck Depression Inventory, State-Trait Anxiety Inventory, and the Neuroticism Scale of the Eysenck Personality Questionnaire. The BSQ has good known-groups validity, significantly discriminating agoraphobic clients from a "normal" control group. The BSQ also is sensitive to changes due to treatment.

PRIMARY REFERENCE Chambless, D. L., Caputo, G. C., Bright, P., and Gallagher, R. (1984). Assessment of fear in agoraphobics: The Body Sensations Questionnaire and the Agoraphobic Cognitions Questionnaire, *Journal of Consulting and Clinical Psychology*, 52, 1090–1097. Instrument reprinted by permission of authors and publisher.

AVAILABILITY Dr. Dianne Chambless, Department of Psychology, University of Pennsylvania, Philadelphia, PA 19104. Email: dchamb@psych.upenn.edu.

Below is a list of specific body sensations that may occur when you are nervous or in a feared situation. Please mark down how afraid you are of these feelings. Use a five-point scale from "not worried" to "extremely frightened." Please rate all items.

1 = Not frightened or worried by this sensation
2 = Somewhat frightened by this sensation
3 = Moderately frightened by this sensation
4 = Very frightened by this sensation
5 = Extremely frightened by this sensation

____ 1. Heart palpitations
____ 2. Pressure or a heavy feeling in chest
____ 3. Numbness in arms or legs
____ 4. Tingling in the fingertips
____ 5. Numbness in another part of your body
____ 6. Feeling short of breath
____ 7. Dizziness
____ 8. Blurred or distorted vision
____ 9. Nausea
____ 10. Having "butterflies" in your stomach
____ 11. Feeling a knot in your stomach
____ 12. Having a lump in your throat
____ 13. Wobbly or rubber legs
____ 14. Sweating
____ 15. A dry throat
____ 16. Feeling disoriented and confused
____ 17. Feeling disconnected from your body: Only partly present
____ 18. Other _____

Please describe _____

_____

_____

Body Shape Questionnaire (BSQ)

PURPOSE To measure concerns about body shape.

AUTHORS P. J. Cooper, M. J. Taylor, Z. Cooper, and C. G. Fairburn

DESCRIPTION The BSQ is a 34-item instrument designed to measure concerns about body shape among young women. The BSQ is based on the notion that disturbance of body image is a central feature of both anorexia nervosa and bulimia. Although a number of assessment procedures have been developed that deal with various aspects of body image, the BSQ is one of the few measures that focus on concerns about body shape. This is especially important because concern about body shape is one of the key dimensions distinguishing the disorder of anorexia. In particular, the BSQ focuses on the phenomenological experience of "feeling fat." The BSQ can be used for both assessment purposes and to evaluate response to treatment.

NORMS The BSQ was developed with four samples of women. These included 38 bulimia patients with a mean age of 22.2 years (SD = 4.1), 85 undergraduate students with a mean age of 20.0 (SD = 1.1), 119 occupational therapy students with a mean age of 21.3 (SD = 3.2), and 331 family planning clinic attenders with a mean age of 23.8 (SD = 6.3). The mean score for bulimia patients was 136.9 (SD = 22.5), and for women in the community the mean score was 81.5 (SD = 28.4).

SCORING The BSQ is scored by simply summing the individual item responses with total scores ranging from 34 to 204. Lower scores indicate lower concerns about body shape.

RELIABILITY No reliability data were reported.

VALIDITY The BSQ has good concurrent and known-groups validity. Concurrent validity was established by significant correlations between the BSQ and the Body Dissatisfaction subscale of the EDI (Eating Disorders Inventory) and significant correlations between the BSQ and the total Eating Attitudes Test score among patients with bulimia nervosa. Known-groups validity was established by showing a significant difference in BSQ scores for bulimia patients and nonpatients.

PRIMARY REFERENCE Cooper, P. J., Taylor, M. J., Cooper, Z., and Fairburn, C. G. (1987). The development and validation of the body shape questionnaire, *International Journal of Eating Disorders*, 6, 485–494.

AVAILABILITY Professor P. J. Cooper, Department of Psychology, University of Reading, Reading, Berkshire, England, R66 6AL, UK. Email: p.j.cooper@reading.ac.uk.

We should like to know how you have been feeling about your appearance over the *past four weeks.* Please read each question and circle the appropriate number to the right. Please answer *all* the questions.

Over the past four weeks:

	Never	Rarely	Some-times	Often	Very often	Always
1. Has feeling bored made you brood about your shape?	1	2	3	4	5	6
2. Have you been so worried about your shape that you have been feeling you ought to diet?	1	2	3	4	5	6
3. Have you thought that your thighs, hips, or bottom are too large for the rest of you?	1	2	3	4	5	6
4. Have you been afraid that you might become fat (or fatter)?	1	2	3	4	5	6
5. Have you worried about your flesh being not firm enough?	1	2	3	4	5	6
6. Has feeling full (e.g., after eating a large meal) made you feel fat?	1	2	3	4	5	6
7. Have you felt so bad about your shape that you have cried?	1	2	3	4	5	6
8. Have you avoided running because your flesh might wobble?	1	2	3	4	5	6
9. Has being with thin women made you feel self-conscious about your shape?	1	2	3	4	5	6
10. Have you worried about your thighs spreading out when sitting down?	1	2	3	4	5	6
11. Has eating even a small amount of food made you feel fat?	1	2	3	4	5	6
12. Have you noticed the shape of other women and felt that your own shape compared unfavorably?	1	2	3	4	5	6
13. Has thinking about your shape interfered with your ability to concentrate (e.g., while watching television, reading, listening to conversations)?	1	2	3	4	5	6
14. Has being naked, such as when taking a bath, made you feel fat?	1	2	3	4	5	6
15. Have you avoided wearing clothes which make you particularly aware of the shape of your body?	1	2	3	4	5	6

continued

	Never	Rarely	Some-times	Often	Very often	Always
16. Have you imagined cutting off fleshy areas of your body?	1	2	3	4	5	6
17. Has eating sweets, cakes, or other high-calorie food made you feel fat?	1	2	3	4	5	6
18. Have you not gone out to social occasions (e.g., parties) because you have felt bad about your shape?	1	2	3	4	5	6
19. Have you felt excessively large and rounded?	1	2	3	4	5	6
20. Have you felt ashamed of your body?	1	2	3	4	5	6
21. Has worry about your shape made you diet?	1	2	3	4	5	6
22. Have you felt happiest about your shape when your stomach has been empty (e.g., in the morning)?	1	2	3	4	5	6
23. Have you thought that you are in the shape you are because you lack self-control?	1	2	3	4	5	6
24. Have you worried about other people seeing rolls of fat around your waist or stomach?	1	2	3	4	5	6
25. Have you felt that it is not fair that other women are thinner than you?	1	2	3	4	5	6
26. Have you vomited in order to feel thinner?	1	2	3	4	5	6
27. When in company have you worried about taking up too much room (e.g., sitting on a sofa, or a bus seat)?	1	2	3	4	5	6
28. Have you worried about your flesh being dimply?	1	2	3	4	5	6
29. Has seeing your reflection (e.g., in a mirror or shop window) made you feel bad about your shape?	1	2	3	4	5	6
30. Have you pinched areas of your body to see how much fat there is?	1	2	3	4	5	6
31. Have you avoided situations where people could see your body (e.g., communal changing rooms or swimming pools)?	1	2	3	4	5	6
32. Have you taken laxatives in order to feel thinner?	1	2	3	4	5	6
33. Have you been particularly self-conscious about your shape when in the company of other people?	1	2	3	4	5	6
34. Has worry about your shape made you feel you ought to exercise?	1	2	3	4	5	6

Boredom Proneness (BP)

PURPOSE To measure proneness to boredom.

AUTHORS Richard Famer and Norman D. Sundberg

DESCRIPTION The BP is a 28-item instrument designed to measure the tendency or predisposition to boredom. The BP is based on the idea that boredom is a widespread and significant problem that has been associated in research with drug use, overeating, truancy in schools, maladjustment ratings in students, job dissatisfaction, and poor functioning on the job. The BP is a useful measure for assessing boredom and then keeping track of changes over time as a result of intervention programs.

NORMS The BP was investigated mainly with a sample of 233 college undergraduates (93 males, 140 females). The overall mean is 9.76 (SD = 4.8). The mean for males was 10.44 (SD = 4.88) and for females 9.30 (SD = 4.72). This difference was not statistically significant.

SCORING The BP is easily scored by summing all "correct" scores. The correct score for items 1, 7, 8, 11, 13, 15, 18, 22–24 is "false." The remaining items are scored "true" to indicate boredom proneness. Higher scores indicate greater proneness to boredom.

RELIABILITY The BP has good internal consistency, with an alpha of .79. The BP also has very good stability, with a one-week test-retest correlation of .83.

VALIDITY The BP has very good construct validity, correlating in predicted ways with self-ratings of boredom, lack of interest in the classroom, the Job Boredom Scale, the Beck Depression Inventory, the Center for Epidemiological Studies—Depression Scale, the Hopelessness Scale, the Perceived Effort Scale, the UCLA Loneliness Scale, the Life Satisfaction Index, and two subscales of the General Causality Orientations Scale.

PRIMARY REFERENCE Famer, R., and Sundberg, N. D. (1986). Boredom proneness—The development and correlates of a new scale, *Journal of Personality Assessment*, 50, 4–17.

AVAILABILITY May be copied from this volume.

Put an "X" below "T" (True) or "F" (False) according to how you would usually describe yourself.

T   F

___ ___   1. It is easy for me to concentrate on my activities.
___ ___   2. Frequently when I am working I find myself worrying about other things.
___ ___   3. Time always seems to be passing slowly.
___ ___   4. I often find myself at "loose ends," not knowing what to do.
___ ___   5. I am often trapped in situations where I have to do meaningless things.
___ ___   6. Having to look at someone's home movies or travel slides bores me tremendously.
___ ___   7. I have projects in mind all the time, things to do.
___ ___   8. I find it easy to entertain myself.
___ ___   9. Many things I have to do are repetitive and monotonous.
___ ___ 10. It takes more stimulation to get me going than most people.
___ ___ 11. I get a kick out of most things I do.
___ ___ 12. I am seldom excited about my work.
___ ___ 13. In any situation I can usually find something to do or see to keep me interested.
___ ___ 14. Much of the time I just sit around doing nothing.
___ ___ 15. I am good at waiting patiently.
___ ___ 16. I often find myself with nothing to do—time on my hands.
___ ___ 17. In situations where I have to wait, such as a line or queue, I get very restless.
___ ___ 18. I often wake up with a new idea.
___ ___ 19. It would be very hard for me to find a job that is exciting enough.
___ ___ 20. I would like more challenging things to do in life.
___ ___ 21. I feel that I am working below my abilities most of the time.
___ ___ 22. Many people would say that I am a creative or imaginative person.
___ ___ 23. I have so many interests, I don't have time to do everything.
___ ___ 24. Among my friends, I am the one who keeps doing something the longest.
___ ___ 25. Unless I am doing something exciting, even dangerous, I feel half-dead and dull.
___ ___ 26. It takes a lot of change and variety to keep me really happy.
___ ___ 27. It seems that the same things are on television or the movies all the time; it's getting old.
___ ___ 28. When I was young, I was often in monotonous and tiresome situations.

Breast Self-Examination Scale (BSE)

PURPOSE To measure attitudes toward breast self-examination.

AUTHORS Kathryn E. H. Race and Jane A. Silverberg

DESCRIPTION The BSE is a 24-item instrument designed to measure women's attitudes toward breast self-examination. Since early detection of breast cancer is critical in providing effective treatment, attitudes toward breast self-examination can help practitioners better understand why women do and do not perform breast self-examination. The scale can be used to assist practitioners in providing services to encourage women to examine their breasts on a regular basis. Although there are six subscales based on a factor analysis as reported in the original article, it appears as though the BSE is best used as a single, intact scale.

NORMS The BSE was originally studied with a sample of 2,000 women randomly selected from a population of outpatients at a large teaching hospital located in a Chicago suburb. From that sample 990 questionnaires were returned; 94% of respondents were Caucasian with a mean age of 51. Seventy percent of respondents were married, 33% had some education at the college level, and 57% reported a household income of $35,000 or more. The mean score on the BSE was 101.17 (SD = 9.55), with higher scores reflecting more positive attitudes toward breast self-examination.

SCORING All BSE items are rated on a 5-point Likert-type scale ranging from "strongly agree" to "strongly disagree." Each item should be scored such that a rating of 5 represents the most positive response (i.e., strongly agree with a positive item or strongly disagree with an item that reflects a negative attitude or behavior). The higher the score, the more positive perception a woman has about the benefits of breast self-examination and related behaviors. The scores are simply summed after recoding so that a range of 24 to 120 is provided. Higher scores represent more positive responses about attitudes toward breast self-examination.

RELIABILITY The internal consistency of the BSE is good with an alpha of .83. All subscale alphas were lower and ranged from .48 to .75. No data on stability were reported.

VALIDITY The BSE has good concurrent validity, with scores on the total scale significantly correlated with self-reported breast self-examination knowledge and performance. Subsequent, unpublished research reveals that total scores on the BSE allowed predictions that indicated that 72% of women could be accurately identified as either performing or not performing breast self-examination based on BSE total scores.

PRIMARY REFERENCE Race, K. H., and Silverberg, J. A. (1996). Toward a reliable measure of breast self-examination, *Evaluation Review*, 20, 541–551.

AVAILABILITY There is no fee for use of the scale. It should be noted, however, that the development of this scale is dynamic. Assistance in evaluating the psychometric properties of this scale, therefore, is encouraged and is available for a fee. Please contact Kathryn E. H. Race, President, Race and Associates, Ltd., 4430 N. Winchester Ave., Chicago, IL 60640, (773) 878-8535. OR www.raceassociates.com.

Please rate each statement by placing the appropriate number in the space next to each item.

1 = Strongly disagree
2 = Disagree somewhat
3 = Disagree a little
4 = Agree a little
5 = Agree somewhat
6 = Strongly agree

____ 1. I am confident I know how to correctly perform a breast exam.
____ 2. I am afraid of examining my breasts for fear of what I might find.
____ 3. I am too embarrassed to touch my breasts.
____ 4. I do not have time to regularly examine my breasts.
____ 5. I do not have the privacy to regularly examine my breasts.
____ 6. I would be embarrassed if I thought I found a problem from my breast self-examination and it turned out to be nothing.
____ 7. I often forget to perform a breast self-examination.
____ 8. My religious or cultural beliefs have taught me that touching myself is wrong.
____ 9. I think that breast self-examinations are too complicated to do correctly.
____ 10. I believe that breast cancer is treatable if detected early.
____ 11. I believe that breast cancer could be a serious threat to my health.
____ 12. If I were to get breast cancer, I believe nothing could be done to save my life and/or my breasts.
____ 13. Daily activities which may involve touching my breasts, such as bathing or sexual activity, cannot take the place of a breast self-examination.
____ 14. I think that breast self-examination may be helpful in detecting breast cancer.
____ 15. Besides a breast self-examination, other health examinations, such as a mammogram or a clinical breast examination, are effective ways to detect breast cancer.
____ 16. My primary health care provider told me of the importance of breast self-examination.
____ 17. Most of my friends and family members think a breast self-examination is a good idea.
____ 18. Doing a breast self-examination serves as a positive role model for other women and girls in my family and my friends' families.
____ 19. I like to be well informed of matters regarding my own health.
____ 20. I am embarrassed to discuss my personal medical issues with my family or my circle of friends.
____ 21. I believe that people who are going to die from a disease will die regardless of what is done.
____ 22. There are many things I can do to help keep a disease from getting worse.
____ 23. I take responsibility for my own health.
____ 24. I am important enough to take good care of myself.

Brief Depression Rating Scale (BDRS)

PURPOSE To measure depression.

AUTHOR Robert Kellner

DESCRIPTION The BDRS is an 8-item rating scale designed to measure depression by clinical observations. The scale was developed through a series of studies beginning with reviews of symptoms of depressed patients, and culminating in a series of validation studies. The BDRS is particularly recommended for its brevity, its sensitivity to measuring changes in depression, and its ability to detect small differences between the effects of two treatments. The BDRS is one of the few rating scales in this book, i.e., it is not a self-report measure. Its ease of use compared to many other rating scales was the primary reason for its inclusion.

NORMS The BDRS has been studied with several samples including depressed in- and outpatients. Specific demographic information is not available nor are actual norms.

SCORING The BDRS is easily scored by summing individual items for a total score.

RELIABILITY The BDRS has excellent interobserver reliability with correlations that range from .91 to .94.

VALIDITY The BDRS has excellent concurrent validity, correlating .83 with the Hamilton Depression Rating Scale. The BDRS also has good known-groups validity, significantly distinguishing between depressed in- and outpatients. The BDRS also has been found to be sensitive to differences between treatments.

PRIMARY REFERENCE Kellner, R. (1986). The Brief Depression Rating Scale, in N. Sartorius and T. A. Ban (eds.), *Assessment of Depression*, pp. 179–183. New York: Springer-Verlag.

AVAILABILITY May be copied from this volume.

Circle the appropriate number

I. Depressive mood. Feeling of despair	Incapacitating	Severe distress	Moderately distressed	Slight	Cheerful*
	9　　8	7　　6	5　　4	3　　2	1
II. Psychophysiologic somatic symptoms**	Incapacitating	Severe symptoms or impairment	Moderate	Slight	Completely absent or normal functions
	9　　8	7　　6	5　　4	3　　2	1
III. Lack of interest, initiative, and activity	Totally inactive	Severe apathy, very few activities	Moderately impaired interest and initiative	Slight loss of interest and initiative	Interested and energetic
	9　　8	7　　6	5　　4	3　　2	1
IV. Sleep disturbance***	Apparently sleeping 1 h or less	Sleeping about 2 h a night	Sleeping 4–5 h	Slight sleep disturbance	Sleeping well*
	9　　8	7　　6	5　　4	3　　2	1
V. Anxiety, worry, tension	Incapacitating	Severe distress	Moderate tension or anxiety	Slight	Calm and relaxed
	9　　8	7　　6	5　　4	3　　2	1
VI. Appearance	Continuous expression of utmost despair	Sad appearance, does not smile at all	Sad appearance, but can be made to smile	Sad appearance at times	Appears cheerful*
	9　　8	7　　6	5　　4	3　　2	1
VII. Depressive beliefs	Most thoughts are delusional	Has some depressive psychotic delusions	Frequent beliefs of no hope or un-worthiness	Occasional brief depressional beliefs	Confident* and optimistic
	9　　8	7　　6	5　　4	3　　2	1
VIII. Suicidal thoughts or behavior	Evidence of serious risk and a recent suicide attempt	Frequent suicidal preoccu-pations and wishes to die	Intermittent thought of suicide. No plans	Occasional thoughts of suicide. Does not want to die	No suicidal thoughts.
	9　　8	7　　6	5　　4	3　　2	1

If excessive, please comment.

** Including appetite, sexual interest, gastric symptoms, etc. Rate the symptom which is most severe.

*** If any of the following is reported: difficulty in falling asleep, waking up early, restless sleep, or nightmares, rate the sleep disturbances as "slightly moderate" or "severe" even if the total number of hours slept is adequate.

If in doubt whether to rate *severity* of the symptoms or behavior or *frequency* of occurrence, rate *severity* of the symptom or behavior.

The usual period rated is the *past* week; the rating period can be made longer or shorter, depending on the design of the study.

For the symptoms which do not have specific rating instructions the rating cues should be interpreted as follows:

9—Incapacitating—The patient is unable to carry out everyday tasks (not only related to his or her occupation) because of the severity of his or her symptoms.

7—Severe—The patient is severely distressed and/or his or her performance is substantially impaired but not to the point of incapacity.

5—Moderate—This rating is made when neither "severe" not "slight" is applicable.

3—Slight—The patient either mentions spontaneously or replies to questioning that the symptom is not troublesome with statements such as "slight" or "only a little."

1—Absent—Total absence of the symptom during the period covered by rating.

Intermediate ratings—(scores 2, 4, 6, and 8) should be used only if the main cues (1, 3, 5, 7, and 9) do not adequately express the rater's opinion.

Brief Screen for Depression (BSD)

PURPOSE To measure depression.

AUTHORS A. Ralph Hakstian and Peter D. McLean

DESCRIPTION The BSD is a 4-item instrument designed to serve as a screening device for depression. The BSD was designed to detect clinical levels of depression, and to tap a full range of response domains. The BSD can be used alone or as part of a battery of measures. The BSD has a cutting score of 21 to distinguish clinical from nonclinical subjects and 24 to distinguish depressed from other psychiatric subjects.

NORMS The BSD was studied with a sample of 196 depressed subjects as diagnosed by the MMPI Depression Scale and the Depression Adjective Checklist; mean age was 39, with 72% of the sample being female; 25% had made a serious suicide attempt. A sample of 161 "normal" subjects was recruited by newspaper ads, and 107 nondepressed psychiatric patients matched with other groups was used as a control. For the depressed group, the mean was 33.88 (SD = 6.6), and for the "normal" group the mean was 13.27 (SD = 5.2).

SCORING The BSD is scored by summing scores for items 2–4 and adding four times the item "1" score to produce an overall score.

RELIABILITY The BSD has fair internal consistency, with alphas that range from .63 to .65. The BSD has good stability, with a one-week test-retest correlation of .73 and a three-month test-retest correlation of .54.

VALIDITY The BSD has very good concurrent validity, correlating with the Beck Depression Inventory and the Depression Adjective Checklist. It also has excellent known-groups validity as evidenced by the cut-off scores described earlier that distinguish between depressed and nondepressed patients and between patients and "normals."

PRIMARY REFERENCE Hakstian, A. R., and McLean, P. D. (1989). Brief Screen for Depression, *Psychological Assessment*, 1, 139–141.

AVAILABILITY May be copied from this volume.

1. How many times during the last 2 days have you been preoccupied by thoughts of hopelessness, helplessness, pessimism, intense worry, unhappiness, and so on? (Circle number)

1	2	3	4	5
Not at all	Rarely	Frequently	Most of the time	All of the time

2. How relaxed have you been during the last 2 days, compared to how you normally are? (Circle number)

1	2	3	4	5	6	7	8	9	10
Quite calm and relaxed physically									Extremely tense (i.e., wringing hands, muscle tremors, etc.)

3. To what extent have you had difficulty starting and following through an ordinary job or task to completion during the last week compared to when you feel things have been going well? (Circle number)

1	2	3	4	5	6	7	8	9	10
Start and finish jobs as well as most other people									Put things off/ starting and not finishing for a long time, if at all

4. How satisfied are you with your ability to perform your usual domestic duties (i.e., shopping, meals, dishes, home repair, cleaning up, child care, etc.)? (Circle number)

1	2	3	4	5	6	7	8	9	10
Very satisfied									Very dissatisfied

Brief Sexual Attitudes Scale (BSAS)

PURPOSE To measure sexual attitudes.

AUTHORS Clyde Hendrick, Susan S. Hendrick, and Darcy A. Reich

DESCRIPTION The BSAS is a 23-item instrument designed to measure sexual attitudes in an easy-to-use, brief format. The BSAS is a more efficient and current version of the Sexual Attitudes Scale (SAS), a 43-item, multi-dimensional scale developed in the early 1980s. While the SAS has been extensively studied nationally and internationally, the authors believed it was time to update the SAS into a briefer and more current format to enhance its utility. The result of that work is the BSAS. The BSAS is comprised of four subscales: Permissiveness (items 1–10); Birth Control (items 11–13); Communion (items 14–18); and Instrumentality (items 19–23).

NORMS The BSAS was developed in research with three samples involving over 1,500 respondents. The third and final sample involved 518 respondents of whom 58% were female, and 96% were age 22 or younger. 76% of the sample was white, 11% Hispanic, 3% African American, 3.5% Asian or Pacific Islander, and 9% "other." All respondents were college students in Texas. 42% of the respondents reported being in a current romantic relationship. Means for the four scales were as follows: Permissiveness = 3.31; Birth Control = 1.83; Communion = 2.09; and Instrumentality = 3.38. There were no gender differences on Birth Control or Instrumentality, but women were less endorsing of Permissiveness and Communion than men.

SCORING The BSAS is easily scored by summing up items responses within each subscale and dividing by the number of items. Lower scores indicate more of a sexual attitude. In scoring the BSAS, substitute "1" for "A" and "5" for "E."

RELIABILITY The BSAS has fair to excellent internal consistency with alphas of .95 for Permissiveness, .88 for Birth Control, .73 for Communion and .77 for Instrumentality. The BSAS has excellent stability with a one month test-retest correlation of .92 for Permissiveness, .57 for Birth Control, .86 for Communion, and .75 for Instrumentality.

VALIDITY Three of four of the subscales of the BSAS have established good concurrent validity correlating significantly and in predicted directions with several other scales of sexuality. Only Birth Control was essentially uncorrelated with other measures.

PRIMARY REFERENCE Hendrick, C., Hendrick, S. S., and Reich, D. A. (in press). *Journal of Sex Research*. Instrument reproduced with permission of Dr. Hendrick.

AVAILABILITY Email Dr. Hendrick at susan.hendrick@ttu.edu.

Listed below are several statements that reflect different attitudes about sex. For each statement fill in the response on the answer sheet that indicates how much you agree or disagree with that statement. Some of the items refer to a specific sexual relationship, while others refer to general attitudes and beliefs about sex. Whenever possible, answer the questions with your current partner in mind. If you are not currently dating anyone, answer the questions with your most recent partner in mind. If you have never had a sexual relationship, answer in terms of what you think your responses would most likely be.

For each statement:

A = Strongly agree with the statement
B = Moderately agree with the statement
C = Neutral—neither agree nor disagree
D = Moderately disagree with the statement
E = Strongly disagree with the statement

1. I do not need to be committed to a person to have sex with him/her.
2. Casual sex is acceptable.
3. I would like to have sex with many partners.
4. One-night stands are sometimes very enjoyable.
5. It is okay to have ongoing sexual relationships with more than one person at a time.
6. Sex as a simple exchange of favors is okay if both people agree to it.
7. The best sex is with no strings attached.
8. Life would have fewer problems if people could have sex more freely.
9. It is possible to enjoy sex with a person and not like that person very much.
10. It is okay for sex to be just good physical release.
11. Birth control is part of responsible sexuality.
12. A woman should share responsibility for birth control.
13. A man should share responsibility for birth control.
14. Sex is the closest form of communication between two people.
15. A sexual encounter between two people deeply in love is the ultimate human interaction.
16. At its best, sex seems to be the merging of two souls.
17. Sex is a very important part of life.
18. Sex is usually an intensive, almost overwhelming experience.
19. Sex is best when you let yourself go and focus on your own pleasure.
20. Sex is primarily the taking of pleasure from another person.
21. The main purpose of sex is to enjoy oneself.
22. Sex is primarily physical.
23. Sex is primarily a bodily function, like eating.

Bulimia Test—Revised (BULIT-R)

PURPOSE To measure bulimia in accordance with the *DSM-III-R*.

AUTHORS Mark H. Thelen and Marcia Smith

DESCRIPTION This 28-item instrument is designed to measure bulimia using the definitions set forth in the *Diagnostic and Statistical Manual, 3rd Edition, Revised*. The BULIT-R revises and replaces the original instrument because five new criteria were adopted in the *DSM-III-R* and two others from the *DSM-III* were dropped. The new criteria are: a persistent overconcern with the shape and weight of one's body; recurring episodes of binge eating; a minimum average of two episodes a week for at least three months; lack of control of overeating behaviors during the episodes; and weight reduction behaviors, including self-induced vomiting, fasting, vigorous exercise, or the use of laxatives. The two criteria dropped in the *DSM-III-R* and the BULIT-R are the reference to depression and the exclusion criterion of anorexia nervosa. The instrument was developed with rigorous psychometric procedures using six separate samples of bulimic and control subjects. It may be used to screen clients for bulimia as well as measure change during treatment. While the BULIT-R was developed on females for whom this disorder is more common, the instrument has clinical utility with males at risk of bulimia, such as high school wrestlers or other competitive athletes who may have weight limits imposed on them.

NORMS The mean BULIT-R score for a sample of 21 females diagnosed with bulimia was 117.95; for a sample of 100 female psychology students, it was 57.50. An independent sample of 23 bulimics and 157 controls reported means of 118.08 and 59.62, respectively.

SCORING There are eight filler items that are not scored. BULIT-R scores are the sum of the responses to items 1, 2*, 3, 4, 5*, 7*, 8*, 9, 10*, 12*, 13*, 14*, 15*, 16*, 17*, 18, 21*, 22, 23*, 24, 25, 26*, 28*, 30*, 32*, 33, 34, 35*. Items with an asterisk are reverse-scored. The instrument has a suggested cutting score of 104, below which one would not be classified as bulimic. To reduce false negatives, a cutting score of 85 is recommended.

RELIABILITY The BULIT-R has excellent internal consistency. From a sample of 23 female bulimics and 157 normal college females, the alpha coefficient was .97. Test-retest over a two-month period was .95 suggesting the instrument is extremely stable.

VALIDITY The validity of the instrument is evidenced with known-group procedures where each item and total scores discriminated between subjects diagnosed with bulimia and college females enrolled in a psychology course. This discrimination was replicated in an independent sample of bulimics and "normals." Concurrent validity is seen by a correlation of .85 between BULIT-R scores and scores on the Binge Scale. Scores on the BULIT-R correlated .99 with the original BULIT.

PRIMARY REFERENCE Thelen, M. H., Farmer, J., Wonderlich, S., and Smith, M. (1991). A revision of the bulimia test: The BULIT-R, *Psychological Assessment*, 3, 119–124. Instrument reproduced with permission of Mark Thelen.

AVAILABILITY Dr. Mark Thelen, 2508 Ridgefield Road, Columbia, MO 65203-1534. Telephone: 573.445.4689.

Answer each question by circling the appropriate number. Please respond to each item as honestly as possible; remember, all of the information you provide will be kept strictly confidential.

1. I am satisfied with my eating patterns.
   1. Agree
   2. Neutral
   3. Disagree a little
   4. Disagree
   5. Disagree strongly

2. Would you presently call yourself a "binge eater"?
   1. Yes, absolutely
   2. Yes
   3. Yes, probably
   4. Yes, possibly
   5. No, probably not

3. Do you feel you have control over the amount of food you consume?
   1. Most or all of the time
   2. A lot of the time
   3. Occasionally
   4. Rarely
   5. Never

4. I am satisfied with the shape and size of my body.
   1. Frequently or always
   2. Sometimes
   3. Occasionally
   4. Rarely
   5. Seldom or never

5. When I feel that my eating behavior is out of control, I try to take rather extreme measures to get back on course (strict dieting, fasting, laxatives, diuretics, self-induced vomiting, or vigorous exercise).
   1. Always
   2. Almost always
   3. Frequently
   4. Sometimes
   5. Never or my eating behavior is never out of control

6. I use laxatives or suppositories to help control my weight.
   1. Once a day or more
   2. 3–6 times a week
   3. Once or twice a week
   4. 2–3 times a month
   5. Once a month or less (or never)

7. I am obsessed about the size and shape of my body.
   1. Always
   2. Almost always

3. Frequently
4. Sometimes
5. Seldom or never

8. There are times when I rapidly eat a very large amount of food.
   1. More than twice a week
   2. Twice a week
   3. Once a week
   4. 2–3 times a month
   5. Once a month or less (or never)

9. How long have you been binge eating (eating uncontrollably to the point of stuffing yourself)?
   1. Not applicable; I don't binge eat
   2. Less than 3 months
   3. 3 months to 1 year
   4. 1–3 years
   5. 3 or more years

10. Most people I know would be amazed if they knew how much food I can consume at one sitting.
    1. Without a doubt
    2. Very probably
    3. Probably
    4. Possibly
    5. No

11. I exercise in order to burn calories.
    1. More than 2 hours per day
    2. About 2 hours per day
    3. More than 1 but less than 2 hours per day
    4. One hour or less per day
    5. I exercise but not to burn calories or I don't exercise

12. Compared with women your age, how preoccupied are you about your weight and body shape?
    1. A great deal more than average
    2. Much more than average
    3. More than average
    4. A little more than average
    5. Average or less than average

13. I am afraid to eat anything for fear that I won't be able to stop.
    1. Always
    2. Almost always
    3. Frequently
    4. Sometimes
    5. Seldom or never

14. I feel tormented by the idea that I am fat or might gain weight.
    1. Always
    2. Almost always
    3. Frequently
    4. Sometimes
    5. Seldom or never

15. How often do you intentionally vomit after eating?
    1. 2 or more times a week
    2. Once a week
    3. 2–3 times a month
    4. Once a month
    5. Less than once a month or never

16. I eat a lot of food when I'm not even hungry.
    1. Very frequently
    2. Frequently
    3. Occasionally
    4. Sometimes
    5. Seldom or never

17. My eating patterns are different from the eating patterns of most people.
    1. Always
    2. Almost always
    3. Frequently
    4. Sometimes
    5. Seldom or never

18. After I binge eat I turn to one of several strict methods to try to keep from gaining weight (vigorous exercise, strict dieting, fasting, self-induced vomiting, laxatives, or diuretics).
    1. Never or I don't binge eat
    2. Rarely
    3. Occasionally
    4. A lot of the time
    5. Most or all of the time

19. I have tried to lose weight by fasting or going on strict diets.
    1. Not in the past year
    2. Once in the past year
    3. 2–3 times in the past year
    4. 4–5 times in the past year
    5. More than 5 times in the past year

20. I exercise vigorously and for long periods of time in order to burn calories.
    1. Average or less than average
    2. A little more than average
    3. More than average
    4. Much more than average
    5. A great deal more than average

21. When engaged in an eating binge, I tend to eat foods that are high in carbohydrates (sweets and starches).
    1. Always
    2. Almost always
    3. Frequently
    4. Sometimes
    5. Seldom or I don't binge

22. Compared to most people, my ability to control my eating behavior seems to be:
    1. Greater than others' ability
    2. About the same

3. Less

4. Much less

5. I have absolutely no control

23. I would presently label myself a "compulsive eater" (one who engages in episodes of uncontrolled eating).
    1. Absolutely
    2. Yes
    3. Yes, probably
    4. Yes, possibly
    5. No, probably not

24. I hate the way my body looks after I eat too much.
    1. Seldom or never
    2. Sometimes
    3. Frequently
    4. Almost always
    5. Always

25. When I am trying to keep from gaining weight, I feel that I have to resort to vigorous exercise, strict dieting, fasting, self-induced vomiting, laxatives, or diuretics.
    1. Never
    2. Rarely
    3. Occasionally
    4. A lot of the time
    5. Most or all of the time

26. Do you believe that it is easier for you to vomit than it is for most people?
    1. Yes, it's no problem at all for me
    2. Yes, it's easier
    3. Yes, it's a little easier
    4. About the same
    5. No, it's less easy

27. I use diuretics (water pills) to help control my weight.
    1. Never
    2. Seldom
    3. Sometimes
    4. Frequently
    5. Very frequently

28. I feel that food controls my life.
    1. Always
    2. Almost always
    3. Frequently
    4. Sometimes
    5. Seldom or never

29. I try to control my weight by eating little or no food for a day or longer.
    1. Never
    2. Seldom
    3. Sometimes
    4. Frequently
    5. Very frequently

30. When consuming a large quantity of food, at what rate of speed do you usually eat?
    1. More rapidly than most people have ever eaten in their lives
    2. A lot more rapidly than most people
    3. A little more rapidly than most people
    4. About the same rate as most people
    5. More slowly than most people (or not applicable)

31. I use laxatives or suppositories to help control my weight.
    1. Never
    2. Seldom
    3. Sometimes
    4. Frequently
    5. Very frequently

32. Right after I binge eat I feel:
    1. So fat and bloated I can't stand it
    2. Extremely fat
    3. Fat
    4. A little fat
    5. OK about how my body looks or I never binge eat

33. Compared to other people of my sex, my ability to always feel in control of how much I eat is:
    1. About the same or greater
    2. A little less
    3. Less
    4. Much less
    5. A great deal less

34. In the last 3 months, on the average how often did you binge eat (eat uncontrollably to the point of stuffing yourself)?
    1. Once a month or less (or never)
    2. 2–3 times a month
    3. Once a week
    4. Twice a week
    5. More than twice a week

35. Most people I know would be surprised at how fat I look after I eat a lot of food.
    1. Yes, definitely
    2. Yes
    3. Yes, probably
    4. Yes, possibly
    5. No, probably not or I never eat a lot of food

36. I use diuretics (water pills) to help control my weight.
    1. 3 times a week or more
    2. Once or twice a week
    3. 2–3 times a month
    4. Once a month
    5. Never

Bulimic Automatic Thoughts Test (BATT)

PURPOSE To measure bulimic cognitions.

AUTHORS Debra L. Franco and David C. Zuroff

DESCRIPTION The BATT is a 20-item instrument designed to measure cognitions that are specific to bulimic individuals. The test was developed in an effort to overcome limitations of other scales in this area, and to obtain a measure of the frequency and type of cognitions common to bulimic patients. In particular, the authors wanted to distinguish between thoughts of bulimic individuals and those of other related but different target groups (e.g., depressed or obese patients). The items of the BATT were derived from examples of cognitive distortions formed in cognitive therapy and from information gathered from bulimic patients' food diaries. The resulting 20 items were devised to identify automatic thoughts associated with bulimia nervosa. The BATT shows promise not only for assessment purposes but also for evaluating change after treatment.

NORMS The BATT was developed with 124 subjects including 64 who met the *DSM-III* criteria for bulimia nervosa, 20 depressed college students, 20 non-binging obese patients in a diet program, and 20 "normal" college students. The mean age for the bulimic subjects was 25.2 years and for the other three groups was 20.6 years. It appears as though all subjects were women. The mean BATT score (and standard deviation) for the bulimic patients was 62.8 (SD = 17.7) and was significantly different from scores of the other three groups.

SCORING The BATT is scored simply by summing scores on the individual items which are arranged on a 5-point scale. Scores range from 20 to 100 with higher scores indicating greater dysfunctional thinking concerning bulimia.

RELIABILITY Split-half reliability for the BATT is .95, with an alpha of .91 for the bulimic patients, suggesting excellent internal consistency. Data on stability were not reported.

VALIDITY The BATT correlated significantly with two other measures of bulimia, the Bulimia Test and the bulimia subscale of the Eating Disorders Inventory, thus indicating very good concurrent validity. The BATT also was correlated significantly with the frequency of binge eating and vomiting, again supporting the concurrent validity of the BATT. The BATT also is sensitive to change as a result of treatment, showing a significant drop in scores (at the .001 level) following cognitive-behavioral intervention.

PRIMARY REFERENCE Franko, D. L., and Zuroff, D. C. (1992). The Bulimic Automatic Thoughts Test: Initial reliability and validity data, *Journal of Clinical Psychology*, 48(4), 505–509. Instrument reprinted by permission of the authors.

AVAILABILITY Debra L. Franko, Ph.D., Department of Counseling and Applied Educational Psychology, Northeastern University, Boston, MA 02115. Email: d.franko@neu.edu.

BATT

Listed below are a variety of thoughts that pop into people's heads. Please read each thought and indicate how frequently, if at all, the thought has occurred to you *over the last week*. Please read each item carefully and circle the appropriate number:

1	2	3	4	5
Not at all	Sometimes	Moderately often	Often	All the time

1. I ought to be thinner than I am.   1   2   3   4   5
2. If only I could reach my "ideal weight," my life would be much happier.   1   2   3   4   5
3. If I gain weight, I will be less competent in my work.   1   2   3   4   5
4. The only way that I can be in control is if I control my eating.   1   2   3   4   5
5. I must avoid carbohydrates or vomit after I eat them in order not to become obese.   1   2   3   4   5
6. Gaining five pounds would push me over the brink.   1   2   3   4   5
7. If I'm not in complete control, I lose all control.   1   2   3   4   5
8. If I gain one pound, I'll go on and gain many pounds.   1   2   3   4   5
9. Others notice even if I gain a pound or two.   1   2   3   4   5
10. If I keep down a sweet, it will be converted quickly into stomach fat.   1   2   3   4   5
11. Either I binge or I fast, there's no middle ground for me.   1   2   3   4   5
12. If I do stop binging, I'll do something else destructive to take its place.   1   2   3   4   5
13. I'm special if I'm at the "right" weight.   1   2   3   4   5
14. I can only be happy if I'm at the right weight.   1   2   3   4   5
15. If others comment about my weight, I can't stand it.   1   2   3   4   5
16. If I can't master this area of my life (binging and vomiting), I'll lose everything.   1   2   3   4   5
17. If I begin to keep down fattening foods, I will become obese.   1   2   3   4   5
18. Binging means I have no control in my life.   1   2   3   4   5
19. If only I could stop this binging and vomiting, my life would be great.   1   2   3   4   5
20. When I see someone who is overweight, I worry that I will be like her.   1   2   3   4   5

Career Decision Self-Efficacy Scale (CDSES)

PURPOSE To measure confidence in making career decisions.

AUTHORS Karen M. O'Brien and Nancy E. Betz et al.

DESCRIPTION The CDSES is a 25-item scale designed to assess confidence in making career-related decisions and engaging in tasks related to career decision-making. The CDSES is used to promote confidence and happiness at work by identifying areas in which adult workers may lack confidence and then developing interventions to increase confidence in the career development process. The CDSES is based on the theory of self-efficacy, and in particular, career self-efficacy, defined as confidence in one's ability to manage career development and work-related tasks. The CDSES is comprised of five subscales: Occupational Information, Goal Selection, Problem-Solving, Planning, and Self-Appraisal. Items on these subscales are available from the author.

NORMS For a sample of college students, mean scores ranged from 34.0 (SD = 6.9) to 36.7 (SD = 7.1) for females to 38.4 (SD = 6.6) for males.

SCORING All items are summed to obtain the total score, while the subscale scores also are summed. Higher scores reflect greater confidence in completing career-related tasks.

RELIABILITY The CDSES has excellent internal consistency with an overall alpha of .94 and alphas for the subscales that range from .73 to .83. Data on stability were not available.

VALIDITY The CDSES has excellent concurrent validity with negative correlations with measures of career indecision and positive correlations with vocational identity, career beliefs related to control, responsibility, and working hard, as predicted.

PRIMARY REFERENCE Betz, N. E., et al. (1996). Evaluation of a short form of the Career Decision-Making Self-Efficacy Scale, *Journal of Career Assessment*, 1, 21–34. Instrument reproduced with permission of Drs. Betz and O'Brien.

AVAILABILITY Email Dr. Betz at betz.3@osu.edu.

Career Questionnaire

Instructions: For each statement below, please read carefully and indicate how much confidence you have that you could accomplish each of these tasks by marking your answer according to the key. Mark your answer by filling in the correct circle on the answer sheet.

No confidence at all	Very little confidence	Moderate confidence	Much confidence	Complete confidence
1	2	3	4	5

Example: How much confidence do you have that you could:

a. Summarize the skills you have developed in the jobs you have held?

If your response was "moderate confidence," you would fill out the number **3** on the sheet.

How much confidence do you have that you could:

— 1. Find information in the library about occupations you are interested in.
— 2. Select one major from a list of potential majors you are considering.
— 3. Make a plan of your goals for the next five years.
— 4. Determine the steps to take if you are having academic trouble with an aspect of your chosen major.
— 5. Accurately assess your abilities.
— 6. Select one occupation from a list of potential occupations you are considering.
— 7. Determine the steps you need to take to successfully complete your chosen major.
— 8. Persistently work at your major or career goal even when you get frustrated.
— 9. Determine what your ideal job would be.
— 10. Find out the employment trends for an occupation over the next ten years.
— 11. Choose a career that will fit your preferred lifestyle.
— 12. Prepare a good resume.
— 13. Change majors if you did not like your first choice.
— 14. Decide what you value most in an occupation.
— 15. Find out about the average yearly earnings of people in an occupation.
— 16. Make a career decision and then not worry about whether it was right or wrong.
— 17. Change occupations if you are not satisfied with the one you enter.
— 18. Figure out what you are and are not ready to sacrifice to achieve your career goals.
— 19. Talk with a person already employed in the field you are interested in.
— 20. Choose a major or career that will fit your interests.
— 21. Identify employers, firms, institutions relevant to your career possibilities.
— 22. Define the type of lifestyle you would like to live.
— 23. Find information about graduate or professional schools.
— 24. Successfully manage the job interview process.
— 25. Identify some reasonable major or career alternatives if you are unable to get your first choice.

Reprinted with permission of Nancy E. Betz and Karen M. Taylor.

Caregiver Strain Index (CSI)

PURPOSE To measure caregiver strain.

AUTHOR Betsy C. Robinson

DESCRIPTION The CSI is a 13-item instrument designed to measure the strain among caregivers of physically ill and functionally impaired older adults. The CSI was developed by systematically identifying the most common stressors named by adult children caring for an elderly parent and by reviewing the literature on caregiver strain. Although most practitioners are aware of the strain involved in providing care for the elderly, this brief, easily administered and scored questionnaire should be useful in preventive clinical practice. The CSI can be read to the respondent or filled out by the respondent as he or she reads it.

NORMS The CSI was studied initially with 85 individuals who had been named as primary caregivers by elderly ex-patients from three San Francisco hospitals. The caregivers included 38% spouses, 22% daughters or daughters-in-law, 11% sons, 14% other relatives, 12% friends, and 4% neighbors. The age range was from 22 to 83 years. The mean score was 3.529 with a standard deviation of 3.5. The authors suggest that positive responses to seven or more items on the CSI indicate a greater level of stress.

SCORING Item scores are summed for a total score that can range from 0 to 13 with higher scores indicating greater strain.

RELIABILITY The CSI has very good internal consistency, with an alpha of .86. No data on stability were provided.

VALIDITY The CSI has demonstrated fairly good construct validity, correlating in the predicted direction with a number of variables measuring expatient characteristics (e.g., ability to perform activities of daily living) subjective perception of the caregiving relationship (e.g., caregiver perceives it is hard to give help), and emotional status of caregivers (e.g., hostility).

PRIMARY REFERENCE Robinson, B. C. (1983), Validation of a Caregiver Strain Index, *Journal of Gerontology*, 38, 344–348.

AVAILABILITY May be copied from this volume.

I am going to read a list of things which other people have found to be difficult in helping out after somebody comes home from the hospital. *Would you tell me whether any of these apply to you by answering "yes" or "no" for each item?*

	Yes = 1	No = 2
Sleep is disturbed (e.g., because _____ is in and out of bed or wanders around at night).	——	——
It is inconvenient (e.g., because helping takes so much time or it's a long drive over to help).	——	——
It is a physical strain (e.g., because of lifting in and out of a chair; effort or concentration is required).	——	——
It is confining (e.g., helping restricts free time or cannot go visiting).	——	——
There have been family adjustments (e.g., because helping has disrupted routine; there has been no privacy).	——	——
There have been changes in personal plans (e.g., had to turn down a job; could not go on vacation).	——	——
There have been other demands on my time (e.g., from other family members).	——	——
There have been emotional adjustments (e.g., because of severe arguments).	——	——
Some behavior is upsetting (e.g., because of incontinence; _____ has trouble remembering things; or _____ accuses people of taking things).	——	——
It is upsetting to find _____ has changed so much from his/her former self (e.g., he/she is a different person than he/she used to be).	——	——
There have been work adjustments (e.g., because of having to take time off).	——	——
It is a financial strain.	——	——
Feeling completely overwhelmed (e.g., because of worry about _____; concerns about how you will manage).	——	——

Total Score (COUNT "YES" RESPONSES)

Caregiver's Burden Scale (CBS)

PURPOSE To measure caregivers' feelings of burden.

AUTHORS Steven H. Zarit, Karen E. Reever, and Julie Bach-Peterson

DESCRIPTION The CBS is a 29-item scale designed to measure feelings of burden experienced by caregivers of elderly persons with senile dementia. The items for the CBS were selected based on clinical experience and prior research, and covered areas most frequently mentioned by caregivers as problems. Because of the increasing aging of the population and the emphasis in the gerontological literature on finding alternatives to institutionalization for the elderly, there is a need to be aware of the potential burden on family members of caring for older relatives, especially those with dementia. The CBS provides the opportunity for a systematic assessment of caregivers' perceptions of these burdens.

NORMS The CBS was initially studied with 29 elderly people with senile dementia and their 29 primary caregivers. The mean age of the elderly was 76 with 16 males and 13 females, all white. Of the 29 caregivers, only four were male; they had a mean age of 65 years. Respondents were recruited from a research and training center offering services to older persons. The mean score for the total sample of caregivers was 30.8 with a standard deviation of 13.3. For daughters as caregivers, the mean score was 28.3 (SD = 14.6) and for spouses as caregivers, the mean was 32.5 (SD = 13.4).

SCORING The CBS is scored on a 5-point sliding scale with scores on the items summed for the total scores. Items 14, 16, 20, and 29 are reverse-scored and subtracted from the total. Where the spouse is not the primary caregiver, the term *spouse* on the CBS can be replaced with the appropriate relationship (father, mother, etc.).

RELIABILITY No data on reliability were reported.

VALIDITY There were no significant correlations between feelings of burden and extent of behavior impairment or duration of illness. There was a low (.48) but significant negative correlation between the CBS and the frequency of family visits, a form of concurrent validity.

PRIMARY REFERENCE Zarit, S. H., Reever, K. E., and Bach-Peterson, J. (1980). Relatives of the impaired elderly: Correlates of feelings of burden, *The Gerontologist*, 20, 649–655.

AVAILABILITY Dr. Steven H. Zarit, Department of Human Development and Family Studies, Pennsylvania State University, University Park, PA 16802. Email: 267@psu.edu.

The following is a list of statements which reflect how people sometimes feel when taking care of another person. In the space to the left of each statement, please indicate how often you feel that way using the following scale:

0 = Never
1 = Rarely
2 = Sometimes
3 = Quite frequently
4 = Nearly always

___ 1. Feel resentful of other relatives who could but who do not do things for my spouse.

___ 2. I feel that my spouse makes requests which I perceive to be over and above what he/she needs.

___ 3. Because of my involvement with my spouse, I don't have enough time for myself.

___ 4. I feel stressed between trying to give to my spouse as well as to other family responsibilities, job, etc.

___ 5. I feel embarrassed over my spouse's behavior.

___ 6. I feel guilty about my interactions with my spouse.

___ 7. I feel that I don't do as much for my spouse as I could or should.

___ 8. I feel angry about my interactions with my spouse.

___ 9. I feel that in the past, I haven't done as much for my spouse as I could have or should have.

___ 10. I feel nervous or depressed about my interactions with my spouse.

___ 11. I feel that my spouse currently affects my relationships with other family members and friends in a negative way.

___ 12. I feel resentful about my interactions with my spouse.

___ 13. I am afraid of what the future holds for my spouse.

___ 14. I feel pleased about my interactions with my spouse.

___ 15. It's painful to watch my spouse age.

___ 16. I feel useful in my interactions with my spouse.

___ 17. I feel my spouse is dependent.

___ 18. I feel strained in my interactions with my spouse.

___ 19. I feel that my health has suffered because of my involvement with my spouse.

___ 20. I feel that I am contributing to the well-being of my spouse.

___ 21. I feel that the present situation with my spouse doesn't allow me as much privacy as I like.

___ 22. I feel that my social life has suffered because of my involvement with my spouse.

___ 23. I wish that my spouse and I had a better relationship.

___ 24. I feel that my spouse doesn't appreciate what I do for him/her as much as I would like.

___ 25. I feel uncomfortable when I have friends over.

___ 26. I feel that my spouse tries to manipulate me.

___ 27. I feel that my spouse seems to expect me to take care of him/her as if I were the only one he/she could depend on.
___ 28. I feel that I don't have enough money to support my spouse in addition to the rest of our expenses.
___ 29. I feel that I would like to be able to provide more money to support my spouse than I am able to now.

Center for Epidemiologic Studies—Depressed Mood Scale (CES-D)

PURPOSE To measure depressive symptomatology in the general population.

AUTHOR L. S. Radloff

DESCRIPTION The CES-D is a 20-item scale that was originally designed to measure depression in the general population for epidemiological research. However it also has been shown to be useful in clinical and psychiatric settings. The scale is very easily administered and scored and was found to be easy to use by respondents in both the clinical and general populations. The CES-D measures current level of depressive symptomatology, with emphasis on the affective component—depressed mood. The CES-D items were selected from a pool of items from previously validated depression scales, from the literature, and from factor analytic studies. Because of the extensive research conducted in its development and its broad applicability, the CES-D is a particularly useful measure.

NORMS Extensive research on the CES-D involved 3,574 white respondents of both sexes from the general population plus a retest involving 1,422 respondents. In addition, 105 psychiatric patients of both sexes were involved in clinical studies. An additional unspecified number of black respondents from the general population were involved in the testing. Means for the general population of white respondents ranged from 7.94 to 9.25. The mean for 70 psychiatric patients was 24.42. All results regarding reliability and validity were reported as being confirmed for subgroups: blacks and whites, both sexes, and three levels of education. No cutting scores were reported.

SCORING The CES-D is easily scored by reverse-scoring items 4, 8, 12, and 16 and then summing the scores on all items. This produces a range of 0 to 60 with higher scores indicating greater depression.

RELIABILITY The CES-D has very good internal consistency with alphas of roughly .85 for the general population and .90 for the psychiatric population. Split-half and Spearman-Brown reliability coefficients ranged from .77 to .92. The CES-D has fair stability with test-retest correlations that range from .51 to .67 (tested over two to eight weeks) and .32 to .54 (tested over 3 months to one year).

VALIDITY The CES-D has excellent concurrent validity, correlating significantly with a number of other depression and mood scales. The CES-D also has good known-groups validity, discriminating well between psychiatric inpatients and the general population, and moderately among levels of severity within patient groups. The CES-D also discriminated between people in the general population who state they "need help" and those that did not, and it was shown to be sensitive to change in psychiatric patients' status after treatment. There was a very small association with social desirability response bias but it does not appear to affect the utility of CES-D.

PRIMARY REFERENCE Radloff, L. S. (1977). The CES-D scale: A self-report depression scale for research in the general population, *Applied Psychological Measurement*, 1, 385–401. Instrument reproduced with permission of Dr. Ben Z. Locke.

AVAILABILITY May be copied from this volume.

Using the scale below, indicate the number which best describes how often you felt or behaved this way—DURING THE PAST WEEK.

1 = Rarely or none of the time (less than 1 day)
2 = Some or a little of the time (1–2 days)
3 = Occasionally or a moderate amount of time (3–4 days)
4 = Most or all of the time (5–7 days)

During the Past Week:

___ 1. I was bothered by things that usually don't bother me.
___ 2. I did not feel like eating; my appetite was poor.
___ 3. I felt that I could not shake off the blues even with help from my family or friends.
___ 4. I felt that I was just as good as other people.
___ 5. I had trouble keeping my mind on what I was doing.
___ 6. I felt depressed.
___ 7. I felt that everything I did was an effort.
___ 8. I felt hopeful about the future.
___ 9. I thought my life had been a failure.
___ 10. I felt fearful.
___ 11. My sleep was restless.
___ 12. I was happy.
___ 13. I talked less than usual.
___ 14. I felt lonely.
___ 15. People were unfriendly.
___ 16. I enjoyed life.
___ 17. I had crying spells.
___ 18. I felt sad.
___ 19. I felt that people disliked me.
___ 20. I could not get "going."

Chabot Emotional Differentiation Scale (CEDS)

PURPOSE To measure intrapsychic individuation

AUTHOR David Chabot

DESCRIPTION The CEDS is a 17-item scale designed to measure emotional differentiation or intrapsychic individuation. Emotional differentiation is based on Murray Bowen's family-of- origin theory and defines differentiation as one's ability to distinguish emotional and intellectual functioning and then use the intellect in emotionally charged circumstances. Differentiation is considered a global personality trait and is the predicate to mature development and psychological health. Emotional differentiation is different from automatic emotional responses that seem innate to humans, but is the adaptive response in a relationship in which one may make intellectual effort. To some degree the CEDS expands the Bowenian concept as the items are not anchored to a family relationship, but differentiation is defined in the context of the integration of thinking and feeling. The CEDS is age appropriate for late teens dealing with identity versus ego diffusion and other emotional conditions and adults.

NORMS The mean CEDS score was 60.07 with a standard deviation of 7.4 (range 40–83) for a sample of 167 undergraduates. From a sample of Italians and a sample of Italian Americans the mean CEDS scores were 58.59 and 60.07, respectively.

SCORING The items with the * are first reverse-scored such that the 5 = 1, 4 = 2, 3= 3, 2 = 4, and 1 =5. Next, sum the item scores for the total score. Scores range from 17 to 85.

RELIABILITY The CEDS has very good reliability estimates. From the sample of 167 undergraduates, the alpha was .80 and from various other samples the mean alpha was .81.

VALIDITY The CEDS has excellent support for its validity. Face validity was evidenced by evaluation of items by a panel of 3 clinicians trained in Bowen's approach. Concurrent validity was evidenced with CEDS scores correlating negatively with depression and anxiety and positively with other measures of differentiation. Scores correlated with social adjustment, college adjustment, and negatively with triangulation.

PRIMARY REFERENCE Licht, C., and Chabot, D. (2006). The Chabot Emotional Differentiation Scale: A theoretically and psychometrically sound instrument for measuring Bowen's intrapsychic aspects of differentiation. *Journal of marital and family therapy, 32*, 167–180.

AVAILABILITY David R. Chabot, Ph.D., 2 Boyce Road, Danbury CT 06811. Email: drchabot@sbcglobal.net.

Please indicate the degree to which the following statements are true of you at the present time. Use the following scale for your answers. Circle the appropriate number for each question.

1	2	3	4	5
Never	Almost Never	Sometimes	Almost	Always

1 2 3 4 5   1. During nonstressful periods, my behavior reflects a good integration between my thinking and my emotions.

1 2 3 4 5 *2. When I am under prolonged stress, I find that my behavior is directed more by my emotions than my reason.

1 2 3 4 5 *3. I have difficulty bringing my feelings and my thoughts into harmony before I act

1 2 3 4 5   4. Even under stress, I can eventually respond in a rational way without denying my emotions.

1 2 3 4 5 *5 In my relationship with my parents, I have a hard time responding in a reasonable yet sympathetic manner.

1 2 3 4 5 *6. I have difficulty changing emotionally close relationships that I know are not conducive to my well-being.

1 2 3 4 5   7. In most matters I can act in a decisive manner and am not bothered by my emotions and/or thoughts.

1 2 3 4 5   8. When I am in a pressured situation, I am still clear about what I feel and what I believe.

1 2 3 4 5   In my significant relationships, I do not like to express my convictions for fear of hurting the other person's feelings.

1 2 3 4 5 10. I conduct myself in a manner that is consistent both with my intellectual convictions and my emotional sentiments.

1 2 3 4 5 *11. During a crisis, conflict between my emotions and my reason will immobilize my behavior.

1 2 3 4 5   2. I can maintain my principles in an intimate relationship without feeling emotionally threatened.

1 2 3 4 5 13. I can maintain internal calmness and clear thinking even when I have to constantly deal with overly demanding and over controlling people.

1 2 3 4 5 *14. I prefer work relationships to intimate relationships because there is a clear separation between feelings for, and responsibilities to, each other.

1 2 3 4 5 15 When I am in a casual relationship, I feel just as balanced between my feelings and my thinking as when I am in a family relationship.

1 2 3 4 5 *16 When I am in an emotionally satisfying relationship, I have difficulty knowing my own mind and asserting myself.

1 2 3 4 5 17 I have had to leave an intimate relationship(s) where my partner needed to define who I am.

* = reverse scored

Chinese Depressive Symptom Scale (CDS)

PURPOSE To measure depression among Chinese in China.

AUTHOR Nan Lin

DESCRIPTION The CDS is a 22-item instrument designed to measure depressive symptoms among Chinese people in China. It was developed by adapting and translating the Center for Epidemiological Studies—Depression Scale and adding six new items based upon discussion with Chinese mental health workers. The added items were intended to tap the common idioms of psychiatric complaints that originated in the past, especially during the Cultural Revolution. The CDS can be usefully applied in cross-cultural studies or in clinical work with Chinese clients. However, its utility with Chinese living outside of China is unknown. It is reproduced here in English and Romanized Chinese.

NORMS The CDS was administered to a random sample of 1,000 adults living in Tianjin, the third largest city in China. Respondents were about equally divided between men and women, with a mean age of 43.2, 94% married, mean education of approximately seven to nine years. The mean score for the 22 items was 7.067.

SCORING Individual items on the 4-point scales are summed to provide a range from 0 to 66 with higher scores indicating greater depressive symptoms.

RELIABILITY The CDS has excellent internal consistency, with an alpha of .89. Data on stability were not provided.

VALIDITY The CDS has good criterion validity, with significant correlations with four quality-of-life factors from a quality-of-life scale. The CDS was viewed as having very good predictive validity, correlating significantly with two life events scales. All validity checks indicated results were very similar to studies in North America.

PRIMARY REFERENCE Lin, N. (1989). Measuring Depressive Symptomatology in China, *Journal of Nervous and Mental Disease*, 177, 121–131.

AVAILABILITY May be copied from this volume.

Please place a number beside each item, to the extent it applies to you, as follows:

3 = Always
2 = From time to time
1 = Occasionally
0 = Never

___ 1. I was bothered by things that usually don't bother me.
Yuan lai bu fan nao de shi, kai shi shi wuo fan nao.

___ 2. I did not feel like eating; my appetite was poor.
Wou bu xiang chi dong xi, wei kou bu jia.

___ 3. I felt that I could not shake off the blues even with the help of my family/friends.
Wou jue de xin fan, qin you de bang zhu ye bu guan yong.

___ 4. I had trouble keeping my mind on what I was doing.
Wou bu neng ji zhong jing li zou wou yao zuo de shi.

___ 5. I felt depressed.
Wou gan dao xie oi.

___ 6. I felt that everything I did was an effort.
Wuo jue de zuo shen mo shi duo hen chi li.

___ 7. I thought my life had been a failure.
Wuo jue de wuo de ren sheng jing li shi chang shi bai.

___ 8. I felt fearful.
Wuo gan dao hai pa.

___ 9. My sleep was restless.
Wuo shui bu hao jiao.

___ 10. I talked less than usual.
Wuo hao xiang shuo hua bi yi qian shao le.

___ 11. I felt lonely.
Wuo gan dao gu du.

___ 12. People were unfriendly.
Wuo gan dao ren men dui wuo bu you hao.

___ 13. I had crying spells.
Wuo ge yi duan shi jian jiu hui ku yi chang.

___ 14. I felt sad.
Wuo gan dao bei shang.

___ 15. I felt that people disliked me.
Wuo jue de bie ren bu xi huan wuo.

___ 16. I could not get "going."
Wuo zuo ren he shi dou bu qi jin.

___ 17. I felt I have a lot to talk about, but can't find the opportunity to say it.
Wuo jue de you hao xie hua yao shuo, dan you mei you hi shi de ji hui shuo.

___ 18. I feel suffocated.
Wuo gan dao hen ku men.

___ 19. I feel suspicious of others.
Wuo dui bei ren qi huai yi xin.

___ 20. I don't think others trust me.
  Wuo jue de bie ren bu xin ren wuo.
___ 21. I don't think I can trust others.
  Wuo jue de bu neng xin ren ta ren.
___ 22. I remember unpleasant things from the past.
  Wuo hui xiang qi yi wang jing li guo de bu yu kuai de shi qing.

Chronic Pain Intrusion and Accommodation Scale (CPIAS)

PURPOSE To measure pain appraisal.

AUTHORS Mary Casey Jacob, Robert D. Kerns, Roberta Rosenberg, and Jennifer Haythornthwaite

DESCRIPTION The CPIAS is a 14-item instrument designed to measure an individual's appraisal of pain problems. The CPIAS measures two aspects of pain appraisal. The first is a factor related to predictability, called intrusion (items 2, 3, 4, 5, 6, 9, 10, and 12); the second factor is called pain accommodation (as opposed to control; items 1, 7, 8, 11, 13, and 14). The intrusion subscale reflects reciprocal relationships between pain and affective distress and the intrusiveness of this predictability. The accommodation subscale reflects a person's ability to live a satisfying life despite having chronic pain. The CPIAS appears to be a valuable tool not only for future research investigating chronic pain, but as a guide for clinicians working with clients who are suffering from chronic pain.

NORMS The CPIAS was developed on two samples of chronic pain patients including 144 patients referred to a pain management center and 105 subsequent referred patients. The mean age for the two samples was about 49 years, with a mean education of 12.2 years; mean pain duration in years for the first sample was 10.2 years; for the second sample it was 14.2 years. Eighty-five percent and 89% of the two samples, respectively, were male, and 25% and 35% of the respondents in the two samples, respectively, were employed. The majority of respondents were currently using pain medication and almost half in each sample had had one pain-related surgery. Actual means and standard deviations were not presented in the original article.

SCORING The CPIAS is easily scored by summing the items for each factor and the total scale.

RELIABILITY The CPIAS has fair to good internal consistency, with alphas for pain intrusion ranging from .71 to .80 and alphas for accommodation ranging from .64 to .82. The CPIAS also has fair to good stability with two-to-three-week test-retest correlations of .61 and .77 for the two samples.

VALIDITY The CPIAS has good concurrent validity, with validity coefficients for the two subscales showing significant correlations with a number of other pain measures and with the Beck Depression Inventory.

PRIMARY REFERENCE Jacob, M. C., Kerns, R. D., Rosenberg, R., and Haythornthwaite, J. (1993). Chronic pain: Intrusion and accommodation, *Behaviour Research and Therapy*, 31, 519–527.

AVAILABILITY Dr. Mary Casey Jacob, Associate Professor, Psychiatry and Obstetrics and Gynecology, Behavioral Medicine MC6228, University of Connecticut Health Center, 263 Farmington Ave., Farmington, CT 06030. Email: jacob@nso1.uchc.edu.

To what extent do you agree or disagree with the following 14 statements? Read each statement carefully and then *circle* a number on the scale under it to indicate how that specific statement applies to you.

0 = Strongly disagree
1 = Moderately disagree
2 = Mildly disagree
3 = Neither agree nor disagree
4 = Mildly agree
5 = Moderately agree
6 = Strongly agree

1. At times I am able to get my mind off my pain.

    0   1   2   3   4   5   6

2. The intensity of my pain is affected by how I am feeling emotionally.

    0   1   2   3   4   5   6

3. I can predict when my pain is going to get worse.

    0   1   2   3   4   5   6

4. At the times that my pain is worst, I usually feel helpless and depressed.

    0   1   2   3   4   5   6

5. My pain is affected by changes in the weather.

    0   1   2   3   4   5   6

6. When I'm too active, I know I'll suffer more later.

    0   1   2   3   4   5   6

7. Despite my pain problem, I still feel that I'm in control of my life.

    0   1   2   3   4   5   6

8. Despite my pain problem, I think I'm quite able to handle my daily affairs and problems.

    0   1   2   3   4   5   6

9. When I'm feeling down or sad my pain usually bothers me more.

    0   1   2   3   4   5   6

10. When I am bothered by daily problems and I feel stressed, my pain is usually worse.

    0   1   2   3   4   5   6

11. I know that I'll be able to overcome my pain problem and live a satisfactory life.

    0   1   2   3   4   5   6

12. When I'm feeling excited or when I'm enjoying myself my pain doesn't bother me as much.

| 0   1   2   3   4   5   6 |

13. All things considered I think of myself as able to deal with life's problems and "hassles."

| 0   1   2   3   4   5   6 |

14. Despite my pain problem, I know how to have a good time and lift my spirits.

| 0   1   2   3   4   5   6 |

Client Experiences Questionnaire (CEQ)

PURPOSE To measure experiences of service satisfaction and quality of life.

AUTHORS James R. Greenley and Jan Steven Greenberg

DESCRIPTION This 42-item measure consists of two instruments designed to assess a client's satisfaction with services (SS) and satisfaction with life, often called quality of life (QL). The SS has three subscales: satisfaction with humanness of staff (SHS: items A2, A4, A6, A8, A9, and A13), satisfaction with perceived technical competence of staff (SPTCS: items A1, A3, A5, A7, A11, and A12), and appropriateness/effectiveness of services (AES: items B1 to B5). SHS and SPTCS scores may be summed and used as a total SS score. Part C of the CES measures a client's life satisfaction in seven domains: living situation (LS: items C1 to C5), finances (F: items C6, C7, and C8), leisure (L: items C9 to C12), family relations (FR: items C13 to C15), social relations (SR: C16 to C20), health (H: items C21 and C22), and access to health care (AHC: items C23 and C24). The subscales of the QL may be used separately or may be summed to form a general measure of quality of life.

NORMS Normative data on the QL subscales are available from a sample of 971 clients with serious mental illness. The means (and standard deviations) were 5.2 (1.22), 4.1 (1.5), 4.9 (1.09), 4.9 (1.41), 4.7 (1.19), 4.6 (1.35), and 5.1 (1.14) for the LS, F, L, SR, H, and AHC subscales, respectively.

SCORING Responses to the CES are assigned a number from 1 to 7 or 1 to 5 for section B. "Extremely dissatisfied" and "definitely no" are assigned 1 and the "extremely satisfied" and "yes definitely" responses are assigned 7 or 5. Scale scores and subscale scores are the sum of all the items answered, divided by the number of items answered. This approach allows for missing responses to an item or two. The scale should not be scored if more than 40% of the items are unanswered.

RELIABILITY In a study of 1,018 persons with serious mental illness, SS had an internal consistency coefficient of .96, and the AES had a reliability coefficient of .88. The subscales of the QL had internal consistency coefficients ranging from .80 to .91 for a sample of 1,864 clients with serious mental illness and their families.

VALIDITY The subscale structure of the CEQ was generally supported with factor analysis. Total QL scores correlated with patient general functioning. Clients reporting more satisfaction with services also reported higher quality of life scores. QL scores differentiated voluntary from nonvoluntary participation. Scores also differentiated employed from unemployed clients. These findings tend to support the criterion-related validity of the CES.

PRIMARY REFERENCE Greenley, J. R., Greenberg, J. S., and Brown, R. (1997). Measuring Quality of Life: A new and practical survey instrument, *Social Work*, 42, 244–254.

AVAILABILITY Jan Greenberg, Ph.D., School of Social Work, University of Wisconsin, Madison, WI 53706. Email: greenberg@WAISMan.WISC.edu.

For each question, write the number of the answer that best corresponds to how you feel in the space to the left of the item.

A. Below are some questions about your satisfaction with the services you receive.

1 = Extremely satisfied
2 = Very satisfied
3 = Somewhat satisfied
4 = Not certain
5 = Somewhat dissatisfied
6 = Very dissatisfied
7 = Extremely dissatisfied

___ 1. The general quality of services you receive in this program?
___ 2. The courtesy and friendliness of the staff?
___ 3. The thoroughness of the staff in gathering all important information about your problem?
___ 4. The staff's warmth and personal interest in you?
___ 5. The degree to which the staff thoroughly explains what you are expected to do?
___ 6. The amount of respect shown to you by the staff?
___ 7. The technical competence of the staff?
___ 8. The consideration shown for your feelings?
___ 9. The amount of concern the staff expresses about your problems?
___ 10. The degree to which the staff seems to be familiar with your kind of problem?
___ 11. How well the staff checks up on the problems you have had before?
___ 12. The comprehensiveness or completeness of services which were provided to you?
___ 13. Attempts by staff to explain how things are done so you won't worry?

B. Below are some questions about the program you are in.

1 = Yes, definitely
2 = Yes, somewhat
3 = Neither yes nor no
4 = No, somewhat
5 = No, definitely

___ 1. Do you like being in this program?
___ 2. Do you feel excellent progress has been made on your problem since you entered this program?
___ 3. Are you getting the kind of help here that you need?
___ 4. Is the help you are receiving in this program appropriate for your problem?
___ 5. Has the condition that led to your being in this program improved a great deal?

C. Below are some additional questions about how satisfied you are with some aspects of your life.

1 = Terrible
2 = Unhappy
3 = Mostly dissatisfied
4 = Equally satisfied/dissatisfied
5 = Mostly satisfied
6 = Pleased
7 = Delighted

Concerning your living arrangements, how do you feel about:

___ 1. The living arrangements where you live?
___ 2. The rules there?
___ 3. The privacy you have there?
___ 4. The amount of freedom you have there?
___ 5. The prospect of staying on where you currently live for a long period of time?

Here are some questions about money. How do you feel about:

___ 6. The amount of money you get?
___ 7. How comfortable and well-off you are financially?
___ 8. How much money you have to spend for fun?

Here are some questions about how you spend your spare time. How do you feel about:

___ 9. The way you spend your spare time?
___ 10. The chance you have to enjoy pleasant or beautiful things?
___ 11. The amount of relaxation in your life?
___ 12. The pleasure you get from the TV or radio?

Here are some questions about your family. How do you feel about:

___ 13. Your family in general?
___ 14. The way you and your family act toward each other?
___ 15. The way things are in general between you and your family?

Here are some questions about your social life. How do you feel about:

___ 16. The things you do with other people?
___ 17. The amount of time you spend with other people?
___ 18. The people you see socially?
___ 19. The chance you have to know people with whom you feel really comfortable?
___ 20. The amount of friendship in your life?

Here are some questions about your health. How do you feel about:

___ 21. Your health in general?
___ 22. Your physical condition?
___ 23. The medical care available to you if you need it?
___ 24. How often you see a doctor?

Client Motivation for Therapy Scale (CMOTS)

PURPOSE To measure motivation for therapy.

AUTHORS Luc G. Pelletier, Kim M. Tuson, and Nagwa K. Haddad

DESCRIPTION The CMOTS is a 24-item instrument designed to measure client motivation for therapy. The scale is based on the theoretical perspective of human motivation and self-determination proposed by Deci and Ryan who postulate the existence of six different types of motivation that are classified along a continuum of increasing autonomy. The six subscales of the CMOTS do indeed correspond to the six different types of motivation postulated by the theory and appear to fall along a self-determination continuum. The subscales are: intrinsic motivation (items 3, 4, 12, 16); integrated regulation (items 17, 18, 23, 24); identified regulation (items 6, 7, 15, 20); introjected regulation (items 5, 9, 10, 19); external regulation (items 1, 11, 21, 22); and amotivation (items 2, 8, 13, 14). The CMOTS is a valuable measure that practitioners can use to address the impact of client motivation on psychotherapy effectiveness and mental health.

NORMS The CMOTS was studied with 138 clients from three outpatient hospital clinics and two university-based clinics in Canada. Eighty-three of the respondents were women whose mean age was 24.8 years and 55 of the respondents were men whose mean age was 28.3 years. Ninety percent of the respondents had more than 12 years of education. Clients reported being in therapy for a number of reasons with interpersonal problems, depression, and low self-esteem being the most common complaints. Means and standard deviations were not reported.

SCORING The CMOTS is easily scored by summing individual items for each subscale.

RELIABILITY The CMOTS has fair to excellent internal consistency, with alphas for the subscales that range from .70 for external regulation to .92 for intrinsic motivation. No data on stability were provided.

VALIDITY The CMOTS has demonstrated good construct validity, with significant correlations between its subscales and perceptions of therapists' interpersonal behaviors (e.g., clients with more self-determined types of motivation reported working with therapists providing relatively more autonomy support, care, and competence feedback and less control than clients with less self-determined types of motivation). Significant correlations also were reported between the CMOTS subscales and motivational consequences (e.g., scales measuring distraction, tension, positive emotions during therapy, etc., plus constructs associated with psychological functioning such as self-esteem, and depression).

PRIMARY REFERENCE Pelletier, L. G., Tuson, K. M., and Haddad, N. K. (1997). Client motivation for therapy scale: A measure of intrinsic motivation, extrinsic motivation, and amotivation for therapy, *Journal of Personality Assessment*, 68, 414–435.

AVAILABILITY Dr. Luc G. Pelletier, School of Psychology, University of Ottawa, Ottawa, Ontario, K1N 6N7, Canada. Reprinted by permission of Dr. Pelletier. Email: luc.pelletier@uottawa.ca.

Why Are You Presently Involved in Therapy?

Using the scale below, please indicate to what extent each of the following items corresponds to the reasons why you are *presently* involved in therapy by circling the appropriate number to the right of each item. We realize that the reasons why you are in therapy at this moment may differ from the reasons that you initially began therapy. However, we are interested to know why you are in therapy *at the present moment*.

	Does not correspond at all		Corresponds moderately			Corresponds exactly	
1. Because other people think that it's a good idea for me to be in therapy.	1	2	3	4	5	6	7
2. Honestly, I really don't understand what I can get from therapy.	1	2	3	4	5	6	7
3. For the pleasure I experience when I feel completely absorbed in a therapy session.	1	2	3	4	5	6	7
4. For the satisfaction I have when I try to achieve my personal goals in the course of therapy.	1	2	3	4	5	6	7
5. Because I would feel guilty if I was not doing anything about my problem.	1	2	3	4	5	6	7
6. Because I would like to make changes to my current situation.	1	2	3	4	5	6	7
7. Because I believe that eventually it will allow me to feel better.	1	2	3	4	5	6	7
8. I once had good reasons for going to therapy; however, now I wonder whether I should quit.	1	2	3	4	5	6	7
9. Because I would feel bad about myself if I didn't continue my therapy.	1	2	3	4	5	6	7
10. Because I should have a better understanding of myself.	1	2	3	4	5	6	7
11. Because my friends think I should be in therapy.	1	2	3	4	5	6	7
12. Because I experience pleasure and satisfaction when I learn new things about myself that I didn't know before.	1	2	3	4	5	6	7
13. I wonder what I'm doing in therapy; actually, I find it boring.	1	2	3	4	5	6	7
14. I don't know; I never really thought about it before.	1	2	3	4	5	6	7
15. Because I believe that therapy will allow me to deal with things better.	1	2	3	4	5	6	7
16. For the interest I have in understanding more about myself.	1	2	3	4	5	6	7

continued

	Does not correspond at all			Corresponds moderately			Corresponds exactly
17. Because through therapy I've come to see a way that I can continue to approach different aspects of my life.	1	2	3	4	5	6	7
18. Because through therapy I feel that I can now take responsibility for making changes in my life.	1	2	3	4	5	6	7
19. Because it is important for clients to remain in therapy until it's finished.	1	2	3	4	5	6	7
20. Because I believe it's a good thing to do to find solutions to my problem.	1	2	3	4	5	6	7
21. To satisfy people close to me who want me to get help for my current situation.	1	2	3	4	5	6	7
22. Because I don't want to upset people close to me who want me to be in therapy.	1	2	3	4	5	6	7
23. Because I feel that changes that are taking place through therapy are becoming part of me.	1	2	3	4	5	6	7
24. Because I value the way therapy allows me to make changes in my life.	1	2	3	4	5	6	7

Client Perception of Therapy (CPT)

PURPOSE To measure a client's perception of successful therapy outcomes

AUTHOR Muriel Singer

DESCRIPTION The CPT is a 10-item qualitative instrument designed to assess the client's view of what is contributing to successful outcomes in therapy. The CPT contrasts with other instruments that ascertain a clinician's perspective. The CPT is not scored but the content of each item is used collaboratively with the client and clinician as a team in the treatment process. The CPT attempts to answer the question "How does a client make sense of the experience of therapy?" The CPT is based on a post-modern, social constructionist school of thought. The CPT items were developed with a panel of 9 therapist-client dyads over the course of treatment where both client and clinician keep case notes.

NORMS There are no norms for the CPT.

SCORING Item 1 is scored on a scale of 1 to 10 with 10 reflecting more successful therapy. Items 2 through 10 have written responses by the client that are used in collaboration with the clinician to determine what seems to be working in therapy.

RELIABILITY There is no quantitative data for internal consistency, which is less of a concern than with other measures as the CPT is designed for the individual client.

VALIDITY There is good evidence of qualitative estimates of accuracy in the primary reference.

PRIMARY REFERENCE Singer, M. (2005). A twice-told tale: A phenomenological inquiry into clients' perceptions of therapy. *Journal of Marital and Family Therapy,* 31, 269–281.

AVAILABILITY Muriel Singer, Ph.D., Psychology Department, Kean University, 1000 Morris Avenue, Union, NJ 07083. Email: msinger@kean.edu.

Client Case Notes

We welcome your participation. One thing we try to do here is provide good care and we would like to learn from your point of view what you think is important about the conversations you have in therapy. We have found this to be useful in previous studies as a way of learning what our clients find helpful or not so helpful. We value your feedback and believe we can only do a better job by getting to know what you think. As to what is written in the notes, there are no rules about what you say or how you say it. You may write any comments about the therapy or the therapist, what you like or dislike, points you wish to remember, or even future goals. Correct grammar and spelling are not important. In short, anything you want recorded is written down.

1. How do you think therapy is going? On a scale of 1-10, how would you rate the session?
2. What ideas do you have about what needs to happen for improvement to occur?
3. How well do you feel you related to the therapist? How well did the therapist relate to you?
4. Did you feel heard, understood and respected?
5. What was helpful to you? What might have been more helpful?
6. Was there anything you expected or hoped would happen or be talked about, but wasn't?
7. How well did you accomplish what you hoped to accomplish?
8. What are some of the most important qualities that you look for in a therapist?
9. Does the treatment being offered here make sense to you?
10. What is the one thing you would change about the therapy sessions?

Client Satisfaction Inventory (CSI)

PURPOSE To measure client satisfaction.

AUTHORS Steven L. McMurty and Walter W. Hudson

DESCRIPTION The CSI is a 25-item instrument designed to measure the degree or magnitude of satisfaction experienced by clients regarding the services that were provided to them. The CSI can be used with a single client or with all clients in a periodic survey of client satisfaction. The CSI involves an effort to develop a psychometrically sound instrument that can be used in a wide range of client situations. The preliminary evidence on the CSI suggests that it can be effectively used to assess client satisfaction in a range of different agencies. One advantage of the CSI is that it is one of several scales of the WALMYR Assessment Scales package reproduced here, all of which are administered and scored the same way.

NORMS Norms are available from the author.

SCORING Like most WALMYR Assessment Scales, the CSI is scored by first reverse-scoring items listed at the bottom of the page (items 4, 7, 16, 18, and 22), summing these and remaining scores, subtracting the number of completed items, multiplying this figure by 100, and dividing by the number of items completed times 6. This will produce a range from 0 to 100 with higher scores indicating greater magnitude or degree of satisfaction with services.

RELIABILITY The CSI has excellent internal consistency, with an alpha of .93. The CSI also has a low SEM of 3.16. Data on stability were not available.

VALIDITY The CSI has been investigated regarding content, construct, and factorial validity. It nearly always achieves validity coefficients of .60 or greater.

PRIMARY REFERENCE Hudson, W. W. (1997). *The WALMYR Assessment Scales Scoring Manual*. Tallahassee, FL: WALMYR Publishing Company.

AVAILABILITY This scale cannot be reproduced or copied in any manner and must be obtained by writing to the WALMYR Publishing Company, P.O. Box 12217, Tallahassee, FL 32317-2217 or WALMYR.com.

CLIENT SATISFACTION INVENTORY (CSI)

Name: _____ Today's Date: _____

This questionnaire is designed to measure the way you feel about the services you have received. It is not a test, so there are no right or wrong answers. Answer each item as carefully and as accurately as you can by placing a number beside each one as follows.

1 = None of the time
2 = Very rarely
3 = A little of the time
4 = Some of the time
5 = A good part of the time
6 = Most of the time
7 = All of the time
8 = Does not apply

1. ___ The services I get here are a big help to me.
2. ___ People here really seem to care about me.
3. ___ I would come back here if I need help again.
4. ___ I feel that no one here really listens to me.
5. ___ People here treat me like a person, not like a number.
6. ___ I have learned a lot here about how to deal with my problems.
7. ___ People here want to do things their way, instead of helping me find my way.
8. ___ I would recommend this place to people I care about.
9. ___ People here really know what they are doing.
10. ___ I get the kind of help here that I really need.
11. ___ People here accept me for who I am.
12. ___ I feel much better now than when I first came here.
13. ___ I thought no one could help me until I came here.
14. ___ The help I get here is really worth what it costs.
15. ___ People here put my needs ahead of their needs.
16. ___ People here put me down when I disagree with them.
17. ___ The biggest help I get here is learning how to help myself.
18. ___ People here are just trying to get rid of me.
19. ___ People who know me say this place has made a positive change in me.
20. ___ People here have shown me how to get help from other places.
21. ___ People here seem to understand how I feel.
22. ___ People here are only concerned about getting paid.
23. ___ I feel I can really talk to people here.
24. ___ The help I get here is better than I expected.
25. ___ I look forward to the sessions I have with people here.

Client Satisfaction Questionnaire (CSQ-8)

PURPOSE To assess client satisfaction with treatment.

AUTHOR C. Clifford Attkisson

DESCRIPTION The CSQ-8 is an 8-item, easily scored and administered measure that is designed to measure client satisfaction with services. The items for the CSQ-8 were selected on the basis of ratings by mental health professionals of a number of items that could be related to client satisfaction and by subsequent factor analysis. The CSQ-8 is unidimensional, yielding a homogeneous estimate of general satisfaction with services. The CSQ-8 has been extensively studied, and while it is not necessarily a measure of a client's perceptions of gain from treatment, or outcome, it does elicit the client's perspective on the value of services received. Items 3, 7, and 8 can be used as a shorter scale.

NORMS The CSQ-8 has been used with a number of populations. The largest single study involved 3,268 clients from 76 clinical facilities including inpatients and outpatients. This study involved 42 Mexican Americans, 96 non-Mexican Hispanics, 361 blacks, and 2,605 whites. Both sexes and a wide range of other demographic variables were included. In essence, the CSQ-8 seems to operate about the same across all ethnic groups. This also is true for a version of the CSQ-8 that was translated into Spanish. The mean scores for the four groups ranged from 26.35 to 27.23 and were not significantly different.

SCORING The CSQ-8 is easily scored by summing the individual item scores to produce a range of 8 to 32, with higher scores indicating greater satisfaction.

RELIABILITY The CSQ-8 has excellent internal consistency, with alphas that range from .86 to .94 in a number of studies. Test-retest correlations were not reported.

VALIDITY The CSQ-8 has very good concurrent validity. Scores on the CSQ-8 are correlated with clients' ratings of global improvement and symptomatology, and therapists' ratings of clients' progress and likability. Scores also are correlated with drop-out rate (less satisfied clients having higher drop-out rates). The CSQ-8 has also demonstrated moderate correlations with a number of other (but not all) outcome variables, thus suggesting a modest correlation between satisfaction and treatment gain.

PRIMARY REFERENCE Larsen, D. L., Attkisson, C. C., Hargreaves, W. A., and Nguyen, T. D. (1979). Assessment of client/patient satisfaction: Development of a general scale, *Evaluation and Program Planning*, 2, 197–207. Instrument reproduced with permission of C. Clifford Attkisson.

AVAILABILITY Dr. C. Clifford Attkisson, at Email: tammatrix@mac.com. Telephone: 415.381.0242.

Please help us improve our program by answering some questions about the services you have received. We are interested in your honest opinions, whether they are positive or negative. *Please answer all of the questions.* We also welcome your comments and suggestions. Thank you very much; we really appreciate your help.

Circle your answer:

1. How would you rate the quality of service you have received?

4	3	2	1
Excellent	Good	Fair	Poor

2. Did you get the kind of service you wanted?

1	2	3	4
No, definitely	No, not really	Yes, generally	Yes, definitely

3. To what extent has our program met your needs?

4	3	2	1
Almost all of my needs have been met	Most of my needs have been met	Only a few of my needs have been met	None of my needs have been met

4. If a friend were in need of similar help, would you recommend our program to him or her?

1	2	3	4
No, definitely not	No, I don't think so	Yes, I think so	Yes, definitely

5. How satisfied are you with the amount of help you have received?

1	2	3	4
Quite dissatisfied	Indifferent or mildly dissatisfied	Mostly satisfied	Very satisfied

6. Have the services you received helped you to deal more effectively with your problems?

4	3	2	1
Yes, they helped	Yes, they helped a great deal	No, they really didn't help	No, they seemed to make things worse

7. In an overall, general sense, how satisfied are you with the service you have received?

4	3	2	1
Very satisfied	Mostly satisfied	Indifferent or mildly dissatisfied	Quite dissatisfied

8. If you were to seek help again, would you come back to our program?

1	2	3	4
No, definitely not	No, I don't think so	Yes, I think so	Yes, definitely

Clinical Anxiety Scale (CAS)

PURPOSE To measure clinical anxiety.

AUTHOR Bruce A. Thyer

DESCRIPTION The CAS is a 25-item scale that is focused on measuring the amount, degree, or severity of clinical anxiety reported by the respondent, with higher scores indicating higher amounts of anxiety. The CAS is simply worded, and easy to administer, score, and interpret. The items for the CAS were psychometrically derived from a larger number of items based on the criteria for anxiety disorders in *DSM-III*. The CAS has a clinical cutting score of 30 (±5) and is designed to be scored and administered in the same way as the scales of the WALMYR Assessment Scales, also reproduced in this book. This instrument is particularly useful for measuring general anxiety in clinical practice.

NORMS Initial study of the CAS was based on 41 women and 6 men (average age 40.9 years) from an agoraphobic support group, 51 men and 32 women from the U.S. Army who were attending courses in health sciences (average age 25.7 years), and 58 female and 15 male university students (average age 26.6 years). No other demographic information was available nor were actual norms.

SCORING Like most WALMYR Assessment Scales instruments, the CAS is scored by first reverse-scoring items listed at the bottom of the page (1, 6, 7, 9, 13, 15, 16), summing these and the remaining scores, subtracting the number of completed items, multiplying this figure by 100, and dividing by the number of items completed times 4. This will produce a range from 0 to 100 with higher scores indicating greater magnitude or severity of problems.

RELIABILITY The CAS has excellent internal consistency, with a coefficient alpha of .94. The SEM of 4.2 is relatively low, suggesting a minimal amount of measurement error. The CAS had good stability, with two-week test-retest correlations that range from .64 to .74.

VALIDITY The CAS has good known-groups validity, discriminating significantly between groups known to be suffering from anxiety and lower-anxiety control groups. Using the clinical cutting score of 30, the CAS had a very low error rate of 6.9% in distinguishing between anxiety and control groups. No other validity information was available. Analysis of the CAS in relation to demographic variables such as age, sex, and education reveals that scores on the CAS are not affected by those factors (ethnicity was not examined).

PRIMARY REFERENCE Hudson, W. W. (1992). *The WALMYR Assessment Scales Scoring Manual.* Tempe, AZ: WALMYR Publishing Co.

AVAILABILITY WALMYR Publishing Co., P.O. Box 12217, Tallahassee, FL 32317-2217, or WALMYR.com.

CLINICAL ANXIETY SCALE (CAS)

Name: _____ Today's Date: _____

This questionnaire is designed to measure how much anxiety you are currently feeling. It is not a test, so there are no right or wrong answers. Answer each item as carefully and as accurately as you can by placing a number beside each one as follows.

1 = Rarely or none of the time
2 = A little of the time
3 = Some of the time
4 = A good part of the time
5 = Most or all of the time

1. ___ I feel calm.
2. ___ I feel tense.
3. ___ I feel suddenly scared for no reason.
4. ___ I feel nervous.
5. ___ I use tranquilizers or antidepressants to cope with my anxiety.
6. ___ I feel confident about the future.
7. ___ I am free from senseless or unpleasant thoughts.
8. ___ I feel afraid to go out of my house alone.
9. ___ I feel relaxed and in control of myself.
10. ___ I have spells of terror or panic.
11. ___ I feel afraid in open spaces or in the streets.
12. ___ I feel afraid I will faint in public.
13. ___ I am comfortable traveling on buses, subways, or trains.
14. ___ I feel nervousness or shakiness inside.
15. ___ I feel comfortable in crowds, such as shopping or at a movie.
16. ___ I feel comfortable when I am left alone.
17. ___ I feel afraid without good reason.
18. ___ Due to my fears, I unreasonably avoid certain animals, objects, or situations.
19. ___ I get upset easily or feel panicky unexpectedly.
20. ___ My hands, arms, or legs shake or tremble.
21. ___ Due to my fears, I avoid social situations, whenever possible.
22. ___ I experience sudden attacks of panic which catch me by surprise.
23. ___ I feel generally anxious.
24. ___ I am bothered by dizzy spells.
25. ___ Due to my fears, I avoid being alone, whenever possible.

Cognitions and Behaviors Scale (CABS)

PURPOSE To measure thoughts, feelings, and behaviors of adult survivors of childhood sexual abuse.

AUTHOR Humberto E. Fabelo-Alcover

DESCRIPTION The CABS is a 58-item multidimensional assessment scale based on the Traumagenic Dynamics Model for use in research and in clinical settings with adult male and female survivors of childhood sexual abuse (CSA). The CABS assesses cognitive and behavioral functioning in four specific areas of symptomatology associated with CSA: betrayal, stigmatization, powerlessness, and sexual traumatization. The resulting four subscale scores are used to assess each of the four dynamics identified above. The total scale score can also be used as a global indication of the respondent's overall functioning in regards to symptomatology often seen in adult survivors of CSA. The CABS can be used as part of the assessment process when working with survivors of CSA to help clinicians identify areas for immediate intervention. It is currently being tested for its efficacy as a treatment outcome measure.

NORMS The CABS was initially normed on an ethnically and racially diverse college sample of male and female undergraduate and graduate students (n = 287). Additional norming has been completed on an ethnically and racially diverse clinical sample of adult female survivors of CSA (n = 148) and with a clinical sample of mostly white non-Hispanic adult male survivors of CSA (n = 67). The CABS scores are standardized so that they range from 0 to 100, with higher scores indicating higher levels of distress or impairment. Mean total scale and betrayal, powerlessness, stigmatization, and sexual traumatization subscales scores for non-survivors in the initial norming sample are: 18.12, 26.96, 16.41, 13.81, 14.17, respectively. Although clinically significant cutting scores have not yet been established, both clinical samples have yielded scores well above 30 points for the total scale and each of the four subscales.

SCORING Each item is rated on a 7-point Likert scale, 1 indicating "None of the Time," and 7 indicating "All of the Time." No item is reverse-scored. Scoring instructions assist respondents or clinicians in scoring each of the subscales and in obtaining a total scale score. Although the current form is hand-scored using a calculator, the author is developing a computer-based form that is completed and automatically scored on a computer.

VALIDITY The CABS has excellent concurrent validity. The CABS correlates highly ($r > .70$) with standardized measures of clinical stress, depression, satisfaction with life, and contentment. It also correlates highly with other trauma-related measures such as the Trauma Symptom Checklist and the Trauma Symptom Inventory ($r > .70$). CABS scores for survivors are significantly higher than for non-survivors.

PRIMARY REFERENCES Fabelo-Alcover, H. E., and Sowers, K. (2003). Cognitions and Behaviors Scale: Development and initial performance of a scale for use with adult survivors of childhood sexual abuse. *Research on Social Work Practice, 13*(1), 43–64.

Fabelo-Alcover, H. E., and Lipton, M. (2003). Further validation of the Cognitions and Behaviors Scale using a clinical sample of adult female survivors of childhood sexual abuse. *Research on Social Work Practice*, 13(2), 166–180. Instrument reproduced with permission of Dr. Fabelo-Alcover.

AVAILABILITY Humberto E. Fabelo-Alcover, Virginia Commonwealth University School of Social Work, P. O. Box 842027, Richmond, VA 23284-2027. email: hefabelo@vcu.edu.

PLEASE INDICATE THE DEGREE TO WHICH YOU EXPERIENCE ANY OF THE FOLLOWING THOUGHTS, FEELINGS, OR BEHAVIORS. MARK YOUR RESPONSE IN THE SPACE TO THE LEFT OF THE ITEM ACCORDING TO THE SCALE PROVIDED BELOW.

1 NONE OF THE TIME

2 VERY RARELY

3 A LITTLE OF THE TIME

4 SOME OF THE TIME

5 A GOOD PART OF THE TIME

6 MOST OF THE TIME

7 ALL OF THE TIME

1. ___ I feel afraid of things
2. ___ I feel nausea
3. ___ I find it hard to be close to my friends
4. ___ I cry when I am alone
5. ___ I feel ashamed
6. ___ I feel scared
7. ___ People think I am bad
8. ___ I like to stay away from people
9. ___ Seeing myself naked scares me
10. ___ I have unpleasant sexual thoughts
11. ___ I feel sick
12. ___ I fear something bad will happen to me
13. ___ I feel like I lead a double life
14. ___ I feel that others let me down
15. ___ I have difficulty experiencing sexual pleasure
16. ___ I need reassurance
17. ___ I think about death
18. ___ I feel like I have lost a lot of time in my life
19. ___ People will hurt you
20. ___ My breathing is troubled
21. ___ I think of hurting myself
22. ___ My sleep is restless
23. ___ Crowds make me feel anxious
24. ___ When you trust others you get hurt
25. ___ I spend money on pornography
26. ___ I feel depressed
27. ___ When I feel sexy it scares me
28. ___ I have anxiety attacks
29. ___ I am afraid at night
30. ___ I feel irritable for no reason at all
31. ___ I regret my past
32. ___ I feel guilty
33. ___ I prefer to be on my own than to be with others
34. ___ People disappoint me
35. ___ I feel guilty after having sex
36. ___ When I was young I thought about having sex
37. ___ I think I would be better off dead
38. ___ I feel I am different from other people
39. ___ Being in open places makes me feel anxious
40. ___ I feel ugly
41. ___ I feel restless or jumpy

42. ___ Bad things happen to me
43. ___ I am easily annoyed by others
44. ___ I feel that I am an unlucky person
45. ___ I feel alone
46. ___ I feel inferior
47. ___ I feel like hurting others
48. ___ I feel like never having sex again
49. ___ Thinking positive scares me
50. ___ I find it difficult to understand what is expected of me
51. ___ I feel that it is better to be on your own than to have a close relationship
52. ___ I cry when I think of the bad things that have happened to me
53. ___ I need to hear my friends and family tell me they like me
54. ___ I can relate to the rejected and downtrodden members of society
55. ___ I think of unpleasant things, even when I do not want to
56. ___ I feel embarrassed when I see people who know secrets about me
57. ___ When I am not in control I feel that others will take advantage of me
58. ___ I feel angrier than most people when I see a bully picking on someone who is less powerful

Cognitive Coping Strategy Inventory (CCSI)

PURPOSE To measure coping strategies in acute pain.

AUTHORS Robert W. Butler, Fred L. Damarin, Cynthia Beaulieu, Andrew Schwebel, and Beverly E. Thorn

DESCRIPTION The CCSI is a 70-item instrument designed to measure cognitive coping strategies and catastrophizing in managing acute pain. Since most other standardized measures are used for measuring chronic pain, the CCSI is one of the few measures, if not the only one, developed for use with nonchronic or acute pain. The CCSI has seven factors; however, it can be used as a two-subscale instrument with one subscale called catastrophizing (C: items 7, 8, 11, 12, 34, 44, 50, 62, 67, 70), and the other called the cognitive coping index (CCI: remainder of items).

NORMS The CCSI has been studied with several samples of postsurgical patients, totaling 264, including 122 men and 142 women. The mean age of the samples ranged from 45.1 to 50.3. The mean score for the CCI was 93.3 (SD = 30.7) and for catastrophizing was 19.6 (SD = 7.0).

SCORING The scores for the CCSI are determined by adding up all items except catastrophizing and subtracting the sum of the catastrophizing items from that total for the CCI score, and simply summing subscale items (noted above) for the catastrophizing score.

RELIABILITY The CCSI has very good internal consistency, with alphas for the subscales that range from .77 to .90. Data on stability were not available.

VALIDITY The CCSI has good concurrent and known-groups validity, correlating with several independent and self-reported measures of pain and use of pain medication.

PRIMARY REFERENCE Butler, R.W. (1989). Assessing cognitive coping strategies for acute postsurgical pain, *Psychological Assessment*, 1, 41–45.

AVAILABILITY Dr. Robert Butler, Division of Child and Adolescent Psychiatry, Oregon Health Science University, Portland, OR 97239-3098. Email: butlerr@ohsu.edu.

The following statements describe different thoughts and behaviors that people engage in when they experience pain. For each statement you are to indicate whether it is never, some of the time, one-half of the time, most of the time, or all of the time true about the way in which you deal with your pain. You may find it helpful to think back to the most recent time you were in some degree of pain and imagine as if you were answering these questions while in pain. If the individual *content* of a test item is not similar, but the *style* in which you deal with the pain is similar to the item, you should mark the item in the true categories. Make only one response per item and try and answer each item.

	1	2	3	4	5
	Never true	Some of the time true	One half of the time true	Most of the time true	All of the time true
1. I use my imagination to change the situation or place where I am experiencing pain in order to try and make the pain more bearable.	—	—	—	—	—
2. I think of photographs or paintings that I have seen in the past.	—	—	—	—	—
3. I might attempt to imagine myself leaving my body and observing my pain in an impartial, detached manner.	—	—	—	—	—
4. I concentrate on things or people around me.	—	—	—	—	—
5. If my pain feels severely throbbing, I might tend to imagine it as only a dull ache.	—	—	—	—	—
6. I might count ceiling tiles or other objects in the room in order to occupy my mind.	—	—	—	—	—
7. I feel like I just want to get up and run away.	—	—	—	—	—
8. I imagine the pain becoming even more intense and hurtful.	—	—	—	—	—
9. I try to imagine myself in a place completely different, such as my hometown.	—	—	—	—	—
10. I attend to and analyze my pain as perhaps a doctor or scientist might.	—	—	—	—	—

continued

	1 Never true	2 Some of the time true	3 One half of the time true	4 Most of the time true	5 All of the time true
11. I begin thinking of all the possible bad things that could go wrong in association with the pain.	—	—	—	—	—
12. If my pain feels stabbing I might try and imagine that it is only pricking.	—	—	—	—	—
13. I describe the pain to myself or tell others about it in order to try and make the pain less hurtful.	—	—	—	—	—
14. I might try and imagine myself "floating off" away from the pain but still realize that my body hurts.	—	—	—	—	—
15. I tell myself that the pain is really not what it seems to be, but rather some other sensation.	—	—	—	—	—
16. I "psych" myself up to deal with the pain, perhaps by telling myself that it won't last much longer.	—	—	—	—	—
17. If possible, I would try and read a book or magazine to take my mind off the pain.	—	—	—	—	—
18. I picture in my "mind's eye" a lush, green forest or other similar peaceful scene.	—	—	—	—	—
19. If a television set was available I would watch TV to distract myself from the pain.	—	—	—	—	—
20. I try and imagine that for some reason it is important for me to endure the pain.	—	—	—	—	—
21. If my pain feels burning I might try and pretend that it is only warm.	—	—	—	—	—
22. I tell myself that I don't think I can bear the pain any longer.	—	—	—	—	—
23. I try and mentally remove the pain from the part of my body that hurts by paying close attention to it.	—	—	—	—	—
24. I try and make myself busy by pretending that I am doing other things.	—	—	—	—	—

	1 Never true	2 Some of the time true	3 One half of the time true	4 Most of the time true	5 All of the time true
25. I use my imagination to develop pictures which help distract me.	—	—	—	—	—
26. I imagine that the pain is really not as severe as it seems to feel.	—	—	—	—	—
27. In general, my ability to see things visually in my "mind's eye" or imagination is quite good.	—	—	—	—	—
28. I develop images or pictures in my mind to try and ignore the pain.	—	—	—	—	—
29. I might concentrate on how attractive certain colors are in the room or place where I am experiencing pain.	—	—	—	—	—
30. I might repeat a phrase such as "It's not that bad" over and over to myself.	—	—	—	—	—
31. I imagine my pain as occurring in a situation completely different from the place where I am experiencing it.	—	—	—	—	—
32. I might imagine that I am with a date/ spouse and feel the pain but don't want to let on that it hurts too much.	—	—	—	—	—
33. I might pay attention to the parts of my body that do not hurt and compare how much better they feel than where the pain is.	—	—	—	—	—
34. I find myself worrying about possibly dying.	—	—	—	—	—
35. I might think of myself as a prisoner who must withhold secrets under torture to protect my friends or country.	—	—	—	—	—
36. I might picture myself as an adventurer who has been hurt while on a journey.	—	—	—	—	—
37. I take myself very far away from the pain by using my imagination.	—	—	—	—	—
38. I might do something such as gently rub a part of my body close to where it hurts and notice the difference in the feelings.	—	—	—	—	—

continued

	1 Never true	2 Some of the time true	3 One half of the time true	4 Most of the time true	5 All of the time true
39. I would focus my attention on something such as a chair or tree and think real hard about it.	___	___	___	___	___
40. I try and pretend that the pain is really only a feeling of pressure.	___	___	___	___	___
41. I would listen to music to help keep my mind off the pain.	___	___	___	___	___
42. I think of jokes that I have heard.	___	___	___	___	___
43. I might begin thinking about my pain as if I were conducting an experiment or writing a biology report.	___	___	___	___	___
44. I find myself expecting the worst.	___	___	___	___	___
45. I try and pretend that I am on the beach, or somewhere else enjoying a summer day.	___	___	___	___	___
46. I might sit down and balance my checkbook, work crossword puzzles, or engage in hobbies if I am able.	___	___	___	___	___
47. I might attend to the pain in much the same way that a sports announcer or reporter would describe an event.	___	___	___	___	___
48. I might try and think of a difficult problem in my life and how it could be solved in order to try and forget the pain.	___	___	___	___	___
49. I concentrate on making the pain feel as if it hurts less.	___	___	___	___	___
50. I tend to think that my pain is pretty awful.	___	___	___	___	___
51. I concentrate on what others might think of me and act as brave as I can.	___	___	___	___	___
52. I concentrate on convincing myself that I will deal with the pain and that it will get better in the near future.	___	___	___	___	___
53. I think of myself as being interested in pain and wanting to describe it to myself in detail.	___	___	___	___	___

	1 Never true	2 Some of the time true	3 One half of the time true	4 Most of the time true	5 All of the time true
54. I try and take my mind off the pain by talking to others, such as family members, about different things.	—	—	—	—	—
55. I might try and imagine being given a pain shot and my body becoming numb.	—	—	—	—	—
56. I think of and picture myself being with my spouse/boyfriend/girlfriend.	—	—	—	—	—
57. I might do mental arithmetic problems to keep my mind occupied.	—	—	—	—	—
58. I might try and think that I'm overreacting and that my pain is really not as severe as it seems.	—	—	—	—	—
59. I try and sort out in my mind problems at work or home.	—	—	—	—	—
60. I describe objects in the room to myself.	—	—	—	—	—
61. I might begin making plans for a future event, such as a vacation, to distract me from thinking about the pain.	—	—	—	—	—
62. I can't help but concentrate on how bad the pain actually feels.	—	—	—	—	—
63. I work at talking myself into believing that the pain is really not all that bad and that there are others who are much worse off than me.	—	—	—	—	—
64. I might pretend that my pain was similar to pain I have felt after a good session of exercise.	—	—	—	—	—
65. I try and preoccupy my mind by daydreaming about various pleasant things such as clouds or sailboats.	—	—	—	—	—
66. If my pain feels shooting I try and pretend that it is only tingling.	—	—	—	—	—
67. I find it virtually impossible to keep my mind off of my pain and how bad it hurts.	—	—	—	—	—

continued

	1 Never true	2 Some of the time true	3 One half of the time true	4 Most of the time true	5 All of the time true
68. I might imagine that the pain is the result of an injury while engaging in my favorite sport.	—	—	—	—	—
69. I tell myself that I can cope with the pain without imagining or pretending anything.	—	—	—	—	—
70. I begin to worry that something might be seriously wrong with me.	—	—	—	—	—

Cognitive Processes Survey (CPS)

PURPOSE To measure components of imaginal life.

AUTHOR Raymond F. Martinetti

DESCRIPTION The CPS is a 39-item instrument designed to measure three components of imaginal life: degree of imaginal life (DIL—the intensity and extensity of imaginal activity), orientation toward imaginal life (OIL—the individual's emotional response to imaginal processes), and degree of suppression (DOS—the tendency to suppress feelings, especially anger and sexual ideation). The CPS may be useful for exploring the continuity of some imaginal processes between waking and sleep, and for evaluating the effectiveness of therapeutic techniques aimed at enhancing dream recall and exploration of inner states of awareness.

NORMS The CPS was standardized on a sample of 350 college students, but actual norms were not provided. A subsequent sample of 45 men and 45 women from college psychology courses provided the following means and standard deviations: DIL—men, 30.31 (SD = 11.9), women, 42.27 (SD = 12.53); OIL—men, 28.76 (SD = 9.22), women, 38.36 (SD = 11.89); and DOS—men, 27.42 (SD = 7.70), women, 25.21 (SD = 7.01).

SCORING The CPS is scored on a 5-point scale with scores for each subscale being a simple sum of the items on the subscale and scores for the total scale being a sum of all 39 items. Following is a guide to the subscales: OIL: items 1, 6, 7, 11, 16, 20, 21, 22, 26, 28, 32, 34, 35. DIL: items 2, 8, 9, 12, 14, 17, 19, 24, 27, 31, 33, 36, 38. DOS: items 3, 4, 5, 10, 13, 15, 18, 23, 25, 29, 30, 37, 39. Items to be reverse-scored are 1, 2, 4, 6, 8, 9, 10, 11, 12, 13, 14, 15, 17, 19, 21, 24, 25, 27, 28, 30, 31, 33, 35–39. The total range per subscale is 13 to 65, and the total range for the entire CPS is 39 to 195.

RELIABILITY Reliability coefficients for the three subscales are reported as .78 for DIL, .75 for OIL, and .72 for DOS. The author does not state what type of reliability these coefficients measure (presumably internal consistency), nor is the reliability for the overall scale reported.

VALIDITY No real validity data are reported. However, the author does report significant positive correlations showing that respondents with the highest imaginal life reported most dreams recalled. This may be viewed as a type of concurrent validity.

PRIMARY REFERENCE Martinetti, R. F. (1989). Sex differences in dream recall and components of imaginal life, *Perceptual and Motor Skills*, 69, 643–649. Instrument reprinted with permission of author and publisher.

AVAILABILITY May be copied from this volume.

Determine the extent to which you agree or disagree with each of the following statements. Place a check in the appropriate space provided to the right of each item. (SA = strongly agree, A = agree, U = undecided, D = disagree, SD = strongly disagree). Try to be as accurate as possible in giving the *first* impression you have for each statement.

	SA	A	U	D	SD
1. I like to contemplate my innermost feelings.	—	—	—	—	—
2. I often dream in color.	—	—	—	—	—
3. I can't stay angry at other people for a long time.	—	—	—	—	—
4. Masturbation is not a topic that should be openly discussed.	—	—	—	—	—
5. A very sad novel or movie can move me to tears.	—	—	—	—	—
6. I enjoy analyzing my own dreams.	—	—	—	—	—
7. ESP and psychic experiences probably do not really occur.	—	—	—	—	—
8. If I think about a song I feel as if I am really *hearing* it.	—	—	—	—	—
9. I often experience *déjà vu* (thinking something has already happened while it is happening).	—	—	—	—	—
10. If I had thoughts of a homosexual nature I would worry about my mental health.	—	—	—	—	—
11. I would enjoy reading about other people's fantasies.	—	—	—	—	—
12. I have a rich fantasy life.	—	—	—	—	—
13. The best way to deal with disturbing thoughts is to concentrate on something completely different.	—	—	—	—	—
14. When I listen to music I can usually visualize what it represents.	—	—	—	—	—
15. Those who try to look deeply into their own feelings are treading on dangerous ground.	—	—	—	—	—
16. I have no patience with people who claim they can predict the future.	—	—	—	—	—
17. I am more idealistic than realistic.	—	—	—	—	—
18. I think I would be sexually aroused by pornographic material.	—	—	—	—	—
19. I have had recurrent dreams at least once during my life.	—	—	—	—	—
20. People who really believe in "ghosts" are somewhat mentally disturbed.	—	—	—	—	—
21. I would rather plan my "dream house" than actually build it.	—	—	—	—	—

	SA	A	U	D	SD
22. A danger of hypnosis is that the hypnotized person loses his/her free will.	—	—	—	—	—
23. A very good way of dealing with your problems is to talk to other people about them.	—	—	—	—	—
24. If I think about a food very intensely I can practically taste it.	—	—	—	—	—
25. If I had a terminal illness I would rather not know about it.	—	—	—	—	—
26. Dreams have no real meanings: They are random thoughts.	—	—	—	—	—
27. I have often wondered what becomes of a person's awareness after death.	—	—	—	—	—
28. I believe that dreams reveal truths about us.	—	—	—	—	—
29. I often think about my own shortcomings.	—	—	—	—	—
30. It is not good to openly reveal your feelings.	—	—	—	—	—
31. My dreams tend to be quite complex.	—	—	—	—	—
32. Daydreaming is unproductive and may even be harmful.	—	—	—	—	—
33. I can recall past experiences in vivid detail.	—	—	—	—	—
34. If an idea does not have practical application, it is worthless.	—	—	—	—	—
35. I can wake up from a dream, go back to sleep, and continue the dream.	—	—	—	—	—
36. The more you explore your motives the better is your self-understanding.	—	—	—	—	—
37. I think everyone has private thoughts which are never publicly revealed.	—	—	—	—	—
38. I like fictional works (books, films, etc.) better than nonfictional works.	—	—	—	—	—
39. If I told people what I really thought of them I'd have very few friends.	—	—	—	—	—

Cognitive Slippage Scale (CSS)

PURPOSE To measure cognitive impairment.

AUTHORS Tracey C. Miers and Michael L. Raulin

DESCRIPTION The CSS is a 35-item scale that is designed to measure cognitive slippage, an aspect of cognitive distortion that is viewed as a primary characteristic of schizophrenia. Cognitive slippage is also viewed as central to a schizotypic personality indicative of a genetic predisposition to schizophrenia. Cognitive slippage can be manifested in several ways such as hallucinations, delusions, speech deficits, confused thinking, and attentional disorders. The CSS focuses mainly on speech deficits and confused thinking. Although the scale was developed to identify schizotypic characteristics, it may also be useful in identifying cognitive disorders among other populations.

NORMS The scale was developed in two series of studies eventually involving 690 male and 516 female undergraduate students in introductory psychology courses. The mean score for males was 7.8 and for females 9.3; actual norms are not reported.

SCORING The CSS is scored by assigning a score of one to the correct response and then summing these scores. The correct response is "true" on items 2, 3–5, 9, 11, 13, 15, 18, 20, 22, 24, 25, 27, 28, 30, 31, 33. The remainder are correct if answered "false."

RELIABILITY The CSS has excellent internal consistency, with alphas of .87 for males and .90 for females. No test-retest correlations are available.

VALIDITY The CSS has good concurrent validity in correlations with several other scales measuring schizotypic characteristics (e.g., perceptual aberration, intense ambivalence, social fear, magical ideation, somatic symptoms, and distrust). The CSS also has fair construct validity, accurately predicting scores on several scales of the MMPI between high and low scorers on the CSS. The CSS is slightly correlated with social desirability response bias suggesting that this factor cannot be totally ruled out.

PRIMARY REFERENCE Miers, T. C., and Raulin, M. L. (1985). The development of a scale to measure cognitive slippage. Paper presented at the Eastern Psychological Association Convention, Boston, Mass., March 1985. Instrument reproduced with permission of Michael L. Raulin.

AVAILABILITY Dr. Michael L. Raulin, SUNY-Buffalo, Psychology Department, Julian Park Hall, Buffalo, NY 14260. Email: raulin@acsu.buffalo.edu.

Please circle either T for true or F for false for each item as it applies to you.

T F 1. My thoughts are orderly most of the time.
T F 2. I almost always feel as though my thoughts are on a different wavelength from 98% of the population.
T F 3. Often when I am talking I feel that I am not making any sense.
T F 4. Often people ask me a question and I don't know what it is that they are asking.
T F 5. Often I don't even know what it is that I have just said.
T F 6. I hardly ever find myself saying the opposite of what I meant to say.
T F 7. I rarely feel so mixed up that I have difficulty functioning.
T F 8. My thoughts are usually clear, at least to myself.
T F 9. My thoughts are more random than orderly.
T F 10. The way I perceive things is much the same as the way in which others perceive them.
T F 11. Sometimes my thoughts just disappear.
T F 12. I can usually keep my thoughts going straight.
T F 13. My thoughts are so vague and hazy that I wish that I could just reach up and pull them into place.
T F 14. I usually feel that people understand what I say.
T F 15. There have been times when I have gone an entire day or longer without speaking.
T F 16. I ordinarily don't get confused about *when* things happened.
T F 17. It's usually easy to keep the point that I am trying to make clear in my mind.
T F 18. My thoughts speed by so fast that I can't catch them.
T F 19. I usually don't feel that I'm rambling on pointlessly when I'm speaking.
T F 20. Sometimes when I try to focus on an idea, so many other thoughts come to mind that I find it impossible to concentrate on just one.
T F 21. I have no difficulty in controlling my thoughts.
T F 22. My thinking often gets "cloudy" for no apparent reason.
T F 23. I think that I am reasonably good at communicating my ideas to other people.
T F 24. I often find myself saying something that comes out completely backwards.
T F 25. My thoughts often jump from topic to topic without any logical connection.
T F 26. I'm pretty good at keeping track of time.
T F 27. Often during the day I feel as though I am being flooded by thoughts.
T F 28. The way that I process information is very different from the way in which other people do.
T F 29. I have no difficulty separating past from present.
T F 30. I often find that people are puzzled by what I say.
T F 31. My thoughts seem to come and go so quickly that I can't keep up with them.
T F 32. I can usually think things through clearly.
T F 33. I often feel confused when I try to explain my ideas.
T F 34. Usually my thoughts aren't difficult to keep track of.
T F 35. I have no difficulty in controlling my thoughts.

Cognitive-Somatic Anxiety Questionnaire (CSAQ)

PURPOSE To measure cognitive and somatic components of anxiety.

AUTHORS Gary E. Schwartz, Richard J. Davidson, and Daniel J. Goleman

DESCRIPTION The CSAQ is a 14-item, simply worded, easy to understand measure of the cognitive and somatic aspects of anxiety. The scale is based on the assumption that there are two different aspects of anxiety—cognitive and somatic. The importance of this for practice is that therapeutic techniques for reducing anxiety may differ in their impact on these two systems. Thus, by providing information on each aspect of anxiety, this measure allows the practitioner to be more precise in selecting intervention techniques. The CSAQ is considered to be a trait measure of anxiety in that it taps relatively enduring patterns.

NORMS The initial study was conducted on 77 respondents consisting of 44 participants in a physical exercise class and 33 volunteers who practiced cognitively-based passive meditation at least once daily. The physical exercisers were predominantly female with an average age of 27.3 years while the meditators were approximately equally divided between males and females and had an average age of 20.86 years. No real effort was made to develop norms due to the size and nature of the samples.

SCORING The cognitive (items 1, 3, 6, 8, 9, 10, 13) and somatic items (the remainder) of the CSAQ appear in random order and are scored by totaling the sums of the scores on each item. Separate scores are computed for the cognitive and somatic scales with a range for each of 7 to 35.

RELIABILITY No data reported.

VALIDITY The CSAQ has good concurrent validity, correlating significantly with the State-Trait Anxiety Inventory. The CSAQ also demonstrated a type of known-groups validity in that respondents who were meditators reported less cognitive and more somatic anxiety than physical exercisers and the exercisers reported more cognitive and less somatic anxiety. The two groups did not differ on overall anxiety, supporting the idea that anxiety may not be a diffuse, undifferentiated state, but may be subdivided into component parts.

PRIMARY REFERENCE Schwartz, G. E., Davidson, R. J., and Goleman, D. J. (1978). Patterning of cognitive and somatic processes in the self-regulation of anxiety: Effects of meditation versus exercise, *Psychosomatic Medicine*, 40, 321–328. Instrument reproduced by permission of Gary E. Schwartz and Daniel J. Goleman and the Elsevier Science Publishing Co., Inc.

AVAILABILITY May be copied from this volume.

Please read the following and rate the degree to which you generally or typically experience each symptom when you are feeling anxious. Rate each item by filling in one number from 1 through 5 in the left-hand column, with 1 representing "not at all" and 5 representing "very much so." Be sure to answer every item and try to be as honest and accurate as possible in your responses.

1	2	3	4	5
Not at all				Very much so

___ 1. Some unimportant thought runs through my mind and bothers me.
___ 2. I perspire.
___ 3. I imagine terrifying scenes.
___ 4. I become immobilized.
___ 5. My heart beats faster.
___ 6. I can't keep anxiety-provoking pictures out of my mind.
___ 7. I nervously pace.
___ 8. I find it difficult to concentrate because of uncontrollable thoughts.
___ 9. I can't keep anxiety-provoking thoughts out of my mind.
___ 10. I feel like I am losing out on things because I can't make up my mind soon enough.
___ 11. I feel tense in my stomach.
___ 12. I get diarrhea.
___ 13. I worry too much over something that doesn't really matter.
___ 14. I feel jittery in my body.

PURPOSE To measure the cognitive triad in depressed persons.

AUTHORS Ernest Edward Beckham, William R. Leber, John T. Watkins, Jenny L. Boyer, and Jacque B. Cook

DESCRIPTION The CTI is a 30-item instrument designed to measure the cognitive triad hypothesized to be present in depressed persons: negative views of themselves, their worlds, and their future. Negative cognitions in these areas are hypothesized as actually leading to feelings of depression. Thus, in cognitive therapy, they would be an important target for change. The items are arranged in three subscales (negative and positive refer to scoring): view of self (items −5, −10, −13, +17, −21, +25, −29, +31, +33, −35); view of world (items +3, +8, +12, −18, +20, −23, +24, −27, −30, −34); and view of future (items +6, +9, +11, −15, −16, −19, −26, +28, −32, +36). The CTI is seen as useful for studying the role of the cognitive triad in the etiology and treatment of depression as well as how these states change over time, including after single therapy sessions.

NORMS The CTI was initially studied on a sample of 54 patients from an outpatient mental health service in Oklahoma. All were diagnosed as depressed with a mean Beck Depression Inventory score of 21.8. The sample comprised 44 women and 10 men with a mean age of 36 years and a mean educational attainment of 13.9 years. All but two of the sample were white (the other two black), with 35.1% married, 35.1% divorced, 20.3% single, and 9.2% separated. Norms were as follows: view of self: 36.96 (SD = 14.86), view of world = 35.11 (SD = 11.21), view of future = 31.93 (SD = 13.56), and total score = 104 (SD = 34.96).

SCORING Items on the CTI are phrased in both positive and negative terms and answered on 7-point Likert-type scales (from 1 = totally agree to 7 = totally disagree). Scores for each subscale are a sum of the items on each subscale, as indicated in the description, adding positive and negative items. To that total, add 48 to view of self, and 40 to the other two subscales. The total score is a sum of all items, with high scores representing positive views and low scores representing negative views. Items 1, 2, 4, 7, 14, and 18 are not scored.

RELIABILITY The CTI has excellent internal consistency, with alphas of .91 for view of self, .81 for view of world, and .93 for view of future. The alpha for the total scale was .95.

VALIDITY The authors report good face validity based on high levels of agreement regarding the meaning of the items by 16 faculty members from a university department of psychiatry and behavioral sciences. The CTI has good concurrent validity, correlating significantly (.77) with the Beck Depression Inventory. All subscales correlated significantly with external raters' ratings of those three dimensions, and the view of self subscale correlated significantly (.90) with a measure of self-esteem, while the view of future subscale correlated significantly (.90) with a measure of hopelessness.

PRIMARY REFERENCE Beckham, E. E., Leber, W. R., Watkins, J. T., Boyer, J. L., and Cook, J. B. (1986). Development of an instrument to measure Beck's cognitive triad: The

Cognitive Triad Inventory, *Journal of Consulting and Clinical Psychology*, 54, 566–567.

AVAILABILITY Dr. E. E. Beckham, 6406 North Santa Fe Ave, Suite A, Oklahoma City, OK 73116. Telephone: 405.755.3540.

This inventory lists different ideas that people sometimes have.

For each of these ideas, show how much you agree with it by circling the answer that best describes your opinion. Be sure to *choose only one answer for each idea.* Answer the items for what you are thinking *right now.*

TA = Totally agree	SD = Slightly disagree
MA = Mostly agree	MD = Mostly disagree
SA = Slightly agree	TD = Totally disagree
N = Neutral	

1. I have many talents and skills.   TA   MA   SA   N   SD   MD   TD

2. My job (housework, schoolwork, daily duties) is unpleasant.   TA   MA   SA   N   SD   MD   TD

3. Most people are friendly and helpful.   TA   MA   SA   N   SD   MD   TD

4. Nothing is likely to work out for me.   TA   MA   SA   N   SD   MD   TD

5. I am a failure.   TA   MA   SA   N   SD   MD   TD

6. I like to think about the good things that lie ahead for me.   TA   MA   SA   N   SD   MD   TD

7. I do my work (job, schoolwork, housework) adequately.   TA   MA   SA   N   SD   MD   TD

8. The people I know help me when need it.   TA   MA   SA   N   SD   MD   TD

9. I expect that things will be going very well for me a few years from now.   TA   MA   SA   N   SD   MD   TD

10. I have messed up almost all the important relationships I have ever had.   TA   MA   SA   N   SD   MD   TD

11. The future holds a lot of excitement for me.   TA   MA   SA   N   SD   MD   TD

12. My daily activities are fun and rewarding.   TA   MA   SA   N   SD   MD   TD

13. I can't do anything right.   TA   MA   SA   N   SD   MD   TD

14. People like me.   TA   MA   SA   N   SD   MD   TD

15. There is nothing left in my life to look forward to.   TA   MA   SA   N   SD   MD   TD

16. My current problems or concerns will always be there in one way or another.   TA   MA   SA   N   SD   MD   TD

17. I am as adequate as other people I know.   TA   MA   SA   N   SD   MD   TD

18. The world is a very hostile place.   TA   MA   SA   N   SD   MD   TD

19. There is no reason for me to be hopeful about my future.   TA   MA   SA   N   SD   MD   TD

20. The important people in my life are helpful and supportive.   TA   MA   SA   N   SD   MD   TD

21. I hate myself.   TA   MA   SA   N   SD   MD   TD

22. I will overcome my problems.   TA   MA   SA   N   SD   MD   TD

23. Bad things happen to me a lot.   TA   MA   SA   N   SD   MD   TD

24.	I have a spouse or friend who is warm and supportive.	TA	MA	SA	N	SD	MD	TD
25.	I can do a lot of things well.	TA	MA	SA	N	SD	MD	TD
26.	My future is simply too awful to think about.	TA	MA	SA	N	SD	MD	TD
27.	My family doesn't care what happens to me.	TA	MA	SA	N	SD	MD	TD
28.	Things will work out well for me in the future.	TA	MA	SA	N	SD	MD	TD
29.	I am guilty of a great many things.	TA	MA	SA	N	SD	MD	TD
30.	No matter what I do, others make it difficult for me to get what I need.	TA	MA	SA	N	SD	MD	TD
31.	I am a worthwhile human being.	TA	MA	SA	N	SD	MD	TD
32.	There is nothing to look forward to in the years ahead.	TA	MA	SA	N	SD	MD	TD
33.	I like myself.	TA	MA	SA	N	SD	MD	TD
34.	I am faced with many difficulties.	TA	MA	SA	N	SD	MD	TD
35.	I have serious flaws in my character.	TA	MA	SA	N	SD	MD	TD
36.	I expect to be content and satisfied as the years go by.	TA	MA	SA	N	SD	MD	TD

Collective Self-Esteem Scale (CSE)

PURPOSE To measure collective (social) self-esteem.

AUTHORS Riia Luhtanen and Jennifer Crocker

DESCRIPTION The CSE is a 16-item scale designed to measure social or collective identity. Social or collective identity refers to the part of the self-concept that is based on membership in social groups or categories. This is in contrast to personal identity, also part of one's self-concept, which includes specific attributes of the individual such as competence and talent. The CSE focuses on respondents' level of social identity based on their membership in groups pertaining to gender, race, religion, ethnicity, and socioeconomic class. Thus the contribution of the CSE, as perhaps the only scale measuring this phenomenon, is not only for future research, but in helping clinical practitioners identify areas of low collective self-esteem in relation to any of the groups described earlier. The CSE is composed of four subscales: membership (items 1, 5, 9, and 13); private (items 2, 6, 10, and 14); public (items 3, 7, 11, and 15); and identity (items 4, 8, 12, and 16).

NORMS The CSE was developed in a series of studies involving 887 introductory psychology students, of whom 91.2% were white and 51% were female; 83 additional students, of whom 65% were female and 85% were white; and 180 undergraduate students, of whom 70% were female and 80% were white. For the largest sample the overall mean for white respondents was 86.25, for African American respondents the mean was 79.90, and for Asian respondents the mean was 82.71. The original article provides means for all the subscales based on the three racial groupings.

SCORING The CSE is easily scored by first reverse-scoring items 2, 4, 5, 10, 12, 13, and 15 and then summing all item responses for the total score or for subscale scores. Higher scores indicate greater collective self-esteem.

RELIABILITY The CSE has very good internal consistency, with alphas ranging from .85 to .88 for the total scale and alphas for the subscales that range from .71 to .86. The CSE also has good stability, with a six-week test-retest correlation of .68 for the total scale and correlations that range from .58 to .68 for the subscales.

VALIDITY The CSE has very good concurrent validity, with correlations between the total scale and most of the subscales with several measures of self-esteem such as the Rosenberg Self-Esteem Scale and with other measures such as the Ego Task Orientation and Ego Task Esteem scales. The total scale and some of the subscales also are significantly correlated with measures of individualism-collectivism, internal orientation, and individuation, including both internal and environmental subscales of the Internal Orientation Scale.

PRIMARY REFERENCE Luhtanen, R., and Crocker, J. (1992). A collective self-esteem scale: Self-evaluation with one's social identity, *Personality and Social Psychology Bulletin*, 18, 302–318.

AVAILABILITY Dr. Riia Luhtanen, Research Center for Group Dynamics, University of Michigan, Ann Arbor, MI 48106. Email: riia@umich.edu.

We are all members of different social groups or social categories. Some of such social groups or categories pertain to *gender, race, religion, nationality, ethnicity, and socioeconomic class*. We would like you to consider your memberships in those particular groups or categories, and respond to the following statements on the basis of how you feel about those groups and your memberships in them. There are no right or wrong answers to any of these statements; we are interested in your honest reactions and opinions. Please read each statement carefully, and respond by using the following scale:

1 = Strongly disagree
2 = Disagree
3 = Disagree somewhat
4 = Neutral
5 = Agree somewhat
6 = Agree
7 = Strongly agree

___ 1. I am a worthy member of the social groups I belong to.
___ 2. I often regret that I belong to some of the social groups I do.
___ 3. Overall, my social groups are considered good by others.
___ 4. Overall, my group memberships have very little to do with how I feel about myself.
___ 5. I feel I don't have much to offer to the social groups I belong to.
___ 6. In general, I'm glad to be a member of the social groups I belong to.
___ 7. Most people consider my social groups, on the average, to be more ineffective than other social groups.
___ 8. The social groups I belong to are an important reflection of who I am.
___ 9. I am a cooperative participant in the social groups I belong to.
___ 10. Overall, I often feel that the social groups of which I am a member are not worthwhile.
___ 11. In general, others respect the social groups that I am a member of.
___ 12. The social groups I belong to are unimportant to my sense of what kind of a person I am.
___ 13. I often feel I'm a useless member of my social groups.
___ 14. I feel good about the social groups I belong to.
___ 15. In general, others think that the social groups I am a member of are unworthy.
___ 16. In general, belonging to social groups is an important part of my self-image.

College Alcohol Problems Scale (CAPS)

PURPOSE To measure problems associated with drinking among college students.

AUTHORS Jason E. Maddock et al.

DESCRIPTION The CAPS is an 8-item scale designed to measure personal and social problems associated with use of alcohol among college students. Based on an earlier CAPS developed by O'Hare, the current, revised scale was modified by reducing items through factor analysis. Given the fact that abuse of alcohol appears to be a major problem for many college students, this scale was developed to measure the negative consequences related to alcohol consumption. One of the advantages of the CAPS, in addition to its brevity, is its use of subfactors involved in these negative consequences. The two subscales of the CAPS are Personal Problems (PP; items 1–4) and Social Problems (SP; items 5–8).

NORMS This version of the CAPS was studied with a sample of 663 undergraduates from an eastern university who reported ever drinking. Of the respondents, 344 were female, 502 reported themselves as regular drinkers, 111 were members of a fraternity or sorority, with the remainder (534) reporting they weren't. Means and standard deviations for these and other categories are available in the Primary Reference. The mean scores for females and males, respectively, were 3.75 (SD = 4.11) and 3.28 (SD = 4.12) for PP; 3.47 (SD = 4.0) and 4.93 (SD = 4.78) for SP; and 7.17 (SD = 7.02) and 8.22 (SD = 7.51) for the CAPS total score. The difference between males and females was significant only for SP.

SCORING The CAPS is easily scored by summing the subscale items with higher scores indicating greater problems. A computerized scoring protocol is available from the authors.

RELIABILITY The CAPS has good internal consistency with alphas of .79 for PP and .75 for SP. Data on stability were not available.

VALIDITY The CAPS has excellent concurrent validity, being strongly correlated with a number of alcohol consumption variables and with the YAAPST, another measure of alcohol consumption in college students. The CAPS also was correlated significantly with a measure of temptation to drink.

PRIMARY REFERENCE Maddock, J. E., et al. (2001). The College Alcohol Problems Scale, *Addictive Behaviors, 26*, 385–398. Instrument reproduced with permission of Dr. Thomas O'Hare.

AVAILABILITY Email Dr. O'Hare at oharet@bc.edu.

COLLEGE ALCOHOL PROBLEMS SCALE—REVISED

Use the scale below to rate HOW OFTEN you have had any of the following problems over the past year as a result of drinking alcoholic beverages.

1. Feeling sad, blue, or depressed

    (1) Never   (2) Yes, but not in the past year   (3) 1–2 times

    (4) 3–5 times   (5) 6–9 times   (6) 10 or more times

2. Nervousness, irritability

    (1) Never   (2) Yes, but not in the past year   (3) 1–2 times

    (4) 3–5 times   (5) 6–9 times   (6) 10 or more times

3. Caused you to feel bad about yourself

    (1) Never   (2) Yes, but not in the past year   (3) 1–2 times

    (4) 3–5 times   (5) 6–9 times   (6) 10 or more times

4. Problems with appetite or sleeping

    (1) Never   (2) Yes, but not in the past year   (3) 1–2 times

    (4) 3–5 times   (5) 6–9 times   (6) 10 or more times

5. Engaged in unplanned sexual activity

    (1) Never   (2) Yes, but not in the past year   (3) 1–2 times

    (4) 3–5 times   (5) 6–9 times   (6) 10 or more times

6. Drove under the influence

    (1) Never   (2) Yes, but not in the past year   (3) 1–2 times

    (4) 3–5 times   (5) 6–9 times   (6) 10 or more times

7. Did not use protection when engaging in sex

    (1) Never   (2) Yes, but not in the past year   (3) 1–2 times

    (4) 3–5 times   (5) 6–9 times   (6) 10 or more times

8. Illegal activities associated with drug use

    (1) Never   (2) Yes, but not in the past year   (3) 1–2 times

    (4) 3–5 times   (5) 6–9 times   (6) 10 or more times

Combat Exposure Scale (CES)

PURPOSE To measure wartime stressors.

AUTHORS Terrence M. Keane, John A. Fairbank, Juesta M. Caddell, Rose T. Zimmering, Kathryn L. Taylor, and Catherine A. Mora

DESCRIPTION The CES is a 7-item instrument designed to measure the subjective report of wartime stressors experienced by combatants. The CES was developed by deriving items from a previous combat scale and by consensus of four clinicians experienced in treating posttraumatic stress disorder (PTSD). The CES is very useful for helping understand the relationship of combat stressors interacting with other factors to produce PTSD.

NORMS The CES was studied with three samples involving a total of 431 male, Vietnam-era veterans, with a mean age between 36.9 and 39.3 years. The mean number of years of education ranged from 13.3 to 16.3 years. The mean for a subsample of PTSD veterans was 29.37 (SD = 6.1) and for a non-PTSD veteran group was 22.8 (SD = 10.4); this difference was statistically significant.

SCORING The CES is scored by subtracting one from the answer given on each item (e.g., an answer of 4 becomes 3). Then, from items 1, 3, 6, and 7, multiply that figure by 2. On item 3 only, if the original response is 5, subtract 2 and multiply by 2. Then sum these results for a total score. The range for the CES is from 0 to 41, with 0–8 indicating light exposure to combat, 9–16 light to moderate, 17–24 moderate, 25–32 moderate to heavy, and 33–41 heavy exposure.

RELIABILITY The CES has very good internal consistency, with an alpha of .85. The CES also has excellent stability, with a one-week test-retest correlation of .97.

VALIDITY The CES has good known-groups validity, significantly discriminating between veterans with and without PTSD.

PRIMARY REFERENCE Keane, T. M., and Caddell, J. M. (1989). Clinical evaluation of a measure to assess combat exposure, *Psychological Assessment*, 1, 53–55.

AVAILABILITY Dr. Terrence Keane, V.A. Medical Center, 150 South Huntington Avenue, Boston, MA 02130. Email: terry.keane@va.gov.

Please circle the answer that comes closest to describing your experiences.

1. Did you ever go on combat patrols or have other very dangerous duty?

1	2	3	4	5
No	1–3X	4–12X	13–50X	51 + times

2. Were you ever under enemy fire?

1	2	3	4	5
Never	< 1 month	1–3 mos	4–6 mos	7 mos or more

3. Were you ever surrounded by the enemy?

1	2	3	4	5
No	1–2X	3–12X	13–25X	26X or more

4. What percentage of the men in your unit were killed (KIA), wounded, or missing in action (MIA)?

1	2	3	4	5
None	1–25%	26–50%	51–75%	76% or more

5. How often did you fire rounds at the enemy?

1	2	3	4	5
Never	1–2X	3–12X	13–50X	51X or more

6. How often did you see someone hit by incoming or outgoing rounds?

1	2	3	4	5
Never	1–2X	3–12X	13–50X	51X or more

7. How often were you in danger or being injured or killed (i.e., pinned down, overrun, ambushed, near miss, etc.)?

1	2	3	4	5
Never	1–2X	3–12X	13–50X	51X or more

Components of Primary Care Index (CPCI)

PURPOSE To measure attributes of primary care.

AUTHOR Susan A. Flocke

DESCRIPTION The CPCI is a 52-item scale designed to measure several key aspects of the delivery of primary care from the perspective of patients visiting their family physician. The main components of primary care were categorized as follows: Comprehensiveness (items 1–5, 11); Accumulated Knowledge (items 6–9, 12–14); Interpersonal Communication (items 15–20); Preference for Regular Physician (items 21–23, 25); Coordination of Care (items 27, 29, 30, 44–46); Advocacy (Items 26, 31–38); Family Context (items 39–41); Community Context (items 42,43); Longitudinality with Physician (item 48); and Usual Provider Continuity (items 50/item 50 + 51 + 52). These clusters were all derived based on the Institute of Medicine definitions. The CPCI can be used to evaluate associations of the attributes of primary care with other health care outcomes or to test the effect of health care system variables on the delivery of these attributes of primary care.

NORMS The CPCI was evaluated with a sample of 2,899 patients visiting their family physicians. The mean age of respondents was 42, 62% were female, and the mean number of problems addressed in the visits was 2.3 with 57% of the problems being acute, 24% being chronic, 13% well care and 6% other. Actual norms for each component were not provided.

SCORING The items within each category are summed ("strongly disagree" = 1 and "strongly agree" = 6) and divided by the number of items, with higher scores indicating greater endorsement of a given attribute as important. Items 10, 16, 18–20, 24, 36 and 47 are reverse-scored.

RELIABILITY The first seven of the dimensions described above have good to excellent internal consistency with alphas that range from .71 (Preference for Regular Doctor) to .92 (Advocacy). Data on the other dimensions and stability were not reported.

VALIDITY The CPCI has good concurrent validity with significant correlations between all of the scales except Longitudinality with Practice and a measure of patient satisfaction with the visit.

PRIMARY REFERENCE Flocke, S. A. (1997). Measuring attributes of primary care: Development of a new instrument, *Journal of Family Practice, 45,* 64–74. Instrument reproduced with permission of Dr. Flocke.

AVAILABILITY Dr. Susan A. Flocke, Department of Family medicine, Case Western Reserve University, 1101 Cedar Road, UCRC 2, Room 306, Cleveland, OH 44106. Email: susan.flocke@case.edu.

CPCI

Please answer the questions to the best of your ability by marking your response.

Mark the response that best describes your *regular doctor*

	Strongly Disagree					Strongly Agree
1. I go to this doctor for almost all of my medical care	O	O	O	O	O	O
2. This doctor handles emergencies	O	O	O	O	O	O
3. This doctor can take care of almost any medical problem I might have	O	O	O	O	O	O
4. I could go to this doctor for help with a personal or emotional problem	O	O	O	O	O	O
5. I could go to this doctor for care of an ongoing problem such as high blood pressure	O	O	O	O	O	O
6. This doctor knows a lot about my family medical history	O	O	O	O	O	O
7. This doctor clearly understands my health needs	O	O	O	O	O	O
8. This doctor and I have been through a lot together	O	O	O	O	O	O
9. This doctor understands what is important to me regarding my health	O	O	O	O	O	O
10. This doctor does not know my medical history very well	O	O	O	O	O	O
11. I could go to this doctor for a check-up to prevent illness	O	O	O	O	O	O
12. This doctor always takes my beliefs and wishes into account in caring for me	O	O	O	O	O	O
13. This doctor knows whether or not I exercise, eat right, smoke, or drink alcohol	O	O	O	O	O	O
14. This doctor knows me well as a person (such as my hobbies, job, etc.)	O	O	O	O	O	O
15. I can easily talk about personal things with this doctor ...	O	O	O	O	O	O
16. Sometimes, this doctor does not listen to me	O	O	O	O	O	O
17. This doctor always explains things to my satisfaction	O	O	O	O	O	O
18. Sometimes, with this doctor, I don't bring up things that I'm worried about	O	O	O	O	O	O
19. I don't always feel comfortable asking questions of this doctor	O	O	O	O	O	O
20. Sometimes, I feel like this doctor ignores my concerns ..	O	O	O	O	O	O

continued

21. If I am sick, I would always contact a doctor in this office first . . . . ○ ○ ○ ○ ○ ○

22. My medical care improves when I see the same doctor that I have seen before . . . . ○ ○ ○ ○ ○ ○

23. It is very important to me to see my regular doctor . . . . . ○ ○ ○ ○ ○ ○

24. I rarely see the same doctor when I go for medical care . . . . ○ ○ ○ ○ ○ ○

25. I can call this doctor if I have a concern and am not sure I need to see a doctor . . . . ○ ○ ○ ○ ○ ○

26. I have tremendous trust in this doctor . . . . ○ ○ ○ ○ ○ ○

27. This doctor knows when I'm due for a check-up . . . . ○ ○ ○ ○ ○ ○

28. I want one doctor to coordinate all of the health care I receive . . . . ○ ○ ○ ○ ○ ○

29. This doctor keeps track of all my health care . . . . ○ ○ ○ ○ ○ ○

30. This doctor always follows up on a problem I've had, either at the next visit or by phone . . . . ○ ○ ○ ○ ○ ○

31. I would recommend this doctor to friends and family . . . ○ ○ ○ ○ ○ ○

32. This doctor always has my best interests at heart . . . . . . ○ ○ ○ ○ ○ ○

33. This doctor takes responsibility for helping me get all the health care I need . . . . ○ ○ ○ ○ ○ ○

34. I am confident this doctor will act as my advocate . . . . . ○ ○ ○ ○ ○ ○

35. This doctor looks out for my interests in dealing with my health insurance . . . . ○ ○ ○ ○ ○ ○

36. I wonder if this doctor is cutting corners on my health care . . . . ○ ○ ○ ○ ○ ○

37. This doctor helps me weigh the pros and cons of my health care decisions . . . . ○ ○ ○ ○ ○ ○

38. This doctor guides me through the steps I need to take to deal with my insurance plan . . . . ○ ○ ○ ○ ○ ○

39. Other members of my family see this doctor . . . . ○ ○ ○ ○ ○ ○

40. This doctor knows a lot about my family . . . . ○ ○ ○ ○ ○ ○

41. This doctor understands how my family affects my health . . . . ○ ○ ○ ○ ○ ○

42. This doctor knows a lot about my community . . . . ○ ○ ○ ○ ○ ○

43. This doctor uses her/his knowledge of my community to take care of me . . . . ○ ○ ○ ○ ○ ○

	Not Applicable	Strongly Disagree				Strongly Agree	

44. This doctor always follows up on my visits
to other health care providers . . . .   ○ ○ ○ ○ ○ ○ ○

45. This doctor helps me interpret my lab tests,
x-rays or visits to other doctors . . . .   ○ ○ ○ ○ ○ ○ ○

46. This doctor communicates with the other
health providers I see . . . .   ○ ○ ○ ○ ○ ○ ○

47. This doctor does not always know
about care I have received at other places . . . . .   ○ ○ ○ ○ ○ ○ ○

Please circle the best answer for the following questions:

48. How many *years* have
you been a patient of
this doctor? . . . .   <1   1–2   3–5   6–10   11–15   16–20   20+

49. How many years have
you been a patient of
this practice? . . . .   <1   1–2   3–5   6–10   11–15   16–20   20+

50. In the *last year*, how
many *visits* have you
had to this doctor?
(including this visit)   1   2   3   4   5   6   7   8   9+

51. In the *last year*, how many
visits have you had to *other
doctors* in this office?   0   1   2   3   4   5   6   7   8   9+

52. In the *last year*, how many
visits have you had to doctors
outside of this office?   0   1   2   3   4   5   6   7   8   9+

Thank you for completing this survey.
Please return the completed survey in the envelope provided.

Compulsiveness Inventory (CI)

PURPOSE To measure nonpathological compulsiveness.

AUTHORS Donna M. Kagan and Rose L. Squires

DESCRIPTION The 11-item CI, based on the Leyton Obsessional Inventory, is designed to measure compulsive behaviors that are common in the "normal" population. Pathological compulsiveness is defined in terms of extreme preoccupation with thoughts or activities, a tendency toward overorganization and difficulty making decisions. This scale focuses specifically on overconcern with decisions and tasks to be completed perfectly according to rigid well-established norms. It measures three aspects of compulsivity: indecision and double checking (IDC), order and regularity (OR), detail and perfection (DP). The total score on the CI can also be used as a general measure of compulsiveness.

NORMS Normative data are not available from the primary references. The CI was developed on a sample of 563 college students. Three hundred and four subjects were males and 259 were female. The average age was 28.2 with a standard deviation of 7.4 years.

SCORING The scores on the CI are the total number of "yes" responses. Items for the subscales are: IDC: 1, 2, 3, 4, 5; DT: 6, 7, 8, 9; OR: 10, 11. Higher scores mean greater compulsiveness.

RELIABILITY The reliability of the CI is presented for each subscale using coefficient alpha. The internal consistency for the subscales was excellent and was .89 for the IDC, .88 for OR, and .85 for DP. Alpha for the total CI was .80. No information on stability was reported.

VALIDITY Criterion validity was estimated by correlating the subscales with numerous personality measures. While the results are not separately presented, the summary indicates that the CI subscales correlate with behavioral dimensions of rigidity in men and women, compulsive eating and dieting, and several other measures.

PRIMARY REFERENCES Kagan, D. M., and Squires, R. L. (1985). Measuring nonpathological compulsiveness, *Psychological Reports*, 57, 559–563; Squires, R. L., and Kagan, D. M. (1985). Personality correlates of disordered eating, *International Journal of Eating Disorders*, 4, 80–85. Reprinted with permission of Donna M. Kagan and John Wiley and Sons, Inc.

AVAILABILITY May be copied from the volume.

Please respond to each question below by circling "yes" or "no."

Yes   No   1. Do you have to turn things over and over in your mind for a long time before being able to decide what to do?

Yes   No   2. Do you often have to check things several times?

Yes   No   3. Do you ever have to do things over again a certain number of times before they seem quite right?

Yes   No   4. Do you have difficulty making up your mind?

Yes   No   5. Do you have to go back and check doors, cupboards, or windows to make sure they are really shut?

Yes   No   6. Do you dislike having a room untidy or not quite clean for even a short time?

Yes   No   7. Do you take great care in hanging and folding your clothes at night?

Yes   No   8. Do you like to keep a certain order to undressing and dressing or washing or bathing?

Yes   No   9. Do you like to put your personal belongings in set places?

Yes   No   10. Do you like to get things done exactly right down to the smallest detail?

Yes   No   11. Are you the sort of person who has to pay a great deal of attention to details?

Concern about Death-Dying (CADD) and Coping (C) Checklists

PURPOSE To measure fears of death and dying and coping responses.

AUTHOR P. S. Fry

DESCRIPTION This instrument combines a 30-item checklist measuring seven aspects of one's fear of death and dying (CADD) and a 27-item checklist measuring six aspects of coping with these fears (C). The seven concerns about death and dying on the CADD are two types of physical pain and suffering (items 1–4 and items 5–7), fear of sensory loss (items 8–11), risk of personal safety (items 12–14), self-esteem concerns (items 15–21), uncertainty of life beyond death (items 22–27), and vacuum beyond death (items 28–30). The six coping methods on the C are internal self-control (items 1–6), two types of social support seeking (items 7–11 and items 12–15), prayer (items 16–20), preoccupying oneself with objects of attachment (items 21–24), and avoidance, denial, and escape (items 25–27). The items of the two checklists were developed from semistructured interviews with 178 elderly persons and were selected for inclusion based on ratings by a panel of experts.

NORMS Normative data are not available.

SCORING The checklists are easily scored by simply counting the total number of items checked as either a fear or a coping method for each of the subscales. Total scores are the sum of subscales scores, and range from 0 to 30 for the concerns about death-dying and 0 to 27 for the coping mechanisms.

RELIABILITY Extensive reliability data are not available for these two checklists. Internal consistency is suggested by the item factor loadings, which ranged from .31 to .71 for the concerns about death-dying checklist and .34 to .94 for the coping checklist.

VALIDITY The items of the checklists were selected based on semi-structured interviews with the homebound elderly and based on the interrater agreement of a panel of seven experts. These two procedures, especially the interrater reliability, suggest the checklists have, at the least, face validity.

PRIMARY REFERENCE Fry, P. S. (1990). A factor analytic investigation of home-bound elderly individuals' concerns about death and dying and their coping responses, *Journal of Clinical Psychology*, 46, 737–748. Instruments reproduced with permission of P. S. Fry and *Journal of Clinical Psychology*.

AVAILABILITY Dr. P. S. Fry, Research Professor, Trinity Western University, Langley, BC V2Y 1Y1, Canada. Email: fry@twu.ca.

CADD CHECKLIST

Below is a list of concerns people might have about death and dying. Check all that are a concern to you.

___ 1. Thoughts of physical pain and being hurt
___ 2. Thoughts of suffocating and choking
___ 3. Thoughts of lingering indefinitely on life-supporting systems
___ 4. Thoughts of being taken off life-supporting systems
___ 5. Thoughts of unsuccessful organ transplant
___ 6. Thoughts of death by violent means
___ 7. Thoughts of being consumed by parasites
___ 8. Fear of paralysis
___ 9. Fear of blindness
___ 10. Fear of inability to hear and communicate
___ 11. Fear of darkness
___ 12. Thoughts that my belongings will be destroyed after my death
___ 13. Thoughts of burglars invading my possessions
___ 14. Thoughts of strangers taking over
___ 15. Thoughts of being permanently forgotten after death
___ 16. Thoughts of no one caring
___ 17. Thoughts that life has been useless
___ 18. Thoughts of no one attending funeral
___ 19. Thoughts of no one paying respect or tribute
___ 20. Thoughts of indignity at the hands of undertakers, bankers, and insurance agents
___ 21. Thoughts of autopsy
___ 22. Rejection by God
___ 23. Thoughts of reincarnation
___ 24. Devil and other punitive elements in life beyond death
___ 25. No admission to Heaven or other place of peace
___ 26. Thoughts of timelessness in life beyond death
___ 27. Loud noises everywhere (wind blowing, thundering) in the life beyond death
___ 28. Stillness, emptiness
___ 29. Shadows everywhere beyond death
___ 30. Darkness everywhere beyond death

Below is a list of ways people cope with death and dying. Check all those things that you do to cope with death and dying.

___ 1. Reminisce on happy events of the past
___ 2. Keep busy in things that are of interest
___ 3. Remind myself that there is nothing to be afraid of
___ 4. Tell myself that everything is going to be OK
___ 5. Think happy and pleasant thoughts for the future
___ 6. Try to relax
___ 7. Call family member(s) into room and ask them to sit close by
___ 8. Telephone friends or relatives and have a prolonged conversation
___ 9. Reminisce about old times with family member or friend
___ 10. Visit doctor or physician and ask questions about physical health problems, physical illness symptoms, or medications
___ 11. Call child in the family (grandchild, niece, nephew) and ask him or her to spend the night
___ 12. Go or ask to be taken to visit family members or relatives
___ 13. Go or ask to be taken to church
___ 14. Go or ask to be taken for a drive
___ 15. Go or ask to be taken to the park
___ 16. Say a prayer
___ 17. Phone a prayer line
___ 18. Listen to religious and sacred music
___ 19. Watch religious programs on TV
___ 20. Read holy books
___ 21. Look at family picture albums
___ 22. Look at family heirlooms
___ 23. Read old letters from family members, relatives, and friends
___ 24. Bring out family will and read and ask questions about it
___ 25. Stay up late till ready to fall asleep
___ 26. Ask for a snack or something to drink
___ 27. Watch TV or listen to radio late into the night

Control Belief Scales (CBS)

PURPOSE To measure control over events.

AUTHORS Miron Zuckerman et al.

DESCRIPTION The CBS is comprised of two 21-item subscales to measure perceived control over controllable events (realistic control belief) and over uncontrollable events (unrealistic control belief). The CBS is based in part on the coping literature that shows that some control beliefs are adaptive and some are not. The CBS is an important development for the field because previous control scales did not make the distinction of realistic and unrealistic control beliefs. Thus, practitioners using the CBS can know what beliefs need reinforcement to encourage their continuation and/or increase (realistic) and what beliefs should not be encouraged (unrealistic). The two subscales of the CBS are presented separately as a Realistic Control Beliefs (RCB) scale and an Unrealistic Control Beliefs (UCB) scale. The two subscales are independent indicating that they really do measure different aspects of control beliefs.

NORMS The CBS was studied over a period of five years with 1,840 undergraduate students. No other demographic data were available in the Primary Reference. The mean score for the RCB was 5.29 (SD = .61) and the mean for the UCB was 3.04 (SD = .68). The difference between the two means was significant indicating that respondents were more likely to report they exercised control over controllable than over uncontrollable beliefs. Higher scores indicate greater control.

SCORING The two subscales are scored the same way by reverse-scoring the items on the scales with asterisks and then summing the item scores and dividing by the number of scores on each subscale.

RELIABILITY The two subscales have fair internal consistency with an alpha of .79 for the RCB and .77 for the UCB. Data on stability were not available.

VALIDITY The CBS has demonstrated very good convergent and discriminative validity. The RCB and UCB correlated with other valid perceived control measures such as Rotter's IE scale. The RCB and UCB also showed different associations with numerous variables such as those related to coping, expectations, and taking responsibility.

PRIMARY REFERENCE Zuckerman, M., et al. (2004). What individuals believe they can and cannot do: Explorations of realistic and unrealistic control beliefs, *Journal of Personality Assessment, 82*, 215–232. Instrument reproduced with permission of Dr. Zuckerman.

AVAILABILITY Email Dr. Zuckerman at miron@psych.rochester.edu, or may be copied from this volume.

Please indicate in this space before each item what comes closest to expressing your actual beliefs. All items are answered on a 7-point scale:

1	2	3	4	5	6	7

| Strongly Disagree | | | Neither Agree Nor Disagree | | | Strongly Agree |

Realistic Control Belief

___ *1. Grades in school are largely a matter of luck or teachers' whims.
___ *2. To be successful, it is essential to be in the right place at the right time.
___ 3. Hard work and following through are the best means of realizing one's goals.
___ 4. If I try very hard, most of my plans will work out.
___ *5. To achieve your goals, you need to know the right people.
___ 6. I have the ability needed to handle life challenges.
___ *7. One's great accomplishments result from good fortune.
___ 8. I am sure I can acquire all the skills necessary to fulfill my career plans.
___ *9. No matter how hard you work, without a lucky break, you will fail.
___ *10. There is very little I can do to influence how much other people like me.
___ 11. I can initiate and maintain friendships.
___ *12. I often find that others misunderstand me when I try to explain myself.
___ *13. It is my impression that in most group situations people ignore me.
___ *14. I am more of a follower than a leader.
___ 15. I can get along with most other people.
___ 16. I can say no even under social pressure.
___ *17. I am often awkward when interacting with others.
___ 18. Couples who work at their relationship are more likely to enjoy their life together than couples who don't.
___ 19. I can get along even with people I dislike.
___ 20. I can usually show others that I am trustworthy.
___ 21. I can discuss many topics without feeling uncomfortable.

Unrealistic Control Belief

___ *1. Some daily hassles cannot be prevented.
___ 2. There is no such thing as misfortune; everything that happens to us is the result of our own doing.
___ 3. When unexpected events happen, it means that the people involved failed to think ahead.
___ 4. People aren't born with personality traits; they are what they wish to be.
___ 5. What people see as inability is invariably a lack of will.
___ 6. In each and every task, not finishing successfully reflects a lack of motivation.
___ 7. Any person who tries can become a world-class scholar.
___ *8. I could work very hard and still lose my job.
___ *9. Some tasks in life require abilities that I do not have.
___ *10. Sometimes I can do my best and still not get the job done.
___ *11. I can be as careful as possible and still make mistakes.

___ *12. I can be a very alert driver and still end up in a serious accident.

___ *13. Even if I do everything I am capable of, some people may not like me.

___ 14. The success of my relations with others is solely up to me.

___ 15. I can keep anyone from getting angry at me.

___ 16. I can keep any friend from engaging in irresponsible behavior (e.g., taking drugs).

___ 17. I am responsible for the well-being and happiness of all my friends.

___ *18. My impressions of others are not always accurate.

___ *19. I don't always know when others deceive me.

___ *20. I cannot make another person love me.

___ *21. Even if I try very hard, I cannot make myself like some people.

Costello-Comrey Depression and Anxiety Scales (CCDAS)

PURPOSE To measure depression and anxiety.

AUTHORS C. G. Costello and Andrew L. Comrey

DESCRIPTION The CCDAS is a 14-item depression scale and a 9-item anxiety scale that can be administered separately or together. These scales were initially developed separately but eventually combined into a package for final psychometric analysis. Based on independent studies utilizing a large number of items and factor analysis, the "best" depression and anxiety items were combined to form the CCDAS. These scales are viewed more as trait than state scales. The depression scale measures a person's tendency to experience a depressive mood, while the anxiety scale measures a predisposition to develop anxious affective states.

NORMS The CCDAS was developed in a number of studies involving several hundred male and female respondents with a wide age range and number of occupations. The sample included nonclinical and clinical populations. Although means are available on earlier versions of the scales, norms were not reported for the latest CCDAS.

SCORING All items are scored on a 1 to 9 scale, with two categories of response depending on the item: "absolutely" to "absolutely not" and "always" to "never." Scores for the anxiety and depression scales are calculated separately by reverse-scoring items 1, 6, 7, 8, 9, and 10 on the depression scale and item 3 on the anxiety scale and then summing the items on each scale. This will produce a range of 14 to 126 on the depression scale and 9 to 81 on the anxiety scale, with higher scores on both scales representing greater depression or anxiety.

RELIABILITY The depression scale has excellent internal consistency, with split-half reliabilities of .90; split-half reliability for the anxiety scale was .70. Both scales are fairly stable, with test-retest correlations after admission and before discharge for psychiatric patients (no time given) of .72 for anxiety and .70 for depression (it is not clear in this case if this finding means the scales are not sensitive to change).

VALIDITY The CCDAS has fair concurrent validity; its anxiety scale is correlated with the Taylor Manifest Anxiety Scales and the depression scale is correlated with the Depression scale of the MMPI. There is small to moderate correlation between the CCDAS and social desirability, suggesting some response bias may be present.

PRIMARY REFERENCE Costello, C. G., and Comrey, A. L. (1967). Scales for measuring depression and anxiety, *Journal of Psychology*, 66, 303–313. Instrument reproduced with permission of the *Journal of Psychology*.

AVAILABILITY May be copied from this volume.

Please circle the number that best describes your response to each item.

Depression Scale

1. I feel that life is worthwhile.

Absolutely	Very definitely	Definitely	Probably	Possibly	Probably not	Definitely not	Very definitely not	Absolutely not
9	8	7	6	5	4	3	2	1

2. When I wake up in the morning I expect to have a miserable day.

Always	Almost always	Very frequently	Frequently	Fairly often	Occasionally	Rarely	Almost never	Never
9	8	7	6	5	4	3	2	1

3. I wish I had never been born.

Absolutely	Very definitely	Definitely	Probably	Possibly	Probably not	Definitely not	Very definitely not	Absolutely not
9	8	7	6	5	4	3	2	1

4. I feel that there is more disappointment in life than satisfaction.

Absolutely	Very definitely	Definitely	Probably	Possibly	Probably not	Definitely not	Very definitely not	Absolutely not
9	8	7	6	5	4	3	2	1

5. I want to run away from everything.

Always	Almost always	Very frequently	Frequently	Fairly often	Occasionally	Rarely	Almost never	Never
9	8	7	6	5	4	3	2	1

6. My future looks hopeful and promising.

Absolutely	Very definitely	Definitely	Probably	Possibly	Probably not	Definitely not	Very definitely not	Absolutely not
9	8	7	6	5	4	3	2	1

7. When I get up in the morning I expect to have an interesting day.

Always	Almost always	Very frequently	Frequently	Fairly often	Occasionally	Rarely	Almost never	Never
9	8	7	6	5	4	3	2	1

8. Living is a wonderful adventure for me.

Always	Almost always	Very frequently	Frequently	Fairly often	Occasionally	Rarely	Almost never	Never
9	8	7	6	5	4	3	2	1

9. I am a happy person.

Always	Almost always	Very frequently	Frequently	Fairly often	Occasionally	Rarely	Almost never	Never
9	8	7	6	5	4	3	2	1

10. Things have worked out well for me.

Absolutely	Very definitely	Definitely	Probably	Possibly	Probably not	Definitely not	Very definitely not	Absolutely not
9	8	7	6	5	4	3	2	1

11. The future looks so gloomy that I wonder if I should go on.

Always	Almost always	Very frequently	Frequently	Fairly often	Occasionally	Rarely	Almost never	Never
9	8	7	6	5	4	3	2	1

12. I feel that life is drudgery and boredom.

Always	Almost always	Very frequently	Frequently	Fairly often	Occasionally	Rarely	Almost never	Never
9	8	7	6	5	4	3	2	1

13. I feel blue and depressed.

Always	Almost always	Very frequently	Frequently	Fairly often	Occasionally	Rarely	Almost never	Never
9	8	7	6	5	4	3	2	1

14. When I look back I think life has been good to me.

Absolutely	Very definitely	Definitely	Probably	Possibly	Probably not	Definitely not	Very definitely not	Absolutely not
9	8	7	6	5	4	3	2	1

Anxiety Scale

1. I get rattled easily.

Always	Almost always	Very frequently	Frequently	Fairly often	Occasionally	Rarely	Almost never	Never
9	8	7	6	5	4	3	2	1

2. When faced with excitement or unexpected situations, I become nervous and jumpy.

Always	Almost always	Very frequently	Frequently	Fairly often	Occasionally	Rarely	Almost never	Never
9	8	7	6	5	4	3	2	1

3. I am calm and not easily upset.

Always	Almost always	Very frequently	Frequently	Fairly often	Occasionally	Rarely	Almost never	Never
9	8	7	6	5	4	3	2	1

4. When things go wrong I get nervous and upset instead of calmly thinking out a solution.

Always	Almost always	Very frequently	Frequently	Fairly often	Occasionally	Rarely	Almost never	Never
9	8	7	6	5	4	3	2	1

5. It makes me nervous when I have to wait.

Always	Almost always	Very frequently	Frequently	Fairly often	Occasionally	Rarely	Almost never	Never
9	8	7	6	5	4	3	2	1

6. I am a tense, "high-strung" person.

Absolutely	Very definitely	Definitely	Probably	Possibly	Probably not	Definitely not	Very definitely not	Absolutely not
9	8	7	6	5	4	3	2	1

7. I am more sensitive than most other people.

Absolutely	Very definitely	Definitely	Probably	Possibly	Probably not	Definitely not	Very definitely not	Absolutely not
9	8	7	6	5	4	3	2	1

8. My hand shakes when I try to do something.

Always	Almost always	Very frequently	Frequently	Fairly often	Occasionally	Rarely	Almost never	Never
9	8	7	6	5	4	3	2	1

9. I am a very nervous person.

Absolutely	Very definitely	Definitely	Probably	Possibly	Probably not	Definitely not	Very definitely not	Absolutely not
9	8	7	6	5	4	3	2	1

Cultural Congruity Scale (CCS)

PURPOSE To measure cultural congruity.

AUTHORS Alberta M. Gloria and Sharon E. Robinson-Kurpius

DESCRIPTION The CCS is a 13-item instrument that was designed to measure Chicano/a students' sense of cultural congruity or cultural fit within the college environment. Cultural congruity is based on the notion that people belonging to two or more cultures may experience cultural incongruity if the cultures are different in values, beliefs, and expectations of behaviors. Beliefs, behaviors, and/or values that differ from established norms, especially in academia, may be considered deviant or abnormal; therefore, the minority student may find himself or herself in an uncomfortable or incongruent situation. Minority students, and in this case, Latino students, often feel unwelcome in higher education because of their cultural or racial/ethnic differences. The CCS is probably the first instrument designed to examine the importance of perceived cultural fit or cultural congruence as one of the variables for examining the academic persistence of minority students, particularly Chicano/a students.

NORMS The CCS was initially developed and validated with several different samples including 158 Chicanos/as at the University of California at Irvine (UCI) and 285 Chicanos/as at Arizona State University (ASU). At UCI, 74% of the students were female with a mean age of 21.07 years (SD = 3.41), and at ASU, 76% of the students were female and the mean age was 22.63 years (SD = 5.51). The mean score for combined samples on the CCS was 71.88 (SD = 12.55).

SCORING The CCS is easily scored by summing individual item responses after reverse-scoring items 1, 2, 3, 4, 6, 7, 9, and 10. Scores range from 13 to 91 with higher scores indicating greater perceived cultural congruity.

RELIABILITY The CCS has good internal consistency, with an alpha for combined samples of .81. No data on stability were reported.

VALIDITY The CCS has established some initial predictive validity, accounting for a significant amount of the variance in academic persistence. There's also a negative correlation between academic persistence and the CCS showing that as students perceive a more positive cultural fit, they make more positive persistence decisions.

PRIMARY REFERENCE Gloria, A. M., and Kurpius, S. E. R. (1996). The validation of the cultural congruity scale and the university environment scale with Chicano/a students, *Hispanic Journal of Behavioral Sciences*, 18, 553–549.

AVAILABILITY May be copied from this volume.

For each of the following items, indicate the extent to which you have experienced the feeling or situation at school. Use the following ratings:

Not at all						A great deal
1	2	3	4	5	6	7

___ 1. I feel that I have to change myself to fit in at school.
___ 2. I try not to show the parts of me that are "ethnically" based.
___ 3. I often feel like a chameleon, having to change myself depending on the ethnicity of the person I am with at school.
___ 4. I feel that my ethnicity is incompatible with other students.
___ 5. I can talk to my friends at school about my family and culture.
___ 6. I feel I am leaving my family values behind by going to college.
___ 7. My ethnic values are in conflict with what is expected at school.
___ 8. I can talk to my family about my friends from school.
___ 9. I feel that my language and/or appearance make it hard for me to fit in with other students.
___ 10. My family and school values often conflict.
___ 11. I feel accepted at school as an ethnic minority.
___ 12. As an ethnic minority, I feel as if I belong on this campus.
___ 13. I can talk to my family about my struggles and concerns at school.

Current Attachment Relationships (CAR)

PURPOSE To assess attachment.

AUTHORS Jon G. Allen et al.

DESCRIPTION The CAR is an instrument designed to measure current attachment relationships among women in treatment for trauma-related problems. The authors believe that attachment theory is very useful for understanding social support, based on their work in trying to help women who have been traumatized. The construct of current attachment relationships was seen as particularly useful for diagnostic and therapeutic work since the information obtained from the CAR helps focus on the importance of making use of relationships to help in emotional regulation, a primary problem for people suffering from PTSD. This instrument works simply by asking clients to list their current attachment figures, and then to rate the degree of security that relationship provides. The CAR provides a global measure of the client's perception of the quantity of emotionally supportive relationships.

NORMS The CAR was developed using a sample of 99 women with a severe trauma history and 154 women from a community sample of non-traumatized women. For the women where the data were available, the combined sample had a mean age of 41.5 (SD = 10.3). 14% had high school degrees, while the majority had college or graduate degrees. The community sample, however, was significantly older than the trauma sample (43.9 years versus 37.8 years) and the community sample also had a significantly higher education level. Although actual means are not available in the Primary Reference, scores on the CAR are presented in comparison to two other measures of attachment style. However, there was a significant difference between the trauma and community samples on CAR scores.

SCORING The CAR can be scored simply by counting the number of attachment figures listed, and also by analyzing those figures that are considered secure and not secure on the 5-point scale. Data also can be analyzed by breaking down the listed figures by categories, such as professional, non-family, family of marriage, and family of origin.

RELIABILITY Data on reliability were not available in the Primary Reference.

VALIDITY The CAR has good known-groups validity, showing significant differences between trauma and community samples. The CAR also has established some degree of construct validity by correlating in predicted directions with the subscales of two measures of attachment style, the Relationship Quality Questionnaire and the Adult Attachment Scale.

PRIMARY REFERENCE Allen, J. G., et al. (2001). A model for brief assessment of attachment and its application to women in inpatient treatment for trauma-related psychiatric disorders, *Journal of Personality Assessment, 76,* 421–447. Instrument reproduced with permission of Dr. Jon Allen.

AVAILABILITY Email Dr. Allen at jallen@menninger.edu.

Please indicate below your relationships that—at least some of the time—give you some feeling of security. List the persons you might seek out for comfort when you are distressed or go to for protection when you feel unsafe. Include those you trust—at least to some degree—not to hurt or abandon you. You may include a pet if your relationship with your pet is important in providing you with a feeling of security and comfort. Write in the individual's name (first name or initials), and indicate the type of relationship (for example, friend, partner, husband, wife, mother, daughter, therapist, psychiatrist, pastor, pet). Then indicate how secure you feel in the relationship at present by circling a number from 1 (very insecure) to 5 (very secure). If the gender of the person is not already obvious (e.g., "mother," "uncle"), please circle M for male or F for female. You may have one, a few, or many relationships that provide some feeling of security. Put down as many or as few as you have at present. If you do not currently have a relationship that—at least sometimes— provides you with a feeling of security, indicate that by putting a checkmark next to the statement below.

___ I do not currently have any relationship that provides any feeling of security.

Name or initials	Type of relationship	Degree of Security					Gender	
		very insecure		somewhat secure		very secure		
_____	_____	1	2	3	4	5	M	F
_____	_____	1	2	3	4	5	M	F
_____	_____	1	2	3	4	5	M	F
_____	_____	1	2	3	4	5	M	F
_____	_____	1	2	3	4	5	M	F
_____	_____	1	2	3	4	5	M	F
_____	_____	1	2	3	4	5	M	F
_____	_____	1	2	3	4	5	M	F
_____	_____	1	2	3	4	5	M	F
_____	_____	1	2	3	4	5	M	F

Dating and Assertion Questionnaire (DAQ)

PURPOSE To measure social competence.

AUTHORS Robert W. Levenson and John M. Gottman

DESCRIPTION The 18-item DAQ was designed to measure social competence with a focus on social skills in two social situations: dating and assertion. Nine items measure the general social skills of dating and nine measure assertion. The measures are sensitive to change resulting from social skills training and, therefore, are clinically useful. The Dating items and Assertion items form two separate measures. One limitation of the DAQ is that two, and possibly three, of the items pertain to social situations for college students and would not be relevant to other clients.

NORMS Normative data on the DAQ are limited. The two subscales were developed on samples of college students, including those volunteering for social skills training in dating ($n = 46$) and assertiveness training ($n = 46$). Posttest scores for the dating skills training group were 2.41 on the Dating subscale and 2.76 on the Assertion subscale; posttest scores for subjects in the assertiveness training were 3.02 for the Dating subscale and 3.02 for the Assertion subscale.

SCORING Half of the items are rated on a 1 to 4 scale of how frequently the respondent performs the specified behavior. The other half are rated on a 1 to 5 scale according to how comfortable the respondent would feel in the specified situation. Separate scores are computed for the dating and assertion subscales, noted by an "A" or a "D" beside the items. To compute the assertion subscale score, add the responses to items 1, 3, 4, and 6, then divide by 4; next add the responses to items 10, 12, 15, 16, and 18, then divide that total by 5; add these two figures to get an assertion subscale score. To compute the dating subscale score add the responses to items 2, 5, 7, 8, and 9 and then divide the sum by 5; next add the responses to items 11, 13, 14, and 17, and then divide by 4. Add these two figures together for a dating subscale score. These scoring procedures are summarized as: Assertion subscale score = [(items 1 + 3 + 4 + 6) $\prod$ 4] + [(items 10 + 12 + 15 + 16 + 18) $\prod$ 5]. Dating subscale score = [(items 2 + 5 + 7 + 8 + 9) $\prod$ 5] + [(items 11 + 13 + 14 + 17) $\prod$ 4]. Both subscale scores range from one to nine.

RELIABILITY These subscales have good to excellent reliability. Their internal consistency using coefficient alpha was .92 and .85 for the Dating and Assertive subscales, respectively. The test-retest reliability correlation was good with both scales correlating .71 over a two-week period. The subscales were only slightly less stable when tested over a six-week test-retest period.

VALIDITY The validity of these subscales is supported by known-groups validity where significantly different scores were found between a clinical sample and a nonclinical ("normal") sample of college students. Scores were also significantly different for people identified as having dating and assertive problems compared to a sample of "normal" college subjects. Both instruments have been shown to be sensitive to measuring change resulting from social skills training.

PRIMARY REFERENCE Levenson, R. W., and Gottman, J. M. (1978). Toward the assessment of social competence, *Journal of Consulting and Clinical Psychology*, 46, 453–462. Instrument reproduced with permission of Robert W. Levenson and the American Psychological Association.

AVAILABILITY May be copied from this volume.

We are interested in finding out something about the likelihood of your acting in certain ways. Below you will find a list of specific behaviors you may or may not exhibit. Use the following rating scale:

1 = I never do this
2 = I sometimes do this
3 = I often do this
4 = I do this almost always

Now, next to each of the items on the following list, place the number which best indicates the likelihood of your behaving in that way. Be as objective as possible.

____ 1. Stand up for your rights (A)
____ 2. Maintain a long conversation with a member of the opposite sex (D)
____ 3. Be confident in your ability to succeed in a situation in which you have to demonstrate your competence (A)
____ 4. Say "no" when you feel like it (A)
____ 5. Get a second date with someone you have dated once (D)
____ 6. Assume a role of leadership (A)
____ 7. Be able to accurately sense how a member of the opposite sex feels about you (D)
____ 8. Have an intimate emotional relationship with a member of the opposite sex (D)
____ 9. Have an intimate physical relationship with a member of the opposite sex (D)

The following questions describe a variety of social situations that you might encounter. In each situation you may feel "put on the spot." Some situations may be familiar to you, and others may not. We'd like you to read each situation and try to imagine yourself actually in the situation. The more vividly you get a mental picture and place yourself into the situation, the better.

After each situation circle one of the numbers from 1 to 5 which best describes you, using the following scale:

1 = I would be so uncomfortable and so unable to handle this situation that I would avoid it if possible.
2 = I would feel very uncomfortable and would have a lot of difficulty handling this situation.
3 = I would feel somewhat uncomfortable and would have some difficulty in handling this situation.
4 = I would feel quite comfortable and would be able to handle this situation fairly well.
5 = I would feel very comfortable and be able to handle this situation very well.

____ 10. You're waiting patiently in line at the checkout when a couple of people cut right in front of you. You feel really annoyed and want to tell them to wait their turn at the back of the line. One of them says, "Look, you don't mind, do you? But we're in a terrible hurry." (A)
____ 11. You have enjoyed this date and would like to see your date again. The evening is coming to a close and you decide to say something. (D)

___ 12. You are talking to a professor about dropping a class. You explain your situation, which you fabricate slightly for effect. Looking at his grade book the professor comments that you are pretty far behind. You go into greater detail about why you are behind and why you'd like to be allowed to withdraw from his class. He then says, "I'm sorry, but it's against university policy to let you withdraw this late in the semester." (A)

___ 13. You meet someone you don't know very well but are attracted to. You want to ask him/her out for a date. (D)

___ 14. You meet someone of the opposite sex at lunch and have a very enjoyable conversation. You'd like to get together again and decide to say something. (D)

___ 15. Your roommate has several obnoxious traits that upset you very much. So far, you have mentioned them once or twice, but no noticeable changes have occurred. You still have 3 months left to live together. You decide to say something. (A)

___ 16 You're with a small group of people who you don't know too well. Most of them are expressing a point of view that you disagree with. You'd like to state your opinion even if it means you'll probably be in the minority. (A)

___ 17. You go to a party where you don't know many people. Someone of the opposite sex approaches you and introduces themself. You want to start a conversation and get to know him/her. (D)

___ 18. You are trying to make an appointment with the dean. You are talking to his secretary face-to-face. She asks you what division you are in and when you tell her, she starts asking you questions about the nature of your problem. You inquire as to why she is asking all these questions and she replies very snobbishly that she is the person who decides if your problem is important enough to warrant an audience with the dean. You decide to say something. (A)

Death Depression Scale (DDS)

PURPOSE To measure death depression.

AUTHORS Donald I. Templer, Michael LaVoie, Hilda Chalgujian, and Shan Thomas-Dobson

DESCRIPTION The DDS is a 17-item instrument designed to measure depression about one's own impending death, the death of others, or death in general. Although there are a number of instruments designed to measure fear or anxiety about death, this is reportedly the first to measure depression about death. The DDS comprises six factors: death despair (items 8, 11, 16), death loneliness (items 4, 9, 10, 13), death dread (items 14, 15, 16), death sadness (items 2, 3), death depression (items 2, 12), and death finality (items 6, 7). The DDS is seen as a useful clinical measure to determine change over time as a function of bereavement, terminal illness, and various life events.

NORMS The DDS was studied initially on 190 psychology course undergraduates in Fresno, California, including 62 males and 128 females with a mean age of 32.2. Actual norms are not reported.

SCORING The DDS can be administered in a true-false format (reproduced here) or in a 5-point Likert-type format (1 = "strongly agree" to 5 = "strongly disagree"). Scores on the two formats correlate .77. Of the 17 items, all but items 11 and 12 are keyed as "true." Each item scored "correctly" (i.e., as keyed) receives a score of 1, with the score for the total scale being simply the sum of all those items. (The Likert-type format is scored the same way, with reverse-scoring of items 11 and 12, and the total score being the sum of all scores on the individual items). Higher scores signify greater death depression.

RELIABILITY The DDS has fair internal consistency, with a Kuder-Richardson coefficient of .77. No information on stability was reported.

VALIDITY The DDS has very good concurrent validity, with significant correlations with the Death Anxiety Scale and the Zuckerman measures of general anxiety and depression.

PRIMARY REFERENCE Templer, D. I., LaVoie, M., Chalgujian, H., and Thomas-Dobson, S. (1990). The measurement of death depression, *Journal of Clinical Psychology*, 46, 834–839.

AVAILABILITY May be copied from this volume.

Please circle T for true or F for false in each item as it applies to you.

T F   1. I get depressed when I think about death.

T F   2. Hearing the word death makes me sad.

T F   3. Passing by cemeteries makes me sad.

T F   4. Death means terrible loneliness.

T F   5. I become terribly sad when I think about friends or relatives who have died.

T F   6. I am terribly upset by the shortness of life.

T F   7. I cannot accept the finality of death.

T F   8. Death deprives life of its meaning.

T F   9. I worry about dying alone.

T F   10. When I die, I will completely lose my friends and loved ones.

T F   11. Death does not rob life of its meaning.

T F   12. Death is not something to be depressed by.

T F   13. When I think of death, I feel tired and lifeless.

T F   14. Death is painful.

T F   15. I dread to think of the death of friends and loved ones.

T F   16. Death is the ultimate failure in life.

T F   17. I feel sad when I dream of death.

Defense Style Questionnaire-40 (DSQ-40)

PURPOSE To measure defense styles.

AUTHORS Gavin Andrews, Michelle Singh, and Michael Bond

DESCRIPTION The DSQ is a 40-item questionnaire designed to measure defense style/defense mechanisms. The DSQ comprises three factors and 20 defense mechanisms as described in the *DSM-III-R*. The first factor is the mature factor, which includes sublimation, humor, anticipation, and suppression. The second is called the neurotic factor, and includes the defenses of undoing, pseudo-altruism, idealization, and reaction formation. The third factor—the immature factor—comprises projection, passive aggression, acting out, isolation, devaluation, autistic fantasy, denial, displacement, dissociation, splitting, rationalization, and somatization. Each of the defenses is represented by two items on the DSQ; these items are described in the primary reference. The DSQ is an important addition for clinical practice among those practitioners who utilize the construct of defense mechanisms and develop differentiated treatments on the basis of the presence or absence of certain defense mechanisms.

NORMS The DSQ-40 was studied with 712 subjects, of whom 64% were female; the mean age was 35 (SD = 13). The 712 subjects included the following subsamples: a normal control sample ($n = 388$); a general practice sample ($n = 67$); a psychiatric outpatient sample ($n = 225$); and a sample of child-abusing parents ($n = 32$). Means and standard deviations for the individual items that make up each of the 20 defenses are available in the primary reference.

SCORING The DSQ is easily scored by averaging the two items for each defense; factor scores are simply the average of the defense scores contributing to each factor. The DSQ thus yields 20 individual defense scores and three factor scores (mature, neurotic, and immature).

RELIABILITY The three factors of the DSQ have fair internal consistency, with alphas of .68, .58, and .80 for the mature, neurotic, and immature factors, respectively. The individual defenses (comprising two items each) have lower reliability, ranging from minus .01 for devaluation to .89 for autistic fantasy. The DSQ has very good stability, with four-week test-retest correlations that range from .75 to .85 for the three factors and from .38 to .80 for the defense mechanisms.

VALIDITY The DSQ has established fair known-groups validity, significantly discriminating anxiety patients from "normal" controls, child-abusing parents from "normal" controls, and child-abusing parents from anxiety patients.

PRIMARY REFERENCE Andrews, G., Singh, M., and Bond, M. (1993). The Defense Style Questionnaire, *Journal of Nervous and Mental Disease*, 181, 246–256.

AVAILABILITY Dr. Gavin Andrews, School of Psychiatry, University of New South Wales at St. Vincent's Hospital, 299 Forbes St., Darlinghurst, Sydney, NSW 2010, Australia. Email: gavina@unsw.edu.au.

This questionnaire consists of a number of statements about personal attitudes. *There are no right or wrong answers.* Using the 9-point scale shown below, please indicate how much you agree or disagree with each statement by *circling* one of the numbers on the scale beside the statement. For example, a score of **5** would indicate that you neither agree nor disagree with the statement, a score of **3** that you moderately disagree, a score of **9** that you strongly agree.

1	2	3	4	5	6	7	8	9

Strongly disagree — Strongly agree

1. I get satisfaction from helping others, and if this were taken away from me I would get depressed.   1 2 3 4 5 6 7 8 9

3. I'm able to keep a problem out of my mind until I have time to deal with it.   1 2 3 4 5 6 7 8 9

5. I work out my anxiety through doing something constructive and creative like painting or woodworking.   1 2 3 4 5 6 7 8 9

6. I am able to find good reasons for everything I do.   1 2 3 4 5 6 7 8 9

8. I'm able to laugh at myself pretty easily.   1 2 3 4 5 6 7 8 9

12. People tend to mistreat me.   1 2 3 4 5 6 7 8 9

13. If someone mugged me and stole my money, I'd rather he be helped than punished.   1 2 3 4 5 6 7 8 9

16. People say I tend to ignore unpleasant facts as if they didn't exist.   1 2 3 4 5 6 7 8 9

23. I ignore danger as if I was Superman.   1 2 3 4 5 6 7 8 9

24. I pride myself on my ability to cut people down to size.   1 2 3 4 5 6 7 8 9

27. I often act impulsively when something is bothering me.   1 2 3 4 5 6 7 8 9

28. I get physically ill when things aren't going well for me.   1 2 3 4 5 6 7 8 9

29. I'm a very inhibited person.   1 2 3 4 5 6 7 8 9

31. I get more satisfaction from my fantasies than from my real life.   1 2 3 4 5 6 7 8 9

37. I've special talents that allow me to go through life with no problems.   1 2 3 4 5 6 7 8 9

38. There are always good reasons when things don't work out for me.   1 2 3 4 5 6 7 8 9

40. I work more things out in my daydreams than in my real life.   1 2 3 4 5 6 7 8 9

42. I fear nothing.   1 2 3 4 5 6 7 8 9

43. Sometimes I think I'm an angel and other times I think I'm a devil.   1 2 3 4 5 6 7 8 9

46. I get openly aggressive when I feel hurt.	1	2	3	4	5	6	7	8	9
51. I always feel that someone I know is like a guardian angel.	1	2	3	4	5	6	7	8	9
53. As far as I'm concerned, people are either good or bad.	1	2	3	4	5	6	7	8	9
54. If my boss bugged me, I might make a mistake in my work or work more slowly so as to get back at him.	1	2	3	4	5	6	7	8	9
58. There is someone I know who can do anything and who is absolutely fair and just.	1	2	3	4	5	6	7	8	9
59. I can keep the lid on my feelings if letting them out would interfere with what I'm doing.	1	2	3	4	5	6	7	8	9
61. I'm usually able to see the funny side of an otherwise painful predicament.	1	2	3	4	5	6	7	8	9
62. I get a headache when I have to do something I don't like.	1	2	3	4	5	6	7	8	9
63. I often find myself being very nice to people who by all rights I should be angry at.	1	2	3	4	5	6	7	8	9
66. I am sure I get a raw deal from life.	1	2	3	4	5	6	7	8	9
68. When I have to face a difficult situation, I try to imagine what it will be like and plan ways to cope with it.	1	2	3	4	5	6	7	8	9
69. Doctors never really understand what is wrong with me.	1	2	3	4	5	6	7	8	9
71. After I fight for my rights, I tend to apologize for my assertiveness.	1	2	3	4	5	6	7	8	9
73. When I'm depressed or anxious, eating makes me feel better.	1	2	3	4	5	6	7	8	9
76. I'm often told that I don't show my feelings.	1	2	3	4	5	6	7	8	9
81. If I can predict that I'm going to be sad ahead of time, I can cope better.	1	2	3	4	5	6	7	8	9
82. No matter how much I complain, I never get a satisfactory response.	1	2	3	4	5	6	7	8	9
83. Often I find that I don't feel anything when the situation would seem to warrant strong emotions.	1	2	3	4	5	6	7	8	9
84. Sticking to the task at hand keeps me from feeling depressed or anxious.	1	2	3	4	5	6	7	8	9
86. If I were in a crisis, I would seek out another person who had the same problem.	1	2	3	4	5	6	7	8	9
88. If I have an aggressive thought, I feel the need to do something to compensate for it.	1	2	3	4	5	6	7	8	9

Dental Anxiety Scale (DAS)

PURPOSE To measure dental anxiety.

AUTHORS Norman L. Corah, Elliot N. Gale, and Stephen J. Illig

DESCRIPTION The DAS is a 4-item instrument designed to measure anxiety about dental treatment. Dental anxiety is conceptualized as the patient's response to the stress that is specific to the dental situation. If the dentist uses this short, easy-to-administer instrument to assess patients' anxiety, he or she will not only be prepared for it, but will be able to take measures to alleviate it.

NORMS The DAS has been normed with two large groups (totaling 2,103) of college students in undergraduate psychology courses (998 men and 1,105 women). No other demographic data were available. The overall mean for the DAS was 9.07, with differences of only .44 between the two groups, though this difference was statistically significant. Women tend to score more highly (more anxiety) than men.

SCORING The DAS is easily scored by summing individual item scores (from a = 1 to e = 5) for a total score (range of 4 to 20).

RELIABILITY The DAS has very good internal consistency, with a reliability coefficient of .86. Data on stability were not provided.

VALIDITY The DAS has good concurrent validity, with significant correlations with several other measures of stress and anxiety related to dental work. The DAS also is reported as being sensitive to changes in dental anxiety as a result of treatment.

PRIMARY REFERENCE Corah, N. L., Gale, E. N., and Illig, S. J. (1969). Assessment of a Dental Anxiety Scale, *Journal of the American Dental Association*, 97, 816–818.

AVAILABILITY May be copied from this volume.

Please circle one letter under each question that most accurately represents your feelings.

1. If you had to go to the dentist tomorrow, how would you feel about it?

    a. I would look forward to it as a reasonably enjoyable experience.
    b. I wouldn't care one way or the other.
    c. I would be a little uneasy about it.
    d. I would be afraid that it would be unpleasant and painful.
    e. I would be very frightened of what the dentist might do.

2. When you are waiting in the dentist's office for your turn in the chair, how do you feel?

    a. Relaxed.
    b. A little uneasy.
    c. Tense.
    d. Anxious.
    e. So anxious that I sometimes break out in a sweat or almost feel physically sick.

3. When you are in the dentist's chair waiting while he gets his drill ready to begin working on your teeth, how do you feel?

    a. Relaxed.
    b. A little uneasy.
    c. Tense.
    d. Anxious.
    e. So anxious that I sometimes break out in a sweat or almost feel physically sick.

4. You are in the dentist's chair to have your teeth cleaned. While you are waiting and the dentist is getting out the instruments which he will use to scrape your teeth around the gums, how do you feel?

    a. Relaxed.
    b. A little uneasy.
    c. Tense.
    d. Anxious.
    e. So anxious that I sometimes break out in a sweat or almost feel physically sick.

Dental Fear Survey (DFS)

PURPOSE To measure fear of dental work.

AUTHORS R. A. Kleinknecht, R. K. Klepac, L. D. Alexander, and D. A. Bernstein

DESCRIPTION The DFS is a 20-item instrument designed to identify the respondent's specific and unique responses to a variety of dental-related stimuli that could produce fear and/or avoidance, plus a global item (item 20) for fear of dentistry. The scale is based on learning theory as being more relevant than traditional formulations in helping both understand and treat the problem of dental fear. Three factors (subscales) were identified in several factor analyses: avoidance of dentistry (items 1 and 2); felt autonomic arousal during dentistry (items 3–7); and fear of situations and stimuli (items 8–20). The DFS is viewed as being well enough established to justify its routine use with people fearful of dental work, perhaps helping match treatments to specific problems.

NORMS The DFS has been studied with several populations including 279 males and 239 females from the practices of dentists in Washington state, and 150 males and 267 females who were college students in Florida. Overall means for these groups ranged from 2.49 (SD = 1.35) to 2.65 (SD = 1.15) for females and 2.06 (SD = 1.07) to 2.29 (SD = .94) for males.

SCORING The DFS is easily scored by summing individual items for subscale and total scores.

RELIABILITY Although exact figures were not available, the DFS was reported as having "uniformly high" alpha coefficients and "robust" eight- to thirteen-week test-retest correlations.

VALIDITY The DFS has good known-groups validity, significantly distinguishing between high and low scores regarding canceled appointments, waiting room activity levels, pain reports, and palmar sweating.

PRIMARY REFERENCE Kleinknecht, R. A., McGlynn, F. D., Thorndike, R. M., and Harkavy, J. (1984). Factor analysis of the Dental Fear Survey with cross validation, *Journal of the American Dental Association*, 108, 59–61. Instrument reproduced with permission of Pergamon Press.

AVAILABILITY Dr. R. A. Kleinknecht, Western Washington University, Bellingham, WA. Email: ronald.kleinknecht@wwu.edu.

The items in this questionnaire refer to various situations, feelings, and reactions related to dental work. Please rate your feeling or reaction to these items by *circling the number* (1, 2, 3, 4, or 5) of the category which most closely corresponds to your reaction.

1. Has fear of dental work ever caused you to put off making an appointment?

1	2	3	4	5
Never	Once or twice	A few times	Often	Nearly every time

2. Has fear of dental work ever caused you to cancel or not appear for an appointment?

1	2	3	4	5
Never	Once or twice	A few times	Often	Nearly every time

When having dental work done:

3. My muscles become tense

1	2	3	4	5
Not at all	A little	Somewhat	Much	Very much

4. My breathing rate increases

1	2	3	4	5
Never	Once or twice	A few times	Often	Nearly every time

5. I perspire

1	2	3	4	5
Never	Once or twice	A few times	Often	Nearly every time

6. I feel nauseated and sick to my stomach

1	2	3	4	5
Never	Once or twice	A few times	Often	Nearly every time

7. My heart beats faster

1	2	3	4	5
Never	Once or twice	A few times	Often	Nearly every time

Following is a list of things and situations that many people mention as being somewhat anxiety or fear producing. Please rate how much fear, anxiety or unpleasantness each of them causes you. Use the numbers 1–5, from the following scale. Make a check in the appropriate space. (If it helps, try to imagine yourself in each of these situations and describe what your common reaction is.)

1	2	3	4	5
None at all	A little	Somewhat	Much	Very much

	1	2	3	4	5
8. Making an appointment for dentistry	—	—	—	—	—
9. Approaching the dentist's office	—	—	—	—	—

	1	2	3	4	5	
	None at all	A little	Somewhat	Much	Very much	
10. Sitting in the waiting room	—	—	—	—	—
11. Being seated in the dental chair	—	—	—	—	—
12. The smell of the dentist's office	—	—	—	—	—
13. Seeing the dentist walk in	—	—	—	—	—
14. Seeing the anesthetic needle	—	—	—	—	—
15. Feeling the needle injected	—	—	—	—	—
16. Seeing the drill	—	—	—	—	—
17. Hearing the drill	—	—	—	—	—
18. Feeling the vibrations of the drill	—	—	—	—	—
19. Having your teeth cleaned	—	—	—	—	—
20. All things considered, how fearful are you of having dental work done?	—	—	—	—	—

Depression Anxiety and Stress Scales (DASS)

PURPOSE To measure depression, anxiety, and stress.

AUTHORS Sydney H. Lovibond and Peter F. Lovibond

DESCRIPTION This 42-item instrument measures three negative emotional states often found in clinical practice: depression, anxiety, and stress. Each scale is composed of 14 primary symptoms, or 7 primary symptoms when using the DASS-21 (see below). Each item is rated on severity for the past week. As such, the DASS ascertains the depression, anxiety, and stress as relatively varying states and not necessarily an enduring trait, unless the observations are stable over time. However, the DASS may be adopted as a trait measure by instructing the respondent to answer each item as he or she characteristically feels or experiences it. The DASS was developed through a series of rigorous procedures beginning in 1979 using a number of samples, including several clinical samples. The result is a clinically reliable, valid, and sensitive instrument that measures three common client experiences. The instrument is accompanied with a useful manual, scoring templates, and permission to reproduce.

NORMS Normative data are available on a number of samples. From a sample of 2,914 adults the means (and standard deviations) were 6.34 (6.97), 4.7 (4.91), and 10.11 (7.91) for the depression, anxiety, and stress scales, respectively. A clinical sample reported means (and standard deviations) of 10.65 (9.3), 10.90 (8.12), and 21.1 (11.15) for the three measures.

SCORING Depression scores are the sum of the responses to items 3*, 5, 10*, 13, 16, 17*, 21, 24, 26*, 31*, 34, 37, 38*, and 42*. Anxiety scores are the sum of items 2*, 4*, 7, 9, 15, 19, 20*, 23, 25*, 28*, 30, 36, 40*, and 41*. Stress scores are the sum of 1, 6*, 8*, 11, 12*, 14, 18*, 22*, 27, 29, 32, 33, 35*, 39*. (Starred items are retained on the DASS-21.)

RELIABILITY From a clinical sample of 437 the DAS scales had excellent internal consistency: .96, .89, and .93, for depression, anxiety, and stress, respectively. Test-retest reliability coefficients over a 2-week period were .71, .79, and .81. A number of studies report similar evidence of reliability.

VALIDITY A number of studies also support the validity of the DASS, including concurrent validity, confirmatory factor analysis, and known-groups validity.

PRIMARY REFERENCES Lovibond, S. H., and Lovibond, P. F. (1995). *Manual for the Depression Anxiety and Stress Scales*. Sydney, Australia: Psychological Foundation of Australia. Lovibond, P. F., and Lovibond, S. H. (1995). The structure of negative emotional states: Comparison of the Depression Anxiety and Stress Scales (DASS) with the Beck Depression and Anxiety Inventories, *Behaviour Research and Therapy*, 33, 335–342.

AVAILABILITY The Psychological Foundation, Room 1017-A Mathews Building, University of New South Wales, Sydney NSW 2052, Australia. www.psy.unsw.edu.au/Groups/Dass/

Please read each statement and circle a number 0, 1, 2, or 3 which indicates how much the statement applied to you *over the past week*. There are no right or wrong answers. Do not spend too much time on any statement.

0 = Did not apply to me at all
1 = Applied to me to some degree, or some of the time
2 = Applied to me to a considerable degree, or a good part of the time
3 = Applied to me very much, or most of the time

1.	I found myself getting upset by quite trivial things.	0	1	2	3
2.	I was aware of dryness of my mouth.	0	1	2	3
3.	I couldn't seem to experience any positive feeling at all.	0	1	2	3
4.	I experienced breathing difficulty (e.g., excessively rapid breathing, breathlessness in the absence of physical exertion).	0	1	2	3
5.	I just couldn't seem to get going.	0	1	2	3
6.	I tended to overreact to situations.	0	1	2	3
7.	I had a feeling of shakiness (e.g., legs going to give way).	0	1	2	3
8.	I found it difficult to relax.	0	1	2	3
9.	I found myself in situations that made me so anxious I was most relieved when they ended.	0	1	2	3
10.	I felt that I had nothing to look forward to.	0	1	2	3
11.	I found myself getting upset rather easily.	0	1	2	3
12.	I felt that I was using a lot of nervous energy.	0	1	2	3
13.	I felt sad and depressed.	0	1	2	3
14.	I found myself getting impatient when I was delayed in any way (e.g., elevators, traffic lights, being kept waiting).	0	1	2	3
15.	I had a feeling of faintness.	0	1	2	3
16.	I felt that I had lost interest in just about everything.	0	1	2	3
17.	I felt I wasn't worth much as a person.	0	1	2	3
18.	I felt that I was rather touchy.	0	1	2	3
19.	I perspired noticeably (e.g., hands sweaty) in the absence of high temperatures or physical exertion.	0	1	2	3
20.	I felt scared without any good reason.	0	1	2	3
21.	I felt that life wasn't worthwhile.	0	1	2	3
22.	I found it hard to wind down.	0	1	2	3
23.	I had difficulty in swallowing.	0	1	2	3
24.	I couldn't seem to get any enjoyment out of the things I did.	0	1	2	3
25.	I was aware of the action of my heart in the absence of physical exertion (e.g., sense of heart rate increase, heart missing a beat).	0	1	2	3
26.	I felt downhearted and blue.	0	1	2	3
27.	I found that I was very irritable.	0	1	2	3
28.	I felt I was close to panic.	0	1	2	3
29.	I found it hard to calm down after something upset me.	0	1	2	3
30.	I feared that I would be "thrown" by some trivial but unfamiliar task.	0	1	2	3
31.	I was unable to become enthusiastic about anything.	0	1	2	3

32. I found it difficult to tolerate interruptions to what I was doing.	0	1	2	3
33. I was in a state of nervous tension.	0	1	2	3
34. I felt I was pretty worthless.	0	1	2	3
35. I was intolerant of anything that kept me from getting on with what I was doing.	0	1	2	3
36. I felt terrified.	0	1	2	3
37. I could see nothing in the future to be hopeful about.	0	1	2	3
38. I felt that life was meaningless.	0	1	2	3
39. I found myself getting agitated.	0	1	2	3
40. I was worried about situations in which I might panic and make a fool of myself.	0	1	2	3
41. I experienced trembling (e.g., in the hands).	0	1	2	3
42. I found it difficult to work up the initiative to do things.	0	1	2	3

Depression-Happiness Scale (DHS)

PURPOSE To measure depression and happiness.

AUTHORS Stephen Joseph and Christopher Alan Lewis

DESCRIPTION The DHS is a 25-item bipolar measure designed to measure depression and happiness. The DHS is a revision of an earlier 40-item scale. The DHS items represent a mix of affective, cognitive, and bodily experiences. The DHS defines happiness as more than the absence of depressive symptoms; happiness is viewed also as the presence of a variety of positive thoughts, feelings, and bodily experiences. A major strength of the DHS is its bipolar nature with lower scores on the scale suggesting the presence of depression and higher scores suggesting the presence of happiness. The DHS, therefore, can be used not only for research but as a guide to clinicians who not only attempt to alleviate depression but also attempt to promote happiness. Thus changes can be documented along the depression-happiness continuum.

NORMS The most recent study of the DHS involved 100 university students in England. The mean age of the students was 24.78 (SD = 7.11). The mean score on the DHS was 48.04 (SD = 10.75).

SCORING After reverse-scoring the negatively worded items (1, 2, 3, 5, 7, 10, 13, 14, 17, 19, 21, 24, and 25), the DHS is easily scored by summing all items. The total score can range from 0 to 75 with higher scores on the scale indicating a higher frequency of positive thoughts, feelings, and bodily experiences and a lower frequency of negative thoughts, feelings, and bodily experiences.

RELIABILITY The internal consistency of the DHS was very good with an alpha of .88. No data on stability were reported.

VALIDITY The DHS has very good concurrent validity correlating positively with the Oxford Happiness Inventory, negatively with the Beck Depression Inventory, and positively with the achievement subscale of the Dysfunctional Attitude Scale.

PRIMARY REFERENCE Joseph, S., and Lewis, C. A. (1998). The Depression-Happiness Scale: Reliability and validity of a bipolar self-report scale, *Journal of Clinical Psychology*, 54, 537–544.

AVAILABILITY Dr. Stephen Joseph, Department of Psychology, University of Warwick, Coventry, CV4 7AL, UK. Email Psychology@warwick.ac.uk.

A number of statements that people have used to describe how they feel are given below. Please read each one and circle the number which best describes how frequently you felt that way in the past seven days, including today. Some statements describe positive feelings and some describe negative feelings. You may have experienced both positive and negative feelings at different times during the past seven days.

0 = Never
1 = Rarely
2 = Sometimes
3 = Often

1.	I felt sad.	0	1	2	3
2.	I felt that I had failed as a person.	0	1	2	3
3.	I felt dissatisfied with my life.	0	1	2	3
4.	I felt mentally alert.	0	1	2	3
5.	I felt disappointed with myself.	0	1	2	3
6.	I felt cheerful.	0	1	2	3
7.	I felt that life wasn't worth living.	0	1	2	3
8.	I felt satisfied with my life.	0	1	2	3
9.	I felt healthy.	0	1	2	3
10.	I felt like crying.	0	1	2	3
11.	I felt that I had been successful.	0	1	2	3
12.	I felt happy.	0	1	2	3
13.	I felt that I couldn't make decisions.	0	1	2	3
14.	I felt unattractive.	0	1	2	3
15.	I felt optimistic about the future.	0	1	2	3
16.	I felt that life was rewarding.	0	1	2	3
17.	I felt cheerless.	0	1	2	3
18.	I felt that life had a purpose.	0	1	2	3
19.	I felt too tired to do anything.	0	1	2	3
20.	I felt pleased with the way I am.	0	1	2	3
21.	I felt lethargic.	0	1	2	3
22.	I found it easy to make decisions.	0	1	2	3
23.	I felt that life was enjoyable.	0	1	2	3
24.	I felt that life was meaningless.	0	1	2	3
25.	I felt run down.	0	1	2	3

Depressive Personality Disorder Inventory (DPDI)

PURPOSE To measure depressive personality disorder.

AUTHORS S. K. Huprich, J. Margrett, K. J. Barthelemy, and M. A. Fine

DESCRIPTION The DPDI is a 41-item instrument designed to assess cognitions that are representative of the *DSM-IV* conceptualization of the depressive personality disorder. The diagnosis of depressive personality disorder, though described in early editions of the *DSM*, was dropped from the *DSM-III* but reinstituted in *DSM-IV* due to its wide use in the literature and recent empirical support. There appear to be no other paper-and-pencil questionnaires to assess the symptoms of depressive personality disorder, so the DPDI is particularly important as a more or less objective way to assess the disorder both for research and practice purposes.

NORMS The DPDI was developed with 89 undergraduates from a private, midwestern, Catholic university, of whom 32 were male and 57 were female. The mean age was 19.09 years; 95.5% of respondents were Caucasian. The mean for all respondents was 127.11 (SD = 33.75); the mean for male was 124.76 (SD = 35.89); and the mean for females was 128.70 (SD = 32.40).

SCORING The DPDI is easily scored by summing the ratings on the 41 items after reverse-scoring items 1, 4, 6–14, 16, 19–26, 28, 29, 31, 37–40. Higher scores reflect endorsement of a greater number of characteristics reflective of depressive personality disorders. Scores can range from 41 to 287.

RELIABILITY The DPDI has excellent internal consistency, with an alpha of .94. No data on stability were provided.

VALIDITY The DPDI has very good concurrent validity as demonstrated by significant correlations between the DPDI and the total scores on the Automatic Thoughts Questionnaire—Revised and the Dysfunctional Attitude Scale. Subsequent research not reported in the original article shows a strong, significant positive correlation between the DPDI and scores on the semistructured interview, the Diagnostic Interview for Depressive Personality Disorder, thereby adding to the concurrent validity of the DPDI.

PRIMARY REFERENCE Huprich, S. K., Margrett, J., Barthelemy, K. J., and Fine, M. A. (1996). The Depressive Personality Disorder Inventory: An initial examination of its psychometric properties, *Journal of Clinical Psychology*, 52, 153–159.

AVAILABILITY Mark A. Fine, Ph.D., Human Development and Family Studies, University of North Carolina at Greensboro, P.O. Box 21670, Greensboro, NC 27402-6170/ Email: mafine@uncg.edu.

This questionnaire lists different attitudes or beliefs which people sometimes hold. Read each statement carefully and decide how much you agree or disagree with the statement. For each of the attitudes, write in the corresponding space the answer that best describes how you think. Be sure to choose only one answer for each attitude. Because people are different, there is no right answer or wrong answer to these statements. To decide whether a given attitude is typical of your way of looking at things, simply keep in mind what you are like most of the time.

> 1 = Totally agree
> 2 = Agree very much
> 3 = Agree slightly
> 4 = Neutral
> 5 = Disagree slightly
> 6 = Disagree very much
> 7 = Totally disagree

___ 1. My mood could frequently be described as gloomy.
___ 2. I feel good about myself.
___ 3. When I make a mistake, I do not come down too hard on myself.
___ 4. I frequently think that something is about to go wrong.
___ 5. I appreciate people who try their hardest, even if I do not think they did a good job.
___ 6. I frequently do not see how things will go my way.
___ 7. It is usually my fault if something goes wrong.
___ 8. More often than not, I am sad and unhappy.
___ 9. No matter what I do, it just does not seem to be good enough.
___ 10. If something goes wrong, it is usually my fault.
___ 11. People say I do not see the positive side very much.
___ 12. People are seldom really interested in helping others.
___ 13. Nothing is ever going to work out for me.
___ 14. I cannot do anything right.
___ 15. My contributions are worthwhile.
___ 16. I find myself thinking about my hardships frequently.
___ 17. People are generally good and well-intentioned.
___ 18. If you are patient, good things will eventually happen to you.
___ 19. I feel guilty much of the time.
___ 20. I feel that it is not right for me to have fun or be happy.
___ 21. I feel disappointed in myself.
___ 22. I have trouble completing the simplest of tasks.
___ 23. I worry constantly about the future.
___ 24. I try not to count on others, because they often do not come through.
___ 25. Trying hard is not worth it because things usually will not turn out the way you want them to.
___ 26. I blame myself when I do not succeed.
___ 27. I am a happy person.
___ 28. I feel like a failure.
___ 29. I have a much harder time than others when I do anything.

___ 30. I am not a worrier.
___ 31. I am often disappointed by others.
___ 32. Things will turn out all right if you just look on the bright side.
___ 33. I have no regrets for what I have done in the past.
___ 34. There is a lot of joy in my life.
___ 35. I am a worthwhile person.
___ 36. I am proud of my accomplishments.
___ 37. I dwell on problems.
___ 38. Even when others are to blame, I still tend to blame myself.
___ 39. I am inadequate.
___ 40. I punish myself when I do not succeed.
___ 41. I do not "mope around" very often.

Detox Fear Survey Schedule-27 (DFSS-27)

PURPOSE To measure detoxification fear.

AUTHORS Mary A. Gentile and Jesse B. Milby

DESCRIPTION The DFSS-27 is a 27-item instrument designed to measure the pathological fear of methadone detoxification, which has been termed detoxification fear. With evidence indicating that methadone treatment interrupts heroin use in criminal behavior, holds clients in treatment, and increases employment in other productive activities, it is clear that data on methadone use and nonuse can provide important information for practitioners in this arena. Prior research also shows that there is a range of difficulties with detoxification employing methadone with evidence suggesting that negative expectancy, anxiety, and fear all have a powerful effect on the withdrawal process. Clients with detoxification fear, therefore, have significantly longer time on methadone maintenance and fewer overall as well as successful detoxification attempts compared to their nonfear counterparts. Thus, ability to assess detoxification fear may be one of the most important ingredients affecting successful methadone maintenance treatment outcome. The DFSS-27 is a more sensitive version of an earlier 14-item measure.

NORMS Several samples were used in the development of the DFSS-27. The first two samples involved 226 subjects from two Veterans Administration methadone maintenance programs, of which almost all were male; 115 were Caucasian, 78 were African American, 23 were Hispanic, 2 were Asian, and 7 were other groups. The mean age of these samples were 40.1 and 44.0, with both samples having a duration of opioid addiction that ranged between 16 and 18 years. The next group involved 159 subjects from two private methadone maintenance programs, of which 83 were male and 76 were female; 144 were Caucasian, 9 were African American, and 6 were Hispanic. The mean ages of the samples from these two programs were 36.3 and 32.1 with a duration of opioid addiction of 11.7 and 11.3 years. A 6-year follow-up was also conducted on a total of 105 subjects for whom demographic data were not provided in the article. The duration of methadone maintenance for the four samples was 7.5 years, 10.5 years, 5.5 years, and 3.0 years, respectively. Although means and standard deviations were not available in the original article, the data showed that a score of 70 would be a useful cut-off score such that scores of 70 and over seem to indicate the greatest detoxification fears. The authors caution, however, that use of the DFSS-27 should be guided by clinical need.

SCORING The total score for the DFSS-27 is calculated by simply summing the item scores for a range of 0 to 101, with higher scores indicating greater fear of detoxification. Three factors also are available using the DFSS-27 with the most important factor by far being the fear of relapse containing most of the items on the DFSS-27; a second factor is fear of withdrawal symptoms such as leg cramps, backache, difficulty in sleeping, and irritability on lower doses. And a third factor comprising two items involves fear of AIDS.

RELIABILITY The subscales of the DFSS-27 have fair to excellent internal consistency, with alphas for the fear of relapse of .96, for fear of withdrawal of .74, and for fear of AIDS of .74. The DFSS-27 also has good stability with a two-week test-retest correlation of .77.

VALIDITY The validity of the DFSS-27 was established by comparing scores on the scale with an assessment by an examiner who assessed respondents' detoxification fear and who participated in a structured interview. Discriminant analysis of the DFSS-27 revealed that it correctly grouped cases 87% of the time using the structured interview as the external criterion for detoxification fear. The DFSS-27 also demonstrated good sensitivity (the percent of positive test results among subjects with criterion fear) and good specificity (the percent of negative test results among those who do not have the criterion fear). These data generated the cut-off score described above in Norms. The DFSS-27 shows a lack of significant respondent bias for producing socially desirable responses.

PRIMARY REFERENCE Gentile, M. A., and Milby, J. B. (1992). Methadone maintenance detoxification fear: A study of its components, *Journal of Clinical Psychology*, 48, 797–807.

AVAILABILITY The authors state the scale is in the public domain. Copies of the scale can be obtained from Dr. Jesse B. Milby, Director of the Consortium for Substance Abuse Research and Training Program, University of Alabama, Birmingham, AL 35294, or may be copied from this volume.

The items in this questionnaire refer to situations and experiences that may cause you fear or other unpleasant feelings. Read each item and decide how much you are disturbed by it. Circle the number next to each item according to the following scale categories:

0 = If you are not disturbed at all
1 = If you are a little disturbed
2 = If you are more disturbed
3 = If you are much more disturbed
4 = If you are very much disturbed

1.	Spending evening alone during detoxification.	0	1	2	3	4
2.	Going to jail.	0	1	2	3	4
3.	Feeling backache.	0	1	2	3	4
4.	Loss of everything accomplished on methadone if I detoxify.	0	1	2	3	4
5.	Irritability on lower doses.	0	1	2	3	4
6.	Feeling leg cramps.	0	1	2	3	4
7.	Will resort to drugs off methadone.	0	1	2	3	4
8.	Lack ability to cope with life off drugs.	0	1	2	3	4
9.	Difficulty sleeping.	0	1	2	3	4
10.	Stress of living will lead me back to drugs.	0	1	2	3	4
11.	Wonder if I can function in society without chemicals.	0	1	2	3	4
12.	Having "goose bumps."	0	1	2	3	4
13.	Unable to hold down a decent job.	0	1	2	3	4
14.	Scared of becoming readdicted.	0	1	2	3	4
15.	Unsure I can say no to people on the street.	0	1	2	3	4
16.	Something will pull me down and get me started on drugs again.	0	1	2	3	4
17.	Feeling unsteady off drugs.	0	1	2	3	4
18.	Concerned that I may have already been exposed to the AIDS virus.	0	1	2	3	4
19.	After I detoxify I may become readdicted to narcotics.	0	1	2	3	4
20.	May be unable to do my job without drugs.	0	1	2	3	4
21.	Unsure if I can cope with my life straight.	0	1	2	3	4
22.	Scared of going back to heroin.	0	1	2	3	4
23.	Feeling bad off drugs will lead me to old friends to get drugs.	0	1	2	3	4
24.	Afraid to fall back to where I was before I began methadone.	0	1	2	3	4
25.	Worried about getting the AIDS virus if I detoxify.	0	1	2	3	4
26.	Uncertainty of making it without drugs.	0	1	2	3	4
27.	Being told at the nursing station you have almost completed detox.	0	1	2	3	4

Dietary Inventory of Eating Temptations (DIET)

PURPOSE To measure competence in situations related to weight control.

AUTHORS David G. Schlundt and Rose T. Zimering

DESCRIPTION The DIET is a 30-item instrument designed to measure behavioral competence in six types of situations related to weight control: overeating (items 6, 9, 10, 12, 14), negative emotional eating (items 24, 25, 28–30), exercise (items 2, 11, 13, 17, 19), resisting temptation (items 3, 15, 16, 20, 26), positive social eating (items 1, 18, 21, 22, 27), and food choice (items 4, 5, 7, 8, 23). The DIET was developed by using statements generated from the work of experienced weight control clinicians regarding commonly reported problem situations. An initial total of 50 situations was grouped by expert judges into the six categories described above. Subsequent research resulted in the current 30-item version. The DIET is a useful measure for assessing behavioral competency in specific energy balance situations and prescribing specific therapeutic activities as competency deficits are found.

NORMS The DIET was studied with 361 respondents recruited from a variety of sources including college students, nurses, subjects in a weight control program, and subjects in a high blood pressure program. The total number of subjects was 193 normal weight and 168 overweight respondents. The mean DIET total score for normal weight subjects was 56.02 (SD = 16.2) and for overweight subjects was 51.16 (SD = 18.0).

SCORING The DIET is scored simply by using the raw data supplied by each respondent who is asked to read each situation and rate the percentage of time he or she would behave as described. That percentage figure is then the score on that item. Scores for each of the six categories are the mean of the percentages for the five items in that category, and the total score is simply the mean for all item percentages.

RELIABILITY The DIET has good to excellent internal consistency, with an alpha for the total score of .93 and alphas for the subscales ranging from .68 to .79. Stability of the DIET is also excellent, with one-week test-retest reliability of .96 for the total scores and subscale coefficients ranging from .81 to .92.

VALIDITY The DIET has very good known-groups validity, significantly distinguishing between normal weight and overweight respondents on the total score and the exercise, overeating, and negative emotional eating subscales. A type of construct validity also was demonstrated for respondents in the weight control program by relating DIET scores to actual behavioral patterns in predicted ways as measured by self-monitoring.

PRIMARY REFERENCE Schlundt, D. G., and Zimering, R. T. (1988). The Dieter's Inventory of Eating Temptations: A measure of weight control competence, *Addictive Behaviors*, 13, 151–164.

AVAILABILITY Dr. David Schlundt, 323 Wilson Hall, Vanderbilt University, Nashville, TN 37274. Email: david.g.schlundt@vanderbilt.edu.

Each item in this questionnaire describes a situation and a behavior that promotes weight loss or weight control. Imagine that you are in the situation described and rate the percent of the time you would behave in the way described. If you would always act in the way described then give a rating of 100%. If you would never act that way give a rating of 0%. If you would sometimes act that way then circle the number at the point on the scale that shows how often you would act as described. If you feel that you never get into a situation like the one described (it does not apply to you), then rate how often you engage in the kind of behavior described in general.

1. You're having dinner with your family and your favorite meal has been prepared. You finish the first helping and someone says, "Why don't you have some more?" What percent of the time would you turn down a second helping?

    0 — 10 — 20 — 30 — 40 — 50 — 60 — 70 — 80 — 90 — 100

2. You would like to exercise every day but it is hard to find the time because of your family and work obligations. What percent of the time would you set aside a daily time for exercise?

    0 — 10 — 20 — 30 — 40 — 50 — 60 — 70 — 80 — 90 — 100

3. You like to eat high calorie snack food (e.g., cookies, potato chips, crackers, cokes, beer, cake) while watching television. What percent of the time would you watch TV without eating a high calorie snack?

    0 — 10 — 20 — 30 — 40 — 50 — 60 — 70 — 80 — 90 — 100

4. When you eat in a good restaurant, you love to order high calorie foods. What percent of the time would you order a low calorie meal?

    0 — 10 — 20 — 30 — 40 — 50 — 60 — 70 — 80 — 90 — 100

5. When planning meals, you tend to choose high calorie foods. What percent of the time would you plan low calorie meals?

    0 — 10 — 20 — 30 — 40 — 50 — 60 — 70 — 80 — 90 — 100

6. You are at a party and there is a lot of fattening food. You have already eaten more than you should and you are tempted to continue eating. What percent of the time would you stop with what you have already eaten?

    0 — 10 — 20 — 30 — 40 — 50 — 60 — 70 — 80 — 90 — 100

7. You like to flavor your vegetables with butter, margarine, ham, or bacon fat. What percent of the time would you choose a low calorie method of seasoning?

    0 — 10 — 20 — 30 — 40 — 50 — 60 — 70 — 80 — 90 — 100

8. You often prepare many of your foods by frying. What percent of the time would your prepare your food in a way that is less fattening?

    0 — 10 — 20 — 30 — 40 — 50 — 60 — 70 — 80 — 90 — 100

9. You allow yourself a snack in the evening, but you find yourself eating more than your diet allows. What percent of the time would you reduce the size of your snack?

    0 — 10 — 20 — 30 — 40 — 50 — 60 — 70 — 80 — 90 — 100

10. Instead of putting foods away after finishing a meal, you find yourself eating the left-overs. What percent of the time would you put the food away without eating any?

$$0 — 10 — 20 — 30 — 40 — 50 — 60 — 70 — 80 — 90 — 100$$

11. You are asked by another person to go for a walk but you feel tired and kind of low. What percent of the time would you overcome these feelings and say "yes" to the walk?

$$0 — 10 — 20 — 30 — 40 — 50 — 60 — 70 — 80 — 90 — 100$$

12. You often overeat at supper because you are tired and hungry when you get home. What percent of the time would you not overeat at supper?

$$0 — 10 — 20 — 30 — 40 — 50 — 60 — 70 — 80 — 90 — 100$$

13. When you have errands to run that are only a couple of blocks away you usually drive the car. What percent of the time would you walk on an errand when it only involves a couple of blocks?

$$0 — 10 — 20 — 30 — 40 — 50 — 60 — 70 — 80 — 90 — 100$$

14. You are invited to someone's house for dinner and your host is an excellent cook. You often overeat because the food tastes so good. What percent of the time would you not overeat as a dinner guest?

$$0 — 10 — 20 — 30 — 40 — 50 — 60 — 70 — 80 — 90 — 100$$

15. You like to have something sweet to eat on your coffee break. What percent of the time would you only have coffee?

$$0 — 10 — 20 — 30 — 40 — 50 — 60 — 70 — 80 — 90 — 100$$

16. When you cook a meal you snack on the food. What percent of the time would you wait until the meal is prepared to eat?

$$0 — 10 — 20 — 30 — 40 — 50 — 60 — 70 — 80 — 90 — 100$$

17. You planned to exercise after work today but you feel tired and hungry when the time arrives. What percent of the time would you exercise anyway?

$$0 — 10 — 20 — 30 — 40 — 50 — 60 — 70 — 80 — 90 — 100$$

18. There is a party at work for a co-worker and someone offers you a piece of cake. What percent of the time would you turn it down?

$$0 — 10 — 20 — 30 — 40 — 50 — 60 — 70 — 80 — 90 — 100$$

19. You would like to climb the stairs instead of taking the elevator. What percent of the time would you take the stairs to go one or two flights?

$$0 — 10 — 20 — 30 — 40 — 50 — 60 — 70 — 80 — 90 — 100$$

20. You are happy and feeling good today. You are tempted to treat yourself by stopping for ice cream. What percent of the time would you find some other way to be nice to yourself?

$$0 — 10 — 20 — 30 — 40 — 50 — 60 — 70 — 80 — 90 — 100$$

21. You are at a friend's house and your friend offers you a delicious looking pastry. What percent of the time would you refuse this offer?

$$0 — 10 — 20 — 30 — 40 — 50 — 60 — 70 — 80 — 90 — 100$$

22. You feel like celebrating. You are going out with friends to a good restaurant. What percent of the time would you celebrate without overeating?

$$0 - 10 - 20 - 30 - 40 - 50 - 60 - 70 - 80 - 90 - 100$$

23. You finished your meal and you still feel hungry. There is cake and fruit available. What percent of the time would you choose the fruit?

$$0 - 10 - 20 - 30 - 40 - 50 - 60 - 70 - 80 - 90 - 100$$

24. You are at home feeling lonely, blue, and bored. You are craving something to eat. What percent of the time would you find another way of coping with these feelings besides eating?

$$0 - 10 - 20 - 30 - 40 - 50 - 60 - 70 - 80 - 90 - 100$$

25. Today you did something to hurt your ankle. You want to get something to eat to make yourself feel better. What percent of the time would you find some other way to take your mind off your mishap?

$$0 - 10 - 20 - 30 - 40 - 50 - 60 - 70 - 80 - 90 - 100$$

26. When you spend time alone at home you are tempted to snack. You are spending an evening alone. What percent of the time would you resist the urge to snack?

$$0 - 10 - 20 - 30 - 40 - 50 - 60 - 70 - 80 - 90 - 100$$

27. You are out with a friend at lunch time and your friend suggests that you stop and get some ice cream. What percent of the time would you resist the temptation?

$$0 - 10 - 20 - 30 - 40 - 50 - 60 - 70 - 80 - 90 - 100$$

28. You just had an upsetting argument with a family member. You are standing in front of the refrigerator and you feel like eating everything in sight. What percent of the time would you find some other way to make yourself feel better?

$$0 - 10 - 20 - 30 - 40 - 50 - 60 - 70 - 80 - 90 - 100$$

29. You are having a hard day at work and you are anxious and upset. You feel like getting a candy bar. What percent of the time would you find a more constructive way to calm down and cope with your feelings?

$$0 - 10 - 20 - 30 - 40 - 50 - 60 - 70 - 80 - 90 - 100$$

30. You just had an argument with your (husband, wife, boyfriend, girlfriend). You are upset, angry, and you feel like eating something. What percent of the time would you talk the situation over with someone or go for a walk instead of eating?

$$0 - 10 - 20 - 30 - 40 - 50 - 60 - 70 - 80 - 90 - 100$$

Dissociative Experiences Scale (DES)

PURPOSE To measure dissociation.

AUTHORS Eve M. Bernstein and Frank W. Putman

DESCRIPTION The DES is a 28-item instrument designed to measure dissociation, the lack of "normal" integration of thoughts, experiences, and feelings into the stream of consciousness and memory. Dissociation is viewed not only as a problem in and of itself, but as related to a number of other psychiatric disorders. The DES is based on the assumption that dissociation lies along a continuum from minor dissociations of everyday life to major psychopathology. The DES was developed by using data from interviews with people meeting *DSM-III* criteria for dissociative disorders and consultations with clinical experts. Items identifying dissociation of moods and impulses were excluded so that experiences of dissociation would not be confused with alternations in mood and impulse related to affective disorders. The DES is viewed as an excellent research and clinical measure, perhaps the only one available to examine dissociation.

NORMS The DES was studied originally with 31 college students (18 to 22 years), 34 "normal" adults, 14 alcoholics, 24 phobic clients, 29 agoraphobics, 10 posttraumatic stress disorder clients, 20 schizophrenics, and 20 clients with multiple personality disorder. The median scores for the eight groups were: "normals"—4.38, alcoholics—4.72, phobics—6.04, agoraphobics—7.41, adolescents—14.11, schizophrenics—20.63, PTSD—31.25, and multiple personality disorder—57.06. Most of these differences were statistically significant from each other.

SCORING The DES originally (as with the median scores above) was scored by measuring the subject's slash mark to the nearest 5mm from the left-hand anchor point of each 100mm line. The overall score reflected in the norms above was simply a sum of the 28 item scores. The newer scale reprinted here is scored by simply adding up the circled figures (percentages) for each item for a total score. Higher scores equal greater dissociation.

RELIABILITY The DES has very good split-half reliability, with coefficients for the eight groups ranging from .71 to .96, and with six of these being .90 or above. The DES also has very good stability, with a four- to eight-week test-retest reliability coefficient of .84.

VALIDITY The DES has fairly good construct validity, not correlating with some theoretically unrelated variables (such as social class and sex), and with significant correlations (using Kendall's coefficient of concordance) to show a high degree of agreement among item scores in the differentiation of diagnostic groups. The DES also yielded a predicted continuum of scores with steady progression from "normal" subjects to multiple personality disorder subjects.

PRIMARY REFERENCE Bernstein, E. M., and Putman, F. W. (1986). Development, reliability, and validity of a dissociation scale, *Journal of Nervous and Mental Disease*, 174, 727–735.

AVAILABILITY May be copied from this volume.

This questionnaire consists of twenty-eight questions about experiences that you may have in your daily life. We are interested in how often you have these experiences. It is important, however, that you answers show how often these experiences happen to you when you *are not* under the influence of alcohol or drugs.

To answer the questions, please determine to what degree the experience described in the question applies to you and circle the number to show what percentage of the time you have the experience.

1. Some people have the experience of driving or riding in a car or bus or subway and suddenly realizing that they don't remember what has happened during all or part of the trip. Circle a number to show what percentage of the time this happens to you.

   0%   10   20   30   40   50   60   70   80   90   100%

2. Some people find that sometimes they are listening to someone talk and they suddenly realize that they did not hear part or all of what was said. Circle a number to show what percentage of the time this happens to you.

   0%   10   20   30   40   50   60   70   80   90   100%

3. Some people have the experience of finding themselves in a place and having no idea how they got there. Circle a number to show what percentage of the time this happens to you.

   0%   10   20   30   40   50   60   70   80   90   100%

4. Some people have the experience of finding themselves dressed in clothes that they don't remember putting on. Circle a number to show what percentage of the time this happens to you.

   0%   10   20   30   40   50   60   70   80   90   100%

5. Some people have the experience of finding new things among their belongings that they do not remember buying. Circle a number to show what percentage of the time this happens to you.

   0%   10   20   30   40   50   60   70   80   90   100%

6. Some people sometimes find that they are approached by people that they do not know who call them by another name or insist that they have met them before. Circle a number to show what percentage of the time this happens to you.

   0%   10   20   30   40   50   60   70   80   90   100%

7. Some people sometimes have the experience of feeling as though they are standing next to themselves or watching themselves do something and they actually see themselves as if they were looking at another person. Circle a number to show what percentage of the time this happens to you.

   0%   10   20   30   40   50   60   70   80   90   100%

8. Some people are told that they sometimes do not recognize friends or family members. Circle a number to show what percentage of the time this happens to you.

   0%   10   20   30   40   50   60   70   80   90   100%

9. Some people find that they have no memory for some important events in their lives (for example, a wedding or graduation). Circle a number to show what percentage of the time this happens to you.

   0%   10   20   30   40   50   60   70   80   90   100%

10. Some people have the experience of being accused of lying when they do not think that they have lied. Circle a number to show what percentage of the time this happens to you.

   0%   10   20   30   40   50   60   70   80   90   100%

11. Some people have the experience of looking in a mirror and not recognizing themselves. Circle a number to show what percentage of the time this happens to you.

   0%   10   20   30   40   50   60   70   80   90   100%

12. Some people have the experience of feeling that other people, objects, and the world around them are not real. Circle a number to show what percentage of the time this happens to you.

   0%   10   20   30   40   50   60   70   80   90   100%

13. Some people have the experience of feeling that their body does not seem to belong to them. Circle a number to show what percentage of the time this happens to you.

   0%   10   20   30   40   50   60   70   80   90   100%

14. Some people have the experience of sometimes remembering a past event so vividly that they feel as if they were reliving that event. Circle a number to show what percentage of the time this happens to you.

   0%   10   20   30   40   50   60   70   80   90   100%

15. Some people have the experience of not being sure whether things that they remember happening really did happen or whether they just dreamed them. Circle a number to show what percentage of the time this happens to you.

   0%   10   20   30   40   50   60   70   80   90   100%

16. Some people have the experience of being in a familiar place but finding it strange and unfamiliar. Circle a number to show what percentage of the time this happens to you.

   0%   10   20   30   40   50   60   70   80   90   100%

17. Some people find that when they are watching television or a movie they become so absorbed in the story that they are unaware of other events happening around them. Circle a number to show what percentage of the time this happens to you.

   0%   10   20   30   40   50   60   70   80   90   100%

18. Some people find that they become so involved in a fantasy or daydream that it feels as though it were really happening to them. Circle a number to show what percentage of the time this happens to you.

   0%   10   20   30   40   50   60   70   80   90   100%

19. Some people find that they sometimes are able to ignore pain. Circle a number to show what percentage of the time this happens to you.

   0%   10   20   30   40   50   60   70   80   90   100%

20. Some people find that they sometimes sit staring off into space, thinking of nothing, and are not aware of the passage of time. Circle a number to show what percentage of the time this happens to you.

    0%   10   20   30   40   50   60   70   80   90   100%

21. Some people sometimes find that when they are alone they talk out loud to themselves. Circle a number to show what percentage of the time this happens to you.

    0%   10   20   30   40   50   60   70   80   90   100%

22. Some people find that in one situation they may act so differently compared with another situation that they feel almost as if they were two different people. Circle a number to show what percentage of the time this happens to you.

    0%   10   20   30   40   50   60   70   80   90   100%

23. Some people sometimes find that in certain situations they are able to do things with amazing ease and spontaneity that would usually be difficult for them (for example, sports, work, social situations, etc.). Circle a number to show what percentage of the time this happens to you.

    0%   10   20   30   40   50   60   70   80   90   100%

24. Some people sometimes find that they cannot remember whether they have done something or have just thought about doing that (for example, not knowing whether they have just mailed a letter or have just thought about mailing it). Circle a number to show what percentage of the time this happens to you.

    0%   10   20   30   40   50   60   70   80   90   100%

25. Some people find evidence that they have done things that they do not remember doing. Circle a number to show what percentage of the time this happens to you.

    0%   10   20   30   40   50   60   70   80   90   100%

26. Some people sometimes find writings, drawings, or notes among their belongings that they must have done but cannot remember doing. Circle a number to show what percentage of the time this happens to you.

    0%   10   20   30   40   50   60   70   80   90   100%

27. Some people sometimes find that they hear voices inside their head that tell them to do things or comment on things that they are doing. Circle a number to show what percentage of the time this happens to you.

    0%   10   20   30   40   50   60   70   80   90   100%

28. Some people sometimes feel as if they are looking at the world through a fog so that people and objects appear far away or unclear. Circle a number to show what percentage of the time this happens to you.

    0%   10   20   30   40   50   60   70   80   90   100%

Drinking Context Scale (DCS)

PURPOSE To measure context for excessive drinking.

AUTHOR Thomas O'Hare

DESCRIPTION The DCS is a 9-item scale designed to assess the relationship between excessive alcohol use in youths and contexts that might encourage that drinking. The DCS was developed out of concern that few, if any, measures were available to assess, in an integrated way, psychological, socioemotional, and situational dimensions of drinking behavior among college students. Although early research on the DCS used more items than described here, the most recent research used confirmatory factor analysis to confirm the original three factors, but with fewer items, leading to greater ease in use of the DCS. The three factors are: Convivial drinking (C; items 1–3); Negative coping (NC; items 4–6); and Intimate drinking (I; items 6–9).

NORMS The most recent study of the DCS involved a sample of 505 undergraduate students at a New England university. All respondents had been adjudicated at the university for underage drinking or use of illicit drugs. The mean age was 18.7 (SD = 1.29), 62.2% were male, most (77%) were in their first undergraduate year, with almost all (95.4%) living on campus. Most were middle or upper middle class, and 93.3% were white, with the remainder distributed across several ethnic groups. Mean scores were as follows: C = 9.23 (SD = 3.42); NC = 4.30 (SD = 2.09); and I = 5.42 (SD = 2.42).

SCORING The DCS is easily scored by summing the item scores within each subscale for the subscale score for a range of 3 to 15 for each subscale. Higher scores suggest a greater likelihood of drinking excessively.

RELIABILITY The DCS has very good internal consistency with alphas of .82, .85, and .81 for the C, NC, and I, respectively. Data on stability were not available.

VALIDITY The DCS has excellent concurrent validity with significant associations with a measure of community problems and the Alcohol Use Disorders Identification Test for all three DCS subscales, and a significant effect of all three subscales on the Socioemotional subscale of the College Alcohol Problem Scale.

PRIMARY REFERENCE O'Hare, T. (2001). The Drinking Context Scale: A confirmatory factor analysis. *Journal of Substance Abuse Treatment*, 20, 129–136. Instrument reproduced with permission of Dr. O'Hare.

AVAILABILITY Email Dr. O'Hare at oharet@bc.edu.

Based on your *personal experience*, how would you **RATE THE CHANCES** that you might find yourself *drinking excessively* in the *following circumstances*? (Use the following scale to rate your responses.)

Extremely high	High	Moderate	Low	Extremely low
5	4	3	2	1

Convivial drinking

1	When I'm at a party, similar other get-together	5	4	3	2	1
2	When I'm at a concert, or other public event	5	4	3	2	1
3	When I'm celebrating something important to me	5	4	3	2	1

Negative coping

4	When I've had a fight with someone close to me	5	4	3	2	1
5	When I'm feeling sad, depressed or discouraged	5	4	3	2	1
6	When I'm angry with myself or someone else	5	4	3	2	1

Intimate drinking

7	When I'm with my lover	5	4	3	2	1
8	When I'm on a date	5	4	3	2	1
9	Before having sex	5	4	3	2	1

PURPOSE To measure attitudes of deviant drivers

AUTHORS David L. Wiesenthal, Dwight Hennessy, and Patrick M. Gibson

DESCRIPTION The DVQ is a 15-item questionnaire designed to assess drivers' use of vengeance when faced with common driving situations. The DVQ was developed out of concern for increasing stress among drivers due to increasing traffic congestion. The increase in driver stress is seen as related to an increase in roadway aggression. Vengeance was conceptualized as a response to a perceived threat to one's safety and/or honor. Since there were no available measures of aggressive reactions of drivers in stressful situations, a series of studies by the authors involving factor analyses of the original 37 items led to the current 15 items involving a single factor, called "Driver Vengeance." The DVQ is seen as useful for identifying situations among drivers that could lead to aggressive responses, and possibly as a marker for changes brought about in aggressive drivers in a therapeutic program.

NORMS The DVQ was studied with 178 female and 74 male college students, with an average age of 23; 179 female and 90 male college students in introductory psychology classes, with an average age of 27; 74 male inmates at a correctional institute, with an average age of 33; and a sample of 123 female and 70 males from a university and business community with an average age of 26; a follow-up psychometric study on the revised questionnaire included 28 females and 28 males from a university and general metropolitan area. Norms were reported on the final scale only for the third of the four samples, analyzed by age and driving experience: age 19, mean score was 57.65; age 20/21, mean score was 57.12; age 22–32 years, mean was 52.50; and >33, the mean score was 47.00 with significant differences between the oldest group and the two youngest. Scores by driving experience also revealed a significant difference between the scores of the most experienced group (>9 years), with all other less experienced groups.

SCORING Each item of the DVQ consists of a common driving response followed by four options for reactions, ranked from most aggressive response to least aggressive. The most aggressive responses are given a value of four and the least aggressive a value of one. Thus, the total score can range from a high of 60 (most aggressive) to a low of 15 (least aggressive). The DVQ also has an "other" category response for each item, allowing a write-in response. That response is then evaluated as to its level of aggressiveness compared to the four standard responses and rated accordingly.

RELIABILITY The DVQ has fair internal consistency with an alpha of .83. Test-retest reliability data were not available.

VALIDITY The DVQ has good concurrent validity, correlating significantly with the Violent Driving Behavior Questionnaire and with the State Driver Aggression Questionnaire, but only when the questions on the latter instrument refer to situations of high traffic congestion. The DVQ total score also was correlated with impulsivity, habitual criminality, escapism, several scales of the MMPI, and the Marlowe-Crowne Social Desirability Scale (suggesting a certain degree of social desirability response bias).

PRIMARY REFERENCE Wiesenthal, D. L., et al. (2000). The driving vengeance question-naire (DVQ): The development of a scale to measure deviant drivers' attitudes. *Violence and Victims*, 15, 115–136. Instrument reproduced with permission of Dr. David Wiesenthal.

AVAILABILITY May be copied from this volume.

Age:___ Sex:___ Years of driving experience:___

The following are some common situations encountered by drivers. Please indicate the response that you would most likely make in that situation.

1. After stopping at a STOP sign, a motorist fails to yield the right of way to you when it is your turn to proceed through the intersection. You would:
   a) Pull out quickly to block their way.
   b) Give the driver an obscene gesture (eg., the finger).
   c) Honk your horn.
   d) Do nothing.
   e) Other:_____ .

2. While driving on an expressway a vehicle cuts in front of you, forcing you to apply the brakes. You would:
   a) Cut in front of their vehicle forcing them to apply the brakes.
   b) Give the driver an obscene gesture.
   c) Honk your horn.
   d) Do nothing.
   e) Other:_____ .

3. A driver passes you and makes an obscene gesture at you. You would:
   a) Force the other vehicle off the road.
   b) Give the driver an obscene gesture.
   c) Honk your horn.
   d) Do nothing.
   e) Other:_____ .

4. Immediately after passing you, the driver slows down or applies his brakes. You would:
   a) Pull in front of their vehicle and slow down.
   b) Give the driver an obscene gesture.
   c) Honk your horn.
   d) Do nothing.
   e) Other:_____ .

5. While driving at night, the vehicle immediately behind you has its high beam headlights on. You would:
   a) Let the vehicle pass and turn on your high beams.
   b) Apply your brakes.
   c) Honk your horn.
   d) Do nothing.
   e) Other:_____ .

6. A driver persistently honks at you. You would:
   a) Force the other vehicle off the road.
   b) Give the driver an obscene gesture.
   c) Honk your horn.
   d) Do nothing.
   e) Other:_____ .

7. A driver gets out of his vehicle at a traffic signal and approaches you in a threatening manner. You would:
   a) Get out of your vehicle and confront him/her.
   b) Give the driver an obscene gesture.

c) Honk your horn.

d) Drive away.

e) Other:_____ .

8. A vehicle bypasses a queue of vehicles and remains in the merge lane until the lane ends, and then tries to cut in front of your vehicle. You would:

a) Block the vehicle so that it can't get in.

b) Give the driver an obscene gesture.

c) Honk your horn.

d) Do nothing.

e) Other:_____ .

9. A slowly moving vehicle is occupying the left lane on an expressway, slowing traffic. You would:

a) Tailgate the vehicle until it moves.

b) Give the driver an obscene gesture.

c) Honk your horn.

d) Do nothing.

e) Other:_____ .

10. The driver in a vehicle directly in front of yours frequently applies the brakes, although no vehicle or pedestrians is in front of it. You would:

a) Pass the vehicle and apply your brakes.

b) Give the driver an obscene gesture.

c) Honk your horn.

d) Do nothing.

e) Other:_____ .

11. Garbage thrown from another vehicle hits your vehicle. You would:

a) Throw garbage at the offending vehicle.

b) Give the driver an obscene gesture.

c) Honk your horn.

d) Do nothing.

e) Other:_____ .

12. Another driver takes a parking space that you have been waiting for. You would:

a) Get out of your vehicle and tell the driver to move his vehicle.

b) Give the driver an obscene gesture.

c) Honk your horn.

d) Do nothing.

e) Other:_____ .

13. The car in front of you doesn't proceed on an advanced green signal. You would:

a) Bump into the other car.

b) Give the driver an obscene gesture.

c) Honk your horn.

d) Do nothing.

e) Other:_____ .

14. You want to turn right at a red light and the car in front of you, also making a right turn, does not proceed when the way is clear. You would:

a) Bump into the other car.

b) Give the driver an obscene gesture.

c) Honk your horn.

d) Do nothing.

e) Other:_____ .

15. A vehicle stops on the roadway to pick up, or let out, a passenger causing a traffic delay. You would:
    a) Stop and tell the driver off.
    b) Give the driver an obscene gesture.
    c) Honk your horn.
    d) Do nothing.
    e) Other:_____ .

Drug Abuse Screening Test (DAST)

PURPOSE To measure drug use and abuse.

AUTHOR Harvey A. Skinner

DESCRIPTION The DAST is a 20-item instrument that yields a quantitative index of the range of problems associated with drug abuse. The items on the DAST parallel items on the Michigan Alcoholism Screening Test, a widely used assessment device for alcohol use and abuse. Factor analysis reveals the DAST to be measuring a dominant single dimension of problems related to drug abuse. The DAST also has low correlations with measures of response bias such as social desirability. The DAST is a convenient measure for assessing the extent of problems related to drug misuse, with a total score providing a quantitative index of problem severity. The 20 items reprinted here are almost perfectly correlated with the 28-item DAST and therefore are feasible to be used as a short-form scale. The DAST also may be shortened by using items 1, 3, 5, 6, 7, 8, 11, 15, 17, and 18 only.

NORMS The DAST was originally studied with a sample of 223 people (72% male, 28% female) who had voluntarily sought help at an addiction research foundation. Of the total sample, 58.6% were referred for alcohol problems, 25.4% for drug problems, and 16.0% for both alcohol and drug problems. The mean age of the sample was 32.47 (SD = 11.17); 39.5% of the respondents were single, 18.4% were married, and 28.5% were divorced or separated. At the time of the study 17.2% of the sample had completed high school, and 47.6% of the sample were unemployed. For the group with alcohol problems only, the mean score was 14.5. For the group with drug and alcohol problems the mean score was 15.2. For the group with drug problems only, the mean score was 17.8. The original article also lists item means for each of the 28 items.

SCORING The DAST total score is computed by summing all items that are endorsed in the direction of increased drug use problems, with items 4, 5, and 7 being scored in the "no" or false direction. The total score on the DAST can range from 0 to 28, with higher scores indicating a greater degree of problems with drug abuse.

RELIABILITY The DAST has excellent internal consistency, with an alpha of .92. No data on stability were presented.

VALIDITY The DAST has good discriminant validity, with the total score significantly differentiating the group with primarily alcohol-related problems from the two groups with drug problems. The DAST also has good concurrent validity, with significant correlations between the DAST total score and all psychopathology items on the Basic Personality Inventory for the total sample and significant correlations on six out of eight of the psychopathology items for the sample excluding subjects with only alcohol problems. The total DAST score was also significantly correlated with the frequency of drug use in past months for seven types of drugs for the total sample and for two types of drugs for the sample excluding subjects with only alcohol problems.

PRIMARY REFERENCE Skinner, H. A. (1983). The Drug Abuse Screening Test, *Journal of Addictive Behaviors*, 7, 363–371.

AVAILABILITY For information on the DAST, contact Dr. Harvey Skinner, Department of Public Health Sciences, University of Toronto, Toronto, Ontario, Canada, M5S 1A8. May be copied from this volume.

The following questions concern information about your potential involvement with drugs *not including alcoholic beverages* during the past 12 months. Carefully read each statement and decide if your answer is "Yes" or "No." Then, circle the appropriate response beside the question.

In the statements "drug abuse" refers to (1) the use of prescribed or over-the-counter drugs in excess of the directions and (2) any nonmedical use of drugs. The various classes of drugs may include: cannabis (e.g., marijuana, hash), solvents, tranquilizers (e.g., Valium), barbiturates, cocaine, stimulants (e.g., speed), hallucinogens (e.g., LSD), or narcotics (e.g., heroin). Remember that the questions *do not* include alcoholic beverages.

Please answer every question. If you have difficulty with a statement, then choose the response that is mostly right. *These questions refer to the past 12 months.*

1.	Have you used drugs other than those required for medical reasons?	Yes	No
2.	Have you abused prescription drugs?	Yes	No
3.	Do you abuse more than one drug at a time?	Yes	No
4.	Can you get through the week without using drugs?	Yes	No
5.	Are you always able to stop using drugs when you want to?	Yes	No
6.	Have you had "blackouts" or "flashbacks" as a result of drug use?	Yes	No
7.	Do you ever feel bad or guilty about your drug use?	Yes	No
8.	Does your spouse (or parents) ever complain about your involvement with drugs?	Yes	No
9.	Has drug abuse created problems between you and your spouse or your parents?	Yes	No
10.	Have you lost friends because of your use of drugs?	Yes	No
11.	Have you neglected your family because of your use of drugs?	Yes	No
12.	Have you been in trouble at work because of drug abuse?	Yes	No
13.	Have you lost a job because of drug abuse?	Yes	No
14.	Have you gotten into fights when under the influence of drugs?	Yes	No
15.	Have you engaged in illegal activities in order to obtain drugs?	Yes	No
16.	Have you been arrested for possession of illegal drugs?	Yes	No
17.	Have you ever experienced withdrawal symptoms (felt sick) when you stopped taking drugs?	Yes	No
18.	Have you had medical problems as a result of your drug use (e.g., memory loss, hepatitis, convulsions, bleeding, etc.)?	Yes	No
19.	Have you gone to anyone for help for a drug problem?	Yes	No
20.	Have you been involved in a treatment program specifically related to drug use?	Yes	No

Duke Health Profile (DUKE) and Duke Anxiety-Depression (DUKE-AD)

PURPOSE To measure health quality of life.

AUTHOR George R. Parkerson, Jr.

DESCRIPTION The DUKE is a 17-item scale designed to measure patient-reported health-related quality of life (HRQOL). The DUKE can be used in a variety of ways, including as separate items, a total scale score, or as 11 subscales. The subscales are Physical Health (items 8, 9, 10, 11, 12); Mental Health (items 1, 4, 5, 13, 14); Social Health (Items 2, 6, 7, 15, 16); General Health (items combined from first three subscales and divided by three); Perceived Health (item 3); Self-Esteem (items 1, 2, 4, 6, 7); Anxiety (items 2, 6, 7, 10, 12, 14); Depression (items 1, 4, 10, 12, 13); Anxiety-Depression (DUKE-AD, also reproduced here; items 4, 5, 7, 10, 12, 13, 14); Pain (item 11); and Disability (item 17). The DUKE and DUKE-AD can be administered easily by an interviewer or by the client filling out the questionnaire (the form reproduced here). These scales have been translated into 17 languages and are very widely studied and used.

NORMS The DUKE and DUKE-AD have been studied extensively in the United States and internationally. Most respondents, totaling well into the many thousands, were medical policy holders and medical out- and in-patients. The DUKE and DUKE-AD also were studied with samples of medical students. The means, standard deviations, and other descriptive statistics for several samples are available in the Primary Reference. These scores can be compared with scores from a given individual. Means for 1,997 patients, of whom 1,335 were female, are as follows: Physical Health = 62.8 (SD = 25.8); Mental Health = 80.7 (SD = 19.5); Social Health = 73.7 (SD = 19.0); General Health = 72.7 (SD = 16.6); Perceived Health = 75.2 (SD = 31.7); Self-Esteem = 82.5 (SD = 18.1); Anxiety = 25.4 (SD = 19.6); Depression = 26.2 (SD = 21.4); DUKE-AD = 24.1 (SD = 19.6); Pain = 46.1 (SD = 34.4); and Disability = 12.5 (SD = 28.3).

SCORING The DUKE and DUKE-AD can be scored by computer (see Primary Reference) or manually. The raw scores of 0, 1, and 2 are simply transformed to 0, 50, and 100, producing a scale from 0 to 100. For multi-item subscales, sum the items and divide by the number of items. For the first six scales in the Norms section (considered to be Positive Function), higher scores are better. For the last four scales (considered to be Dysfunction), lower scores are better.

RELIABILITY The DUKE and DUKE-AD have fair internal consistency with alphas available for several different samples that are in .60s and .70s. Alphas for single-item scales are lower. The DUKE and DUKE-AD also have very good stability with test-retest correlations available for several samples and time periods; these correlations range from the .50s to the .70s, with lower correlations for single-item measures.

VALIDITY The DUKE and DUKE-AD have extensive evidence of concurrent, predictive, discriminative, and construct validity in a number of samples. The DUKE and DUKE-AD have been shown to be correlated with many other valid health and QOL measures, can be used as indicators of clinical outcomes, and have demonstrated convergent and divergent validity (construct validity) by correlating with multiple other measures where the DUKE and DUKE-AD should be correlated, and not correlating with other measures where it is predicted that the DUKE and DUKE-AD should not be correlated.

PRIMARY REFERENCE Parkerson, G. R. (2002). *User's Guide for Duke Health Measures*. Durham, NC: Department of Community and Family Medicine, Duke University Medical Center.

AVAILABILITY Email Dr. Parkerson at parke001@mc.duke.edu.

DUKE

Date Today: _____   Name: _____   ID Number:_____

Date of Birth: _____   Female _____   Male _____

INSTRUCTIONS: Here are some questions about your health and feelings. Please read each question carefully and check (✔) your best answer. You should answer the questions in your own way. There are no right or wrong answers. (Please ignore the small scoring numbers next to each blank.)

	Yes, describes me exactly	Somewhat describes me	No, doesn't describe me at all
1. I like who I am.	_____ 12	_____ 11	_____
2. I am not an easy person to get along with. . .	_____ 20	_____ 21	_____
3. I am basically a healthy person	_____ 32	_____ 31	_____
4. I give up too easily.	_____ 40	_____ 41	_____
5. I have difficulty concentrating	_____ 50	_____ 51	_____
6. I am happy with my family relationships	_____ 62	_____ 61	_____
7. I am comfortable being around people	_____ 72	_____ 71	_____

TODAY would you have any physical trouble or difficulty:

	None	Some	A Lot
8. Walking up a flight of stairs.	_____ 82	_____ 81	_____
9. Running the length of a football field	_____ 92	_____ 91	_____

DURING THE PAST WEEK: How much trouble have you had with:

	None	Some	A Lot
10. Sleeping	_____ 102	_____ 101	_____
11. Hurting or aching in any part of your body. . .	_____ 112	_____ 111	_____
12. Getting tired easily	_____ 122	_____ 121	_____
13. Feeling depressed or sad	_____ 132	_____ 131	_____
14. Nervousness	_____ 142	_____ 141	_____

DURING THE PAST WEEK: How often did you:

	None	Some	A Lot
15. Socialize with other people (talk or visit with friends or relatives)	_____ 150	_____ 151	_____
16. Take part in social, religious, or recreation activities (meetings, church, movies, sports, parties).	_____ 160	_____ 161	_____

DURING THE PAST WEEK: How often did you:

	None	1–4 Days	5–7 Days
17. Stay in your home, a nursing home, or hospital because of sickness, injury, or other health problem	_____ 172	_____ 171	_____

DUKE-AD

INSTRUCTIONS: Here are some questions about your health and feelings. Please read each question carefully and check (✓) your best answer. You should answer the questions in your own way. There are no right or wrong answers.

	Yes, describes me exactly	Somewhat describes me	No, doesn't describe me at all
1. I give up too easily.	_____ 2	_____ 1	_____ 0
2. I have difficulty concentrating	_____ 2	_____ 1	_____ 0
3. I am comfortable being around people	_____ 0	_____ 1	_____ 2

DURING THE PAST WEEK:

How much trouble have you had with:

	None	Some	A Lot
4. Sleeping.	_____ 0	_____ 1	_____ 2
5. Getting tired easily	_____ 0	_____ 1	_____ 2
6. Feeling depressed or sad	_____ 0	_____ 1	_____ 2
7. Nervousness.	_____ 0	_____ 1	_____ 2

Duke Social Support and Stress Scale (DUSOCS)

PURPOSE To measure social support and stress.

AUTHOR George R. Parkerson, Jr.

DESCRIPTION The DUSOCS is a 24-item measure designed to assess both social support and social stress. The DUSOCS was developed because of the well-documented relationships between family/social support and stress and health. Social Support (SS) is measured by 12 items (1–12) and Social Stress (ST) is measured by 12 items (13–24). The DUSOCS provides four separate scores: Family Support (FS), Family Stress (FST), Non-Family Support (NFS), and Non-Family Stress (NFST). Total social support and total social stress scores can be derived by simply combining family and non-family components. The DUSOCS can be administered by an interviewer or can be filled out by the client (the form reproduced here).

NORMS The DUSOCS has been studied with a wide range of samples, mainly involving primary care patients, but also some end-stage renal disease patients. The total number of people involved in developing norms for the DUSOCS was 413, of whom 242 were female. The means on the six DUSCOS subscales were as follows: SS=55.6 (SD=22.8); FS=52.5 (SD=25.0); NFST=48.0 (SD=24.8); SST=19.0 (SD=16.6); FST=20.1 (SD=18.9); and NFST=13.0 (SD=16.6).

SCORING The DUSOCS can be scored by computer (see Primary Reference) or manually. Each of the four subscales is scored slightly differently. For all scales, assign the following values: "None"=0, "Some"=1, "A lot"=2, "Yes"=2, "No"=0, "There is no such person"=0. As an example of scoring of Family Support: sum the scores for the six family categories (items 1–6); if the person in item 12 is a family member, add a score of 2 to the sum of the first six items (and add nothing if not a family member); and divide by 14 and multiply by 100 to obtain the Family Support score on a scale of 0 to 100. The remaining scales are scored in a similar fashion with specific instructions available in the Primary Reference. On support scales, higher scores are better, while on stress scales lower scores are better.

RELIABILITY The DUSOCS has fair to good internal consistency with alphas as follows: Family Support=.71, Non-Family Support=.70; Family Stress=.69; and Non-Family Stress=.53. The DUCOS has good stability with test-retest correlations of .67 to .76 for all scales except Family Stress with a correlation of .40.

VALIDITY Numerous studies, available in the Primary Reference, establish excellent concurrent and discriminative validity for the DUSOCS. The DUSOCS has significant correlations with several other family support and stress instruments and discriminates between patient groups with different clinical profiles, functional health status, and severity of illness.

PRIMARY REFERENCE Parkerson, G. R. (2002). *User's Guide for Duke Health Measures*. Durham, NC: Department of Community and Family Medicine, Duke University Medical Center.

AVAILABILITY Email Dr. Parkerson at parke001@mc.duke.edu.

DUSOCS

Date Today:_____   Name:_____   ID#:_____

Date of Birth:_____   Female_____   Male_____

SUPPORT

I. People Who Give Personal *Support*

[A *supportive person* is one who is helpful, who will listen to you, or who will back you up when you are in trouble.]

INSTRUCTIONS: Please look at the following list and decide how much each person (or group of persons) is supportive of you at this time in your life. Check (✓) your answer.

How supportive are these people now:	None	Some	A Lot	There is No Such Person
1. Your wife, husband, or significant other person	_____	_____	_____	_____
2. Your children or grandchildren	_____	_____	_____	_____
3. Your parents or grandparents	_____	_____	_____	_____
4. Your brothers or sisters	_____	_____	_____	_____
5. Your other blood relatives	_____	_____	_____	_____
6. Your relatives by marriage (for example: in-laws, ex-wife, ex-husband)	_____	_____	_____	_____
7. Your neighbors	_____	_____	_____	_____
8. Your co-workers	_____	_____	_____	_____
9. Your church members	_____	_____	_____	_____
10. Your other friends	_____	_____	_____	_____

	Yes	No	
11. Do you have one particular person whom you trust and to whom you can go with personal difficulties?	_____	_____	

12. If you answered "yes," which of the above types of person is he or she? (for example: child, parent, neighbor). . . . . _____

STRESS (DUSOCS FORM A)

II. People Who Cause Personal *Stress*

[A person who *stresses* you is one who causes problems for you or makes your life more difficult.]

INSTRUCTIONS: Please look at the following list and decide how much each person (or group of persons) is a stress for you at this time in your life. Check (✓) your answer.

How supportive are these people now:	None	Some	A Lot	There is No Such Person
1. Your wife, husband, or significant other person....................	————	————	————	————
2. Your children or grandchildren	————	————	————	————
3. Your parents or grandparents	————	————	————	————
4. Your brothers or sisters	————	————	————	————
5. Your other blood relatives	————	————	————	————
6. Your relatives by marriage (for example: in-laws, ex-wife, ex-husband)	————	————	————	————
7. Your neighbors	————	————	————	————
8. Your co-workers	————	————	————	————
9. Your church members............	————	————	————	————
10. Your other friends...............	————	————	————	————

	Yes	No
11. Is there one particular person who is causing you the most personal stress now?....................	————	————

12. If you answered "yes," which of the above types of person is he or she? (for example: child, parent, neighbor)...................... ————————————————————

Dysfunctional Attitude Scale (DAS)

PURPOSE To measure cognitive distortion.

AUTHOR Arlene Weissman

DESCRIPTION The DAS is a 40-item instrument designed to identify cognitive distortions—particularly the distortions that may underlie or cause depression. Based on the cognitive therapy model of Aaron Beck, the items on the DAS were constructed so as to represent seven major value systems: approval, love, achievement, perfectionism, entitlement, omnipotence, and autonomy. Two 40-item parallel forms of the DAS, which are highly correlated and have roughly the same psychometric properties, were derived from an original pool of 100 items. Although the overall score on the DAS is considered the key measure, practitioners can also examine areas where the respondent is emotionally vulnerable or strong by analyzing responses to specific items. Clinical work can then be directed at correcting the distortions underlying the depression, rather than only at the depressive symptoms per se.

NORMS The DAS was developed in a series of studies ultimately involving some 216 male and 485 female, predominantly white, undergraduate students. Other research involved 105 depressed out-patients, 30 manic-depressive outpatients and their spouses, and 107 depressed patients. No actual norms were reported since the number of DAS items varied among these studies. For nonclinical respondents, the mean score is approximately 113.

SCORING The DAS is easily scored by using zeros for items omitted, assigning a score of 1 (on a 7-point scale) to the adaptive end of the scale, and simply summing up the scores on all items. With no items omitted, scores on the DAS range from 40 to 280 with lower scores equaling more adaptive beliefs (few cognitive distortions).

RELIABILITY The DAS has very good internal consistency, with alphas on the form of the DAS reproduced here ranging from .84 to .92. The DAS also has excellent stability, with test-retest correlations over eight weeks of .80 to .84.

VALIDITY The DAS has excellent concurrent validity, significantly correlating with a number of other measures of depression and depressive-distortions such as the Beck Depression Inventory, the Profile of Mood States, and the Story Completion Test. The DAS also has good known-groups validity, significantly distinguishing between groups diagnosed as depressed or not depressed on the Beck Depression Inventory. The DAS also was found to be sensitive to change following clinical intervention with depressed outpatients.

PRIMARY REFERENCE Weissman, A. N. (1980). Assessing depressogenic attitudes: A validation study. Paper presented at the 51st Annual Meeting of the Eastern Psychological Association, Hartford, CT. Instrument reproduced with permission of Arlene N. Weissman.

AVAILABILITY Dr. Arlene Weissman, Towers, Perrin, Forster, and Crosby, 1500 Market Street, Philadelphia, PA 19102.

This questionnaire lists different attitudes or beliefs which people sometimes hold. Read *each* statement carefully and decide how much you agree or disagree with the statement.

For each of the attitudes, indicate to the left of the item the number that *best describes how you think*. Be sure to choose only one answer for each attitude. Because people are different, there is no right answer or wrong answer to these statements. Your answers are confidential, so please do not put your name on this sheet.

To decide whether a given attitude is typical of your way of looking at things, simply keep in mind what you are like *most of the time*.

1 = Totally agree
2 = Agree very much
3 = Agree slightly
4 = Neutral
5 = Disagree slightly
6 = Disagree very much
7 = Totally disagree

___ 1. It is difficult to be happy unless one is good looking, intelligent, rich, and creative.
___ 2. Happiness is more a matter of my attitude towards myself than the way other people feel about me.
___ 3. People will probably think less of me if I make a mistake.
___ 4. If I do not do well all the time, people will not respect me.
___ 5. Taking even a small risk is foolish because the loss is likely to be a disaster.
___ 6. It is possible to gain another person's respect without being especially talented at anything.
___ 7. I cannot be happy unless most people I know admire me.
___ 8. If a person asks for help, it is a sign of weakness.
___ 9. If I do not do as well as other people, it means I am a weak person.
___ 10. If I fail at my work, then I am a failure as a person.
___ 11. If you cannot do something well, there is little point in doing it at all.
___ 12. Making mistakes is fine because I can learn from them.
___ 13. If someone disagrees with me, it probably indicates he does not like me.
___ 14. If I fail partly, it is as bad as being a complete failure.
___ 15. If other people know what you are really like, they will think less of you.
___ 16. I am nothing if a person I love doesn't love me.
___ 17. One can get pleasure from an activity regardless of the end result.
___ 18. People should have a chance to succeed before doing anything.
___ 19. My value as a person depends greatly on what others think of me.
___ 20. If I don't set the highest standards for myself, I am likely to end up a second-rate person.
___ 21. If I am to be a worthwhile person, I must be the best in at least one way.
___ 22. People who have good ideas are better than those who do not.
___ 23. I should be upset if I make a mistake.
___ 24. My own opinions of myself are more important than others' opinions of me.
___ 25. To be a good, moral, worthwhile person I must help everyone who needs it.
___ 26. If I ask a question, it makes me look stupid.

___ 27. It is awful to be put down by people important to you.
___ 28. If you don't have other people to lean on, you are going to be sad.
___ 29. I can reach important goals without pushing myself.
___ 30. It is possible for a person to be scolded and not get upset.
___ 31. I cannot trust other people because they might be cruel to me.
___ 32. If others dislike you, you cannot be happy.
___ 33. It is best to give up your own interests in order to please other people.
___ 34. My happiness depends more on other people than it does on me.
___ 35. I do not need the approval of other people in order to be happy.
___ 36. If a person avoids problems, the problems tend to go away.
___ 37. I can be happy even if I miss out on many of the good things in life.
___ 38. What other people think about me is very important.
___ 39. Being alone leads to unhappiness.
___ 40. I can find happiness without being loved by another person.

Eating Attitudes Test (EAT)

PURPOSE To measure symptoms of anorexia nervosa.

AUTHORS David M. Garner and Paul E. Garfinkel

DESCRIPTION The 40-item EAT was designed to measure a broad range of behaviors and attitudes characteristic of anorexia nervosa. Each item is a symptom frequently observed in the disorder. The instrument has a rough cutting score of 30, above which scores indicate anorectic eating concerns. The EAT is helpful in identifying clients with serious eating concerns even if they do not show the weight loss classic to this disorder.

NORMS The EAT was developed using two samples of patients diagnosed with anorexia nervosa ($n = 32$ and $n = 34$). The average age of the onset of the disorder was 18.4 years. Two "normal" control groups were also used which were composed of Canadian college students ($n = 34$ and $n = 59$). The "normal" control subjects and anorectics were from similar socioeconomic backgrounds, and the average age for the four groups was approximately 22.4 years. Average EAT scores for one of the anorectic samples was 58.9 with a standard deviation of 13.3. The "normal" control sample of 59 had a mean of 15.6 with a standard deviation of 9.3. A group of clinically recovered anorectics ($n = 9$) had a mean of 11.4 and a standard deviation of 5.1.

SCORING The 40 items are scored in terms of frequencies of the experience. Items 1, 18, 19, 23, and 39 are scored as follows: $6 = 3$, $5 = 2$, $4 = 1$, and 3, 2, and $1 = 0$. The remaining items are scored as follows: $1 = 2$, $2 = 2$, $3 = 1$, and 4, 5, and $6 = 0$. Items 2–17, 20–22, 24–26, 28–38, 40 when marked "Always" and items 1, 18, 19, 23, and 39 when marked "Never" indicate anorexia. Total scores are the sum of the item values, and range from 0 to 120.

RELIABILITY This instrument has excellent internal consistency, with a coefficient alpha of .94 for a combined sample of anorectics and normals. For the anorectic subjects alone, the coefficient was .79.

VALIDITY A 23-item prototype of this instrument was tested for known-groups validity. Scores differed significantly for a sample of anorectics and "normals." This finding was replicated in a separate sample. The EAT was shown to be independent of the Restraint Scale, weight fluctuation, extroversion, and neuroticism. Post hoc analysis of a group of recovered anorectics indicated that scores were in the normal range, suggesting the scale is sensitive to change.

PRIMARY REFERENCE Garner, D. M., and Garfinkel, P. E. (1979). The Eating Attitudes Test: An index of the symptoms of anorexia nervosa, *Psychological Medicine*, 9, 273–279. Instrument reproduced with permission of David M. Garner.

AVAILABILITY Dr. David M. Garner, River Centre Clinic, 5465 Main Street, Sylvania, Ohio 43560. May be copied from this volume.

Please indicate on the line at left the answer which applies best to each of the numbered statements. All of the results will be *strictly* confidential. Most of the questions directly relate to food or eating, although other types of questions have been included. Please answer each question carefully. Thank you.

1 = Always
2 = Very often
3 = Often
4 = Sometimes
5 = Rarely
6 = Never

____ 1. Like eating with other people.
____ 2. Prepare foods for others but do not eat what I cook.
____ 3. Become anxious prior to eating.
____ 4. Am terrified about being overweight.
____ 5. Avoid eating when I am hungry.
____ 6. Find myself preoccupied with food.
____ 7. Have gone on eating binges where I feel that I may not be able to stop.
____ 8. Cut my food into small pieces.
____ 9. Aware of the calorie content of foods that I eat.
____ 10. Particularly avoid foods with a high carbohydrate content (e.g., bread, potatoes, rice, etc.).
____ 11. Feel bloated after meals.
____ 12. Feel that others would prefer if I ate more.
____ 13. Vomit after I have eaten.
____ 14. Feel extremely guilty after eating.
____ 15. Am preoccupied with a desire to be thinner.
____ 16. Exercise strenuously to burn off calories.
____ 17. Weigh myself several times a day.
____ 18. Like my clothes to fit tightly.
____ 19. Enjoy eating meat.
____ 20. Wake up early in the morning.
____ 21. Eat the same foods day after day.
____ 22. Think about burning my calories when I exercise.
____ 23. Have regular menstrual periods.
____ 24. Other people think that I am too thin.
____ 25. Am preoccupied with the thought of having fat on my body.
____ 26. Take longer than others to eat my meals.
____ 27. Enjoy eating at restaurants.
____ 28. Take laxatives.
____ 29. Avoid foods with sugar in them.
____ 30. Eat diet foods.
____ 31. Feel that food controls my life.
____ 32. Display self-control around food.
____ 33. Feel that others pressure me to eat.
____ 34. Give too much time and thought to food.

_____ 35. Suffer from constipation.
_____ 36. Feel uncomfortable after eating sweets.
_____ 37. Engage in dieting behavior.
_____ 38. Like my stomach to be empty.
_____ 39. Enjoy trying new rich foods.
_____ 40. Have the impulse to vomit after meals.

Eating Disorder Diagnostic Scale (EDDS)

PURPOSE To measure eating disorders.

AUTHORS Eric Stice, Christy F. Telch, and Shireen L. Rizvi

DESCRIPTION The EDDS is a 22-item scale designed to diagnose three eating disorders: anorexia nervosa, bulimia nervosa and binge-eating disorder according to DSM-IV criteria. Combining all three disorders, in a brief measure, was seen by the researchers as a very convenient way to avoid far more time-consuming diagnostic assessments. The authors argue that no parallel measure for actually diagnosing the three eating disorders exists. The EDDS also can be used to monitor outcomes of prevention and treatment programs for these three eating disorders. The three eating disorders are diagnosed by examining answers to specific items for each disorder. For anorexia, the items involved are: 19 and 20 that result in a body mass index of less than 17.5; items 2, 3 and 4, and 21. For bulimia, the pertinent items are: 5, 6, 8, 15–18, and 3 and 4. For binge-eating disorder, the items are: 5–7, 9–13, 14, 15–18.

NORMS The EDDS has been studied with a sample of 367 females between the ages of 13 and 46 who were recruited mainly from several eating disorder studies and treatment programs as well as some nonspecific psychiatric treatment programs ($n=41$). The sample was 80% white, 9% "other," 6% Hispanic, 2% African American, 2% Asian or Pacific Islander and 1% Native American. The mean age was 29.7 (SD$=13.2$). 22% of the sample had some high school, 17% had graduate or professional degrees, and the modal education response was "some college education." The EDDS does not provide norms because of the complicated scoring algorithms described below.

SCORING The EDDS is scored in a fairly complicated way, with specific steps required for each disorder. These procedures are described in detail in the Primary Reference. As an example, bulimia is diagnosed if the client responds "yes" to items 5 and 6, greater than 2 on item 7, "yes" to at least three out of four of items 9–13, "yes" to item 14, and 0 to items 15–18. The rationale for the scoring algorithms is presented in the Primary Reference. Also, the author will provide the computer code for computerized scoring.

RELIABILITY The EDDS has excellent internal consistency with an alpha of .91 for the items that are standardized. The EDDS also has very good stability with 1-week test-retest correlations of .95 for anorexia, .71 for bulimia, and .75 for binge-eating disorder.

VALIDITY The EDDS has excellent discriminant validity, accurately distinguishing between individuals identified in a structured interview as with or without eating disorders; the accuracy coefficient ranged from .93 for binge-eating disorder to .99 for anorexia. The EDDS also has excellent convergent validity, with the composite score correlating significantly with several other validated measures of eating disorders.

PRIMARY REFERENCE Stice, E., Telch, C. F., and Rizvi, S. L. (2000). Development and validation of the Eating Disorder Diagnostic Scale: A brief self-report measure of anorexia, bulimia, and binge-eating disorder, *Psychological Assessment*, 2, 123–131. Instrument reproduced by permission of Dr. Eric Stice.

AVAILABILITY Dr. Eric M. Stice Oregon Research Institute, 1715 Franklin Blvd.. Eugene OR. 97403-1983, Telephone: 541.484.2123.

EDDS:

Please carefully complete all questions.

Over the *past 3 MONTHS* . . .	Not at all		Slightly		Moderately		Extremely
1. Have you felt fat? . . .	0	1	2	3	4	5	6
2. Have you had a definite fear that you might gain weight or become fat? . . .	0	1	2	3	4	5	6
3. Has your weight influenced how you think about (judge) yourself as a person? . . .	0	1	2	3	4	5	6
4. Has your shape influenced how you think about (judge) yourself as a person? . . .	0	1	2	3	4	5	6

5. During the **past 6 MONTHS** have there been times when you felt you have eaten what other people would regard as an unusually large amount of food (e.g., a quart of ice cream) given the circumstances?. . . . . YES   NO

6. During the times when you ate an unusually large amount of food, did you experience a loss of control (feel you couldn't stop eating or control what or how much you were eating)? . . . . YES   NO

7. How many **DAYS per week** on average over the **past 6 MONTHS** have you eaten an unusually large amount of food and experienced a loss of control?
   0 1 2 3 4 5 6 7

8. How many **TIMES per week** on average over the **past 3 MONTHS** have you eaten an unusually large amount of food and experienced a loss of control?
   0 1 2 3 4 5 6 7 8 9 10 11 12 13 14

During these episodes of overeating and loss of control did you. . .

9. Eat much more rapidly than normal? . . . . YES   NO

10. Eat until you felt uncomfortably full? . . . . YES   NO

11. Eat large amounts of food when you didn't feel physically hungry? . . . . YES   NO

12. Eat alone because you were embarrassed by how much you were eating?. . . . . YES   NO

13. Feel disgusted with yourself, depressed, or very guilty after overeating? . . . YES   NO

14. Feel very upset about your uncontrollable overeating or resulting weight gain? . . . . YES   NO

15. How many **TIMES per week** on average over the **past 3 MONTHS** have you made yourself vomit to prevent weight gain or counteract the effects of eating?
   0 1 2 3 4 5 6 7 8 9 10 11 12 13 14

16. How many *TIMES per week* on average over the *past 3 MONTHS* have you used laxatives or diuretics to prevent weight gain or to counteract the effects of eating?
    0   1   2   3   4   5   6   7   8   9   10   11   12   13   14

17. How many *TIMES per week* on average over the *past 3 MONTHS* have you fasted (skipped at least two meals in a row) to prevent weight gain or to counteract the effects of eating?   0   1   2   3   4   5   6   7   8   9   10   11   12   13   14

18. How many *TIMES per week* on average over the *past 3 MONTHS* have you engaged in excessive exercise specifically to counteract the effects of overeating episodes?
    0   1   2   3   4   5   6   7   8   9   10   11   12   13   14

19. How much do you weigh? If uncertain, please give your best estimate. _____ lbs.

20. How tall are you? _____ ft. _____ in.

21. Over the *past 3 MONTHS,* how many menstrual periods have you **missed?**
    0   1   2   3   n/a

22. Have you been taking birth control pills during the *past 3 MONTHS*? . . . . .YES   NO

Eating Questionnaire—Revised (EQ-R)

PURPOSE To measure bulimia.

AUTHORS Donald A. Williamson, C. J. Davis, Anthony J. Goreczny, Sandra J. McKenzie, and Philip Watkins

DESCRIPTION The EQ-R is a 15-item instrument designed to assess the symptoms of bulimia. The EQ-R is in a symptom checklist format that allows documentation of eating and purging habits, and can be used to differentiate binge eaters and obesity. The EQ-R is short, easy to utilize, can be used with total score or individual items, and can be used both to screen for bulimia and binge eating or to assess treatment outcome.

NORMS The EQ-R was studied with 561 women, including 104 diagnosed with bulimia nervosa, 45 bulimic binge eaters, 36 diagnosed as obese, and 376 diagnosed as "normal" (with no eating disorders). The "normal" group was recruited from undergraduate psychology classes, while the clinical subjects were referred to an outpatient eating disorders program for treatment of bulimia or obesity. The means for the groups were: 32.18 for the nonclinical group, 47.98 for the bulimia nervosa group, 45.53 for the simple bulimia group, and 37.94 for the obese group.

SCORING The EQ-R is easily scored by summing the item scores (from a = 1 to e = 5) for a total score. Items 7 and 10 are reverse-scored.

RELIABILITY The EQ-R has very good internal consistency, with an alpha of .87. The EQ-R has excellent stability, with a two-week test-retest correlation of .90.

VALIDITY The EQ-R has very good concurrent validity, correlating with the Eating Attitudes Test and the BULIT. The EQ-R also has good known-groups validity, significantly distinguishing between the bulimic groups, the obese group, and the nonclinical group.

PRIMARY REFERENCE Williamson, D. A., Davis, C. J., Goreczny, A. J., McKenzie, S. J., and Watkins, P. (1989). The Eating Questionnaire—Revised: A symptom checklist for bulimia, in P. A. Keller and S. R. Heyman (eds.), *Innovations in clinical practice*, Vol. 8, pp. 321–326. Sarasota, FL: Professional Resource Exchange, Inc. Instrument reprinted by permission.

AVAILABILITY Professional Resource Exchange, Inc., P.O. Box 15560, Sarasota, FL 34277-1560, or www.prpress.com.

In the space provided indicate the letter of the answer that best describes your eating behavior.

___ 1. How often do you binge eat? (a) seldom; (b) once or twice a month; (c) once a week; (d) almost every day; (e) every day.

___ 2. What is the average length of a bingeing episode? (a) less than 15 minutes; (b) 15–30 minutes; (c) 30 minutes to 1 hour; (d) 1 hour to 2 hours; (e) more than 2 hours (if e, please indicate length of episode _____).

___ 3. Which of the following statements best applies to your binge eating? (a) I don't eat enough to satisfy me; (b) I eat until I've had enough to satisfy me; (c) I eat until my stomach feels full; (d) I eat until my stomach is painfully full; (e) I eat until I can't eat anymore.

___ 4. Do you ever vomit after a binge? (a) never; (b) about 25% of the time; (c) about 50% of the time; (d) about 75% of the time; (e) about 100% of the time.

___ 5. Which of the following best applies to your eating behavior when binge eating? (a) I eat much more slowly than usual; (b) I eat somewhat more slowly than usual; (c) I eat at about the same speed as I usually do; (d) I eat somewhat faster than usual; (e) I eat very rapidly.

___ 6. How much are you concerned about your binge eating? (a) not bothered at all; (b) bothers me a little; (c) moderately concerned; (d) a major concern; (e) the most important concern in my life.

___ 7. Which best describes the control you feel over your eating during a binge? (a) never in control; (b) in control about 25% of the time; (c) in control about 50% of the time; (d) in control about 75% of the time; (e) always in control.

___ 8. Which of the following describes your feelings immediately after a binge? (a) I feel very good; (b) I feel good; (c) I feel fairly neutral, not too nervous or uncomfortable; (d) I am moderately nervous and/or uncomfortable; (e) I am very nervous and/or uncomfortable.

___ 9. Which most accurately describes your mood immediately after a binge? (a) very happy; (b) moderately happy; (c) neutral; (d) moderately depressed; (e) very depressed.

___ 10. Which of the following best describes the situation in which you typically binge? (a) always completely alone; (b) alone but around unknown others (e.g., restaurant); (c) only around others who know about my bingeing; (d) only around friends and family; (e) in any situation.

___ 11. Which of the following best describes any weight changes you have experienced in the last year? (a) 0–5 lbs; (b) 5–10 lbs; (c) 10–20 lbs; (d) 20–30 lbs; (e) more than 30 lbs.

___ 12. On a day that you binge, how many binge episodes typically occur during that day? (a) 0; (b) 1; (c) 2; (d) 3; (e) 4 or more.

___ 13. How often do you use restrictive diets/fasts? (a) never; (b) one time per month; (c) two times per month; (d) one time per week; (e) almost always.

___ 14. How often do you use laxatives to lose weight? (a) never; (b) 1–3 times per month; (c) one time per week; (d) one time per day; (e) more than one time per day (if e, please indicate frequency _____).

___ 15. How often do you use diuretics to lose weight? (a) never; (b) 1–3 times per month; (c) one time per week; (d) one time per day; (e) more than one time per day (if e, please indicate frequency _____).

Eating Self-Efficacy Scale (ESES)

PURPOSE To measure eating self-efficacy.

AUTHORS Shirley M. Glynn and Audrey J. Ruderman

DESCRIPTION The ESES is a 25-item instrument designed to assess the individual's self-efficacy regarding eating (and overeating) behavior. Eating self-efficacy refers to the individual's confidence in his or her ability to cope, in this instance, in the area of eating. Previous research suggests that people's perceptions of self-efficacy with regard to eating may be an important influence on dieting and weight loss success. The ESES has two factors, eating as a function of negative affects (NA: items 2, 4, 5, 8, 11–15, 17, 18, 20, 22, 23, and 25) and eating as a function of socially acceptable circumstances (SA: remaining 10 items). Since few, if any, other scales on eating self-efficacy are available, the ESES may have important predictive and therapeutic applications.

NORMS The ESES was first studied with 328 college introductory psychology students to reduce an original 79-item version to the current 25-item version. The ESES was then studied with 484 female undergraduates in introductory psychology courses. No other demographic data were provided. The mean on the ESES was 80.9 (SD=26.5, median=80). The NA mean was 42.15 (SD=20.03) and the SA mean was 38.92 (SD=11.47). The possible range of the total scale is 25–185. In a separate study of 618 subjects (303 male and 315 females), the mean for males was 74.24 (SD=30.28) and for females 88.43 (SD=29.39). The difference was statistically significant, with females reporting greater difficulty controlling their eating.

SCORING The ESES is scored by simply adding up item scores (1 to 7) for the subscale scores (NA=15 items, SA=10 items) and summing all items for a total score. The higher the score, the greater the problem with self-efficacy for eating.

RELIABILITY The ESES has excellent internal consistency, with an alpha of .92 for the entire scale, .94 for NA, and .85 for SA. The ESES also has very good stability, with a test-retest correlation of .70.

VALIDITY The ESES has good predictive and construct validity. Scores on the ESES were significantly related to weight loss among weight loss program participants. The ESES also was significantly related in predicted directions with percentage overweight, Restraint Scale scores, previous and current dieting experience and to self-esteem.

PRIMARY REFERENCE Glynn, S. M., and Ruderman, A. J. (1986). The development and validation of an Eating Self-Efficacy Scale, *Cognitive Therapy and Research*, 10, 403–420.

AVAILABILITY May be copied from this volume.

For numbers 1–25 you should rate the likelihood that you would have difficulty controlling your overeating in each of the situations, using this scale:

1	2	3	4	5	6	7

No difficulty controlling eating		Moderate difficulty controlling eating		Most difficulty controlling eating

Please complete every item and record your answer in the space to the left.

How difficult is it to control your . . .

— 1. Overeating after work or school
— 2. Overeating when you feel restless
— 3. Overeating around holiday time
— 4. Overeating when you feel upset
— 5. Overeating when tense
— 6. Overeating with friends
— 7. Overeating when preparing food
— 8. Overeating when irritable
— 9. Overeating as part of a social occasion dealing with food—like at a restaurant or dinner party
— 10. Overeating with family members
— 11. Overeating when annoyed
— 12. Overeating when angry
— 13. Overeating when you are angry at yourself
— 14. Overeating when depressed
— 15. Overeating when you feel impatient
— 16. Overeating when you want to sit back and enjoy some food
— 17. Overeating after an argument
— 18. Overeating when you feel frustrated
— 19. Overeating when tempting food is in front of you
— 20. Overeating when you want to cheer up
— 21. Overeating when there is a lot of food available to you (refrigerator is full)
— 22. Overeating when you feel overly sensitive
— 23. Overeating when nervous
— 24. Overeating when hungry
— 25. Overeating when anxious or worried

Ego Identity Scale (EIS)

PURPOSE To measure ego identity.

AUTHORS Allen L. Tan, Randall J. Kendis, Judith Fine, and Joseph Porac

DESCRIPTION The EIS is a 12-item scale that measures Erik Erikson's concept of ego identity. The authors reviewed Erikson's characterization of ego identity achievement and developed 41 pairs of forced-choice items with one item representing ego identity and one representing ego diffusion. Ego identity was defined as acceptance of self, a sense of direction. Identity diffusion implies doubts about one's self, lack of sense of continuity over time, and inability to make decisions and commitments. This pool of 41 items was reduced to 12 on the basis of their ability to discriminate between higher and lower scorers across all 41 items, and imperviousness to social desirability response set.

NORMS A series of studies to develop the EIS was conducted involving 249 undergraduate students. No other demographic data or norms were reported.

SCORING The EIS is scored by assigning a score of 1 to each statement that reflects ego identity and that is circled by the respondent, then summing the scores. The items that reflect ego identity are 1a, 2b, 3b, 4a, 5b, 6b, 7b, 8a, 9b, 10b, 11a, 12a.

RELIABILITY The EIS has only fair internal consistency, with a split-half reliability coefficient of .68. No other reliability information was reported.

VALIDITY The EIS correlated significantly and in predicted directions with four personality variables: internal control, intimacy, dogmatism, and extent to which an individual derives his or her values from his or her own life experiences. These correlations provide some evidence of construct validity. The EIS also correlated significantly with indices of political and occupational commitment.

PRIMARY REFERENCE Tan, A. L., Kendis, R. J., Fine, J. T., and Porac, J. (1977). A short measure of Eriksonian ego identity, *Journal of Personality Assessment*, 41, 279–284. Instrument reproduced with permission of Allen Tan, Randall Kendis, and Judith Fine.

AVAILABILITY May be copied from this volume.

On these pages, you will see 12 PAIRS of statements. Each pair consists of an *a* statement and a *b* statement. Read each of them carefully and choose which of the two describes you better. If it is statement *a,* then circle the letter *a* that appears before the statement. If it is statement *b*, then circle the letter *b* that precedes the statement. Make sure that you make a choice on every one of the 12 pairs of statements.

1. a. I enjoy being active in clubs and youth groups.
    b. I prefer to focus on hobbies which I can do on my own time, at my own pace.

2. a. When I daydream, it is primarily about my past experiences.
    b. When I daydream, it is primarily about the future and what it has in store for me.

3. a. No matter how well I do a job, I always end up thinking that I could have done better.
    b. When I complete a job that I have seriously worked on, I usually do not have doubts as to its quality.

4. a. I will generally voice an opinion, even if I appear to be the only one in a group with that point of view.
    b. If I appear to be the only one in a group with a certain opinion, I try to keep quiet in order to avoid feeling self-conscious.

5. a. Generally speaking, a person can keep much better control of himself and of situations if he maintains an emotional distance.
    b. A person need not feel loss of control, of himself, and of situations simply because he becomes intimately involved with another person.

6. a. I have doubts as to the kind of person my abilities will enable me to become.
    b. I try to formulate ideas now which will help me achieve my future goals.

7. a. My evaluation of self-worth depends on the success or failure of my behavior in a given situation.
    b. My self-evaluation, while flexible, remains about the same in most situations.

8. a. While there may be disadvantages to competition, I agree that it is sometimes necessary and even good.
    b. I do not enjoy competition.

9. a. There are times when I don't know what is expected of me.
    b. I have a clear vision of how my life will unfold ahead of me.

10. a. What I demand of myself and what others demand of me are often in conflict.
    b. Most of the time, I don't mind doing what others demand of me because they are things I would probably have done anyway.

11. a. When confronted with a task that I do not particularly enjoy, I find that I usually can discipline myself enough to perform them.
    b. Often, when confronted with a task, I find myself expending my energies on other interesting but unrelated activities instead of concentrating on completing the task.

12. a. Because of my philosophy of life, I have faith in myself, and in society in general.
    b. Because of the uncertain nature of the individual and society, it is natural for me not to have a basic trust in society, in others, or even in myself.

Emotional Assessment Scale (EAS)

PURPOSE To measure emotional reactivity.

AUTHORS Charles R. Carlson, Frank L. Collins, Jean F. Stewart, James Porzelius, Jeffrey A. Nitz, and Cheryl O. Lind

DESCRIPTION The EAS is a 24-item instrument designed to measure immediate emotional responses to a full range of emotions at the same time. Based on work involving emotional responses in psychophysiological research, the EAS examines eight emotional states that are viewed as fundamental and consistent across cultures. The eight emotions are anger (items 4, 12, 20), anxiety (items 6, 14, 22), disgust (items 3, 11, 19), fear (items 2, 9, 17), guilt (items 5, 13, 15), happiness (items 8, 16, 24), sadness (items 7, 21, 23), and surprise (items 1, 10, 18). The EAS is a very useful instrument for measuring momentary levels and changes in emotions. It can be filled out in less than a minute and can be used in a variety of clinical settings and situations.

NORMS The EAS was studied initially with 120 persons from an undergraduate psychology course with an age range of 18 to 34 and 62% female, 38% male. The following means and standard deviations were reported: anger—mean = 14.6 (SD = 18.9); anxiety—mean = 32.4 (SD = 24.5); disgust—mean = 9.7 (SD = 13.3); fear—mean = 13.0 (SD = 14.5); guilt—mean = 12.6 (SD = 14.5); happiness—mean = 38.8 (SD = 23.8); sadness—mean = 19.1 (SD = 19.6); and surprise—mean = 10.7 (SD = 10.4).

SCORING The EAS is scored by simply measuring the number of millimeters from the left endpoint to the slash mark located along the 100 mm line. The three items composing each emotion are then summed for the score for that emotion. No total score is used.

RELIABILITY The EAS has good to excellent reliability, with interitem reliability for the emotions ranging from .70 to .91 and split-half reliability for the entire measure of .94. No data on stability were reported.

VALIDITY The EAS has very good concurrent validity, with several of the subscales correlating with existing measures, such as the Profile of the Mood States, the Beck Depression Inventory, and the State-Trait Anxiety Inventory (State form). Subscales of the EAS also were found in subsequent research to be sensitive to changes in externally induced stress levels.

PRIMARY REFERENCE Carlson, C. R., Collins, F. L., Stewart, J. F., Porzelius, J., Nitz, J. A., and Lind, C. O. (1989). The assessment of emotional reactivity: A scale development and validation study, *Journal of Psychopathology and Behavioral Assessment*, 11, 313–325.

AVAILABILITY Dr. Charles Carlson, Department of Psychology, University of Kentucky, Lexington, KY 40506. Email: ccarl@email.uky.edu.

EAS

For each word listed, place a slash (/) somewhere on the appropriate line to indicate how you are feeling at this moment.

Least possible   Most possible

1. Surprised _____
2. Afraid _____
3. Disgusted _____
4. Angry _____
5. Guilty _____
6. Anxious _____
7. Sad _____
8. Delighted _____
9. Scared _____
10. Astonished _____
11. Repulsed _____
12. Mad _____
13. Ashamed _____
14. Worried _____
15. Disturbed _____
16. Joyful _____
17. Frightened _____
18. Amazed _____
19. Sickened _____
20. Annoyed _____
21. Humiliated _____
22. Nervous _____
23. Hopeless _____
24. Happy _____

Emotional Contagion Scale (ECS)

PURPOSE To measure susceptibility to ìcatchingî and sharing the emotions of others

AUTHORS Darcy Siebert, Carl Siebert and Alicia Taylor-McLaughlin

DESCRIPTION The ECS is a 5-item instrument designed to measure the vulnerability of ìcatchingî which is the emotional experience of another when in fact there is little or no interaction to warrant having the shared emotions. Emotional contagion contrasts with social interactional emotional experience which results from two people having a common experience and common emotion shared via social interaction. It also is distinguishable from empathy which is defined as sensing another experience as if it was your own, but without losing the "as if" quality. Emotional contagion is when only one person has the emotional experience and it is shared by another without much social interaction. Emotional contagion has an association with depression, burnout, professional impairments, and is useful in clinical supervision. The ECS is also useful when working with the moodiness of the teenage years, some personality disorders and persons vulnerable to vicarious and secondary traumatization.

NORMS Based on a sample of 376 clinical social workers, ECS scores had a mean score of 11.21 with a standard deviation of 4.13.

SCORING Items 1 and 2 are reverse-scored and then item scores are summed for the five items. Scores range from 0 to 25.

RELIABILITY The internal consistency of the ECS was .72.

VALIDITY The validity of the unidimensionality of the ECS was supported with exploratory and confirmatory factor analysis. Concurrent validity was evidenced with correlations between ECS scores and depression, burnout, and professional impairment.

PRIMARY REFERENCE Siebert, D. C, Siebert, C. F. and Taylor-McLaughin, A. (2007). Susceptibility to emotional contagion: Its measurement and importance to social work. *Journal of social service research. 33*, 47–56.

AVAILABILITY Darcy Siebert, Ph.D., Florida State University, College of Social Work, University Center C, Tallahassee, FL 32306–2570. Email: dsiebert@fsu.edu.

Please indicate how much you disagree or agree with each of the following statements.

1. I often find that I can remain cool in spite of excitement around me.

Strongly disagree	Disagree	Neither disagree nor agree	Agree	Strongly Agree
1	2	3	4	5

2. I am able to remain calm even though those around me worry.

Strongly disagree	Disagree	Neither disagree nor agree	Agree	Strongly Agree
1	2	3	4	5

3. I cannot continue to feel okay if people around me are depressed.

Strongly disagree	Disagree	Neither disagree nor agree	Agree	Strongly Agree
1	2	3	4	5

4. I become nervous if others around me seem to be nervous.

Strongly disagree	Disagree	Neither disagree nor agree	Agree	Strongly Agree
1	2	3	4	5

5. The people around me have great influence on my moods.

Strongly disagree	Disagree	Neither disagree nor agree	Agree	Strongly Agree
1	2	3	4	5

Emotional/Social Loneliness Inventory (ESLI)

PURPOSE To measure emotional and social loneliness and isolation.

AUTHORS Harry Vincenzi and Fran Grabosky

DESCRIPTION The ESLI is a 15-item instrument designed to measure both loneliness and isolation from social and emotional points of view. The 15 items are presented in a paired format to contrast one's perception of his/her social network with his/her feelings about it. The ESLI has four factors that differentiate social loneliness (items 1–8, first set of questions), emotional loneliness (items 1–8, second set), social isolation (items 9–15, first set), and emotional isolation (items 9–15, second set). The ESLI can be used to help researchers and clinicians distinguish between social and emotional components of loneliness and isolation.

NORMS The ESLI was studied initially with two samples. The first contained 95 respondents, including 33 masters-level psychology students, 33 high school students, and 26 in an adult psychotherapy program. The second sample included 229 respondents, 65 from a clinical population, 65 undergraduates, and 99 high school students. Both samples contained males and females. No other demographic data were reported. The following means were reported for the second sample ($n=228$), with the scores for the clinical sample ($n=65$) in parentheses: emotional isolation—5.3 (12.0), social isolation—7.3 (11.0), emotional loneliness—8.4 (14.0), and social loneliness—7.0 (11.9).

SCORING Scores for the subscales and the total scale are obtained by simply summing the pertinent score items.

RELIABILITY The ESLI has good internal consistency, with alphas for the subscales that range from .80 to .86. The ESLI has very good stability, with a two-week test-retest reliability of .80 for the total score.

VALIDITY The ESLI has good known-groups validity, significantly distinguishing between the clinical and nonclinical groups on all four subscales. No other validity data were reported.

PRIMARY REFERENCE Vincenzi, H., and Grabosky, F. (1987). Measuring the emotional/ social aspects of loneliness and isolation, *Journal of Social Behavior and Personality*, 2, 257–270.

AVAILABILITY May be copied from this volume.

The purpose of this questionnaire is to help you explore what is TRUE in your life versus how you FEEL at this time. For example, you may have a mate, but due to a poor relationship you don't feel like you have a mate. Please use the last two weeks as a guideline to answer these questions.

Please respond to each question by circling the response that best describes you. Please respond to *both* categories for each questions.

Usually true = 3   Often true = 2   Sometimes true = 1   Rarely true = 0

WHAT IS TRUE IN MY LIFE AT THIS TIME

WHAT I FEEL IN MY LIFE AT THIS TIME

1. I don't have a close friend.

   0   1   2   3

   I don't feel like I have a close friend.

   0   1   2   3

2. People take advantage of me when I'm involved with them.

   0   1   2   3

   I'm afraid to trust others.

   0   1   2   3

3. I don't have a mate (or boyfriend/girlfriend).

   0   1   2   3

   I don't feel like I have a mate (or boyfriend/girlfriend).

   0   1   2   3

4. I don't want to burden others with my problems.

   0   1   2   3

   Those close to me feel burdened by me when I share my problems.

   0   1   2   3

5. There is nobody in my life who depends on me.

   0   1   2   3

   I don't feel needed or important to others.

   0   1   2   3

6. I don't have any relationships that involve sharing personal thoughts.

   0   1   2   3

   I don't feel I can share personal thoughts with anyone.

   0   1   2   3

7. There is no one in my life that tries to understand me.

   0   1   2   3

   I don't feel understood.

   0   1   2   3

8. Nobody in my life really wants to be involved with me.

   0   1   2   3

   I don't feel safe reaching out to others.

   0   1   2   3

9. I spend a lot of time alone.

   0   1   2   3

   I feel lonely.

   0   1   2   3

10. I am not part of a social group or organization.

    0   1   2   3

    I don't feel part of a social group or organization.

    0   1   2   3

11. I haven't spoken to anyone today.

    0   1   2   3

I don't feel like I made contact with anyone today.

    0   1   2   3

12. I don't have much in common to talk about with those around me.

    0   1   2   3

I don't feel I have anything to say to people.

    0   1   2   3

13. When I'm with others I don't disclose much about myself.

    0   1   2   3

I don't feel I'm being myself with others.

    0   1   2   3

14. I don't take social risks.

    0   1   2   3

I fear embarrassing myself around others.

    0   1   2   3

15. People don't see me as an interesting person.

    0   1   2   3

I don't feel I am interesting.

    0   1   2   3

Erectile Dysfunction Quality of Life (EDQoL)

PURPOSE To measure quality of life (QoL) for men with erectile dysfunction (ED).

AUTHORS R. P. MacDonagh et al.

DESCRIPTION The EDQoL is a 15-item questionnaire designed to measure the impact on QoL of men suffering from ED. Despite the apparent widespread prevalence of ED, and the likely impact of this problem on QoL, there are no questionnaires that utilize a simple, straightforward assessment of the extent of QoL issues in men with ED. Items for the EDQoL were generated from a review of the literature, consultations with health care professionals, and interviews with men with ED. Using specific criteria for excluding items (described in the Primary Reference), the authors developed the EDQoL. The authors believe that the combination of quantitative and qualitative methods used to develop the EDQoL have led to a questionnaire that is both relevant and psychometrically sound.

NORMS The EDQoL was studied with a sample of 40 men with ED attending clinics in the UK. The mean age of the sample was 52. A number of the sample also had MS; these patients had a mean age of 35 compared to non-MS patients with a mean age of 56. No other demographic information was provided. The mean score on the EDQoL for all respondents was 22 (SD=14). The range of scores was from 0 to 58, suggesting that the EDQoL has a good ability to reflect the wide range of QoL effects.

SCORING The EDQoL is easily scored by summing item responses. The range of possible scores is from 0 to 60, with lower scores indicating better QoL.

RELIABILITY The EDQoL has very good internal consistency, with an alpha of .94. Data on stability were not available.

VALIDITY Data on validity were not available in the Primary Reference, but will be available in subsequent publications. The authors might argue that the EDQoL has good face and content validity.

PRIMARY REFERENCE MacDonagh, R. P., et al. (2004). The EDQoL: The development of a new quality of life measure for patients with erectile dysfunction, *Quality of Life Research, 13,* 361–368. Instrument reproduced with the permission of Dr. R. P. MacDonagh.

AVAILABILITY Email Dr. MacDonagh at Ruaraidh.MacDonagh@tst.nhs.uk.

EDQoL

Instructions: Please check the one response for each question that comes closest to describing you.

Question	Response		
1. As a result of your erectile difficulties, do you blame yourself for being unable to satisfy your partner?	☐ Not at all ☐ Quite a lot	☐ A little ☐ A great deal	☐ Somewhat
2. Does your inability to produce an erection with your partner make you feel guilty?	☐ Not at all ☐ Quite a lot	☐ A little ☐ A great deal	☐ Somewhat
3. Do you feel less desirable as a result of your erectile difficulties?	☐ Not at all ☐ Quite a lot	☐ A little ☐ A great deal	☐ Somewhat
4. Do you feel hurt by your partner's response to your erectile difficulties?	☐ Not at all ☐ Quite a lot	☐ A little ☐ A great deal	☐ Somewhat
5. Does the fact that you are unable to produce an erection make you feel less of a man?	☐ Not at all ☐ Quite a lot	☐ A little ☐ A great deal	☐ Somewhat
6. Do you feel angry or bitter that you cannot produce an erection?	☐ Not at all ☐ Quite a lot	☐ A little ☐ A great deal	☐ Somewhat
7. Do you feel a failure because of your erectile difficulties?	☐ Not at all ☐ Quite a lot	☐ A little ☐ A great deal	☐ Somewhat
8. Does your partner feel let down by your inability to produce an erection?	☐ Not at all ☐ Quite a lot	☐ A little ☐ A great deal	☐ Somewhat
9. Are you worried that your erectile problems have affected the closeness between you and your partner?	☐ Not at all ☐ Quite a lot	☐ A little ☐ A great deal	☐ Somewhat
10. Does your erectile problem make you worry about how your life will develop in the future?	☐ Not at all ☐ Quite a lot	☐ A little ☐ A great deal	☐ Somewhat
11. Is your sense of identity altered by your lack of erectile function?	☐ Not at all ☐ Quite a lot	☐ A little ☐ A great deal	☐ Somewhat
12. Are you preoccupied by your erection problems?	☐ Not at all ☐ Quite a lot	☐ A little ☐ A great deal	☐ Somewhat
13. Do you feel sad or tearful as a result of your erectile difficulties?	☐ Not at all ☐ Quite a lot	☐ A little ☐ A great deal	☐ Somewhat

14. Do you feel that other people are happier than you because they are sexually fulfilled?

☐ Not at all   ☐ A little   ☐ Somewhat
☐ Quite a lot   ☐ A great deal

15. Is your self-esteem damaged by your erectile problems?

☐ Not at all   ☐ A little   ☐ Somewhat
☐ Quite a lot   ☐ A great deal

Experience of Heterosexual Intercourse Scale (EHIS)

PURPOSE To measure components of heterosexual intercourse.

AUTHORS Gurit E. Birnbaum and Dafna Laser-Brandt

DESCRIPTION The EHIS is a 79-item instrument designed to assess various aspects of heterosexual experience, including feelings, thoughts, and motives involved in the experience. The purpose of developing of this questionnaire, a refined version of the authors' Women's Experience of Heterosexual Intercourse Questionnaire, included in this book, was to make available a questionnaire on sexual experiences that could be used for both men and women. The EHIS is comprised of three major subscales and several subfactors (factors within each of the subscales): Relationship-Centered Sexual Experience (RC; 29 items, 4 subfactors); Worry-Centered Sexual Experience (WC; 26 items, 4 subfactors); and Pleasure-Centered Sexual Experience (PC; 24 items, 3 subfactors). The items in each subscale are available in the Primary Reference. While the EHIS has more items than most of the scales in this book, it is easily administered and completed; hence, its inclusion.

NORMS The EHIS was developed with a sample of 178 Israeli men and 181 Israeli women (mean age=25.15). The mean age and years of education (approximately 13.70 years) showed no significant differences between the men and women. 28.02% of the men were married and 71.98% were single, while 35.23% of women were married and 64.77% were single. The means for the subscales in relation to subfactors are available in the Primary Reference.

SCORING The EHIS is easily scored by taking the mean of the items within each subscale. Higher scores indicate greater adherence to that subscale. Men and women differed in their responses, with women being more centered on the aversive and positive relational aspects of heterosexual intercourse than men.

RELIABILITY The EHIS has fair to very good internal consistency with alphas of .67 to .86 for the subscales. The overall alpha for all items was .87. Data on stability were not reported.

VALIDITY The EHIS has established some degree of concurrent validity with significant correlations between most of the subfactors and the Israeli Sexual Behavior Inventory.

PRIMARY REFERENCE Birnbaum, G. E., and Laser-Brandt, D. (2002). Gender differences in the experience of heterosexual intercourse, *Canadian Journal of Human Sexuality, 11*, 143–158. Instrument reproduced with permission of Dr. Birnbaum.

AVAILABILITY Email Dr. Birnbaum at birnbag@mail.biu.as.il.

The objective of this questionnaire is to describe the experience of sexual intercourse.

Try to recall a situation or a number of situations in which you had sexual intercourse, and imagine to yourself, in as much detail as possible, what happened to you during the entire experience, and try to recreate in your mind the things that occurred during those moments.

On the following pages, you will find a list of sentences dealing with the situation/s that you have brought to your awareness.

Please circle, next to each sentence, the degree to which it matches the experience/s you had.

For each sentence, there is a scale of numbers from 1, which indicates total lack of fit, to 9 which represents a total match. If the sentence matches the experience closely, mark a higher number; if it does not match, mark a lower number.

It is important to us that your answers be based on an experience or experiences of sexual intercourse that you have had during your life, therefore try to answer the questions from your own personal-subjective point of view, and ignore things you have heard or read about the topic.

Please try not to skip any questions.

At this point, we wish to note that these questionnaires are anonymous and confidential.

We greatly appreciate the effort you are willing to make.

Thank you for your cooperation.

Next to each sentence, mark the degree to which it matches your experience/s during sexual intercourse.

During sexual intercourse . . .	Closely matches						Does not match		
1. I feel my partner is considerate of me	9	8	7	6	5	4	3	2	1
2. I'm focused on satisfying my partner	9	8	7	6	5	4	3	2	1
3. I'm afraid of the outcomes of my actions	9	8	7	6	5	4	3	2	1
4. I feel desired	9	8	7	6	5	4	3	2	1
5. I feel special	9	8	7	6	5	4	3	2	1
6. I think that it can't be better than this	9	8	7	6	5	4	3	2	1
7. I feel my partner knows me	9	8	7	6	5	4	3	2	1
8. I feel guilty	9	8	7	6	5	4	3	2	1
9. I feel loss of control	9	8	7	6	5	4	3	2	1
10. I feel warmth toward my partner	9	8	7	6	5	4	3	2	1
11. I'm afraid of disappointing my partner	9	8	7	6	5	4	3	2	1
12. I think about good things only	9	8	7	6	5	4	3	2	1
13. I feel power and strength	9	8	7	6	5	4	3	2	1
14. I feel disconnected from the world	9	8	7	6	5	4	3	2	1
15. I want there to be more foreplay	9	8	7	6	5	4	3	2	1
16. I'm jealous of my partner	9	8	7	6	5	4	3	2	1
17. I feel that I'm not "good" enough in bed	9	8	7	6	5	4	3	2	1
18. I'm in a state of ecstasy	9	8	7	6	5	4	3	2	1
19. I want to receive attention from my partner	9	8	7	6	5	4	3	2	1
20. I feel a sort of fogginess in my thinking	9	8	7	6	5	4	3	2	1
21. I feel a sense of conquest	9	8	7	6	5	4	3	2	1
22. I feel I am important to my partner	9	8	7	6	5	4	3	2	1
23. I feel a lack of communication with my partner	9	8	7	6	5	4	3	2	1
24. I try to please my partner	9	8	7	6	5	4	3	2	1
25. I'm focused on enjoying my partner	9	8	7	6	5	4	3	2	1

continued

During sexual intercourse . . .	Closely matches								Does not match
26. I feel distress	9	8	7	6	5	4	3	2	1
27. I think about what my partner thinks/feels	9	8	7	6	5	4	3	2	1
28. I feel relaxed	9	8	7	6	5	4	3	2	1
29. I feel that my partner accepts me	9	8	7	6	5	4	3	2	1
30. I feel embarrassed	9	8	7	6	5	4	3	2	1
31. I feel it is difficult for me to reach orgasm	9	8	7	6	5	4	3	2	1
32. I'm using my partner to fulfill my needs	9	8	7	6	5	4	3	2	1
33. I feel satisfied	9	8	7	6	5	4	3	2	1
34. I feel attracted to my partner	9	8	7	6	5	4	3	2	1
35. I feel sadness	9	8	7	6	5	4	3	2	1
36. I'm focused on my own needs	9	8	7	6	5	4	3	2	1
37. I feel love toward my partner	9	8	7	6	5	4	3	2	1
38. I feel lonely	9	8	7	6	5	4	3	2	1
39. I feel pleasure	9	8	7	6	5	4	3	2	1
40. I feel familiar with my body	9	8	7	6	5	4	3	2	1
41. I feel intimacy and closeness to my partner	9	8	7	6	5	4	3	2	1
42. I feel that I am merging with my partner	9	8	7	6	5	4	3	2	1
43. I feel that I'm slave of my body and desire	9	8	7	6	5	4	3	2	1
44. I feel alienated and detached	9	8	7	6	5	4	3	2	1
45. I feel disgust	9	8	7	6	5	4	3	2	1
46. I feel secure	9	8	7	6	5	4	3	2	1
47. I think of how to entice my partner	9	8	7	6	5	4	3	2	1
48. Bothersome thoughts disturb my concentration	9	8	7	6	5	4	3	2	1
49. I feel a sensation of wholeness	9	8	7	6	5	4	3	2	1
50. I want to feel loved	9	8	7	6	5	4	3	2	1
51. I feel a floating sensation	9	8	7	6	5	4	3	2	1
52. I feel that I'm doing something impure	9	8	7	6	5	4	3	2	1

During sexual intercourse . . .	Closely matches								Does not match
53. I'm preoccupied in seducing my partner	9	8	7	6	5	4	3	2	1
54. I'm afraid of penetration	9	8	7	6	5	4	3	2	1
55. My thoughts wander to other things	9	8	7	6	5	4	3	2	1
56. I feel that I'm doing something forbidden	9	8	7	6	5	4	3	2	1
57. I feel as if I have melted	9	8	7	6	5	4	3	2	1
58. I want my partner to express warmth towards me	9	8	7	6	5	4	3	2	1
59. I feel relief	9	8	7	6	5	4	3	2	1
60. I feel anger toward my partner	9	8	7	6	5	4	3	2	1
61. I feel something is missing	9	8	7	6	5	4	3	2	1
62. I feel self-hatred	9	8	7	6	5	4	3	2	1
63. My partner's pleasure satisfies me	9	8	7	6	5	4	3	2	1
64. I feel emptiness	9	8	7	6	5	4	3	2	1
65. I feel feminine/masculine	9	8	7	6	5	4	3	2	1
66. I feel calmness	9	8	7	6	5	4	3	2	1
67. I feel I'm responding to my partner's needs	9	8	7	6	5	4	3	2	1
68. I feel self-pity	9	8	7	6	5	4	3	2	1
69. I feel excitement	9	8	7	6	5	4	3	2	1
70. I allow myself to do things I do not in daily life	9	8	7	6	5	4	3	2	1
71. I feel that my partner is focused on me	9	8	7	6	5	4	3	2	1
72. I feel wanted	9	8	7	6	5	4	3	2	1
73. I concentrate solely on myself	9	8	7	6	5	4	3	2	1
74. I want to be alone	9	8	7	6	5	4	3	2	1
75. I feel understood	9	8	7	6	5	4	3	2	1
76. I want there to be more feeling	9	8	7	6	5	4	3	2	1
77. I feel my partner doesn't know how to excite me	9	8	7	6	5	4	3	2	1
78. It is hard for me to concentrate during the act itself	9	8	7	6	5	4	3	2	1
79. I feel that my behavior is spontaneous	9	8	7	6	5	4	3	2	1

Fear-of-Intimacy Scale (FIS)

PURPOSE To measure fear of intimacy.

AUTHORS Carol J. Descutner and Mark H. Thelen

DESCRIPTION The FIS is a 35-item instrument designed to measure fear of intimacy, defined as the inhibited capacity of an individual, because of anxiety, to exchange thoughts and feelings of personal significance with another individual who is highly valued. The FIS is based on the idea that intimacy exists only with the communication of personal information about which one has strong feelings and with high regard for the intimate other. The FIS is viewed as useful for research on this topic as well as for evaluating treatment outcomes when problems with intimacy are the focus.

NORMS The FIS was studied initially in several stages involving 175 male and 285 female introductory psychology students. The mean age for the subsample of 129 from this group was 19.1 years. The mean score on the FIS was 78.75 (SD=21.82); there was no statistically significant difference between men and women.

SCORING The FIS is easily scored by summing individual item responses for a total score. Items 3, 6–8, 10, 14, 17–19, 21, 22, 25, 27, 29, and 30 are reverse-scored.

RELIABILITY The FIS has excellent internal consistency, with an alpha of .93. The FIS also has excellent stability, with a one-month test-retest correlations of .89.

VALIDITY The FIS has good construct validity in comparison with a number of measures with which it should and should not be correlated. These included positive correlations with the UCLA Loneliness Scale and negative correlations with the Jourard Self-Disclosure Questionnaire, the Miller Social Intimacy Scale, and the Need for Cognition, as well as several items of self-report data on relationships. The FIS is correlated significantly with social desireability.

PRIMARY REFERENCE Descutner, C. J., and Thelen, M. H. (1991). Development and validation of a Fear-of-Intimacy Scale, *Psychological Assessment*, 3, 218–225.

AVAILABILITY Dr. Mark Thelen, University of Missouri, 210 McAlester Hall, Columbia, MO 65211. Email: thelenm@missouri.edu.

Part A Instructions: Imagine you are in a *close, dating* relationship. Respond to the following statements as you would *if you were in that close relationship*. Rate how characteristic each statement is of you on a scale of 1 to 5 as described below, and put your response in the space to the left of the statement.

1 = Not at all characteristic me
2 = Slightly characteristic of me
3 = Moderately characteristic of me
4 = Very characteristic of me
5 = Extremely characteristic of me

Note. In each statement "O" refers to the person who would be in the close relationship with you.

____ 1. I would feel uncomfortable telling O about things in the past that I have felt ashamed of.
____ 2. I would feel uneasy talking with O about something that has hurt me deeply.
____ 3. I would feel comfortable expressing my true feelings to O.
____ 4. If O were upset I would sometimes be afraid of showing that I care.
____ 5. I might be afraid to confide my innermost feelings to O.
____ 6. I would feel at ease telling O that I care about him/her.
____ 7. I would have a feeling of complete togetherness with O.
____ 8. I would be comfortable discussing significant problems with O.
____ 9. A part of me would be afraid to make a long-term commitment to O.
____ 10. I would feel comfortable telling my experiences, even sad ones, to O.
____ 11. I would probably feel nervous showing O strong feelings of affection.
____ 12. I would find it difficult being open with O about my personal thoughts.
____ 13. I would feel uneasy with O depending on me for emotional support.
____ 14. I would not be afraid to share with O what I dislike about myself.
____ 15. I would be afraid to take the risk of being hurt in order to establish a closer relationship with O.
____ 16. I would feel comfortable keeping very personal information to myself.
____ 17. I would not be nervous about being spontaneous with O.
____ 18. I would feel comfortable telling O things that I do not tell other people.
____ 19. I would feel comfortable trusting O with my deepest thoughts and feelings.
____ 20. I would sometimes feel uneasy if O told me about very personal matters.
____ 21. I would be comfortable revealing to O what I feel are my shortcomings and handicaps.
____ 22. I would be comfortable with having a close emotional tie between us.
____ 23. I would be afraid of sharing my private thoughts with O.
____ 24. I would be afraid that I might not always feel close to O.
____ 25. I would be comfortable telling O what my needs are.
____ 26. I would be afraid that O would be more invested in the relationship than I would be.
____ 27. I would feel comfortable about having open and honest communication with O.
____ 28. I would sometimes feel uncomfortable listening to O's personal problems.
____ 29. I would feel at ease to completely be myself around O.
____ 30. I would feel relaxed being together and talking about our personal goals.

Part B Instructions: Respond to the following statements as they apply to your past relationships. Rate how characteristic each statement is of you on a scale of 1 to 5 as described in the instructions for Part A.

___ 31. I have shied away from opportunities to be close to someone.
___ 32. I have held back my feelings in previous relationships.
___ 33. There are people who think that I am afraid to get close to them.
___ 34. There are people who think that I am not an easy person to get to know.
___ 35. I have done things in previous relationships to keep me from developing closeness.

Fear of Negative Evaluation (FNE)

PURPOSE To measure social anxiety.

AUTHORS David Watson and Ronald Friend

DESCRIPTION This 30-item instrument was designed to measure one aspect of social anxiety, the fear of receiving negative evaluations from others. Scores on the FNE essentially reflect a fear of the loss of social approval. Items on the measure include signs of anxiety and ineffective social behaviors that would incur disapproval by others. The FNE is also available in a shorter, 12-item form (Leary, 1983). Both versions are reproduced here. The Brief FNE is composed of the original FNE items which correlated above .50 with the total FNE score. The Brief FNE and the original FNE are highly correlated.

NORMS The FNE was originally developed on a sample of 298 college students, of which 92 were excluded from data analysis because of attrition or missing information. No demographic data are presented. The mean FNE score was 13.97 for males ($n=60$) and 16.1 for females ($n=146$). The Brief FNE has a different scoring system. The mean Brief FNE score was 35.7 with a standard deviation of 8.1 for a sample of 150 college students.

SCORING The FNE items are answered "true" or "false." Items 2, 3, 5, 7, 9, 11, 13, 14, 17, 19, 20, 22, 24, 25, 28, 29, and 30 are keyed "true" while the other items are keyed for "false" responses. A value of 1 is assigned to each item answer which matches the key and 0 for answers which do not match the key. Scores are the sum of all item values and range from 0 to 30. The Brief FNE is rated on a five point scale in terms of how characteristic each item is of the respondent. Items 2, 4, 7, and 10 are reverse-scored. Total scores are the sum of the item responses and range from 12 to 60.

RELIABILITY Internal consistency of the FNE was first determined by correlating each item with the total FNE score. The average item-to-total-score correlation was .72. Internal consistency using Kuder-Richardson formula 20 was excellent, with correlations of .94 for a sample of 205 college students and .96 for a separate sample of 154 subjects. The FNE was shown to be stable with a test-retest correlation of .78 over a one-month period and .94 from a separate sample of 29 subjects. The Brief FNE has excellent internal consistency, with a Cronbach's alpha of .90. The Brief FNE is also considered stable with a test-retest correlation of .75 over a four-week period.

VALIDITY A type of known-groups validity was demonstrated by comparing a sample of subjects who scored in the upper 25 percentile of the FNE with subjects from the lower 25 percentile. The results, which only approach statistical significance, suggest that the high FNE group sought more approval from others and avoided disapproval. The groups also differed on measures of uneasiness. Scores on the FNE correlated with measures of social approval, locus of control, desirability, autonomy, dependence, dominance, abasement, exhibitionism, and other measures of anxiety. The Brief FNE was evaluated for validity first by correlating scores with the full-length FNE; this correlation was .96. Criterion-related validity was shown with scores on the Brief FNE correlating with anxiety, avoidance, the degree to which respondents said they were well presented, and the degree to which respondents were bothered by an unfavorable evaluation from others.

PRIMARY REFERENCES Watson, D., and Friend, R. (1969). Measurement of social-evaluative anxiety, *Journal of Consulting and Clinical Psychology*, 33, 448–457. Leary, M. R. (1983). A brief version of the Fear of Negative Evaluation scale, *Personality and Social Psychology Bulletin*, 9, 371–375. Instrument reproduced with permission of D. Watson and the American Psychological Association.

AVAILABILITY May be copied from this volume.

For the following statements, please answer each in terms of whether it is true or false for you. Circle T for true or F for false.

T F   1. I rarely worry about seeming foolish to others.
T F   2. I worry about what people will think of me even when I know it doesn't make any difference.
T F   3. I become tense and jittery if I know someone is sizing me up.
T F   4. I am unconcerned even if I know people are forming an unfavorable impression of me.
T F   5. I feel very upset when I commit some social error.
T F   6. The opinions that important people have of me cause me little concern.
T F   7. I am often afraid that I may look ridiculous or make a fool of myself.
T F   8. I react very little when other people disapprove of me.
T F   9. I am frequently afraid of other people noticing my shortcomings.
T F   10. The disapproval of others would have little effect on me.
T F   11. If someone is evaluating me I tend to expect the worst.
T F   12. I rarely worry about what kind of impression I am making on someone.
T F   13. I am afraid that others will not approve of me.
T F   14. I am afraid that people will find fault with me.
T F   15. Other people's opinions of me do not bother me.
T F   16. I am not necessarily upset if I do not please someone.
T F   17. When I am talking to someone, I worry about what they may be thinking about me.
T F   18. I feel that you can't help making social errors sometimes, so why worry about it.
T F   19. I am usually worried about what kind of impression I make.
T F   20. I worry a lot about what my superiors think of me.
T F   21. If I know someone is judging me, it has little effect on me.
T F   22. I worry that others will think I am not worthwhile.
T F   23. I worry very little about what others may think of me.
T F   24. Sometimes I think I am too concerned with what other people think of me.
T F   25. I often worry that I will say or do the wrong things.
T F   26. I am often indifferent to the opinions others have of me.
T F   27. I am usually confident that others will have a favorable impression of me.
T F   28. I often worry that people who are important to me won't think very much of me.
T F   29. I brood about the opinions my friends have about me.
T F   30. I become tense and jittery if I know I am being judged by my superiors.

For the following statements please indicate how characteristic each is of you using the following rating scale:

1 = Not at all characteristic of me
2 = Slightly characteristic of me
3 = Moderately characteristic of me
4 = Very characteristic of me
5 = Extremely characteristic of me

Please record your answers in the spaces to the left of the items.

____ 1. I worry about what other people will think of me even when I know it doesn't make any difference.
____ 2. I am unconcerned even if I know people are forming an unfavorable impression of me.
____ 3. I am frequently afraid of other people noticing my shortcomings.
____ 4. I rarely worry about what kind of impression I am making on someone.
____ 5. I am afraid that people will not approve of me.
____ 6. I am afraid that people will find fault with me.
____ 7. Other people's opinions of me do not bother me.
____ 8. When I am talking to someone, I worry about what they may be thinking about me.
____ 9. I am usually worried about what kind of impression I make.
____ 10. If I know someone is judging me, it has little effect on me.
____ 11. Sometimes I think I am too concerned with what other people think of me.
____ 12. I often worry that I will say or do the wrong things.

Fear Questionnaire (FQ)

PURPOSE To measure fear in phobic patients.

AUTHORS I. M. Marks and A. M. Mathews

DESCRIPTION This 24-item instrument was developed in three research and treatment facilities in order to assess the outcome of work with phobic patients. The form is general enough to be useful with any phobic disorder, but has added precision because it allows the practitioner to specify the phobia that is the focus of treatment, which is called the main target phobia rating. The form includes fifteen questions on different types of phobias, which can be used as subscales measuring agoraphobia (Ag), blood-injury phobia (BI), and social phobia (SP). The FQ also includes 5 items measuring anxiety and depression symptoms (ADS) associated with phobia. Finally, along with the target phobia at the beginning of the form, the FQ ends with another global phobia index.

NORMS Normative data are reported on all aspects of the FQ. For the main target phobia, the mean score for a sample of 20 phobic inpatients was 7. The mean score on the 15-item total phobia scale was 47 for the 20 patients. Extensive additional data on large samples are available.

SCORING All items are rated on a scale from 1 to 8 with higher scores reflecting more severe phobic responses. The total phobia rating is the sum of the scores for items 2 through 16. The three subscales are composed of the following items: Ag: 5, 6, 8, 12, 15; BI: 2, 4, 10, 13, 16; SP: 3, 7, 9, 11, 14. The ADS score is the sum of items 18 through 22.

RELIABILITY This instrument has good test-retest reliability. For the three subscales combined the correlation was .82 for a one-week period. The test-retest correlation was also excellent for the Main Target Phobia (.93), and good for the global phobia rating (.79) and the anxiety-depression subscale (.82). Internal consistency data are not reported.

VALIDITY The validity of the FQ has been supported by several studies. The FQ has been shown to discriminate between phobics and nonphobics on all aspects of the measure. Most important for the purposes of monitoring clients, the FQ has been shown to be sensitive, with scores changing over the course of intervention.

PRIMARY REFERENCE Marks, I. M., and Mathews, A. M. (1978). Brief standard self-rating for phobic patients, *Behaviour Research and Therapy*, 17, 263–267. Instrument reproduced with permission of I. M. Marks and A. M. Mathews.

AVAILABILITY May be copied from this volume.

Choose a number from the scale below to show how much you would avoid each of the situations listed below because of fear or other unpleasant feelings. Then write the number you chose in the blank opposite each situation.

0	1	2	3	4	5	6	7	8
Would not avoid it		Slightly avoid it		Definitely avoid it		Markedly avoid it		Always avoid it

___ 1. Main phobia you want treated (describe in your own words)
___ 2. Injections or minor surgery
___ 3. Eating or drinking with other people
___ 4. Hospitals
___ 5. Traveling alone by bus or coach
___ 6. Walking alone on busy streets
___ 7. Being watched or stared at
___ 8. Going into crowded shops
___ 9. Talking to people in authority
___ 10. Sight of blood
___ 11. Being criticized
___ 12. Going alone far from home
___ 13. Thought of injury or illness
___ 14. Speaking or acting to an audience
___ 15. Large open spaces
___ 16. Going to the dentist
___ 17. Other situations (describe)

Now choose a number from the scale below to show how much you are troubled by each problem listed, and write the number in the blank.

0	1	2	3	4	5	6	7	8
Hardly at all		Slightly troublesome		Definitely troublesome		Markedly troublesome		Very severely troublesome

___ 18. Feeling miserable or depressed
___ 19. Feeling irritable or angry
___ 20. Feeling tense or panicky
___ 21. Upsetting thoughts coming into your mind
___ 22. Feeling you or your surroundings are strange or unreal
___ 23. Other feelings (describe)

How would you rate the present state of your phobic symptoms on the scale below? Please circle one number between 0 and 8.

0	1	2	3	4	5	6	7	8
No phobias present		Slightly disturbing/not really disturbing		Definitely disturbing/ disabling		Markedly disturbing/ disabling		Very severely disturbing/ disabling

Fear Survey Schedule-II (FSS-II)

PURPOSE To measure responses to commonly occurring fears.

AUTHOR James H. Geer

DESCRIPTION The 51-item FSS-II is designed to measure fear responses. The FSS-II is one of the most widely-used fear schedules in the behavior therapy literature. The instrument lists potential fear-evoking situations and stimuli. A client rates his or her level of discomfort or distress. The items included on the FSS-II were first empirically selected from a pool of 111. Each item was then examined to determine its correlation with total scores. All items, except number 15, correlated with total scores for male and female college students, with item 15 reaching significance for females. Total scores on this FSS reflect general fear.

NORMS Mean scores on the sample mentioned above were 75.78 with a standard deviation of 33.84, for males and 100.16 with a standard deviation of 36.11 for females. These means were significantly different. In a separate study, 1814 college students enrolled in an introductory psychology class had means and standard deviations of 81.81 and 33.64 for males and 108.47 and 36.78 for females. These means were also significantly different.

SCORING Each item is rated on a 7-point scale of intensity of fear. Scores are the sum of the item scores and range from 51 to 357. Higher scores indicate greater fear.

RELIABILITY The FSS-II is a very reliable instrument, with an internal consistency coefficient of .94 using Kuder-Richardson formula 20. The instrument is reported to be stable, although the reliability data are not as direct as test-retest reliability data.

VALIDITY The FSS has good concurrent validity, with significant correlations between the FSS and emotionality and anxiety, while the scores are not associated with scores on measures of introversion and extroversion. Known-groups validity data indicate that groups categorized according to FSS scores differ on five relevant criteria: the time it took subjects to approach a frightening stimulus, the distance between the subjects and the stimulus, subjects' ratings of experienced fear, experimenter's rating of the fear the subjects presented, and an affect adjective checklist completed by the subjects.

PRIMARY REFERENCE Geer, J. H. (1965). The development of a scale to measure fear, *Behaviour Research and Therapy*, 3, 45–53. Instrument reproduced with permission of James H. Geer.

AVAILABILITY May be copied from this volume.

Below are 51 different stimuli that can cause fear in people. Please rate how much fear you feel using the following rating scale and record your answer in the space provided:

1 = None
2 = Very little fear
3 = A little fear
4 = Some fear
5 = Much fear
6 = Very much fear
7 = Terror

___ 1. Sharp objects
___ 2. Being a passenger in a car
___ 3. Dead bodies
___ 4. Suffocating
___ 5. Failing a test
___ 6. Looking foolish
___ 7. Being a passenger on an airplane
___ 8. Worms
___ 9. Arguing with parents
___ 10. Rats and mice
___ 11. Life after death
___ 12. Hypodermic needles
___ 13. Being criticized
___ 14. Meeting someone for the first time
___ 15. Roller coasters
___ 16. Being alone
___ 17. Making mistakes
___ 18. Being misunderstood
___ 19. Death
___ 20. Being in a fight
___ 21. Crowded places
___ 22. Blood
___ 23. Heights
___ 24. Being a leader
___ 25. Swimming alone
___ 26. Illness
___ 27. Being with drunks
___ 28. Illness or injury to loved ones
___ 29. Being self-conscious
___ 30. Driving a car
___ 31. Meeting authority
___ 32. Mental illness
___ 33. Closed places
___ 34. Boating
___ 35. Spiders

___ 36. Thunderstorms
___ 37. Not being a success
___ 38. God
___ 39. Snakes
___ 40. Cemeteries
___ 41. Speaking before a group
___ 42. Seeing a fight
___ 43. Death of a loved one
___ 44. Dark places
___ 45. Strange dogs
___ 46. Deep water
___ 47. Being with a member of the opposite sex
___ 48. Stinging insects
___ 49. Untimely or early death
___ 50. Losing a job
___ 51. Auto accidents

Five Facet Mindfulness Questionnaire (FFMQ)

AUTHORS Ruth A. Baer, Gregory T. Smith, Emily Lykins, Daniel Button, Jennifer Krietemeyer, Sharon Sauer, Erin Walsh, Danielle Duggan, L. Toney and J. Mark G. Williams

PURPOSE To measure five aspects of mindfulness

DESCRIPTION The 39-item instrument assesses five interrelated dimensions of mindfulness: Observing, where one attends to the label of inner experiences and those in the social environment; Describing, the labels in one's inner experience and social environmental experiences; Acting with Awareness, where one attends to the here-and-now experience; Nonjudgmentalness of one's inner experiences; and Non-reactivity where one allows thoughts, emotions and experience to come and go and not to press the situation or get carried away by the experience. The FFMQ is useful in evaluating treatments using mindfulness-based interventions such as Buddhist meditation, yoga, thi chi and some relaxation interventions for anxiety. It is also useful when evaluating a wellness and health promotion program. Since mindfulness is so highly associated with psychological well being and the absence of mental health symptoms, it is a useful goal to monitor with most interventions.

NORMS The FFMQ has excellence norms using four different samples: students (n = 259), community sample of non-mediators (n = 293), highly-educated non-mediators (n = 252) and meditator (n = 213) who have at least one year experience (45% reported 10 years or more of meditation) and do so at least once a week (the average was 3-4 times a week and 44% indicated they meditated for 21-30 minutes each time; it is safe to say that the mediators were quite experienced. The means and (standard deviations) of Observe Score (OS), Describe Score (DS), Act Aware Score (AAS),NonJudgmental Score (NJS), and NonReactive Score (NRS) were 31.96 (4.16), 31.84 (5.3)28.08 (5.1)32.44 (5.63)and 25.70 (4.01) for the sample of meditators, and 27.04 (5.63), 30.01 (5.63), 28.32 (5.21), 29.13 (5.79), and 22.82, (4.19) for the sample of well-educated non-meditators. The student means and (standard deviations) were 24.324.84, 26.46 6.01, 25.315.77 27.75 5.9, 20.5 3.82 for the OS, DS, AAS, NJS and NRS, respectively. The community sample of non-mediators had means and (standard deviations) of 24.32 (5.48), 24.63 (7.06), 24.57 (6.57), 23.85, (7.33), 19.53 (4.88) on the OS, DS, AAS, NJS and NRS, respectively.

SCORING The OS is obtained by summing items 1, 6, 11, 15, 20, 26, 31, 36. The DS is obtained by summing items 2, 7, 12R, 16, 22, 27, 32, 37 with 16 and 22 requiring reversing the scores due to the directionality of the items. AAS is obtained by reverse-scoring all the items and then summing 5, 8, 13, 18, 23, 28, 34, 38. NJS is obtained by first reversing all responses and then summing items 3, 10, 14, 17, 25, 30, 35, 39. Finally, the NRS is obtained by summing items 4, 9, 19, 21, 24, 29, 33.

RELIABILITY The FFMQ has adequate to good reliability with alpha coefficients ranging from .72 to .91 for all scales except NRS which was .67; however, in other samples the NRS had alpha coefficients ranging from .81 to .86.

VALIDITY The FFMQ has excellent evidence of validity. The five-facet structure was supported by factor analysis, with the scale scores having moderate correlations to suggest they are independent but are interrelated constructs. Meditation experiences are also associated with each scale, except for AAS, in a sample of 1,107. The FFMS also has very strong evidence of known-groups validity with the meditators having significantly higher scores than all three of the non-meditating samples. Convergent and concurrent validity are evidenced with correlations between psychological well-being on all of the FFMs scales; the student sample was not associated with well-being. The FFMS also has evidence of predictive validity as meditation experiences were predictor variables for well-being in regression analyses.

PRIMARY REFERENCES Baer, R. A., Smith, G. T., Hopkins, J., Krietemeyer, J, and Toney, L (2006). Using self-report assessment methods to explore facets of mindfulness. *Assessment*, *13*, 27–45. Baer, R. A., Smith G. T., Lykins, E., Button, D., Krietemeyer, J., Sauer, S., Walsh, E., Duggan, D. and Williams, J. M. G. (2008). Construct validity of the Five Facet Mindfulness Questionnaire in meditating and nonmeditating samples. *Assessment*, *15*, 329–342.

AVAILABILITY Ruth Baer, Ph.D, Department of Psychololgy, 115 Kastle Hall, University of Kentucky, Lexington, KY 40506-0044.

5-FACET M QUESTIONNAIRE

Please rate each of the following statements using the scale provided. Write the number in the blank that best describes your own opinion of what is generally true for you.

1	2	3	4	5
never or very rarely true	rarely true	sometimes true	often true	very often or always true

—— 1. When I'm walking, I deliberately notice the sensations of my body moving.

—— 2. I'm good at finding words to describe my feelings.

—— 3. I criticize myself for having irrational or inappropriate emotions.

—— 4. I perceive my feelings and emotions without having to react to them.

—— 5. When I do things, my mind wanders off and I'm easily distracted.

—— 6. When I take a shower or bath, I stay alert to the sensations of water on my body.

—— 7. I can easily put my beliefs, opinions, and expectations into words.

—— 8. I don't pay attention to what I'm doing because I'm daydreaming, worrying, or otherwise distracted.

—— 9. I watch my feelings without getting lost in them.

—— 10. I tell myself I shouldn't be feeling the way I'm feeling.

—— 11. I notice how foods and drinks affect my thoughts, bodily sensations, and emotions.

—— 12. It's hard for me to find the words to describe what I'm thinking.

—— 13. I am easily distracted.

—— 14. I believe some of my thoughts are abnormal or bad and I shouldn't think that way.

—— 15. I pay attention to sensations, such as the wind in my hair or sun on my face.

—— 16. I have trouble thinking of the right words to express how I feel about things

—— 17. I make judgments about whether my thoughts are good or bad.

—— 18. I find it difficult to stay focused on what's happening in the present.

—— 19. When I have distressing thoughts or images, I "step back" and am aware of the thought or image without getting taken over by it.

—— 20. I pay attention to sounds, such as clocks ticking, birds chirping, or cars passing.

—— 21. In difficult situations, I can pause without immediately reacting.

—— 22. When I have a sensation in my body, it's difficult for me to describe it because I can't find the right words.

—— 23. It seems I am "running on automatic" without much awareness of what I'm doing.

—— 24. When I have distressing thoughts or images, I feel calm soon after.

—— 25. I tell myself that I shouldn't be thinking the way I'm thinking.

—— 26. I notice the smells and aromas of things.

—— 27. Even when I'm feeling terribly upset, I can find a way to put it into words.

1	2	3	4	5
never or very rarely true	rarely true	sometimes true	often true	very often or always true

—— 28. I rush through activities without being really attentive to them.

—— 29. When I have distressing thoughts or images I am able just to notice them without reacting.

—— 30. I think some of my emotions are bad or inappropriate and I shouldn't feel them.

—— 31. I notice visual elements in art or nature, such as colors, shapes, textures, or patterns of light and shadow.

—— 32. My natural tendency is to put my experiences into words.

—— 33. When I have distressing thoughts or images, I just notice them and let them go.

—— 34. I do jobs or tasks automatically without being aware of what I'm doing.

—— 35. When I have distressing thoughts or images, I judge myself as good or bad, depending what the thought/image is about.

—— 36. I pay attention to how my emotions affect my thoughts and behavior.

—— 37. I can usually describe how I feel at the moment in considerable detail.

—— 38. I find myself doing things without paying attention.

—— 39. I disapprove of myself when I have irrational ideas.

Frequency of Self-Reinforcement Questionnaire (FSRQ)

PURPOSE To measure skill at self-reinforcement.

AUTHOR Elaine M. Heiby

DESCRIPTION The FSRQ (also known as the Self-Reinforcement Questionnaire or SRQ) is a 30-item instrument designed to assess respondents' encouraging, supporting, and valuing themselves and their own efforts. Self-reinforcement is seen as a generalized response set with a low frequency of self-reinforcement viewed as a possible causative factor in depression. Thus, use of this measure would be in conjunction with clinical work on increasing a client's skills at, and the frequency of, self-reinforcement. Items on the FSRQ were initially selected from a pool of 100 items, based on judgments of content validity by 10 clinicians. Research on the FSRQ is continuing with a shorter form available from the author.

NORMS The FSRQ has been studied with several samples of educated adults and undergraduate college students. Actual norms on the latest version of the FSRQ are not available.

SCORING The FSRQ is easily scored by reverse-scoring negatively worded items and summing the individual items to obtain an overall score. The range of scores is from 0 to 90 with higher scores indicating greater frequency of self-reinforcement. Scores below 17 suggest deficits in self-reinforcement skills, dependence on others for approval, and possible vulnerability to depression.

RELIABILITY The FSRQ has very good internal consistency, with split-half reliability of .87. The FSRQ has excellent stability, with an eight-week test-retest correlation of .92.

VALIDITY The FSRQ has good concurrent validity as demonstrated by correlations between FSRQ scores and self-monitoring of self-reinforcement and experimenter ratings of respondents' tendency to engage in self-reinforcement. The FSRQ is not correlated with social desirability response set, and is sensitive to change following training in self-reinforcement skills. The FSRQ is also reported as having good construct validity as demonstrated by negative correlations with self-punishment, the Beck Depression Inventory, and measures of cognitive distortion.

PRIMARY REFERENCE Heiby, E. M. (1983). Assessment of frequency of self-reinforcement, *Journal of Personality and Social Psychology*, 44, 263–270. Instrument reproduced with permission of Elaine M. Heiby and the American Psychological Association.

AVAILABILITY Dr. Elaine M. Heiby, Department of Psychology, University of Hawaii, Honolulu, HI 96822. Email: heiby@hawaii.edu.

Below are a number of statements about beliefs or attitudes people have. Indicate how descriptive the statements are for you by rating each item, as indicated below. There are no right or wrong answers. Your answers are confidential, so do not put your name on this sheet. Thank you!

Rate each item for how much of the time it is descriptive for you. In the blank before each item, rate:

0 = Never descriptive of me
1 = A little of the time descriptive of me
2 = Some of the time descriptive of me
3 = Most of the time descriptive of me

____ 1. When I fail at something, I am still able to feel good about myself.
____ 2. I can stick to a boring task that I need to finish without someone pushing me.
____ 3. I have negative thoughts about myself.
____ 4. When I do something right, I take time to enjoy the feeling.
____ 5. I have such high standards for what I expect of myself that I have a hard time meeting my standards.
____ 6. I seem to blame myself and be very critical of myself when things go wrong.
____ 7. I can have a good time doing some things alone.
____ 8. I get upset with myself when I make mistakes.
____ 9. My feelings of self-confidence go up and down.
____ 10. When I succeed at small things, it helps me to go on.
____ 11. If I do not do something absolutely perfectly, I don't feel satisfied.
____ 12. I get myself through hard things mostly by thinking I'll enjoy myself afterwards.
____ 13. When I make mistakes, I take time to criticize myself.
____ 14. I encourage myself to improve at something by feeling good about myself.
____ 15. I put myself down so that I will do things better in the future.
____ 16. I think talking about what you've done right is bragging.
____ 17. I find that I feel better when I silently praise myself.
____ 18. I can keep working at something hard to do when I stop to think of what I've already done.
____ 19. The way I keep up my self-confidence is by remembering any successes I have had.
____ 20. The way I achieve my goals is by rewarding myself every step along the way.
____ 21. Praising yourself is being selfish.
____ 22. When someone criticizes me, I lose my self-confidence.
____ 23. I criticize myself more often than others criticize me.
____ 24. I feel I have a lot of good qualities.
____ 25. I silently praise myself even when other people do not praise me.
____ 26. Any activity can provide some pleasure no matter how it comes out.
____ 27. If I don't do the best possible job, I don't feel good about myself.
____ 28. I should be upset if I make a mistake.
____ 29. My happiness depends more on myself than it depends on other people.
____ 30. People who talk about their own better points are just bragging.

Friendliness–Unfriendliness Scale (SACRAL)

PURPOSE To measure friendliness as related to self-concept, accessibility, rewardingness, and alienation.

AUTHOR John M. Reisman

DESCRIPTION This 20-item instrument measures friendliness–unfriendliness. Friendliness is a complex set of skills and beliefs about one's self that relates to loneliness, shyness, social skills deficits, and feelings of alienation. For some clients whose problems relate to loneliness and depression, friendliness is a more important assessment than the actual number of friends. Items in the SACRAL were selected from a pool of 40 items based on the ability to discriminate between respondents categorized into high-SACRAL and low-SACRAL groups according to total scores. The short form reported here correlated .94 with the 40-item version. There are four subscales composed of the following items: self-concept (S: items 1, 5, 9, 13, 17); accessibility (AC: items 2, 6, 10, 14, 18); rewardingness (R: items 3, 7, 11, 15, 19); and alienation (AL: items 4, 8, 12, 16, 20). The total score measuring overall friendliness is derived by adding scores for S, AC, R, and AL.

NORMS A sample of 25 undergraduates had a mean and standard deviation of 42.2 and 15.0, respectively. Scores tended to range from 27 to 57. For a subsample of respondents categorized as high in friendliness, the mean was 113 and the standard deviation was 8.8 ($n = 17$). A subsample of respondents considered low in friendliness had a mean of 81 and a standard deviation of 9.0. Both sets of norms are based on the 40-item version and not the 20-item version.

SCORING Items 9, 10, 11, 14, 15, 17, 18, and 19 are scored in the positive direction. Responses of 0 or 1 are scored as 0. All other items are reverse-scored, with responses of 3 or 4 both being scored as 0.

RELIABILITY Reliability data are not presented in the Primary Reference.

VALIDITY There is evidence of construct validity. This is seen in a 94% agreement rate between subjects' SACRAL scores and the assessment of raters of subject responses in a laboratory setting. Concurrent validity is seen by associations between SACRAL subscale scores and ratings of satisfaction with oneself and one's friends and by scores on a measure of the value of friends for being supportive, helpful, and stimulating. Respondents with high and low scores on the SACRAL had significantly different ratings on interpersonal judgment.

PRIMARY REFERENCE Reisman, J. M., and Billingham, S. (1989). SACRAL: Additional correlates of a self-report measure of friendliness-unfriendliness, *Journal of Personality Assessment*, 53, 113–121. Instrument reproduced with permission of John M. Reisman.

AVAILABILITY May be copied from this volume.

The following statements sample how people feel about themselves and other people. There are no right or wrong answers. *What is important is what you personally believe or feel is true of yourself.* Read each statement carefully, then mark how much you agree or disagree with it. Circle 4 if you agree very much. Circle 3 if you somewhat agree. Circle 1 if you somewhat disagree. Circle 0 if you disagree very much.

1. There are many times when you don't think well of yourself.	4	3	1	0
2. A lot of the ideas and opinions of other people don't make much sense.	4	3	1	0
3. You often don't give compliments to someone who might deserve them.	4	3	1	0
4. You find it hard to be really yourself, even with your friends.	4	3	1	0
5. You are a shy person.	4	3	1	0
6. Even if you don't hear from a friend for several days and don't know why, you don't try to get in touch.	4	3	1	0
7. When your friends need advice, it is not always easy for you to give them suggestions or ideas about what to do.	4	3	1	0
8. You like to spend your time alone and to be by yourself.	4	3	1	0
9. You are very pleasant and agreeable.	4	3	1	0
10. If someone comes to talk with you, you always stop whatever it is you're doing and give your attention to the person.	4	3	1	0
11. If there is a new person around, you introduce yourself and your friends.	4	3	1	0
12. If you have time for fun and relaxation, you prefer to read or watch television or do something by yourself.	4	3	1	0
13. You lose your temper easily.	4	3	1	0
14. It's easy for you to start a conversation with a stranger and keep it going.	4	3	1	0
15. When your friends are sick, you always send them a little present or give them a call.	4	3	1	0
16. People often take your actions and comments the wrong way.	4	3	1	0
17. You think of yourself as a very friendly person.	4	3	1	0
18. People often come to you with their personal problems.	4	3	1	0
19. If you see someone who needs help, you drop whatever you're doing and lend a hand.	4	3	1	0
20. Good friends are hard for you to find.	4	3	1	0

Frost Multidimensional Perfectionism Scale (FMPS)

PURPOSE To measure perfectionism.

AUTHORS Randy O. Frost, Patricia Martin, Cathleen Lahart, and Robin Rosenblate

DESCRIPTION The FMPS is a 35-item instrument designed to measure the several components of perfectionism. Since few if any existing measures tap all major dimensions of perfectionism, the FMPS was developed. Perfectionism in general was viewed as having high standards of performance accompanied by overly critical evaluations of one's own behavior. Perfectionism also was viewed as either underlying or being related to several other psychological disorders. A total of 67 items was generated from other measures, and reduced to 35 items in a series of studies. The 35 items comprise six factors: concern over mistakes (CM, items 9, 10, 13, 14, 18, 21, 23, 25, 34); personal standards (PS, items 4, 6, 12, 16, 19, 24, 30); parental expectations (PE, items 1, 11, 15, 20, 26); parental criticism (PC, items 3, 5, 22, 35); doubts about actions (D, items 17, 28, 32, 33); and organization (O, items 2, 7, 8, 27, 29, 31). The FMPS is viewed as a useful measure both for research and therapeutic practice in helping pinpoint and evaluate change in the different components of perfectionism.

NORMS A series of four studies was undertaken to develop the FMPS. The total number of subjects involved 576 female undergraduate students. No other demographic information was provided, nor were actual norms (means and standard deviations).

SCORING The subscale and total scores are derived simply by summing individual item scores. The possible range from the 35 5-point Likert-type items is from 35 to 175, with higher scores suggesting greater amounts of perfectionism.

RELIABILITY The FMPS has good to excellent reliability, with alphas that range from .77 to .93 for the subscales. The alpha for the total scale was .90. No test-retest data were provided.

VALIDITY The FMPS has good concurrent validity, significantly correlating with three other perfectionism scales, the BURNS, EDI, and IBT. The overall FMPS and/or several of its subscales have good construct validity, correlating with a variety of measures of psychopathology including the Brief Symptom Inventory, the Depressive Experiences Questionnaire, and several measures of compulsivity, and with procrastination.

PRIMARY REFERENCE Frost, R. O., Martin, P., Lahart, C., and Rosenblate, R. (1990). The dimensions of perfectionism, *Cognitive Therapy and Research*, 14, 449–468. Instrument reprinted with permission of Randy O. Frost and Plenum Publishing Corp.

AVAILABILITY Dr. Randy O. Frost, Department of Psychology, Smith College, Northampton, MA 01063. Email: rfrost@smith.edu.

Please circle the number that best corresponds to your agreement with each statement below. Use this rating system:

Strongly disagree   1   2   3   4   5   Strongly agree

	Strongly disagree				Strongly agree
1. My parents set very high standards for me.	1	2	3	4	5
2. Organization is very important to me.	1	2	3	4	5
3. As a child, I was punished for doing things less than perfectly.	1	2	3	4	5
4. If I do not set the highest standards for myself, I am likely to end up a second-rate person.	1	2	3	4	5
5. My parents never tried to understand my mistakes.	1	2	3	4	5
6. It is important to me that I be thoroughly competent in everything I do.	1	2	3	4	5
7. I am a neat person.	1	2	3	4	5
8. I try to be an organized person.	1	2	3	4	5
9. If I fail at work/school, I am a failure as a person.	1	2	3	4	5
10. I should be upset if I make a mistake.	1	2	3	4	5
11. My parents wanted me to be the best at everything.	1	2	3	4	5
12. I set higher goals than most people.	1	2	3	4	5
13. If someone does a task at work/school better than I, then I feel like I failed the whole task.	1	2	3	4	5
14. If I fail partly, it is as bad as being a complete failure.	1	2	3	4	5
15. Only outstanding performance is good enough in my family.	1	2	3	4	5
16. I am very good at focusing my efforts on attaining a goal.	1	2	3	4	5
17. Even when I do something very carefully, I often feel that it is not quite right.	1	2	3	4	5
18. I hate being less than best at things.	1	2	3	4	5
19. I have extremely high goals.	1	2	3	4	5

	Strongly disagree				Strongly agree
20. My parents have expected excellence from me.	1	2	3	4	5
21. People will probably think less of me if I make a mistake.	1	2	3	4	5
22. I never felt like I could meet my parents' expectations.	1	2	3	4	5
23. If I do not do as well as other people, it means I am an inferior human being.	1	2	3	4	5
24. Other people seem to accept lower standards from themselves than I do.	1	2	3	4	5
25. If I do not do well all the time, people will not respect me.	1	2	3	4	5
26. My parents have always had higher expectations for my future than I have.	1	2	3	4	5
27. I try to be a neat person.	1	2	3	4	5
28. I usually have doubts about the simple everyday things I do.	1	2	3	4	5
29. Neatness is very important to me.	1	2	3	4	5
30. I expect higher performance in my daily tasks than most people.	1	2	3	4	5
31. I am an organized person.	1	2	3	4	5
32. I tend to get behind in my work because I repeat things over and over.	1	2	3	4	5
33. It takes me a long time to do something "right."	1	2	3	4	5
34. The fewer mistakes I make, the more people will like me.	1	2	3	4	5
35. I never felt like I could meet my parents' standards.	1	2	3	4	5

Gambling Attitudes Scale (GAS)

PURPOSE To measure attitudes toward gambling.

AUTHOR Jeffrey I. Kassinove

DESCRIPTION The GAS is a 59-item instrument designed to measure general attitudes toward gambling and attitudes toward gambling in casinos, betting on horse races, and playing the lottery. In comparison with other questionnaires, the focus of the GAS is on attitudes toward gambling, as opposed to behaviors related to gambling. This is important because attitudes suggest a readiness to act, and people may act differently toward different forms of gambling. Thus, the GAS can be used to help predict which people may be more likely to engage in gambling. For example, highly positive attitudes toward gambling in youth may predict development of pathological gambling. The results of the GAS could be used in schools to develop educational programs to prevent problem gambling. The GAS has four subscales: GAS-general (items 1, 3, 25, 28, 30, 35, 38, 45, and 57); GAS-casino (items 8, 11, 14, 18, 24, 42, 46, 51, and 55); GAS-horse races (items 7, 10, 13, 19, 21, 33, 40, 43, and 48); GAS-lottery (items 4, 16, 27, 32, 36, 47, 50, 53, and 59); and two related scales: a risk-taking scale (items 29 and 54) and a liberal-conservative scale involving the remainder of the items.

NORMS The GAS was developed with 170 college students in undergraduate psychology classes. Norms are as follows: GAS-general, mean 31.77 (SD = 9.69); GAS-casino, mean 35.80 (SD = 9.99); GAS-horse races, mean 27.18 (SD = 9.58); GAS-lottery, mean 39.28 (SD = 8.51); liberal-conservative mean 80.20 (SD = 16.02); and risk-taking, mean 8.17 (SD = 2.51). Means and standard deviations are available in the primary reference for males and females separately.

SCORING The following items are reverse-scored: 1, 2, 3, 4, 5, 7, 8, 11, 12, 13, 15, 16, 18, 19, 20, 21, 24, 25, 27, 28, 29, 30, 32, 33, 34, 35, 36, 38, 40, 41, 42, 43, 45, 46, 48, 49, 53, 54, 55, 56, 57, 58. The scores for the individual subscales are then determined by simply summing up scores on the individual items on that subscale after reverse-scoring.

RELIABILITY The GAS has very good internal consistency with alphas on all subscales that range from .82 to .90. The GAS also has good stability with 2-week test-retest correlations that range from .62 to .94.

VALIDITY The GAS does not appear to be strongly affected by social desirability responses; correlations are very low between the GAS subscales and the Marlowe-Crowne Social Desirability Scale. The GAS has established a fair degree of validity with significant correlations between the four GAS scales and the risk-taking scale. There do not appear to be strong relationships between the GAS scales and religious affiliation, religiosity, or liberal or conservative political attitudes.

PRIMARY REFERENCE Kassinove, J. I. (1998). Development of a gambling attitude scale: Preliminary findings, *Journal of Clinical Psychology*, 54, 763–771.

AVAILABILITY May be copied from this volume.

GAS

This is a questionnaire about general attitudes toward gambling and about specific attitudes toward gambling on horse races, on lotteries, and at casinos. There are also questions about the role of women in society, health care, and so on about which we would like your opinion. Please give your personal opinions about each item by writing the appropriate number in the space to the left of the item. Thank you.

1 = Strongly agree
2 = Moderately agree
3 = Mildly agree
4 = Mildly disagree
5 = Moderately disagree
6 = Strongly disagree

___ 1. I enjoy gambling.
___ 2. I am a liberal thinker.
___ 3. I think gambling is good for America.
___ 4. I enjoy buying lottery tickets.
___ 5. I tend to act like a Democrat and approve of Democratic Party policies.
___ 6. I feel happy that people on welfare will now have to work for their money.
___ 7. I enjoy betting on horse races.
___ 8. I support the right of Americans to gamble in casinos as often as they want.
___ 9. I tend to think conservatively.
___ 10. I detest betting on horse races.
___ 11. I gamble in casinos when the opportunity arises.
___ 12. I approve of increased federal taxes to provide more social welfare programs.
___ 13. I want to bet on horse races.
___ 14. I detest gambling casinos.
___ 15. I am in favor of abortion rights for women.
___ 16. I want to buy lottery tickets.
___ 17. Many people on welfare are simply lazy.
___ 18. I enjoy gambling in casinos.
___ 19. I think betting on horse races is good for America.
___ 20. We need more presidents like Jimmy Carter and Lyndon Johnson.
___ 21. I feel excited when I am around people who bet on horse races.
___ 22. I tend to favor the Republican Party way of thinking.
___ 23. I am in favor of capital punishment (by lethal injection, etc.) for murderers.
___ 24. Gambling in casinos is acceptable.
___ 25. I gamble when the opportunity arises.
___ 26. I think our government in Washington is too big and too controlling.
___ 27. I feel comfortable around people who frequently play the lottery.
___ 28. I support the right of Americans to gamble as often as they want.
___ 29. I am a thrill seeker.
___ 30. I want to gamble.
___ 31. I think that gay and lesbian marriages are a bad idea.
___ 32. Buying lottery tickets is acceptable.
___ 33. When people talk about betting on horses, I want to bet.
___ 34. Catholic priests deserve freedom to marry, just like anyone else.

___ 35.   I feel excited when I am around people who gamble.
___ 36.   When people talk about buying a lottery ticket, I want to buy one.
___ 37.   We need more presidents like Ronald Reagan and George Bush.
___ 38.   When people talk about gambling, I want to gamble.
___ 39.   When possible, I vote for Republicans.
___ 40.   Betting on horse races is acceptable.
___ 41.   It would be a good idea if there were sex education classes in elementary schools.
___ 42.   I feel comfortable around people who frequently gamble in casinos.
___ 43.   I bet on horse races when the opportunity arises.
___ 44.   Certain occupations, like firefighting, should be restricted to men.
___ 45.   It's OK if there is gambling in my town.
___ 46.   I want to gamble in casinos.
___ 47.   I feel upset when I see advertisements that promote the state lottery.
___ 48.   It's OK if there is betting at horse racing tracks in my town.
___ 49.   I would vote for a woman to become president of the U.S.
___ 50.   The state lottery is detrimental to our society.
___ 51.   It would be better if casino gambling was banned in my state.
___ 52.   I feel happy when there is a Republican in office.
___ 53.   I buy lottery tickets when the opportunity arises.
___ 54.   I like to take risks.
___ 55.   It's OK if there is casino gambling in my town.
___ 56.   All Americans are entitled to government-sponsored free or low-cost health care.
___ 57.   Gambling is acceptable.
___ 58.   I tend to vote for Democrats.
___ 59.   I detest state lotteries.

General Emotional Dysregulation Measure (GEDM)

PURPOSE To measure emotional dysregulation.

AUTHORS Christina E. Newhill, Edward P. Mulvey, and Paul A. Pilkonis

DESCRIPTION The GEDM is a 13-item scale designed to assess emotional dysregulation, erratic, emotional and unpredictable behavior that is characteristic of four personality disorders in the Cluster B grouping of DSM-IV-TR. The authors state that emotional dysregulation is comprised of low threshold or high sensitivity to emotional stimuli, high amplitude of emotional response, and a slow return to emotional baseline. Despite emotional dysregulation being central to the understanding of certain personality disorders, and the clinical face validity of the construct, there are no empirically based measures of emotional dysregulation. The GEDM can be filled out by the client or read to the client with the interviewer filling in responses for the client.

NORMS The GEDM was developed with a sample of 100 people in in- or out-patient mental health facilities. 81% of the sample was female, 62% white, and the remainder "non-white." The mean age was 36 (SD = 9.5). 54% of the sample was recruited from inpatient units and 46% from outpatient clinics. The total scores from this sample ranged from 33 to 65 (the highest possible score is 65) with a mean of 55 (SD = 7.4).

SCORING The GEDM is easily scored by summing the items for a total score with higher scores reflecting greater emotional dysregulation.

RELIABILITY The GEDM has good internal consistency with an alpha of .82. The GEDM also has very good stability with a 3-week test-retest correlation of .81.

VALIDITY The GEDM has established excellent concurrent and divergent validity with significant correlations with several other measures in predicted directions, including the Affect Intensity Scale, The Negative Affect Scale of the PANAS, and the Personality Disorder subscales of the Inventory of Interpersonal Problems.

PRIMARY REFERENCE Newhill, C. E., Mulvey, E. P., and Pilkonis, P. A. (2004). Initial development of a measure of emotional dysregulation for individuals with Cluster B personality disorders, *Research on Social Work Practice*, 6, 443–449. Instrument reproduced with permission of Dr. Christine Newhill.

AVAILABILITY Dr. Christine E. Newhill, School of Social Work, University of Pittsburgh, 2326 Cathedral of Learning, Pittsburgh, PA 15260. Email: newhill@pitt.edu.

INSTRUCTIONS

We are trying to find out how different people see themselves. The following questions ask for ratings about how you handle emotions. "Emotions" are defined as feelings, both positive and negative, like love, anger, sadness, fear, joy and so forth. There are no right or wrong answers about this topic, since everyone handles emotions differently.

1	2	3	4	5
Strongly disagree	Moderately disagree	Neither agree nor disagree	Moderately agree	Strongly agree

___ 1.   In general, I have a hard time handling my emotions.

___ 2.   I often feel overwhelmed by my emotions.

___ 3.   I see myself as more sensitive to emotions than other people.

___ 4.   When I get emotional, it's a long time before I feel normal again.

___ 5.   My feelings tend to be stronger than other people's.

___ 6.   Other people tell me I'm "too sensitive" or that I "over-react" to emotional issues.

___ 7.   Being sad can stick with me much longer than with other people.

___ 8.   When I feel happy, it is more intense than the way that other people seem to feel.

___ 9.   Feeling sad can overwhelm me.

___ 10.   Small things that might not bother others often make me feel bad.

___ 11.   My emotional responses to events in my life tend to be high.

___ 12.   When I get emotional about something, I have a hard time settling down.

___ 13.   When I feel an emotion, my feelings tend to be strong.

There is no fee for the use of the GEDM for research or practice purposes.

Generalized Contentment Scale (GCS)

PURPOSE To measure nonpsychotic depression.

AUTHOR Walter W. Hudson

DESCRIPTION The GCS is a 25-item scale that is designed to measure the degree, severity, or magnitude of nonpsychotic depression. In contrast to many measures of depression, the GCS focuses largely on affective aspects of clinical depression, examining respondents' feelings about a number of behaviors, attitudes, and events associated with depression. The GCS has three cutting scores. The first is a score of 30 (±5); scores below this point indicate absence of a clinically significant problem in this area. Scores above 30 suggest the presence of a clinically significant problem. The second cutting score is 50 (±5), with clients scoring above 50 often found to have some suicidal ideation. The third cutting score is 70. Scores above this point nearly always indicate that clients are experiencing severe stress with a clear possibility that suicide may be being considered. The practitioner should be aware of and investigate this possibility. Another advantage of the GCS is that it is one of several scales of the WALMYR Assessment Scales package reproduced here, all of which are administered and scored the same way.

NORMS This scale was developed with 2,140 respondents, including single and married individuals, clinical and nonclinical populations, high school and college students and nonstudents. Respondents were primarily Caucasian, but also included Japanese and Chinese Americans, and a smaller number of members of other ethnic groups. The GCS is not recommended for use with children under the age of 12. Actual norms are not available.

SCORING Like most WALMYR Assessment Scales instruments, the GCS is scored by first reverse-scoring items listed at the bottom of the page (5, 8, 9, 11–13, 15, 16, 21–24), summing these and the remaining scores, subtracting the number of completed items, multiplying this figure by 100, and dividing by the number of items completed times 6. This will produce a range from 0 to 100 with higher scores indicating greater magnitude or severity of problems.

RELIABILITY The GCS has a mean alpha of .92, indicating excellent internal consistency, and an excellent (low) SEM of 4.56. The GCS also has excellent short-term stability, with a two-hour test-retest correlation of .94.

VALIDITY The GCS has good concurrent validity, correlating in two studies .85 and .76 with the Beck Depression Inventory and .92 and .81 for two samples using the Zung Depression Inventory. The GCS has excellent known-groups validity, discriminating significantly between members of a group judged to be clinically depressed and those judged not to be depressed. The GCS also has good construct validity, correlating poorly with a number of measures with which it should not correlate, and correlating at high levels with several measures with which it should, such as self-esteem, happiness, and sense of identity.

PRIMARY REFERENCE Hudson, W. W. (1997). *The WALMYR Assessment Scales scoring manual*. Tallahassee, FL: WALMYR Publishing Co.

AVAILABILITY This scale may not be reproduced or copied in any manner and must be obtained by writing to the WALMYR Publishing Company, P.O. Box 12217, Tallahassee, FL 32317-2217 or WALMYR.com.

GENERALIZED CONTENTMENT SCALE (GCS)

Name: _____ Today's Date: _____

This questionnaire is designed to measure the way you feel about your life and surroundings. It is not a test, so there are no right or wrong answers. Answer each item as carefully and as accurately as you can by placing a number besides each one as follows.

1 = None of the time
2 = Very rarely
3 = A little of the time
4 = Some of the time
5 = A good part of the time
6 = Most of the time
7 = All of the time

1. ___ I feel powerless to do anything about my life.
2. ___ I feel blue.
3. ___ I think about ending my life.
4. ___ I have crying spells.
5. ___ It is easy for me to enjoy myself.
6. ___ I have a hard time getting started on things that I need to do.
7. ___ I get very depressed.
8. ___ I feel there is always someone I can depend on when things get tough.
9. ___ I feel that the future looks bright for me.
10. ___ I feel downhearted.
11. ___ I feel that I am needed.
12. ___ I feel that I am appreciated by others.
13. ___ I enjoy being active and busy.
14. ___ I feel that others would be better off without me.
15. ___ I enjoy being with other people.
16. ___ I feel that it is easy for me to make decisions.
17. ___ I feel downtrodden.
18. ___ I feel terribly lonely.
19. ___ I get upset easily.
20. ___ I feel that nobody really cares about me.
21. ___ I have a full life.
22. ___ I feel that people really care about me.
23. ___ I have a great deal of fun.
24. ___ I feel great in the morning.
25. ___ I feel that my situation is hopeless.

5, 8, 9, 11, 12, 13, 15, 16, 21, 22, 23, 24.

Generalized Expectancy for Success Scale—Revised (GESS-R)

PURPOSE To measure optimism.

AUTHORS W. Daniel Hale and C. D. Cochran

DESCRIPTION The GESS-R is a 25-item measure designed to assess dispositional optimism. Working within the framework of Rotter's social learning theory, the generalized expectancy for success (or dispositional optimism) is conceptualized as the belief held by a person that he/she is likely to attain his/her valued goals or outcomes in most situations encountered. The current version is a modification of the original 30-item scale (Fibel & Hale, 1978). People with a high generalized expectancy for success not only report higher level of self-esteem and general well-being, but also are more likely to risk engaging in behaviors that may to lead to desired outcomes.

NORMS The original development of the GESS-R utilized 199 college students. Since that time, additional normative data have been collected on samples including 400 college students, 100 middle-class individuals employed full time (ages 18–60), and 100 retired elderly individuals (ages 55–85). GESS-R means are relatively stable across these three groups. For one sample of college students the mean was 99.16 (SD = 13.06); for employed individuals and an elderly sample the means were 103.33 (SD = 9.08) and 97.97 (SD = 12.75), respectively.

SCORING The GESS-R is easily scored by reverse scoring (1 = 5, 2 = 4, 3 = 3, 4 = 2, 5 = 1) negatively worded items (9, 13, 17, 20, and 23) and then summing the individual item scores. Higher scores reflect greater optimism.

RELIABILITY Internal consistency reliability is very good; with coefficient alphas of .93 and .94. The split half reliability coefficient was also high, r = .92 (with the Spearman-Brown correction), and a test-retest study showed stability over six weeks to be good with a coefficient of .69.

VALIDITY Construct validity: The GESS-R shows very good discriminant and convergent validity. Research findings include significant correlations with the Life Orientation Test (a measure of dispositional optimism), Rosenberg Self-Esteem Scale, Rotter's Internal-External Locus of Control Scale, self-ratings of health, measures of unique invulnerability, and other related measures. Criterion-related validity: Concurrent validity also appears to be good. With regard to predictive validity, the GESS-R seems to be a good predictor of the kinds of behavioral outcomes expected of optimists.

PRIMARY REFERENCE Hale, W. D., and Cochran, C. D. (1992). The revised generalized expectancy for success scale: A validity and reliability study, *Journal of Clinical Psychology*, 48, 517–521.

AVAILABILITY W. Daniel Hale, Ph.D., Department of Psychology, Stetson University, DeLand, FL 32720. Email: dhale@stetson.edu.

Please indicate the degree to which you believe each statement would apply to you personally by circling the appropriate number, according to the following key:

1 = Highly improbable
2 = Improbable
3 = Equally improbable and probable, not sure
4 = Probable
5 = Highly probable

In the future I expect that I will

1. succeed at most things I try.	1	2	3	4	5
2. be listened to when I speak.	1	2	3	4	5
3. carry through my responsibilities successfully.	1	2	3	4	5
4. get the promotions I deserve.	1	2	3	4	5
5. have successful close personal relationships.	1	2	3	4	5
6. handle unexpected problems successfully.	1	2	3	4	5
7. make a good impression on people I meet for the first time.	1	2	3	4	5
8. attain the career goals I set for myself.	1	2	3	4	5
9. experience many failures in my life.	1	2	3	4	5
10. have a positive influence on most of the people with whom I interact.	1	2	3	4	5
11. be able to solve my own problems.	1	2	3	4	5
12. acquire most of the things that are important to me.	1	2	3	4	5
13. find that no matter how hard I try, things just don't turn out the way I would like.	1	2	3	4	5
14. be a good judge of what it takes to get ahead.	1	2	3	4	5
15. handle myself well in whatever situation I'm in.	1	2	3	4	5
16. reach my financial goals.	1	2	3	4	5
17. have problems working with others.	1	2	3	4	5
18. discover that the good in life outweighs the bad.	1	2	3	4	5
19. be successful in my endeavors in the long run.	1	2	3	4	5
20. be unable to accomplish my goals.	1	2	3	4	5
21. be very successful in working out my personal life.	1	2	3	4	5
22. succeed in the projects I undertake.	1	2	3	4	5
23. discover that my plans don't work out too well.	1	2	3	4	5
24. achieve recognition in my profession.	1	2	3	4	5
25. have rewarding intimate relationships.	1	2	3	4	5

Geriatric Depression Scale (GDS)

PURPOSE To measure depression in the elderly.

AUTHORS T. L. Brink, J. A. Yesavage, O. Lum, P. Heersema, V. Huang, T. L. Rose, M. Adey, and V. O. Leirer

DESCRIPTION The GDS is a 30-item instrument to rate depression in the elderly. The GDS is written in simple language and can be administered in an oral or written format. If administered orally, the practitioner may have to repeat the question in order to get a response that is clearly yes or no. Translations are available in Spanish, Hebrew, Romanian, Russian, and French. The main purpose for development of the GDS was to provide a screening test for depression in elderly populations that would be simple to administer and not require special training for the interviewer. The GDS has been used successfully with both physically healthy and ill samples of the elderly.

NORMS The initial data for the GDS came from two groups of elderly people. The first ($n = 40$) were individuals recruited from senior centers and housing projects who were functioning well with no history of mental problems. The second group ($n = 60$) comprised elderly under treatment—inpatient and outpatient—for depression. No other demographic data are reported. The authors state that 0 to 10 on the GDS is normal; 11 to 20 indicates moderate or severe depression.

SCORING Of the 30 items, 20 indicate the presence of depression when answered positively while 10 (items 1, 5, 7, 9, 15, 19, 21, 27, 29, 30) indicate depression when answered negatively. The GDS is scored by totaling one point counted for each depressive answer and zero point counted for each nondepressed answer.

RELIABILITY The GDS has excellent internal consistency with an alpha of .94 and split-half reliability of .94. The GDS also has excellent stability, with a one-week test-retest correlation of .85.

VALIDITY The GDS has excellent concurrent validity, with correlations of .83 between the GDS and Zung's Self-Rating Depression Scale and .84 with the Hamilton Rating Scale for Depression. The GDS also has good known-groups validity in distinguishing significantly among respondents classified as normal, mildly depressed, and severely depressed. The GDS also has distinguished between depressed and nondepressed physically ill elderly and between depressed and nondepressed elderly undergoing cognitive treatment for senile dementia.

PRIMARY REFERENCE Yesavage, J. A., Brink, T. L., Rose, T. L., and Leirer, V. O. (1983). Development and validation of a geriatric depression screening scale: A preliminary report, *Journal of Psychiatric Research*, 17, 37–49. Instrument reproduced with permission of T. L. Brink and Jerome Yesavage.

AVAILABILITY In public domain. May be copied from this volume.

Please circle the best answer for how you felt over the past week.

Yes	No	1. Are you basically satisfied with your life?
Yes	No	2. Have you dropped many of your activities and interests?
Yes	No	3. Do you feel that your life is empty?
Yes	No	4. Do you often get bored?
Yes	No	5. Are you hopeful about the future?
Yes	No	6. Are you bothered by thoughts you can't get out of your head?
Yes	No	7. Are you in good spirits most of the time?
Yes	No	8. Are you afraid that something bad is going to happen to you?
Yes	No	9. Do you feel happy most of the time?
Yes	No	10. Do you often feel helpless?
Yes	No	11. Do you often get restless and fidgety?
Yes	No	12. Do you prefer to stay at home, rather than going out and doing new things?
Yes	No	13. Do you frequently worry about the future?
Yes	No	14. Do you feel you have more problems with memory than most?
Yes	No	15. Do you think it is wonderful to be alive now?
Yes	No	16. Do you often feel downhearted and blue?
Yes	No	17. Do you feel pretty worthless the way you are now?
Yes	No	18. Do you worry a lot about the past?
Yes	No	19. Do you find life very exciting?
Yes	No	20. Is it hard for you to get started on new projects?
Yes	No	21. Do you feel full of energy?
Yes	No	22. Do you feel that your situation is hopeless?
Yes	No	23. Do you think that most people are better off than you are?
Yes	No	24. Do you frequently get upset over little things?
Yes	No	25. Do you frequently feel like crying?
Yes	No	26. Do you have trouble concentrating?
Yes	No	27. Do you enjoy getting up in the morning?
Yes	No	28. Do you prefer to avoid social gatherings?
Yes	No	29. Is it easy for you to make decisions?
Yes	No	30. Is your mind as clear as it used to be?

Goldfarb Fear of Fat Scale (GFFS)

PURPOSE To measure the fear of gaining weight.

AUTHOR Lori A. Goldfarb

DESCRIPTION The 10-item GFFS measures one of the underlying emotional experiences of eating disorders, the fear of becoming fat. The instrument can also be used to assess weight phobia. It is also useful in identifying clients at risk of bulimia or anorexia as well as in assessing the state of those already suffering from these disorders.

NORMS The GFFS was developed on student and clinical samples. The mean score was 25.5 for 98 high school females. A sample of randomly selected college students had a mean of 18.33, while a small sample of anorectic patients ($N=7$) had a mean of 35.0. A third sample of college females has a mean of 30 for a group of diagnosed bulimics, 23.9 for "repeat dieters," and 17.3 for nondieting females.

SCORING Each item is rated on a scale from 1 to 4, "very untrue" to "very true." Scores are the sum of each item, and range from 10 to 40 with high scores indicating more fear of gaining weight.

RELIABILITY The GFFS has been shown to have very good reliability. The internal consistency reliability using coefficient alpha was .85. Over a one-week period, the GFFS has excellent stability, with a test-retest correlation of .88.

VALIDITY The validity data generally are positive. There were significantly different scores for samples of anorectic patients and college females; the scores also differed between bulimic and repeat dieters and nondieters. Both of these studies reflect known-groups validity. Correlations between the GFFS and state-trait anxiety, depression, neuroticism, maladjustment, and control and achievement orientations demonstrate concurrent validity. The GFFS was negatively correlated with self-esteem.

PRIMARY REFERENCE Goldfarb, L. A., Dykens, E. M., and Gerrard, M. (1985). The Goldfarb Fear of Fat Scale, *Journal of Personality Assessment*, 49, 329–332. Instrument reproduced with permission of Lori A. Goldfarb and the *Journal of Personality Assessment*.

AVAILABILITY May be copied from this volume.

Please read each of the following statements and select the number which best represents your feelings and beliefs.

1 = Very untrue
2 = Somewhat untrue
3 = Somewhat true
4 = Very true

____ 1. My biggest fear is of becoming fat.
____ 2. I am afraid to gain even a little weight.
____ 3. I believe there is a real risk that I will become overweight someday.
____ 4. I don't understand how overweight people can live with themselves.
____ 5. Becoming fat would be the worst thing that could happen to me.
____ 6. If I stopped concentrating on controlling my weight, chances are I would become very fat.
____ 7. There is nothing that I can do to make the thought of gaining weight less painful and frightening.
____ 8. I feel like all my energy goes into controlling my weight.
____ 9. If I eat even a little, I may lose control and not stop eating.
____ 10. Staying hungry is the only way I can guard against losing control and becoming fat.

Harder Personal Feelings Questionnaire (PFQ2)

PURPOSE To measure shame and guilt.

AUTHOR David W. Harder

DESCRIPTION The PFQ2 is a 22-item instrument designed to measure proneness to shame and guilt. The PFQ2 is composed of two subscales, one for measuring shame and one for measuring guilt. The shame subscale comprises items 1, 3, 6, 7, 10, 12, 14, 16, 18, and 21. The guilt subscale comprises items 2, 4, 8, 11, 17, and 22. The PFQ2 is particularly valuable for assessment and clinical practice in its inclusion of subscales for both shame and guilt, distinct emotional states that are not always easy to differentiate clinically or experientially. The PFQ2 can be used to assess these states as they relate to depression in particular, and to track changes in shame and guilt over time as a result of clinical interventions.

NORMS The PFQ2 and its predecessor scale, the PFQ, have been examined in a number of studies. Some major data are based on a sample of 63 college students, 90% freshmen, with 37 male and 26 female, aged 17–22 with a mean of 18.46 years. Mean age for the shame subscale was 16.13 (SD=4.51) and for the guilt subscale, was 9.76 (SD=3.11).

SCORING The PFQ2 is easily scored by summing the items on each subscale. Scores on the shame subscale range from 0 to 40 and on the Guilt subscale from 0 to 24. Higher scores on both subscales mean greater amounts of shame and guilt.

RELIABILITY The PFQ2 has fair to good internal consistency with alphas of .72 for guilt and .78 for shame. Both subscales demonstrate good to excellent test stability with 2-week, test-retest correlations of .85 for guilt and .91 for shame.

VALIDITY The PFQ2 has established good construct validity. A number of predicted relationships with 11 construct validity variables were made including predictions of moderate correlations, high correlations, negative correlations, and no correlations. The construct validity variables included a number of well-known scales, such as the Beck Depression Inventory. Many of the predicted relationships were established for both the guilt and shame subscales, suggesting that the PFQ2 is a valuable indicator of proneness to guilt and shame that has established validity.

PRIMARY REFERENCE Harder, D. W., and Zalma, A. (1990). Two promising shame and guilt scales: A construct validity comparison, *Journal of Personality Assessment*, 55, 729–745.

AVAILABILITY David W. Harder, Ph.D., Psychology Department, Tufts University, Medford, MA 02155. Permission to print the PFQ2 in this and future editions of this book was granted by David W. Harder, Ph.D. Email: david.harder@tufts.edu.

For each of the following listed feelings, to the left of the item number, please place a number from 0 to 4, reflecting how common the feeling is for you.

$$4 = \text{Continuously or almost continuously.}$$
$$3 = \text{Frequently but not continuously.}$$
$$2 = \text{Some of the time}$$
$$1 = \text{Rarely}$$
$$0 = \text{Never}$$

___ 1. Embarrassment
___ 2. Mild guilt
___ 3. Feeling ridiculous
___ 4. Worry about hurting or injuring someone
___ 5. Sadness
___ 6. Self-consciousness
___ 7. Feeling humiliated
___ 8. Intense guilt
___ 9. Euphoria
___ 10. Feeling "stupid"
___ 11. Regret
___ 12. Feeling "childish"
___ 13. Mild happiness
___ 14. Feeling helpless, paralyzed
___ 15. Depression
___ 16. Feelings of blushing
___ 17. Feeling you deserve criticism for what you did
___ 18. Feeling laughable
___ 19. Rage
___ 20. Enjoyment
___ 21. Feeling disgusting to others
___ 22. Remorse

Hardiness Scale (HS)

PURPOSE To measure resiliency to stress.

AUTHORS Paul T. Bartone, Robert J. Ursano, Kathleen M. Wright, and Larry H. Ingraham

DESCRIPTION The HS is a 45-item instrument designed to measure dispositional resilience, the hardiness of one's personality. Hardiness is considered to relate to how one approaches and interprets experiences. Three components of hardiness serve as subscales of the HS: commitment, which refers to imputed meaning and purpose to self, others, and work; control, a sense of autonomy and influence on one's future; and challenge, a zest and excitement for life which is perceived as opportunities for growth. Hardiness has been shown to relate to how people process and cope with stressful events. In stressful situations, hardiness has been shown to be associated with high levels of well-being.

NORMS Normative data are currently being developed by Paul Bartone. Published norms are not available, though the HS was studied originally with 164 military disaster assistance officers, 93% of whom were male, 85% white, with a median age of 34.

SCORING The HS is scored by first reverse-scoring items 3–7, 9–12, 14, 16, 18, 20, 23, 24, 26, 29, 31, 32, 34, 35, 37, 38, 40, 41, and 43–45. Each subscale is then scored by summing the subscale items as follows: Commitment = 1 + 7 + 8 + 9 + 17 + 18 + 23 + 24 + 25 + 31 + 37 + 39 + 41 + 44 + 45. Control = 2 + 3 + 4 + 10 + 11 + 13 + 14 + 19 + 22 + 26 + 28 + 29 + 34 + 42 + 43. Challenge = 5 + 6 + 12 + 15 + 16 + 20 + 21 + 27 + 30 + 32 + 33 + 35 + 36 + 38 + 40. An HS short form is available by deleting items 3, 9, 11, 12, 14, 16, 18, 23, 28, 35, 37, 38, 40, 43, and 44. Higher scores indicate more hardiness.

RELIABILITY The internal consistency (alpha) coefficients were .62, .66, and .82 for the challenge, control, and commitment subscales, respectively. As a total summated scale, the HS had an alpha of .85. The internal consistency of the 30-item short form ranged from .56 to .82 for the subscales. Internal consistency of the summated 30-item form was .83. Data on stability are not available.

VALIDITY The 45-item HS was developed from a pool of 76 items. Scale scores correlated .93 with total scores on the 76-item version. The three-subscale structure was supported with principal components factor analysis. Scores on the 30-item short form correlated .82 with scores on the 45-item version. HS scores were predictive of mental and physical health. Scores are sensitive to measuring change due to the level of stressful events.

PRIMARY REFERENCE Bartone, P., Ursano, R. J., Wright, K. M., and Ingraham, L. H. (1989). The impact of a military air disaster on the health of assistance workers, *Journal of Nervous and Mental Disease*, 177, 317–328. Instrument is in the public domain and reprinted with permission of Paul T. Bartone.

AVAILABILITY Captain Paul T. Bartone, Ph.D., National Defense University, 300 5th Avenue, Bldg 62, Fort McNair, DC 20319-5066. Email: bartone@ndu.edu.

Below are statements about life that people often feel differently about. Circle a number to show how you feel about each one. Read the items carefully, and indicate how much you think each one is true in general. There are no right or wrong answers; just give your own honest opinions.

Not at all true	A little true	Quite true	Completely true
0	1	2	3

1. Most of my life gets spent doing things that are worthwhile.   1   2   3   4   5

2. Planning ahead can help avoid most future problems.   1   2   3   4   5

3. Trying hard doesn't pay, since things still don't turn out right.   1   2   3   4   5

4. No matter how hard I try, my efforts usually accomplish nothing.   1   2   3   4   5

5. I don't like to make changes in my everyday schedule.   1   2   3   4   5

6. The "tried and true" ways are always best.   1   2   3   4   5

7. Working hard doesn't matter, since only the bosses profit by it.   1   2   3   4   5

8. By working hard you can always achieve your goals.   1   2   3   4   5

9. Most working people are simply manipulated by their bosses.   1   2   3   4   5

10. Most of what happens in life is just meant to be.   1   2   3   4   5

11. It's usually impossible for me to change things at work.   1   2   3   4   5

12. New laws should never hurt a person's paycheck.   1   2   3   4   5

13. When I make plans, I'm certain I can make them work.   1   2   3   4   5

14. It's very hard for me to change a friend's mind about something.   1   2   3   4   5

15. It's exciting to learn something about myself.   1   2   3   4   5

16. People who never change their minds usually have good judgment.   1   2   3   4   5

17. I really look forward to my work.   1   2   3   4   5

18. Politicians run our lives.   1   2   3   4   5

19. If I'm working on a difficult task, I know when to seek help.   1   2   3   4   5

20. I won't answer a question until I'm really sure I understand it.   1   2   3   4   5

21. I like a lot of variety in my work.   1   2   3   4   5

22. Most of the time, people listen carefully to what I say.   1   2   3   4   5

23. Daydreams are more exciting than reality for me.   1   2   3   4   5

24. Thinking of yourself as a free person just leads to frustration. 1 2 3 4 5

25. Trying your best at work really pays off in the end. 1 2 3 4 5

26. My mistakes are usually very difficult to correct. 1 2 3 4 5

27. It bothers me when my daily routine gets interrupted. 1 2 3 4 5

28. It's best to handle most problems by just not thinking of them. 1 2 3 4 5

29. Most good athletes and leaders are born, not made. 1 2 3 4 5

30. I often wake up eager to take up my life wherever it left off. 1 2 3 4 5

31. Lots of times, I don't really know my own mind. 1 2 3 4 5

32. I respect rules because they guide me. 1 2 3 4 5

33. I like it when things are uncertain or unpredictable. 1 2 3 4 5

34. I can't do much to prevent it if someone wants to harm me. 1 2 3 4 5

35. People who do their best should get full support from society. 1 2 3 4 5

36. Changes in routine are interesting to me. 1 2 3 4 5

37. People who believe in individuality are only kidding themselves. 1 2 3 4 5

38. I have no use for theories that are not closely tied to facts. 1 2 3 4 5

39. Most days, life is really interesting and exciting for me. 1 2 3 4 5

40. I want to be sure someone will take care of me when I'm old. 1 2 3 4 5

41. It's hard to imagine anyone getting excited about working. 1 2 3 4 5

42. What happens to me tomorrow depends on what I do today. 1 2 3 4 5

43. If someone gets angry at me, it's usually no fault of mine. 1 2 3 4 5

44. It's hard to believe people who say their work helps society. 1 2 3 4 5

45. Ordinary work is just too boring to be worth doing. 1 2 3 4 5

Hassles Assessment Scale for Students in College (HASS/Col)

PURPOSE To measure students' stress.

AUTHORS Edward P. Sarafino and Maureen Ewing

DESCRIPTION The HASS/Col is a 54-item instrument designed to measure college students' hassles, defined as the frequency of stressor occurrence, the unpleasantness (intensity) of the stressor, and the extent of rumination or dwelling on the stressor. The latter characteristics make the HASS/Col unique among instruments designed to assess college students' stress. Factor analyses revealed that the items each appeared to contribute independently to the overall scale so that subscales, other than Frequency, Unpleasantness and Dwelled, were not used.

NORMS The HASS/Col was developed using a sample of 132 undergraduate students of whom 108 were female. The age range of participants was from 18 to 24. Forty-four of the respondents were 1st-year students, 39 were sophomores, 33 were juniors, and 13 were seniors. No other demographic data were reported. The mean score for Frequency was 105.72 (SD=28.35), 81.98 (SD=27.84) for Unpleasantness, and 109.89 (SD=28.32) for Dwelling. There were no significant differences between males and females on the Frequency dimension, but females had significantly higher scores on the Unpleasantness and Dwelling dimensions. The means for women and men on these two dimensions, respectively, were 84.22 for women and 70.66 for men and 113.8 for women and 93.09 for men.

SCORING The HASS/Col is easily scored by simply summing up the scores on each of the scale's dimensions. Higher scores indicate greater amounts of each dimension.

RELIABILITY The dimensions of the HASS/Col have excellent internal consistency with alphas that range from .90 to .93. Data on stability were not reported.

VALIDITY The HASS/Col has good concurrent validity, with significant correlations between each dimension of the HASS/Col and the already validated Inventory of College Students' Recent Life Experiences.

PRIMARY REFERENCE Sarafino, E. P., and Ewing, M. (1999). The Hassles Assessment Scale for Students in College: Measuring the frequency and unpleasantness of and dwelling on stressful events, *Journal of American College Health*, 4, 75–83. Instrument reproduced with permission of Dr. Sarafino.

AVAILABILITY May be copied from this volume.

HASSLES ASSESSMENT SCALE FOR STUDENTS IN COLLEGE (HASS/Col)

INSTRUCTIONS

The items below describe circumstances you may sometimes find unpleasant if they make you frustrated, irritated, or anxious. Think of them as **events**—they happen and end. For your experiences in the **past month or so**, darken the circled ratings next to each event to describe its **frequency**, the **degree of unpleasantness** it usually produced for you, and the extent to which you **dwelled** on or were bothered by it when the actual event was not present (before or after). Use **all three** rating scales, which are defined to the right.

RATING SCALE DEFINITIONS

FREQUENCY—rate how often in the past month or so the event occurred, using a scale that ranges from 0 = "never" to 5 = "extremely often."

UNPLEASANTNESS—rate how unpleasant the event usually was when it actually happened, using a scale that ranges from 0 = "not at all" to 4 = "extremely" unpleasant. Mark 0 if the event didn't occur.

DWELLED—rate the extent to which you usually were **bothered** by each event when it was not actually present, before or after it occurred. Use a scale from 1 to 5, where **1** means you dwelled on it either *not at all or very little* (thinking about it *briefly for less than an hour*) and **5** means you dwelled on it *very often and for more than a week.* Mark 1 if the event didn't occur.

GENERAL INFORMATION

Please complete the following items about yourself:

Sex: (circle)   Age: _____
    Male   Female

Major: _____

Ethnic Background: (circle)

Caucasian   African-American
Hispanic   Asian
Other: (specify) _____

EVENTS	FREQUENCY						UNPLEASANTNESS					DWELLED				
	Never	Rarely	Occasion-ally	Often	Very Often	Extremely Often	Not at all	Mildly	Moder-ately	Very	Extremely	Very little/ not at all	Some-what	Moder-ately	A lot	A great deal
1. Annoying social behavior of others (e.g., rude, inconsiderate, sexist/racist)	⓪	①	②	③	④	⑤	⓪	①	②	③	④	①	②	③	④	⑤
2. Annoying behavior of self (e.g., habits, temper)	⓪	①	②	③	④	⑤	⓪	①	②	③	④	①	②	③	④	⑤
3. Appearance of self (e.g., noticing unattractive features, grooming)	⓪	①	②	③	④	⑤	⓪	①	②	③	④	①	②	③	④	⑤

(continued)

EVENTS	FREQUENCY						UNPLEASANTNESS					DWELLED				
	Never	Rarely	Occasion-ally	Often	Very Often	Extremely Often	Not at all	Mildly	Moder-ately	Very	Extremely	Very little/not at all	Some-what	Moder-ately	A lot	A great deal
4. Accidents/clumsiness/ mistakes of self (e.g., spilling beverage, tripping)	⓪	①	②	③	④	⑤	⓪	①	②	③	④	①	②	③	④	⑤
5. Athletic activities of self (e.g., aspects of own performance, time demands)	⓪	①	②	③	④	⑤	⓪	①	②	③	④	①	②	③	④	⑤
6. Bills/overspending: seeing evidence of	⓪	①	②	③	④	⑤	⓪	①	②	③	④	①	②	③	④	⑤
7. Boredom (e.g., nothing to do, current activity uninteresting)	⓪	①	②	③	④	⑤	⓪	①	②	③	④	①	②	③	④	⑤
8. Car problems (e.g., breaking down, repairs)	⓪	①	②	③	④	⑤	⓪	①	②	③	④	①	②	③	④	⑤
9. Crowds/large social groups (e.g., at parties, while shopping)	⓪	①	②	③	④	⑤	⓪	①	②	③	④	①	②	③	④	⑤
10. Dating (e.g., noticing lack of, uninteresting partner)	⓪	①	②	③	④	⑤	⓪	①	②	③	④	①	②	③	④	⑤
11. Environment (e.g., noticing physical living or working conditions)	⓪	①	②	③	④	⑤	⓪	①	②	③	④	①	②	③	④	⑤
12. Extracurricular groups (e.g., activities, responsibilities)	⓪	①	②	③	④	⑤	⓪	①	②	③	④	①	②	③	④	⑤

13. Exams (e.g., preparing for, taking)	⓪	①	②	③	④	⑤		⓪	①	②	③	④		①	②	③	④	⑤
14. Exercising (e.g., unpleasant routines, time to do)	⓪	①	②	③	④	⑤		⓪	①	②	③	④		①	②	③	④	⑤
16. Family: obligations or activities	⓪	①	②	③	④	⑤		⓪	①	②	③	④		①	②	③	④	⑤
18. Fears of physical safety (e.g., while walking alone, being on a plane or in a car)	⓪	①	②	③	④	⑤		⓪	①	②	③	④		①	②	③	④	⑤
20. Food (e.g., unappealing or unhealthful meals)	⓪	①	②	③	④	⑤		⓪	①	②	③	④		①	②	③	④	⑤
22. Friends/peers: relationship issues, annoyances	⓪	①	②	③	④	⑤		⓪	①	②	③	④		①	②	③	④	⑤

(continued)

341

EVENTS	FREQUENCY						UNPLEASANTNESS					DWELLED				
	Never	Rarely	Occasionally	Often	Very Often	Extremely Often	Not at all	Mildly	Moderately	Very	Extremely	Very little/not at all	Somewhat	Moderately	A lot	A great deal
24. Getting up early (e.g., for class or work)	⓪	①	②	③	④	⑤	⓪	①	②	③	④	①	②	③	④	⑤
25. Girl/boy friend: relationship issues, annoyances	⓪	①	②	③	④	⑤	⓪	①	②	③	④	①	②	③	④	⑤
26. Goals/tasks: not completing enough	⓪	①	②	③	④	⑤	⓪	①	②	③	④	①	②	③	④	⑤
27. Grades (e.g., getting a low grade)	⓪	①	②	③	④	⑤	⓪	①	②	③	④	①	②	③	④	⑤
28. Health/physical symptoms of self (e.g., flu, PMS, allergies, headaches)	⓪	①	②	③	④	⑤	⓪	①	②	③	④	①	②	③	④	⑤
29. Schoolwork (e.g., working on term papers, reading tedious/hard material, low motivation)	⓪	①	②	③	④	⑤	⓪	①	②	③	④	①	②	③	④	⑤
30. Housing: finding/getting or moving	⓪	①	②	③	④	⑤	⓪	①	②	③	④	①	②	③	④	⑤
31. Injustice: seeing examples or being a victim of	⓪	①	②	③	④	⑤	⓪	①	②	③	④	①	②	③	④	⑤
32. Job: searching for or interviews	⓪	①	②	③	④	⑤	⓪	①	②	③	④	①	②	③	④	⑤
33. Job/work issues (e.g., demands or annoying aspects of)	⓪	①	②	③	④	⑤	⓪	①	②	③	④	①	②	③	④	⑤

	Item																
34.	Lateness of self (e.g., for appointment or class)	⓪ ① ② ③ ④ ⑤						⓪ ① ② ③ ④					① ② ③ ④ ⑤			
35.	Losing or misplacing things (e.g., keys, books)	⓪ ① ② ③ ④ ⑤						⓪ ① ② ③ ④					① ② ③ ④ ⑤			
36.	Medical/dental treatment (e.g., unpleasant, time demands)	⓪ ① ② ③ ④ ⑤						⓪ ① ② ③ ④								
37.	Money: noticing lack of	⓪ ① ② ③ ④ ⑤						⓪ ① ② ③ ④					① ② ③ ④ ⑤			
38.	New experiences or challenges: engaging in	⓪ ① ② ③ ④ ⑤						⓪ ① ② ③ ④					① ② ③ ④ ⑤			
39.	Noise of other people or animals	⓪ ① ② ③ ④ ⑤						⓪ ① ② ③ ④					① ② ③ ④ ⑤			
40.	Oral presentations/public speaking	⓪ ① ② ③ ④ ⑤						⓪ ① ② ③ ④					① ② ③ ④ ⑤			
41.	Parking problems (e.g., on campus, at work, at home)	⓪ ① ② ③ ④ ⑤						⓪ ① ② ③ ④					① ② ③ ④ ⑤			
42.	Privacy: noticing lack of	⓪ ① ② ③ ④ ⑤						⓪ ① ② ③ ④					① ② ③ ④ ⑤			
43.	Professors/coaches (e.g., unfairness, demands of, unavailability)							⓪ ① ② ③ ④					① ② ③ ④ ⑤			
44.	Registering for or selecting classes to take	⓪ ① ② ③ ④ ⑤						⓪ ① ② ③ ④					① ② ③ ④ ⑤			
45.	Roommate(s)/housemate(s): relationship issues, annoyances	⓪ ① ② ③ ④ ⑤						⓪ ① ② ③ ④					① ② ③ ④ ⑤			

(continued)

343

EVENTS	FREQUENCY						UNPLEASANTNESS					DWELLED				
	Never	Rarely	Occasion-ally	Often	Very Often	Extremely Often	Not at all	Mildly	Moder-ately	Very	Extremely	Very little/ not at all	Some-what	Moder-ately	A lot	A great deal
46. Sexually transmitted diseases (e.g., concerns about, efforts to reduce risk of STDs/HIV)	⓪	①	②	③	④	⑤	⓪	①	②	③	④	①	②	③	④	⑤
47. Sports team/celebrity performance (e.g., favorite athlete or team losing)	⓪	①	②	③	④	⑤	⓪	①	②	③	④	①	②	③	④	⑤
48. Tedious everyday chores (e.g., shopping, cleaning apartment)	⓪	①	②	③	④	⑤	⓪	①	②	③	④	①	②	③	④	⑤
49. Time demands/deadlines	⓪	①	②	③	④	⑤	⓪	①	②	③	④	①	②	③	④	⑤
50. Traffic problems (e.g., inconsiderate or careless drivers, traffic jams)	⓪	①	②	③	④	⑤	⓪	①	②	③	④	①	②	③	④	⑤
51. Traffic tickets getting (e.g., for moving or parking violations)	⓪	①	②	③	④	⑤	⓪	①	②	③	④	①	②	③	④	⑤
52. Waiting (e.g., for appointments, in lines)	⓪	①	②	③	④	⑤	⓪	①	②	③	④	①	②	③	④	⑤
53. Weather problems (e.g., snow, heat/humidity, storms)	⓪	①	②	③	④	⑤	⓪	①	②	③	④	①	②	③	④	⑤
54. Weight/dietary management (e.g., not sticking to plans)	⓪	①	②	③	④	⑤	⓪	①	②	③	④	①	②	③	④	⑤

Health Survey Short Forms (SF-36 and SF-12)

PURPOSE To measure physical and mental health status.

AUTHOR John E. Ware, Jr.

DESCRIPTION The Health Survey Short Form—36 (SF-36) and Short Form—12 (SF-12) measure perceived physical and mental health. Both instruments produce two composite scores: a physical health composite score (PCS) and a mental health composite score (MCS). For the SF-36 the PCS is the summation of scores on four aspects of physical health: physical functioning (items 3a, 3b, 3c, 3d, 3e, 3f, 3g, 3h, 3i, and 3j), physical role (items 4a, 4b, 4c, and 4d), bodily pain (items 7 and 8), and general health (items 1*, 11a, 11b*, 11c, and 11d*). MCS scores are the summation of vitality (9a, 9e, 9g*, and 9i*), social functioning (items 6* and 10), emotional role (5a, 5b*, and 5c*), and general mental health (9b*, 9c*, 9d, 9f*, and 9h). (Item numbers with an asterisk are reverse-scored.) The SF-12 scores are derived from the same physical and mental health domains, but use only one or two items. PCS and MCS scores on the SF-36 and SF-12 are highly associated, with correlations ranging between .93 and .97. The SF-36 and SF-12 have been administered widely in the United States and throughout much of the world. This provides for valuable and rich normative data useful in interpreting a wide variety of respondents' scores. Both ascertain physical and mental health with an acute version, using a one-week period of recall, and a standard version which uses a four-week recall period; the acute version is particularly useful when assessing the impact of a specific intervention on a patient's physical or mental health, while the standard version is useful when comparing a patient to a general population. The standard version is reproduced here.

NORMS The SF-36 and SF-12 have a number of useful normative data from the United States and over 40 countries. The norms are reported as T scores which have a mean of 50 and a standard deviation of 10. The average T scores (and standard deviations) for the PCS and MCS for a sample of adult males from the United States ($n = 1055$) are 51.05 (9.4) and 50.73 (9.6), respectively. A sample of adult females ($n = 1412$) had an average PCS score of 49.07 (10.4) and an average MCS score of 49.33 (10.3). The mean and standard deviation scores for the SF-12 were quite similar.

SCORING The SF-36 and SF-12 are computer scored, which includes standardizing the scores for each item into a Z-score, weighing the score by a factor analytic weight, and aggregating the scores into T scores. Fortunately, these procedures are computerized and readily available with the user's manual.

RELIABILITY The SF-36 has excellent internal consistency reliability with alpha coefficients of .93 and .88 for the PCS and MCS, respectively. Similar internal consistency coefficients were found from European countries. The SF-12 PCS has good test-retest reliability, correlating .89 over a two-week period; the SF-12 MCS correlated .76 for a two-week period.

VALIDITY The SF-36 and SF-12 have extensive empirical support for their validity. For example, the PCS scores have been shown to be associated with a number of health criteria, including diabetes, health symptomatology, reported change in general health and physical health. MCS scores are associated with self-reported change in mental health and clinical depression. PCS scores distinguished subjects with minor from those with serious health conditions, and MCS scores distinguished persons with psychiatric conditions from those with minor health conditions. Additional validity estimates are available in the primary references.

PRIMARY REFERENCES Ware, J. E., Kosinski, M., and Keller, S. D. (1994). *SF-36 Physical and Mental Health Summary scales: A user's manual*. Boston: Medical Outcomes Trust. Ware, J. E., Kosinski, M., and Keller, S. D. (1996). A 12-item Short-Form Health Survey (SF-12): Construction of scales and preliminary tests of reliability and validity. *Medical Care*, 32, 220–233.

AVAILABILITY Medical Outcomes Trust, 20 Park Plaza, Suite 1014, Boston, MA 02116. Website: www.outcomes-trust.org.

This survey asks for your views about your health. This information will help keep track of how you feel and how well you are able to do your usual activities.

Answer every question by marking the answer as indicated. If you are unsure about how to answer a question, please give the best answer you can.

1. In general, how would you describe your health? (Circle one.)

Excellent	1
Very good	2
Good	3
Fair	4
Poor	5

2. *Compared to one year ago*, how would you rate your health in general *now*? (Circle one.)

Much better now than one year ago	1
Somewhat better now than one year ago	2
About the same as one year ago	3
Somewhat worse now than one year ago	4
Much worse now than one year ago	5

3. The following items are about activities you might do during a typical day. Does *your health now limit you* in these activities? If so, how much? (Circle one number on each line.)

Activities	Yes, limited a lot	Yes, limited a little	No, not limited at all
a. **Vigorous activities**, such as running, lifting heavy objects, participating in strenuous sports	1	2	3
b. **Moderate activities**, such as moving a table, pushing a vacuum cleaner, bowling, or playing golf	1	2	3
c. Lifting or carrying groceries	1	2	3
d. Climbing **several** flights of stairs	1	2	3
e. Climbing **one** flight of stairs	1	2	3
f. Bending, kneeling, or stooping	1	2	3
g. Walking **more than a mile**	1	2	3
h. Walking **several blocks**	1	2	3
i. Walking **one block**	1	2	3
j. Bathing or dressing yourself	1	2	3

4. During the *past 4 weeks*, have you had any of the following problems with your work or other regular daily activities *as a result of your physical health*? (Circle one number on each line.)

	Yes	No
a. Cut down on the **amount of time** you spent on work or other activities	2	1
b. **Accomplished less** than you would like	1	2

		Yes	No
c.	Were limited in the **kind** of work or other activities	1	2
d.	Had **difficulty** performing the work or other activities (for example, it took extra effort)	1	2

5. During the *past 4 weeks*, have you had any of the following problems with your work or other regular daily activities *as a result of any emotional problems* (such as feeling depressed or anxious)? (Circle one number on each line.)

		Yes	No
a.	Cut down the **amount of time** you spent on work or other activities	1	2
b.	**Accomplished less** than you would like	1	2
c.	Didn't do work or other activities as **carefully** as usual	1	2

6. During the *past 4 weeks*, to what extent has your physical health or emotional problems interfered with your normal social activities with family, friends, neighbors, or groups? (Circle one.)

Not at all	1
Slightly	2
Moderately	3
Quite a bit	4
Extremely	5

7. How much *bodily* pain have you had during the *past 4 weeks*? (Circle one.)

None	1
Very mild	2
Mild	3
Moderate	4
Severe	5
Very severe	6

8. During the *past 4 weeks*, how much did *pain* interfere with your normal work (including both work outside the home and housework)? (Circle one.)

Not at all	1
A little bit	2
Moderately	3
Quite a bit	4
Extremely	5

9. These questions are about how you feel and how things have been with you *during the past 4 weeks*. For each question, please give the one answer that comes closest to the way you have been feeling. How much of the time during the *past 4 weeks*: (Circle one number on each line.)

		All of the time	Most of the time	A good bit of the time	Some of the time	A little of the time	None of the time
a.	Did you feel full of pep?	1	2	3	4	5	6
b.	Have you been a very nervous person?	1	2	3	4	5	6

		All of the time	Most of the time	A good bit of the time	Some of the time	A little of the time	None of the time
c.	Have you felt so down in the dumps that nothing could cheer you up?	1	2	3	4	5	6
d.	Have you felt calm and peaceful?	1	2	3	4	5	6
e.	Did you have a lot of energy?	1	2	3	4	5	6
f.	Have you felt downhearted and blue?	1	2	3	4	5	6
g.	Did you feel worn out?	1	2	3	4	5	6
h.	Have you been a happy person?	1	2	3	4	5	6
i.	Did you feel tired?	1	2	3	4	5	6

10. During the *past 4 weeks*, how much of the time has your *physical health or emotional problems* interfered with your social activities (like visiting with friends, relatives, etc.)? (Circle one.)

All of the time	1
Most of the time	2
Some of the time	3
A little of the time	4
None of the time	5

11. How TRUE or FALSE is *each* of the following statements for you? (Circle one number on each line.)

		Definitely true	Mostly true	Don't know	Mostly false	Definitely false
a.	I seem to get sick a little easier than other people	1	2	3	4	5
b.	I am as healthy as anybody I know	1	2	3	4	5
c.	I expect my health to get worse	1	2	3	4	5
d.	My health is excellent	1	2	3	4	5

This questionnaire asks for your views about your health. This information will help keep track of how you feel and how well you are able to do your usual activities.

Please answer every question by marking one box. If you are unsure about how to answer, please give the best answer you can.

1. In general, would you say your health is:

☐	☐	☐	☐	☐
Excellent	Very good	Good	Fair	Poor

The following items are about activities you might do during a typical day. Does *your health now limit you* in these activities? If so, how much?

	Yes, limited a lot	Yes, limited a little	No, not limited at all
2. **Moderate activities**, such as moving a table, pushing a vacuum cleaner, bowling, or playing golf	☐	☐	☐
3. Climbing **several** flights of stairs	☐	☐	☐

During the *past 4 weeks*, have you had any of the following problems with your work or other regular daily activities *as a result of your physical health*?

	Yes	No
4. **Accomplished less** than you would like	☐	☐
5. Were limited in the **kind** of work or other activities	☐	☐

During the *past 4 weeks*, have you had any of the following problems with your work or other regular daily activities *as a result of any emotional problems* (such as feeling depressed or anxious)?

	Yes	No
6. **Accomplished less** than you would like	☐	☐
7. Didn't do work or other activities as **carefully** as usual	☐	☐

8. During the *past 4 weeks*, how much did *pain* interfere with your normal work (including both work outside the home and housework)?

☐	☐	☐	☐	☐
Not at all	A little bit	Moderately	Quite a bit	Extremely

These questions are about how you feel and how things have been with you *during the past 4 weeks*. For each question, please give the one answer that comes closest to the way you have been feeling. How much of the time during the *past 4 weeks*:

	All of the time	Most of the time	A good bit of the time	Some of the time	A little of the time	None of the time
9. Have you felt clam and peaceful?	☐	☐	☐	☐	☐	☐
10. Did you have a lot of energy?	☐	☐	☐	☐	☐	☐

11. Have you felt downhearted
    and blue?   ☐   ☐   ☐   ☐   ☐   ☐

12. During the *past 4 weeks*, how much of the time has your *physical health or emotional
    problems* interfered with your social activities (like visiting with friends, relatives, etc.)?

☐	☐	☐	☐	☐
All of the time	Most of the time	Some of the time	A little of the time	None of the time

Health Value (HV) and Health Locus of Control (HLC)

PURPOSE To measure the value one places on health (HV) and health locus of control (HLC).

AUTHORS Richard R. Lau, Karen A. Hartman, and John E. Ware, Jr.

DESCRIPTION The HV is a 4-item scale designed to measure the value an individual places on health. Health value is an important concept in the study of health behaviors, but one that is surprisingly underutilized in health research. The HV scale is one of the first measures, if not the first, to measure health as a value. The HV is short and easily administered, and should be useful not only in health research, but in clinical practice when trying to assess individual barriers to obtaining health care. The HV is comprised of items 6*, 17, 20*, and 27.

The HV is embedded in the 26-item HLC, a scale that measures the extent to which one believes one can control one's health. The reason for integrating the two scales is because of the authors' assumption that it is not reasonable to expect a measure of health locus of control to predict healthy behavior, i.e., taking steps to maintain good health, unless the individual values health. Thus, the two scales can be used together. The HLC is comprised of four subscales: Self Control over Health (items 1*, 5, 7*, 9*, 14, 18*, 24, 28*); Provider Control Over Health (items 4, 8, 10*, 12, 15, 19*, 23*, 26*); Chance Health Outcomes (items 3*, 11, 16*, 21*, 25, 30); and General Health Threat (items 2*, 13, 22*, 29*). It is recommended that the HLC be used only as subscales, and that the subscales not be combined into a single scale. Further information on the HLC regarding reliability and validity, etc., is available in the second of the Primary References.

NORMS The HV was developed using several samples including 326 undergraduate college students of whom 69% were white and 60% female, 97 11- to 16-year-old girls, 95 parents of the young girls, 74 ulcer clinic patients, 1,026 students entering a university, and 940 of the parents of those entering students. Norms are available for all those groups in the Primary Reference; however, it might be noted that, as expected, younger people tended to score lower on the HV than did adults, with mean scores on the HV ranging from 13.43 (SD=2.96) for the youngest sample to 22.95 (SD=4.18) for the parents of the entering college students.

SCORING The HLC and HV are scored the same way, by first reverse-scoring the items with asterisks noted above, and then simply adding up the results. Thus, the HV has scores that can range from 4 to 28 with higher scores indicating higher value placed on health.

RELIABILITY The HV has fair internal consistency with alphas that range from .63 to .72. The HV has very good stability with a 6-week test-retest correlation of .78.

VALIDITY The HV has fair concurrent validity and discriminative validity, particularly when divided into groups with high and low scores on the HV. In that way, the HV high and low scores are correlated in predicted directions with a number of health behaviors and beliefs and with the subscales of the HLC.

PRIMARY REFERENCE Lau, R. R., Hartman, K. A., and Ware, J. E., Jr. (1986). Health as a value: Methodological and theoretical considerations, *Health Psychology*, 5, 25–43;

Lau, R. R., & Ware, J. E., Jr. (1981). The conceptualization and measurement of a multi-dimensional health-specific locus of control scale, *Medical Care, 19,* 1147–1158. Instruments reproduced with the permission of Dr. Richard Lau.

AVAILABILITY Professor Richard Lau, Department of Political Science, Rutgers University, 89 George Street, New Brunswick, NJ. Email: ricklau@rutgers.edu.

Now we want to ask some questions concerning your beliefs about health and illness. Indicate the extent to which you agree with the following statements, using the scale below. Write the appropriate number in the blank to the right of each statement.

Strongly Agree		Moderately Agree		Moderately Disagree		Strongly Disagree
1	2	3	4	5	6	7

1. If I get sick, it's usually my own fault.

2. Some kinds of illness are so bad that nothing can be done about them. ____

3. Whether or not people get well is often a matter of chance. ____

4. Doctors can rarely do very much for people who are sick. ____

5. Healthwise, there isn't much you can do for yourself when you get sick. ____

6. There is nothing more important than good health. ____

7. Anyone can learn a few basic health principles which can go a long way in preventing illness. ____

8. Many times doctors do not help their patients to get well. ____

9. I have a lot of confidence in my ability to cure myself once I get sick. ____

10. Recovery from illness requires good medical care more than anything else. ____

11. When it comes to health, there is no such thing as "bad luck." ____

12. Doctors can do very little to prevent illness. ____

13. In today's world, few diseases are totally debilitating (crippling). ____

14. "Taking care of yourself" has little or no relation to whether you get sick. ____

15. Doctors relieve or cure only a few of the medical problems their patients have. ____

16. People who never get sick are just plain lucky. ____

17. Good health is of only minor importance in a happy life. ____

18. In the long run, people who take care of themselves stay healthy and get well quick. ____

19. Most sick people are helped a great deal when they go to a doctor. ____

20. If you don't have your health, you don't have anything. ____

21. Good health is largely a matter of fortune. ____

22. No matter what anybody does, there are many diseases that can just wipe you out. ____

23. Seeing a doctor for regular check-ups is a key factor in staying healthy. ____

24. There is little one can do to prevent illness. ____

25. Staying well has little or nothing to do with chance. ____

26. Doctors can almost always help their patients feel better. ____

27. There are many things I care about more than my health. ____

28. People's ill health results from their own carelessness. ____

29. There are a lot of medical problems that can be very serious or even fatal (can kill you). ____

30. Recovery from illness has nothing to do with luck. ____

Helping Relationship Inventory-Client (HRI-C) version and-Provider version (HRI-P)

PURPOSE To measure structural and interpersonal dimensions of an effective helping relationship

AUTHORS John Poulin and Thomas Young

DESCRIPTION The HRI-C and HRI-P are 7 and 20-item instruments designed to measure the magnitude of a positive structure of the helping relationship, such as Planning, and the interpersonal components of the helping relationship as perceived by the client and the provider. Each of the HRI has subscales for the Structure and the Interpersonal aspects (see scoring). While originally written for clinical social workers, the practicality of the HRIs is enhanced by the general terms provider. The importance of these instruments is underscored by the fact that the helping relationship is the sine quo non of all clinical practices, including manualized treatment. Moreover, there is a strong association between the quality of the helping relationship and positive treatment outcome, a finding applicable to behavioral, cognitive-behavioral and interpersonal therapies. The magnitudes of the associations tend to be higher for clients than for psychotherapists. The instrument can be used as a total scale score of the helping relationship, or with the subscales of quality structure and affective interpersonal practices.

NORMS The instruments were developed with a sample of 42 clients and 14 clinical social workers. No norms are reported.

SCORING The HRI-C has two subscales (Structural, HRI-CS) which is the sum of items 1 through 10, and the Interpersonal dimension (HRI-CI), which is the sum of items 11-20. Similarly, providers have the same subscales, and the HRI-PS is the sum of items 1 through 10, and the HRI-PI is the sum of items 11–20.

RELIABILITY The HRI total scores have excellent internal consistency with an alpha coefficient of .96 for the client version and .93 for the provider version. Both subscales on the HRI-C had coefficients of .96, and the provider version had an alpha of .86 for the HRI-PS and .91 for the HRI-PI.

VALIDITY There are numerous supports for the validity of the HRIs. Items were selected from factor analysis and had appropriate loadings on the structural and interpersonal dimensions for clients; this was then tested for a small sample of clinical social workers. There is excellent support for the concurrent validity of the HRIs with scores correlating with the Working Alliance Inventory, which is included in this volume; the correlation was .84 for clients and .87 for providers and WAI scores. There is support for known-groups validity with scores distinguishing between the highest and lowest quality of the helping relationship. Finally, scores on the HRI-C and those of their providers (HRI-P) were correlated with a coefficient of .52, suggesting there is 25 per cent commonality in the observations.

PRIMARY REFERENCE Poulin, J. and Young, T. (1997). Development of a Helping Relationship Inventory for social work practice. *Research on social work practice, 7,* 463–489.

AVAILABILITY John Pouline, Ph.D. or Thomas Young, Ph.D., Center for Social Work Education, Weidner University, Chester PA 19013. Emails: jepoulin@widener.edu and tmyoung@ widener.edu.

Below are questions about your helping relationship with_____. Please answer each question by recording the degree the ìnot at allî present to a ìgreat deal.î Use the following rating scale and record your answers in the space to the right of each question. Please be honest with your answers as we want to better understand the helping relationship.

1 = Not at all present
2 = Slightly
3 = Somewhat
5 = Considerably
5 = Great deal

1. How much input have you had in determining how the two of you will work together?_____

2. How much have you and your clinician discussed the specific problem(s) with which you want help?_____

3. How much input have you had in determining the specific problem(s) you are addressing in your work together?_____

4. To what extent have you and your clinician discussed the specific goal(s) you hope to accomplish in your work together?_____

5. How much input have you had in determining the goal(s) you are working on?_____

6. To what extent have you and your clinician discussed the specific actions you will take to address your difficulties?_____

7. To what extent have you and your clinician discussed the specific actions your clinician will take to address your difficulties?_____

Below are questions about your helping relationship with_____. Please answer each question by recording the degree the ìnot at allî present to a ìgreat deal. Use the following rating scale and record your answers in the space to the right of each question. Please be honest with your answers as we want to better understand the helping relationship.

1 = Not at all present
2 = Slightly
3 = Somewhat
6 = Considerably
6 = Great deal

1. How much input does your client have in determining how your work together will be approached?_____

2. How much have you and your client discussed the specific problem(s) with which he or she wants help?_____

3. How clear are you about the specific problem(s) you and your client are addressing?_____

4. To what extent have you and your client discussed the specific goal(s) you hope to accomplish in your work together?_____

5. How much input does your client have in determining the goal(s) he or she is working on?_____

6. How clear are you about your client's goals?_____

7. To what extent have you and your client discussed the specific actions he or she will take to address his or her difficulties?_____

8. How clear are you about the actions you are taking?_____

9. How much input does your client have in determining how you and your client will assess your progress?_____

10. How clear are you about how you and your client are assessing his or her progress?_____

11. Do you explain to your client your understanding of his or her difficulties?_____

12. Is your client's understanding of his or her difficulties similar to your own?_____

13. Does talking to your client help you get more organized about resolving your difficulties?_____

14. Do you enjoy meeting and talking with your client?_____

15. Does talking with you have a calming, soothing effect on your client?_____

16. Are you able to handle the emotional aspects of your client's difficulties?_____

17. Does talking with you give your client hope?_____

18. In general, do you feel you and your client see things in a similar way?_____

19. Do you help your client think more clearly about himself or herself?_____

20. Do you feel that you and your client are alike in some ways?_____

21. How much have you and your clinician discussed how your progress is going to be assessed?_____

22. How much input do you have in determining how you and your clinician will assess your progress?_____

23. To what extent have you and your clinician discussed your progress?_____

24. Do you feel your clinician pays attention to you?_____

25. Is your clinician's understanding of your difficulties similar to your own?_____

26. Does talking to your clinician help you get more organized about resolving your difficulties?_____

27. Does talking with your clinician have a calming, soothing effect on you?_____

28. Does talking with your clinician give you hope?_____

29. Does your clinician help you think more clearly about your difficulties?_____

30. Does talking with your clinician help you to believe more in yourself?_____

31. In general, do you feel you and your clinician see things in a similar way?_____

32. Does your clinician help you think more dearly about yourself?_____

33. Do you feel that you and your clinician are alike in some ways?_____

Helpless Behavior Questionnaire (HBQ)

PURPOSE To measure helpless behavior.

AUTHOR Christopher Peterson

DESCRIPTION The HBQ is a 24-item instrument designed to measure helpless behavior. Helpless behavior is seen as a primary component of a helplessness model that has been used to explain a variety of failures of human adaptation including depression, academic failure, victimization, athletic setbacks, poor work performance, illness, and even early death. The strategy underlying the HBQ was to define helplessness in terms of the extent to which helpless behaviors are displayed; to say that someone is helpless, then, is to say that he or she displays a high frequency of helpless acts over a given period of time. It is assumed that the helplessness measured by this questionnaire leads to inappropriate passivity in the face of stresses and other uncontrollable events. In the HBQ, of the 24 items, 7 are filler items. The items on the questionnaire which form the score for the HBQ include 2, 3, 5, 6, 8–11, 14–18, and 20–23.

NORMS The HBQ was studied with 165 undergraduate, introductory psychology students. The study included 89 females and 76 males; no other demographic data were provided. The mean score on the HBQ was 47.65 (SD=41.23).

SCORING The HBQ is easily scored by summing respondents' answers on the 17 items described above. Each item refers to how many times a respondent performed that behavior during the past month, with higher scores indicating greater helplessness.

RELIABILITY The HBQ has fair internal consistency, with an alpha of .69. No data on stability were reported.

VALIDITY The HBQ has good known-groups validity, significantly discriminating between generally happy and generally unhappy individuals. The HBQ also has what may be described as some degree of predictive validity in that research showed that the willingness of subjects' friends to go along with subjects decreased as the extent of helpless behavior increased.

PRIMARY REFERENCE Peterson, C. (1993). Helpless behavior, *Behaviour Research and Therapy*, 31, 289–295.

AVAILABILITY Chris M. Peterson, Department of Psychology, University of Michigan, 525 East University, Ann Arbor, MI 48109-1109. Reprinted by permission of the author. Email: chrispet@umich.edu.

Listed below are a number of specific behaviors. In the space next to each behavior, write a number that corresponds to *how many times* you performed this behavior *during the past month*.

____ 1. I told several jokes in a row.
____ 2. I gave up in the middle of doing something.
____ 3. I didn't study because it didn't matter.
____ 4. I got people together to play a sport.
____ 5. I didn't change a strategy that does not work.
____ 6. I failed to make an important decision.
____ 7. I addressed a group of people.
____ 8. I was unable to fix a broken object.
____ 9. I didn't cook for myself.
____ 10. I cried.
____ 11. I let someone else make a decision for me.
____ 12. I went to a bar to socialize.
____ 13. I threw a big party.
____ 14. I didn't stand up for myself.
____ 15. I didn't leave my house/apartment all day.
____ 16. I said negative things about myself.
____ 17. I asked others to do something for me.
____ 18. I did not compete when given the opportunity.
____ 19. I sang loudly in the street.
____ 20. I refused to do something on my own.
____ 21. I used another person as a crutch.
____ 22. I stayed in an abusive relationship.
____ 23. I let someone take advantage of me.
____ 24. I organized a group gathering.

Hendrick Sexual Attitude Scale (HSAS)

PURPOSE To measure four attitudes of sexuality.

AUTHORS Susan Hendrick and Clyde Hendrick

DESCRIPTION The HSAS is a 43-item instrument which measures four dimensions of sexuality: permissiveness (HSAS-P); sexual practices (HSAS-SP); communion in the relationship (HSAS-C); and instrumentality (HSAS-I). The instrument was developed from a pool of 150 items. The four-subscale structure was supported by two independent factor analyses with two samples. When using this scale one needs to be mindful of gender differences on some scores, such as HSAS-P and HSAS-I, and differences on all four subscales due to race and ethnicity. With couples in treatment, it is important to compare their scores with those of the gender-specific norms before determining if the discrepancies between their scores are meaningful.

NORMS Because of the differences due to gender and race/ethnicity, extensive norms for men and women are reported in the Primary Reference. From a sample of 341 women, the mean scores on the HSAS-P, HSAS-SP, HSAS-C, and HSAS-I were 4.0, 2.1, 1.9, and 2.6, respectively. From a sample of 466 men, mean scores for the same subscales were 3.0, 2.0, 1.9, and 3.2, respectively. The Primary Reference also provides additional normative data categorized by ethnicity.

SCORING After reverse-scoring items 19, 20, and 21, subscale scores are the sum of the item ratings, divided by the number of items in each subscale (HSAS-P: items 1–21, HSAS-SP: items 22–28, HSAS-C: 29–37, and HSAS-I: 38–43). Higher scores reflect more permissive sexual attitudes.

RELIABILITY The four subscales of the HSAS have good to excellent internal consistency and test-retest reliability. In a study of 807 subjects the standardized alpha was .94, .71, .80, and .80 for the HSAS-P, HSAS-SP, HSAS-C, and HSAS-I, respectively. Test-retest correlations over a four-week period were .88, .80, .67 and .66 for the same subscales.

VALIDITY The validity of the HSAS has been estimated with concurrent validity procedures. Scores on the subscales tend to correlate with other measures of sex and love and sensation seeking. Known-groups validity is suggested by differences in scores between persons reporting to be currently in love with those not currently in love on three of the four subscales.

PRIMARY REFERENCE Hendrick, S., and Hendrick, C. (1987). Multidimensionality of sexual attitudes, *The Journal of Sex Research*, 23, 502–526. Instrument reproduced with permission of *The Journal of Sex Research*, a publication for the scientific study of sex.

AVAILABILITY Susan Hendrick, Ph.D., Department of Psychology, Texas Tech University, Lubbock, TX 79409. Email: s.hendrick@ttu.edu.

Using the following scale, please rate each item and record your response on the space next to that item.

> 1 = Strongly agree
> 2 = Moderately agree
> 3 = Neutral
> 4 = Moderately disagree
> 5 = Strongly disagree

___ 1. I do not need to be committed to a person to have sex with him/her.
___ 2. Casual sex is acceptable.
___ 3. I would like to have sex with many partners.
___ 4. One-night stands are sometimes very enjoyable.
___ 5. It is okay to have ongoing sexual relationships with more than one person at a time.
___ 6. It is okay to manipulate someone into having sex as long as no future promises are made.
___ 7. Sex as a simple exchange of favors is okay if both people agree to it.
___ 8. The best sex is with no strings attached.
___ 9. Life would have fewer problems if people could have sex more freely.
___ 10. It is possible to enjoy sex with a person and not like that person very much.
___ 11. Sex is more fun with someone you don't love.
___ 12. It is all right to pressure someone into having sex.
___ 13. Extensive premarital sexual experience is fine.
___ 14. Extramarital affairs are all right as long as one's partner doesn't know about them.
___ 15. Sex for its own sake is perfectly all right.
___ 16. I would feel comfortable having intercourse with my partner in the presence of other people.
___ 17. Prostitution is acceptable.
___ 18. It is okay for sex to be just good physical release.
___ 19. Sex without love is meaningless.
___ 20. People should at least be friends before they have sex together.
___ 21. In order for sex to be good, it must also be meaningful.
___ 22. Birth control is part of responsible sexuality.
___ 23. A woman should share responsibility for birth control.
___ 24. A man should share responsibility for birth control.
___ 25. Sex education is important for young people.
___ 26. Using "sex toys" during lovemaking is acceptable.
___ 27. Masturbation is all right.
___ 28. Masturbating one's partner during intercourse can increase the pleasure of sex.
___ 29. Sex gets better as a relationship progresses.
___ 30. Sex is the closest form of communication between two people.
___ 31. A sexual encounter between two people deeply in love is the ultimate human interaction.
___ 32. Orgasm is the greatest experience in the world.
___ 33. At its best, sex seems to be the merging of two souls.
___ 34. Sex is a very important part of life.

___ 35. Sex is usually an intensive, almost overwhelming experience.
___ 36. During sexual intercourse, intense awareness of the partner is the best frame of mind.
___ 37. Sex is fundamentally good.
___ 38. Sex is best when you let yourself go and focus on your own pleasure.
___ 39. Sex is primarily the taking of pleasure from another person.
___ 40. The main purpose of sex is to enjoy oneself.
___ 41. Sex is primarily physical.
___ 42. Sex is primarily a bodily function, like eating.
___ 43. Sex is mostly a game between males and females.

HIV/AIDS Provider Stigma Inventory (HAPSI)

AUTHORS Scott Rutlege, James Whyte, Neil Abell, Kristin Brown and Nicole Cesnales

PURPOSE To measure stigma towards HIV/AIDS care providers

DESCRIPTION The HAPSI is an 81-item inventory which is designed to assess personal stigma about providing health and social services to persons living with HIA/AIDS. It has three scales measuring Awareness (a 42-item scale), Acceptance (20-item scale) and Action (a 19-item scale) with each scale having subscales. It is helpful for providers of all disciplines to measure their own bias and prejudice in order to facilitate personal and professional understanding and insight; moreover, understanding stigma toward persons living with AIDS/HIV will help remedy the adverse impact of stigma on best medical and social service practices. The HAPSI is based on social psychology theory that stigma is designed to separate one group from another group which in turn positions the stigmatizing group to have power over the other; the theory asserts that stigma consists of labeling, stereotyping, out-grouping and the discrimination. The instrument is also based on mindfulness theory which has three levels of Awareness, Acceptance and Action. The first level concerns examining one's inner thoughts and feelings about the other group, in order to have Acceptance of the impact of stigmatized the HIV/AIDS patient population; and finally, out of Awareness and Acceptance one takes internal Action to eliminate the stigma and to remedy the adverse impact in order to provide best practices.

NORMS Normative data are not reported in the primary reference.

SCORING Scale scores range from 1 to 7 and are calculated using the scoring template that follows the instrument.

RELIABILITY The HAPI scales have excellent internal consistency reliability. The global measure of Awareness had a consistency coefficient of. 97. The Acceptance global measure was. 98, and the Action scale had a coefficient of. 96. All are excellent. The subscales had acceptable reliability estimates with coefficents ranging from .69 to .98.

VALIDITY The HAPSI has very good content validity and convergent validity. The structure of the HAPSI was supported by the ratings of each item by 15 experts, and confirmatory factor analysis. Scale scores correlated with the AIDS Attitude Scale and prejudicial attitudes toward HIV positive persons.

PRIMARY REFERENCE Rutledge, S. E., Whyte, J. Abell, N, Brown, K. and Cesnales, N. I. (2011). Measuring stigma among health care and social service providers: The HIV/AIDS Provider Stigma Inventory. *AIDS patient care and STDS, 25,* 673-682.

AVAILABILITY Scott Edward Rutledge, Ph. D. School of Social Work, Temple University, 301 Cecil B Moore Avenue, Philadelphia, PA 19122-6091.

AWARENESS

Defined as: "looking deeply," noticing the full range of our experiences when encountering or thinking of people living with HIV/AIDS (PLHA).

Drawing from your own experiences, please circle the number that fits best where 1 = Completely Disagree and 7 = Completely Agree

The first "awareness" items focus on how people may use names for PLHA when thinking or talking about them.

If I know or suspect a patient or client has HIV, I am more likely to:

1) think of negative names to describe them. _____ 1 2 3 4 5 6 7

2) think of them in scornful terms. _____ 1 2 3 4 5 6 7

3) think they are a bad person. _____ 1 2 3 4 5 6 7

4) think of them as a "junkie," "whore," or "pervert." _____ 1 2 3 4 5 6 7

If I am concerned that I might get HIV from a patient or client, I am more likely to:

5) think of them in language I wouldn't want others to hear me say. __ 1 2 3 4 5 6 7

6) imagine names for them that are angry or blaming. _____ 1 2 3 4 5 6 7

7) think they are disgusting. _____ 1 2 3 4 5 6 7

8) think of them as contagious to justify avoiding them. _____ 1 2 3 4 5 6 7

If I am concerned that others in my life will think of or treat me differently because I work with PLHA, I am more likely to:

9) use scornful language when describing them. _____ 1 2 3 4 5 6 7

10) imagine them in terms I'd be embarrassed to say out loud. _____ 1 2 3 4 5 6 7

11) call them names behind their back that I wouldn't say to
their face. _____ 1 2 3 4 5 6 7

12) think they are "low lifes." _____ 1 2 3 4 5 6 7

The next "awareness" items focus on how people may judge PLHA based on personal characteristics or qualities. If I know or suspect a PLHA is also gay, I am more likely to think he or she:

13) is immoral. _____ 1 2 3 4 5 6 7

14) is a sinner. _____ 1 2 3 4 5 6 7

15) got HIV through bad behavior. _____ 1 2 3 4 5 6 7

16) is disgusting. _____ 1 2 3 4 5 6 7

If I know or suspect a PLHA is also an injection drug user (IDU), I am more likely to think he or she:

17) is a thief. _____ 1 2 3 4 5 6 7

18) is an addict. _____ 1 2 3 4 5 6 7

19) is a criminal. _____ 1 2 3 4 5 6 7

20) is weak. _____ 1 2 3 4 5 6 7

21) cannot be trusted. _____ 1 2 3 4 5 6 7

22) is hiding important information from me. _____ 1 2 3 4 5 6 7

23) will not follow through on recommendations or instructions. _____ 1 2 3 4 5 6 7

24) will say anything to get what he or she wants. _____ 1 2 3 4 5 6 7

If I know or suspect a PLHA has many sex partners, I am more likely to think he or she:

25) is desperate. _____ 1 2 3 4 5 6 7

26) is immoral. _____ 1 2 3 4 5 6 7

27) is a sinner. _____ 1 2 3 4 5 6 7

28) has no self-control. _____ 1 2 3 4 5 6 7

29) has made a mess of his or her life. _____ 1 2 3 4 5 6 7

30) is bringing trouble on himself or herself. _____ 1 2 3 4 5 6 7

31) is filthy. . _____ 1 2 3 4 5 6 7

The next "awareness" items focus on how people may reinforce differences between themselves and PLHA.

If I know or suspect a PLHA is gay, an injection drug user, or has many sex partners, I am more likely to:

32) make sure others know I think their behavior is unacceptable. _____ 1 2 3 4 5 6 7

33) remind myself that I'm not like them. _____ 1 2 3 4 5 6 7

34) think of my life as different from theirs. _____ 1 2 3 4 5 6 7

35) keep quiet when others say hurtful or mean things about PLHA ___ 1 2 3 4 5 6 7

36) avoid spending my free time around people like PLHA. _____ 1 2 3 4 5 6 7

If I am concerned that I might get HIV from a patient or client, I am more likely to:

37) make my interactions with them as brief as possible. _____ 1 2 3 4 5 6 7

38) let volunteers or family members provide care that I should
provide. _____ 1 2 3 4 5 6 7

39) ask a colleague to take over their case. _____ 1 2 3 4 5 6 7

If I am concerned that others in my life will think of or treat me differently because I work with PLHA, I am more likely to:

40) put them down for the way they live. _____ 1 2 3 4 5 6 7

41) blame them for bringing problems on themselves. _____ 1 2 3 4 5 6 7

42) gossip about them. _____ 1 2 3 4 5 6 7

ACCEPTANCE

Defined as fully acknowledging the potential impact, intended or not, of our thoughts about and interactions with PLHA.

The first "acceptance" items focus on how people may harm PLHA if they use names for them when thinking or talking about them.

If I think of or use unpleasant names (e. g., queer, junkie, hooker, etc.) to describe my patients or clients, I am more likely to:

1) think of them as a "case" rather than as a unique human being. _____ 1 2 3 4 5 6 7

2) think of them based on their program of care (e. g., Ryan White, Medicare Part B or C, or Medicaid) rather than their individual identity and life experiences _____ 1 2 3 4 5 6 7

3) think of them as a disease rather than a person. _____ 1 2 3 4 5 6 7

4) oversimplify their experiences or problems. _____ 1 2 3 4 5 6 7

The next "acceptance" items focus on how people may harm PLHA if they judge them based on personal characteristics or qualities.

If I let my opinions about PLHAs being injection drug users, gay, or promiscuous shape how I think or feel about them, I am more likely to:

5) think of them as immoral. _____ 1 2 3 4 5 6 7

6) think of them as lazy. _____ 1 2 3 4 5 6 7

7) give up on being creative, and just try to get through the day at work. _____ 1 2 3 4 5 6 7

8) think of them as having brought their problems on themselves. ___ 1 2 3 4 5 6 7

9) feel they won't come back for test results or other follow-up. ____ 1 2 3 4 5 6 7

10) feel that people like them are not worth the trouble. _____ 1 2 3 4 5 6 7

The next "acceptance" items focus on how people may harm PLHA if they reinforce differences between themselves and PLHA.

If I try to make sure others will see I am not like my PLHA patients or clients, I am more likely to:

11) reinforce that as a professional I know better than they do. _____ 1 2 3 4 5 6 7

12) tell degrading jokes about them. _____ 1 2 3 4 5 6 7

13) make sure that others know that I do not approve of the way PLHA live _____ 1 2 3 4 5 6 7

14) talk about how other people make better lifestyle choices than PLHA do _____ 1 2 3 4 5 6 7

The last "acceptance" items focus on how people may harm PLHA if they respond differently to them based on their personal characteristics or qualities.

If I treat my clients or patients differently because I think or know they have HIV, I am more likely to:

15) forget to remind colleagues to maintain confidentiality _____ 1 2 3 4 5 6 7

16) keep quiet when others speak badly of them _____ 1 2 3 4 5 6 7

17) overlook practices at work that may make PLHA feel put down
or disrespected _____ 1 2 3 4 5 6 7

18) rush through things rather than take the time to understand
their feelings _____ 1 2 3 4 5 6 7

19) not advocate for changing the way things are done _____ 1 2 3 4 5 6 7

20) have them wait, sit or receive treatment in a separate area from
other people _____ 1 2 3 4 5 6 7

ACTION

Defined as intentionally expressed constructive and compassionate behavior.

Drawing from your own experiences, please circle the number that fits best, where: 1 = Completely Disagree and 7 = Completely Agree

If I always try to act in ways that meet PLHA's needs rather than reacting to negative feelings I have about their behaviors, I am more likely to:

1) attend events designed to bring awareness to AIDS _____ 1 2 3 4 5 6 7

2) belong to coalitions of HIV/AIDS service providers _____ 1 2 3 4 5 6 7

3) encourage my own friends and family to get tested _____ 1 2 3 4 5 6 7

4) stop negative talk about PLHA when I hear it_____ 1 2 3 4 5 6 7

5) remind co-workers to maintain confidentiality _____ 1 2 3 4 5 6 7

6) advocate for PLHA to get services or welfare benefits that
   are hard to get _____ 1 2 3 4 5 6 7

7) speak publicly about my work _____ 1 2 3 4 5 6 7

8) work to maximize services and referrals for each individual PLHA __ 1 2 3 4 5 6 7

9) talk with my family about AIDS stigma _____ 1 2 3 4 5 6 7

10) do my best to be more compassionate with PLHA_____ 1 2 3 4 5 6 7

11) educate my colleagues about appropriate care for PLHA _____ 1 2 3 4 5 6 7

12) question policies that seem to leave some PLHA in the cracks _____ 1 2 3 4 5 6 7

13) keep on top of developments in treating PLHA (e. g., reading
    journals, going to conferences). _____ 1 2 3 4 5 6 7

14) write or call people in power to change stigmatizing HIV policies
    and practices_____ 1 2 3 4 5 6 7

15) encourage my church, synagogue or temple to sponsor HIV
    services _____ 1 2 3 4 5 6 7

16) push my supervisor to address problems with confidentiality _____ 1 2 3 4 5 6 7

17) report my colleagues who violate patient confidentiality _____ 1 2 3 4 5 6 7

18) contribute to a compassionate environment in the workplace _____ 1 2 3 4 5 6 7

19) contribute to a happier, less tense atmosphere on the job _____ 1 2 3 4 5 6 7

HAPSI SCORING TEMPLATE

- All scores range from 1-7.
- For Awareness and Acceptance (and their respective subscales), higher scores mean greater tendencies to stigmatize or discriminate in specific ways.
- For Action, higher scores mean greater tendencies to act compassionately rather than re-act unintentionally.

Scale	Sum	Score
Awareness (Global):		
Sum responses to items 1-42; divide by 42.		
Awareness Label:		
Sum responses to items 1-12; divide by 12.		
Awareness Label Associate:		
Sum responses to Items 1-4; divide by 4.		
Awareness Label Instrumental:		
Sum responses to items 5-8; divide by 4.		
Awareness Label Symbolic:		
Sum responses to items 9-12; divide by 4.		
Awareness Stereotype:		
Sum responses to items 13-31; divide by 19.		
Awareness Stereotype Gay:		
Sum responses to items 13-16; divide by 4.		
Awareness Stereotype IDU:		
Sum responses to items 17-24; divide by 8.		
Awareness Stereotype MSP:		
Sum responses to items 25-31; divide by 7.		
Awareness Outgroup:		
Sum responses to items 32-36; divide by 6.		
Awareness Discriminate:		
Sum responses to items 37-42; divide by 7.		
Awareness Discriminate Instrumental:		
Sum responses to items 37-39; divide by 3.		

Scale	Sum	Score
Awareness Discriminate Symbolic:		
Sum responses to items 40-42; divide by 3.		
Acceptance (Global):		
Sum responses to items 1-20; divide by 20.		
Acceptance Label:		
Sum responses to items 1-4; divide by 4.		
Acceptance Stereotype:		
Sum responses to items 5-10; divide by 6.		
Acceptance Stereotype:		
Sum responses to items 11-14; divide by 4.		
Acceptance Stereotype:		
Sum responses to items 15-20; divide by 6.		
Action:		
Sum responses to items 1-19; divide by 19.		

Homesickness and Contentment Scale (HC)

PURPOSE To measure adjustment to a new culture for Asians.

AUTHORS Heajong Shin and Neil Abell

DESCRIPTION The HC is a 20-item instrument designed to be culturally sensitive to an Asian population in measuring emotional and psychological adjustment to a new culture. The scale evolved from a 30-item Homesickness, Loneliness, and Depression scale. The HC was developed to aid in assessing the problems that international students in the United States encounter, including academic and cultural challenges. The HC scale also is intended to be sensitive to the private nature of Asians when examining symptoms of homesickness and contentment. The HC has been translated into Chinese and Korean; the translated scale is available from the authors. The HC has two subscales: homesickness (items 1–10) and contentment (items 11–20). The HC can be used not only to study new immigrants and assess their adjustment to a new culture, but can be used as an outcome measure of intervention helping immigrants face the pressures of adjustment to a new culture.

NORMS The HC was studied with 201 university students in the southeastern United States. Of the sample 144 were Chinese and 57 were Korean students and their spouses; 101 were women and 100 were men. Mean age of the subjects was 31 (SD = 3.7). Sixty-six percent of the subjects were enrolled in university programs, the majority in graduate programs. The mean for the global HC scale was 3.09 (SD = .53). The homesickness subscale had a mean of 2.52 (SD = .82), and the contentment subscale had a mean of 3.62 (SD = .88).

SCORING The HC is easily scored by simply summing all items for the total scale and individual items for each of the subscales and then dividing by the number of items totaled. The higher the score on the total scale the better adjusted is the individual; a high score on the homesickness subscale reflects the individual's low level of homesickness; and a high score on the contentment subscale reflects the participant's high state of contentment.

RELIABILITY The HC has fair to good internal consistencies with alphas of .79, .86, and .93, for the global scale, the homesickness subscale and the contentment subscale, respectively. Data on stability were not available.

VALIDITY The HC has fair construct validity, as demonstrated by a lack of correlations as predicted with variables with which the scale should not be correlated such as sex and number of months married, and correlations in predicted directions with some variables with which the HC should be correlated including number of months in the United States, the PCTUS (Perception of Coming to the United States Scale) and PSNAS (Personality and Social Network Adjustment Scale), although the main correlations were with the homesickness subscale and these three variables. The authors report very good factorial validity.

PRIMARY REFERENCE Shin, H., and Abell, N. (1999). The Homesickness and Contentment Scale: Developing a culturally sensitive measure of adjustment for Asians, *Research on Social Work Practice*, 9, 45–60.

AVAILABILITY Dr. Neil Abell, School of Social Work, Florida State University, Tallahassee, FL 32306-2570. Email: nabell@fsu.edu.

Please read each item carefully and circle the number that best reflects your response.

1 = Very often
2 = Often
3 = Sometimes
4 = Rarely
5 = Never

1. I want to go back to my home country.

   1   2   3   4   5

2. I write letters to my family and friends back home.

   1   2   3   4   5

3. I am very interested in current situations in my country.

   1   2   3   4   5

4. I remember birthdays of my family back home.

   1   2   3   4   5

5. I forget my country's national holidays.

   1   2   3   4   5

6. I think about what I would do if I were back home.

   1   2   3   4   5

7. I remember special occasions happening back home.

   1   2   3   4   5

8. I feel homesick.

   1   2   3   4   5

9. I miss my friends and family back home.

   1   2   3   4   5

10. I wish I had a friend with whom I could do many things.

    1   2   3   4   5

11. I feel left alone in this world.

    1   2   3   4   5

12. I feel that nobody understands me.

    1   2   3   4   5

13. I feel lonely.

    1   2   3   4   5

14. I feel that I am not close to anyone.

    1   2   3   4   5

15. I feel excluded by others.

| | 1 | 2 | 3 | 4 | 5 |

16. I feel that my situation is hopeless.

| | 1 | 2 | 3 | 4 | 5 |

17. I am unhappy with myself.

| | 1 | 2 | 3 | 4 | 5 |

18. I feel depressed.

| | 1 | 2 | 3 | 4 | 5 |

19. I feel overwhelmed and defeated.

| | 1 | 2 | 3 | 4 | 5 |

20. I get upset very easily.

| | 1 | 2 | 3 | 4 | 5 |

Homosexual Experiences Survey (HSES)

PURPOSE To measure unwanted sexual contacts.

AUTHORS Barbara Krahe et al.

DESCRIPTION The HSES is a 6-item measure designed to assess unwanted sexual contacts among men. These contacts include differing means of coercion, sexual acts and victim-perpetrator acts. The HSES basically examines the extent of sexual aggression in male to male contacts. The HSES contains 3 items (1–3) from the point of view of the victim and three (4–6) from the point-of-view of the perpetrator. Thus, the HSES allows exploration of sexual victimization and perpetration of sexually aggressive acts.

NORMS The HSES was developed with a sample of 310 men with a mean age of 21.79 (SD = 3.56). The study took place in Germany; 92.3% of the sample were German nationals, 2.3% were Turkish, and the rest were other ethnicities. The educational characteristics of the sample were: 61.9% had completed or were aiming to complete 13 years of formal education (university entrance qualification) while 37.5% had completed 10 or fewer years of formal schooling. The sample was recruited from settings frequented by gay men. All respondents reported sexual contacts with a male partner. The prevalence of sexual victimization by coercive strategy and the prevalence of sexual aggression by coercive strategy are available in the Primary Reference. Overall, just over 15% of the sample reported some form of sexual victimization, and over 5% reported they had used, or threatened to use, physical force to make a man comply with their sexual demands.

SCORING The HSES isn't scored in the traditional sense. Each item, in a "yes"/"no" format can be used individually to indicate the existence of victimization or perpetration.

RELIABILITY The HSES has excellent internal consistency with the victimization items having an alpha of .90 and perpetration having an alpha of .88. Data on stability were not provided.

VALIDITY The items on the HSES are assumed to have face validity. Other data on validity were not available.

PRIMARY REFERENCE Krahe, B., et al. (2000). The prevalence of sexual aggression and victimization among homosexual men, *Journal of Sex Research*, 37, 142–150. Instrument reproduced with permission of Dr. Krahe.

AVAILABILITY Email Dr. Krahe at krahe@rz.uni-potsdam.de.

VICTIMIZATION ITEMS

Preface:

The following questions are about whether or not you have ever been made by a man to engage in nonconsensual sexual acts, i.e., sexual acts against your will.

Please note: The questions do not refer to sexual abuse in childhood or to sexual contacts with women who were in a position of authority over you (e.g., teachers). Instead, we want to know about sexual contacts in which you engaged against your will with men who could, in principle, have been partners in a consensual relationship.

By "nonconsensual" we mean sexual contacts where you were made to engage in sexual acts with another man **against your will** because the man

— used or threatened to use physical force (e.g., holding you down, threatening you with a weapon),

— exploited the fact that you were unable to resist (e.g., because you had consumed too much alcohol or drugs or because you were incapacitated for some other reason), or

— put verbal pressure on you (e.g., by threatening to end your relationship, by calling you a failure).

You can tick more than one box!

Item 1:

> Has a man ever made you have sex with him against your will *by using physical force or threatening to do so*?

Item 2:

> Has a man ever made you have sex with him against your will *by exploiting the fact that you could not resist* (e.g., after too much alcohol or drugs)?

Item 3:

> Has a man ever made you have sex with you against your will *by using verbal pressure?*

PERPETRATION ITEMS

Preface:

The following questions are about whether or not you have ever made a man engage in nonconsensual sexual acts, i.e., sexual acts against his will.

By "nonconsensual" we mean sexual contacts where you

— used or threatened to use physical force (e.g., holding him down, threatening him with a weapon),

— exploited the fact that he was unable to resist (e.g., because he had consumed too much alcohol or drugs or because he was incapacitated for some other reason), or

— put verbal pressure on him (e.g., by threatening to end your relationship, by calling him a failure).

You can tick more than one box!

Item 1:

Have you ever made a man have sex with you against his will *by using physical force or threatening to do so?*

Item 2:

Have you ever made a man have sex with you against his will *by exploiting the fact that he could not resist* (e.g., after too much alcohol or drugs)?

Item 3:

Have you ever made a man have sex with you against his will *by using verbal pressure?*

Response format for each item:

☐   No

☐   Yes, . . .
. . . my (ex-) partner:

       ☐   Touching (Kissing, stroking)

       ☐   Masturbating ("Wanking")

       ☐   Oral sex ("Sucking")

       ☐   Anal sex ("Fucking")

. . . a friend or acquaintance:

       ☐   Touching

       ☐   Masturbating

       ☐   Oral sex

       ☐   Anal sex

. . . an unknown man:

       ☐   Touching

       ☐   Masturbating

       ☐   Oral sex

       ☐   Anal sex

Hope Index (HI)

PURPOSE To measure hope.

AUTHORS Sara Staats and Christie Partlo

DESCRIPTION The HI is a 16- item instrument designed to measure hope, defined as the interactions of wishes and expectations. All items are scored twice by the respondent, once for "Wish" and once for "Expect." These are each considered to be subscales of the HI. The other two subscales are HopeSelf (items 1, 3–8, 15) and HopeOther (items 2, 9–14, 16). The HI has been shown to be sensitive to cultural events or threats such as war or economic prosperity.

NORMS The HI has been studied with several samples. One of these studies involved three samples totaling 276 parents and students obtained at a regional commuter campus of a large midwestern university. The three samples were collected over a period of four years. The first (N=87) had 29 mothers (mean age=44), 29 fathers (mean age=46), and 29 students (mean age=19.1). The second sample (N=99) included 33 mothers (mean age=43.9), 33 fathers (mean age=46.4), and 33 students (mean age=20.2). The third sample (N=90) had mean ages of 45.5, 47.6 and 19.2 for the mothers, fathers, and students respectively. The mean total score for the mothers over the three time periods was approximately 225, 245, and 235; for fathers, the means were 215, 255 and 240; and for the students, the means were approximately 217, 240, and 237. College women tend to have higher scores than college men, and older respondents tend to have higher HopeOther than HopeSelf scores.

SCORING The HI is scored in the following way: The score for Wish (0 to 5) is multiplied by the score for expect (0 to 5) for each item and then summed. The range of scores for the total HI is from 0 to 400. The Wish subscale and Expect subscales are scored by simply summing the item scores for ranges of 0 to 80. The HopeSelf scale and HopeOther scales are scored by multiplying the eight wish items in each subscale and multiplying them by the eight expect items. These scores are then summed for a range from 0 to 200.

RELIABILITY The HI has fair to good internal consistency with alphas for the subscales that range from the upper .70s to the mid .80s across several samples. Data on stability were not available.

VALIDITY The HI has established some construct and discriminative validity with several of the subscales showing significant differences across time depending on external conditions.

PRIMARY REFERENCE Staats, S., and Partlo, C. (1992). A brief report on hope in peace and war, and in good times and bad, *Social Indicators Research*, 24, 229–243. Instrument reproduced with permission of Dr. Staats.

AVAILABILITY Instrument is in the public domain and may be reproduced from this volume with permission of Dr. Staats who can be reached at staats1@osu.edu.

Instructions

Read the item below and circle 0, 1, 2, 3, 4 or 5 on the left hand side to indicate the extent that you would wish for the item mentioned. Then circle 0, 1, 2, 3, 4, or 5 on the right hand side to indicate the extent to which you expect the thing mentioned to occur.

To what extent would you wish for this? 0=not at all 5=very much	[Insert proper time frame here]	To what extent do you expect this? 0=not at all 5=very much

Item

		To what extent do you expect this?
0 1 2 3 4 5	1. To do well in school, in job, or in daily tasks.*	0 1 2 3 4 5
0 1 2 3 4 5	2. To have more friends.	0 1 2 3 4 5
0 1 2 3 4 5	3. To have good health.	0 1 2 3 4 5
0 1 2 3 4 5	4. To be competent.	0 1 2 3 4 5
0 1 2 3 4 5	5. To achieve long range goals.	0 1 2 3 4 5
0 1 2 3 4 5	6. To be happy.	0 1 2 3 4 5
0 1 2 3 4 5	7. To have money.	0 1 2 3 4 5
0 1 2 3 4 5	8. To have leisure time.	0 1 2 3 4 5
0 1 2 3 4 5	9. Other people to be helpful.	0 1 2 3 4 5
0 1 2 3 4 5	10. The crime rate to go down.	0 1 2 3 4 5
0 1 2 3 4 5	11. The country to be more productive.	0 1 2 3 4 5
0 1 2 3 4 5	12. Understanding by my family.	0 1 2 3 4 5
0 1 2 3 4 5	13. Justice in the world.	0 1 2 3 4 5
0 1 2 3 4 5	14. Peace in the world.	0 1 2 3 4 5
0 1 2 3 4 5	15. Personal freedom.	0 1 2 3 4 5
0 1 2 3 4 5	16. Resources for all.	0 1 2 3 4 5

* Use the item most appropriate to sample, e.g. daily tasks for retired persons

Hunger-Satiety Scales (H-SS)

PURPOSE To measure the sensation of hunger and satiety.

AUTHOR Paul E. Garfinkel

DESCRIPTION The H-SS is composed of two 9-item measures developed for research on anorexia. The point of departure for the instrument is that anorectic patients have a distorted view of hunger signals—they become unable to perceive hunger and therefore eat less frequently; because they feel unable to stop eating, they are unable to recognize satiation. The hunger scale measures one's response to signs of hunger, and the satiety scale assesses one's response to signs to stop eating. The instruments do not provide continuous scores, so comparison must be in terms of change from misperception to correct perception on each item.

NORMS The instrument was originally developed on a sample of 11 female anorexia nervosa patients who had a weight loss greater than 25 percent. These subjects ranged in age from 16 to 23 years. Eleven undergraduate females were selected to serve as a comparison group. These subjects were matched with the clinical sample on age, religion, social class, and height.

SCORING Scores are not summed on the H-SS. Each item is an individual index. Comparisons can be made by examining changes in the alternatives chosen as indicative of respondent's "feelings at the moment."

RELIABILITY Reliability data are not available.

VALIDITY Known-groups validity is evident from the fact that the anorectics and matched controls responded differently. Anorectics tended to have a stronger urge to eat and to be more preoccupied with food and more anxious when hungry. The control group experienced satiety as a fullness in the stomach while anorectic patients experienced satiety without appropriate physical sensations.

PRIMARY REFERENCE Garfinkel, P. E. (1974). Perception of hunger and satiety in anorexia nervosa, *Psychological Medicine*, 4, 309–315. Instruments reproduced with permission of Paul Garfinkel.

AVAILABILITY May be copied from this volume.

This questionnaire is about hunger. For each heading circle as many of the answers as are appropriate to how you feel now. You may leave a section out or answer more than once. At the end add any general comments about your usual feelings of hunger.

I. Gastric sensations:
1. feeling of emptiness
2. rumbling
3. ache
4. pain
5. tenseness
6. nausea
7. no gastric sensations to provide information for hunger

II. Mouth and throat sensations:
1. emptiness
2. dryness
3. salivation
4. unpleasant taste or sensation
5. pleasant
6. tightness

III. Cerebral sensations:
1. headache
2. dizziness
3. faintness
4. spots before the eyes
5. ringing in ears

IV. General overall sensations:
1. weakness
2. tiredness
3. restlessness
4. cold
5. warmth
6. muscular spasms

V. Mood when hungry:
1. nervous
2. irritable
3. tense
4. depressed
5. apathetic
6. cheerful
7. excited
8. calm
9. relaxed
10. contented

VI. Urge to eat:
1. no urge to eat
2. mild—would eat if food were available but can wait comfortably
3. fairly strong—want to eat soon, waiting is fairly uncomfortable
4. so strong you want to eat now, waiting is very uncomfortable

VII. Preoccupation with thoughts of food.
1. not at all—no thoughts of food
2. mild—only occasional thoughts of food
3. moderate—many thoughts of food but can concentrate on other things
4. very preoccupied—most of thoughts are of food and it is difficult to concentrate on other things

VIII. Time of day or night when hungriest:

IX. Other comments about hunger:

This questionnaire is about fullness. For each heading circle as many answers as are appropriate to how you've felt since completing the meal. You may leave a section out or answer more than once. At the end add any general comments about your feelings of fullness.

I. One most important reason for stopping eating:
   1. no more food available
   2. eat until feeling of satisfaction
   3. "diet-limit" set for figure or health

II. Gastric sensation at end of eating:
   1. full stomach
   2. distended
   3. bloated
   4. nausea
   5. ache
   6. pain
   7. feeling of emptiness
   8. no stomach sensations to provide information for stopping

III. Cerebral sensations at end of eating:
   1. headache
   2. dizziness
   3. faintness
   4. spots before the eyes
   5. ringing in ears

IV. General overall sensations at end of eating:
   1. weakness
   2. tiredness
   3. restlessness
   4. cold
   5. warmth
   6. muscular spasms

V. Mood at end of eating:
   1. nervous
   2. irritable
   3. tense
   4. depressed
   5. apathetic
   6. cheerful
   7. excited
   8. calm
   9. relaxed
   10. contented

VI. Urge to eat at end of eating:
   1. no urge to eat
   2. mild—would eat if food were available
   3. moderate—want to eat again soon, waiting is fairly uncomfortable
   4. strong—want to eat again now, waiting is very uncomfortable

VII. Preoccupation with thoughts of food:
   1. not at all—no thoughts of food
   2. mild—only occasional thoughts of food
   3. moderate—many thoughts of food but can concentrate on other things
   4. very preoccupied—most of thoughts are of food and it is difficult to concentrate on other things

VIII. Will power required to stop eating:
   1. none—stopping is an abrupt process
   2. none—stopping a gradual process
   3. some—will power required since the urge to eat is still present
   4. considerable will power is required.

IX. Other comments about feeling full:

Hypercompetitive Attitude Scale (HAS)

PURPOSE To measure hypercompetitiveness.

AUTHORS Richard M. Ryckman, Max Hammer, Linda M. Kaczor, and Joel A. Gold

DESCRIPTION The HAS is a 26-item instrument designed to measure hypercompetitiveness—the need to compete and win at any cost as a way of maintaining self-worth. The construct includes manipulation, aggressiveness, and exploitation and denigration of others across a wide range of situations. The HAS is based on psychoanalyst Karen Horney's construct of hypercompetitiveness. Based on an initial pool of 65 items, subsequent research produced the current 26-item scale. The HAS is seen as useful in business and industry as either a screening instrument or as a way of singling out individuals who may need special help. The HAS also may prove useful in clinical situations as both an assessment and an evaluation device.

NORMS The HAS has been evaluated in a series of studies ultimately involving 642 subjects. All were undergraduates in psychology classes at the University of Maine. The one study that reported mean scores involved 53 male and 51 female students. No other demographic data were provided. The mean scores for the HAS ranged from 71.87 to 72.07 (with standard deviations ranging from 12.18 to 14.12).

SCORING The HAS is scored on a 5-point scale with the total score being a sum of all item scores. The following items are reverse-scored: 3, 5, 6, 10, 13, 15, 16, 18–20, 24–26. Higher scores indicate stronger hypercompetitive attitudes.

RELIABILITY The HAS has excellent internal consistency, with an alpha of .91. The HAS also has very good stability, with a six-week test-retest correlation of .81.

VALIDITY The HAS has good concurrent and construct validity. It is correlated with the Win-at-Any-Cost Sports Competition Scale, is positively correlated with neuroticism, and is negatively correlated with self-esteem and self-actualization. The HAS also was positively correlated with mistrust, dogmatism, calloused sexual attitudes toward women, and to perceptions that violence is manly. The HAS is not correlated with social desirability response set.

PRIMARY REFERENCE Ryckman, R. M., Hammer, M., Kaczor, L. M., and Gold, J. A. (1990). Construction of a Hypercompetitive Attitude Scale, *Journal of Personality Assessment*, 55, 630–639.

AVAILABILITY May be copied from this volume.

Please read each of the statements very carefully so that you understand what is being asked. Then ask yourself how true the statement is as it applies to you. Rate your answer to that statement on the 5-point scale and record your answer in the space to the left of the item. The categories for each score are as follows:

1 = Never true of me
2 = Seldom true of me
3 = Sometimes true of me
4 = Often true of me
5 = Always true of me

___ 1. Winning in competition makes me feel more powerful as a person.
___ 2. I find myself being competitive even in situations which do not call for competition.
___ 3. I do not see my opponents in competition as my enemies.
___ 4. I compete with others even if they are not competing with me.
___ 5. Success in athletic competition does not make me feel superior to others.
___ 6. Winning in competition does not give me a greater sense of worth.
___ 7. When my competitors receive rewards for their accomplishment, I feel envy.
___ 8. I find myself turning a friendly game or activity into a serious contest or conflict.
___ 9. It's a dog-eat-dog world. If you don't get the better of others, they will surely get the better of you.
___ 10. I do not mind giving credit to someone for doing something that I could have done just as well or better.
___ 11. If I can disturb my opponent in some way in order to get the edge in competition, I will do so.
___ 12. I really feel down when I lose in athletic competition.
___ 13. Gaining praise from others is not an important reason why I enter competitive situations.
___ 14. I like the challenge of getting someone to like me who is already going with someone else.
___ 15. I do not view my relationships in competitive terms.
___ 16. It does not bother me to be passed by someone while I am driving on the roads.
___ 17. I can't stand to lose an argument.
___ 18. In school, I do not feel superior whenever I do better on tests than other students.
___ 19. I feel no need to get even with a person who criticizes or makes me look bad in front of others.
___ 20. Losing in competition has little effect on me.
___ 21. Failure or loss in competition makes me feel less worthy as a person.
___ 22. People who quit during competition are weak.
___ 23. Competition inspires me to excel.
___ 24. I do not try to win arguments with members of my family.
___ 25. I believe that you can be a nice guy and still win or be successful in competition.
___ 26. I do not find it difficult to be fully satisfied with my performance in a competitive situation.

Hypochondriasis Scale for Institutional Geriatric Patients (HSIG)

PURPOSE To measure beliefs about physical health in geriatric patients.

AUTHORS T. L. Brink, J. Bryant, J. Belanger, D. Capri, S. Jasculca, C. Janakes, and C. Oliveira

DESCRIPTION The HSIG is a 6-item scale that can be administered in written or oral form. The practitioner may have to repeat questions in order to get a clear yes or no answer. The HSIG is actually a test of attitudes rather than behavior so that it is possible for a respondent to score high on the HSIG (higher scores indicating higher hypochondriasis), and yet have no somatic complaints. The 6 items for the scale were selected from a pool of 27 questions on the basis of their ability to distinguish between respondents known to be hypochondriacal and those known not to be. The scale is available in Spanish and French.

NORMS Initial study was conducted on a sample of 69 patients at three extended-care facilities for the elderly. The mean score for those identified by staff as hypochondriacal was 3.9 and the mean score for nonhypochondriacal patients was 1.56. No other demographic data were available.

SCORING Each item is answered yes or no. For each hypochondriacal answer, the item is scored as one point; these items are then summed for a total score with a range from 0 to 6. Hypochondriacal answers are "yes" to items 3, 5, and 6 and "no" to items 1, 2, and 4. Scores under 3 are considered nonhypochondriacal.

RELIABILITY No reliability data were reported.

VALIDITY The HSIG significantly distinguished between geriatric patients identified by staff consensus as hypochondriacal and those not so identified. No other validity data are available.

PRIMARY REFERENCE Brink, T. L., Bryant, J., Belanger, J., Capri, D., Jasculca, S., Janakes, C., and Oliveira, C. (1978). Hypochondriasis in an institutional geriatric population: Construction of a scale (HSIG), *Journal of the American Geriatrics Society*, 26, 552–559. Instrument reproduced with permission of T. L. Brink.

AVAILABILITY Dr. T. L. Brink, Professor of Psychology, Crafton Hills College, Yucaipa, CA 92391. Email: tlbrink@sbccd.cc.ca.us. Telephone: 909.389.3343.

Please circle either "Yes" or "No" for each question as it applies to you.

Yes No 1. Are you satisfied with your health most of the time?

Yes No 2. Do you ever feel completely well?

Yes No 3. Are you tired most of the time?

Yes No 4. Do you feel your best in the morning?

Yes No 5. Do you frequently have strange aches and pains that you cannot identify?

Yes No 6. Is it hard for you to believe it when the doctor tells you that there is nothing physically wrong with you?

Illness Attitude Scale (IAS)

PURPOSE To measure hypochondriasis.

AUTHOR Robert Kellner

DESCRIPTION The IAS is a 28-item instrument designed to measure attitudes, fears and beliefs associated with the psychopathology of hypochondriasis and that of abnormal illness behavior. The IAS comprises several subscales: worry about illness (W: items 1–3); concern about pain (CP: items 4–6); health habits (HH: items 7–9); hypochondriacal beliefs (HB: items 10–12); thanatophobia (Th: items 13–15); disease phobia (DP: items 16–18); bodily preoccupation (BP: items 19–21); treatment experience (TE: items 22–24); and effects of symptoms (ES: items 26–28). Items 15a and 25 are not scored. The IAS is a useful measure for monitoring changes in hypochondriacal attitudes and fears due to treatment.

NORMS The IAS has been studied with a number of samples involving several hundred people. These included hundreds of nonsymptomatic or "normal" respondents, samples of hypochondriacal patients, nonhypochondriacal psychiatric patients, a sample of elderly, and several samples of students. A wide range of demographic characteristics were reported including variations in income and employment, both genders, and different ethnicities. Mean scores are available from the author for most of these groups. Several of the subscales significantly distinguish among groups based on sex, medical problem, presence of hypochondriasis, and so on.

SCORING The IAS is easily scored by summing item responses for each subscale. Subscale scores range from 3 to 15; higher scores indicate more pathology.

RELIABILITY The IAS has fair to excellent stability, with one- to four-week test-retest correlations for the subscales for "normal" respondents that range from .62 to .92. All correlations except one were .75 or higher. Data on internal consistency are not available.

VALIDITY The IAS has good known-groups validity, significantly distinguishing between patients known to have hypochondriacal symptoms and those known not to have such symptoms. The IAS also has fair concurrent validity, with significant correlations between most subscales and self-ratings of depression, anxiety, and anger. The IAS also is sensitive to changes due to treatment.

PRIMARY REFERENCE Kellner, R., Slocumb, J., Wiggins, R. N., Abbott, P. J., Winslow, W. W., and Pathak, D. (1985). Hostility, somatic symptoms and hypochondriacal fears and beliefs, *Journal of Nervous and Mental Disease*, 173, 554–560.

AVAILABILITY May be copied from this volume.

Please answer all questions which can be checked by circling the response that is best for you. Circle one answer even if you cannot answer accurately. Answer the other few questions with a few words or sentences. Do not think long before answering. Work quickly!

	1	2	3	4	5
1. Do you worry about your health?	No	Rarely	Some-times	Often	Most of the time
2. Are you worried that you may get a serious illness in the future?	No	Rarely	Some-times	Often	Most of the time
3. Does the thought of a serious illness scare you?	No	Rarely	Some-times	Often	Most of the time
4. If you have a pain, do you worry that it may be caused by a serious illness?	No	Rarely	Some-times	Often	Most of the time
5. If a pain lasts for a week or more, do you see a physician?	No	Rarely	Some-times	Often	Most of the time
6. If a pain lasts a week or more, do you believe that you have a serious illness?	No	Rarely	Some-times	Often	Most of the time
7. Do you avoid habits which may be harmful to you such as smoking?	No	Rarely	Some-times	Often	Most of the time
8. Do you avoid foods which may not be healthy?	No	Rarely	Some-times	Often	Most of the time
9. Do you examine your body to find whether there is something wrong?	No	Rarely	Some-times	Often	Most of the time
10. Do you believe that you have a physical disease but the doctors have not diagnosed it correctly?	No	Rarely	Some-times	Often	Most of the time
11. When your doctor tells you that you have no physical disease to account for your symptoms, do you refuse to believe him?	No	Rarely	Some-times	Often	Most of the time
12. When you have been told by a doctor what he found, do you soon begin to believe that you may have developed a new illness?	No	Rarely	Some-times	Often	Most of the time
13. Are you afraid of news which reminds you of death (such as funerals, obituary notices)?	No	Rarely	Some-times	Often	Most of the time

14. Does the thought of death scare you?	No	Rarely	Some-times	Often	Most of the time
15. Are you afraid that you may die soon?	No	Rarely	Some-times	Often	Most of the time
15a. Has your doctor told you that you have an illness now?	Yes	No			
If yes, what illness? _____					
15b. How often do you worry about this illness?	Not at all	Rarely	Some-times	Often	Most of the time
16. Are you afraid that you may have cancer?	No	Rarely	Some-times	Often	Most of the time
17. Are you afraid that you may have heart disease?	No	Rarely	Some-times	Often	Most of the time
18. Are you afraid that you may have another serious illness?	No	Rarely	Some-times	Often	Most of the time
Which illness? _____					
19. When you read or hear about an illness, do you get symptoms similar to those of the illness?	No	Rarely	Some-times	Often	Most of the time
20. When you notice a sensation in your body, do you find it difficult to think of something else?	No	Rarely	Some-times	Often	Most of the time
21. When you feel a sensation in your body do you worry about it?	No	Rarely	Some-times	Often	Most of the time
22. How often do you see a doctor?	Almost never	Only very rarely	About 4 times a year	About once a month	About once a week
23. How many different doctors, chiropractors or other healers have you seen in the past year?	None	1	2 or 3	4 or 5	6 or more
24. How often have you been treated during the past year? (for example, drugs, change of drugs, surgery, etc.)	Not at all	Once	2 or 3 times	4 or 5 times	6 or more times
25. If yes, what were the treatments? _____ _____					

The next three questions concern your bodily symptoms (for example, pain, aches, pressure in your body, breathing difficulties, tiredness, etc.).

26.	Do your bodily symptoms stop you from working?	No	Rarely	Some-times	Often	Most of the time
27.	Do your bodily symptoms stop you from concentrating on what you are doing?	No	Rarely	Some-times	Often	Most of the time
28.	Do your bodily symptoms stop you from enjoying yourself?	No	Rarely	Some-times	Often	Most of the time

Illness Behavior Inventory (IBI)

PURPOSE To measure illness behavior.

AUTHORS Ira Daniel Turkat and Loyd S. Pettegrew

DESCRIPTION The IBI is a 20-item scale designed to assess the behaviors performed or reported by a respondent that indicate he or she is physically ill or in physical discomfort. The items were initially developed based on observations of patients in inpatient and ambulatory clinical settings. Two dimensions of illness behavior are measured by this instrument: work-related illness behavior with items related to the curtailment of work behaviors and activities when ill, and social illness behavior with items related to frequent discussion or complaints about being ill and acting more ill than one feels. This measure may be useful in work with clients who exhibit excessive or inappropriate illness behavior and as a screening device for clinical practice since it correlates well with a variety of factors related to medical utilization.

NORMS Several different samples were used to examine aspects of this measure including 40 graduate nursing students, 32 undergraduate linguistic students, 50 lower back pain patients, a group of diabetic neuropathy patients (number unknown), 152 healthy college students, and 63 female undergraduates. No other demographic information was provided. The IBI is in a relatively early stage of development and work on standardization is only beginning.

SCORING Scores on each of the six-point Likert-type scales are simply totaled to provide a range from 20 to 120. Higher scores indicate greater illness behavior.

RELIABILITY The IBI has excellent internal consistency; the work items have an alpha of .89 and the 11 social items have an alpha of .88. No data for the measure as a whole were reported. The IBI also has excellent stability, with two-week test-retest reliabilities of .97 for work-related items, .93 for social items, and .90 overall.

VALIDITY The IBI has good concurrent validity in that it correlates significantly with a number of illness behavior measures and treatment outcome measures in chronically ill samples. The IBI also has good known-groups validity in distinguishing between patients independently assessed as either high- or low-illness behavior patients. Finally, the IBI also demonstrates good predictive validity by predicting several illness behaviors in a healthy sample.

PRIMARY REFERENCE Turkat, I. D., and Pettegrew, L. S. (1983). Development and validation of the Illness Behavior Inventory, *Journal of Behavioral Assessment*, 5, 35–45. Instrument reproduced with permission of Ira D. Turkat and L. S. Pettegrew and Plenum Press.

AVAILABILITY Dr. Loyd S. Pettegrew, Department of Communications, University of South Florida, Tampa, FL 33620. Email: lpettegr@usf.edu.

Please put a number beside each item indicating the extent to which you agree or disagree as follows:

1 = Strongly disagree
2 = Disagree
3 = Somewhat disagree
4 = Somewhat agree
5 = Agree
6 = Strongly agree

___ 1. I see doctors often.
___ 2. When ill, I have to stop work completely.
___ 3. I stay in bed when I feel ill.
___ 4. I work fewer hours when I'm ill.
___ 5. I do fewer chores around the house when I'm ill.
___ 6. I seek help from others when I'm ill.
___ 7. When ill, I work slower.
___ 8. I leave work early when I'm ill.
___ 9. I complain about being ill when I feel ill.
___ 10. I avoid certain aspects of my job when I'm ill.
___ 11. I take rest periods when I'm ill.
___ 12. Most people who know me are aware that I take medication.
___ 13. Even if I don't feel ill at certain times, I find that I talk about my illness anyway.
___ 14. Others often behave towards me as if I'm ill.
___ 15. Although I very seldom bring up the topic of my illness, I frequently find myself involved in conversation about my illness with others.
___ 16. Others seem to act as if I am more ill than I really am.
___ 17. My illness or aspects of it are a frequent topic of conversation.
___ 18. When I'm ill people can tell by the way I act.
___ 19. Often I act more ill than I really am.
___ 20. I have large medical bills.

D-No	Yes	No	27. Except for your illness, do you have any problems in your life?
	Yes	No	28. Do you care whether or not people realize you are sick?
GH-Yes	Yes	No	29. Do you find that you get jealous of other people's good health?
GH-Yes	Yes	No	30. Do you ever have silly thoughts about your health which you can't get out of your mind, no matter how hard you try?
D-No	Yes	No	31. Do you have any financial problems?
GH-Yes	Yes	No	32. Are you upset by the way people take your illness?
	Yes	No	33. Is it hard for you to believe the doctor when he tells you there is nothing for you to worry about?
	Yes	No	34. Do you often worry about the possibility that you have got a serious illness?
DC-No	Yes	No	35. Are you sleeping well?
AI-Yes	Yes	No	36. When you are angry, do you tend to bottle up your feelings?
GH-Yes	Yes	No	37. Do you often think that you might suddenly fall ill?
GH-Yes	Yes	No	38. If a disease is brought to your attention (through the radio, television, newspapers, or someone you know), do you worry about getting it yourself?
	Yes	No	39. Do you get the feeling that people are not taking your illness seriously enough?
	Yes	No	40. Are you upset by the appearance of your face or body?
DC-Yes	Yes	No	41. Do you find that you are bothered by many different symptoms?
	Yes	No	42. Do you frequently try to explain to others how you are feeling?
D-No	Yes	No	43. Do you have any family problems?
P/S-Yes	Yes	No	44. Do you think there is something the mater with your mind?
	Yes	No	45. Are you eating well?
P/S-No	Yes	No	46. Is your bad health the biggest difficulty of your life?
AD-Yes	Yes	No	47. Do you find that you get sad easily?
	Yes	No	48. Do you worry or fuss over small details that seem unimportant to others?
	Yes	No	49. Are you always a cooperative patient?
	Yes	No	50. Do you often have the symptoms of a very serious disease?
	Yes	No	51. Do you find that you get angry easily?
	Yes	No	52. Do you have any work problems?
AI-Yes	Yes	No	53. Do you prefer to keep your feelings to yourself?
Ad-Yes	Yes	No	54. Do you often find that you get depressed?
D-Yes	Yes	No	55. Would all your worries be over if you were physically healthy?

I-Yes	Yes	No	56. Are you more irritable towards other people?
P/S-Yes	Yes	No	57. Do you think that your symptoms may be caused by worry?
AI-Yes	Yes	No	58. Is it easy for you to let people know when you are cross with them?
AD-Yes	Yes	No	59. Is it hard for you to relax?
D-No	Yes	No	60. Do you have personal worries which are not caused by physical illness?
I-Yes	Yes	No	61. Do you often find that you lose patience with other people?
AI-Yes	Yes	No	62. Is it hard for you to show people your personal feelings?

Impact of Event Scale (IES)

PURPOSE To measure the stress associated with traumatic events.

AUTHOR Mardi J. Horowitz

DESCRIPTION The 15-item IES assesses the experience of posttraumatic stress for any specific life event and its context, such as the death of a loved one. The instructions intentionally do not define the traumatic event. This is to be done by the practitioner and the respondent during the course of treatment. The IES is a relatively direct measure of the stress associated with a traumatic event. The IES measures two categories of experience in response to stressful events: intrusive experience, such as ideas, feelings, or bad dreams; and avoidance, the recognized avoidance of certain ideas, feelings, and situations. Because the IES has been shown to be sensitive to change, it is appropriate for monitoring clients' progress in treatment.

NORMS Normative data are available on two samples. One was a sample of 35 outpatients who sought treatment to cope with the death of a parent. The second was a field sample of 37 adult volunteers who had a recently deceased parent. The average age of the outpatient sample was 31.4 with a standard deviation of 8.7 years. The mean score and standard deviation on the intrusive subscale was 21.02 and 7.9, respectively. Mean score on the avoidance subscale was 20.8 with a standard deviation of 10.2. The mean intrusive subscale score for the field sample was 13.5 with a standard deviation of 9.1. The avoidance subscale mean was 9.4 with a standard deviation of 9.6. All of the above data were assessed two months after the stressful event had occurred.

SCORING Items are rated according to how frequently the intrusive or avoidance reaction occurred. Responses are scored from 0 to 5 with higher scores reflecting more stressful impact. Scores for the intrusive subscale range from 0 to 35 and are the sum of the ratings on the following items: 1, 4, 5, 6, 10, 11, 14. Scores range from 0 to 40 for the avoidance subscale, computed by adding the ratings on the following items: 2, 3, 7, 8, 9, 12, 13, 15. A cutoff point of 26 is suggested, with scores above that suggesting moderate to severe impact.

RELIABILITY Based on two separate samples, the subscales of the IES show very good internal consistency, with coefficients ranging from .79 to .92, with an average of .86 for the intrusive subscale and .90 for the avoidance subscale. No data on stability were reported.

VALIDITY The known-groups validity of the IES has been supported with significant differences in the scores of outpatients seeking treatment for bereavement and three field samples. The subscales indicate the IES is sensitive to change as scores changed over the course of the treatment.

PRIMARY REFERENCES Horowitz, M. J., Wilner, N., and Alvarez, W. (1979). Impact of Event Scale: A measure of subjective stress. *Psychosomatic Medicine*, 41, 209–218; Zilberg, N. J., Weiss, D. S., and Horowitz, M. J. (1982). Impact of event scale: A cross-validation study and some empirical evidence supporting a conceptual model of stress response syndromes, *Journal of Consulting and Clinical Psychology*, 50, 407–414. Instrument reproduced with permission of M. J. Horowitz and the American Psychological Association.

AVAILABILITY Mardi J. Horowitz, M.D., Professor of Psychiatry, University of California, 401 Parnassus Avenue, San Francisco, CA 94143. Email: mardih@lppi.ucsf.edu.

Below is a list of comments made by people about stressful life events and the context surrounding them. Read each item and decide how frequently each item was true for you during the past seven (7) days, for the event and its context, about which you are dealing in treatment. If the item did not occur during the past seven days, choose the "Not at all" option. Indicate on the line at the left of each comment the number that best describes that item. Please complete each item.

$$0 = \text{Not at all}$$
$$1 = \text{Rarely}$$
$$3 = \text{Sometimes}$$
$$5 = \text{Often}$$

___ 1. I thought about it when I didn't mean to.
___ 2. I avoided letting myself get upset when I thought about it or was reminded of it.
___ 3. I tried to remove it from memory.
___ 4. I had trouble falling asleep or staying asleep, because of pictures or thoughts that came into my mind.
___ 5. I had waves of strong feelings about it.
___ 6. I had dreams about it.
___ 7. I stayed away from reminders of it.
___ 8. I felt as if it hadn't happened or wasn't real.
___ 9. I tried not to talk about it.
___ 10. Pictures about it popped into my mind.
___ 11. Other things kept making me think about it.
___ 12. I was aware that I still had a lot of feelings about it, but I didn't deal with them.
___ 13. I tried not to think about it.
___ 14. Any reminder brought back feelings about it.
___ 15. My feelings about it were kind of numb.

Imposter Phenomenon Scale (IPS)

PURPOSE To measure self-perception of being an imposter.

AUTHOR Pauline Rose Clance

DESCRIPTION This 20-item instrument assesses the internal experience of phoniness, theoretically a result of an inability to internalize successful experiences. For a person with the imposter phenomenon, the feelings of phoniness are fairly chronic and continue even though there is demonstrated competence. The imposter believes that each new challenge will finally expose him or her as a fraud. The imposter phenomenon is associated with social anxieties and was first identified in high-achieving women, but is experienced by men at a similar rate. The IPS is not gender specific and may be used by men and women alike. The IPS uses total scores, with a cutting score of 62 or above suggesting the respondent has a problem with feelings of phoniness and a lack of internalized sense of success or competence.

NORMS Normative data are reported for a clinical sample ($n = 32$) and a non-clinical sample ($n = 30$). Each sample had persons who experience the imposter phenomenon. The "imposters" in the clinical sample had an average IPS score of 86.87 (SD = 5.38), while the "non-imposters" had an average score of 45.5 (SD = 11.09). The nonclinical sample was made up of college students with a grade point average of B or better. Ten were classified as having feelings of being an imposter, and had an average IPS score of 70.30 (SD = 8.5). Those not experiencing the imposter phenomenon in the nonclinical sample had an average IPS score of 49.65 (SD = 8.66).

SCORING Total scores on IPS are the sum of the item scores. Scores range from 20 to 100, and higher scores evidence more intense experiences of the imposter phenomenon.

RELIABILITY The IPS has excellent internal consistency reliability, with an alpha coefficient of .96. The correlation between item scores and the total score ranged from .41 to .89.

VALIDITY The IPS had good concurrent validity, as seen by the correlation of scores with another measure of the imposter phenomenon. Scores also differentiated persons with the imposter phenomenon from non-imposters in clinical and nonclinical samples, illustrating known-groups validity.

PRIMARY REFERENCES Clance, P. R. (1985). *The imposter phenomenon: Overcoming the fears that haunt your success*. Atlanta, GA: Peachtree Publishers. Holmes, S. W., Kertay, L., Adamson, L. B., Holland, C. L., and Clance, P. R. (1993). Measuring the imposter phenomenon: A comparison of Clance's IP Scale with Harvey's I-P Scale. *Journal of Personality Assessment*, 60, 48–59.

AVAILABILITY Dr. Pauline Rose Clance, Department of Psychology, Georgia State University, University Plaza, Atlanta, GA 30303. Telephone: (404) 593-3128. Email: drpaulinerose@comcast.net.

It is best to give the first response that enters your mind rather than dwelling on each statement and thinking about it over and over.

1 = Not at all true
2 = Rarely
3 = Sometimes
4 = Often
5 = Very true

1. I have often succeeded on a test or task even though I was afraid that I would not do well before I undertook the task.

   1   2   3   4   5

2. I can give the impression that I'm more competent than I really am.

   1   2   3   4   5

3. I avoid evaluations if possible and have a dread of others evaluating me.

   1   2   3   4   5

4. When people praise me for something I've accomplished. I'm afraid I won't be able to live up to their expectations of me in the future.

   1   2   3   4   5

5. I sometimes think I obtained my present position or gained my present success because I happened to be in the right place at the right time or knew the right people.

   1   2   3   4   5

6. I'm afraid people important to me may find out that I'm not as capable as they think I am.

   1   2   3   4   5

7. I tend to remember the incidents in which I have not done my best more than those times I have done my best.

   1   2   3   4   5

8. I rarely do a project or task as well as I'd like to do it.

   1   2   3   4   5

9. Sometimes I feel or believe that my success in my life or in my job has been the result of some kind of error.

   1   2   3   4   5

10. It's hard for me to accept compliments or praise about my intelligence or accomplishments.

    1   2   3   4   5

11. At times, I feel my success was due to some kind of luck.

    1   2   3   4   5

12. I'm disappointed at times in my present accomplishments and think I should have accomplished much more.

1	2	3	4	5

13. Sometimes I'm afraid others will discover how much knowledge or ability I really lack.

1	2	3	4	5

14. I'm often afraid that I may fail at a new assignment or undertaking even though I generally do well at what I attempt.

1	2	3	4	5

15. When I've succeeded at something and received recognition for my accomplishments, I have doubts that I can keep repeating that success.

1	2	3	4	5

16. If I receive a great deal of praise and recognition for something I've accomplished, I tend to discount the importance of what I have done.

1	2	3	4	5

17. I often compare my ability to those around me and think they may be more intelligent than I am.

1	2	3	4	5

18. I often worry about not succeeding with a project or on an examination, even though others around me have considerable confidence that I will do well.

1	2	3	4	5

19. If I'm going to receive a promotion or gain recognition of some kind, I hesitate to tell others until it is an accomplished fact.

1	2	3	4	5

20. I feel bad and discouraged if I'm not "the best" or at least "very special" in situations that involve achievement.

1	2	3	4	5

Indecisiveness Scale (IS)

PURPOSE To measure indecisiveness.

AUTHORS Randy O. Frost and Deanna L. Shows

DESCRIPTION The IS is a 15-item instrument designed to measure indecisiveness as a symptom of obsessive-compulsive disorder (OCD). The concept of indecisiveness appears to be related to worries about making mistakes. Indecisiveness among individuals with OCD may also be seen as a product of the need to do things correctly so that unless actions are correct or mistake-free, people with OCD will hesitate to act (i.e., are indecisive). Thus, only if one's actions are perfect, that is, not subject to criticism from others, will engaging in the act be free from indecision. Some authors also see indecisiveness as a formal cognitive characteristic stemming from a problem with the structuring of input. Therefore, obsessive individuals may overstructure information during input, impairing their ability to use the information leading to uncertainty and problems with decision making.

NORMS The IS was developed in a series of several studies reported in the original article. All subjects were females and undergraduate college students. No other demographic data were provided. The sample for the first study was 112 subjects; for the second study it was 52 subjects selected based on their extreme scores in the first study, and for the third study 88 different female college students. No actual norms were provided in the original article.

SCORING The IS is easily scored by reverse-scoring items 2, 3, 5, 6, 8, and 9, and then summing all item responses.

RELIABILITY The IS has very good internal consistency, with alphas of at least .87. No data on stability were provided.

VALIDITY The IS has established good concurrent and discriminant validity. The IS is correlated with other measures as predicted including measures of perfectionism, hoarding, compulsivity, and procrastination. In addition, subjects who scored high on the IS took longer to make a series of decisions and had higher scores on another measure of decision making than did subjects with low IS scores. The IS also was related to the number of psychopathological symptoms experienced during the previous month, although the average intensity of any given symptom was not different from that of the decisive subjects. The measures used in the validation studies included the Maudsley Obsessive-Compulsive Inventory, the Compulsive Activity Checklist—Revised, the Obsessional Thoughts Questionnaire, Frost et al.'s Multidimensional Perfectionism Scale, Hewitt and Flett's Multidimensional Perfectionism Scale, and the decision making subscale of the Social Problem-Solving Inventory.

PRIMARY REFERENCE Frost, R. O., and Shows, D. L. (1993). The nature and measurement of compulsive indecisiveness, *Behaviour Research and Therapy*, 31, 683–692.

AVAILABILITY Professor Randy Frost, Department of Psychology, Smith College, Northampton, MA 01063. Reprinted with permission of the authors. Email: rfrost@smith.edu.

Please circle the number that best corresponds to your agreement with each statement below.

		Strongly disagree				Strongly agree
1.	I try to put off making decisions.	1	2	3	4	5
2.	I always know exactly what I want.	1	2	3	4	5
3.	I find it easy to make decisions.	1	2	3	4	5
4.	I have a hard time planning my free time.	1	2	3	4	5
5.	I like to be in a position to make decisions.	1	2	3	4	5
6.	Once I make a decision, I feel fairly confident that it is a good one.	1	2	3	4	5
7.	When ordering from a menu, I usually find it difficult to decide what to get.	1	2	3	4	5
8.	I usually make decisions quickly.	1	2	3	4	5
9.	Once I make a decision, I stop worrying about it.	1	2	3	4	5
10.	I become anxious when making a decision.	1	2	3	4	5
11.	I often worry about making the wrong choice.	1	2	3	4	5
12.	After I have chosen or decided something, I often believe I've made the wrong choice or decision.	1	2	3	4	5
13.	I do not get assignments done on time because I can not decide what to do first.	1	2	3	4	5
14.	I have trouble completing assignments because I can't prioritize what is more important.	1	2	3	4	5
15.	It seems that deciding on the most trivial thing takes me a long time.	1	2	3	4	5

Index of Alcohol Involvement (IAI)

PURPOSE To measure alcohol abuse.

AUTHOR Gordon MacNeil

DESCRIPTION The IAI is a 25-item instrument designed to measure the degree or magnitude of problems of alcohol abuse. The items of the IAI were constructed to be a sample of all possible items that would indicate the presence or absence of difficulties regarding alcohol use. The IAI is a very easy-to-use measure for assessing self-reported alcohol abuse. Another advantage of the IAI is that it is one of some 20 instruments of the WALMYR Assessment Scales (WAS) package reproduced here, all of which are administered and scored the same way.

NORMS The IAI was studied with 305 undergraduate students at a large western university. The mean age was 24 years; 87% were white, 13% were minorities. Females were approximately 60% of the sample. Actual norms are not available.

SCORING Like most WAS instruments, the IAI is scored by first reverse-scoring items listed at the bottom of the page (5, 20, 23), summing these and the remaining scores, subtracting the number of completed items, multiplying this figure by 100, and dividing by the number of items completed times 6. This will produce a range from 0 to 100 with higher scores indicating greater problems with alcohol.

RELIABILITY The IAI has excellent internal consistency, with an alpha of .90. Data on stability were not reported.

VALIDITY The IAI has very good factorial and construct validity. It was correlated in predicted directions and amounts with a number of other scales of the WAS including the Generalized Contentment Scale, the Index of Clinical Stress, the Partner Abuse Scale (Physical and Non-Physical), the Non-Physical Abuse of Partner Scale, and the Physical Abuse of Partner Scale.

PRIMARY REFERENCE MacNeil, G. (1991). A short-form scale to measure alcohol abuse, *Research on Social Work Practice*, 1, 68–75.

AVAILABILITY This scale cannot be reproduced or copied in any manner and must be obtained by writing to the WALMYR Publishing Co., P.O. Box 12217, Tallahassee, FL 32317-2217 or WALMYR.com.

INDEX OF ALCOHOL INVOLVMENT (IAH)

Name: _____ Today's Date: _____

This questionnaire is designed to measure your use of alcohol. It is not a test so there are no right or wrong answers. Answer each item as carefully and as accurately as you can by placing a number beside each one as follows.

> 1 = Never
> 2 = Very rarely
> 3 = A little of the time
> 4 = Some of the time
> 5 = A good part of the time
> 6 = Most of the time
> 7 = Always

1. ___ When I have a drink with friends, I usually drink more than they do.
2. ___ My family or friends tell me I drink too much.
3. ___ I feel that I drink too much alcohol.
4. ___ After I've had one or two drinks, it is difficult for me to stop drinking.
5. ___ When I am drinking, I have three or fewer drinks.
6. ___ I feel guilty about what happened when I have been drinking.
7. ___ When I go drinking, I get into fights.
8. ___ My drinking causes problems with my family or friends.
9. ___ My drinking causes problems with my work.
10. ___ After I have been drinking, I cannot remember things that happened when I think about them the next day.
11. ___ After I have been drinking, I get the shakes.
12. ___ My friends think I have a drinking problem.
13. ___ I drink to calm my nerves or make me feel better.
14. ___ I drink when I am alone.
15. ___ I drink until I go to sleep or pass out.
16. ___ My drinking interferes with obligations to my family or friends.
17. ___ I have one or more drinks when things are not going well for me.
18. ___ It is hard for me to stop drinking when I want to.
19. ___ I have one or more drinks before noon.
20. ___ My friends think my level of drinking is acceptable.
21. ___ I get mean and angry when I drink.
22. ___ My friends avoid me when I am drinking.
23. ___ I avoid drinking to excess.
24. ___ My personal life gets very troublesome when I drink.
25. ___ I drink 3 to 4 times a week.

Index of Attitudes Toward Homosexuals (IAH)

PURPOSE To measure homophobia.

AUTHORS Walter W. Hudson and Wendell A. Ricketts

DESCRIPTION The IAH is a 25-item instrument designed to measure the degree or magnitude of a problem clients may have with homophobia, the fear of being in close quarters with homosexuals. Unlike most of the other scales in this book, the IAH is not designed to measure necessarily a personal or social problem; scores on the IAH are not indicative of a clinical disorder. The score on the IAH reflects the degree of comfort the respondent feels when in the presence of homosexuals. An advantage of the IAH is that it is one of some 20 instruments of the WALMYR Assessment Scales package reproduced here, all of which are administered and scored the same way.

NORMS Not available. The IAH has a cutting point of 50; scores below 50 reflect an increasingly nonhomophobic response and scores over 50 represent increasing degrees of a homophobic response.

SCORING Like most WALMYR Assessment Scales instruments, the IAH is scored by first reverse-scoring items listed at the bottom of the page (3, 4, 6, 9, 10, 12–15, 17, 19, 21, 24), summing these and the remaining scores, subtracting the number of completed items, multiplying this figure by 100, and dividing by the number of items completed times 4. This will produce a range from 0 to 100 with higher scores indicating greater magnitude or severity of problems.

RELIABILITY The IAH has excellent internal consistency, with alphas in excess of .90. Data on stability were not available.

VALIDITY The IAH is reported to have excellent content, construct, and factorial validity, with most validity correlations over .60.

PRIMARY REFERENCE Hudson, W. W. (1997). *The WALMYR Assessment scales scoring manual.* Tallahassee, FL: WALMYR Publishing Co.

AVAILABILITY This scale cannot be reproduced or copied in any manner and must be obtained by writing to the WALMYR Publishing Co., P.O. Box 12217, Tallahassee, FL 32317-2217 or WALMYR.com.

INDEX OF ATTITUDES TOWARD HOMOSEXUALS (IAI)

Name: _____ Today's Date: _____

This questionnaire is designed to measure the way you feel about working or associating with homosexuals. It is not a test so there are no right or wrong answers. Answer each item as carefully and as accurately as you can by placing a number beside each one as follows.

    1 = Strongly Agree
    2 = Agree
    3 = Neither agree nor disagree
    4 = Disagree
    5 = Strongly disagree

1. ___ I would feel comfortable working closely with a male homosexual.
2. ___ I would enjoy attending social functions at which homosexuals were present.
3. ___ I would feel uncomfortable if I learned that my neighbor was homosexual.
4. ___ If a member of my sex made a sexual advance toward me I would feel angry.
5. ___ I would feel comfortable knowing that I was attractive to members of my sex.
6. ___ I would feel uncomfortable being seen in a gay bar.
7. ___ I would feel comfortable if a member of my sex made an advance toward me.
8. ___ I would be comfortable if I found myself attracted to a member of my sex.
9. ___ I would feel disappointed if I learned that my child was homosexual.
10. ___ I would feel nervous being in a group of homosexuals.
11. ___ I would feel comfortable knowing that my clergyman was homosexual.
12. ___ I would be upset if I learned that my brother or sister was homosexual.
13. ___ I would feel that I had failed as a parent if I learned that my child was gay.
14. ___ If I saw two men holding hands in public I would feel disgusted.
15. ___ If a member of my sex made an advance toward me I would be offended.
16. ___ I would feel comfortable if I learned that my daughter's teacher was a lesbian.
17. ___ I would feel uncomfortable if I learned that my spouse or partner was attracted to members of his or her sex.
18. ___ I would feel at ease talking with a homosexual person at a party.
19. ___ I would feel uncomfortable if I learned that my boss was homosexual.
20. ___ It would not bother me to walk through a predominantly gay section of town.
21. ___ It would disturb me to find out that my doctor was homosexual.
22. ___ I would feel comfortable if I learned that my best friend of my sex was homosexual.
23. ___ If a member of my sex made an advance toward me I would feel flattered.
24. ___ I would feel uncomfortable knowing that my son's male teacher was homosexual.
25. ___ I would feel comfortable working closely with a female homosexual.

Index of Clinical Stress (ICS)

PURPOSE To measure subjective stress.

AUTHOR Neil Abell

DESCRIPTION The ICS is a 25-item instrument designed to measure the degree or magnitude of problems clients have with personal stress. The items were designed to reflect the range of perceptions associated with subjective stress the items were developed not as responses to specifically identified stressed events, but as general indicators of affective states associated with the experience of stress. The ICS enables a practitioner to explore perceived stress without the problems associated with life events indices. Another advantage of the ICS is that it is one of some 20 instruments of the WALMYR Assessment Scales (WAS) package reproduced here, all of which are administered and scored the same way.

NORMS The ICS was studied initially with 205 patients and family member recruited at a family practice residency program in a regional medical center in a midsized southern community. The mean age was 33 years, 72.1% were female, 27.9% were male, 62.6% were married, and the rest were single, divorced, or widowed; 81.9% were white, 16.2% were black, and the rest were other minorities. The mean ICS score was 28.96 (SD = 18.73). However, this score was based on 5-point scales for responses; currently 7-point responses are recommended.

SCORING Like most WALMYR Assessment Scales instruments, the ICS is scored by first reverse-scoring items listed at the bottom of the page (5, 8, 11, 13), summing these and the remaining scores, subtracting the number of completed items, multiplying this figure by 100, and dividing by the number of items completed times 6. This will produce a range from 0 to 100 with higher scores indicating greater magnitude or severity of problems.

RELIABILITY The ICS has excellent internal consistency, with an alpha of .96 Data on stability were not reported.

VALIDITY The ICS has good factorial validity and fair beginning construct validity, correlating in the predicted direction with the Generalized Contentment Scale and the Index of Family Relations.

PRIMARY REFERENCE Abell, N. (1991). The Index of Clinical Stress: A brief measure of subjective stress for practice and research, *Social Work Research and Abstracts*, 27, 12–15.

AVAILABILITY This scale cannot be reproduced or copied in any manner and must be obtained by writing to the WALMYR Publishing Co., P.O. Box 12217, Tallahassee, FL 32317-2217 or www.walmyr.com.

INDEX OF CLINICAL STRESS (ICS)

Name: _____ Today's Date: _____

This questionnaire is designed to measure the way you feel about the amount of personal stress that you experience. It is not a test so there are no right or wrong answers. Answer each item as carefully and as accurately as you can by placing a number beside each one as follows.

1 = None of the time
2 = Very rarely
3 = A little of the time
4 = Some of the time
5 = A good part of the time
6 = Most of the time
7 = All of the time

1. ___ I feel extremely tense.
2. ___ I feel very jittery.
3. ___ I feel like I want to scream.
4. ___ I feel overwhelmed.
5. ___ I feel very relaxed.
6. ___ I feel so anxious I want to cry.
7. ___ I feel so stressed that I'd like to hit something.
8. ___ I feel very calm and peaceful.
9. ___ I feel like I am stretched to the breaking point.
10. ___ I feel it is hard for me to relax.
11. ___ It is very easy for me to fall asleep at night.
12. ___ I feel an enormous sense of pressure on me.
13. ___ I feel like my life is going very smoothly.
14. ___ I feel very panicked.
15. ___ I feel like I am on the verge of a total collapse.
16. ___ I feel that I am losing control of my life.
17. ___ I feel that I am near a breaking point.
18. ___ I feel wound up like a coiled spring.
19. ___ I feel that I can't keep up with all the demands on me.
20. ___ I feel very much behind in my work.
21. ___ I feel tense and angry with those around me.
22. ___ I feel I must race from one task to the next.
23. ___ I feel that I just can't keep up with everything.
24. ___ I feel as tight as a drum.
25. ___ I feel very much on edge.

Index of Drug Involvement (IDI)

PURPOSE To measure the degree or magnitude of drug-related problems.

AUTHORS Anna C. Faul and Walter W. Hudson

DESCRIPTION The IDI is a 25-item scale designed to measure the degree or magnitude of the problems of an individual using drugs. The IDI measures the extent to which the problems associated with drug abuse are present or absent based on the perceptions of the respondent and then reflects the intensity of these problems. The IDI was designed to follow principles of the domain sampling model of measurement. Items were selected based on those behaviors and emotions that were associated with extensive drug use based on reports in the literature. Then the items were scaled to indicate the degree or the extent of such problems. The IDI is a very easy-to-use measure for assessing problems with self-reported drug abuse. Another advantage of the IDI is that it is one of several instruments of the WALMYR Assessment Scales (WAS) package reproduced here, all of which are administered and scored the same way.

NORMS The IDI was initially studied on a sample of 357 people including 265 graduate students at Arizona State University with the remaining 92 from an undergraduate program at Randafrikaans University in South Africa. The IDI was designed largely for people who had grown up or lived in what can be regarded as a Western culture. The age of respondents ranged from 17 to 51 years with a mean of 21.8 years. The respondents had a mean of 13.1 years of school attendance. The scores on the IDI ranged from 0 to 86 with a mean of 3.1 (SD=10.8). The sample on which the IDI was initially studied in most instances did not report use of drugs; therefore, scores in this initial study were relatively low.

SCORING The IDI is scored by first reverse-scoring items 5, 18, 20 and 23. Then, like most WAS instruments, the total score is computed by summing all item scores, subtracting the number of completed items, multiplying this figure by 100, and dividing by the number of items completed times 6. This will produce a range from 0–100 with higher scores indicating greater problems associated with drug use.

RELIABILITY The IDI has excellent internal consistency, with an alpha of .969. The IDI has a standard error of measurement (SEM) of 2.8, suggesting that a person's obtained score will fall within ±6 points of the true scores approximately 95% of the time. This suggests excellent reliability for the IDI.

VALIDITY The IDI has excellent criterion validity and excellent construct validity. It significantly distinguished between a group with known drug-use problems and a group without. The IDI also was reported to be highly correlated with other measures of the WAS with which it should be correlated, with lower and moderate correlations with other measures and demographic variables with which it should not be correlated, thus supporting the measure's construct validity. The IDI was also shown to have a clinical cutting point of 30, with scores above 30 indicating a problem with drug use and scores below 30 suggesting the absence of such a problem. The IDI had a misclassification error of only 1% for the problem group (false positives) and 4% for the nonproblem group (false negatives).

PRIMARY REFERENCE Faul, A. C., and Hudson, W. W. (1997). The Index of Drug Involvement: A partial validation, *Social Work*, 42, 565–572.

AVAILABILITY This scale cannot be reproduced or copied in any manner and must be obtained by writing to the WALMYR Publishing Co., P.O. Box 12217, Tallahassee, FL 32317-2217 or WALMYR.com.

INDEX OF DRUG INVOLVEMENT (IDI)

Name: _____ Today's Date: _____

This questionnaire is designed to measure your use of drugs. It is not a test so there are no right or wrong answers. Answer each item as carefully and as accurately as you can by placing a number beside each one as follows.

> 1 = None of the time
> 2 = Very rarely
> 3 = A little of the time
> 4 = Some of the time
> 5 = A good part of the time
> 6 = Most of the time
> 7 = All of the time

1. ___ When I do drugs with friends, I usually have more than they do.
2. ___ My family or friends tell me I take too many or too much drugs.
3. ___ I feel that I use too much drugs.
4. ___ After I've begun using drugs, it is difficult for me to stop.
5. ___ I do not use drugs.
6. ___ I feel guilty about my use of drugs.
7. ___ When I do drugs, I get into fights.
8. ___ My drug use causes problems with my family or friends.
9. ___ My drug use causes problems with my work.
10. ___ After I have been using drugs I cannot remember things that happened.
11. ___ After I have been using drugs, I get the shakes.
12. ___ My friends think I have a drug problem.
13. ___ I do drugs to calm my nerves or make me feel better.
14. ___ I do drugs when I am alone.
15. ___ I do drugs so much that I pass out.
16. ___ My drug use interferes with obligations to my family or friends.
17. ___ I do drugs when things are not going well for me.
18. ___ I can stop using drugs whenever I want to.
19. ___ I do drugs before noon.
20. ___ My friends think my level of drug use is acceptable.
21. ___ I get mean and angry when I do drugs.
22. ___ My friends avoid me when I am using drugs.
23. ___ I avoid excessive use of drugs.
24. ___ My personal life gets very troublesome when I do drugs.
25. ___ I use drugs several times a week.

Index of Job Satisfaction (IJS)

PURPOSE To measure job satisfaction.

AUTHORS Cathy King Pike and Walter W. Hudson

DESCRIPTION The IJS is a 25-item instrument designed to provide information about job satisfaction among employees. This type of information is sought for use in many different types of reports and research undertakings. Despite the need for such information, it is often difficult to obtain with use of standardized, reliable, and valid measurement tools. The IJS appears to be a measure that can meet some of the gaps in the current literature. The IJS also may be used as an index of change for clients who are experiencing job dissatisfaction. That is, scores that improve over time may reflect positive results due to clinical interventions or to interventions by organizations. One advantage of the IJS is that it is one of several scales of the WALMYR Assessment Scales package reproduced here, all of which are administered and scored the same way.

NORMS Available from the author.

SCORING Like most WALMYR Assessment Scales instruments, the IJS is scored by first reverse-scoring items listed at the bottom of the instrument (items 1, 2, 4, 5, 6, 9, 11, 15, 18, 19, 21, 22), summing these and the remaining scores, subtracting the number of completed items, multiplying this figure by 100, and dividing by the number of items completed times 6. This will produce a range from 0 to 100 with higher scores indicating greater magnitude or degree of job satisfaction.

RELIABILITY The IJS has excellent internal consistency with an alpha of .94. The IJS also has a good, low SEM of 3.46. The data on stability were not available.

VALIDITY The IJS has been investigated with regard to content, construct, and factorial validity. It nearly always achieves validity coefficients of .60 or greater.

PRIMARY REFERENCE Hudson, W. W. (1997). *The WALMYR Assessment Scale scoring manual*. Tallahassee, FL: WALMYR Publishing Co.

AVAILABILITY This scale cannot be reproduced or copied in any manner and must be obtained by writing to the WALMYR Publishing Co., P.O. Box 12217, Tallahassee, FL 32317-2217 or WALMYR.com.

INDEX OF JOB SATISFACTION (IJS)

Job Title/Description: _____

The IJS scale is designed to measure the way you feel about your job or place of employment. It is not a test, so there are no right or wrong answers. Answer each item as carefully and as accurately as you can by placing a number beside each one as follows.

1 = None of the time
2 = Very rarely
3 = A little of the time
4 = Some of the time
5 = A good part of the time
6 = Most of the time
7 = All of the time

1. ___ My job is very boring.
2. ___ I hate my job.
3. ___ I really like my job.
4. ___ If I won a lottery, I would quit this job.
5. ___ I like to "goof off" on the job.
6. ___ The best part of my job is coffee breaks, lunch, and vacations.
7. ___ I work very hard at my job and I am very conscientious about doing it well.
8. ___ I enjoy thinking about my job when I'm not at work.
9. ___ I don't like to think about work when I'm at home.
10. ___ The work I do is important to me, personally.
11. ___ My job is just a way to make a living.
12. ___ I enjoy taking on new responsibilities in my job.
13. ___ My job is more than just a way to make a living.
14. ___ I enjoy thinking of ways to improve the work I do in my job.
15. ___ The best part of my day is leaving work.
16. ___ I get personal rewards from the work I do.
17. ___ My organization provides the resources and tools I need to do my job.
18. ___ I get through the day by planning what I'll do when I retire.
19. ___ I think about looking for another job.
20. ___ My job is interesting to me.
21. ___ I don't have enough to do in my job.
22. ___ My organization does not support my work.
23. ___ My organization makes it easier to accomplish my work.
24. ___ I believe I have job security.
25. ___ Organizational rewards are distributed fairly.

Index of Self-Esteem (ISE)

PURPOSE To measure problems with self-esteem.

AUTHOR Walter W. Hudson

DESCRIPTION The ISE is a 25-item scale designed to measure the degree, severity, or magnitude of a problem the client has with self-esteem. Self-esteem is considered as the evaluative component of self-concept. The ISE is written in very simple language, is easily administered, and easily scored. Because problems with self-esteem are often central to social and psychological difficulties, this instrument has a wide range of utility for a number of clinical problems. The ISE has two cutting scores. The first is a score of 30 (±5); scores below this point indicate absence of a clinically significant problem in this area. Scores above 30 suggest the presence of a clinically significant problem. The second cutting score is 70. Scores above this point nearly always indicate that clients are experiencing severe stress with a clear possibility that some type of violence could be considered or used to deal with problems. The practitioner should be aware of this possibility. Another advantage of the ISE is that it is one of some 20 scales of the WALMYR Assessment Scales (WAS) package reproduced here, all of which are administered and scored the same way.

NORMS This scale was derived from tests involving 1,745 respondents, including single and married individuals, clinical and nonclinical populations, college students and nonstudents. Respondents included Caucasians, Japanese and Chinese Americans, and a smaller number of members of other ethnic groups. The ISE is not recommended for use with children under the age of 12. Actual norms are not available.

SCORING Like most WALMYR Assessment Scales instruments, the ISE is scored by first reverse-scoring items listed at the bottom of the page (3–7, 14, 15, 18, 21–23, 25), summing these and the remaining scores, subtracting the number of completed items, multiplying this figure by 100, and dividing by the number of items completed times 6. This will produce a range from 0 to 100 with higher scores indicating greater magnitude or severity of problems.

RELIABILITY The ISE has a mean alpha of .93, indicating excellent internal consistency, and an excellent (low) SEM of 3.70. The ISE also has excellent short-term stability with a two-hour test-retest correlation of .92.

VALIDITY The ISE has good known-groups validity, significantly distinguishing between clients judged by clinicians to have problems in the area of self-esteem and those judged not to. Further, the ISE has very good construct validity, correlating poorly with measures with which it should not and correlating well with a range of other measures with which it should correlate highly, e.g., depression, happiness, sense of identity, and scores on the Generalized Contentment Scale (depression).

PRIMARY REFERENCE Hudson, W. W. (1997). *The WALMYR Assessment Scales scoring manual*. Tallahassee, FL: WALMYR Publishing Co.

AVAILABILITY This scale cannot be reproduced or copied in any manner and must be obtained by writing to the WALMYR Publishing Co., P.O. Box 12217, Tallahassee, FL 32317-2217 or WALMYR.com.

INDEX OF SELF-ESTEEM (ISE)

Name: _____ Today's Date: _____

This questionnaire is designed to measure how you see yourself. It is not a test so there are no right or wrong answers. Answer each item as carefully and as accurately as you can by placing a number beside each one as follows.

1 = None of the time
2 = Very rarely
3 = A little of the time
4 = Some of the time
5 = A good part of the time
6 = Most of the time
7 = All of the time

1. ___ I feel that people would not like me if they really knew me well.
2. ___ I feel that others get along much better than I do.
3. ___ I feel that I am a beautiful person.
4. ___ When I am with others I feel they are glad I am with them.
5. ___ I feel that people really like to talk to me.
6. ___ I feel that I am a very competent person.
7. ___ I think I make a good impression on others.
8. ___ I feel that I need more self-confidence.
9. ___ When I am with strangers I am very nervous.
10. ___ I think that I am a dull person.
11. ___ I feel ugly.
12. ___ I feel that others have more fun than I do.
13. ___ I feel that I bore people.
14. ___ I think my friends find me interesting.
15. ___ I think I have a good sense of humor.
16. ___ I feel very self-conscious when I am with strangers.
17. ___ I feel that if I could be more like other people I would have it made.
18. ___ I feel that people have a good time when they are with me.
19. ___ I feel like a wallflower when I go out.
20. ___ I feel I get pushed around more than others.
21. ___ I think I am a rather nice person.
22. ___ I feel that people really like me very much.
23. ___ I feel that I am a likeable person.
24. ___ I am afraid I will appear foolish to others.
25. ___ My friends think very highly of me.

Index of Sexual Harassment (ISH)

PURPOSE To measure sexual harassment.

AUTHORS Walter W. Hudson and Adrienne L. Decker

DESCRIPTION The ISH is a 19-item questionnaire designed to measure the degree or magnitude of harassment experienced by an individual in the workplace or in any group setting where harassment can occur. The ISH can be used with a single client or with all members of an agency, company, business, plant, school, or department. The 19 items of the ISH represent harassment behavior that has been found illegal in a court of law. The ISH can be used by examining each item response as well as the total score. A score of 0 indicates that the respondent is not experiencing any form of sexual harassment that is represented by the ISH. Higher scores on the ISH indicate increasingly greater degrees of sexual harassment; the larger the score the greater the reported problem. It should be remembered that while it is possible to obtain a low total score on the ISH, positive scores on one or two of the items indicate that harassment behavior is taking place. One advantage of the ISH is that it is one of several scales of the WALMYR Assessment Scales package reproduced here, all of which are administered and scored the same way.

NORMS Available from the author.

SCORING The ISH is easily scored by summing item scores, subtracting the number of completed items, multiplying this figure by 100, and dividing by the number of items completed times 6. This will produce a range from 0 to 100 with higher scores indicating greater magnitude or severity of problems.

RELIABILITY The ISH has excellent internal consistency, with an alpha of .90. The ISH also has a low SEM of 2.97. Data on stability were not reported.

VALIDITY The authors report that the scale has been investigated with respect to content, construct, and factorial validity. It nearly always achieves validity coefficients of .60 or greater.

PRIMARY REFERENCE Hudson, W. W. (1997). *The WALMYR Assessment Scales scoring manual*. Tallahassee, FL: WALMYR Publishing Co.

AVAILABILITY This scale cannot be reproduced or copied in any manner and must be obtained by writing to the WALMYR Publishing Co., P.O. Box 12217, Tallahassee, FL 32317-2217 or WALMYR.com.

INDEX OF SEXUAL HARASSMENT (ISH)

Name: _____ Today's Date: _____

This questionnaire is designed to measure the level of sexual harassment in the workplace. It is not a test, so there are no right or wrong answers. Answer each item as carefully and as accurately as you can by placing a number beside each one as follows.

1 = None of the time
2 = Very rarely
3 = A little of the time
4 = Some of the time
5 = A good part of the time
6 = Most of the time
7 = All of the time

1. __ My peer or supervisor tells sexually explicit jokes at work.
2. __ My peer or supervisor describes me or a coworker using sexually explicit terminology.
3. __ My peer or supervisor creates offensive rumors concerning the appearance or sexual behavior of me or a coworker.
4. __ My peer or supervisor uses subtle questioning to determine my or my coworker's sexual behavior or availability.
5. __ My peer or supervisor repeatedly asks me or a coworker for a date.
6. __ My peer or supervisor asks me or a coworker for sexual favors.
7. __ My peer or supervisor places obscene phone calls to me or a coworker.
8. __ My peer or supervisor offers me or a coworker compensation or work benefits in exchange for sexual favors.
9. __ My peer or supervisor demands sexual favors from me or a coworker to maintain job security.
10. __ My peer or supervisor displays sexually explicit photographs and pictures at work.
11. __ My peer or supervisor produces sexually explicit graffiti for display at work.
12. __ My peer or supervisor shows pornographic videotapes at work.
13. __ My peer or supervisor sends sexually explicit letters, cards or other written material to me or a coworker.
14. __ My peer or supervisor uses gestures or staring considered sexually offensive by me or a coworker.
15. __ My peer or supervisor stalks me or a coworker to pressure a personal relationship.
16. __ My peer or supervisor blocks my or a coworker's pathway to force physical contact.
17. __ My peer or supervisor touches self sexually in the presence of me or a coworker.
18. __ My peer or supervisor touches me or a coworker in a sexually offensive manner.
19. __ My peer or supervisor initiates unwelcome sexual activity with me or a coworker.

Index of Sexual Satisfaction (ISS)

PURPOSE To measure problems in sexual satisfaction.

AUTHOR Walter W. Hudson

DESCRIPTION The ISS is a 25-item measure of the degree, severity or magnitude of a problem in the sexual component of a couple's relationship. The ISS measures the respondent's feelings about a number of behaviors, attitudes, events, affect states, and preferences that are associated with the sexual relationship between partners. The items were written with special concern about being nonoffensive and not imposing on the rights or privacy of the client. The ISS has two cutting scores. The first is a score of 30 (±5); scores below this point indicate absence of a clinically significant problem in this area. Scores above 30 suggest the presence of a clinically significant problem. The second cutting score is 70. Scores above this point nearly always indicate that clients are experiencing severe stress with a clear possibility that some type of violence could be considered or used to deal with problems. The practitioner should be aware of this possibility. Another advantage of the ISS is that it is one of some 20 scales of the WALMYR Assessment Scales instrument package reproduced here, all of which are administered and scored the same way.

NORMS The scale was developed from tests involving 1,738 respondents, including single and married individuals, clinical and nonclinical populations, high school and college students and nonstudents. Respondents were primarily Caucasian, but also include Japanese and Chinese Americans, and a smaller number of members of other ethnic groups. Actual norms are not available.

SCORING Like most WALMYR Assessment Scales instruments, the ISS is scored by first reverse-scoring items listed at the bottom of the page (1–3, 9, 10, 12, 16, 17, 19, 21–23), summing these and the remaining scores, subtracting the number of completed items, multiplying this figure by 100, and dividing by the number of items completed times 6. This will produce a range from 0 to 100 with higher scores indicating greater magnitude or severity of problems.

RELIABILITY The ISS has a mean alpha of .92, indicating excellent internal consistency, and a (low) SEM of 4.24. The ISS also has excellent short-term stability, with a two-hour test-retest correlation of .94.

VALIDITY The ISS has excellent concurrent validity, correlating significantly with the Locke-Wallace Marital Adjustment Scale and the Index of Marital Satisfaction. It has excellent known-groups validity, significantly distinguishing between people known to have problems with sexual satisfaction and those known not to. The ISS also has excellent construct validity, correlating poorly with those measures with which it should not correlate and correlating highly with several measures with which it should correlate such as measures of marital satisfaction and problems.

PRIMARY REFERENCE Hudson, W. W. (1997). *The WALMYR Assessment Scales scoring manual*. Tallahassee, FL: WALMYR Publishing Co.

AVAILABILITY This scale cannot be reproduced or copied in any manner and must be obtained by writing to the WALMYR Publishing Co., P.O. Box 12217, Tallahassee, FL 32317-2217 or WALMYR.com.

INDEX OF SEXUAL SATISFACTION (ISS)

Name: _____ Today's Date: _____

This questionnaire is designed to measure the degree of satisfaction you have in the sexual relationship with your partner. It is not a test, so there are no right or wrong answers. Answer each item as carefully and as accurately as you can by placing a number beside each one as follows.

1 = None of the time
2 = Very rarely
3 = A little of the time
4 = Some of the time
5 = A good part of the time
6 = Most of the time
7 = All of the time

1. ___ I feel that my partner enjoys our sex life.
2. ___ Our sex life is very exciting.
3. ___ Sex is fun for my partner and me.
4. ___ Sex with my partner has become a chore for me.
5. ___ I feel that our sex is dirty and disgusting.
6. ___ Our sex life is monotonous.
7. ___ When we have sex it is too rushed and hurriedly completed.
8. ___ I feel that my sex life is lacking in quality.
9. ___ My partner is sexually very exciting.
10. ___ I enjoy the sex techniques that my partners like or uses.
11. ___ I feel that my partner wants too much sex from me.
12. ___ I think that our sex is wonderful.
13. ___ My partner dwells on sex too much.
14. ___ I try to avoid sexual contact with my partner.
15. ___ My partner is too rough or brutal when we have sex.
16. ___ My partner is a wonderful sex mate.
17. ___ I feel that sex is a normal function of our relationship.
18. ___ My partner does not want sex when I do.
19. ___ I feel that our sex life really adds a lot to our relationship.
20. ___ My partner seems to avoid sexual contact with me.
21. ___ It is easy for me to get sexually excited by my partner.
22. ___ I feel that my partner is sexually pleased with me.
23. ___ My partner is very sensitive to my sexual needs and desires.
24. ___ My partner does not satisfy me sexually.
25. ___ I feel that my sex life if boring.

Insight and Treatment Attitudes Questionnaire (ITAQ)

PURPOSE To assess the recognition of the need for treatment by people who are diagnosed with schizophrenia.

AUTHORS Joseph P. McEvoy et al.

DESCRIPTION The ITAQ is an 11-item instrument designed to assess the extent to which people with a diagnosis of schizophrenia can recognize their illness and their need for care. The ITAQ addresses three themes: "Do you have a mental illness?' "Do you need treatment?" "Do you need medications?" The ITAQ is one of the few available instruments to measure the insight of patients diagnosed as schizophrenic. Low insight scores can be used as indicators for the kind of treatment clinicians will have to provide.

NORMS The ISS was studied with 52 patients admitted to the schizophrenia unit of a psychiatric unit, and who were diagnosed as in an acute psychotic episode due to medication non-compliance. The mean age of the sample was 34; 28 were men and 24 were women. The sample had 5 to 6 previous hospitalizations; 28 were admitted voluntarily, and 24 were committed involuntarily. The average length of hospitalization was 34 days (+or– 16 days). Actual norms on the ITAQ were not provided.

SCORING The ITAQ can be easily scored since each item ranges from 0 (no insight) to 2 (good insight). Total scores than are categorized into three groups: good insight (scores from 15 to 22); fair insight (8 to 14); and poor insight (0 to 7). However, the authors recommend that the items be read to the subject and then the subject should be asked to clarify his/her response. The responses should be recorded verbatim and then scored according to the criteria shown on the scale template, available from the author.

RELIABILITY Data on reliability were not available.

VALIDITY The ITAQ has fair predictive validity, with patients with higher insight scores being less likely to be readmitted for psychiatric hospitalization in a long-term follow-up study of discharged patients. Scores on the ITAQ also approached significance with patients with higher scores being more compliant with treatment 30 days after discharge.

PRIMARY REFERENCE McEvoy, J. P., et al. (1989). Insight and the clinical outcome of schizophrenic patients, *Journal of Nervous and Mental Disease*, 177, 48–51. Instrument reproduced with permission of Dr. Bauer.

AVAILABILITY For more information, contact Dr. Bauer at John Umstead Hospital, 103 12th Street, Butner, NC 27509. May be copied from this volume.

ITAQ

Rater: . . . . Date: . . . .

PATIENT'S PERSONAL DETAILS

Name: . . . . Age: . . . . Gender: M/F

Questions 1 and 2

1. *Have you at any time had mental problems (ie, 'nerves' or 'worries')
   that were different from most other individual's?*   **Rating:** . . . . .
2. *Have you at any time needed treatment (eg, hospitalization or
   out-patient care) for mental problems (ie, 'nerves' or 'worries')?*   **Rating:** . . . . .

Coding instructions for questions 1 and 2:

The patient states that no problem existed and that treatment was completely unnecessary or gives nonsensical answers (eg, 'I came for coffee')	0
The patient acknowledges only anxiety, sleep disturbances, arguing or being upset, and believes that treatment may not have been necessary; or states that important others (eg, family) felt he/she was ill and should be treated	1
The patient acknowledges the presence of delusional beliefs, hallucinatory experiences or disorganised thoughts, and views these as serious problems that require substantial interventions	2

Notes: . . . .
. . . .

Questions 3 and 4

3. *Do you have mental problems (ie, 'nerves' or 'worries') now?*   **Rating:** . . . . .
4. *Do you need treatment (hospitalization or out-patient care)
   for mental problems (ie, 'nerves' or 'worries') now?*   **Rating:** . . . . .

Coding instructions for questions 3 and 4:

The patient believes there never were any problems; there are no problems now; and there is certainly no need for treatment	0
The patient states that all problems, which have been present in the past, are now completely gone and that there is no more need for concern. He/she is unclear as to why treatment is continuing, but willing to comply if told to do so by family or physician	1
The patient acknowledges that some psychopathology is still present or, if symptoms have cleared, that the illness has been controlled, but not completely cured. He/she views imminent recovery as the happy result of successful treatment.	2

Notes: . . . .
. . . .

Questions 5 and 6

5. *Is it possible that in the future you may have mental problems (ie, 'nerves' or 'worries')?*   **Rating:** . . . . .

6. *Will you need continued treatment (eg, out-patient care or, possibly, hospitalization) for mental problems (ie, 'nerves' or 'worries') in the future?*   **Rating:** . . . . .

Coding instructions for questions 5 and 6:

The patient assures us that there will be no mental problems in his/her future, and that aftercare treatment is completely unnecessary   0

The patient is unsure about the possibility of relapse or the need for maintenance treatment, but will participate if told to do so by his family or physician   1

The patient is aware that schizophrenia is a chronic illness, similar to diabetes mellitus or hypertension, and that maintenance treatment, including attendance at out-patient follow-up appointments, is required to prevent relapse   2

Notes: . . . .
. . . .

Questions 7, 8 and 9

7. *Have you at any time needed to take medication for mental problems (ie, 'nerves' or 'worries')?*   **Rating:** . . . . .

8. *Do you need to take medications for mental problems (ie, 'nerves' or 'worries') now?*   **Rating:** . . . . .

9. *Will you need to take medications for mental problems (ie, 'nerves' or 'worries') in the future?*   **Rating:** . . . . .

Coding instructions for questions 7, 8 and 9:

The patient believes that medications have not been indicated and certainly are not required in the future   0

The patient states that medications were helpful in relieving anxieties, improving sleep or diminishing irritability. He/she is unsure as to whether medications will be required on a regular basis in the future   1

The patient views antipsychotic medications as having favourable therapeutic effects in alleviating delusions, hallucinations or disorganized thoughts, and states that continued treatment will be required to prevent a recurrence of these symptoms   2

Notes: . . . .
. . . .

Questions 10 and 11

10. *Will you take the recommended medication?*   **Rating:** . . . . .

11. *Does the medication do you any good?*   **Rating:** . . . . .

Coding instructions for questions 10 and 11:

The patient states that medications are unnecessary and does no good, and that he/she will not take them after discharge   0

The patient states that he/she probably will take medications after discharge because they help him/her to sleep or because his family or physician tell him/her to   1

The patient states that he/she will take medications after discharge because he/she has a chronic psychiatric illness that the medication controls (or prevents relapse)   2

Notes: . . . .
. . . .

Total score: . . . .

Interaction and Audience Anxiousness Scales (IAS and AAS)

PURPOSE To measure social anxiety.

AUTHOR Mark R. Leary

DESCRIPTION The IAS (15 items) and AAS (12 items) are designed to measure two forms of social anxiety. These two measures of anxiety deviate from other instruments that assess anxious feelings and anxious behavior. They start from the position that a person who has anxious feelings may still interact socially despite feeling distressed. These instruments define social anxiety as the experiential state of anxiety resulting from being evaluated in social settings. Two classes of social anxiety are measured: interaction anxiety (IA), which concerns social responses that are contingent upon others' behavior, and audience anxiousness (AA), when social responses are not contingent upon others' behaviors. The measures can be used separately or together.

NORMS A sample of 363 college students was used to develop the IAS and AAS. Demographic data and norms are not reported in the Primary Reference. Data are reported for a clinical sample of 13 students seeking professional help for interpersonal problems, speech majors ($n = 12$), and students selected from a pool of volunteers ($n = 17$). The mean IAS and AAS scores were 54.9 and 43.1, respectively, for those seeking professional help. The speech majors had mean IAS and AAS scores of 33.6 and 28.2 respectively, while the third sample's means were 38.1 and 39.3. Little information is available on sampling procedures or demographic characteristics.

SCORING Each item is rated on a 5-point scale from "uncharacteristic or not true" to "characteristic or true." Items 3, 6, 10, and 15 on the IAS and 2 and 8 on the AAS are reverse-scored. Scores are the sum of the item ratings. For the IAS, scores range from 15 to 75. For the AAS, scores range from 12 to 60.

RELIABILITY The reliability of these two instruments is excellent. The internal consistency using coefficient alphas was .88 for both the IAS and AAS. Both measures had very good test-retest reliability, correlating .80 for the IAS and .84 for the AAS over a four-week period.

VALIDITY These instruments also have strong evidence of validity. Concurrent validity was indicated with IAS scores correlating with the Social Avoidance and Distress Scale, social anxiety, shyness, confidence as a speaker, fear of negative evaluation, sociability, public self-consciousness, and self-esteem. The AAS scores also correlated with these criteria. There is also evidence of known-groups validity with differences between IAS and AAS scores for the clinical sample and the other two samples presented in the section on Norms. Scores are fairly independent of social desirability.

PRIMARY REFERENCE Leary, M. R. (1983). Social anxiousness: The construct and its measurement, *Journal of Personality Assessment*, 47, 66–75. Instruments reproduced with permission of Mark R. Leary.

AVAILABILITY May be copied from this volume.

Below are fifteen statements. Please read each one and consider how characteristic it is of you. Rate each statement using the following scale and record your answer in the space to the left of the statement.

1 = Uncharacteristic of me or not true
2 = Somewhat uncharacteristic of me or somewhat not true
3 = Neither uncharacteristic nor characteristic
4 = Somewhat characteristic of me or somewhat true
5 = Characteristic of me or true

___ 1. I often feel nervous even in casual get-togethers.

___ 2. I usually feel uncomfortable when I am in a group of people I don't know.

___ 3. I am usually at ease when speaking to a member of the opposite sex.

___ 4. I get nervous when I must talk to a teacher or boss.

___ 5. Parties often make me feel anxious and uncomfortable.

___ 6. I am probably less shy in social interactions than most people.

___ 7. I sometimes feel tense when talking to people of my own sex if I don't know them very well.

___ 8. I would be nervous if I was being interviewed for a job.

___ 9. I wish I had more confidence in social situations.

___ 10. I seldom feel anxious in social situations.

___ 11. In general, I am a shy person.

___ 12. I often feel nervous when talking to an attractive member of the opposite sex.

___ 13. I often feel nervous when calling someone I don't know very well on the telephone.

___ 14. I get nervous when I speak to someone in a position of authority.

___ 15. I usually feel relaxed around other people, even people who are quite different from me.

AAS

Below are twelve statements. Please read each one and consider how characteristic it is of you. Rate each statement using the following scale and record your answer in the space to the left of the statement.

1 = Uncharacteristic of me or not true
2 = Somewhat uncharacteristic of me or somewhat not true
3 = Neither uncharacteristic nor characteristic
4 = Somewhat characteristic or somewhat true
5 = Characteristic of me or true

—— 1.   I usually get nervous when I speak in front of a group.

—— 2.   I enjoy speaking in public.

—— 3.   I tend to experience "stage fright" when I must appear before a group.

—— 4.   I would be terrified if I had to appear before a large audience.

—— 5.   I get "butterflies" in my stomach when I must speak or perform before others.

—— 6.   I would feel awkward and tense if I knew someone was filming me with a movie camera.

—— 7.   My thoughts become jumbled when I speak before an audience.

—— 8.   I don't mind speaking in front of a group if I have rehearsed what I am going to say.

—— 9.   I wish I did not get so nervous when I speak in front of a group.

—— 10.   If I was a musician, I would probably get "stage fright" before a concert.

—— 11.   When I speak in front of others, I worry about making a fool out of myself.

—— 12.   I get nervous when I must make a presentation at school or work.

Internal Control Index (ICI)

PURPOSE To measure locus of control.

AUTHOR Patricia Duttweiler

DESCRIPTION The ICI is a 28-item instrument designed to measure where a person looks for, or expects to obtain, reinforcement. An individual with an external locus of control believes that reinforcement is based on luck or chance, while an individual with an internal locus of control believes that reinforcement is based on his or her own behavior. Locus of control is viewed as a personality trait that influences human behavior across a wide range of situations related to learning and achievement. There are two factors contained in the ICI, one that is called self-confidence, and a second that is called autonomous behavior (behavior independent of social pressure).

NORMS The ICI was developed and tested using several samples of junior college, university undergraduate, and continuing education students. The total N involved 1365 respondents of both sexes. Means are available that are broken down by age, group, sex, race, and educational and socioeconomic level and range from 99.3 to 120.8.

SCORING Each item is scored on a 5-point scale from A ("rarely") to E ("usually"). Half of the items are worded so that high internally oriented respondents are expected to answer half at the "usually" end of the scale and the other half at the "rarely" end. The "rarely" response is scored as 5 points on items 1, 2, 4, 6, 8, 11, 14, 17, 19, 22, 23, 24, 26, and 27; for the remainder of the items, the response "usually" is scored as 5 points. This produces a possible range of scores from 28 to 140 with higher scores reflecting higher internal locus of control.

RELIABILITY The ICI has very good internal consistency, with alphas of .84 and .85. No test-retest correlations were reported.

VALIDITY The ICI has fair concurrent validity, with a low but significant correlation with Mirels' Factor I of the Rotter I-E Scale.

PRIMARY REFERENCE Duttweiler, P. C. (1984). The Internal Control Index: A newly developed measure of locus of control, *Educational and Psychological Measurement*, 44, 209–221. Instrument reproduced with permission of Patricia Duttweiler and *Educational and Psychological Measurement*.

AVAILABILITY May be copied from this volume.

Please read each statement. Where there is a blank, decide what your normal or usual attitude, feeling, or behavior would be:

> A = Rarely (less than 10% of the time)
> B = Occasionally (about 30% of the time)
> C = Sometimes (about half the time)
> D = Frequently (about 70% of the time)
> E = Usually (more than 90% of the time)

Of course, there are always unusual situations in which this would not be the case, but think of what you would do or feel in most normal situations.

Write the letter that describes your usual attitude or behavior in the *space provided on the response sheet.*

1. When faced with a problem I _____ try to forget it.

2. I _____ need frequent encouragement from others for me to keep working at a difficult task.

3. I _____ like jobs where I can make decisions and be responsible for my own work.

4. I _____ change my opinion when someone I admire disagrees with me.

5. If I want something I _____ work hard to get it.

6. I _____ prefer to learn the facts about something from someone else rather than have to dig them out for myself.

7. I _____ will accept jobs that require me to supervise others.

8. I _____ have a hard time saying "no" when someone tries to sell me something I don't want.

9. I _____ like to have a say in any decisions made by any group I'm in.

10. I _____ consider the different sides of an issue before making any decisions.

11. What other people think _____ has a great influence on my behavior.

12. Whenever something good happens to me I _____ feel it is because I've earned it.

13. I _____ enjoy being in a position of leadership.

14. I _____ need someone else to praise my work before I am satisfied with what I've done.

15. I _____ am sure enough of my opinions to try and influence others.

16. When something is going to affect me I _____ learn as much about it as I can.

17. I _____ decide to do things on the spur of the moment.

18. For me, knowing I've done something well is _____ more important than being praised by someone else.

19. I _____ let other people's demands keep me from doing things I want to do.

20. I _____ stick to my opinions when someone disagrees with me.

21. I _____ do what I feel like doing not what other people think I ought to do.

22. I _____ get discouraged when doing something that takes a long time to achieve results.

23. When part of a group I _____ prefer to let other people make all the decisions.

24. When I have a problem I _____ follow the advice of friends or relatives.

25. I _____ enjoy trying to do difficult tasks more than I enjoy trying to do easy tasks.

26. I _____ prefer situations where I can depend on someone else's ability rather than just my own.

27. Having someone important tell me I did a good job is _____ more important to me than feeling I've done a good job.

28. When I'm involved in something I _____ try to find out all I can about what is going on even when someone else is in charge.

Internal State Scale (ISS)

PURPOSE To assess mood state.

AUTHOR Mark S. Bauer

DESCRIPTION The ISS is a 15-item measure that is designed to assess clients' mood states, and that can be used at frequent intervals and away from clinical sites. The ISS is particularly useful because it assesses both depressed and manic states. The ISS has been studied in a number of contexts and with a wide variety of respondents. The ISS is comprised of four subscales: Perceived Conflict (items 1, 2, 4, 11, and 14); Well Being (items 3, 5, and 15); Activation (items 6, 8, 10, 11, and 12); and Depression (items 7 and 9). The last item is not included in the scoring, although it can provide a sort of validity check. The ISS has two main uses. The first is to discriminate mood state in bipolar disorders. This is accomplished by use of two subscales, Activation and Well-Being, that have rough cutoff scores that should be standardized by each user: Hypomania is considered to be indicated by scores over 155 on Activation and over 125 on Well-Being. Mixed State is over 155 on Activation and less than 125 on Well-Being. Euthymia is less than 155 on Activation and greater than 125 on Well-Being. Depression is indicated by scores less than 155 on Activation and less than 125 on Well-Being. The second use is for symptom severity, and that involves use of three subscales: Activation for manic symptoms, Depression for depressive symptoms, and Perceived Conflict for global psychopathology. The ISS has been translated into Spanish, German, and French.

NORMS The ISS has been studied with a number of samples. In the original development study, the sample was composed of 89 patients with bipolar disorder or major depressive disorder, and 24 "normal" control subjects. Subjects did not differ in age, ethnicity, gender, or education in analyses comparing the experimental and control groups. However, the exact demographic characteristics of the sample were not provided. Actual norms were not provided although all subscales differentiated significantly between the experimental and control groups.

SCORING The ISS is scored like a Likert scale with each circle representing increments of 10 in the scores. The subscale scores are simply the sums of the item scores for each subscale.

RELIABILITY The ISS has good internal consistency with alphas that range from .81 to .92 for the subscales. The ISS also has some degree of stability with no significant changes for control subjects in test-retest situations.

VALIDITY The ISS has excellent convergent validity with scores on the subscales correlating in predicted ways with clinician ratings, Hamilton Depression Rating Scale scores, and the Brief Psychiatric Rating Scale. The ISS also has good discriminative validity distinguishing significantly between diagnosed patients and "normal" subjects.

PRIMARY REFERENCE Bauer, M. S., et al. (1991). Independent assessment of manic and depressive symptoms by self-rating, *Archives of General Psychiatry*, 48, 807–812. Instrument reproduced with permission of Dr. Bauer.

AVAILABILITY The ISS may be reproduced from this book with permission of Dr. Bauer. Please notify Dr. Bauer of results of research using the ISS at Mark_ Bauer@brown.edu

ISS

Name:_____

Date: _____

For each of the following statements, please blacken the circle on the line that best describes the way you have felt *over the past 24 hours*. While there may have been some change during that time, try to give a single summary rating for each item.

Today my mood is changeable.

0   100

○   ○   ○   ○   ○   ○   ○   ○   ○   ○   ○

Not at all   Very much so
Rarely   Much of the time

Today I feel irritable.

0   100

○   ○   ○   ○   ○   ○   ○   ○   ○   ○   ○

Not at all   Very much so
Rarely   Much of the time

Today I feel like a capable person.

0   100

○   ○   ○   ○   ○   ○   ○   ○   ○   ○   ○

Not at all   Very much so
Rarely   Much of the time

Today I feel like people are out to get me.

0   100

○   ○   ○   ○   ○   ○   ○   ○   ○   ○   ○

Not at all   Very much so
Rarely   Much of the time

Today I actually feel great inside.

0   100

○   ○   ○   ○   ○   ○   ○   ○   ○   ○   ○

Not at all   Very much so
Rarely   Much of the time

Today I feel impulsive.

0   100

○   ○   ○   ○   ○   ○   ○   ○   ○   ○   ○

Not at all   Very much so
Rarely   Much of the time

Today I feel depressed.

0   100

○   ○   ○   ○   ○   ○   ○   ○   ○   ○   ○

Not at all   Very much so

Rarely   Much of the time

Today my thoughts are going fast.

0   100

○   ○   ○   ○   ○   ○   ○   ○   ○   ○   ○

Not at all   Very much so

Rarely   Much of the time

Today it seems like nothing will ever work out for me.

0   100

○   ○   ○   ○   ○   ○   ○   ○   ○   ○   ○

Not at all   Very much so

Rarely   Much of the time

Today I feel overactive.

0   100

○   ○   ○   ○   ○   ○   ○   ○   ○   ○   ○

Not at all   Very much so

Rarely   Much of the time

Today I feel as if the world is against me.

0   100

○   ○   ○   ○   ○   ○   ○   ○   ○   ○   ○

Not at all   Very much so

Rarely   Much of the time

Today I feel "sped up" inside.

0   100

○   ○   ○   ○   ○   ○   ○   ○   ○   ○   ○

Not at all   Very much so

Rarely   Much of the time

Today I feel restless.

0   100

○   ○   ○   ○   ○   ○   ○   ○   ○   ○   ○

Not at all   Very much so

Rarely   Much of the time

Today I feel argumentative.

0   100

○   ○   ○   ○   ○   ○   ○   ○   ○   ○   ○

Not at all   Very much so

Rarely   Much of the time

Today I feel energized.

0   100
○   ○   ○   ○   ○   ○   ○   ○   ○   ○   ○
Not at all   Very much so
Rarely   Much of the time

Today I feel:

0   100
○   ○   ○   ○   ○   ○   ○   ○   ○   ○   ○
Depressed   Normal   Manic
Down   High

434

Internal Versus External Control of Weight Scale (IECW)

PURPOSE To measure locus of control pertaining to weight loss.

AUTHORS Lester L. Tobias and Marian L. MacDonald

DESCRIPTION The 5-item IECW is similar to other measures of locus of control in that it attempts to measure the degree to which respondents consider achievement of a goal as contingent or noncontingent on their own behavior. The scale was initially developed to test the effectiveness of internal perceptions to facilitate weight reduction. The instrument is relevant to weight reduction treatment that emphasizes clients' taking responsibility for their treatment. While the IECW registers change toward an internal control orientation as a consequence of treatment, the perceived responsibility itself is insufficient to facilitate weight loss. Consequently, the IECW needs to be used along with other measures of treatment effectiveness.

NORMS The IECW was developed on 100 undergraduate females whose weights were at least 10% more than their desirable weight, who expressed a belief that the weight problem was related to eating and activity patterns, and declared a desire to change. The sample's average age was 19.2 years, ranging from 17 to 26. The average weight of the sample was 161.8 pounds. The average IECW score before any experimental manipulation was approximately 1.04.

SCORING Items are arranged in a forced-choice format; one alternative reflects an internal orientation and the other reflects an external orientation. External choices (the first alternative in items 1, 3, and 5, the second alternative in items 2 and 4) are scored as "1." Total scores are the sum of the internal alternatives selected by the respondent. Scores range from 0 to 5.

RELIABILITY The reliability of the IECW was determined using test-retest correlations over a ten-week period. The correlation coefficient was .52, which is low but acceptable because of the long period between administrations. Internal consistency data were not reported.

VALIDITY The instrument lacks validity data. Scores did not differ between pre- and post-weight reduction program. Criterion validity to determine if scores actually correlate with weight reduction has not been established.

PRIMARY REFERENCE Tobias, L. L., and MacDonald, M. L. (1977). Internal locus of control and weight loss: An insufficient condition, *Journal of Consulting and Clinical Psychology*, 45, 647–653.   Instrument reproduced with permission of the American Psychological Association.

AVAILABILITY May be copied from this volume.

Each item consists of two statements; choose the statement with which you *agree most* by placing a check in the blank to the left of that statement.

1. ___ Overweight problems are mainly a result of hereditary or physiological factors.
   ___ Overweight problems are mainly a result of lack of self-control.
2. ___ Overweight people will lose weight only when they can generate enough internal motivation.
   ___ Overweight people need some tangible external motivation in order to reduce.
3. ___ Diet pills can be a valuable aid in weight reduction.
   ___ A person who loses weight with diet pills will gain the weight back eventually.
4. ___ In overweight people, hunger is caused by the expectation of being hungry.
   ___ In overweight people, hunger is caused by stomach contractions and low blood sugar levels.
5. ___ Overweight problems can be traced to early childhood and are very resistant to change.
   ___ Overweight problems can be traced to poor eating habits which are relatively simple to change.

Internalized Homophobia Scale (IHS)

PURPOSE To measure internalized homophobia.

AUTHORS Michael W. Ross and B. R. Simon Rosser

DESCRIPTION The IHS is a 26-item instrument designed to measure internalized homophobia. Internalized homophobia is thought to be a key construct in the symptomatology and treatment of gay men and lesbians. Internalized homophobia can be conceptualized as reaction to the stigma associated with being homosexual. A number of psychological characteristics are associated with internalized homophobia including lower self-acceptance, lower ability to self-disclose, low self-esteem, self-hatred, self-doubt, belief in one's inferiority, and acceptance of popular myths about homosexuality. The IHS, therefore, has great utility in helping clinicians identify internalized homophobia among clients and identifying areas of that internalized homophobia that would be responsive to intervention. The IHS comprises four subscales: public identification as gay (items 1, 3, 8, 10, 11, 12, 19, 21, 23, and 25); perception of stigma associated with being gay (items 13, 15, 17, 18, 20, and 24); social comfort with gay men (items 2, 4, 5, 6, 7, and 9); and moral and religious acceptability of being gay (items 14, 16, 22, and 26).

NORMS The IHS was initially studied with 184 men who directly or indirectly self-identified as being gay. The mean age was 37 years (SD=9.3); 33.7% were college graduates, and 31.7% had a graduate degree or professional qualifications. While overall means were not available in the original article, means are available for the four subscales based on whether respondents are HIV seropositive and belong or do not belong to gay groups.

SCORING The IHS is scored by summing all items after reverse-scoring items 1, 2, 5, 7, 8, 9, 12, 13, 15, 17, and 19. Higher scores equal greater internalized homophobia.

RELIABILITY The IHS has fair to good internal consistencies, with alphas of .85, .69, .64, and .62 for the factors presented in the order above, respectively. Data on stability were not available.

VALIDITY The IHS has fair concurrent validity, with three out of four of the subscales being significantly correlated with a number of variables relating to relationships with and attraction to men, amount of time spent with gays, and the extent to which the respondents were openly gay.

PRIMARY REFERENCE Ross, M. W., and Rosser, B. R. S. (1996). Measurement and correlates of internalized homophobia: A factor analytic study, *Journal of Clinical Psychology*, 52, 15–21.

AVAILABILITY Dr. Michael W. Ross, Center for Health Education Research and Development, School of Public Health, University of Texas, P.O. Box 20186, Houston, TX 77225. Telephone: 713-500-9652. Email: michael.w.ross@uth.tmc.edu.

Fill out this scale by writing the number that best describes your response in the space to the left of each statement. Give your first response and don't spend too much time on any item. The responses are

1 = Strongly agree
2 = Moderately agree
3 = Slightly agree
4 = Neither agree nor disagree
5 = Slightly disagree
6 = Moderately disagree
7 = Strongly disagree

___ 1. Obviously effeminate homosexual men make me feel uncomfortable.
___ 2. I prefer to have anonymous sexual partners.
___ 3. It would not be easier in life to be heterosexual.
___ 4. Most of my friends are homosexual.
___ 5. I do not feel confident about making an advance toward another man.
___ 6. I feel comfortable in gay bars.
___ 7. Social situations with gay men make me feel uncomfortable.
___ 8. I don't like thinking about my homosexuality.
___ 9. When I think about other homosexual men, I think of negative situations.
___ 10. I feel comfortable being seen in public with an obviously gay person.
___ 11. I feel comfortable discussing homosexuality in a public situation.
___ 12. It is important to me to control who knows about my homosexuality.
___ 13. Most people have negative reactions to homosexuality.
___ 14. Homosexuality is not against the will of God.
___ 15. Society still punishes people for being gay.
___ 16. I object if an anti-gay joke is told in my presence.
___ 17. I worry about becoming old and gay.
___ 18. I worry about becoming unattractive.
___ 19. I would prefer to be more heterosexual.
___ 20. Most people don't discriminate against homosexuals.
___ 21. I feel comfortable being homosexual.
___ 22. Homosexuality is morally acceptable.
___ 23. I am not worried about anyone finding out that I am gay.
___ 24. Discrimination against gay people is still common.
___ 25. Even if I could change my sexual orientation, I wouldn't.
___ 26. Homosexuality is as natural as heterosexuality.

Interpersonal Dependency Inventory (IDI)

PURPOSE To measure interpersonal dependency.

AUTHORS Robert M. A. Hirschfield, G. L. Klerman, H. G. Gough, J. Barrett, S. J. Korchin, and P. Chodoff.

DESCRIPTION The IDI is a 48-item instrument designed to measure the thoughts, behaviors, and feelings revolving around the need to associate closely with valued people. The theoretical base for the IDI is a blend of psychoanalytic, social learning, and attachment theories emphasizing the importance of excess dependency for a range of emotional and behavioral disorders. Based on an initial pool of 98 items, the 48-item scale was developed using factor analysis. This resulted in three subscales: Emotional reliance on others (items 3, 6, 7, 9, 12, 15, 16, 19, 22, 26, 29, 33, 35, 38, 40, 43, 45, 47), lack of self-confidence (items 2, 5, 10, 13, 17, 19, 20, 23, 24, 27, 30, 32, 36, 29, 41, 44, 46) and assertion of autonomy (items 1, 4, 8, 11, 14, 18, 21, 25, 28, 31, 34, 37, 42, 48).

NORMS Research on the IDI has involved three samples. The first is a predominantly white group of 88 university males and 132 university females with a mean age of 24. The second involved 76 male and 104 female psychiatric patients, predominantly white. The third involved 19 male and 47 female psychiatric patients (mean age of 31) and 64 male and 57 female nonpsychiatric community residents (mean age of 41). Means for these groups on the IDI ranged from 176.3 to 210.3; however, a new scoring system has replaced the one used in determining these figures so that the mean for "normal" samples averages around 50.

SCORING The IDI is scored by summing the responses from each of the three subscales to yield scores for each one. Items 10, 23, and 44 on the self-confidence subscale are rescored by subtracting the item response from 5. The scores on the three subscales can be summed for the overall score. A new, more complicated scoring system for the total score, utilizing weighted scores and producing means of around 50 for normal samples, is available from the author.

RELIABILITY The IDI has good internal consistency, with split-half reliabilities that range from .72 to .91. No test-retest data were reported.

VALIDITY The IDI has fairly good concurrent validity, with the first two subscales correlating significantly with measures of general neuroticism (the Maudley Personality Inventory) and anxiety, interpersonal sensitivity, and depression (Symptom Checklist-90). The IDI also distinguishes between psychiatric patients and normals. However, the first two subscales are also correlated with the social desirability scale of the MMPI, suggesting that respondents tend to respond based on what they believe is socially desirable.

PRIMARY REFERENCE Hirschfield, R. M. A., Klerman, G. L., Gough, H. G., Barrett, J., Korchin, S. J., and Chodoff, P. (1977). A measure of interpersonal dependency, *Journal of Personality Assessment*, 41, 610–618. Instrument reproduced by permission of the authors and the *Journal of Personality Assessment*.

AVAILABILITY Dr. Harrison G. Gough, Institute of Personality Assessment and Research, University of California, Berkeley, CA 94720. Email: jparibm@berkeley.edu.

Please read each statement and decide whether or not it is characteristic of your attitudes, feelings, or behaviors. Then assign a rating to every statement, using the values given below:

4 = very characteristic of me
3 = quite characteristic of me
2 = somewhat characteristic of me
1 = not characteristic of me

___ 1. I prefer to be by myself.
___ 2. When I have a decision to make, I always ask for advice.
___ 3. I do my best work when I know it will be appreciated.
___ 4. I can't stand being fussed over when I am sick.
___ 5. I would rather be a follower than a leader.
___ 6. I believe people could do a lot more for me if they wanted to.
___ 7. As a child, pleasing my parents was very important to me.
___ 8. I don't need other people to make me feel good.
___ 9. Disapproval by someone I care about is very painful for me.
___ 10. I feel confident of my ability to deal with most of the personal problems I am likely to meet in life.
___ 11. I'm the only person I want to please.
___ 12. The idea of losing a close friend is terrifying to me.
___ 13. I am quick to agree with the opinions expressed by others.
___ 14. I rely only on myself.
___ 15. I would be completely lost if I didn't have someone special.
___ 16. I get upset when someone discovers a mistake I've made.
___ 17. It is hard for me to ask someone for a favor.
___ 18. I hate it when people offer me sympathy.
___ 19. I easily get discouraged when I don't get what I need from others.
___ 20. In an argument, I give in easily.
___ 21. I don't need much from people.
___ 22. I must have one person who is very special to me.
___ 23. When I go to a party, I expect that the other people will like me.
___ 24. I feel better when I know someone else is in command.
___ 25. When I am sick, I prefer that my friends leave me alone.
___ 26. I'm never happier than when people say I've done a good job.
___ 27. It is hard for me to make up my mind about a TV show or movie until I know what other people think.
___ 28. I am willing to disregard other people's feelings in order to accomplish something that's important to me.
___ 29. I need to have one person who puts me above all others.
___ 30. In social situations I tend to be very self-conscious.
___ 31. I don't need anyone.
___ 32. I have a lot of trouble making decisions by myself.
___ 33. I tend to imagine the worst if a loved one doesn't arrive when expected.
___ 34. Even when things go wrong I can get along without asking for help from my friends.

___ 35. I tend to expect too much from others.
___ 36. I don't like to buy clothes by myself.
___ 37. I tend to be a loner.
___ 38. I feel that I never really get all that I need from people.
___ 39. When I meet new people, I'm afraid that I won't do the right thing.
___ 40. Even if most people turned against me, I could still go on if someone I love stood by me.
___ 41. I would rather stay free of involvements with others than to risk disappointments.
___ 42. What people think of me doesn't affect how I feel.
___ 43. I think that most people don't realize how easily they can hurt me.
___ 44. I am very confident about my own judgment.
___ 45. I have always had a terrible fear that I will lose the love and support of people I desperately need.
___ 46. I don't have what it takes to be a good leader.
___ 47. I would feel helpless if deserted by someone I love.
___ 48. What other people say doesn't bother me.

Intimacy Scale (IS)

PURPOSE To assess intimacy.

AUTHORS Alexis J. Walker and Linda Thompson

DESCRIPTION The IS is a 17-item instrument designed to measure general intimacy or affection. The IS is actually part of a broader instrument that taps several dimensions of intimacy but is reported on by its authors as a separate scale. Intimacy is defined simply as family members' caring about each other, and includes such elements of emotional closeness as affection, altruism, enjoyment, satisfaction, a feeling that the relationship is important, openness, respect, solidarity, and commitment.

NORMS The IS was studied initially with 166 female college undergraduates of whom 68% were aged 20 to 25; 166 mothers of the students, most of whom were aged 40 to 49 (63%) and were middle class, with 73% on their first marriages; and 148 grandmothers, 40% of whom were between the ages of 60 and 69 and 40% of whom were between the ages of 70 and 79, 52% of whom were married and 45% widowed. The mean IS score for mothers was 6.21 (SD = .69), and the mean IS score for daughters was 6.04 (SD = 1.00).

SCORING The IS is scored by summing and then averaging (dividing by 17) item scores to create individual scores. The possible range is 1 to 7 with higher scores reflecting greater intimacy.

RELIABILITY The IS has excellent internal consistency, with alphas that range from .91 to .97. No stability data were reported.

VALIDITY Although actual validity data are not reported in the Primary Reference, the IS was correlated with distal and proximal aid to the mother from the mother's report and with proximal aid to the mother from the daughter's report.

PRIMARY REFERENCE Walker, A. J., and Thompson, L. (1983). Intimacy and intergenerational aid and contact among mothers and daughters, *Journal of Marriage and the Family*, 45, 841–849, a publication of the National Council on Family Relations.

AVAILABILITY May be copied from this volume.

Please indicate your perception of your relationship using the following scale:

1 = Never
2 = Occasionally
3 = Sometimes
4 = Often
5 = Frequently
6 = Almost always
7 = Always

Record your perception in the space to the left of each item.

___ 1. We want to spend time together.
___ 2. She shows that she loves me.
___ 3. We're honest with each other.
___ 4. We can accept each other's criticism of our faults and mistakes.
___ 5. We like each other.
___ 6. We respect each other.
___ 7. Our lives are better because of each other.
___ 8. We enjoy the relationship.
___ 9. She cares about the way I feel.
___ 10. We feel like we are a unit.
___ 11. There's a great amount of unselfishness in our relationship.
___ 12. She always thinks of my best interest.
___ 13. I'm lucky to have her in my life.
___ 14. She always makes me feel better.
___ 15. She is important to me.
___ 16. We love each other.
___ 17. I'm sure of this relationship.

Intrinsic Spirituality Scale (ISS)

PURPOSE To measure spirituality.

AUTHOR David Hodges

DESCRIPTION The ISS is a 6-item instrument designed to measure intrinsic spirituality. Spirituality is distinguishable from intrinsic religion as it is a wider construct than religion, which tends to be external behaviors and community-based. Spirituality is considered an internal function that serves as an individual's master motivator. The ISS is not derived from a theistic view and, in fact, it does not reference God. Consequently, the ISS is useful with a wide variety of populations. Spirituality has been shown to be a protective factor associated with lower rates of alcohol, drugs and tobacco use. The ISS is useful when monitoring coping by caregivers or caregiver burden and stress.

NORMS A sample of adult caregivers of Alzheimer members had a mean of 7. 5 and a standard deviation of 2. 14.

SCORING Scores on the ISS are the sum of the item responses, divided by the number of items answered and range from 0 to 100. Higher scores reflect greater spirituality.

RELIABILITY From a sample of 172 students from a Baptist affiliated college, the internal consistency coefficient was excellent at. 96. From a sample of caregivers, the internal consistency coefficient was. 91 using split half reliability.

VALIDITY The ISS has excellent concurrent validity with scores correlating with intrinsic religion, secure attachment, and inversely associated with tobacco, alcohol and drug use, binge drinking, insecurity, avoidance and ambivalence.

PRIMARY REFERENCE

Hodge, D. R. (2003). The intrinsic spirituality scale: A new six-item instrument for assessing salience of spirituality as a motivational construct. *Journal of Social Service Research, 30*, 41-61.

Gough, H. R., Wilks, S. and Prattini, R. J. (2010). Spirituality among Alzheimer's caregivers: Psychometric reevaluation of the Intrinsic Spirituality Scale. *Journal of Social Services Research, 36*, 278-288.

AVAILABILITY David R. Hodge, Social of Social Work, Mail Code 3920, 411N. Central Avenue, Suite 800, Arizona State University, Phoenix AZ 85004-0689. Email: david-hodge@asu.edu.

For the following six questions, *spirituality* is defined as one's relationship to God, or whatever you perceive to be Ultimate Transcendence.

The questions use a sentence completion format to measure various attributes associated with spirituality. An incomplete sentence fragment is provided, followed directly below by two phrases that are linked to a scale ranging from 0 to 10. The phrases, which complete the sentence fragment, anchor each end of the scale. The 0 to 10 range provides you with a continuum on which to reply, with 0 corresponding to absence or zero amount of the attribute, while 10 corresponds to the maximum amount of the attribute. In other words, the end points represent extreme values, while five corresponds to a medium, or moderate, amount of the attribute. Please circle the number along the continuum that best reflects your initial feeling.

1. In terms of the questions I have about life, my spirituality answers

no										**absolutely all**
questions										**my questions**
0	*1*	*2*	*3*	*4*	*5*	*6*	*7*	*8*	*9*	*10*

2. Growing spiritually is

more important than										**of no**
anything else										**importance**
in my life										**to me**
10	*9*	*8*	*7*	*6*	*5*	*4*	*3*	*2*	*1*	*0*

3. When I am faced with an important decision, my spirituality

plays										**is always**
absolutely										**the overriding**
no role										**consideration**
0	*1*	*2*	*3*	*4*	*5*	*6*	*7*	*8*	*9*	*10*

4. Spirituality is

the master motive of my										
life, directing every other										**not part**
aspect of my life										**of my life**
10	*9*	*8*	*7*	*6*	*5*	*4*	*3*	*2*	*1*	*0*

5. When I think of the things that help me to grow and mature as a person, my spirituality

has no effect										**is absolutely the most**
on my personal										**important factor in**
growth										**my personal growth**
0	*1*	*2*	*3*	*4*	*5*	*6*	*7*	*8*	*9*	*10*

6. My spiritual beliefs affect

absolutely every										**no aspect**
aspect of my life										**of my life**
10	*9*	*8*	*7*	*6*	*5*	*4*	*3*	*2*	*1*	*0*

Inventory of Depression and Anxiety Symptoms (IDAS)

PURPOSE To measure the symptoms of major depression and related anxiety

AUTHORS David Watson, Michael O'Hara, Leonard Simms, Roman Kotov, Michael Chmielewski, Elizabeth McDade-Montez, Wakiza Gamez and Scott Stuart.

DESCRIPTION The IDAS is a 64-item instrument designed to measure the symptoms of major depression and the anxiety particularly related to it. The items of the IDAS were all based directly from the DSM-IV criteria for major depression and the final items were derived from a pool of 180 items. The IDAS was developed on a number of large samples including psychiatric patients (n = 369 and n = 139), college students (n = 673 and n = 499), youth adults and adults from the general population (n = 271 and n= 370), women diagnosed with postpartum depression (n = 832), and numerous samples of high school students. The IDAS produces a General Depression scale scores and 11 subscales scores, Dysphoria (D), Lassitude (L), Insomnia (I), Suicidality (S), Appetite Loses (AL), Appetite Gain, (AG), I Temper (IT), Well-Being (WB), Social Anxiety (SA), Panic (P) and Traumatic Intrusions (TI). The IDAS used impeccable and advanced psychometric procedures using these samples separately and in various combinations, and then replicated the finding with two additional samples, one of 306 college students and one of 605 adult psychiatric patients. In many respects, the IDAS is the successor to the Mood and Anxiety Symptoms Questionnaire, which is also in this volume. The IDAS is useful with adolescents and adults of all ages.

NORMS There are numerous norms in the primary references. A sample of adult psychiatric patient had means and (standard deviations) for the scores of: GD 56.04 (15.42), D 28.80 (9.27) L 16.5 (5.79), I114.92 (6.26), S 10.73 (5.58) AL 6.57 (2.99), AG 6.97 (3.48), IT 10.59 (5.17) WB 18.3 (6.70) SA 12.59 (5.50), P 15. 09 (6.10) and TI 9.92 (4.79). Following the same order as above, the mean and standard deviations for a sample of adults from the general population were: GD (44.9914.75), D 22. 33 (8.66), L 14.54 (5.87), I112. 72 (5.71), S 8.15 (3.73), AL 5.25 (2.59), AG 6. 87 (3.38), IT 9. 61 (4.66), WB 22.43 (7. 22), SA 10. 04 (4.86), P 12. 58 (5.26), and TI 7. 60 (4.20).

SCORING The GD is the sum of items 2, 3, 4, 6, 7, 10, 11, 12, 13, 15, 16, 17, 24*, 35*, 42, 47, 48, 49, 51 and 53, with the * items reverse-scored. D scores are the sum of items 3, 4, 6, 11, 13, 42, 47, 48, 49 and 51. L scores are the sum of items 2, 8, 44, 45, 50 and 53. I scores are the sum of items 5, 10, 12, 46, 52 and 54. S scores are the sum of items 7, 9, 14, 15, 41 and 43. AL scores are the sum of items 16, 17 and 19, while AG scores are the sum of items 18, 20 and 22. IT scores are the sum of 25, 28, 30, 31 and 33. WB scores are the sum of items 1, 21, 23, 24, 26, 27, 34 and 35. SA scores are the sum of items 37, 39, 56, 58 and 61. P scores are the sum of items 38, 40, 55, 57, 59, 62, 63 and 64. And TI scores are the sum of items 29, 32, 36 and 60.

RELIABILITY Based on the various samples, the IDAS has very good to excellent internal consistency reliability. For example, the internal consistency coefficients were GD = .89, D = .89, WB = .84, P = .83, 1 = .81, S = .80, SA = .82, IT = .85, Tl = .82 AL = .78 AG = .77 for a sample of college students. The GD had very good test-retest reliability (r =.. 84) for a one-week period; the subscales had test-retest coefficients ranging between. 72 to. 82 and averaging 79.

VALIDITY The IDAS has exceptional validity estimates evidenced from the large number of samples noted above. This include factor analyses supporting the subscale structure, correlations between the scale scores and DSM-IV-based diagnostic interviews, and concurrent validity with scores correlating with the Beck Depression Inventory and the Beck Anxiety Inventory. Scores also correlated with mood and anxiety assessment interviews, the Hamilton Depression Scale, and there is also evidence of known group validities as evidenced by the differences between the various patients and adults samples.

PRIMARY REFERENCES Watson, D., O'Hara, M. W., Simms, L L. J., Kotov, R, Chmielewski, M, McDade-Montez, E. A., Gamez, W. and Stuart, S. (2007). Development and validation of the Inventory of Depression and Anxiety Symptoms (IDAS). *Psychological Assessment. 19*, 253-268. Watson, D., O'Hara, M. W., Chmielewski, M, McDade-Montez, E. A., Koffel, E, Naragon, K. and Stuart, S. (2007). Future validation of the IDAS: Evidence of convergent, discriminant, criterion, and incremental validity. *Psychological Assessment, 20*, 248-259.

AVAILABILITY David Watson, Ph. D., Department of Psychology, Ell Seashore Hall, University of Iowa, Iowa City, IA 52242-1407. Email: david.watson@uiowa.edu.

Below is a list of feelings, sensations, problems, and experiences that people sometimes have. Read each item to determine how well it describes your recent feelings and experiences. Then select the option that best describes how much you have felt or experienced tilings this way during the past two weeks, including today. Use this scale when answering:

1	2	3	4	5
Not at all	A little bit	Moderately	Quite a bit	Extremely

_____ 1. I was proud of myself

_____ 2. I felt exhausted

_____ 3. I felt depressed

_____ 4. I felt inadequate

_____ 5. I slept less than usual

_____ 6. I felt fidgety, restless

_____ 7. I had thoughts of suicide

_____ 8. I slept more than usual

_____ 9. I hurt myself purposely

_____ 10. I slept very poorly

_____ 11. I blamed myself for things

_____ 12. I had trouble falling asleep

_____ 13. I felt discouraged about things

_____ 14. I thought about my own death

_____ 15. I thought about hurting myself

_____ 16. I did not have much of an appetite

_____ 17. I felt like eating less than usual

_____ 18. I thought a lot about food

_____ 19. I did not feel much like eating

_____ 20. I ate when I wasn't hungry

_____ 21. I felt optimistic

_____ 22. I ate more than usual

_____ 23. I felt that I had accomplished a lot

_____ 24. I looked forward to things with enjoyment

_____ 25. I was furious

_____ 26. I felt hopeful about the future

_____ 27. I felt that I had a lot to look forward to

_____ 28. I felt like breaking things

_____ 29. I had disturbing thoughts of something bad that happened to me

_____ 30. Little things made me mad

_____ 31. I felt enraged

_____ 32. I had nightmares that reminded me of something bad that happened

_____ 33. I lost my temper and yelled at people

_____ 34. I felt like I had a lot of interesting things to do

_____ 35. I felt like I had a lot of energy

_____ 36. I had memories of something scary that happened

_____ 37. I felt self-conscious knowing that others were watching me

_____ 38. I felt a pain in my chest

_____ 39. I was worried about embarrassing myself socially

_____ 40. I felt dizzy or light headed

____ 41. I cut or burned myself on purpose

____ 42. I had little interest in my usual hobbies or activities

____ 43. I thought that the world would be better off without me

____ 44. I felt much worse in the morning than later in the day

____ 45. I felt drowsy, sleepy

____ 46. I woke up early and could not get back to sleep

____ 47. I had trouble concentrating

____ 48. I had trouble making up my mind

____ 49. I talked more slowly than usual

____ 50. I had trouble waking up in the morning

____ 51. I found myself worrying all the time

____ 52. I woke up frequently during the night

____ 53. It took a lot of effort for me to get going

____ 54. I woke up much earlier than usual

____ 55. I was trembling or shaking

____ 56. I became anxious in a crowded public setting

____ 57. I felt faint

____ 58. I found it difficult to make eye contact with people

____ 59. My heart was racing or pounding 60.

____ 60. I got upset thinking about something bad that happened

____ 61. I found it difficult to talk with people did not know well

____ 62. I had a very dry mouth

____ 63. I was short of breath

____ 64. I felt like I was choking

Inventory to Diagnose Depression (IDD)

PURPOSE To measure major depression disorder.

AUTHORS Mark Zimmerman, William Coryell, Caryn Corenthal, and Sheila Wilson

DESCRIPTION The IDD is a 22-item instrument designed to diagnose major depressive disorder (MDD). The IDD differs from other depression scales in three ways. First, it covers the entire range of symptoms used in DSM-III to diagnose MDD. Second, the IDD not only can quantify the severity of depression but can be used to decide the presence or absence of a symptom. And third, the IDD assesses symptom duration.

NORMS The IDD was studied initially with 220 psychiatric inpatients and 15 "normal" controls including 94 men and 141 women; 42.1% were single, 31.9% married, and the rest divorced, separated, or widowed. The mean number of years of education was 12.7 (81.3% high school graduates and 16.2% college graduates); 62.1% were diagnosed with MDD, 11.1% with schizophrenia, and the rest scattered among several diagnoses (including 15 "normals"). The mean score on the IDD for patients diagnosed as MDD was 42.6 (SD = 11.8) and for nondepressed subjects 19.0 (SD = 15.7). This difference was statistically significant.

SCORING To quantify the severity of depression, the item scores are totaled, with higher scores showing greater severity. A score of 0 or 1 on each item represents no disturbance (0) or subclinical severity (1), and a score of 2 or more is counted as a symptom.

RELIABILITY The IDD has excellent internal consistency, with an alpha of .92. The IDD also has excellent stability, with a one-day test-retest correlation of .98.

VALIDITY The IDD has excellent concurrent validity, correlating significantly with other scales of depression (Beck Depression Inventory, Carrol Rating Scale, and the HRS). The IDD also discriminates significantly between different levels of depression and was highly accurate (over 80% in diagnostic sensitivity). The IDD also was sensitive to clinical change.

PRIMARY REFERENCE Zimmerman, M., Coryell, W., Corenthal, C., and Wilson, S. (1986). A self-report scale to diagnose major depressive disorder, *Archives of General Psychiatry*, 43, 1076–1081.

AVAILABILITY Dr. Mark Zimmerman, Brown University, Department of Psychiatry and Human Behavior, Providence R.I. 02912. Email: mark-zimmerman@brown.edu, or mzimmerman@lifespon.org.

On this questionnaire are groups of 5 statements.

Read each group of statements carefully. Then pick out the one statement in each group that best describes the way you have been feeling the PAST WEEK. Circle the number next to the statement you picked.

For every group in which you circled #1, 2, 3, or 4, answer the follow-up question as to whether you have been feeling that way for more or less than 2 weeks by circling either "more" or "less" as appropriate.

1. 0   I do not feel sad or depressed.
    1   I occasionally feel sad or down.
    2   I feel sad most of the time, but I can snap out of it.
    3   I feel sad all the time, and I can't snap out of it.
    4   I am so sad or unhappy that I can't stand it.

    If you circled #1, 2, 3, or 4: Have you been feeling sad or down for more or less
    than 2 weeks?   more   less

2. 0   My energy level is normal.
    1   My energy level is occasionally a little lower than normal.
    2   I get tired more easily or have less energy than usual.
    3   I get tired from doing almost anything.
    4   I feel tired or exhausted almost all of the time.

    If you circled #1, 2, 3, or 4: Has your energy level been lower than usual for
    more or less than 2 weeks?   more   less

3. 0   I have not been feeling more restless and fidgety than usual.
    1   I feel a little more restless or fidgety than usual.
    2   I have been very fidgety, and I have some difficulty sitting still in a chair.
    3   I have been extremely fidgety, and I have been pacing a little bit almost every day.
    4   I have been pacing more than an hour per day, and I can't sit still.

    If you circled #1, 2, 3, or 4: Have you felt restless and fidgety for more
    or less than 2 weeks?   more   less

4. 0   I have not been talking or moving more slowly than usual.
    1   I am talking a little slower than usual.
    2   I am speaking slower than usual, and it takes me longer to respond to questions, but
        I can still carry on a normal conversation.
    3   Normal conversations are difficult because it is hard to start talking.
    4   I feel extremely slowed down physically, like I am stuck in mud.

    If you circled #1, 2, 3, or 4: Have you felt slowed down for more
    or less than 2 weeks?   more   less

5. 0   I have not lost interest in my usual activities.
    1   I am a little less interested in 1 or 2 of my usual activities.
    2   I am less interested in several of my usual activities.
    3   I have lost most of my interest in almost all of my usual activities.
    4   I have lost all interest in all of my usual activities.

    If you circled #1, 2, 3, or 4: Has your interest in your usual activities been
    low for more or less than 2 weeks?   more   less

6. 0   I get as much pleasure out of my usual activities as usual.
    1   I get a little less pleasure from 1 or 2 of my usual activities.
    2   I get less pleasure from several of my usual activities.
    3   I get almost no pleasure from most of the activities which I usually enjoy.
    4   I get no pleasure from any of the activities which I usually enjoy.

    If you circled #1, 2, 3, or 4: Has your enjoyment in your usual activities been
    low for more or less than 2 weeks?   more   less

7. 0   I have not noticed any recent change in my interest in sex.
    1   I am only slightly less interested in sex than usual.
    2   There is a noticeable decrease in my interest in sex.
    3   I am much less interested in sex now.
    4   I have lost all interest in sex.

    If you circled #1, 2, 3, or 4: Has your interest in sex been low for more
    or less than 2 weeks?   more   less

8. 0   I have not been feeling guilty.
    1   I occasionally feel a little guilty.
    2   I often feel guilty.
    3   I feel quite guilty most of the time.
    4   I feel extremely guilty most of the time.

    If you circled #1, 2, 3, or 4: Have you had guilt feelings for more or
    less than 2 weeks?   more   less

9. 0   I do not feel like a failure.
    1   My opinion of myself is occasionally a little low.
    2   I feel I am inferior to most people.
    3   I feel like a failure.
    4   I feel I am a totally worthless person.

    If you circled #1, 2, 3, or 4: Have you been down on yourself for more
    or less than 2 weeks?   more   less

10. 0   I haven't had any thoughts of death or suicide.
    1   I occasionally think life is not worth living.
    2   I frequently think of dying in passive ways (such as going to sleep and not waking up),
        or that I'd be better off dead.
    3   I have frequent thoughts of killing myself, but I would not carry them out.
    4   I would kill myself if I had the chance.

    If you circled #1, 2, 3, or 4: Have you been thinking about dying or killing
    yourself for more or less than 2 weeks?   more   less

11. 0   I can concentrate as well as usual.
    1   My ability to concentrate is slightly worse than usual.
    2   My attention span is not as good as usual and I am having difficulty collecting my
        thoughts, but this hasn't caused any problems.
    3   My ability to read or hold a conversation is not as good as it usually is.
    4   I cannot read, watch TV, or have a conversation without great difficulty.

    If you circled #1, 2, 3, or 4: Have you had problems concentrating for more
    or less than 2 weeks?   more   less

12. 0   I make decisions as well as I usually do.
    1   Decision making is slightly more difficult than usual.
    2   It is harder and takes longer to make decisions, but I do make them.
    3   I am unable to make some decisions.
    4   I can't make any decisions at all.

If you circled #1, 2, 3, or 4: Have you had problems making decisions for more or less than 2 weeks?   more   less

13. 0   My appetite is not less than normal.
    1   My appetite is slightly worse than usual.
    2   My appetite is clearly not as good as usual, but I still eat.
    3   My appetite is much worse now.
    4   I have no appetite at all, and I have to force myself to eat even a little.

If you circled #1, 2, 3, or 4: Has your appetite been decreased for more or less than 2 weeks?   more   less

14. 0   I haven't lost any weight.
    1   I've lost less than 5 pounds.
    2   I've lost between 5 and 10 pounds.
    3   I've lost between 11 and 25 pounds.
    4   I've lost more than 25 pounds.

If you circled #1, 2, 3, or 4: Have you been dieting and deliberately trying to lose weight?   Y or N

If you circled #1, 2, 3, or 4: Have you been losing weight for more or less than 2 weeks?   more   less

15. 0   My appetite is not greater than normal.
    1   My appetite is slightly greater than usual.
    2   My appetite is clearly greater than usual.
    3   My appetite is much greater than usual.
    4   I feel hungry all the time.

If you circled #1, 2, 3, or 4: Has your appetite been increased for more or less than 2 weeks?   more   less

16. 0   I haven't gained any weight.
    1   I've gained less than 5 pounds.
    2   I've gained between 5 and 10 pounds.
    3   I've gained between 11 and 25 pounds.
    4   I've gained more than 25 pounds.

If you circled #1, 2, 3, or 4: Have you been gaining weight for more or less than 2 weeks?   more   less

17. 0   I am not sleeping less than normal.
    1   I occasionally have slight difficulty sleeping.
    2   I clearly don't sleep as well as usual.
    3   I sleep about half my normal amount of time.
    4   I sleep less than 2 hours per night.

If you circled #1, 2, 3, or 4: Which of these sleep problems have you experienced? (circle all which apply)

1   I have difficulty falling asleep.
2   My sleep is fitful and restless in the middle of the night.
3   I wake up earlier than usual and cannot fall back to sleep.

If you circled #1, 2, 3, or 4: Have you been having sleep problems for more or less than 2 weeks?   more   less

18. 0   I am not sleeping more than normal.
     1   I occasionally sleep more than usual.
     2   I frequently sleep at least 1 hour more than usual.
     3   I frequently sleep at least 2 hours more than usual.
     4   I frequently sleep at least 3 hours more than usual.

If you circled #1, 2, 3, or 4: Have you been sleeping extra for more or less than 2 weeks?   more   less

19. 0   I do not feel anxious, nervous, or tense.
     1   I occasionally feel a little anxious.
     2   I often feel anxious.
     3   I feel very anxious most of the time.
     4   I feel terrified and near panic.

If you circled #1, 2, 3, or 4: Have you been feeling anxious, nervous, or tense for more or less than 2 weeks?   more   less

20. 0   I do not feel discouraged about the future.
     1   I occasionally feel a little discouraged about the future.
     2   I often feel discouraged about the future.
     3   I feel very discouraged about the future most of the time.
     4   I feel that the future is hopeless and that things will never improve.

If you circled #1, 2, 3, or 4: Have you been feeling discouraged than usual for more or less than 2 weeks?   more   less

21. 0   I do not feel irritated or annoyed.
     1   I occasionally get a little more irritated than usual.
     2   I get irritated or annoyed by things that usually don't bother me.
     3   I feel irritated or annoyed almost all the time.
     4   I feel so depressed that I don't get irritated at all by things that used to bother me.

If you circled #1, 2, 3, or 4: Have you been feeling more irritable than usual for more or less than 2 weeks?   more   less

22. 0   I am not worried about my physical health.
     1   I am occasionally concerned about bodily aches and pains.
     2   I am worried about my physical health.
     3   I am very worried about my physical health.
     4   I am so worried about my physical health that I cannot think about anything else.

If you circled #1, 2, 3, or 4: Have you been worried about your physical health for more or less than 2 weeks?   more   less

Inventory of Dyadic Heterosexual Preferences (IDHP)

PURPOSE To measure preferences for specific sexual behaviors.

AUTHORS Daniel M. Purnine, Michael P. Carey, and Randall S. Jorgensen

DESCRIPTION The IDHP is a 27-item instrument designed to measure preferences for specific sexual behaviors of heterosexual men and women in a dyadic context. The IDHP is perhaps the first empirically derived instrument for assessing the multidimensional nature of preferred heterosexual practices among men and women. The IDHP assesses several domains of sexual preferences in a relatively brief inventory, thereby allowing practitioners and researchers to obtain a comprehensive profile of individuals' heterosexual preferences. The IDHP has six subscales: use of drugs/alcohol (items 12, 20, 15, and 14); use of erotica (items 27, 9, 24, and 4); erotophilia (items 1, 17, 8, 16, 7, 11, and 18); use of contraception (items 6, 3, 26, and 13); romantic foreplay (items 2, 21, 25, and 18); and conventionality (items 5, 10, 23, and 22).

NORMS The IDHP was initially studied with two samples involving a total of 496 undergraduate and graduate students. The samples had a mean age of approximately 22 years with a range from 17 to 59 years; 310 subjects were female. The mean number of previous and current intimate relationships was 3.7 with 57.5% of subjects currently involved in a relationship. The mean scores on the subscales were as follows: erotophilia, M=4.48 (SD=.71); use of contraception, M=4.49 (SD=.89); conventionality, M=3.07 (SD=.88); use of erotica, M=3.57 (SD=1.13); use of drugs/alcohol, M=2.73 (SD=1.30); and romantic foreplay, M=4.71 (SD=.75). There were statistically significant differences between men and women on all subscales except for conventionality, as described in the original article.

SCORING The IDHP is easily scored by summing individual item scores on each subscale after reverse-scoring items 3, 24, and 26.

RELIABILITY The IDHP has fair to good internal consistency, with alphas on the subscales that range from .62 for romantic foreplay to .87 for use of drugs/alcohol (mean alpha=.72). The IDHP is very stable with two-week test-retest reliability on the subscales that ranges from .73 for romantic foreplay to .92 for use of erotica (mean=.84).

VALIDITY The IDHP has very good construct validity. Of 42 predictions regarding the presence or absence of correlations between the IDHP and seven other measures such as the Sexual Irrationality Questionnaire and the Sexual Opinion Survey, 34 (81%) were confirmed (e.g., 5 of 6 predicted positive relationships between criterion measures and a specific IDHP scale were significant). Social desirability response bias does not appear to affect IDHP subscales in a systematic way.

PRIMARY REFERENCE Purnine, D. M., Carey, M. P. and Jorgensen, R. S. (1996). The inventory of dyadic heterosexual preferences: Development and psychometric evaluation, *Behaviour Research and Therapy*, 34, 375–387.

AVAILABILITY Dr. Daniel Purnine, Syracuse VA Medical Center, 800 Irving Avenue, Syracuse, NY 13210. Telephone: 315-425-4400. Reprinted with permission of the authors. May be copied from this volume.

Please read the following statements carefully and indicate how much **you** agree or disagree that the statement is **true for you.** Respond to each item as you would actually like things to be in relations with you partner. Feel free to ask the investigator about any statement that is not clear to you. **Please respond to all items.** There are no right or wrong answers; respond as truthfully as possible.

1 = Strongly disagree
2 = Disagree
3 = Somewhat disagree
4 = Somewhat agree
5 = Agree
6 = Strongly agree

1. I would like to initiate sex.

    1   2   3   4   5   6

2. An intimate, romantic dinner together would be a real turn-on to me.

    1   2   3   4   5   6

3. Using spermacide would spoil sex for me.

    1   2   3   4   5   6

4. I would like to use a vibrator or other sexual toy (or aid) during sex.

    1   2   3   4   5   6

5. I would prefer to have sex under the bedcovers and with the lights off.

    1   2   3   4   5   6

6. Having myself or my partner use a condom would not spoil sex for me.

    1   2   3   4   5   6

7. Having sex in rooms other than the bedroom would turn me on.

    1   2   3   4   5   6

8. I would prefer to have sex every day.

    1   2   3   4   5   6

9. Looking at sexually explicit books and movies would turn me on.

    1   2   3   4   5   6

10. I would not enjoy looking at my partner's genitals.

    1   2   3   4   5   6

11. I would like to have sex after a day at the beach.

    1   2   3   4   5   6

12. I would like to mix alcohol and sex.

    1   2   3   4   5   6

13. Using a contraceptive would not affect my sexual satisfaction or pleasure.

     1   2   3   4   5   6

14. I would enjoy having sex after smoking marijuana.

     1   2   3   4   5   6

15. I would prefer to have sex while using drugs that make me feel aroused.

     1   2   3   4   5   6

16. I would enjoy having sex outdoors.

     1   2   3   4   5   6

17. My preferred time for having sex is in the morning.

     1   2   3   4   5   6

18. Swimming in the nude with my partner would be a turn-on.

     1   2   3   4   5   6

19. I would enjoy dressing in sexy/revealing clothes to arouse my partner.

     1   2   3   4   5   6

20. I would like to mix drugs and sex.

     1   2   3   4   5   6

21. I would get turned on if my partner touched my chest and nipples.

     1   2   3   4   5   6

22. I would prefer to avoid having sex during my (partner's) period.

     1   2   3   4   5   6

23. I would not enjoy having my partner look at my genitals.

     1   2   3   4   5   6

24. Sexually explicit books and movies are disgusting to me.

     1   2   3   4   5   6

25. I would find deep kissing with the tongue quite arousing to me.

     1   2   3   4   5   6

26. Using a vaginal lubricant (KY jelly) would spoil sex for me.

     1   2   3   4   5   6

27. Watching erotic movies with my partner would turn me on.

     1   2   3   4   5   6

Irrational Values Scale (IVS)

PURPOSE To measure endorsement of irrational values.

AUTHOR A. P. MacDonald

DESCRIPTION The IVS is a 9-item scale that was designed to measure a respondent's endorsement of nine irrational values that are based on the work of Albert Ellis. The underlying assumption is the belief that high endorsement of certain values or ideas would lead to neurosis. (Although eleven values were studied, two values were dropped because they did not possess adequate psychometric properties.) The IVS was seen as providing construct validity for Ellis's ideas because it was related to several measures of psychopathology. The scale might prove useful in clinical programs where the goal is to challenge and refute the clients' unrealistic, dysfunctional, or irrational ideas.

NORMS Initial study of the IVS was based on three samples of undergraduates including 101 males and 80 females. No work on standardization was reported.

SCORING The scores on 9-point Likert-type scales are totaled, producing a range of 9 to 81.

RELIABILITY Internal consistency of the IVS is fairly good, with alphas of .73 and .79 reported. No test-retest data were reported.

VALIDITY The IVS has good concurrent validity, correlating significantly with several measures including the California Personality Inventory, Eysenck Neuroticism Scale, Taylor Manifest Anxiety Scale, and the MacDonald-Tseng Internal-External Locus of Control Scale. Also, the IVS was not correlated with the Marlowe-Crowne Social Desirability Scale, indicating the IVS is free from social desirability response set.

PRIMARY REFERENCE MacDonald, A. P., and Games, Richard G. (1972). Ellis' irrational values, *Rational Living*, 7, 25–28. Instrument reproduced with permission of Dr. A. P. MacDonald.

AVAILABILITY May be copied from this volume

People have different opinions. We are interested in knowing your opinions concerning the following issues. There are no right or wrong answers for the items; we are interested in opinions only. Please indicate your own opinion by circling a number from one to nine on the scale provided for each statement. In case of doubt, circle the number which comes closest to representing your true opinion. Please do not leave any blanks.

1. It is essential that one be loved or approved by virtually everyone in his community.

Completely disagree								Completely agree
1	2	3	4	5	6	7	8	9

2. One must be perfectly competent, adequate, and achieving to consider oneself worthwhile.

Completely disagree								Completely agree
1	2	3	4	5	6	7	8	9

3. Some people are bad, wicked, or villainous and therefore should be blamed and punished.

Completely disagree								Completely agree
1	2	3	4	5	6	7	8	9

4. It is a terrible catastrophe when things are not as one wants them to be.

Completely disagree								Completely agree
1	2	3	4	5	6	7	8	9

5. Unhappiness is caused by outside circumstances and the individual has no control over it.

Completely disagree								Completely agree
1	2	3	4	5	6	7	8	9

6. Dangerous or fearsome things are causes for great concern, and their possibility must be continually dwelt upon.

Completely disagree								Completely agree
1	2	3	4	5	6	7	8	9

7. One should be dependent on others and must have someone stronger on whom to rely.

Completely disagree								Completely agree
1	2	3	4	5	6	7	8	9

8. One should be quite upset over people's problems and disturbances.

Completely disagree								Completely agree
1	2	3	4	5	6	7	8	9

9. There is always a right or perfect solution to every problem, and it must be found or the results will be catastrophic.

	Completely disagree								Completely agree
	1	2	3	4	5	6	7	8	9

Irritability/Apathy Scale (IAS)

PURPOSE To measure apathy and irritability in Alzheimer and Huntington's disease patients.

AUTHORS Alistair Burns, Susan Folstein, Jason Brandt, and Marshall Folstein

DESCRIPTION The IAS is composed of two 5-item rating scales, an irritability scale and an apathy scale. These two characteristics are seen as prominent in a number of psychiatric disorders, but also in diseases such as Alzheimer and Huntington's. However, most previous measures of these constructs were not useful for severely cognitively impaired patients. The IAS is viewed as an advance in measurement since it utilizes a rating system by relevant others and focuses on measuring specific defined tracts.

NORMS The IAS was studied with 31 Alzheimer (AD) and 26 Huntington's (HD) patients from clinics at the Johns Hopkins Hospital. The AD subjects were 93% white and 7% black with 18 women and 13 men with a mean age of 70.3. HD patients were 69% white and 31% black with 11 women and 15 men and a mean age of 48.3. The mean irritability score for the AD group was 9.6, with 58% scoring above the cut-off point, and the mean score for the HD group was 8.2, with 58% scoring above the cut-off point. The mean apathy score for the AD group was 14.7 with 48% above the cut-off point, while the mean apathy score for the HD group was 15.1 with 48% above the cut-off point.

SCORING Irritability is scored by summing all items for a maximum total of 17. Irritability was defined as present (the cut-off point) if the patient was rated at 2 or above on the 5-point irritability scale. Apathy is scored by summing all items for a maximum total of 25. Apathy was defined as present (the cut-off point) if a majority of the items were endorsed (a rating of 3 or above on questions 2, 4, and 5 and a rating of 4 or 5 on questions 1 and 3).

RELIABILITY Both scales have fair to good internal consistency. The alpha for all 5 items on the irritability scale is .82 and for all 5 items on apathy is .78. Interrater reliabilities were excellent: 1.00 for irritability and .85 for apathy. Both scales are also very stable with one- to two-week test-retest reliabilities of .81 for irritability and .76 for apathy.

VALIDITY The IAS has good concurrent validity, correlating .87 for the HD group with the behavioral abnormalities scale of the Psychogeriatric Dependency Rating Scale. The IAS also has good known-groups validity, significantly distinguishing both the AD and HD group on both scales from a group of "normals." Neither scale was correlated with a measure of aggression.

PRIMARY REFERENCE Burns, A., Folstein, S., Brandt, J., and Folstein, M. (1990). Clinical assessment of irritability, aggression and apathy in Huntington and Alzheimer Disease, *Journal of Nervous and Mental Disease*, 178, 20–26.

AVAILABILITY May be copied from this volume.

Please answer the following questions about your _____ according to how he/she is now, compared with how he/she was before his/her health problems began. (It may be necessary to emphasize that the questionnaire relates to behavior since the onset of the illness and not in the very recent past. An open-ended question such as "what effect has your _____ illness had on him/her" may be used.)

Irritability

1. How irritable would you say he/she was?   *Score*

1	2	3	4	5
Not at all irritable				Extremely irritable

_____

		Never (score=1)	Some-times (score=2)	Always (score=3)
2. Does he/she sulk after he/she is angry?		_____	_____	_____
3. Does he/she "pout" if he/she does not get his/her own way?		_____	_____	_____
4. Does he/she get into arguments?		_____	_____	_____
5. Does he/she raise his/her voice in anger?		_____	_____	_____

Apathy

1. Has his/her interest in everyday events changed?   *Score*

1	2	3	4	5
Much more interested		Just the same		Much less interested

_____

2. How long does he/she stay lying in bed or sitting in a chair doing nothing during the day?   *Score*

1	2	3	4	5
No more than anyone else				All the time

_____

3. How active is he/she in day to day activities?   *Score*

1	2	3	4	5
Very active		Normal		Very inactive

_____

4. How busy does he/she keep himself/herself?   *Score*

1	2	3	4	5
Same hobbies as usual	Less so but still has hobbies	Prefers doing nothing but does with prompting	Prefers watching TV or watches others doing things	If left alone does nothing

_____

5. Does the patient seem withdrawn from things?   *Score*

1	2	3	4	5
Not at all	A little more than usual	More than usual	Much more than usual	Yes, definitely

_____

Jewish Religious Coping Scale (JCOPE)

PURPOSE To measure the use of religion to cope with stress

AUTHORS David Rosmarin, Kenneth Pargament, Elizabeth Krumrei and Kevin Flannelly

DESCRIPTION The JCOPE is a 16-item instrument designed to measure the use of Jewish customs, beliefs and practices to cope with stressful situations. The role of religion in psychological health, well-being, and illness is generally a protective factor to prevent drug and alcohol and tobacco use. This has chiefly been studied in Christian populations, and recently with Hindus and Muslim worshippers. No instrument was available to monitor the impact of Jewish religious beliefs and coping. The JCOPE is the first, and it is useful in working with faith-based interventions, and in treating depression and anxiety. The JCOPE was developed with two excellent studies. The first (n = 468) used exploratory factor analysis, and the results were supported in a second study (n = 234) using confirmatory factor analysis. The JCOPE has two subscales, Positive Religious Coping (PRC) and Negative Religious Coping (NRC).

NORMS From a sample of adult Jews (n = 234), the PRC had a mean of 43.0 and a standard deviation of 10.6, and the NRC had a mean of 8.3 and a standard deviation of 3.0.

SCORING The PRC scale score is the sum of items, 1, 3, 4, 5, 6, 7, 8, 9, 11, 12, 14, and 15. Scores on the NRC are the sum of items 2, 10, 13, and 16. The other items are decoys and are not scored, or may be deleted.

RELIABILITY The PRC has excellent internal consistency at .93, but the NRC is only .69 due chiefly to the fact that there are so few items.

VALIDITY The PRC has very good estimates of validity as seen with scores correlating with religious doctrinal belief (r = .61), weekly religious practices (r = .48), and cultural practices (r = .55). NRC had moderate validity with scores correlating between −.17 and −.27 on the above variables. Both subscales had very good discriminant validity on income, age, education and income, while having convergent validity with general religiosity. Both subscales had concurrent validity estimates with associations with worrying, anxiety and depression.

PRIMARY REFERENCE Rosmarin, D. H., Pargament, K. I, Krumrei, E. J. and Flannelly, K. J. (2009). Relgious coping among Jews: Development and initial validation of the JCOPE. *Journal of Clinical Psychology, 65,* 670–683.

AVAILABILITY David Rosmarin, Ph.D., Department of Psychology, Bowling Green State University, Bowling Green, OH 43403; email: drosmar@bgsu.edu

Dealing with Stress: This questionnaire asks about different ways in which you might rely on religion to deal with stress. Choose the answer that best describes how often you do the following things when you have a stressful problem.

1 – Never
2 – Hardly
3 – Ever Sometimes
4 – Most of the Time
5 – Always

WHEN I HAVE STRESSFUL PROBLEMS:

1. I ask G-d to forgive me for things I did wrong.
2. I get mad at G-d.
3. I try to be an inspiration to others.
4. I try to see how G-d may be trying to teach me something.
5. I think about what Judaism has to say about how to handle the problem.
6. I do the best I can and know the rest is G-d's will.
7. I look forward to Shabbat.
8. I talk to my rabbi.
9. I look for a stronger connection with G-d.
10. I question whether G-d can really do anything.
11. I pray for the well-being of others.
12. I pray for G-d's love and care.
13. I wonder if G-d cares about me
14. I try to do Mitzvot (good deeds).
15. I try to remember that my life is part of a larger spiritual force.
16. I question my religious beliefs, faith and practices.

PURPOSE To measure social-evaluative anxiety in job interviews.

AUTHORS Richard G. Heimberg, Kevin E. Keller, and Theresa Peca-Baker

DESCRIPTION The JISSS is a 50-item instrument designed to measure positive and negative cognitions and their relations to evaluative anxiety in job interview situations. The JISSS is based on the idea that social-evaluative anxiety about performance in job interviews may inhibit effective performance, and that internal dialogues (self-statements) contribute to the presence or absence of anxiety. Thus, the JISSS uses an essentially cognitive perspective to examine self-statements that could affect job interview performance. The JISSS has two subscales, negative self-statement (items 1, 4, 9, 11, 13, 15, 16, 20–24, 26, 27, 29, 34, 37, 38, 40, 42–46, 48) and positive self-statement (items 2, 3, 5–8, 10, 12, 14, 17–19, 25, 28, 30–33, 35, 36, 39, 41, 47, 49, 50). It also provides two scores, one for assessing the frequency of occurrence of self-statements ("how often") and the other for assessing the impact of self-statements ("help or hinder").

NORMS The JISSS was studied with two samples of undergraduate psychology students totaling 303 (200 women, 103 men), with a mean age of 18+. No other demographic information was provided. Means on the positive subscale ranged from 308.72 to 337.70 (SD=74.5 to 80.3) and the negative subscale ranged from 190.77 to 205.08 (SD=62.2 to 71.8). In one out of three trials, women had a significantly higher negative score than men.

SCORING The two scores for the JISSS are derived by multiplying frequency ratings by impact ratings and summing across all subscale items.

RELIABILITY The JISSS has excellent internal consistency, with alphas of .91 and .92 for both subscales. The JISSS has fair to good stability, with three- to four-week test-retest correlations of .57 for the negative subscale and .73 for the positive subscale.

VALIDITY The JISSS has good concurrent validity, with significant correlations in predicted directions with interview anxiety as measured by the A-State portion of the State-Trait Anxiety Inventory. The JISSS was not related to social desirability or general fears of negative evaluation. The JISSS also has good known-groups validity, significantly distinguishing between groups of high- and low-interview-anxious subjects.

PRIMARY REFERENCE Heimberg, R. G., Keller, K. E., and Peca-Baker, T. (1986). Cognitive assessment of social-evaluative anxiety in the job interview: Job Interview Self-Statement Schedule, *Journal of Counseling Psychology*, 33, 190–195.

AVAILABILITY Dr. Richard Heimberg, Temple University, School of Medicine, Philadelphia, PA 19140. Email: heimberg@temple.edu.

While you answer this questionnaire, you are to imagine that you are being interviewed for a job and that you and the interviewer are the only persons present. Items in this questionnaire were made up to be like thoughts you may have during the job interview. Answer the following two questions about each item:

a. How often

How often would this thought occur to you in a job interview?

1 = Never
2 = Seldom
3 = Sometimes
4 = Often
5 = Constantly

b. Help or Hinder

Should this thought occur to you, to what extent would it help or hinder your interview performance?

1 = Not at all
2 = A little
3 = Some
4 = A lot
5 = A great deal

Use the key above in marking your answers on the blanks next to each question.

1. I am being humiliated.
   ___ a. How often?
   ___ b. Help or hinder?
2. I really have good qualifications for this job.
   ___ a. How often?
   ___ b. Help or hinder?
3. I'm usually better at things than most people so I have a better chance of getting hired.
   ___ a. How often?
   ___ b. Help or hinder?
4. I can't think of a thing to say.
   ___ a. How often?
   ___ b. Help or hinder?
5. I feel like I dressed right for this interview.
   ___ a. How often?
   ___ b. Help or hinder?
6. When I leave I will feel like I have done my best.
   ___ a. How often?
   ___ b. Help or hinder?

7. I would be very happy in this job.
   ___ a. How often?
   ___ b. Help or hinder?

8. I would be very good at this job.
   ___ a. How often?
   ___ b. Help or hinder?

9. I'm not expressing myself clearly.
   ___ a. How often?
   ___ b. Help or hinder?

10. I make a good impression on people.
    ___ a. How often?
    ___ b. Help or hinder?

11. I feel less qualified when I think about the other applicants.
    ___ a. How often?
    ___ b. Help or hinder?

12. I am feeling and coming across as confident.
    ___ a. How often?
    ___ b. Help or hinder?

13. I am afraid that I'll never be hired for anything.
    ___ a. How often?
    ___ b. Help or hinder?

14. I am really looking my best today.
    ___ a. How often?
    ___ b. Help or hinder?

15. I am not coming across as knowing enough about the position.
    ___ a. How often?
    ___ b. Help or hinder?

16. The interviewer has already made up his/her mind.
    ___ a. How often?
    ___ b. Help or hinder?

17. I am looking forward to meeting the people who work here.
    ___ a. How often?
    ___ b. Help or hinder?

18. This job would give me a good chance to get ahead.
    ___ a. How often?
    ___ b. Help or hinder?

19. The interviewer and I are on the same wavelength.
    ___ a. How often?
    ___ b. Help or hinder?

20. I wish I had more interview experience.
    ___ a. How often?
    ___ b. Help or hinder?

21. My voice is shaky
    ___ a. How often?
    ___ b. Help or hinder?

22. The interviewer doesn't like "people like me."
    ___ a. How often?
    ___ b. Help or hinder?

23. I am saying all the wrong things.
    ___ a. How often?
    ___ b. Help or hinder?

24. This interview is not going well.
    ___ a. How often?
    ___ b. Help or hinder?

25. The interviewer is pleased with my qualifications.
    ___ a. How often?
    ___ b. Help or hinder?

26. I am freezing up under the pressure.
    ___ a. How often?
    ___ b. Help or hinder?

27. I am afraid that they will find out later that I'm not as competent as I have claimed.
    ___ a. How often?
    ___ b. Help or hinder?

28. I am expressing myself well.
    ___ a. How often?
    ___ b. Help or hinder?

29. I'm nervous and the interviewer knows it.
    ___ a. How often?
    ___ b. Help or hinder?

30. I'm doing a good job answering the interviewer's questions.
    ___ a. How often?
    ___ b. Help or hinder?

31. I will be myself and that should be plenty.
    ___ a. How often?
    ___ b. Help or hinder?

32. This sounds interesting and exciting.
    ___ a. How often?
    ___ b. Help or hinder?

33. I expect the interviewer to like me.
    ___ a. How often?
    ___ b. Help or hinder?

34. I don't know what this person wants from me.
    ___ a. How often?
    ___ b. Help or hinder?

35. I really can do this job.
    ___ a. How often?
    ___ b. Help or hinder?

36. The more interviews I go on, the better I get.
    ___ a. How often?
    ___ b. Help or hinder?

37. I sound like I don't know what I am taking about.
    ___ a. How often?
    ___ b. Help or hinder?

38. I won't be able to say what I want before the interview ends.
    ___ a. How often?
    ___ b. Help or hinder?

39. The future looks promising.
    ___ a. How often?
    ___ b. Help or hinder?

40. I forgot the questions I was going to ask.
    ___ a. How often?
    ___ b. Help or hinder?

41. This place needs someone like me.
    ___ a. How often?
    ___ b. Help or hinder?

42. I won't be able to answer an important question.
    ___ a. How often?
    ___ b. Help or hinder?

43. I will cost myself this job by doing something stupid.
    ___ a. How often?
    ___ b. Help or hinder?

44. I am not qualified.
    ___ a. How often?
    ___ b. Help or hinder?

45. This is stressful.
    ___ a. How often?
    ___ b. Help or hinder?

46. I am not going to get this job.
    ___ a. How often?
    ___ b. Help or hinder?

47. This is what I want and my attitude shows it.
    ___ a. How often?
    ___ b. Help or hinder?

48. I sound stupid.
    ___ a. How often?
    ___ b. Help or hinder?

49. This job is perfect for me and I am perfect for this job.
    ___ a. How often?
    ___ b. Help or hinder?

50. I would feel terrific if I got this job.
    ___ a. How often?
    ___ b. Help or hinder?

Life Events Questionnaire (LEQ)

PURPOSE To measure stressful life events.

AUTHOR T. S. Brugha

DESCRIPTION The LEQ is a 12-item instrument measuring common life events that tend to be threatening. The instrument was designed to overcome the labor-intense time and expense of more lengthy interviews. The LEQ is useful in making an assessment for an Axis IV diagnosis with the DSM-IV. The instrument is acceptable to psychiatric patients and the general population. The instrument has high sensitivity and is more likely to produce false positives (identify as a stressful event one that may not be) than false negatives (failing to identify a stressful event that is present). The client identifies stressful events over the past six months, with the specific months written in at the top of the questionnaire. Once a client has successfully identified the stressful events, the specific LEQ items may serve as a good point of departure in developing a self-anchored rating scale.

NORMS No normative data are available.

SCORING Each item of the LEQ may be scored 1 if it is checked and 0 if not. A total score would be the sum of all items, although scores will tend to be skewed due to the nature of the instrument.

RELIABILITY The test-retest reliability of the LEQ is reported as .84 for a three-month period and .66 for a six-month period. Data on internal consistency are not available.

VALIDITY Concurrent validity estimates were derived from the concordance between inpatient psychotic patients' identification of stressful events and those identified by a significant other; there was a 90% agreement when assessed at a three-month period and a 70% agreement when assessed at six months. The authors also used an extensive interview of stressful events as a base rate and showed that the LEQ was sensitive to the identification of stressful events.

PRIMARY REFERENCE Brugha, T. S., and Cragg, D. (1990). The list of threatening experiences: The reliability and validity of a brief Life Events Questionnaire, *Acta Psychiatrica Scandinavica*, 82, 77–81.   Instrument reproduced with permission of T. S. Brugha.

AVAILABILITY Dr. T. S. Brugha, Leicester General Hospital, Gwendolen Road, Leicester, LES 4PW United Kingdom. Email: tsb@le.ac.uk.

LEQ

Have any of the following life events or problems happened to you during the last 6 months? Please check the box or boxes corresponding to the month or months in which any event happened or began.

Months

You yourself suffered a serious illness, injury, or an assault.						
A serious illness, injury, or assault happened to a close relative.						
Your parent, child, or spouse died.						
A close family friend or another relative (aunt, cousin, grandparent) died.						
You had a separation due to marital difficulties.						
You broke off a steady relationship.						
You had a serious problem with a close friend, neighbor, or relative.						
You became unemployed or you were seeking work unsuccessfully for more than one month.						
You were sacked from your job.						
You had a major financial crisis.						
You had problems with the police and a court appearance.						
Something you valued was lost or stolen.						

Life Satisfaction Index-Z (LSIZ)

PURPOSE To measure the psychological well-being of the elderly.

AUTHORS Bernice Neugarten, Robert J. Havighurst, and Sheldon S. Tobin

DESCRIPTION The LSIZ is an 18-item instrument designed to measure the life satisfaction of older people. The LSIZ was developed from a rating scale that was designed to be used by interviewers rating respondents, and it may be administered as a self-report instrument orally or in writing. Items for the LSIZ were selected on the basis of their correlations with the original rating scale and their ability to discriminate between high and low scorers on the rating scale. Based on research on this instrument, it is recommended that the LSIZ be used mainly with individuals over 65.

NORMS Initial study of the LSIZ was conducted with a sample of 60 people reported to represent a wide range of ages from 65 years, both sexes, and all social classes. The mean score on the original instrument was 12.4; however, this instrument included two more items than the current LSIZ.

SCORING The LSIZ is easily scored by assigning one point to each item that is "correctly" checked and summing these scores. A correct score is "agree" on items 1, 2, 4, 6, 8, 9, 11, 12, 13, 14, 17. Other items are correct if the respondent answers "disagree."

RELIABILITY No data were reported, but the rating scales from which the LSIZ was developed had excellent inter-observer agreement.

VALIDITY The LSIZ showed a moderate correlation with the instrument from which it was developed, the Life Satisfaction Rating Scale, indicating some degree of concurrent validity. The LSIZ also demonstrated a form of known-groups validity by successfully discriminating between high and low scorers on the Life Satisfaction Rating Scale.

PRIMARY REFERENCE Neugarten, B. L., Havighurst, R. J, and Tobin, S. S. (1961). The measurement of life satisfaction, *Journal of Gerontology*, 16, 134–143. Instrument reproduced with permission of Bernice Neugarten and Robert J. Havighurst.

AVAILABILITY May be copied from this volume.

Here are some statements about life in general that people feel different ways about. Read each statement on the list and indicate at left the number that best describes how you feel about the statement.

1 = Agree
2 = Disagree
3 = Unsure

___ 1. As I grow older, things seem better than I thought they would be.
___ 2. I have gotten more of the breaks in life than most of the people I know.
___ 3. This is the dreariest time of my life.
___ 4. I am just as happy as when I was younger.
___ 5. My life could be happier than it is now.
___ 6. These are the best years of my life.
___ 7. Most of the things I do are boring or monotonous.
___ 8. I expect some interesting and pleasant things to happen to me in the future.
___ 9. The things I do are as interesting to me as they ever were.
___ 10. I feel old and somewhat tired.
___ 11. As I look back on my life, I am fairly well satisfied.
___ 12. I would not change my past life even if I could.
___ 13. Compared to other people my age, I make a good appearance.
___ 14. I have made plans for things I'll be doing in a month or a year from now.
___ 15. When I think back over my life, I didn't get most of the important things I wanted.
___ 16. Compared to other people, I get down in the dumps too often.
___ 17. I've gotten pretty much what I expected out of life.
___ 18. In spite of what some people say, the lot of the average man is getting worse, not better.

Liking People Scale (LPS)

PURPOSE To measure interpersonal orientation.

AUTHOR Erik E. Filsinger

DESCRIPTION This 15-item instrument measures one aspect of interpersonal orientation, the general liking of other people. Interpersonal orientation plays a significant role in one's social development and adjustment. The theoretical point of departure of the LPS is that the degree of liking people influences whether one approaches or avoids social interaction. The instrument has utility, then, for monitoring intervention in cases of social isolation, shyness, and antisocial behavior. Scores on the instrument do not appear to be significantly different for males and females, although females score slightly higher than males.

NORMS Normative data are reported for three samples. One hundred and forty college students (57 males and 83 females) from diverse demographic backgrounds had a mean of 59.4 with a standard deviation of 8.14. A second sample of college students had mean scores of 57.64 for males ($n = 15$) and 59.86 for females ($n = 58$). A third sample of randomly selected adults had a mean score of 52.27 for males and 55.35 for females.

SCORING Respondents rate each item in terms of their agreement or disagreement. Ratings are quantified from 1 to 5 as follows: $a = 1$, $b = 2$, $c = 3$, $d = 4$, and $e = 5$. Items 4, 6, 8, 9, 10, and 15 are reverse-scored; total scores are the sum of all the items, with a range of 15 to 75. Higher scores indicate greater liking of people.

RELIABILITY The reliability of the LPS was estimated using Cronbach's alpha to test internal consistency. The LPS had good to very good internal consistency from two samples of college students (.85 and .75, respectively). Coefficient alpha was .78 from the random sample of adults. No data on stability were reported.

VALIDITY The instrument generally has good validity evidence. In three separate samples the LPS was shown to have good concurrent validity, correlating with the amount of time spent alone, the number of close friends, scores on a misanthropy measure, and social anxiety. The instrument has also been shown to correlate with four measures of affiliation motivation, with social self-esteem, and with the ability to judge others.

PRIMARY REFERENCE Filsinger, E. E. (1981). A measure of interpersonal orientation: The Liking People Scale, *Journal of Personality Assessment*, 45, 295–300. Instrument reproduced with permission of Erik E. Filsinger.

AVAILABILITY May be copied from this volume.

The following questions ask your feeling about a number of things. Since we are all different, some people may think and feel one way; other people think and feel another way. There is no such thing as a "right" or "wrong" answer. The idea is to read each question and then fill out your answer. Try to respond to every question, even if it does not apply to you very well. The possible answers for each question are:

a = Strongly agree
b = Moderately agree
c = Neutral
d = Moderately disagree
e = Strongly disagree

___ 1. Sometimes when people are talking to me, I find myself wishing that they would leave.
___ 2. My need for people is quite low.
___ 3. One of the things wrong with people today is that they are too dependent upon other people.
___ 4. My happiest experiences involve other people.
___ 5. People are not important for my personal happiness.
___ 6. Personal character is developed in the stream of life.
___ 7. I could be happy living away from people.
___ 8. It is important to me to be able to get along with other people.
___ 9. No matter what I am doing, I would rather do it in the company of other people.
___ 10. There is no question about it—I like people.
___ 11. Personal character is developed in solitude.
___ 12. In general, I don't like people.
___ 13. Except for my close friends, I don't like people.
___ 14. A person only has a limited amount of time and people tend to cut into it.
___ 15. People are the most important thing in my life.

Loneliness Rating Scale (LRS)

PURPOSE To measure affective components of loneliness.

AUTHORS Joseph J. Scalise, Earl J. Ginter, and Lawrence H. Gerstein

DESCRIPTION The LRS is a 40-item instrument in two parts: Part A measures the frequency of certain affects and Part B measures the intensity or impact of the affective experience. The LRS is composed of four factors derived from factor analysis: depletion (a loss of vigor, exhaustion), isolation (an interpersonal segregation), agitation (restlessness, frustration, antagonism). and dejection (a feeling of discouragement or despondency). The original items for the LRS were based on a list of words solicited from students about how they felt when they were lonely, plus review of the loneliness literature. The LRS thus allows measurement both of how often a respondent experiences each of the four dimensions, and of the impact the experience.

NORMS The LRS was developed with a sample of 277 males and 486 females. largely university students. The median age was 21 years with a range of 11 to 72 years. Means and standard deviations are reported for all four subscales for both men and women. There is a significant difference between male and female scores on all of the subscales except agitation. In all instances, women scored higher suggesting greater frequency and intensity of loneliness.

SCORING Eight separate scores are derived from the LRS, four frequency scores and four intensity scores. Scores for each factor are obtained by simply adding up the numbers circled for the items of each factor (depletion: 4, 9, 11, 14, 18, 21, 22, 25, 26, 37; isolation: 6, 7, 20, 23, 28, 29, 31, 35, 39, 40; agitation: 3, 8, 12, 13, 15, 17, 24, 32, 33, 34; dejection: 1, 25, 10, 16, 19, 27, 30, 36, 38). If a person circles "never" for frequency, the corresponding intensity (Part B) portion should not be completed. Scores range from 0 to 30 for the frequency dimensions and 0 to 50 for intensity.

RELIABILITY The frequency dimensions have very good internal consistency, with alphas that range from .82 to .89. Stability of the LRS is also good with six-week test-retest reliabilities ranging from .61 to .71 for frequency and .65 to .70 for intensity while four-week test-retest reliability was .72 to .81 for frequency and .73 to .78 for intensity.

VALIDITY Available validity information shows correlations of .25 to .46 with the UCLA Loneliness Scale, thus suggesting moderate concurrent validity.

PRIMARY REFERENCE Scalise, J. J., Ginter, E. J., and Gerstein, L. H. (1984). A multidimensional loneliness measure: The Loneliness Rating Scale (LRS), *Journal of Personality Assessment*, 48, 525–530. Instrument reproduced with permission of J. J. Scalise.

AVAILABILITY May be copied from this volume.

This is not a test. We are only interested in finding out how you feel when you experience loneliness.

There are 40 two-part questions. In the first part of the question, several words are used to describe loneliness. Indicate which word most describes how you feel by placing the appropriate number of the following scale to the left of each statement.

$$0 = \text{Never}$$
$$1 = \text{Occasionally}$$
$$2 = \text{Frequently}$$
$$3 = \text{Always}$$

In the second part, you are asked to indicate on a scale of 1 to 5 how much this feeling affects you by writing the appropriate number on the right-hand side of the statement.

1	2	3	4	5
Bothersome				Overwhelming

If your answer to the first part of the statement is "never," skip the second part of the statement.

____ 1. When I experience loneliness, I feel *low*.
The feeling of being *low* is: ____

____ 2. When I experience loneliness, I feel *sad*.
The feeling of being *sad* is: ____

____ 3. When I experience loneliness, I feel *angry*.
The feeling of being *angry* is: ____

____ 4. When I experience loneliness, I feel *depressed*.
The feeling of being *depressed* is: ____

____ 5. When I experience loneliness, I feel *drained*.
The feeling of being *drained* is: ____

____ 6. When I experience loneliness, I feel *unloved*.
The feeling of being *unloved* is: ____

____ 7. When I experience loneliness, I feel *worthless*.
The feeling of being *worthless* is: ____

____ 8. When I experience loneliness, I feel *nervous*.
The feeling of being *nervous* is: ____

____ 9. When I experience loneliness, I feel *empty*.
The feeling of being *empty* is: ____

____ 10. When I experience loneliness, I feel *blue*.
The feeling of being *blue* is: ____

____ 11. When I experience loneliness, I feel *hollow*.
The feeling of being *hollow* is: ____

____ 12. When I experience loneliness, I feel *humiliated*.
The feeling of being *humiliated* is: ____

____ 13. When I experience loneliness, I feel *guilty*.
The feeling of being *guilty* is: ____

—— 14. When I experience loneliness, I feel *secluded*.
The feeling of being *secluded* is: ——

—— 15. When I experience loneliness, I feel *tormented*.
The feeling of being *tormented* is: ——

—— 16. When I experience loneliness, I feel *self-pity*.
The feeling of *self-pity* is: ——

—— 17. When I experience loneliness, I feel *aggressive*.
The feeling of being *aggressive* is: ——

—— 18. When I experience loneliness, I feel *alienated*.
The feeling of being *alienated* is: ——

—— 19. When I experience loneliness, I feel *hurt*.
The feeling of being *hurt* is: ——

—— 20. When I experience loneliness, I feel *hopeless*.
The feeling of being *hopeless* is: ——

—— 21. When I experience loneliness, I feel *broken*.
The feeling of being *broken* is: ——

—— 22. When I experience loneliness, I feel *withdrawn*.
The feeling of being *withdrawn* is: ——

—— 23. When I experience loneliness, I feel *disliked*.
The feeling of being *disliked* is: ——

—— 24. When I experience loneliness, I feel *hostile*.
The feeling of being *hostile* is: ——

—— 25. When I experience loneliness, I feel *numb*.
The feeling of being *numb* is: ——

—— 26. When I experience loneliness, I feel *passive*.
The feeling of being *passive* is: ——

—— 27. When I experience loneliness, I feel *confused*.
The feeling of being *confused* is: ——

—— 28. When I experience loneliness, I feel *abandoned*.
The feeling of being *abandoned* is: ——

—— 29. When I experience loneliness, I feel *unacceptable*.
The feeling of being *unacceptable* is: ——

—— 30. When I experience loneliness, I *feel discouraged*.
The feeling of being *discouraged* is: ——

—— 31. When I experience loneliness, I feel *faceless*.
The feeling of being *faceless* is: ——

—— 32. When I experience loneliness, I feel *sick*.
The feeling of being *sick* is: ——

—— 33. When I experience loneliness, I feel *scared*.
The feeling of being *scared* is: ——

—— 34. When I experience loneliness, I feel *tense*.
The feeling of being *tense* is: ——

—— 35. When I experience loneliness, I feel *deserted*.
The feeling of being *deserted* is: ——

___ 36. When I experience loneliness, I feel *miserable*.
         The feeling of being *miserable* is: ___

___ 37. When I experience loneliness, I feel *detached*.
         The feeling of being *detached* is: ___

___ 38. When I experience loneliness, I feel *unhappy*.
         The feeling of being *unhappy* is: ___

___ 39. When I experience loneliness, I feel *excluded*.
         The feeling of being *excluded* is: ___

___ 40. When I experience loneliness, I feel *useless*.
         The feeling of being *useless* is: ___

Love Attitudes Scale (LAS)

PURPOSE To measure love styles/attitudes.

AUTHORS Clyde Hendrick and Susan S. Hendrick

DESCRIPTION The LAS is a 42-item instrument designed to measure attitudes about love. Six styles of love form the subscales of the LAS: Eros (E: passionate love, items 1–7), Ludus (L: game-playing love, items 8–14), Storge (S: friendship love, items 15–21), Pragma (P: logical, "shopping list" love, items 22–28), Mania (M: possessive, dependent love, items 29–35), and Agape (A: all-giving selfless love, items 36–42). The LAS has two versions, the most recent (reprinted here) being relationship-specific. The LAS is a useful measure for both research and practice focusing on issues involving love.

NORMS The LAS has been studied with several samples involving a total of 536 male and 607 female college students taking introductory psychology courses. For the current version of the LAS, means were: E=2.08, L=3.56, S=2.42, P=3.09, M=2.94, A=2.20. There are significant differences between men and women on all but the eros and agape subscales.

SCORING The LAS is scored by summing the 5-point Likert-type item responses, with A ("strongly agree") 1 point scored as and E ("strongly disagree") given 5 points. Lower scores indicate greater agreement with the scale. It is recommended that only the subscale scores be used.

RELIABILITY The LAS has good internal consistency, with alphas for the subscales that range from .74 to .84. Data on stability were not reported on the new scale, but four- to six-week test-retest correlations on the older version of the LAS were reported as ranging from .70 to .82.

VALIDITY Although no data on validity were reported for the relationship-specific version of the LAS, the older, more general version, which is very similar to the newer version, is reported as having good concurrent validity. The LAS is related to sex-role attitudes, self-disclosure and sensation-seeking, sexual attitudes, religious beliefs, and whether individuals currently are in love.

PRIMARY REFERENCE Hendrick, C., and Hendrick, S. S. (1990). A relationship-specific version of the Love Attitudes Scale, *Journal of Social Behavior and Personality*, 5, 239–254. Instrument reprinted by permission of authors and the American Psychological Association.

AVAILABILITY May be copied from this volume. Email: susan.hendrick@ttu.edu.

Listed below are several statements that reflect different attitudes about love. For each statement fill in the blank using the response that indicates how much you agree or disagree with that statement. The items refer to a specific love relationship. Whenever possible, answer the questions with your current partner in mind. If you are not currently dating anyone, answer the questions with your most recent partner in mind. If you have never been in love, answer in terms of what you think your responses would most likely be.

For each statement:

A = Strongly agree with the statement
B = Moderately agree with the statement
C = Neutral—neither agree nor disagree
D = Moderately disagree with the statement
E = Strongly disagree with the statement

___ 1. My partner and I were attracted to each other immediately after we first met.
___ 2. My partner and I have the right physical "chemistry" between us.
___ 3. Our lovemaking is very intense and satisfying.
___ 4. I feel that my partner and I were meant for each other.
___ 5. My partner and I became emotionally involved rather quickly.
___ 6. My partner and I really understand each other.
___ 7. My partner fits my ideal standards of physical beauty/handsomeness.
___ 8. I try to keep my partner a little uncertain about my commitment to him/her.
___ 9. I believe that what my partner doesn't know about me won't hurt him/her.
___ 10. I have sometimes had to keep my partner from finding out about other partners.
___ 11. I could get over my affair with my partner pretty easily and quickly.
___ 12. My partner would get upset if he/she knew of some of the things I've done with other people.
___ 13. When my partner gets too dependent on me, I want to back off a little.
___ 14. I enjoy playing the "game of love" with my partner and a number of other partners.
___ 15. It is hard for me to say exactly when our friendship turned into love.
___ 16. To be genuine, our love first required *caring* for a while.
___ 17. I expect to always be friends with my partner.
___ 18. Our love is the best kind because it grew out of a long friendship.
___ 19. Our friendship merged gradually into love over time.
___ 20. Our love is really a deep friendship, not a mysterious, mystical emotion.
___ 21. Our love relationship is the most satisfying because it developed from a good friendship.
___ 22. I considered what my partner was going to become in life before I committed myself to him/her.
___ 23. I tried to plan my life carefully before choosing my partner.
___ 24. In choosing my partner, I believed it was best to love someone with a similar background.
___ 25. A main consideration in choosing my partner was how he/she would reflect on my family.

___ 26. An important factor in choosing my partner was whether or not he/she would be a good parent.

___ 27. One consideration in choosing my partner was how he/she would reflect on my career.

___ 28. Before getting very involved with my partner, I tried to figure out how compatible his/her hereditary background would be with mine in case we ever had children.

___ 29. When things aren't right with my partner and me, my stomach gets upset.

___ 30. If my partner and I break up, I would get so depressed that I would even think of suicide.

___ 31. Sometimes I get so excited about being in love with my partner that I can't sleep.

___ 32. When my partner doesn't pay attention to me, I feel sick all over.

___ 33. Since I've been in love with my partner, I've had trouble concentrating on anything else.

___ 34. I cannot relax if I suspect that my partner is with someone else.

___ 35. If my partner ignores me for a while, I sometimes do stupid things to try to get his/her attention back.

___ 36. I try to always help my partner through difficult times.

___ 37. I would rather suffer myself than let my partner suffer.

___ 38. I cannot be happy unless I place my partner's happiness before my own.

___ 39. I am usually willing to sacrifice my own wishes to let my partner achieve his/hers.

___ 40. Whatever I own is my partner's to use as he/she chooses.

___ 41. When my partner gets angry with me, I still love him/her fully and unconditionally.

___ 42. I would endure all things for the sake of my partner.

Love Attitudes Scale—Short Form (LAS-SF)

PURPOSE To measure components of love.

AUTHORS Clyde Hendrick and Susan Hendrick

DESCRIPTION The LAS-SF is a 24-item scale designed to measure six major components of love: Eros (items 1–4); Ludus (items 5–8); Storge (items 9–12); Pragma (items 13–16); Mania (items 17–20); and Agape (items 21–24). These love styles or attitudes (defined in the Primary Reference) are based on theory developed by Lee in the mid-seventies about the basic love styles. The goal of development of the LAS-SF was to further development of a theory of love by empirically demonstrating that the theory has firm empirical referents. The LAS-SF also can be used by practitioners in work with individuals and couples to examine these characteristics in their clients and conduct evaluations of the relationship between these characteristics and other variables.

NORMS The 24-item LAS-SF was developed using two samples of 834 and 847 undergraduate psychology students at a Texas university. No other demographic data or actual norms were provided, although men and women differed significantly on several of the six love styles.

SCORING The LAS-SF is scored by summing the item scores within each component and dividing by the number of items to obtain the mean subscale score. For purposes of analysis, "A" on the response = 1 and "E" = 5.

RELIABILITY The six components of the LAS-SF have very good internal consistency with alphas that range from .75 to .88. The LAS-SF also has very good seven-week stability with test-retest correlations that range from .70 to .82.

VALIDITY The LAS-SF has some degree of discriminative validity with a number of differences on the scales according to the degree of self-esteem and whether a respondent had ever been in love, or was in love now.

PRIMARY REFERENCE Hendrick, C., and Hendrick, S. (1998). The Love Attitude Scale: Short Form, *Journal of Social and Personal Relationships*, 147–159. Instrument reproduced with permission of Dr. Susan Hendrick.

AVAILABILITY Email Dr. Hendrick at susan.hendrick@ttu.edu.

Listed below are several statements that reflect different attitudes about love. For each statement fill in the response on the answer sheet that indicates how much you agree or disagree with that statement. The items refer to a specific love relationship. Whenever possible, answer the questions with your current partner in mind. If you are not currently dating anyone, answer the questions with your most recent partner in mind. If you have never been in love, answer in terms of what you think your responses would most likely be.

For each statement:

A = Strongly agree with the statement
B = Moderately agree with the statement
C = Neutral—neither agree nor disagree
D = Moderately disagree with the statement
E = Strongly disagree with the statement

___ 1. My partner and I have the right physical "chemistry" between us.

___ 2. I feel that my partner and I were meant for each other.

___ 3. My partner and I really understand each other.

___ 4. My partner fits my ideal standards of physical beauty/handsomeness.

___ 5. I believe that what my partner doesn't know about me won't hurt him/her.

___ 6. I have sometimes had to keep my partner from finding out about other partners.

___ 7. My partner would get upset if he/she knew of some of the things I've done with other people.

___ 8. I enjoy playing the "game of love" with my partner and a number of other partners.

___ 9. Our love is the best kind because it grew out of a long friendship.

___ 10. Our friendship merged gradually into love over time.

___ 11. Our love is really a deep friendship, not a mysterious, mystical emotion.

___ 12. Our love relationship is the most satisfying because it developed from a good friendship.

___ 13. A main consideration in choosing my partner was how he/she would reflect on my family.

___ 14. An important factor in choosing my partner was whether or not he/she would be a good parent.

___ 15. One consideration in choosing my partner was how he/she would reflect on my career.

___ 16. Before getting very involved with my partner, I tried to figure out how compatible his/her hereditary background would be with mine in case we ever had children.

___ 17. When my partner doesn't pay attention to me, I feel sick all over.

___ 18. Since I've been in love with my partner, I've had trouble concentrating on anything else.

___ 19. I cannot relax if I suspect that my partner is with someone else.

____ 20. If my partner ignores me for a while, I sometimes do stupid things to try to get his/her attention back.

____ 21. I would rather suffer myself than let my partner suffer.

____ 22. I cannot be happy unless I place my partner's happiness before my own.

____ 23. I am usually willing to sacrifice my own wishes to let my partner achieve his/hers.

____ 24. I would endure all things for the sake of my partner.

Magical Ideation Scale (MIS)

PURPOSE To measure magical thinking.

AUTHORS Mark Eckblad and Loren J. Chapman

DESCRIPTION This 30-item instrument was designed to measure the magical ideations characteristic of schizotypical disorders. The MIS is also considered to be a general measure of proneness to psychosis. Magical ideation is defined as the belief in what general Western culture would consider invalid causation, such as superstitiousness, clairvoyance, telepathy, and so on. The focus of the MIS is not on the credibility of these forms of causation, but the respondent's personal beliefs and experiences.

NORMS The MIS has normative data from a total of 1,512 undergraduate college students. The mean score was 8.56 with a standard deviation of 5.24 for males ($n=682$). Females ($n=830$) have a mean of 9.69 and a standard deviation of 5.93.

SCORING Respondents indicate whether the item is true or false regarding their personal experience. Items 7, 12, 13, 16, 18, 22, 23 are scored 1 if answered false. All other items are scored 1 if answered true. Total scores range from 0 to 30; higher scores reflect more reported experiences of magical ideation.

RELIABILITY The MIS has very good internal consistency, with correlations of .82 and .85 for males and females respectively. Data on stability were not available.

VALIDITY The items of the MIS were first judged as to whether or not they were congruent with a specified definition of magical ideation; this represents logical content validity. The instrument then went through several revisions in order to make certain it was not associated with social desirability and an acquiescence response set. Concurrent validity is supported with correlations between scores on the MIS and measures of perceptual aberration, physical anhedonia, and psychoticism. Known-groups validity was evident with differences on psychotic and psychotic-like symptoms for subjects whose MIS scores were two standard deviations above the mean and a control group.

PRIMARY REFERENCE Eckblad, M., and Chapman, L. J. (1983). Magical ideation as an indicator of schizotypy, *Journal of Consulting and Clinical Psychology* 51, 215–225. Instrument reproduced with permission of Mark Eckblad and Loren Chapman and the American Psychological Association.

AVAILABILITY May be copied from this volume.

Indicate whether each item is true or false of your experiences by circling the T or the F to the left of the item.

T F   1. Some people can make me aware of them just by thinking about me.
T F   2. I have had the momentary feeling that I might not be human.
T F   3. I have sometimes been fearful of stepping on sidewalk cracks.
T F   4. I think I could learn to read others' minds if I wanted to.
T F   5. Horoscopes are right too often for it to be a coincidence.
T F   6. Things sometimes seem to be in different places when I get home, even though no one has been there.
T F   7. Numbers like 13 and 7 have no special powers.
T F   8. I have occasionally had the silly feeling that a TV or radio broadcaster knew I was listening to him.
T F   9. I have worried that people on other planets may be influencing what happens on earth.
T F 10. The government refuses to tell us the truth about flying saucers.
T F 11. I have felt that there were messages for me in the way things were arranged, like in a store window.
T F 12. I have never doubted that my dreams are the products of my own mind.
T F 13. Good luck charms don't work.
T F 14. I have noticed sounds on my records that are not there at other times.
T F 15. The hand motions that strangers make seem to influence me at times.
T F 16. I almost never dream about things before they happen.
T F 17. I have had the momentary feeling that someone's place has been taken by a look-alike.
T F 18. It is not possible to harm others merely by thinking bad thoughts about them.
T F 19. I have sometimes sensed an evil presence around me, although I could not see it.
T F 20. I sometimes have a feeling of gaining or losing energy when certain people look at me or touch me.
T F 21. I have sometimes had the passing thought that strangers are in love with me.
T F 22. I have never had the feeling that certain thoughts of mine really belonged to someone else.
T F 23. When introduced to strangers, I rarely wonder whether I have known them before.
T F 24. If reincarnation were true, it would explain some unusual experiences I have had.
T F 25. People often behave so strangely that one wonders if they are part of an experiment.
T F 26. At times I perform certain little rituals to ward off negative influences.
T F 27. I have felt that I might cause something to happen just by thinking too much about it.
T F 28. I have wondered whether the spirits of the dead can influence the living.
T F 29. At times I have felt that a professor's lecture was meant especially for me.
T F 30. I have sometimes felt that strangers were reading my mind.

Mathematics Anxiety Rating Scale—Revised (MARS-R)

PURPOSE To measure anxiety about math.

AUTHORS Barbara S. Plake and Clair S. Parker

DESCRIPTION This 24-item instrument is designed to measure anxiety related to involvement in statistics and mathematic courses. The instrument is a revised version of a 98-item scale by F. C. Richardson and R. M. Suinn (1972). The current version is more focused on situation-specific (state) anxiety, general (trait) anxiety, and test anxiety. The instrument forms two subscales: learning math anxiety (LMA), which pertains to the process of learning math and statistics, and mathematic evaluation anxiety (MEA), which measures anxiety over being tested about math and statistics.

NORMS Data are reported on 170 college students enrolled in three introductory statistics classes at a large, urban, midwestern university. The mean MARS-R score was 59.84 with a standard deviation of 20.55.

SCORING Respondents rate each item on a 5-point scale from "low anxiety" to "high anxiety." Scores are the sum of the item ratings and range from 24 to 120 for the total scale.

RELIABILITY The reliability of the revised form has been tested for internal consistency using coefficient alpha. The scale has excellent reliability, with an alpha of .98. No data are presented on stability.

VALIDITY There are mixed findings regarding the MARS-R. Scores were not correlated with achievement anxiety, but were correlated with Spielberger's State-Trait Anxiety measures. Concurrent validity was established with correlations between the MARS-R and math achievement, and with significant correlations with the 98-item version.

PRIMARY REFERENCES Plake, B. S., and Parker, C. S. (1982). The development and validation of a revised version of the Mathematics Anxiety Rating Scale, *Educational and Psychological Measurement*, 42, 551–557. Instruments reproduced with permission of Richard M. Suinn, the Rocky Mountains Behavioral Science Institute, Inc., and *Educational and Psychological Measurement*.

AVAILABILITY May be copied from this volume.

Please rate each item in terms of how anxious you feel during the event specified. Use the following scale and record your answer in the space to the left of the item:

1 = Low anxiety
2 = Some anxiety
3 = Moderate anxiety
4 = Quite a bit of anxiety
5 = High anxiety

Learning Mathematics Anxiety

___ 1. Watching a teacher work an algebraic equation on the blackboard.
___ 2. Buying a math textbook.
___ 3. Reading and interpreting graphs or charts.
___ 4. Signing up for a course in statistics.
___ 5. Listening to another student explain a math formula.
___ 6. Walking into a math class.
___ 7. Looking through the pages in a math text.
___ 8. Starting a new chapter in a math book.
___ 9. Walking on campus and thinking about a math course.
___ 10. Picking up a math textbook to begin working on a homework assignment.
___ 11. Reading the word "statistics."
___ 12. Working on an abstract mathematical problem, such as: "if x=outstanding bills, and y=total income, calculate how much you have left for recreational expenditures."
___ 13. Reading a formula in chemistry.
___ 14. Listening to a lecture in a math class.
___ 15. Having to use the tables in the back of a math book.
___ 16. Being told how to interpret probability statements.

Mathematics Evaluation Anxiety

___ 1. Being given a homework assignment of many difficult problems which is due the next class meeting.
___ 2. Thinking about an upcoming math test one day before.
___ 3. Solving square root problem.
___ 4. Taking an examination (quiz) in a math course.
___ 5. Getting ready to study for a math test.
___ 6. Being given a "pop" quiz in a math class.
___ 7. Waiting to get a math test returned in which you expected to do well.
___ 8. Taking an examination (final) in a math course.

Maudsley Obsessional-Compulsive Inventory (MOC)

PURPOSE To measure obsessional-compulsive complaints.

AUTHORS R. J. Hodgson and S. Rachman

DESCRIPTION The MOC is a 30-item inventory designed to measure different types of obsessive-compulsive ritual. Sixty-five items based on a review of the literature and interviews with obsessive-compulsive patients made up the first questionnaire. Following pretesting, the current 30-item questionnaire was developed. Factor analysis revealed four factors: checking (C: items 6, 8, 14, 15, 20, 22, 26); cleaning (CL: items 1, 4, 5, 9, 13, 17, 19, 21, 24, 26, 27); slowness (S: items 2, 4, 8, 16, 23, 25, 29); and doubting (D: items 3, 7, 10–12, 18, 30). (Items 2 and 8 on the S factor are negatively related to the factor; some items load on more than one factor.) The MOC is viewed as a valuable measure for evaluating change in therapy on specific obsessive-compulsive dimensions.

NORMS The MOC was studied initially with 100 obsessional patients in England, Scotland, and Wales, plus 50 nonobsessional neurotic individuals. No other demographic data were provided. The total mean score for the obsessional patients was 18.86 (SD=4.92) and for the neurotics 9.27 (SD=5.43). The mean checking score was 6.10 (SD=2.21) for obsessionals and 2.84 (SD=2.29) for neurotics. The mean for cleaning was 5.55 (SD=3.04) for obsessionals and 2.38 (SD=1.97) for neurotics. The slowness mean was 3.63 (SD=1.93) for obsessionals and 2.27 (SD=1.09) for neurotics, and the doubting mean was 5.39 (SD=1.60) for obsessionals and 3.69 (SD=1.99) for neurotics.

SCORING The MOC is scored by totaling the number of questions that are answered in the obsessional direction for each factor and then summing these for the total score. For example, a "true" response for item 1 would count as one point because it is in the "obsessional direction" whereas a "false" response to item 1 would not count in the score.

RELIABILITY The MOC has fair internal consistency, with an alpha of .80 for the cleaning subscale and alphas of .70 for the remaining subscales. No overall alpha was reported. The MOC has very good stability, with a one-month test-retest reliability coefficient of .80.

VALIDITY The MOC has fair concurrent validity, correlating .60 with the Leyton Obsessional Inventory. The MOC is reported to be sensitive to change as a result of therapy and has good known-groups validity in distinguishing between patients with obsessive-compulsive and neurotic disorders.

PRIMARY REFERENCE Hodgson, R. J., and Rachman, S. (1977). Obsessional-compulsive complaints, *Behavior Research and Therapy*, 15, 389–395. Instrument reprinted with permission of Pergamon Press.

AVAILABILITY May be copied from this volume.

Please answer each question by putting a circle around T for "true" or F for "false" in response to each question. There are no right or wrong answers, and no trick questions. Work quickly and do not think too long about the exact meaning of the question.

T F   1. I avoid using public telephones because of possible contamination.
T F   2. I frequently get nasty thoughts and have difficulty in getting rid of them.
T F   3. I am more concerned than most people about honesty.
T F   4. I am often late because I can't seem to get through everything on time.
T F   5. I don't worry unduly about contamination if I touch an animal.
T F   6. I frequently have to check things (e.g., gas or water taps, doors, etc.) several times.
T F   7. I have a very strict conscience.
T F   8. I find that almost every day I am upset by unpleasant thoughts that come into my mind against my will.
T F   9. I do not worry unduly if I accidently bump into somebody.
T F   10. I usually have serious doubts about the simple everyday things I do.
T F   11. Neither of my parents was very strict during my childhood.
T F   12. I tend to get behind in my work because I repeat things over and over again.
T F   13. I use only an average amount of soap.
T F   14. Some numbers are extremely unlucky.
T F   15. I do not check letters over and over again before mailing them.
T F   16. I do not take a long time to dress in the morning.
T F   17. I am not excessively concerned about cleanliness.
T F   18. One of my major problems is that I pay too much attention to detail.
T F   19. I can use well-kept toilets without any hesitation.
T F   20. My major problem is repeated checking.
T F   21. I am not unduly concerned about germs and diseases.
T F   22. I do not tend to check things more than once.
T F   23. I do not stick to a very strict routine when doing ordinary things.
T F   24. My hands do not feel dirty after touching money.
T F   25. I do not usually count when doing a routine task.
T F   26. I take rather a long time to complete my washing in the morning.
T F   27. I do not use a great deal of antiseptics.
T F   28. I spend a lot of time every day checking things over and over again.
T F   29. Hanging and folding my clothes at night does not take up a lot of time.
T F   30. Even when I do something very carefully I often feel that it is not quite right.

McGill Pain Questionnaire (MPQ)

PURPOSE To measure pain.

AUTHOR Ronald Melzack

DESCRIPTION The MPQ is a 21-item instrument designed to obtain quantitative measures of complex qualitative pain experiences. It consists of 78 adjectives arranged into 20 groups: 10 groups measure the sensory quality of pain (SQ: items 1–10), 5 groups measure the affective quality of pain (AQ: items 11–15), 1 set of adjectives measures the evaluative quality of pain, the overall intensity of the pain experience (EQ: item 16), and 4 groups measure miscellaneous pain (MP: items 17–20); 1 item measures present pain intensity (PPI: item 21). The human figure on the MPQ is used to indicate the location of one's pain, and additional items provide useful qualitative information. A French version also is available.

NORMS Norms are available in the Primary References for several samples presenting different types of pain, such as menstrual pain, arthritis, and back pain.

SCORING Several methods of scoring the MPQ are described in the Primary References. The most important is the pain rating index (PRI) that is obtained for the SQ, AQ, EQ, and MP separately as well as for a total score. The PRI is obtained by adding the rank values of the words selected by the respondent in each set and for the total of the first 20 items. A second score is the overall intensity of pain (PPI, item 21). A third score is simply the total of the number of items checked for each set; scores are the total of the items, divided by the number of items composing the subscales. The total score—the sum of the subscales—also can be used.

RELIABILITY The author notes that several studies have shown the MPQ to provide a reliable measure of pain experience.

VALIDITY There is strong support for the validity of the MPQ. The different scoring procedures have moderate to high correlations, and the subscales also are correlated. The MPQ also is sensitive to changes due to pain management training, and has shown known-groups validity by distinguishing among different forms of pain (e.g., low back pain in people with and without organic symptoms).

PRIMARY REFERENCES Melzack, R. (1975). The McGill Pain Questionnaire: Major properties and scoring methods, *Pain*, 1, 277–299. Melzack, R. (1983). *Pain measurement and assessment*. New York: Raven Press. Instrument reproduced with permission of Ronald Melzack.

AVAILABILITY Ronald Melzack, Ph.D., Professor, Department of Psychology, McGill University, 1205 Dr. Penfield Avenue, Montreal, Quebec, Canada H3A 1B1. Email: ronold.melzack@mcgill.ca.

Check every item that describes your pain. Indicate on the figure the areas where you are experiencing pain.

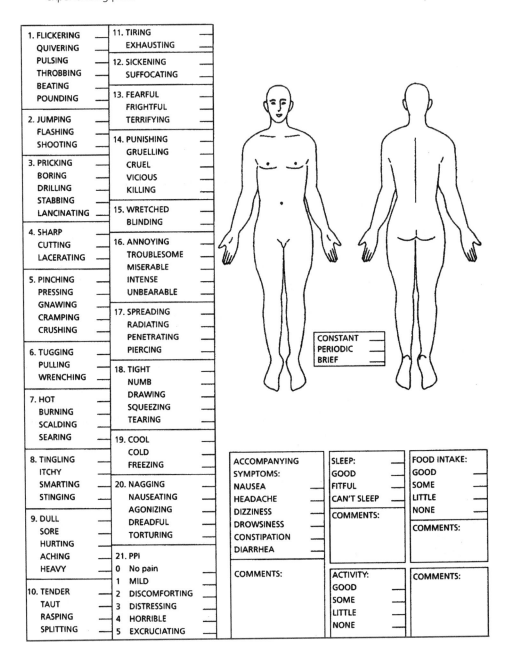

1. FLICKERING	11. TIRING
QUIVERING	EXHAUSTING
PULSING	12. SICKENING
THROBBING	SUFFOCATING
BEATING	13. FEARFUL
POUNDING	FRIGHTFUL
2. JUMPING	TERRIFYING
FLASHING	14. PUNISHING
SHOOTING	GRUELLING
3. PRICKING	CRUEL
BORING	VICIOUS
DRILLING	KILLING
STABBING	15. WRETCHED
LANCINATING	BLINDING
4. SHARP	16. ANNOYING
CUTTING	TROUBLESOME
LACERATING	MISERABLE
5. PINCHING	INTENSE
PRESSING	UNBEARABLE
GNAWING	17. SPREADING
CRAMPING	RADIATING
CRUSHING	PENETRATING
6. TUGGING	PIERCING
PULLING	18. TIGHT
WRENCHING	NUMB
7. HOT	DRAWING
BURNING	SQUEEZING
SCALDING	TEARING
SEARING	19. COOL
8. TINGLING	COLD
ITCHY	FREEZING
SMARTING	20. NAGGING
STINGING	NAUSEATING
	AGONIZING
9. DULL	DREADFUL
SORE	TORTURING
HURTING	
ACHING	21. PPI
HEAVY	0 No pain
	1 MILD
10. TENDER	2 DISCOMFORTING
TAUT	3 DISTRESSING
RASPING	4 HORRIBLE
SPLITTING	5 EXCRUCIATING

CONSTANT
PERIODIC
BRIEF

ACCOMPANYING SYMPTOMS:	SLEEP:	FOOD INTAKE:
NAUSEA	GOOD	GOOD
HEADACHE	FITFUL	SOME
DIZZINESS	CAN'T SLEEP	LITTLE
DROWSINESS	COMMENTS:	NONE
CONSTIPATION		COMMENTS:
DIARRHEA		
COMMENTS:	ACTIVITY:	COMMENTS:
	GOOD	
	SOME	
	LITTLE	
	NONE	

McMullin Addiction Thought Scale (MAT)

PURPOSE To measure irrational thoughts in chemically dependent clients.

AUTHOR Rian E. McMullin

DESCRIPTION The MAT is a 42-item instrument designed to measure irrational cognitions of chemically dependent clients both for assessment and evaluation purposes. The MAT has five core types: not my fault (I: items 1, 4, 8, 11, 17, 19, 28, 29); I am powerful enough to control it (II: items 2, 14–16, 18, 23, 26, 30, 36, 39); drinking is good, pleasant, fun (III: items 3, 6, 10, 13, 22, 27, 31, 38, 41); I am not an alcoholic/don't have a problem (IV: items 5, 7, 25, 32, 35, 42); and I need to drink (V: items 9, 12, 20, 21, 24, 33, 34, 37, 40). The MAT is a very useful measure for keeping track of changes over time, especially as a result of cognitive-behavioral treatment.

NORMS The MAT was studied with several samples in chemical dependency treatment centers in the United States and Australia: 275 subjects participated; 75% were male with ages ranging from 17 to 78. Norms are divided into very high, high, average, low, and very low scores for each factor. Very high (a) and high (b) scores were as follows for each subscale: I = 8 (a) and 6, 7 (b); II = 8–10 (a) and 5–7 (b); III = 8, 9 (a) and 6, 7 (b); IV = 5, 6 (a) and 3, 4 (b); and V = 8, 9 (a) and 6, 7 (b). Very low scores were 0 on subscales II and IV and 0, 1 on the other subscales.

SCORING The MAT is easily scored by summing item responses for each subscale score and the total score.

RELIABILITY Data were not available.

VALIDITY The MAT has good predictive validity, showing significant reductions in irrational thoughts given longer periods of sobriety. The MAT also has good known-groups validity, significantly distinguishing between a recovered and nonrecovered sample. The MAT also is sensitive to changes due to treatment.

PRIMARY REFERENCE McMullin, R. E., and Gehlaar, P. (1990). *Thinking and drinking: An exposé of drinkers' distorted beliefs.* Wheelers Hill, Victoria, Australia: Marlin Publications.

AVAILABILITY Dr. Rian McMullin, 46-090 Puulena Street, Suite 1312, Kaneoha, HI 96744. Email: rian@hgea.net.

Using the following scale, record your answer in the space to the left of each item:

0 = Strongly disagree
1 = Disagree
2 = Neutral
3 = Agree
4 = Strongly agree

How many of the following thoughts do you believe right now?

___ 1. I am not responsible for my drinking or drugging.
___ 2. I can stop drinking or drugging through will power alone.
___ 3. A little booze is good for me.
___ 4. I can't stop drinking or drugging, so why bother trying?
___ 5. A couple of drinks or a little drug can't hurt me.
___ 6. I need to drink or drug to have fun.
___ 7. It's normal to drink alcohol or use drugs the way I have in the past.
___ 8. Bad feelings (fear, sadness, anger, etc.) caused me to drink or drug too much.
___ 9. The best way to stop feeling bad is to take a drink or drug.
___ 10. Being intoxicated or high feels good.
___ 11. I can't hold my liquor or my drug as well as others.
___ 12. I need to drink or drug to be more self-confident.
___ 13. Drinking or drugging is a good way to remove boredom.
___ 14. I can cure my drinking or drugging by a *little* self-discipline.
___ 15. I can become a social drinker or a social user, if I try hard enough.
___ 16. It's my fault that I am an alcoholic or an addict.
___ 17. Something inside of me took over and made me drink or drug.
___ 18. Addiction is just a bad habit.
___ 19. Outside catastrophes (losing a job, spouse leaving, etc.) causes people to drink or drug.
___ 20. I can cope better with life by drinking or drugging.
___ 21. Drinking or drugging is a good way to get back at someone.
___ 22. Wanting a drink or drug is the same as needing one.
___ 23. One can be cured of any addiction.
___ 24. It's necessary to stop withdrawal symptoms by taking another drink or drug.
___ 25. My drinking or drugging problem was not that serious.
___ 26. I can predict what I will do when I drink or drug.
___ 27. I am a better lover when I drink or drug.
___ 28. Social pressure made me use drink or drugs too much.
___ 29. I needed to take a drink or drug to keep emotions from overpowering me.
___ 30. I can be sober without help if I try hard enough.
___ 31. I needed a drink or drug to feel better.
___ 32. A person who works hard earns a drink or drug.
___ 33. Drinking or drugging is a good way to escape from life's stresses.
___ 34. I should be happy all the time.
___ 35. I am not an alcoholic or an addict.
___ 36. You can't tell me anything about my drinking or drugging that I don't know.

___ 37. We should get what we want in life.
___ 38. Intoxication or getting high uncovers an individual's real personality.
___ 39. Psychological problems cause alcoholism and addiction.
___ 40. The best way to handle problems is not to think about them.
___ 41. I am more creative when I am drinking or drugging.
___ 42. There are more important things in life than my drinking or drugging problem.

Medical Avoidance Survey (MAS)

PURPOSE To measure avoidance of medical treatment.

AUTHOR Ronald A. Kleinknecht

DESCRIPTION The MAS is a 21-item instrument designed to measure the extent to which respondents have avoided medical treatment due to fear of various procedures or anticipated outcomes. Avoidance of medical treatment is a significant problem in that it has serious potential consequences that could place an individual's life at risk. The phobia of avoidance of medical treatment requires the attention of medical care providers since they may be able to counteract avoidance of treatment with appropriate intervention and education. The MAS can be used not only to provide the warning to medical care providers, but also as an outcome measure to evaluate change and avoidance as a result of treatment. The MAS has three subscales: avoidance of medical treatment due to fear that serious illness might be found (items 3, 4, 10, 11, 12, 17, 18, and 19); avoidance of medical treatment due to fear that blood might be drawn or injections given (items 5, 7, 8, 14, and 15); avoidance due to logistical considerations and cost (items 2, 6, 13, 16, and 21).

NORMS The MAS was initially studied with 934 undergraduate students of whom 628 were female, 305 were male, and one did not specify gender. The mean age was 20.43 (SD=4.36). Thirty percent of the respondents reported a history of fainting or almost fainting in the presence of various medical stimuli such as blood, injury, and injections. Mean scores on each of the subscales are available for respondents who were fainters and who were nonfainters. For the fear of finding a serious illness subscale, the mean for fainters was 2.77 (SD=3.33) and for nonfainters the mean was 2.31 (SD=2.8); for the fear of injection or pain, the mean for fainters was 17.24 (SD=10.9) and for nonfainters the mean was 8.39 (SD=8.1); for cost and logistics, the mean for fainters was 1.99 (SD=2.4) and the mean for non-fainters was 2.08 (SD=2.2). On all but the cost and logistics subscales, the mean for females was higher than for males though the difference was significant only on the fear of injections and pain subscale.

SCORING The MAS is easily scored by simply summing the individual item scores for each subscale.

RELIABILITY The MAS has poor to good internal consistency. The alpha for fear of finding a serious illness was .81, for fear of injections and pain it was .73, and for cost and logistics, the alpha was .55. Data on stability were not provided.

VALIDITY The MAS has good predictive validity with two of three MAS subscales—the fear of finding serious illness and, especially, fear of injections and blood draws—contributing significantly to the prediction of fainting. The MAS also has good concurrent validity with all three subscales significantly correlated with the Dental Fear Survey and two of the three subscales significantly correlated with a mutilation questionnaire.

PRIMARY REFERENCE Kleinknecht, R. A., Thorndike, R. M. and Walls, M. M. (1996). Factorial dimensions and correlates of blood, injury, injection and related medical fears: Cross validation of the Medical Fear Survey, *Behavior Research and Therapy*, 34, 323–331.

AVAILABILITY Dr. Ronald A. Kleinknecht, Professor and Chair, Department of Psychology, Western Washington University, Bellingham, WA 98225-9089. Reprinted with permission of the author. Email: ronald.kleinknecht@wwu.edu.

Below are listed some reasons that people give for not going to see doctors and for not seeking medical care. After carefully reading the scales below, please indicate if and how much you have ever avoided medical treatment due to the listed reason.

0 = I have never, and I would not avoid medical treatment for this reason. (I always seek treatment when needed)

1 = I have not avoided due to this reason but have seriously thought about it. (I go, but have hesitated)

2 = I have avoided due to this reason but I usually go when necessary.

3 = I have avoided several times for this reason in the past, but would probably go if it meant life or death.

4 = I have avoided for this reason in the past and at this time I do not think I can go because of it.

Have you ever avoided going to the doctor or seeking health care due to:

		0	1	2	3	4
1.	Embarrassment over having to expose your body?	—	—	—	—	—
2.	Finding the time in your day to get there and then the waiting?	—	—	—	—	—
3.	Embarrassment that others will find out what possible diagnosis you have?	—	—	—	—	—
4.	Fear that you would find that you have a serious illness or injury?	—	—	—	—	—
5.	Fear that you might experience too much pain or discomfort?	—	—	—	—	—
6.	The cost of doctor's appointments?	—	—	—	—	—
7.	Fear that you might have to receive a hypodermic needle injection?	—	—	—	—	—
8.	Fear that you would have blood drawn from you?	—	—	—	—	—
9.	Not having a regular doctor who knows you and your health?	—	—	—	—	—
10.	Fear that you might need surgery?	—	—	—	—	—
11.	Fear that the doctor or nurse might think badly of you for not taking better care of yourself physically?	—	—	—	—	—
12.	Fear that you would have to see the various types of medical equipment?	—	—	—	—	—
13.	The difficulty in arranging transportation?	—	—	—	—	—
14.	Fear that you might faint when having an injection or having blood taken?	—	—	—	—	—
15.	Fear that you might need stitches?	—	—	—	—	—
16.	The cost of medicine?	—	—	—	—	—
17.	Fear that you might have cancer?	—	—	—	—	—
18.	Fear that you might be found to have AIDS?	—	—	—	—	—
19.	Fear that you might have to undergo lengthy treatment?	—	—	—	—	—
20.	Fear that you might have to have an X-ray?	—	—	—	—	—
21.	The difficulty in getting an appointment?	—	—	—	—	—

Medical Fear Survey (MFS)

PURPOSE To measure medical fears.

AUTHOR Ronald A. Kleinknecht

DESCRIPTION The MFS is a 50-item instrument designed to measure blood, injection, and injury fear and phobias (BII). BII is one of the more prevalent of the specific phobias and frequently results in avoidance and delay in seeking medical care; this can have serious health consequences. The MFS was specifically designed to measure several components of BII fear and phobia not found in other measures of this phenomenon. The MFS has value as a possible screen for medical patients to provide valuable information to physicians and lab technicians; the MFS also could be administered as a pre- and post-treatment measure, thereby serving as an outcome measure for treatment of BII phobic patients. There are five subscales of the MFS: injections and blood draws (items 1, 6, 16, 20, 24, 27, 31, 34, 45, and 47); sharp objects (items 2, 3, 7, 15, 21, 26, 29, 32, 42, and 44); examinations and symptoms as intimation of illness (items 4, 8, 13, 17, 22, 28, 37, 39, 43, and 48); blood (items 5, 9, 10, 19, 23, 25, 33, 35, 40, and 49); and mutilation (items 11, 12, 14, 18, 30, 36, 38, 41, 46, and 50).

NORMS The MFS has been developed over 10 years with the most research being conducted on two university student samples totaling 1085 respondents. The larger of these samples included 782 respondents, of whom 309 were male and 473 were female. No other demographic data were provided. The means for the five subscales are: mutilation—male $M=10.75$ ($SD=6.56$), female $M=18.17$ ($SD=8.31$); sharp objects—male $M=2.47$ ($SD=3.05$), female $M=6.10$ ($SD=5.38$); examinations and symptoms—male $M=5.93$ ($SD=4.08$), female $M=8.12$ ($SD=5.04$); injections— male $M=6.86$ ($SD=5.70$), female $M=10.74$ ($SD=7.73$); blood—male $M=2.34$ ($SD=3.74$), female $M=6.21$ ($SD=6.44$). On all subscales females scored higher than males.

SCORING The MFS is easily scored by summing item scores on the subscale items. Higher scores indicate greater fears on each dimension.

RELIABILITY The MFS has very good to excellent internal consistency, with alphas that range from .84 on examinations and symptoms to .93 on blood. No data on stability were provided.

VALIDITY The MFS has very good concurrent and predictive validity. The MFS is significantly correlated with other related fear scales such as the Injection Phobia Scale. The MFS also predicts a history of BII-related fainting at injections or blood draws and correlates with avoidance of medical treatment and of blood donation.

PRIMARY REFERENCE Kleinknecht, R. A. et al. (1999). The medical fear survey: Psychometric properties (in press); Kleinknecht, R. A. et al. (1996). Factorial dimensions and correlates of blood, injury, injection and related medical fears: Cross validation of the Medical Fear Survey, *Behaviour Research and Therapy*, 34, 323–331.

AVAILABILITY Dr. Ronald A. Kleinknecht, Professor and Chair, Department of Psychology, Western Washington University, Bellingham, WA 98225-9089. Reprinted with permission of the author. Email: Ronald.kleinknecht@wwu.edu.

The following situations are known to cause some people to experience fear and apprehension. Please use the following scale to evaluate each situation and place a mark (X) in the space corresponding to how much fear or tension you would experience in the listed situation.

$$0 = \text{No fear or tension at all}$$
$$1 = \text{Mild fear}$$
$$2 = \text{Considerable fear}$$
$$3 = \text{Intense fear}$$
$$4 = \text{Terror}$$

How much fear or discomfort would you experience from:

	0	1	2	3	4
1. Handling a hypodermic needle	—	—	—	—	—
2. Cutting with a hunting knife	—	—	—	—	—
3. Operating a power saw	—	—	—	—	—
4. Seeing a nurse for an illness	—	—	—	—	—
5. Seeing a small vial of your own blood	—	—	—	—	—
6. Receiving an anesthetic injection in the mouth	—	—	—	—	—
7. Observing someone chop with an ax	—	—	—	—	—
8. Feeling like you will faint	—	—	—	—	—
9. Seeing a small test tube of animal blood	—	—	—	—	—
10. Seeing a large beaker of animal blood	—	—	—	—	—
11. Seeing a preserved brain in a jar	—	—	—	—	—
12. Seeing a bleeding wound to a person's arm	—	—	—	—	—
13. Feeling pains in your chest	—	—	—	—	—
14. Observing a surgical amputation	—	—	—	—	—
15. Observing someone cut with a butcher knife	—	—	—	—	—
16. Receiving a hypodermic injection in the arm	—	—	—	—	—
17. Having a severe headache	—	—	—	—	—
18. Seeing a mutilated body on TV	—	—	—	—	—
19. Seeing a small bottle of human blood on TV	—	—	—	—	—
20. Having blood drawn from your arm	—	—	—	—	—
21. Observing someone operate a power saw	—	—	—	—	—
22. Feeling dizzy	—	—	—	—	—
23. Seeing a photo of a large blood vein	—	—	—	—	—
24. Observing someone getting their finger stitched	—	—	—	—	—
25. Seeing a large bottle of your own blood	—	—	—	—	—
26. Handling a butcher knife	—	—	—	—	—
27. Having a blood sample drawn from your finger tip	—	—	—	—	—
28. Going to a doctor for an illness	—	—	—	—	—
29. Observing someone operate a meat cutter	—	—	—	—	—
30. Seeing a dead person, unknown to you	—	—	—	—	—
31. Seeing blood being drawn from someone's arm	—	—	—	—	—
32. Handling an open pocket knife	—	—	—	—	—
33. Observing blood pulse through a vein	—	—	—	—	—

	0	1	2	3	4
34. Seeing someone receiving an injection in the arm	—	—	—	—	—
35. Seeing a large bottle of human blood on TV	—	—	—	—	—
36. Seeing a bleeding wound to a person's eye	—	—	—	—	—
37. Feeling your heart race for no obvious reason	—	—	—	—	—
38. Seeing the mutilated body of a dog that had been run over by a car	—	—	—	—	—
39. Receiving a diagnosis from a doctor	—	—	—	—	—
40. Seeing a large bottle of human blood	—	—	—	—	—
41. Observing an open heart surgery operation	—	—	—	—	—
42. Chopping wood with an ax	—	—	—	—	—
43. Feeling odd tingling in your arm	—	—	—	—	—
44. Operating a meat slicer	—	—	—	—	—
45. Seeing someone receiving an injection in the mouth	—	—	—	—	—
46. Seeing photos of wounded soldiers from war	—	—	—	—	—
47. Seeing someone handling a hypodermic needle	—	—	—	—	—
48. Feeling nauseated	—	—	—	—	—
49. Seeing a small vial of human blood	—	—	—	—	—
50. Seeing the remains of bodies following an airline crash	—	—	—	—	—

Menstrual Symptom Questionnaire (MSQ)

PURPOSE To measure spasmodic and congestive menstrual pain.

AUTHOR Margaret Chesney

DESCRIPTION This 25-item instrument is designed to measure two types of menstrual pain: spasmodic, which begins on the first day of menstruation and is experienced as spasms, and congestive, which occurs during the premenstrual cycle and is experienced as heaviness or dull aching pains in abdomen, breasts, and ankles. The MSQ supports the theory that there are two types of dysmenorrhea. The instrument is very useful in classifying types of menstrual pain and selecting appropriate interventions. Since these two types of menstrual pain occur separately, once the client's pain is classified, the half of the items that assess the particular type of dysmenorrhea should be used.

NORMS The MSQ was developed on a sample of 56 undergraduate college students who described themselves as having menstrual discomfort. Normative data are not presented.

SCORING On the first 24 items respondents are asked to indicate the degree to which they experience the symptom by selecting one of the five alternatives. Spasmodic items (2, 4, 6, 7, 8, 10, 12, 14, 15, 18, 21, 24) are scored from 1 to 5 for each alternative as indicated on the instrument. Congestive items (1, 3, 5, 9, 11, 13, 16, 17, 19, 20, 22, 23) are reverse-scored. Item 25 is scored by assigning 5 points if the respondent checked Type 1 and 1 point if she checked Type 2. Total scores are the sum of all 25 items. Higher MSQ scores reflect spasmodic menstrual pain, while lower scores reflect congestive menstrual pain. Scores range from 29 to 125 with 77 as a mid-point between the two types of pain. Scores closer to 77 indicate an absence of either type of menstrual pain.

RELIABILITY Test-retest correlations provide the primary support for reliability. Over a two-week period, items 1 through 24 had a test-retest correlation of .78. The test-retest correlation for item 25 was .93. Total MSQ scores correlated .87 for this same period, indicating that the instrument is stable. No internal consistency data were reported.

VALIDITY The MSQ was developed from a pool of 51 items. Based on factor analysis, items were included on the MSQ if they had factor loadings of .35 or greater. Twelve items were related to spasmodic pain and 12 were related to congestive pain. Scores on the forced-choice item, number 25, correlated .49 with spasmodic pain scores and −.39 with congestive pain scores, suggesting moderate concurrent validity.

PRIMARY REFERENCE Chesney, M. A. and Tasto, D. L. (1975). The development of the Menstrual Symptom Questionnaire, *Behaviour Research and Therapy*, 13, 237–244. Instrument reproduced with permission of Margaret Chesney.

AVAILABILITY May be copied from this volume.

For each of the 24 items below please indicate how often you have had the experience, using the following scale. Please record your answers in the space to the left of the items.

1 = Never
2 = Rarely
3 = Sometimes
4 = Often
5 = Always

___ 1. I feel irritable, easily agitated, and am impatient a few days *before* my period.
___ 2. I have cramps that *begin* on the first day of my period.
___ 3. I feel depressed for several days *before* my period.
___ 4. I have abdominal pain or discomfort which begins one day *before* my period.
___ 5. For several days *before* my period I feel exhausted, lethargic, or tired.
___ 6. I only know that my period is coming by looking at the calendar.
___ 7. I take a prescription drug for the pain *during* my period.
___ 8. I feel weak and dizzy *during* my period.
___ 9. I feel tense and nervous *before* my period.
___ 10. I have diarrhea *during* my period.
___ 11. I have backaches several days *before* my period.
___ 12. I take aspirin for the pain *during* my period.
___ 13. My breasts feel tender and sore a few days *before* my period.
___ 14. My lower back, abdomen, and the inner sides of my thighs *begin* to hurt or be tender on the first day of my period.
___ 15. *During* the first day or so of my period, I feel like curling up in bed, using a hot water bottle on my abdomen, or taking a hot bath.
___ 16. I gain weight *before* my period.
___ 17. I am constipated *during* my period.
___ 18. *Beginning* on the first day of my period, I have pains which may diminish or disappear for several minutes and then reappear.
___ 19. The pain I have with my period is not intense, but a continuous dull aching.
___ 20. I have abdominal discomfort for more than one day *before* my period.
___ 21. I have backaches which *begin* the same day as my period.
___ 22. My abdominal area feels bloated for a few days *before* my period.
___ 23. I feel nauseous *during* the first day or so of my period.
___ 24. I have headaches for a few days *before* my period.

For the final question please read each of the two descriptions and indicate the type most closely experienced by you.

25. TYPE 1 The pain begins on the first day of menstruation, often coming within an hour of the first signs of menstruation. The pain is most severe the first day and may or may not continue on subsequent days. Felt as spasms, the pain may lessen or subside for awhile and then reappear. A few women find this pain so severe as to cause vomiting, fainting or dizziness; some others report that they are most comfortable in bed or taking a hot bath. This pain is limited to the lower abdomen, back and inner sides of the thighs.

TYPE 2 There is advanced warning of the onset of menstruation during which the woman feels an increasing heaviness, and a dull aching pain in the lower abdomen. This pain is sometimes accompanied by nausea, lack of appetite, and constipation. Headaches, backaches, and breast pain are also characteristic of this type of menstrual discomfort.

The type that most closely fits my experience is TYPE ____

Michigan Alcoholism Screening Test (MAST)

PURPOSE To detect alcoholism.

AUTHOR Melvin L. Selzer

DESCRIPTION The MAST is a 24-item instrument designed to detect alcoholism. The items on the MAST were selected on the basis of review of several other approaches to investigating alcohol abuse. A few items were developed to be sufficiently neutral that persons reluctant to see themselves as problem drinkers may reveal their alcoholic symptoms. The MAST was developed with the understanding that lack of candor of respondents may be a problem, and was validated in a way that attempted to minimize such failures. Although the MAST was originally designed to be administered orally by professionals and nonprofessionals, it may also be completed by the respondent, although it is not known what effect this may have on its validity. The MAST has been found to be superior as a screening device to a search of records from medical, legal, and social agencies. Where the MAST is used for screening purposes, clinical confirmation is suggested. A short form of 13 items also is available (items 1, 3, 5, 6, 7, 8, 10, 13, 15, 19, 20, 23, and 24).

NORMS The MAST was administered to several groups: 103 controls, 116 hospitalized alcoholics, 99 people arrested for drunk driving, 110 people arrested for being drunk and disorderly, and 98 people under review for revocation of their driver's licenses because of excessive accidents and moving violations. The groups were largely white and male with mean ages that ranged from 25 to 44 years. Scores on the MAST for all five groups are available in the primary references.

SCORING Although the scoring of the MAST appears complicated, it is fairly easy once mastered. Each item on the MAST is assigned a weight of 0 to 5, with 5 considered diagnostic of alcoholism. Weights for the items are listed in the left-hand column of the instrument. Negative responses to items 1, 4, 6, and 7 are considered alcoholic responses, and positive responses to the other items are considered alcoholic responses. An overall score of 3 points or less is considered to indicate nonalcoholism, 4 points is suggestive of alcoholism, and 5 points or more indicates alcoholism.

RELIABILITY The long and short forms of the MAST have excellent internal consistencies, with alphas of .95 and .93, respectively. No data on stability were reported.

VALIDITY The MAST has excellent known-groups validity, being able to classify most respondents as alcoholic or nonalcoholic; only 15 out of 526 people originally classified as nonalcoholic subsequently were found to be alcoholic. In fact, even when respondents were instructed in advance to lie about their drinking problems, the MAST correctly identified 92% of 99 hospitalized alcoholics as having severe alcoholic problems. Low correlations with the Deny-Bad subscale of the Crowne-Marlowe Social Desirability Scale suggest the effect of denial on MAST scores is weak.

PRIMARY REFERENCES Selzer, M. L. (1971). The Michigan Alcoholism Screening Test: The quest for a new diagnostic instrument, *American Journal of Psychiatry*, 127, 89–94. Selzer, M. L., Vinokur, A., and van Rooijen, L. (1975). A self-administered Short Michigan Alcoholism Screening Test, *Journal of Studies on Alcohol*, 36, 117–126. Instrument reproduced with permission of *American Journal of Psychiatry*.

AVAILABILITY May be copied from this volume.

Please circle either Yes or No for each item as it applies to you.

Yes   No   (2)   1. Do you feel you are a normal drinker?

Yes   No   (2)   2. Have you ever awakened the morning after some drinking the night before and found that you could not remember a part of the evening before?

Yes   No   (1)   3. Does your wife, husband, a parent, or other near relative ever worry or complain about your drinking?

Yes   No   (2)   4. Can you stop drinking without a struggle after one or two drinks?

Yes   No   (1)   5. Do you ever feel guilty about your drinking?

Yes   No   (2)   6. Do friends or relatives think you are a normal drinker?

Yes   No   (2)   7. Are you able to stop drinking when you want to?

Yes   No   (5)   8. Have you ever attended a meeting of Alcoholics Anonymous (AA)?

Yes   No   (1)   9. Have you ever gotten into physical fights when drinking?

Yes   No   (2)   10. Has drinking ever created problems between you and your wife, husband, a parent, or other near relative?

Yes   No   (2)   11. Has your wife, husband, a parent, or other near relative ever gone to anyone for help about your drinking?

Yes   No   (2)   12. Have you ever lost friends or girlfriends/boyfriends because of your drinking?

Yes   No   (2)   13. Have you ever gotten into trouble at work because of drinking?

Yes   No   (2)   14. Have you ever lost a job because of drinking?

Yes   No   (2)   15. Have you ever neglected your obligations, your family, or your work for two or more days in a row because you were drinking?

Yes   No   (1)   16. Do you drink before noon fairly often?

Yes   No   (2)   17. Have you ever been told you have liver trouble? Cirrhosis?

Yes   No   (5)   18. After heavy drinking, have you ever had delirium tremens (DTs) or severe shaking, or heard voices, or seen things that weren't really there?

Yes   No   (5)   19. Have you ever gone to anyone for help about your drinking?

Yes   No   (5)   20. Have you ever been in a hospital because of drinking?

Yes   No   (2)   21. Have you ever been a patient in a psychiatric hospital or on a psychiatric ward of a general hospital where drinking was part of the problem that resulted in hospitalization?

Yes   No   (2)   22. Have you ever been seen at a psychiatric or mental health clinic, or gone to a doctor, social worker, or clergyman for help with any emotional problem where drinking was part of the problem?

Yes   No   (2)   23. Have you ever been arrested for drunken driving while intoxicated or driving under the influence of alcoholic beverages?

Yes   No   (2)   24. Have you ever been arrested, even for a few hours, because of other drunken behavior?

Miller Social Intimacy Scale (MSIS)

PURPOSE To measure the level of social intimacy.

AUTHORS Rickey S. Miller and Herbert M. Lefcourt

DESCRIPTION The MSIS is a 17-item instrument (items 4–20) designed to measure closeness with others. It is based on the findings of several studies that show intimacy to be an important predictor of healthy psychological and physical functioning, especially in regard to marriage, relationships with others, bereavement, and response to stress. The initial item pool of 30 was generated by intensive interviews with university undergraduates; subsequent tests produced the current 17 items, 6 of which are frequency items and 11 of which measure intensity. The MSIS is structured to permit an assessment of intimacy in the context of friendship or marriage.

NORMS The 252 respondents who participated in the developmental research on the MSIS included 72 male and 116 female unmarried undergraduate students (mean age 21.3 years), 17 ($n = 34$) married couples (mean age 24.3) who were also students, and a married clinic sample of 15 couples ($n = 30$) seeking conjoint marital therapy (mean age 36.3 years). Mean scores for the groups were: unmarried males 134.9, unmarried females 139.3, married males 152.5, married females 156.2, clinic males 124.5, and clinic females 133.8.

SCORING The original instrument, scored on a 10-point scale, has been revised to the 5-point scale reproduced here. Items 1, 2, 3, 21, and 22 are not scored. Items 5 and 17 are reverse-scored, then the individual items are summed (A = 1, E = 5) to produce an overall score for the MSIS, with higher scores indicating greater amounts of social intimacy.

RELIABILITY The MSIS has excellent internal consistency; with alphas in two samples of .86 and .91. The MSIS is also extremely stable, with a two-month test-retest correlation of .96 and .84 over a one-month interval.

VALIDITY The MSIS has good known-groups validity, significantly distinguishing between couples seeking marital therapy and those not seeking it, and between married and unmarried students. It also has established construct validity by correlating or not correlating in predicted directions with several other measures such as the UCLA Loneliness Scale, the Interpersonal Relationship Scale, the Tennessee Self-Concept Scale, and the Personality Research Form. Responses on the MSIS are not affected by social desirability response set.

PRIMARY REFERENCE Miller, R. S. and Lefcourt, H. M. (1982). The assessment of social intimacy, *Journal of Personality Assessment*, 46, 514–518. Instrument reproduced with permission of Rickey S. Miller and Herbert M. Lefcourt.

AVAILABILITY Dr. Herbert M. Lefcourt, ww.peckyou/_lefcourt or linkin.com/pub/herbert-lefcourt/1b/409/892.

A number of phrases are listed below that describe the kind of relationships people have with others. Indicate, by circling the appropriate letters in the answer field, how you would describe your current relationship with your closest friend. This friend can be of either sex and should be someone whom you consider to be your closest friend at this time. While it is not necessary to specify the name of this friend, please indicate his/her sex in question 1.

Remember that you are to indicate the kind of relationship you have *now* with your *closest friend*.

1. Sex of your closest friend: M _____   F _____

2. Your marital status: single _____   married _____   common-law _____
                              separated or divorced _____   widowed _____

3. Is the friend you describe your spouse?   Yes _____   No _____

	Very rarely		Some of the time		Almost always
4. When you have leisure time how often do you choose to spend it with him/her alone?	A	B	C	D	E
5. How often do you keep very personal information to yourself and do not share it with him/her?	A	B	C	D	E
6. How often do you show him/her affection?	A	B	C	D	E
7. How often do you confide very personal information to him/her?	A	B	C	D	E
8. How often are you able to understand his/her feelings?	A	B	C	D	E
9. How often do you feel close to him/her?	A	B	C	D	E

	Not much		A little		A great deal
10. How much do you like to spend time alone with him/her?	A	B	C	D	E
11. How much do you feel like being encouraging and supportive to him/her when he/she is unhappy?	A	B	C	D	E
12. How close do you feel to him/her most of the time?	A	B	C	D	E
13. How important is it to you to listen to his/her personal disclosures?	A	B	C	D	E
14. How satisfying is your relationship with him/her?	A	B	C	D	E

		Not much		A little		A great deal
15. How affectionate do you feel towards him/her?		A	B	C	D	E
16. How important is it to you that he/she understand your feelings?		A	B	C	D	E
17. How much damage is caused by a typical disagreement in your relationship with him/her?		A	B	C	D	E
18. How important is it to you that he/she be encouraging and supportive to you when you are unhappy?		A	B	C	D	E
19. How important is it to you that he/she show you affection?		A	B	C	D	E
20. How important is your relationship with him/her in your life?		A	B	C	D	E

21. You have just described the relationship you have now with your closest friend. We are interested in knowing *how long* this person has been your closest friend. Please check the appropriate category:

    less than a month _____ 1–4 months _____ 5–8 months _____
    9–12 months _____ over a year _____

22. Recall your *previous* closest friend. Are you less close _____ just as close _____ or closer _____ with the current friend you described on this scale?

Milwaukee Psychotherapy Expectations Questionnaire (MPEQ)

PURPOSE To measure the process and outcome expectations of therapy.

AUTHOR Melissa Norberg, Chad Wetterneck and Daniel Sass

DESCRIPTION The MPEQ is a 13-item instrument designed to measure two domains of a client's expectation of being in psychotherapy, Process Expectation (PE) and Outcome Expectation (OE). PE refers to what the client believes about what the clinician and client will do and what will happen in treatment. OE refers to the prognostic expectations for improvement as a result of psychotherapy. The importance of assessing the clients, expectations is supported by the fact that psychotherapy outcomes are enhanced by 15% when the expectations are considered at intake or the initial session of therapy. Expectation also impacts the strength of the therapeutic alliance and overall treatment effectiveness. The MPEQ is particularly useful in structuring realistic roles of the patient and the clinician and to identify clients likely to drop out of treatment because of unrealistic expectations. The MPEW has considerable support for its consistency and accuracy having been developed on 3 nonclinical samples and one clinical sample. The MPEQ is written at an 8th grade reading level and is therefore useful with adolescents and adults.

NORMS From three samples of undergraduates the mean PE and (standard deviations) for men were 7.51 (1.52), 7 .75 (1.37), 7.44 (1.53). The OE had scores of 6.47 (2.04), 6.81 (1.91) and 6.33 (1.83) for undergraduate males. Males from the clinical sample have means of 7.97 (.91) on the PE and 7.17 (1.59) on the OE. For females from the three samples the PE mean scores were 7.94 (1.31), 7.97 (1.23), 7.98 (1.50). OE means were 7.23 (1.64), 7.34 (1.45), 7.23 (1.87). Females from the clinical sample had means of 8.4 (1.11) on the PE and 7.46 (1.67) on the OE.

SCORING PE scores are the sum of items 1 through 8 plus 13, divided by 9. The OE scores are the sum of items 9,10,11 and 12 divided by 4. Both scales have scores from 0 to 10. Total scores are the sum of the PE and OE scales scores; to keep with the same matrix as the PE and OE, which is recommended, it is necessary to divide by 2.

RELIABILITY The MPEQ has very good internal consistency with alpha coefficients ranging from .86 to .91 from the non-clinical samples and .83 for the clinical sample. The test-retest reliability was .83 for the PE and .76 for OE which indicates the scales are stable in the short term.

VALIDITY The MPEQ has a wide range of support for its validity. The instrument was assessed for face validity using a panel of experts rating the original item pool. The 2-dimension structure of the MPEQ was supported with exploratory and confirmatory factor analyses. Concurrent validity strong with as scores on the MPEQ correlated with self-efficacy, other measures of expectations, and scores on an outcomes questionnaire. The PE but not the OE, has predictive validity with scores correlating with continuing or terminating treatment.

PRIMARY REFERENCE Norberg, M M ., Wetterneck, C. T. and Sass, D A. (2011). Development and psychometric evaluation of the Milwaukee Psychotherapy Expectations Questionnaire. *Journal of Clinical Psychology*, 67, 574–590.

AVAILABILITY Melissa Norberg, Ph.D., National Cannabis Prevention and Information Centre, University of New South Wales, PO Box684, Randwick, NSW, 2031, Australia. Email: m_norberg@unsw.

Below is a list of statements describing expectations about therapy that you may have. These statements cover expectations regarding your own behavior in therapy, your future therapist, and the therapy setting. Some of these expectations you may not have considered previously; however, we would like for you to think about them now. Read each statement carefully and circle the number that indicates the strength with which you find yourself expecting what is described in the statement.

	Not at all			Somewhat					Very much so	
1. I expect my therapist will provide support	0	1 2 3		4 5	6	7 8			9	10
2. My therapist will provide me feedback	0	1 2 3		4 5	6	7 8			9	10
3. I will be able to express my true thoughts and feelings	0	1 2 3		4 5	6	7 8			9	10
4. I will feel comfortable with my therapist	0	1 2 3		4 5	6	7 8			9	10
5. My therapist will be sincere	0	1 2 3		4 5	6	7 8			9	10
6. My therapist will be interested in what I have to say	0	1 2 3		4 5	6	7 8			9	10
7. My therapist will be sympathetic	0	1 2 3		4 5	6	7 8			9	10
8. I expect that I will come to every appointment	0	1 2 3		4 5	6	7 8			9	10
9. Therapy will provide me with an increased level of self-respect	0	1 2 3		4 5	6	7 8			9	10
10. After therapy, I will have the strength needed to avoid feelings of distress in the future	0	1 2 3		4 5	6	7 8			9	10
11. I anticipate being a better person as a result of therapy	0	1 2 3		4 5	6	7 8			9	10
12. After therapy, I will be a much more optimistic person	0	1 2 3		4 5	6	7 8			9	10
13. I expect that I will tell my therapist if I have concerns about therapy	0	1 2 3		4 5	6	7 8			9	10

Mississippi Scale (MS)

PURPOSE To assess combat-related posttraumatic stress disorder.

AUTHORS Terrance Keane, J. M. Caddell, and K. L. Taylor

DESCRIPTION The MS is a 35-item instrument designed to measure posttraumatic stress disorder (PTSD) resulting from combat. The MS covers the full domain of PTSD symptoms and various associated features as delineated in the *DSM-III-R*. Factor analysis suggests the MS assesses six aspects of combat-related PTSD: intrusive memories and depression, problems with interpersonal adjustment, lability of affect and memory, ruminative features, problems sleeping, and other interpersonal problems. The MS is also available in forms appropriate for spouses and civilians.

NORMS Means and standard deviations are available from three samples of Vietnam veterans: combat veterans with PTSD ($n=30$), noncombat psychiatric patients ($n=30$), and well-adjusted veterans ($n=32$). The means (and standard deviations) are 130 (18), 86 (26), and 76 (18) for the respective three samples.

SCORING Items 2, 6, 11, 17, 19, 22, 24, 27, 30, and 34 are reverse-scored. Total scores are the sum of all item scores. Scores range from 35 to 175 with higher scores reflecting higher PTSD symptoms.

RELIABILITY The MS has excellent reliability. The alpha coefficient of internal consistency is .94 and the average item-to-total correlation is .58. Test-retest reliability over a one-week period is .97.

VALIDITY The MS has some evidence of concurrent validity. Scores on the MS correlated .25 with combat exposure, which may seem low but may suggest there is a threshold of exposure sufficient to become the antecedent of PTSD. From this perspective, a correlation of this magnitude is acceptable. The MS has excellent evidence of known-groups validity, with scores differentiating PTSD patients from psychiatric patients and a well-adjusted sample; MS scores correctly classified 90% of the subjects. There was agreement between the MS and the structured clinical interview of the *DSM-III-R*, with a coefficient of agreement (kappa) of .75. The concordance rate between the MS and diagnosis in the community was .53, indicating a greater likelihood of a false positive score with the MS (i.e., failing to identify a patient who indeed is suffering from PTSD).

PRIMARY REFERENCE Keane, T. M., Caddell, J. M., and Taylor K. L. (1988) Mississippi Scale for combat-related posttraumatic stress disorder: Three studies in reliability and validity, *Journal of Consulting and Clinical Psychology*, 56, 85–90. Instrument reproduced with permission of Terrance Keane.

AVAILABILITY Terrance Keane, Ph.D., Boston University, Dpt of Behavioral neuroscience, Boston, MA 02118. Email: tmkeane@bu.edu.

Please circle the number that best describes how you feel about each statement.

1. Before I entered the military, I had more close friends than I have now.

1	2	3	4	5
Not at all true	Slightly true	Somewhat true	Very true	Extremely true

2. I do not feel guilt over things that I did in the military.

1	2	3	4	5
Never true	Rarely true	Sometimes true	Usually true	Always true

3. If someone pushes me too far, I am likely to become violent.

1	2	3	4	5
Very unlikely	Unlikely	Somewhat unlikely	Very likely	Extremely likely

4. If something happens that reminds me of the military, I become very distressed and upset.

1	2	3	4	5
Never	Rarely	Sometimes	Frequently	Very frequently

5. The people who know me best are afraid of me.

1	2	3	4	5
Never true	Rarely true	Sometimes true	Usually true	Always true

6. I am able to get emotionally close to others.

1	2	3	4	5
Never	Rarely	Sometimes	Frequently	Very frequently

7. I have nightmares over experiences in the military that really happened.

1	2	3	4	5
Never	Rarely	Sometimes	Frequently	Very frequently

8. When I think of some of the things I did in the military, I wish I were dead.

1	2	3	4	5
Never true	Rarely true	Sometimes true	Usually true	Always true

9. It seems as if I have no feelings.

1	2	3	4	5
Not at all true	Slightly true	Somewhat true	Very true	Extremely true

10. Lately, I have felt like killing myself.

1	2	3	4	5
Not at all true	Slightly true	Somewhat true	Very true	Extremely true

11. I fall asleep, stay asleep, and awaken only when the alarm goes off.

1	2	3	4	5
Never	Rarely	Sometimes	Frequently	Very frequently

12. I wonder why I am still alive when others died in the military.

1	2	3	4	5
Never	Rarely	Sometimes	Frequently	Very frequently

13. Being in certain situations makes me feel as though I am back in the military.

1	2	3	4	5
Never	Rarely	Sometimes	Frequently	Very frequently

14. My dreams at night are so real that I waken in a cold sweat and force myself to stay awake.

1	2	3	4	5
Never	Rarely	Sometimes	Frequently	Very frequently

15. I feel like I cannot go on.

1	2	3	4	5
Not at all true	Slightly true	Somewhat true	Very true	Extremely true

16. I do not laugh or cry at the same things other people do.

1	2	3	4	5
Not at all true	Slightly true	Somewhat true	Very true	Extremely true

17. I still enjoy doing many things that I used to enjoy.

1	2	3	4	5
Never true	Rarely true	Sometimes true	Usually true	Always true

18. Daydreams are very real and frightening.

1	2	3	4	5
Never true	Rarely true	Sometimes true	Usually true	Always true

19. I have found it easy to keep a job since my separation from the military.

1	2	3	4	5
Not at all true	Slightly true	Somewhat true	Very true	Extremely true

20. I have trouble concentrating on tasks.

1	2	3	4	5
Never true	Rarely true	Sometimes true	Usually true	Always true

21. I have cried for no good reason.

1	2	3	4	5
Never	Rarely	Sometimes	Frequently	Very frequently

22. I enjoy the company of others.

1	2	3	4	5
Never	Rarely	Sometimes	Frequently	Very frequently

23. I am frightened by my urges.

1	2	3	4	5
Never	Rarely	Sometimes	Frequently	Very frequently

24. I fall asleep easily at night.

1	2	3	4	5
Never	Rarely	Sometimes	Frequently	Very frequently

25. Unexpected noises make me jump.

1	2	3	4	5
Never	Rarely	Sometimes	Frequently	Very frequently

26. No one understands how I feel, not even my family.

1	2	3	4	5
Not at all true	Slightly true	Somewhat true	Very true	Extremely true

27. I am an easy-going, even-tempered person.

1	2	3	4	5
Never	Rarely	Sometimes	Frequently	Very frequently

28. I feel there are certain things that I did in the military that I can never tell anyone, because no one would ever understand.

1	2	3	4	5
Not at all true	Slightly true	Somewhat true	Very true	Extremely true

29. There have been times when I used alcohol (or other drugs) to help me sleep or to make me forget about things that happened while I was in the service.

1	2	3	4	5
Never	Rarely	Sometimes	Frequently	Very frequently

30. I feel comfortable when I am in a crowd.

1	2	3	4	5
Never	Rarely	Sometimes	Frequently	Very frequently

31. I lose my cool and explode over minor everyday things.

1	2	3	4	5
Never	Rarely	Sometimes	Frequently	Very frequently

32. I am afraid to go to sleep at night.

1	2	3	4	5
Never	Rarely	Sometimes	Frequently	Very frequently

33. I try to stay away from anything that will remind me of things which happened while I was in the military.

1	2	3	4	5
Never	Rarely	Sometimes	Frequently	Very frequently

34. My memory is as good as it ever was.

1	2	3	4	5
Not at all true	Slightly true	Somewhat true	Very true	Extremely true

35. I have a hard time expressing my feelings, even to the people I care about.

1	2	3	4	5
Not at all true	Slightly true	Somewhat true	Very true	Extremely true

Mobility Inventory for Agoraphobia (MI)

PURPOSE To measure severity of agoraphobic avoidance behavior.

AUTHORS Dianne L. Chambless, G. Craig Caputo, Susan E. Jasin, Edward Gracely, and Christine Williams

DESCRIPTION The MI is a 27-item instrument designed to measure agoraphobic avoidance behavior and frequency of panic attacks. Twenty-six of the items measure avoidance, with each item rated for avoidance both when the client is alone and when accompanied. The final item gives a definition of panic and asks the respondent to report the number of panic experiences during the previous week. The MI was developed by using items from the Fear Survey Schedule, items obtained in interviews with agoraphobic clients, and from observations of avoidance behavior and panic attacks in agoraphobic clients. The MI provides clinically useful information both in total score form as well as in interpretation of scores on individual items.

NORMS Two samples were used in development of the MI. The first consistent of 159 clients applying for treatment at a clinic specializing in agoraphobia and anxiety (88% female, mean age 34.6) and 23 nonagoraphobic control with similar demographic characteristics. The second sample involved 83 agoraphobic clients, including significantly more males. Norms for all of these groups on each item are available in the primary reference. When averaged across all situations, the mean score for agoraphobics for avoidance when accompanied ranges from 2.41 to 2.64 and the mean score for avoidance when alone ranges from 3.30 to 3.35

SCORING Each item on the MI is scored on a 1 to 5 basis and each item can be interpreted independently. The MI does not use a mean score averaged across all situations for avoidance when accompanied by another and avoidance when alone. To derive these scores simply add the rating for the "when accompanied" column and divide by the number of items answered. Do the same procedures for the items in the "when alone" column.

RELIABILITY The MI has excellent internal consistency, with alphas that range from .91 to .97. The MI also has excellent stability, with overall test-retest reliabilities over 31 days of .89 and .90 for avoidance when alone and .75 and .86 for avoidance when accompanied.

VALIDITY The MI has very good concurrent validity, correlating significantly with the agoraphobic factor of the Fear Questionnaire, the Beck Depression Inventory, and the Trait form of the State-Trait Anxiety Inventory. The MI also has good known-groups validity, significantly distinguishing between agoraphobic and non-clinical and social phobic respondents. Finally, the MI also has been found in two studies to be sensitive to changes following treatment for agoraphobia.

PRIMARY REFERENCE Chambless, D. L., Caputo, G. C., Jasin, S. E., Gracely, E. J., and Williams, C. (1985). The Mobility Inventory for Agoraphobia, *Behavioral Research and Therapy*, 23, 35–44. Instrument reproduced with permission of Pergamon Press.

AVAILABILITY May be copied from this volume.

Please indicate the degree to which you avoid the following places or situations because of discomfort or anxiety. Rate your amount of avoidance when you are with a trusted companion and when you are alone. Do this by using the following scale.

1 = Never avoid
2 = Rarely avoid
3 = Avoid about half the time
4 = Avoid most of the time
5 = Always avoid

(You may use numbers halfway between those listed when you think it is appropriate. For example, 3-1/2 or 4-1/2.)

Write your score in the blanks for each situation or place under both conditions: when accompanied, and when alone. Leave blank those situations that do not apply to you.

Places	When accompanied	When alone
Theaters	—	—
Supermarkets	—	—
Classrooms	—	—
Department stores	—	—
Restaurants	—	—
Museums	—	—
Elevators	—	—
Auditoriums or stadiums	—	—
Parking garages	—	—
High places	—	—
Tell how high _____	—	—
Enclosed spaces (e.g., tunnels)	—	—
Open spaces	—	—
Outside (e.g., fields, wide streets, courtyards)	—	—
Inside (e.g., large rooms, lobbies)	—	—
Riding in:		
Buses	—	—
Trains	—	—
Subways	—	—
Airplanes	—	—
Boats	—	—
Driving or riding in car:		
At any time	—	—
On expressways	—	—
Situations:		
Standing in lines	—	—
Crossing bridges	—	—
Parties or social gatherings	—	—
Walking on the street	—	—

Places	When accompanied	When alone
Staying at home alone	NA	—
Being far way from home	—	—
Other (specify)	—	—

We define a *panic attack* as:

(1) a high level of anxiety accompanied by
(2) strong body reactions (heart palpitations, sweating, muscle tremors, dizziness, nausea) with
(3) the temporary loss of the ability to plan, think, or reason and
(4) the intense desire to escape or flee the situation. (Note, this is different from high anxiety or fear alone.)

Please indicate the total number of panic attacks you have had in the last 7 days. _____

Mood Disorder Questionnaire (MDQ)

PURPOSE To measure bipolar spectrum disorder.

AUTHORS Robert M. A. Hirschfield et al.

DESCRIPTION The MDQ is a 13-item questionnaire (all contained in item 1 on the questionnaire) consisting of a series of simple "yes/no" questions that is designed to measure the presence or absence of bipolar disorder, both among individuals and in the general population. The 13 items were derived from the DSM-IV and clinical experience. This is an extremely useful instrument because a cut-off score of seven "yes" responses has been established. Plus, in answer to other questions on the MDQ, the respondent also must indicate that several of the symptoms co-occurred and that they caused at least moderate psychological impairment. The MDQ can be administered by phone, by mail or in person.

NORMS A very large number of respondents were used to establish norms, including a 2001 national prevalence study of 127,800 people aged 18 and over. The subjects were fairly even in sex distribution, 89% were white, 5% were African-American, and 1% or less were Asian/Pacific Islander or Native American; 5% were other ethnicities or unknown. Age of the subjects ranged from 18 to over 65 (17%). Using a random sample of 3,059 of the large sample, with a return rate of 80%, a positive MDQ was validated as endorsement of seven or more symptoms, co-occurrence of two or more symptoms and moderate or severe symptom-related impairment on the measures that are part of the MDQ.

SCORING The 13 items are very easily scored by simply summing the "yes" scores to see if they total seven or more.

RELIABILITY The MDQ has excellent internal consistency with an alpha of .90. Test-retest data were not reported.

VALIDITY The MDQ has excellent validity demonstrated in several studies. The sensitivity of the MDQ is very good (.73, meaning that 7 out of 10 people with bipolar disorder would be correctly identified), and excellent specificity (.90, meaning that 9 out of 10 people without bipolar disorder would be screened out). The MDQ has excellent discriminant validity, successfully discriminating between people with positive (high) MDQ scores and those with negative MDQ scores on several co-morbid physical and psychiatric symptoms. Finally, the MDQ has excellent concurrent validity, with several demographic subgroups showing correlations between the MDQ and the Sheehan Disability Scale and the Social Adjustment Scale.

PRIMARY REFERENCE Calabrese, J.R. et al. (2003). Impact of bipolar disorder on a U.S community sample. *Journal of Clinical Psychiatry*, 64, 425–432. Instrument reproduced with the permission of Dr. Robert M.A. Hirschfield. Adapted from Hirschfield, R.M., Williams, J.B., Spitzer, R.L., Calabrese, J.R., Flynn, L., Keck, P.E., Lewis, L., McElroy, S.L., Post, R.M., Rapport, D.J., Russell, J.M., Sachs, G.S., Zajecka, J. (2000). The development and validation of a screening instrument for bipolar spectrum disorder: The Mood Disorder Questionnaire, *American Journal of Psychiatry*, 157; 1873–1875.

AVAILABILITY May be copied from this volume.

MDQ

> **Instructions:** This questionnaire is an important part of providing you with the best health care possible. Your answers will help in understanding problems that you may have. Please answer each question as best you can.

1 Has there ever been a period of time when you were not your usual self and . . .

	YES	NO
. . . you felt so good or so hyper that other people thought you were not your normal self or you were so hyper that you got into trouble?	☐	☐
. . . you were so irritable that you shouted at people or started fights or arguments?	☐	☐
. . . you felt much more self-confident than usual?	☐	☐
. . . you got much less sleep than usual and found you didn't really miss it?	☐	☐
. . . you were much more talkative or spoke much faster than usual?	☐	☐
. . . thoughts raced through your head or you couldn't slow your mind down?	☐	☐
. . . you were so easily distracted by things around you that you had trouble concentrating or staying on track?	☐	☐
. . . you had much more energy than usual?	☐	☐
. . . you were much more active or did many more things than usual?	☐	☐
. . . you were much more social or outgoing than usual, for example, you telephoned friends in the middle of the night?	☐	☐
. . . you were much more interested in sex than usual?	☐	☐
. . . you did things that were unusual for you or that other people might have thought were excessive, foolish or risky?	☐	☐
. . . spending money got you or your family into trouble?	☐	☐

2 If you checked YES to more than one of the above, have several of these ever happened during the same period of time? ☐ ☐

3 How much of a problem did any of these cause you—like being unable to work; having family, money or legal troubles; getting into arguments or fights? *Please circle one response only.*

No problem   Minor problem   Moderate problem   Serious problem

4 Have any of your blood relatives (i.e. children, siblings, parents, grandparents, aunts, uncles) had manic-depressive illness or bipolar disorder? ☐ ☐

5 Has a health professional ever told you that you have manic-depressive illness or bipolar disorder? ☐ ☐

Thank you for completing this questionnare. Please return this form to your Doctor.

Mood-Related Pleasant Events Schedule (MRPES)

PURPOSE To measure frequency and enjoyment of pleasant events.

AUTHORS Douglas J. MacPhillamy and Peter M. Lewinsohn

DESCRIPTION The MRPES is a 49-item instrument designed to measure how frequently one engages in pleasant events and how much enjoyment one derives from those events. As part of the 320-item Pleasant Event Schedule (PES), the MRPES contains events that are related to mood. The frequency and enjoyment scores may be used separately or by multiplying the frequency by the enjoyment to create a product score. In addition to these total scores, the MRPES has two useful subscales, the pleasant social interactions subscale (items 12, 14, 15, 42, and 49) and the competence and independence subscale (items 11, 19, 25, 28, 33, 35, and 45). The MRPES is useful in identifying pleasant events that may serve as reinforcement in behavior therapy and as an assessment of change in enjoyment, as would be relevant when working with a person who is depressed.

NORMS Normative data are available for males and females from a sample of 464 normal adults. The mean frequency score for males was 1.31 with a standard deviation of .27. For females, the mean and standard deviation were 1.37 and .25, respectively. For males, total enjoyment scores had a mean and standard deviation of 1.47 and .29, respectively; for females, 1.54 and .26. The mean and standard deviation of the total product score were 2.06 and .63 for males and 2.18 and .59 for females.

SCORING The frequency and enjoyment scores are derived by simply summing the item scores and dividing by the total number of items. Product scores are derived by multiplying the item frequency score by the enjoyment score, summing the results, and dividing by the number of items. Computerized scoring procedures are available from the authors. Frequency and enjoyment scores have a range of 0 to 2 and product scores have a range of 0 to 4. Higher scores reflect more frequent participation in pleasant events and more enjoyment derived from those events.

RELIABILITY Internal consistency information is not available for the MRPES, but is reported for the 320-item PES. This longer version has excellent internal consistency, with alpha coefficients of .96, .98, and .97 for the frequency, enjoyment, and product scores, respectively. Test-retest reliability is available for the MRPES for one-month (.69), two-month (.49), and three-month (.50) periods. The test-retest reliability suggests adequate stability for the MRPES.

VALIDITY Most of the validity data available examine the 320-item PES, which has excellent construct and concurrent validity. The 320-item PES also has known-groups validity, with scores discriminating people who are depressed from those who are not. The MRPES itself seems slightly affected by an irrelevant response set, most likely a "yea-saying" response set. Scoring procedures are available from the authors which help minimize this limitation.

PRIMARY REFERENCE MacPhillamy, D. J. and Lewinsohn, P. M. (1982). The Pleasant Events Schedule: Studies on reliability, validity and scale inter-correlation, *Journal of Consulting and Clinical Psychology*, 50, 363–380. Instrument reproduced with permission of Peter Lewinsohn.

AVAILABILITY Peter M. Lewinsohn, Ph.D., Research Scientist, Oregon Research Institute, 1715 Franklin Blvd., Eugene, OR 97403-1983. Email: pcl@uoregon.edu. Telephone: 541.484.2123.

This schedule is designed to find out about the things you have enjoyed during the past month. The schedule contains a list of events or activities that people sometimes enjoy. You will be asked to go over the list twice, the first time rating each event on how many times it has happened in the past month and the second time rating each event on how pleasant it has been for you. Please rate every event. There are no right or wrong answers.

Below is a list of activities, events, and experiences. HOW OFTEN HAVE THESE EVENTS HAPPENED IN YOUR LIFE IN THE PAST MONTH? Please answer this question by rating each item on the following scale:

0 = This has not happened in the past 30 days.
1 = This has happened *a few times* (1 to 6) in the past 30 days.
2 = This has happened *often* (7 or more) in the past 30 days.

Place your rating in the space to the far left of the item, under the column headed "Frequency." Important: Some items will list *more than one event*; for those items, mark how often you have done *any* of the listed events.

Frequency   Enjoyment

—	—	1. Being in the country
—	—	2. Meeting someone new of the same sex
—	—	3. Planning trips or vacations
—	—	4. Reading stories, novels, poems, or plays
—	—	5. Driving skillfully
—	—	6. Breathing clean air
—	—	7. Saying something clearly
—	—	8. Thinking about something good in the future
—	—	9. Laughing
—	—	10. Being with animals
—	—	11. Having a frank and open conversation
—	—	12. Going to a party
—	—	13. Combing or brushing my hair
—	—	14. Being with friends
—	—	15. Being popular at a gathering
—	—	16. Watching wild animals
—	—	17. Sitting in the sun
—	—	18. Seeing good things happen to my family or friends
—	—	19. Planning or organizing something
—	—	20. Having a lively talk
—	—	21. Having friends come to visit
—	—	22. Wearing clean clothes
—	—	23. Seeing beautiful scenery
—	—	24. Eating good food
—	—	25. Doing a good job
—	—	26. Having spare time
—	—	27. Being noticed as sexually attractive
—	—	28. Learning to do something new
—	—	29. Complimenting or praising someone

Frequency	Enjoyment	
—	—	30. Thinking about people I like
—	—	31. Kissing
—	—	32. Feeling the presence of the Lord in my life
—	—	33. Doing a project in my own way
—	—	34. Having peace and quiet
—	—	35. Being relaxed
—	—	36. Sleeping soundly at night
—	—	37. Petting, necking
—	—	38. Amusing people
—	—	39. Being with someone I love
—	—	40. Having sexual relations with a partner
—	—	41. Watching people
—	—	42. Being with happy people
—	—	43. Smiling at people
—	—	44. Being with my husband or wife
—	—	45. Having people show interest in what I have said
—	—	46. Having coffee, tea, a Coke, etc., with friends
—	—	47. Being complimented or told I have done well
—	—	48. Being told I am loved
—	—	49. Seeing old friends

Now please go over the list once again. This time the question is, HOW PLEASANT, EN-JOYABLE, OR REWARDING WAS EACH EVENT DURING THE PAST MONTH? Please answer this question by rating each event on the following scale:

> 0 = This was *not* pleasant. (Use this rating for events
> that were either neutral or unpleasant.)
> 1 = This event was *somewhat* pleasant. (Use this rating
> for events that were *mildly* or *moderately* pleasant.)
> 2 = This event was *very* pleasant. (Use this rating for events
> that were *strongly or extremely* pleasant.)

Important: If an event has happened to you *more than once* in the past month, try to rate roughly how pleasant it was *on the average*. If an event has *not* happened to you during the past month, then rate it according to how much fun you *think* it would have been. (If you haven't done any of the events in such an item, give it the average rating of the events in that item which you *would like to have done*.)

Place your ratings in the space immediately to the left of each item, under the column headed "Enjoyment." Now go back to the list of events, start with item 1, and go through the entire list rating each event on *roughly how pleasant it was (or would have been) during the past 30 days*. Please make sure that you rate each item.

Mood Survey (MS)

PURPOSE To measure happy and sad moods.

AUTHORS Bill Underwood and William J. Froming

DESCRIPTION The MS is an 18-item instrument that assesses happy and sad moods as traits, that is, as long-term personality characteristics. Happy and sad moods are treated as endpoints on a continuum in an attempt to identify people who differ in average mood level taken over a long period of time. Conceptual analysis of moods suggested three dimensions on which initial construction of the MS was based: the average level of a person's mood, frequency of mood change, and the intensity with which people react to mood experiences. The MS actually possesses two primary subscales: level of mood (LM) and reactivity to situations (RS).

NORMS Several studies were carried out to identify the psychometric properties of the MS. All were based on undergraduate students in an introductory psychology class (796 females and 591 males). No additional demographic data were reported nor were specific norms.

SCORING Individual item scores on the 6-point Likert scales are simply totaled along with the responses to three questions asking respondents to estimate mood level, frequency of mood change, and intensity of mood reactions on 99-point scales. The LM subscale consists of items 2, 4, 6, 8, 10, 11, 13, 15, and 16 with items 6, 11, 13, and 15 reverse-scored. The RS subscale consists of items 1, 5, 7, 9, 12, 14, 17, and 18 with items 5, 9, and 14 reverse-scored.

RELIABILITY Test-retest reliability over three weeks is .80 for the level subscale and .85 for reactivity, indicating good stability. For a seven-week period, test-retest reliability was .63 for level and .83 for reactivity. No data on internal consistency were available.

VALIDITY The MS has good concurrent validity, correlating significantly with a number of other measures such as the Beck Depression Inventory and the Mood Adjective Checklist. The MS also showed stronger correlations with personality measures than did other, state measures of mood. Further, the subscales of the MS were found to correlate or not correlate in the predicted directions with other mood scales, establishing a form of construct validity.

PRIMARY REFERENCE Underwood, B. and Froming, W. J. (1980). The Mood Survey: A personality measure of happy and sad moods, *Journal of Personality Assessment*, 44, 404–414. Instrument reproduced with permission of William J. Froming and *Journal of Personality Assessment*.

AVAILABILITY Dr. William J. Froming, Vice President of Academic Affairs, Pacific Graduate School of Psychology, 1791 Arastradeo Rd., Palo Alto, CA 94303. Telephone: 650.433.3830.

Below are a number of statements about your experience of moods. We would like you to consider your usual behavior when you respond. Using the scale, indicate the appropriate number to the left of each question and try to be as honest as you can.

1 = Strongly disagree
2 = Moderately disagree
3 = Somewhat disagree
4 = Somewhat agree
5 = Moderately agree
6 = Strongly agree

___ 1. I may change from happy to sad and back again several times in a single week.
___ 2. I usually feel quite cheerful.
___ 3. I'm frequently "down in the dumps."
___ 4. I generally look at the sunny side of life.
___ 5. Compared to my friends, I'm less up and down in my mood states.
___ 6. I'm not often really elated.
___ 7. Sometimes my moods swing back and forth very rapidly.
___ 8. I usually feel as though I'm bubbling over with joy.
___ 9. My moods are quite consistent; they almost never vary.
___ 10. I consider myself a happy person.
___ 11. Compared to my friends, I think less positively about life in general.
___ 12. I'm a very changeable person.
___ 13. I am not as cheerful as most people.
___ 14. I'm not as "moody" as most people I know.
___ 15. My friends often seem to feel I am unhappy.
___ 16. If 1=extremely sad, 50=neutral, and 99=extremely happy, how happy are you in general?
___ 17. If 1=hardly ever and 99=extremely frequently, how frequently do your moods change?
___ 18. If 1=not at all and 99=extremely intensely, how intensely do you react to mood experiences?

Multidimensional Body-Self Relations Questionnaire (MBSRQ)

PURPOSE To measure body image.

AUTHOR Thomas F. Cash

DESCRIPTION The MBSRQ is a 69-item instrument designed to measure self-attitudinal aspects of the body-image construct. The MBSRQ contains a number of subscales based on factor analysis: appearance evaluation (AE: items 5, 11, 21, 30, 39, *42, *48), appearance orientation (AO: items 1, 2, 12, 13, 22, *23, 31, *32, *40, 41, *49, 50), fitness evaluation (FE: items 24, *33, 51), fitness orientation (FO: items 3, 4, *6, 14, *15, *16, *25, 26, *34, 35, *43, 44, 53), health evaluation (HE: items 7, *17, 27, *30, *45, 54), health orientation (HO: items 8, 9, 18, 19, *28, 29, *38, 52), illness orientation (IO: items *37, 46, *47, 55, 56), body areas satisfaction (BAS: items 61–68), subjective weight (SW: items 59 and 60), and weight preoccupation (WP: items 10, 28, 57, 58). The MBSRQ offers a wide range of information that can be useful in assessing a number of dimensions of body image.

NORMS The MBSRQ was studied with a sample of 2066 (996 males, 1070 females) based upon a stratified random sample of the U.S. population. The means for the factors described above are as follows: AE—males 3.49, females 3.36; AO—males 3.60, females 3.91; FE—males 3.72, females 3.48; FO—males 3.41, females 3.20; HE—males 3.95, females 3.86; HO—males 3.61, females 3.75; IO—males 3.18, females 3.21; BAS—males 4.12, females 3.80; SW—males 3.26, females 3.53; WP—males 9.87, females 12.14.

SCORING All items with asterisks as noted above are reverse-scored, then items on the respective factors are summed for the subscale scores. Subjective weight is scored by summing items 59 and 60 and dividing by 2. Weight preoccupation is scored by summing items 10, 20, 57, 58 and dividing by 4.

RELIABILITY The first seven factors of the MBSRQ have very good internal consistency, with alphas that range from .75 to .90. All subscales have good to excellent stability, with test-retest correlations that range from .49 to .91.

VALIDITY The MBSRQ has demonstrated its validity in numerous studies in which subscales have been correlated with a number of other health and body image instruments.

PRIMARY REFERENCE Cash, T. F. and Pruzinsky, T. (eds.). (1990). *Body Images: Development, Deviance and Change*. New York: Guilford.

AVAILABILITY Dr. Thomas Cash, Department of Psychology, Old Dominion University, Norfolk, VA 23529. Email: tcash@odu.edu.

The following pages contain a series of statements about how people might think, feel, or behave. You are asked to indicate *the extent to which each statement pertains to you personally.*

Your answers to the items in the questionnaire are anonymous, so please do not write your name on any of the materials. In order to complete the questionnaire, read each statement carefully and decide how much it pertains to you personally. Using the scale below, indicate your answer by entering it to the left of the number of the statement.

1	2	3	4	5
Definitely disagree	Mostly disagree	Neither agree nor disagree	Mostly agree	Definitely agree

There are no right or wrong answers. Just give the answer that is most accurate for you. Remember, your responses are anonymous, so please be *completely honest*. Please give an answer to all of the items.

1. Before going out in public, I always notice how I look.
2. I am careful to buy clothes that will make me look my best.
3. I would pass most physical-fitness tests.
4. It is important that I have superior physical strength.
5. My body is sexually appealing.
6. I am not involved in a regular exercise program.
7. I am in control of my health.
8. I know a lot about things that affect my physical health.
9. I have deliberately developed a healthy life-style.
10. I constantly worry about being or becoming fat.
11. I like my looks just the way they are.
12. I check my appearance in a mirror whenever I can.
13. Before going out, I usually spend a lot of time getting ready.
14. My physical endurance is good.
15. Participating in sports is unimportant to me.
16. I do not actively do things to keep physically fit.
17. My health is a matter of unexpected ups and downs.
18. Good health is one of the most important things in my life.
19. I don't do anything that I know might threaten my health.
20. I am very conscious of even small changes in my weight.
21. Most people would consider me good looking.
22. It is important that I always look good.
23. I use very few grooming products.
24. I easily learn physical skills.
25. Being physically fit is not a strong priority in my life.
26. I do things to increase my physical strength.
27. I am seldom physically ill.
28. I take my health for granted.
29. I often read books and magazines that pertain to health.
30. I like the way I look without my clothes.
31. I am self-conscious if my grooming isn't right.

___ 32. I usually wear whatever is handy without caring how it looks.
___ 33. I do poorly in physical sports or games.
___ 34. I seldom think about my athletic skills.
___ 35. I work to improve my physical stamina.
___ 36. From day to day, I never know how my body will feel.
___ 37. If I am sick, I don't pay much attention to my symptoms.
___ 38. I make no special effort to eat a balanced and nutritious diet.
___ 39. I like the way my clothes fit me.
___ 40. I don't care what people think about my appearance.
___ 41. I take special care with my hair grooming.
___ 42. I dislike my physique.
___ 43. I don't care to improve my abilities in physical activities.
___ 44. I try to be physically active.
___ 45. I often feel vulnerable to sickness.
___ 46. I pay close attention to my body for any signs of illness.
___ 47. If I'm coming down with a cold or flu, I just ignore it and go on as usual.
___ 48. I am physically unattractive.
___ 49. I never think about my appearance.
___ 50. I am always trying to improve my physical appearance.
___ 51. I am very well coordinated.
___ 52. I know a lot about physical fitness.
___ 53. I play a sport regularly throughout the year.
___ 54. I am a physically healthy person.
___ 55. I am very aware of small changes in my physical health.
___ 56. At the first sign of illness, I seek medical advice.
___ 57. I am on a weight-loss diet.

For the remainder of the items use the response scale given with the item, and enter your answer in the space beside the item.

___ 58. I have tried to lose weight by fasting or going on crash diets.

1. Never
2. Rarely
3. Sometimes
4. Often
5. Very often

___ 59. I think I am:

1. Very underweight
2. Somewhat underweight
3. Normal weight
4. Somewhat overweight
5. Very overweight

___ 60. From looking at me, most other people would think I am:

1. Very underweight
2. Somewhat underweight
3. Normal weight
4. Somewhat overweight
5. Very overweight

61–69. Use this 1–5 scale to indicate how satisfied you are with each of the following areas of your body:

1	2	3	4	5
Very dissatisfied	Mostly dissatisfied	Neither satisfied nor dissatisfied	Mostly satisfied	Very satisfied

___ 61. Face (facial features, complexion)
___ 62. Hair (color, thickness, texture)
___ 63. Lower torso (buttocks, hips, thighs, legs)
___ 64. Mid torso (waist, stomach)
___ 65. Upper torso (chest or breasts, shoulders, arms)
___ 66. Muscle tone
___ 67. Weight
___ 68. Height
___ 69. Overall appearance

Multidimensional Desire for Control Scales (MDCS)

PURPOSE To measure desire for control in clinical health care interactions.

AUTHOR Lynda A. Anderson

DESCRIPTION This 17-item instrument is designed to measure three dimensions of clients' desire for control in clinical interactions, which is considered facilitative in promoting effective patient-health care. While the development of the MDCS was based on patients in diabetes management, the instrument has utility in other health care contexts. It helps determine whether one's patient prefers a prescriptive clinician-directed clinical interaction or a participatory role in his or her health care. The MDCS assesses three dimensions of control: personal control (PC), clinician control (CC), and shared control (SC) between patient and clinician.

NORMS Normative data are available for three samples of males in treatment for non-insulin dependent diabetes mellitus. The three samples had ns of 110, 50, and 109; for all three samples, the majority of respondents were African-American. For the sample of 110 men, the PC, CC, and SC have the following means and standard deviations: 2.20 (SD = .95), 4.19 (SD = .78), 4.02 (SD = .99), respectively. The sample of 50 had the following means and standard deviations for PC, CC, and SC: 2.14 (SD = 1.01); 4.11 (SD = .88); and 4.06 (SD = .97). The sample of 109 had similar scores.

SCORING Each item is rated on a 7-point Likert-type scale ranging from "strongly agree" to "strongly disagree." The three scales are the sum of each item score as follows: PC = 5 + 9 + 10 + 12 + 13 + 15 + +16; CC = 1 + 2 + 3 + 4 + 8 + 11; SC = 6 + 7 + 14 + 17. Lower scores reflect more control by the patient, clinician, or shared control by patient and clinician.

RELIABILITY Internal consistency of the MDCS is fair to good. For the sample of 110 patients, the alpha coefficients were .79, .76, .75 for PC, CC, and SC, respectively. For the sample of 109 the alpha coefficients were .81, .80, and .75 for the three scales. Data on stability were not available.

VALIDITY The MDCS has good factorial validity supported by an exploratory factor analysis on the sample of 110 patients and a confirmatory factor analysis from the sample of 109 patients. Concurrent validity is evidenced by correlations with the Multidimensional Health Locus of Control Scales. The PC was slightly associated with social desirability, although social desirability was uncorrelated with scores on the CC and SC. PC scores also correlated with a measure of the role of patient while the CC and SC correlated with scores on a measure of the role of the doctor, and shared roles between the patient and clinician. The PC correlated with measures of affective and behavioral satisfaction, and CC scores correlated with affective, behavioral, and cognitive satisfaction. The SC was unassociated with satisfaction.

PRIMARY REFERENCE Anderson, L. A., DeVellis, R. F., Boyles, B., and Feussner, J. R. (1989). Patients' perception of their clinical interactions: Development of the Multidimensional Desire for Control Scales, *Health Education Research*, 4, 383–397.

AVAILABILITY Lynda A. Anderson, Ph.D., University of Michigan, School of Public Health, 1420 Washington Heights, Ann Arbor, MI 48109-2029. Email: lindasa@umich.edu.

The following items ask about your beliefs regarding your clinical care. Please answer each item by rating your degree of agreement or disagreement using the following scale, and record your answer in the space to the left of each item.

1 = Strongly agree
2 = Somewhat agree
3 = Slightly agree
4 = Neither agree nor disagree
5 = Slightly disagree
6 = Somewhat disagree
7 = Strongly disagree

___ 1. The doctor, not I, will decide what information I receive about my medical care.
___ 2. The doctor will make the decisions for me regarding a treatment program for my diabetes.
___ 3. The doctor, not I, will direct my medical care.
___ 4. I will defer decisions about my treatment to the expert advice of the doctor.
___ 5. I, not the doctor, will decide what type of diet program I need to follow.
___ 6. The doctor and I will make decisions about my medical care together, on an equal basis.
___ 7. The doctor and I will be equal partners in establishing the treatment goals for my illness.
___ 8. The doctor will try to influence the choices I make about my treatment program.
___ 9. I, not the doctor, will decide what information I get about my treatment program.
___ 10. If my diabetes gets out of control, I will decide what should be done to change my treatment program.
___ 11. The doctor, not I, will begin discussions of my laboratory test results.
___ 12. I will decide the best way to meet my treatment goals, regardless of how they are established.
___ 13. I will decide what my medical care program is going to be.
___ 14. The doctor and I will supervise my treatment program together.
___ 15. I, not the doctor, will be in charge of my medical care.
___ 16. Even in a medical crisis, I will make the decision about my medical care.
___ 17. The doctor will give me a choice about what glucose testing method I should use at home.

Multidimensional Health Locus of Control Scales (MHLC)

PURPOSE To measure locus of control of health-related behavior.

AUTHORS Kenneth A. Wallston, Barbara Studler Wallston, and Robert DeVellis

DESCRIPTION This 18-item instrument measures three dimensions of locus of control of reinforcement as it pertains to health. Specifically, the MHLC assesses people's belief that their health is or is not determined by their own behavior. These issues of internal and external control have been extensively studied in regard to numerous clinical problems. The MHLC looks at beliefs about three sources of control over health, with each subscale containing six items: internality of health locus of control (IHLC), powerful other locus of control (POLC), and chance locus of control (CHLC). The MHLC has parallel forms (Forms A and B) designed to be alternated for use as repeated measures, or the two forms may be combined to create longer (12 items) and more reliable subscales. Further information on scoring and application of the scales is available from the authors.

NORMS Normative data are available on samples of chronic patients ($n = 609$), college students ($n = 749$), healthy adults ($n = 1287$) and persons involved in preventive health behaviors ($n = 720$). The IHLC, CHLC, and POLC scales had average scores of 25.78, 17.64, and 22.54 for the chronic patients, and 26.68, 16.72, and 17.87 for college students. Healthy adults had average scores of 25.55, 16.21, and 19.16 for the IHLC, CHLC, and POLC, respectively, while the sample of persons involved in preventive health behaviors had average scores of 27.38, 15.52, and 18.44.

SCORING All items are arranged on 6-point Likert scales ranging from "strongly agree" to "strongly disagree." Scores for each subscale are the sums of the following items: IHLC: 1, 6, 8, 12, 13, 17; POLC: 3, 5, 7, 10, 14, 18; CHLC: 2, 4, 9, 11, 15, 16. Higher scores reflect externality.

RELIABILITY The items were empirically selected from a pool of 88 items, with fairly stringent criteria. The internal consistency reliability using Cronbach's alpha ranged from .67 to .77 for all six scales, the three dimensions, and two parallel forms. When the parallel forms were combined to make 12-item scales the alphas ranged from .83 to .86 for the three scales. Data on stability were not available.

VALIDITY The MHLC scales have fairly good criterion validity, correlating with subjects' state of health. The scales also correlate with other measures of locus of control, including the Multidimensional Locus of Control Scales for Psychiatric Patients. Except for the chance locus of control scale, the scales were not correlated with social desirability.

PRIMARY REFERENCE Wallston, K. A., Wallston, B. S., and DeVellis, R. (1978). Development of the Multidimensional Health Locus of Control (MHLC) Scales, *Health Education Monographs*, 6, 160–170. Instrument reproduced with permission of Kenneth A. Wallston, Ph.D.

AVAILABILITY Kenneth A. Wallston, Professor, Health Care Research Project, Vanderbilt University, School of Nursing, Nashville, TN 37240. Email: ken.wallston@vanderbilt.edu.

MHLC

Form A

This is a questionnaire designed to determine the way in which different people view certain important health-related issues. Each item is a belief statement with which you may agree or disagree. Each statement can be rated on a scale which ranges from strongly disagree (1) to strongly agree (6). For each item we would like you to record the number that represents the extent to which you disagree or agree with the statement. The more strongly you agree with a statement, then the higher will be the number you record. The more strongly you disagree with a statement, then the lower will be the number you record. Please make sure that you answer every item and that you record *only one* number per item. This is a measure of your personal beliefs; obviously, there are no right or wrong answers.

Please answer these items carefully, but do not spend too much time on any one item. As much as you can, try to respond to each item independently. When making your choice, do not be influenced by your previous choices. It is important that you respond according to your actual beliefs and not according to how you feel you should believe or how you think we want you to believe.

1 = Strongly disagree
2 = Moderately disagree
3 = Slightly disagree
4 = Slightly agree
5 = Moderately agree
6 = Strongly agree

___ 1. If I get sick, it is my own behavior which determines how soon I get well again.
___ 2. No matter what I do, if I am going to get sick, I will get sick.
___ 3. Having regular contact with my physician is the best way for me to avoid illness.
___ 4. Most things that affect my health happen to me by accident.
___ 5. Whenever I don't feel well, I should consult a medically trained professional.
___ 6. I am in control of my health.
___ 7. My family has a lot to do with my becoming sick or staying healthy.
___ 8. When I get sick, I am to blame.
___ 9. Luck plays a big part in determining how soon I will recover from an illness.
___ 10. Health professionals control my health.
___ 11. My good health is largely a matter of good fortune.
___ 12. The main thing which affects my health is what I myself do.
___ 13. If I take care of myself, I can avoid illness.
___ 14. When I recover from an illness, it's usually because other people (for example, doctors, nurses, family, friends) have been taking good care of me.
___ 15. No matter what I do, I'm likely to get sick.
___ 16. If it's meant to be, I will stay healthy.
___ 17. If I take the right actions, I can stay healthy.
___ 18. Regarding my health, I can only do what my doctor tells me to do.

Form B

This is a questionnaire designed to determine the way in which different people view certain important health-related issues. Each item is a belief statement with which you may agree or disagree. Each statement can be rated on a scale which ranges from strongly disagree (1) to strongly agree (6). For each item we would like you to record the number that represents the extent to which you disagree or agree with the statement. The more strongly you agree with a statement, then the higher will be the number you record. The more strongly you disagree with a statement, then the lower will be the number you record. Please make sure that you answer every item and that you record *only one* number per item. This is a measure of your personal beliefs; obviously, there are no right or wrong answers.

Please answer these items carefully, but do not spend too much time on any one item. As much as you can, try to respond to each item independently. When making your choice, do not be influenced by your previous choices. It is important that you respond according to your actual beliefs and not according to how you feel you should believe or how you think we want you to believe.

1 = Strongly disagree
2 = Moderately disagree
3 = Slightly disagree
4 = Slightly agree
5 = Moderately agree
6 = Strongly agree

____ 1. If I become sick, I have the power to make myself well again.
____ 2. Often I feel that no matter what I do, if I am going to get sick, I will get sick.
____ 3. If I see an excellent doctor regularly, I am less likely to have health problems.
____ 4. It seems that my health is greatly influenced by accidental happenings.
____ 5. I can only maintain my health by consulting health professionals.
____ 6. I am directly responsible for my health.
____ 7. Other people play a big part in whether I stay healthy or become sick.
____ 8. Whatever goes wrong with my health is my own fault.
____ 9. When I am sick, I just have to let nature run its course.
____ 10. Health professionals keep me healthy.
____ 11. When I stay healthy, I'm just plain lucky.
____ 12. My physical well-being depends on how well I take care of myself.
____ 13. When I feel ill, I know it is because I have not been taking care of myself properly.
____ 14. The type of care I receive from other people is what is responsible for how well I recover from an illness.
____ 15. Even when I take care of myself, it's easy to get sick.
____ 16. When I become ill, it's a matter of fate.
____ 17. I can pretty much stay healthy by taking good care of myself.
____ 18. Following doctor's orders to the letter is the best way for me to stay healthy.

Multidimensional Locus of Control Scales for Psychiatric Patients (MLOCP)

PURPOSE To measure locus of control of adjustment and empowerment.

AUTHOR Hanna Levenson

DESCRIPTION This 24-item multidimensional instrument measures the belief that reinforcement is contingent upon one's own behavior or on events which are not contingent upon one's behavior, such as chance or luck. A person who has an internal locus of control is viewed as more adjusted than one who considers consequences the result of external events. Moreover, the author of this instrument believes that one of the goals of treatment is the development of internal control, signifying competence and mastery. The three dimensions of locus of control assessed are internal locus of control (ILC), powerful others control (POC) and chance control (CC). Factor analysis has generally supported the dimensionality of the instrument.

NORMS Normative data are based on 165 consecutively admitted psychiatric patients. Ninety-five were male and approximately 66 percent of the sample was white, while the rest were black. The average age of the sample was 37 years old. Data also are available on 96 "normal" subjects, although little demographic information is reported. The mean scores for the ILC, POC, and CC were 35.4, 23.8, and 21.7, respectively, for the sample of psychiatric patients. The ILC, POC, and CC average scores were 35.5, 16.7, and 13.9 for the nonclinical sample. Males and females do not seem to score differently on the subscales.

SCORING Each item is rated on a 6-point scale from "strongly disagree" to "strongly agree." The three subscales are summed separately, and the items grouped according to scales. Total scale scores range from 8 to 48. Higher scores reflect more externality. Scale items are: ILC: 1, 4, 5, 9, 18, 19, 21, 23; POC: 3, 8, 11, 13, 15, 17, 20, 22; CC: 2, 6, 7, 10, 12, 14, 16, 24.

RELIABILITY For two of the three scales, the internal consistency reliability was good. Alphas were .67, .82, and .79 for the ILC, POC, and CC, respectively. Test-retest reliability over a five-day interval was .74 and .78 for the POC and CC, but only .08 for the ILC.

VALIDITY The validity of this instrument is established primarily through known-groups procedures. Scores on the POC and CC scales discriminated between neurotic and psychotic patients, with a range of specific differences occurring between specific types of disorders.

PRIMARY REFERENCE Levenson, H. (1973). Multidimensional locus of control in psychiatric patients, *Journal of Consulting and Clinical Psychology*, 41, 397–404. Instrument reproduced with permission of the American Psychological Association.

AVAILABILITY May be copied from this volume.

Indicate the extent to which you agree with each of the statements below using the following scale:

1 = Strongly agree
2 = Moderately agree
3 = Slightly agree
4 = Slightly disagree
5 = Moderately disagree
6 = Strongly disagree

___ 1. Whether or not I get to be a leader depends mostly on my ability.
___ 2. To a great extent my life is controlled by accidental happenings.
___ 3. I feel like what happens in my life is mostly determined by powerful people.
___ 4. My behavior will determine when I am ready to leave the hospital.
___ 5. When I make plans, I am almost certain to make them work.
___ 6. Often there is no chance of protecting my personal interests from bad luck happenings.
___ 7. When I get what I want it's usually because I'm lucky.
___ 8. Even if I were a good leader, I would not be made a leader unless I play up to those in positions of power.
___ 9. How many friends I have depends on how nice a person I am.
___ 10. I have often found that what is going to happen will happen.
___ 11. My life is chiefly controlled by powerful others.
___ 12. It is impossible for anyone to say how long I'll be in the hospital.
___ 13. People like myself have very little chance of protecting our interests when they conflict with those of powerful other people.
___ 14. It's not always wise for me to plan too far ahead because many things turn out to be a matter of good or bad fortune.
___ 15. Getting what I want means I have to please those people above me.
___ 16. Whether or not I get to be a leader depends on whether I'm lucky enough to be in the right place at the right time.
___ 17. If important people were to decide they didn't like me, I probably wouldn't make many friends.
___ 18. I can pretty much determine what will happen in my life.
___ 19. I am usually able to protect my personal interests.
___ 20. How soon I leave the hospital depends on other people who have power over me.
___ 21. When I get what I want, it's usually because I worked hard for it.
___ 22. In order to have my plans work, I make sure that they fit in with the desires of people who have power over me.
___ 23. My life is determined by my own actions.
___ 24. It's chiefly a matter of fate whether or not I have a few friends or many friends.

Multidimensional Scale of Perceived Social Support (MSPSS)

PURPOSE To measure perceived social support.

AUTHORS Gregory D. Zimet, Nancy W. Dahlem, Sara G. Zimet, and Gordon K. Farley

DESCRIPTION The MSPSS is a 12-item instrument designed to measure perceived social support from three sources: family, friends, and a significant other. The MSPSS assesses the extent to which respondents perceive social support from each of those sources and is divided into three subscales: family (items 3, 4, 8, 11); friends (items 1, 2, 5, 6, 7, 9, 12); and significant other (items 1, 2, 5, 10). The MSPSS is short, easy to use, self-explanatory, and time effective.

NORMS The MSPSS has been studied with a variety of diverse samples. The most recent study involves 154 students in a two- or four-year college on a large urban campus. The mean age of the 122 women and 32 men was 26.5 (range from 18 to 51 years); the students were characterized as from ethnically and socioeconomically diverse backgrounds. Means for this group were 5.58 (SD = 1.07) for the total score, 5.31 (SD = 1.46) for the family subscale, 5.50 (SD = 1.25) for the friends subscale, and 5.94 (SD = 1.34) for the significant-other subscale.

SCORING The MSPSS is easily scored by summing individual item scores for the total and subscale scores and dividing by the number of items. Higher scores reflect higher perceived support.

RELIABILITY The MSPSS has excellent internal consistency, with alphas of .91 for the total scale and .90 to .95 for the subscales. The authors claim good test-retest reliability as well.

VALIDITY The MSPSS has good factorial validity and has good concurrent validity, correlating with depression, and with degree of coronary artery disease in Type A patients (inverse correlations). The authors also claim good construct validity for the MSPSS. The MSPSS is not correlated with the Marlow-Crowne Social Desirability Scale.

PRIMARY REFERENCE Zimet, G. D., Dahlem, N. W., Zimet, S. G., and Farley, G. K. (1988). The Multidimensional Scale of Perceived Social Support, *Journal of Personality Assessment*, 52, 30–41.

AVAILABILITY Dr. Gregory D. Zimet, Riley Hospital for Children, Indiana University, School of Medicine, Indianapolis, IN 46202. Email: gzimet@iupui.edu.

We are interested in how you feel about the following statements. Read each statement carefully. Indicate how you feel about each statement by circling the appropriate number using the following scale:

1 = Very strongly disagree
2 = Strongly disagree
3 = Mildly disagree
4 = Neutral
5 = Mildly agree
6 = Strongly agree
7 = Very strongly agree

1. There is a special person who is around when I am in need.	1	2	3	4	5	6	7
2. There is a special person with whom I can share joys and sorrows.	1	2	3	4	5	6	7
3. My family really tries to help me.	1	2	3	4	5	6	7
4. I get the emotional help and support I need from my family.	1	2	3	4	5	6	7
5. I have a special person who is a real source of comfort to me.	1	2	3	4	5	6	7
6. My friends really try to help me.	1	2	3	4	5	6	7
7. I can count on my friends when things go wrong.	1	2	3	4	5	6	7
8. I can talk about my problems with my family.	1	2	3	4	5	6	7
9. I have friends with whom I can share my joys and sorrows.	1	2	3	4	5	6	7
10. There is a special person in my life who cares about my feelings.	1	2	3	4	5	6	7
11. My family is willing to help me make decisions.	1	2	3	4	5	6	7
12. I can talk about my problems with my friends.	1	2	3	4	5	6	7

Multidimensional Sense of Humor Scale (MSHS)

PURPOSE To measure sense of humor.

AUTHORS James A. Thorson and F. C. Powell

DESCRIPTION The MSHS is a 24-item scale designed to measure personal sense of humor as one mechanism for helping people cope with life. The MSHS has been widely used and translations of the scale are available in a number of languages at the address listed below. The MSHS was deliberately designed to include a number of elements that are central to the basic concept of sense of humor, ranging from the ability to be humorous to the appreciation of others' humor to being able to laugh at problems or master difficult situations through the uses of humor. The MSHS, in the largest sample tested so far involving 612 respondents, was shown to comprise four factors: humor, creativity, and social use of humor (items 1–11 and 19); use of coping humor (items 21–24); attitudes toward humorous people (items 12, 13, 15, 16, 20, and 22); and attitudes toward humor itself (items 14, 17, and 18). However studies have shown some variation in the factor structure in the MSHS across samples; therefore, it may be best to use the MSHS as an overall score rather than the scores of the individual subscales.

NORMS The MSHS has been studied with a number of samples in a number of countries. In one study in the United States, a sample of 199 young adults comprising 94 males and 100 females, with a mean age of 19.5 years (SD=1.0) was compared to a sample of 214 older persons, including 123 males and 91 females, with a mean age of 77.9 (SD=7.4). The mean MSHS score for the younger sample was 66.6 (SD=11.7) as compared to a mean of 57.2 (SD=14.6) for the older sample.

SCORING The MSHS is scored on a 5-point Likert scale with higher scores indicating a stronger sense of humor. Items left blank are scored as 2, and items 4, 8, 11, 13, 17, and 20 are reverse-scored. Then simply add up individual item scores. The subscales are scored in the same way.

RELIABILITY The MSHS has shown very good internal consistency, with alphas across a number of samples that have ranged from the mid-.80s to the mid-.90s. Data on stability were not available.

VALIDITY The MSHS has established good construct validity, with correlations with other psychological tests in the directions that are hypothesized. The MSHS is positively correlated with exhibition, dominance, warmth, gregariousness, assertiveness, excitement-seeking, creativity, intrinsic religiosity, arousability, positive emotions, extroversion, and cheerfulness. The MSHS is negatively correlated with neuroticism, pessimism, avoidance, negative self-esteem, deference, order, endurance, aggression, depression, death anxiety, seriousness, perception of daily hassles, and bad mood.

PRIMARY REFERENCE Thorson, J. A., Powell, F. C., Sarmany-Shuller, I., and Hampes, W. P. (1997). Psychological health and sense of humor, *Journal of Clinical Psychology*, 53, 605–619.

AVAILABILITY Copyright James A. Thorson, 1993; used by permission. May be copied from this volume.

We are conducting a study of attitudes and would appreciate your help. This is an anonymous survey; please don't write your name on the questionnaire. If answering these items threatens you in any way, please just turn in a blank questionnaire. Please go through these items quickly, marking the response that is appropriate for you going from left to right: "strongly disagree," "disagree," "neutral," "agree," or "strongly agree."

	Strongly disagree				Strongly agree
1. Sometimes I think up jokes or funny stories.	—	—	—	—	—
2. Uses of wit or humor help me master difficult situations.	—	—	—	—	—
3. I'm confident that I can make other people laugh.	—	—	—	—	—
4. I dislike comics.	—	—	—	—	—
5. Other people tell me that I say funny things.	—	—	—	—	—
6. I can use wit to help adapt to many situations.	—	—	—	—	—
7. I can ease a tense situation by saying something funny.	—	—	—	—	—
8. People who tell jokes are a pain in the neck.	—	—	—	—	—
9. I can often crack people up with the things I say.	—	—	—	—	—
10. I like a good joke.	—	—	—	—	—
11. Calling somebody a "comedian" is a real insult.	—	—	—	—	—
12. I can say things in such a way as to make people laugh.	—	—	—	—	—
13. Humor is a lousy coping mechanism.	—	—	—	—	—
14. I appreciate those who generate humor.	—	—	—	—	—
15. People look to me to say amusing things.	—	—	—	—	—
16. Humor helps me cope.	—	—	—	—	—
17. I'm uncomfortable when everyone is cracking jokes.	—	—	—	—	—
18. I'm regarded as something of a wit by my friends.	—	—	—	—	—
19. Coping by using humor is an elegant way of adapting.	—	—	—	—	—
20. Trying to master situations through uses of humor is really dumb.	—	—	—	—	—
21. I can actually have some control over a group by my uses of humor.	—	—	—	—	—
22. Uses of humor help to put me at ease.	—	—	—	—	—
23. I use humor to entertain my friends.	—	—	—	—	—
24. My clever sayings amuse others.	—	—	—	—	—

Multidimensional Support Scale (MDSS)

PURPOSE To measure social support in young adults.

AUTHORS Helen R. Winefield, Anthony H. Winefield, and Marika Tiggemann

DESCRIPTION The MDSS is a 19-item instrument designed to measure social support—including frequency and adequacy of emotional, practical, and informational support—in young adults. The MDSS is structured to examine support from three sources—confidants, peers, and supervisors. The MDSS has five factors reflecting sources of support rather than types: confidant availability (section A: items 1a, 2a, 4a, 4b, 5a, 6a, 7a), supervisor adequacy (section C: items 1b, 2b, 3b, 4b, 5b, 6b), supervisor availability (section C: items 1a, 2a, 4a, 5a, 6a), peer adequacy (section B: items 1b, 2b, 3b, 4b, 5b, 6b), and peer availability (section B: items 1a, 2a, 4a, 5a, 6a). On the items above "a" refers to frequency/availability rating and "b" is the adequacy/satisfaction rating.

NORMS The MDSS was studied with 483 adults living in Australia, with a mean age of 23.6 years (SD = 1.1), 51.3% female, with 24.3% of the males and 42.7% of the females being married; 84.4% of the sample was employed, the remainder being either students (10.1%) or unemployed (4.8%). Actual norms were not reported.

SCORING The MDSS is scored by simply summing item scores for the individual factors and total scores, using a 4-point scale for frequency and a 3-point scale for satisfaction.

RELIABILITY The MDSS has very good internal consistency, with alphas for the subscales that range from .81 to .90. No data on stability were reported.

VALIDITY The MDSS has good concurrent validity, with significant correlations with three measures of psychological well-being: Rosenberg's Self-Esteem and Depressive Affect scales and the General Health Questionnaire. The MDSS was a better predictor of psychological well-being than measures of health, financial distress, and stressful life events.

PRIMARY REFERENCE Winefield, H. R., Winefield, A. H., and Tiggemann, M. (1992). Social support and psychological well-being in young adults: The Multidimensional Support Scale, *Journal of Personality Assessment*, 58, 198–210.

AVAILABILITY May be copied from this volume.

Below are some questions about the kind of help and support you have available to you in coping with your life at present. The questions refer to three different groups of people who might have been providing support to you IN THE LAST MONTH. For each item, please *circle the alternative* which shows your answer.

A. Firstly, think of your *family and close friends, especially the 2–3 who are most important to you.*

		Never	Some-times	Often	Usually/always	WOULD HAVE LIKED THEM TO DO THIS		
						More often	Less often	Just right
1.	How often did they really listen to you when you talked about your concerns or problems?	1	2	3	4	1	2	3
2.	How often did you feel that they were really trying to understand your problems?	1	2	3	4	1	2	3
3.	How often did they try to take your mind off your problems by telling jokes or chattering about other things?	1	2	3	4	1	2	3
4.	How often did they really make you feel loved?	1	2	3	4	1	2	3
5.	How often did they help you in practical ways, like doing things for you or lending you money?	1	2	3	4	1	2	3
6.	How often did they answer your questions or give you advice about how to solve your problems?	1	2	3	4	1	2	3
7.	How often could you use them as examples of how to deal with your problems?	1	2	3	4	1	2	3

B. Now, think of *other people of about your age that you know, who are like you in being employed, unemployed, or studying.*

1.	How often did they really listen to you when you talked about your concerns or problems?	1	2	3	4	1	2	3

					WOULD HAVE LIKED THEM TO DO THIS		
		Never	Some-times	Often	Usually/always	More often	Less often	Just right

		Never	Some-times	Often	Usually/ always	More often	Less often	Just right
2.	How often did you feel that they were really trying to understand your problems?	1	2	3	4	1	2	3
3.	How often did they try to take your mind off your problems by telling jokes or chattering about other things?	1	2	3	4	1	2	3
4.	How often did they help you in practical ways, like doing things for you or lending you money?	1	2	3	4	1	2	3
5.	How often did they answer your questions or give you advice about how to solve your problem?	1	2	3	4	1	2	3
6.	How often could you use them as examples of how to deal with your problems?	1	2	3	4	1	2	3

C. Lastly, think about the *people in some sort of* authority over you. If you are employed, this means your supervisors at work. If you are unemployed, it means your local employment service staff. If you are a fulltime student, it means your lecturers and tutors. Depending on which ones are relevant for you, answer for the 2–3 that you see most.

		Never	Some-times	Often	Usually/ always	More often	Less often	Just right
1.	How often did they really listen to you when you talked about your concerns or problems?	1	2	3	4	1	2	3
2.	How often did you feel that they were really trying to understand your problems?	1	2	3	4	1	2	3
3.	How often did they try to take your mind off your problems by telling jokes or chattering about other things?	1	2	3	4	1	2	3
4.	How often did they fulfill their responsibilities towards you in helpful practical ways?	1	2	3	4	1	2	3

continued

		Never	Some-times	Often	Usually/always	WOULD HAVE LIKED THEM TO DO THIS		
						More often	Less often	Just right
5.	How often did they answer your questions or give you advice about how to solve your problems?	1	2	3	4	1	2	3
6.	How often could you use them as examples of how to deal with your problems?	1	2	3	4	1	2	3

Negative Attitudes Toward Masturbation Inventory (NAMI)

PURPOSE To measure guilt over masturbation.

AUTHORS Paul R. Abramson and Donald L. Mosher

DESCRIPTION This 30-item instrument measures negative attitudes toward masturbation. Negative attitudes can emerge from a lack of information or from inadequate information about sexuality; additionally, negative attitudes may develop from conditioned emotional reactions. Negative attitudes tend to be related to a lower frequency of masturbation and to sexual inexperience. Negative attitudes are considered evidence of guilt over masturbation. Knowledge of negative attitudes toward masturbation can assist in therapeutic work on sexuality and the treatment of some orgasmic disorders.

NORMS Normative data are reported on 95 male and 99 female college students. The mean NAMI was 72.06 with a standard deviation of 15.29 for males and 72.44 with a standard deviation of 16.36 for females. The difference between males and females on NAMI scores was not significant.

SCORING Each item is rated on a 5-point Likert-type scale by recording a number from (1) strongly disagree to (5) strongly agree in the space to the left of the item. Items 3, 5, 8, 11, 13, 14–17, 22, 27, 29, are reverse-scored. Total scores are the sum of all items and range from 30 to 150 with higher scores indicating more negative attitudes.

RELIABILITY This instrument has acceptable evidence of internal consistency. The reliability, calculated according to the Spearman-Brown formula was .75. All items except one had significant correlations with total scores. Estimates of test-retest reliability are not available.

VALIDITY The NAMI shows strong evidence of concurrent validity. Correlations were found between NAMI and sexual guilt, sexual experiences, and frequency of masturbation for females. For males the NAMI only correlated with two of the criteria, sexual guilt and frequency of masturbation.

PRIMARY REFERENCE Abramson, P. R. and Mosher, D. L. (1975). Development of a measure of negative attitudes toward masturbation, *Journal of Consulting and Clinical Psychology*, 43, 485–490. Instrument reproduced with permission of Dr. Paul R. Abramson and the American Psychological Association.

AVAILABILITY Dr. Paul R. Abramson, Department of Psychology, UCLA, Los Angeles, CA 90024. Email: abramson@psych.ucla.edu.

Below are thirty statements regarding masturbation. Please indicate the extent to which you agree with each by placing the appropriate number to the left of the statement. The numbers are based on the following scale:

1 = Strongly disagree
2 = Disagree
3 = Neither agree nor disagree
4 = Agree
5 = Strongly agree

___ 1. People masturbate to escape from feelings of tension and anxiety.
___ 2. People who masturbate will not enjoy sexual intercourse as much as those who refrain from masturbation.
___ 3. Masturbation is a private matter which neither harms nor concerns anyone else.
___ 4. Masturbation is a sin against yourself.
___ 5. Masturbation in childhood can help a person develop a natural, healthy attitude toward sex.
___ 6. Masturbation in an adult is juvenile and immature.
___ 7. Masturbation can lead to homosexuality.
___ 8. Excessive masturbation is physically impossible, as it is a needless worry.
___ 9. If you enjoy masturbating too much, you may never learn to relate to the opposite sex.
___ 10. After masturbating, a person feels degraded.
___ 11. Experience with masturbation can potentially help a woman become orgastic in sexual intercourse.
___ 12. I feel guilty about masturbating.
___ 13. Masturbation can be a "friend in need" when there is no "friend in deed."
___ 14. Masturbation can provide an outlet for sex fantasies without harming anyone else or endangering oneself.
___ 15. Excessive masturbation can lead to problems of impotence in men and frigidity in women.
___ 16. Masturbation is an escape mechanism which prevents a person from developing a mature sexual outlook.
___ 17. Masturbation can provide harmless relief from sexual tensions.
___ 18. Playing with your own genitals is disgusting.
___ 19. Excessive masturbation is associated with neurosis, depression, and behavioral problems.
___ 20. Any masturbation is too much.
___ 21. Masturbation is a compulsive, addictive habit which once begun is almost impossible to stop.
___ 22. Masturbation is fun.
___ 23. When I masturbate, I am disgusted with myself.
___ 24. A pattern of frequent masturbation is associated with introversion and withdrawal from social contacts.
___ 25. I would be ashamed to admit publicly that I have masturbated.
___ 26. Excessive masturbation leads to mental dullness and fatigue.

___ 27. Masturbation is a normal sexual outlet.
___ 28. Masturbation is caused by an excessive preoccupation with thoughts about sex.
___ 29. Masturbation can teach you to enjoy the sensuousness of your own body.
___ 30. After I masturbate, I am disgusted with myself for losing control of my body.

Network Orientation Scale (NOS)

PURPOSE To measure negative network orientation.

AUTHORS Alan Vaux, Philip Burda, and Doreen Stewart

DESCRIPTION The NOS is a 20-item instrument designed to measure negative network orientation—the perspective that it is inadvisable, useless, or risky to seek help from others. The NOS is based on social support theory, but does not focus on the fact that a person may suffer from lack of social support; rather, the NOS measures the individual's unwillingness to maintain, nurture, or utilize those supports that he or she has. Items for the NOS were generated rationally after clarification of the basic construct of negative network orientation and were intended to reflect beliefs that it is useless, inadvisable, or dangerous to draw on network resources. The NOS is seen as not only a useful research device, but one that could be valuable in assessing client potential for involvement in therapy or in other community helping resources.

NORMS The NOS initially was studied on four samples of college students and one of community adults. Ethnicity/cultural characteristics were mixed, including U.S. whites and blacks and foreign students. The mean age of the students ranged from 22 to 25 and of the community adults ranged from 30 to 60. The proportion of women in the samples ranged from 30% to 73%. Actual norms were not provided.

SCORING Items using both positive and negative wording are used to minimize acquiescence in responding. Items 3, 5, 8, 10, 12, 13, 15, 17, 18, and 20 are negatively worded and are reverse-scored. All items are then summed for a total score, with higher scores indicating a more negative orientation.

RELIABILITY The NOS has very good internal consistency, with alphas that range from .60 to .88 (mean alpha = .74). Stability was shown to be good in two of three tests including test-retest correlations of .85, .87, and .18 over one-, two-, and three-week intervals, respectively.

VALIDITY The NOS has good concurrent validity and fair construct validity. Negative network expectations were associated with reports of smaller support networks, less available supportive behavior, and less positive appraisals of support. Positive network orientations were associated with personality factors such as nurturance, affiliation, trust, and a feminine sex-role orientation.

PRIMARY REFERENCE Vaux, A., Burda, P., and Stewart, D. (1986). Orientation toward utilization of support resources, *Journal of Community Psychology*, 11, 159–170.

AVAILABILITY May be copied from this volume.

Below is a list of statements concerning relationships with other people. Please indicate the extent to which you agree or disagree with each statement. (Using the scale below, circle one number corresponding to each statement.)

1 = Strongly agree
2 = Agree
3 = Disagree
4 = Strongly disagree

		SA	A	D	SD
1.	Sometimes it is necessary to talk to someone about your problems.	1	2	3	4
2.	Friends often have good advice to give.	1	2	3	4
3.	You have to be careful who you tell personal things to.	1	2	3	4
4.	I often get useful information from other people.	1	2	3	4
5.	People should keep their problems to themselves.	1	2	3	4
6.	It's easy for me to talk about personal and private matters.	1	2	3	4
7.	In the past, friends have really helped me out when I've had a problem.	1	2	3	4
8.	You can never trust people to keep a secret.	1	2	3	4
9.	When a person gets upset they should talk it over with a friend.	1	2	3	4
10.	Other people never understand my problems.	1	2	3	4
11.	Almost everyone knows someone they can trust with a personal secret.	1	2	3	4
12.	If you can't figure out your problems, nobody can.	1	2	3	4
13.	In the past, I have rarely found other people's opinions helpful when I have a problem.	1	2	3	4
14.	It really helps when you are angry to tell a friend what happened.	1	2	3	4
15.	Some things are too personal to talk to anyone about.	1	2	3	4
16.	It's fairly easy to tell who you can trust, and who you can't.	1	2	3	4
17.	In the past, I have been hurt by people I confided in.	1	2	3	4
18.	If you confide in other people, they will take advantage of you.	1	2	3	4
19.	It's okay to ask favors of people.	1	2	3	4
20.	Even if I need something, I would hesitate to borrow it from someone.	1	2	3	4

Neurotic Perfectionism Questionnaire (NPQ)

PURPOSE To measure neurotic perfectionism in persons with eating disorders.

AUTHORS Susan F. Mitzman, Peter Slade, and Michael E. Dewey

DESCRIPTION This 42-item instrument measures the experiences of perfectionism that have become neurotic or self-defeating to a client. In contrast to functional perfectionism where realistic targets are met by the reinforcement associated with success, neurotic perfectionism includes unobtainable standards, overpricing and exaggerating the adverse effects of failure, and feelings of dissatisfaction. Neurotic perfectionism is associated with feelings of inferiority, depression, shame and guilt, and self-depreciation. Neurotic perfectionism is considered a predicate to the emergence and maintenance of eating disorders, and is a useful concept when working with clients with bulimia and anorexia.

NORMS The NPQ was developed on a sample of 32 women in their late teens and early 20s who attended self-help groups for persons with eating disorders, and 255 undergraduate females. The control subjects who were classified as "real control" (i.e., no eating problems) had NPQ scores below 144. The combined sample of self-help group members was classified as nonperfectionists, normal perfectionists, or neurotic perfectionists; means (and standard deviations) for these groups were 112.80 (28.88), 107.86 (1973), and 146.10 (27.69).

SCORING The NPQ is a unidimensional measure where items are summed to produce a total scale score. The scale is scored 1 = "Strongly disagree" to 5 = "Strongly agree." Total scores range from 42 to 210, and a score of 145 or below is a cutting score suggesting little trouble with the problem of self-defeating perfectionism. Higher scores indicate more neurotic perfectionism.

RELIABILITY The instrument has excellent internal consistency, with an alpha coefficient of .95 for the total sample of persons with eating disorders and the "real control" group of undergraduates.

VALIDITY The NPQ has very good known-groups validity where scores differentiate persons with eating problems from undergraduates with no eating disorders. Scores also distinguished subjects with different levels of perfectionism and research participants above and below the cutting scores on another measure of eating disorders.

PRIMARY REFERENCE Mitzman, S. F., Slade, P., and Dewey, M. E. (1994). Preliminary development of a questionnaire designed to measure neurotic perfectionism in the eating disorders. *Journal of Clinical Psychology*, 50, 516–522.

AVAILABILITY Susan F. Mitzman, Clinical Psychologist, Department of Clinical Psychology, The Whelan Building, University of Liverpool, P.O.B. 147, Liverpool, L69 3BX England. Email: sfm@liverpool.ac.uk.

Please place an (X) under the column which applies best to each of the numbered statements. All replies are strictly confidential. Thank you for your help.

	Strongly agree	Agree	Don't know	Disagree	Strongly disagree
1. I set impossibly high standards for myself.	( )	( )	( )	( )	( )
2. No matter how well I do, I never feel satisfied with my performance.	( )	( )	( )	( )	( )
3. At times I feel empty and hollow inside.	( )	( )	( )	( )	( )
4. If one is to attempt anything, one should do it perfectly or not at all.	( )	( )	( )	( )	( )
5. I constantly monitor my performance/ behavior.	( )	( )	( )	( )	( )
6. I often feel lonely/isolated.	( )	( )	( )	( )	( )
7. Sometimes I feel as though I don't really know who I am.	( )	( )	( )	( )	( )
8. I am harshly critical of myself.	( )	( )	( )	( )	( )
9. As soon as I succeed in reaching a goal, I have to set myself an even more difficult target to work toward.	( )	( )	( )	( )	( )
10. At times my emotions get so confused, I can't make any sense of them.	( )	( )	( )	( )	( )
11. I often experience feelings of self-contempt or worthlessness.	( )	( )	( )	( )	( )
12. I believe if I fail someone they will cease to respect me, or care for me.	( )	( )	( )	( )	( )
13. Unless I am constantly working toward achieving a goal, I feel dissatisfied.	( )	( )	( )	( )	( )
14. I have a clear idea of the kind of person I would like to be, or ought to be, but I feel that I always fall short of this.	( )	( )	( )	( )	( )
15. I find it difficult to obtain excitement/ pleasure from life.	( )	( )	( )	( )	( )
16. On occasions I feel if people could "see through me" they would expose me for the fraud that I sometimes feel I am.	( )	( )	( )	( )	( )
17. I measure myself by other people's standards.	( )	( )	( )	( )	( )
18. It feels as if my best is never good enough.	( )	( )	( )	( )	( )
19. When I get what I want (i.e., achieve my goal) I feel dissatisfied or disillusioned.	( )	( )	( )	( )	( )
20. I often feel ashamed.	( )	( )	( )	( )	( )
21. When I most need to be close to a person, I often find myself deliberately trying to reject or push them away.	( )	( )	( )	( )	( )

continued

	Strongly agree	Agree	Don't now	Disagree	Strongly disagree
22. As a child, however well I did, it felt as if it were never enough to please others.	( )	( )	( )	( )	( )
23. If I do less than my best I feel guilty and ashamed.	( )	( )	( )	( )	( )
24. I tend to think in extremes, i.e., feeling "all good or all bad," "all successful or all failing."	( )	( )	( )	( )	( )
25. I try to avoid the disapproval of others at all costs.	( )	( )	( )	( )	( )
26. I constantly compare myself with people I consider to be better than me.	( )	( )	( )	( )	( )
27. It often feels as if people make impossible/ excessive demands of me.	( )	( )	( )	( )	( )
28. No matter how successful my performance, I still feel that I could/should have done better.	( )	( )	( )	( )	( )
29. In order to feel O.K. about myself, I have to be what others expect me to be.	( )	( )	( )	( )	( )
30. Important others (i.e., mother, father) seemed to love me more for *how well I did* rather than for *who* I was.	( )	( )	( )	( )	( )
31. As a child I couldn't understand what others expected or required of me.	( )	( )	( )	( )	( )
32. At times my anger toward other people seems so intense, it feels destructive and unsafe.	( )	( )	( )	( )	( )
33. I often feel anxious or confused before beginning a task.	( )	( )	( )	( )	( )
34. I feel O.K. if I lapse or make mistakes.	( )	( )	( )	( )	( )
35. I feel guilty a lot of the time.	( )	( )	( )	( )	( )
36. I sometimes feel blaming and hostile toward other people.	( )	( )	( )	( )	( )
37. I am oversensitive to criticism.	( )	( )	( )	( )	( )
38. I often feel like withdrawing from people and social gatherings.	( )	( )	( )	( )	( )
39. If I do badly in something, I feel like a total failure.	( )	( )	( )	( )	( )
40. I am always punishing myself.	( )	( )	( )	( )	( )
41. I am usually good at making decisions.	( )	( )	( )	( )	( )
42. I feel I have to be perfect in order to gain approval.	( )	( )	( )	( )	( )

Noncontingent Outcome Instrument (NOI)

PURPOSE To measure pessimism regarding uncontrolled events.

AUTHOR Jeremy P. Shapiro

DESCRIPTION The NOI is a 10-item instrument designed as an index of the respondent's pessimism regarding the occurrence of relatively uncontrolled events in the lives of people in general. The respondent is asked to estimate the frequency or probability of 10 events whose occurrence is basically beyond the control of individuals. This measure may be used as an estimate of the extent of pessimism and negativity in an individual's perceptions of the lives of others, and may be especially useful with depressed clients.

NORMS The NOI was initially studied with 65 men and 49 women who were students in an introductory college psychology class. The age range was from 18 to 23. No other demographic data are provided. Means and standard deviations for each item are reported for men and women separately in the original article, but no overall norms for the measure as a whole are provided.

SCORING Each item provides an exact percentage figure for each client. Presumably, these items can be tallied across subjects. In addition, the scores on each item could be totaled for an overall score which could range hypothetically from 0 to 1000.

RELIABILITY Split-half reliability for the NOI was very good for women with a correlation of .87, but poor for men (.40).

VALIDITY There was a significant correlation for men with scores on a self-criticism scale. For women, the NOI was significantly correlated with scales measuring dependency, self-criticism, and efficacy. The NOI was not correlated with overall depression for either group.

PRIMARY REFERENCE Shapiro, J. P. (1988). Relationships between dimensions of depressive experience and perceptions of the lives of people in general, *Journal of Personality Assessment*, 52, 297–308.

AVAILABILITY May be copied from this volume.

Please answer the following questions. It is impossible to know the exact right answers, so just state your best judgment. All the questions refer to people of all ages in America.

1. What percentage of people do you think will have cancer at some time in their lives? _____%

2. What percentage of people do you think will at some time get into an automobile accident that is not their fault? _____%

3. What percentage of people do you think will be the victim of a violent crime at some time in their lives? _____%

4. What do you think the probability is that there will be a major economic depression in the next 25 years? _____%

5. What percentage of married couples do you think have experienced or will experience infertility (inability to have a child)? _____%

6. What percentage of people do you think will be the victim of a nonviolent crime (e.g., burglary) at some time in their lives? _____%

7. What percentage of people do you think have one or more serious medical problems? _____%

8. What do you think the probability is that there will be a nuclear war in the next 50 years? _____%

9. What percentage of people do you think will die before the age of 50? _____%

10. What percentage of people do you think will at some time have an accident in their home that will require a trip to a doctor? _____%

Obsessive-Compulsive Inventory (OCI)

PURPOSE To measure the frequency and distress of obsessive-compulsiveness.

AUTHORS Edna B. Foa, Michael J. Kazak, and Paul M. Salkovskis

DESCRIPTION This 42-item instrument is designed to measure the severity of obsessive-compulsive symptoms and to facilitate the diagnosis of obsessive-compulsive disorder. The OCI was developed to include a range of obsessions and compulsions, to allow comparisons of the severity between clusters of the symptoms, and to be useful with clinical and nonclinical populations. The OCI has seven subscales: washing (W: items 2, 4, 8, 21, 22, 27, 38, and 42); checking (C: items 3, 7, 9, 10, 19, 24, 31, 32, and 40); doubting (D: items 26, 37, and 41); ordering (O: items 14, 15, 23, 29, and 35); obsession (OB: items 1, 12, 13, 17, 20, 28, 30, and 33); hoarding (H: items 6, 11, and 34); neutralizing (N: items 5, 16, 18, 25, 36, and 39). These seven subscales reflect the major symptoms of obsessive-compulsive disorder. The OCI ascertains the frequency of obsessive-compulsive symptoms and the magnitude of distress associated with the symptoms, producing total scores on frequency and distress, with a cutting score of 40 and above on the distress scale as an indicator of a likely diagnosis of obsessive-compulsive disorder.

NORMS Normative data are reported on four samples: 114 persons with the diagnosis of obsessive-compulsive disorder, 44 persons with the diagnosis of posttraumatic stress disorder, 58 persons with the diagnosis of a general social phobia, and 194 persons with no mental health condition. The norms for the obsessive-compulsive and nonpatient samples are reported here, and the others are found in the primary reference. The patients with an obsessive-compulsive diagnosis had a mean of 66.33 with a standard deviation of 31.9 for the total distress ratings, and a mean of 66.36 and standard deviation of 29.4 for the frequency ratings. The nonpatient sample had a mean of 25.25 (SD = 20.8) for the distress ratings and a mean of 34.15 (SD = 21.2) for the frequency ratings. The clinical sample reported a mean (and standard deviation) of 1.44 (1.3), 1.51 (.9), 1.84 (1.3), 1.87 (1.2), 1.79 (1.1), 1.24 (1.3), and 1.38 (1.0) for the distress ratings on W, C, D, O, OB, H, and N subscales, respectively. The clinical sample had a mean (and standard deviation) of 1.44 (1.4), 1.51 (.9), 2.01 (1.1), 1.87 (1.1), 1.67 (.8), 1.22 (1.1), and 1.49 (.9) for the frequency ratings of the W, C, D, O, OB, H, and N subscales. The nonpatients reported a mean (and standard deviation) of .55 (.7), .52 (5), .65 (.8), .80 (.8), .60 (60), 1.06 (.8), and .41 (.5) for the distress ratings on the W, C, D, O, OB, H, and N subscales. The nonpatients reported a mean (and standard deviation) of .76 (.7), .72 (.5), .78 (.8), 1.08 (.8), .69 (.6), 1.52 (.9), and .64 (.6) for the frequency ratings of the W, C, D, O, OB, H, and N subscales.

SCORING Total scores for the frequency ratings and distress ratings are the sum of the items. Scores range from 0 to 168. Subscale scores are the sum of the item scores divided by the number of items in each subscale. Subscale scores range from 0 to 4. A higher score indicates greater obsessive-compulsiveness.

RELIABILITY The internal consistency of the OCI is excellent for the total scores, with alpha coefficients ranging from .86 to .95 for the four samples mentioned above. Internal consistency was satisfactory for the subscale scores, with alpha coefficients ranging from .59 to .96. Forty-one persons with a diagnosis of obsessive-compulsive disorder and 57 nonpatients provided data to estimate the test-retest reliability of the OCI. The correlation between the first and second administration ranged from .68 to .97 for the subscales, and between .84 to .90 for the total scores. These results indicate the OCI scores are quite stable over a one-to-two-week period.

VALIDITY The OCI has excellent evidence of validity. Total distress scores and subscale scores discriminated persons with an obsessive-compulsive diagnosis from persons with posttraumatic stress, general social phobia, and nonpatients. Total scores and subscale scores on the frequency of the symptoms also distinguished persons with obsessive-compulsive disorders from the other two mental health conditions and the nonpatients. OCI total scores correlated with other measures of obsessive-compulsiveness for the persons diagnosed with an obsessive-compulsive disorder and for the nonpatient sample. Distress and frequency total scores also correlated with measures of anxiety and depression for the nonpatients, and with anxiety for the sample of persons with an obsessive-compulsive diagnosis.

PRIMARY REFERENCE Foa, E. B., Kozak, M. J., Salkovskis, P. M., Coles, M. E., and Amir, N. (1998). The validation of a new obsessive-compulsive disorder scale: The Obsessive-Compulsive Inventory, *Psychological Assessment*, 10, 206–214.

AVAILABILITY Edna B. Foa, Ph.D., Director, A Center for the Treatment and Study of Anxiety, University of Pennsylvania, 3200 Henry Avenue, Philadelphia, PA 19129. Email: foa@mail.med.upenn.edu.

The following statements refer to experiences that many people have in their everyday lives. Under the column labeled FREQUENCY, circle the number next to each statement that best describes how *frequently you have had the experience in the past month*. The numbers in this column refer to the following verbal labels:

0 = Never
1 = Almost never
2 = Sometimes
3 = Often
4 = Almost always

Then in the column labeled DISTRESS, circle the number that best describes *how much* that experience has *distressed or bothered you during the past month*. The numbers in this column refer to the following verbal labels:

0 = Not at all
1 = A little
2 = Moderately
3 = A lot
4 = Extremely

	Frequency	Distress
1. Unpleasant thoughts come into my mind against my will and I cannot get rid of them.	0 1 2 3 4	0 1 2 3 4
2. I think contact with bodily secretions (perspiration, saliva, blood, urine, etc.) may contaminate my clothes or somehow harm me.	0 1 2 3 4	0 1 2 3 4
3. I ask people to repeat things to me several times, even though I understood them the first time.	0 1 2 3 4	0 1 2 3 4
4. I wash and clean obsessively.	0 1 2 3 4	0 1 2 3 4
5. I have to review mentally past events, conversations, and actions to make sure that I didn't do something wrong.	0 1 2 3 4	0 1 2 3 4
6. I have saved up so many things that they get in the way.	0 1 2 3 4	0 1 2 3 4
7. I check things more often than necessary.	0 1 2 3 4	0 1 2 3 4
8. I avoid using public toilets because I am afraid of disease or contamination.	0 1 2 3 4	0 1 2 3 4
9. I repeatedly check doors, windows, drawers, etc.	0 1 2 3 4	0 1 2 3 4
10. I repeatedly check gas and water taps and light switches after turning them off.	0 1 2 3 4	0 1 2 3 4
11. I collect things I don't need.	0 1 2 3 4	0 1 2 3 4

continued

561

	Frequency					Distress				
12. I have thoughts of hurting someone and not knowing it.	0	1	2	3	4	0	1	2	3	4
13. I have thoughts that I might want to harm myself or others.	0	1	2	3	4	0	1	2	3	4
14. I get upset if objects are not arranged properly.	0	1	2	3	4	0	1	2	3	4
15. I feel obliged to follow a particular order in dressing, undressing, and washing myself.	0	1	2	3	4	0	1	2	3	4
16. I feel compelled to count while I am doing things.	0	1	2	3	4	0	1	2	3	4
17. I am afraid of impulsively doing embarrassing or harmful things.	0	1	2	3	4	0	1	2	3	4
18. I need to pray to cancel bad thoughts or feelings.	0	1	2	3	4	0	1	2	3	4
19. I keep on checking forms or other things I have written.	0	1	2	3	4	0	1	2	3	4
20. I get upset at the sight of knives, scissors, and other sharp objects in case I lose control with them.	0	1	2	3	4	0	1	2	3	4
21. I am excessively concerned with cleanliness.	0	1	2	3	4	0	1	2	3	4
22. I find it difficult to touch an object when I know it has been touched by strangers or certain people.	0	1	2	3	4	0	1	2	3	4
23. I need things to be arranged in a particular order.	0	1	2	3	4	0	1	2	3	4
24. I get behind in my work because I repeat things over and over again.	0	1	2	3	4	0	1	2	3	4
25. I feel I have to repeat certain numbers.	0	1	2	3	4	0	1	2	3	4
26. After doing something carefully, I still have the impression that I have not finished it.	0	1	2	3	4	0	1	2	3	4
27. I find it difficult to touch garbage or dirty things.	0	1	2	3	4	0	1	2	3	4
28. I find it difficult to control my own thoughts.	0	1	2	3	4	0	1	2	3	4
29. I have to do things over and over again until it feels right.	0	1	2	3	4	0	1	2	3	4
30. I am upset by unpleasant thoughts that come into my mind against my will.	0	1	2	3	4	0	1	2	3	4
31. Before going to sleep I have to do certain things in a certain way.	0	1	2	3	4	0	1	2	3	4
32. I go back to places to make sure that I have not harmed anyone.	0	1	2	3	4	0	1	2	3	4
33. I frequently get nasty thoughts and have difficulty in getting rid of them.	0	1	2	3	4	0	1	2	3	4

	Frequency					Distress				
34. I avoid throwing things away because I am afraid I might need them later.	0	1	2	3	4	0	1	2	3	4
35. I get upset if others change the way I have arranged things.	0	1	2	3	4	0	1	2	3	4
36. I feel that I must repeat certain words or phrases in my mind in order to wipe out bad thoughts, feelings, or actions.	0	1	2	3	4	0	1	2	3	4
37. After I have done things, I have persistent doubts about whether I really did them.	0	1	2	3	4	0	1	2	3	4
38. I sometimes have to wash or clean myself simply because I feel contaminated.	0	1	2	3	4	0	1	2	3	4
39. I feel that there are good and bad numbers.	0	1	2	3	4	0	1	2	3	4
40. I repeatedly check anything which might cause a fire.	0	1	2	3	4	0	1	2	3	4
41. Even when I do something very carefully I feel that it is not quite right.	0	1	2	3	4	0	1	2	3	4
42. I wash my hands more often and longer than necessary.	0	1	2	3	4	0	1	2	3	4

Obsessive-Compulsive Scale (OCS)

PURPOSE To measure degree of compulsivity.

AUTHORS Gerald D. Gibb, James R. Bailey, Randall H. Best, and Thomas T. Lambirth

DESCRIPTION This 20-item instrument measures a concept that is widely discussed in clinical practice, but for which there are few systematic measurement tools. The focus of the OCS is on a general tendency toward obsessive thoughts and compulsive behaviors. The scale is a general measure of this disorder, and does not provide separate scores for obsessive thoughts and compulsive behaviors. The true-false format makes the OCS easy to complete, and the instrument has a validity check (see below).

NORMS The OCS was developed using 114 college students with mean scores of 11.15 and 11.24 for males and females, respectively. The mean for a clinical sample ($n=57$) was 11.22.

SCORING Items 1, 2, 4, 6, 7, 8, 16, 17, 18, and 21 are assigned 1 point if answered "true." Items 5, 9, 10, 11, 12, 13, 14, 19, 20, and 22 are assigned 1 point if answered "false." Scores range from 0 to 20, with higher scores indicating more compulsivity. Items 3 and 15 are validity checks, and if answered incorrectly, the OCS score should not be considered valid.

RELIABILITY This instrument has evidence of internal consistency and test-retest reliability. The internal consistency was estimated by correlating each item with the total, and these correlations were significant. The test-retest reliability correlation was .82 over a three-week period, indicating good stability.

VALIDITY The OCS has several estimates of concurrent validity: scores correlated with clinicians' ratings of clients' compulsivity, with Comrey's Order Scale, and with a measure of flexibility.

PRIMARY REFERENCE Gibb, G. D., Bailey, J. R., Best, R. H., and Lambirth, T. T. (1983). The measurement of the obsessive-compulsive personality, *Educational and Psychological Measurement*, 43, 1233–1237. Instrument reproduced with permission of Gerald D. Gibb.

AVAILABILITY Lt. Gerald D. Gibb, MSC, USNR, Psychological Sciences Department, Naval Aerospace Medical Research Library, Naval Air Station, Pensacola, FL 32508.

Please indicate whether each statement below is true or false for you by circling the T or the F to the left of the question.

T F   1. I feel compelled to do things I don't want to do.
T F   2. I usually check things that I know I have already done.
T F   3. I can walk 30 miles in an hour.
T F   4. I often do things I don't want to do because I cannot resist doing them.
T F   5. I seldom keep a daily routine.
T F   6. I feel compelled always to complete what I am doing.
T F   7. I often feel the need to double check what I do.
T F   8. I'd rather do things the same way all the time.
T F   9. I seldom have recurring thoughts.
T F   10. I seldom am compelled to do something I don't want to do.
T F   11. I don't feel uncomfortable and uneasy when I don't do things my usual way.
T F   12. If I don't feel like doing something it won't bother me not to do it.
T F   13. I usually never feel the need to be organized.
T F   14. I am uneasy about keeping a rigid time schedule.
T F   15. My birthday comes once a year.
T F   16. I am often compelled to do some things I do not want to do.
T F   17. I like to keep a rigid daily routine.
T F   18. I believe there is a place for everything and everything in its place.
T F   19. I seldom check things I know I have already done.
T F   20. I am not obsessed with details.
T F   21. I often have recurring thoughts.
T F   22. I like to do things differently each time.

Organizational Climate Scale (OCS)

PURPOSE To measure problem-solving and communication patterns in the workplace.

AUTHORS Anne Thompson and Hamilton McCubbin

DESCRIPTION The OCS is a 30-item scale designed to measure the problem-solving and communication patterns of individuals in the workplace that are sensitive to organizational change. The OCS has two problem-solving and two communication factors. The challenge factor is defined as the organization's emphasis on working together to solve problems, planning, and defining difficulties as challenges (items 2, 4, 6, 8, 10, 12, 14, 16, 18, and 20). The control dimension characterizes problem solving with the organization's emphasis on an internal locus of control, having a shared belief that problem solving is within the employee's and the organization's control and abilities (items 1, 3, 5, 7, 9, 11, 13, 15, 17, and 19). The conflictual communications dimension assesses the degree to which the organization emphasizes confrontation, embarrassment, becoming strained, and ultimately making matters more incendiary (items 21, 23, 25, 27, and 29). The supportive communication dimension focuses on the degree to which the organization emphasizes respect, sensitivity, affirmation, listening, and seeking of positive conclusions (items 22, 24, 26, 28, and 30). The OCS is one of the few available measures to focus on these organizational dimensions and as such is an important measure to aid in determining the impact of organizational interventions.

NORMS The OCS was studied with 1346 employees of a national insurance company of whom males constituted approximately 28%. Combining scores on the two problem-solving subscales produced a mean of 40.2 (SD = 7.3). Combining the two subscales for organizational communication produced a mean of 20.9 (SD = 4.5). Scores also are available for each of the individual subscales for men and for women.

SCORING After reverse-scoring items 1, 3, 4, 5, 7, 9, 15, 17, 19, and 29, the scores for the total scale as well as the subscales can be determined easily by summing the items on the total scale or each subscale. The reverse scoring ensures that all items are weighted in the same positive direction.

RELIABILITY The OCS has very good internal consistency with alphas of .82, .83, .87, and .89 for the challenge, control, conflictual communication, and supportive communication subscales, respectively. The OCS has excellent stability, with one-year test-retest correlations that range from .49 to .68.

VALIDITY The OCS has good concurrent validity as established through significant correlations among all of the OCS subscales with both work-environment subscales of the Work Pressure and Supervisor Support measure.

PRIMARY REFERENCE Thompson, A. I., and McCubbin, H. I. Organizational Climate Scale (OCS). In H. I. McCubbin, A. I. Thompson, and M.A. McCubbin (1996). *Family Assessment: Resiliency, Coping and Adaptation—Inventories for Research and Practice*. Madison: University Wisconsin System, 791–821.

AVAILABILITY After purchase of the primary reference, use instructions available in the book to register by telephone at (608) 262–5070 and to obtain permission to use the instrument.

Please read each statement below and decide to what degree each describes your work-place.

	False	Mostly false	Mostly true	True
1. Trouble we experience is caused by the decisions we make.	0	1	2	3
2. People make an extra effort to understand the organization's purposes and goals.	0	1	2	3
3. It is not wise to plan ahead and hope because things don't turn out anyway.	0	1	2	3
4. My work seems dull and meaningless.	0	1	2	3
5. Most of the unhappy things that happen to us are due to things beyond our control.	0	1	2	3
6. We believe that things will work out for the better if we work together.	0	1	2	3
7. Our work and efforts are not appreciated no matter now hard we try and work.	0	1	2	3
8. When our organization tries to solve problems we try new and exciting ways.	0	1	2	3
9. Our work situation is determined by factors over which we have little influence.	0	1	2	3
10. We work together to solve problems.	0	1	2	3
11. In the long run, the bad things that happen to us are balanced by the good things that happen.	0	1	2	3
12. We encourage each other to try new things and experiences.	0	1	2	3
13. Success is determined by the decisions we make.	0	1	2	3
14. We trust that policies and changes are really in everyone's best interest.	0	1	2	3
15. It is better to keep things the same rather than to make changes.	0	1	2	3
16. We have a sense of being strong even when we face big problems.	0	1	2	3
17. Top management makes all the decisions, we just react.	0	1	2	3
18. We are dedicated to do the best job possible.	0	1	2	3
19. We will experience a major disruption if we have another problem or change.	0	1	2	3
20. New challenges improve morale.	0	1	2	3

continued

When we struggle with problems or conflicts in our workplace, I would describe the way we work in the following way:

	False	Mostly false	Mostly true	True
21. We confront and embarrass each other in meetings.	0	1	2	3
22. We are respectful of each others' feelings.	0	1	2	3
23. We are not open and honest with each other.	0	1	2	3
24. We work hard to be sure colleagues/co-workers are not offended or hurt emotionally.	0	1	2	3
25. We walk away from disagreements and heated discussions feeling frustrated.	0	1	2	3
26. We affirm each other's opinions and viewpoints, even when we may disagree.	0	1	2	3
27. We make matters more difficult by getting emotionally upset and stirring up old problems.	0	1	2	3
28. We take the time to hear what each other has to say or feel.	0	1	2	3
29. We work to be calm and talk things through.	0	1	2	3
30. We get upset, but we try to end our differences on a positive note.	0	1	2	3

Orthogonal Cultural Identification Scale (OCIS)

PURPOSE To measure identification with cultures.

AUTHORS Fred Beauvais and E. R. Oetting

DESCRIPTION This 6-item instrument is designed to measure the magnitude of identification with a number of cultures. Cultural identification is the extent to which a person views himself or herself as involved and invested in an identified group. Cultural identification contrasts sharply with cultural identity, which is one's affiliation with a specific group. Strong cultural identification reflects a person's ability to meet the expectations of other cultural groups while the groups concomitantly meet one's own personal needs. The OCIS is based on a model of multiculturalism where identification with any one culture is independent from identification with another culture. As such, the instrument allows for monocultural, bicultural, and multicultural identification. The OCIS measures three aspects of cultural identification: identification with the way of life, perceived and expected success in the culture, and involvement in cultural activities and traditions. Each aspect of cultural identification is ascertained in terms of the respondent and the respondent's perception of his or her family. The OCIS assesses identification for five ways of life: Asian/Asian-American, white American/Anglo, Mexican-American or Spanish, Black or African-American, and American Indian. The OCIS is useful when working with parent-child conflict for persons of the identified cultures, biracial couples and families, and individuals struggling with cultural conflicts.

NORMS Norms are not available on the 6-item version reprinted here. The instrument was tested, however, on a sample of 2048 Mexican-American and American Indian youth.

SCORING The OCIS is scored by summing the item responses to each culture separately. Responses are scored "A lot"=4, "Some"=3, "Not much"=2, and "None at all"=1. The sum of the items is then divided by the number of items answered, producing a score ranging from 1 to 6. The OCIS should not be scored if more than 2 items are left unanswered. Higher scores reflect more cultural identification.

RELIABILITY The reliability of the OCIS was originally tested on only four of the six items. The 4-item version has an internal consistency coefficient of .80.

VALIDITY The 4-item version of the OCIS had good construct validity, with scores correlating with self-esteem and family relationships. As theorized, higher scores on the OCIS were correlated with better school adjustment. For American Indian youth, scores were associated with the practice of traditional, native ways, such as following tribal customs. Indian youths' scores on identification with Anglo values were not correlated with school adjustment or practicing traditional ways.

PRIMARY REFERENCE Oetting, E. R., Swaim, R. C., and Chiarella, M. C. (1998). Factor structure and invariance of the Orthogonal Cultural Identification Scale among American Indian and Mexican American youth. *Hispanic Journal of Behavioral Sciences*, 20, 131–154.

AVAILABILITY May be copied from this volume.

The following questions ask how close you are to different cultures. You may identify with more than one culture, so please mark all responses that apply to you.

	A lot	Some	A few	None at all

1. Some families have special activities or traditions that take place every year at particular times (such as holiday parties, special meals, religious activities, trips, or visits). How many of these special activities or traditions did your family of origin have when you were growing up that are based on . . .

	A lot	Some	A few	None at all
White American or Anglo culture	( )	( )	( )	( )
Asian or Asian-American culture	( )	( )	( )	( )
Mexican-American or Spanish culture	( )	( )	( )	( )
Black or African-American culture	( )	( )	( )	( )
American Indian culture	( )	( )	( )	( )

2. When you are an adult and have your own family, will you do special things together or have special traditions that are based on . . .

	A lot	Some	A few	None at all
Mexican-American or Spanish culture	( )	( )	( )	( )
Asian or Asian-American culture	( )	( )	( )	( )
White American or Anglo culture	( )	( )	( )	( )
Black or African-American culture	( )	( )	( )	( )
American Indian culture	( )	( )	( )	( )

3. Does your family live by or follow the . . .

	A lot	Some	A few	None at all
American Indian way of life	( )	( )	( )	( )
White American or Anglo way of life	( )	( )	( )	( )
Mexican-American or Spanish way of life	( )	( )	( )	( )
Black or African-American way of life	( )	( )	( )	( )
Asian or Asian-American way of life	( )	( )	( )	( )

4. Do *you* live by or follow the . . .

	A lot	Some	A few	None at all
Asian or Asian-American way of life	( )	( )	( )	( )
White American or Anglo way of life	( )	( )	( )	( )
Mexican-American or Spanish way of life	( )	( )	( )	( )
Black or African-American way of life	( )	( )	( )	( )
American Indian way of life	( )	( )	( )	( )

5. Is your family a success in the . . .

	A lot	Some	A few	None at all
Black or African-American way of life	( )	( )	( )	( )
Mexican-American or Spanish way of life	( )	( )	( )	( )
American Indian way of life	( )	( )	( )	( )
White American or Anglo way of life	( )	( )	( )	( )
Asian or Asian-American way of life	( )	( )	( )	( )

	A lot	Some	A few	None at all
6. Are you a success in the . . .				
American Indian way of life	( )	( )	( )	( )
Asian or Asian-American way of life	( )	( )	( )	( )
Mexican-American or Spanish way of life	( )	( )	( )	( )
Black or African-American way of life	( )	( )	( )	( )
White American or Anglo way of life	( )	( )	( )	( )

Padua Inventory (PI)

PURPOSE To measure common obsessional thoughts and compulsive behaviors.

AUTHOR Ezio Sanavio

DESCRIPTION The PI is a 60-item list of common obsessional thoughts and compulsive behaviors. The PI has an advantage over many other measures of symptoms of obsessive-compulsive disorders (OCD) by providing two distinct obsessional scales in addition to traditional checking and contamination scales. Research in several countries has provided cross-cultural support for the reliability and validity of the PI. The PI is one of the most widely used self-report measures of OCD in both research and clinical endeavors. (A revised version of the PI which removes the concept of worry from the obsessional subscales is available in the second reference below.) The PI comprises four subscales: impaired control over mental activities (items, in order of factor loadings, 32, 33, 31, 36, 35, 26, 28, 37, 27, 29, 38, 43, 59, 11, 34, 44, and 30); becoming contaminated (items 8, 7, 9, 3, 10, 5, 2, 4, 6, 1, and 60); checking behaviors (items 21, 22, 20, 19, 25, 23, 24, and 18); and urges and worries of losing control over motor behaviors (items 53, 46, 57, 47, 54, 55, and 49). (The remaining 17 items should not be used to calculate factor scores.) Perhaps the best use of the PI is as a measure of the impact of therapy as an index of change.

NORMS The PI has been studied on samples in a number of countries and has established a range of norms in those countries. The original study of the PI involved 967 nonclinical subjects residing in Italy and ranging in age from 16 to 70 years; 489 were male, 478 were female. Other groups in the original study included 198 male and 192 females in higher education institutes in Italy with an age range from 16 to 19 years. Data on 35 male and 70 female clinical subjects also are available. For the nonclinical subjects the mean score ranged from 46.8 to 70.1 in relation to six age groups. For the clinical sample, for males with OCD, the mean was 83.6 (SD = 34.8) and for females the mean was 98.6 (SD = 32.3). For clinical samples with other neurotic disorders, the mean on the PI for males was 50.2 (SD = 28.9) and for females the mean was 66.5 (SD = 32.4).

SCORING The PI is easily scored by summing all item scores for the total scores, with higher scores indicating greater psychopathology. The total scores range from 0 to 240. To obtain mean scores for each subscale the scores of the items on the subscales are divided by the number of items.

RELIABILITY The PI has excellent internal consistency, with alphas for males of .90 and for females of .94. The PI also has very good stability with 30-day test-retest correlations of .78 for males and .83 for females.

VALIDITY The PI has good concurrent and known-groups validity. Concurrent validity is evidenced by high correlations between the PI and a number of other measures including the Fear Survey Schedule, the Leyton Obsessional-Compulsive Inventory, and the Maudsley Obsessional-Compulsive Questionnaire. The known-groups validity of the PI was established with significant differences between respondents who had been diagnosed as obsessional and those who had been diagnosed with other neurotic disorders.

PRIMARY REFERENCES Sanavio, E. (1988). Obsessions and compulsions: The Padua Inventory, *Behaviour Research and Therapy*, 26, 169–177. Burns, G. L., et al. (1996). Revision of the Padua Inventory of obsessive compulsive disorder symptoms: Distinctions between worry, obsessions, and compulsions, *Behaviour Research and Therapy*, 34, 163–173.

AVAILABILITY May be copied from this volume. Reprinted by permission of Dr. Sanavio.

The following statements refer to thoughts and behaviors which may occur to everyone in everyday life. For each statement, choose the reply which best seems to fit you and the degree of disturbance which such thoughts or behaviors may create. Rate your replies as follows:

0 = Not at all
1 = A little
2 = Quite a lot
3 = A lot
4 = Very much

	0	1	2	3	4
1. I feel my hands are dirty when I touch money.	☐	☐	☐	☐	☐
2. I think even slight contact with bodily secretions (perspirations, saliva, urine, etc.) may contaminate my clothes or somehow harm me.	☐	☐	☐	☐	☐
3. I find it difficult to touch an object when I know it has been touched by strangers or by certain people.	☐	☐	☐	☐	☐
4. I find it difficult to touch rubbish or dirty things.	☐	☐	☐	☐	☐
5. I avoid using public toilets because I am afraid of disease and contamination.	☐	☐	☐	☐	☐
6. I avoid using public telephones because I am afraid of contagion and disease.	☐	☐	☐	☐	☐
7. I wash my hands more often and longer than necessary.	☐	☐	☐	☐	☐
8. I sometimes have to wash or clean myself simply because I think I may be dirty or "contaminated."	☐	☐	☐	☐	☐
9. If I touch something I think is "contaminated" I immediately have to wash or clean myself.	☐	☐	☐	☐	☐
10. If an animal touches me, I feel dirty and immediately have to wash myself or change my clothing.	☐	☐	☐	☐	☐
11. When doubts and worries come to my mind, I cannot rest until I have talked them over with a reassuring person.	☐	☐	☐	☐	☐
12. When I talk I tend to repeat the same things and the same sentences several times.	☐	☐	☐	☐	☐
13. I tend to ask people to repeat the same things to me several times consecutively, even though I did understand what they said the first time.	☐	☐	☐	☐	☐
14. I feel obliged to follow a particular order in dressing, undressing, and washing myself.	☐	☐	☐	☐	☐
15. Before going to sleep I have to do certain things in a certain order.	☐	☐	☐	☐	☐
16. Before going to bed I have to hang up or fold my clothes in a special way.	☐	☐	☐	☐	☐
17. I feel I have to repeat certain numbers for no reason.	☐	☐	☐	☐	☐
18. I have to do things several times before I think they are properly done.	☐	☐	☐	☐	☐
19. I tend to keep on checking things more often than necessary.	☐	☐	☐	☐	☐

20. I check and recheck gas and water taps and light switches after turning them off. ☐ ☐ ☐ ☐ ☐

21. I return home to check doors, windows, drawers, etc., to make sure they are properly shut. ☐ ☐ ☐ ☐ ☐

22. I keep on checking forms, documents, checks, etc., in detail, to make sure I have filled them in correctly. ☐ ☐ ☐ ☐ ☐

23. I keep on going back to see that matches, cigarettes, etc., are properly extinguished. ☐ ☐ ☐ ☐ ☐

24. When I handle money I count and recount it several times. ☐ ☐ ☐ ☐ ☐

25. I check letters carefully many times before posting them. ☐ ☐ ☐ ☐ ☐

26. I find it difficult to make decisions, even about unimportant matters. ☐ ☐ ☐ ☐ ☐

27. Sometimes I am not sure I have done things which in fact I know I have done. ☐ ☐ ☐ ☐ ☐

28. I have the impression that I will never be able to explain things clearly, especially when talking about important matters that involve me. ☐ ☐ ☐ ☐ ☐

29. After doing something carefully, I still have the impression I have either done it badly or not finished it. ☐ ☐ ☐ ☐ ☐

30. I am sometimes late because I keep on doing certain things more often than necessary. ☐ ☐ ☐ ☐ ☐

31. I invent doubts and problems about most of the things I do. ☐ ☐ ☐ ☐ ☐

32. When I start thinking of certain things, I become obsessed with them. ☐ ☐ ☐ ☐ ☐

33. Unpleasant thoughts come into my mind against my will and I cannot get rid of them. ☐ ☐ ☐ ☐ ☐

34. Obscene or dirty words come into my mind and I cannot get rid of them. ☐ ☐ ☐ ☐ ☐

35. My brain constantly goes its own way and I find it difficult to attend to what is happening round me. ☐ ☐ ☐ ☐ ☐

36. I imagine catastrophic consequences as a result of absent-mindedness or minor errors which I make. ☐ ☐ ☐ ☐ ☐

37. I think or worry at length about having hurt someone without knowing it. ☐ ☐ ☐ ☐ ☐

38. When I hear about a disaster, I think it is somehow my fault. ☐ ☐ ☐ ☐ ☐

39. I sometimes worry at length for no reason that I have hurt myself or have some disease. ☐ ☐ ☐ ☐ ☐

40. I sometimes start counting objects for no reason. ☐ ☐ ☐ ☐ ☐

41. I feel I have to remember completely unimportant numbers. ☐ ☐ ☐ ☐ ☐

42. When I read I have the impression I have missed something important and must go back and reread the passage at least two or three times. ☐ ☐ ☐ ☐ ☐

43. I worry about remembering completely unimportant things and make an effort not to forget them. ☐ ☐ ☐ ☐ ☐

44. When a thought or doubt comes into my mind, I have to examine it from all points of view and cannot stop until I have done so. ☐ ☐ ☐ ☐ ☐

45. In certain situations I am afraid of losing my self-control and doing embarrassing things. ☐ ☐ ☐ ☐ ☐

continued

	0	1	2	3	4
46. When I look down from a bridge or a very high window, I feel an impulse to throw myself into space.	☐	☐	☐	☐	☐
47. When I see a train approaching I sometimes think I could throw myself under its wheels.	☐	☐	☐	☐	☐
48. At certain moments I am tempted to tear off my clothes in public.	☐	☐	☐	☐	☐
49. While driving I sometimes feel an impulse to drive the car into someone or something.	☐	☐	☐	☐	☐
50. Seeing weapons excites me and makes me think violent thoughts.	☐	☐	☐	☐	☐
51. I get upset and worried at the sight of knives, daggers, and other pointed objects.	☐	☐	☐	☐	☐
52. I sometimes feel something inside me which makes me do things which are really senseless and which I do not want to do.	☐	☐	☐	☐	☐
53. I sometimes feel the need to break or damage things for no reason.	☐	☐	☐	☐	☐
54. I sometimes have an impulse to steal other people's belongings, even if they are of no use to me.	☐	☐	☐	☐	☐
55. I am sometimes almost irresistibly tempted to steal something from the supermarket.	☐	☐	☐	☐	☐
56. I sometimes have an impulse to hurt defenseless children or animals.	☐	☐	☐	☐	☐
57. I feel I have to make special gestures or walk in a certain way.	☐	☐	☐	☐	☐
58. In certain situations I feel an impulse to eat too much, even if I am then ill.	☐	☐	☐	☐	☐
59. When I hear about a suicide or a crime, I am upset for a long time and find it difficult to stop thinking about it.	☐	☐	☐	☐	☐
60. I invent useless worries about germs and diseases.	☐	☐	☐	☐	☐

Pain Catastrophizing Scale (PCS)

PURPOSE To measure pain catastrophizing.

AUTHORS Michael J. L. Sullivan, Scott R. Bishop, and Jayne Pivik

DESCRIPTION The PCS is a 13-item instrument designed to measure the role of catastrophizing in mediating responses to pain. Prior research has demonstrated a consistent relationship between catastrophizing and distress reactions to painful stimulation. The PCS appears to be a useful research instrument in efforts to understand the psychological processes that lead to heightened physical and emotional distress in response to pain. The PCS also may be useful in identifying individuals who may be susceptible to heightened distress responses to aversive medical procedures such as chemotherapy or surgery. The knowledge of individuals' level of catastrophizing may facilitate the application of coping interventions that will be most effective in promoting recovery from or adaptation to aversive medical procedures. The PCS comprises three subscales: rumination (items 8–11); magnification (items 6, 7, 13); and helplessness (items 1–5 and 12).

NORMS The PCS was initially developed in a series of four studies. The largest of these was the development and psychometric evaluation of the PCS. The study comprised 429 introductory psychology students of whom 127 were men and 302 were women with a mean age of 20.1 (SD=5.1). Means were reported by gender and showed significant gender differences on the total scale and on the rumination and helplessness scales, with women reporting higher levels of catastrophizing on all three. The mean for the total scale for women was 19.5 (SD=8.5) and for men was 16.4 (SD=7.3). The mean for rumination for women was 2.2 (SD=.9) and for men was 1.8 (SD=.8); for helplessness the mean for women was 1.2 (SD=.6) and for men was 1.0 (SD=.6); on magnification the mean for women was 1.1 (SD=.7) and for men was 1.0 (SD=.6).

SCORING The PCS is easily scored by summing scores on the individual items for the total scale and for the subscales. Higher scores suggest greater catastrophizing.

RELIABILITY The PCS has very good internal consistency, with an alpha for the total scale of .87. Alphas for the subscales were .87 for rumination, .79 for helplessness, and a low .60 for magnification. The PCS shows very good stability, with a 6-week test-retest correlation of .75.

VALIDITY The PCS has good concurrent and discriminant validity. The PCS distinguishes significantly between groups of catastrophizers and noncatastrophizers, and is a good predictor of the intensity of physical and emotional distress experienced by participants undergoing experimental pain situations; these data have been validated both with nonclinical and clinical samples. The PCS is also significantly correlated with a number of measures of psychopathology including depression, trait anxiety, negative affectivity, and fear of pain.

PRIMARY REFERENCE Sullivan, M. J. L., Bishop, S. R., and Pivik, J. (1995). The Pain Catastrophizing Scale: Development and validation, *Psychological Assessment*, 7, 524–532.

AVAILABILITY Dr. Michael Sullivan, Department of Psychology, Dalhousie University, Halifax, NS, Canada, B3H 4JI. Reprinted by permission of the author. Email: michael.osullivan@dal.ca. Telephone: (902) 494.6776.

Everyone experiences painful situations at some point in their lives. Such experiences may include headaches, tooth pain, joint or muscle pain. People are often exposed to situations that may cause pain such as illness, injury, dental procedures, or surgery.

We are interested in the types of thoughts and feelings that you have when you are in pain. Listed below are thirteen statements describing different thoughts and feelings that may be associated with pain. Using the following scale, please indicate the degree to which you have these thoughts and feelings when you are experiencing pain.

0 = Not at all
1 = To a slight degree
2 = To a moderate degree
3 = To a great degree
4 = All the time

When I'm in pain . . .

___ 1. I worry all the time about whether the pain will end.
___ 2. I feel I can't go on.
___ 3. It's terrible and I think it's never going to get any better.
___ 4. It's awful and I feel that it overwhelms me.
___ 5. I feel I can't stand it anymore.
___ 6. I become afraid that the pain will get worse.
___ 7. I keep thinking of other painful events.
___ 8. I anxiously want the pain to go away.
___ 9. I can't seem to keep it out of my mind.
___ 10. I keep thinking about how much it hurts.
___ 11. I keep thinking about how badly I want the pain to stop.
___ 12. There's nothing I can do to reduce the intensity of the pain.
___ 13. I wonder whether something serious may happen.

Pain-Related Self-Statements Scale (PRSS)
Pain-Related Control Scale (PRCS)

PURPOSE To measure pain-related cognitions.

AUTHORS Herta Flor, Deborah J. Behle, and Niels Birbaumer

DESCRIPTION The PRSS is an 18-item questionnaire designed to measure situation-specific aspects of a patient's cognitive coping with pain. The PRCS is a 15-item instrument designed to measure general attitudes toward pain. These two scales were developed to overcome apparent deficiencies of other scales in measuring cognitions about pain. The PRCS assesses underlying cognitive schemata of pain patients, especially beliefs of the pain's controllability and predictability. The PRSS, on the other hand, measures situation-specific cognitions that either promote or hinder attempts to cope with pain. These scales are useful not only in conducting basic research, but as evaluation measures regarding patients' responses to cognitive-behavioral therapeutic programs relating to patients' pain management. The PRSS comprises two factors: catastrophizing (items 2, 4, 7, 9, 10, 13, 14, 15, and 16) and active coping (items 1, 3, 5, 6, 8, 11, 12, 17, and 18). The PRCS also comprises two factors: helplessness (items 2, 5, 8, 9, 10, 12, and 13) and resourcefulness (items 1, 3, 4, 6, 7, 11, 14, and 15).

NORMS The PRCS and PRSS were developed in a series of two studies. The first consisted of 120 pain-clinic patients suffering from different types of chronic pain, and the second involved 213 patients who suffered from chronic back pain plus 44 patients who suffered from chronic jaw pain and 38 healthy subjects who were comparable demographically. The sample 1 subjects included 72 females and 48 males with a mean age of 49 and a mean number of months of pain duration of 126. The sample 2 subjects (chronic back pain) included 120 females and 93 males, with a mean age of 43.7 and a mean pain duration of 129.6 months. The means and standard deviations of the four subscales for sample 2 and the healthy sample are as follows: For PRSS catastrophizing, the sample 2 mean was 2.03 (SD = 1.22) and for the healthy group the mean was .85 (SD = .80); for PRSS coping, the sample 2 mean was 2.96 (SD = .91) and for the healthy group it was 3.37 (SD = 1.13); for PRCS helplessness, the sample 2 mean was 2.15 (SD = 1.09) and the healthy group mean was 1.09 (SD = .91); and for PRCS resourcefulness, the sample 2 mean was 2.78 (SD = .75) and the healthy sample mean was 2.87 (SD = 1.07). The means for all items also are available in the original article.

SCORING All subscales are scored the same way: the item responses are summed and divided by the number of items within each subscale.

RELIABILITY The two scales have good to excellent internal consistency, with alphas for the PRSS subscales of .88 and .92 and for the PRCS subscales of .77 and .83. The scales also have good stability with one-week test-retest coefficients that range from .77 to .88.

VALIDITY Both scales are reported to have excellent factorial construct validity in a series of factor analyses involving the PCRS and the PSRS and other scales of pain and the Hopelessness Scale. The PRSS and PRCS also have good known-groups validity, significantly distinguishing between chronic pain patients and healthy subjects. Both scales are also sensitive to change as a result of clinical intervention, particularly on the catastrophizing and helplessness subscales.

PRIMARY REFERENCE Flor, H., Behle, D. J., and Birbaumer, N. (1992). Assessment of pain-related cognitions in chronic pain patients, *Behaviour Research and Therapy*, 31, 63–73.

AVAILABILITY Herta Flor, Ph.D., Department of Psychology, Humboldt University, Hausvogteiplatz 5-7, D-10117, Berlin, Germany; Email: hflor@rz.hu-berlin.de. Reprinted with permission of Dr. Flor.

Most of the time, we have an internal conversation with ourselves. We ask ourselves, for example, to do certain things, we blame ourselves if we make a mistake, and we reward ourselves for our accomplishments. When we are in pain, we also say certain things to ourselves that are different from what we say when we are feeling good. Below, we have listed typical thoughts of people in pain. Please read each of the statements, and then mark how often you have this thought when your pain is severe. Please circle the appropriate number on the scale ranging from 0 = Almost never to 5 = Almost always.

	Almost never					Almost always
1. If I stay calm and relax, things will be better.	0	1	2	3	4	5
2. I cannot stand this pain any longer.	0	1	2	3	4	5
3. I can do something about my pain.	0	1	2	3	4	5
4. No matter what I do, my pain doesn't change anyway.	0	1	2	3	4	5
5. I need to relax.	0	1	2	3	4	5
6. I'll manage.	0	1	2	3	4	5
7. I need to take some pain medication.	0	1	2	3	4	5
8. I will soon be better again.	0	1	2	3	4	5
9. This will never end.	0	1	2	3	4	5
10. I am a hopeless case.	0	1	2	3	4	5
11. There are worse things than my pain.	0	1	2	3	4	5
12. I'll cope with it.	0	1	2	3	4	5
13. When will it get worse again?	0	1	2	3	4	5
14. This pain is killing me.	0	1	2	3	4	5
15. I can't go on anymore.	0	1	2	3	4	5
16. The pain drives me crazy.	0	1	2	3	4	5
17. A distraction helps my pain.	0	1	2	3	4	5
18. I can help myself.	0	1	2	3	4	5

Below, we have listed attitudes and reactions towards chronic pain we hear from other patients. Please indicate if you agree or disagree with each statement by circling the appropriate number on the scale ranging from 0 = Completely disagree to 5 = Completely agree.

	Completely disagree					Completely agree
1. I can predict my pain, there are warning signals.	0	1	2	3	4	5
2. No matter what I try, I cannot influence my pain.	0	1	2	3	4	5
3. Psychological stress aggravates my pain.	0	1	2	3	4	5
4. I can do something to reduce my pain.	0	1	2	3	4	5
5. When I am in pain, only painkillers or a doctor visit will help.	0	1	2	3	4	5
6. Pain is a challenge for me.	0	1	2	3	4	5
7. I do not let the pain get the best of me but try to fight it.	0	1	2	3	4	5
8. I am powerless towards my pain.	0	1	2	3	4	5
9. Pain is a matter of fate that must be tolerated.	0	1	2	3	4	5
10. I do not believe that there is anything that I myself can do about my pain.	0	1	2	3	4	5
11. I try to forget about my pain as often as possible.	0	1	2	3	4	5
12. I worry about the future because of my pain.	0	1	2	3	4	5
13. I have tried to cope with my pain but I have given it up because I had no success.	0	1	2	3	4	5
14. The best way to cope with my pain is to distract myself.	0	1	2	3	4	5
15. I have learned to live with my pain.	0	1	2	3	4	5

Panic Attack Cognitions Questionnaire (PACQ)

PURPOSE To measure cognitions associated with panic attacks.

AUTHORS George A. Clum, Susan Broyles, Janet Borden, and Patti Lou Watkins

DESCRIPTION The PACQ is a 23-item instrument designed to measure negative or catastrophic cognitions associated with panic attacks. The items for the PACQ were derived from the *DSM-III*, the Agoraphobic Cognition Questionnaire, and interviews with clients. Since negative cognitions are viewed as a key part of the problem in panic disorders, the PACQ is viewed as especially useful for clinical and research work with panic attacks.

NORMS The PACQ was studied initially with 103 subjects including 63 females and 40 males, with a mean age of 32 years. All subjects responded to an offer for a free evaluation of problem anxiety, and met *DSM-III* criteria for at least one anxiety disorder diagnosis. The group was divided into those with and without panic attacks. The means for subjects with and without panic attacks were not reported although there were significant differences between the groups.

SCORING The PACQ is easily scored by summing the ratings across all items. The potential range for the scale is 23 to 92, with higher scores indicating more domination of negative cognitions during or after a panic attack.

RELIABILITY The PACQ has very good internal consistency, with an alpha of .88. No data on stability were reported.

VALIDITY The PACQ has fair known-groups validity, significantly distinguishing between individuals suffering from panic attacks and those with anxiety disorders not suffering from panic attacks.

PRIMARY REFERENCE Clum, G. A., Broyles, S., Borden, J., and Watkins, P. L. (1990). Validity and reliability of the Panic Attack Symptoms and Cognitions Questionnaires, *Journal of Psychopathology and Behavioral Assessment*, 12, 233–245, Plenum Publishing Corp.

AVAILABILITY Dr. George A. Clum, Psychology Department, Virginia Tech, Blacksburg, VA 24011. Email: gclum@vt.edu.

Frightening thoughts often accompany or follow panic attacks. Think of your last panic attack. Using the scale below, rate each of the following thoughts according to the degree to which you thought it during and after this panic attack. Remember to rate each thought twice, once for during and once for after your last attack.

1 = Not at all
2 = Some, but not much
3 = Quite a lot
4 = Totally dominated your thoughts

	During	After
1. I am going to die.	_____	_____
2. I am going insane.	_____	_____
3. I am losing control.	_____	_____
4. This will never end.	_____	_____
5. I am really scared.	_____	_____
6. I am having a heart attack.	_____	_____
7. I am going to pass out.	_____	_____
8. I don't know what people will think.	_____	_____
9. I won't be able to get out of here.	_____	_____
10. I don't understand what is happening to me.	_____	_____
11. People will think I am crazy.	_____	_____
12. I will always be this way.	_____	_____
13. I am going to throw up.	_____	_____
14. I must have a brain tumor.	_____	_____
15. I am going to act foolish.	_____	_____
16. I am going blind.	_____	_____
17. I will hurt someone.	_____	_____
18. I am going to have a stroke.	_____	_____
19. I am going to scream.	_____	_____
20. I will be paralyzed by fear.	_____	_____
21. Something is really physically wrong with me.	_____	_____
22. I will not be able to breathe.	_____	_____
23. Something terrible will happen.	_____	_____

Panic Attack Symptoms Questionnaire (PASQ)

PURPOSE To measure symptoms of a panic attack.

AUTHORS George A. Clum, Susan Broyles, Janet Borden, and Patti Lou Watkins

DESCRIPTION The PASQ is a 33-item (plus one open-ended item) instrument designed to measure duration of symptoms (and, hence, severity) experienced during panic attacks. The items for the PASQ were taken from the DSM-III description of panic disorder symptoms, from symptoms reported in the literature, and from interviews with clients. Given the recent proliferation of research and clinical work with clients who suffer from panic attacks, the PASQ is viewed as very useful for both research and clinical work.

NORMS The PASQ was studied initially with 103 subjects including 63 females and 40 males, with a mean age of 32 years. All subjects responded to an offer for a free evaluation of problem anxiety, and met DSM-III criteria for at least one anxiety disorder diagnosis. The group was divided into those with panic attacks and those without. The mean for subjects with panic attacks was 87.53 and for those without panic attacks was 70.1. This difference was statistically significant.

SCORING The PASQ is easily scored by summing the ratings across all items. The potential range for the 33 items is 0 to 165, with higher scores indicating greater duration of symptoms.

RELIABILITY The PASQ has very good internal consistency, with an alpha of .88. No data on stability were reported.

VALIDITY The PASQ has excellent known-groups validity, significantly distinguishing between individuals suffering from panic attacks and those with anxiety disorders not suffering from panic attacks.

PRIMARY REFERENCE Clum, G. A., Broyles, S., Borden, J., and Watkins, P. L. (1990). Validity and reliability of the Panic Attack Symptoms and Cognitions Questionnaires, *Journal of Psychopathology and Behavioral Assessment*, 12, 233-245, Plenum Publishing Corp.

AVAILABILITY Dr. George A. Clum, Psychology Department, Virginia Tech, Blacksburg, VA 24061. Email: gclum@vt.edu.

The symptoms listed below are frequently experienced during a panic attack. Using the scale below for your most recent attack, circle the number corresponding to the length of time you experienced any of the symptoms listed.

0 = Did not experience this
1 = Fleetingly (1 second to 1 minute)
2 = Briefly (1 minute to 10 minutes)
3 = Moderately (10 minutes to 1 hour)
4 = Persistently (1 hour to 24 hours)
5 = Protractedly (1 day to 2 days or longer)

1. Heart beating rapidly	0 1 2 3 4 5
2. Pain in chest	0 1 2 3 4 5
3. Heart pounding in chest	0 1 2 3 4 5
4. Difficulty in swallowing (lump in throat)	0 1 2 3 4 5
5. Feeling of suffocation	0 1 2 3 4 5
6. Choking sensation	0 1 2 3 4 5
7. Hands or feet tingle	0 1 2 3 4 5
8. Face feels hot	0 1 2 3 4 5
9. Sweating	0 1 2 3 4 5
10. Trembling or shaking inside	0 1 2 3 4 5
11. Hands or body trembling or shaking	0 1 2 3 4 5
12. Numbness in hands or feet	0 1 2 3 4 5
13. Feeling that you are not really you or are disconnected from your body	0 1 2 3 4 5
14. Feeling that things around you are unreal, as if in a dream	0 1 2 3 4 5
15. Nausea	0 1 2 3 4 5
16. Breathing rapidly (as if unable to catch your breath)	0 1 2 3 4 5
17. Cold hands or feet	0 1 2 3 4 5
18. Dry mouth	0 1 2 3 4 5
19. Sinking feeling in stomach	0 1 2 3 4 5
20. Nerves feeling "wired"	0 1 2 3 4 5
21. Feeling physically immobilized	0 1 2 3 4 5
22. Blurred or distorted vision	0 1 2 3 4 5
23. Pressure in chest	0 1 2 3 4 5

24. Shortness of breath	0	1	2	3	4	5
25. Dizziness	0	1	2	3	4	5
26. Feeling faint	0	1	2	3	4	5
27. Butterflies in stomach	0	1	2	3	4	5
28. Stomach knotted	0	1	2	3	4	5
29. Tightness in chest	0	1	2	3	4	5
30. Legs feeling wobbly or rubbery	0	1	2	3	4	5
31. Feeling disoriented or confused	0	1	2	3	4	5
32. Cold clamminess	0	1	2	3	4	5
33. Sensitivity to loud noises	0	1	2	3	4	5

34. Other (please list) _____

_____

How many times have you experienced these attacks:

in the past week _____

in the past month _____

in the past six months _____

in the past year _____

Patient Reactions Assessment (PRA)

PURPOSE To measure perceived qualities of health care providers.

AUTHORS John P. Galassi, Rachel Schanberg, and William B. Ware

DESCRIPTION The PRA is a 15-item instrument composed of three subscales designed to measure perceived quality of information (I; items 1, 5, 10, 11, 14), affective behaviors of health care providers (A; items 3, 6, 9, 12, 15), and the client's perceived ability to initiate communication (C; items 2, 4, 7, 8, 13). The PRA is based on the assumption that provider information giving and affective behaviors are related to clients' satisfaction, compliance, and understanding of their condition. Client communication is also viewed as important in overall health care provision. The PRA can be viewed as a measure of the perceived quality of the relationship in a medical setting.

NORMS The PRA was studied with 197 patients at a cancer center in North Carolina including 79 men, 116 women, and 2 who did not specify gender. The sample was 86.3% white, 7.6% black, and .6% Native American. Seventy-eight percent of the sample was married. The most frequent types of cancer were melanoma, breast, and lymphoma. The mean for the total PRA was 88.16 (SD=12.85); for the I subscale, 29.24 (SD=4.54); for the A subscale, 30.49 (SD=4.95); and for the C subscale, 28.43 (SD=6.32).

SCORING The PRA is scored by first reverse-scoring items 2, 4, 7, 8, 12, 13, and 15 and then summing item responses for a total score and subscale scores.

RELIABILITY The PRA has excellent internal consistency, with an overall alpha of .91 and alphas that range from .87 to .91 for the subscales. There were no data on stability.

VALIDITY The PRA has fair known-groups validity, significantly distinguishing a group of caregivers perceived by counseling professionals as having more effective relationships from those seen as having less effective relationships.

PRIMARY REFERENCE Galassi, J. P., Schanberg, R., and Ware, W. B. (1992). The Patient Reactions Assessment: A brief measure of quality of the patient-provider relationship, *Psychological Assessment*, 4, 346–351.

AVAILABILITY May be copied from this volume.

Think about your *recent* contacts with the medical professional who *primarily* examined you in clinic today. Then answer the following questions by circling the number that best describes how you feel about your *recent* contacts with that person. Use the following key to guide your answers:

1 = Very strongly disagree
2 = Strongly disagree
3 = Disagree
4 = Unsure
5 = Agree
6 = Strongly agree
7 = Very strongly agree

1. I understand the possible side effects of treatment.　　1　2　3　4　5　6　7

2. If this person tells me something that is different from what I was told before, it is difficult for me to ask about it in order to get it straightened out.　　1　2　3　4　5　6　7

3. He/she is warm and caring toward me.　　1　2　3　4　5　6　7

4. If I don't understand something the person says, I have difficulty asking for more information.　　1　2　3　4　5　6　7

5. The person told me what he/she hopes the treatment will do for me.　　1　2　3　4　5　6　7

6. This person makes me feel comfortable about discussing personal or sensitive issues.　　1　2　3　4　5　6　7

7. It is hard for me to tell the person about new symptoms.　　1　2　3　4　5　6　7

8. It is hard for me to ask about how my treatment is going.　　1　2　3　4　5　6　7

9. This person really respects me.　　1　2　3　4　5　6　7

10. I understand pretty well the medical plan for helping me.　　1　2　3　4　5　6　7

11. After talking to this person, I have a good idea of what changes to expect in my health over the next weeks and months.　　1　2　3　4　5　6　7

12. When I talk to this person, I sometimes end up feeling insulted.　　1　2　3　4　5　6　7

13. I have difficulty asking this person questions.　　1　2　3　4　5　6　7

14. The treatment procedure was clearly explained to me.　　1　2　3　4　5　6　7

15. This individual *doesn't* seem interested in me as a person.　　1　2　3　4　5　6　7

Penn State Worry Questionnaire (PSWQ)

PURPOSE To measure worry.

AUTHORS T. J. Meyer, M. L. Miller, R. L. Metzger, and T. D. Borkovec

DESCRIPTION The PSWQ is a 16-item instrument designed to measure the trait of worry. The process of worry is pervasive throughout all of the anxiety disorders, and chronic worry is a major defining characteristic of generalized anxiety disorder (GAD). Although worry is a predominant feature of the anxiety disorders, there are few if any scales available to measure worry; most measures in this area have been developed to tap other aspects of anxiety and stress. The PSWQ measures worry as a construct independent of anxiety and depression among moderately severe cases of GAD. It is therefore an important measure for the assessment of worry as well as a good device for tracking changes in worry as a result of clinical treatment.

NORMS The PSWQ has been studied in a series of studies involving hundreds of undergraduate students and some clinical samples. One of the major studies involved a group of 405 introductory psychology college students of whom 228 were female. No other demographic data were available. The mean of the PSWQ for the total group was 48.8 (SD = 13.8), with the mean for females being 51.2 and for males 46.1. Females scored significantly higher on the PSWQ than males. Means and standard deviations for a number of different samples are available in the original article.

SCORING The PSWQ is easily scored by reverse-scoring items 1, 3, 8, 10, and 11, and then summing individual items for the total score. Higher scores suggest a stronger tendency to worry.

RELIABILITY Reliability data on the number of samples is available in the original article. In the sample described above the internal consistency of the PSWQ was excellent, with an alpha of .93. The PSWQ also has excellent stability, with a one-month test-retest correlation on a separate sample of 73 undergraduate students of .93.

VALIDITY The PSWQ has excellent concurrent and known-groups validity. In several studies, the PSWQ has been shown to correlate in predicted directions with other emotional-disturbance questionnaires, with assessments of other psychological constructs meaningfully related to pervasive worries such as self-esteem and perfectionism, and with specific maladaptive ways of coping with environmental stress. The PSWQ also distinguishes levels of diagnosable GAD and produced higher scores among individuals with GAD than among diagnosable posttraumatic stress disorder cases. In a clinical sample the PSWQ was shown to be sensitive to changes as a result of clinical treatment. The PSWQ does not appear to be affected by social desirability response conditions.

PRIMARY REFERENCE Meyer, T. J., Miller, M. L., Metzger, R. L., and Borkovec, T. D. (1990). Development and validation of the Penn State Worry Questionnaire, *Behaviour Research and Therapy*, 28, 487–495.

AVAILABILITY Dr. T. D. Borkovec, Department of Psychology, Penn State University, University Park, PA 16802. Reprinted with permission of Dr. Borkovec. Email: tdb@psu.edu.

PSWQ

Enter the number from the scale below that best describes how typical or characteristic each of the 16 items is of you, putting the number next to the item.

1	2	3	4	5
Not at all typical		Somewhat typical		Very typical

___ 1. If I don't have enough time to do everything, I don't worry about it.

___ 2. My worries overwhelm me.

___ 3. I don't tend to worry about things.

___ 4. Many situations make me worry.

___ 5. I know I shouldn't worry about things, but I just can't help it.

___ 6. When I am under pressure, I worry a lot.

___ 7. I am always worrying about something.

___ 8. I find it easy to dismiss worrisome thoughts.

___ 9. As soon as I finish one task, I start to worry about everything else I have to do.

___ 10. I never worry about anything.

___ 11. When there is nothing more I can do about a concern, I don't worry about it any more.

___ 12. I've been a worrier all my life.

___ 13. I notice that I have been worrying about things.

___ 14. Once I start worrying, I can't stop.

___ 15. I worry all the time.

___ 16. I worry about projects until they are all done.

Perceived Efficacy in Patient-Physician Interactions (PEPPI)

PURPOSE To measure older patients' self-efficacy in obtaining medical information.

AUTHORS Rose C. Maly et al.

DESCRIPTION The PEPPI is a 5-item questionnaire that was designed to assess the self-efficacy of older patients in their efforts to obtain from physicians medical information and attention to their medical concerns. The PEPPI was developed out of concerns that sociocultural factors specific to the elderly may have an adverse impact on their interactions with physicians (and, by extension, other medical personnel). In addition, research has shown that self-efficacy mediates health outcomes. Thus, the PEPPI can be used to assess the extent of problems a patient may have in this area so that some effort can be expended to produce more self-efficacious behaviors in the patient. The PEPPI is very easy to administer and takes less than a minute to complete. Adding to its utility is the fact that the PEPPI has two forms, one for self-report and one for interviewer administration, both of which are reproduced here.

NORMS The PEPPI was developed with two samples of convenience at a number of senior multipurpose centers in Los Angeles County. The total sample size was 163 (59 in sample 1 and 104 in sample 2) with 76% of sample 1 and 57.7% in sample 2 being women. The mean age in both samples was approximately 77. Ethnic breakdown for sample 1 was 76.3% white, 15.3% African American, and 8.5% Asian or Pacific Islander while the same figures for sample 2 were 57.7% women, 75% white, 8.7% African American, 3.9% Hispanic, 10.6% Asian or Pacific Islander and 1.9% other. There were significant differences between the two samples with re: gender, ethnicity, and college education with sample 2 having significantly more college graduates than sample 1. Approximately half of the respondents in both samples were widowed. Mean scores for each sample for each item are available in the Primary Reference. The overall mean on the PEPPI for sample 1 was 18.93 and for sample 2 was 18.72.

SCORING The PEPPI is very easily scored by simply summing all the item scores. The range of scores on the PEPPI is from 5 to 50 with higher scores representing greater self-efficacy.

RELIABILITY The PEPPI has good internal consistency with alphas of .82 and .83 for the two samples respectively. Data on stability were not reported.

VALIDITY The PEPPI demonstrated good construct validity through establishing convergent and discriminative validity. As predicted, the PEPPI was significantly correlated in expected directions with active coping (a scale from the Medical Outcomes Scale), patient satisfaction (the Patient Satisfaction Questionnaire), and a general self-efficacy measure, Pearlin's Self-Mastery Scale.

PRIMARY REFERENCE Maly, R. C., et al. (1998). Perceived efficacy in physician-patient interactions (PEPPI): Validation of an instrument in older persons, *Journal of the American Geriatric Society, 46*, 889–894. Instrument reproduced with the permission of Dr. Maly.

AVAILABILITY The instrument is in the public domain per Dr. Maly. Dr. Maly can be contacted at the School of Medicine, UCLA, Department of Family Medicine, 10880 Wilshire Blvd., Suite 1800, Los Angeles, CA 90024. Email: rmaly@modnet.ucla.edu.

The following 5 questions are about how you interact with doctors as a patient. **Please circle the number** that tells me how CONFIDENT you feel in your ability to do each of the following things. Remember, these questions are about your ability to do these things *in general* and not about any particular doctor.

Rate your confidence on a scale of 0 to 10, with 10 meaning extremely confident and 0 meaning not confident at all.

How *confident* are you in your *ability*:
1. To know what questions to ask a doctor:

[0 = not confident at all, 10 = extremely confident]

| 1 | 2 | 3 | 4 | 5 | 6 | 7 | 8 | 9 | 10 |

How *confident* are you in your *ability*:
2. To get a doctor to answer all of your questions:

[0 = not confident at all, 10 = extremely confident]

| 1 | 2 | 3 | 4 | 5 | 6 | 7 | 8 | 9 | 10 |

How *confident* are you in your *ability*:
3. To make the most of your visits with your doctors:

[0 = not confident at all, 10 = extremely confident]

| 1 | 2 | 3 | 4 | 5 | 6 | 7 | 8 | 9 | 10 |

How *confident* are you in your *ability*:
4. To get a doctor to take your chief health concern seriously:

[0 = not confident at all, 10 = extremely confident]

| 1 | 2 | 3 | 4 | 5 | 6 | 7 | 8 | 9 | 10 |

How *confident* are you in your *ability*:
5. To get a doctor to do something about your chief health concern:

[0 = not confident at all, 10 = extremely confident]

| 1 | 2 | 3 | 4 | 5 | 6 | 7 | 8 | 9 | 10 |

Interviewer:

"The following 5 questions are about how you interact with doctors as a patient. Please tell me how CONFIDENT you feel in your ability to do each of the following things. Remember, these questions are about your ability to do these things *in general* and not about any particular doctors.

Rate your confidence on a scale of 0 to 10, with 10 meaning extremely confident and 0 meaning not confident at all."

How *confident* are you in your *ability*:
1. To know what questions to ask a doctor:

CONFIDENCE LEVEL, 0–10 _____   [0 = not confident at all,
                                    10 = extremely confident]

How *confident* are you in your *ability*:
2. To get a doctor to answer all of your questions:

CONFIDENCE LEVEL, 0–10 _____   [0 = not confident at all,
                                    10 = extremely confident]

How *confident* are you in your *ability*:
3. To make the most of your visits with your doctors:

CONFIDENCE LEVEL, 0–10 _____   [0 = not confident at all,
                                    10 = extremely confident]

How *confident* are you in your *ability*:
4. To get a doctor to take your chief health concern seriously:

CONFIDENCE LEVEL, 0–10 _____   [0 = not confident at all,
                                    10 = extremely confident]

How *confident* are you in your *ability*:
5. To get a doctor to do something about your chief health concern:

CONFIDENCE LEVEL, 0–10 _____   [0 = not confident at all,
                                    10 = extremely confident]

Perceived Guilt Index—State (PGI-S)
Perceived Guilt Index—Trait (PGI-T)

PURPOSE To measure the state and trait of guilt.

AUTHORS John R. Otterbacher and David C. Munz

DESCRIPTION The PGI-S and the PGI-T make up an instrument that measures the emotional experience of guilt as a state at the moment (PGI-S) and as a generalized self-concept (PGI-T). The instruments are quite different from others in this volume as they are scored as a single index and the score value is based on ratings from a sample of college students. The instrument was developed by having undergraduates ($n=80$) develop an item pool of adjectives and phrases describing guilt. A second sample of college students rated each item in terms of its intensity of guilt, and 83 items were selected based on the median ratings. A final sample of college students then rated the items on a semantic differential and 11 items were selected as a unidimensional index of the emotional experience of guilt. The instrument is particularly useful in settings where one needs to monitor a client's guilt reaction to specific events or situations. When the PGI-T and PGI-S instruments are used together, the trait scale should be administered first.

NORMS Normative data are not available. The score values for all the items were based on a sample of 55 undergraduate students.

SCORING There are two ways to score the PGI, as single indexes for the specific trait and state word selected, and as a score assessing one's guilt reaction to a particular situation which is compared to how one "normally" feels. Scores for the PGI-S and PGI-T are determined by assigning the item score value. The score values for each item are: 1=6.8, 2=1.1, 3=4.3, 4=9.4, 5=2.0, 6=7.8, 7=5.9, 8=3.4, 9=8.6, 10=5.3, 11=10.4. Since the respondent is instructed to select one item, the score is simply the item score value corresponding to the item.

The second method of scoring the PGI is more complicated. First assign the respondent the appropriate item scores as described above, then subtract the PGI-T from the PGI-S score, and add 10 to the result. The constant 10 is used to eliminate confusion over minus and positive signs. Moreover, scores above 10 indicate an intensity of guilt greater than what one normally feels, while scores below 10 represent a guilt reaction less than one's usual experience.

RELIABILITY Reliability for the two scales is reported in terms of test-retest correlations over a four-week period. Scores were not correlated for the PGI-S scale, as would be expected of a state measurement. The PGI-T was only slightly correlated (.30). Data on internal consistency were not available.

VALIDITY As a measure of one's guilt reaction (i.e., the second scoring method), the PGI-S and PGI-T have been shown to be sensitive to assessing changes occurring as a consequence of sacramental confession. Concurrent validity is demonstrated by differences in the relationship between state and trait guilt scores for groups where guilt increased and decreased over a four-week period.

PRIMARY REFERENCE Otterbacher, J. R., and Munz, D. C. (1973). State-trait measure of experiential guilt, *Journal of Consulting and Clinical Psychology*, 40, 115–121. Instruments reproduced with permission of David C. Munz and the American Psychological Association.

AVAILABILITY David C. Munz, Ph.D., Department of Psychology, St. Louis University, St. Louis, MO 63104. Email: munzdc@slu.edu.

Below is a list of words and phrases people use to describe how they feel at different times. Please check the word or phrase that best describes the way you feel *at this moment.* So that you will become familiar with the general range of feeling that they cover or represent, carefully read the entire list before making your selection. Again, check only *one* word or phrase, that which best describes the way you feel *at this moment.*

___ 1. Reproachable
___ 2. Innocent
___ 3. Pent up
___ 4. Disgraceful
___ 5. Undisturbed
___ 6. Marred
___ 7. Chagrined
___ 8. Restrained
___ 9. Degraded
___ 10. Fretful
___ 11. Unforgivable

Below is a list of words and phrases people use to describe how *guilty* they feel at different times. Please check the word or phrase which best describes the way you *normally feel*. So that you will become familiar with the general range of feeling that they cover or represent, carefully read this entire list before making your selection. Again, check only *one* word or phrase, that which best describes how *guilty* you *normally feel*.

___ 1. Reproachable
___ 2. Innocent
___ 3. Pent up
___ 4. Disgraceful
___ 5. Undisturbed
___ 6. Marred
___ 7. Chagrined
___ 8. Restrained
___ 9. Degraded
___ 10. Fretful
___ 11. Unforgivable

Perceived Social Support—Friend Scale (PSS-Fr)
Perceived Social Support—Family Scale (PSS-Fa)

PURPOSE To measure fulfillment of social support from friends and family.

AUTHORS Mary E. Procidano and Kenneth Heller

DESCRIPTION The PSS-Fr and PSS-Fa are two 20-item instruments designed to measure the degree one perceives his/her needs for support as fulfilled by friends and family. Social support varies between friends and family in that one's network of friends is comparatively less long-term than the family networks and requires more social competence in maintenance than is demanded of one's family network. In part, this difference is because people assume the family network is their birthright. The items of the instruments presented here were developed from a pool of 84 items and were selected by magnitude of items to total correlations. Factor analysis suggests the instruments each measure a single domain.

NORMS Normative data were derived from a sample of 222 (mean age=19 years) undergraduate psychology students. The mean and standard deviation for the PSS-Fr and PSS-Fa were 15.15 (SD=5.08) and 13.40 (SD=4.83).

SCORING The PSS-Fr and PSS-Fa are scored "yes," "no," and "don't know" ("don't know" is scored 0 on both scales). On the PSS-Fr an answer of "no" is scored +1 for items 2, 6, 7, 15, 18, and 20. For the remaining items "yes" is scored +1. For the PSS-Fa, answers of "no" to items 3, 4, 16, 19, and 20 are scored +1, and for all other items a "yes" answer is scored +1. Scale scores are the total of item scores and range from 0 to 20 for the PSS-Fr and the PSS-Fa. Higher scores reflect more perceived social support.

RELIABILITY The PSS has excellent internal consistency, with an alpha of .90. The test-retest coefficient of stability over a one-month period was .83. The reliability data are based on the original 20-item PSS before the items were anchored for separate perceived support from friends and family. Alphas for the final PSS-Fa ranged from .88 to .91 and .84 to .90 for the PSS-Fr.

VALIDITY Both the PSS-Fr and PSS-Fa have good concurrent validity. Scores are correlated with psychological distress and social competence. Both measures were associated with psychological symptoms. Scores on the PSS-Fr were predicted by length of time one was a member of one's social network and the degree of reciprocity in the relationship. Scores on the PSS-Fa were predicted by intangible and tangible support from family members. Correlations also were noted with the California Personality Inventory and interpersonal dependency. Subjects categorized as high and low in perceived support differed in the verbal disclosure which supports the instruments' known-groups validity. Clinical and nonclinical samples also differed on both measures.

PRIMARY REFERENCE Procidano, M. E., and Heller, K. (1983). Measures of perceived social support from friends and from family: Three validation studies, *American Journal of Community Psychology*, 11, 1–24. Instrument reprinted with permission of Mary Procidano and Plenum Publishing Corp.

AVAILABILITY Dr. Mary Procidano, Department of Psychology, Fordham University, Bronx, NY 10458-5198. Email: procidano@fordham.edu.

The statements which follow refer to feelings and experiences which occur to most people at one time or another in their relationships with *friends*. For each statement there are three possible answers: Yes, No, Don't know. Please circle the answer you choose for each item.

Yes	No	Don't know	1.	My friends give me the moral support I need.
Yes	No	Don't know	2.	Most other people are closer to their friends than I am.
Yes	No	Don't know	3.	My friends enjoy hearing about what I think.
Yes	No	Don't know	5.	I rely on my friends for emotional support.
Yes	No	Don't know	6.	If I felt that one or more of my friends were upset with me, I'd just keep it to myself.
Yes	No	Don't know	7.	I feel that I'm on the fringe in my circle of friends.
Yes	No	Don't know	8.	There is a friend I could go to if I were just feeling down, without feeling funny about it later.
Yes	No	Don't know	9.	My friends and I are very open about what we think about things.
Yes	No	Don't know	10.	My friends are sensitive to my personal needs.
Yes	No	Don't know	11.	My friends come to me for emotional support.
Yes	No	Don't know	12.	My friends are good at helping me solve problems.
Yes	No	Don't know	13.	I have a deep sharing relationship with a number of friends.
Yes	No	Don't know	14.	My friends get good ideas about how to do things or make things from me.
Yes	No	Don't know	15.	When I confide in friends, it makes me feel uncomfortable.
Yes	No	Don't know	16.	My friends seek me out for companionship.
Yes	No	Don't know	17.	I think that my friends feel that I'm good at helping them solve problems.
Yes	No	Don't know	18.	I don't have a relationship with a friend that is as intimate as other people's relationships with friends.
Yes	No	Don't know	19.	I've recently gotten a good idea about how to do something from a friend.
Yes	No	Don't know	20.	I wish my friends were much different.

The statements which follow refer to feelings and experiences which occur to most people at one time or another in their relationships with their *families*. For each statement there are three possible answers: Yes, No, Don't know. Please circle the answer you choose for each item.

Yes   No   Don't know   1.   My family gives me the moral support I need.

Yes   No   Don't know   2.   I get good ideas about how to do things or make things from my family.

Yes   No   Don't know   3.   Most other people are closer to their family than I am.

Yes   No   Don't know   4.   When I confide in the members of my family who are closest to me, I get the idea that it makes them uncomfortable.

Yes   No   Don't know   5.   My family enjoys hearing about what I think.

Yes   No   Don't know   6.   Members of my family share many of my interests.

Yes   No   Don't know   7.   Certain members of my family come to me when they have problems or need advice.

Yes   No   Don't know   8.   I rely on my family for emotional support.

Yes   No   Don't know   9.   There is a member of my family I could go to if I were just feeling down, without feeling funny about it later.

Yes   No   Don't know   10.   My family and I are very open about what we think about things.

Yes   No   Don't know   11.   My family is sensitive to my personal needs.

Yes   No   Don't know   12.   Members of my family come to me for emotional support.

Yes   No   Don't know   13.   Members of my family are good at helping me solve problems.

Yes   No   Don't know   14.   I have a deep sharing relationship with a number of members of my family.

Yes   No   Don't know   15.   Members of my family get good ideas about how to do things or make things from me.

Yes   No   Don't know   16.   When I confide in members of my family, it makes me uncomfortable.

Yes   No   Don't know   17.   Members of my family seek me out for companionship.

Yes   No   Don't know   18.   I think that my family feels that I'm good at helping them solve problems.

Yes   No   Don't know   19.   I don't have a relationship with a member of my family that is as close as other people's relationships with family members.

Yes   No   Don't know   20.   I wish my family were much different.

Perceived Stress Scale (PSS)

PURPOSE To measure stressful situations.

AUTHORS Sheldon Cohen, Tom Kamarck, and Robin Mermelstein

DESCRIPTION The PSS is a 10-item instrument designed to measure the degree to which situations in one's life are appraised as stressful. The PSS assesses global perceptions of stress with a rationale that stressful events can increase risk of health problems when they are appraised as threatening or otherwise demanding. The PSS provides information about the process through which stressful events influence pathology, and also can be used to assess whether a factor known to moderate stress-illness relations, such as social support, operates through its influence on stress appraisal or through some other pathway. The scale can be used to investigate the role of overall stress appraisal and situations in which the objective sources of stress are difficult to measure. The PSS also can be viewed as an outcome measure examining the experienced level of stress as a function of objective stressful events, coping processes, and personality factors.

NORMS The current version of the PSS was studied with a national probability sample of 2388 respondents, which was compared to census data for the entire United States. In all categories, the sample was similar to that of the U.S. Census, thereby suggesting the generalizability of the data generated from this study of the PSS. The overall mean for the PSS was 13.02 (SD=6.35); the mean for males was 12.1 (SD=5.9) and for females was 13.7 (SD=6.6). Mean scores for a variety of other demographic variables ranging from age to race to income are available in the original article.

SCORING After reverse-scoring items 4, 5, 7, and 8, the score for the PSS is obtained by summing all item scores. Higher scores suggest greater levels of perceived stress.

RELIABILITY The PSS has good internal consistency, with an alpha of .78. No data on stability were reported.

VALIDITY The PSS has established good construct validity. The PSS scores were moderately related to responses on other measures of appraised stress as well as to measures of potential sources of stress as assessed by stress-event frequency. Small but significant correlations were also found between higher PSS scores and some self-reports of health behaviors. The PSS was also related to scores on the Health Youth Services Utilization Scale and the three factors of the Psychosomatic Index. The frequency of physical illness and symptoms of physical illness also were positively related to reports of stress. The PSS was significantly correlated with the Life Satisfaction Scale and with measures of help-seeking behaviors.

PRIMARY REFERENCES Cohen, S., and Williamson, G. M. (1988). Perceived stress in a probability sample of the United States. In S. Spacapan and S. Oskamp (eds.), *The Social Psychology of Health*. Newbury Park, CA: Sage, 31–67. Cohen, S., Kamarck, T., and Mermelstein, R. (1983). A global measure of perceived stress, *Journal of Health and Social Behavior*, 24, 385–396.

AVAILABILITY Reprinted with permission of the authors. Shelton Cohen, Carnegie Mellon, Department of Psychology, Baker Hall 3426, Pittsburgh, PA 15213. Email: scohen@cmu.edu.

The questions in this scale ask you about your feelings and thoughts during *the last month*. In each case, please indicate by writing a number in the space *how often* you felt or thought a certain way.

$$0 = \text{Never}$$
$$1 = \text{Almost never}$$
$$2 = \text{Sometimes}$$
$$3 = \text{Fairly often}$$
$$4 = \text{Very often}$$

___ 1. In the last month, how often have you been upset because of something that happened unexpectedly?

___ 2. In the last month, how often have you felt you were unable to control the important things in your life?

___ 3. In the last month, how often have you felt nervous and "stressed"?

___ 4. In the last month, how often have you felt confident about your ability to handle your personal problems?

___ 5. In the last month, how often have you felt that things were going your way?

___ 6. In the last month, how often have you found that you could not cope with all the things that you had to do?

___ 7. In the last month, how often have you been able to control irritations in your life?

___ 8. In the last month, how often have you felt that you were on top of things?

___ 9. In the last month, how often have you been angered because of things that were outside of your control?

___ 10. In the last month, how often have you felt difficulties were piling up so high that you could not overcome them?

Perfectionism Inventory (PI)

PURPOSE To measure perfectionism.

AUTHORS Robert W. Hill et al.

DESCRIPTION The PI is a 59-item questionnaire designed to assess the multidimensional aspects of the construct of perfectionism. The authors argue that to capture all of these dimensions, one would have to use at least two previous perfectionism measures. Thus, the PI can be used as a single measure with multiple subscales, making it a more efficient application than previous measures. These subscales are: Concern over Mistakes (CM; items 6, 14, 22, 30, 38, 46, 53, 57); High Standards for Others (HSO; items 3, 11, 19, 27, 35, 43, 50); Need for Approval (NA; items 2, 10, 18, 26, 34, 42, 49, 59); Organization (O; items 4, 12, 20, 28, 36, 44, 51, 56); Perceived Parental Pressure (PP; items 7, 15, 23, 31, 39, 47, 54, 58); Planfulness (P; items 5, 13, 21, 29, 37, 45, 52); Rumination (R; items 8, 16, 24, 32, 40, 458, 55); Striving for Excellence (SE; items 1, 9, 17, 25, 33, 41). In addition, the total score may be used as well as two composite factors, Conscientious Perfectionism (CE; subscales HSO, O, P, SE) and Self-Evaluative Perfectionism (SEP; subscales CM, NA, PP, R).

NORMS The PI was developed with several samples of undergraduate students. In the study for norming purposes, 366 students, with a mean age of 20.2 years (SD = 1.6) were used. Sixty-two percent of the respondents were women, 30% men, and the rest did not indicate gender. Ninety-six percent of respondents were white, and the rest were other ethnicities. The means (SD) for the subscales and total PI are as follows: CM = 2.46 (SD = .75); HSO = 2.83 (.78); NA = 3.22 (.77); O = 3.5 (.86); PP = 3.5 (.86); P = 3.4 (.76); R = 2.83 (.82); SE = 3.1 (.80); CP = 12.83 (2.41); SEP = 11.68 (2.61); and for the total PI, 24.51 (4.40).

SCORING The PI is easily scored by simply summing item scores for the subscales scores and summing the appropriate subscale scores for the composite scores. Scores 1 SD above the mean represent higher perfectionism scores while scores 1 SD below the mean reflect lower scores.

RELIABILITY The PI has very good internal consistency with alphas for the subscales that range from .83 to .91. The PI also has excellent stability with mean 4.5-week test-retest correlations for the 8 subscales that range from .71 to .91.

VALIDITY The PI has established excellent convergent validity with significant correlations among the PI subscales and the subscales of two other valid multidimensional perfectionism inventories, the MPS-HF and the MPS-F. The PI also is correlated in predicted directions with the Fear of Negative Evaluations Scale and the Brief Symptom Inventory.

PRIMARY REFERENCE Hill, R. W., et al. (2004). A new measure of perfectionism: The Perfectionism Inventory, *Journal of Personality Assessment, 82,* 80–91. Instrument reproduced with permission of copyright holder, Dr. Robert W. Hill.

AVAILABILITY Email Dr. Hill at hillrw@appstate.edu.

Please use the following options to rate how much you generally agree with each statement.

1	2	3	4	5
strongly disagree	disagree somewhat	neither agree nor disagree	agree somewhat	strongly agree

___ 1. My work needs to be perfect, in order for me to be satisfied.

___ 2. I am over-sensitive to the comments of others.

___ 3. I usually let people know when their work isn't up to my standards.

___ 4. I am well-organized.

___ 5. I think through my options carefully before making a decision.

___ 6. If I make mistakes, people might think less of me.

___ 7. I've always felt pressure from my parent(s) to be the best.

___ 8. If I do something less than perfectly, I have a hard time getting over it.

___ 9. All my energy is put into achieving a flawless result.

___ 10. I compare my work to others and often feel inadequate.

___ 11. I get upset when other people don't maintain the same standards I do.

___ 12. I think things should be put away in their place.

___ 13. I find myself planning many of my decisions.

___ 14. I am particularly embarrassed by failure.

___ 15. My parents hold me to high standards.

___ 16. I spend a lot of time worrying about things I've done, or things I need to do.

___ 17. I can't stand to do something halfway.

___ 18. I am sensitive to how others respond to my work.

___ 19. I'm not very patient with people's excuses for poor work.

___ 20. I would characterize myself as an orderly person.

___ 21. Most of my decisions are made after I have had time to think about them.

___ 22. I over-react to making mistakes.

___ 23. My parent(s) are difficult to please.

___ 24. If I make a mistake, my whole day is ruined.

___ 25. I have to be the best in every assignment I do.

___ 26. I'm concerned with whether or not other people approve of my actions.

___ 27. I'm often critical of others.

___ 28. I like to always be organized and disciplined.

___ 29. I usually need to think things through before I know what I want.

___ 30. If someone points out a mistake I've made, I feel like I've lost that person's respect in some way.

___ 31. My parent(s) have high expectations for achievement.

___ 32. If I say or do something dumb I tend to think about it for the rest of the day.

___ 33. I drive myself rigorously to achieve high standards.

___ 34. I often don't say anything, because I'm scared I might say the wrong thing.

___ 35. I am frequently aggravated by the lazy or sloppy work of others.

___ 36. I clean my home often.

___ 37. I need time to think up a plan before I take action.

___ 38. If I mess up on one thing, people might start questioning everything I do.

___ 39. Growing up, I felt a lot of pressure to do everything right.

___ 40. When I make an error, I generally can't stop thinking about it.
___ 41. I must achieve excellence in everything I do.
___ 42. I am self-conscious about what others think of me.
___ 43. I have little tolerance for other people's careless mistakes.
___ 44. I make sure to put things away as soon as I'm done using them.
___ 45. I tend to deliberate before making up my mind.
___ 46. To me, a mistake equals failure.
___ 47. My parent(s) put a lot of pressure on me to succeed.
___ 48. I often obsess over some of the things I have done.
___ 49. I am often concerned that people will take what I say the wrong way.
___ 50. I often get frustrated over other people's mistakes.
___ 51. My closet is neat and organized.
___ 52. I usually don't make decisions on the spot.
___ 53. Making mistakes is a sign of stupidity.
___ 54. I always felt that my parent(s) wanted me to be perfect.
___ 55. After I turn a project in, I can't stop thinking of how it could have been better.
___ 56. My workspace is generally organized.
___ 57. If I make a serious mistake, I feel like I'm less of a person.
___ 58. My parent(s) have expected nothing but my best.
___ 59. I spend a great deal of time worrying about other people's opinion of me.

PURPOSE To distinguish among passive, aggressive, and assertive behavior.

AUTHORS Bonnie L. Hedlund and Carol U. Lindquist

DESCRIPTION The PAA is a 30-item instrument designed to assess passive, aggressive, and assertive behavior and to help determine an individual's need for assertion training. The PAA asks respondents to report what they actually do rather than what they know how to do. A pool of 87 items was collected from a number of available assertion inventories. Through use of factor analysis, the PAA was reduced to 30 items and three factors, each with 10 items; three factor analyses with different samples confirm the presence of the three factors—passive (items 3, 6, 11, 13, 16, 21, 25, 26, 27, 29), aggressive (items 5, 7, 10, 12, 15, 17, 22, 23, 24, 30), and assertive (items 1, 2, 4, 8, 9, 14, 18, 19, 20, 28).

NORMS Three separate samples were used in developing and validating the PAA. The first was a sample of 120 undergraduates (mean age 19); the second was a sample of 200 undergraduates (mean age 23.3); the third sample of 275 included 68 male and 76 female adolescents (mean age 17.5), 25 male and 32 female alcoholics (mean age 43), 5 females and 7 males involved in spouse abuse, and 10 males and 17 females who reported they were satisfied in their marriages (mean age 40). The means for the second sample were 23.45 for aggression, 18.97 for assertion, and 21.20 for passivity. The means for the third sample were 29.23 for aggression, 22.12 for assertion, and 27.37 for passivity. There were no differences between males and females.

SCORING The individual items are summed for each subscale; a low score indicates more of that type of behavior. Each subscale ranges from 0 to 40.

RELIABILITY The PAA has fairly good stability with a one-week test-retest correlation of .70 for aggression and assertion and .82 for passivity. No internal consistency data were reported.

VALIDITY The PAA demonstrates a fair degree of construct validity. The PAA subscales correlated in predicted directions with some measures with which they should correlate, including a number of personality tests of assertion and aggression, taped role-play situations, peer ratings, and global self-ratings. There were small but significant correlations between the assertion and aggression subscales and the Marlowe-Crowne Social Desirability Scale, indicating a small effect of social desirability on responses to the PAA.

PRIMARY REFERENCE Hedlund, B. L., and Lindquist, C. U. (1984). The development of an inventory for distinguishing among passive, aggressive, and assertive behavior, *Behavioral Assessment*, 6, 379–390. Instrument reproduced with permission of Bonnie L. Hedlund and Carol U. Lindquist.

AVAILABILITY Dr. Carol U. Lindquist, Department of Psychology, California State University, Fullerton, CA 92634. Email: clindquist@fullerton.edu.

Please read the following statements: Each one describes a situation and a response. Try to imagine a situation in your life that is as close to the one described as possible, then rate the response according to its similarity with what you *might* do in the actual situation.

1 = Just like me
2 = Sometimes like me
3 = Not usually like me
4 = Not at all like me

____ 1. You'd like a raise, so you make an appointment with your boss to explain the reasons you feel you should receive one.

____ 2. You usually take the lead when you are in a group of people.

____ 3. Because of a high-pressure salesperson, you buy a camera that meets most but not all of your requirements.

____ 4. You're working on a project with a friend but you seem to be doing all the work. You say, "I'd like to see if we could find a different way to divide the responsibility. I feel I'm doing most of the work."

____ 5. After waiting in a restaurant for 20 minutes, you loudly tell the host of your dissatisfaction and leave.

____ 6. A very important person you have long admired comes to speak in your town. Afterwards you are too hesitant to go and meet him/her.

____ 7. Your parents have been after you to spend more time with them. You tell them to stop nagging you.

____ 8. Your neighbor's stereo is disturbing you. You call and ask if he/she would please turn it down.

____ 9. A repairman overcharges you. You explain that you feel the charges are excessive and ask for the bill to be adjusted.

____ 10. A person cuts in front of you in line, so you push him/her out of line.

____ 11. When you're feeling warm towards your parent/spouse, it is difficult for you to express this to them.

____ 12. You are delayed getting home because you stayed at a friend's too long. When your parent/spouse is angry, you tell him/her it's none of his/her business.

____ 13. When trying to talk to someone of the opposite sex, you get nervous.

____ 14. In a job interview you are able to state your positive points as well as your negative points.

____ 15. You are driving to an appointment with a friend and she/he has a flat tire. While she/he is changing the tire, you tell her/him how dumb it was to let the tires get worn.

____ 16. You accept your boss's opinion about your lack of ability to handle responsibility, but later complain to some friends about his/her unfairness.

____ 17. You are arguing with a person and she/he pushes you, so you push her/him back.

____ 18. In a discussion with a small group of people, you state your position and are willing to discuss it, but you don't feel that you have to win.

____ 19. The person next to you in a movie is explaining the plot of the movie to his/her companion. You ask them to please be quiet because they are distracting you from the movie.

___ 20. When you see a new person you would like to meet, you usually try to start a conversation with him/her.

___ 21. Your neighbor wants to use your car. Even though you'd rather she/he didn't, you say yes.

___ 22. A friend of yours is arguing with someone much larger than she/he is. You decide to help your friend by saying, "I'm really tired of listening to you mouth off."

___ 23. A person cuts in front of you in line, so you say, "Who do you think you are? Get out of my way."

___ 24. You are talking to a friend and she/he doesn't appear to be listening. You tell her/him that you are sick and tired of her/him not listening to you.

___ 25. Speaking before a group makes you so nervous that you have a great deal of trouble speaking clearly.

___ 26. You are waiting for a car to pull out of a parking place so that you can park. Someone comes up behind you and honks. You drive on.

___ 27. You find it hard to express contradictory opinions when dealing with an authority figure.

___ 28. Your spouse/boyfriend/girlfriend is supposed to take you out. Fifteen minutes before you are to leave, she/he calls and cancels. You tell her/him that you are very disappointed.

___ 29. In a group situation, you usually wait to see what the majority of the people want before giving your opinion.

___ 30. You have arranged to meet a friend, but she/he doesn't arrive. At the first opportunity, you call her/him and demand an explanation.

Personal Style Inventory (PSI)

PURPOSE To measure sociotropy and autonomy in depression.

AUTHORS Clive J. Robins and Alice G. Luten

DESCRIPTION The PSI is a 60-item instrument designed to measure sociotropy and autonomy as they are related to depression. Sociotropy is defined as social dependency, a person's investment in positive interchange with others. Autonomy, or individuality, is defined as a person's investment in preserving and increasing his or her independence. Each characteristic is hypothesized to be related to different clinical presentations among depressed clients. Highly sociotropic individuals, when depressed, primarily feel deprived and exhibit clinical features consistent with this sense of deprivation (e.g., thoughts of loss, crying). This pattern is consistent with the concept of reactive depression. When highly autonomous people are depressed, they primarily feel defeated (e.g., pessimistic about treatment, self-blaming, feeling like a failure). This pattern is consistent with the picture of endogenous depression. The PSI is very useful for understanding depression and perhaps for keeping track over time of differentially targeted intervention efforts. The PSI consists of six subscales that comprise the two main subscales, sociotropy and autonomy. Sociotropy includes subscales for concern about what others think (items 1, 7, 13, 19, 25, 31, 36, 43, 49, 55), dependency (items 3, 9, 15, 21, 27, 33, 39, 45, 51, 57), and pleasing others (items 5, 11, 17, 23, 29, 35, 41, 47, 53, 59). Autonomy includes the subscales perfectionism/self-criticism (items 2, 8, 14, 20, 26, 32, 38, 44, 50, 56), need for control/freedom from outside control (items 4, 10, 16, 22, 28, 34, 44, 46, 52, 58), and defensive separation (items 6, 12, 18, 24, 30, 36, 42, 48, 54, 60).

NORMS The PSI was studied with 13 male and 37 female psychiatric inpatients diagnosed with some variation of depression. The mean age was 44.12 years, 58% were married, 26% were separated or divorced, 4% widowed, and 12% never married. Twenty percent had less than a high school diploma, 18% completed high school, and 62% had some college or a college degree. The mean score on the sociotropy scale was 127.65 (SD=18.36) and on autonomy was 117.27 (SD=17.29). There were no significant differences between men and women.

SCORING The PSI subscales are easily scored by summing item scores, with "strongly disagree" equaling a score of 1 to "strongly agree" equaling a score of 6. Scores on each of the sets of three subscales can be summed to produce overall sociotropy and autonomy scores. Obtaining a single total score is not recommended.

RELIABILITY The PSI has very good internal consistency, with alphas of .88 for sociotropy and .83 for autonomy. The PSI has very good stability, with five- to thirteen-week test-retest reliabilities of .80 for sociotropy and .76 for autonomy.

VALIDITY The PSI has very good concurrent and predictive validity, correlating in predicted directions with an Index of Clinical Features that comprised 19 clinical features that are hypothesized to be differentially related to sociotropy or autonomy.

PRIMARY REFERENCE Robins, C. J., and Luten, A. G. (1991). Sociotropy and autonomy: Differential patterns of clinical presentation in unipolar depression, *Journal of Abnormal Psychology*, 100, 71–77.

AVAILABILITY Dr. Clive Robins, Duke University Medical Center, Box 3903, Durham, NC 27710. Email: robin026@mc.dnke.edu.

Here are a number of statements about personal characteristics. Please read each one carefully, and indicate whether you agree or disagree, and to what extent, by circling a number.

	Strongly disagree	Disagree	Slightly disagree	Slightly agree	Agree	Strongly agree
1. I am very sensitive to criticism by others.	1	2	3	4	5	6
2. I often find that I don't live up to my own standards and ideals.	1	2	3	4	5	6
3. I find it difficult to be separated from people I love.	1	2	3	4	5	6
4. I resent it when people try to direct my behavior or activities.	1	2	3	4	5	6
5. I often put other people's needs before my own.	1	2	3	4	5	6
6. I don't like relying on others for help.	1	2	3	4	5	6
7. I worry a lot that people may criticize me.	1	2	3	4	5	6
8. The standards and goals I set for myself are usually higher than those of other people.	1	2	3	4	5	6
9. It is hard for me to break off a relationship even if it is making me unhappy.	1	2	3	4	5	6
10. I rarely trust the advice of others when making a big decision.	1	2	3	4	5	6
11. I am very sensitive to the effects I have on the feelings of other people.	1	2	3	4	5	6
12. When I'm feeling blue, I don't like to be offered sympathy.	1	2	3	4	5	6
13. I am very sensitive to signs of possible rejection by others.	1	2	3	4	5	6

	Strongly disagree	Disagree	Slightly disagree	Slightly agree	Agree	Strongly agree
14. It is hard for me to accept my own weaknesses and limitations.	1	2	3	4	5	6
15. It is hard for me to take charge of my own affairs without help from other people.	1	2	3	4	5	6
16. I am very upset when other people or circumstances interfere with my plans.	1	2	3	4	5	6
17. I worry a lot about hurting or offending people.	1	2	3	4	5	6
18. I don't like people to invade my privacy.	1	2	3	4	5	6
19. I am easily persuaded by others.	1	2	3	4	5	6
20. I tend to be very self-critical.	1	2	3	4	5	6
21. I need other people's help in order to cope with life's problems.	1	2	3	4	5	6
22. I try to maintain control over my feelings at all times.	1	2	3	4	5	6
23. I try to please other people too much.	1	2	3	4	5	6
24. It is hard for me to have someone dependent on me.	1	2	3	4	5	6
25. It is very important to me to be liked or admired by others.	1	2	3	4	5	6
26. I believe in doing something well or not doing it at all.	1	2	3	4	5	6
27. I never really feel secure in a close relationship because I am concerned that I might lose the other person.	1	2	3	4	5	6
28. I am easily bothered by other people making demands of me.	1	2	3	4	5	6

continued

	Strongly disagree	Disagree	Slightly disagree	Slightly agree	Agree	Strongly agree
29. I often feel responsible for solving other people's problems.	1	2	3	4	5	6
30. I can be completely independent of other people.	1	2	3	4	5	6
31. I am very concerned with how people react to me.	1	2	3	4	5	6
32. I should be able to excel at anything if I try hard enough.	1	2	3	4	5	6
33. I find it difficult if I have to be alone all day.	1	2	3	4	5	6
34. I often try to change other people's behavior.	1	2	3	4	5	6
35. I feel I have to be nice to other people.	1	2	3	4	5	6
36. I tend to keep other people at a distance.	1	2	3	4	5	6
37. I get very uncomfortable when I'm not sure whether or not someone likes me.	1	2	3	4	5	6
38. I usually view my performance as either a complete success or a complete failure.	1	2	3	4	5	6
39. It is very hard for me to get over the feeling of loss when a relationship has ended.	1	2	3	4	5	6
40. It is hard for me to take instructions from people who have authority over me.	1	2	3	4	5	6
41. I am too apologetic to other people.	1	2	3	4	5	6
42. It is hard for me to open up and talk about my feelings and other personal things.	1	2	3	4	5	6
43. I often censor what I say because the other person may disapprove or disagree.	1	2	3	4	5	6

	Strongly disagree	Disagree	Slightly disagree	Slightly agree	Agree	Strongly agree
44. I judge myself as a person based on the quality of the work that I do.	1	2	3	4	5	6
45. I like to be certain that there is somebody close I can contact in case something unpleasant happens to me.	1	2	3	4	5	6
46. When making a big decision, I usually feel that advice from others is intrusive.	1	2	3	4	5	6
47. It is hard for me to say "no" to other people's requests.	1	2	3	4	5	6
48. It is hard for me to express admiration or affection.	1	2	3	4	5	6
49. It is hard for me to be a nonconformist.	1	2	3	4	5	6
50. It bothers me when I feel that I am only average and ordinary.	1	2	3	4	5	6
51. I become upset when something happens to me and there's nobody around to talk to.	1	2	3	4	5	6
52. I become upset more than most people I know when limits are placed on my personal independence and freedom.	1	2	3	4	5	6
53. I often let people take advantage of me.	1	2	3	4	5	6
54. It is difficult for me to make a long-term commitment to a relationship.	1	2	3	4	5	6
55. I am most comfortable when I know my behavior is what others expect of me.	1	2	3	4	5	6
56. I feel bad about myself when I am not actively accomplishing things.	1	2	3	4	5	6
57. I become very upset when a friend breaks a date or forgets to call me as planned.	1	2	3	4	5	6

continued

	Strongly disagree	Disagree	Slightly disagree	Slightly agree	Agree	Strongly agree
58. I resent it when others assume responsibility for my plans.	1	2	3	4	5	6
59. It is hard for me to let people know when I am angry with them.	1	2	3	4	5	6
60. In relationships, people are often too demanding of one another.	1	2	3	4	5	6

Physical Self-Efficacy Scale (PSE)

PURPOSE To measure perceived physical competence.

AUTHORS Richard M. Ryckman, Michael A. Robbins, Billy Thornton, and Peggy Cantrell

DESCRIPTION The PSE is a 22-item instrument that is based on the assumption that people's expectations about their own efficacy have important effects on cognitive, affective, and behavioral patterns. The PSE also is based on the assumption that there are a variety of arenas in which individuals must achieve mastery if they are to perceive themselves as efficacious. One of these arenas is physical self-concept. The PSE is designed to measure individual differences in perceived physical competence and feelings of confidence in displaying physical skills to others. The instrument was based on a pool of 90 items; those items that were not highly correlated with social desirability response set but were related to two primary factors were selected to form the PSE. The final form has two subscales, perceived physical ability (PPA: items 1, 2, 4, 6, 8, 12, 13, 19*, 21*, 22*) and physical self-presentation confidence (PSPC: items 3*, 5, 7, 9*, 10, 11*, 14*, 15, 16, 17*, 18, 20*), plus an overall PSE scale. The PSE is useful for diagnostic and assessment purposes in medical and clinical settings and in athletic programs.

NORMS A series of studies was conducted in the development of the PSE, eventually involving some 950 undergraduate students. Demographic data and actual norms were not reported.

SCORING The PSE is scored by first reverse-scoring the items with asterisks (noted above), then summing the scores on the individual items within each factor for the subscale scores and summing the two subscale scores for the overall PSE score. The scores on the PPA range from 10 to 60, on PSPC from 12 to 72, and overall scores from 22 to 132. Higher scores on all three indicate greater self-efficacy.

RELIABILITY The PSE has good internal consistency, with alphas of .84 for PPA, .74 for PSPC, and .81 for the overall PSE. The PSE is also a very stable instrument with six-week test-retest correlations of .89 for PPA, .69 for PSPC, and .80 for the PSE as a whole.

VALIDITY The PSE has good concurrent validity, correlating significantly with a number of other measures such as the Tennessee Physical Self-Concept Scale, the Texas Social Behavior Inventory (self-esteem), the Self-Consciousness Scale, and the Taylor Manifest Anxiety Scale. The PSE also has good predictive validity, predicting a number of scores on other instruments as well as sports and physically related activities (e.g., respondents with higher PSE scores outperform respondents with lower PSE scores).

PRIMARY REFERENCE Ryckman, R. M., Robbins, M. A., Thornton, B., and Cantrell, P. (1982). Development and validation of a Physical Self-Efficacy Scale, *Journal of Personality and Social Psychology*, 42, 891–900. Instrument reproduced with permission of Richard M. Ryckman and the American Psychological Association.

AVAILABILITY Dr. Richard M. Ryckman, Department of Psychology, University of Maine, Orono, ME 04469. Email: richard.ryckman@umit.mine.edu.

Please place one number to the left of the column for each item as follows:

1 = Strongly agree
2 = Agree
3 = Somewhat agree
4 = Somewhat disagree
5 = Disagree
6 = Strongly disagree

___ 1. I have excellent reflexes.
___ 2. I am not agile and graceful.
___ 3. I am rarely embarrassed by my voice.
___ 4. My physique is rather strong.
___ 5. Sometimes I don't hold up well under stress.
___ 6. I can't run fast.
___ 7. I have physical defects that sometimes bother me.
___ 8. I don't feel in control when I take tests involving physical dexterity.
___ 9. I am never intimidated by the thought of a sexual encounter.
___ 10. People think negative things about me because of my posture.
___ 11. I am not hesitant about disagreeing with people bigger than I.
___ 12. I have poor muscle tone.
___ 13. I take little pride in my ability in sports.
___ 14. Athletic people usually do not receive more attention than I.
___ 15. I am sometimes envious of those better looking than myself.
___ 16. Sometimes my laugh embarrasses me.
___ 17. I am not concerned with the impression my physique makes on others.
___ 18. Sometimes I feel uncomfortable shaking hands because my hand is clammy.
___ 19. My speed has helped me out of some tight spots.
___ 20. I find that I am not accident prone.
___ 21. I have a strong grip.
___ 22. Because of my agility, I have been able to do things that many others could not do.

Positive and Negative Suicide Ideation Inventory (PANSI)

PURPOSE To measure positive and negative thoughts about suicide.

AUTHORS Augustine Osman, Beverly A. Kopper, Francisco X. Barrios, and Peter M. Gutierrez

DESCRIPTION This 14-item instrument is designed to measure ideations about suicide. The PANSI has two subscales: positive ideation (PI: items 2, 6, 8, 12, 13, and 14), which are thoughts that are buffers against the possibility of suicide or parasuicidal behaviors, and negative ideations (NI: items 1, 3, 4, 5, 7, 9, 10, and 11), which are thoughts about committing suicide. The clinical assumption of the PANSI is that many negative thoughts coupled with few positive thoughts present a risk of suicide. The PANSI was developed from a pool of 165 items evaluated for content validity and eventually reduced to 20 items, which were submitted to more rigorous psychometric research on the construct validity and factor structure. This resulted in the final 14-item version. It was designed for use with young adults, including youth in the late teens.

NORMS For a sample of college students, the mean PI score was 4.0 (SD = .6) for a sample of 84 men and 3.9 (SD = .7) for a sample of 202 women. The average for the NI subscale was 1.2 (SD = .5) for women and 1.9 (SD = .4) for men. There appear to be no gender differences.

SCORING Scores on the PI and the NI are the sum of the item scores, divided by the number of items. Scores range from 1 to 5 with higher scores indicating more positive and negative ideations of suicide on the respective subscales.

RELIABILITY The reliability of the NI is very good, with internal consistency coefficients of .91 and .93 from samples of college students. The PI has good test-retest reliability, with coefficients of consistency of .80 and .81.

VALIDITY The validity of the PANSI is very good. Concurrent validity is evidenced by scores on the PI correlating negatively with other measures of suicide and scores on the NI correlating positively. Additionally, scores on both subscales were associated with measures of hopelessness, depression, and general psychological distress. The final 14-item version of the PANSI was supported with factor analysis, and scores on the NI and PI are negatively correlated ($r = -.51$).

PRIMARY REFERENCE Osman, A., Gutierrez, P. M., Kopper, B. A., Barrios, F. X., and Chiros, C. E. (in press). The Positive and Negative Suicide Ideation Inventory: Development and validation. *Psychological Reports*.

AVAILABILITY Augustine Osman, Ph.D., The University of Texas at San Antonio, One UTSA Circle, MH 4.01.23, San Antonio, Texas 78249-0641. Email: angustine.osman@utsa.edu.

Below is a list of statements that may or may not apply to you. Please read each statement carefully and then place your answer in the space to the left of that statement. Use the five-point scale as follows:

1 = None of the time
2 = Very rarely
3 = Some of the time
4 = A good part of the time
5 = Most of the time

During the *past two weeks*, including today, *how often* have you:

___ 1. Seriously considered killing yourself because you could not live up to the expectations of other people?
___ 2. Felt that you were in control of most situations in your life?
___ 3. Felt hopeless about the future and you wondered if you should kill yourself?
___ 4. Felt so unhappy about your relationship with someone you wished you were dead?
___ 5. Thought about killing yourself because you could not accomplish something important in your life?
___ 6. Felt hopeful about the future because things were working out well for you?
___ 7. Thought about killing yourself because you could not find a solution to a personal problem?
___ 8. Felt excited because you were doing well at school or at work?
___ 9. Thought about killing yourself because you felt like a failure in life?
___ 10. Thought that your problems were so overwhelming that suicide was seen as the only option to you?
___ 11. Felt so lonely or sad you wanted to kill yourself so that you could end your pain?
___ 12. Felt confident about your ability to cope with most of the problems in your life?
___ 13. Felt that life was worth living?
___ 14. Felt confident about your plans for the future?

Primary Care Evaluation of Mental Disorders-Patient Questionnaire (PRIME-MD.PQ)

PURPOSE to assess common mental disorders

AUTHOR Robert L. Spitzer

DESCRIPTION This 26-item instrument measures the presence of the most common mental disorders that are seen in primary care settings. It was designed as an initial screen for use by primary care providers working with outpatients. The PRIME-MD ascertains five domains of mental disorders: somatoform (items 1-16), eating disorders (item 15), mood disorders (item 17 +18) anxiety (item 19–21), alcohol problems (items 22–25) and one general health item, which is unnumbered. The instrument is designed for use with a clinician's guide, a 12-page semi-structured interview, which is then used to probe more thoroughly for those mental health problems initially identified by the patient questionnaire. When used with the follow-up interview, the PRIME-MD provides a broad consideration of 18 possible mental disorders, nine of which correspond to disorders found in the *Diagnostic and Statistical Manual of the American Psychiatric Association*. The instrument is intended for use at any time in the treatment process, from an initial screen at an intake or anytime the clinician suspects the presence of a mental health problem. With the semi-structured interview the assessment takes about 10 minutes.

NORMS The instrument was developed at five different clinical sites, and included 1,360 adult patients, of which 386 were identified as having a psychiatric disorder. Additional norms are not available.

SCORING The PRIME-MD is designed to facilitate accurate diagnoses. It is used as a screen to be used in conjunction with the semi-structured interview. Endorsement of any three items of the somatic items (items 1-16) warrants further assessment. Endorsement of the eating disorder item is sufficient to warrant further diagnostic assessment.

RELIABILITY The chief evidence of reliability is the agreement between raters using the PRIME-MD, called inter-rater reliability. Of these patients assessed by a primary care physician and a mental health professional, the kappa coefficient of agreement was. 71 for identifying any mental disorder. The kappa coefficients ranged from a very low. 15 for diagnosing minor depression to. 73 for diagnosing an eating disorder or major depression. These coefficients represent about 19% agreement for minor depression to 80% agreement for eating disorders and major depression.

VALIDITY The PRIME- MD has very good evidence of validity. First of all, the agreement rates between the primary care physicians and mental health professionals indicate the instrument not only allows for some accuracy when used by providers of primary care, but that the instrument does not over-diagnosis a particular problem. The instrument also has concurrent validity estimates, correlating with subscales on the Health Survey (SF-36), the Zung Depression scale, and a measure of somatic symptomatology. The instrument also distinguished patients on the number of visits to physicians and emergency facilities, and the number of days when poor health was an impediment to one's usual daily activities. These differences support the instrument's known-groups validity. Support for the PRIME-MD's utility is its ability to recognize the presence of a mental disorder which would likely have gone undetected; this is evidenced by 48% of those cases with a mental disorder which were unrecognized by the primary care physicians when the instrument was not used.

PRIMARY REFERENCE Spitzer, R. L., Williams, J. B. W., Kroenke, K., Linzer, M. deGruy, III, F. V., Hahn, S. R., Brody, D. and Johnson, J. G. (1994). Utility of a new procedure for diagnosing mental disorders in primary care: The PRIME-MD 1000 study. *Journal of the American Medical Association. 272*, 1749-1756.

AVAILABILITY Email: Dr. Spitzer at Spitzer8@verizon.net or Dr. Janet Williams at jbw5©columbia.edu.

PATIENT QUESTIONNAIRE

NAME: _____   AGE: _____

SEX: ☐ Male   ☐ Female   TODAY'S DATE: _____

INSTRUCTIONS: This questionnaire will help in understanding problems that you may have. It may be necessary to ask you more questions about some of these items. Please make sure to check a box for every item.

During the **PAST MONTH**, have you been bothered **A LOT** by...		During the **PAST MONTH**...
Yes No	**Yes No**	**Yes No**
1. stomach pain ☐ ☐	12. constipation, loose bowels, or diarrhea ☐ ☐	21. have you had an anxiety attack (suddenly feeling fear or panic) ☐ ☐
2. back pain ☐ ☐		
3. pain in your arms, legs, or joints (knees, hips, etc) ☐ ☐	13. nausea, gas, or indigestion ☐ ☐	22. have you thought you should cut down on your drinking of alcohol ☐ ☐
	14. feeling tired or having low energy ☐ ☐	
4. menstrual pain or problems ☐ ☐		
	15. trouble sleeping ☐ ☐	23. has anyone complained about your drinking ☐ ☐
5. pain or problems during sexual intercourse ☐ ☐	16. your eating being out of control ☐ ☐	24. have you felt guilty or upset about your drinking ☐ ☐
6. headaches ☐ ☐	17. little interest or pleasure in doing things ☐ ☐	
7. chest pain ☐ ☐		25. was there ever a single day in which you had five or more drinks of beer, wine, or liquor ☐ ☐
8. dizziness ☐ ☐	18. feeling down, depressed, or hopeless ☐ ☐	
9. fainting spells ☐ ☐		
10. feeling your heart pound or race	19. "nerves" or feeling anxious or on edge ☐ ☐	
		Overall, would you say your health is:
11. shortness of breathYes No ☐ ☐	20. worrying about a lot of different things ☐ ☐	Excellent ☐ Very good ☐ Good ☐ Fair ☐ Poor ☐

Problem-Solving Inventory (PSI)

PURPOSE To assess respondents' perception of their problem-solving behaviors and attitudes.

AUTHOR P. Paul Heppner

DESCRIPTION The PSI is a 35-item instrument designed to measure how individuals believe they generally react to personal problems in their daily lives. The term "problems" refers to personal problems such as getting along with friends, feeling depressed, choosing a career, or deciding whether to get divorced. Although the PSI does not measure actual problem-solving skills, it does measure the evaluative awareness of one's problem-solving abilities or style. The PSI comprises three subscales based on factor analysis: problem-solving confidence (items 5, 10, 11*, 12, 19, 23, 24, 27, 33, 34*, 35), approach-avoidance style (items 1*, 2*, 4*, 6, 7, 8, 13*, 15*, 16, 17*, 18, 20, 21*, 28, 30, 31), and personal control (3*, 14*, 25*, 26*, 32*). In addition, the total score is viewed as a single, general index of problem-solving perception. This is one of the few standardized measures that addresses this central concern of helping professionals with clients' coping and problem-solving skills.

NORMS The PSI was developed and tested with several samples of white, introductory psychology students (402 males, 498 females); 25 black male and 59 black female students; 26 male and 42 female counseling center clients; 306 undergraduates across all four academic years; and four populations of adults including 101 "normals," 77 inpatient alcoholic males, 29 elderly, and 90 female university extension staff members. Norms for all these groups are available. The means on the total PSI range from 74.0 for the female extension staff members to 98.0 for male counseling center clients.

SCORING The PSI can be self-scored by the client, or scored by the practitioner either directly or using a computer (computer answer sheets are available). Items with asterisks (see above) are reverse-scored. Then the scores for the items on each factor are summed. The three factor scores are summed for the total score. Items 9, 22, and 29 are filler items and not scored. Lower scores reflect greater perceived problem-solving abilities.

RELIABILITY The PSI has good to excellent internal consistency, with alphas ranging from .72 to .85 on the subscales and .90 for the total measure. The PSI has excellent stability with two-week test-retest correlations for the subscales and total measure that range from .83 to .89.

VALIDITY Extensive testing of the PSI reveals good validity in several areas. Concurrent validity was established by significant correlations between the PSI and scores on a self-rating scale of one's problem-solving skill. Construct validity has been demonstrated in a number of studies by establishing that the PSI is correlated with other measures with which it should be correlated and is not correlated with those with which it theoretically should not be. Several personality measures were used in these studies, such as Rotter's Internal-External Scale and the Myers-Briggs Type Indicator. The PSI has been found to distinguish significantly between groups such as clinical and nonclinical, or those with higher and lower scores on measures of psychological disturbance, thus establishing known-groups validity. The PSI is sensitive to clinical changes and also is not affected by social desirability response set.

PRIMARY REFERENCE Heppner, P. P., and Petersen. C. H. (1982). The development and implications of a personal problem-solving inventory, *Journal of Counseling Psychology*, 29, 66–75. Instrument reproduced with permission of P. Paul Heppner.

AVAILABILITY Dr. P. Paul Heppner, University of Missouri-Columbia, Psychology Department, 210 McAlester Hall, Columbia, MO 65211. Email: heppnerp@missouri.edu.

Read each statement, and indicate the extent to which you agree or disagree with that statement, using the following options:

1 = Strongly agree
2 = Moderately agree
3 = Slightly agree
4 = Slightly disagree
5 = Moderately disagree
6 = Strongly disagree

___ 1. When a solution to a problem was unsuccessful, I did not examine why it didn't work.

___ 2. When I am confronted with a complex problem, I do not bother to develop a strategy to collect information so I can define exactly what the problem is.

___ 3. When my first efforts to solve a problem fail, I become uneasy about my ability to handle the situation.

___ 4. After I have solved a problem, I do not analyze what went right or what went wrong.

___ 5. I am usually able to think up creative and effective alternatives to solve a problem.

___ 6. After I have tried to solve a problem with a certain course of action, I take time and compare the actual outcome to what I think should have happened.

___ 7. When I have a problem, I think up as many possible ways to handle it as I can until I can't come up with any more ideas.

___ 8. When confronted with a problem, I consistently examine my feelings to find out what is going on in a problem situation.

___ 9. When I am confused with a problem, I do not try to define vague ideas or feelings into concrete or specific terms.

___ 10. I have the ability to solve most problems even though initially no solution is immediately apparent.

___ 11. Many problems I face are too complex for me to solve.

___ 12. I make decisions and am happy with them later.

___ 13. When confronted with a problem, I tend to do the first thing that I can think to solve it.

___ 14. Sometimes I do not stop and take time to deal with my problems, but just kind of muddle ahead.

___ 15. When deciding on an idea or possible solution to a problem, I do not take time to consider the chances of each alternative being successful.

___ 16. When confronted with a problem, I stop and think about it before deciding on a next step.

___ 17. I generally go with the first good idea that comes to my mind.

___ 18. When making a decision, I weight the consequences of each alternative and compare them against each other.

___ 19. When I make plans to solve a problem, I am almost certain that I can make them work.

___ 20. I try to predict the overall result of carrying out a particular course of action.

___ 21. When I try to think up possible solutions to a problem, I do not come up with very many alternatives.

___ 22. In trying to solve a problem, one strategy I often use is to think of past problems that have been similar.

___ 23. Given enough time and effort, I believe I can solve most problems that confront me.

___ 24. When faced with a novel situation I have confidence that I can handle problems that may arise.

___ 25. Even though I work on a problem, sometimes I feel like I am groping or wandering, and am not getting down to the real issue.

___ 26. I make snap judgments and later regret them.

___ 27. I trust my ability to solve new and difficult problems.

___ 28. I have a systematic method for comparing alternatives and making decisions.

___ 29. When I try to think of ways of handling a problem, I do not try to combine different ideas together.

___ 30. When confronted with a problem, I don't usually examine what sort of external things in my environment may be contributing to my problem.

___ 31. When I am confronted by a problem, one of the first things I do is survey the situation and consider all the relevant pieces of information.

___ 32. Sometimes I get so charged up emotionally that I am unable to consider many ways of dealing with my problem.

___ 33. After making a decision, the outcome I expected usually matches the actual outcome.

___ 34. When confronted with a problem, I am unsure of whether I can handle the situation.

___ 35. When I become aware of a problem, one of the first things I do is to try to find out exactly what the problem is.

Procrastination Assessment Scale—Students (PASS)

PURPOSE To measure procrastination.

AUTHORS Linda J. Solomon and Esther D. Rothblum

DESCRIPTION The PASS is a 44-item instrument designed to measure the frequency of cognitive-behavioral antecedents of procrastination. The PASS was developed to measure three areas: (1) the prevalence of academic procrastination, (2) the reasons for academic procrastination, and (3) to compare scores on the PASS with behavioral indices of procrastination and other related constructs. The PASS is divided into two parts; the first part measures the prevalence of procrastination in six academic areas, and the second part assesses reasons for procrastination. The PASS is useful in both identifying potential focal areas for intervention and tracking changes in procrastination over time.

NORMS The PASS was investigated with 323 university students (101 males, 222 females) enrolled in introductory psychology courses; 90% were between the ages of 18 to 21; 85% were freshmen, 13% were sophomores, and the remaining subjects were juniors and seniors. Norms were reported in percentages: 46% always or nearly always procrastinate on a paper, 27.6% procrastinate on studying for exams, 30.1% procrastinate on reading weekly assignments, 10.6% procrastinate on administrative tasks, 23% on attendance tasks, and 10.2% on school activities in general. In addition, 23.7% reported that procrastination was always or nearly always a problem when writing a paper, 21.2% said it was a problem when studying for exams, and 23.7% said it was a problem when doing weekly readings. There were no significant sex differences in procrastination. Regarding reasons for procrastination, 49.5% of the variance reflects fear of failure, and 18% reflects aversiveness of the task and laziness. Females were more likely to fear failure than were males.

SCORING Scores on the 5-point Likert-type scale (a = 1 to e = 5) are summed for each academic task (scores range from 2 to 10) and across the six areas of academic functioning (ranging from 12 to 60). Scores on reasons for procrastination and interest in changing are summed as separate subscales. A total score can be obtained by summing all subscale scores.

RELIABILITY The most recent research shows low levels of internal consistency for the PASS with split-half correlations of .58 for men and .31 for women regarding procrastination frequency. The correlation for procrastination as a problem was .26 overall and for reasons for procrastination was .80. The stability of the PASS was fair with one-month test-retest correlations of .74 for prevalence and .56 for reasons for procrastination. For the total score, the test-retest correlation was .80.

VALIDITY The PASS has very good concurrent validity, with significant correlations with the Beck Depression Inventory, Ellis Scale of Irrational Cognitions, Rosenberg Self-Esteem Scale, and the Delay Avoidance Scale. Significant correlations also were found between the number of self-paced quizzes and PASS scores and between the PASS and total grade point averages (higher PASS scores correlated with lower GPAs).

PRIMARY REFERENCE Solomon, L. J., and Rothblum, E. D. (1984). Academic Procrastination: Frequency and cognitive behavioral correlates, *Journal of Counseling Psychology*, 31, 503–509.

AVAILABILITY May be copied from this volume.

AREAS OF PROCRASTINATION

For each of the following activities, please rate the degree to which you delay or procrastinate. Rate each item on an a to e scale according to how often you wait until the last minute to do the activity. Then, indicate on an a to e scale the degree to which you feel procrastination on that task is a problem. Finally, indicate on an a to e scale the degree to which you would like to decrease your tendency to procrastinate on each task. Mark your answers by circling the appropriate letter below each question.

I. *Writing a Term Paper*

1. To what degree do you procrastinate on this task?

Never procrastinate	Almost never	Sometimes	Nearly always	Always Procrastinate
a	b	c	d	e

2. To what degree is procrastination on this task a problem for you?

Not at all a problem	Almost never	Sometimes	Nearly always	Always a problem
a	b	c	d	e

3. To what extent do you want to decrease your tendency to procrastinate on this task?

Do not want to decrease		Somewhat		Definitely want to decrease
a	b	c	d	e

II. *Studying for Exams*

4. To what degree do you procrastinate on this task?

Never procrastinate	Almost never	Sometimes	Nearly always	Always Procrastinate
a	b	c	d	e

5. To what degree is procrastination on this task a problem for you?

Not at all a problem	Almost never	Sometimes	Nearly always	Always a problem
a	b	c	d	e

6. To what extent do you want to decrease your tendency to procrastinate on this task?

Do not want to decrease		Somewhat		Definitely want to decrease
a	b	c	d	e

III. *Keeping Up Weekly Reading Assignments*

7. To what degree do you procrastinate on this task?

Never procrastinate	Almost never	Sometimes	Nearly always	Always Procrastinate
a	b	c	d	e

8. To what degree is procrastination on this task a problem for you?

Not at all a problem	Almost never	Sometimes	Nearly always	Always a problem
a	b	c	d	e

9. To what extent do you want to decrease your tendency to procrastinate on this task?

Do not want to decrease		Somewhat		Definitely want to decrease
a	b	c	d	e

IV. *Academic Administrative Tasks: Filling Out Forms, Registering for Classes, Getting ID Card, etc.*

10. To what degree do you procrastinate on this task?

Never procrastinate	Almost never	Sometimes	Nearly always	Always Procrastinate
a	b	c	d	e

11. To what degree is procrastination on this task a problem for you?

Not at all a problem	Almost never	Sometimes	Nearly always	Always a problem
a	b	c	d	e

12. To what extent do you want to decrease your tendency to procrastinate on this task?

Do not want to decrease		Somewhat		Definitely want to decrease
a	b	c	d	e

V. *Attendance Tasks: Meeting with Your Advisor, Making an Appointment with a Professor, etc.*

13. To what extent do you procrastinate on this task?

Never procrastinate	Almost never	Sometimes	Nearly always	Always Procrastinate
a	b	c	d	e

14. To what extent is procrastination on this task a problem for you?

Not at all a problem	Almost never	Sometimes	Nearly always	Always a problem
a	b	c	d	e

15. To what extent do you want to decrease your tendency to procrastinate on this task?

Do not want to decrease		Somewhat		Definitely want to decrease
a	b	c	d	e

VI. *School Activities in General*

16. To what extent do you procrastinate on these activities?

Never procrastinate	Almost never	Sometimes	Nearly always	Always Procrastinate
a	b	c	d	e

17. To what extent is procrastination on these activities a problem for you?

Not at all a problem	Almost never	Sometimes	Nearly always	Always a problem
a	b	c	d	e

18. To what extent do you want to decrease your tendency to procrastinate on these activities?

Do not want to decrease		Somewhat		Definitely want to decrease
a	b	c	d	e

REASONS FOR PROCRASTINATION

Think of the last time the following situation occurred. It's near the end of the semester. The term paper you were assigned at the beginning of the semester is due very soon. You have not begun work on this paper. There are reasons why you have been procrastinating on this task.

Rate each of the following reasons on a 5-point scale according to how much it reflects why you procrastinated at the time. Mark your answers by writing the letter a to e in the space to the left of each statement.

Use the scale:

Not at all reflects why I procrastinated		Somewhat reflects		Definitely reflects why I procrastinated
a	b	c	d	e

____ 19. You were concerned the professor wouldn't like your work.
____ 20. You had a hard time knowing what to include and what not to include in your paper.
____ 21. You waited until a classmate did his/hers, so that he/she could give you some advice.
____ 22. You had too many other things to do.
____ 23. There's some information you needed to ask the professor, but you felt uncomfortable approaching him/her.
____ 24. You were worried you would get a bad grade.

___ 25. You resented having to do things assigned by others.

___ 26. You didn't think you knew enough to write the paper.

___ 27. You really disliked writing term papers.

___ 28. You felt overwhelmed by the task.

___ 29. You had difficulty requesting information from other people.

___ 30. You looked forward to the excitement of doing this task at the last minute.

___ 31. You couldn't choose among all the topics.

___ 32. You were concerned that if you did well, your classmates would resent you.

___ 33. You didn't trust yourself to do a good job.

___ 34. You didn't have enough energy to begin the task.

___ 35. You felt it just takes too long to write a term paper.

___ 36. You liked the challenge of waiting until the deadline.

___ 37. You knew that your classmates hadn't started the paper either.

___ 38. You resented people setting deadlines for you.

___ 39. You were concerned you wouldn't meet your own expectations.

___ 40. You were concerned that if you got a good grade, people would have higher expectations of you in the future.

___ 41. You waited to see if the professor would give you some more information about the paper.

___ 42. You set very high standards for yourself and you worried that you wouldn't be able to meet those standards.

___ 43. You just felt too lazy to write a term paper.

___ 44. Your friends were pressuring you to do other things.

Procrastination Scale (PS)

PURPOSE To measure procrastination.

AUTHOR Bruce W. Tuckman

DESCRIPTION The PS is a 35-item instrument designed to measure tendencies of procrastination. Procrastination is viewed as the lack or absence of self-regulated performance, the tendency to put off or completely avoid an activity under one's control. From an original 72 items, factor analysis resulted in the present 35-item scale. Subsequent factor analysis revealed 16 items that could be used as a short form PS (items 1, 2, 3, 4, 7, 9, 11, 18, 22–25, 28, 29, 32, 34). The PS is a useful scale for research or for evaluating changes in clients being treated for problems involving procrastination.

NORMS The PS was studied with 183 college juniors and seniors between the ages of 19 and 22 who were preparing to become teachers. Actual norms were not provided.

SCORING The PS is easily scored by summing the item responses on a scale from 1 to 4 ("That's me for sure"=4) for a total score, with higher scores equaling greater tendencies to procrastination. Items 6, 8, 13, 17, 25, 27, 29, 30, 33, 34 are reverse-scored.

RELIABILITY The PS has excellent internal consistency, with an alpha of .90 for the 35-item scale and .86 for the 16-item scale. No data on stability were reported.

VALIDITY The PS has good concurrent validity, correlating negatively with the General Self-Efficacy Scale and a behavioral measure of self-regulated performance.

PRIMARY REFERENCE Tuckman, B. W. (1991). The development and concurrent validity of the Procrastination Scale, *Educational and Psychological Measurement*, 51, 473–480.

AVAILABILITY May be copied from this volume.

Indicate how you feel about each statement by placing the appropriate letter in the blank.

> A = That's me for sure
> B = That's my tendency
> C = That's *not* my tendency
> D = That's *not* me for sure

___ 1. I needlessly delay finishing jobs, even when they're important.
___ 2. I postpone starting in on things I don't like to do.
___ 3. When I have a deadline, I wait till the last minute.
___ 4. I delay making tough decisions.
___ 5. I stall on initiating new activities.
___ 6. I'm on time for appointments.
___ 7. I keep putting off improving my work habits.
___ 8. I get right to work, even on life's unpleasant chores.
___ 9. I manage to find an excuse for not doing something.
___ 10. I avoid doing those things which I expect to do poorly.
___ 11. I put the necessary time into even boring tasks, like studying.
___ 12. When I get tired of an unpleasant job, I stop.
___ 13. I believe in "keeping my nose to the grindstone."
___ 14. When something's not worth the trouble, I stop.
___ 15. I believe that things I don't like doing should not exist.
___ 16. I consider people who make me do unfair and difficult things to be rotten.
___ 17. When it counts, I can manage to enjoy even studying.
___ 18. I am an incurable time waster.
___ 19. I feel that it's my absolute right to have other people treat me fairly.
___ 20. I believe that other people don't have the right to give me deadlines.
___ 21. Studying makes me feel entirely miserable.
___ 22. I'm a time waster now but I can't seem to do anything about it.
___ 23. When something's too tough to tackle, I believe in postponing it.
___ 24. I promise myself I'll do something and then drag my feet.
___ 25. Whenever I make a plan of action, I follow it.
___ 26. I wish I could find an easy way to get myself moving.
___ 27. When I have trouble with a task, it's usually my own fault.
___ 28. Even though I hate myself if I don't get started, it doesn't get me going.
___ 29. I always finish important jobs with time to spare.
___ 30. When I'm done with my work, I check it over.
___ 31. I look for a loophole or shortcut to get through a tough task.
___ 32. I still get stuck in neutral even though I know how important it is to get started.
___ 33. I never met a job I couldn't "lick."
___ 34. Putting something off until tomorrow is not the way I do it.
___ 35. I feel that work burns me out.

Provision of Social Relations (PSR)

PURPOSE To measure social support.

AUTHORS R. Jay Turner, B. Gail Frankel, and Deborah M. Levin

DESCRIPTION The PSR is a 15-item instrument designed to measure components of social support. Based initially on the conceptualization by Weiss of five components of social support (attachment, social integration, reassurance of worth, reliable alliance, and guidance), factor analysis revealed the PSR to have essentially two dimensions, family support (items 4, 7, 10, 11, 12, 14) and friend support (items 1, 2, 3, 5, 6, 8, 9, 13, 15). The PSR is one of the few instruments that examines the environmental variable of social support (or, at least, the respondent's perceptions of it), a key element for assessment and intervention in many clinical approaches.

NORMS The PSR was developed in a series of studies involving 200 university students, 523 discharged psychiatric patients in Canada (59% female), and 989 (54% female) psychiatrically disabled community residents located in interviews with 11,000 households in Ontario, Canada. Actual norms are not available.

SCORING The PSR is scored by reverse-scoring items 7 and 15 and then summing the item scores on each of the subdimensions to get a score for that dimension. A total score can be obtained by summing the scores on the two subdimensions. Higher scores reflect more social support.

RELIABILITY The PSR has good internal consistency, with alphas that range from .75 to .87. No test-retest correlations were reported.

VALIDITY The PSR has good concurrent validity, correlating significantly with the Kaplan Scale of Social Support. The PSR is negatively correlated with several measures of psychological distress, indicating that the PSR is not confounded by item content measuring psychological distress.

PRIMARY REFERENCE Turner, R. J., Frankel, B. G., and Levin, D. M. (1983). Social support: Conceptualization, measurement, and implications for mental health, *Research in Community and Mental Health*, 3, 67–111. Instrument reproduced with permission of JAI Press, Inc. and B. Gail Frankel.

AVAILABILITY May be copied from this volume.

We would like to know something about your relationships with other people. Please read each statement below and decide how well the statement describes you. For each statement, show your answer by indicating to the left of the item the number that best describes how you feel. The numbers represent the following answers.

1 = Very much like me
2 = Much like me
3 = Somewhat like me
4 = Not very much like me
5 = Not at all like me

—— 1. When I'm with my friends, I feel completely able to relax and be myself.
—— 2. I share the same approach to life that many of my friends do.
—— 3. People who know me trust me and respect me.
—— 4. No matter what happens, I know that my family will always be there for me should I need them.
—— 5. When I want to go out to do things I know that many of my friends would enjoy doing these things with me.
—— 6. I have at least one friend I could tell anything to.
—— 7. Sometimes I'm not sure if I can completely rely on my family.
—— 8. People who know me think I am good at what I do.
—— 9. I feel very close to some of my friends.
—— 10. People in my family have confidence in me.
—— 11. My family lets me know they think I am a worthwhile person.
—— 12. People in my family provide me with help in finding solutions to my problems.
—— 13. My friends would take the time to talk over my problems, should I ever want to.
—— 14. I know my family will always stand by me.
—— 15. Even when I am with my friends I feel alone.

Psychological and Interpersonal Relationship Scales (PAIRS)

PURPOSE To measure treatment outcomes for erectile dysfunction.

AUTHORS Ralph W. Swindle, Ann E. Cameron, et al.

DESCRIPTION The PAIRS is a 23-item scale designed to measure the complex psychological and interpersonal outcomes associated with the treatment of erectile dysfunction (ED). Because ED can have a profound impact on men's lives, and because there were no other measures available that contained sufficient specificity regarding quality of life and other psychological domains related to ED, the authors developed the PAIRS. The conceptual foundation for the PAIRS was self-efficacy theory, which focuses on the development of task-specific constructs rather than broad traits. The PAIRS is composed of three subscales or domains: Sexual Self-Confidence (items 4, 8, 11, 18, 21, 23); Spontaneity (items 3, 9, 10, 12, 13, 14, 16, 17, 22); and Time Concerns (items 1, 2, 5, 6, 7, 15, 19, 20). Only subscale scores are used with the PAIRS, not the total score.

NORMS The PAIRS was initially studied with four, nonoverlapping samples of men including those diagnosed with ED and community controls. The first sample is comprised of 73 men from a multicenter study of ED in the United States, with a mean age of 58 years. Sample 2 involved 201 men in a Canadian-Australian study of medication for ED, with a mean age of 60 years. Sample 3 consisted of 139 men with ED with a mean age of 57 recruited from a multinational (Argentina, Brazil, France, Germany, and the United Kingdom) study of medication for ED. The fourth sample consisted of 801 men from the United States who were recruited from a nationally representative panel, and ranged in age from 40 to 70. The latter sample comprised 589 men without ED (mean age of 50) and 212 men with ED (mean age of 54.75). The Primary Reference presents other demographic data and scores on several measures for all samples. The Primary Reference also provides the mean scores and standard deviations on the three subscales for all of the samples.

SCORING The PAIRS is easily scored by computing the means for each domain. For respondents who are not using medication for ED, the Time Concerns subscale is computed without the three medication-related items.

RELIABILITY The PAIRS has good to excellent internal consistency with alphas ranging from .90 to .96 on Sexual Self-Confidence, .88 to .92 on Spontaneity, and .73 to .81 on Time Concerns. The PAIRS also has very good stability with 2-week test-retest reliability of .77 for sexual Self-Confidence, .66 for Spontaneity and .63 for time Concerns.

VALIDITY The PAIRS has excellent construct validity, with the subscales correlating in expected directions with numerous measures of sexual satisfaction and not correlating in predicted way with unrelated measures. The PAIRS also discriminated between the scores of men who were successfully treated for ED and men who were not successfully treated.

PRIMARY REFERENCE Swindle, R. W., et al (2004). The Psychological and Interpersonal Scales: Assessing psychological and relationship outcomes associated with erectile dysfunction and its treatment. *Archives of Sexual Behavior, 33,*

19–30. Instrument reproduced with the permission of Dr. Ann Cameron and Eli Lilly.

AVAILABILITY Dr. Ann Cameron, Outcomes Research, USMD, Eli Lilly and Co., Lily Corporate Center, Drop Code 5024, Indianapolis, IN 46285.

Now, please answer some questions regarding the relationship between you and your partner. Please answer these questions based on your personal experience.

Using the following 4-point scale where *1 equals "Strongly Disagree"* and *4 equals "Strongly Agree,"* how much do you agree or disagree with each of the statements? (Please circle the responses below.) *Also, please note: date can be defined as going out to dinner together, seeing a movie, shopping, taking a walk together—any activity you do as a couple that is usually enjoyable for you both.*

	Strongly Disagree	Disagree	Agree	Strongly Agree
1. The dating experience feels rushed when we are planning to have sex later.	1	2	3	4
2. I am very aware that if I wait too long after taking my medication, it may not work.	1	2	3	4
3. We are able to relax on dates and not worry.	1	2	3	4
4. I am able to have sex like I used to.	1	2	3	4
5. Once I take my medication, I want to have sex as soon as it takes effect.	1	2	3	4
6. Dates feel programmed in order to have sex on schedule.	1	2	3	4
7. My partner sometimes feels some pressure to have sex with me.	1	2	3	4
8. I feel very comfortable about my sexual abilities.	1	2	3	4
9. Before having sex, we have plenty of time to snuggle and be close.	1	2	3	4
10. We are able to have a good time together without worrying about the time.	1	2	3	4
11. I feel fantastic about my sex life.	1	2	3	4
12. When out together we feel free to change plans as we go.	1	2	3	4
13. Before we have sex, our time together can be spontaneous.	1	2	3	4
14. When we are alone before having sex, we can talk freely without feeling rushed.	1	2	3	4
15. Sometimes I ruin the mood by having to worry about the time.	1	2	3	4

	Strongly Disagree	Disagree	Agree	Strongly Agree
16. We are able to be easygoing when we are out together.	1	2	3	4
17. Before we have sex, I feel I can "go with the flow" with my partner when we are alone together.	1	2	3	4
18. I am confident I can achieve an erection when the mood is right.	1	2	3	4
19. I find myself feeling hurried when I think we will have sex later on.	1	2	3	4
20. I find myself worrying whether my medication will wear off before I can use it.	1	2	3	4
21. I am confident that I can enjoy spontaneous sexual activity.	1	2	3	4
22. When we will probably have sex later, we have time to be romantic and easygoing together.	1	2	3	4
23. It is very easy to have fulfilling sexual intercourse.	1	2	3	4

Psychosocial Well-Being Scale (PSWS)

PURPOSE To measure client outcomes in substance abuse cases.

AUTHORS Thomas O'Hare et al.

DESCRIPTION The PSWS is a 12-item scale designed for easy and efficient ratings of client well-being during and at the end of treatment. Unlike most measures in this book, the PSWS requires the practitioner to make judgments about the client's well-being as opposed to client self-report. The items for the PSWS were generated from a thorough review of the empirical and measurement literature regarding people with mental illness and substance abuse problems. The resulting scale is an assessment instrument with two major 4-item subscales: Psychological (P; items 1, 2, 3, & 4) and Social (S; items 5, 6, 7, 8). The remaining items are used as stand-alone indices.

NORMS The PSWS was developed with a sample of 297 clients, of whom 55.9% were female; the median age was 43, 91.2% were white, and 93.2% were taking psychoactive medications. Other demographic characteristics are described in the Primary Reference. The data were reported by case managers about whom no other data were reported. The mean for P was 12.9 (SD = 3.3) and the mean for S was 12.5 (SD = 3.3).

SCORING The PSWS is easily scored by summing up the item scores for the two subscales. The scores on the subscales run from 0 to 16 with higher scores indicating greater well-being.

RELIABILITY The PSWS has good internal consistency with alphas of .84 for P and .79 for S. Data on stability were not reported.

VALIDITY The PSWS has good concurrent validity with significant correlations between the subscales and a number of treatment variables such as Global Assessment of Functioning, psychiatrists' ratings, and a 1-item Global Substance Abuse Index. Subsequent research showed the PSWS associated with a number of other valid assessment tools.

PRIMARY REFERENCE O'Hare, T., et al. (2002). Validating the Psychosocial Well-being Scale (PSWS) with community clients, *Social Work in Mental Health*, 1, 15–30. Instrument reproduced with permission of Dr. O'Hare.

AVAILABILITY May be copied from this volume.

PSWS

RATE YOUR CLIENT'S WELL-BEING **OVER THE LAST 30 DAYS** USING THE SCALE BELOW. SCORE EACH OF THE FOLLOWING AREAS. *USE EVERYTHING YOU KNOW ABOUT THIS CLIENT.* (If you provide treatment as part of a team, give a score based on team consensus.)

POOR	IMPAIRED	MARGINAL	GOOD	EXCELLENT
0	1	2	3	4

1. *MENTAL STATUS: COGNITIVE FUNCTIONING*: Consider the client's level of hallucinations, delusions, disorientation, bizarre behavior or speech, memory problems, serious confusion or other symptoms of serious cognitive impairment. How would you rate their overall mental status? **RATING** ___

2. *MENTAL STATUS: EMOTIONAL STATE:* Consider the client's level of depression, anxiety, obsessional thinking and overall emotional state . . . How would you rate their overall emotional condition? **RATING** ___

3. *IMPULSE CONTROL*: Think about your client's overall behavior. Consider things such as their ability to express themselves effectively, ability to work at things patiently, tendencies to verbally or physically lash out at others, run away, harm themselves or proneness to impulsive, criminal, or drug-abusing behavior. How would you rate their overall impulse control? **RATING** ___

4. *COPING SKILLS:* Think about your client's ability to cope with problems and everyday stresses. How would you rate their ability to assess problem situations, deal with "triggers," use stress reduction strategies, consider possible solutions to problems, perhaps reach out to others for help in order to deal effectively with their difficulties? **RATING** ___

5. *IMMEDIATE SOCIAL NETWORK* (close friends, spouse, family): Consider the quality of your client's relationships with those available friends, family, spouse (as applicable). How would you rate the quality of the interaction overall between your client and them with respect to closeness, intimacy, general interpersonal satisfaction, effective communications, conflict, level of hostility, aggression, abuse? **RATING** ___

6. *EXTENDED SOCIAL RELATIONSHIPS/NETWORK* (local community): Think about your client's relationships with persons outside their immediate family and social group. Consider their relationship to others in the community, their involvement in social groups, organizations, and general feeling of integration into the wider community in which they live. How would you rate their overall relationship with the community right now? **RATING** ___

7. *RECREATIONAL ACTIVITIES:* Consider what the client does for fun (alone or social), hobbies, relaxation (reading, TV, video games, playing cards, etc. . . .) and physical exercise (walking, jogging, biking, etc. . . .). How would you rate the client's overall involvement in recreational activities? **RATING** ___

8. *LIVING ENVIRONMENT:* Think about your client's current living environment. Consider such things as adequacy of food, clothing, shelter, safety, and level of restrictiveness. How would you rate their overall living environment? **RATING** ___

9. *USE OF ALCOHOL AND OTHER DRUGS:* Consider the clients use of alcohol, illicit substances (cocaine, heroin, marijuana, PCP, hallucinogens, etc. . . .) and illicit prescription medication. Consider the following: how often do they use them, in what quantity, and what are the psychological, physical and social consequences associated with their use? How would you rate the client's overall functioning with regard to the use of alcohol and other drugs? **RATING** ___

10. *HEALTH:* Consider the client's overall health. Aside from normal, transient illnesses, think about health habits, chronic primary health disorders, their opinion of their own health, ability to engage in their usual activities relatively free from discomfort, overall energy level, hospitalizations and treatments for illness other than psychiatric ones. How would you rate their health overall? **RATING** ___

11. *INDEPENDENT LIVING/SELF CARE:* Consider how your client manages their household, takes care of personal hygiene, eats, sleeps and otherwise cares for themselves. How would you rate their performance in this area? **RATING** ___

12. *WORK SATISFACTION:* Consider if the client works outside the home, or is a homemaker, student, retired, level of disability and so forth. Think for a moment about their productivity in their respective role relative to other people their age. How would you rate their overall role productivity? **RATING** ___

Pursuing-Distancing Scale (P-D)

PURPOSE To measure interpersonal pursuing and distancing.

AUTHORS Donald M. Bernstein, John Santelli, Karen Alter-Reid, and Vincent Androsiglio

DESCRIPTION The P-D is an 80-item scale designed to measure the construct of interpersonal pursuing and distancing. Although the scale is longer than almost all in this book, it is included here because of its easy and speedy administration. Pursuing and distancing are related to the general construct of interpersonal contact or preferred amount of "space" among people. Pursuing is said to represent the forces of connectedness and togetherness, while distancing represents the forces of individuality and depends upon privacy and avoidance of emotional involvement for self-protection. The P-D reflects the manner in which pursuing and distancing are expressed behaviorally. The P-D is viewed as useful not only for research on these constructs but as a tool for clinicians who explore these topics with their clients.

NORMS The P-D has been studied with several samples, including 36 pairs of twins, 95 psychology students, 203 Indians, 161 Thais (all English speaking), and 61 nonstudent American adults. The mean age of the samples ranged from 23 to 39. The scores were fairly equally distributed. Across all American samples, pursuing scores average 22 (SD=5.5) and distancing scores average 19.5 (SD=5.7). There were no significant differences due to sex.

SCORING The P-D is easily responded to by circling "Yes" next to an item if it applies to the respondent, or "No" if it does not. The scores for pursuing and distancing are easily obtained by summing the number of items of each type found self-descriptive by the subject. The pursuing items are 1, 2, 3, 6, 8, 11, 12, 13, 16, 19, 21, 22, 24, 26, 27, 31, 32, 34, 37, 38, 44, 45, 47, 49, 50, 54, 55, 57, 58, 60, 63, 65, 68, 69, 70, 73, 75, 76, 79, 80. The remaining items are distancing. The scale has six subscales for which scoring keys are available from the authors. The subscales are: cognitive style, emotional style, social style, communicative style, sensation selling, and anality.

RELIABILITY Internal consistency for the P-D was determined by finding the correlation of each item with the total score for that item's form (pursuing and distancing). The mean correlation for all items was .31, suggesting rather weak internal consistency. No data on stability are available.

VALIDITY The P-D is said to have very good construct validity, as revealed by significant correlations in predicted ways with instruments measuring sex role, assertiveness, sensation-seeking, introversion-extraversion, and by clinicians' ratings of client characteristics.

PRIMARY REFERENCE Bernstein, D. M., Santelli, J., Alter-Reid, K., and Androsiglio, V. (1985). Pursuing and distancing: The construct and its measurement, *Journal of Personality Assessment*, 49, 273–281.

AVAILABILITY Dr. Donald M. Bernstein, 278 Pines Lake Drive East, Wayne NJ 07470. Telephone: 973.839.6074.

Please circle "Yes" on the answer sheet for each item that applies to you, and circle "No" if the item does not apply to you. You must pick one or the other; *never mark both "Yes" and "No" for the same item*. On occasion, you may feel that two seemingly contradictory items apply or do not apply to you. In those instances make the response that best describes you for each separate item regardless of the apparent contradiction. That is, it's OK to make the same response to contradictory statements if you see both statements as characterizing you.

Yes No 1. When I talk to people I like to make frequent eye contact.
Yes No 2. If my feelings were badly hurt I would not hesitate to show them.
Yes No 3. When something good happens to me, I can't wait to tell someone about it.
Yes No 4. When I greet family and friends I'm glad when the hugging and kissing are over.
Yes No 5. After a fight I usually remain silent and aloof.
Yes No 6. I enjoy gambling.
Yes No 7. I tend to hold back praise or compliments.
Yes No 8. I usually talk to the person sitting next to me on the train or bus.
Yes No 9. I am more comfortable when situations are clear-cut and unambiguous.
Yes No 10. I find it difficult to say "I love you" to someone.
Yes No 11. I am inclined to be optimistic.
Yes No 12. I like to spend a lot of my time playing games that involve other people.
Yes No 13. I often prefer to buy things on impulse.
Yes No 14. When I come home from work or school I relax by watching a good TV program.
Yes No 15. I tend to avoid disclosing information of a personal nature.
Yes No 16. I like to take spontaneous vacations with as little planning as possible.
Yes No 17. I find entertaining at my house a burden.
Yes No 18. When I listen to a song I focus my attention mainly on the lyrics.
Yes No 19. I can easily say "I'm sorry."
Yes No 20. I tend to avoid using intuition.
Yes No 21. I prefer not to wear a watch.
Yes No 22. I find it easy to trust people.
Yes No 23. When I recall a work of art it is mainly in terms of its technical aspects.
Yes No 24. I tend to speak my mind even if feelings get ruffled.
Yes No 25. I tend to describe events as the orderly sequence of specific details.
Yes No 26. I prefer to initiate sexual activity with my partner.
Yes No 27. I make friends quickly.
Yes No 28. When I take a trip I'm mainly interested in reaching my destination.
Yes No 29. I think a great deal about the past and future.
Yes No 30. I prefer to save my money.
Yes No 31. If someone owed me money I would ask for it back.
Yes No 32. At a party I rapidly become involved with other people.
Yes No 33. I like movies with clear-cut plots.
Yes No 34. If I disagree with someone I will let them know what I think.
Yes No 35. I find it difficult to say "I'm angry with you" to someone.
Yes No 36. After a heated argument I usually refrain from discussing the topic more.

Yes	No	37.	I enjoy movies that make me cry.
Yes	No	38.	I prefer to try new things.
Yes	No	39.	If a restaurant served me something ill-prepared I would probably not send it back.
Yes	No	40.	I become uncomfortable when people around me are emotional.
Yes	No	41.	I often find myself looking elsewhere while talking to someone.
Yes	No	42.	If I were badly injured I would control my feelings.
Yes	No	43.	When something good happens to me I often wait awhile before telling someone about it.
Yes	No	44.	When I greet family and friends I like to hug and kiss.
Yes	No	45.	I usually make up soon after a fight.
Yes	No	46.	I don't enjoy gambling.
Yes	No	47.	I give praise or compliments freely.
Yes	No	48.	When I take a train or bus I read the paper or a book during the trip.
Yes	No	49.	I have little difficulty dealing with ambiguity and uncertainty.
Yes	No	50.	I would find it easy to say "I love you" to someone.
Yes	No	51.	I'm inclined to be pessimistic.
Yes	No	52.	I like to spend most of my time reading good books.
Yes	No	53.	I consider my finances and research prices before making most purchases.
Yes	No	54.	When I come home from work or school I unwind by engaging in conversation.
Yes	No	55.	I find it easy to tell people about myself.
Yes	No	56.	I like to take planned vacations where I know what will happen in advance.
Yes	No	57.	I like to entertain people at my house.
Yes	No	58.	When I hear a song it is mainly the melody that holds my attention.
Yes	No	59.	I find it difficult to say "I'm sorry."
Yes	No	60.	I am inclined to be intuitive.
Yes	No	61.	I prefer to wear a watch.
Yes	No	62.	I find it difficult to trust people.
Yes	No	63.	When I recall a work of art it is in terms of the impression it made on me.
Yes	No	64.	I avoid telling people what's on my mind if I think it may hurt their feelings.
Yes	No	65.	I tend to describe events in terms of general impressions.
Yes	No	66.	I would rather have my partner initiate sexual activity.
Yes	No	67.	I make friends slowly.
Yes	No	68.	Traveling to a destination is as enjoyable as getting there.
Yes	No	69.	I am mainly concerned with the present.
Yes	No	70.	I prefer to spend my money.
Yes	No	71.	If someone owed me money I would be hesitant to ask for it back.
Yes	No	72.	At a party I wait to be approached by people.
Yes	No	73.	I prefer impressionistic, abstract movies.
Yes	No	74.	I avoid making waves.
Yes	No	75.	I would find it easy to say "I'm angry with you" to someone.
Yes	No	76.	After a heated argument I often continue discussing the topic.
Yes	No	77.	I rarely react emotionally to a movie.
Yes	No	78.	I prefer to do things I'm familiar with.
Yes	No	79.	If a restaurant served me something ill-prepared I would send it back.
Yes	No	80.	I remain at ease when people around me are emotional.

Questionnaire of Experiences of Dissociation (QED)

PURPOSE To measure dissociation.

AUTHOR Kevin C. Riley

DESCRIPTION The QED is a 26-item instrument designed to measure dissociation or the failure to integrate thoughts, feelings, and actions into consciousness. Dissociation is viewed as the mechanism underlying the syndrome of hysteria and symptoms such as conversion reaction, fugue states, and multiple personality. The items for the QED were drawn from the clinical literature on people suffering from the above problems. The QED is viewed as a useful measure for clinicians working with problems related to dissociation.

NORMS The QED has been studied with large, nonclinical samples (760 women, 450 men), and smaller samples of clinical respondents (somatization disorder, $n=21$, and multiple personality disorder, $n=3$). No other demographic information is available. The "normal" group had a mean of 9.92, the somatization disorder group's mean was 13.9, and the multiple personality group's mean was 24.6.

SCORING The QED is scored by simply scoring one point for each dissociation response and summing these up. Higher scores show greater dissociation. "Correct" (dissociative) answers are "true" for all items except items 7, 10, 15, 17, 18, 20, 21, and 23–26.

RELIABILITY The QED has fairly good internal consistency, with an alpha of .77. No data on stability are available.

VALIDITY The QED has good face validity. There are no other real validity data; however, the fact that the two clinical groups, somatization and multiple personality disorder as described above, believed to be at risk for dissociation, have elevated scores on the QED suggests some degree of known-groups validity.

PRIMARY REFERENCE Riley, K. C. (1988). Measurement of dissociation, *Journal of Nervous and Mental Disease*, 176, 449–450.

AVAILABILITY May be copied from this volume.

Listed below are a number of statements about experiences you may or may not have had. Read each one and indicate your response by circling the appropriate letter (T = True, F = False). There are no "right" or "wrong" answers.

T F   1. I often feel as if things were not real.
T F   2. Occasionally, I feel like someone else.
T F   3. Sometimes my mind blocks, goes totally empty.
T F   4. I often wonder who I really am.
T F   5. At one or more times, I have found myself staring intently at myself in the mirror as though looking at a stranger.
T F   6. I often feel that I am removed from my thoughts and actions.
T F   7. I rarely feel confused, like in a daze.
T F   8. I have had periods where I could not remember where I had been the day (or days) before.
T F   9. When I try to speak words, they don't come out right.
T F 10. I have never come to without knowing where I was or how I got there.
T F 11. As I was growing up, people often said that I seemed to be off in a world of my own.
T F 12. Sometimes I feel like my body is undergoing a transformation.
T F 13. Sometimes I feel as if there is someone inside of me directing my actions.
T F 14. Sometimes my limbs move on their own.
T F 15. When I was a child, I rarely sat and daydreamed in school.
T F 16. Sometimes I have problems understanding others' speech.
T F 17. I am rarely bothered by forgetting where I put things.
T F 18. My mind has never gone blank on me.
T F 19. I have a rich and exciting fantasy life.
T F 20. I never find myself staring off into space without thinking of anything.
T F 21. I daydream very little.
T F 22. My soul sometimes leaves my body.
T F 23. I do not think that I would be able to hypnotize myself.
T F 24. When I was a child, I never had imaginary companions.
T F 25. I have never gone into a trance, like hypnosis.
T F 26. I have never had periods of déjà vu, that is, found myself in a new position with the distinct sense that I had been there or experienced it before.

Race-Related Stressor Scale (RRSS)

PURPOSE To measure the exposure to race-related stressors in the military and war zone.

AUTHORS Chalsa M. Loo et al.

DESCRIPTION The RRSS is a 33-item scale designed to assess the exposure of military personnel to stressors that are related to race among Asian American Vietnam War veterans. Based in part on the need for more precise analyses of the large number of PTSD cases among Vietnam War veterans, this scale focuses on a model of race-related stressors that might have affected veterans from Asian minority groups. Items for the scale were generated from the literature, clinical interviews, focus groups, and input from clinicians. Factor analysis revealed three factors: Racial Prejudice and Stigmatization (19 items), Bicultural Identification and Conflict (7 items) and Racist Environment (7 items). The items that loaded on each factor are available in the original article.

NORMS The RRSS was validated on a sample of 300 Asian American Vietnam War veterans, of whom 37% were of mixed Asian and/or Polynesian ancestry, 21% were Japanese ancestry, 14% were of Chinese ancestry, 13% were Chamoro, 12% were of Filipino ancestry, and 3% were of Korean ancestry. 70% of the veterans were from the Army with 10% from each of the other branches of the military. 71% were married and only 39% were employed full time. The mean age of the sample was 55 years with an average of 14.8 years of schooling. Actual norms for the scale were not provided, although the mean total RRSS score on this sample was 56.5 (SD = 29.9).

SCORING The RRSS is easily scored by simply summing the item scores. The range for the scale is from 0 to 132, with higher scores indicating a higher degree of race-related stress. The three subscales are scored and interpreted in the same way.

RELIABILITY The RRSS has excellent internal consistency with an overall alpha of .97 and alphas for the three subscales that range from .93 to .97. The RRSS also has excellent stability with a 5- to 16-week test-retest correlation of .85 for the total scale, .84 for the Racial Prejudice and Bicultural Environment subscales and .60 for Racist Environment.

VALIDITY The RRSS has excellent construct validity with predictions in specific directions between the overall scale and all three subscales validated by significant correlations with the Mississippi Scale (for assessing PTSD), the Brief Symptom Inventory, and the Combat Exposure Scale. In this sample, 37% of respondents were found to be over the empirically derived cut-off on the Mississippi Scale indicating the presence of PTSD.

PRIMARY REFERENCE Loo, C. M., et al. (2001). Measuring exposure to racism: Development and validation of a Race-Related Stressor Scale (RRSS) for Asian American Vietnam veterans, *Psychological Assessment, 13*, 503–520.

AVAILABILITY Dr. Chalsa Loo, National Center for PTSD, 1132 Bishop Street, Suite 307, Honolulu, HI 96813. Telephone: 802.296.6300.

Please answer the following questions about your experiences while you served in the Vietnam War or served in the military during the Vietnam War. These questions describe events that may have occurred in the field or in base camps or other rear areas. The term "military personnel" refers to American military personnel. The term "in Vietnam" refers to any duty on the ground, in the air over or in the waters contiguous to South or North Vietnam or Cambodia, or in or over Laos. Please *circle the answer* that best describes your experiences.

In the military . . .

1. How often, if ever, did you *hear* military personnel describe Asian lives as having no value or lesser value than American lives?

0	1	2	3	4
Never	Rarely	Sometimes	Frequently	Very Frequently

2. Did you ever *observe* military personnel treat Asians as if their lives were of no value or of lesser value than white American lives?

0	1	2	3	4
Never	Rarely	Sometimes	Frequently	Very Frequently

3. How often, if ever, could you identify with the people or culture of Vietnam?

0	1	2	3	4
Never	Rarely	Sometimes	Frequently	Very Frequently

4. How often, if ever, were you concerned that other American soldiers might question your loyalty if you interacted with Vietnamese civilians?

0	1	2	3	4
Never	Rarely	Sometimes	Frequently	Very Frequently

5. As an American of Asian ancestry, did you ever feel a stronger identification with Vietnamese civilians than with American soldiers of white or black ancestry?

0	1	2	3	4
Never	Rarely	Sometimes	Frequently	Very Frequently

6. How often, if ever, did military personnel refer to Asians as "gooks," "slant eyes," "slopes," or some other racially insulting or insensitive name?

0	1	2	3	4
Never	Rarely	Sometimes	Frequently	Very Frequently

7. Were you ever singled out for different or harsher treatment than persons of another race but of the same rank?

0	1	2	3	4
Never	Rarely	Sometimes	Frequently	Very Frequently

8. How often, if ever, did you hear military personnel express hatred toward Asians?

0	1	2	3	4
Never	Rarely	Sometimes	Frequently	Very Frequently

649

9. Were you ever pointed out as an example of what the enemy looked like?

0	1	2	3	4
Never	Rarely	Sometimes	Frequently	Very Frequently

10. Did other Americans ever keep their physical distance from you or tell you to get away from them because you were Asian?

0	1	2	3	4
Never	Rarely	Sometimes	Frequently	Very Frequently

11. Did other Americans ever do or say things that led you to believe that they thought you looked like a Vietnamese?

0	1	2	3	4
Never	Rarely	Sometimes	Frequently	Very Frequently

12. Did you ever observe Asian American military personnel being stared at in ways that non-Asian Americans were not?

0	1	2	3	4
Never	Rarely	Sometimes	Frequently	Very Frequently

13. How often, if ever, did you feel you were more like the Vietnamese than like the Americans?

0	1	2	3	4
Never	Rarely	Sometimes	Frequently	Very Frequently

14. Compared to persons of other races but of the same rank, were you ever ignored or treated disrespectfully?

0	1	2	3	4
Never	Rarely	Sometimes	Frequently	Very Frequently

15. How often, if ever, was your authority questioned for reasons you suspect had to do with your being Asian?

0	1	2	3	4
Never	Rarely	Sometimes	Frequently	Very Frequently

16. How often, if ever, did military personnel treat Asians as inferior?

0	1	2	3	4
Never	Rarely	Sometimes	Frequently	Very Frequently

17. How often, if ever, were you called a "gook," "slope," "slant eyes," "Jap," "kamikaze," "Chink," "boy," "pineapple," or "coconut head" in a way that felt hostile or insulting?

0	1	2	3	4
Never	Rarely	Sometimes	Frequently	Very Frequently

18. Did military personnel ever make racially insensitive remarks about your doing things like eating rice, using chopsticks, or squatting?

0	1	2	3	4
Never	Rarely	Sometimes	Frequently	Very Frequently

19. Did you ever feel like you "stood out" (in a negative way) or were looked at as if you did not belong there?

0	1	2	3	4
Never	Rarely	Sometimes	Frequently	Very Frequently

20. Were you ever in situations where you felt isolated because you were the only or one of few Asian Americans in your platoon or other small group?

0	1	2	3	4
Never	Rarely	Sometimes	Frequently	Very Frequently

21. How often, if ever, did other Americans treat you with racial hatred or hostility?

0	1	2	3	4
Never	Rarely	Sometimes	Frequently	Very Frequently

22. Were you ever denied access to certain areas or hassled before being given access to certain areas because you were Asian?

0	1	2	3	4
Never	Rarely	Sometimes	Frequently	Very Frequently

23. Did you ever feel like you did not really fit in with the rest of the Americans in your unit?

0	1	2	3	4
Never	Rarely	Sometimes	Frequently	Very Frequently

24. How often, if ever, did military personnel make insulting remarks about the South Vietnamese, related to their size, smell, intelligence, diet, or abilities?

0	1	2	3	4
Never	Rarely	Sometimes	Frequently	Very Frequently

25. How often, if ever, did a *living* Vietnamese *male* remind you of a family member, relative, or friend?

0	1	2	3	4
Never	Rarely	Sometimes	Frequently	Very Frequently

26. How often, if ever, did a *living* Vietnamese *woman or child* remind you of a family member, relative, or friend?

0	1	2	3	4
Never	Rarely	Sometimes	Frequently	Very Frequently

27. How often, if ever, did a *wounded or dead* Vietnamese *male* remind you of a family member, relative, or friend?

0	1	2	3	4
Never	Rarely	Sometimes	Frequently	Very Frequently

28. How often, if ever, did any *wounded or dead* Vietnamese *woman or child* remind you of a family member, relative, or friend?

0	1	2	3	4
Never	Rarely	Sometimes	Frequently	Very Frequently

29. Did you ever feel like you had to express anti-Asian sentiments in front of other Americans even if you did not really feel that way?

0	1	2	3	4
Never	Rarely	Sometimes	Frequently	Very Frequently

30. How often, if ever, did you feel your presence in the military was resented because you were Asian?

0	1	2	3	4
Never	Rarely	Sometimes	Frequently	Very Frequently

31. How often, if ever, did you feel you were treated unfairly because of your race or ethnicity?

0	1	2	3	4
Never	Rarely	Sometimes	Frequently	Very Frequently

32. Did other Americans ever treat you like an outsider or a foreigner?

0	1	2	3	4
Never	Rarely	Sometimes	Frequently	Very Frequently

33. How often, if ever, did you try to prove, or feel the need to prove, that you were American?

0	1	2	3	4
Never	Rarely	Sometimes	Frequently	Very Frequently

Rape Aftermath Symptom Test (RAST)

PURPOSE To measure responses to rape.

AUTHOR Dean G. Kilpatrick

DESCRIPTION The RAST is a 70-item instrument designed to measure fear and other symptoms commonly experienced by female victims after a rape experience. The RAST was constructed using items from instruments that were considered successful in detecting rape-related symptoms—the Derogatis SCL-9O-R and the Veronen-Kilpatrick Modified Fear Survey. A major value of the RAST is it is relatively brief (in comparison to the other measures) and thus may enhance assessment and evaluation efficiency.

NORMS The RAST was studied initially with 204 adult, female rape victims and 173 nonvictims, matched for age, race, and residential neighborhood. Roughly 56–57% of each group was white, 40–43% black, and 0.6–2% other. There was a broad range of educational and marital status represented in the samples. The means for the RAST varied dramatically for the rape group depending on the length of time that had transpired since the rape. From 6 to 21 days after the rape ($n = 131$), the mean was 101.80 (SD = 43.17). Six months after the rape ($n = 103$), the mean was 60.70 (SD = 38.17). One year after the rape ($n = 75$), the mean was 60.73 (SD = 40.57), and three years after the rape ($n = 12$), the mean was 46.00 (SD = 32.57).

SCORING The RAST is easily scored by simply summing individual item scores for a total score. The possible range is from 0 to 280 with higher scores indicating more psychological symptoms and fear-producing stimuli.

RELIABILITY The RAST has excellent internal consistency, with an alpha of .95. It also has excellent stability, with a 2.5-month test-retest correlation of .85 (for nonvictims).

VALIDITY The RAST has excellent known-groups validity, significantly distinguishing between victims and nonvictims at all the time periods described above. No other validity data were available.

PRIMARY REFERENCE Kilpatrick, D. G., Best, C. L., Veronen, L. J., Ruff, M. H., Ruff, G. A., and Allison, J. C. (1985). The aftermath of rape: A 3-year longitudinal study. Paper presented at the annual convention of the American Psychological Association, Los Angeles, California.

AVAILABILITY Dr. Dean Kilpatrick, Crime Victims Research and Treatment Center, Department of Psychiatry and Behavioral Sciences, Medical University of South Carolina, Charleston, SC 29425. Email: kilpatdg@musc.edu.

Using the following key, complete the two sections below:

> 0 = Not at all
> 1 = A little
> 2 = A fair amount
> 3 = Much
> 4 = Very much

Section 1

The items in this section refer to things and experiences that may cause fear or unpleasant feelings. Circle the number that describes how much you are disturbed by each item nowadays.

1.	Parking lots	0	1	2	3	4
2.	Being in a car alone	0	1	2	3	4
3.	Being on an elevator alone	0	1	2	3	4
4.	Automobiles	0	1	2	3	4
5.	Darkness	0	1	2	3	4
6.	Strange shapes	0	1	2	3	4
7.	Closed spaces	0	1	2	3	4
8.	Going out with new people	0	1	2	3	4
9.	Entering room where people are seated	0	1	2	3	4
10.	Answering the phone	0	1	2	3	4
11.	Seeing other people injected	0	1	2	3	4
12.	Journeys by bus	0	1	2	3	4
13.	Enclosed places	0	1	2	3	4
14.	Being criticized	0	1	2	3	4
15.	Being awakened at night	0	1	2	3	4
16.	Being in a strange place	0	1	2	3	4
17.	Walking on a dimly lit street	0	1	2	3	4
18.	Being alone	0	1	2	3	4
19.	Sound of doorbell	0	1	2	3	4
20.	Sudden noises	0	1	2	3	4
21.	A man's penis	0	1	2	3	4
22.	Sexual intercourse	0	1	2	3	4
23.	Stopping at a stoplight	0	1	2	3	4
24.	Blind dates	0	1	2	3	4
25.	Dreams	0	1	2	3	4
26.	Strangers	0	1	2	3	4
27.	Door slamming	0	1	2	3	4

28.	People talking about you	0	1	2	3	4
29.	Sleeping alone	0	1	2	3	4
30.	People behind you	0	1	2	3	4
31.	Shadows	0	1	2	3	4
32.	Testifying in court	0	1	2	3	4
33.	Journeys by train	0	1	2	3	4
34.	Journeys by car	0	1	2	3	4
35.	Crowds	0	1	2	3	4
36.	Angry people	0	1	2	3	4
37.	Talking to police	0	1	2	3	4
38.	Large open spaces	0	1	2	3	4
39.	Nude men	0	1	2	3	4
40.	Voices	0	1	2	3	4

Section 2

Below is a list of problems and complaints that people sometimes have. Read each one carefully and circle the number from the previous key (0=not at all, 1=a little, 2=a fair amount, 3=much, 4=very much) that best describes how much discomfort that problem has caused you during the past _____, including today.

1.	Feeling low in energy or slowed down	0	1	2	3	4
2.	Feeling of being caught or trapped	0	1	2	3	4
3.	Feeling lonely	0	1	2	3	4
4.	Feelings of worthlessness	0	1	2	3	4
5.	Feeling afraid in open spaces or in the streets	0	1	2	3	4
6.	Feeling afraid to go out of your house alone	0	1	2	3	4
7.	Feeling afraid to travel on buses, subways, or trains	0	1	2	3	4
8.	Having to avoid certain things, places, or activities because they frighten you	0	1	2	3	4
9.	Feeling uneasy in crowds such as shopping or at a movie	0	1	2	3	4
10.	Feeling nervous when you are left alone	0	1	2	3	4
11.	Trouble falling asleep	0	1	2	3	4
12.	Awakening in the early morning	0	1	2	3	4
13.	Sleep that is restless or disturbed	0	1	2	3	4
14.	Suddenly scared for no reason	0	1	2	3	4
15.	Feeling fearful	0	1	2	3	4
16.	Spells of terror or panic	0	1	2	3	4
17.	Feeling so restless you couldn't sit still	0	1	2	3	4
18.	The feeling that something bad is going to happen to you	0	1	2	3	4
19.	Thoughts and images of a frightening nature	0	1	2	3	4
20.	Feeling that most people cannot be trusted	0	1	2	3	4

21. Feeling that you are watched or talked about by others	0	1	2	3	4
22. Feeling that people will take advantage of you if you let them	0	1	2	3	4
23. Feeling shy or uneasy with the opposite sex	0	1	2	3	4
24. Feeling others do not understand you or are unsympathetic	0	1	2	3	4
25. Feeling uneasy when people are watching or talking about you	0	1	2	3	4
26. Feeling very self-conscious with others	0	1	2	3	4
27. Hearing voices other people do not hear	0	1	2	3	4
28. Feeling lonely even when you are with people	0	1	2	3	4
29. Having thoughts about sex that bother you a lot	0	1	2	3	4
30. The idea that something is wrong with your mind	0	1	2	3	4

Rathus Assertiveness Schedule (RAS)

PURPOSE To measure assertiveness.

AUTHOR Spencer A. Rathus

DESCRIPTION This 30-item instrument was designed to measure assertiveness, or what the author called social boldness. Respondents are asked to rate 30 social situations according to how characteristic each is of their own experience. This widely used instrument provides the practitioner with clients' impressions of their own assertiveness and frankness, and can be used to provide positive feedback to clients during treatment, which is especially important in working with assertiveness problems. The RAS does not seem to be affected by social desirability.

NORMS Data are reported for a sample of 68 undergraduates which also were used in the reliability analysis. The subjects had an age range from 17 to 27 years. The mean RAS was .294 with a standard deviation of 29.121. At an eight-week post-test the mean was 1.62 with a standard deviation of 27.632.

SCORING Items are rated in terms of how descriptive the item is of the respondent. Ratings are from +3 to −3. Seventeen items, indicated by an asterisk on the scale, are reverse-scored. Scores are determined by summing item ratings, and can range from −90 to +90. Negative scores reflect nonassertiveness and positive scores reflect assertiveness.

RELIABILITY The RAS has evidence of good internal consistency and stability. Split-half reliability was .77. Test-retest reliability over an eight-week period was .78.

VALIDITY The RAS has good concurrent validity. Scores on the instrument have been shown to correlate with measures of boldness, outspokenness, assertiveness, aggressiveness, and confidence. Strong concurrent validity also is seen in the correlation between RAS scores and trained raters' rankings of assertiveness. Also, the RAS has been shown to possess construct validity: 19 of the 30 items correlated with external measures of assertiveness and 28 were negatively correlated with a measure of niceness.

PRIMARY REFERENCE Rathus, S. A. (1973). A 30-item schedule for assessing assertive behavior, *Behavior Therapy*, 4, 398–406. Instrument reproduced with permission of Academic Press.

AVAILABILITY May be copied from this volume.

Indicate how characteristic or descriptive each of the following statements is of you by using the code given below.

+3 = Very characteristic of me, extremely descriptive
+2 = Rather characteristic of me, quite descriptive
+1 = Somewhat characteristic of me, slightly descriptive
−1 = Somewhat uncharacteristic of me, slightly nondescriptive
−2 = Rather uncharacteristic of me, quite nondescriptive
−3 = Very uncharacteristic of me, extremely nondescriptive

___ 1. Most people seem to be more aggressive and assertive than I am.*
___ 2. I have hesitated to make or accept dates because of "shyness."*
___ 3. When the food served at a restaurant is not done to my satisfaction, I complain about it to the waiter or waitress.
___ 4. I am careful to avoid hurting other people's feelings, even when I feel that I have been injured.*
___ 5. If a salesman has gone to considerable trouble to show me merchandise that is not quite suitable, I have a difficult time saying "No."*
___ 6. When I am asked to do something, I insist upon knowing why.
___ 7. There are times when I look for a good, vigorous argument.
___ 8. I strive to get ahead as well as most people in my position.
___ 9. To be honest, people often take advantage of me.*
___ 10. I enjoy starting conversations with new acquaintances and strangers.
___ 11. I often don't know what to say to attractive persons of the opposite sex.*
___ 12. I will hesitate to make phone calls to business establishments and institutions.*
___ 13. I would rather apply for a job or for admission to a college by writing letters than by going through with personal interviews.*
___ 14. I find it embarrassing to return merchandise.*
___ 15. If a close and respected relative were annoying me, I would smother my feelings rather than express my annoyance.*
___ 16. I have avoided asking questions for fear of sounding stupid.*
___ 17. During an argument I am sometimes afraid that I will get so upset that I will shake all over.*
___ 18. If a famed and respected lecturer makes a statement which I think is incorrect, I will have the audience hear my point of view as well.
___ 19. I avoid arguing over prices with clerks and salesmen.*
___ 20. When I have done something important or worthwhile, I manage to let others know about it.
___ 21. I am open and frank about my feelings.
___ 22. If someone has been spreading false and bad stories about me, I see him/her as soon as possible to "have a talk" about it.
___ 23. I often have a hard time saying "No."*
___ 24. I tend to bottle up my emotions rather than make a scene.*
___ 25. I complain about poor service in a restaurant and elsewhere.
___ 26. When I am given a compliment, I sometimes just don't know what to say.*

—— 27. If a couple near me in a theater or at a lecture were conversing rather loudly, I would ask them to be quiet or to take their conversation elsewhere.
—— 28. Anyone attempting to push ahead of me in a line is in for a good battle.
—— 29. I am quick to express an opinion.
—— 30. There are times when I just can't say anything.*

Rational Behavior Inventory (RBI)

PURPOSE To measure irrational and absolutist beliefs.

AUTHORS Clayton T. Shorkey and Victor C. Whiteman

DESCRIPTION The RBI is a 37-item instrument that provides an overall index of irrationality, or the tendency to hold irrational and absolutist beliefs. The RBI is based on the work of Albert Ellis on cognitive therapy and the assumption that irrational beliefs underlie emotional disorders. The RBI was specifically constructed to be used for assessment, treatment planning, and evaluation in rational-behavior and cognitive-behavior therapy. It has been extensively studied by a number of investigators. The RBI presents one overall score plus 11 factors: (1) catastrophizing, (2) guilt, (3) perfectionism, (4) need for approval, (5) caring and helping, (6) blame and punishment, (7) inertia and avoidance, (8) independence, (9) self-downing, (10) projected misfortune, and (11) control of emotions. Each factor has three or four items, and separate factor scores as well as the overall score give a clear picture of the extent of an individual's irrational or dysfunctional beliefs in several areas.

NORMS The RBI has been studied with a number of different clinical and nonclinical samples. The initial studies were conducted on 414 undergraduate students and 127 mental health professionals attending workshops by Albert Ellis. For undergraduates, the mean total rationality score was 26.35. There were no statistically significant differences between males and females except on one subscale. For the two groups of mental health professionals, total RBI scores prior to the Ellis workshop were 28.45 and 27.62. Normative data are available for other groups as well.

SCORING The RBI is somewhat difficult to score and it is recommended that the scoring guide available with the instrument be used. Basically, each item on the RBI is assigned a cutting point of 3 or 4, and the number of points assigned to that item is based on that cutting point. Once the score for each factor is determined by summing the scores on each item on the factor, the overall score is determined by summing the scores for all eleven factors. This results in a possible range of 0 to 37 with higher scores indicating greater irrationality.

RELIABILITY The RBI has good internal consistency and homogeneity. Each factor was measured by a Guttman scale with a coefficient of reproducibility of .60 or more. The total RBI had a split-half reliability of .73. The RBI has good stability, with a .82 test-retest correlation after three days and .71 after ten days.

VALIDITY A number of studies have demonstrated good concurrent and known-groups validity for the RBI. The RBI is significantly correlated in predicted directions with several measures of trait and state anxiety in clinical and nonclinical samples. The RBI has been found to be significantly correlated to several other personality measures, such as anomie, authoritarianism, dogmatism, and self-esteem, and to measures of psychiatric symptomatology. Further, the RBI has been found to distinguish between clinical and nonclinical samples in several studies, and is also sensitive to changes from both workshops and therapy. Finally, the RBI does not appear to be influenced by social desirability response set.

PRIMARY REFERENCE Shorkey, C. T., and Whiteman, V. L. (1977). Development of the Rational Behavior Inventory: Initial validity and reliability, *Educational and Psychological Measurement*, 37, 527–534. Instrument reproduced with permission of Clayton T. Shorkey.

AVAILABILITY Clayton T. Shorkey, Ph.D., School of Social Work, 1925 San Jacinto Boulevard, The University of Texas, Austin, TX 78712-1203. Email: cshorkeu@mail.utexas.edu.

For each of the following questions, please follow the scale and indicate the numbered response that most clearly reflects your opinion. Work quickly and answer each question.

1 = Strongly disagree
2 = Disagree
3 = Neutral
4 = Agree
5 = Strongly agree

___ 1. Helping others is the very basis of life.
___ 2. It is necessary to be especially friendly to new colleagues and neighbors.
___ 3. People should observe moral laws more strictly than they do.
___ 4. I find it difficult to take criticism without feeling hurt.
___ 5. I often spend more time trying to think of ways of getting out of things than it would take me to do them.
___ 6. I tend to become terribly upset and miserable when things are not the way I would like them to be.
___ 7. It is impossible at any given time to change one's emotions.
___ 8. It is sinful to doubt the Bible.
___ 9. Sympathy is the most beautiful human emotion.
___ 10. I shrink from facing a crisis or difficulty.
___ 11. I often get excited or upset when things go wrong.
___ 12. One should rebel against doing unpleasant things, however necessary, if doing them is unpleasant.
___ 13. I get upset when neighbors are very harsh with their little children.
___ 14. It is realistic to expect that there should be no incompatibility in marriage.
___ 15. I frequently feel unhappy with my appearance.
___ 16. A person should be thoroughly competent, adequate, talented, and intelligent in all possible respects.
___ 17. What others think of you is most important.
___ 18. Other people should make things easier for us, and help with life's difficulties.
___ 19. I tend to look to others for the kind of behavior they approve as right or wrong.
___ 20. I find that my occupation and social life tend to make me unhappy.
___ 21. I usually try to avoid doing chores which I dislike doing.
___ 22. Some of my family and/or friends have habits that bother and annoy me very much.
___ 23. I tend to worry about possible accidents and disasters.
___ 24. I like to bear responsibility alone.
___ 25. I get terribly upset and miserable when things are not the way I like them to be.
___ 26. I worry quite a bit over possible misfortunes.
___ 27. Punishing oneself for all errors will prevent future mistakes.
___ 28. One can best help others by criticizing them and sharply pointing out the error of their ways.
___ 29. Worrying about a possible danger will help ward it off or decrease its effects.
___ 30. I worry about little things.
___ 31. Certain people are bad, wicked, or villainous and should be severely blamed and punished for their sins.

—— 32. A large number of people are guilty of bad sexual conduct.
—— 33. One should blame oneself severely for all mistakes and wrongdoings.
—— 34. It makes me very uncomfortable to be different.
—— 35. I worry over possible misfortunes.
—— 36. I prefer to be independent of others in making decisions.
—— 37. Because a certain thing once strongly affected one's life, it should indefinitely affect it.

Raulin Intense Ambivalence Scale (RIAS)

PURPOSE To measure intense ambivalence.

AUTHOR Michael L. Raulin

DESCRIPTION The RIAS is a 45-item scale designed to measure intense ambivalence. Ambivalence is defined as the existence of simultaneous or rapidly interchangeable positive and negative feelings toward the same object or activity, with both positive and negative feelings being strong. Although the RIAS was developed on the assumption that intense ambivalence is an important feature in schizophrenia, development of the instrument with diverse populations suggests broader utility. The 45 true/false items were chosen from a wide range of potential items. In designing the scale, particular attention was placed on minimizing social desirability response set.

NORMS Several studies were carried out in the development of RIAS. The first set involved 384 male and 475 female undergraduate students. The second involved 89 male and 8 female inpatients diagnosed as schizophrenic, 13 male and 18 female inpatients diagnosed as depressed, 66 male and 131 female psychology clinic clients with a range of nonpsychotic disorders, and a "normal" control group of 104 male and 39 females from the general population. Mean scores on the RIAS were 16.23 for the depressed patients, 13.93 for the clinic clients, and 10.82 for the "normal" controls. For the college students, mean scores ranged from 8.45 to 10.51.

SCORING The RIAS is scored by assigning a score of 1 to the correct responses and summing them. The correct responses are "true" to items 1, 4, 5, 7–22, 24, 26, 27, 30–32, 34, 35, 37, 38, 40, 42, 43, 45, and "false" for the remainder of the items.

RELIABILITY The RIAS has excellent internal consistency, with alphas that range from .86 to .94. It also has excellent stability, with test-retest correlations of .81 for time periods of ten to twelve weeks.

VALIDITY The RIAS was not correlated with age, education, and social class suggesting these variables do not affect responses. The RIAS has good known-groups validity, distinguishing between college students rated as ambivalent or not ambivalent and among depressed, schizophrenic and clinic clients, and "normal" controls. The RIAS also has some concurrent validity, correlating with two other scales of schizotypy (indicating a genetic predisposition for schizophrenia).

PRIMARY REFERENCE Raulin, M. L. (1984). Development of a scale to measure intense ambivalence, *Journal of Consulting and Clinical Psychology*, 52, 63–72. Instrument reproduced with permission of Michael L. Raulin and the American Psychological Association.

AVAILABILITY Dr. Michael L. Raulin, SUNY-Buffalo, Psychology Department, Julian Park Hall, Buffalo, NY 14260. Telephone: 716.645.3650.

Circle either T for true or F for false for each item as it applies to you.

T F 1. Very often, even my favorite pastimes don't excite me.
T F 2. I feel I can trust my friends.
T F 3. Small imperfections in a person are rarely enough to change love into hatred.
T F 4. There have been times when I have hated one or both of my parents for the affection they have expressed for me.
T F 5. Words of affection almost always make people uncomfortable.
T F 6. I don't mind too much the faults of people I admire.
T F 7. Love and hate tend to go together.
T F 8. Honest people will tell you that they often feel chronic resentment toward the people they love.
T F 9. Everything I enjoy has its painful side.
T F 10. Love never seems to last very long.
T F 11. My strongest feelings of pleasure usually seem to be mixed with pain.
T F 12. Whenever I get what I want, I usually don't want it at all any more.
T F 13. I have always experienced dissatisfaction with feelings of love.
T F 14. I worry the most when things are going the best.
T F 15. I often get very angry with people just because I love them so much.
T F 16. I start distrusting people if I have to depend on them too much.
T F 17. I can think of someone right now whom I thought I liked a day or two ago, but now strongly dislike.
T F 18. The people around me seem to be very changeable.
T F 19. It is hard to imagine two people loving one another for many years.
T F 20. The closer I get to people, the more I am annoyed by their faults.
T F 21. I find that the surest way to start resenting someone is to just start liking them too much.
T F 22. Often I feel like I hate even my favorite activities.
T F 23. I usually know when I can trust someone.
T F 24. Everyone has a lot of hidden resentment toward his loved ones.
T F 25. I usually know exactly how I feel about people I have grown close to.
T F 26. I have noticed that feelings of tenderness often turn into feelings of anger.
T F 27. I always seem to be the most unsure of myself at the same time that I am most confident of myself.
T F 28. My interest in personally enjoyed hobbies and pastimes has remained relatively stable.
T F 29. I can usually depend on those with whom I am close.
T F 30. My experiences with love have always been muddled with great frustration
T F 31. I usually find that feelings of hate will interfere when I have grown to love someone.
T F 32. A sense of shame has often interfered with my accepting words of praise from others.
T F 33. I rarely feel rejected by those who depend on me.
T F 34. I am wary of love because it is such a short-lived emotion.
T F 35. I usually experience doubt when I have accomplished something that I have worked on for a long time.

T F 36. I rarely doubt the appropriateness of praise that I have received from others in the past.

T F 37. I often feel as though I cannot trust people whom I have grown to depend on.

T F 38. I usually experience some grief over my own feelings of pleasure.

T F 39. It is rare for me to love a person one minute and hate them the next minute.

T F 40. I doubt if I can ever be sure exactly what my true interests are.

T F 41. I can't remember ever feeling love and hate for the same person at the same time.

T F 42. Love is always painful for me.

T F 43. Close relationships never seem to last long.

T F 44. I never had much trouble telling whether my parents loved me or hated me.

T F 45. Most people disappoint their friends.

Reaction Inventory Interference (RII)

PURPOSE To measure obsessional thoughts and compulsive acts.

AUTHORS David R. Evans and Shahe S. Kazarian

DESCRIPTION The RII is a 40-item instrument designed to identify obsessional thoughts and compulsive acts that interfere with an individual's daily activities. Items for the RII were selected empirically by asking students in an introductory psychology class to identify bothersome obsessional ruminations and compulsive acts. Those on which there was agreement were included as items on the RII. Although factor analysis revealed nine factors, the overall score of the scale appears to have the most value for identifying obsessive-compulsive behavior. The RII is considered a state measure in that it does not assume that the obsessive-compulsive thoughts and acts are enduring dispositions.

NORMS An initial study, used to refine the RII, was conducted with 25 male and 25 female undergraduate students in an introductory psychology class in Canada. A second study was conducted with 172 members of another introductory psychology class in Canada. No other demographic data or norms were presented.

SCORING The items are rated on a scale of 0 to 4 and those individual scores are simply totaled to produce the "degree of obsessionality" for each respondent. Scores can range from 0 to 160.

RELIABILITY The RII demonstrates excellent internal consistency using item-test correlations to produce an overall reliability figure of .95. Data on test-retest reliability were not reported.

VALIDITY The RII was significantly correlated with the Leyton Obsessional Inventory, suggesting good concurrent validity. No other validity data were available.

PRIMARY REFERENCE Evans, D. R., and Kazarian, S. S. (1977). Development of a state measure of obsessive compulsive behavior, *Journal of Clinical Psychology*, 33, 436–439. Instrument reproduced with permission of David R. Evans, Shahe S. Kazarian, and the American Psychological Association.

AVAILABILITY Dr. David R. Evans, Psychology Department, University of Western Ontario, London, Ontario, Canada N6A 5C2. Email: evans@uwo.ca.

The items in this questionnaire describe thoughts or acts that may interfere with other things or waste your time. Please indicate how much each problem bothers you by writing the appropriate number in the space next to each item.

1 = Not at all
2 = A little
3 = A fair amount
4 = Much
5 = Very much

___ 1. Eating many times a day
___ 2. Constantly checking your watch
___ 3. Repeatedly worrying about finishing things on time
___ 4. Continually thinking about the future
___ 5. Worrying about your appearance over and over again
___ 6. Repeatedly wondering if you are capable
___ 7. Always worrying about your work piling up
___ 8. Constantly wondering whether you will fail at things
___ 9. Repeatedly worrying about your job situation
___ 10. Continually worrying about catching up with your work
___ 11. Frequently being concerned about how you interact with others
___ 12. Always wasting time wandering around
___ 13. Worrying about everyday decisions over and over again
___ 14. Continually worrying about how well you are doing
___ 15. Worrying about being evaluated all the time
___ 16. Always doubting your intelligence or ability
___ 17. Wondering if you are doing the right thing over and over again
___ 18. Continually pondering about the world at large
___ 19. Repeatedly worrying about how you are performing
___ 20. Always checking several times whether you have done something like locking a door
___ 21. Often worrying about your cleanliness or tidiness
___ 22. Always being indecisive
___ 23. Washing your hands many times each day
___ 24. Repeatedly experiencing a tune (number, word) running through your mind
___ 25. Brooding all the time
___ 26. Constantly counting unimportant things
___ 27. Repeatedly asking people for advice
___ 28. Spending time worrying about trivial details all the time
___ 29. Repeatedly being unable to get started on things
___ 30. Constantly thinking about your family
___ 31. Swearing all the time
___ 32. Continually playing with an object (pen, pencil, keys)
___ 33. Repeatedly thinking about things you don't do well
___ 34. Always thinking about the "rat race"

—— 36. Constantly worrying about what people above you think about you
—— 37. Frequently thinking about getting to sleep
—— 38. Always being concerned about improving yourself
—— 39. Repeatedly checking to see if you have done something correctly
—— 40. Constantly thinking about yourself

Reasons for Living Inventory (RFL)

PURPOSE To measure adaptive characteristics in suicide.

AUTHOR Marsha M. Linehan

DESCRIPTION This 48-item inventory assesses a range of beliefs that differentiate suicidal from nonsuicidal individuals and can be viewed as a measure of an individual's commitment to various reasons for not committing suicide. The RFL is one of the few instruments that approach the topic from the perspective of adaptive coping skills that are absent in the suicidal person. It is based on a cognitive-behavioral theory which assumes that cognitive patterns mediate suicidal behavior. While slightly longer than other instruments in this book, the RFL has six short subscales that are potentially very useful in working with suicidal clients: suicidal and coping belief (SCB), responsibility to family (RF), child-related concerns (CRC), fear of suicide (FS), fear of social disapproval (FSD), and moral objections (MO). Total scores may be used, although more value in guiding intervention is found by using the subscales.

NORMS The scale was developed on a sample of 193 nonclinical adults and a sample of 244 psychiatric inpatients. The nonclinical sample had an average age of 36 years. Mean scores on the SCB, RF, CRC, FS, FSD, and MO were 4.55, 3.86, 3.66, 2.38, 2.34, and 3.02, respectively. The clinical sample was categorized into three subsamples according to past suicidal behaviors: nonsuicidal ($n=78$), suicidal ideations ($n=89$), and parasuicidal ($n=77$). The average scores on the SCB, RF, CC, FS, FSD, and MO were as follows for each of the three subsamples: nonsuicidal subjects: 4.82, 4.49, 3.89, 3.07, 3.13, and 3.54; suicidal ideation: 4.82, 4.49, 3.89, 3.07, 3.13, and 3.54; parasuicidal: 3.56, 3.55, 2.69, 2.94, 2.82, and 2.73. Mean scores on the total RFL scale were 4.25, 3.28, and 3.28 for the nonsuicidal, suicidal ideation, and parasuicidal subsamples. Scores are not significantly different for men and women.

SCORING Each subscale score is calculated by averaging the individual item ratings within that subscale; for example, on the SCB the item total is divided by 24. The total score is obtained by summing each item score and dividing by 48. By using average scores for each subscale, comparison across subscales is possible. Subscale items are: SCB: 2, 3, 4, 8, 10, 12, 13, 14, 17, 19, 20, 22, 24, 25, 29, 32, 35, 36, 37, 39, 40, 42, 44, 45; RF: 1, 7, 9, 16, 30, 47, 48; CC: 11, 21, 28; FS: 6, 15, 18, 26, 33, 38, 46; FSD: 31, 41, 43; MO: 5, 24, 27, 34. Higher scores indicate more reasons for living.

RELIABILITY Reliability was based on a variety of samples and estimated using Cronbach's alpha. Correlations ranged from .72 to .89, indicating fairly high internal consistency. No data on stability were reported.

VALIDITY Probably the biggest limitation of this inventory is a lack of predictive validity. The subscale with the strongest concurrent validity is the SCB, which correlated with suicidal ideation and likelihood of suicide in the "normal" sample. In the clinical sample the SCB correlated with suicidal ideation, likelihood of suicide, suicidal threats, and suicidal solutions. The RF also correlated with these suicidal behaviors in the clinical sample, but showed less evidence of validity with the nonclinical sample. The CC was correlated with three of the four criteria for the clinical sample. Evidence of known-groups validity also supports the instrument.

PRIMARY REFERENCE Linehan, M. M., Goldstein, J. L., Nielsen, S. L., and Chiles, J. A. (1983). Reasons for staying alive when you are thinking of killing yourself: The Reasons for Living Inventory, *Journal of Consulting and Clinical Psychology*, 51, 276–286. Instrument reproduced with permission of Marsha M. Linehan and the American Psychological Association.

AVAILABILITY Dr. Marsha M. Linehan, Department of Psychology NI-25, University of Washington, Seattle, WA 98195. Email: linehan@uw.edu. Telephone: 206.685.2037.

Many people have thought of suicide at least once. Others have never considered it. Whether you have considered it or not, we are interested in the reasons you would have for *not* committing suicide if the thought were to occur to you or if someone were to suggest it to you.

Below are reasons people sometimes give for not committing suicide. We would like to know how important each of these possible reasons would be to you at this time in your life as a reason to *not* kill yourself. Please rate this in the space at the left on each question.

Each reason can be rated from 1 (not at all important) to 6 (extremely important). If a reason does not apply to you or if you do not believe the statement is true, then it is not likely important and you should put a 1. Please use the whole range of choices so as not to rate only at the middle (2, 3, 4, 5) or only at the extremes (1, 6).

Even if you never have considered suicide or firmly believe you never would seriously consider killing yourself, it is still important that you rate each reason. In this case, rate on the basis of why killing yourself is not or would never be an alternative for you.

In each space put a number to indicate the importance to you of each for *not* killing yourself.

1 = Not at all *important*
2 = Quite *unimportant*
3 = Somewhat *unimportant*
4 = Somewhat *important*
5 = Quite *important*
6 = Extremely *important*

____ 1. I have a responsibility and commitment to my family.
____ 2. I believe I can learn to adjust or cope with my problems.
____ 3. I believe I have control over my life and destiny.
____ 4. I have a desire to live.
____ 5. I believe only God has the right to end a life.
____ 6. I am afraid of death.
____ 7. My family might believe I did not love them.
____ 8. I do not believe that things get miserable or hopeless enough that I would rather be dead.
____ 9. My family depends upon me and needs me.
____ 10. I do not want to die.
____ 11. I want to watch my children as they grow.
____ 12. Life is all we have and is better than nothing.
____ 13. I have future plans I am looking forward to carrying out.
____ 14. No matter how badly I feel, I know that it will not last.
____ 15. I am afraid of the unknown.
____ 16. I love and enjoy my family too much and could not leave them.
____ 17. I want to experience all that life has to offer and there are many experiences I haven't had yet which I want to have.
____ 18. I am afraid that my method of killing myself would fail.

___ 19. I care enough about myself to live.
___ 20. Life is too beautiful and precious to end it.
___ 21. It would not be fair to leave the children for others to take care of.
___ 22. I believe I can find other solutions to my problems.
___ 23. I am afraid of going to hell.
___ 24. I have a love of life.
___ 25. I am too stable to kill myself.
___ 26. I am a coward and do not have the guts to do it.
___ 27. My religious beliefs forbid it.
___ 28. The effect on my children could be harmful.
___ 29. I am curious about what will happen in the future.
___ 30. It would hurt my family too much and I would not want them to suffer.
___ 31. I am concerned about what others would think of me.
___ 32. I believe everything has a way of working out for the best.
___ 33. I could not decide where, when, and how to do it.
___ 34. I consider it morally wrong.
___ 35. I still have many things left to do.
___ 36. I have the courage to face life.
___ 37. I am so inept that my method would not work.
___ 38. I am afraid of the actual "act" of killing myself (the pain, blood, violence).
___ 39. I believe killing myself would not really accomplish or solve anything.
___ 40. I have hope that things will improve and the future will be happier.
___ 41. Other people would think I am weak and selfish.
___ 42. I have an inner drive to survive.
___ 43. I would not want people to think I did not have control over my life.
___ 44. I believe I can find a purpose in life, a reason to live.
___ 45. I see no reason to hurry death along.
___ 46. I am so inept that my method would not work.
___ 47. I would not want my family to feel guilty afterwards.
___ 48. I would not want my family to think I was selfish or a coward.

Reid-Gundlach Social Service Satisfaction Scale (R-GSSSS)

PURPOSE To assess the extent of consumer satisfaction with social services.

AUTHORS P. Nelson Reid and James P. Gundlach

DESCRIPTION The R-GSSSS is a 34-item instrument that provides an overall satisfaction-with-service score plus three subscales dealing with consumers' reactions to social services regarding the following: (1) relevance (the extent to which a service corresponds to the client's perception of his or her problem and needs); (2) impact (the extent to which services reduce the problem); and (3) gratification (the extent to which services enhance the client's self-esteem and contribute to a sense of power and integrity). The relevance subscale consists of items 1 through 11; the impact subscale is composed of items 12 through 21; and the gratification subscale consists of items 22 through 34. The R-GSSSS is designed for use with a wide range of social services. When necessary, the term "social worker" on individual items can be replaced by the appropriate professional designation.

NORMS The initial study was conducted with 166 heads of households of low-income families who had a high rate of use of social services. The respondents were 81% female, 47% married, and 52.5% between the ages of 19 and 29. The sample contained fairly equal numbers of white and black respondents; 2.4% were Mexican-American. Actual norms were not available.

SCORING The instrument is scored by adding the individual item scores and dividing by the number of items in the scale. Thus, the sum of all scores is divided by 34 for the total score, the relevance subscale is divided by 11, the impact subscale is divided by 10, and the gratification subscale is divided by 13. This results in all scales having a range of scores of 1 (minimum satisfaction) to 5 (maximum satisfaction). Items 3, 6, 9, 10, 13, 16, 17, 18, 20, 22, 23, 26, 27, 28, 29, 30, 31, and 33 are reverse-scored.

RELIABILITY Internal consistency of the scale was very good with a total alpha of .95; the three subscales had alphas ranging from .82 to .86. The authors' analyses reveal the three subscales to be sufficiently independent to justify using all three as measures of different aspects of consumer satisfaction. Data on stability were not available.

VALIDITY The scales have high face validity. Other forms of validity information are not reported. However, race, marital status, and type of service utilized were significantly related to satisfaction in predictable ways. Blacks and Mexican-Americans, single consumers, and those utilizing AFDS and Medicaid reported lower satisfaction levels.

PRIMARY REFERENCE Reid, P. N., and Gundlach, J. H. (1983). A scale for the measurement of consumer satisfaction with social services, *Journal of Social Service Research*, 7, 37–54. Instrument reproduced with permission of P. N. Reid and Haworth Press.

AVAILABILITY Dr. Nelson Reid, University of North Carolina Wilmington, Department of Social Work, Wilmington, NC 27965. Email: reidn@uncw.edu.

Using the scale from one to five described below, please indicate on the line at the left of each item the number that comes closest to how you feel.

1 = Strongly agree
2 = Agree
3 = Undecided
4 = Disagree
5 = Strongly disagree

___ 1. The social worker took my problems very seriously.
___ 2. If I had been the social worker I would have dealt with my problems in just the same way.
___ 3. The worker I had could never understand anyone like me.
___ 4. Overall the agency has been very helpful to me.
___ 5. If a friend of mine had similar problems I would tell them to go to the agency.
___ 6. The social worker asks a lot of embarrassing questions.
___ 7. I can always count on the worker to help if I'm in trouble.
___ 8. The social agency will help me as much as they can.
___ 9. I don't think the agency has the power to really help me.
___ 10. The social worker tries hard but usually isn't too helpful.
___ 11. The problem the agency tried to help me with is one of the most important in my life.
___ 12. Things have gotten better since I've been going to the agency.
___ 13. Since I've been using the agency my life is more messed up than ever.
___ 14. The agency is always available when I need it.
___ 15. I got from the agency exactly what I wanted.
___ 16. The social worker loves to talk but won't really do anything for me.
___ 17. Sometimes I just tell the social worker what I think she wants to hear.
___ 18. The social worker is usually in a hurry when I see her.
___ 19. No one should have any trouble getting some help from this agency.
___ 20. The worker sometimes says things I don't understand.
___ 21. The social workers are always explaining things carefully.
___ 22. I never looked forward to my visits to the social agency.
___ 23. I hope I'll never have to go back to the agency for help.
___ 24. Every time I talk to my worker I feel relieved.
___ 25. I can tell the social worker the truth without worrying.
___ 26. I usually feel nervous when I talk to my worker.
___ 27. The social worker is always looking for lies in what I tell her.
___ 28. It takes a lot of courage to go to the agency.
___ 29. When I enter the agency I feel very small and insignificant.
___ 30. The agency is very demanding.
___ 31. The social worker will sometimes lie to me.
___ 32. Generally the social worker is an honest person.
___ 33. I have the feeling that the worker talks to other people about me.
___ 34. I always feel well treated when I leave the social agency.

PURPOSE To measure efforts to control eating.

AUTHOR C. Peter Herman

DESCRIPTION This 10-item instrument measures one aspect of dieting behavior, the ability to restrain from eating in order to maintain a particular weight. The scale ranges from the extreme of someone who has never given a moment's thought about dieting to someone who is overly concerned with dieting. The instrument may be useful with both obese clients attempting to reduce weight and with anorectic and bulimic clients.

NORMS The instrument was developed on a sample of 57 female college students. Normative data are not presented.

SCORING The RS score is the sum of all 10 items. For items 1 through 4 and item 10 the alternatives are scored as follows: a=0, b=1, c=2, d=3, e=4. Items 5 through 9 are scored as follows: a=0, b=1, c=2, d=3. Scores can range from zero to 35 with higher scores indicating more concern over dieting.

RELIABILITY Reliability data are not available from primary reference.

VALIDITY This instrument was tested for criterion validity by creating two groups, one of restrained eaters and one of nonrestrained eaters. Different eating patterns were then observed for the two groups. The findings tend to be consistent for men and women, with slightly higher scores found for women. Similar differences in eating patterns were found with subjects who were categorized as obese, normal, and skinny according to their scores on the RS. These findings are evidence of known-groups validity. Concurrent validity is evidenced by an association between weight gain and the RS.

PRIMARY REFERENCE Herman, C. P. (1978). Restrained eating. *Psychiatric Clinics of North America*, 1, 593–607. Instrument reproduced with permission of C. P. Herman.

AVAILABILITY May be copied from this volume.

Please answer the following items by circling the alternatives below the question.

1. How often are you dieting?

      a. Never   b. Rarely   c. Sometimes   d. Often   e. Always

2. What is the maximum amount of weight (in pounds) that you have ever lost in one month?

      a. 0–4   b. 5–9   c. 10–14   d. 15–19   e. 20+

3. What is your maximum weight gain within a week?

      a. 0–1   b. 1.1–2   c. 2.1–3   d. 3.1–5   e. 5.1+

4. In a typical week, how much does your weight fluctuate?

      a. 0–1   b. 1.1–2   c. 2.1–3   d. 3.1–5   e. 5.1+

5. Would a weight fluctuation of 5 pounds affect the way you live your life?

      a. Not at all   b. Slightly   c. Moderately   d. Very Much

6. Do you eat sensibly in front of others and splurge alone?

      a. Never   b. Rarely   c. Often   d. Always

7. Do you give too much time and thought to food?

      a. Never   b. Rarely   c. Often   d. Always

8. Do you have feelings of guilt after overeating?

      a. Never   b. Rarely   c. Often   d. Always

9. How conscious are you of what you are eating?

      a. Not at all   b. Slightly   c. Moderately   d. Extremely

10. How many pounds over your desired weight were you at your maximum weight?

      a. 0–1   b. 1–5   c. 6–10   d. 11–20   e. 21+

Revised Kinship Scale (KS)

PURPOSE To measure psychological kinship.

AUTHORS Kent G. Bailey and Gustavo R. Nava

DESCRIPTION The KS is a 20-item instrument designed to measure feelings of deep affiliation and love in interpersonally close relationships. The instrument is based on the notion that feelings of kinship with family members and genetically unrelated significant others derive from a human heritage of attachment, bonding, and sociality. Respondents complete the KS in relation to any person as a stimulus by filling in the blanks on the instrument. This person could be a family member, partner in an interpersonal relationship, or even the clinician, since clinicians are incorporated into a client's psychological kinship. The current KS was revised from an original 60-item instrument. Based on a sample of female college students, factor analyses suggest that there are four subscales of the KS: family love (FL = 1 + 3 + 4 + 6 + 7 + 10 + 11 + 16 + 19 + 20); practical support (PS = 5 + 8 + 15 + 18); emotional intimacy (EI = 12 + 13 + 14 + 17); and intellectual intimacy (II = 2 + 9). The FL can be used as a short-form measure of psychological kinship.

NORMS Norms are reported separately for women and men, and, of course, vary according to the stimulus person. A sample of 144 unmarried college women had a mean KS score of 84.8 with a standard deviation of 9.7 when evaluating their relationship with the parent to whom they were closest, and a mean and standard deviation of 86.6 and 9.3 for the boyfriend. A sample of single college men had means (and standard deviations) of 80.6 (9.6) and 84.6 (8.8) for their closest parent and girlfriend. Means are not reported for the short form or other subscales.

SCORING Each item is rated on a 1-to-5 scale, ranging from "unimportant" to "very important." Total scores are the sum of each item, and range from 20 to 100 for the KS and 10 to 50 for the short form.

RELIABILITY Reliability of the revised KS is not reported; however, the 60-item version had excellent internal consistency, with an odd-even correlation of .95.

VALIDITY This instrument has good concurrent validity, as seen in its correlations with measures of love, liking, and attachment for both samples of women and men when evaluating their closest parent and boyfriend/girlfriend. With the exception of the practical support factor, the subscales also correlated with those measures for both closest parent and boyfriend/girlfriend. Further, mean total scores correlated with four measures of the relationship, of time spent together, time one would want to spend together, reliance on others for emotional support, and perceived caring. For women the total KS scores correlated with two of these four variables.

PRIMARY REFERENCE Nava, G. R., and Bailey, K. G. (1991). Measuring psychological kinship: Scale refinement and validation, *Psychological Reports*, 68, 215–227. Instrument reprinted with permission of Kent G. Bailey and Clinical Psychology Publishing Company, Inc.

AVAILABILITY Dr. Kent G. Bailey, Facebook.com/people/kent-bailey/100001694913127.

This questionnaire is about what you consider important in your relations with other people. Think about _____. Then consider how important each of the following items is in your relationship with this person. Use the following scale and record your rating in the space next to each item:

$$5 = \textit{Very important} \text{ to you}$$
$$4 = \textit{Important} \text{ to you}$$
$$3 = \text{You are } \textit{not sure}$$
$$2 = \textit{Unimportant} \text{ to you}$$
$$1 = \textit{Very unimportant} \text{ to you}$$

How important is it for _____:

___ 1. To hug me if I need it.
___ 2. To share my beliefs and values.
___ 3. To feel love for me.
___ 4. To remember me ten years from now.
___ 5. To give me a birthday present.
___ 6. To still like me even if I do something wrong.
___ 7. To be available when I need him/her.
___ 8. To care about my financial situation.
___ 9. To make specific suggestions about how to deal with my personal problems.
___ 10. To treat me like a member of the family.
___ 11. To be a loving person.
___ 12. To be someone I could cry in front of.
___ 13. To be concerned about my health.
___ 14. To be willing to accept a loan from me.
___ 15. To post bail for me if I am in jail.
___ 16. To feel that I am important in his/her life.
___ 17. To be willing to care for me if I am sick.
___ 18. To lend me money if I am in need.
___ 19. To think of me as a "loved one."
___ 20. To share a strong feeling of "kinship" with me.

PURPOSE To measure the need for approval from others.

AUTHOR Harry J. Martin

DESCRIPTION This 20-item instrument assesses the need for favorable evaluations from others. It is considered revised because the present form controls for an acquiescence response bias, which has a problem with earlier forms of the instrument. It is similar to the Marlowe-Crowne Social Desirability Scale, although the RMLAM more directly taps the construct in terms of the desire to receive positive evaluations and social reinforcement (approval) as well as the need to avoid negative evaluations and social punishment (criticism and rejection.). The instrument focuses on social situations and interpersonal behaviors. The RMLAM also is available in a shorter 10-item form (items 2, 4, 5, 6, 10, 12, 13, 16, 18, and 19).

NORMS Mean and standard deviation scores are available from a sample of college students ($n = 123$). The average score was 53.6 with a standard deviation of 9.02. The mean and standard deviation for the shorter 10-item version was 26.3 and 5.37, respectively. Scores do not seem to be influenced by gender.

SCORING Items are rated on a 5-point scale from "disagree strongly" to "agree strongly." Items 2, 12, 13, 16, and 19 are reverse-scored. Total scores are the sum of the items and range from 20 to 100 for the 20-item version; higher scores indicate stronger need for social approval.

RELIABILITY The reliability of the RMLAM was estimated in terms of internal consistency and test-retest reliability. For the long and short forms alpha was .75 and .67, respectively. Test-retest correlations for a one-week period were .72 and .94 for the two forms.

VALIDITY Scores on the long version correlated with faking on the MMPI and clinical defensiveness. The short form correlated with clinical defensiveness but was not associated with faking on the MMPI. Both long and short forms correlated with neuroticism and the Marlowe-Crowne Social Desirability Scale.

PRIMARY REFERENCE Martin, H. J. (1984). A revised measure of approval motivation and its relationship to social desirability, *Journal of Personality Assessment*, 48, 508–519. Instrument reproduced with permission of the *Journal of Personality Assessment*.

AVAILABILITY May be copied from this volume.

Below are twenty statements. Please rate how much you agree with each using the following scale. Please record your answer in the space to the left of the statement.

1 = Disagree strongly
2 = Disagree
3 = No opinion
4 = Agree
5 = Agree strongly

—— 1. Depending upon the people involved, I react to the same situation in different ways.

—— 2. I would rather be myself than be well thought of.

—— 3. Many times I feel like just flipping a coin in order to decide what I should do.

—— 4. I change my opinion (or the way that I do things) in order to please someone else.

—— 5. In order to get along and be liked, I tend to be what people expect me to be.

—— 6. I find it difficult to talk about my ideas if they are contrary to group opinion.

—— 7. One should avoid doing things in public which appear to be wrong to others, even though one knows that he/she is right.

—— 8. Sometimes I feel that I don't have enough control over the direction that my life is taking.

—— 9. It is better to be humble than assertive when dealing with people.

—— 10. I am willing to argue only if I know that my friends will back me up.

—— 11. If I hear that someone expresses a poor opinion of me, I do my best the next time that I see this person to make a good impression.

—— 12. I seldom feel the need to make excuses or apologize for my behavior.

—— 13. It is not important to me that I behave "properly" in social situations.

—— 14. The best way to handle people is to agree with them and tell them what they want to hear.

—— 15. It is hard for me to go on with my work if I am not encouraged to do so.

—— 16. If there is any criticism or anyone says anything about me, I can take it.

—— 17. It is wise to flatter important people.

—— 18. I am careful at parties and social gatherings for fear that I will do or say things that others won't like.

—— 19. I usually do not change my position when people disagree with me.

—— 20. How many friends you have depends on how nice a person you are.

Revised UCLA Loneliness Scale (RULS)

PURPOSE To measure loneliness.

AUTHORS Dan Russell, Letitia Peplau, and Carolyn Cutrona

DESCRIPTION The RULS is a 20-item scale designed to measure loneliness in a variety of populations. This and earlier versions have been used in a number of studies that show loneliness is a common and distressing problem for many people. Loneliness has been linked with any number of other problems, including personality characteristics (shyness, feelings of alienation), alcohol abuse, adolescent delinquent behavior, suicide, and physical illness. This version of the scale was undertaken to eliminate response bias, social desirability response set, and lack of clarity regarding distinctiveness from related constructs. The RULS has a number of potential uses for practice in identifying lonely individuals whose loneliness is a problem in and of itself or as related to other problems.

NORMS A number of studies have been carried out with earlier versions of the RULS. With this version, 399 undergraduate students (171 males, 228 females) from three campuses provided the basis for the research. The mean for male students was 37.06 and for females, 128. The mean for students who were not dating was 43.1, which was significantly different from students who were dating casually (34.0) and romantically involved (32.7).

SCORING After reverse-scoring items 1, 4–6, 9, 10, 15, 16, 19, 20, the scores on all 20 items are summed, producing a possible range of 20 to 80 with higher scores indicating greater loneliness.

RELIABILITY The RULS has excellent internal consistency, with an alpha of .94. No test-retest data are reported.

VALIDITY The RULS has good concurrent validity, correlating with a number of mood and personality measures (e.g., the Beck Depression Inventory, the Texas Social Behavior Inventory) and particularly with a self-labeling loneliness index. In addition, people who were more lonely on the RULS reported more limited social activities and relationships and more emotions theoretically linked to loneliness. Finally, results showed the RULS to be unaffected by social desirability response set as measured by the Marlowe-Crowne Social Desirability Inventory.

PRIMARY REFERENCE Russell, D., Peplau, L. A., and Cutrona, C. E. (1980). The Revised UCLA Loneliness Scale: Concurrent and discriminant validity evidence, *Journal of Personality and Social Psychology*, 39, 472–480. Instrument reproduced with permission of Letitia A. Peplau.

AVAILABILITY Professor Letitia A. Peplau, Department of Psychology, UCLA, Los Angeles, CA 90024. Email: lapeplau@ucla.edu.

Indicate how often you have felt the way described in each statement using the following scale:

$$4 = \text{"I have felt this way } \textit{often.}\text{"}$$
$$3 = \text{"I have felt this way } \textit{sometimes.}\text{"}$$
$$2 = \text{"I have felt this way } \textit{rarely.}\text{"}$$
$$1 = \text{"I have } \textit{never} \text{ felt this way."}$$

___ 1. I feel in tune with the people around me.

___ 2. I lack companionship.

___ 3. There is no one I can turn to.

___ 4. I do not feel alone.

___ 5. I feel part of a group of friends.

___ 6. I have a lot in common with the people around me.

___ 7. I am no longer close to anyone.

___ 8. My interests and ideas are not shared by those around me.

___ 9. I am an outgoing person.

___ 10. There are people I feel close to.

___ 11. I feel left out.

___ 12. My social relationships are superficial.

___ 13. No one really knows me well.

___ 14. I feel isolated from others.

___ 15. I can find companionship when I want it.

___ 16. There are people who really understand me.

___ 17. I am unhappy being so withdrawn.

___ 18. People are around me but not with me.

___ 19. There are people I can talk to.

___ 20. There are people I can turn to.

Role Perception Scale (RPS)

PURPOSE To measure perception of roles.

AUTHORS Mary Sue Richardson and Judith Landon Alpert

DESCRIPTION This 40-item instrument is designed to measure four aspects of one's perception of roles: innovation (items 1–10), involvement (items 11–20), affectivity (items 21–30), and competition (31–40). The instrument is intended to be used in conjunction with a projective technique where the respondent first writes brief stories in response to the roles of work, marriage, parenting, the combination of work and marriage roles, and the combination of the work and parenting roles. Respondents are given the first sentence and instructed to write a brief story (in 5 minutes or less) which addresses four concerns: what led up to the event in the story, a description of what is happening at the moment, a description of what the character is thinking and feeling at the moment, and the outcome of the story. Respondents answer the RPS in response to the character in the story; the RPS has two forms, one for male and one for female characters in the story. The RPS can be used with any role, such as a client in an identity crisis or struggling to adapt to a change in life. The RPS is particularly useful to clinicians working with clients troubled by role transitions, including marriage, parenthood, divorce, retirement, widowhood, or caring for a sick loved one. Evidence of the RPS's reliability and validity, however, is limited to the roles mentioned above.

NORMS Norms are reported for role engagement (RE), which combines the scores on innovation, involvement, and affectivity. Norms are based on 88 female and 46 male college students. For males, RE means (and standard deviations) were −.532 (.89), −.058 (.92), −.174 (.95), −.213 (.91), and .374 (.74) for the roles of work, marriage, parenting, work-marriage, and work-parenting, respectively. The means (and standard deviations) for the competition subscale were .129 (1.0), .02 (.84), .041 (.96), .022 (.96), and .232 (.76) for the same five roles. Female means (and standard deviations) for the RE were −.298 (.95), .089 (.93), −.200 (.98), .38 (.77), and .344 (.92) for the roles of work, marriage, parenting, work-marriage, and work-parenting, respectively. Competition means (and standard deviations) for females were .085 (92), −.11 (.86), −.26 (86), .235 (.88), and −.188 (.84) for the same five roles.

SCORING Items 1, 4–6, 10, 12, 15, 18–20, 21, 25–27, 30, 33, 34, 36, 39, and 40 are scored 1 if the respondent answered "false." A "true" response on the other items is scored as 1. Scores are then summed for each subscale and divided by the number of items answered. Higher scores reflect more innovation, involvement, affectivity, and competition in the particular role.

RELIABILITY A prototype of the RPS had an internal consistency coefficient of .91. No other reliability information is available.

VALIDITY The validity of the RPS is primarily supported with factor analysis where items of the affectivity, innovation, and involvement subscales loaded together to form the RE, which was independent of the competition subscale.

PRIMARY REFERENCE Richardson, M. S., and Alpert, J. L. (1980). Role perceptions: Variations by sex and roles, *Sex Roles*, 6, 783–793. Instrument reproduced with permission of Mary Sue Richardson and Judith Landon Alpert.

AVAILABILITY Mary Sue Richardson, Ph.D., NYU Department of Applied Psychology, 400 East Building, Washington Square, New York, NY 10003. Email: msr1@nyu.edu.

Please indicate whether each statement is True or False for the main character in your story. Record your answer in the space to the left of each statement by writing "T" if it is true of the main character or "F" if the statement is false for the main character.

—   1.   She (he) has very little to say about how her (his) day is spent.

—   2.   What she (he) does is different on different days.

—   3.   Her (his) activities from day to day are varied.

—   4.   She (he) is not able to do unusual things.

—   5.   She (he) is expected to follow set rules.

—   6.   She (he) seldom tries out new ideas.

—   7.   She (he) thinks up unusual activities for others to do.

—   8.   She (he) thinks about different ideas every day.

—   9.   She (he) can choose what she (he) will do each day.

—   10.   She (he) is involved in the same kind of activities every day.

—   11.   She (he) seldom feels bored.

—   12.   She (he) probably wouldn't be there if she (he) didn't have to be.

—   13.   She (he) is often curious.

—   14.   She (he) puts a lot of energy into what she (he) does.

—   15.   She (he) only does what she (he) has to do.

—   16.   She (he) wants to do what she (he) is doing.

—   17.   She (he) seldom daydreams.

—   18.   She (he) is thinking about something else.

—   19.   She (he) would rather be doing something other than what she (he) is doing.

—   20.   She (he) doesn't really care.

—   21.   She (he) feels discouraged.

—   22.   She (he) enjoys her (his) life.

—   23.   She (he) feels happy.

—   24.   She (he) often feels like smiling.

—   25.   She (he) is often thinking "it's unfair."

—   26.   She (he) thinks it's hopeless.

—   27.   Something is troubling her (him).

—   28.   She (he) often thinks that her (his) life is good.

—   29.   She (he) seldom has headaches.

—   30.   She (he) often feels like arguing.

—   31.   She (he) tries hard to be best.

—   32.   Winning is very important to her (him).

—   33.   She (he) doesn't mind losing.

—   34.   She (he) seldom competes with others.

___ 35. She (he) tries to do things better than other people.

___ 36. She (he) doesn't care about whether others get things done first.

___ 37. She (he) usually tries to get things done before others.

___ 38. She (he) compares what she (he) does with what others do.

___ 39. She (he) doesn't care if she (he) wins or loses.

___ 40. She (he) doesn't feel pressured to compete.

Note: Parentheses indicate changes for male form.

Ruminations on Sadness Scale (RSS)

PURPOSE To measure rumination on sadness.

AUTHORS Michael Conway et al.

DESCRIPTION The RSS is a 13-item measure designed to assess repetitive thoughts concerning a person's present distress and the circumstances concerning the sadness. The focus is on current sadness; such rumination is of negative content, does not help in problem resolution, is solitary, and can be intrusive. The authors state that the RSS overcomes some of the conceptual and psychometric problems with other rumination scales. The RSS can be very useful in tracking such rumination and as a tool for evaluating change in therapeutic programs aiming to decrease ruminations about sadness and associated problems.

NORMS The RSS was developed in a series of studies at a Canadian university. 220 students completed the RSS; 133 were women, 82 were men, and 5 did not report gender. The mean age of respondents was 24.94. Other demographic data were not reported. Means for each of the items are available in the Primary Reference. The total mean score was 35.41 (SD = 10.61). The difference between male and female scores was not significant.

SCORING The RSS is easily scored by summing item scores for a total score. The range of scores is from 13 to 65 with higher scores indicating greater rumination.

RELIABILITY The RSS has excellent internal consistency with an alpha of .91. The RSS also has excellent stability with a 2- to 3-week test-retest correlation of .70.

VALIDITY The RSS has excellent concurrent validity, correlating significantly with several other scales such as the Beck Depression Inventory, the Ruminative Responses Scale of the Response Styles Questionnaire, and several other measures of personality, negative thinking and emotional expressiveness.

PRIMARY REFERENCE Conway, M., et al. (2000). On assessing individual differences in rumination on sadness, *Journal of Personality Assessment, 75,* 404–425. Instrument reproduced with permission of Dr. Conway.

AVAILABILITY Email Dr. Conway at michael.conway@concordia.ca.

The statements below describe some thoughts that people may have when they are feeling sad or down. Please read each statement and decide how much you do what the statement describes when you are feeling sad. Indicate the degree to which you do what is described by circling the appropriate number on the scale.

When I am Sad, Down, or Feel Blue . . .

A. I have difficulty getting myself to stop thinking about how sad I am.

1	2	3	4	5
NOT AT ALL	RARELY	SOMETIMES	QUITE A BIT	VERY MUCH

B. I repeatedly analyze and keep thinking about the reasons for my sadness.

1	2	3	4	5
NOT AT ALL	RARELY	SOMETIMES	QUITE A BIT	VERY MUCH

C. I search my mind many times to try and figure out if there is anything about my personality that may have led me to feel this way.

1	2	3	4	5
NOT AT ALL	RARELY	SOMETIMES	QUITE A BIT	VERY MUCH

D. I get absorbed in thinking about why I am sad and find it difficult to think about other things.

1	2	3	4	5
NOT AT ALL	RARELY	SOMETIMES	QUITE A BIT	VERY MUCH

E. I search my mind repeatedly for events or experiences in my childhood that may help me understand my sad feelings.

1	2	3	4	5
NOT AT ALL	RARELY	SOMETIMES	QUITE A BIT	VERY MUCH

F. I keep wondering about how I was able to be happy at other points in my life.

1	2	3	4	5
NOT AT ALL	RARELY	SOMETIMES	QUITE A BIT	VERY MUCH

G. I lie in bed and keep thinking about my lack of motivation and wonder about whether it will ever return.

1	2	3	4	5
NOT AT ALL	RARELY	SOMETIMES	QUITE A BIT	VERY MUCH

When I am Sad, Down, or Feel Blue . . .

H. If people try to talk to me or ask me questions it feels as though they are interrupting an ongoing silent conversation I am having with myself about my sadness.

1	2	3	4	5
NOT AT ALL	RARELY	SOMETIMES	QUITE A BIT	VERY MUCH

I. I question and keep wondering about the meaning of life to find clues that may help me understand my sadness.

1	2	3	4	5
NOT AT ALL	RARELY	SOMETIMES	QUITE A BIT	VERY MUCH

J. I repeatedly think about what sadness really is by concentrating on my feelings and trying to understand them.

1	2	3	4	5
NOT AT ALL	RARELY	SOMETIMES	QUITE A BIT	VERY MUCH

K. I get the feeling that if I think long enough about my sadness I will find that it has some deeper meaning and that I will be able to understand myself better because of it.

1	2	3	4	5
NOT AT ALL	RARELY	SOMETIMES	QUITE A BIT	VERY MUCH

L. I keep thinking about my problems to try and examine where things went wrong.

1	2	3	4	5
NOT AT ALL	RARELY	SOMETIMES	QUITE A BIT	VERY MUCH

M. I exhaust myself by thinking so much about myself and the reasons for my sadness.

1	2	3	4	5
NOT AT ALL	RARELY	SOMETIMES	QUITE A BIT	VERY MUCH

Satisfaction with Appearance Scale (SWAP)

PURPOSE To measure body image among burn survivors.

AUTHORS John W. Lawrence et al.

DESCRIPTION The SWAP is a 14-item questionnaire designed to assess both the subjective appraisal and social/behavioral components of body image among burn survivors. The SWAP is perhaps the only instrument available to directly measure burn survivors' body image. As such it has great value not only as a basic research instrument for investigating body image, but the SWAP can be useful clinically in identifying patients who can benefit from therapy following a burn, and also can be used to monitor patients' improvement in body image over time. The SWAP has four factors, the first two of which address a subjective component of body image and the second two of which address the behavioral/social component of body image. Factor one is subjective satisfaction with appearance (items 4–7); factor two is satisfaction with nonfacial features (items 8–11); factor three is social discomfort due to appearance (items 1–3); and factor four is perceived social impact (items 12–14).

NORMS The SWAP was initially studied with 165 adult burn patients, including 121 men and 44 women, with a mean age of 41.5 years (SD = 14.7). All participants required hospitalization in a burn treatment center. Sixty-five percent of the sample was European American, 32% was African American, and 3% was other. The mean number of years of education was 11.68 (SD = 2.28). Burn size ranged from 1% to 77% of total skin area with an average burn size of 13% (SD = 12.72). The mean score on the SWAP was 17.0 (SD = 15.3) with a median of 12.

SCORING The total SWAP score is calculated by subtracting one from each of the items (in order to anchor each item at zero) and then totaling the items. Questions 4–11 are reverse-scored. Higher scores indicate greater dissatisfaction with appearance and poor body image.

RELIABILITY The SWAP has very good internal consistency, with an alpha of .87. The SWAP also has good stability with a two-month test-retest correlation of .59 in a subsample of 84 participants.

VALIDITY The SWAP has established good construct validity on the basis of correlations in the predicted directions with a number of other measures including the Davidson Trauma Scale, the Beck Anxiety Inventory, the Beck Depression Inventory, the SF-36 Health Survey, and the Physical Appearance State and Trait Anxiety Scale.

PRIMARY REFERENCE Lawrence, J. W., et al. (1998). Development and validation of the Satisfaction with Appearance Scale: Assessing body image among burn-injured patients, *Psychological Assessment*, 10, 64–70.

AVAILABILITY Dr. John W. Lawrence, College of Staten Island, Department of Psychology, Building 45, Room 212, States Island, NY 10314. Email: john.lawrence@CSI.cuny.edu. Telephone: 718.982.4136.

In each of the following statements, circle the most correct responses for you according to the following scale:

1 = Strongly disagree
2 = Disagree
3 = Somewhat disagree
4 = Neutral
5 = Somewhat agree
6 = Agree
7 = Strongly agree

1. Because of changes in my appearance caused by my burn, I am uncomfortable in the presence of my family. 1 2 3 4 5 6 7

2. Because of changes in my appearance caused by my burn, I am uncomfortable in the presence of my friends. 1 2 3 4 5 6 7

3. Because of changes in my appearance caused by my burn, I am uncomfortable in the presence of strangers. 1 2 3 4 5 6 7

4. I am satisfied with my overall appearance. 1 2 3 4 5 6 7
5. I am satisfied with the appearance of my scalp. 1 2 3 4 5 6 7
6. I am satisfied with the appearance of my face. 1 2 3 4 5 6 7
7. I am satisfied with the appearance of my neck. 1 2 3 4 5 6 7
8. I am satisfied with the appearance of my hands. 1 2 3 4 5 6 7
9. I am satisfied with the appearance of my arms. 1 2 3 4 5 6 7
10. I am satisfied with the appearance of my legs. 1 2 3 4 5 6 7
11. I am satisfied with the appearance of my chest. 1 2 3 4 5 6 7
12. Changes in my appearance have interfered with my relationships. 1 2 3 4 5 6 7
13. I feel that my burn is unattractive to others. 1 2 3 4 5 6 7
14. I don't think people would want to touch me. 1 2 3 4 5 6 7

Satisfaction with Life Scale (SWLS)

PURPOSE To assess subjective life satisfaction.

AUTHORS Ed Diener, Robert A. Emmons, Randy J. Larsen, and Sharon Griffin

DESCRIPTION The 5-item SWLS, as part of a body of research on subjective well-being, refers to the cognitive-judgmental aspects of general life satisfaction. Thus, in contrast to measures that apply some external standard, the SWLS reveals the individual's own judgment of his or her quality of life. This instrument is very short and unidimensional. Because satisfaction with life is often a key component of mental well-being, the SWLS may have clinical utility with a wide range of clients, including adolescents undergoing identity crises or adults experiencing midlife crisis.

NORMS The SWLS was developed on a sample of 176 undergraduates from the University of Illinois. The mean was 23.5 with a standard deviation of 6.43. The researchers also report a mean of 25.8 for a sample of 53 elderly citizens from a midwestern city; the mean age for this sample was 75 years, and 32 of the 53 were female.

SCORING Each item is scored from 1 to 7 in terms of "strongly disagree" to "strongly agree." Item scores are summed for a total score, which ranges from 5 to 35, with higher scores reflecting more satisfaction with life.

RELIABILITY The 5 items on the SWLS were selected from a pool of 48 based on factor analysis. The instrument's internal consistency is very good, with an alpha of .87. The instrument appears to have excellent test-retest reliability, with a correlation of .82 for a two-month period, suggesting it is very stable.

VALIDITY The SWLS has been tested for concurrent validity using two samples of college students. Scores correlated with nine measures of subjective well-being for both samples. The scale was not correlated with a measure of affect intensity. The SWLS has also been shown to correlate with self-esteem, a checklist of clinical symptoms, neuroticism, and emotionality. Scores on the SWLS also correlated with independent ratings of life satisfaction among the elderly.

PRIMARY REFERENCE Diener, E., Emmons, R. A., Larsen, R. J., and Griffin, S. (1985). The Satisfaction with Life Scale, *Journal of Personality Assessment*, 49, 71–75. Instrument reproduced with permission of Ed Diener.

AVAILABILITY Dr. Ed Diener, Associate Professor, Psychology Department, University of Illinois, 603 E. Daniel, Champaign, IL 61820. Email: ediener@illinois.edu.

Below are five statements with which you may agree or disagree. Using the scale below, indicate your agreement with each item by placing the appropriate number on the line preceding that item. Please be open and honest in your responding.

1 = Strongly disagree
2 = Disagree
3 = Slightly disagree
4 = Neither agree nor disagree
5 = Slightly agree
6 = Agree
7 = Strongly agree

____ 1. In most ways my life is close to my ideal.
____ 2. The conditions of my life are excellent.
____ 3. I am satisfied with my life.
____ 4. So far I have gotten the important things I want in life.
____ 5. If I could live my life over, I would change almost nothing.

Scale for the Assessment of Negative Symptoms (SANS)
Scale for the Assessment of Positive Symptoms (SAPS)

PURPOSE To assess negative and positive symptoms of psychopathology.

AUTHOR Nancy C. Andreasen

DESCRIPTION These two instruments assess negative and positive symptoms of psychopathology, primarily the symptomatology of schizophrenia. Both are rating scales, used by practitioners to assess clients. The SANS is a 25-item scale that has five subscales: affective flattening, alogia, avolition and apathy, anhedonia and asociality, and impairment of attention. The SAPS is a 35-item scale with four subscales: hallucination, delusions, bizarreness, and positive formal thought disorder; the SAPS concludes with a global assessment of inappropriate affect. For both instruments, each subscale also contains a global rating index. The symptoms are considered within the time frame of one month, although this may be changed to measure more immediate responses to treatment (e.g., a one-week period in response to medication). The SANS and SAPS are designed to be used in conjunction with structured interviews, although information may be derived from direct clinical observations, observations by family members, reports from treatment personnel or the patient himself or herself.

NORMS Means and standard deviations reported by Schuldberg et al. (1991) are from a sample of more than 390 outpatients from a mental health center and are for composite or total scores on a 22-item version of the SANS and composite scores on the first 34 items of the SAPS. The SANS had a mean of 25.5 and a standard deviation of 16.1; at a two-year follow-up the mean was 17.6 and the standard deviation was 9.0. The SAPS had a mean of 4.8 and a standard deviation of 9.3; at the two-year follow-up the mean was 8.2 with a standard deviation of 11.7. For patients with a diagnosis of schizophrenia the mean on the SANS was 32.4 and the standard deviation was 15.9, and the SAPS had a mean of 18.9 and a standard deviation of 12.9.

SCORING The SANS and SAPS may be scored in a variety of ways. Subscale scores are the sum of all items, including the global rating item. Global items may be used by summing each to form the global summary score. Total scores for negative and positive symptoms are the sum of all items in each of the instruments to form the composite score. Total scores for the SANS range from 0 to 125 and from 0 to 175 for the SAPS. Higher scores reflect more severe negative and positive symptomatology.

RELIABILITY The reliability is very good for both the SANS and the SAPS. Using intraclass correlations coefficients on the bases of 19 patients rated, using from three to five raters, reliabilities ranged from .83 to .92 for the global summary and total scores (Schuldberg et al., 1991). Internal consistency for the global summary scores was moderate, .47 for the SANS and .58 for the SAPS, due in part to the limited number of items. Internal consistency for the total scores was .90 for the SANS and .86 for the SAPS. Test-retest reliability over a two-year period was also very good considering the long time period, ranging from .40 to .50.

VALIDITY Factor analysis suggests the SANS and SAPS measure two fairly independent dimensions of schizophrenic symptomatology. Outpatients diagnosed with schizophrenia had less severe negative and positive symptoms than persons hospitalized for schizophrenia, while patients without a diagnosis of schizophrenia had less severe symptoms than either group of persons with schizophrenia.

PRIMARY REFERENCES Andreasen, N. C. (1982). Negative symptoms of schizophrenia: Definition and reliability, *Archives of General Psychiatry*, 39, 784–788. Andreasen, N. C., and Olsen, S. (1982). Negative v. positive schizophrenia: Definition and validation, *Archives of General Psychiatry*, 39, 789–794. Schuldberg, D., Quinlan, D. M., Morgenstern, H., and Glazer, W. (1990). Positive and negative symptoms in chronic psychiatric outpatients: Reliability, stability, and factor structure, *Psychological Assessment*, 2, 262–268. Instruments reproduced with permission of Nancy C. Andreasen.

AVAILABILITY Nancy C. Andreasen, M.D., Ph.D., University of Iowa Hospitals and Clinics, MH-CRC 2911 JPP, 200 Hawkins Drive, Iowa City, IA 52242-1057. Email: nancy-andreasen@uiowa.edu.

Rate the patient on each item using the following scale:

0 = None
1 = Questionable
2 = Mild
3 = Moderate
4 = Marked
5 = Severe

Affective Flattening or Blunting

1. *Unchanging Facial Expression*   0 1 2 3 4 5
   The patient's face appears wooden, changes less than
   expected as emotional content of discourse changes.

2. *Decreased Spontaneous Movements*   0 1 2 3 4 5
   The patient shows few or no spontaneous movements,
   does not shift position, move extremities, etc.

3. *Paucity of Expressive Gestures*   0 1 2 3 4 5
   The patient does not use hand gestures, body position,
   etc., as an aid to expressing his ideas.

4. *Poor Eye Contact*   0 1 2 3 4 5
   The patient avoids eye contact or "stares through"
   interviewer even when speaking.

5. *Affective Nonresponsivity*   0 1 2 3 4 5
   The patient fails to smile or laugh when prompted.

6. *Lack of Vocal Inflections*   0 1 2 3 4 5
   The patient fails to show normal vocal emphasis
   patterns, is often monotonic.

7. *Global Rating of Affective Flattening*   0 1 2 3 4 5
   This rating should focus on overall severity of symptoms, especially unresponsiveness, eye contact, facial
   expression, and vocal inflections.

Alogia

8. *Poverty of Speech*   0 1 2 3 4 5
   The patient's replies to questions are restricted in
   amount, tend to be brief, concrete, and unelaborated.

9. *Poverty of Content of Speech*   0 1 2 3 4 5
   The patient's replies are adequate in amount but tend
   to be vague, overconcrete, or overgeneralized, and
   convey little information.

10. *Blocking*   0 1 2 3 4 5
    The patient indicates, either spontaneously or with
    prompting, that his train of thought was interrupted.

11. *Increased Latency of Response*   0 1 2 3 4 5
    The patient takes a long time to reply to questions; prompting indicates the patient is aware of the question.

12. *Global Rating of Alogia*   0 1 2 3 4 5
    The core features of alogia are poverty of speech and poverty of content.

Avolition-Apathy

13. *Grooming and Hygiene*   0 1 2 3 4 5
    The patient's clothes may be sloppy or soiled, and he may have greasy hair, body odor, etc.

14. *Impersistence at Work or School*   0 1 2 3 4 5
    The patient has difficulty seeking or maintaining employment, completing school work, keeping house, etc. If an inpatient, cannot persist at ward activities, such as OT, playing cards, etc.

15. *Physical Anergia*   0 1 2 3 4 5
    The patient tends to be physically inert. He may sit for hours and does not initiate spontaneous activity.

16. *Global Rating of Avolition-Apathy*   0 1 2 3 4 5
    Strong weight may be given to one or two prominent symptoms if particularly striking.

Anhedonia-Asociality

17. *Recreational Interests and Activities*   0 1 2 3 4 5
    The patient may have few or no interests. Both the quality and quantity of interests should be taken into account.

18. *Sexual Activity*   0 1 2 3 4 5
    The patient may show a decrease in sexual interest and activity, or enjoyment when active.

19. *Ability to Feel Intimacy and Closeness*   0 1 2 3 4 5
    The patient may display an inability to form close or intimate relationships, especially with the opposite sex and family.

20. *Relationships with Friends and Peers*   0 1 2 3 4 5
    The patient may have few or no friends and may prefer to spend all of his time isolated.

21. *Global Rating of Anhedonia-Asociality*   0 1 2 3 4 5
    This rating should reflect overall severity, taking into account the patient's age, family status, etc.

continued

Attention

22. *Social Inattentiveness*   0   1   2   3   4   5
 The patient appears uninvolved or unengaged. He may
 seem "spacy."

23. Inattentiveness During Mental Status Testing   0   1   2   3   4   5
 Tests of "serial 7s" (at least five subtractions) and
 spelling "world" backwards:
 Score: 2 = 1 error; 3 = 2 errors; 4 = 3 errors

24. *Global Rating of Attention*   0   1   2   3   4   5
 This rating should assess the patient's overall concentration, clinically and on tests.

Hallucinations

1. *Auditory Hallucinations*　　　　　0　1　2　3　4　5
   The patient reports voices, noises, or other sounds that
   no one else hears.

2. *Voices Commenting*　　　　　0　1　2　3　4　5
   The patient reports a voice which makes a running
   commentary on his behavior or thoughts.

3. *Voices Conversing*　　　　　0　1　2　3　4　5
   The patient reports hearing two or more voices
   conversing.

4. *Somatic or Tactile Hallucinations*　　　　　0　1　2　3　4　5
   The patient reports experiencing peculiar physical
   sensations in the body.

5. *Olfactory Hallucinations*　　　　　0　1　2　3　4　5
   The patient reports experiencing unusual smells which
   no one else notices.

6. *Visual Hallucinations*　　　　　0　1　2　3　4　5
   The patient sees shapes or people that are not actually
   present.

7. *Global Rating of Hallucinations*　　　　　0　1　2　3　4　5
   This rating should be based on the duration and severity of the hallucinations and their effects on the
   patient's life.

Delusions

8. *Persecutory Delusions*　　　　　0　1　2　3　4　5
   The patient believes he is being conspired against or
   persecuted in some way.

9. *Delusions of Jealousy*　　　　　0　1　2　3　4　5
   The patient believes his spouse is having an affair with
   someone.

10. *Delusions of Guilt or Sin*　　　　　0　1　2　3　4　5
    The patient believes that he has committed some terri-
    ble sin or done something unforgivable.

11. *Grandiose Delusions*　　　　　0　1　2　3　4　5
    The patient believes he has special powers or abilities.

12. *Religious Delusions*　　　　　0　1　2　3　4　5
    The patient is preoccupied with false beliefs of a reli-
    gious nature.

13. *Somatic Delusions*　　　　　0　1　2　3　4　5
    The patient believes that somehow his body is dis-
    eased, abnormal, or changed.

continued

14. *Delusions of Reference*   0 1 2 3 4 5
    The patient believes that insignificant remarks or
    events refer to him or have some special meaning.

15. *Delusions of Being Controlled*   0 1 2 3 4 5
    The patient feels that his feelings or actions are con-
    trolled by some outside force.

16. *Delusions of Mind Reading*   0 1 2 3 4 5
    The patient feels that people can read his mind or
    know his thoughts.

17. *Thought Broadcasting*   0 1 2 3 4 5
    The patient believes that his thoughts are broadcast so
    that he himself or others can hear them.

18. *Thought Insertion*   0 1 2 3 4 5
    The patient believes that thoughts that are not his own
    have been inserted into his mind.

19. *Thought Withdrawal*   0 1 2 3 4 5
    The patient believes that thoughts have been taken
    away from his mind.

20. *Global Rating of Delusions*   0 1 2 3 4 5
    This rating should be based on the duration and persis-
    tence of the delusions and their effect on the patient's
    life.

Bizarre Behavior

21. *Clothing and Appearance*   0 1 2 3 4 5
    The patient dresses in an unusual manner or does
    other strange things to alter his appearance.

22. *Social and Sexual Behavior*   0 1 2 3 4 5
    The patient may do things considered inappropriate
    according to usual social norms (e.g., masturbating in
    public).

23. *Aggressive and Agitated Behavior*   0 1 2 3 4 5
    The patient may behave in an aggressive, agitated
    manner, often unpredictably.

24. *Repetitive or Stereotyped Behavior*   0 1 2 3 4 5
    The patient develops a set of repetitive action or rituals
    that he must perform over and over.

25. *Global Rating of Bizarre Behavior*   0 1 2 3 4 5
    This rating should reflect the type of behavior and the
    extent to which it deviates from social norms.

Positive Formal Thought Disorder

26. *Derailment*   0 1 2 3 4 5
    A pattern of speech in which ideas slip off track onto
    ideas obliquely related or unrelated.

27. *Tangentiality*
Replying to a question in an oblique or irrelevant manner.

0 1 2 3 4 5

28. *Incoherence*
A pattern of speech which is essentially incomprehensible at times.

0 1 2 3 4 5

29. *Illogicality*
A pattern of speech in which conclusions are reached which do not follow logically.

0 1 2 3 4 5

30. *Circumstantiality*
A pattern of speech which is very indirect and delayed in reaching its goal idea.

0 1 2 3 4 5

31. *Pressure of Speech*
The patient's speech is rapid and difficult to interrupt; the amount of speech produced is greater than that considered normal.

0 1 2 3 4 5

32. *Distractible Speech*
The patient is distracted by nearby stimuli which interrupt his flow of speech.

0 1 2 3 4 5

33. *Clanging*
A pattern of speech in which sounds rather than meaningful relationships govern word choice.

0 1 2 3 4 5

34. *Global Rating of Positive Formal Thought Disorder*
This rating should reflect the frequency of abnormality and degree to which it affects the patient's ability to communicate.

0 1 2 3 4 5

Inappropriate Affect

35. *Inappropriate Affect*
The patient's affect is inappropriate or incongruous, not simply flat or blunted.

0 1 2 3 4 5

Scale of Dissociative Activities (SODAS)

PURPOSE To measure dissociative behaviors.

AUTHORS Jennifer L. Mayer and Richard F. Farmer

DESCRIPTION The SODAS is a 35-item instrument that was designed to measure the degree to which individuals experience mild to severe dissociative activities. The foundation for this scale was a conceptualization of dissociation as occurring on a continuum of severity as indicated by number of symptoms present and their frequency of occurrence. From a pool of 83 items generated by the literature on dissociation, a pilot study on 215 undergraduates led to the present 35-item measure. The authors believe the literature on dissociation was lacking a psychometrically sound measure, and believe they have developed one with the SODAS.

NORMS The SODAS was studied using 533 predominantly white college students. The sample included 157 men and 376 women with a mean age of 23.3 years. Actual norms were not available in the Primary Reference although the authors note that there was no difference in scores between males and females.

SCORING Scores on the SODAS are easily obtained by assigning numbers (1 for "Never" to 5 for "Very Frequently") to the responses on the scale and simply summing them. Scores range from 35 (never endorsing any of the experiences) to 175 (very frequently having all of the experiences). Higher scores equal greater experience of dissociative activities.

RELIABILITY The SODAS has excellent internal consistency with an alpha of .95. The SODAS also has very good stability with a 38-day test-retest reliability of .77.

VALIDITY The SODAS has very good concurrent validity, correlating significantly with two other measures of dissociation. The SODAS was significantly negatively correlated with a measure of social desirability, i.e., as scores increased on social desirability, scores decreased on the SODAS.

PRIMARY REFERENCE Mayer, J. L., and Farmer, R.F. The development and psychometric evaluation of a new measure of dissociative activities, *Journal of Personality Assessment, 80*, 185–196. Instrument reproduced with permission of Drs. Mayer and Farmer.

AVAILABILITY Instrument may be reproduced from this volume with permission of Drs. Mayer and Farmer.

Directions: This questionnaire asks you to indicate how often you have certain experiences. Indicate the frequency by circling the "N" if the statement NEVER happens to you, "R" if the statement RARELY happens to you, "O" if the statement OCCASIONALLY happens to you, "F" if the statement FREQUENTLY happens to you, or "VF" if the statement VERY FREQUENTLY happens to you.

N=NEVER   R=RARELY   O=OCCASIONALLY   F=FREQUENTLY
VF=VERY FREQUENTLY

1. I have difficulty staying mentally engaged when I participate in routine tasks.   N   R   O   F   VF

2. My mind wanders off.   N   R   O   F   VF

3. I have periods when I feel like I am detached or separate from my body.   N   R   O   F   VF

4. There are occasions when I discover that I have done something even though I have no recollection of doing it.   N   R   O   F   VF

5. There are times when places that were once familiar to me appear strange or different.   N   R   O   F   VF

6. There are periods when I experience myself as having different personalities.   N   R   O   F   VF

7. I take comfort in retreating into my own inner world.   N   R   O   F   VF

8. There are times when I feel I have little control over my actions or behavior.   N   R   O   F   VF

9. When I listen to people speak, I "space out" or have difficulty attending to what they say.   N   R   O   F   VF

10. There are times when I feel like I am in a daze or trance   N   R   O   F   VF

11. There are times when I have difficulty distinguishing what I thought about doing from what I actually did do.   N   R   O   F   VF

12. There are periods during which I "lose time," or am unaware of what happened during extended periods of time.   N   R   O   F   VF

13. I engage in daydreaming.   N   R   O   F   VF

14. I feel numb.   N   R   O   F   VF

15. I find things in my possession which I don't remember acquiring.   N   R   O   F   VF

16. There are times when I feel a deep, dark void within me.   N   R   O   F   VF

17. There are periods when I lose my sense of how much time has gone by.   N   R   O   F   VF

18. There are occasions when people who I know momentarily seem unfamiliar to me.   N   R   O   F   VF

19. I have difficulty focusing my attention or concentration for long periods of time.   N   R   O   F   VF

20. There are times when I find myself emerged from a period during which I had clearly been doing something, but I cannot remember what it was that I was doing.   N   R   O   F   VF

21. I have feelings of emptiness.   N   R   O   F   VF

22. I am bothered by not having a clear sense of who I really am.   N   R   O   F   VF

23. There are occasions when I have the experience of hearing sounds associated with my past, even though there is nothing in my present environment that produced those sounds.   N R O F VF

24. I have experiences where I find myself questioning if aspects of the environment I am in are real.   N R O F VF

25. When I imagine experiences or events or when I daydream, it seems like what I am imagining is actually occurring.   N R O F VF

26. I have difficulty describing what I am experiencing on the inside because those experiences are so mixed up or confused.   N R O F VF

27. There are times when I am overcome by feelings of non-existence or nothingness.   N R O F VF

28. When I walk, drive, or ride a bicycle, I have the experience of wondering what I was doing during the various points along the way.   N R O F VF

29. There have been times when I had difficulty deciding whether my environment was real or part of a dream.   N R O F VF

30. When I perceive my situation as threatening, punishing, or dangerous, I respond by "spacing out" or by mentally "checking out" from the situation.   N R O F VF

31. There are occasions when I have the experience of watching myself and feeling like I am watching another person.   N R O F VF

32. When I engage in some type of behavior or activity, I am mentally disconnected from what I am doing.   N R O F VF

33. I or others have noticed that at times I stare off into space and seem disconnected from what is going on around me. N R O F VF

34. I have had the feeling that my body was an empty shell.   N R O F VF

35. When alone, I have difficulty focusing my attention in the present.   N R O F VF

Schwartz Outcome Scale (SOS-10)

PURPOSE To measure the effectiveness of mental health treatment.

AUTHORS Mark A. Blais et al.

DESCRIPTION The SOS is a 10-item scale designed to evaluate the effectiveness of treatment across a wide range of mental health services and populations. Given the pressure on individuals and organizations to provide evaluation data, a single, easy-to-use self report measure that cuts across a wide variety of services and problems, and could be used appropriately by all mental health workers using virtually all theories and systems of intervention, could conceivably be a major boon to the field.

NORMS The SOS was initially studied with patient and practitioner focus groups and over 100 patients from various mental health sites. Once the final 10 items were selected, the SOS was studied with 57 patients from a variety of mental health sites and 28 nonpatients. There were no other demographic data about these respondents reported nor were norms. However, 20 inpatients undergoing treatment on a locked psychiatric ward were given pre- and post-tests using the SOS. These patients had a mean age of 50 (SD = 16), and included 11 women and nine men. Mean length of treatment was 11 days (SD = 11). The pretest scores on the SOS had a mean of 42 (SD = 12) and a post-test mean score of 42 (SD = 12).

SCORING The SOS is scored easily by summing all the item scores for a range of 0 to 60. Higher scores suggest more positive outcomes.

RELIABILITY The SOS has excellent internal consistency with an alpha of .96. Data on stability were not reported.

VALIDITY The SOS has excellent construct validity as established through convergent and divergent validity with positive and negative correlations in predicted ways with numerous scales including the Psychiatric Symptom Scale, Beck Hopelessness Scale, and measures of well-being and life satisfaction such as the Satisfaction with Life Scale. The SOS also is sensitive to change as noted above in the Norms section.

PRIMARY REFERENCE Blais, M. A., et al. (1999). Development and initial validation of a brief mental health outcome measure, *Journal of Personality Assessment, 73*, 359–373. Instrument reproduced with permission of Dr. Blais and Massachusetts General Hospital.

AVAILABILITY May be copied from this volume.

SOS-10

Instructions: Below are 10 statements about you and your life that help us see how you feel you are doing. Please respond to each statement by circling the response number that best fits how you have generally been over the last seven days (1 week). There are no right or wrong responses and it is important that your responses reflect how you feel you are doing. Often the first answer that comes to mind is best. Thank you for your thought effort. Please be sure to respond to each statement.

1) Give my current physical condition, I am satisfied with what I can do.

    0   1   2   3   4   5   6
    Never   All of the time or nearly all of the time

2) I have confidence in my ability to sustain important relationships.

    0   1   2   3   4   5   6
    Never   All of the time or nearly all of the time

3) I feel hopeful about my future.

    0   1   2   3   4   5   6
    Never   All of the time or nearly all of the time

4) I am often interested and excited about things in my life.

    0   1   2   3   4   5   6
    Never   All of the time or nearly all of the time

5) I am able to have fun.

    0   1   2   3   4   5   6
    Never   All of the time or nearly all of the time

6) I am generally satisfied with my psychological health.

    0   1   2   3   4   5   6
    Never   All of the time or nearly all of the time

7) I am able to forgive myself for my failures.

    0   1   2   3   4   5   6
    Never   All of the time or nearly all of the time

8) My life is progressing according to my expectations.

    0   1   2   3   4   5   6
    Never   All of the time or nearly all of the time

9) I am able to handle conflicts with others.

    0   1   2   3   4   5   6
    Never   All of the time or nearly all of the time

10) I have peace of mind.

    0   1   2   3   4   5   6
    Never   All of the time or nearly all of the time

Self-Administered Alcoholism Screening Test (SAAST and SAAST-Form II)

PURPOSE To measure alcohol abuse.

AUTHORS Wendell M. Swenson and Robert M. Morse

DESCRIPTION The SAAST is a 35-item instrument designed to measure the presence of alcohol abuse. The SAAST is based on the Michigan Alcoholism Screening Test, which is a 15-minute structured interview. Items on the Michigan Alcoholism Screening Test, were revised and placed in a self-report format by the authors. The SAAST has been studied with thousands of patients in a number of separate empirical investigations. It has been found to be a considerably more sensitive indicator of alcoholism than laboratory testing or physical examination. The SAAST-II was developed as a companion measure with responses obtained from the spouses of patients who were abusing alcohol. Results from the SAAST-II show that alcohol abuse could have been diagnosed in 90% of inpatient alcoholics by information from the spouse alone. Thus the SAAST and SAAST-II are excellent companion measures for both diagnosing alcohol abuse and monitoring the effectiveness of treatment for alcohol abuse.

NORMS The original study of the SAAST was conducted with 100 patients in an alcoholism treatment unit as well as 50 spouses, counselors of the 100 patients, and 100 control group members who were medical-psychiatric patients selected at random. Seventy of the patients were male and 30 of the patients were female; the mean age was 48.5 years. Seventy-five of the patients were married, 11 were single, 10 were divorced or separated, and 4 were widowed. In this original sample of patients, the total mean score for all patients was 16.68 (SD=6.06); the mean score for males was 17.12 (SD=6.03); and the mean score for females was 15.63 (SD=6.06). Scores for spouses and counselors in assessing the patients' level of alcohol abuse were M=17.96 for spouses and M=21.78 for counselors. The mean for controls was 4.03. (SD=3.46).

SCORING The basic summary index of the SAAST is the total score, which is a count of the items on the SAAST that are endorsed in the "alcoholic" direction. The scorable answer is "yes" for all items except items 2, 5, 7, and 8 for which "no" is the scorable response. Items 1b and 4a are not scored. If the total score is 7 or greater it is likely that the patient has alcoholism. A short form SAAST includes items 2, 4b, 8, 11, 17, 18, 25, 27, and 31. Items 4b and 18 are each given a weighted score of 2 as opposed to the score of 1 given to the remaining items. The maximum short form score is 11, and a score of 4 or greater is suggestive of possible alcoholism. The "alcoholic" response is positive responses to all items except 2, 5, 7 and 8. The SAAST has a cutoff score of 7, suggesting that scores of 7 or greater indicate probable alcohol abuse.

RELIABILITY No data on reliability were available in the original article.

VALIDITY The SAAST has excellent validity in identifying and differentiating individuals with alcohol abuse problems from those without alcohol abuse problems. In a study of 520 alcoholic patients and 636 nonalcoholic patients, SAAST was found to have both high sensitivity (95%) and high specificity (96%) as a screening test for alcohol abuse. In another study, SAAST-II information from the patients' spouses correctly classified 98% of the alcoholic patients.

PRIMARY REFERENCE Swenson, W. M., and Morse, R. M. (1975). The use of a self-administered alcoholism screening test (SAAST) in a medical center, *Mayo Clinic Proceedings*, 50, 204–208.

AVAILABILITY Dr. R. M. Morse, Department of Psychiatry and Psychology, W-11, Mayo Clinic and Foundation, Rochester, MN 55905. Reprinted by permission of Dr. Morse. Copies of the SAAST, SAAST-II, or a manual for the SAAST are available from the author for no charge. Email: morse.robert@mayo.edu.

	Yes	No
1. Do you have a drink now and then?	☐	☐

> (If you never drink alcoholic beverages, and have no previous experiences with drinking, do not continue this questionnaire.)

	Yes	No
If you don't drink now, did you stop drinking because of problems with alcohol? (*If you* do *drink now*, leave this item blank.)	☐	☐
2. Do you feel you are a normal drinker? (That is, drink no more than average.)	☐	☐
3. Have you ever awakened the morning after some drinking the night before and found that you could not remember a part of the evening?	☐	☐
4. Does your spouse ever worry or complain about your drinking?	☐	☐
Do close relatives ever worry or complain about your drinking?	☐	☐
5. Can you stop drinking without a struggle after one or two drinks?	☐	☐
6. Do you ever feel guilty about your drinking?	☐	☐
7. Do friends or relatives think you are a normal drinker?	☐	☐
8. Are you always able to stop drinking when you want to?	☐	☐
9. Have you ever attended a meeting of Alcoholics Anonymous (AA) because of your drinking?	☐	☐
10. Have you gotten into physical fights when drinking?	☐	☐
11. Has your drinking ever created problems between you and your wife, husband, parents, or other near relative?	☐	☐
12. Has your wife, husband, or other family member ever gone to anyone for help about your drinking?	☐	☐
13. Have you ever lost friendships because of your drinking?	☐	☐
14. Have you ever gotten into trouble at work because of your drinking?	☐	☐
15. Have you ever lost a job because of your drinking?	☐	☐
16. Have you ever neglected your obligations, your family, or your work for two or more days in a row because of drinking?	☐	☐
17. Do you ever drink in the morning?	☐	☐
18. Have you ever felt the need to cut down on your drinking?	☐	☐
19. Have there been times in your adult life when you found it necessary to completely avoid alcohol?	☐	☐
20. Have you ever been told you have liver trouble? Cirrhosis?	☐	☐
21. Have you ever had delirium tremens (DTs)?	☐	☐
22. Have you ever had severe shaking, heard voices, or seen things that weren't there after heavy drinking?	☐	☐
23. Have you ever gone to anyone for help about your drinking?	☐	☐
24. Have you ever been in a hospital because of your drinking?	☐	☐
25. Have you ever been told by a doctor to stop drinking?	☐	☐
26. Have you ever been a patient in a psychiatric hospital or on a psychiatric ward of a general hospital? (If the answer to #26 is No, skip to #28.)	☐	☐

continued

27. If you answered Yes to #26, was drinking part of the problem that
    resulted in your hospitalization?   ☐   ☐
28. Have you ever been a patient at a psychiatric or mental health clinic
    or gone to any doctor, social worker, or member of the clergy
    for help with any emotional problem?   ☐   ☐
    (If the answer to #28 is No, skip to #30.)
29. If you answered Yes to #28, was your drinking part of the problem? ☐   ☐
30. Have you ever been arrested, even for a few hours,
    because of drunken behavior (not driving)?   ☐   ☐
31. Have you ever been arrested, even for a few hours,
    because of driving while intoxicated?   ☐   ☐
32. Has either of your parents ever had problems with alcohol?   ☐   ☐
33. Have any of your brothers or sisters ever had problems with alcohol? ☐   ☐
34. Has your husband or wife ever had problems with alcohol?   ☐   ☐
35. Have any of your children ever had problems with alcohol?   ☐   ☐

SAAST-Form II

Yes   No

1. Does the patient have a drink now and then?   ☐   ☐

> (If the patient never drinks alcoholic beverages, and has no previous
> experience with drinking, do not continue this questionnaire.)

If the patient doesn't drink now, did he/she stop drinking because of
problems with alcohol? (*If the patient* does *drink now*, leave this
item blank.)   ☐   ☐
2. Do you feel the patient is a normal drinker?
   (That is, drinks no more than average.)   ☐   ☐
3. Has the patient ever awakened the morning after some drinking
   the night before and found that he or she could not remember
   a part of the evening?   ☐   ☐
4. Do you ever worry or complain about the patient's drinking?   ☐   ☐
   Do close relatives ever worry or complain about the patient's drinking? ☐   ☐
5. Can the patient stop drinking without a struggle after one or
   two drinks?   ☐   ☐
6. Does the patient ever feel guilty about his/her drinking?   ☐   ☐
7. Do friends or relatives think the patient is a normal drinker?   ☐   ☐
8. Is the patient always able to stop drinking when he or she wants to? ☐   ☐
9. Has the patient ever attended a meeting of Alcoholics Anonymous (AA)
   because of his or her drinking?   ☐   ☐
10. Has the patient gotten into physical fights when drinking?   ☐   ☐
11. Has the patient's drinking ever created problems between the patient
    and you, parents, or other near relative?   ☐   ☐
12. Have you or other family members ever gone to anyone for help about
    the patient's drinking?   ☐   ☐
13. Has the patient ever lost friendships because of his/her drinking? ☐   ☐

14. Has the patient ever gotten into trouble at work because of his/her drinking?   □   □
15. Has the patient ever lost a job because of his/her drinking?   □   □
16. Has the patient ever neglected obligations, the family, or work for two or more days in a row because of his/her drinking?   □   □
17. Does the patient ever drink in the morning?   □   □
18. Has the patient ever felt the need to cut down on his/her drinking?   □   □
19. Have there been times in the patient's adult life when he/she found it necessary to completely avoid alcohol?   □   □
20. Has the patient ever been told he/she had liver trouble? Cirrhosis?   □   □
21. Has the patient ever had delirium tremens (DTs)?   □   □
22. Has the patient ever had severe shaking, heard voices, or seen things that weren't there after heavy drinking?   □   □
23. Has the patient ever gone to anyone for help about his/her drinking?   □   □
24. Has the patient ever been in a hospital because of his/her drinking?   □   □
25. Has the patient ever been told by a doctor to stop drinking?   □   □
26. Has the patient ever been a patient in a psychiatric hospital or on a psychiatric ward of a general hospital?   □   □
    (If the answer to #26 is No, skip to #28.)
27. If you answered Yes to #26, was drinking part of the problem that resulted in the patient's hospitalization?   □   □
28. Has the patient ever been a patient at a psychiatric or mental health clinic or gone to any doctor, social worker, or member of the clergy for help with any emotional problem?   □   □
    (If the answer to #28 is No, skip to #30.)
29. If you answered Yes to #28, was the patient's drinking part of the problem?   □   □
30. Has the patient ever been arrested, even for a few hours, because of drunken behavior (not driving)?   □   □
31. Has the patient ever been arrested, even for a few hours, because of driving while intoxicated?   □   □
32. Has either of the patient's parents ever had problems with alcohol?   □   □
33. Have any of the patient's brothers or sisters ever had problems with alcohol?   □   □
34. Have you ever had problems with alcohol?   □   □
35. Have any of the patient's children ever had problems with alcohol?   □   □

Self-Attitude Inventory (SAI)

PURPOSE To measure self-esteem.

AUTHORS Maurice Lorr and Richard A. Wunderlich

DESCRIPTION The SAI is a 32-item instrument designed to measure self-esteem. The SAI actually is composed of two subscales: confidence (items 1A, 3A, 5B, 7A, 9A, 11A, 13B, 15A, 17B, 19A, 21B, 23B, 25A, 27B, 29A, 31B) and popularity or social approval (items 2A, 4B, 6B, 8B, 10B, 12B, 14A, 16A, 18A, 20A, 22A, 24B, 26B, 28B, 30A, 32B). The SAI is presented in a paired-choice format to minimize response bias. Because of the importance of self-esteem to a number of theoretical formulations of problematic behaviors, activities, and feelings, these two brief subscales that focus on specific components of self-esteem are viewed as particularly useful, especially in evaluating the effectiveness of counseling for disturbed children.

NORMS The SAI was studied with several samples of high school boys totaling 924, plus a sample of 45 psychiatric patients and 50 "normal" adults. No other demographic data are available nor are actual norms.

SCORING The SAI is easily scored by simply adding up the number of items circled that agree with items described above (i.e., if 1A is circled, it is one point toward the total confidence score). The maximum score on each scale is 16, with higher scores showing greater self-esteem.

RELIABILITY The SAI has good internal consistency, with alphas that range from .80 to .86 for confidence and from .69 to .81 for popularity. No test-retest data are reported.

VALIDITY The SAI has good concurrent validity, correlating with the Rosenberg Self-Esteem Scale. The SAI also has good known-groups validity, significantly distinguishing between psychiatric patients and "normal" adults.

PRIMARY REFERENCE Lorr, M., and Wunderlich, R. A. (1986). Two objective measures of self-esteem, *Journal of Personality Assessment*, 50, 18–23.

AVAILABILITY May be copied from this volume.

Below are a number of statements that describe how people feel about themselves and how they relate to others. You will notice that each numbered item has two possible answers labeled A and B. Read each statement and select the one (either A or B) you agree with most. Then draw a circle around the A or the B, whichever describes you best. Be sure to circle *one* answer for each item.

1. A.   I usually feel confident in my abilities.
   B.   I often lack confidence in my abilities.

2. A.   I have few doubts that I am popular.
   B.   I have real doubts about my popularity.

3. A.   I usually expect to succeed in things I try.
   B.   Only occasionally do I expect to succeed in things I try.

4. A.   Not many people think well of me.
   B.   Most people think well of me.

5. A.   There are only a few things I can do that I am proud of.
   B.   There are a fair number of things I can do that I am proud of.

6. A.   I seldom feel approved or noticed by people I like.
   B.   I usually get both approval and attention from people I like.

7. A.   I feel sure of myself in most circumstances.
   B.   I feel sure of myself only in a few situations.

8. A.   Few people say they like being with me.
   B.   Most people say they like being with me.

9. A.   I can usually accomplish everything I set out to do.
   B.   Often I am unable to accomplish what I set out to do.

10. A.   People seldom go out of their way to include me in their affairs.
    B.   People often go out of their way to include me in their affairs.

11. A.   I feel as capable as most people I know.
    B.   I feel less capable than a fair number of people I know.

12. A.   Few people consider me to be an interesting person.
    B.   I feel that a lot of people consider me to be an interesting person.

13. A.   I feel unsure whether I can handle what the future brings.
    B.   I feel sure I can handle whatever the future is likely to bring.

14. A.   A fair number of people seem to look up to me.
    B.   Very few people seem to look up to me.

15. A.   I tend to be optimistic when I take on a new job.
    B.   I tend to expect failure when I take on a new job.

16. A.   A fair number of persons say positive things about me.
    B.   Relatively few people say nice things about me.

17. A. I seldom feel satisfied with myself.
    B. I usually feel pleased with myself.

18. A. I feel accepted by most people important to me.
    B. I feel accepted only by some people important to me.

19. A. Most people I know would rate me as a self-assured person.
    B. Few people I know would rate me as a self-assured person.

20. A. I seem to get more social invitations than my friends do.
    B. I seem to get fewer social invitations than my friends do.

21. A. I often feel I can't do anything right.
    B. Usually I can do whatever I set my mind to.

22. A. Often people confide in me.
    B. It is seldom that people confide in me.

23. A. I have a record of fewer successes than failures.
    B. I have a record of more successes than failures.

24. A. Only a few people enjoy associating with me.
    B. Many people like to associate with me.

25. A. I usually expect to win when competing with others.
    B. I seldom expect to win when competing with others.

26. A. Few people tell me they enjoy my company.
    B. Most people say they enjoy my company.

27. A. I probably think less favorably of myself than the ordinary person does.
    B. I think more favorably of myself than the ordinary person does.

28. A. Not many people seem to value my friendship.
    B. Quite a few persons appear to value my friendship.

29. A. There are very few things I would change about myself.
    B. There are many things about myself I wish I could change.

30. A. I am often asked to voice my opinion in a group discussion.
    B. I am seldom asked to express an opinion in a group discussion.

31. A. I seldom reach the goals I set for myself.
    B. I usually reach the goals I set for myself.

32. A. My acquaintances don't seem to follow my suggestions.
    B. My acquaintances usually follow my suggestions.

Self-Consciousness Scale (SCS)

PURPOSE To measure individual differences in private and public self-consciousness and social anxiety.

AUTHOR Michael F. Scheier

DESCRIPTION The SCS is a 22-item scale that was revised from an earlier version to make it appropriate for non-college populations. The SCS is focused on the assessment of an individual's self-consciousness in both public and private situations. Public self-consciousness refers to the tendency to think about those aspects of oneself that are matters of public display (items 2, 5, 10, 13, 16, 18, 20); private self-consciousness refers to the tendency to think about more covert or hidden aspects of the self (items 1, 4, 6, 8, 12, 14, 17, 19, 21). The scale also includes a measure of social anxiety, an apprehensiveness about being evaluated by others (items 3, 7, 9, 11, 15, 22). Extensive research on the original instrument shows that public and private self-consciousness mediate a wide range of behaviors and cognitions.

NORMS Norms for the revised SCS are based on a sample of 213 undergraduate men, 85 undergraduate women, 42 middle-aged men who had recently undergone coronary artery bypass surgery, and 396 women between the ages of 45 and 50 who were involved in a longitudinal study of menopause. For the undergraduate students, means for the men were 15.5 on private self-consciousness, 13.5 on public self-consciousness, and 8.8 on social anxiety. Means for the undergraduate women were 17.3 for private, 14.2 for public and 8.6 for social anxiety. The means were significantly different for men and women on private self-consciousness. For middle-aged men the mean for private self-consciousness was 13.5; for middle-aged women, the mean was 10.8 for public self-consciousness and 7.3 for social anxiety.

SCORING The SCS is scored by summing scores, which range from 0 to 3, for each item. This produces a total possible range of 0 to 66.

RELIABILITY The SCS has fairly good internal consistency, with an alpha of .75 for private self-consciousness, .84 for public self-consciousness, and .79 for social anxiety. The scale also demonstrates good stability, with test-retest correlations of .76 for private, .74 for public, and .77 for social anxiety.

VALIDITY Since the original scale had demonstrated good validity, the main source of validity information to date is a form of concurrent validity, correlations of the revised scale with the original. All three subscales correlate in the low to mid .80s with the original scale.

PRIMARY REFERENCE Scheier, M. F., and Carver, C. S. (1985). The Self-Consciousness Scale: A revised version for use with the general population, *Journal of Applied Social Psychology*, 15, 687–699. Instrument reproduced by permission of Dr. Michael F. Scheier.

AVAILABILITY Dr. Michael F. Scheier, Department of Psychology, Carnegie-Mellon University, Pittsburgh, PA 15213. Email: Scheier@cmu.edu.

Please put a number next to each item indicating the extent to which that item is like you.

0 = Not at all like me
1 = A little like me
2 = Somewhat like me
3 = A lot like me

___ 1. I'm always trying to figure myself out.
___ 2. I'm concerned about my style of doing things.
___ 3. It takes me time to get over my shyness in new situations.
___ 4. I think about myself a lot.
___ 5. I care a lot about how I present myself to others.
___ 6. I often daydream about myself.
___ 7. It's hard for me to work when someone is watching me.
___ 8. I never take a hard look at myself.
___ 9. I get embarrassed very easily.
___ 10. I'm self-conscious about the way I look.
___ 11. It's easy for me to talk to strangers.
___ 12. I generally pay attention to my inner feelings.
___ 13. I usually worry about making a good impression.
___ 14. I'm constantly thinking about my reasons for doing things.
___ 15. I feel nervous when I speak in front of a group.
___ 16. Before I leave my house, I check how I look.
___ 17. I sometimes step back (in my mind) in order to examine myself from a distance.
___ 18. I'm concerned about what other people think of me.
___ 19. I'm quick to notice changes in my mood.
___ 20. I'm usually aware of my appearance.
___ 21. I know the way my mind works when I work through a problem.
___ 22. Large groups make me nervous.

Self-Control Questionnaire (SCQ)

PURPOSE To measure self-control behaviors and cognitions.

AUTHOR Lynn P. Rehm

DESCRIPTION The SCQ is a 40-item instrument designed to measure depression-related self-control behaviors and cognitions. The SCQ was developed to evaluate the effectiveness of a self-control therapy program for depression. Items for the SCQ were derived from deficits in self-control behavior that are hypothesized to be contributory factors in depression. The SCQ is not only useful as an outcome measure, but may be useful as an assessment of vulnerability to depression.

NORMS The SCQ has been studied with a sample of 101 clinically depressed community volunteers and with undefined samples of "normal" and pregnant women. No other demographic data are available nor are actual norms.

SCORING The SCQ is scored on a 5-point scale (0 to 4) from A ("very characteristic of me, extremely descriptive") to E ("very uncharacteristic of me, extremely undescriptive"). As shown on the questionnaire, 19 items (marked "A") are phrased to reflect positive, nondepressive attitudes and 21 items (marked "E") to reflect negative, depressive attitudes. The latter should be reverse-scored (A=4, E=0). The total score is then the sum of all items.

RELIABILITY The SCQ has very good internal consistency, with alphas that range from .82 to .88. The SCQ also is very stable with a five-week, test-retest correlation of .86.

VALIDITY The SCQ has fair concurrent validity, with a correlation of .42 with the more general Rosenberg Self-Control Schedule. Correlations with the Beck Depression Inventory range from .16 to .31. The SCQ has good predictive validity, predicting post-partum depression in pregnant women. The SCQ also is very sensitive to changes due to clinical treatment.

PRIMARY REFERENCE O'Hara, M. W., Rehm, L. P., and Campbell, S. B. (1982), Predicting depressive symptomatology: Cognitive-behavioral models and post-partum depression, *Journal of Abnormal Psychology*, 91 457–461.

AVAILABILITY Dr. Lynn P. Rehm, Department of Psychology, University of Houston, TX 77204. Email: lprehm@uh.edu.

SCQ

Please read each of the following statements and indicate just how characteristic or descriptive of you the statement is by using the letters of the code given below:

A = *Very characteristic of me, extremely descriptive*
B = Rather characteristic of me, quite descriptive
C = Somewhat characteristic of me, slightly undescriptive
D = Rather uncharacteristic of me, quite undescriptive
E = *Very uncharacteristic of me, extremely undescriptive*

(E) ___ 1. Rewarding myself for progress toward a goal is unnecessary and may actually spoil me.

(A) ___ 2. Concentrating on the final goals as well as the immediate results of my efforts can help me feel better about my work.

(E) ___ 3. When things are going well, I often feel that something bad is just around the corner and there's nothing I can do about it.

(A) ___ 4. I am aware of my accomplishments each day.

(A) ___ 5. Thinking about how well I'm doing so far is what keeps me trying.

(A) ___ 6. When I do something right, I take time to enjoy the feeling.

(A) ___ 7. It usually works best for me to save my special treats until after I carry out what I intended to accomplish.

(A) ___ 8. What is most important is how I feel about my actions, not what other think.

(E) ___ 9. There is nothing I can do to change things that are upsetting me.

(A) ___ 10. The way to achieve my goals is to reward myself along the way, in order to keep up my own efforts.

(E) ___ 11. Punishing myself for only making partial gains toward a goal is the smart way to keep pressure on and get the job done.

(A) ___ 12. I get myself through hard things largely by planning on enjoying myself afterwards.

(E) ___ 13. I depend heavily on other people's opinions to evaluate objectively what I do.

(A) ___ 14. When I don't feel like doing anything, sometimes it helps if I take time out to do something I really enjoy.

(E) ___ 15. I always seem to remember the bad things that happen to me more than the good.

(A) ___ 16. It's success at the little things that encourages me to go on trying.

(A) ___ 17. To get good results, I have to observe what I'm actually doing in order to decide what I need to do next.

(E) ___ 18. The things in life that are most important depend on chance more than anything I can do.

(A) ___ 19. Planning each step of what I have to do helps me to get things done well.

(E) ___ 20. It's no use trying to change most of the things that make me miserable.

(E) ___ 21. My mood is unrelated to my behavior.

(E) ___ 22. There isn't anything to do when I want something important other than be patient and hope for good luck.

(E) ___ 23. Activities which fail to lead to something immediately should be dropped in favor of those that do so.

(E) ___ 24. My goals seem distant and unreachable.

(E) ___ 25. I think talking about what you've done right or well is just boastful and tooting your own horn.

(E) ___ 26. Unless I set and reach very high goals, my efforts are likely to be wasted.

(E) ___ 27. When I feel blue, the best thing to do is focus on all the negative things happening to me.

(A) ___ 28. Judging what I've done realistically is necessary for me to feel good about myself.

(E) ___ 29. How I feel about myself has a lot to do with what I'm accomplishing.

(E) ___ 30. I shouldn't dwell on things I've done well in hopes of feeling good about myself.

(A) ___ 31. When there is some goal I'd like to reach, I find it best to list specifically what I have to do to get there.

(A) ___ 32. My mood changes in relation to what I'm doing.

(A) ___ 33. It's just as important to think about what will happen later as a result of my actions, as it is to watch for immediate effects.

(E) ___ 34. I'd just be fooling myself if I tried to judge my reactions myself.

(E) ___ 35. Keeping watch on what I do wrong is more helpful than watching what I do correctly.

(E) ___ 36. Criticizing myself is often the best way to help me get through a difficult task.

(A) ___ 37. Not only what goes on around us, but also the things we say and do to ourselves determine how we feel from day to day.

(A) ___ 38. I encourage myself to improve by treating myself to something special whenever I make progress.

(E) ___ 39. It's more helpful to receive criticism than praise for my actions.

(A) ___ 40. I'd be unlikely to change for the better if I didn't silently praise myself or feel good for every step in the right direction.

Self-Control Schedule (SCS)

PURPOSE To measure self-control.

AUTHOR Michael Rosenbaum

DESCRIPTION The SCS is a 36-item instrument designed to assess individual tendencies to apply self-control methods to the solution of behavioral problems. The SCS was developed on the basis of a cognitive-behavioral formulation of self-control in which self-controlling responses were assumed to be cued by an internal event (e.g., anxiety, disruptive thought) that affects the effective performance of some behavior. The behaviors for the measure were derived from the literature on stress-handling methods and coping-skills therapies. The initial list of 60 items was pared down to the current 36 by expert opinion and initial research on the SCS. The SCS can be used to predict success in cognitive-behavior therapy, as an indicator of changes in therapy, as a predictor of adherence to prescribed medical regimens, and to assess the client's repertoire of self-control skills.

NORMS The SCS has been studied with several samples of Israeli and American college students amounting to several hundred subjects and including males and females. The SCS also was administered to a group of 105 Israeli men (mean age of 50.5 years) randomly selected from a group of men who were having their driver's licenses renewed and 290 male and 356 female residents of Eugene, Oregon (mean age = 63.7). The means for all samples ranged from 23 to 27 (with standard deviations from 15.2 to 25). For "normal" populations, the norm is approximately 25 (SD = 20).

SCORING The SCS is scored by first reverse-scoring items 4, 6, 8, 9, 14, 16, 18, 19, 21, 29, and 35, and then summing all individual items. The total score of the scale could range from −108 (36×−3) to +108 (36×+3).

RELIABILITY The SCS has good to excellent internal consistency, with alphas that range from .72 to .91. The SCS also has good to excellent stability, with test-retest correlations for 11 months of .77 and for four weeks of .86.

VALIDITY The SCS has good construct validity with correlations in predicted directions with Rotter's Internal-External Scale, the Irrational Beliefs Test, and some subscales of the MMPI and the G Factor (measuring self-control as a personality pattern) of the 16 PF.

PRIMARY REFERENCE Rosenbaum, M. (1980). A schedule for assessing self-control behaviors: Preliminary findings, *Behavior Therapy*, 11, 109–121. Instrument reprinted by permission of publisher and author.

AVAILABILITY Dr. Michael Rosenbaum, Department of Psychology, Tel Aviv University, Tel Aviv 69978, Israel. Email: miker@post.tau.ac.il.

Indicate how characteristic or descriptive each of the following statements is of you by using the code given below.

+3 = Very characteristic of me
+2 = Rather characteristic of me
+1 = Somewhat characteristic of me
−1 = Somewhat uncharacteristic of me
−2 = Rather uncharacteristic of me
−3 = Very uncharacteristic of me

Thank you for your cooperation

1. When I do a boring job, I think about the less boring parts of the job and about the reward I will receive when I finish.   −3 −2 −1 +1 +2 +3

2. When I have to do something that makes me anxious, I try to visualize how I will overcome my anxiety while doing it.   −3 −2 −1 +1 +2 +3

3. By changing my way of thinking, I am often able to change my feelings about almost anything.   −3 −2 −1 +1 +2 +3

4. I often find it difficult to overcome my feelings of nervousness and tension without outside help.   −3 −2 −1 +1 +2 +3

5. When I am feeling depressed, I try to think about pleasant events.   −3 −2 −1 +1 +2 +3

6. I cannot help thinking about mistakes I made.   −3 −2 −1 +1 +2 +3

7. When I am faced with a difficult problem, I try to approach it in a systematic way.   −3 −2 −1 +1 +2 +3

8. I usually do what I am supposed to do more quickly when someone is pressuring me.   −3 −2 −1 +1 +2 +3

9. When I am faced with a difficult decision, I prefer to postpone it even if I have all the facts.   −3 −2 −1 +1 +2 +3

10. When I have difficulty concentrating on my reading, I look for ways to increase my concentration.   −3 −2 −1 +1 +2 +3

11. When I plan to work, I remove everything that is not relevant to my work.   −3 −2 −1 +1 +2 +3

12. When I try to get rid of a bad habit, I first try to find out all the reasons why I have the habit.   −3 −2 −1 +1 +2 +3

13. When an unpleasant thought is bothering me, I try to think about something pleasant.   −3 −2 −1 +1 +2 +3

14. If I smoked two packs of cigarettes a day, I would need outside help to stop smoking.   −3 −2 −1 +1 +2 +3

15. When I feel down, I try to act cheerful so that my mood will change.   −3 −2 −1 +1 +2 +3

16. If I have tranquilizers with me, I would take one whenever I feel tense and nervous.　　−3 −2 −1 +1 +2 +3

17. When I am depressed, I try to keep myself busy with things I like.　　−3 −2 −1 +1 +2 +3

18. I tend to postpone unpleasant tasks even if I could perform them immediately.　　−3 −2 −1 +1 +2 +3

19. I need outside help to get rid of some of my bad habits.　　−3 −2 −1 +1 +2 +3

20. When I find it difficult to settle down and do a task, I look for ways to help me settle down.　　−3 −2 −1 +1 +2 +3

21. Although it makes me feel bad, I cannot help thinking about all sorts of possible catastrophes.　　−3 −2 −1 +1 +2 +3

22. I prefer to finish a job that I have to do before I start doing things I really like.　　−3 −2 −1 +1 +2 +3

23. When I feel physical pain, I try not to think about it.　　−3 −2 −1 +1 +2 +3

24. My self-esteem increases when I am able to overcome a bad habit.　　−3 −2 −1 +1 +2 +3

25. To overcome bad feelings that accompany failure, I often tell myself that it is not catastrophic and I can do anything.　　−3 −2 −1 +1 +2 +3

26. When I feel that I am too impulsive, I tell myself to stop and think before I do something about it.　　−3 −2 −1 +1 +2 +3

27. Even when I am terribly angry at someone, I consider my actions very carefully.　　−3 −2 −1 +1 +2 +3

28. Facing the need to make a decision, I usually look for different alternatives instead of deciding quickly and spontaneously.　　−3 −2 −1 +1 +2 +3

29. Usually, I first do the thing I really like to do even if there are more urgent things to do.　　−3 −2 −1 +1 +2 +3

30. When I realize that I am going to be unavoidably late for an important meeting, I tell myself to keep calm.　　−3 −2 −1 +1 +2 +3

31. When I feel pain in my body, I try to divert my thoughts from it.　　−3 −2 −1 +1 +2 +3

32. When I am faced with a number of things to do, I usually plan my work.　　−3 −2 −1 +1 +2 +3

33. When I am short of money, I decide to record all my expenses in order to budget more carefully in the future.　　−3 −2 −1 +1 +2 +3

34. If I find it difficult to concentrate on a task, I divide it into smaller segments.　　−3 −2 −1 +1 +2 +3

35. Quite often, I cannot overcome unpleasant thoughts that bother me.　　−3 −2 −1 +1 +2 +3

36. When I am hungry and I have no opportunity to eat, I try to divert my thoughts from my stomach or try to imagine that I am satisfied.　　−3 −2 −1 +1 +2 +3

Self-Efficacy Scale (SES)

PURPOSE To measure general levels of belief in one's own competence.

AUTHORS Mark Sherer, James E. Maddux, Blaise Mercandante, Steven Prentice-Dunn, Beth Jacobs, and Ronald W. Rogers.

DESCRIPTION The SES is a 30-item instrument that measures general expectations of self-efficacy that are not tied to specific situations or behavior. The assumptions underlying this instrument are that personal expectations of mastery are a major determinant of behavioral change, and that individual differences in past experiences and attributions of success lead to different levels of generalized self-efficacy expectations. Thus, this instrument may be useful in tailoring the course of clinical intervention to the client's needs, and also as an index of progress since expectations of self-efficacy should change during the course of intervention. The SES consists of two subscales, general self-efficacy (items 2, 3, 4, 7, 8, 11, 12, 15, 16, 18, 20, 22, 23, 26, 27, 29, 30) and social self-efficacy (items 6, 10, 14, 19, 24, 28).

NORMS The initial studies of the SES involved 376 undergraduate students in introductory psychology classes and 150 inpatients from a Veterans Administration alcohol treatment unit. No other demographic data were provided nor were actual norms for these groups.

SCORING Seven items (1, 5, 9, 13, 17, 21, 25) are filler items and are not scored. After items presented in a negative fashion (3, 6, 7, 8, 11, 14, 18, 20, 22, 24, 26, 29, 30) are reverse-scored, the scores for all items are summed. Before reverse-scoring, the answers are keyed as follows: A=1, B=2, C=3, D=4, E=5. The higher the score, the higher the self-efficacy expectations.

RELIABILITY The SES has fairly good internal consistency, with alphas of .86 for the general subscale and .71 for the social subscale. No test-retest data were reported.

VALIDITY The SES was shown to have good criterion-related validity by accurately predicting that people with higher self-efficacy would have greater success than those who score low in self-efficacy in past vocational, educational, and monetary goals. The SES also has demonstrated construct validity by correlating significantly in predicted directions with a number of measures such as the Ego Strength Scale, the Interpersonal Competency Scale, and the Rosenberg Self-Esteem Scale.

PRIMARY REFERENCE Sherer, M., Maddox, J. E., Mercandante, B., Prentice-Dunn, S., Jacobs, B., and Rogers, R. W. (1982). The Self-Efficacy Scale: Construction and validation, *Psychological Reports*, 51, 663–671. Instrument reproduced with permission of Mark Sherer and Ronald W. Rogers and Psychological Reports.

AVAILABILITY Dr. Mark Sherer, Methodist Rehabilitation Center, 1350 E. Woodrow Wilson Blvd., Jackson, MS, 39216. Telephone: 601.981.2611 or 800.223.6672.

This questionnaire is a series of statements about your personal attitudes and traits. Each statement represents a commonly held belief. Read each statement and decide to what extent it describes you. There are no right or wrong answers. You will probably agree with some of the statements and disagree with others. Please indicate your own personal feelings about each statement below by marking the letter that best describes your attitude or feeling. Please be very truthful and describe yourself as you really are, not as you would like to be.

A = Disagree strongly
B = Disagree moderately
C = Neither agree nor disagree
D = Agree moderately
E = Agree strongly

___ 1. I like to grow house plants.
___ 2. When I make plans, I am certain I can make them work.
___ 3. One of my problems is that I cannot get down to work when I should.
___ 4. If I can't do a job the first time, I keep trying until I can.
___ 5. Heredity plays the major role in determining one's personality.
___ 6. It is difficult for me to make new friends.
___ 7. When I set important goals for myself, I rarely achieve them.
___ 8. I give up on things before completing them.
___ 9. I like to cook.
___ 10. If I see someone I would like to meet, I go to that person instead of waiting for him or her to come to me.
___ 11. I avoid facing difficulties.
___ 12. If something looks too complicated, I will not even bother to try it.
___ 13. There is some good in everybody.
___ 14. If I meet someone interesting who is very hard to make friends with, I'll soon stop trying to make friends with that person.
___ 15. When I have something unpleasant to do, I stick to it until I finish it.
___ 16. When I decide to do something, I go right to work on it.
___ 17. I like science.
___ 18. When trying to learn something new, I soon give up if I am not initially successful.
___ 19. When I'm trying to become friends with someone who seems uninterested at first, I don't give up very easily.
___ 20. When unexpected problems occur, I don't handle them well.
___ 21. If I were an artist, I would like to draw children.
___ 22. I avoid trying to learn new things when they look too difficult for me.
___ 23. Failure just makes me try harder.
___ 24. I do not handle myself well in social gatherings.
___ 25. I very much like to ride horses.
___ 26. I feel insecure about my ability to do things.
___ 27. I am a self-reliant person.
___ 28. I have acquired my friends through my personal abilities at making friends.
___ 29. I give up easily.
___ 30. I do not seem capable of dealing with most problems that come up in my life.

Self-Efficacy Scale for Schizophrenics (SESS)

PURPOSE To measure self-efficacy for persons with schizophrenia.

AUTHOR Barbara McDermott

DESCRIPTION This 57-item instrument assesses self-efficacy in persons with schizophrenia or schizophrenic-like disorders. Self-efficacy is defined with the SESS as an individual's belief that he or she has the psychological, biological, cognitive, and social capacity to execute a desired behavior. The theory of self-efficacy holds that the expectation of being efficacious is related to social skills and competence. Self-efficacy, in turn, is enhanced by the reciprocal determinism found with accomplishments. Self-efficacy has been shown to moderate the effects of depression and coping responses for persons with severe and persistent schizophrenic disorders. The SESS was developed from a pool of 91 items, and items were selected by consensus in a panel of mental health professionals. The SESS is composed of three subscales: positive symptoms (PS), negative symptoms (NS), and social skills (SS). The SESS may be used as a total score or subscale scores.

NORMS Normative data are available from a sample of 42 persons assessed on two occasions. The averages for the PS, NS, and SS at the first assessment period were 74.46, 76.95, and 71.75, respectively. The scores were 77.96, 78.91, and 74.84 for the PS, NS, and SS at a second assessment two weeks later. The average total score was 74.39 at the first administration and 77.23 at the second.

SCORING Scores on the PS subscale are the average of items 8, 11, 12, 15–18, 25, 27–29, 31, 33, 42, 43, 46, 50, 54, and 56. NS subscale scores are the average of items 2, 6, 9, 10, 14, 19, 20, 21, 23, 32, 35, 36, 37, 39, 45, 48, 49, 53, and 57. SS subscale scores are the average of items 1, 3, 4, 5, 7, 13, 21, 24, 26, 30, 34, 38, 40, 41, 44, 47, 51, 52, and 55. Scores range from 0 to 100, and higher scores indicate more self-efficacy.

RELIABILITY The internal consistency coefficients of the PS, NS, and SS are excellent: .95, .93, and .92, respectively. The test-retest reliability ranged from .799 to .862 for the subscale scores and .876 for total scores, suggesting the SESS is stable over a two-week period.

VALIDITY The SESS has good criterion-related validity. Scores on the PS, NS, and SS correlated with the number of hospitalizations, and the NS and SS correlated with length of one's illness. SESS subscale scores also correlated with self-esteem, while PS scores were associated with locus of control.

PRIMARY REFERENCE McDermott, B. E. (1995). Development of an instrument for assessing self-efficacy in schizophrenic spectrum disorders, *Journal of Clinical Psychology*, 51, 320–331. The SESS was developed with support from the Ohio Department of Mental Health, grant number 88.1011.

AVAILABILITY Barbara McDermott, Ph.D., School of Medicine, Tulane University Medical Center, 1440 Canal Street, New Orleans, LA 70122-2715.

On the following pages are descriptions of behaviors. People with emotional disorders (past or present) sometimes consider these behaviors to be difficult for them. You will be asked to read each statement and circle the number that best describes how confident you are in your ability to do each one, on a scale from 0 to 100 in the following manner:

0 - - - 10 - - - 20 - - - 30 - - - 40 - - - 50 - - - 60 - - - 70 - - - 80 - - - 90 - - - 100

No
confidence

Total
confidence

A score of 0% means that you have no confidence in your ability to do the task or behavior. A score of 100% means that you feel totally confident in your ability. All listed numbers between 0 and 100 may be used to accurately express your feeling of confidence in your abilities. For example, if you think that you can *probably* do the specific task with a great deal of effort, and you are still unsure, you might rate your confidence as 10 or 20%. In contrast, if you are generally fairly sure, but are not 100% certain, you might rate your confidence as 70 or 80%. Remember, all numbers between 0 and 100 listed on the scale may be used. Try to rate each item according to how you feel about your ability to do it, whether or not you are doing each one at this time.

Please read each statement carefully and circle the number that most accurately describes your feeling of confidence in your ability to do each one. Although you may feel that some items do not apply to you, try to imagine how you would rate your confidence if they did apply. REMEMBER: all listed numbers between 0 and 100 can be used.

How confident are you in your ability to:

1. Go out on a date.

   0 — 10 — 20 — 30 — 40 — 50 — 60 — 70 — 80 — 90 — 100

2. Use your free time for activities other than watching TV.

   0 — 10 — 20 — 30 — 40 — 50 — 60 — 70 — 80 — 90 — 100

3. Go to a party with friends.

   0 — 10 — 20 — 30 — 40 — 50 — 60 — 70 — 80 — 90 — 100

4. Ask someone out on a date.

   0 — 10 — 20 — 30 — 40 — 50 — 60 — 70 — 80 — 90 — 100

5. Go out when a friend calls and invites you.

   0 — 10 — 20 — 30 — 40 — 50 — 60 — 70 — 80 — 90 — 100

6. Get regular exercise.

   0 — 10 — 20 — 30 — 40 — 50 — 60 — 70 — 80 — 90 — 100

7. Ask a friend for advice.

   0 — 10 — 20 — 30 — 40 — 50 — 60 — 70 — 80 — 90 — 100

8. Stop thoughts that others are controlling what you think.

   0 — 10 — 20 — 30 — 40 — 50 — 60 — 70 — 80 — 90 — 100

9. Go to a job interview.

   0 — 10 — 20 — 30 — 40 — 50 — 60 — 70 — 80 — 90 — 100

10. Go shopping for clothes.

    0 — 10 — 20 — 30 — 40 — 50 — 60 — 70 — 80 — 90 — 100

11. Stop feelings of being frightened of people.

    0 — 10 — 20 — 30 — 40 — 50 — 60 — 70 — 80 — 90 — 100

12. Stop any feeling that your insides are rotting.

    0 — 10 — 20 — 30 — 40 — 50 — 60 — 70 — 80 — 90 — 100

13. Have your family visit you.

    0 — 10 — 20 — 30 — 40 — 50 — 60 — 70 — 80 — 90 — 100

14. Go shopping for groceries.

    0 — 10 — 20 — 30 — 40 — 50 — 60 — 70 — 80 — 90 — 100

15. Stop any feeling that your mind is racing.

    0 — 10 — 20 — 30 — 40 — 50 — 60 — 70 — 80 — 90 — 100

16. Ignore feelings of wanting to kill yourself.

    0 — 10 — 20 — 30 — 40 — 50 — 60 — 70 — 80 — 90 — 100

17. Stop yourself from hurting someone.

    0 — 10 — 20 — 30 — 40 — 50 — 60 — 70 — 80 — 90 — 100

18. Stop any feeling that the TV is communicating with you.

    0 — 10 — 20 — 30 — 40 — 50 — 60 — 70 — 80 — 90 — 100

19. Attend classes.

    0 — 10 — 20 — 30 — 40 — 50 — 60 — 70 — 80 — 90 — 100

20. Concentrate when you read.

    0 — 10 — 20 — 30 — 40 — 50 — 60 — 70 — 80 — 90 — 100

21. Remember to pay your bills.

    0 — 10 — 20 — 30 — 40 — 50 — 60 — 70 — 80 — 90 — 100

22. Trust your friends.

    0 — 10 — 20 — 30 — 40 — 50 — 60 — 70 — 80 — 90 — 100

23. Go out even if you don't want to.

    0 — 10 — 20 — 30 — 40 — 50 — 60 — 70 — 80 — 90 — 100

24. Trust your family.

    0 — 10 — 20 — 30 — 40 — 50 — 60 — 70 — 80 — 90 — 100

25. Get rid of bad thoughts or ideas.

    0 — 10 — 20 — 30 — 40 — 50 — 60 — 70 — 80 — 90 — 100

26. Get along with your neighbors.

    0 — 10 — 20 — 30 — 40 — 50 — 60 — 70 — 80 — 90 — 100

27. Stop feelings of fearfulness.

    0 — 10 — 20 — 30 — 40 — 50 — 60 — 70 — 80 — 90 — 100

28. Stop feelings of nervousness or shakiness.

    0 — 10 — 20 — 30 — 40 — 50 — 60 — 70 — 80 — 90 — 100

29. Stop thoughts that you can control what others think.

    0 — 10 — 20 — 30 — 40 — 50 — 60 — 70 — 80 — 90 — 100

30. Visit your family.

    0 — 10 — 20 — 30 — 40 — 50 — 60 — 70 — 80 — 90 — 100

31. Ignore bad thoughts or ideas.

    0 — 10 — 20 — 30 — 40 — 50 — 60 — 70 — 80 — 90 — 100

32. Accomplish your occupational goals.

    0 — 10 — 20 — 30 — 40 — 50 — 60 — 70 — 80 — 90 — 100

33. Stop feelings of irritability or anger.

    0 — 10 — 20 — 30 — 40 — 50 — 60 — 70 — 80 — 90 — 100

34. Find someone to talk to when you feel lonely.

    0 — 10 — 20 — 30 — 40 — 50 — 60 — 70 — 80 — 90 — 100

35. Look for a job in the newspaper.

    0 — 10 — 20 — 30 — 40 — 50 — 60 — 70 — 80 — 90 — 100

36. Remember to take your medications.

    0 — 10 — 20 — 30 — 40 — 50 — 60 — 70 — 80 — 90 — 100

37. Enroll in a class you are interested in.

    0 — 10 — 20 — 30 — 40 — 50 — 60 — 70 — 80 — 90 — 100

38. Make friends.

    0 — 10 — 20 — 30 — 40 — 50 — 60 — 70 — 80 — 90 — 100

39. Concentrate on your work.

    0 — 10 — 20 — 30 — 40 — 50 — 60 — 70 — 80 — 90 — 100

40. Begin a conversation with a friend.

    0 — 10 — 20 — 30 — 40 — 50 — 60 — 70 — 80 — 90 — 100

41. Talk to people in a group.

    0 — 10 — 20 — 30 — 40 — 50 — 60 — 70 — 80 — 90 — 100

42. Get rid of feelings of wanting to kill yourself.

    0 — 10 — 20 — 30 — 40 — 50 — 60 — 70 — 80 — 90 — 100

43. Stop any feeling that others are watching you.

    0 — 10 — 20 — 30 — 40 — 50 — 60 — 70 — 80 — 90 — 100

44. Call and ask a friend to go out.

    0 — 10 — 20 — 30 — 40 — 50 — 60 — 70 — 80 — 90 — 100

45. Get out of the house enough to stay active.

      0 — 10 — 20 — 30 — 40 — 50 — 60 — 70 — 80 — 90 — 100

46. Ignore voices you might hear.

      0 — 10 — 20 — 30 — 40 — 50 — 60 — 70 — 80 — 90 — 100

47. Have sex with someone in a way that you and the other person can enjoy.

      0 — 10 — 20 — 30 — 40 — 50 — 60 — 70 — 80 — 90 — 100

48. Make decisions.

      0 — 10 — 20 — 30 — 40 — 50 — 60 — 70 — 80 — 90 — 100

49. Keep your living quarters clean.

      0 — 10 — 20 — 30 — 40 — 50 — 60 — 70 — 80 — 90 — 100

50. Stop thoughts that outside forces are controlling your behavior.

      0 — 10 — 20 — 30 — 40 — 50 — 60 — 70 — 80 — 90 — 100

51. Introduce yourself to someone you don't know.

      0 — 10 — 20 — 30 — 40 — 50 — 60 — 70 — 80 — 90 — 100

52. Shake hands when you meet someone.

      0 — 10 — 20 — 30 — 40 — 50 — 60 — 70 — 80 — 90 — 100

53. Maintain interest in your job or schoolwork.

      0 — 10 — 20 — 30 — 40 — 50 — 60 — 70 — 80 — 90 — 100

54. Ignore any feeling that someone may be trying to hurt you.

      0 — 10 — 20 — 30 — 40 — 50 — 60 — 70 — 80 — 90 — 100

55. Begin a conversation with a stranger.

      0 — 10 — 20 — 30 — 40 — 50 — 60 — 70 — 80 — 90 — 100

56. Control your temper.

      0 — 10 — 20 — 30 — 40 — 50 — 60 — 70 — 80 — 90 — 100

57. Enjoy things as much as others do.

      0 — 10 — 20 — 30 — 40 — 50 — 60 — 70 — 80 — 90 — 100

Self-Esteem Rating Scale (SERS)

PURPOSE To measure self-esteem.

AUTHORS William R. Nugent and Janita W. Thomas

DESCRIPTION The SERS is a 40-item instrument that was developed to provide a clinical measure of self-esteem that can indicate not only problems in self-esteem but also positive or nonproblematic levels. The items were written to tap into a range of areas of self-evaluation including overall self-worth, social competence, problem-solving ability, intellectual ability, self-competence, and worth relative to other people. The SERS is a very useful instrument for measuring both positive and negative aspects of self-esteem in clinical practice.

NORMS The SERS was studied initially with two samples. Sample 1 contained 246 people, of whom 91 were male and 155 female, with an average age of 32.5 years and an average of 15.7 years of formal education. Thirty-one percent were white, 11.8% black, 4.5% Hispanic, 7.7% Asian, and the rest were mixed or other groups. Sample 2 involved 107 people including 23 males and 84 females, with an average of 15.3 years of education; 93.5% were white, 4.7% black, and the rest in other groups. Actual norms were not available.

SCORING The SERS is scored by scoring the items shown at the bottom of the measure as p/+ positively, and scoring the remaining items (N/–) negatively by placing a minus sign in front of the item score. The items are summed to produce a total score ranging from –120 to +120. Positive scores indicate more positive self-esteem and negative scores indicate more negative levels of self-esteem.

RELIABILITY The SERS has excellent internal consistency, with an alpha of .97. The standard error of measurement was 5.67. Data on stability were not reported.

VALIDITY The SERS was reported as having good content and factorial validity. The SERS has good construct validity, with significant correlations with the Index of Self-Esteem and the Generalized Contentment Scale (a measure of depression) as predicted, and generally low correlations with a variety of demographic variables, also as predicted.

PRIMARY REFERENCE Nugent, W. R., and Thomas J. W. (1993). Validation of the Self-Esteem Rating Scale, *Research on Social Work Practice*, 3, 191–207.

AVAILABILITY May be copied from this volume.

This questionnaire is designed to measure how you feel about yourself. It is not a test, so there are no right or wrong answers. Please answer each item as carefully and accurately as you can by placing a number by each one as follows:

1 = Never
2 = Rarely
3 = A little of the time
4 = Some of the time
5 = A good part of the time
6 = Most of the time
7 = Always

Please begin.

___ 1. I feel that people would *NOT* like me if they really knew me well.
___ 2. I feel that others do things much better than I do.
___ 3. I feel that I am an attractive person.
___ 4. I feel confident in my ability to deal with other people.
___ 5. I feel that I am likely to fail at things I do.
___ 6. I feel that people really like to talk with me.
___ 7. I feel that I am a very competent person.
___ 8. When I am with other people I feel that they are glad I am with them.
___ 9. I feel that I make a good impression on others.
___ 10. I feel confident that I can begin new relationships if I want to.
___ 11. I feel that I am ugly.
___ 12. I feel that I am a boring person.
___ 13. I feel very nervous when I am with strangers.
___ 14. I feel confident in my ability to learn new things.
___ 15. I feel good about myself.
___ 16. I feel ashamed about myself.
___ 17. I feel inferior to other people.
___ 18. I feel that my friends find me interesting.
___ 19. I feel that I have a good sense of humor.
___ 20. I get angry at myself over the way I am.
___ 21. I feel relaxed meeting new people.
___ 22. I feel that other people are smarter than I am.
___ 23. I do *NOT* like myself.
___ 24. I feel confident in my ability to cope with difficult situations.
___ 25. I feel that I am *NOT* very likeable.
___ 26. My friends value me a lot.
___ 27. I feel afraid I will appear stupid to others.
___ 28. I feel that I am an OK person.
___ 29. I feel that I can count on myself to manage things well.
___ 30. I wish I could just disappear when I am around other people.
___ 31. I feel embarrassed to let others hear my ideas.
___ 32. I feel that I am a nice person.

___ 33. I feel that if I could be more like other people then I would feel *better* about myself.

___ 34. I feel that I get pushed around more than others.

___ 35. I feel that people like me.

___ 36. I feel that people have a good time when they are with me.

___ 37. I feel confident that I can do well in whatever I do.

___ 38. I trust the competence of others more than I trust my own abilities.

___ 39. I feel that I mess things up.

___ 40. I wish that I were someone else.

(p/+)   3,4,6,7,8,9,10,14,15,18,19,21,24,26,28,29,32,35,36,37.

(N/−)   1,2,5,11,12,13,16,17,20,22,23,25,27,30,31,33,34,38,39,40.

Self-Harm Behavior Questionnaire (SHBQ)

PURPOSE To measure suicidal behaviors and thoughts.

AUTHORS Peter M. Gutierrez et al.

DESCRIPTION The SHBQ is a 5-item questionnaire, with numerous secondary items, for a total of 26 items, that is designed to measure suicide-related behaviors and thoughts about suicide. The SHBQ was developed as a compromise between information obtained in interviews and other less efficient standardized measures. The SHBQ is divided into four sections: intentional self-harm questions not identified by the respondent as suicidal, suicide attempts, suicide threats, and suicide ideation. Each section contains follow-up questions to determine the specific type of behavior, thought, or verbalization being reported, along with information on intent, lethality and outcome. The four sections of the SHBQ correspond to four factors: Self Harm Behavior (SHB; the questions in item 1); Past Suicide Attempts (SA; the questions in items 2 and 3); Suicide Threat (ST; the questions in item 4); and Suicide Ideation (SI; the questions in item 5). The SHBQ was developed for both research and clinical purposes.

NORMS The SHBQ was developed on a sample of 202 female and 140 male undergraduate psychology students. The mean age was 19.48 (SD=1.52), with 98.2% of the sample being single and 95.9% being white. Actual norms were not provided. There were small but significant differences between male and female respondents on three of the four subscales, with women scoring higher on all but the SHB.

SCORING The SHBQ has specific instructions for scoring responses including coding of the written responses. These instructions and score sheets are available from the authors (see "Availability").

RELIABILITY The SHBQ has excellent internal consistency, with alphas on three scales in the mid-.90s and an alpha for ST of .89. Data on stability were not provided.

VALIDITY The SHBQ has excellent convergent validity with significant correlations among the subscales of the SHBQ and several other measures of suicide behavior and ideation as well as the Beck Depression Inventory. The ST and SI also significantly predicted scores on the Suicide Probability Scale.

PRIMARY REFERENCE Gutierrez, P. M., et al. (2001). Development and initial validation of the Self-Harm Behavior Questionnaire, *Journal of Personality Assessment, 77,* 475–490. Instrument reproduced with permission of Dr. Gutierrez.

AVAILABILITY Dr. Peter M. Gutierrez, Department of Psychology, Northern Illinois University, DeKalb, IL 60115-2892, or email pqut@niu.edu.

SHBQ

A lot of people do things which are dangerous and might get them hurt. There are many reasons why people take these risks. Often people take risks without thinking about the fact that they might get hurt. Sometimes, however, people hurt themselves on purpose. We are interested in learning more about the ways in which you may have intentionally or unintentionally hurt yourself. We are also interested in trying to understand why people your age may do some of these dangerous things. It is important for you to understand that if you tell us about things you've done which may have been unsafe or make it possible that you may not be able to keep yourself safe, we will encourage you to discuss this with a counselor or other confidant in order to keep you safe in the future. Please circle **YES** or **NO** in response to each question and answer the follow-up questions. For questions where you are asked whom you told something to, do not give specific names. We only want to know if it was someone like a parent, teacher, doctor, etc.

Things you may have actually done to yourself on purpose.

1. Have you ever hurt yourself on purpose? (e.g., scratched yourself with finger nails or sharp object.) **YES**   **NO**

    If no, go on to question #2.

    If yes, what did you do? _____

    _____

    _____

    _____

    a. Approximately how many times did you do this? _____

    b. Approximately when did you first do this to yourself? *(write your age)* _____

    c. When was the last time you did this to yourself? *(write your age)* _____

    d. Have you ever told anyone that you had done these things?   **YES**   **NO**

        If yes, whom did you tell?_____

    e. Have you ever needed to see a doctor after doing these things? **YES**   **NO**

Times you hurt yourself badly on purpose or tried to kill yourself.

2. Have you ever attempted suicide? **YES**   **NO**

    If no, go on to question # 4.

    If yes, how? _____

    _____

    (**Note:** if you took pills, what kind? _____; how many? _____; over how long a period of time did you take them? _____)

continued

a. How many times have you attempted suicide? _____

b. When was the most recent attempt? *(write your age)* _____

c. Did you tell anyone about the attempt?   **YES**   **NO**

  Who? _____

d. Did you require medical attention after the attempt?   **YES**   **NO**

   If yes, were you hospitalized overnight or longer?   **YES**   **NO**

   How long were you hospitalized? _____

e. Did you talk to a counselor or some other person like that after your attempt?

   YES   **NO**   Who? _____

3. If you attempted suicide, please answer the following:

   a. What other things were going on in your life around the time that you tried to kill yourself? _____

   _____

   _____

   b. Did you actually want to die?   **YES**   **NO**

   c. Were you hoping for a specific reaction to your attempt?   **YES**   **NO**

      If yes, what was the reaction you were looking for? _____

      _____

      _____

      _____

   d. Did you get the reaction you wanted?   **YES**   **NO**

      If you *didn't*, what type of reaction was there to your attempt? _____

      _____

      _____

   e. Who knew about your attempt? _____

Times you threatened to hurt yourself badly or try to kill yourself.

4. Have you ever threatened to commit suicide?   **YES**   **NO**

   If no, go on to question # 5.

   If yes, what did you threaten to do? _____

   _____

   a. Approximately how many times did you do this? _____

   b. Approximately when did you first do this? *(write your age)* _____

c. When was the last time you did this? *(write your age)* _____

d. Whom did you make the threats to? (e.g., mom, dad) _____

e. What other things were going on in your life during the time that you were threatening to kill yourself? _____

_____

_____

f. Did you actually want to die?   **YES**   **NO**

g. Were you hoping for a specific reaction to your threat?   **YES**   **NO**

If yes, what was the reaction you were looking for? _____

_____

_____

_____

h. Did you get the reaction you wanted?   **YES**   **NO**

If you didn't, what type of reaction was there to your attempt? _____

_____

_____

5. Have you ever talked or thought about:

—wanting to die   **YES**   **NO**

—committing suicide   **YES**   **NO**

a. What did you talk about doing? _____

_____

_____

b. With whom did you discuss this? _____

c. What made you feel like doing that? _____

_____

_____

_____

d. Did you have a specific plan for how you would try to kill yourself?

YES   **NO**

If yes, what plan did you have? _____

_____

_____

_____

continued

736

f. In looking back, how did you imagine people would react to your attempt? _____

_____

_____

_____

g. Did you think about how people would react if you did succeed in killing yourself?

YES   NO

If yes, how did you think they would react? _____

_____

_____

h. Did you ever take steps to prepare for this plan?   **YES   NO**

If yes, what did you do to prepare? _____

_____

_____

Self-Help Agency Satisfaction Scale (SHASS)

PURPOSE To measure client satisfaction with self-help agencies.

AUTHORS Steven P. Segal, Dina Redman, and Carol Silverman

DESCRIPTION The SHASS is an 11-item scale designed to measure consumers' satisfaction with self-help services and their involvement in treatment decisions. Because of the increasing use of mental health agencies operated largely by consumers with psychiatric disabilities, the authors believed that it is important to develop an outcome tool that was specific to such agencies. Prior research has shown that there are two essential factors in outcomes from the point of view of psychiatric consumers: behavioral autonomy (helping consumers become actively involved in their own care) and supportive care. The SHASS thus was designed to reflect these two dimensions. The SHASS can be used as an overall scale or as two subscales: Involvement, which measures satisfaction with active involvement in the agency (items 7–11), and Service, which measures satisfaction with the services or support received (items 1–6).

NORMS The SHASS was developed in a study of 310 baseline and 248 follow-up interviews with clients of four urban self-help agencies. The mean age of the 310 participants was 38 (SD=8.4). 222 (72%) of the respondents were male and 269 (87%) had confirmed DSM-III-R diagnoses. Almost half of the respondents (44%) were living in a shelter or on the streets while many of the remaining respondents were in "unstable" housing. Actual norms were not reported.

SCORING The SHASS is scored by simply summing individual items on the subscales and the total scale. The range for the total scale is from 11 to 55, and on all scales, higher scores mean greater satisfaction.

RELIABILITY The SHASS has excellent internal consistency with alphas that range from .87 to .93 across the total scale and subscales. The SHASS also has excellent stability with 6-month test-retest correlations that range from .44 for the Involvement subscale to .61 for the total scale.

VALIDITY The SHASS has good concurrent and predictive ability with baseline scores of the Service subscale significantly correlated with four measures of social functioning, psychiatric symptoms, and personal empowerment. The Involvement subscale was significantly correlated with one social functioning scale and personal empowerment.

PRIMARY REFERENCE Segal, S. P., Redman, D., & Silverman, C. (2000). Measuring clients' satisfaction with self-help agencies. *Psychiatric Services, 51*, 1148–1152. Instrument reproduced by permission of Dr. Steven Segal.

AVAILABILITY Dr. Steven Segal, Professor and Director, Mental Health and Social Welfare Research Group, School of Social Welfare, 120 Haviland Hall, Berkeley, CA 94720. Email: spsegal@berkeley.edu.

Keep thinking about your experiences at (agency name) and tell me how satisfied you are (about):

1. How much you get to make decisions about the services at (agency name).
   5. Very satisfied
   4. Satisfied
   3. About equally satisfied/dissatisfied
   2. Dissatisfied
   1. Very dissatisfied

2. How much you get to make decisions about the rules at (agency name).
   5. Very satisfied
   4. Satisfied
   3. About equally satisfied/dissatisfied
   2. Dissatisfied
   1. Very dissatisfied

3. How much you get to make decisions about the activities at (agency name).
   5. Very satisfied
   4. Satisfied
   3. About equally satisfied/dissatisfied
   2. Dissatisfied
   1. Very dissatisfied

4. How much opportunity you get to do a job at (agency name).
   5. Very satisfied
   4. Satisfied
   3. About equally satisfied/dissatisfied
   2. Dissatisfied
   1. Very dissatisfied

5. How much opportunity you get to make suggestions to the staff at (agency name).
   5. Very satisfied
   4. Satisfied
   3. About equally satisfied/dissatisfied
   2. Dissatisfied
   1. Very dissatisfied

6. With help from (agency name).
   5. Very satisfied
   4. Satisfied
   3. About equally satisfied/dissatisfied
   2. Dissatisfied
   1. Very dissatisfied

7. With extent that (agency name) meets your needs.
   5. Very satisfied
   4. Satisfied
   3. About equally satisfied/dissatisfied
   2. Dissatisfied
   1. Very dissatisfied

8. With the help you get from (agency name) coping with problems.
   5. Very satisfied
   4. Satisfied
   3. About equally satisfied/dissatisfied
   2. Dissatisfied
   1. Very dissatisfied

9. With the emotional support you get from (agency name).
   5. Very satisfied
   4. Satisfied
   3. About equally satisfied/dissatisfied
   2. Dissatisfied
   1. Very dissatisfied

10. With the material support you get from (agency name).
    5. Very satisfied
    4. Satisfied
    3. About equally satisfied/dissatisfied
    2. Dissatisfied
    1. Very dissatisfied

11. With counseling you get at (agency name).
    5. Very satisfied
    4. Satisfied
    3. About equally satisfied/dissatisfied
    2. Dissatisfied
    1. Very dissatisfied

Self-Rating Anxiety Scale (SAS)

PURPOSE To assess anxiety as a clinical disorder and quantify anxiety symptoms.

AUTHOR William W. K. Zung

DESCRIPTION The SAS is a 20-item instrument consisting of the most commonly found characteristics of an anxiety disorder (5 affective and 15 somatic symptoms). Five of the items are worded symptomatically positive and 15 are worded symptomatically negative; respondents use a 4-point scale to rate how each item applied to himself or herself during the past week. The author has also developed a rating scale based on the same symptoms to be used by the clinician to rate the client (Anxiety Status Inventory or ASI), thus allowing two sources of data on the same symptoms.

NORMS The initial study was carried out on 225 psychiatric patients including 152 male inpatients and 23 male and 50 female outpatients with a mean age of 41 years. An additional 100 male and female "normal" (nonpatient) subjects were part of the study. However, little formal standardization work has been carried out on the SAS.

SCORING The SAS is scored by summing the values on each item to produce a raw score ranging from 20 to 80. An SAS index is derived by dividing the raw score by 80, producing an index that ranges from .25 to 1.00 (higher scores equal more anxiety). A cutoff score of 50 is recommended, with scores over 50 suggesting the presence of clinically meaningful anxiety.

RELIABILITY Data are not available.

VALIDITY The SAS has fair concurrent validity, correlating significantly with the Taylor Manifest Anxiety Scale and with the clinician rating scale developed by the author (ASI). The SAS also has good known-groups validity, distinguishing between patients diagnosed as having anxiety disorders and those with other psychiatric diagnoses and between nonpatient and patient groups.

PRIMARY REFERENCE Zung, W. K. (1971). A rating instrument for anxiety disorders, *Psychosomatics*, 12, 371–379. Instrument reproduced by permission of W. K. Zung and *Psychosomatics*, all rights reserved.

AVAILABILITY Psykey, Inc., P.O. Box 58051, Salt Lake City, UT 84158-8051, or psykey.com. Telephone: 801.755.6339.

SAS

Below are twenty statements. Please rate each using the following scale:

1 = Some or a little of the time
2 = Some of the time
3 = Good part of the time
4 = Most or all of the time

Please record your rating in the space to the left of each item.

___ 1. I feel more nervous and anxious than usual.
___ 2. I feel afraid for no reason at all.
___ 3. I get upset easily or feel panicky.
___ 4. I feel like I'm falling apart and going to pieces.
___ 5. I feel that everything is all right and nothing bad will happen.
___ 6. My arms and legs shake and tremble.
___ 7. I am bothered by headaches, neck and back pains.
___ 8. I feel weak and get tired easily.
___ 9. I feel calm and can sit still easily.
___ 10. I can feel my heart beating fast.
___ 11. I am bothered by dizzy spells.
___ 12. I have fainting spells or feel like it.
___ 13. I can breathe in and out easily.
___ 14. I get feelings of numbness and tingling in my fingers, toes.
___ 15. I am bothered by stomachaches or indigestion.
___ 16. I have to empty my bladder often.
___ 17. My hands are usually dry and warm.
___ 18. My face gets hot and blushes.
___ 19. I fall asleep easily and get a good night's rest.
___ 20. I have nightmares.

Self-Rating Depression Scale (SDS)

PURPOSE To assess depression as a clinical disorder and quantify the symptoms of depression.

AUTHOR William W. K. Zung

DESCRIPTION The SDS is a 20-item instrument developed to examine three basic aspects of depression: (1) pervasive affect, (2) physiological concomitants, and (3) psychological concomitants. The SDS consists of 10 items worded symptomatically positive and 10 items worded symptomatically negative. Items on the SDS were specifically selected to tap one of the three aspects of depression described above and include cognitive, affective, psychomotor, somatic, and social-interpersonal items. Respondents are asked to rate each of the 20 items on a sliding scale as to how it applies to them at the time of testing. Individual item scores as well as overall scores are considered meaningful. The author suggests the following clinical cutting scores to estimate the degree of depression: 50 to 59 (mild to moderate); 60 to 69 (moderate to severe); 70 and over (severe). A test booklet is available.

NORMS Initial study of the SDS was conducted on 56 patients admitted to the psychiatric service of a hospital with a primary diagnosis of depression and 100 "normal" (nonpatient) subjects. Subsequent study of 22 samples reveals some support for the clinical cutting scores. However, little formal effort at standardization has been made.

SCORING The SDS is scored by summing the values obtained on each item to produce a raw score ranging from 20 to 80. An SDS index is produced by dividing the raw score by 80 to produce a range of .25 to 1.00 (higher scores equal greater depression).

RELIABILITY The SDS has fair internal consistency, with a split-half reliability of .73.

VALIDITY The SDS has good known-groups validity in distinguishing between depressed and nondepressed samples, and has good concurrent validity in regard to correlations with other depression measures, such as the Beck Depression Inventory and the Hamilton Rating Scale for Depression. The SDS also is reported to be sensitive to clinical changes.

PRIMARY REFERENCE Zung, W. K. (1965). A Self-Rating Depression Scale, *Archives of General Psychiatry*, 12, 63–70. Instrument reproduced with permission of W. K. Zung, all rights reserved.

AVAILABILITY Psykey, Inc., P.O. Box 58051, Salt Lake City, UT 84158-8051, or psykey.com. Telephone: 801.755.6339.

Below are twenty statements. Please rate each using the following scale:

> 1 = Some or a little of the time
> 2 = Some of the time
> 3 = Good part of the time
> 4 = Most or all of the time

Please record your rating in the space to the left of each item.

___ 1. I feel down-hearted, blue, and sad.
___ 2. Morning is when I feel the best.
___ 3. I have crying spells or feel like it.
___ 4. I have trouble sleeping through the night.
___ 5. I eat as much as I used to.
___ 6. I enjoy looking at, talking to, and being with attractive women/men.
___ 7. I notice that I am losing weight.
___ 8. I have trouble with constipation.
___ 9. My heart beats faster than usual.
___ 10. I get tired for no reason.
___ 11. My mind is as clear as it used to be.
___ 12. I find it easy to do the things I used to.
___ 13. I am restless and can't keep still.
___ 14. I feel hopeful about the future.
___ 15. I am more irritable than usual.
___ 16. I find it easy to make decisions.
___ 17. I feel that I am useful and needed.
___ 18. My life is pretty full.
___ 19. I feel that others would be better off if I were dead.
___ 20. I still enjoy the things I used to do.

Self-Righteousness Scale (SRS)

PURPOSE To measure self-righteousness.

AUTHOR Toni Falbo

DESCRIPTION This 7-item instrument measures the conviction that one's beliefs or behavior are correct, especially in comparison to alternative beliefs or behaviors. It excludes self-righteousness about political issues and focuses not on specific beliefs, but on the general characteristic of self-righteousness. The SRS is not associated with anxiety, thereby distinguishing it from similar variables such as dogmatism, which assumes the presence of anxiety. Two subscales can be formed, one measuring general self-righteousness (SR) and another measuring its opposite, acceptance (A). The SRS can be reworded to measure self-righteousness about a particular belief or behavior. It is useful in assessing communication style in clinical intervention with families and dyads as well as individuals.

NORMS One hundred and twenty respondents were involved in the development of the SRS. Fifty-four were male and 66 were female, and the subjects' ages ranged from 17 to 63 years. The total SRS scores ranged from 4 to 18 with a mean of 7.45. A second sample consisted of 70 respondents (45 males and 25 females). This sample had an age range from 17 to 45 and all were involved in a demanding 10-kilometer foot race. Pretest mean scores were 9.82. The average SRS score after completing the race was 9.07.

SCORING Each item is rated on a 5-point scale, ranging from "strongly agree" to "strongly disagree." The SR items (1, 2, 3, 4) are summed to form a total score ranging from 4 to 20. Items 3 and 4 are reverse-scored. Higher scores reflect more self-righteousness. Items 5, 6, and 7 are summed to obtain an acceptance score (A). Scores range from 3 to 15 with higher scores indicating more acceptance of others.

RELIABILITY Reliability was separately determined for the two subscales and was generally only moderate. Internal consistency using coefficient alpha was .60 and .58 for the SR and A subscales, although all items significantly correlated with subscale scores. Stability of the SR was moderate (.54) using test-retest correlations after a ten-kilometer race. While this magnitude of a test-retest reliability coefficient is only moderate, a higher correlation would not be expected since major accomplishments, such as completing a foot race, could impact upon one's level of self-righteousness.

VALIDITY Items of the SRS were selected from a pool of 100, based on ratings by 15 judges. Items were also selected on the basis of a lack of association with a measure of social desirability. Concurrent validity was evidenced with correlations between the SR and measures of dogmatism, intolerance for ambiguity, and state-trait anxiety. The acceptance subscale was not found to correlate with these validity criteria. Based on the theoretical notion that self-righteousness is a defense mechanism which is utilized less when one has accomplished a goal, scores on the SRS were found to be lower for subjects who were winners in the 10-kilometer race compared to subjects who simply completed the race or lost the race. The change from pretest to posttest for winners in the race was significant, suggesting the SRS is sensitive to measuring change.

PRIMARY REFERENCE Falbo, T., and Belk, S. S. (1985). A short scale to measure self-righteousness, *Journal of Personality Assessment*, 49, 72–77. Instrument reproduced with permission of Toni Falbo and the *Journal of Personality Assessment*.

AVAILABILITY May be copied from this volume.

Answer each item according to the following scale and record your answer to the left of each statement.

1 = Strongly agree
2 = Agree
3 = Neutral
4 = Disagree
5 = Strongly disagree

___ 1. People who disagree with me are wrong.
___ 2. I can benefit other people by telling them the right way to live.
___ 3. I am excited by the free exchange of ideas.
___ 4. I enjoy having different points of view.
___ 5. One person's opinions are just as valid as the next.
___ 6. Most people naturally do the right thing.
___ 7. People generally make few mistakes because they do know what is right or wrong.

Selfism (NS)

PURPOSE To measure narcissism.

AUTHORS E. Jerry Phares and Nancy Erskine

DESCRIPTION The NS is a 28-item scale designed to measure narcissism, referred to by developers of this instrument as "selfism." Selfism is viewed as an orientation, belief, or set affecting how one construes a whole range of situations that deal with the satisfaction of needs. A person who scores high on the NS views a large number of situations in a selfish or egocentric fashion. At the opposite end of the continuum are individuals who submerge their own satisfaction in favor of others. The NS samples beliefs across a broad range of situations and is not targeted toward a specific need area. Based on a review of the literature, impressionistic sources, and the work of cultural observers, the original 100 items were narrowed down to 28 based on low correlations with the Marlowe-Crowne Social Desirability Scale, high correlations with NS total scores, and a reasonable spread over the five response categories.

NORMS A series of studies was conducted in development of the NS. The respondents included some 548 undergraduate males and 675 undergraduate females, 71 city police, and 11 campus police. No other demographic data are available. Means for 175 college females were 76.50; for 150 college males, 77.91; for 71 city police, 75.33; and for 11 campus police, 74.73. None of these differences was statistically significant.

SCORING The NS is scored by summing the individual item scores, each of which is on a 5-point Likert-type scale, to produce a range of 28 to 140. The following are filler items, included to disguise the purpose of the scale, and are not scored: 1, 6, 8, 12, 15, 19, 23, 26, 30, 34, 38, 39.

RELIABILITY The NS has very good internal consistency, with split-half reliabilities of .84 for males and .83 for females. The NS also has excellent stability, with a four-week test-retest correlation of .91.

VALIDITY The NS has fair concurrent validity, correlating significantly with the Narcissistic Personality Inventory and the Religious Attitude Scale. Also, the NS demonstrated a form of known-groups validity by correlating positively with observers' judgments of their close friends' narcissistic characteristics. The NS also distinguished between respondents who were high and low on cynicism regarding the motives of individuals in need of help.

PRIMARY REFERENCE Phares, E. J., and Erskine, N. (1984). The measurement of selfism, *Educational and Psychological Measurement*, 44, 597–608. Instrument reproduced with permission of E. Jerry Phares.

AVAILABILITY May be copied from this volume.

Listed below are 40 statements that deal with personal attitudes and feelings about a variety of things. Obviously, there are no right or wrong answers—only opinions. Read each item and then decide how you *personally* feel. Mark your answers to the left of each item according to the following scheme:

5 = Strongly agree
4 = Mildly agree
3 = Agree and disagree equally
2 = Mildly disagree
1 = Strongly disagree

___ 1. The widespread interest in professional sports is just another example of escapism.

___ 2. In times of shortages it is sometimes necessary for one to engage in a little hoarding.

___ 3. Thinking of yourself first is no sin in this world today.

___ 4. The prospect of becoming very close to another person worries me a good bit.

___ 5. The really significant contributions in the world have very frequently been made by people who were preoccupied with themselves.

___ 6. Every older American deserves a guaranteed income to live in dignity.

___ 7. It is more important to live for yourself rather than for other people, parents, or for posterity.

___ 8. Organized religious groups are too concerned with raising funds these days.

___ 9. I regard myself as someone who looks after his/her personal interests.

___ 10. The trouble with getting too close to people is that they start making emotional demands on you.

___ 11. Having children keeps you from engaging in a lot of self-fulfilling activities.

___ 12. Many of our production problems in this country are due to the fact that workers no longer take pride in their jobs.

___ 13. It's best to live for the present and not to worry about tomorrow.

___ 14. Call it selfishness if you will, but in this world today we all have to look out for ourselves first.

___ 15. Education is too job oriented these days; there is not enough emphasis on basic education.

___ 16. It seems impossible to imagine the world without me in it.

___ 17. You can hardly overestimate the importance of selling yourself in getting ahead.

___ 18. The difficulty with marriage is that it locks you into a relationship.

___ 19. Movies emphasize sex and violence too much.

___ 20. If it feels right, it is right.

___ 21. Breaks in life are nonsense. The real story is pursuing your self-interests aggressively.

___ 22. An individual's worth will often pass unrecognized unless that person thinks of himself or herself first.

___ 23. Consumers need a stronger voice in governmental affairs.

___ 24. Getting ahead in life depends mainly on thinking of yourself first.

___ 25. In general, couples should seek a divorce when they find the marriage is not a fulfilling one.

___ 26. Too often, voting means choosing between the lesser of two evils.

_____ 27. In striving to reach one's true potential, it is sometimes necessary to worry less about other people.

_____ 28. When choosing clothes I generally consider style before matters such as comfort or durability.

_____ 29. I believe people have the right to live any damn way they please.

_____ 30. Too many people have given up reading to passively watch TV.

_____ 31. Owing money is not so bad if it's the only way one can live without depriving oneself of the good life.

_____ 32. Not enough people live for the present.

_____ 33. I don't see anything wrong with people spending a lot of time and effort on their personal appearance.

_____ 34. Physical punishment is necessary to raise children properly.

_____ 35. The Peace Corps would be a good idea if it did not delay one's getting started along the road to a personal career.

_____ 36. It simply does not pay to become sad or upset about friends, loved ones, or events that don't turn out well.

_____ 37. A definite advantage of birth control devices is that they permit sexual pleasure without the emotional responsibilities that might otherwise result.

_____ 38. Doctors seem to have forgotten that medicine involves human relations and not just prescriptions.

_____ 39. I believe that some unidentified flying objects have actually been sent from outer space to observe our culture here on earth.

_____ 40. In this world one has to look out for oneself first because nobody else will look out for you.

Semantic Differential Feeling and Mood Scales (SDFMS)

PURPOSE To measure mood states.

AUTHORS Maurice Lorr and Richard A. Wunderlich

DESCRIPTION The SDFMS is a 35-item semantic differential scale for measuring feeling and mood states. A semantic differential scale takes into account the bipolar language of nature and mood. The respondent simply checks off on a one-to-five scale which mood is closer to how he or she feels at the current time. The SDFMS has five factors with items on each factor indicated on the instrument: A=elated–depressed, B=relaxed–anxious, C=confident–unsure, D=energetic–fatigued, and E=good natured–grouchy.

NORMS The SDFMS was studied initially on two samples of high school boys totaling 210 students. No other demographic data are given nor are norms.

SCORING Each scale point is scored from 1 to 5 (from left to right on the scale). The scores on the individual scales within each factor are totaled and then divided by 7 (number of items in each factor). The scores on the five factors can be summed for an overall score.

RELIABILITY The SDFMS has fair internal consistency, with average reliability coefficients of .74. No data on stability are available.

VALIDITY The SDFMS has fair concurrent validity, with support from findings on the (unipolar) POMS that show four of the five mood states found with the SDFMS, and five out of six (bipolar) POMS scales, corresponding closely to the SDFMS.

PRIMARY REFERENCE Lorr, M., and Wunderlich, R. A. (1988). A Semantic Differential Mood Scale, *Journal of Clinical Psychology*, 44, 33–35.

AVAILABILITY May be copied from this volume.

Below are some scales that describe the feelings and moods people have. Think how you feel RIGHT NOW, that is, at the present moment. Suppose the scale contrasts *sad* and *happy*. *To which* mood are you closer? Place a check mark, ✓, in the space that describes how you feel. You can rate yourself as *quite* happy or *slightly* happy. Or, you can rate yourself *slightly* or *quite* sad. If neither word describes how you feel, place a check mark under *neutral*.

Place your check mark in the *middle* of spaces, not on the boundaries.

			Quite	Slightly	Neutral	Slightly	Quite	
(A)	1.	Dejected						Cheerful
(C)	2.	Bold						Timid
(D)	3.	Fresh						Tired
(B)	4.	Anxious						Relaxed
(E)	5.	Friendly						Hostile
(A)	6.	Low-spirited						High-spirited
(C)	7.	Strong						Weak
(D)	8.	Lively						Weary
(B)	9.	Tense						Serene
(E)	10.	Agreeable						Grouchy
(A)	11.	Gloomy						Jolly
(C)	12.	Confident						Unsure
(D)	13.	Vigorous						Exhausted
(B)	14.	Nervous						Tranquil
(E)	15.	Good-natured						Bad-tempered
(A)	16.	Sad						Happy
(C)	17.	Self-assured						Uncertain
(D)	18.	Energetic						Fatigued
(B)	19.	Shaky						Composed
(E)	20.	Sympathetic						Quarrelsome
(A)	21.	Depressed						Jubilant
(C)	22.	Forceful						Inadequate

continued

			Quite	Slightly	Neutral	Slightly	Quite	
(D)	23.	Ready-to-go						Sluggish
(B)	24.	Uneasy						Untroubled
(E)	25.	Genial						Irritable
(A)	26.	Despondent						Delighted
(C)	27.	Powerful						Incompetent
(D)	28.	Full of pep						Worn out
(B)	29.	Jittery						Calm
(E)	30.	Cordial						Angered
(A)	31.	Unhappy						Lighthearted
(C)	32.	Assertive						Docile
(D)	33.	Alert						Drowsy
(B)	34.	Worried						Carefree
(E)	35.	Amiable						Annoyed

Sensation Scale (SS)

PURPOSE To measure subjective experience of physical changes following alcohol use.

AUTHORS S. A. Maisto, V. J. Adesso, and R. Lauerman

DESCRIPTION The SS is a 26-item instrument designed to measure respondents' perceptions of physiological changes following alcohol consumption. The main purpose of the SS is to examine individuals' ability to estimate their own level of intoxication. The SS generally is used as a six-category (or factor) measure: gastrointestinal (items 1, 2, 12, 18), anesthetic (items 7, 8, 13, 14, 16, 17, 22, 23, 26), central stimulant (items 3, 9, 11, 15), impaired function (items 19, 20, 24), warmth/glow (items 4, 10, 25), and dynamic peripheral (items 5, 6, 21). The SS is recommended for use in studying changes induced by moderate alcohol intoxication, especially if a treatment goal is controlled drinking.

NORMS The SS has been studied with several samples, including 16 males and 10 females in health-related professions who claimed no drinking-related problems and 124 male undergraduates classified as moderate to heavy drinkers. No other demographic data are reported nor are actual norms.

SCORING The SS is scored easily by summing individual item scores for each of the six factors.

RELIABILITY A type of stability was determined by having subjects sort the adjectives on the SS into the six categories or factors of the instrument. This resulted in agreement ratings that ranged from 76% for the dynamic peripheral factor to 97% for the gastrointestinal factor.

VALIDITY The SS has good known-groups validity, significantly distinguishing between subjects who have consumed an alcoholic or a nonalcoholic beverage.

PRIMARY REFERENCE Maisto, S. A., Connors, G. J., Tucker, J. A., McCollam, J. B., and Adesso, V. J. (1980). Validation of the Sensation Scale: A measure of subjective physiological responses to alcohol, *Behavior Research and Therapy*, 18, 17–43.

AVAILABILITY Dr. Stephen A. Maisto, Syracuse University, Department of Psychology, 430 Huntington Hall, Syracuse, NY 13244; 960 Belmont Street, Brockton, MA 02401. Email: samaisto@syr.edu.

Please circle the number that comes closest to describing how often you've experienced each sensation.

	Not at all				Moderately				A great deal		
	0	1	2	3	4	5	6	7	8	9	10
1. Nauseous	0	1	2	3	4	5	6	7	8	9	10
2. Stomach growling	0	1	2	3	4	5	6	7	8	9	10
3. Ringing, buzzing	0	1	2	3	4	5	6	7	8	9	10
4. Face flush	0	1	2	3	4	5	6	7	8	9	10
5. Breathing changing	0	1	2	3	4	5	6	7	8	9	10
6. Body rushes	0	1	2	3	4	5	6	7	8	9	10
7. Limbs heavy	0	1	2	3	4	5	6	7	8	9	10
8. Drowsy	0	1	2	3	4	5	6	7	8	9	10
9. Light-headed	0	1	2	3	4	5	6	7	8	9	10
10. Warm	0	1	2	3	4	5	6	7	8	9	10
11. Head spinning	0	1	2	3	4	5	6	7	8	9	10
12. Burning in stomach	0	1	2	3	4	5	6	7	8	9	10
13. Face numb	0	1	2	3	4	5	6	7	8	9	10
14. Relaxed	0	1	2	3	4	5	6	7	8	9	10
15. Dizzy	0	1	2	3	4	5	6	7	8	9	10
16. Numb all over	0	1	2	3	4	5	6	7	8	9	10
17. Lips numb	0	1	2	3	4	5	6	7	8	9	10
18. Stomach bloated	0	1	2	3	4	5	6	7	8	9	10
19. Impaired writing	0	1	2	3	4	5	6	7	8	9	10
20. Impaired vision	0	1	2	3	4	5	6	7	8	9	10
21. Heartbeat changing	0	1	2	3	4	5	6	7	8	9	10
22. Heavy	0	1	2	3	4	5	6	7	8	9	10
23. Head numb	0	1	2	3	4	5	6	7	8	9	10
24. Difficulty with thinking	0	1	2	3	4	5	6	7	8	9	10
25. Cheeks warm	0	1	2	3	4	5	6	7	8	9	10
26. Tongue thicker	0	1	2	3	4	5	6	7	8	9	10

Sense of Social Support (SSS)

PURPOSE To measure social support.

AUTHORS Christyn L. Dolbier and Mary A. Steinhardt

DESCRIPTION The SSS is a 21-item scale designed to assess an individual's sense of social support, a construct that is somewhat different than other social support measures. The SSS is intended to provide a global view of a respondent's social environment, and whether that view is generally positive or negative. The SSS measures an individual's sense of both quantitative and qualitative aspects of support.

NORMS After an initial study on an earlier version of the SSS, a sample of 120 physical activity students in courses at a southwestern university was developed. Twenty-three percent of the sample was female, and the mean age was 20.9. Sixty-four point six percent of the sample were white, 16% were Hispanic, 10.1% were Asian, 5.9% were African-American, and 3.4% were other ethnicities. The mean score for this sample was 49.3 (SD = 8.8).

SCORING The SSS is easily scored by reverse-scoring items 4, 6, 12, 15, 18, 20 and 21 and then summing the scores for the total score. The scores can range from 0 to 63, with higher scores indicating a stronger (more positive) sense of social support.

RELIABILITY The SSS has very good internal consistency with an alpha of .86. The SSS also has excellent stability with 2-week test-retest reliability coefficient of .91.

VALIDITY The SSS has very good construct validity with scores correlating in predicted directions, positively and negatively, with a number of other measures including the subscales of the Social Provisions Scale, the Interpersonal Support Evaluation List and the Negative Affectivity Scale from the Positive and Negative Affect Schedule.

PRIMARY REFERENCE Dolbier, C. L., and Steinhardt, M. A. (2000). The development and validation of the Sense of Support Scale, *Behavioral Medicine, 25,* 169–179. Instrument reproduced with permission of Dr. Steinhardt.

AVAILABILITY May be copied from this volume.

Please read each of the following questions carefully. Circle the number which best describes what is generally true using the following scale:

0 = Not at all true
1 = A little true
2 = Somewhat true
3 = Completely true

1.	I participate in volunteer/service projects.	0	1	2	3
2.	I have meaningful conversations with my parents and/or siblings.	0	1	2	3
3.	I have a mentor(s) in my life I can go to for support/advice.	0	1	2	3
4.	I seldom invite others to join me in my social and/or recreational activities.(A)	0	1	2	3
5.	There is at least one person I feel a strong emotional tie with.	0	1	2	3
6.	There is no one I can trust to help solve my problems.(A)	0	1	2	3
7.	I take time to visit with my neighbors.	0	1	2	3
8.	If a crisis arose in my life, I would have the support I need from family and/or friends.	0	1	2	3
9.	I belong to a club (e.g., sports, hobbies, support group, special interests).	0	1	2	3
10.	I have friends from work that I see socially (e.g., movie, dinner, sports, etc.).	0	1	2	3
11.	I have friendships that are mutually fulfilling.	0	1	2	3
12.	There is no one I can talk to when making important decisions in my life.(A)	0	1	2	3
13.	I make an effort to keep in touch with friends.	0	1	2	3
14.	My friends and family feel comfortable asking me for help.	0	1	2	3
15.	I find it difficult to make new friends.(A)	0	1	2	3
16.	I look for opportunities to help and support others.	0	1	2	3
17.	I have a close friend(s) whom I feel comfortable sharing deeply about myself.	0	1	2	3
18.	I seldom get invited to do things with others.(A)	0	1	2	3
19.	I feel well supported by my friends and/or family.	0	1	2	3
20.	I wish I had more people in my life that enjoy the same interests and activities as I do.(A)	0	1	2	3
21.	There is no one that shares my beliefs and attitudes.(A)	0	1	2	3

Sense of Symbolic Immortality Scale (SSIS)

PURPOSE To measure the sense of one's immortality.

AUTHOR Jean-Louis Drolet

DESCRIPTION This 26-item instrument is designed to measure one's inner realization of death's inevitability as a way of deriving meaning in life. The scale is based on Robert Lifton's theory that, in contrast to viewing death as the antithesis of life, asserts that developmentally one transcends denial and fear of death and senses it as part of a continuum of life. A sense of immortality is defined as an adaptive response to the frightening reality of death. The absence of a sense of symbolic immortality is considered to thwart the capacity to derive meaning in life. The SSIS consists of five subscales in accord with Lifton's theory of the modes of experiencing symbolic immortality: biosocial mode (B=items $5+11+12+14+19+21+23+25$); creation mode (C=items $4+6+7+9+20+22+24$); spiritual mode (S=items $1+8+10+15$); transcendence mode (T=items $3+13+17+16$); and natural mode (N=items $2+16+18$). Total scale scores of the SSIS may also be used and seem to be the most valid. The SSIS may be useful for a client with an identity crisis and depression. A French version is also available.

NORMS Total scores on the SSIS have a mean of 5.1 for a sample of 151 Canadian college students. Means for the B and C subscales were 4.9 and 5.3, respectively.

SCORING Items 3, 4, 5, 6, 11, 12, 14, 17, 19, 23, and 26 are reverse-scored. Subscale scores are the sum of the subscale items divided by the number of items in the subscale. A total score is the sum of all item scores divided by 26. Scores range from 1 to 7 with higher scores indicating stronger sense of one's symbolic immortality.

RELIABILITY The 26 items of the SSIS have excellent internal consistency, with an alpha of .91. The internal consistencies of the B, C, S, T, and N subscales were .75, .82, .64, .63, and .53, respectively. Test-retest reliability of total scores was .97 for a - three-week period.

VALIDITY The SSIS has good concurrent validity, correlating negatively with death anxiety and positively with one's sense of purpose in life. As suggested by the theory, older adults have higher scores than younger adults, which supports the known-groups validity of the SSIS.

PRIMARY REFERENCE Drolet, J. L. (1990). Transcending death during early adulthood: Symbolic immortality, death anxiety, and purpose in life, *Journal of Clinical Psychology*, 46, 148–160. Instrument reproduced with permission of Jean-Louis Drolet.

AVAILABILITY Dr. Jean-Louis Drolet, Department de Counseling et Orientation, Sciences de l'Education, Universite Laval, Quebec, Canada G1K-7P4. Email: Jean-Louis.Drolet@fse.ulaval.ca.

For each of the following statements, circle the number which most corresponds to *your feelings, way of seeing things, or way of living* at this stage in your life. Please note that the numbers always range from one to seven, number 1 indicating strong disagreement with the statement and number 7 indicating strong agreement with the statement. Try to use number 4 ("neutral") as little as possible, since this position indicates absence of judgment in either direction.

1 = Strongly disagree
2 = Disagree
3 = Slightly disagree
4 = Neutral
5 = Slightly agree
6 = Agree
7 = Strongly agree

1. I have developed a personal understanding of existence which helps me appreciate life fully.

| 1 | 2 | 3 | 4 | 5 | 6 | 7 |

2. The physical surroundings in which I live are very healthy.

| 1 | 2 | 3 | 4 | 5 | 6 | 7 |

3. Nothing interesting happens in my life.

| 1 | 2 | 3 | 4 | 5 | 6 | 7 |

4. I don't have any influence on my surroundings.

| 1 | 2 | 3 | 4 | 5 | 6 | 7 |

5. I am of no value in the eyes of society.

| 1 | 2 | 3 | 4 | 5 | 6 | 7 |

6. If I died today, I feel that absolutely no trace or influence of myself would remain.

| 1 | 2 | 3 | 4 | 5 | 6 | 7 |

7. I participate in the development of many others.

| 1 | 2 | 3 | 4 | 5 | 6 | 7 |

8. I feel that, in spite of my inevitable death, I will always be an integral part of the world.

| 1 | 2 | 3 | 4 | 5 | 6 | 7 |

9. I feel that I am doing what I want in life.

| 1 | 2 | 3 | 4 | 5 | 6 | 7 |

10. I have certain values or beliefs that help me accept or rise above my mortal condition.

| 1 | 2 | 3 | 4 | 5 | 6 | 7 |

11. I have the feeling that human nature is doomed to destruction.

| 1 | 2 | 3 | 4 | 5 | 6 | 7 |

12. Intimate relationships scare me.

      1   2   3   4   5   6   7

13. Once I've decided to do something, I do it with sustained interest.

      1   2   3   4   5   6   7

14. I often feel very lonely.

      1   2   3   4   5   6   7

15. The eventuality of my death contributes towards giving meaning and structure to my life.

      1   2   3   4   5   6   7

16. My sex life contributes greatly to my well-being.

      1   2   3   4   5   6   7

17. I have difficulty undertaking new things.

      1   2   3   4   5   6   7

18. I feel comfortable in my body.

      1   2   3   4   5   6   7

19. My love life brings me little joy.

      1   2   3   4   5   6   7

20. I feel competent in what I do.

      1   2   3   4   5   6   7

21. If I died today, I have the feeling that I would live on in certain people I would leave behind.

      1   2   3   4   5   6   7

22. I am full of energy and vitality.

      1   2   3   4   5   6   7

23. I am not sure of who I am.

      1   2   3   4   5   6   7

24. I am satisfied with my life so far.

      1   2   3   4   5   6   7

25. I have good contact with others.

      1   2   3   4   5   6   7

26. I feel that I do not use my time well.

      1   2   3   4   5   6   7

Separation-Individuation Process Inventory (S-IPI)

PURPOSE To assess disturbances in the separation-individuation process.

AUTHORS R. M. Christenson and William P. Wilson

DESCRIPTION The S-IPI is a 39-item instrument designed to measure disturbances in the childhood processes of separation and individuation as manifested in adult pathology. Disturbances in this developmental process are manifested in a lack of boundaries between self and others, intolerance of aloneness, as well as trust and control issues in interpersonal relationships. Items on the S-IPI were selected from a pool of 65 items because each significantly differentiated a sample of patients with borderline personality disorder and a control sample of university employees. Because of the theoretical relationship with borderline personality disorder, the S-IPI is particularly useful in monitoring progress with this clinically challenging client.

NORMS The mean and standard deviation of S-IPI scores for a sample of 20 patients diagnosed with borderline personality disorder were 201.0 and 65.6, respectively. A sample of 180 "normal" university employees had a mean S-IPI score of 120.6 with a standard deviation of 40.0. The authors suggest a cutting score of 190 to distinguish persons with separation-individuation problems from those without that problem.

SCORING Items 7, 15, and 18 are reverse-scored. Total S-IPI scores are the sum of all items. Scores range from 39 to 390, with higher scores indicating more problems with individuation-separation.

RELIABILITY The S-IPI has excellent internal consistency, with an alpha of .92. Data on stability are not available.

VALIDITY The S-IPI has demonstrated known-groups validity with scores differentiating a sample of persons with *DSM-III* diagnoses of borderline personality disorder from a sample of "normal" university employees. There was some overlap in the instrument's specificity in detecting the borderline personality, with 30% of the borderline sample and 7% of the "normals" scoring as false positives and false negatives, respectively.

PRIMARY REFERENCE Christenson, R. M., and Wilson, W. P. (1985). Assessing pathology in the separation-individuation process by an inventory: A preliminary report, *Journal of Nervous and Mental Disease*, 173, 561–565. Reproduced with permission of Randall M. Christenson, M.D.

AVAILABILITY Randall M. Christenson, M.D., Pine Rest Christian Hospital, 300 68th Street, S.E., Grand Rapids, MI 49501-0165.

In this section, you are asked to rate how characteristic the following statements are about people in general. The rating is on a scale of 1 to 10 with 1 being not characteristic and 10 being very characteristic. Your rating is your opinion of how people in general feel about themselves and others, so there are no right or wrong answers. Since people's attitudes about themselves and others vary considerably, the questions vary considerably; some questions may seem a little strange or unusual to you. Please answer all the questions as best you can. Answer them fairly quickly without putting a lot of thought into them. Please write your answers in the spaces to the left.

____ 1. When people really care for someone, they often feel worse about themselves.
____ 2. When someone gets too emotionally close to another person, he/she often feels lost.
____ 3. When people really get angry at someone, they often feel worthless.
____ 4. It is when people start getting emotionally close to someone that they are most likely to get hurt.
____ 5. People need to maintain control over others to keep from being harmed.

In this section you are asked to rate whether you think the following statements are characteristic of your feelings about yourself and other people. The rating is on a scale of 1 to 10 with 1 being not characteristic and 10 being very characteristic. Again, these are your opinions so there are no right or wrong answers. As different people often have very different thoughts about themselves and others, the statements vary considerably. Some of them may seem strange or unusual to you, but please answer all of them the best you can. Rate each statement fairly quickly without giving a lot of thought to them. Write your rating in the spaces to the left.

____ 6. I find that people seem to change whenever I get to know them.
____ 7. It is easy for me to see both good and bad qualities that I have at the same time.
____ 8. I find that people either really like me or they hate me.
____ 9. I find that others often treat me as if I am just there to meet their every wish.
____ 10. I find that I really vacillate between really liking myself and really disliking myself.
____ 11. When I am by myself, I feel that something is missing.
____ 12. I need other people around me to not feel empty.
____ 13. I sometimes feel that part of me is lost whenever I agree with someone else.
____ 14. Like others, whenever I see someone I really respect and to whom I look up, I often feel worse about myself.
____ 15. I find it easy to see myself as a distinct individual.
____ 16. Whenever I realize how different I am from my parents, I feel very uneasy.
____ 17. In my experience, I almost always consult my mother before making an important decision.
____ 18. I find it relatively easy to make and keep commitments to other people.
____ 19. I find that when I get emotionally close to someone, I occasionally feel like hurting myself.
____ 20. I find that either I really like someone or I can't stand them.
____ 21. I often have dreams about falling that make me feel anxious.
____ 22. I find it difficult to form mental pictures of people significant to me.
____ 23. I have on more than one occasion seemed to wake up and find myself in a relationship with someone, and not be sure of how or why I am in the relationship.

___ 24. I must admit that when I feel lonely, I often feel like getting intoxicated.
___ 25. Whenever I am very angry with someone, I feel worthless.
___ 26. If I were to tell my deepest thoughts, I would feel empty.
___ 27. In my experience, people always seem to hate me.
___ 28. Whenever I realize how similar I am to my parents, I feel very uneasy.
___ 29. Often, when I am in a close relationship, I find that my sense of who I am gets lost.
___ 30. I find it difficult for me to see others as having both good and bad qualities at the same time.
___ 31. I find that the only way I can be me is to be different from other people.
___ 32. I find that when I get emotionally too close to someone, I sometimes feel that I have lost a part of who I am.
___ 33. Whenever I am away from my family, I feel very uneasy.
___ 34. Getting physical affection itself seems more important to me than who gives it to me.
___ 35. I find it difficult to really know another person well.
___ 36. I find that it is important for me to have my mother's approval before making a decision.
___ 37. I must admit that whenever I see someone else's faults, I feel better.
___ 38. I am tempted to try to control other people in order to keep them close to me.
___ 39. I must admit that whenever I get emotionally close to someone, I sometimes want to hurt them.

Session Evaluation Questionnaire (SEQ)

PURPOSE To measure the impact of clinical sessions.

AUTHOR William B. Stiles

DESCRIPTION The SEQ consists of 24 bipolar adjective scales presented in a 7-point semantic differential format. It is designed to measure clients' perceptions of two dimensions of clinical sessions, depth and smoothness, and two dimensions of post-session mood, positivity and arousal. Depth refers to a session's perceived power and value, and smoothness refers to a session's comfort, relaxation, and pleasantness. Positivity refers to feelings of confidence and clarity as well as happiness, while arousal refers to feeling active and excited as opposed to quiet and calm. The four dimensions were constructed on the basis of factor analyses.

NORMS Several studies have been conducted using several different forms of the SEQ. A recent one included 72 clients and 17 counselors. The clients included 59 undergraduate students, 5 graduate students, and 8 community residents. Of these, 97% were white, 67% were female, and 33% were male. The clients' problems most typically included depression, relationship problems, low self-esteem, and insecurity. The counselors were graduate students in clinical psychology, including 9 males and 8 females. Both clients and counselors used the SEQ to rate each session. No real norms are available, although means for client and counselor ratings are reported.

SCORING The four dimensions are scored separately. Scores are the sum of the item ratings, divided by the number of items that make up each dimension. Thus, depth includes four items: deep–shallow, valuable–worthless, full–empty, powerful–weak, and special–ordinary. Smoothness includes smooth–rough, comfortable–uncomfortable, easy–difficult, pleasant–unpleasant, and relaxed–tense. Positivity includes happy–sad, confident–afraid, pleased–angry, definite–uncertain, and friendly–unfriendly. Arousal includes aroused–quiet, fast–slow, moving–still, and excited–calm. Higher scores indicate greater depth, smoothness, positivity, and arousal.

RELIABILITY The four dimensions of the SEQ have good internal consistency, with alphas that range from .78 to .91. No test-retest reliabilities are reported.

VALIDITY No real validity data are reported, although data comparing the dimensions to each other and counselor and client ratings to each other are reported. In essence, the depth and smoothness dimensions are independent of each other, while positivity and arousal were moderately correlated. Both counselor and client ratings varied greatly from session to session.

PRIMARY REFERENCE Stiles, W. B., and Snow, J. S. (1984). Counseling session impact as seen by novice counselors and their clients, *Journal of Counseling Psychology*, 31, 3–12. Instrument reproduced with permission of William B. Stiles and the American Psychological Association.

AVAILABILITY Dr. William B. Stiles, Department of Psychology, Miami University, Oxford, OH 45056. Email: Stileswb@muchio.edu.

SEQ

Please place an "X" on each line to show how you feel about this session.

This session was:

Bad	___ : _ : _ : _ : _ : ___	Good
Safe	___ : _ : _ : _ : _ : ___	Dangerous
Difficult	___ : _ : _ : _ : _ : ___	Easy
Valuable	___ : _ : _ : _ : _ : ___	Worthless
Shallow	___ : _ : _ : _ : _ : ___	Deep
Relaxed	___ : _ : _ : _ : _ : ___	Tense
Unpleasant	___ : _ : _ : _ : _ : ___	Pleasant
Full	___ : _ : _ : _ : _ : ___	Empty
Weak	___ : _ : _ : _ : _ : ___	Powerful
Special	___ : _ : _ : _ : _ : ___	Ordinary
Rough	___ : _ : _ : _ : _ : ___	Smooth
Comfortable	___ : _ : _ : _ : _ : ___	Uncomfortable

Right now I feel:

Happy	___ : _ : _ : _ : _ : ___	Sad
Angry	___ : _ : _ : _ : _ : ___	Pleased
Moving	___ : _ : _ : _ : _ : ___	Still
Uncertain	___ : _ : _ : _ : _ : ___	Definite
Calm	___ : _ : _ : _ : _ : ___	Excited
Confident	___ : _ : _ : _ : _ : ___	Afraid
Wakeful	___ : _ : _ : _ : _ : ___	Sleepy
Friendly	___ : _ : _ : _ : _ : ___	Unfriendly
Slow	___ : _ : _ : _ : _ : ___	Fast
Energetic	___ : _ : _ : _ : _ : ___	Peaceful
Involved	___ : _ : _ : _ : _ : ___	Detached
Quiet	___ : _ : _ : _ : _ : ___	Aroused

Severity of Symptoms Scale (SSS)

PURPOSE To measure severity of compulsive behavior in the developmentally disabled.

AUTHORS Benedetto Vitiello, Scott Spreat, and David Behar

DESCRIPTION The SSS is a 9-item rating scale to measure the severity of symptoms of compulsive behavior in the developmentally disabled. Compulsive behaviors are often a major problem among the developmentally disabled, and include repetitive, ritualistic behaviors that pose problems for the people performing them. The SSS is used by observers not to identify the behaviors themselves but to rate their severity. Thus, the SSS is a good measure for determining the need for treatment and for monitoring treatment success.

NORMS The SSS was studied initially with a group of 283 mildly to profoundly developmentally disabled, all of whom were patients in a residential facility in Philadelphia. The mean age was 29.5. Patients were referred by staff members on the basis of presence of repetitive behaviors. From this group, 10 were identified as compulsive, 9 as noncompulsive but high in stereotyped behaviors, and 10 who were low in both. Overall norms are not available, although the mean for the 10 subjects identified as compulsive was 13.0.

SCORING The SSS is easily scored by summing item scores for a total score.

RELIABILITY The SSS has very good interrater reliability with a kappa for differential diagnosis of .82 and intraclass correlation coefficient of .82.

VALIDITY The SSS has fair known-groups validity, significantly distinguishing between subjects previously identified as compulsive and those with neither stereotypes nor compulsive behavior.

PRIMARY REFERENCE Vitiello, B., Spreat, S., and Behar, D. (1989). Obsessive-compulsive disorder in mentally retarded patients, *Journal of Nervous and Mental Disease*, 177, 232–236.

AVAILABILITY Dr. B. Vitiello, NIMH, NIH 10/3D-41, Bethesda, MD 20892. Email: bvitiell@mail.nih.gov.

Rate the following aspects of severity of the repetitive behaviors by circling the appropriate number.

During the last week:

1. Time spent with all symptoms daily
   - 0 = Less than 15 minutes
   - 1 = 15 to 30 minutes
   - 2 = 30 minutes to 1 hour
   - 3 = 1 to 3 hours
   - 4 = More than 3 hours

   0   1   2   3   4

2. Subjective resistance or attempt to stop the symptoms
   - 0 = Not interested in stopping
   - 1 = Would like to stop, but didn't try
   - 2 = Has tried a little
   - 3 = Has tried hard
   - 4 = Has tried very hard

   0   1   2   3   4

3. Ability to stop symptoms when desired
   - 0 = Always
   - 1 = Most of the time
   - 2 = Only in front of other people
   - 3 = Very little, even when with other people
   - 4 = Not at all

   0   1   2   3   4

4. Interference with work/school
   - 0 = No work/school missed
   - 1 = Often late arriving at work/school
   - 2 = Often late completing tasks at work/school
   - 3 = Unable to complete tasks at work/school
   - 4 = Completely unable to attend work/school

   0   1   2   3   4

5. Interference with self-care
   - 0 = No interference with daily self-care
   - 1 = Hygiene poor occasionally
   - 2 = Frequent delays in hygiene and/or dressing and/or emptying bladder or bowels
   - 3 = Has to be showered and/or dressed by others and/or constipated often
   - 4 = Completely dependent on other people for survival functions such as feeding

   0   1   2   3   4

6. Interference with social contacts and leisure activities
   0 = No interference
   1 = Has sometimes given up opportunities to see friends or play sports/hobbies
   2 = Has often refused to meet friends or to enjoy sports/hobbies
   3 = Needs to be constantly pushed in order to have any social contact
   4 = Unable to engage in any social or leisure time activities

   0   1   2   3   4

7. Slowness of walking, talking, or moving in general:
   0 = None at all
   1 = Sometimes slow in movements
   2 = Often slowed
   3 = Constantly slowed
   4 = Extremely slow, often needs help to move

   0   1   2   3   4

8. Interventions by others required:
   0 = No external intervention required
   1 = Verbal intervention from other people is sometimes necessary
   2 = Verbal intervention is often necessary
   3 = Physical intervention is necessary
   4 = Strenuous physical intervention with struggling is necessary

   0   1   2   3   4

9. Suffering and distress from symptoms or their consequences:
   0 = None at all
   1 = A little, or occasional
   2 = Moderately, often
   3 = A lot, every day
   4 = Intense, unremitting distress

   0   1   2   3   4

Total severity score = _____

Sexual Behavioral System Subgoals Scale (SBSSS)

PURPOSE To measure subgoals of the sexual system.

AUTHORS Gurit E. Birnbaum and Omri Gillath

DESCRIPTION The SBSSS is an 18-item measure designed to assess individual differences in sex behaviors and beliefs related to the pursuit of various subgoals of the sexual system. This scale is based on concepts from evolutionary psychology regarding variations in the emphasis individuals may place on particular sexual-system subgoals and the psychological mechanisms that may be associated with them. These individual differences can be seen as corresponding to differences in behavioral intentions and actual sexual behavior. The SBSSS is said to be the first psychometrically sound measure designed to examine those differences. The SBSSS examines four subgoals that correspond to four factors or subscales: Relationship Initiation (RI; items 5, 11, 12, 16, 17); Negative Reactions (NR; items 3, 9, 10, 15); Maintaining the Bond (MB; items 7, 8, 13, 14, 18); and Sexual Pleasure and Motivation (SPM; items 1, 2, 4, 6).

NORMS The SBSSS was developed in a series of four studies in the United State and Israel involving almost 1200 respondents. In the U.S. study, 319 women and 157 men who were taking introductory psychology in a West Coast university, participated. The median age was 19; 49.2% were white, 25.2% Asian, 6.9% Hispanic, 3.6% African American, and 13% other ethnicities. Actual norms were not provided for the U.S. sample, but are available for men and women in an Israeli sample in the Primary Reference.

SCORING The SBSSS is scored easily by taking the mean of the item scores for each subscale. The SBSSS focuses mainly on the subscales rather than the total score.

RELIABILITY The subscales of the SBSSS have fair to good internal consistencies with alphas of .68, .76, .84, and .82 for SPM, MB, NR, and RI, respectively. Data on stability were not reported.

VALIDITY The SBSSS has very good construct validity using convergent and discriminative validity methods. As predicted, subscales of the SBSSS were positively, negatively, or not correlated with a number of other scales of sexuality and personality. The SBSSS is not significantly associated with social desirability.

PRIMARY REFERENCE Birnbaum, G. E., and Gillath, O. (in press). Measuring subgoals of the sexual behavioral system: What is sex good for? *Journal of Social and Personal Relationships*. Instrument reproduced with permission of Dr. Birnbaum.

AVAILABILITY Email Dr. Birnbaum at birnbag@mail.biu.ac.il.

Next to each sentence, please mark the degree to which it characterizes your feelings, expectations and beliefs about sexual activity with a partner

Not at all Characteristic	1	2	3	4	5	6	7	8	9	Very Characteristic

___ 1. Many people feel intense sexual need or desire almost all the time.

___ 2. Having sex can bring me to a state of ecstasy.

___ 3. I feel bored while having sex.

___ 4. Sexual intercourse is great fun.

___ 5. I have sometimes initiated romantic relationships by having sex.

___ 6. Sex is a major source of pleasure in my life.

___ 7. Having sex helps me maintain a romantic relationship.

___ 8. Without adequate sex, a romantic relationship is likely to deteriorate.

___ 9. I feel indifferent or apathetic during sexual activity.

___ 10. Having sex often leaves me frustrated, both physically and emotionally.

___ 11. I've had no difficulty using sex to establish romantic relationships.

___ 12. I have gotten involved in relationships in order to have sex.

___ 13. Sexual intercourse maintains partners' interest in their relationship.

___ 14. Having sex helps me feel secure in a relationship.

___ 15. It's difficult for me to enjoy sexual intercourse.

___ 16. Having sex is way to begin romantic relationships.

___ 17. In my experience, sexual intercourse has been a good foundation on which to build a relationship.

___ 18. Sexual attraction is a necessity for maintaining a long-term relationship.

Sexual Inhibition (SIS) and Sexual Excitation (SES) Scales

PURPOSE To measure sexual inhibition and sexual excitation.

AUTHORS Erick Janssen et al.

DESCRIPTION The SES/SIS is a 45-item scale developed to measure the propensity for sexual inhibition and excitation in men. The SIS/SES differs from many other scales in that it focuses on sexual response patterns rather than values, attitudes, and behavioral tendencies. Items initially were developed by researchers affiliated with the Kinsey Institute, with inhibition items written to reflect situations in which existing sexual arousal is lost due to introduction of some intra- or interpersonal threat (e.g., related to negative consequences or performance). The excitation items were written to include a variety of stimuli including social interactions. The SIS/SES is comprised of three factors/scales: excitation (SES); inhibition-1 (SIS1); and inhibition-2 (SES2). Each of these scales also has subscales. The items in these subscales are identified in the Primary Reference.

NORMS The SIS/SES was developed with four samples. The first was comprised of 408 undergraduate students in a psychology class (mean age=22.8, 89% white), the second was comprised of 459 undergraduate psychology students (mean age=20.9, 82% white), the third was composed of 312 men (mean age=46.2, predominantly white) working on the university campus where the SIS/SES was developed, and the fourth was comprised of 50 undergraduate psychology students (mean age=21.1; used for test-retest reliability). SIS/SES scores were relatively comparable across the first three samples, with small but significant differences between sample 1 and 2 on SES and between samples 1 and 3 on SIS1 & SIS2. For purposes of illustration, the means on the three scales for sample 2 are as follows: SES=58.5; SIS1=27.1; SIS2=27.6. The means for all samples are available in the Primary Reference.

SCORING The first scale is SES, which has 20 items and four subscales. The highest possible score on SES is 80 (20 items×scale minimum of 4). The SIS1 has 14 items and 3 subscales, one of which contains 3 items related to inhibitions due to concerns during sexual interaction with a partner (low partner arousal, concerns about pleasing one's partner) and is reverse-scored. The highest possible score on SIS1 is 56 (14 items×4). The third scale is SIS2, which has 11 items and 3 subscales. The highest possible score on SIS2 is 44 (11 items×4). Once items are reverse-scored, the scores on the items within the subscales are summed for the subscale scores.

RELIABILITY The SIS/SES has very good internal consistency, with alphas that range around .89 for SES, .78 for SIS1, and .69 for SIS2. The SIS/SES also has very good stability with mean seven-week test-retest correlations of .78 for SES, .67 for SIS1, and .74 for SES2.

VALIDITY The SES and SIS1 have no correlation with the Social Desirability Scale, but there is a weak correlation with social desirability and SIS2. The SIS/SES has demonstrated both convergent and discriminant validity with small but significant correlations with a number of other valid measures and no correlations where none would be expected. Some of these other measures were the Sexual Opinion Survey, the Harm Avoidance Scale, subscales of the Eysenck Personality Questionnaire, the Frequency of Sexual Activity Questionnaire, and the Sociosexual Orientation Inventory.

PRIMARY REFERENCE Janssen, E. et al. (2002). The Sexual Inhibition (SIS) and Sexual Excitation (SES) Scales: I. Measuring sexual inhibition and excitation proneness in men, *Journal of Sex Research, 39,* 114–126. Instrument reproduced with permission of Dr. Janssen.

AVAILABILITY Email Dr. Janssen at ejanssen@indiana.edu.

INSTRUCTION

In this questionnaire you will find statements about how you might react to various sexual situations, activities, or behaviors. Obviously, how you react will often depend on the circumstances, but we are interested in what would be the *most likely* reaction for you.

Please read each statement carefully and decide how you would be most likely to react. Then circle the number that corresponds with your answer.

Please try to respond to every statement.

Sometimes you may feel that none of the responses seems *completely* accurate. **Sometimes you may read a statement which you feel is 'not applicable'. In these cases, please circle a response which you would choose *if it were* applicable to you.**

In many statements you will find words describing reactions such as 'sexually aroused', or sometimes just 'aroused'. With these words we mean to describe 'feelings of sexual excitement', feeling 'sexually stimulated', 'horny', 'hot', or turned on'.

Don't think too long before answering, please give your first reaction.

Try to not skip any questions. Try to be as honest as possible.

SIS/SES QUESTIONNAIRE
VERSION 1.0

	Strongly Agree	Agree	Disagree	Strongly Disagree
1. When I look at erotic pictures, I easily become sexually aroused.	1	2	3	4
2. If I feel that I am being rushed, I am unlikely to get very aroused.	1	2	3	4
3. If I am on my own watching a sexual scene in a film, I quickly become sexually aroused.	1	2	3	4
4. Sometimes just lying in the sun sexually arouses me.	1	2	3	4
5. Using condoms or other safe-sex products can cause me to lose my arousal.	1	2	3	4
6. When a sexually attractive stranger accidentally touches me, I easily become aroused.	1	2	3	4
7. When I have a quiet candlelight dinner with someone I find sexually attractive, I get aroused.	1	2	3	4
8. If there is a risk of unwanted pregnancy, I am unlikely to get sexually aroused.	1	2	3	4
9. I need my clitoris to be stimulated to continue feeling aroused.	1	2	3	4
10. When I am having sex, I have to focus on my own sexual feelings in order to stay aroused.	1	2	3	4
11. When I feel sexually aroused, I usually have a genital response (e.g., vaginal lubrication, being wet).	1	2	3	4
12. If I am having sex in a secluded, outdoor place and I think that someone is nearby, I am not likely to get very aroused.	1	2	3	4
13. When I see someone I find attractive dressed in a sexy way, I easily become sexually aroused.	1	2	3	4
14. When I think someone sexually attractive wants to have sex with me, I quickly become sexually aroused.	1	2	3	4
15. If I discovered that someone I find sexually attractive is too young, I would have difficulty getting sexually aroused with him/her.	1	2	3	4
16. When I talk to someone on the telephone who has a sexy voice, I become sexually aroused.	1	2	3	4
17. When I notice that my partner is sexually aroused, my own arousal becomes stronger.	1	2	3	4
18. If my new sexual partner does not want to use a condom/safe-sex product, I am unlikely to stay aroused.	1	2	3	4

continued

	Strongly Agree	Agree	Disagree	Strongly Disagree
19. I cannot get aroused unless I focus exclusively on sexual stimulation.	1	2	3	4
20. If I feel that I'm expected to respond sexually, I have difficulty getting aroused.	1	2	3	4
21. If I am concerned about pleasing my partner sexually, it interferes with my arousal.	1	2	3	4
22. If I am masturbating on my own and I realize that someone is likely to come into the room at any moment, I will lose my sexual arousal.	1	2	3	4
23. It is difficult to become sexually aroused unless I fantasize about a very arousing situation.	1	2	3	4
24. If I can be heard by others while having sex, I am unlikely to stay sexually aroused.	1	2	3	4
25. Just thinking about a sexual encounter I have had is enough to turn me on sexually.	1	2	3	4
26. When I am taking a shower or a bath, I easily become sexually aroused.	1	2	3	4
27. If I realize there is a risk of catching a sexually transmitted disease, I am unlikely to stay sexually aroused.	1	2	3	4
28. If I can be seen by others while having sex, I am unlikely to stay sexually aroused.	1	2	3	4
29. If I am with a group of people watching an X-rated film, I quickly become sexually aroused.	1	2	3	4
30. When a sexually attractive stranger makes eye-contact with me, I become aroused.	1	2	3	4
31. If I think that having sex will cause me pain, I will lose my arousal.	1	2	3	4
32. When I wear something I feel attractive in, I am likely to become sexually aroused.	1	2	3	4
33. If I am worried about being too dry, I am less likely to get lubricated.	1	2	3	4
34. If having sex will cause my partner pain, I am unlikely to stay sexually aroused.	1	2	3	4
35. When I think of a very attractive person, I easily become sexually aroused.	1	2	3	4
36. Once I am sexually aroused, I want to start inter-course right away before I lose my arousal.	1	2	3	4
37. When I start fantasizing about sex, I quickly become sexually aroused.	1	2	3	4
38. When I see others engaged in sexual activities, I feel like having sex myself.	1	2	3	4

	Strongly Agree	Agree	Disagree	Strongly Disagree
39. When I see an attractive person, I start fantasizing about having sex with him/her.	1	2	3	4
40. When I have a distracting thought, I easily lose my arousal.	1	2	3	4
41. I often rely on fantasies to help me maintain my sexual arousal.	1	2	3	4
42. If I am distracted by hearing music, television, or a conversation, I am unlikely to stay aroused.	1	2	3	4
43. When I feel interested in sex, I usually have a genital response (e.g., vaginal lubrication, being wet).	1	2	3	4
44. When an attractive person flirts with me, I easily become sexually aroused.	1	2	3	4
45. During sex, pleasing my partner sexually makes me more aroused.	1	2	3	4

Sexual Modes Questionnaire (SMQ)

PURPOSE To measure cognitive and emotional factors of sexual function.

AUTHORS Pedro J. Nobre and Jose Pinto-Gouveia

DESCRIPTION The SMQ is a 33-item scale for women and a 30-item scale for men, both of which are displayed here, designed to assess the interaction between automatic thoughts and the related emotions and sexual responses. The SMQ is based on a recent theory by Aaron Beck that features the concept of "mode" as a composite of schemas (emotional, cognitive, and behavioral) interacting together. The SMQ was developed specifically to assess those integrated and interdependent processes in the field of sexuality. The female version is comprised of six factors: Sexual Abuse Thoughts (items 1–4, 6 15, 32, 33); Failure/Disengagement Thoughts (items 19, 22, 26, 30); Partner's Lack of Affection (items 7, 12, 24, 27, 28); Sexual Passivity and Control (10, 14, 17, 21, 23, 29); Lack of Erotic thoughts (5, 8, 11, 25, 31); and Low Self-Body Image Thoughts (items 9, 16, 20). The men's scale is comprised of five factors: Failure Anticipation Thoughts (items 1, 2, 3, 4, 6, 7); Erection Concern Thoughts (items 5, 8–12); Age and Body Related Thoughts (items 19, 21, 22, 28); Negative thoughts Toward Sex (items 20, 23, 24, 25, 30); and Lack of Erotic Thoughts (items 14, 17, 18, 26). The SMQ assesses three different areas: Frequency of Types of Automatic Thoughts, Types of Emotions (emotional response), and Intensity of Sexual Response.

NORMS The SQM was developed with a sample of 456 subjects, of whom 154 were female and 206 were male. 360 people were recruited from the community and 90 were recruited from a sex clinic in a university hospital. All subjects were residents of Portugal. The demographic breakdowns by gender, clinical versus general samples, marital status and education level are available in the Primary Reference. Generally, both female samples were younger than the male samples (mean age for females was around 29 versus 43 for the males). The men generally had lower educational levels than the women and roughly similar marital status. The means, standard deviations, median, and range of scores for men and women are available in the Primary Reference.

SCORING The Automatic Thoughts subscale (AT) is scored by reverse-scoring all items with erotic cues, and then summing up the items within each factor. The Emotional Response subscale (ER) is scored using the following formula: total number of each emotion endorsed/total number of emotions endorsed. This index represents the ratio at which respondents usually experience each emotion during sexual activity, with scores ranging from 0 to 1. The Sexual Response subscale (SR) is scored using the following formula: sum of the sexual response for each item / total number of sexual items endorsed. This index ranges from 1 to 5.

RELIABILITY The SMQ has very good internal consistency with alphas for the factors ranging from .69 for the male version of Lack of Erotic Thoughts to .83 for the male version of Erection Concern Thoughts. The total alphas for the SMQ are .87 for the female version and .88 for the male version. The SMQ also has very good stability with 4-week test-retest coefficients for the entire scale that range from .65 for the male version to .95 for the female.

VALIDITY The SMQ has good convergent validity with several of the subscales correlating significantly with the International Index of Erectile Functioning (for men) and the Female Sexual Function Index (for women). The SMQ also has good discriminative ability, discriminating significantly between the clinical and general samples on sadness, pleasure and satisfaction for men and hurt, pleasure, and satisfaction for women.

PRIMARY REFERENCE Nobre, P. J., and Pinto-Gouveia, J. (2003). *Journal of Sex Research*, 40, 368–382. Instrument reproduced with permission of Dr. Nobre.

AVAILABILITY Email Dr. Nobre at pedro.j.nobre@clix.pt.

SMQ—FEMALE VERSION

The items presented below are a list of thoughts one can have during sexual activity. In the first column, please indicate the frequency of which you experience these **thoughts** by circling a number (1-never to 5-always). Next, indicate the **types of emotions** you typically experience when having these thoughts by marking an X in the columns for the appropriate emotions. Finally, in the last column, for each thought experienced indicate the intensity of your typical **sexual response** (arousal) while you are having that thought by circling a number (1-very low to 5-very high).

NOTE: For thoughts that you indicate as never experiencing, you do not need to fill out the emotion or sexual response column.

Example: Imagine that the thought "making love is wonderful" comes to your mind often whenever you are engaged in a sexual activity, and that this idea is accompanied by pleasurable emotions, and your sexual arousal becomes very high. In this case your answer should be:

THOUGHTS	FREQUENCY				
TYPE OF THOUGHTS	Never	Seldom	Sometimes	Often	Always
Example: Making love is wonderful	1	2	3	X	5

EMOTIONS										
TYPES OF EMOTIONS	Worry	Sadness	Disillusioned	Fear	Guilt	Shame	Anger	Regret	Pleasure	Satisfaction
									X	

SEXUAL RESPONSE					
INTENSITY	Very low	Low	Middling	High	Very high
	1	2	3	4	X

THOUGHTS	FREQUENCY				
TYPE OF THOUGHTS	Never	Seldom	Sometimes	Often	Always
1. He is abusing me	1	2	3	4	5
2. How can I get out of this situation?	1	2	3	4	5
3. He only wants to satisfy himself	1	2	3	4	5

EMOTIONS										
TYPES OF EMOTIONS	Worry	Sadness	Disillusioned	Fear	Guilt	Shame	Anger	Regret	Pleasure	Satisfaction

SEXUAL RESPONSE					
INTENSITY	Very low	Low	Middling	High	Very high
	1	2	3	4	5
	1	2	3	4	5
	1	2	3	4	5

THOUGHTS	FREQUENCY					EMOTIONS — TYPES OF EMOTIONS										SEXUAL RESPONSE — INTENSITY				
TYPE OF THOUGHTS	Never	Seldom	Sometimes	Often	Always	Worry	Sadness	Disillusioned	Fear	Guilt	Shame	Anger	Regret	Pleasure	Satisfaction	Very low	Low	Middling	High	Very high
4. Sex is all he thinks about	1	2	3	4	5											1	2	3	4	5
5. The way he is talking turns me on	1	2	3	4	5											1	2	3	4	5
6. He is violating me	1	2	3	4	5											1	2	3	4	5
7. This way of having sex is immoral	1	2	3	4	5											1	2	3	4	5
8. These movements and positions are fabulous	1	2	3	4	5											1	2	3	4	5
9. I'm getting fat/ugly	1	2	3	4	5											1	2	3	4	5
10. If I let myself go he is going to think I'm promiscuous	1	2	3	4	5											1	2	3	4	5
11. Making love is wonderful	1	2	3	4	5											1	2	3	4	5
12. He is not being as affectionate as he used to be	1	2	3	4	5											1	2	3	4	5
13. I'm not satisfying my partner	1	2	3	4	5											1	2	3	4	5
14. I must not show that I'm interested	1	2	3	4	5											1	2	3	4	5
15. This is disgusting	1	2	3	4	5											1	2	3	4	5
16. I'm not as physically attractive as I used to be	1	2	3	4	5											1	2	3	4	5
17. I should not take the lead in sexual activity	1	2	3	4	5											1	2	3	4	5
18. He only cares about me when he wants sex	1	2	3	4	5											1	2	3	4	5
19. I'm not getting turned on	1	2	3	4	5											1	2	3	4	5

Continued

THOUGHTS

TYPE OF THOUGHTS	FREQUENCY				
	Never	Seldom	Sometimes	Often	Always
20. I'm not feeling physically attractive	1	2	3	4	5
21. These activities shouldn't be planned ahead of time	1	2	3	4	5
22. I can't feel anything	1	2	3	4	5
23. I don't want to get hurt emotionally	1	2	3	4	5
24. Why doesn't he kiss me?	1	2	3	4	5
25. My body turns him on	1	2	3	4	5
26. When will this be over?	1	2	3	4	5
27. If only he'd whisper something romantic in my ear	1	2	3	4	5
28. He only loves me if I'm good in bed	1	2	3	4	5
29. I should wait for him to make the first move	1	2	3	4	5
30. I am only doing this because he asked me to	1	2	3	4	5
31. I'm the happiest woman on earth	1	2	3	4	5
32. I have other more important matters to deal with	1	2	3	4	5
33. If I refuse to have sex, he will cheat on me	1	2	3	4	5

EMOTIONS

TYPES OF EMOTIONS

Worry	Sadness	Disillusioned	Fear	Guilt	Shame	Anger	Regret	Pleasure	Satisfaction

SEXUAL RESPONSE

INTENSITY

Very low	Low	Middling	High	Very high
1	2	3	4	5
1	2	3	4	5
1	2	3	4	5
1	2	3	4	5
1	2	3	4	5
1	2	3	4	5
1	2	3	4	5
1	2	3	4	5
1	2	3	4	5
1	2	3	4	5
1	2	3	4	5
1	2	3	4	5
1	2	3	4	5
1	2	3	4	5

SMQ—MALE VERSION

The items presented below are a list of thoughts one can have during sexual activity. In the first column, please indicate the frequency of which you experience these **thoughts** by circling a number (1-never to 5-always). Next, indicate the **types of emotions** you typically experience when having these thoughts by marking an X in the columns for the appropriate emotions. Finally, in the last column, for each thought experienced indicate the intensity of your typical **sexual response** (arousal) while you are having that thought by circling a number (1-very low to 5-very high).

NOTE: For thoughts that you indicate as never experiencing, you do not need to fill out the emotion or sexual response column.

Example: Imagine that the thought "making love is wonderful" comes to your mind very often whenever you are engaged in a sexual activity, and that this idea is accompanied by pleasurable emotions, and your sexual arousal becomes very high. In this case your answer should be:

THOUGHTS TYPE OF THOUGHTS	FREQUENCY					EMOTIONS TYPES OF EMOTIONS										SEXUAL RESPONSE INTENSITY				
	Never	Seldom	Sometimes	Often	Always	Worry	Sadness	Disillusioned	Fear	Guilt	Shame	Anger	Hurt	Pleasure	Satisfaction	Very low	Low	Moderate	High	Very high
Example: Making love is wonderful	1	2	3	X	5									X		1	2	3	4	X

THOUGHTS TYPE OF THOUGHTS	FREQUENCY					EMOTIONS TYPES OF EMOTIONS										SEXUAL RESPONSE INTENSITY				
	Never	Seldom	Sometimes	Often	Always	Worry	Sadness	Disillusioned	Fear	Guilt	Shame	Anger	Hurt	Pleasure	Satisfaction	Very low	Low	Moderate	High	Very high
1. It would be better to die than to be like this	1	2	3	4	5											1	2	3	4	5
2. This time I cannot disappoint my partner	1	2	3	4	5											1	2	3	4	5

Continued

THOUGHTS

TYPE OF THOUGHTS	Never	Seldom	Sometimes	Often	Always
3. She will replace me with another guy	1	2	3	4	5
4. I'm condemned to failure	1	2	3	4	5
5. I must be able to have intercourse	1	2	3	4	5
6. This is not going anywhere	1	2	3	4	5
7. I'm not satisfying her	1	2	3	4	5
8. I must achieve an erection	1	2	3	4	5
9. I'm not penetrating my partner	1	2	3	4	5
10. My penis is not responding	1	2	3	4	5
11. Why isn't this working?	1	2	3	4	5
12. I wish this could last longer	1	2	3	4	5
13. What is she thinking about me?	1	2	3	4	5
14. These movements and positions are fabulous	1	2	3	4	5
15. What if others knew I'm not capable	1	2	3	4	5
16. If I fail again I am a lost cause	1	2	3	4	5
17. I'm the happiest man on earth	1	2	3	4	5

EMOTIONS

TYPES OF EMOTIONS

Worry	Sadness	Disillusioned	Fear	Guilt	Shame	Anger	Hurt	Pleasure	Satisfaction

SEXUAL RESPONSE

INTENSITY

Very low	Low	Moderate	High	Very high
1	2	3	4	5
1	2	3	4	5
1	2	3	4	5
1	2	3	4	5
1	2	3	4	5
1	2	3	4	5
1	2	3	4	5
1	2	3	4	5
1	2	3	4	5
1	2	3	4	5
1	2	3	4	5
1	2	3	4	5
1	2	3	4	5
1	2	3	4	5
1	2	3	4	5

THOUGHTS

TYPE OF THOUGHTS	FREQUENCY Never	Seldom	Sometimes	Often	Always
18. This is turning me on	1	2	3	4	5
19. If I don't climax now, I won't be able to later	1	2	3	4	5
20. She is not being as affectionate as she used to	1	2	3	4	5
21. She doesn't find my body attractive anymore	1	2	3	4	5
22. I'm getting old	1	2	3	4	5
23. This is disgusting	1	2	3	4	5
24. This way of having sex is immoral	1	2	3	4	5
25. Telling her what I want sexually would be unnatural	1	2	3	4	5
26. She is really turned on	1	2	3	4	5
27. I must show my virility	1	2	3	4	5
28. It will never be the same again	1	2	3	4	5
29. If I can't get an erection, I will be embarrassed	1	2	3	4	5
30. I have other more important matters to deal with	1	2	3	4	5

EMOTIONS — TYPES OF EMOTIONS

Worry	Sadness	Disillusioned	Fear	Guilt	Shame	Anger	Hurt	Pleasure	Satisfaction

SEXUAL RESPONSE — INTENSITY

Very low	Low	Moderate	High	Very high
1	2	3	4	5
1	2	3	4	5
1	2	3	4	5
1	2	3	4	5
1	2	3	4	5
1	2	3	4	5
1	2	3	4	5
1	2	3	4	5
1	2	3	4	5
1	2	3	4	5
1	2	3	4	5
1	2	3	4	5
1	2	3	4	5

Short Acculturation Scale for Hispanics (SASH)

PURPOSE To measure acculturation in Hispanics.

AUTHOR Gerardo Marin

DESCRIPTION The SASH is a 12-item instrument designed to measure acculturation among Hispanics. Acculturation is defined as modification in the values, norms, attitudes, and behaviors of Hispanics as they become exposed to mainstream cultural patterns of the United States. Measurement of acculturation is important not only as a way of identifying individual or personality differences, but also because it has been reported to be related to other important variables such as mental health, levels of social support, alcohol and drug use, and suicide. The SASH comprises three factors: language use and ethnic loyalty (items 1, 2, 3, 4, and 5); media (items 6, 7, and 8); and ethnic social relations (items 9, 10, 11, and 12). The SASH can be reduced to five items (1, 2, 3, 4, and 5) without sacrificing predictive value, validity, or reliability.

NORMS The SASH was initially studied with 363 Hispanics of whom 44% were Mexican-American, 6% Cuban-American, 47% other Hispanics (almost all of whom were Central American), and 2% Puerto Rican. The mean age was 31.2 years and mean level of education 12.3 years. Sixty-two percent of the respondents were female. Seventy percent of respondents were foreign born who had lived an average of 14.7 years in the United States. A score of 2.99 is used to differentiate the less acculturated respondents (average score between 1 and 2.99) and the more acculturated respondents (average score above 2.99). A midpoint in the scale should not be construed to represent biculturalism.

SCORING Scores on the SASH are easily determined by summing items across the total scale or the subscales and dividing by the number of items.

RELIABILITY The SASH has very good to excellent internal consistency, with an alpha for all items of .92, and alphas that range from .78 for the third factor to .90 for the first factor. No data on stability were provided.

VALIDITY The SASH has established good concurrent and predictive validity, with high correlations in the expected direction between scores on the SASH and generation of the respondents, length of residence, self-evaluation, an acculturative index, and age of arrival in the United States. The SASH also has good known-groups validity, significantly distinguishing between the responses of Hispanic and non-Hispanic respondents. There is no significant difference between the scores of Mexican-American Hispanics and Central-American Hispanics.

PRIMARY REFERENCE Marin, G., et al. (1987). Development of a short acculturation scale for Hispanics, *Hispanic Journal of Behavioral Sciences*, 9, 183–205.

AVAILABILITY The scale is in the public domain and no permission is required to use it. Researchers are asked to provide copies of their report to G. Marin, Department of Psychology, University of San Francisco, San Francisco, CA 94117-1080. Reprinted by permission of Dr. Marin.

A. English

1. In general, what language(s) do you read and speak?

1	2	3	4	5
Only Spanish	Spanish better than English	Both equally	English better than Spanish	Only English

2. What was the language(s) you used as a child?

1	2	3	4	5
Only Spanish	More Spanish than English	Both equally	More English than Spanish	Only English

3. What language(s) do you usually speak at home?

1	2	3	4	5
Only Spanish	More Spanish than English	Both equally	More English than Spanish	Only English

4. In which language(s) do you usually think?

1	2	3	4	5
Only Spanish	More Spanish than English	Both equally	More English than Spanish	Only English

5. What language(s) do you usually speak with your friends?

1	2	3	4	5
Only Spanish	More Spanish than English	Both equally	More English than Spanish	Only English

6. In what language(s) are the TV programs you usually watch?

1	2	3	4	5
Only Spanish	More Spanish than English	Both equally	More English than Spanish	Only English

7. In what language(s) are the radio programs you usually listen to?

1	2	3	4	5
Only Spanish	More Spanish than English	Both equally	More English than Spanish	Only English

continued

8. In general, in what language(s) are the movies, TV, and radio programs you *prefer* to watch and listen to?

1	2	3	4	5
Only Spanish	More Spanish than English	Both equally	More English than Spanish	Only English

9. Your close friends are:

1	2	3	4	5
All Latinos/ Hispanics	More Latinos than Americans	About half and half	More Americans than Latinos	All Americans

10. You prefer going to social gatherings/parties at which the people are:

1	2	3	4	5
All Latinos/ Hispanics	More Latinos than Americans	About half and half	More Americans than Latinos	All Americans

11. The persons you visit or who visit you are:

1	2	3	4	5
All Latinos/ Hispanics	More Latinos than Americans	About half and half	More Americans than Latinos	All Americans

12. If you could choose your children's friends, you would want them to be:

1	2	3	4	5
All Latinos/ Hispanics	More Latinos than Americans	About half and half	More Americans than Latinos	All Americans

B. Spanish

1. Por lo general, qué idioma(s) leé y habla usted?

1	2	3	4	5
Solo Español	Español mejor que Inglés	Ambos por igual	Inglés mejor que Español	Solo Inglés

2. Cuál fué el idioma(s) que habló cuando era niño(a)?

1	2	3	4	5
Solo Español	Más Español que Inglés	Ambos por igual	Más Inglés que Español	Solo Inglés

3. Por lo general, en qué idioma(s) habla en su casa?

1	2	3	4	5
Solo Español	Más Español que Inglés	Ambos por igual	Más Inglés que Español	Solo Inglés

4. Por lo general, en qué idioma(s) piensa?

1	2	3	4	5
Solo Español	Más Español que Inglés	Ambos por igual	Más Inglés que Español	Solo Inglés

5. Por lo general, en qué idioma(s) habla con sus amigos(as)?

1	2	3	4	5
Solo Español	Más Español que Inglés	Ambos por igual	Más Inglés que Español	Solo Inglés

6. Por lo general, en qué idioma(s) son los programas de televisión que usted ve?

1	2	3	4	5
Solo Español	Más Español que Inglés	Ambos por igual	Más Inglés que Español	Solo Inglés

7. Por lo general, en qué idioma(s) son los programas de radio que usted escucha?

1	2	3	4	5
Solo Español	Más Español que Inglés	Ambos por igual	Más Inglés que Español	Solo Inglés

8. Por lo general, en qué idioma(s) *prefiere oir y* ver peliculas, y programas de radio y televisión?

1	2	3	4	5
Solo Español	Más Español que Inglés	Ambos por igual	Más Inglés que Español	Solo Inglés

9. Sus amigos y amigas mas cercanos son:

1	2	3	4	5
Solo Latinos	Más Latinos que Americanos	Casi mitad y mitad	Más Americanos que Latinos	Solo Americanos

10. Usted prefiere ir a reuniones sociales/fiestas en las cuales las personas son:

1	2	3	4	5
Solo Latinas	Más Latinas que Americanas	Casi mitad y mitad	Más Americanas que Latinas	Solo Americanas

11. Las personas que usted visita o que le visitan son:

1	2	3	4	5
Solo Latinas	Más Latinas que Americanas	Casi mitad y mitad	Más Americanas que Latinas	Solo Americanas

continued

12. Si usted pudiera escoger los amigos(as) de sus hijos(as), quisiera cue ellos(as) fueran:

1	2	3	4	5
Solo Latinos	Más Latinos que Americanos	Casi mitad y mitad	Más Americanos que Latinos	Solo Americanos

Simpatia Scale (SS)

PURPOSE To measure simpatia.

AUTHORS James D. Griffith, George W. Joe, Lois R. Chatham, and D. Dwayne Simpson

DESCRIPTION The SS is a 17-item scale developed to measure the concept of simpatia in Hispanics entering drug treatment. Simpatia is a cultural factor often cited as being potentially important in the treatment of Hispanics. Simpatia refers to a Hispanic cultural script that promotes smooth social relations; people who embody this concept show a certain level of conformity and empathy for the feelings of others, behave with dignity and respect toward others, and strive to achieve harmony in their interpersonal relations. Thus simpatia is seen as a general tendency toward avoiding interpersonal conflict by emphasizing positive behaviors in agreeable situations and de-emphasizing negative behaviors in conflictive circumstances. The SS comprises three factors: agreeableness (items 2, 3, 5, 8, 9, 14, and 15); respect (items 1, 4, 10, 12, 16, and 17); and politeness (items 6, 7, 11, and 13). The SS provides a way for practitioners to be sensitive to the cultural script of simpatia when treating Hispanic substance abusers.

NORMS The SS was developed and validated in a series of studies, the last of which involved 144 daily opioid drug users in a methadone treatment clinic in Texas. The mean age was 41 years (SD=9.12), and 65% were male. Fifty-nine percent were Hispanic, 19% were Caucasian, and 22% were African-American. Of the subjects, 35% were married, and 47% were separated, divorced, or widowed. Ninety-nine percent of the subjects had a history of previous arrest. All were daily opioid drug users (usually heroin), with cocaine being the second drug of choice. The actual means and standard deviations were not presented in the primary reference.

SCORING After reverse-scoring items 2, 3, 5, 8, 9, 14, and 15, the scores for the total scale and the three subscales are simply sums of the items on the scales.

RELIABILITY The SS has good internal consistency with an alpha of .80 for the overall scale. The three subscales had alphas of .72, .71, and .70 for agreeableness, respect, and politeness, respectively.

VALIDITY The SS has established very good construct validity. The SS and its subscales were positively correlated, mainly to a significant level, with a number of other measures as predicted, including measures of social support, social conformity, counselor skills, staff efficiency, convenience scheduling, program organization, and program satisfaction. The SS showed negative correlations, as predicted, with acculturation, hostility, needle exposure, and risky sex. And as predicted, there were no significant relationships between problem indicators and psychological reasons.

PRIMARY REFERENCE Griffith, J. D., et al. (1998). The development and validation of a simpatia scale for Hispanics entering drug treatment, *Hispanic Journal of Behavioral Sciences*, 20, 468–482.

AVAILABILITY Dr. James D. Griffith, Institute of Behavioral Research, Texas Christian University, TCU Box 298740, Fort Worth, TX 76129, or email: Dr. Griffith at ibr.@tcu.edu.

Please circle the number that best reflects your answer.

During the past 3 months, how often:

	Never	Rarely	Sometimes	Often	Always
1. Did you think that your counselor said positive things to you?	0	1	2	3	4
2. Did you put down the culture of others?	0	1	2	3	4
3. Did you openly disagree with others?	0	1	2	3	4
4. Did you trust the judgment of your counselor?	0	1	2	3	4
5. Did the counselor do things that you thought were rude or insulting?	0	1	2	3	4
6. Did you treat others as your equal?	0	1	2	3	4
7. Did you try to avoid conflict with others?	0	1	2	3	4
8. Did you think about disagreeing with your counselor?	0	1	2	3	4
9. Did you think your counselor should have been more polite?	0	1	2	3	4
10. Did you say good things about your counselor when talking to others?	0	1	2	3	4
11. Were you polite to others?	0	1	2	3	4
12. Did you point out the positive qualities of others?	0	1	2	3	4
13. Did you do favors for others?	0	1	2	3	4
14. Did you disagree with what the counselor said?	0	1	2	3	4
15. Did you think that your counselor's opinions were different from yours?	0	1	2	3	4
16. Did you think that your counselor treated others with respect?	0	1	2	3	4
17. Did your counselor do things that made you feel comfortable?	0	1	2	3	4

Simple Rathus Assertiveness Schedule (SRAS)

PURPOSE To measure assertiveness for persons with low reading ability.

AUTHOR Iain A. McCormick

DESCRIPTION This 30-item measure of assertiveness is based on the Rathus Assertiveness Schedule (also reproduced in this book) and is designed for persons with poor reading ability. Care was taken to make certain item content equivalent with that of the original instrument. Because it is shorter and easier to read, the SRAS is useful in clinical work with adolescents and children as well as adults. The SRAS is more useful with teenagers than the original RAS.

NORMS The SRAS was tested on a sample of 116 graduate students. The mean score was 94.6 with a standard deviation of 25.4 for females ($n=82$), and 99.8 with a standard deviation of 20.1 for males ($n=34$).

SCORING Each item is rated on a 6-point scale from "very much like me" to "very unlike me." Items 1, 2, 4, 5, 9, 11, 12–17, 19, 23, 24, 26, and 30 are reverse-scored. The total score is the sum of all items, and can range from 30 to 180 with higher scores reflecting more assertion.

RELIABILITY Reliability of this instrument is very good. Internal consistency was determined with odd-even correlations and was .90. The SRAS correlated .94 with the original, suggesting the two may be used as parallel forms. Data on stability were not available.

VALIDITY There is very little validity data for this instrument. As a parallel form, much of the validity of the Rathus Assertiveness Schedule would apply. The parallel form reliability correlation can also be seen as concurrent validity data.

PRIMARY REFERENCE McCormick, I. A. (1984). A simple version of the Rathus Assertiveness Schedule, *Behavioral Assessment* 7, 95–99, Instrument reproduced with permission of Dr. McCormick.

AVAILABILITY Dr. I. A. McCormick, Psychology Department, Victoria University of Wellington, Private Bay, Wellington, New Zealand.

Read each sentence carefully. Write down on each line whatever number is correct for you.

6 = Very much like me
5 = Rather like me
4 = Somewhat like me
3 = Somewhat unlike me
2 = Rather unlike me
1 = Very unlike me

____ 1. Most people stand up for themselves more than I do.
____ 2. At times I have not made or gone on dates because of my shyness.
____ 3. When I am eating out and the food I am served is not cooked the way I like it, I complain to the person serving it.
____ 4. I am careful not to hurt other people's feelings, even when I feel hurt.
____ 5. If a person serving in a store has gone to a lot of trouble to show me something which I do not really like, I have a hard time saying "No."
____ 6. When I am asked to do something, I always want to know why.
____ 7. There are times when I look for a good strong argument.
____ 8. I try as hard to get ahead in life as most people like me do.
____ 9. To be honest, people often get the better of me.
____ 10. I enjoy meeting and talking with people for the first time.
____ 11. I often don't know what to say to good looking people of the opposite sex.
____ 12. I do not like making phone calls to businesses or companies.
____ 13. I would rather apply for jobs by writing letters than by going to talk to the people.
____ 14. I feel silly if I return things I don't like to the store that I bought them from.
____ 15. If a close relative that I like was upsetting me, I would hide my feelings rather than say that I was upset.
____ 16. I have sometimes not asked questions for fear of sounding stupid.
____ 17. During an argument I am sometimes afraid that I will get so upset that I will shake all over.
____ 18. If a famous person were talking in a crowd and I thought he/she was wrong, I would get up and say what I thought.
____ 19. I don't argue over prices with people selling things.
____ 20. When I do something important or good, I try to let others know about it.
____ 21. I am open and honest about my feelings.
____ 22. If someone has been telling false and bad stories about me, I see him/her as soon as possible to "have a talk" about it.
____ 23. I often have a hard time saying "No."
____ 24. I tend not to show my feelings rather than upsetting others.
____ 25. I complain about poor service when I am eating out or in other places.
____ 26. When someone says I have done very well, I sometimes just don't know what to say.
____ 27. If a couple near me in the theater were talking rather loudly, I would ask them to be quiet or to go somewhere else and talk.
____ 28. Anyone trying to push ahead of me in a line is in for a good battle.
____ 29. I am quick to say what I think.
____ 30. There are times when I just can't say anything.

Smoking Self-Efficacy Questionnaire (SSEQ)

PURPOSE To measure beliefs about one's ability to resist the urge to smoke.

AUTHORS Gep Colletti and Jay A. Supnick

DESCRIPTION The SSEQ is a 17-item instrument designed to assess the application of self-efficacy theory to smoking, that is, whether a change in one's belief about one's ability to execute a given action successfully can bring about behavior change (smoking reduction or completely quitting). Respondents are asked to read each of 17 situations and then to assess whether they could expect to control their smoking behavior and remain on a smoking reduction program in that situation. The instrument yields a total score indicating the overall strength of the self-efficacy judgment. Although still in an early stage of development, the SSEQ shows potential for clinical and research applications.

NORMS Initial development of the SSEQ was based on 128 male and female respondents with a mean age of 39.7, who were participants in an ongoing, behaviorally oriented smoking reduction program. Twenty-nine additional respondents participated in earlier stages in the development of the scale. Means for the sample of 128 are available and broken down by sex and pre- and posttreatment scores. The overall pretreatment mean was 42.13, which rose to 72.53 after treatment.

SCORING The SSEQ is scored by totaling respondents' confidence ratings (on a scale from 10 to 100) on each of the 17 items that apply to that respondent's personal situation. Scores are then divided by the number of items answered. This yields a mean rated confidence score with a range of 0% to 100%.

RELIABILITY The SSEQ has an alpha coefficient of better than .90, indicating excellent internal consistency. Test-retest reliabilities were lower but significant, ranging from .41 to .62. However, these results were confounded by the fact that respondents were undergoing treatment for smoking at the time.

VALIDITY Correlations between smoking rate and the SSEQ were statistically significant, suggesting good concurrent and predictive validity.

PRIMARY REFERENCE Colletti, G., Supnick, J. A., and Payne, T. J. (1985). The Smoking Self-Efficacy Questionnaire (SSEQ): Preliminary scale development and validation, *Behavioral Assessment*, 7, 249–260. Instrument reproduced with permission of J. Supnick and G. Colletti.

AVAILABILITY Dr. Jay Supnick, Department of Psychiatry, University of Rochester, Medical Center, Rochester, NY 14642. Email: jsupnick@rochester.rr.com.

The following paragraphs are descriptions of situations in which people with smoking problems often find it very difficult not to smoke. If you are trying to stop, they may be the situations in which you are likely to give up.

First, read each description and as vividly as possible try to imagine yourself in that situation. Then assess whether you expect that in this situation you could control your smoking behavior and remain on your reduction program. Write down "Yes," meaning "I could control my smoking behavior" or "No," meaning "I could not control my smoking behavior" in the blank marked "Can Do."

If you answer "Yes," then please assess how confident you are that you could control your smoking behavior. Using the numbers from the scale 10 to 100 printed below, choose one that expresses your degree of confidence, and write that number down in the blank marked "Confidence."

Some of the exact details of a situation may not apply to you, such as smoking while drinking coffee, but the description may be similar to a situation you do experience, for example, smoking while drinking alcohol. You can assess that instead. If the situation is not one you would ever experience, you can place an X in the "Can Do" blank and go on to the next item.

Confidence Scale

10	20	30	40	50	60	70	80	90	100

| Quite uncertain | | | | Moderately certain | | | | | Certain |

	Can Do	Confidence
1. You just returned from an important exam and you "know" you have done poorly.	——	——
2. A planned date stands you up. You are disappointed and begin to blame yourself.	——	——
3. You have had a fight with your boyfriend, girlfriend, spouse, or any friend and you are angry and upset.	——	——
4. You have been out for an evening, you feel relaxed and want to end the evening with a smoke.	——	——
5. You have just finished dinner in a good restaurant on a special occasion. Everyone orders coffee and your friends all sit back to enjoy a cigarette.	——	——
6. You are out with friends who are smoking a lot. You don't want them to know that you are on a smoking reduction program.	——	——
7. You just came home from a really rough day at school or work. The whole day was filled with anxiety, frustration, and failure.	——	——
8. You are sitting at home alone, in a bad mood, thinking about the problems and failures in your life.	——	——

	Can Do	Confidence
9. Watching television (e.g., sport event).	_____	_____
10. Studying.	_____	_____
11. Reading a novel or magazine.	_____	_____
12. Attending a sports or entertainment event.	_____	_____
13. Talking on the phone.	_____	_____
14. Drinking coffee or other nonalcoholic beverages.	_____	_____
15. After a meal.	_____	_____
16. Talking or socializing.	_____	_____
17. Playing cards.	_____	_____

Social Adjustment Scale-Self Report (SAS-SR)

PURPOSE To measure adaptive social functioning.

AUTHORS Myrna M. Weissman and Eugene S. Paykel

DESCRIPTION The SAS-SR is a 54-item instrument designed to measure adaptive functioning within a variety of social contexts. The SAS-SR actually is based on an earlier version involving a structured interview developed by the authors. The SAS-SR can be completed by the client, or a relevant other about the client. The authors recommend having someone knowledgeable about the measure be available to instruct a respondent about its use. The SAS-SR is a very useful way of operationalizing social adjustment. In addition to the global score, it includes subscales providing information about a number of role areas: work outside home (items 1–6), work at home (items 7–12), work as a student (items 13–18), social and leisure (items 19–29), extended family (items 30–37), marital (items 38–46), parental (items 47–50), family unit (items 51–53), and economic (item 54).

NORMS The SAS-SR has been studied with a number of clinical and nonclinical groups. For a community sample of 399 (272 female), the overall mean was 1.59 (SD = .33). For a sample of 172 acute depressives (148 female), the overall mean was 2.53 (SD = .46). For a sample of 26 alcoholics (17 female), the mean was 2.23 (SD = .61). And for a sample of 39 schizophrenics (35 females), the mean was 1.96 (SD = .62).

SCORING The overall adjustment score is the sum of all items divided by the number of items actually scored; the role area mean score is a sum of the items in a role area divided by the number of items actually scored in that area. For the total adjustment score, only one work area is used (one of the first three subscales). Higher scores reflect greater impairment.

RELIABILITY The SAS-SR has fair internal consistency, with an alpha of .74. The SAS-SR has good stability, with a one-month test-retest correlation of .74.

VALIDITY The SAS-SR has fair concurrent validity as demonstrated by correlations with the social adjustment structured interview upon which it is based. The SAS-SR has good known-groups validity, distinguishing a nonclinical, community sample from three psychiatric samples and distinguishing acutely depressed from recovered patients.

PRIMARY REFERENCE Weissman, M. M., and Bothwell, S. (1976). Assessment of social adjustment by patient self-report, *Archives of General Psychiatry*, 33, 1111–1115.

AVAILABILITY Dr. Myrna Weissman, College of Physicians and Surgeons, Columbia University, 722 W. 168th Street, Box 14, New York, NY 10032. Email: mmw3@columbia.edu.

We are interested in finding out how you have been doing in the last *two weeks*. We would like you to answer some questions about your work, spare time, and your family life. There are no right or wrong answers to these questions, check the answers that best describe how you have been in the last *two weeks*.

Work Outside the Home

Please describe the situation that best describes you.

I am   1. ☐   a worker for pay   4. ☐   retired
        2. ☐   a housewife   5. ☐   unemployed
        3. ☐   a student

Do you usually work for pay more than 15 hours per week?
        1. ☐   Yes   2. ☐   No

Did you work any hours for pay in the last 2 weeks?
        1. ☐   Yes   2. ☐   No

Check the answer that best describes how you have been in the last 2 weeks.

1. How many days did you miss from work in the last 2 weeks?
   1. ☐   No days missed.
   2. ☐   One day.
   3. ☐   I missed about half the time.
   4. ☐   Missed more than half the time but did make at least one day.
   5. ☐   I did not work any days.
   6. ☐   I was on vacation the last two weeks.

If you have not worked any days in the past 2 weeks, go on to Question 7.

2. Have you been able to do any work in the last 2 weeks?
   1. ☐   I did my work very well.
   2. ☐   I did my work but had some minor problems.
   3. ☐   I needed help with work and did not do well about half the time.
   4. ☐   I did my work poorly most of the time.
   5. ☐   I did my work poorly all the time.

3. Have you been ashamed of how you do your work in the past 2 weeks?
   1. ☐   I never felt ashamed.
   2. ☐   Once or twice I felt a little ashamed.
   3. ☐   About half the time I felt ashamed.
   4. ☐   I felt ashamed most of the time.
   5. ☐   I felt ashamed all the time.

4. Have you had any arguments with people at work in the last 2 weeks?
   1. ☐   I had no arguments and got along very well.
   2. ☐   I usually got along well but had minor arguments.
   3. ☐   I had more than one argument.
   4. ☐   I had many arguments.
   5. ☐   I was constantly in arguments.

5. Have you felt upset, worried or uncomfortable while doing your work during the last 2 weeks?
   1. ☐   I never felt upset.
   2. ☐   Once or twice I felt upset.
   3. ☐   Half the time I felt upset
   4. ☐   I felt upset most of the time.
   5. ☐   I felt upset all of the time.

6. Have you found your work interesting these last 2 weeks?
   1. ☐   My work was almost always interesting.
   2. ☐   Once or twice my work was not interesting.
   3. ☐   Half the time my work was uninteresting.
   4. ☐   Most of the time my work was uninteresting.
   5. ☐   My work was always uninteresting.

Work Outside the Home—Housewives Answer Questions 7–12. Otherwise, Go on to Question 13.

7. How many days did you do some housework during the last 2 weeks?
   1. ☐   Every day.
   2. ☐   I did the housework almost every day.
   3. ☐   I did the housework about half the time.
   4. ☐   I usually did not do the housework.
   5. ☐   I was completely unable to do housework.
   6. ☐   I was away from home all of the past two weeks.

8. During the last 2 weeks, have you kept up with your housework? This includes cooking, cleaning, laundry, grocery shopping, and errands.
   1. ☐   I did my work very well.
   2. ☐   I did my work but had some minor problems.
   3. ☐   I needed help with work and did not do well about half the time.
   4. ☐   I did my work poorly most of the time.
   5. ☐   I did my work poorly all the time.

9. Have you been ashamed of how you did your housework during the last 2 weeks?
   1. ☐   I never felt ashamed.
   2. ☐   Once or twice I felt a little ashamed.
   3. ☐   About half the time I felt ashamed.
   4. ☐   I felt ashamed most of the time.
   5. ☐   I felt ashamed all the time.

10. Have you had any arguments with salespeople, tradesmen, or neighbors in the last 2 weeks?
   1. ☐   I had no arguments and got along very well.
   2. ☐   I usually got along well but had minor arguments.
   3. ☐   I had more than one argument.
   4. ☐   I had many arguments.
   5. ☐   I was constantly in arguments.

11. Have you felt upset while doing your housework during the last 2 weeks?
   1. ☐   I never felt upset.
   2. ☐   Once or twice I felt upset.

3. ☐ Half the time I felt upset
4. ☐ I felt upset most of the time.
5. ☐ I felt upset all of the time.

12. Have you found your housework interesting these last 2 weeks?
1. ☐ My work was almost always interesting.
2. ☐ Once or twice my work was not interesting.
3. ☐ Half the time my work was uninteresting.
4. ☐ Most of the time my work was uninteresting.
5. ☐ My work was always uninteresting.

For Students

Answer Questions 13–18 if you go to school half time or more. Otherwise go to Question 19.

What best describes your school program? (Choose one)
1. ☐ Full time
2. ☐ 3/4 time
3. ☐ Half time

Check the answer that best describes how you have been the last 2 weeks.

13. How many days of classes did you miss in the last 2 weeks?
1. ☐ No days missed.
2. ☐ A few days missed.
3. ☐ I missed about half the time.
4. ☐ Missed more than half time but did make at least one day.
5. ☐ I did not go to classes at all.
6. ☐ I was on vacation all of the last two weeks.

14. Have you kept up with your class work in the last 2 weeks?
1. ☐ I did my work very well.
2. ☐ I did my work but had some minor problems.
3. ☐ I needed help with work and did not do well about half the time.
4. ☐ I did my work poorly most of the time.
5. ☐ I did my work poorly all the time.

15. During the last 2 weeks have you been ashamed of how you do your schoolwork?
1. ☐ I never felt ashamed.
2. ☐ Once or twice I felt a little ashamed.
3. ☐ About half the time I felt ashamed.
4. ☐ I felt ashamed most of the time.
5. ☐ I felt ashamed all the time.

16. Have you had any arguments with people at school in the last 2 weeks?
1. ☐ I had no arguments and got along very well.
2. ☐ I usually got along well but had minor arguments.
3. ☐ I had more than one argument.
4. ☐ I had many arguments.
5. ☐ I was constantly in arguments.

17. Have you felt upset at school during the last 2 weeks?
    1. ☐ I never felt upset.
    2. ☐ Once or twice I felt upset.
    3. ☐ Half the time I felt upset
    4. ☐ I felt upset most of the time.
    5. ☐ I felt upset all of the time.

18. Have you found your school work interesting these last 2 weeks?
    1. ☐ My work was almost always interesting.
    2. ☐ Once or twice my work was not interesting.
    3. ☐ Half the time my work was uninteresting.
    4. ☐ Most of the time my work was uninteresting.
    5. ☐ My work was always uninteresting.

Spare Time—Everyone Answer Questions 19–27.

Check the answer that best describes the way you have been in the last 2 weeks.

19. How many friends have you seen or spoken to on the telephone in the last 2 weeks?
    1. ☐ Nine or more friends.
    2. ☐ Five to eight friends.
    3. ☐ Two to four friends.
    4. ☐ One friend.
    5. ☐ No friends.

20. Have you been able to talk about your feelings and problems with at least one friend during the last 2 weeks?
    1. ☐ I can always talk about my innermost feelings.
    2. ☐ I usually can talk about my feelings.
    3. ☐ About half the time I felt able to talk about my feelings.
    4. ☐ I usually was not able to talk about my feelings.
    5. ☐ I was never able to talk about my feelings.
    6. ☐ Not applicable; I have no friends.

21. How many times in the last 2 weeks have you gone out socially with other people? For example, visited friends, gone to movies, bowling, church, restaurants, invited friends to your home?
    1. ☐ More than 3 times.
    2. ☐ Three times.
    3. ☐ Twice.
    4. ☐ Once.
    5. ☐ None.

22. How much time have you spent on hobbies or spare time interests during the last 2 weeks? For example, bowling, sewing, gardening, sports, reading?
    1. ☐ I spent most of my spare time on hobbies almost every day.
    2. ☐ I spent some spare time on hobbies some of the days.
    3. ☐ I spent a little time on hobbies.
    4. ☐ I usually did not spend any time on hobbies but did watch TV.
    5. ☐ I did not spend any spare time on hobbies or watching TV.

23. Have you had open arguments with your friends in the past 2 weeks?
    1. ☐ I had no arguments and got along very well.
    2. ☐ I usually got along but had minor arguments.
    3. ☐ I had more than one argument.
    4. ☐ I had many arguments.
    5. ☐ I was constantly in arguments.
    6. ☐ Not applicable; I have no friends.

24. If your feelings were hurt or offended by a friend during the last 2 weeks, how badly did you take it?
    1. ☐ It did not affect me or it did not happen.
    2. ☐ I got over it in a few hours.
    3. ☐ I got over it in a few days.
    4. ☐ I got over it in a week.
    5. ☐ It will take me months to recover.
    6. ☐ Not applicable; I have no friends.

25. Have you felt shy or uncomfortable with people in the last 2 weeks?
    1. ☐ I always felt comfortable.
    2. ☐ Sometimes I felt uncomfortable but could relax after a while.
    3. ☐ About half the time I felt uncomfortable.
    4. ☐ I usually felt uncomfortable.
    5. ☐ I always felt uncomfortable.
    6. ☐ Not applicable; I was never with people.

26. Have you felt lonely and wished for more friends during the last 2 weeks?
    1. ☐ I have not felt lonely.
    2. ☐ I have felt lonely a few times.
    3. ☐ About half the time I felt lonely.
    4. ☐ I usually felt lonely.
    5. ☐ I always felt lonely and wished for more friends.

27. Have you felt bored in your spare time during the last 2 weeks?
    1. ☐ I never felt bored.
    2. ☐ I usually did not feel bored.
    3. ☐ About half the time I felt bored.
    4. ☐ Most of the time I felt bored.
    5. ☐ I was constantly bored.

Are you a single, separated, or divorced person not living with a person of opposite sex? Please answer below:
    1. ☐ Yes; answer questions 28 and 29.
    2. ☐ No; go to question 30.

28. How many times have you been with a date these last 2 weeks?
    1. ☐ More than 3 times.
    2. ☐ Three times.
    3. ☐ Twice.
    4. ☐ Once.
    5. ☐ Never.

29. Have you been interested in dating during the last 2 weeks? If you have not dated, would you have liked to?
    1. ☐ I was always interested in dating.
    2. ☐ Most of the time I was interested.
    3. ☐ About half the time I was interested.
    4. ☐ Most of the time I was not interested.
    5. ☐ I was completely uninterested.

Family

Answer questions 30–37 about your parents, brothers, sisters, in-laws, and children not living at home. Have you been in contact with any of them in the last 2 weeks?
    1. ☐ Yes; answer questions 30–37
    2. ☐ No; go to question 36.

30. Have you had open arguments with your relatives in the past 2 weeks?
    1. ☐ We always got along very well.
    2. ☐ We usually got along very well but had some minor arguments.
    3. ☐ I had more than one argument with at least one relative.
    4. ☐ I had many arguments.
    5. ☐ I was constantly in arguments.

31. Have you been able to talk about your feelings and problems with at least one friend during the last 2 weeks?
    1. ☐ I can always talk about my feelings with at least one relative.
    2. ☐ I usually can talk about my feelings.
    3. ☐ About half the time I felt able to talk about my feelings.
    4. ☐ I usually was not able to talk about my feelings.
    5. ☐ I was never able to talk about my feelings.

32. Have you avoided contacts with your relatives these last 2 weeks?
    1. ☐ I have contacted relatives regularly.
    2. ☐ I have contacted a relative at least once.
    3. ☐ I have waited for my relatives to contact me.
    4. ☐ I avoided my relatives, but they contacted me.
    5. ☐ I have no contacts with any relatives.

33. Did you depend on your relatives for help, advice, money, or friendship during the last 2 weeks?
    1. ☐ I never need to depend on them.
    2. ☐ I usually did not need to depend on them.
    3. ☐ About half the time I needed to depend on them.
    4. ☐ Most of the time I depend on them.
    5. ☐ I depend completely on them.

34. Have you wanted to do the opposite of what your relatives wanted in order to make them angry during the last 2 weeks?
    1. ☐ I never wanted to oppose them.
    2. ☐ Once or twice I wanted to oppose them.
    3. ☐ About half the time I wanted to oppose them.
    4. ☐ Most of the time I wanted to oppose them.
    5. ☐ I always opposed them

35. Have you been worried about things happening to your relatives without good reason in the last 2 weeks?
   1. ☐ I have not worried without reason.
   2. ☐ Once or twice I worried.
   3. ☐ About half the time I worried.
   4. ☐ Most of the time I worried.
   5. ☐ I have worried the entire time.

Everyone answer questions 36 and 37, even if your relatives are not living.

36. During the last 2 weeks, have you been thinking that you have let any of your relatives down or have been unfair to them at any time?
   1. ☐ I did not feel that I let them down at all.
   2. ☐ I usually did not feel that I let them down.
   3. ☐ About half the time I felt that I let them down.
   4. ☐ Most of the time I have felt that I let them down.
   5. ☐ I always felt that I let them down.

37. During the last 2 weeks, have you been thinking that any of your relatives have let you down or have been unfair to you at any time?
   1. ☐ I never felt that they let me down.
   2. ☐ I felt that they usually did not let me down.
   3. ☐ About half the time I felt they let me down.
   4. ☐ I usually have felt that they let me down.
   5. ☐ I am very bitter that they let me down.

Are you living with your spouse or have you been living with a person of the opposite sex in permanent relationship?
   1. ☐ Yes; please answer questions 38–46.
   2. ☐ No; go to question 47.

38. Have you had open arguments with your partner in the past 2 weeks?
   1. ☐ We had no arguments and we got along very well.
   2. ☐ We usually got along very well but had some minor arguments.
   3. ☐ We had more than one argument.
   4. ☐ We had many arguments.
   5. ☐ We were constantly in arguments.

39. Have you been able to talk about your feelings and problems with your partner during the last 2 weeks?
   1. ☐ I could always talk about my feelings.
   2. ☐ I usually could talk about my feelings.
   3. ☐ About half the time I felt able to talk about my feelings.
   4. ☐ I usually was not able to talk about my feelings.
   5. ☐ I was never able to talk about my feelings.

40. Have you been demanding to have your own way at home during the last 2 weeks?
   1. ☐ I have not insisted on always having my own way.
   2. ☐ I usually have not insisted on having my own way.
   3. ☐ About half the time I insisted on having my own way.

continued

4. □ I usually insisted on having my own way.
5. □ I always insisted on having my own way.

41. Have you been bossed around by your partner these last 2 weeks?
    1. □ Almost never.
    2. □ Once in a while.
    3. □ About half the time.
    4. □ Most of the time.
    5. □ Always.

42. How much have you felt dependent on your partner these last 2 weeks?
    1. □ I was independent.
    2. □ I was usually independent.
    3. □ I was somewhat dependent.
    4. □ I was usually dependent.
    5. □ I depended on my partner for everything.

43. How have you felt about your partner during the last 2 weeks?
    1. □ I always felt affection.
    2. □ I usually felt affection.
    3. □ About half the time I felt dislike and half the time affection.
    4. □ I usually felt dislike.
    5. □ I always felt dislike.

44. How many times have you and your partner had intercourse?
    1. □ More than twice a week.
    2. □ Once or twice a week.
    3. □ Once every two weeks.
    4. □ Less than once every two weeks but at least once in the past month.
    5. □ Not at all in a month or longer.

45. Have you had any problems during intercourse, such as pain, these last 2 weeks?
    1. □ None.
    2. □ Once or twice.
    3. □ About half the time.
    4. □ Most of the time.
    5. □ Always.
    6. □ Not applicable; no intercourse in the last two weeks.

46. How have you felt about intercourse during the last 2 weeks?
    1. □ I always enjoyed it.
    2. □ I usually enjoyed it.
    3. □ About half the time I did and half the time I did not enjoy it.
    4. □ I usually did not enjoy it.
    5. □ I never enjoyed it.

Children

Have you had unmarried children, stepchildren, or foster children living at home during the last 2 weeks?
1. □ Yes; answer questions 47–50.
2. □ No; go to question 51.

47. Have you been interested in what your children are doing—school, play, or hobbies during the last 2 weeks?
    1. ☐ I was always interested and actively involved.
    2. ☐ I was usually interested and involved.
    3. ☐ About half the time interested and half the time not interested.
    4. ☐ I usually was disinterested.
    5. ☐ I was always disinterested.

48. Have you been able to talk and listen to your children during the last 2 weeks? Include only children over the age of 2.
    1. ☐ I was always able to communicate with them.
    2. ☐ I usually was able to communicate with them.
    3. ☐ About half the time I could communicate.
    4. ☐ I was usually not able to communicate.
    5. ☐ I was completely unable to communicate.
    6. ☐ Not applicable; no children over the age of 2.

49. How have you been getting along with the children during the last 2 weeks?
    1. ☐ I had no arguments and we got along very well.
    2. ☐ I usually got along very well but had some minor arguments.
    3. ☐ I had more than one argument.
    4. ☐ I had many arguments.
    5. ☐ I was constantly in arguments.

50. How have you felt towards your children these last 2 weeks?
    1. ☐ I always felt affection.
    2. ☐ I mostly felt affection.
    3. ☐ About half the time I felt affection.
    4. ☐ Most of the time I did not feel affection.
    5. ☐ I never felt affection toward them.

Family Unit

Have you ever been married, ever lived with a person of the opposite sex, or ever had children? Please check.
    1. ☐ Yes; please answer questions 51–53.
    2. ☐ No; go to question 54.

51. Have you worried about your partner or any of your children without any reason during the last 2 weeks, even if you are not living together now?
    1. ☐ I never worried.
    2. ☐ Once or twice I worried.
    3. ☐ About half the time I worried.
    4. ☐ Most of the time I worried.
    5. ☐ I always worried.
    6. ☐ Not applicable; partner and children not living.

52. During the last 2 weeks, have you been thinking that you have let down your partner or any of your children at any time?
    1. ☐ I did not feel I let them down.
    2. ☐ I usually did not feel that I let them down.

continued

3. ☐ About half the time I felt I let them down.
4. ☐ Most of the time I felt I let them down.
5. ☐ I let them down completely.

Financial

Everyone please answer question 54.

54. Have you had enough money to take care of your own and your family's financial needs during the last 2 weeks?
1. ☐ I had enough money for needs
2. ☐ I usually had enough money, with minor problems.
3. ☐ About half the time I did not have enough money but did not have to borrow money.
4. ☐ I usually did not have enough money and had to borrow from others.
5. ☐ I had great financial difficulty.

Social Anxiety Thoughts Questionnaire (SAT)

PURPOSE To measure the cognitive component of social anxiety.

AUTHOR Lorne M. Hartman

DESCRIPTION The SAT is a 21-item instrument designed to measure the frequency of cognitions that accompany social distress or anxiety. The basis for this instrument is the notion that cognitive factors (thoughts, images, memories, feelings) such as negative self-evaluations and evaluation of feedback from others play a role in the development, maintenance, and treatment of disorders such as social anxiety. From a pool of 117 self-statements collected from university students, the 21 items that showed the best psychometric properties were selected. Factor analysis revealed four factors, but the overall score on the SAT appears to be the most useful indicator of cognitive components of social anxiety. The four factors are (1) thoughts of general discomfort and social inadequacy, (2) concern with others' awareness of distress, (3) fear of negative evaluations, and (4) perceptions of autonomic arousal and performance anxiety.

NORMS Initial study of the SAT involved 28 male and 74 female undergraduates with a mean age of 21.6. No other demographic data or samples were reported. The mean score for those respondents was 42.3.

SCORING The SAT is scored by summing the individual item scores, producing a range of 21 to 105, with higher scores indicating higher frequency of cognitions accompanying social anxiety.

RELIABILITY The SAT has excellent internal consistency, with an alpha of .95. Test-retest correlations were not reported.

VALIDITY The SAT has fairly good concurrent validity, showing significant correlations with the Social Avoidance and Distress Scale and the Fear of Negative Evaluation Scale. No other forms of validity were reported.

PRIMARY REFERENCE Hartman, L. M. (1984). Cognitive components of anxiety, *Journal of Clinical Psychology*, 40, 137–139. Instrument reproduced with permission of Lorne Hartman.

AVAILABILITY Dr. L. M. Hartman, Addiction Research Foundation, University of Toronto, 33 Russell Street, Toronto, Ontario, Canada.

We are interested in the thoughts people have in social situations. Listed below are a variety of thoughts that pop into peoples' heads in situations that involve being with other people or talking to them. Please read each thought and indicate how frequently, if at all, the thought occurred to you *over the last week*. Please read each item carefully and, following the scale, indicate to the left of the question the number that best applies to you. Please answer each question very carefully. *In social or interpersonal situations during the past week, how often did you have the following thoughts?*

1 = Never
2 = Rarely
3 = Sometimes
4 = Often
5 = Always

___ 1. I feel tense and uncertain.
___ 2. I don't know what to say.
___ 3. Maybe I sound stupid.
___ 4. I am perspiring.
___ 5. What will I say first?
___ 6. Can they tell I am nervous?
___ 7. I feel afraid.
___ 8. I wish I could just be myself.
___ 9. What are they thinking of me?
___ 10. I feel shaky.
___ 11. I'm not pronouncing well.
___ 12. Will others notice my anxiety?
___ 13. I feel defenseless.
___ 14. I will freeze up.
___ 15. Now they know I am nervous.
___ 16. I don't like being in this situation.
___ 17. I am inadequate.
___ 18. Does my anxiety show?
___ 19. I feel tense in my stomach.
___ 20. Others will not understand me.
___ 21. What do they think of me?

Social Avoidance and Distress Scale (SAD)

PURPOSE To measure social anxiety.

AUTHORS David Watson and Ronald Friend

DESCRIPTION This 28-item measure was developed to assess anxiety in social situations. The SAD assesses two aspects of anxiety: one's experience of distress, discomfort, fear, and anxiety; and the deliberate avoidance of social situations. The SAD, however, is a unidimensional measure and does not have subscales. The items are phrased to reflect anxiety and non-anxiety symptoms in an effort to control for response bias. The SAD is appropriate for general social situations rather than specific problems such as test anxiety or simple phobia.

NORMS The SAD was developed on a sample of 297 college students. Demographic data are not available. The mean for males ($n=60$) was 11.2, and for females ($n=145$) the mean was 8.24. There was a significant difference between males and females, indicating that females report more social anxiety.

SCORING Each item is answered either "true" or "false." Items 2, 5, 8, 10, 11, 13, 14, 16, 18, 20, 21, 23, 24, and 26 are keyed for "true" answers, while the other items are keyed "false." Answers which match the keyed response are given the value of 1 and answers which do not match the key are assigned the value of 0. Total scores are the sum of the item values. Scores range from 0 to 28 with higher scores indicating more anxiety.

RELIABILITY The internal consistency of the instrument was assessed by correlating each item with the total score on the SAD. The average item-to-total-score correlation was .77. Reliability was also determined using Kuder-Richardson Formula 20 and was excellent, with a correlation of .94. Test-retest reliability for a one-month period was .68 using a sample of 154 college students enrolled in summer school and .79 for a separate sample.

VALIDITY The validity of the SAD was assessed by testing to see if subjects with high scores demonstrated more discomfort in a social situation than did subjects with lower scores. Additionally, comparisons were made to determine if subjects with high scores demonstrated a greater preference for being alone than did subjects with lower scores. Differences were found between the groups on these variables and are evidence of known-groups validity.

PRIMARY REFERENCE Watson, D., and Friend, R. (1969). Measurement of social-evaluation anxiety, *Journal of Consulting and Clinical Psychology*, 33, 448–457. Instrument reprinted with permission of David Watson and the American Psychological Association.

AVAILABILITY May be copied from this volume.

For the following statements, please answer each in terms of whether it is true or false for you. Circle T for true or F for false.

T F   1. I feel relaxed even in unfamiliar social situations.
T F   2. I try to avoid situations which force me to be very sociable.
T F   3. It is easy for me to relax when I am with strangers.
T F   4. I have no particular desire to avoid people.
T F   5. I often find social occasions upsetting.
T F   6. I usually feel calm and comfortable at social occasions.
T F   7. I am usually at ease when talking to someone of the opposite sex.
T F   8. I try to avoid talking to people unless I know them well.
T F   9. If the chance comes to meet new people, I often take it.
T F 10. I often feel nervous or tense in casual get-togethers in which both sexes are present.
T F 11. I am usually nervous with people unless I know them well.
T F 12. I usually feel relaxed when I am with a group of people.
T F 13. I often want to get away from people.
T F 14. I usually feel uncomfortable when I am in a group of people I don't know.
T F 15. I usually feel relaxed when I meet someone for the first time.
T F 16. Being introduced to people makes me tense and nervous.
T F 17. Even though a room is full of strangers, I may enter it anyway.
T F 18. I would avoid walking up and joining a large group of people.
T F 19. When my superiors want to talk with me, I talk willingly.
T F 20. I often feel on edge when I am with a group of people.
T F 21. I tend to withdraw from people.
T F 22. I don't mind talking to people at parties or social gatherings.
T F 23. I am seldom at ease in a large group of people.
T F 24. I often think up excuses in order to avoid social engagements.
T F 25. I sometimes take the responsibility for introducing people to each other.
T F 26. I try to avoid formal social occasions.
T F 27. I usually go to whatever social engagement I have.
T F 28. I find it easy to relax with other people.

Social Fear Scale (SFS)

PURPOSE To measure social fear.

AUTHORS Michael L. Raulin and Jennifer L. Wee

DESCRIPTION The SFS is a 36-item instrument designed to measure the particular type of social fear that is believed to be a common characteristic of schizotypic individuals, those who have a possible genetic predisposition to schizophrenia. The SFS was developed to measure interpersonal aversiveness, characteristics such as social inadequacy, and a dearth of interpersonal relationships that might be present in preschizophrenics in the general population. The 36 items were selected from an item pool of 120 items based on descriptions of social fear as a schizotypic symptom.

NORMS Development of the SFS was carried out with separate samples of undergraduate students, totaling 792 females and 670 males. No actual norms or other demographic information were reported.

SCORING Respondents are asked to indicate whether each item is true or false as it applies to them. Items 3, 8, 16, 18, 19, 31, and 32 are considered "correct" if marked "false"; all others are "correct" if marked "true." Correct answers are assigned 1 point, and the scores are summed. The higher the score, the greater the degree of social fear.

RELIABILITY The SFS has very good internal consistency, with alphas ranging from .85 to .88. No test-retest correlations are reported.

VALIDITY The SFS has fair concurrent validity, correlating moderately with several other scales measuring schizotypic characteristics (e.g., perceptual aberration, intense ambivalence, somatic symptoms). High, medium, and low scores on the SFS also significantly distinguished among groups independently rated on social fear and sociability, thus suggesting some degree of known-groups validity. The SFS is slightly correlated with social desirability response bias, so this condition cannot be totally ruled out.

PRIMARY REFERENCE Raulin, M. L., and Wee, J. L. (1984). The development and validation of a scale to measure social fear, *Journal of Clinical Psychology*, 40, 780–784. Instrument reproduced with permission of Michael L. Raulin.

AVAILABILITY Dr. Michael L. Raulin, SUNY Buffalo, Psychology Department, Julian Park Hall, Buffalo, NY 14260. Email: raulin@acsu.buffalo.edu. Telephone: 716.645.3801.

Circle either T for true or F for false for each item as it applies to you.

T F   1. I like staying in bed so that I won't have to see anyone.

T F   2. I enjoy being a loner.

T F   3. I usually prefer being with friends to being by myself.

T F   4. Upon entering a crowded room, I often feel a strong urge to leave immediately.

T F   5. Honest people will admit that socializing is a burden.

T F   6. I find I can't relax unless I am alone.

T F   7. I feel more comfortable being around animals than being around people.

T F   8. I think I would enjoy a job that involved working with a lot of different people.

T F   9. I like to go for days on end without seeing anyone.

T F 10. I stay away from other people whenever possible.

T F 11. All my favorite pastimes are things I do by myself.

T F 12. I often tell people that I am not feeling well just to get out of doing things with them.

T F 13. The only time I feel really comfortable is when I'm off by myself.

T F 14. Being around other people makes me nervous.

T F 15. I would rather eat alone than with other people.

T F 16. I prefer traveling with friends to traveling alone.

T F 17. I really prefer going to movies alone.

T F 18. I almost always enjoy being with people.

T F 19. It is rare for me to prefer sitting home alone to going out with a group of friends.

T F 20. I often dream of being out in the wilderness with only animals as friends.

T F 21. While talking with people I am often overwhelmed with a desire to be alone.

T F 22. Pets are generally safer to be with than people.

T F 23. I usually find that being with people is very wearing.

T F 24. I often feel like leaving parties without saying goodbye.

T F 25. Even when I am in a good mood, I prefer being alone to being with people.

T F 26. Often I can't wait until the day is over so I can be by myself.

T F 27. I wish people would just leave me alone.

T F 28. I feel most secure when I am by myself.

T F 29. When seated in a crowded place I have often felt the urge to get up suddenly and leave.

T F 30. I often need to be totally alone for a couple of days.

T F 31. I feel most comfortable when I am with people.

T F 32. I like spending my spare time with other people.

T F 33. Whenever I make plans to be with people I always regret it later.

T F 34. The strain of being around people is so unbearable that I have to get away.

T F 35. I would consider myself a loner.

T F 36. I wish that I could be alone most of the time.

Social Interaction Self-Statement Test (SISST)

PURPOSE To assess self-statements about social anxiety.

AUTHORS Carol R. Glass, Thomas V. Merluzzi, Joan L. Biever, and Kathryn H. Larsen

DESCRIPTION The SISST is a 30-item instrument designed to measure cognitions (self-statements) associated with anxiety about social interaction. This instrument is designed for men and women who tend to have low self-confidence, inappropriate fears, worry over negative experiences, and concern about physical appearance. The SISST is based on the assumption that self-statements in specific stressful social situations are related to anxiety and competence. Thus, the SISST assesses thoughts reported by anxious individuals prior to, during, or after social interaction. The items in the SISST were derived empirically from a sample of individuals who were viewed as having high social anxiety. It consists of 15 positive (facilitative) self-statements (items 2, 4, 6, 9, 10, 12, 13, 14, 17, 18, 24, 25, 27, 28, 30) and 15 negative (inhibitory) self-statements (the remaining items). The gender of pronouns and references to males and females can be changed to produce appropriate forms for men and women.

NORMS Initial study of the SISST was conducted on two samples. The first consisted of 40 high and 40 low socially anxious undergraduate women and the second included 32 men and 32 women selected on the basis of a random sample of undergraduate introductory psychology students, stratified by scores on the Bem Sex-Role Inventory. Means for the several subcategories of the sample are reported and range from 38.82 to 58.43 on the SISST-positive and 28.43 to 51.91 on the SISST-negative.

SCORING The SISST is scored by summing scores (scored from 1 to 5) for the 15 positive and 15 negative items separately. Each subscale has a range of 15 to 75.

RELIABILITY The SISST has good internal consistency, with split-half reliability coefficients of .73 for the positive and .86 for the negative subscales. No test-retest data were available.

VALIDITY The SISST has good concurrent validity, with the subscales correlating with the Social Avoidance and Distress Scale and the Survey of Heterosocial Interactions. In addition, the SISST significantly correlated with respondents' self-evaluations of skill and anxiety immediately after role-played situations. The SISST also has good known-groups validity, with both subscales distinguishing between high and low socially anxious respondents based on scores on other measures.

PRIMARY REFERENCE Glass, C. R., Merluzzi, T. V., Biever, J. O., and Larsen, K. H. (1982). Cognitive assessment of social anxiety: Development and validation of a self-statement questionnaire, *Cognitive Therapy and Research*, 6, 37–55. Instrument reproduced with permission of Carol R. Glass and Plenum Publishing Corporation.

AVAILABILITY Dr. Carol R. Glass, Department of Psychology, Catholic University, Washington, DC 20064. Email: glass@cua.edu.

It is obvious that people think a variety of things when they are involved in different social situations. Below is a list of things which you may have thought to yourself at some time before, during, and after the interaction in which you were engaged. Read each item and decide how frequently you may have been thinking a similar thought before, during, and after the interaction. Indicate to the left of the item the appropriate number. The scale is interpreted as follows:

1 = Hardly ever had the thought
2 = Rarely had the thought
3 = Sometimes had the thought
4 = Often had the thought
5 = Very often had the thought

Please answer as honestly as possible.

____ 1. When I can't think of anything to say I can feel myself getting very anxious.
____ 2. I can usually talk to women pretty well.
____ 3. I hope I don't make a fool of myself.
____ 4. I'm beginning to feel more at ease.
____ 5. I'm really afraid of what she'll think of me.
____ 6. No worries, no fears, no anxieties.
____ 7. I'm scared to death.
____ 8. She probably won't be interested in me.
____ 9. Maybe I can put her at ease by starting things going.
____ 10. Instead of worrying I can figure out how best to get to know her.
____ 11. I'm not too comfortable meeting women so things are bound to go wrong.
____ 12. What the heck, the worst that can happen is that she won't go for me.
____ 13. She may want to talk to me as much as I want to talk to her.
____ 14. This will be a good opportunity.
____ 15. If I blow this conversation, I'll really lose my confidence.
____ 16. What I say will probably sound stupid.
____ 17. What do I have to lose? It's worth a try.
____ 18. This is an awkward situation but I can handle it.
____ 19. Wow—I don't want to do this.
____ 20. It would crush me if she didn't respond to me.
____ 21. I've just got to make a good impression on her or I'll feel terrible.
____ 22. You're such an inhibited idiot.
____ 23. I'll probably "bomb out" anyway.
____ 24. I can handle anything.
____ 25. Even if things don't go well it's no catastrophe.
____ 26. I feel awkward and dumb; she's bound to notice.
____ 27. We probably have a lot in common.
____ 28. Maybe we'll hit it off real well.
____ 29. I wish I could leave and avoid the whole situation.
____ 30. Ah! Throw caution to the wind.

Social Problem-Solving Inventory (SPSI)

PURPOSE To measure problem-solving ability.

AUTHORS Thomas J. D'Zurilla and Arthur M. Nezu

DESCRIPTION The SPSI is a 70-item multidimensional measure based on a prescriptive model of problem solving that characterizes social problem solving as a complex, cognitive-affective-behavioral process that consists of a number of different components, including general motivational variables and a set of specific skills. The SPSI consists of two major scales—the Problem Orientation Scale (POS; 30 items) and the Problem-Solving Skills Scale (PSSS; 40 items)—and seven subscales (each with 10 items, as indicated on the instrument). Subsumed under the POS are the cognition subscale (CS), the emotion subscale (ES), and the behavior subscale (BS). Subsumed under the PSSS are the problem definition and formulation subscale (PDFS), the generation of alternatives subscale (GASS), the decision making subscale (DMS), and the solution implementation and verification subscale (SIVS). Although the SPSI has more items than most measures in this book, it was included because of its excellent potential for clinical use, and the centrality of the problem-solving process to many different approaches to clinical practice.

NORMS The 70-item version of the SPSI was administered to three samples: (A) 192 undergraduates at SUNY-Stony Brook (60% female, 30% male, mean age of 19.8, 72% Caucasian, 12% Asian, 8% black, 5% Hispanic); (B) 107 undergraduates from Fairleigh Dickinson University (53% male, 47% female, mean age of 21.3, 90% Caucasian, 10% black); and (C) 45 high-stressed community residents who volunteered to participate in a stress-management research program (28 females, 17 males, mean age of 44.3, all Caucasian). The means (and standard deviation) on the SPSI and two major subscales were: (A) SPSI = 165.2 (SD = 33.24), POS = 73.56 (SD = 20.15), PSSS = 91.31 (SD = 19.88); (B) SPSI = 171.08 (SD = 35.73), POS = 77.76 (SD = 19.58), PSSS = 96.41 (SD = 25.85); and (C) SPSI = 144.64 (SD = 40.43), POS = 62.66 (SD = 17.88), PSSS = 81.96 (SD = 26.96).

SCORING The SPSI is scored by simply summing the scores on the relevant items for each subscale, the two major scales, and the SPSI itself. The range for each subscale is from 0 to 40; for the POS, 0 to 120; for the PSSS, 0 to 160; and for the SPSI as a whole, 0 to 280. Items to be reverse-scored are indicated with an asterisk on the measure.

RELIABILITY The SPSI has excellent internal consistency, with alphas of .94 for the POS and SPSI and .92 for the PSSS. The measure also has very good stability, with three-week test-retest correlations of .87 for the SPSI as a whole and .83 and .88 for the POS and PSSS respectively.

VALIDITY The SPSI has excellent concurrent validity, with significant correlations between the SPSI as a whole and its two major subscales with two other problem-solving measures, the Problem-Solving Inventory and the Means-Ends Problem-Solving Procedure. The SPSI also has very good construct validity, correlating in predicted ways with several other measures, including the Internal-External Locus of Control Scale and the Scholastic Aptitude Test. The SPSI also was found to be sensitive to changes due to training in problem-solving skills, and demonstrated good predictive ability, negatively correlating with several measures of stress level, life problems, and psychological symptoms.

PRIMARY REFERENCE D'Zurilla, T. J., and Nezu, A. M. (1992). Development and preliminary evaluation of the Social Problem-Solving Inventory (SPSI), *Psychological Assessment*, 2, 156–163.

AVAILABILITY May be copied from this volume.

Below is a series of statements that describe the way some people might think, feel, and behave when they are faced with problems in everyday living. We are talking about important problems that could have a significant effect on your well-being or the well-being of your loved ones, such as a health-related problem, a dispute with a family member, or a problem with your performance at work or in school. Please read each statement and carefully select one of the numbers below which indicates the extent to which the statement is true of you. Consider yourself as you *typically* think, feel, and behave when you are faced with problems in living *these days* and place the appropriate number in the parentheses ( ) next to the number of the statement.

0 = Not at all true of me
1 = Slightly true of me
2 = Moderately true of me
3 = Very true of me
4 = Extremely true of me

CS   *1.   ( )   When I cannot solve a problem quickly and without much effort, I tend to think that I am stupid or incompetent.

PDFS   2.   ( )   When I have a problem to solve, one of the things I do is examine all the information that I have about the problem and try to decide what is most relevant or important.

BS   *3.   ( )   I spend too much time worrying about my problems instead of trying to solve them.

ES   *4.   ( )   I usually feel threatened and afraid when I have an important problem to solve.

DMS   *5.   ( )   When making decisions, I do *not* usually evaluate and compare the different alternatives carefully enough.

CS   *6.   ( )   When I have a problem, I often doubt that there is a solution for it.

DMS   *7.   ( )   When I am attempting to decide what is the best solution to a problem, I often fail to take into account the effect that each alternative is likely to have on the well-being of other people.

GASS   8.   ( )   When I am trying to find a solution to a problem, I often think of a number of possible solutions and then try to combine different solutions to make a better solution.

ES   *9.   ( )   I usually feel nervous and unsure of myself when I have an important decision to make.

CS   10.   ( )   When my first efforts to solve a problem fail, I usually think that if I persist and do not give up too easily, I will be able to find a good solution eventually.

GASS   *11.   ( )   When I am attempting to solve a problem, I usually act on the first idea that comes to mind.

CS   12.   ( )   When I have a problem, I usually believe that there is a solution for it.

PDFS   13.   ( )   When I am faced with a large, complex problem, I often try to break it down into smaller problems that I can solve one at a time.

SIVS   *14. ( )   After carrying out a solution to a problem, I do *not* usually take the time to compare the actual outcome with the outcome that I had anticipated when I decided on that particular solution.

BS   *15. ( )   I usually wait to see if a problem will resolve itself first, before trying to solve it myself.

PDFS   16. ( )   When I have a problem to solve, one of the things I do is analyze the situation and try to identify what obstacles are keeping me from getting what I want.

ED   *17. ( )   When my first efforts to solve a problem fail, I get very angry and frustrated.

CS   *18. ( )   When I am faced with a difficult problem, I often doubt that I will be able to solve it on my own no matter how hard I try.

SIVS   19. ( )   I am usually quite satisfied with the outcome of my problem solutions after I carry them out.

PDFS   20. ( )   Before trying to solve a problem, I often try to find out if the problem is being caused by some other more important problem that should be solved first.

BS   *21. ( )   When a problem occurs in my life, I usually put off trying to solve it for as long as possible.

SIVS   *22. ( )   After carrying out a solution to a problem, I do *not* usually take the time to evaluate all of the results carefully.

BS   *23. ( )   I usually go out of my way to avoid having to deal with problems in my life.

ES   *24. ( )   Difficult problems make me very upset.

DMS   25. ( )   When I am attempting to decide what is the best solution to a problem, I try to predict the overall outcome of carrying out each alternative course of action.

BS   26. ( )   I usually confront my problems "head on," instead of trying to avoid them.

GASS   27. ( )   When I am attempting to solve a problem, I often try to be creative and think of original or unconventional solutions.

GASS   *28. ( )   When I am attempting to solve a problem, I usually go with the first good idea that comes to mind.

GASS   29. ( )   When I am trying to find a solution to a problem, I often think of a number of possible solutions and then later go back over them and consider how different solutions can be modified to make a better solution.

GASS   *30. ( )   When I attempt to think of possible solutions to a problem, I cannot usually come up with many alternatives.

BS   *31. ( )   I usually prefer to avoid problems instead of confronting them and being forced to deal with them.

DMS   32. ( )   When making decisions, I usually consider not only the immediate consequences of each alternative course of action, but also the long-term consequences.

SIVS   33. ( )   After carrying out a solution to a problem, I usually try to analyze what went right and what went wrong.

GASS	34. ( )	When I am attempting to find a solution to a problem, I usually try to think of as many different ways to approach the problem as possible.
SIVS	35. ( )	After carrying out a solution to a problem, I usually examine my feelings and evaluate how much they have changed for the better.
SIVS	36. ( )	Before carrying out a solution to a problem in the actual problematic situation, I often practice or rehearse the solution in order to increase my chances of success.
CS	37. ( )	When I am faced with a difficult problem, I usually believe that I will be able to solve the problem on my own if I try hard enough.
PDFS	38. ( )	When I have a problem to solve, one of the first things I do is get as many facts about the problem as possible.
PDFS	39. ( )	Before trying to solve a problem, I often try to find out if the problem is only one part of a bigger, more important problem that I should deal with.
BS	*40. ( )	I often put off solving problems until it is too late to do anything about them.
PDFS	41. ( )	Before trying to solve a problem, I usually evaluate the situation to determine how important the problem is for my well-being or the well-being of my loved ones.
BS	*42. ( )	I think that I spend more time avoiding my problems than solving them.
ES	*43. ( )	When I am attempting to solve a problem, I often get so upset that I cannot think clearly.
PDFS	44. ( )	Before I try to think of a solution to a problem, I usually set a specific goal that makes clear exactly what I want to accomplish.
DMS	*45. ( )	When I am attempting to decide what is the best solution to a problem, I do *not* usually take the time to consider the pros and cons of each solution alternative.
SIVS	46. ( )	When the outcome of my solution to a problem is not satisfactory, I usually try to find out what went wrong and then I try again.
ES	*47. ( )	When I am working on a difficult problem, I often get so upset that I feel confused and disoriented.
ES	*48. ( )	I hate having to solve the problems that occur in my life.
SIVS	49. ( )	After carrying out a solution to a problem, I usually try to evaluate as carefully as possible how much the situation has changed for the better.
ES	*50. ( )	I am generally able to remain "cool, calm, and collected" when I am solving problems.
CS	51. ( )	When I have a problem, I usually try to see it as a challenge, or opportunity to benefit in some positive way from having the problem.
GASS	52. ( )	When I am attempting to solve a problem, I usually think of as many alternative solutions as possible until I cannot come up with any more ideas.
DMS	53. ( )	When I am attempting to decide what is the best solution to a problem, I usually try to weigh the consequences of each solution alternative and compare them against each other.

ES   *54.   ( )   I often become depressed and immobilized when I have an important problem to solve.

SIVS   55.   ( )   My problem solutions are usually successful in achieving my problem-solving goals.

BS   *56.   ( )   When I am faced with a difficult problem, I usually try to avoid the problem or I go to someone else for help in solving it.

DMS   57.   ( )   When I am attempting to decide what is the best solution to a problem, I usually consider the effect that each alternative course of action is likely to have on my personal feelings.

PDFS   58.   ( )   When I have a problem to solve, one of the things I do is examine what sort of external circumstances in my environment might be contributing to the problem.

CS   *59.   ( )   When a problem occurs in my life, I usually blame myself for causing it.

DMS   *60.   ( )   When making decisions, I usually go with my "gut feeling" without thinking too much about the consequences of each alternative.

DMS   61.   ( )   When making decisions, I generally use a systematic method for judging and comparing alternatives.

GASS   62.   ( )   When I am attempting to find a solution to a problem, I try to keep in mind what my goal is at all times.

CS   *63.   ( )   When my first efforts to solve a problem fail, I usually think that I should give up and go look for help.

BS   *64.   ( )   When I have negative feelings, I tend to just go along with the mood, instead of trying to find out what problem might be causing these feelings.

GASS   65.   ( )   When I am attempting to find a solution to a problem, I try to approach the problem from as many different angles as possible.

PDFS   66.   ( )   When I am having trouble understanding a problem, I usually try to get more specific and concrete information about the problem to help clarify it.

CS   *67.   ( )   When I have a problem, I tend to dwell on the harm or loss that will result if I do not solve the problem successfully.

ES   *68.   ( )   When my first efforts to solve a problem fail, I tend to get discouraged and depressed.

SIVS   *69.   ( )   When a solution that I have carried out does not solve my problem satisfactorily, I do *not* usually take the time to examine carefully why it did not work.

DMS   *70.   ( )   I think that I am too impulsive when it comes to making decisions.

Social Rhythm Metric (SRM)

PURPOSE To measure daily social rhythm.

AUTHORS Timothy Monk, Joseph F. Flaherty, Ellen Frank, and David J. Kupfer

DESCRIPTION This 17-item instrument is designed to measure the social rhythms that are important to structuring one's day. The SRM is useful when working with depressed clients. Fifteen events or behaviors are listed which are typical daily events; two items ("Activity A" and "Activity B") are left blank in order to isolate specific events or behaviors relevant to the respondent. The 15 events or behaviors were derived from a list of 37 daily activities. The theoretical basis for the SRM is that regularity of one's social rhythms is important to well-being. The SRM is considered useful in monitoring a patient's decline in depression and recovery from depression in terms of the regularity of events and behaviors of the day. To determine regularity of social rhythms, the SRM should be completed daily for an entire week, then averaged, with regularity defined as the average regularity of events. The SRM appears to be accurate whether completed throughout the day or retrospectively at the end of the day.

NORMS Twelve activities occurred at least three times a week for a sample of 50 paid "normal" respondents. Scale scores of events had a mean of 3.44 and a standard deviation of .91. A small sample of seven patients with recurrent depression reported a mean of 3.20 and a standard deviation of 1.03.

SCORING Scores are based on those items which occurred at least three times per week; items occurring less than three times per week are excluded. From those items occurring at least three times, the "habitual time" of occurrence is determined by excluding any extreme exceptions (such as going to bed one night at 5 a.m. when the rest of the week one retires much earlier. Next, compare the times at which each event occurred; if it is within 45 minutes of the "habitual time," count it as a "hit" and score it 1. Now add the number of hits for all events occurring more than three times a week and divide by the number of events. Scores range from 1 to 7.

RELIABILITY Test-retest reliability for a one-week period was .44, which is low but statistically significant. There were no differences in the mean scores for the first and second testing period. Data on internal consistency were not available.

VALIDITY Validity data is limited to a comparison of SRM scores for four subjects with interruptions in routine. The means and standard deviations before the disruptive events were 1.95 and .78 and were 3.06 and .95 when they returned to their normal routines.

PRIMARY REFERENCE Monk, T. H., Flaherty, J. F., Frank, E., Hoskinson, M. A., and Kupfer, D. J. (1990). The Social Rhythm Metric: An instrument to quantify the daily rhythms of life, *Journal of Nervous and Mental Disease*, 178, 120–126. Instrument reproduced with permission of Timothy H. Monk.

AVAILABILITY Dr. T. H. Monk, Sleep Evaluation Center, Western Psychiatric Institute, 3811 O'Hara Street, Pittsburgh, PA 15213. Email: monkth/at/upmc.edu, or monkth@msx.upmc.edu.

Fill out at end of day

ACTIVITY	Check if DID NOT DO	TIME			Check if ALONE	PEOPLE 1 = Just present 2 = Actively involved			
		Clock time	A.M.	P.M.		Spouse/ Partner	Children	Other Family Members	Other
Out of bed									
First contact (in person or by phone) with another person									
Have morning beverage									
Have breakfast									
Go outside for the first time									
Start work, school, housework, volunteer activities, child or family care									
Have lunch									
Take an afternoon nap									
Have dinner									
Physical exercise									
Have an evening snack/drink									
Watch evening TV news program									
Watch another TV program									
Activity A _____									
Activity B _____									
Return home (last time)									
Go to bed									

Social Support Appraisals Scale (SSA)

PURPOSE To measure subjective appraisals of support.

AUTHORS Alan Vaux, Jeffrey Phillips, Lori Holley, Brian Thompson, Deirdre Williams, and Doreen Stewart

DESCRIPTION The SSA is a 23-item instrument based on the idea that social support is in fact support only if the individual believes it is available. These subjective appraisals also are viewed as related to overall psychological well-being. The SSA taps the extent to which the individual believes he or she is loved by, esteemed by, and involved with family, friends, and others.

NORMS The SSA was studied with 10 undergraduate and community samples involving 979 respondents. The mean age ranged from mid-teens to 48. The samples were approximately 60% female, predominantly white (roughly 8% black), and roughly 50% married. Actual norms (means and standard deviations) are not reported in the primary reference.

SCORING The SSA is scored by reverse-scoring items 3, 10, 13, 21, and 22 and adding up the individual items for a total score, with lower scores indicating a stronger subjective appraisal of social support. In addition to the total score, the 8 "family" items make up an SSA-Family subscale and the 7 "friend" items make up a friend subscale. The remaining items refer to people or others in general.

RELIABILITY The SSA has very good internal consistency, with alpha coefficients that range from .81 to .90. No data on stability were reported.

VALIDITY The SSA was subjected to considerable evaluation of its validity resulting in very good concurrent, predictive, known-groups, and construct validity. The SSA is significantly correlated in predicted ways with a variety of measures of social support and psychological well-being, including network satisfaction, perceived support, family environment, depression, positive affect, negative affect, loneliness, life satisfaction, the SCL-90, and happiness.

PRIMARY REFERENCE Vaux, A., Phillips, J., Holly, L., Thomson, B., Williams, D., and Stewart, D. (1986). The Social Support Appraisals (SSA) Scale: Studies of reliability and validity, *American Journal of Community Psychology*, 14, 195–219.

AVAILABILITY May be copied from this volume.

Below is a list of statements about your relationships with family and friends. Please indicate how much you agree or disagree with each statement as being true.

(Circle one number in each row)

	Strongly agree	Agree	Disagree	Strongly disagree
1. My friends respect me.	1	2	3	4
2. My family cares for me very much.	1	2	3	4
3. I am not important to others.	1	2	3	4
4. My family holds me in high esteem.	1	2	3	4
5. I am well liked.	1	2	3	4
6. I can rely on my friends.	1	2	3	4
7. I am really admired by my family.	1	2	3	4
8. I am respected by other people.	1	2	3	4
9. I am loved dearly by my family.	1	2	3	4
10. My friends don't care about my welfare.	1	2	3	4
11. Members of my family rely on me.	1	2	3	4
12. I am held in high esteem.	1	2	3	4
13. I can't rely on my family for support.	1	2	3	4
14. People admire me.	1	2	3	4
15. I feel a strong bond with my friends.	1	2	3	4
16. My friends look out for me.	1	2	3	4
17. I feel valued by other people.	1	2	3	4
18. My family really respects me.	1	2	3	4
19. My friends and I are really important to each other.	1	2	3	4
20. I feel like I belong.	1	2	3	4
21. If I died tomorrow, very few people would miss me.	1	2	3	4
22. I don't feel close to members of my family.	1	2	3	4
23. My friends and I have done a lot for one another.	1	2	3	4

Social Support Behaviors Scale (SSB)

PURPOSE To measure modes of social support.

AUTHORS Alan Vaux, Sharon Riedel, and Doreen Stewart

DESCRIPTION The SSB is a 45-item instrument designed to assess five modes of social support: emotional (items 3, 8, 12, 16, 20, 23, 27, 30, 31, 36), socializing (items 1, 2, 5, 9, 13, 18, 24), practical assistance (items 4, 6, 7, 11, 34, 37, 40, 43), financial assistance (items 14, 21, 26, 29, 32, 38, 41, 45), and advice/guidance (items 10, 15, 17, 19, 22, 25, 28, 33, 35, 39, 42, 44). The SSB is designed to assess available supportive behavior and to do so separately for family and friends. With slight changes in wording, the SSB can be used to tap supportive behaviors actually enacted in the face of some stressor. The five subscales have been confirmed through factor analysis. This is an important measure not only for the study of social support networks, but for use in clinical practice as a way of understanding real and potential supports available for clients.

NORMS The SSB was studied initially in a series of five developmental studies involving over 300 undergraduate students. Males and females were roughly equally represented; most respondents were white with about 25% being black. Overall norms are not available since the testing strategy was to ask respondents to respond to the SSB in the face of particular stimulus problem conditions rather than as a general report of social support behaviors.

SCORING Scores for the subscales and total scales are simply computed by summing individual item scores on the 5-point scales (possible range of 45–225). However, if the SSB is to be used to determine enacted social support, the scale is changed to a 2-point scale (0=no, 1=yes) and those item scores are summed as indicated above.

RELIABILITY The SSB has very good internal consistency, with alphas that exceed .85 for several college samples. Data on stability are not available.

VALIDITY The SSB has good concurrent validity, with significant correlations with social support network associations, support appraisals, and the Inventory of Socially Supportive Behaviors. The SSB subscales also are differentially sensitive to different types of support related to each mode of support.

PRIMARY REFERENCE Vaux, A., Riedel, S., and Stewart, D. (1987). Modes of social support: The Social Support Behaviors (SSB) Scale, *American Journal of Community Psychiatry*, 15, 209–237.

AVAILABILITY May be copied from this volume.

People help each other out in a lot of different ways. Suppose you had some kind of problem (were upset about something, needed help with a practical problem, were broke, or needed some advice or guidance), *how likely* would (a) members of your *family*, and (b) your *friends* be to help you out in each of the specific ways listed below. We realize you may rarely need this kind of help, but *if you did* would family and friends help in the ways indicated. Try to base your answers on your past experience with these people. Use the scale below, and circle one number under family, and one under friends, in each row.

1 = *No one* would do this
2 = *Someone might* do this
3 = *Some* family member/friend would *probably* do this
4 = *Some* family member/friend would *certainly* do this
5 = *Most* family members/friends would *certainly* do this

	(a) Family	(b) Friends
1. Would suggest doing something, just to take my mind off my problems.	1 2 3 4 5	1 2 3 4 5
2. Would visit with me, or invite me over.	1 2 3 4 5	1 2 3 4 5
3. Would comfort me if I was upset.	1 2 3 4 5	1 2 3 4 5
4. Would give me a ride if I needed one.	1 2 3 4 5	1 2 3 4 5
5. Would have lunch or dinner with me.	1 2 3 4 5	1 2 3 4 5
6. Would look after my belongings (house, pets, etc.) for a while.	1 2 3 4 5	1 2 3 4 5
7. Would loan me a car if I needed one.	1 2 3 4 5	1 2 3 4 5
8. Would joke around or suggest doing something to cheer me up.	1 2 3 4 5	1 2 3 4 5
9. Would go to a movie or concert with me.	1 2 3 4 5	1 2 3 4 5
10. Would suggest how I could find out more about a situation.	1 2 3 4 5	1 2 3 4 5
11. Would help me out with a move or other big chore.	1 2 3 4 5	1 2 3 4 5
12. Would listen if I needed to talk about my feelings.	1 2 3 4 5	1 2 3 4 5
13. Would have a good time with me.	1 2 3 4 5	1 2 3 4 5
14. Would pay for my lunch if I was broke.	1 2 3 4 5	1 2 3 4 5
15. Would suggest a way I might do something.	1 2 3 4 5	1 2 3 4 5
16. Would give me encouragement to do something difficult.	1 2 3 4 5	1 2 3 4 5
17. Would give me advice about what to do.	1 2 3 4 5	1 2 3 4 5
18. Would chat with me.	1 2 3 4 5	1 2 3 4 5

	(a) Family	(b) Friends
19. Would help me figure out what I wanted to do.	1 2 3 4 5	1 2 3 4 5
20. Would show me that they understood how I was feeling.	1 2 3 4 5	1 2 3 4 5
21. Would buy me a drink if I was short of money.	1 2 3 4 5	1 2 3 4 5
22. Would help me decide what to do.	1 2 3 4 5	1 2 3 4 5
23. Would give me a hug, or otherwise show me I was cared about.	1 2 3 4 5	1 2 3 4 5
24. Would call me just to see how I was doing.	1 2 3 4 5	1 2 3 4 5
25. Would help me figure out what was going on.	1 2 3 4 5	1 2 3 4 5
26. Would help me out with some necessary purchase.	1 2 3 4 5	1 2 3 4 5
27. Would not pass judgment on me.	1 2 3 4 5	1 2 3 4 5
28. Would tell me who to talk to for help.	1 2 3 4 5	1 2 3 4 5
29. Would loan me money for an indefinite period.	1 2 3 4 5	1 2 3 4 5
30. Would be sympathetic if I was upset.	1 2 3 4 5	1 2 3 4 5
31. Would stick by me in a crunch.	1 2 3 4 5	1 2 3 4 5
32. Would buy me clothes if I was short of money.	1 2 3 4 5	1 2 3 4 5
33. Would tell me about the available choices and options.	1 2 3 4 5	1 2 3 4 5
34. Would loan me tools, equipment, or appliances if I needed them.	1 2 3 4 5	1 2 3 4 5
35. Would give me reasons why I should or should not do something.	1 2 3 4 5	1 2 3 4 5
36. Would show affection for me.	1 2 3 4 5	1 2 3 4 5
37. Would show me how to do something I didn't know how to do.	1 2 3 4 5	1 2 3 4 5
38. Would bring me little presents of things I needed.	1 2 3 4 5	1 2 3 4 5
39. Would tell me the best way to get something done.	1 2 3 4 5	1 2 3 4 5
40. Would talk to other people to arrange something for me.	1 2 3 4 5	1 2 3 4 5
41. Would loan me money and want to "forget about it."	1 2 3 4 5	1 2 3 4 5
42. Would tell me what to do.	1 2 3 4 5	1 2 3 4 5

continued

	(a) Family	(b) Friends
43. Would offer me a place to stay for a while.	1 2 3 4 5	1 2 3 4 5
44. Would help me think about a problem.	1 2 3 4 5	1 2 3 4 5
45. Would loan me a fairly large sum of money (say the equivalent of a month's rent or mortgage).	1 2 3 4 5	1 2 3 4 5

Sociopolitical Control Scale (SPCS)

PURPOSE To measure sociopolitical control.

AUTHORS Marc A. Zimmerman and James H. Zahniser

DESCRIPTION The SPCS is a 17-item instrument that attempts to distinguish sociopolitical control from other types of perceived control. The SPCS is based on the assumption that perceived control includes personality, cognitive, and motivational variables, all of which are built into this scale, and differs across different life spheres. The SPCS has two subscales, leadership competence (items 5–8, 14–17) and policy control (items 1–4, 9–13). This scale is especially useful for clinicians involved in some form of community practice, wherein the scale can be used to measure the sense of empowerment in clients or help in understanding the experiences of volunteers, activists, and community isolates.

NORMS The SPCS was studied with three samples: sample 1 involved 390 undergraduates (50% female, 88% white) enrolled in an introductory psychology class; sample 2 involved 205 community residents recruited at voluntary organization meetings (55% female, 92% white, mean age=42); sample 3 involved 143 people from four Methodist churches (52% female, 96% white, mean age=38). On the original scales, scores were standardized and then summed producing means of 0 with deviations from 0 indicating responses above or below the average respondent.

SCORING To simplify scoring, items on each subscale can simply be summed for a subscale score after reverse-scoring items 9–17. Thus, higher scores would indicate higher leadership competence and policy control.

RELIABILITY The SPCS has fairly good internal consistency, with alphas for the subscales that range from .75 to .78. No data on stability were reported.

VALIDITY The SPCS has good construct validity, with correlations in the predicted directions with locus of control measures, alienation measures, and a measure of willingness to lead. Both subscales differed across groups with different levels of participation in community activities.

PRIMARY REFERENCE Zimmerman, M. A., and Zahniser, J. H. (1991). Refinements of sphere-specific measures of perceived control: Development of a Sociopolitical Control Scale, *Journal of Community Psychology*, 19, 189–204.

AVAILABILITY Dr. Marc Zimmerman, Department of Health Behavior and Health Education, University of Michigan School of Public Health, Ann Arbor, MI 48109-2029. Email: marcz@umich.edu.

Please use the 6-point scale below to indicate how strongly you agree or disagree with each of the following statements as they apply to you. Place the number from 1–6 in the blank to the left of each statement.

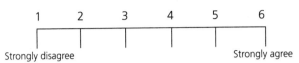

	1	2	3	4	5	6
Strongly disagree						Strongly agree

___ 1. There are plenty of ways for people like me to have a say in what our government does.

___ 2. People like me are generally well qualified to participate in the political activity and decision making in our country.

___ 3. I feel like I have a pretty good understanding of the important political issues which confront our society.

___ 4. I enjoy political participation because I want to have as much say in running government as possible.

___ 5. I am often a leader in groups.

___ 6. I can usually organize people to get things done.

___ 7. I would prefer to be a leader rather than a follower.

___ 8. Other people usually follow my ideas.

___ 9. A good many local elections aren't important enough to bother with.

___ 10. So many other people are active in local issues and organizations that it doesn't matter much to me whether I participate or not.

___ 11. It hardly makes any difference who I vote for because whoever gets elected does whatever he wants to do anyway.

___ 12. Most public officials wouldn't listen to me no matter what I did.

___ 13. Sometimes politics and government seem so complicated that a person like me can't really understand what's going on.

___ 14. I like to wait and see if someone else is going to solve a problem so that I don't have to be bothered by it.

___ 15. I would rather not try something I'm not good at.

___ 16. I find it very hard to talk in front of a group.

___ 17. I would rather someone else took over the leadership role when I'm involved in a group project.

Solution Building Inventory (SBI)

PURPOSE To measure solution building experiences

AUTHORS Sara Smock, Eric McCollum and Michele Stevenson

DESCRIPTION The SBI is a 6-item scale that measures solution building from the perspective of solution-focused brief treatment. Solution building treatment is distinguishable from problem-solving therapy in that the latter considers the basis of the problem in an effort to develop new and workable skills. Solution building, in contrast, focuses on what the client would like to see in the future and then to observe how to some degree the desired life already exists. Problem solving treatments are more cause and effect, while solution-focused brief treatment is more a motivational-teleological theory where the client is drawn to the solution. The SBI was developed with impeccable psychometric procedures, including using a panel of experts trained in solution-focused brief treatment to develop a pool of items, and two research samples (n = 97 and n = 302) using factor analysis to develop the 6-item version. The instrument is one-dimensional indicating that solution building is more of a single set of experiences and not multidimensional as the theory would suggest.

NORMS The SBI has average item means ranging from 3. 64 to 4. 31 with standard deviations range from .494 to .882. Complete item norms are available from Sara Smock.

SCORING Scores on the SBI are the sum of the item scores, divided by the number of items answered. The scale range is 1 to 5.

RELIABILITY The SBI has very good reliability estimates; the internal consistency was .87.

VALIDITY The is strong support for the validity of the SBI from factor analytic procedures. Scores on the SBI also were correlated with scores on the Dispositional Hope Scale and the Life-Orientation Test; suggesting strong concurrent validity.

PRIMARY REFERENCE Smock, S. A., McCollum, E. E., Stevenson, M. L (2010). The development of the Solution Building Inventory. *Journal of Marital and Family Therapy.* *36,* 499-510.

AVAILABILITY Sara A. Smock, Ph. D. Applied and Professional Studies, Texas Tech University, Lubbock, Texas 79409-1162. Email: Sara.smock@ttu. edu

For the following items, please respond by stating strongly agree, agree, neutral, disagree, or strongly disagree, and record the rating in the space using the scale

5 = Strongly agree

4 = Agree

3 = Neutral

2 = Disagree

1 = Strongly disagree

1. I can think about things that have made a positive difference for me. _____

2. I am able to focus on times when my situation is not so overwhelming, even a little bit. _____

3. There are times in my life when I am able to handle difficulties well. _____

4. I am aware of small positive changes that I make. _____

5. I have successfully overcome challenges in the past. _____

6. I have made steps towards improving my life. _____

Somatic, Cognitive, Behavioral Anxiety Inventory (SCBAI)

PURPOSE To measure the components of anxiety.

AUTHORS Paul M. Lehrer and Robert L. Woolfolk

DESCRIPTION The SCBAI is a 36-item instrument designed to measure the three key components of anxiety: behavior (social avoidance), cognition (worrying), and somatic (hyperventilation). This inventory was based on previous research that showed that different types or components of anxiety do not necessarily correlate highly with each other. Items for this inventory were derived from a variety of already well-established anxiety measures as well as from the authors' clinical experiences. Separate studies decreased the size of the measure from 112 to the current items. All items load over .5 on their respective factors. The three subscales are somatic (items 1, 2, 4, 7, 10, 13, 14, 18, 20, 23, 29, 30, 31, 33, 34, 35), behavioral (items 3, 6, 9, 12, 17, 22, 25, 26, 28), and cognitive (items 5, 8, 11, 15, 16, 19, 21, 24, 27, 32, 36). This measure is viewed as particularly valuable for therapeutic work since various types of anxiety might respond differentially to different kinds of treatment.

NORMS The SCBAI was developed in a series of five studies. A total of 621 subjects were involved, most of whom were male and female college students, plus 70 neurotic psychiatric patients, 67 participants in a stress workshop, and 67 nonpsychotic anxious clients of several psychotherapists. Actual norms (means and standard deviations) are not reported.

SCORING The SCBAI is scored by adding up item scores for scores on subscales as well as the total score. The higher the score, the greater the level of anxiety. Since the purpose of this measure is to focus on the components of anxiety, the total score is less a point of focus than the three subscales.

RELIABILITY The SCBAI has excellent internal consistency, with split-half reliability coefficients of .93 for the somatic factor, .92 for the behavioral factor, and .92 for the cognitive factor. Test-retest data are not reported.

VALIDITY The SCBAI has very good concurrent validity, with the three subscales correlating significantly with several relevant measures: the Spielberger Trait Anxiety, Eysenck Neuroticism, Eysenck Introversion, SCL-90, and the IPAT Anxiety Inventory. The SCBAI also is sensitive to change in clinical practice with the behavior subscale showing significant change following a behavioral treatment group and the cognitive subscale showing significant change following a cognitive therapy group. However, the SCBAI is also highly correlated with the Edwards Social Desirability Scale, indicating that some 25–35% of the variance in each subscale is due to social desirability.

PRIMARY REFERENCE Lehrer, P. M., and Woolfolk, R. L. (1982). Self-report assessment of anxiety: Somatic, cognitive, and behavioral modalities, *Behavioral Assessment*, 4, 167–177.

AVAILABILITY Dr. Paul Lehrer, Department of Psychiatry, Rutgers Medical School, Piscataway, NJ 08854. Email: lehrer@umdnj.edu.

Please circle the number that indicates how you feel for each item. *For example*, if you feel happy often, but not all the time, put:

I feel happy.

0	1	2	3	4	5	⑥	7	8
Never								Extremely often

1. My throat gets dry.

0	1	2	3	4	5	6	7	8
Never								Extremely often

2. I have difficulty in swallowing.

0	1	2	3	4	5	6	7	8
Never								Extremely often

3. I try to avoid starting conversations.

0	1	2	3	4	5	6	7	8
Never								Extremely often

4. My heart pounds.

0	1	2	3	4	5	6	7	8
Never								Extremely often

5. I picture some future misfortune.

0	1	2	3	4	5	6	7	8
Never								Extremely often

6. I avoid talking to people in authority (my boss, policemen).

0	1	2	3	4	5	6	7	8
Never								Extremely often

7. My limbs tremble.

0	1	2	3	4	5	6	7	8
Never								Extremely often

8. I can't get some thoughts out of my mind.

0	1	2	3	4	5	6	7	8
Never								Extremely often

9. I avoid going into a room by myself where people are already gathered and talking.

0	1	2	3	4	5	6	7	8
Never								Extremely often

10. My stomach hurts.

0	1	2	3	4	5	6	7	8
Never								Extremely often

11. I dwell on mistakes that I have make.

0	1	2	3	4	5	6	7	8
Never								Extremely often

12. I avoid new or unfamiliar situations.

| 0 | 1 | 2 | 3 | 4 | 5 | 6 | 7 | 8 |
Never   Extremely often

13. My neck feels tight.

| 0 | 1 | 2 | 3 | 4 | 5 | 6 | 7 | 8 |
Never   Extremely often

14. I feel dizzy.

| 0 | 1 | 2 | 3 | 4 | 5 | 6 | 7 | 8 |
Never   Extremely often

15. I think about possible misfortunes to my loved ones.

| 0 | 1 | 2 | 3 | 4 | 5 | 6 | 7 | 8 |
Never   Extremely often

16. I cannot concentrate at a task or job without irrelevant thoughts intruding.

| 0 | 1 | 2 | 3 | 4 | 5 | 6 | 7 | 8 |
Never   Extremely often

17. I pass by school friends, or people I know but have not seen me for a long time, unless they speak to me first.

| 0 | 1 | 2 | 3 | 4 | 5 | 6 | 7 | 8 |
Never   Extremely often

18. I breathe rapidly.

| 0 | 1 | 2 | 3 | 4 | 5 | 6 | 7 | 8 |
Never   Extremely often

19. I keep busy to avoid uncomfortable thoughts.

| 0 | 1 | 2 | 3 | 4 | 5 | 6 | 7 | 8 |
Never   Extremely often

20. I can't catch my breath.

| 0 | 1 | 2 | 3 | 4 | 5 | 6 | 7 | 8 |
Never   Extremely often

21. I can't get some pictures or images out of my mind.

| 0 | 1 | 2 | 3 | 4 | 5 | 6 | 7 | 8 |
Never   Extremely often

22. I try to avoid social gatherings.

| 0 | 1 | 2 | 3 | 4 | 5 | 6 | 7 | 8 |
Never   Extremely often

23. My arms or legs feel stiff.

| 0 | 1 | 2 | 3 | 4 | 5 | 6 | 7 | 8 |
Never   Extremely often

24. I imagine myself appearing foolish with a person whose opinion of me is important.

| 0 | 1 | 2 | 3 | 4 | 5 | 6 | 7 | 8 |
Never   Extremely often

continued

25. I find myself staying home rather than involving myself in activities outside.

0	1	2	3	4	5	6	7	8
Never							Extremely often	

26. I prefer to avoid making specific plans for self-improvement.

0	1	2	3	4	5	6	7	8
Never							Extremely often	

27. I am concerned that others might not think well of me.

0	1	2	3	4	5	6	7	8
Never							Extremely often	

28. I try to avoid challenging jobs.

0	1	2	3	4	5	6	7	8
Never							Extremely often	

29. My muscles twitch or jump.

0	1	2	3	4	5	6	7	8
Never							Extremely often	

30. I experience a tingling sensation somewhere in my body.

0	1	2	3	4	5	6	7	8
Never							Extremely often	

31. My arms or legs feel weak.

0	1	2	3	4	5	6	7	8
Never							Extremely often	

32. I have to be careful not to let my real feelings show.

0	1	2	3	4	5	6	7	8
Never							Extremely often	

33. I experience muscular aches and pains.

0	1	2	3	4	5	6	7	8
Never							Extremely often	

34. I feel numbness in my face, limbs, or tongue.

0	1	2	3	4	5	6	7	8
Never							Extremely often	

35. I experience chest pains.

0	1	2	3	4	5	6	7	8
Never							Extremely often	

36. I have an uneasy feeling.

0	1	2	3	4	5	6	7	8
Never							Extremely often	

Somatoform Dissociation Questionnaire (SDQ-20)

PURPOSE To measure severity of somatoform symptomatology.

AUTHORS Ellert R. S. Nijenhuis, Onno van der Hart, and Johan Vanderlinden

DESCRIPTION This 20-item instrument is designed to evaluate the severity of somatoform symptomatology, which generally is found with dissociative disorders. These symptoms include anesthesia (i.e., the loss of proprioceptual, visual, auditive, gustatoric, and olfactory perception), amnesia (i.e., the loss of the capacity to retrieve information), and abulia (i.e., the loss of will-power or volition and a restriction of the range of emotional experiences and expression). The SDQ-20 was developed from a pool of 77 items and evaluated by a panel of experts for face validity. An item was included if it discriminated between a sample of patients with a dissociative disorder from a sample of patients with other mental health conditions. The 20 items surviving are a unidimensional measure. A shorter version of the instrument, including only items 4, 8, 13, 15, and 18, can be used for initial clinical screening purposes. The short version has a cutting score of 8 or higher, which indicates sufficient severity of symptoms to warrant further assessment for a dissociative disorder.

NORMS Scores on the SDQ-20 for patients diagnosed with a dissociative disorder averaged 40.8 (SD=11) for men and 49.1 (SD=15.56) for women. Male patients with mental health conditions other than a dissociative disorder had a mean of 23.8 (SD=3.0), while female patients had a mean of 23.4 (SD=4.2).

SCORING The SDQ-20 is scored by adding the item responses. Scores range from 20 to 100 for the SDQ-20 and from 5 to 25 for the SDQ-5. Higher scores indicate more severe somatoform symptoms.

RELIABILITY The internal consistency of the SDQ-20 is excellent, with an alpha coefficient of .95. The internal consistency for the SDQ-5 is .80, which is quite good for such a short instrument.

VALIDITY The validity was estimated with known-groups procedures comparing scores of 50 patients diagnosed with a dissociative disorder with scores from 50 psychiatric patients without a dissociative disorder. Scores were significantly different. Differences also were found for some subtypes of dissociative disorders, such as dissociative identity disorder compared to depersonalization disorder. Scores on the SDQ-20 correlated .71 with scores on a measure of psychological dissociation, evidencing concurrent validity.

PRIMARY REFERENCES Nijenhuis, E. R. S., Spinhoven, P., van Dyck, R., van der Hart, O., and Vanderlinden, J. (1996). The development and psychometric characteristics of the Somatoform Dissociation Questionnaire (SDQ-20), *The Journal of Nervous and Mental Disease*, 184, 688–694. Nijenhuis, E. R. S., Spinhoven, P., van Dyck, R., van der Hart, O., and Vanderlinden, J. (1997). The development of the Somatoform Dissociation Questionnaire (SDQ-5) as a screening instrument for dissociative disorders. *Acta Psychiatrica Scandinavica*, 96, 311–318.

AVAILABILITY Dr. Ellert R. S. Nijenhuis, Cats-Polm Institute, Zeist, Mental Health Care Drenthe, Assen, The Netherlands. Email: e.nijenhuis@home.nl.

This questionnaire asks about different physical symptoms or body experiences, which you may have had either briefly or for a longer time. Please indicate to what extent these experiences apply to you *in the past year*.

For each statement, please circle the number in the first column that best applies to YOU. The possibilities are:

1 = This applies to me NOT AT ALL
2 = This applies to me A LITTLE
3 = This applies to me MODERATELY
4 = This applies to me QUITE A BIT
5 = This applies to me EXTREMELY

If a symptom or experience applies to you, please indicate whether a **physician** has connected it with a **physical disease** by circling the word YES or NO in the column "Is the physical cause known?" If you wrote YES, please write the physical cause (if you know it) on the line. Please do not skip any of the 20 questions.

Thank you for your cooperation.

	Extent to which the symptom or experience applies to you	Is the physical cause known?
Sometimes:		
1. I have trouble urinating.	1 2 3 4 5	NO YES, namely ___
2. I dislike tastes that I usually like (women: at times OTHER THAN pregnancy or monthly periods).	1 2 3 4 5	NO YES, namely ___
3. I hear sounds from nearby as if they were coming from far away.	1 2 3 4 5	NO YES, namely ___
4. I have pain while urinating.	1 2 3 4 5	NO YES, namely ___
5. My body, or a part of it, feels numb.	1 2 3 4 5	NO YES, namely ___
6. People and things look bigger than usual.	1 2 3 4 5	NO YES, namely ___
7. I have an attack that resembles an epileptic seizure.	1 2 3 4 5	NO YES, namely ___
8. My body, or a part of it, is insensitive to pain.	1 2 3 4 5	NO YES, namely ___
9. I dislike smells that I usually like.	1 2 3 4 5	NO YES, namely ___
10. I feel pain in my genitals (at times OTHER THAN sexual intercourse).	1 2 3 4 5	NO YES, namely ___
11. I cannot hear for a while (as if I am deaf).	1 2 3 4 5	NO YES, namely ___
12. I cannot see for a while (as if I am blind).	1 2 3 4 5	NO YES, namely ___

	Extent to which the symptom or experience applies to you	Is the physical cause known?
13. I see things around me differently than usual (for example, as if looking through a tunnel, or seeing merely a part of an object).	1 2 3 4 5	NO YES, namely ___
14. I am able to smell much BETTER or WORSE than I usually do (even though I do not have a cold).	1 2 3 4 5	NO YES, namely ___
15. It is as if my body, or a part of it, has disappeared.	1 2 3 4 5	NO YES, namely ___
16. I cannot swallow, or can swallow only with great effort.	1 2 3 4 5	NO YES, namely ___
17. I cannot sleep for nights on end, but remain very active during daytime.	1 2 3 4 5	NO YES, namely ___
18. I cannot speak (or only with great effort) or I can only whisper.	1 2 3 4 5	NO YES, namely ___
19. I am paralyzed for a while.	1 2 3 4 5	NO YES, namely ___
20. I grow stiff for a while.	1 2 3 4 5	NO YES, namely ___

South Oaks Gambling Screen (SOGS)

PURPOSE To measure pathological gambling.

AUTHORS Henry R. Lesieur and Sheila B. Blume

DESCRIPTION The SOGS is a 20-item instrument designed to identify pathological gamblers. The SOGS was originally developed from DSM-III criteria and is reported as being highly correlated with DSM-III-R. Because of the severity of possible consequences of problem gambling, it is crucial to have an easily administered instrument for early identification of problem gamblers. Unfortunately, many cases are currently overlooked in counseling and in a variety of different professional helping programs. Thus this instrument, perhaps the only well-established measure for identifying problem gamblers, is an important tool in work with the large number of problem gamblers that have been identified in epidemiological research. The SOGS has been translated into numerous languages, with references available from the authors.

NORMS The SOGS was originally studied with a total of 1616 subjects of whom 867 were patients with diagnoses of substance abuse and pathological gambling, 213 members of Gamblers Anonymous, 384 university students, and 152 hospital employees. Of 297 inpatients, 214 received scores of zero, 44 received scores ranging from 1 to 4, and 39 received scores of 5 or more, placing them in the pathological gambling category.

SCORING Scores on the SOGS are determined by adding up the number of questions which show an "at-risk" response. Questions 1, 2, 3, 12, 16j, and 16k are not counted, leaving 20 questions that are counted. Answering none of the questions positively equals no problem; 1–4 "yes" answers equals some problem; and 5 or more "yes" responses indicates probable pathological gambling.

RELIABILITY The SOGS has excellent internal consistency, with an alpha of .97. The SOGS also has good stability, with a thirty-day test-retest correlation of .71.

VALIDITY The SOGS has established excellent validity, identifying 96.7% of pathological gamblers from a Gamblers Anonymous sample as determined by agreement with DSM-III-R diagnoses with a false positive rating of only 1.4% and a false negative rating of only .5%. Scores on the SOGS also showed high and significant correlations with counselors' independent assessment and family members' assessments of gambling problems of the subjects.

PRIMARY REFERENCE Lesieur, H. R., and Blume, S. B. (1987). The South Oaks Gambling Screen (SOGS): A new instrument for the identification of pathological gamblers, *American Journal of Psychiatry*, 144, 1184–1188.

AVAILABILITY The SOGS is copyrighted only so someone doesn't call it the "Jones Gambling Screen." Its use is free but on condition that anyone who uses it in research or in a publication send a copy of that research report or publication to the authors of the SOGS: Dr. Sheila B. Blume, State University of New York at Stony Brook, 284 Green Ave., Sayville, NY 11782, and Henry R. Lesieur, Ph.D., Institute for Problem Gambling, 124 Hillside Ave., Pawtucket, RI 02860. Reprinted with permission of the authors.

SOGS

1. Please indicate which of the following types of gambling you have done in your lifetime. For each type, mark one answer: "Not at all," "Less than once a week," or "Once a week or more."

	Not at all	Less than once a week	Once a week or more
a. Play cards for money	—	—	—
b. Bet on horses, dogs, or other animals (at OTB, the track, or with a bookie)	—	—	—
c. Bet on sports (parlay cards, with a bookie, or at Jai Alai)	—	—	—
d. Played dice games (including craps, over and under, or other dice games) for money	—	—	—
e. Gambled in a casino (legal or otherwise)	—	—	—
f. Played the numbers or bet on lotteries	—	—	—
g. Played bingo for money	—	—	—
h. Played the stock, options, and/or commodities market	—	—	—
i. Played slot machines, poker machines, or other gambling machines	—	—	—
j. Bowled, shot pool, played golf, or some other game of skill for money	—	—	—
k. Pull tabs or "paper" games other than lotteries	—	—	—
m. Some form of gambling not listed above (please specify)	—	—	—

2. What is the largest amount of money you have ever gambled with on any one day?
   ___ never have gambled
   ___ $1 or less
   ___ more than $1 up to $10
   ___ more than $10 up to $100
   ___ more than $100 up to $1,000
   ___ more than $1,000 up to $10,000
   ___ more than $10,000

3. Check which of the following people in your life has (or had) a gambling problem.
   _____ father _____ mother _____ brother or sister _____ grandparent
   _____ my spouse/partner _____ my child(ren) _____ another relative
   _____ a friend or someone else important in my life

4. When you gamble, how often do you go back another day to win back money you lost?
   ___ never
   ___ some of the time (less than half the time I lost)
   ___ most of the time I lost
   ___ every time I lost

5. Have you ever claimed to be winning money gambling but weren't really? In fact, you lost?
   ___ never (or never gamble)

continued

___ yes, less than half the time I lost
___ yes, most of the time

6. Do you feel you have ever had a problem with betting money or gambling?
   ___ no
   ___ yes, in the past but not now
   ___ yes

7. Did you ever gamble more than you intended to?   ___ yes   ___ no

8. Have people criticized your betting or told you that you had a gambling problem, regardless of whether or not you thought it was true?   ___ yes   ___ no

9. Have you ever felt guilty about the way you gamble or what happens when you gamble?   ___ yes   ___ no

10. Have you ever felt like you would like to stop betting money or gambling but didn't think you could?   ___ yes   ___ no

11. Have you ever hidden betting slips, lottery tickets, gambling money, I.O.U.s, or other signs of betting or gambling from your spouse, children, or other important people in your life?   ___ yes   ___ no

12. Have you ever argued with people you live with over how you handle money?   ___ yes   ___ no

13. (If you answered yes to question 12): Have money arguments ever centered on your gambling?   ___ yes   ___ no

14. Have you ever borrowed from someone and not paid them back as a result of your gambling?   ___ yes   ___ no

15. Have you ever lost time from work (or school) due to betting money or gambling?   ___ yes   ___ no

16. If you borrowed money to gamble or to pay gambling debts, who or where did you borrow from? (Check "yes" or "no" for each)

		no	yes
a.	from household money	( )	( )
b.	from your spouse	( )	( )
c.	from other relatives or in-laws	( )	( )
d.	from banks, loan companies, or credit unions	( )	( )
e.	from credit cards	( )	( )
f.	from loan sharks	( )	( )
g.	you cashed in stocks, bonds, or other securities	( )	( )
h.	you sold personal or family property	( )	( )
i.	you borrowed on your checking account (passed bad checks)	( )	( )
j.	you have (had) a credit line with a bookie	( )	( )
k.	you have (had) a credit line with a casino	( )	( )

Splitting Scale (SS)

PURPOSE To measure the characterological use of splitting as a defense mechanism.

AUTHOR Mary-Joan Gerson

DESCRIPTION This 14-item instrument draws from the theories of Kernberg and Kohut who view splitting as a symptom of borderline and narcissistic personality disorders. The function of splitting is to keep ambivalence at bay. Splitting is manifested in radical shifts in evaluations both of self and other, merging of self and other, disassociated grandiosity, and exhibitionism. The defense of splitting is defined as the separation of "good" or idealized objects from "bad" or devalued objects. There does not appear to be a gender difference on the SS, even though females are diagnosed as borderline personality more frequently than males. The SS score is reportedly not associated with age.

NORMS The SS was developed on a sample of 41 female and 34 male graduate students in psychology. The average age was 27.7 years for men and 30 for women. The mean SS was 52.97 with a standard deviation of 11.46, and ranged from 26 to 79. The SS was also developed on a sample of 113 female and 75 male patients from an urban health clinic. The age of this sample ranged from 21 to 42. Normative data are not presented.

SCORING All items are phrased to reflect the splitting defense mechanism. Respondents are asked to rate how "true" each item is to him or her. Ratings range from 1, "not at all," to 7, "very true." Scores are the total of each item rating and range from 14 to 98. Higher scores reflect characterological use of splitting.

RELIABILITY The reliability of the SS has been estimated through internal consistency and test-retest. The alpha coefficient was moderate (.70) but acceptable for an instrument tapping such an elusive concept. The SS was quite stable, with a test-retest correlation of .84 over a three-week period.

VALIDITY The SS has fairly good concurrent validity evidence, with scores correlating positively with a measure of narcissistic personality, and negatively with self-esteem. The negative and positive criterion-related validity coefficients are consistent with the ego-oriented theory of this borderline defense.

PRIMARY REFERENCE Gerson, M.-J. (1984). Splitting: The development of a measure, *Journal of Clinical Psychology*, 40, 157–162. Instrument reproduced with permission of Mary-Joan Gerson.

AVAILABILITY May be copied from this volume.

Below are fourteen questions. Please read each question and indicate in the space to the left how true each is for you using the following scale:

1 = Not at all true
2 = A little true
3 = Slightly true
4 = Somewhat true
5 = Moderately true
6 = Considerably true
7 = Very true

__ 1. I hate to hear someone close to me being criticized.
__ 2. When I'm with someone really terrific, I feel dumb.
__ 3. When I'm angry, everyone around me seems rotten.
__ 4. My friends don't know how much I'd like to be admired by people.
__ 5. It's hard for me to get angry at people I like.
__ 6. It's very painful when someone disappoints me.
__ 7. I have absolutely no sympathy for people who abuse their children.
__ 8. Sometimes I feel I could do anything in the world.
__ 9. There are times my wife (husband)/girlfriend (boyfriend) seems as strong as iron, and at other times as helpless as a baby. (Consider your most recent relationship in the absence of an ongoing relationship.)
__ 10. I often feel that I can't put the different parts of my personality together, so that there is one "me."
__ 11. Sometimes I feel my love is dangerous.
__ 12. When I'm in a new situation, there's often one person I really dislike.
__ 13. It's hard for me to become sexually excited when I'm depressed.
__ 14. Some people have too much power over me.

State Hope Scale (SHS)

PURPOSE To measure hope.

AUTHORS C. R. Snyder et al.

DESCRIPTION The SHS is a 6-item scale designed to measure hope. As a state measure, the SHS measures hope as a temporal state that is related to the ongoing events in people's lives. Thus the SHS provides a snapshot of a person's current goal-directed thinking. Hope is defined as a cognitive set comprising agency (belief in one's capacity to initiate and sustain actions) and pathways (belief in one's capacity to generate roots) to reach goals. The agency subscale comprises the three even-numbered items of the SHS and the pathways subscale comprises the three odd-numbered items. The SHS is useful as an instrument for research on hope and goal-related activities, and also as an outcome measure for interventions in which the focus is on change in goal-directed thinking.

NORMS The SHS was developed in a series of four studies. The initial study with the largest sample involved 444 university students enrolled in an introductory psychology course at the University of Kansas. From this group 168 students were selected from the top, middle, and bottom portions of the distribution of scores on the SHS. The sample involved 28 low-hope men, 28 low-hope women, 28 medium-hope men, 29 medium-hope women, 26 high-hope men, and 29 high-hope women. For the mass testing, the overall mean of the SHS was 37.15 (SD = 6.33). When administered to the smaller sample over a period of 29 consecutive days, the overall mean of the SHS was 33.99 (SD = 7.02). There were no significant differences in the scores for men and women.

SCORING The SHS is easily scored by summing the responses on the six items for a total scale score. Scores can range from a low of 6 to a high of 48, with higher scores indicating greater amounts of hope. The subscales are scored by summing the items on each subscale.

RELIABILITY The SHS has excellent internal consistency, with an alpha of .93 for the total scale, .91 for the agency subscale, and .91 for the pathways subscale. The SHS has variable stability with correlations across any two days in the four-week period of the study ranging from .48 to .93.

VALIDITY The SHS has established very good construct validity, correlating in predicted directions with the Dispositional Hope Scale and State Self-Esteem, State Positive Affect, and State Negative Affect scales.

PRIMARY REFERENCE Snyder, C. R., et al. (1996). Development and validation of the State Hope Scale, *Journal of Personality and Social Psychology*, 70, 321–335.

AVAILABILITY Dr. C. R. Snyder, 305 Fraser Hall, Graduate Training Program in Clinical Psychology, University of Kansas, Lawrence, KS 66045-2462. Reproduced by permission of the senior author and the American Psychological Association. Email: crsynder@ku.edu.

Read each item carefully. Using the scale shown below, please select the number that best describes *how you think about yourself right now* and put that number in the blank before each sentence. Please take a few moments to focus on yourself and what is going on in *your life at this moment*. Once you have this "here and now" set, go ahead and answer each item according to the following scale:

> 1 = Definitely false
> 2 = Mostly false
> 3 = Somewhat false
> 4 = Slightly false
> 5 = Slightly true
> 6 = Somewhat true
> 7 = Mostly true
> 8 = Definitely true

___ 1. If I should find myself in a jam, I could think of many ways to get out of it.
___ 2. At the present time, I am energetically pursuing my goals.
___ 3. There are lots of ways around any problem that I am facing now.
___ 4. Right now, I see myself as being pretty successful.
___ 5. I can think of many ways to reach my current goals.
___ 6. At this time, I am meeting the goals that I have set for myself.

State-Trait Anger Scale (STAS)

PURPOSE To measure the state and trait of anger.

AUTHORS Charles Spielberger and Perry London

DESCRIPTION The 30 items that make up this instrument assess anger both as an emotional state that varies in intensity and as a relatively stable personality trait. State anger is defined as an emotional condition consisting of subjective feelings of tension, annoyance, irritation, or rage. Trait anger is defined in terms of how frequently a respondent feels state anger over time. A person high in trait anger would tend to perceive more situations as anger provoking and respond with higher state-anger scores. In this framework, anger differs from hostility, which connotes a set of attitudes that mediate aggressive behavior. The instruments were developed with rigorous psychometric procedures, including the development of long and short forms which were highly correlated, ranging from .95 for state anger to .99 for trait anger. A short form of the state-anger scale (SAS) is composed of the following items: 1, 2, 3, 7, 8, 9, 10, 11, 12, and 13. A short form of the trait-anger scale (TAS) is composed of items 1, 2, 3, 5, 6, 7, 8, 9, 11, and 14. Trait anger can also be assessed with two subscales: anger temperament and anger reaction.

NORMS Extensive normative data are available from samples of high school students ($n = 3016$), college students ($n = 1621$), working adults ($n = 1252$), and military recruits ($n = 2360$). For a subsample of working adult women who were between 23 and 32 years old, the mean scores for the state anger, trait anger, angry temperament, and angry reaction were 13.71, 18.45, 5.99, and 9.48, respectively. For a subsample of working adult men with ages ranging from 23 to 32, the mean scores for the same scales were 14.28, 18.49, 5.9, and 9.5.

SCORING The trait-anger items are rated on 4-point scales from "almost never" (1) to "almost always" (4). Scores are the sum of the item ratings. Subscale items are: anger temperament, 1, 2, 3, and 8; anger reaction, 5, 6, 7, and 9. The state-anger items are rated on intensity of feelings from "not at all" (1) to "very much so" (4). Scores are the sum of the state-anger items. For both state and trait anger, scores range from 10 to 40 for the 10-item short forms and from 15 to 60 for the long forms. Higher scores reflect greater anger.

RELIABILITY The STAS has very good reliability. The internal consistency of the original 15-item trait-anger measure was .87 for a sample of 146 college students. The trait-anger measure had an internal consistency of .87 for male navy recruits and .84 for female navy recruits. The original state-anger measure has excellent internal consistency, with correlations of .93 for male and female navy recruits. The anger temperament subscale had internal consistency coefficients ranging from .84 to .89 for male and female college students and navy recruits. The angry reaction subscale had internal consistency coefficients ranging from .70 to .75 for the same samples. Internal consistency, reported for the 10-item forms using the same samples, is good to excellent. All internal consistency results are based on Cronbach's alpha.

VALIDITY Concurrent validity support is evidenced by correlations with three measures of hostility and measures of neuroticism, psychotism, and anxiety. Scores were not associated with state-trait curiosity or extraversion. Additional validity findings are reported in the primary reference.

PRIMARY REFERENCES Spielberger, C. D., Jacobs, G., Russel, S., and Crane, R. S. (1983). Assessment of anger: The State-Trait Anger Scale. In J. N. Butcher and C. D. Spielberger (eds.), *Advances in Personality Assessment*, Vol. 2, pp. 159–187. Hillsdale, N.J.: Lawrence Erlbaum Associates, Inc. See also London, P., and Spielberger, C. (1983). Job stress, hassles and medical risk, *American Health*, March, 58–63. Instruments reproduced with permission of C. D. Spielberger, *American Health* and Lawrence Erlbaum Associates, Inc.

AVAILABILITY May be copied from this volume.

A number of statements that people have used to describe how they feel are given below. Read the statements below and indicate how you feel *at the moment* by placing the appropriate number next to each item.

$$1 \ = \ \text{Not at all}$$
$$2 \ = \ \text{Somewhat}$$
$$3 \ = \ \text{Moderately so}$$
$$4 \ = \ \text{Very much so}$$

___ 1.   I am mad.
___ 2.   I feel angry.
___ 3.   I am burned up.
___ 4.   I feel irritated.
___ 5.   I feel frustrated.
___ 6.   I feel aggravated.
___ 7.   I feel like I'm about to explode.
___ 8.   I feel like banging on the table.
___ 9.   I feel like yelling at somebody.
___ 10. I feel like swearing.
___ 11. I am furious.
___ 12. I feel like hitting someone.
___ 13. I feel like breaking things.
___ 14. I am annoyed.
___ 15. I am resentful.

TAS

A number of statements that people have used to describe themselves are given below. Read the statements below and indicate how you *generally* feel by placing the appropriate number next to each item.

1 = Almost never
2 = Sometimes
3 = Often
4 = Almost always

___ 1. I have a fiery temper.
___ 2. I am quick tempered.
___ 3. I am a hotheaded person.
___ 4. I get annoyed when I am singled out for correction.
___ 5. It makes me furious when I am criticized in front of others.
___ 6. I get angry when I'm slowed down by others' mistakes.
___ 7. I feel infuriated when I do a good job and get a poor evaluation.
___ 8. I fly off the handle.
___ 9. I feel annoyed when I am not given recognition for doing good work.
___ 10. People who think they are always right irritate me.
___ 11. When I get mad, I say nasty things.
___ 12. I feel irritated.
___ 13. I feel angry.
___ 14. When I get frustrated, I feel like hitting someone.
___ 15. It makes my blood boil when I am pressured.

Stress-Arousal Checklist (SACL)

PURPOSE To measure stress and arousal.

AUTHORS Colin Mackay and Tom Cox

DESCRIPTION The 30-item SACL consists of adjectives commonly used to describe one's psychological experience of stress. The model of stress is two-dimensional. One dimension consists of feelings ranging from pleasant to unpleasant. This is a general sense of well-being. The second dimension of stress ranges from feelings of wakefulness to drowsiness, or vigorousness. The first dimension is labeled as stress while the second is labeled arousal. The stress dimension is considered a subjective experience in response to the external environment, while the arousal dimension represents ongoing somatic or autonomic activity.

NORMS The SACL was originally tested with a sample of 145 undergraduates, although no demographic data are reported. More recent research tested the factor structure of the SACL with 72 male and 131 female second year college students. Normative data were not reported.

SCORING The respondent rates each adjective in terms of the intensity of his or her feelings about the adjective. For the positive adjectives, the double-plus and plus ratings are scored 1 and the question mark and minus ratings are scored 0. For the negative adjectives, the question mark and minus ratings are scored 1 and the plus and double-plus ratings are scored 0. The stress subscale consists of eight negative adjectives (2, 3, 15, 21, 22, 25, 27, 28) and ten positive stress adjectives (1, 5, 6, 9, 10, 11, 12, 13, 18, 23). The arousal subscale consists of seven positive adjectives (4, 7, 14, 19, 20, 29, 30) and five negative adjectives (8, 16, 17, 24, 26). Scores are the sum of negative and positive adjectives. Stress scores range from 0 to 18; arousal scores from 0 to 12. Higher scores reflect more stress and arousal.

RELIABILITY Reliability data are not available. Evidence of internal consistency is provided, though, by studies using factor analysis, which generally showed adjectives were correlated with other adjectives from the same subscale of stress or arousal.

VALIDITY The SACL has evidence of known-groups validity such that scores on the stress dimension increased as a consequence of a stressful situation. Additionally, a prolonged, monotonous, and repetitive task resulted in increases in stress scores and decreases in arousal scores. The SACL has also been shown to have concurrent validity, with scores correlating with various physiological measures.

PRIMARY REFERENCES Mackay, C., Cox, T., Burrows, G., and Lazzerini, T. (1978). An inventory for the measurement of self-reported stress and arousal, *British Journal of Social and Clinical Psychology*, 17, 283–284. McCormick, I. A., Walkey, F. H., and Taylor, A. J. W. (1985). The Stress Arousal Checklist: An independent analysis, *Educational and Psychological Measurement*, 45, 143–146. Instrument reproduced with permission of Dr. Tom Cox.

AVAILABILITY Dr. Tom Cox, Stress Research, Department of Psychology, University of Nottingham, Nottingham, N.G. 72 RD, United Kingdom. Email: Tom.cox@nottingham.ac.uk.

The words shown below describe different feelings and moods. Please use this list to describe your feelings *at this moment*.

If the word *definitely* describes your feelings, circle the double plus (++). If the word *more or less* describes your feelings circle the plus (+). If you do not understand the word, or *you cannot decide* whether or not it describes how you feel, circle the question mark (?). If the word *does not describe* the way you feel, circle the minus (–).

First reactions are most reliable; therefore do not spend too long thinking about each word. Please be as honest and accurate as possible.

1. Tense	++ + ? –		16. Tired	++ + ? –
2. Relaxed	++ + ? –		17. Idle	++ + ? –
3. Restful	++ + ? –		18. Up-tight	++ + ? –
4. Active	++ + ? –		19. Alert	++ + ? –
5. Apprehensive	++ + ? –		20. Lively	++ + ? –
6. Worried	++ + ? –		21. Cheerful	++ + ? –
7. Energetic	++ + ? –		22. Contented	++ + ? –
8. Drowsy	++ + ? –		23. Jittery	++ + ? –
9. Bothered	++ + ? –		24. Sluggish	++ + ? –
10. Uneasy	++ + ? –		25. Pleasant	++ + ? –
11. Dejected	++ + ? –		26. Sleepy	++ + ? –
12. Nervous	++ + ? –		27. Comfortable	++ + ? –
13. Distressed	++ + ? –		28. Calm	++ + ? –
14. Vigorous	++ + ? –		29. Stimulated	++ + ? –
15. Peaceful	++ + ? –		30. Activated	++ + ? –

Stressful Situations Questionnaire (SSQ)

PURPOSE To measure apprehension and concern in stressful situations.

AUTHORS William F. Hodges and James P. Felling

DESCRIPTION This 40-item instrument was originally developed to test hypotheses regarding stress in trait anxious subjects. It measures the level of reported apprehension or concern (anxiety) in various social situations relevant to college students. The situations are those believed to involve a loss of self-esteem. Factor analysis of the instrument produced four factors which may be used as subscales to measure apprehension in physical danger (APD), apprehension in classroom and speech situations (ACSS), apprehension of social and academic failure (ASAF), and apprehension in dating situations (ADS). The last three subscales may be summed to form one measure of apprehension in ego-threatening situations, that is, situations where one fears failure. Females and males score differently only on the APD subscale.

NORMS The SSQ was developed on a sample of 228 undergraduate college students: 141 males and 87 females. Means and standard deviations are not reported.

SCORING Each item is rated in terms of degree of apprehensiveness or concern from none (1) to extreme (5). Scores are the sums of the item scores. The subscales and items are APD: 3, 7, 10, 11, 12, 13, 14, 16, 17, 18, 28, 32, 45; ACSS: 4, 5, 20, 22, 24, 29, 37, 42; ASAD: 6, 9, 44, 15, 19, 21, 23, 25, 27, 33, 35, 38; ADS: 1, 2, 34, 41. Higher scores reflect more apprehension or concern.

RELIABILITY No reliability data were reported.

VALIDITY The validity of the SSQ has had some support through concurrent validity procedures. Scores on the APD were not correlated with trait anxiety, but the three subscales concerning ego-threatening situations were moderately correlated. These correlations conform to the predictions of state-trait anxiety theory. A stronger concurrent validity correlation was found between the trait anxiety measure and the combined ego-threatening stressful situations than with the state anxiety measure.

PRIMARY REFERENCE Hodges, W. F., and Felling, F. P. (1970). Types of stressful situations and their relation to trait anxiety and sex, *Journal of Consulting and Clinical Psychology*, 34, 333–337. Instrument reproduced with permission of William F. Hodges and the American Psychological Association.

AVAILABILITY May be copied from this volume.

Everyone is faced with situations in life that make them feel more or less apprehensive. Below is a list of situations which you may have experienced, or might be placed in some day. First, read through the entire list; then, for each situation, indicate at left the number that best describes the degree of apprehensiveness or concern you have felt or believe you would feel if in that situation. Do not skip any items. Work rapidly and put down your first impression.

1 = None at all
2 = Slight
3 = Moderate
4 = Considerable
5 = Extreme

___ 1. Going on a blind date.
___ 2. Asking someone for a date to a party.
___ 3. Seeing someone bleed profusely from a cut arm.
___ 4. Asking a teacher to clarify an assignment in class.
___ 5. Giving a speech in front of class.
___ 6. Introducing a friend and forgetting his name.
___ 7. Putting iodine on an open cut.
___ 8. Having someone angry at you.
___ 9. Taking a test that you expect to fail.
___ 10. Seeing a dog run over by a car.
___ 11. Walking in a slum alone at night.
___ 12. Giving blood at the Blood Bank.
___ 13. Riding in an airplane in a storm.
___ 14. Being present at an operation or watching one in a movie.
___ 15. Belching aloud in class.
___ 16. Having a tooth cavity filled.
___ 17. Climbing too steep a mountain.
___ 18. Paying respects at the open coffin of an acquaintance.
___ 19. Being refused membership in a social club.
___ 20. Asking a question in class.
___ 21. Doing poorly in a course that seems easy to others.
___ 22. Reciting a poem in class.
___ 23. Having your date leave a dance with someone else.
___ 24. Reciting in language class.
___ 25. Finding the questions on a test extremely difficult.
___ 26. Having to ask for money that was borrowed from you.
___ 27. Forgetting lines in a school play.
___ 28. Riding a car going 95 miles per hour.
___ 29. Asking a teacher to explain the grading of your test.
___ 30. Getting hurt in a fight.
___ 31. Telling an uninvited guest to leave a party.
___ 32. Passing a very bad traffic accident.
___ 33. Being the only person at a party not dressed up.
___ 34. Introducing yourself to someone attractive of the opposite sex.

____ 35. Spilling your drink on yourself at a formal dinner party.
____ 36. Having an interview for a job.
____ 37. Volunteering an answer to a question in class.
____ 38. Getting back a test you think you may have failed.
____ 39. Skiing out of control.
____ 40. Asking the person behind you to stop kicking your seat.
____ 41. Kissing a date for the first time.
____ 42. Asking a teacher to explain a question during a test.
____ 43. Asking people in a study room to make less noise.
____ 44. Being in a difficult course for which you have inadequate background.
____ 45. Participating in a psychology experiment in which you receive electric shock.

Student Jenkins Activity Survey (SJAS)

PURPOSE To measure Type A behavior.

AUTHORS Paul R. Yarnold and Fred B. Bryant

DESCRIPTION The SJAS is a 21-item instrument designed to measure Type A behaviors: coronary-prone behaviors that consist of time urgent/impatient, hard-driving/competitive, and aggressive/hostile behaviors. The SJAS has three factors or subscales: hard-driving/competitive (items 1, 8–12, 15, 16, 19–21), rapid eating (items 3, 4), and rapid speaking (items 5, 6). The three factors explain roughly 82% of the variance in SJAS scores. Because of the importance of Type A behavior as an established risk factor for coronary-artery disease and heart disease, this measure is viewed as an especially important predictor for physical health and for monitoring clinical changes in Type A behaviors. The SJAS is recommended for use primarily with young adults, particularly those in college.

NORMS The SJAS has been extensively studied with a wide variety of college age samples. These include undergraduate samples of 1248, 4072, and 1810 American students, and 117 students in Greece. Males and females were represented in roughly equal proportions. The mean total score for 4072 undergraduates was 7.77 (SD = 3.25), while the mean for the hard-driving/competitive subscale was 2.24 (SD = 1.56). Whites have higher scores on the SJAS (more Type A) than nonwhites.

SCORING The SJAS is scored by assigning one point for each "correct" response: 1a or b, 2a, 3a or b, 4a, 5a, 6a, 7c, 8a or b, 9a or b, 10a or b, 11c, 12d, 13a or b, 14a, 15c, 16c, 17a, 18c, 19c, 20a, 21a. The total score is just a sum of all item scores with a range of 0 to 21. For the subscale scores, simply sum the items on the appropriate subscale as described above. To classify respondents as Type A or Type B, find the median and classify all subjects above the median as Type A and below the median as Type B. The cutting point for the total score, above which subjects are classified as Type A is 10, and for the hard-driving/competitive subscale, the cutting point is 3.

RELIABILITY The SJAS has only fair internal consistency, with alphas that range from .40 to .72. However, the SJAS has excellent stability, with test-retest reliabilities for two weeks that range from .90 to .96 and for three months, from .74 to .86.

VALIDITY Although not a great deal of information on validity is available, the adult version of the SJAS has been shown to be a predictor of clinical coronary disease, suggesting good predictive validity.

PRIMARY REFERENCE Yarnold, P. R., Mueser, K. T., Grav, B. W., and Grimm, L. G. (1986). The reliability of the student version of the Jenkins Activity Survey, *Journal of Behavioral Medicine*, 9, 401–414.

AVAILABILITY Dr. Paul R. Yarnold, Northwestern University Medical School, 750 N. Lake Shore Drive, Room 626, Chicago, IL 60611.

In the questions which follow there are no "correct" or "incorrect" answers; the important thing is to answer each question AS IT IS TRUE FOR YOU. Your answers are considered strictly confidential—for research purposes only. In addition, your responses are valuable only if you complete each and every question, so be sure to complete every question.

1. Is your everyday life filled mostly by:
   a. Problems needing solutions
   b. Challenges needing to be met
   c. A rather predictable routine of events
   d. Not enough things to keep me interested or busy

2. When you are under pressure or stress, do you usually:
   a. Do something about it immediately
   b. Plan carefully before taking any action

3. Ordinarily, how rapidly do you eat?
   a. I'm usually the first one finished
   b. I eat a little faster than average
   c. I eat at about the same speed as most people
   d. I eat more slowly than most people

4. Has your spouse or some friend ever told you that you eat too fast?
   a. Yes, often
   b. Yes, once or twice
   c. No, no one has told me this

5. When you listen to someone talking, and this person takes too long to come to the point, do you feel like hurrying them along?
   a. Frequently
   b. Occasionally
   c. Almost never

6. How often do you actually "put words in his mouth" in order to speed things up?
   a. Frequently
   b. Occasionally
   c. Almost never

7. If you tell your spouse or a friend that you will meet them somewhere at a definite time, how often do you arrive late?
   a. Once in a while
   b. Rarely
   c. I am never late

8. Do most people consider you to be:
   a. Definitely hard-driving and competitive
   b. Probably hard-driving and competitive
   c. Probably more relaxed and easy going
   d. Definitely more relaxed and easy going

9. Nowadays, do you consider yourself to be:

   a. Definitely hard-driving and competitive
   b. Probably hard-driving and competitive
   c. Probably more relaxed and easy going
   d. Definitely more relaxed and easy going

10. How would your spouse (or closest friend) rate you?

    a. Definitely hard-driving and competitive
    b. Probably hard-driving and competitive
    c. Probably more relaxed and easy going
    d. Definitely more relaxed and easy going

11. How would your spouse (or best friend) rate your general level of activity?

    a. Too slow. Should be more active.
    b. About average. Is busy most of the time.
    c. Too active. Needs to slow down.

12. Would people who know you well agree that you have less energy than most people?

    a. Definitely yes
    b. Probably yes
    c. Probably no
    d. Definitely no

13. How was your "temper" when you were younger?

    a. Fiery and hard to control
    b. Strong, but controllable
    c. I almost never get angry

14. How often are there deadlines in your courses?

    a. Daily or more often
    b. Weekly
    c. Monthly
    d. Never

15. Do you ever set deadlines or quotas for yourself in courses or other things?

    a. No
    b. Yes, but only occasionally
    c. Yes, regularly

16. In school, do you ever keep two projects moving forward at the same time by shifting back and forth rapidly from one to the other?

    a. No, never
    b. Yes, but only in emergencies
    c. Yes, regularly

17. Do you maintain a regular study schedule during vacations such as Thanksgiving, Christmas, and Easter?

    a. Yes
    b. No
    c. Sometimes

18. How often do you bring your work home with you at night or study materials related to your courses?

    a. Rarely or never
    b. Once a week or less often
    c. More than once a week

19. When you are in a group, do the other people tend to look to you to provide leadership?

    a. Rarely
    b. About as often as they look to others
    c. More often than they look to others

In the two questions immediately following, please compare yourself with the average student at your university.

20. In sense of responsibility, I am:

    a. Much more responsible
    b. A little more responsible
    c. A little less responsible
    d. Much less responsible

21. I approach life in general

    a. Much more seriously
    b. A little more seriously
    c. A little less seriously
    d. Much less seriously

Survey of Heterosexual Interactions (SHI)

PURPOSE To measure heterosexual avoidance in males.

AUTHORS Craig T. Twentyman and Richard M. McFall

DESCRIPTION The SHI is a 20-item instrument designed to evaluate males' ability to handle social situations involving interaction with women. Several studies have shown the SHI to be a useful device for identifying individuals who tend to experience difficulties in heterosocial interactions. It can also be used clinically to examine changes in clients' abilities to deal with specific heterosexual problems.

NORMS The SHI has been used in a series of studies with samples consisting solely of undergraduate males, mainly from introductory psychology classes, with the total number of subjects exceeding 2200. No other demographic data were reported. The mean SHI score for the first 604 respondents was 88.21. However, respondents rated as daters were reported as scoring above 100 on the SHI while nondaters scored below 70.

SCORING The SHI is scored by summing the individual items (on a 1 to 7 scale) to produce the overall score, which can range from 20 to 140. Higher scores indicate more heterosocial competence or less heterosocial avoidance.

RELIABILITY The SHI has very good internal consistency, with split-half correlations of .85, and excellent stability with a four-month test-retest correlation of .85.

VALIDITY The SHI has very good concurrent validity, correlating significantly with reported anxiety in heterosocial situations and with self-reported behavior in social situations. The SHI also has good known-groups validity, distinguishing significantly between dating and nondating and shy and nonshy respondents. The SHI also has been found to be sensitive to changes following counseling.

PRIMARY REFERENCE Twentyman, C., Boland, T., and McFall, R. M. (1981). Heterosocial avoidance in college males, *Behavior Modification*, 5, 523–552. Instrument reproduced with permission of Craig Twentyman and Sage Publications.

AVAILABILITY May be copied from this volume.

This questionnaire is concerned with the social behavior of college males. We are interested in what might be broadly defined as "dating behavior." The term "date" used here is to mean any behavior in which some social activity was participated in and planned with a member of the opposite sex. Examples of this type of behavior might include going to the movies, a football game, a party, or even just getting together with some friends.

1. How many "dates" have you had in the last four weeks? Please be exact. _____
2. Estimate the average number of "dates" per month during the past year. _____
3. How many different women have you "dated" during the past year? _____
4. How would you compare yourself with other persons your age with regard to the amount of social behavior you participate in with the opposite sex?

1	2	3	4	5	6	7
Participate in less than an average amount of social behavior			Participate in an average amount of social behavior		Participate in more than an average amount of social behavior	

Items

1. You want to call a woman up for a date. This is the first time you are calling her up as you only know her slightly. When you get ready to make the call, your roommate comes into the room, sits down on his bed, and begins reading a magazine. In this situation you would

1	2	3	4	5	6	7
be unable to call in every case			be able to call in some cases		be able to call in every case	

2. You are at a dance. You see a very attractive woman whom you do not know. She is standing *alone* and you would like to dance with her. You would

1	2	3	4	5	6	7
be unable to ask her in every case			be able to ask her in some cases		be able to ask her in every case	

3. You are at a party and you see two women talking. You do not know these women but you would like to know one of them better. In this situation you would

1	2	3	4	5	6	7
be unable to initiate a conversation			be able to initiate a conversation in some cases		be able to initiate a conversation in every case	

4. You are at a bar where there is also dancing. You see a couple of women sitting in a booth. One, whom you do not know, is talking with a fellow who is standing by the booth. These two go over to dance leaving the other woman sitting alone. You have seen this woman around, but do not really know her. You would like to go over and talk with her (but you wouldn't like to dance). In this situation you would

1	2	3	4	5	6	7
be unable to go over and talk to her			be able to go over and talk to her in some cases		be able to go over and talk to her in every case	

continued

5. In a work break at your job you see a woman who also works there and is about your age. You would like to talk to her, but you do not know her. You would

1	2	3	4	5	6	7
be unable to talk to her in every case			be able to talk to her in some cases		be able to talk to her in every case	

6. You are on a crowded bus. A woman you know only *slightly* is sitting in front of you. You would like to talk to her but you notice that the fellow sitting next to her is watching you. You would

1	2	3	4	5	6	7
be unable to talk to her in every case			be able to talk to her in some cases		be able to talk to her in every case	

7. You are at a dance. You see an attractive woman whom you do not know, standing *in a group* of four women. You would like to dance. In this situation you would

1	2	3	4	5	6	7
be unable to ask her in every case			be able to ask her in some cases		be able to ask her in every case	

8. You are at a drugstore counter eating lunch. A woman whom you do not know sits down beside you. You would like to talk to her. After her meal comes she asks you to pass the sugar. In this situation you would pass the sugar

1	2	3	4	5	6	7
but be unable to initiate a conversation with her			and be able to initiate a conversation in some cases		and be able to initiate a conversation in every case	

9. A friend of yours is going out with his girlfriend this weekend. He wants you to come along and gives you the name and phone number of a woman he says would be a good date. You are not doing anything this weekend. In this situation you would

1	2	3	4	5	6	7
be unable to call in every case			be able to call in some cases		be able to call in every case	

10. You are in the library. You decide to take a break, and as you walk down the hall you see a girl whom you know only casually. She is sitting at a table and appears to be studying. You decide that you would like to ask her to get a coke with you. In this situation you would

1	2	3	4	5	6	7
be unable to ask her in every case			be able to ask her in some cases		be able to ask her in every case	

11. You want to call a woman for a date. You find this woman attractive but you do not know her. You would

1	2	3	4	5	6	7
be unable to call in every case			be able to call in some cases		be able to call in every case	

12. You are taking a class at the university. After one of your classes you see a woman whom you know. You would like to talk to her; however, she is walking with a couple of other women you do not know. You would

1	2	3	4	5	6	7
be unable to talk to her in every case			be able to talk to her in some cases		be able to talk to her in every case	

13. You have been working on a committee for the past year. There is a banquet at which you are assigned a particular seat. On one side of you there is a woman you do not know, on the other is a man you do not know. In this situation you would

1	2	3	4	5	6	7
be unable to initiate a conversation with the woman and talk only with the man			be able to initiate a conversation with the woman in some cases but talk mostly to the man		be able to initiate a conversation in every case and be able to talk equally as freely with the woman as with the man	

14. You are in the lobby of a large apartment complex waiting for a friend. As you are waiting for him to come down, a woman whom you know well walks by with another woman whom you have never seen before. The woman you know says hello and begins to talk to you. Suddenly she remembers that she left something in her room. Just before she leaves you she tells you the other woman's name. In this situation you would

1	2	3	4	5	6	7
find it very difficult to initiate a conversation with the other woman			find it only slightly difficult		find it easy to initiate and continue a conversation	

15. You are at a party at a friend's apartment. You see a woman who has come alone. You don't know her, but you would like to talk to her. In this situation you would

1	2	3	4	5	6	7
be unable to go over and talk to her			be able to go over and talk to her in some cases		be able to go over and talk to her in every case	

16. You are walking to your mailbox in the large apartment building where you live. When you get there you notice that two women are putting their names on the mailbox of the vacant apartment beneath yours. In this situation you would

1	2	3	4	5	6	7
be unable to go over and initiate a conversation			be able to go over and initiate a conversation in some cases		be able to go over and initiate a conversation in every case	

17. You are at a record store and see a woman that you once were introduced to. That was several months ago and now you have forgotten her name. You would like to talk to her. In this situation you would

1	2	3	4	5	6	7
be unable to start a conversation with her in every case			be able to start a conversation with her in some cases		be able to start a conversation with her in every case	

18. You are at the student union or local cafeteria where friends your age eat lunch. You have gotten your meal and are now looking for a place to sit down. Unfortunately, there are no empty tables. At one table, however, there is a woman sitting alone. In this situation you would

1	2	3	4	5	6	7
wait until another place was empty and then sit down			ask the woman if you could sit at the table but not say anything more to her		ask the woman if you could sit at the table and then initiate a conversation	

19. A couple of weeks ago you had a first date with a woman you now see walking on the street toward you. For some reason you haven't seen each other since then. You would like to talk to her but you aren't sure of what she thinks of you. In this situation you would

1	2	3	4	5	6	7
walk by without saying anything			walk up to her and say something to her in some cases		walk up to her and say something in every case	

20. Generally, in most social situations involving women whom you do not know, you would

1	2	3	4	5	6	7
be unable to initiate a conversation			be able to initiate a conversation in some cases		be able to initiate a conversation in every case	

Symptom Questionnaire (SQ)

PURPOSE To measure four aspects of psychopathology and well-being.

AUTHOR Robert Kellner

DESCRIPTION This 92-item instrument measures four major aspects of psychopathology: depression, anxiety, somatization, and anger-hostility. The SQ also has subscales of well-being that correspond to these four aspects, namely relaxed, contented, somatic well-being, and friendly. While longer than other instruments in the book, the checklist format and subscale structure actually provide separate and useful tools that may be administered quickly. A total of the four subscales may be used to assess total distress. Respondents simply and rapidly circle "yes" or "no" for each symptom. Some items request "true" or "false" responses in order to avoid double negatives. The SQ is quite sensitive to change over the course of treatment for persons with psychiatric disorders. It also has utility for assessing the psychological effects of persons with physical diseases. The SQ has an additional feature of assessing different time-frames of the symptoms. A respondent may indicate how he/she feels "right now," "today," or "during the past week." This is particularly useful when diurnal variations are of interest. Users need to cross-out the inappropriate time-frames that appear on the first sentence of the instructions. The SQ also is available in Spanish.

NORMS From a sample of "normals" ($N=50$) the means (and standard deviations) for the four symptom scales and corresponding well-being subscales are as follows: anxiety=2.54 (2.85); relaxed=4.7 (1.47); depression=1.77 (2.16); contented=5.21 (1.11); somatic=2.82 (2.91); somatic well-being=3.88 (1.76); hostility=3.43 (3.32); friendly=5.53 (1.06). For a sample of nonpsychotic-psychiatric patients, the means (and standard deviations) were: anxiety=11.24 (5.52); relaxed=2.53 (1.95); depressed=10.6 (5.9); contented=2.70 (2.16); somatic symptoms=7.56 (5.47); somatic well-being=2.27 (1.97); hostility=8.0 (5.88); friendly=3.37 (1.67).

SCORING The SQ may be scored by hand, with transparent scoring stencils, or by a computer program. "No" is scored 0 and "yes" is scored 1. The sums of the "yes" or "true" responses compose the four symptom subscales, while the sums of the "no" or "false" responses compose the corresponding well-being subscales. Anxiety and relaxed items are: 1, 5, 8, 9*, 16*, 18, 23*, 29*, 30, 34, 36, 42, 49, 50*, 54, 59, 62, 63, 64, 68, 86, 87, 89*. Depression and contented items are: 2, 4*, 6, 7*, 24, 27, 39, 40*, 43*, 45, 47, 51*, 58, 60, 61, 66, 67, 71*, 73, 75, 76, 84, 91. Somatic and somatic well-being items are: 10*, 12, 14*, 15, 19*, 21*, 22, 28, 33, 41, 44, 46*, 52, 53, 57, 65, 72, 74, 77, 78*, 79, 85, 92. Hostility and friendly subscale items are: 3, 11, 13*, 17*, 20, 25, 26, 31*, 32, 35*, 37, 38*, 48, 55, 56, 69, 70, 80, 81, 82, 83*, 88, 90. Items with an asterisk are for the well-being subscales.

RELIABILITY The reliability of the SQ has been estimated with several samples. Test-retest coefficients of stability over a four-week period for anxiety, depression, somatic, and hostility subscales were .71, .95, .77, and .82, respectively. Internal consistency has been assessed using split-half correlations and ranged from .75 to .95 for anxiety, .74 to .93 for depression, .57 to .84 for somatic, and .78 to .95 for hostility. These reliability estimates are based on assessing feelings over a one-week period.

VALIDITY The SQ and subscales have excellent validity estimates determined from a variety of samples. Known-groups validity is shown by scores discriminating between psychiatric patients and "normals" in eleven different studies, as well as discriminating between different subgroups of psychiatric disorders, psychosomatic disorders, and physical diseases. Criterion-referenced validity is also reported. The SQ has been shown to be sensitive to change due to treatment, as well as to changes due to different stages of pregnancy for women undergoing amniocentesis.

PRIMARY REFERENCE Kellner, R. (1987). A symptom questionnaire, *The Journal of Clinical Psychiatry*, 48, 268–274. Instrument reproduced with permission of Robert Kellner, M.D., Ph.D., and Physician Post-graduate Press. Copyright © 1987, Physicians Post-graduate Press.

AVAILABILITY May be copied from this volume.

Please describe how you have felt DURING THE PAST WEEK/TODAY/RIGHT NOW by circling the appropriate response for each word. A few times you have the choice of answering either TRUE or FALSE. Do not think long before answering. Work quickly!

1.	Nervous	Yes	No
2.	Weary	Yes	No
3.	Irritable	Yes	No
4.	Cheerful	Yes	No
5.	Tense, tensed up	Yes	No
6.	Sad, blue	Yes	No
7.	Happy	Yes	No
8.	Frightened	Yes	No
9.	Feeling calm	Yes	No
10.	Feeling healthy	Yes	No
11.	Losing temper easily	Yes	No
12.	Feeling of not enough air	True	False
13.	Feeling kind toward people	Yes	No
14.	Feeling fit	Yes	No
15.	Heavy arms or legs	Yes	No
16.	Feeling confident	Yes	No
17.	Feeling warm toward people	Yes	No
18.	Shaky	Yes	No
19.	No pains anywhere	True	False
20.	Angry	Yes	No
21.	Arms and legs feel strong	Yes	No
22.	Appetite poor	Yes	No
23.	Feeling peaceful	Yes	No
24.	Feeling unworthy	Yes	No
25.	Annoyed	Yes	No
26.	Feeling of rage	Yes	No
27.	Cannot enjoy yourself	True	False
28.	Tight head or neck	Yes	No
29.	Relaxed	Yes	No
30.	Restless	Yes	No
31.	Feeling friendly	Yes	No
32.	Feeling of hate	Yes	No
33.	Choking feeling	Yes	No
34.	Afraid	Yes	No
35.	Patient	Yes	No
36.	Scared	Yes	No
37.	Furious	Yes	No
38.	Feeling charitable, forgiving	Yes	No
39.	Feeling guilty	Yes	No
40.	Feeling well	Yes	No
41.	Feeling of pressure in head or body	Yes	No
42.	Worried	Yes	No
43.	Contented	Yes	No

continued

44. Weak arms or legs	Yes	No
45. Feeling desperate, terrible	Yes	No
46. No aches anywhere	True	False
47. Thinking of death or dying	Yes	No
48. Hot tempered	Yes	No
49. Terrified	Yes	No
50. Feeling of courage	Yes	No
51. Enjoying yourself	Yes	No
52. Breathing difficult	Yes	No
53. Parts of the body feel numb or tingling	Yes	No
54. Takes a long time to fall asleep	Yes	No
55. Feeling hostile	Yes	No
56. Infuriated	Yes	No
57. Heart beating fast or pounding	Yes	No
58. Depressed	Yes	No
59. Jumpy	Yes	No
60. Feeling a failure	Yes	No
61. Not interested in things	True	False
62. Highly strung	Yes	No
63. Cannot relax	True	False
64. Panicky	Yes	No
65. Pressure on head	Yes	No
66. Blaming yourself	Yes	No
67. Thoughts of ending your life	Yes	No
68. Frightening thoughts	Yes	No
69. Enraged	Yes	No
70. Irritated by other people	Yes	No
71. Looking forward toward the future	Yes	No
72. Nauseated, sick to stomach	Yes	No
73. Feeling that life is bad	Yes	No
74. Upset bowels or stomach	Yes	No
75. Feeling inferior to others	Yes	No
76. Feeling useless	Yes	No
77. Muscle pains	Yes	No
78. No unpleasant feeling in head or body	True	False
79. Headaches	Yes	No
80. Feel like attacking people	Yes	No
81. Shaking with anger	Yes	No
82. Mad	Yes	No
83. Feeling of goodwill	Yes	No
84. Feel like crying	Yes	No
85. Cramps	Yes	No
86. Feeling that something bad will happen	Yes	No
87. Wound up, uptight	Yes	No
88. Get angry quickly	Yes	No
89. Self-confident	Yes	No
90. Resentful	Yes	No
91. Feeling of hopelessness	Yes	No
92. Head pains	Yes	No

Symptoms Checklist (SC)

PURPOSE To measure psychiatric symptoms.

AUTHORS Paul T. Bartone, Robert J. Ursano, Kathleen M. Wright, and Larry H. Ingraham

DESCRIPTION The SC is a 20-item instrument designed to measure frequency of psychiatric symptoms. The SC is based on items taken from previous measures including Stouffer's psychosomatic complaints scale and the Hopkins Symptoms Checklist. Although factor analysis showed four factors accounting for 48% of the variance (depression/withdrawal, hyperalertness, generalized anxiety, and somatic complaints), the SC typically is used as a single scale. The simplicity and brevity of the SC make it especially useful for monitoring changes in overall psychiatric symptoms.

NORMS The SC was studied with 164 military survivor assistance officers of whom 93% were male, 85% white, 79% married, with a median age of 34. Actual norms were not provided.

SCORING The SC is easily scored by summing item responses for a total score.

RELIABILITY The SC has excellent internal consistency, with alphas that ranged from .90 to .93. Data on stability were not reported.

VALIDITY The SC has good predictive validity, with respondents who had greater exposure to families affected by an air disaster and who had fewer social supports showing significantly higher SC scores.

PRIMARY REFERENCE Bartone, P. T., Ursano, R. J., Wright, K. M., and Ingraham, L. H. (1989). The impact of a military air disaster on the health of assistance workers, *Journal of Nervous and Mental Disease*, 177, 317–328.

AVAILABILITY May be copied from this volume.

Following is a list of various troubles or complaints people sometimes have. Please indicate whether or not you experienced any of these over the past few weeks, by circling the appropriate number.

		None	A little	Often	Very often
1.	Common cold or flu.	0	1	2	3
2.	Dizziness.	0	1	2	3
3.	General aches and pains.	0	1	2	3
4.	Hands sweat and feel damp and clammy.	0	1	2	3
5.	Headaches.	0	1	2	3
6.	Muscle twitches or trembling.	0	1	2	3
7.	Nervous or tense.	0	1	2	3
8.	Rapid heart beat (not exercising).	0	1	2	3
9.	Shortness of breath (not exercising).	0	1	2	3
10.	Skin rashes.	0	1	2	3
11.	Upset stomach.	0	1	2	3
12.	Trouble sleeping.	0	1	2	3
13.	Depressed mood.	0	1	2	3
14.	Difficulty concentrating.	0	1	2	3
15.	Crying easily.	0	1	2	3
16.	Lack of appetite / loss of weight.	0	1	2	3
17.	Taking medication to sleep or calm down.	0	1	2	3
18.	Overly tired / lack of energy.	0	1	2	3
19.	Loss of interest in TV, movies, news, friends.	0	1	2	3
20.	Feeling life is pointless, meaningless.	0	1	2	3

TCU Depression (TCU-D) and TCU Decision-Making (TCU-DM) Scales

PURPOSE To measure depression and decision-making in intravenous drug users.

AUTHORS George W. Joe, LaVerne Knezek, Deena Watson, and D. Dwayne Simpson

DESCRIPTION The TCU-D and TCU-DM are two parts of a 15-item instrument designed to measure depression and decision-making in intravenous drug users. Depression is recognized as a very important problem among intravenous drug users, while the importance of decision-making is increasing in view of the use of cognitively oriented therapies for drug use problems. The 15-item scale actually can be used as a single scale or divided into the two subscales: depression (items 3, 6, 10–12, 15) and decision-making (items 1, 2, 4, 5, 7–9, 13, 14). The TCU-D and TCU-DM are viewed as useful measures for treatment planning with drug use problems; they may also have implications for use with other problem populations as well, especially because of their brevity and ease of administration. These scales are part of a package of scales of the TCU/Datar Self-Rating Scales for drug users.

NORMS The TCU-D and TCU-DM were studied initially with 154 intravenous drug users who participated in an intravenous drug users project in Dallas, Texas. Roughly half were black, 42% white, and 10% Hispanic; 72% were men and 57% were unmarried. Most (54%) were unemployed. The mean for the TCU-D was 11.4 (SD=4.4) and for the TCU-DM was 21.3 (SD=5.1).

SCORING The TCU-D and TCU-DM are easily scored by summing the item scores for each subscale. Items 3, 4, and 13 are reverse-scored.

RELIABILITY The TCU-D and TCU-DM have fairly good internal consistency, with an alpha of .78 for depression and .77 for decision-making. No data on stability were reported.

VALIDITY The TCU-D has good concurrent validity, correlating .75 with the Beck Depression Inventory. Both scales have an additional degree of concurrent validity in correlating with several behaviors: the TCU-D was positively correlated with intravenous drug use and the TCU-DM was negatively correlated with drug use. AIDS sex-risk behavior was positively correlated with TCU-D and negatively correlated with TCU-DM.

PRIMARY REFERENCE Joe, G. W., Knezek, L., Watson, D., and Simpson, D. D. (1991). Depression and decision-making among intravenous drug users, *Psychological Reports*, 68, 339–347. Instrument reproduced with permission of authors and publisher.

AVAILABILITY Dr. D. Dwayne Simpson, Institute of Behavioral Research, O.P.D. Box 32880, Texas Christian University, Ft. Worth, TX 76129. Or Contact Tami L. Joyce at t.joyce@tcu.edu or Dr. Simpson at d.simpson@tcu.edu.

These questions ask about the way you feel or how you are. Circle the answer that tells *how much of the time* each item describes the way you have been feeling during the past week (including today).

	Never	Rarely	Some-times	Often	Almost always
1. You make good decisions.	0	1	2	3	4
2. You think of several different ways to solve a problem.	0	1	2	3	4
3. You feel interested in life.	0	1	2	3	4
4. You make decisions without thinking about consequences.	0	1	2	3	4
5. You think about probable results of your actions.	0	1	2	3	4
6. You feel extra tired or run down.	0	1	2	3	4
7. You think about what causes your current problems.	0	1	2	3	4
8. You plan ahead.	0	1	2	3	4
9. You consider how your actions will affect others.	0	1	2	3	4
10. You worry or brood a lot.	0	1	2	3	4
11. You have thoughts of committing suicide.	0	1	2	3	4
12. You feel sad or depressed.	0	1	2	3	4
13. You have trouble making decisions.	0	1	2	3	4
14. You analyze problems by looking at all the choices.	0	1	2	3	4
15. You feel lonely.	0	1	2	3	4

Templer Death Anxiety Scale (TDAS)

PURPOSE To measure death anxiety.

AUTHOR Donald I. Templer

DESCRIPTION The TDAS is a 15-item instrument that is designed to measure respondents' anxiety about death. The TDAS includes a broad range of items and concerns about death. The instrument was carefully developed from an original pool of 40 items and has been found to be relatively free of response bias and social-desirability response set. Several factor analytic studies of the TDAS have identified a number of different factors, although essentially, the overall score is what is considered meaningful. A major advantage of the TDAS is that it has been studied and used extensively with a variety of populations. Information is available demonstrating the relationship between the TDAS and age, sex, religion, specific environmental influences, personality, physical and mental health, life expectancy, and a variety of behaviors.

NORMS The TDAS has been tested with a variety of samples including males and females, adolescents and adults, psychiatric patients, and a number of occupational groups. Respondents total in the several thousands. Norms for some groups have been reported: means of "normal" respondents vary from 4.5 to 7.0 with TDAS scores being higher for females and psychiatric patients. For a cross-sectional sample of middle-class people, the means reported were 7.50 for youths, 7.25 for young adults, 6.85 for middle-aged, and 5.74 for elderly respondents.

SCORING The TDAS is scored by assigning a score of one to each item correctly answered ($1 = T$, $2 = F$, $3 = F$, $4 = T$, $5 = F$, $6 = F$, $7 = F$, $8 - 14 = T$, $15 = F$), and then totaling across items.

RELIABILITY The TDAS has fairly good internal consistency, with a Kuder-Richardson formula coefficient of .76. The TDAS also has good stability, with a three-week test-retest correlation of .83.

VALIDITY The TDAS has good concurrent validity, correlating .74 with the Fear of Death Scale. It also has demonstrated good known-groups validity, distinguishing significantly between a group of psychiatric patients who verbalized high death anxiety and a control group.

PRIMARY REFERENCE Lonetto, R., and Templer, D. I. (1983). The nature of death anxiety, in C. D. Spielberger and J. N. Butcher (eds.), *Advances in Personality Assessment*, Vol 3. Hillsdale, N.J.: Lawrence Erlbaum, pp. 14–174. Instrument reproduced with permission of Donald I. Templer.

AVAILABILITY Dr. Donald I. Templer, California School of Professional Psychology, Alliant International University, 1350 M Street, Fresno, CA 93721.

If a statement is true or mostly true as applied to you, circle "T." If a statement is false or mostly false as applied to you, circle "F."

T F 1. I am very much afraid to die.

T F 2. The thought of death seldom enters my mind.

T F 3. It doesn't make me nervous when people talk about death.

T F 4. I dread to think about having to have an operation.

T F 5. I am not at all afraid to die.

T F 6. I am not particularly afraid of getting cancer.

T F 7. The thought of death never bothers me.

T F 8. I am often distressed by the way time flies so very rapidly.

T F 9. I fear dying a painful death.

T F 10. The subject of life after death troubles me greatly.

T F 11. I am really scared of having a heart attack.

T F 12. I often think about how short life really is.

T F 13. I shudder when I hear people talking about a World War III.

T F 14. The sight of a dead body is horrifying to me.

T F 15. I feel that the future holds nothing for me to fear.

Temporal Satisfaction with Life Scale (TSWLS)

PURPOSE To measure temporal satisfaction with life.

AUTHORS William Pavot, Ed Diener, and Eunkook Suh

DESCRIPTION The TSWLS is a 15-item instrument designed to measure an individual's past, present, and future life satisfaction. The TSWLS was developed from the original Satisfaction with Life Scale as an attempt to clarify for respondents to the scale whether questions are about their past, present, or future expectations of life satisfaction. This temporal focus therefore allows for a more comprehensive examination among present, past, and future levels of global life satisfaction. This is particularly useful in examining the experience of life satisfaction across different portions of the life span, or examining life satisfaction in people who have experienced or anticipate significant life changes. The first five items of the TSWLS refer to past life satisfaction, the next five items (6–10) refer to current life satisfaction, and the last five items refer to expectations of future life satisfaction. In several studies, the three temporal dimensions are significantly different from each other.

NORMS The TSWLS has been studied with three samples including 157 university students, 294 adults with a mean age of 59, and 66 older adults with a mean age of 79. The mean scores of the TSWLS for the college students range from 63.61 to 69.96 over three administrations with standard deviations that range from 16.03 to 16.42. The mean score for the general adult sample was 70.80 (SD=14.83). The mean scores for the older adults in two administrations were 72.89 and 74.28 (SD=19.3 and 15.9). For past life satisfaction, the mean scores were 20.98 (SD=6.58) for college students, 22.52 (SD=6.81) for the general adult sample, and 23.34 (SD=7.24) for older adults. For present life satisfaction the mean score for college students was 21.79 (SD=5.96), for the general adult sample the mean was 24.49 (SD=6.37), and for older adults the mean was 25.93 (SD=5.54). For future life satisfaction, for college students the mean was 26.32 (SD=4.81), for the general adult sample the mean was 23.79 (SD=5.93), and for older adults, the mean was 24.83 (SD=5.94).

SCORING All items are positively keyed, so scoring the TSWLS simply involves summing scores on the 15 items or on the five items for each subscale. For the total scale, scores range from 15 to 105, with higher scores considered as indicating greater life satisfaction.

RELIABILITY The TSWLS has excellent internal consistency with alphas for most administrations above .90. The TSWLS also has excellent stability, with four- to nine-week test-retest correlations that range from .82 to .88.

VALIDITY The TSWLS has established excellent concurrent validity, with moderate to strong correlations with numerous other measures of well-being, positive affect, negative affect, personality, and optimism.

PRIMARY REFERENCE Pavot, W., Diener, E., and Suh, E. (1998). The Temporal Satisfaction with Life Scale, *Journal of Personality Assessment*, 70, 340–354.

AVAILABILITY William Pavot, Ph.D, Department of Psychology, Southwest Minnesota State University, Marshall, MN 56258. Use of this scale is free. Users will please seek permission from the author. Email: pavot@southwestmsu.edu.

Below are fifteen statements with which you may agree or disagree. These statements concern either your past, present, or future. Using the 1–7 scale below, indicate your agreement with each item by placing the appropriate number on the line preceding that item. Please be open and honest in your responding. The 7-point scale is:

1 = Strongly disagree
2 = Disagree
3 = Slightly disagree
4 = Neither agree nor disagree
5 = Slightly agree
6 = Agree
7 = Strongly agree

___ 1. If I had my past to live over, I would change nothing.
___ 2. I am satisfied with my life in the past.
___ 3. My life in the past was ideal for me.
___ 4. The conditions of my life in the past were excellent.
___ 5. I had the important things I wanted in my past.
___ 6. I would change nothing about my current life.
___ 7. I am satisfied with my current life.
___ 8. My current life is ideal for me.
___ 9. The current conditions of my life are excellent.
___ 10. I have the important things I want right now.
___ 11. There will be nothing that I will want to change about my future.
___ 12. I will be satisfied with my life in the future.
___ 13. I expect my future life will be ideal for me.
___ 14. The conditions of my future life will be excellent.
___ 15. I will have the important things I want in the future.

Test of Negative Social Exchange (TENSE)

PURPOSE To measure negative social interactions.

AUTHORS Linda S. Ruehlman and Paul Karoly

DESCRIPTION The TENSE is a 16-item instrument designed to measure negative social exchange (social interactions). It is based on the idea that the positive side of social ties—social support—has been disproportionately examined compared to negative social interactions and that few if any instruments are available that can be used in a wide variety of contexts. The TENSE was designed to measure a number of different dimensions of social interactions and applies to the general social network (not just families or peers). The TENSE has four subscales: hostility/impatience (items 1, 3, 10, 15), interference (items 5, 7, 9, 12), insensitivity (items 4, 6, 8, 11, 13), and ridicule (items 2, 14, 16).

NORMS The TENSE was investigated with two samples involving 878 undergraduates enrolled in introductory psychology classes. Demographic information was not available for many subjects though both sexes were well represented. Means for the four subscales were 1.23 (SD = .72) for hostility/impatience (this mean is not currently valid because this subscale had 2 additional items at the time of this report), 1.07 (SD = .77) for insensitivity, .96 (SD = .80) for interference, and .88 (SD = .81) for ridicule.

SCORING The TENSE is easily scored by summing items on each subscale and taking the mean for that subscale. Total scores are not used.

RELIABILITY The TENSE has fair to good internal consistency, with alphas of .87 for hostility/impatience, .82 for insensitivity, .75 for interference, and .70 for ridicule. The TENSE has fair stability, with two-day test-retest correlations of .80 for hostility/impatience, .72 for insensitivity, .65 for interference, and .70 for ridicule.

VALIDITY The TENSE has good construct validity with significant correlations in predicted directions with the Revised UCLA Loneliness Scale, Social Support and Hindrance Inventory, Inventory of Socially Supportive Behaviors, Satisfaction with Life Scale, Self-Rating Anxiety Scale, and the Beck Depression Inventory. The TENSE is negatively correlated with the Social Desirability Scale, though subsequent analyses ruled out social desirability as a potential confound.

PRIMARY REFERENCE Ruehlman, L. S., and Karoly, P. (1991). With a little flack from my friends: Development and preliminary validation of the Test of Negative Social Exchange (TENSE), *Psychological Assessment*, 3, 97–104.

AVAILABILITY Dr. Linda Ruehlman, Department of Psychology, Arizona State University, Tempe, AZ 85287-1104, or Paul Karoly at karoly@asu.edu.

The following survey concerns different types of NEGATIVE INTERACTIONS you might have had with the IMPORTANT PEOPLE IN YOUR LIFE over the PAST MONTH. Please begin by listing the first names of every *adult who currently has an impact on your life*. These important people may be those you see frequently or infrequently, they may be family or nonfamily, people you care about and/or who care about you, people you are close to, those who have some power or control over you, people you like or dislike, etc. Remember to only include ADULTS (persons 18 years of age or older) in your list.

After you have listed the names of the *important people* in your life, take a few moments to think about your interactions with them over the *past month*. Then, use the scale below to rate how often you experienced each of the following types of negative interaction with *one or more of these important people* during the past month. We are *not* concerned with how you were treated by any *one* person in particular. We'd like you to estimate *how often each negative interaction occurred* with one or more of the important people on your list. Using the following scale, select either "0," "1," "2," "3," or "4" depending on how often if happened. Write the number of your choice in the spaces to the left.

$$0 = \text{Not at all}$$
$$1 = \text{Once or twice during the month}$$
$$2 = \text{About once a week}$$
$$3 = \text{Several times a week}$$
$$4 = \text{About every day}$$

___ 1. Lost his or her temper with me
___ 2. Made fun of me
___ 3. Nagged me
___ 4. Took advantage of me
___ 5. Distracted me when I was doing something important
___ 6. Took my feelings lightly
___ 7. Was too demanding of my attention
___ 8. Took me for granted
___ 9. Invaded my privacy
___ 10. Yelled at me
___ 11. Ignored my wishes or needs
___ 12. Prevented me from working on my goals
___ 13. Was inconsiderate
___ 14. Gossiped about me
___ 15. Was angry with me
___ 16. Laughed at me

Thought Control Questionnaire (TCQ)

PURPOSE To measure control of unwanted thoughts.

AUTHORS Adrian Wells and Mark I. Davies

DESCRIPTION The TCQ is a 30-item instrument designed to assess strategy for controlling unpleasant and unwanted thoughts. Unwanted, uncontrollable thoughts are a central feature of numerous anxiety disorders such as obsessive-compulsive disorder, generalized anxiety disorder, and post-traumatic stress disorder. A number of treatment approaches focus on controlling unwanted thoughts through such techniques as thought stopping, distraction, and cognitive reappraisal. The TCQ measures or assesses different dimensions of thought control and is therefore an important instrument to investigate the relationship between control strategies and the maintenance of unwanted thoughts. The TCQ also can be used as a measure to track progress at developing therapeutic strategies for controlling unwanted thoughts. The TCQ comprises five factors that correspond to different strategies for controlling unwanted thoughts: distraction (items 1, 9, 16, 19, 21, and 30); social (items 5, 8, 12, 17, 25, and 29); worry (items 4, 7, 18, 22, 24, and 26); punishment (items 2, 6, 11, 13, 15, and 28); and reappraisal (items 3, 10, 14, 20, 23, and 27).

NORMS The TCQ was developed in a series of studies including administration to 229 undergraduate and postgraduate students between 18 and 47 years of age. Of the 229 students, 96 were male and 133 were female. Scores on the total TCQ were $M = 49.22$ ($SD = 7.27$) for men and $M = 48.29$ ($SD = 6.21$) for women. Means and standard deviations on the subscales are available in the original article.

SCORING After reverse-scoring items 5, 8, and 12, the individual subscales are scored simply by summing the numbers on each item. The total TCQ score is obtained by summing the individual subscales.

RELIABILITY The subscales of the TCQ have fair internal consistency, with alphas that range from .64 to .79. The alpha for the total scale is not reported. The TCQ also has good stability with six-week test-retest correlations on the subscales that range from .67 to .83 for three of the subscales.

VALIDITY The TCQ has established concurrent validity, with correlations in predicted directions with the subscales of a number of other measures such as the Padua Inventory, the Penn State Worry Questionnaire, and the Anxious Thoughts Inventory. The complex pattern of correlations between the TCQ and subscales of the other measures shows in particular that the punishment and worry subscales of the TCQ were correlated with various measures of emotional vulnerability and perceptions of impaired control over cognition.

PRIMARY REFERENCE Wells, A., and Davies, M. I. (1994). The Thought Control Questionnaire: A measure of individual differences in the control of unwanted thoughts, *Behaviour Research and Therapy*, 32, 871–878.

AVAILABILITY Dr. Adrian Wells, University of Manchester, Department of Clinical Psychology, Rawnsley Building, MRI, Manchester, M13 9W, United Kingdom. Copyright, A. Wells, 1994; reprinted by permission of Dr. Wells. Email: Adrian.wells@mar.ac.uk.

Most people experience unpleasant and/or unwanted thoughts (in verbal and/or picture form), which can be difficult to control. We are interested in the techniques that you *generally* use to control such thoughts.

Below are a number of things that people do to control these thoughts. Please read each statement carefully, and indicate how often you use each technique by *circling* the appropriate number. There are no right or wrong answers. Do not spend too much time thinking about each one.

When I experience an unpleasant/unwanted thought:

	Never	Sometimes	Often	Almost always
1. I call to mind positive images instead.	1	2	3	4
2. I tell myself not to be so stupid.	1	2	3	4
3. I focus on the thought.	1	2	3	4
4. I replace the thought with a more trivial bad thought.	1	2	3	4
5. I don't talk about the thought to anyone.	1	2	3	4
6. I punish myself for thinking the thought.	1	2	3	4
7. I dwell on other worries.	1	2	3	4
8. I keep the thought to myself.	1	2	3	4
9. I occupy myself with work instead.	1	2	3	4
10. I challenge the thought's validity.	1	2	3	4
11. I get angry at myself for having the thought.	1	2	3	4
12. I avoid discussing the thought.	1	2	3	4
13. I shout at myself for having the thought.	1	2	3	4
14. I analyze the thought rationally.	1	2	3	4
15. I slap or pinch myself to stop the thought.	1	2	3	4
16. I think pleasant thoughts instead.	1	2	3	4
17. I find out how my friends deal with these thoughts.	1	2	3	4
18. I worry about more minor things instead.	1	2	3	4
19. I do something that I enjoy.	1	2	3	4
20. I try to reinterpret the thought.	1	2	3	4
21. I think about something else.	1	2	3	4
22. I think more about the more minor problems I have.	1	2	3	4
23. I try a different way of thinking about it.	1	2	3	4
24. I think about past worries instead.	1	2	3	4
25. I ask my friends if they have similar thoughts.	1	2	3	4
26. I focus on different negative thoughts.	1	2	3	4
27. I question the reasons for having the thought.	1	2	3	4

	Never	Sometimes	Often	Almost always
28. I tell myself that something bad will happen if I think the thought.	1	2	3	4
29. I talk to a friend about the thought.	1	2	3	4
30. I keep myself busy.	1	2	3	4

Threat Appraisal Scale (TAS)

PURPOSE To measure threat appraisal.

AUTHOR Kenneth E. Hart

DESCRIPTION The TAS is a 12-item situation-specific measure of the extent to which respondents perceive a situation as holding potential for harm to self. The TAS is rooted in cognitive-relational theory that holds that threat-appraisals are stress-relevant cognitions concerning the possibility that a taxing situation may result in damage to one's well-being. Threat appraisals are viewed as primary and secondary appraisals. Primary appraisals concern assessment of the degree to which something of personal significance is at stake and how demanding that situation may be. Secondary appraisal is the judgment of the individual's resources for coping with a stressful situation. The TAS has two subscales: primary appraisal (PA; items 1, 3, 5, 7, 9, 11) and secondary appraisal (SA; items 2, 4, 6, 8, 10, 12). The TAS may be useful in understanding the cognitions that accompany stress and as a way of monitoring changes in those cognitions as a result of therapy.

NORMS The TAS was initially studied with 135 introductory psychology students in a large university in Houston, Texas. There were 67 men and 68 women, with a mean age of 19.8 for the entire sample. No other demographic data were reported. The means for the sample were 3.8 for both subscales with standard deviations of 1.1 for PA and 1.2 for SA. The PA/SA ratio (see "Scoring") mean was 1.1 (SD=0.5).

SCORING The TAS is scored by simply summing the individual item scores (1 to 4) for each subscale. Since the cognitive-relational model proposes that perceptions of threat vary as a function of the balance between PA and SA, a PA/SA ratio score is determined by simply dividing PA scores by SA scores.

RELIABILITY The TAS has only fair internal consistency, with an alpha of .65 for PA and .77 for SA. The alpha for the total scale was .62. No stability data were reported.

VALIDITY The TAS has fair construct validity. It is largely uncorrelated with a variety of theoretically unrelated variables, and as a ratio measure (PA/SA) is correlated with overutilization of maladaptive coping strategies, underutilization of adaptive coping strategies, and exaggerated levels of negative emotional reactivity.

PRIMARY REFERENCE Hart, E. K. Threat appraisals and emotional and coping responses to anger-provoking situations (unpublished manuscript).

AVAILABILITY Dr. Kenneth E. Hart, University of Windsor, Windsor, Ontario, Canada N9B 3P4. Email: kenhart@uwindsor.ca.

With special reference to the stressful situation or event that you described previously, indicate the degree to which you agree or disagree with the following statements.

	Strongly disagree	Moderately disagree	Moderately agree	Strongly agree
1. The situation was one of great importance to me.	1	2	3	4
2. I felt in control of my emotions.	1	2	3	4
3. The situation mattered a great deal to me.	1	2	3	4
4. I felt in control of what it was that I was doing.	1	2	3	4
5. The possibility existed that I might have appeared incompetent to others.	1	2	3	4
6. I felt in control of the situation.	1	2	3	4
7. I felt I was somehow in jeopardy.	1	2	3	4
8. I felt confident that by putting in a lot of effort, things would be OK.	1	2	3	4
9. The possibility existed that I might have lost the respect or approval of others.	1	2	3	4
10. I had a great deal of confidence in my ability to solve the problem.	1	2	3	4
11. The possibility existed that others might have thought less of me.	1	2	3	4
12. I was confident that because of my high level of skill and general ability to solve most problems, things would be OK.	1	2	3	4

Time Urgency and Perpetual Activation Scale (TUPA)

PURPOSE To measure Type A characteristics associated with coronary heart disease.

AUTHORS Logan Wright, Susan McCurdy, and Grace Rogoll

DESCRIPTION This 72-item instrument measures two components of Type A behavior patterns that are associated with coronary heart disease: time urgency and perpetual activation. While appearing to be longer than most instruments in this volume, the TUPA contains 25 decoy items and the scale score consists of only 47 items. The TUPA has 7 items that ascertain only time urgency (items 34, 49, 55, 63, 66, 69, 72), 9 that assess only perpetual activation (items 13, 14, 15, 18, 28, 36, 40, 45, 50), and 31 items that tap both dimensions (items 2, 3, 4, 6, 8, 9, 10, 16, 17, 20, 21, 22, 23, 25, 26, 27, 29, 31, 32, 33, 38, 41, 43, 47, 52, 57, 58, 61, 65, 67, 79). Time urgency refers to the time pressures one imposes on oneself, such as meeting deadlines and arriving on time or early for events; perpetual activation refers to excessive energy levels and being overly active, such as seen in difficulty sitting still, fast-paced behaviors, or being a "workaholic." One strong feature of the TUPA is that the items were developed from a list of time urgent and perpetual activation behaviors recorded by a sample of coronary heart disease patients; the items were then rated by another sample of patients receiving inpatient coronary care, and selected based on the correlations with structured interview assessments of time urgency and perpetual activation.

NORMS Scores for a sample of 40 white, middle-class male noncoronary patients who were considered by their physicians as "destined" for heart disease had a mean TUPA score of 168.35 and a standard deviation of 30.14. Subjects' wives rated them slightly higher using the TUPA, with a mean of 181.06 and a standard deviation of 28.81.

SCORING The TUPA is scored by adding the item scores for all 47 items. Total scores range from 47 to 282 with higher scores reflecting more time urgency and perpetual activation.

RELIABILITY The 47-item TUPA has excellent internal consistency and test-retest reliability. The alpha coefficient was .91, and the coefficient of stability for a two-week interval was .90. The items forming the separate TU and PA were not sufficiently internally consistent (i.e., .54 and .73, respectively) to warrant using them as subscales.

VALIDITY The correlations between patient ratings of the items and interview assessments of time urgency and perpetual activation may be seen as supporting the scale's concurrent validity. Scale scores correlated .43 and .45 with structured interview assessments of time urgency and perpetual activation, respectively. The sample of patients "destined" for heart disease in the opinion of their physicians had scores that correlated .61 with the physicians' rating of them on the TUPA and .57 with their wives' ratings. Total scores on two prototypes of the scale correlated with frequency of physical illness, sleep problems, respiratory illnesses, and frequency of visits to a physician. Scores on one of the prototypes were different for those who set their watches ahead from those who do not, and scores varied by the length of time it took to complete the instrument; setting a watch ahead and completion times are considered *in vivo* indicators of time urgency.

PRIMARY REFERENCE Wright, L., McCurdy, S., and Rogoll G. (1992). The TUPA Scale: A self-report measure for the Type A subcomponent of time urgency and perpetual activation, *Psychological Assessment*, 4, 352–356. Instrument reproduced with permission of Logan Wright and the American Psychological Association.

AVAILABILITY May be copied from this volume.

The following questionnaire should be completed according to how you feel at the present and as it applies to you throughout your entire life (and not just your recent past). Circle the true or untrue choice which *most* accurately describes you, the respondent. Use the following scale:

1 = *Extremely untrue* for me
2 = *Moderately untrue* for me
3 = *Slightly untrue* for me
4 = *Slightly true* for me
5 = *Moderately true* for me
6 = *Extremely true* for me

1. I am seldom understood.   1 2 3 4 5 6

2. During one appointment, I am already thinking about my next appointment.   1 2 3 4 5 6

3. I schedule activities as close as possible to both sides of an appointment in order not to waste time.   1 2 3 4 5 6

4. I hate to make a mistake dialing a phone number and have to start all over again.   1 2 3 4 5 6

5. I have a problem with appetite.   1 2 3 4 5 6

6. I experience a surge of energy at the beginning of a work task.   1 2 3 4 5 6

7. The idea of speaking in front of a large crowd bothers me.   1 2 3 4 5 6

8. I get angry, because I feel that nothing gets done at work until I get there and take control.   1 2 3 4 5 6

9. People I know well agree that I tend to do most things in a hurry.   1 2 3 4 5 6

10. I become impatient with people who are able to operate at a slower, less structured pace.   1 2 3 4 5 6

11. I often have a problem saying no.   1 2 3 4 5 6

12. I believe everyone should be required to give to charity.   1 2 3 4 5 6

13. I find it difficult to sit still and do nothing.   1 2 3 4 5 6

14. When I was in school, I held two or more offices in groups such as student council, glee club, 4-H club, sorority, or team sports.   1 2 3 4 5 6

15. People say I chew food or gum more vigorously than most people.   1 2 3 4 5 6

16. I sometimes go up stairs two at a time.   1 2 3 4 5 6

17. When driving around town, I wait until the last minute to leave and therefore must move with haste to avoid being late.   1 2 3 4 5 6

18. It is difficult for me to sit down to a long meal.   1 2 3 4 5 6

19. I seldom feel in tune with people around me.   1 2 3 4 5 6

20. In traffic, I change lanes rather than staying in a slow one.   1 2 3 4 5 6

21. I often have trouble finding time to get my hair cut or styled.   1 2 3 4 5 6

22. I have the sense that I am falling behind or that things are gaining on me.
1 2 3 4 5 6

23. I am careful to run errands in an orderly sequence, so as to do them in a minimum amount of time.
1 2 3 4 5 6

24. Living is a wonderful experience.
1 2 3 4 5 6

25. When other people talk, if they do not come to the point, I try to direct the conversation toward the central issue or otherwise keep things on track.
1 2 3 4 5 6

26. I get frustrated when fellow workers want to "visit" or casually talk with me while on the job.
1 2 3 4 5 6

27. I will take a business related phone call during a personal conversation.
1 2 3 4 5 6

28. When picking something out of a container, I dig for it quickly.
1 2 3 4 5 6

29. I usually put in an extremely full day.
1 2 3 4 5 6

30. I am not an important person.
1 2 3 4 5 6

31. I make sure the other person knows that I have another appointment or that I am a busy person during an appointment, thereby moving our meeting along more crisply.
1 2 3 4 5 6

32. I find it necessary to hurry much more of the time than my co-workers do.
1 2 3 4 5 6

33. I open things quickly and forcefully, sometimes ripping boxes or letters open rather than easing things open, or cutting them open gently with an opener.
1 2 3 4 5 6

34. When moving about with a group, I go first and lead the way, rather than standing around waiting for someone else to go first or figure out when to move.
1 2 3 4 5 6

35. There are times when people have control over me.
1 2 3 4 5 6

36. It is difficult for me to sit around and talk after finishing a meal.
1 2 3 4 5 6

37. I am sometimes a little envious of those better looking than me.
1 2 3 4 5 6

38. When the plans I make for the day do not go smoothly, I start changing them.
1 2 3 4 5 6

39. I am deeply moved by an eloquent speech.
1 2 3 4 5 6

40. More than once a week, I bring my work home with me at night or study materials related to my job.
1 2 3 4 5 6

41. I get angry with drivers who sit at a red light in the right-hand lane when I am behind them and want to turn right on a red light.
1 2 3 4 5 6

42. I usually have good luck in whatever I do.
1 2 3 4 5 6

43. I anticipate a green light by looking at the yellow light for the opposing traffic.
1 2 3 4 5 6

44. I believe most children deserve more discipline than they get.
1 2 3 4 5 6

45. When I must sit still, I handle an object (like a pencil), produce finger movements, move my teeth, or otherwise do not keep completely still.
1 2 3 4 5 6

46. I believe it is natural to make mistakes. 1 2 3 4 5 6

47. The only time I feel really comfortable when moving slowly is when I am sick. 1 2 3 4 5 6

48. I hate to cook. 1 2 3 4 5 6

49. I find that automated doors open too slowly, and that I often have to slow down to avoid running into them. 1 2 3 4 5 6

50. I keep my teeth pressed together, without grinding, but with my jaw muscle tense. 1 2 3 4 5 6

51. People who are lonely are lonely by choice. 1 2 3 4 5 6

52. I have more than one iron in the fire at a time. 1 2 3 4 5 6

53. There really isn't some good in everyone. 1 2 3 4 5 6

54. I sometimes forget to brush my teeth. 1 2 3 4 5 6

55. I change my route of travel on streets depending on whether or not I hit a red light (i.e., if I come to a red light and I can turn right and go a different route instead of wait through the red light, I will). 1 2 3 4 5 6

56. There is always one right solution for every problem. 1 2 3 4 5 6

57. I am demanding or hard on machinery, mechanical items, or vehicles. 1 2 3 4 5 6

58. I ease through yellow lights or edge forward when waiting for a green light. 1 2 3 4 5 6

59. I often worry about terrible things that may happen in the future. 1 2 3 4 5 6

60. I often doubt that my dreams will come true. 1 2 3 4 5 6

61. I find myself competing with fellow workers. 1 2 3 4 5 6

62. I don't enjoy gifts as much as I think I should. 1 2 3 4 5 6

63. I may be inclined to interrupt people if they are not responding in the way they should be. 1 2 3 4 5 6

64. The government refuses to tell the truth about flying saucers. 1 2 3 4 5 6

65. I have people say that I am a very busy person, one of the busiest that they have ever known. 1 2 3 4 5 6

66. I seem to anticipate that certain jobs will take less time than they eventually wind up taking. 1 2 3 4 5 6

67. I work considerably more than eight hours per day. 1 2 3 4 5 6

68. I can't take people poking fun at me. 1 2 3 4 5 6

69. When I arrive early for a meeting, I get impatient waiting for the meeting to start. 1 2 3 4 5 6

70. I have a facial grimace which I exhibit when exerting myself. 1 2 3 4 5 6

71. I enjoy pain. 1 2 3 4 5 6

72. I prepare for activities ahead of time, so I won't waste time or have to go back and get things I forgot. 1 2 3 4 5 6

Trauma Practice Questionnaire (TPQ)

PURPOSE To measure best practices behaviors when working with trauma patients.

AUTHORS Carlton Craig and Ginny Sprang

DESCRIPTION The TPQ is a 19-item instrument designed to measure the best practices of working with clients with trauma, such as PTSD or acute stress disorder. It was derived from the standards of evidence-based practices as identified by the International Society for Traumatic Stress Studies. As a self-report, the TPQ delineates provider-preferred practice patterns. The PTQ was develop from panel of 8 focus groups. It has six subscales of best practices from different treatment orientations, Eye Movement Desensitization Reprocessing (EMDR, items 3, 9, 15, 19), Cognitive Therapy (CT, items 1, 7, 13), Behavior Therapy (BT, items 4, 10, 16), Eclectic Therapy (ET, items 6, 12, 18), Psychodynamic Therapy (PT, items 5, 11, 17) and Solution Focused Therapy (SFT, items 2, 8, 14).

NORMS Based on a sample of 304 clinical psychologists and social workers, the mean total score was 2. 96 with a standard deviation of 1. 57.

SCORING The items of the TPQ are rated on the frequency of use with higher scores reflecting more use of evidence-based practices. Scores are the sum of the items scores and may be scores with subscales or total socres. A scoring template follows this instrument.

RELIABILITY The internal consistency coefficient for total scales scores was. 75. The internal consistency coefficients for the subscales ranged from .72 for PT to .82 for EMDR.

VALIDITY There is good support for estimating the validity of the TPQ with exploratory and confirmatory factor analysis. The subscales appear to be fairly independent of each other.

PRIMARY REFERENCE Craig, C. D. and Sprang, G. (2009). Exploratory and confirmatory analysis of the Trauma Practices Questionnaire. *Research on Social Work Practice. 19*, 221-233.

AVAILABILITY Carlton Craig, Ph. D., College of Social Work, 661 Patterson Office Tower, Lexington, KY 40506-0027. Email: Carlton.Craig@ukv.edu.

TRAUMA PRACTICES QUESTIONNAIRE

The following items are indications of what you as a clinician/therapist may do when providing therapy/intervening with a client/patient who has been traumatized. Please refer to the boxes below and then place a number by the corresponding item indicating the extent to which you use that respective technique when working with a client who has been traumatized.

Never	Rarely	Occasionally	Sometimes	Often	Almost Always	Always
0	1	2	3	4	5	6

In my work with traumatized individuals I. . .
1) ____ identify the client's irrational beliefs.
2) ____ shift the focus as soon as possible onto current solutions (versus client problems or symptoms).
3) ____ have the individual picture a scene that represents an aspect of the trauma while having them move their eyes from side to side.
4) ____ complete the task of counter-conditioning.
5) ____ identify the individual's core conflicts that make them vulnerable to regression.
6) ____ integrate multiple theories and techniques to develop individualized treatment plans.
7) ____ dispute irrational thoughts.
8) ____ identify what is working and prescribe more of the same.
9) ____ have the client move their eyes from side to side while picturing a traumatic image.
10) ____ work to weaken the bond between a traumatic stimulus and anxiety through reciprocal inhibition.
11) ____ facilitate transference and employ interpretation.
12) ____ use multiple techniques not necessarily adhering to a prescribed theory.
13) ____ replace irrational cognitions with more adaptive beliefs.
14) ____ use solution-focused techniques.
15) ____ desensitize the individual's experience of the traumatic material by prolonged exposure accompanied with eye movements from side to side.
16) ____ use behavioral techniques such as: relaxation training and systematic desensitization.
17) ____ use psychodynamic techniques such as: uncovering of past traumas, catharsis.
18) ____ utilize an eclectic approach versus a purist approach.
19) ____ use EMDR.

Scoring Directions -

This is an analogue measure that assesses basic assumptions of six major intervention theories. Below is the scoring instructions for the items. The respective items should be summed to obtain a total score for each subscale. Except for the EMDR subscale, all other measures have a range of 0 to 18. The EMDR sub-scale has a range of 0 to 24. The higher the individual scores on a subscale, the more likely they are to use that form of therapy when intervening with a traumatized client/patient. If a person scores above 10 (above 14 for EMDR) on a subscale, that individual should be considered as having a strong orientation towards using that form of therapeutic response. A score of 8 to 10 suggests a moderate proclivity to use that form of therapy and a score below 8 suggests a low amount of use of that form of therapy. It is possible for an individual to score high on multiple dimensions, especially if they score high on the eclectic subscale.

Add numbers 1, 7, 13 =   Cognitive Therapy
Add numbers 2, 8, 14 =   Solution Focused Therapy
Add numbers 3, 9, 15, 19 =   Eye Movement Desensitization and Reprocessing Therapy
Add numbers 4, 10, 16 =   Behavior Therapy
Add numbers 5, 11, 17 =   Psychodynamic Therapy
Add numbers 6, 12, 18 =   Eclectic Therapy

Supplemental items for psychopharmacology

The supplementary items have the same scoring as the other three item sub-scales with a range of 0 to 18. However, the supplemental scale only had a moderate internal consistency and should be used with caution.

S1) _____ exclusively use psychopharmacology.
S2) _____ exclusively use psychopharmacology and refer to psychotherapy as needed.
S3) _____ use psychopharmacology and conduct a form of psychotherapy.

Add numbers SI, S2, S3 = Psychopharmacology (supplemental use with caution).

Trust in Physician Scale (TPS)

PURPOSE To measure patients' trust in their physicians.

AUTHORS Lynda A. Anderson and Robert F. Dedrick

DESCRIPTION The TPS is an 11-item scale designed to measure patients' interpersonal trust in their primary-care physicians. This measure is based on the assumption that trust is a key ingredient defining the patient-physician relationship. Trust is defined as a person's belief that the physician's words and actions are credible, and can be relied upon, and that the physician is working in the patient's best interests. The concept of trust is recognized as dualistic, in that too little or too much may be negative. The TPS is useful in understanding patients' desires for control as well as for explaining patients' behaviors related to management of illness.

NORMS The TPS was studied with two samples of patients at V.A. clinics in two cities in North Carolina. Sample 1 = 160 men, mean of 11.8 years of education, mean age of 55.2, 78% married, 56.3% white. Sample 2 = 106 men, mean of 10.3 years of education, mean age of 60.9 years, 84% married and 62% white. Means ranged from 48.13 (SD = 9.86) to 57.32 (SD = 7.32).

SCORING The TPS is scored by reverse-scoring items 1, 5, 7, and 11 and summing all items for the total score. Higher scores reflect more of the construct (i.e., trust).

RELIABILITY The TPS has good to excellent internal consistency, with alphas that range from .85 to .90. No data on stability were reported.

VALIDITY The TPS has good construct validity, correlating in predicted directions with subscales of the Health Locus of Control Scale, with the Multidimensional Desire for Control subscales, and with patient satisfaction. The TPS also is moderately correlated with social desirability.

PRIMARY REFERENCE Anderson, L. A., and Dedrick, R. F. (1990). Development of the Trust in Physician Scale: A measure to assess interpersonal trust in patient-physician relationships, *Psychological Reports*, 67, 1091–1100. Instrument reproduced with permission of authors and publisher.

AVAILABILITY Dr. Lynda Anderson, School of Public Health, University of Michigan, 1420 Washington Heights, Ann Arbor, MI 48109. Telephone: 734.764.5425.

Each item below is a statement with which you may agree or disagree. Beside each statement is a scale that ranges from strongly agree (1) to strongly disagree (5). For each item please circle the number that represents the extent to which you agree or disagree with the statement.

Please make sure that you answer every item and that you circle only one number per item. It is important that you respond according to what you actually believe and not according to how you feel you should believe or how you think we may want you to respond.

1 = Strongly agree
2 = Agree
3 = Neutral
4 = Disagree
5 = Strongly disagree

1. I doubt that my doctor really cares about me as a person.   1 2 3 4 5

2. My doctor is usually considerate of my needs and puts them first.   1 2 3 4 5

3. I trust my doctor so much I always try to follow his/her advice.   1 2 3 4 5

4. If my doctor tell me something is so, then it must be true.   1 2 3 4 5

5. I sometimes distrust my doctor's opinion and would like a second one.   1 2 3 4 5

6. I trust my doctor's judgments about my medical care.   1 2 3 4 5

7. I feel my doctor does *not* do everything he/she should for my medical care.   1 2 3 4 5

8. I trust my doctor to put my medical needs above all other considerations when treating my medical problems.   1 2 3 4 5

9. My doctor is a real expert in taking care of medical problems like mine.   1 2 3 4 5

10. I trust my doctor to tell me if a mistake was made about my treatment.   1 2 3 4 5

11. I sometimes worry that my doctor may not keep the information we discuss totally private.   1 2 3 4 5

Undergraduate Stress Questionnaire (USQ)

PURPOSE To measure life event stress.

AUTHORS Christian S. Crandall, Jeanne J. Preisler, and Julie Aussprung

DESCRIPTION The USQ is an 83-item instrument designed to measure life event stress among undergraduates. Although the USQ contains more items than most of the scales in this book, it is very efficient to administer, requiring only a checkmark next to those events an individual has experienced. The items for the USQ were generated by actual undergraduates; the number of items is intended to ensure that stressful events that commonly occur with undergraduates are not overlooked. The USQ is valuable for clinical as well as research purposes as it allows examination of these stresses in relation to other problems such as eating disorders, substance abuse, and health behaviors.

NORMS The USQ was developed in a series of six studies, all of which used undergraduates as their samples. In one norming study, 86 students in introductory psychology in a Florida university, of whom 45 were female, filled out the USQ. Other demographic data were not reported. The mean score for this sample was 17.63 (SD=7.93). Women scored significantly higher than men (19.3 versus 15.8). The severity and frequency of each item is available in the Primary Reference.

SCORING The USQ is very easily scored by simply totaling the number of items checked off. Item frequency is the proportion of people checking off each item. Higher scores reflect greater life event stress.

RELIABILITY The USQ has good internal consistency with a KR-21 coefficient of .80 and split-half reliability using the Spearman-Brown formula of .83. The USQ has very good stability with a 4-week test-retest coefficient (with a different sample) of .59.

VALIDITY The USQ has excellent concurrent validity with significant negative correlations, as expected, with the Brief Mood Introspection Scale and positive correlations, as expected with Pennebaker's symptom checklist, the PILL.

PRIMARY REFERENCE Crandall, C. S., Preisler, J. J., and Aussprung, J. (1992). Measuring life event stress in the lives of undergraduates: The Undergraduate Stress Questionnaire (USQ), *Journal of Behavioral Medicine, 15,* 627–662. Instrument reproduced with permission of Dr. Crandall.

AVAILABILITY May be copied from this volume for non-commercial use.

Below are a number of events that are considered stressful. Please read each statement one at a time. Has this stressful event happened to you at any time during the last week? If it has, please check the space next to it. If it has not, then please leave it blank.

Note. School-related items marked with a Y, nonschool items marked with an N, and between items marked with a B.

___ Death (family member or friend)	N
___ Had a lot of tests	Y
___ It's finals week	Y
___ Applying to graduate school	Y
___ Victim of a crime	N
___ Assignments in all classes due the same day	Y
___ Breaking up with boy-/girlfriend	N
___ Found out boy-/girlfriend cheated on you	N
___ Lots of deadlines to meet	N
___ Property stolen	N
___ You have a hard upcoming week	B
___ Went into a test unprepared	Y
___ Lost something (especially wallet)	N
___ Death of a pet	N
___ Did worse than expected on test	Y
___ Had an interview	N
___ Had projects, research papers due	Y
___ Did badly on a test	Y
___ Parents getting divorce	N
___ Dependent on other people	N
___ Having roommate conflicts	B
___ Car/bike broke down, flat tire, etc.	N
___ Got a traffic ticket	N
___ Missed your period and waiting	N
___ Coping with addictions	N
___ Thoughts about future	N
___ Lack of money	N
___ Dealt with incompetence at the Registrar's office	N
___ Thought about unfinished work	B
___ No sleep	B
___ Sick, injury	N
___ Had a class presentation	Y
___ Applying for a job	N
___ Fought with boy-/girlfriend	N
___ Working while in school	Y
___ Arguments, conflict of values with friends	N

___ Bothered by having no social support of family	N
___ Performed poorly at a task	N
___ Can't finish everything you needed to do	N
___ Heard bad news	N
___ Had confrontation with an authority figure	N
___ Maintaining a long-distance boy-/girlfriend	N
___ Crammed for a test	Y
___ Feel unorganized	N
___ Trying to decided on major	Y
___ Feel isolated	N
___ Parents controlling with money	B
___ Couldn't find a parking space	B
___ Noise disturbed you while trying to study	Y
___ Someone borrowed something without permission	N
___ Had to ask for money	B
___ Ran out of typewriter ribbon while typing	B
___ Erratic schedule	N
___ Can't understand your professor	Y
___ Trying to get into your major or college	Y
___ Registration for classes	Y
___ Stayed up late writing a paper	Y
___ Someone you expected to call did not	N
___ Someone broke a promise	N
___ Can't concentrate	N
___ Someone did a "pet peeve" of yours	N
___ Living with boy-/girlfriend	N
___ Felt need for transportation	N
___ Bad haircut today	N
___ Job requirements changed	N
___ No time to eat	B

___ Felt some peer pressure	N
___ You have a hangover	N
___ Problems with your computer	B
___ Problem getting home from bar when drunk	N
___ Used a fake ID	N
___ No sex in a while	N
___ Someone cut ahead of you in line	N
___ Checkbook didn't balance	N
___ Visit from a relative and entertaining them	N

___ Decision to have sex on your mind	N
___ Talked with a professor	Y
___ Change of environment (new doctor, dentist, etc.)	N
___ Exposed to upsetting TV show, book, or movie	N
___ Got to class late	Y
___ Holiday	N
___ Sat through a boring class	Y
___ Favorite sporting team lost	B

University Environment Scale (UES)

PURPOSE To measure perceptions of the university environment.

AUTHORS Alberta M. Gloria and Sharon E. Robinson Kurpius

DESCRIPTION The UES is a 14-item scale designed to measure university students' perceptions of the university environment. The UES is developed specifically to identify minority students' perceptions, with emphasis on students who are Chicano/a. The basis for evaluating the university environment is that this appears to be a major factor in accounting for students' persistence at the university level, because the social support system at the university can influence students' attitudes about staying in school. For minority students in particular, perceptions that the university is hostile and/or uncaring are related to nonpersistence, whereas perceptions that the university is supportive and caring are related to persistence at the university level. This scale was developed for use with racial/ethnic students, specifically Chicano/a undergraduates.

NORMS The UES was developed with several samples of university students including 158 Chicanos/as at University of California at Irvine (UCI) and 285 Chicanos/as at Arizona State University (ASU). At UCI, 74% of the students were female with a mean age of 21.07 years, and at ASU, 76% of the students were female with a mean age of 22.63 years. The mean on the UES for the combined sample was 64.49 (SD = 13.92).

SCORING Scores on the UES are easily obtained by summing individual responses after reverse-scoring items 1, 4, 5, 11, and 13. Scores can range from 14 to 98 with higher scores reflecting a more positive perception of a university's environment.

RELIABILITY The UES has good internal consistency, with an alpha for the combined sample of .84. No data on stability were reported.

VALIDITY The UES has developed beginning evidence of its predictive validity; scores on the UES accounted for a significant amount of the variance in academic persistence. A negative correlation between the UES and academic persistence indicated that the more positively students view the university environment, the more likely they were to make positive decisions regarding academic persistence.

PRIMARY REFERENCE Gloria, A. M., and Kurpius, S. E. R. (1996). The validation of the Cultural Congruity Scale and the University Environment Scale with Chicano/a students, *Hispanic Journal of Behavioral Sciences*, 18, 533–549.

AVAILABILITY May be copied from this volume.

Please respond to these statements using the following scale:

Not at all   Very true

  1   2   3   4   5   6   7

___ 1. Class sizes are so large that I feel like a number.

___ 2. The library staff is willing to help me find materials/books.

___ 3. University staff have been warm and friendly.

___ 4. I do not feel valued as a student on campus.

___ 5. Faculty have not been available to discuss my academic concerns.

___ 6. Financial aid staff has been willing to help me with financial concerns.

___ 7. The university encourages/sponsors ethnic groups on campus.

___ 8. There are tutoring services available for me on campus.

___ 9. The university seems to value minority students.

___ 10. Faculty have been available for help outside of class.

___ 11. The university seems like a cold, uncaring place to me.

___ 12. Faculty have been available to help me make course choices.

___ 13. I feel as if no one cares about me personally on this campus.

___ 14. I feel comfortable in the university environment.

University of Texas at San Antonio Future Disposition Inventory (UTSA-FDI)

PURPOSE To measure hopelessness as a suicide risk

AUTHORS Augustine Osman, Peter Gutierrez, Frank Barrios, Jane Wong, Stacey Freedenthal, and Gregorio Lazano

DESCRIPTION The UTSA-FDI is a 24-item instrument designed to measure three future related dimensions of hopelessness (i. e, future disposition) as a suicide risk: Positive Focus (PF) which includes optimism and satisfaction with life, Suicide Orientation (SO) which includes beliefs that suicide is a solution and suicidal rumination, thoughts and a wish to die, and Negative Focus (NF), such as worry, rigidity and dissatisfaction with life. The UTSA-FDI attempts to overcome some of the limitations of other suicide risk instruments, and does so exceptionally. It was developed in three phases: item construction where 85 items of suicide risk were generated by two panels of experts, including 13 psychiatric patients; a content analysis phase where all the items were reviewed for relevancy, clarity and specificity; and an empirical evaluation using two samples and advanced psychometric procedures which support the structure of three distinguishable dimensions of suicide risk. The result is an excellent instrument that assesses three separate dimensions of suicide risk. The UTSA-FDI has a 5th grade reading level.

NORMS From a sample of 350 undergraduates, the mean and (standard deviations) for the PF, SO, and NF were 31. 46 (5. 63), 10. 46 (5. 05), and 16. 79 (6. 59), respectively. In a separate validation study, the means they were 31. 34 (5. 13), 10. 26 (4. 29), and 16. 28 (5. 77) for the PR, SO, and NF, respectively. A clinical sample (n = 40) was selected from the validation group using scores on the Suicide Behavior Questionnaire. The means and standard deviations for the PF, SO, and NF were 32. 25 (4. 10), 15. 78 (7. 63) and 29. 88 (6. 32).

SCORING The subscale scores are the sum of the subscale items. Subscale items are: PF = 1, 2, 5, 7, 10, 11, 13 and 15; SO = 3, 6, 8, 9, 17, 18, 22 and 23; NF = 4, 12, 14, 16, 19, 20, 21, and 24. The scale score range is 8 to 40.

RELIABILITY The UTSA-FDI has very good to excellent internal consistency with reliability coefficients of .86, .93 and .88 for the PF, SO, and NF.

VALIDITY Due chiefly to the three-phase development process, the UTSA-FDI has excellent support for its validity. Scores on the UTSA-FDI correlated with scores on the Suicidal Behavior Questionnaire, Positive and Negative Suicide Ideation Inventory (which is found in this volume), the Beck Hopelessness Scale and general psychopathology. There was also evidence of criterion-related known groups validity with scores from the clinical subsample distinguishable from a nonclinical subsample.

PRIMARY REFERENCE Osman, A., Gutierrez, P. M., Barrios, F., Wong, J. L, Freedenthal, S, and Lozano, G. (2010). Development and initial psychometric properties of the University of Texas at San Antonio Future Disposition Inventory. *Journal of Clinical Psychology*, 66, 410–429.

AVAILABILITY Augustine Osman, Ph. D., The University of Texas at San Antonio, Department of Psychology, One UTSA Circle, San Antonio Texas 78249–0652 or Email: Augustine.osman@utsa.edu.

UTSA-FDI

GENDER: MALE FEMALE   AGE:_____   MARITAL STATUS:_____

ETHNIC BACKGROUND:_____   EDUCATION:_____

INSTRUCTIONS:

This is a list of thoughts, feelings, and attitudes about the future. Using the scale to the right, please circle the number that best describes your thoughts, feelings, and attitude in the past 2-3 weeks.

	1 = Not at all true of me	2 = Slightly true of me	3 = Moderately true of me	4 = Very true of me	5 = Extremely true of me
When I look ahead to future...					
1. I expect things to turn out better for me in life.	1	2	3	4	5
2. I plan to work harder to make things better in my life.	1	2	3	4	5
3. I sometimes think that by ending my life, all the problems ahead of me will go away.	1	2	3	4	5
4. I worry that things will never go well for me no matter what I do.	1	2	3	4	5
5. I plan to deal better with most of the setbacks or losses that I have experienced in my life.	1	2	3	4	5
6. I sometimes think that my life is not worth living.	1	2	3	4	5
7. I expect to enjoy the results or outcomes of all my hard work in life.	1	2	3	4	5
8. I sometimes think that things will actually get better if I were dead.	1	2	3	4	5
9. I think that people close to me would be better off without me.	1	2	3	4	5
10. I remain determined to deal better with most of the demands on me.	1	2	3	4	5
11. I expect to be happier and more content with my life.	1	2	3	4	5
12. I usually get confused and uncertain about what I want to do.	1	2	3	4	5
13. I plan to look at the positive side of most hardships or difficulties that I might face again in my life.	1	2	3	4	5
14. I doubt whether things will ever get better for me in life.	1	2	3	4	5

15. I intend to succeed in working through most personal
    problems I might face in life. 1 2 3 4 5

16. I have a hard time imagining that things will ever get better
    for me. 1 2 3 4 5

17. I sometimes wish I were dead. 1 2 3 4 5

18. I often think that I would be better off dead. 1 2 3 4 5

19. I usually wonder whether I would ever be satisfied or content
    with my life. 1 2 3 4 5

20. I fear that I will run into more difficulties in the years ahead. 1 2 3 4 5

21. All I can see ahead of me are hardships, failures and setbacks. 1 2 3 4 5

22. I wish I could succeed at attempts to kill myself. 1 2 3 4 5

23. I feel I have nothing to lose by ending my life. 1 2 3 4 5

24. I often doubt whether I will ever have control over the way
    that my life is going. 1 2 3 4 5

Values Conflict Resolution Assessment (VCRA)

PURPOSE To measure resolution of values conflict.

AUTHOR Richard T. Kinnier

DESCRIPTION The VCRA is a 17-item instrument designed to assess the extent to which an individual is resolved about a specific values conflict. The items were constructed based on theoretical criteria found in values clarification, decision making, and related literature. The respondent first writes out an important values conflict (e.g., abortion versus adoption) that he or she is experiencing, then the decision that he or she would make at that point if forced to. Then the decision is evaluated on the 17-item scale. This is perhaps the only standardized instrument that can be used to help individuals assess their decisions and should be of value in a wide range of helping situations.

NORMS The VCRA was studied initially with 104 graduate students (70 female and 34 male) ranging in age from 21 to 55 years (median = 32). Although actual norms are not reported, two factors were revealed: ethical-emotional resolution (items 1, 2, 6, 7, 8, 10, 11, 12, 14, 16, 17) and rational-behavioral resolution (items 3, 4, 5, 9, 13, 15).

SCORING The VCRA is scored simply by summing item scores for the two factors and for the total score on the scale. High scores indicate better conflict resolution.

RELIABILITY The VCRA has very good internal consistency, with alphas of .81 for ethical-emotional resolution, .76 for rational-behavioral, and .84 for the total score. The VCRA has excellent stability, with one-week test-retest correlation of .84 for ethical-emotional, .88 for rational-behavioral, and .92 for the total score.

VALIDITY The VCRA has good construct validity, correlating significantly in predicted directions with anxiety about the conflict, self-report of conflict being resolved, and self-esteem. The VCRA also discriminates between successfully resolved conflicts and currently unresolved ones.

PRIMARY REFERENCE Kinnier, R. T. (1987). Development of a Values Conflict Resolution Assessment, *Journal of Counseling Psychology*, 34, 34–37.

AVAILABILITY Dr. R. T. Kinnier, Division of Psychology in Education, Payne Hall 42514, Arizona State University, Tempe, AZ 85287. Email: kinnier@asu.edu.

I. CONFLICT DESCRIPTION

Read the following definitions of *values* and *values conflicts* and then describe a values conflict in your life.

Values

A person's values are his or her *beliefs about what is important in life*. Some values refer to how one should act (i.e., to be . . . honest, altruistic, competitive, self-disciplined, courageous, kind, etc.). Other values refer to what one wants to accomplish or obtain in life (i.e., to want . . . a lot of money, security, fame, a large family, meaningful friendships, world peace, equality, peace of mind, physical health, salvation, wisdom, etc.). Your values exist as a complex set of interweaving personal policies or priorities that serve as a guide for decision making. Some examples of personal value statements are: "My family always comes first," "I would rather be honest and unpopular than dishonest and popular," "I do not need to be wealthy—just comfortable," "My physical health is relatively important to me but maintaining my ideal weight is not a priority at all," "The most meaningful thing I can do with my life is to help others."

Values Conflicts

A person cannot "have it all" or "be all things." Priorities must be established and choices made. An *intrapersonal* values conflict occurs when an individual experiences *uncertainty about what he or she really believes or wants* and (or) when two or more *priorities or beliefs conflict or seem incompatible* to the person. The following are examples:

"I want to be very successful in my career, but I also want a more relaxing lifestyle and more time to spend with my family and friends."

"On the one hand, I don't believe in being materialistic and don't want to be. Yet, on the other hand, I am attracted to and want expensive things. I do want a bigger house, high quality car, etc."

"Generally, I want a comfortable and secure life—I want a secure job and a permanent home in a close-knit community. Yet part of me is attracted to the excitement of change, new challenges, and risk."

These are just a few general examples. Of course there are numerous idiosyncratic values conflicts. In the space provided below please describe an *important values conflict issue that you are experiencing in your life now*.

II. CONFLICT RESOLUTION

You described a values conflict in your life. Pretend that you have to resolve that conflict or make a clear decision right now. In the space provided below write the best resolution that you can *at this particular point in time*. Avoid vague responses like "I would compromise." Rather, write a concise decision or resolution so that it is clear what you would do if you were to carry it out.

_____

_____

III. QUESTIONNAIRE

The following questions refer to the specific conflict you just described and resolution you wrote. Do not change what you wrote. Evaluate *that particular resolution* exactly as written and as objectively as you can. Please respond honestly to each question by circling *one* number for each continuum.

1. *How satisfied are you* with the resolution as written?

0	1	2	3	4
Completely dissatisfied		Moderately		Very satisfied

2. To what extent is this resolution *compatible with your basic ethical, spiritual, or moral standards and principles?*

0	1	2	3	4
Not at all		Somewhat compatible		Very compatible

3. To what extent *has your actual behavior during the past few months been consistent with this resolution?*

0	1	2	3	4
Not consistent at all		Somewhat consistent		Very consistent

4. Resolving conflicts or making decisions usually involves gathering information, considering various alternatives, and critically thinking about options. During your life to what extent do you think you *have carefully analyzed and thought about your alternatives or options for this conflict?*

0	1	2	3	4
I need to do much more thinking		I need to do some more thinking		I have thought about them sufficiently

5. All decisions carry consequences. During your life to what extent have you *carefully considered possible positive and negative consequences* of living in accordance with this resolution?

0	1	2	3	4
I have not thought about possible consequences		I have thought about them to some extent		I have carefully considered possible consequences

6. Assuming that every act or decision has a positive or negative effect on society and the improvement of humankind—in your opinion what *effect (no matter how small) would this resolution have on society?*

0	1	2	3	4
More negative		Equally positive and negative		More positive

7. To what extent does the thought of carrying out this resolution *make you feel bad about yourself?*

0	1	2	3	4
Very		Somewhat		Not at all

8. Imagine, however unlikely it may seem, being in a public meeting and hearing this resolution criticized as being selfish and unhumanitarian. To what extent *could you defend that resolution in good conscience?*

0	1	2	3	4
Not defend it at all		Defend it to some extent		Defend it whole-heartedly

9. To what extent *have you thought about or made plans* regarding what you need to do in order to carry out this resolution?

0	1	2	3	4
I have not made any plans or thought about it		I have done some planning and thinking		I have planned or thought about it sufficiently

10. If most people lived in accordance with the values implied in this resolution, *how do you think the world would be changed?*

0	1	2	3	4
A worse world		No better no worse		A better world

11. To what extent *would you experience feelings of guilt* if you actually carried out this resolution?

0	1	2	3	4
Very guilty		Somewhat guilty		Not guilty at all

12. To what extent would you feel embarrassed if people who you cared about knew you wrote this particular resolution? Overall, *how embarrassed would you feel?*

0	1	2	3	4
Very embarrassed		Somewhat embarrassed		Not embarrassed at all

13. In general, how do you think people who know you well would judge *how consistent your behavior has been* with this resolution?

0	1	2	3	4
Not consistent at all		Somewhat consistent		Very consistent

continued

14. Sometimes people make certain decisions because they feel pressured, influenced, or manipulated by others. In such cases the decisions are not really theirs. To what extent do you think that the resolution you wrote is truly what you want or believe?

0	1	2	3	4
Not at all		Somewhat		Very much

15. To what extent do you feel committed to carrying out this resolution *during the next year*?

0	1	2	3	4
Not com- mitted at all		Somewhat committed		Very committed

16. People often tell themselves that a certain decision is better than it really is in order to avoid feeling bad about having made a mistake. To what extent do you think you are *being honest with yourself* about your evaluation of this resolution?

0	1	2	3	4
Not honest at all		Somewhat honest		Very honest

17. Try to imagine the following situation. It is sometime in the future and you only have a few months to live. Pretend that you have lived in accordance with that resolution and are now thinking about your decision and your impending death. In that context to what extent do you believe you would *regret having lived in accordance* with that resolution?

0	1	2	3	4
I would probably have many regrets		I would probably have some regrets		I would prob- ably have few (if any) regrets

Vancouver Obsessional-Compulsive Inventory-Revised (VOCI-R)

PURPOSE To measure five dimensions of obsessive compulsive behaviors

AUTHORS Sasha Gonner, Willi Ecker, Rainer Leonhart, and Klaus Limbacher

DESCRIPTION The VOCI-R is a 30-item instrument that measures five dimensions of obsessive compulsive disorders: Contamination/Washing (CW), Checking Behaviors (CB), Hoarding (H), Symmetry and Ordering (SO) and two types of Obsessive Thoughts (OT) with two subscales, Immoral Obsession (IO) and Harming Obsessions (HO). The instrument is a revision of other measures that had far more items and lacked support for some psychometric properties, such as dimensionality. The VOCI-R delineates the dimensionality of obsessive compulsive disorders, and therefore has the potential of improving mental health screening and diagnosis. The subscales may be used separately or as a total score for a broadband measure. The VOCI-R has excellent confirmatory factor analysis. It is available in English and German.

NORMS Based on a sample of 226 adult patients (mean age was 36. 6 and the standard deviation was 10.8) diagnosed with Obsessive Compulsive Disorders using the International Classification of disease, the mean and (standard deviation) was 39.71 and (20.27) for total scores on the VOCI-R. The CB had a mean of 13. 48 (sd = 8.06). The CW had a mean of 8. 66 (sd = 7.91). The SO had a mean of 8.74 (sd = 7.64). HB had a mean of 5.38 (sd = 5.63). OT had a mean of 3.91 (sd = 4.81), and the subscales IO and HO had means of 1.84 (sd = 2.85) and 20. 4 (sd = 2.60), respectively.

SCORING The scale scores are the sum of the items, and total scores are the sum of all five subscales. The CW items are 1, 11, 14, 21, 25, and 30. CB items are 2, 7, 13, 17, 22, and 28. H items are 4, 9, 15, 18, 24, and 27. SO items are 5, 10, 19, 23, 26 and 29. IO items are 3, 8 and 16, and HO items are 6, 12 and 20.

RELIABILITY The total scores of the VOCI-R had an internal consistency coefficient of .90, and the subscales had coefficients ranging from .82 to .95, although the HO subscale of the OT had a coefficient of .70.

VALIDITY The VOCI-R had very good to excellent convergent and discriminant validity. The dimensionality was supported by confirmatory factor analysis and structural equation modeling. Total scores and scale scores also correlated with depression and anxiety.

PRIMARY REFERENCE Gonner S, Ecker, W, Leonhart, R. and Limbacher, K. (2010). Revision of the Vancouver Obsessional-Compulsive Inventory and the Systematic Ordering and Arranging Questionnaire. *Journal of Clinical Psychology*, 66, 739–57.

AVAILABILITY Dr. Sasha Gonner, Email: sgoenner@yahoo.de.

VOCI-R

Please rate each statement by putting a circle around the number that best describes how much the statement is true of you. Please answer every item, without spending too much time on any particular item.

How much is each of the following statements true of you?	Not at all	A little	Some	Much	Very much
1. I spend far too much time washing my hands.	0	1	2	3	4
2. I repeatedly check and recheck things like taps and switches after turning them off.	0	1	2	3	4
3. I am often upset by my unwanted thoughts or images of sexual acts	0	1	2	3	4
4. I have trouble carrying out normal household activities because my home is so cluttered with things 1 have collected.	0	1	2	3	4
5. I feel upset if my furniture or other possessions are not always m exactly the same position.	0	1	2	3	4
6. I am often upset by my unwanted thoughts of using a sharp weapon.	0	1	2	3	4
7. I repeatedly check that my doors or windows are locked, even though I try to resist the urge to do so.	0	1	2	3	4
8. I repeatedly experience upsetting and unacceptable thoughts of a religiousnature.	0	1	2	3	4
9. I become very tense or upset when I think about throwing anything away.	0	1	2	3	4
10. If someone accidentally disturbs my belongings - however slightly, I become bothered or upset.	0	1	2	3	4
11. Touching the bottom of my shoes makes me very anxious	0	1	2	3	4
12. I am often frightened by unwanted urges to drive or run into oncoming traffic.	0	1	2	3	4
13. One of my major problems is repeated checking.	0	1	2	3	4
14. I find it very difficult to touch garbage or garbage bins.	0	1	2	3	4
15. I find it almost impossible to decide. what to keep and what to throw away	0	1	2	3	4

How much is each of the following statements true of you?	Not at all	A little	Some	Much	Very much
16. I repeatedly experience upsetting and unwanted immoral thoughts.	0	1	2	3	4
17. I repeatedly check that my stove is turned off. even though I resist the urge to do so.	0	1	2	3	4
18. I have great trouble throwing anything away because I am very afraid of being wasteful.	0	1	2	3	4
19. I feel calm and relaxed only when objects around me are organized and placed correctly.	0	1	2	3	4
20. I am often very upset by my unwanted impulses to harm other people.	0	1	2	3	4
21. I avoid using public telephones because of possible contamination.	0	1	2	3	4
22. I spend a lot of time every day checking things over and over again.	0	1	2	3	4
23. When I see that my belongings are out of place. I become anxious until I can arrange them properly.	0	1	2	3	4
24. I feel compelled to keep far too many things like old magazines, newspapers, and receipts because I am afraid I might need them in the future.	0	1	2	3	4
25. I am very afraid of having even slight contact with bodily secretions (blood,urine, sweat, etc.).	0	1	2	3	4
26. I feel compelled to arrange objects so that they are balanced and evenly spaced	0	1	2	3	4
27. Although I try to resist. I feel compelled to collect a large quantity of things I never actually use.	0	1	2	3	4
28. I frequently have to check things like switches, faucets, appliances and doors several times.	0	1	2	3	4
29. I cannot concentrate unless things arc in the right place	0	1	2	3	4
30. I am afraid to use even well kept public toilets because I am so concerned about germs.	0	1	2	3	4

VOCI-R (Gönner et al., 2010)

Verbal Aggressiveness Scale (VAS)

PURPOSE To measure verbal aggressiveness.

AUTHORS Dominic A. Infante and Charles J. Wigley, III

DESCRIPTION The VAS is a 20-item instrument designed to measure verbal aggressiveness as a trait that predisposes people to attack the self-concepts of others instead of, or in addition to, their positions on topics of communication. The VAS is unidimensional, with 10 items worded negatively. Its main focus is interpersonal; verbal aggressiveness is viewed as an exchange of message between two people where at least one person in the dyad attacks the other in order to hurt him or her psychologically. Thus, the VAS appears to hold promise in the area of family and couple counseling.

NORMS Research on the VAS was conducted on approximately 660 undergraduate students in communication courses. Other demographic information and actual norms were not reported. However, in one study, the mean of 51.97 for males ($N=195$) was significantly different from the mean of 46.38 for females ($N=202$).

SCORING The VAS is scored by reverse-scoring items 1, 3, 5, 8, 10, 12, 14, 15, 17, and 20 and then totaling the scores. This produces a range of 20 to 100.

RELIABILITY The VAS has good internal consistency, with an alpha of .81. The VAS also has excellent stability, with a four-week test-retest correlation of .82.

VALIDITY The VAS has fairly good concurrent validity, correlating at moderate levels with five other trait measures. Further, the VAS was significantly correlated with predicted performance for verbally aggressive messages in a variety of social influence situations, suggesting good predictive validity.

PRIMARY REFERENCE Infante, D. A., and Wigley, C. J., III. (1986). Verbal aggressiveness: An interpersonal model and measure, *Communication Monographs*, 53, 61–69. Instrument reproduced with permission of Dominic A. Infante.

AVAILABILITY May be copied from this volume.

This survey is concerned with how we try to get people to comply with our wishes. Indicate how often each statement is true for you personally when you try to influence other persons. Use the following scale:

    1 = Almost never true
    2 = Rarely true
    3 = Occasionally true
    4 = Often true
    5 = Almost always true

—— 1. I am extremely careful to avoid attacking individuals' intelligence when I attack their ideas.

—— 2. When individuals are very stubborn, I use insults to soften the stubbornness.

—— 3. I try very hard to avoid having other people feel bad about themselves when I try to influence them.

—— 4. When people refuse to do a task I know is important, without good reason, I tell them they are unreasonable.

—— 5. When others do things I regard as stupid, I try to be extremely gentle with them.

—— 6. If individuals I am trying to influence really deserve it, I attack their character.

—— 7. When people behave in ways that are in very poor taste, I insult them in order to shock them into proper behavior.

—— 8. I try to make people feel good about themselves even when their ideas are stupid.

—— 9. When people simply will not budge on a matter of importance I lose my temper and say rather strong things to them.

—— 10. When people criticize my shortcomings, I take it in good humor and do not try to get back at them.

—— 11. When individuals insult me, I get a lot of pleasure out of really telling them off.

—— 12. When I dislike individuals greatly, I try not to show it in what I say or how I say it.

—— 13. I like poking fun at people who do things that are very stupid in order to stimulate their intelligence.

—— 14. When I attack peoples' ideas, I try not to damage their self-concepts.

—— 15. When I try to influence people, I make a great effort not to offend them.

—— 16. When people do things that are mean or cruel, I attack their character in order to help correct their behavior.

—— 17. I refuse to participate in arguments when they involve personal attacks.

—— 18. When nothing seems to work in trying to influence others, I yell and scream in order to get some movement from them.

—— 19. When I am not able to refute others' positions, I try to make them feel defensive in order to weaken their positions.

—— 20. When an argument shifts to personal attacks, I try very hard to change the subject.

Way of Life Scale (WOLS)

PURPOSE To measure exaggerated social control.

AUTHORS Logan Wright, Kurt von Bussmann, Alice Friedman, Mary Khoury, Fredette Owens, and Wayne Paris

DESCRIPTION The WOLS is a 43-item instrument designed to measure non-mutuality, a measure of exaggerated social control thought to be related to the Type A behavior pattern. Nonmutuality involves a tendency to control others inappropriately in social situations. Reports of this type of behavior among Type A patients have been made mainly in clinical settings (coronary care), but include reports on domestic behaviors. The WOLS appears to have potential not only in its focus on Type A behavior, but as a measure for evaluating clinical interventions where the goal is to decrease inappropriate, social controlling behavior.

NORMS The WOLS has been studied with several samples including 62 white, married male university faculty members, 52 middle-aged adults with chronic heart disease, 45 male undergraduates, and 30 hospitalized male patients (ages 40–55) with serious chronic heart disease. No other demographic data are available. Actual norms were not available.

SCORING The WOLS is easily scored by scoring one point for a "true" response on items 2, 3, 7, 9, 10, 12, 15, 17–19, 21, 24, 28–30, 32, 35, and 37–40, and then summing these for the total score. The remaining items are not scored.

RELIABILITY The WOLS has fair internal consistency, with an alpha of .63. The WOLS has very good stability, with three-week and three-month test-retest correlations of .77.

VALIDITY The WOLS has good concurrent validity, correlating with the Jenkins Activity Scale (Type A behavior) and the Burger/Cooper Desirability of Control Scale.

PRIMARY REFERENCE Wright, L., von Bussmann, K., Friedman, A., Khoury, M., Owens, F., and Paris, W. (1990). Exaggerated social control and its relationship to the Type A behavior pattern, *Journal of Research in Personality*, 24, 258–269.

AVAILABILITY May be copied from this volume.

The following questionnaire should be filled out according to how you feel at the present. Respond by circling the True or False choice which *most accurately* describes you, the respondent. The time should not exceed 5 minutes. Thank you for your time and cooperation.

True False   1. I am easily awakened by noise.
True False   2. When it's time to make a major decision like purchasing a house or a car I usually make that decision.
True False   3. When it's time to make a major decision about moving, I usually make that decision.
True False   4. My daily life is full of things that are interesting.
True False   5. I enjoy detective or mystery stories.
True False   6. I work under a great deal of tension.
True False   7. When it's time to discipline the children I make that decision.
True False   8. No one seems to understand me.
True False   9. When it's time to decide about social events with friends or family I usually make that decision.
True False 10. I like to be bossy.
True False 11. At times I feel like swearing.
True False 12. I like to get in the last word.
True False 13. I find it hard to keep my mind on a task.
True False 14. At times I feel like smashing things.
True False 15. I like to know the details about other people's phone conversations.
True False 16. I do not always tell the truth.
True False 17. I like to have rules and structure for handling most or all situations.
True False 18. I like to monitor other people to make sure things are going the way they should be.
True False 19. I like to make sure everything goes according to plan.
True False 20. I am a good mixer.
True False 21. I like to lead conversations or group discussions.
True False 22. I am liked by most people.
True False 23. I get angry sometimes.
True False 24. I may be inclined to interrupt people if they are not responding in the way they should be.
True False 25. I think most people would lie to get ahead.
True False 26. I am lacking in self-confidence.
True False 27. I am an important person.
True False 28. I have a tendency to manipulate, maneuver, or control other people.
True False 29. I am a good leader but not particularly a good follower.
True False 30. I like to give directions about driving or other activities.
True False 31. I am happy most of the time.
True False 32. I am a person who, if I am going out for an evening, likes to decide where to eat, what movie to attend.
True False 33. My hardest battles are with myself.
True False 34. I seem to be about as capable and smart as most others around me.
True False 35. I tend to overstructure spontaneous times such as vacations, etc., and turn them into controlled events.

True   False   36. I feel useless at times.

True   False   37. I have ideas about controlling other things with the children and other people such as how much food they should have on their plate, etc.

True   False   38. I am seen by relatives as being a dominant member of our extended family.

True   False   39. I am the one who usually decides which television channel to watch.

True   False   40. I am the one who usually controls the thermostat in the house.

True   False   41. Criticism or scolding hurts me terribly.

True   False   42. I would rather win than lose in a game.

True   False   43. I do not tire quickly.

West Haven–Yale Multidimensional Pain Inventory (WHYMPI)

PURPOSE To measure chronic pain.

AUTHORS Robert D. Kerns, Dennis C. Turk, and Thomas E. Rudy

DESCRIPTION The WHYMPI is a three-part inventory designed to assess the impact of pain on people's lives (20 items), the responses of others to the individual's communication of pain (14 items), and the extent to which pain sufferers participate in daily activities (18 items). The WHYMPI comprises 12 subscales/factors. For the first scale, the factors are: interference (items 2, 3, 4, 8, 9, 13, 14, 17, 19), support (items 5, 10, 15), pain severity (items 1, 7, 12), self-control (items 11, 16), and negative mood (items 6, 18, 20). The second scale has three subscales: punishing responses (items 1, 4, 7, 11), solicitous responses (items 2, 5, 8, 12, 14, 15), and distracting responses (items 3, 9, 10, 13). On the third scale, there are four subscales: household chores (items 1, 5, 9, 13, 17), outdoor work (items 2, 6, 10, 14, 18), activities away from home (items 3, 7, 11, 15), and social activities (items 4, 8, 12, 16). Because of its brevity, clarity, ease of administration, and multidimensional nature, the WHYMPI is viewed as an excellent measure both for research into chronic pain and to monitor practice endeavors aimed at reducing pain.

NORMS The WHYMPI initially was studied with 120 chronic pain patients (81.5% male) at two Veterans Administration hospitals. The mean age of the patients was 50.8 years, with a mean duration of 10.2 years of chronic pain; 68% of the patients were married. Means for subscales were as follows: interference=3.74, support=4.31, pain severity=3.55, self-control=3.63, negative mood=3.23, punishing responses=0.97, solicitous responses=2.57, distracting responses=1.72, household chores=2.71, outdoor work=1.19, activities away from home=1.79, and social activities=1.94.

SCORING The WHYMPI is easily scored by summing item responses for the overall score and the subscale scores.

RELIABILITY The WHYMPI has very good internal consistency, with subscale alphas that range from .70 to .90. The WHYMPI also has very good stability, with two-week test-retest correlations that range from .62 to .86.

VALIDITY The WHYMPI was viewed as having good construct validity, based on evidence obtained from factor analysis (factorial validity). The WHYMPI also has been used as an outcome measure in several clinical studies and has been shown to be sensitive to change, predictive of depressive symptom severity, and predictive of expressions of pain and affective distress.

PRIMARY REFERENCE Kerns, R. D., Turk, D. C., and Rudy, T. E. (1985). The West Haven–Yale Multidimensional Pain Inventory (WHYMPI), *Pain*, 23, 345–356.

AVAILABILITY Dr. Robert D. Kerns, Psychology Service, Veterans Administration Medical Center, West Haven, CT 06516. Department of Psychiatry, Yale University School of Medicine, New Haven, CT 06510. Email: robert.kerns@yale.edu.

SECTION 1

In the following 20 questions, you will be asked to describe your pain and how it affects your life. Under each question is a scale to record your answer. Read each question carefully and then *circle* a number on the scale under that question to indicate how that specific question applies to you.

1. Rate the level of your pain at the present moment.

0	1	2	3	4	5	6
No pain						Very intense pain

2. In general, how much does your pain problem interfere with your day-to-day activities?

0	1	2	3	4	5	6
No interference						Extreme interference

3. Since the time you developed a pain problem, how much has your pain changed your ability to work?

0	1	2	3	4	5	6
No change						Extreme change

___ Check here if you have retired for reasons other than your pain problem.

4. How much has your pain changed the amount of satisfaction or enjoyment you get from participating in social and recreational activities?

0	1	2	3	4	5	6
No change						Extreme change

5. How supportive or helpful is your spouse (significant other) to you in relation to your pain?

0	1	2	3	4	5	6
Not at all supportive						Extremely supportive

6. Rate your overall mood during the *past week*.

0	1	2	3	4	5	6
Extremely low mood						Extremely high mood

7. On the average, how severe has your pain been during the last week?

0	1	2	3	4	5	6
Not at all severe						Extremely severe

8. How much has your pain changed your ability to participate in recreational and other social activities?

0	1	2	3	4	5	6
No change						Extreme change

9. How much has your pain changed the amount of satisfaction you get from family-related activities?

0	1	2	3	4	5	6
No change						Extreme change

10. How worried is your spouse (significant other) about you in relation to your pain problem?

0	1	2	3	4	5	6
Not at all worried						Extremely worried

11. During the *past week* how much control do you feel that you have had over your life?

0	1	2	3	4	5	6
Not at all in control						Extremely in control

12. How much *suffering* do you experience because of your pain?

0	1	2	3	4	5	6
No suffering						Extreme suffering

13. How much has your pain changed your marriage and other family relationships?

0	1	2	3	4	5	6
No change						Extreme change

14. How much has your pain changed the amount of satisfaction or enjoyment you get from work?

0	1	2	3	4	5	6
No change						Extreme change

___ Check here if you are not presently working.

15. How attentive is your spouse (significant other) to your pain problem?

0	1	2	3	4	5	6
Not at all attentive						Extremely attentive

16. During the *past week* how much do you feel that you've been able to deal with your problems?

0	1	2	3	4	5	6
Not at all						Extremely well

17. How much has your pain changed your ability to do household chores?

0	1	2	3	4	5	6
No change						Extreme change

continued

18. During the past week how irritable have you been?

0	1	2	3	4	5	6
Not at all irritable						Extremely irritable

19. How much has your pain changed your friendships with people other than your family?

0	1	2	3	4	5	6
No change						Extreme change

20. During the past week how tense or anxious have you been?

0	1	2	3	4	5	6
Not at all tense or anxious						Extremely tense or anxious

SECTION 2

In this section, we are interested in knowing how your spouse (or significant other) responds to you when he or she knows that you are in pain. On the scale listed below each question, *circle* a number to indicate *how often* your spouse (or significant other) generally responds to you in that particular way *when you are in pain*. Please answer *all* of the 14 questions.

Please identify the relationship between you and the person you are thinking of _____.

1. Ignores me.

0	1	2	3	4	5	6
Never						Very often

2. Asks me what he/she can do to help.

0	1	2	3	4	5	6
Never						Very often

3. Reads to me.

0	1	2	3	4	5	6
Never						Very often

4. Expresses irritation at me.

0	1	2	3	4	5	6
Never						Very often

5. Takes over my jobs or duties.

0	1	2	3	4	5	6
Never						Very often

6. Talks to me about something else to take my mind off the pain.

0	1	2	3	4	5	6
Never						Very often

7. Expresses frustration at me.

0	1	2	3	4	5	6
Never						Very often

8. Tries to get me to rest.

0	1	2	3	4	5	6
Never						Very often

9. Tries to involve me in some activity.

0	1	2	3	4	5	6
Never						Very often

10. Expresses anger at me.

0	1	2	3	4	5	6
Never						Very often

11. Gets me some pain medication.

0	1	2	3	4	5	6
Never						Very often

12. Encourages me to work on a hobby.

0	1	2	3	4	5	6
Never						Very often

13. Gets me something to eat or drink.

0	1	2	3	4	5	6
Never						Very often

14. Turns on the TV to take my mind off my pain.

0	1	2	3	4	5	6
Never						Very often

SECTION 3

Listed below are 18 common daily activities. Please indicate *how often* you do each of these activities by *circling* a number on the scale listed below each activity. Please complete *all* 18 questions.

1. Wash dishes.

0	1	2	3	4	5	6
Never						Very often

2. Mow the lawn.

0	1	2	3	4	5	6
Never						Very often

3. Go out to eat.

0	1	2	3	4	5	6
Never						Very often

continued

4. Play cards or other games.

0	1	2	3	4	5	6
Never						Very often

5. Go grocery shopping.

0	1	2	3	4	5	6
Never						Very often

6. Work in the garden.

0	1	2	3	4	5	6
Never						Very often

7. Go to a movie.

0	1	2	3	4	5	6
Never						Very often

8. Visit friends.

0	1	2	3	4	5	6
Never						Very often

9. Help with the house cleaning.

0	1	2	3	4	5	6
Never						Very often

10. Work on the car.

0	1	2	3	4	5	6
Never						Very often

11. Take a ride in a car.

0	1	2	3	4	5	6
Never						Very often

12. Visit relatives.

0	1	2	3	4	5	6
Never						Very often

13. Prepare a meal.

0	1	2	3	4	5	6
Never						Very often

14. Wash the car.

0	1	2	3	4	5	6
Never						Very often

15. Take a trip.

0	1	2	3	4	5	6
Never						Very often

16. Go to a park or beach.

0	1	2	3	4	5	6
Never						Very often

17. Do a load of laundry.

0	1	2	3	4	5	6
Never						Very often

18. Work on a needed house repair.

0	1	2	3	4	5	6
Never						Very often

White Bear Suppression Inventory (WBSI)

PURPOSE To measure thought suppression.

AUTHORS Daniel M. Wegner and Sophia Zanakos

DESCRIPTION The WBSI is a 15-item questionnaire designed to measure thought suppression. Chronic thought suppression is a variable that is related to reports of obsessive thinking and expression of negative affect such as depression and anxiety. The WBSI is a very useful measure to identify individuals who may develop obsessive thoughts (but not necessarily compulsive behavior), to identify whether individuals who report wishing they were not depressed are in fact depressed, and to identify whether individuals exposed to emotion-producing thoughts will fail to habituate to them over time. Thus the WBSI can identify people who may suffer negative consequences of trying not to think about certain issues and also can be used by practitioners to evaluate change over time in the tendency to suppress thoughts.

NORMS The WBSI has been studied with thousands of respondents, mainly university students; detailed demographic data were not available in the original reference. The mean score in five samples of university men was 45.8 and in five samples of university women was 47.6. The mean standard deviation across all groups is 9.68. The difference between men and women was significant in four out of the five samples.

SCORING The WBSI is easily scored on a five-point scale from Strongly disagree=1 to Strongly agree=5; the item scores are simply summed for the total score on the WBSI, which ranges from 15 to 75, with higher scores indicating greater tendency to suppress thoughts.

RELIABILITY The WBSI has very good internal consistency, with alphas that range from .87 to .89. The WBSI also has good stability with a one-week test-retest correlation of .92 and a test-retest correlation of .69 when the administrations were separated by times varying from three weeks to three months.

VALIDITY The WBSI has excellent convergent validity with significant correlations between the WBSI and the Beck Depression Inventory, the Maudsley Obsessive-Compulsive Inventory, the Sensitization Subscale of the Repression-Sensitization Scale, the State-Trait Anxiety Inventory, and the Anxiety Sensitivity Inventory. The WBSI was negatively correlated with repression, suggesting that the WBSI measures a characteristic that is unlike repression as traditionally conceived.

PRIMARY REFERENCE Wegner, D. M., and Zanakos, S. (1994). Chronic thought suppression, *Journal of Personality*, 62, 615–640.

AVAILABILITY Dr. Daniel M. Wegner, Department of Psychology, Gilmer Hall, University of Virginia, Charlottesville, VA 22903. Email: dwegner@virginia.edu.

This survey is about thoughts. There are no right or wrong answers, so please respond honestly to each of the items below. Be sure to answer every item by circling the appropriate letter beside each.

A = Strongly disagree
B = Disagree
C = Neutral or don't know
D = Agree
E = Strongly agree

1.	There are things I prefer not to think about.	A	B	C	D	E
2.	Sometimes I wonder why I have the thoughts I do.	A	B	C	D	E
3.	I have thoughts that I cannot stop.	A	B	C	D	E
4.	There are images that come to mind that I cannot erase.	A	B	C	D	E
5.	My thoughts frequently return to one idea.	A	B	C	D	E
6.	I wish I could stop thinking of certain things.	A	B	C	D	E
7.	Sometimes my mind races so fast I wish I could stop it.	A	B	C	D	E
8.	I always try to put problems out of mind.	A	B	C	D	E
9.	There are thoughts that keep jumping into my head.	A	B	C	D	E
10.	There are things that I try not to think about.	A	B	C	D	E
11.	Sometimes I really wish I could stop thinking.	A	B	C	D	E
12.	I often do things to distract myself from my thoughts.	A	B	C	D	E
13.	I have thoughts that I try to avoid.	A	B	C	D	E
14.	There are many thoughts that I have that I don't tell anyone.	A	B	C	D	E
15.	Sometimes I stay busy just to keep thoughts from intruding on my mind.	A	B	C	D	E

Willingness to Care Scale (WTC)

PURPOSE To measure attitudes toward providing emotional, instrumental, and nursing support.

AUTHOR Neil Abell

DESCRIPTION The WTC is a 30-item instrument designed to measure informal caregivers' attitudes toward providing emotional, physical, and instrumental support to persons living with AIDS (PLAs). Informal caregivers are defined as blood kin, spouses, partners, and lovers. There are no other scales designed to measure informal caregivers' attitudes toward providing the variety of types of care and support to the PLA. This assessment is similar to that of caregiver burden, but different in that the caregiver may be asked to anticipate his or her responses to the ill person's current or future needs. A primary concern is whether the relationship can be sustained over time, and what issues or perceptions may need to be addressed to make it mutually functional for caregiver and care recipient. The WTC is composed of a global scale as well as three subscales: emotional (items 1–10), instrumental (items 11–20), and nursing (items 21–30). The WTC reflects two distinct and related components of caregiving: ability (which represents the tasks caregivers believe they could perform if necessary) and willingness (which represents the tasks caregivers would perform). The WTC can be used as an assessment of the needs of caregivers as well as a possible outcome measure to help aid case managers or other practitioners in developing and supporting those caregivers' needs. A Spanish version of the scale is available.

NORMS The WTC was developed with 155 caregivers from two AIDS service organizations in Florida. Forty-seven percent of the subjects were male and 53% were female; 67% were Caucasian, 21% African-American, and 10% Hispanic. Caregiving experience ranged from 3 months to 10 years of primary responsibility. The mean on the global WTC was 4.64 (SD=4.3); on the instrumental subscale, M=4.60 (SD=.50); on the emotional subscale, M=4.68 (SD=.53); and on the nursing subscale, M=4.61 (SD=.64).

SCORING The WTC is easily scored by simply summing item responses on each subscale or on the total scale and dividing by the number of items summed to produce the mean.

RELIABILITY The WTC has good to excellent internal consistency, with an alpha of .92 for the total WTC and alphas of .88, .84, and .91 for the emotional, instrumental, and nursing subscales, respectively. No data on stability were reported.

VALIDITY The author reports good factorial validity for the WTC. In addition, the WTC has fair construct validity. Discriminant validity was established, with the WTC being uncorrelated with demographic variables with which the WTC should not be correlated; convergent validity was established with the WTC being positively correlated with variables with which it was predicted to be correlated (such as perceived social support).

PRIMARY REFERENCE Abell, N. (in press). Assessing willingness to care for persons with AIDS: Validation of a new measure, *Research on Social Work Practice*.

AVAILABILITY Dr. Neil Abell, Florida State University, School of Social Work, Tallahassee, FL 32306-2570. Email: nabell@fsu.edu.

AIDS caregiving can be a demanding and sometimes overwhelming experience. Caregivers may differ in the tasks they feel able and/or willing to perform.

Being *able* to perform a task means that you believe you *could do it* if necessary.

Being *willing* to perform a task means that you feel you *would do it* if it had to be done.

As you read the statements below, think about the person with AIDS you know who is in need of care. FIRST, place an "X" by each one of the tasks *you feel able* to do for him or her. SECOND, reread the items, and CIRCLE THE NUMBER which best shows *how willing you are* to do each one, where:

1 = Completely unwilling
2 = Somewhat unwilling
3 = Not sure
4 = Somewhat willing
5 = Completely willing

		Able?	How Willing?
1.	Listen to someone who is sad.	___	1 2 3 4 5
2.	Comfort someone who is upset.	___	1 2 3 4 5
3.	Help someone deal with anxiety about the future.	___	1 2 3 4 5
4.	Hold hands with someone who is afraid.	___	1 2 3 4 5
5.	Encourage someone who feels hopeless.	___	1 2 3 4 5
6.	Listen to someone's concerns about death or dying.	___	1 2 3 4 5
7.	Help someone keep his or her spirits up.	___	1 2 3 4 5
8.	Hold someone who is crying.	___	1 2 3 4 5
9.	Listen to someone who is angry.	___	1 2 3 4 5
10.	Be patient with someone who is disoriented or confused.	___	1 2 3 4 5
11.	Take someone to a medical appointment.	___	1 2 3 4 5
12.	Bring home groceries for someone.	___	1 2 3 4 5
13.	Help pay for someone's medicine.	___	1 2 3 4 5
14.	Prepare meals for someone.	___	1 2 3 4 5
15.	Clean someone's room or home.	___	1 2 3 4 5
16.	Wash someone's dishes.	___	1 2 3 4 5
17.	Do someone's laundry.	___	1 2 3 4 5
18.	Help pay for someone's food or housing.	___	1 2 3 4 5
19.	Have someone live in your home.	___	1 2 3 4 5
20.	Negotiate someone's health care options with a doctor.	___	1 2 3 4 5
21.	Help someone take medicine.	___	1 2 3 4 5
22.	Change dirty bed sheets.	___	1 2 3 4 5
23.	Help someone take a bath.	___	1 2 3 4 5
24.	Clean up after someone who has lost bowel or bladder control.	___	1 2 3 4 5
25.	Help someone eat a meal.	___	1 2 3 4 5

26. Clean up when someone has thrown up.   —   1 2 3 4 5
27. Turn someone in bed.   —   1 2 3 4 5
28. Change dressings on someone's sores.   —   1 2 3 4 5
29. Help someone in the bathroom.   —   1 2 3 4 5
30. Help someone move in and out of bed.   —   1 2 3 4 5

Women's Experience of Heterosexual Intercourse Scale (WEHI)

PURPOSE To measure women's experience of heterosexual intercourse.

AUTHORS Gurit E. Birnbaum, Hannayah Glaubman, and Mario Mikulincer

DESCRIPTION The WEHI is a 96-item scale designed to assess the variety of experiences women report about heterosexual intercourse. The WEHI is substantially longer than other scales in this book, but takes only 15 minutes to complete and is unique enough to warrant inclusion. The WEHI is based on the notion that there are several possible explanations about women's sexual dysfunction, but few systematic attempts to describe empirically and map the components of women's sexual experience. The WEHI is an attempt to provide a comprehensive profile of the relevant emotional, cognitive, and motivational aspects of women's sexual experience. The WEHI is comprised of three subscales: Relationship-Centered (RC; 32 items); Worry-Centered (WC; 36 items); and Pleasure-Centered (PC; 28 items). The items on each subscale are available in the Primary Reference.

NORMS The WEHI was developed in a series of studies, all with women in Israel. The major norming study involved 564 women, with a mean age of 30.67. The women were recruited from universities, community centers, and sport clubs. 56.7% of the sample was single, 38.5% married, and 4.8% divorced or widowed. The mean years of education were 14.4. Means for each item are available in the Primary Reference, including means for different subgroups in later studies, such as clinical sexual dysfunction groups and controls.

SCORING Each item is scored on a 9-point scale ranging from 1 = "does not match at all" to 9 = "closely matches." The WEHI is easily scored by simply summing item scores within each subscale.

RELIABILITY The WEHI has excellent internal consistency with alphas as follows: RC = .92; WC = .95; and PC = .91. Data on stability were not available.

VALIDITY The WEHI has very good concurrent validity with significant correlations between the WEHI subscales and reports of sexual functioning from the Israeli Sexual Behavior Inventory. The WEHI also has very good known-groups validity differentiating significantly between women with clinical and women with subclinical sexual disorders.

PRIMARY REFERENCE Birnbaum, G. E., Glaubman, H., and Mikulincer, M. Women's Experience of Heterosexual Intercourse Scale: Construction, factor structure, and relations to orgasmic disorders, *Journal of Sex Research, 38*, 191–204. Instrument reproduced with permission of Dr. Birnbaum.

AVAILABILITY Email Dr. Birnbaum at birmbag@mail.biu.ac.il or may be copied from this volume.

The objective of this questionnaire is to describe the experience of sexual intercourse, as women experience it.

Try to recall a situation or a number of situations in which you had sexual intercourse, and imagine to yourself, in as much detail as possible, what happened to you during the entire experience, and try to recreate in your mind the things that occurred during those moments.

On the following pages, you will find a list of sentences dealing with the situation/s that you have brought to your awareness.

Please circle, next to each sentence, the degree to which it matches the experience(s) you had.

For each sentence, there is a scale of numbers from 1, which indicates total lack of fit, to 9, which represents a total match. If the sentence matches the experience closely, mark a higher number; if it does not match, mark a lower number.

It is important to us that your answers be based on an experience or experiences of sexual intercourse that you have had during your life, therefore try to answer the questions from your own personal-subjective point of view, and ignore things you have heard or read about the topic.

Please try not to skip any questions.

At this point, we wish to note that these questionnaires are anonymous and confidential.

We greatly appreciate the effort you are willing to make.

Thank you for your cooperation.

Next to each sentence, mark the degree to which it matches your experience/s during sexual intercourse.

During sexual intercourse . . .

		Closely matches								Does not match
1. I feel my partner is considerate of me	9	8	7	6	5	4	3	2	1
2. I'm focused on satisfying my partner	9	8	7	6	5	4	3	2	1
3. I'm afraid of the outcomes of my actions	9	8	7	6	5	4	3	2	1
4. I feel apathetic	9	8	7	6	5	4	3	2	1
5. I feel grateful to my partner	9	8	7	6	5	4	3	2	1
6. I think that it can't be better than this	9	8	7	6	5	4	3	2	1
7. I feel my partner knows me	9	8	7	6	5	4	3	2	1
8. I feel guilty	9	8	7	6	5	4	3	2	1
9. I feel loss of control	9	8	7	6	5	4	3	2	1
10. I feel warmth toward my partner	9	8	7	6	5	4	3	2	1
11. I'm afraid of disappointing my partner	9	8	7	6	5	4	3	2	1
12. I think about good things only	9	8	7	6	5	4	3	2	1
13. I feel power and strength	9	8	7	6	5	4	3	2	1
14. I feel disconnected from the world	9	8	7	6	5	4	3	2	1
15. I feel my partner is focused on me	9	8	7	6	5	4	3	2	1
16. I feel impatient	9	8	7	6	5	4	3	2	1
17. I feel that I'm not "good" enough in bed	9	8	7	6	5	4	3	2	1
18. I'm in a state of ecstasy	9	8	7	6	5	4	3	2	1
19. I want to receive attention from my partner	9	8	7	6	5	4	3	2	1
20. I feel a sort of fogginess in my thinking	9	8	7	6	5	4	3	2	1
21. I feel a sense of conquest	9	8	7	6	5	4	3	2	1
22. I feel I am important to my partner	9	8	7	6	5	4	3	2	1
23. I feel lack of communication with my partner	9	8	7	6	5	4	3	2	1
24. I'm tired	9	8	7	6	5	4	3	2	1
25. I'm focused on enjoying my partner	9	8	7	6	5	4	3	2	1
26. I feel distress	9	8	7	6	5	4	3	2	1
27. I feel that I'm taking advantage of my partner	9	8	7	6	5	4	3	2	1
28. I feel relaxed	9	8	7	6	5	4	3	2	1

continued

29. I feel that my partner accepts me	9	8	7	6	5	4	3	2	1
30. I feel embarrassed	9	8	7	6	5	4	3	2	1
31. I feel it is difficult for me to reach orgasm	9	8	7	6	5	4	3	2	1
32. I feel ashamed	9	8	7	6	5	4	3	2	1
33. I feel satisfied	9	8	7	6	5	4	3	2	1
34. I feel attracted to my partner	9	8	7	6	5	4	3	2	1
35. I feel a sense of belonging	9	8	7	6	5	4	3	2	1
36. I'm frustrated and disappointed	9	8	7	6	5	4	3	2	1
37. I feel a rising sensation	9	8	7	6	5	4	3	2	1
38. I feel understood	9	8	7	6	5	4	3	2	1
39. I feel pleasure	9	8	7	6	5	4	3	2	1
40. I feel familiar with my body	9	8	7	6	5	4	3	2	1
41. I feel intimacy and closeness to my partner	9	8	7	6	5	4	3	2	1
42. I feel that I am merging with my partner	9	8	7	6	5	4	3	2	1
43. I think about how much I need my partner	9	8	7	6	5	4	3	2	1
44. I feel alienated and detached	9	8	7	6	5	4	3	2	1
45. I feel disgust	9	8	7	6	5	4	3	2	1
46. I feel secure	9	8	7	6	5	4	3	2	1
47. I want to escape from there	9	8	7	6	5	4	3	2	1
48. Bothersome thoughts disturb my concentration	9	8	7	6	5	4	3	2	1
49. I feel a sensation of wholeness	9	8	7	6	5	4	3	2	1
50. I want to feel loved	9	8	7	6	5	4	3	2	1
51. I feel a floating sensation	9	8	7	6	5	4	3	2	1
52. I feel that I'm doing something impure	9	8	7	6	5	4	3	2	1
53. I'm preoccupied in seducing my partner	9	8	7	6	5	4	3	2	1
54. I feel bored	9	8	7	6	5	4	3	2	1
55. I feel vulnerable	9	8	7	6	5	4	3	2	1
56. I feel that I'm doing something forbidden	9	8	7	6	5	4	3	2	1
57. I feel as if I have melted	9	8	7	6	5	4	3	2	1

	Closely matches								Does not match
58. I want my partner to express warmth towards me	9	8	7	6	5	4	3	2	1
59. I feel relief	9	8	7	6	5	4	3	2	1
60. I feel anger toward my partner	9	8	7	6	5	4	3	2	1
61. I feel something is missing	9	8	7	6	5	4	3	2	1
62. I feel calmness	9	8	7	6	5	4	3	2	1
63. My partner's pleasure satisfies me	9	8	7	6	5	4	3	2	1
64. I feel emptiness	9	8	7	6	5	4	3	2	1
65. I feel feminine	9	8	7	6	5	4	3	2	1
66. I feel self-hatred	9	8	7	6	5	4	3	2	1
67. I feel I'm responding to my partner's needs	9	8	7	6	5	4	3	2	1
68. I feel self-pity	9	8	7	6	5	4	3	2	1
69. I feel excitement	9	8	7	6	5	4	3	2	1
70. I allow myself to do things I do not do in daily life	9	8	7	6	5	4	3	2	1
71. I feel that my partner is focused on me	9	8	7	6	5	4	3	2	1
72. I feel wanted	9	8	7	6	5	4	3	2	1
73. I concentrate solely on myself	9	8	7	6	5	4	3	2	1
74. I want to be alone	9	8	7	6	5	4	3	2	1
75. I'm focused on reaching orgasm	9	8	7	6	5	4	3	2	1
76. I want there to be more feeling	9	8	7	6	5	4	3	2	1
77. I feel my partner doesn't know how to excite me	9	8	7	6	5	4	3	2	1
78. I don't think about anything	9	8	7	6	5	4	3	2	1
79. I feel that my behavior is spontaneous	9	8	7	6	5	4	3	2	1
80. I feel lonely	9	8	7	6	5	4	3	2	1
81. I feel love towards my partner	9	8	7	6	5	4	3	2	1
82. I'm focused on my own needs	9	8	7	6	5	4	3	2	1
83. I think of how to entice my partner	9	8	7	6	5	4	3	2	1
84. My thoughts wander to other things	9	8	7	6	5	4	3	2	1
85. I'm jealous of my partner	9	8	7	6	5	4	3	2	1

continued

	Closely matches								Does not match
86. I feel special	9	8	7	6	5	4	3	2	1
87. It is hard for me to concentrate during the act itself	9	8	7	6	5	4	3	2	1
88. I try to please my partner	9	8	7	6	5	4	3	2	1
89. I feel sadness	9	8	7	6	5	4	3	2	1
90. I feel that I'm slave of my body and desire	9	8	7	6	5	4	3	2	1
91. I think about what my partner thinks/feels	9	8	7	6	5	4	3	2	1
92. I want there to be more foreplay	9	8	7	6	5	4	3	2	1
93. I'm afraid of penetration	9	8	7	6	5	4	3	2	1
94. I feel desired	9	8	7	6	5	4	3	2	1
95. I want my partner to finish as fast as possible	9	8	7	6	5	4	3	2	1
96. I'm using my partner for fulfill my needs	9	8	7	6	5	4	3	2	1

Women's Sexual Working Models Scale (WSWMS)

PURPOSE To measure women's sexual working models.

AUTHORS Gurit E. Birnbaum and Harry T. Reis

DESCRIPTION The WSWMS is a 24-item instrument designed to assess variations and individual differences in the sexual working models women may use. This measure is based on evolutionary psychology, particularly, attachment theory. That literature provided the basis for development of items that assessed mental representations of adaptive psychological mechanisms, cognitions, and emotions that may contribute to reproductive success in the context of a long-term adult romantic relationship. The WSWMS contains five factors or subscales: Guilt and Shame (GS; items 4, 7, 10, 16, 18, 22); Maintaining the Bond (MB; items 2, 8, 11, 14, 17, 24); Distancing/Distraction (DD; items 3, 19, 13, 23); Caring Partner (CP; items 1, 6, 12, 21); and Excitement (E; items 5, 9, 15, 20).

NORMS The WSWMS was developed in a series of studies with over 1200 North American and Israeli women. In an early study of 248 North American women, with a mean age of 33.7 (SD=9.85), participants from community centers, sports clubs and university sites volunteered to participate. 54.8% of the sample was married or cohabiting, 31% were single and never married, and 12.1% were divorced, widowed, or separated. The mean education level was 16.1 years (SD=2.35); 79.8% of the sample was white, 7.7% African American, 4.0% Asian, and 2.0% Hispanic. Means for this sample were not available in the Primary Reference, but may be obtained from the author.

SCORING The WSWMS is easily scored by taking the means of the items on each subscale. Higher scores indicate stronger adherence to the subscale.

RELIABILITY The WSWMS has good to very good internal consistency with alphas of .90, .85, .72, .87, and .76 for GS, MB, DD, CP, and E, respectively. Data on stability were not reported.

VALIDITY The WSWMS has established construct validity with subscale correlations in expected directions for North American and Israeli samples with numerous other measures of relationship, love, intimacy, self-esteem, and cognitive, behavioral and affective measures of sexuality. The WSWMS was not correlated significantly with social desirability.

PRIMARY REFERENCE Birnbaun, G. E., and Reis, H.T. (in press). Women's sexual working models: An evolutionary-attachment perspective, *Journal of Sex Research*. Instrument reproduced with permission of Dr. Birnbaum.

AVAILABILITY Email Dr. Birnbaum at birnbag@mail.biu.ac.il.

This survey deals with feelings, expectations, and beliefs about sexual activity with a partner, as perceived by women. The list of sentences describes different feelings, expectations, and beliefs about sexual activity with a partner.

*Thinking over your personal experiences, indicate the extent to which the following items describe **your** feelings, expectations, and beliefs about sexual activity with a partner.*

Try to respond to this questionnaire only from your own personal, subjective viewpoint, and to ignore what you may have heard from others or have read about this subject.

While filling out this questionnaire, you may come across thoughts or feelings you would rather not think about, or would prefer to keep to yourself. If this occurs, you may stop answering this questionnaire at any time.

But if you do complete the questionnaire, it is important not to skip any of the items.

Please DO NOT put your name or any other identifying information on this questionnaire.

We greatly appreciate your effort.
Thank you for your cooperation.

Next to each sentence, please mark the degree to which it characterizes your feelings, expectations, and beliefs about sexual activity with a partner

	not at all characteristic							very characteristic
1. I feel that my partner is concerned and caring during sex	1 2 3 4 5 6 7 8 9							
2. To me, sex is an important part of becoming really close to my partner	1 2 3 4 5 6 7 8 9							
3. During sexual activity, intruding thoughts often distract me	1 2 3 4 5 6 7 8 9							
4. I often feel critical of myself during or after sex for doing something morally wrong	1 2 3 4 5 6 7 8 9							
5. During sexual activity, I feel pleasantly excited	1 2 3 4 5 6 7 8 9							
6. When I have sex, I feel that my partner is responsive to my needs	1 2 3 4 5 6 7 8 9							
7. Sexual activity feels like something impure	1 2 3 4 5 6 7 8 9							
8. To me, sexual activity can strengthen a committed relationship	1 2 3 4 5 6 7 8 9							

	not at all characteristic								very characteristic

9. During sexual activity my physical desires are very intense	1	2	3	4	5	6	7	8	9
10. Sexual activity makes me feel sinful	1	2	3	4	5	6	7	8	9
11. Sexual activity is a way to strengthen the relationship between two people	1	2	3	4	5	6	7	8	9
12. During sexual activity, I feel that my partner accepts me as I am	1	2	3	4	5	6	7	8	9
13. During sexual activity, I sometimes feel apathetic	1	2	3	4	5	6	7	8	9
14. Sexual activity gives me the feeling of being loved	1	2	3	4	5	6	7	8	9
15. During sexual activity, I feel a sense of adventure	1	2	3	4	5	6	7	8	9
16. Sexual activity makes me feel guilty	1	2	3	4	5	6	7	8	9
17. Sexual activity helps me feel understood by my partner	1	2	3	4	5	6	7	8	9
18. To me, sexual activity feels like something forbidden	1	2	3	4	5	6	7	8	9
19. During sexual activity, my thoughts often wander to other unrelated things	1	2	3	4	5	6	7	8	9
20. During sexual activity, I lose control of my inhibitions	1	2	3	4	5	6	7	8	9
21. My partner is considerate of me during sexual activity	1	2	3	4	5	6	7	8	9
22. Sexual activity makes me feel ashamed	1	2	3	4	5	6	7	8	9
23. While having sex, I sometimes feel like I am not involved but instead I am watching myself from outside	1	2	3	4	5	6	7	8	9
24. To me, sexual activity is a way of forming an affectionate relationship	1	2	3	4	5	6	7	8	9

Working Alliance Inventory (WAI)

PURPOSE To measure the working alliance between a client and clinician.

AUTHOR Adam O. Horvath

DESCRIPTION This 36-item instrument measures three aspects of the working alliance between a client and a clinician. The aspects are (1) tasks, where the clinician and client both see in-session action and cognition as relevant and efficacious; (2) goals, where clinician and client mutually endorse and value the anticipated treatment outcome; and (3) bonds, the mutual personal attachment between the client and clinician which includes trust, acceptance, and confidence. Since these three aspects are considered to be common to all clinical treatment, the WAI may be used to evaluate treatment, regardless of theory or techniques. However, the WAI emphasizes the quality of mutuality between the clinician and the client as a primary component of effectiveness. The WAI was developed with excellent psychometric procedures from a pool of 91 items. There are two forms of the WAI, one for the clinician and one for the client. The client form is illustrated here. Each item contains a blank which is filled with either the name of the client or the clinician. A short form of the WAI is available by using only items 2, 4, 8, 12, 21, 22, 23, 24, 26, 27, 32, and 35.

NORMS Norms are not reported in the primary references.

SCORING Individual item responses are summed for a total score.

RELIABILITY The WAI has very good reliability in terms of internal consistency. For example, from a sample of 29 clinician and client dyads involved in short-term treatment, the client form of the WAI had alphas of .87, .82, and .68 for the goals, tasks, and bonds subscales. A separate study of 25 clinicians from a wide range of theoretical orientations reported item homogeneity coefficients ranging from .89 to .93. For the short form of the WAI, the alphas were .90 for tasks, .92 for bonds, and .90 for the goals. The composite scale of the short form has an internal consistency coefficient of .98 using Cronbach's alpha. Data on stability were not available.

VALIDITY The WAI has very good validity. Discriminant and convergent validity were tested with the multimethod-multitrait procedure where the results support the construct validity of the WAI. The goal subscale seems to have the best discriminant validity. Concurrent validity is supported by correlations between the three subscale scores and measures of perceived attractiveness, expertness, and trustworthiness that clients feel towards clinicians, and correlates with clinicians' empathy. Scores on the tasks and goals subscales correlated with client reported outcome. Tasks subscales scores were associated with a measure of client indecision, state-trait anxiety, and change in the client's target complaint as rated by the clinician and the client.

PRIMARY REFERENCES Horvath, A. O., and Greenberg, L. S. (1989). Development and validation of the Working Alliance Inventory, *Journal of Counseling Psychology*, 36, 223–233. Tracey, T. J., and Kokotovic, A. M. (1989). Factor structure of the Working Alliance Inventory, *Psychological Assessment*, 1, 207–210. Instrument reproduced with permission of Adam O. Horvath.

AVAILABILITY Dr. Adam O. Horvath, Counseling Psychology Program, Faculty of Education, Simon Fraser University, Burnaby, British Columbia, Canada V5A 1S6. Email: horvath@sfu.ca.

Below are 36 questions about your relationship with your therapist. Using the following scale rate the degree to which you agree with each statement, and record your answer in the space to the left of the item.

1 = Not at all true
2 = A little true
3 = Slightly true
4 = Somewhat true
5 = Moderately true
6 = Considerably true
7 = Very true

___ 1. I feel uncomfortable with _____.
___ 2. _____ and I agree about the things I will need to do in therapy to help improve my situation.
___ 3. I am worried about the outcome of these sessions.
___ 4. What I am doing in therapy gives me new ways of looking at my problem.
___ 5. _____ and I understand each other.
___ 6. _____ perceives accurately what my goals are.
___ 7. I find what I am doing in therapy confusing.
___ 8. I believe _____ likes me.
___ 9. I wish _____ and I could clarify the purpose of our sessions.
___ 10. I disagree with _____ about what I ought to get out of therapy.
___ 11. I believe the time _____ and I are spending together is not spent efficiently.
___ 12. _____ does not understand what I am trying to accomplish in therapy.
___ 13. I am clear on what my responsibilities are in therapy.
___ 14. The goals of these sessions are important to me.
___ 15. I find what _____ and I are doing in therapy are unrelated to my concerns.
___ 16. I feel that the things I do in therapy will help me to accomplish the changes that I want.
___ 17. I believe _____ is genuinely concerned for my welfare.
___ 18. I am clear as to what _____ wants me to do in these sessions.
___ 19. _____ and I respect each other.
___ 20. I feel that _____ is not totally honest about his/her feelings toward me.
___ 21. I am confident in _____'s ability to help me.
___ 22. _____ and I are working towards mutually agreed upon goals.
___ 23. I feel that _____ appreciates me.
___ 24. We agree on what is important for me to work on.
___ 25. As a result of these sessions I am clearer as to how I might be able to change.
___ 26. _____ and I trust one another.
___ 27. _____ and I have different ideas on what my problems are.
___ 28. My relationship with _____ is very important to me.
___ 29. I have the feeling that if I say or do the wrong things, _____ will stop working with me.
___ 30. _____ and I collaborate on setting goals for my therapy.
___ 31. I am frustrated by the things I am doing in therapy.

___ 32. We have established a good understanding of the kind of changes that would be good for me.

___ 33. The things that _____ is asking me to do don't make sense.

___ 34. I don't know what to expect as the result of my therapy.

___ 35. I believe the way we are working with my problem is correct.

___ 36. I feel _____ cares about me even when I do things that he/she does not approve of.

Young Adult Family Inventory of Life Events and Changes (YA-FILES)

PURPOSE To measure stress in young adults.

AUTHORS Hamilton I. McCubbin, Joan M. Patterson, and Janet R. Grochowski

DESCRIPTION The YA-FILES is a 77-item instrument designed to measure the stressors and strains of young adults. This instrument is a modification of the Adolescent-FILES, especially with regard to 31 items referring to "College Changes." While the YA-FILES has 13 factors, the total score is recommended for use.

NORMS The YA-FILES was studied with 184 college students, including 79 women and 82 men. No other demographic information is available. The overall mean was 196.93 (SD = 18.42).

SCORING Scoring procedures are available from the primary reference for this and other McCubbin scales.

RELIABILITY The YA-FILES has very good internal consistency, with an alpha of .85. The measure also has very good stability, with a test-retest correlation of .85.

VALIDITY The YA-FILES has fair concurrent validity, with correlations with adolescent substance use and adolescent health locus of control. The YA-FILES also is a good predictor of college GPA.

PRIMARY REFERENCE McCubbin, L.D., McCubbin, H.I. and Sievers, J.A. (Eds.) (2012). Family wellbeing: Stress, coping, resilence-Assessment Measures for Research and Practice. Pullman, WA: Washington State University Press.

AVAILABILITY Permission to use this instrument may be obtained by writing to any of the Editors at Department of Counseling and Leadership, Washington State University, Pullman, Washington. There emails are as follows: Dr. Laurie D. McCubbin: (mcubbin@wsu.edu); Dr. Hamilton I. McCubbin (him@wsu.edu); Dr. Jason A. Sievers (jasievers@wsu.edu). Additional instruments are also available from the primary reference and its accompanying CD.

Part I—Family Life Changes

Read each family life change and decide if it happened in your family during the last 6 months. Mark one of the following responses:

Yes, the change happened to me personally
Yes, the change happened to another family member (not me)
No, the change did not happen to any member of my family

Part II—College Changes

Read each college change and decide if it happened to YOU during the last 6 months. Check YES or NO.

"Family" means a group of persons who are related to each other by marriage, blood, or adoption, who may or may not live with you. Family includes step-parents, step-brothers, step-sisters, and foster parents.

Remember: Anytime the words *parent, mother, brother,* etc., are used, they also mean step-parent, step-mother, foster parent, guardian, etc.

PART I: FAMILY LIFE CHANGES

Did this change happen in your family during the past 6 months?

	YES, Happened to me personally	YES, Happened to another family member	NO, Did not happen in my family
1. Family member started new business (farm, store, etc.)	☐	☐	☐
2. Parent quit or lost a job	☐	☐	☐
3. Parents separated or divorced	☐	☐	☐
4. Parent remarried	☐	☐	☐
5. Family member was married	☐	☐	☐
6. Family member was found to have a learning disorder	☐	☐	☐
7. Parents adopted a child	☐	☐	☐
8. A member started junior high or high school	☐	☐	☐
9. Child or teenage member entered college, vocational training, or armed forces	☐	☐	☐
10. Parent started school	☐	☐	☐
11. Brother or sister moved away from home	☐	☐	☐
12. Young adult member entered college, vocational training, or armed forces	☐	☐	☐
13. Parent(s) started or changed to a new job	☐	☐	☐
14. Family moved to a new home	☐	☐	☐
15. Unmarried family member became pregnant	☐	☐	☐
16. Family member had an abortion	☐	☐	☐
17. Birth of a brother or sister	☐	☐	☐

	YES, Happened to me personally	YES, Happened to another family member	NO, Did not happen in my family
18. Unmarried young adult member began having sexual intercourse	☐	☐	☐
19. Family went on welfare	☐	☐	☐
20. Damage to or loss of family property due to fire, burglary, or other disaster	☐	☐	☐
21. Brother or sister died	☐	☐	☐
22. Parent died	☐	☐	☐
23. Close family relative died	☐	☐	☐
24. Death of a close friend or family member	☐	☐	☐
25. Family member or close family friend attempted or committed suicide	☐	☐	☐
26. Family member became seriously ill or injured	☐	☐	☐
27. Family member was hospitalized	☐	☐	☐
28. Family member became physically disabled or was found to have a long-term health problem (e.g., asthma)	☐	☐	☐
29. Family member has emotional problems	☐	☐	☐
30. Grandparent(s) became seriously ill	☐	☐	☐
31. Parent(s) have more responsibility to take care of grandparent(s)	☐	☐	☐
32. Family member ran away	☐	☐	☐
33. More financial debts due to use of credit cards or charges	☐	☐	☐
34. Increased family living expenses for medical care, food, clothing, energy costs (gasoline, heating)	☐	☐	☐
35. Increase of parent's time away from family	☐	☐	☐
36. Young adult member resists doing things with family	☐	☐	☐
37. Increase in arguments between parents	☐	☐	☐
38. Teens/young adults have more arguments with one another	☐	☐	☐
39. Parent(s) and young adult(s) have increased arguments (hassles) over personal appearance (clothes, hair, etc.)	☐	☐	☐
40. Increased arguments about getting the jobs done at home	☐	☐	☐
41. Family member uses drugs (not given by doctor)	☐	☐	☐
42. Family member drinks too much alcohol	☐	☐	☐
43. Teen/young adult was suspended from or dropped out of school	☐	☐	☐
44. Parent(s) and young adults have increased arguments (hassles) over use of cigarettes, alcohol, or drugs	☐	☐	☐
45. Family member went to jail, juvenile detention, or was placed on court probation	☐	☐	☐
46. Family member was robbed or attacked (physically or sexually)	☐	☐	☐

continued

PART II: COLLEGE CHANGES

Did this change happen in your family
during the past 6 months?   YES   NO

47.	Felt pressure to get good grades	☐	☐
48.	Had difficulty getting needed information and help from your college advisor	☐	☐
49.	Had difficulty finding a college counselor for your personal needs (e.g. academic, career, emotional, etc.)	☐	☐
50.	Had difficulty getting the help you needed from a college counselor	☐	☐
51.	Felt pressure to make a career choice	☐	☐
52.	Felt pressure from your parents to make a career choice	☐	☐
53.	Felt pressure from your parents to succeed in college	☐	☐
54.	Been unable to find a quiet place to study	☐	☐
55.	Been unable to use the library to study	☐	☐
56.	Been unable to use the athletic and recreational facilities when you wanted to	☐	☐
57.	Felt financial pressures regarding how to pay for tuition, books, etc.	☐	☐
58.	Had conflict or hassles with your roommate(s)	☐	☐
59.	Felt the need to have more privacy	☐	☐
60.	Felt uncertainty regarding how to act as a college student in social settings	☐	☐
61.	Had difficulty making friends with on-campus students	☐	☐
62.	Had difficulty making friends with commuting students	☐	☐
63.	Had difficult making friends with students living in apartments	☐	☐
64.	Felt lonely because you missed your family	☐	☐
65.	Felt conflict between time to study and time to make friends and party	☐	☐
66.	Worried about driving to class in bad weather	☐	☐
67.	Worried about finding a place to park at school	☐	☐
68.	Felt isolated from the college community	☐	☐
69.	Felt your being in college has placed added strain on your family	☐	☐
70.	Had difficult participating in social activities held at the college during evening hours or on weekends	☐	☐
71.	Felt strain from missing contact with your high school friends	☐	☐
72.	Been unable to study when you wanted to for as long as you wanted	☐	☐
73.	Felt pressure to drink when you didn't want to	☐	☐
74.	Felt pressure to use non-prescription drugs when you didn't want to	☐	☐
75.	Worried about being sexually attractive	☐	☐
76.	Worried about how sexually attractive to be	☐	☐
77.	Felt confused about your priorities, values, beliefs	☐	☐

Young Adult Social Support Inventory (YA-SSI)

PURPOSE To measure social support.

AUTHORS Hamilton I. McCubbin, Joan M. Patterson, and Janet R. Grochowski

DESCRIPTION The YA-SSI is a 54-item instrument designed to measure social support in young adults, particularly entering college freshmen. Although the YA-SSI has not been studied with other samples, it appears to have face validity for use with young adult populations other than college students. The YA-SSI has 11 factors, but can easily serve as an overall measure of social support by using the total score.

NORMS The YA-SSI has been studied with two samples of college students for a total of 361 subjects including both men and women. No other demographic data are available. The overall means ranged from 135.49 (SD = 16.1) to 145.4 (SD = 19.3).

SCORING Scoring procedures are available from the primary reference for this and other McCubbin scales.

RELIABILITY The YA-SSI has excellent internal consistency, with an alpha of .89. The YA-SSI also has excellent stability, with a test-retest correlation of .90.

VALIDITY The YA-SSI has fair predictive validity, significantly correlating with academic GPA and ratings of college friends and other relatives.

PRIMARY REFERENCE McCubbin, L.D., McCubbin, H.I. and Sievers, J.A. (Eds.) (2012). Family wellbeing: Stress, coping, resilence-Assessment measurements for research and practice. Pullman, WA: Washington State University Press.

AVAILABILITY Permission to use this instrument may be obtained by writing any of the Editors at Department of Counseling Psychology and Leadership, Washington State University, Pullman, Washington. The emails are as follows: Dr. Laurie D. McCubbin: (mccubin@wsu.edu); Dr. Hamilton I. McCubbin: (him@was.edu); Dr. Jason A. Sievers (jasievers@wsu.edu). Additional instruments are also available from the primary reference and its accompanying CD.

Please answer the following questions:

	YES	NO
1. Are one or both of your PARENTS living?	☐	☐
2. Do you have SIBLINGS? (i.e., BROTHERS AND/OR SISTERS)	☐	☐
3. Do you have OTHER RELATIVES such as grandparents, aunts, uncles, cousins?	☐	☐
4. Do you have HIGH SCHOOL FRIENDS? (friendships developed during high school years)	☐	☐
5. Do you have COLLEGE FRIENDS? (friendships developed during college)	☐	☐
6. Do you have a paying ($) job where you have CO-WORKERS?	☐	☐
7. Do you belong to a CHURCH OR SYNAGOGUE?	☐	☐
8. Do you have SPIRITUAL BELIEFS?	☐	☐
9. Do you have contact with COLLEGE FACULTY, COUNSELORS, ADMINISTRATORS?	☐	☐
10. Do you have contacts with PROFESSIONALS OR SERVICE PROVIDERS such as doctors, nurses, barbers, diet counselors, etc.?	☐	☐
11. Do you belong to any SPECIAL ORGANIZED GROUPS such as groups for minorities, hobbies, fitness, athletics, etc.?	☐	☐
12. Do you watch TELEVISION, listen to the RADIO or read NEWSPAPERS, MAGAZINES, PAMPHLETS or NON-REQUIRED BOOKS?	☐	☐

Please read each statement and then indicate how much support you receive from each of the sources listed by checking NO, YES, or YES A LOT.

I. I Have a Feeling of Being Loved or Cared About From:

	NO	YES	YES A LOT
13. My parents	☐	☐	☐
14. My siblings	☐	☐	☐
15. Other relatives	☐	☐	☐
16. High school friends	☐	☐	☐
17. College friends	☐	☐	☐
18. Co-workers	☐	☐	☐
19. Church/synagogue groups	☐	☐	☐
20. My spiritual health	☐	☐	☐
21. College faculty, counselors, administrators	☐	☐	☐
22. Other professionals of service providers	☐	☐	☐
23. Special groups I belong to	☐	☐	☐
24. Reading books, watching TV, listening to music	☐	☐	☐
25. Other	☐	☐	☐

II. I Feel I Am Valued or Respected for Who I Am and What I Can Do By:

	YES	NO	YES A LOT
26. My parents	☐	☐	☐
27. My siblings	☐	☐	☐
28. Other relatives	☐	☐	☐
29. High school friends	☐	☐	☐
30. College friends	☐	☐	☐
31. Co-workers	☐	☐	☐
32. Church/synagogue groups	☐	☐	☐
33. My spiritual health	☐	☐	☐
34. College faculty, counselors, administrators	☐	☐	☐
35. Other professionals or service providers	☐	☐	☐
36. Special groups I belong to	☐	☐	☐
37. Reading books, watching TV, listening to music	☐	☐	☐
38. Other	☐	☐	☐

III. I Have a Sense of Trust or Security From the "GIVE and TAKE" of Being Involved With:

	YES	NO	YES A LOT
39. My parents	☐	☐	☐
40. My siblings	☐	☐	☐
41. Other relatives	☐	☐	☐
42. High school friends	☐	☐	☐
43. College friends	☐	☐	☐
44. Co-workers	☐	☐	☐
45. Church/synagogue groups	☐	☐	☐
46. My spiritual health	☐	☐	☐
47. College faculty, counselors, administrators	☐	☐	☐
48. Other professionals or service providers	☐	☐	☐
49. Special groups I belong to	☐	☐	☐
50. Reading books, watching TV, listening to music	☐	☐	☐
51. Other	☐	☐	☐

IV. When I Need To Talk or Think About How I'm Doing With My Life, I Feel Understood and Get Help From:

	YES	NO	YES A LOT
52. My parents	☐	☐	☐
53. My siblings	☐	☐	☐
54. Other relatives	☐	☐	☐
55. High school friends	☐	☐	☐
56. College friends	☐	☐	☐
57. Co-workers	☐	☐	☐

	YES	NO	YES A LOT
58. Church/synagogue groups	☐	☐	☐
59. My spiritual health	☐	☐	☐
60. College faculty, counselors, administrators	☐	☐	☐
61. Other professionals or service providers	☐	☐	☐
62. Special groups I belong to	☐	☐	☐
63. Reading books, watching TV, listening to music	☐	☐	☐
64. Other	☐	☐	☐

V. I Feel Good About Myself When I Am Able to Do Things For and Help:

	YES	NO	YES A LOT
65. My parents	☐	☐	☐
66. My siblings	☐	☐	☐
67. Other relatives	☐	☐	☐
68. High school friends	☐	☐	☐
69. College friends	☐	☐	☐
70. Co-workers	☐	☐	☐
71. Church/synagogue groups	☐	☐	☐
72. My spiritual health	☐	☐	☐
73. College faculty, counselors, administrators	☐	☐	☐
74. Other professionals or service providers	☐	☐	☐
75. Special groups I belong to	☐	☐	☐
76. Reading books, watching TV, listening to music	☐	☐	☐
77. Other	☐	☐	☐